ESSENTIALS OF PSYCHOLOGY

SECOND EDITION

ESSENTIALS OF PSYCHOLOGY

Concepts and Applications

Josh R. Gerow

Indiana University-Purdue University at Fort Wayne

HarperCollins*CollegePublishers*

Acquisitions Editor: Catherine Woods
Developmental Editor: Ann Marie Kirby
Project Coordination and Text Design: Ruttle, Shaw & Wetherill, Inc.
Cover Designer: Kay Petronio
Cover Photograph: Tony Demin/Adventure Photo & Film
Photo Researcher: Sandy Schneider
Electronic Production Manager: Christine Pearson
Manufacturing Manager: Helene G. Landers
Electronic Page Makeup: Ruttle, Shaw & Wetherill, Inc.
Printer and Binder: R. R. Donnelley & Sons Company
Cover Printer: New England Book Components, Inc.

For permission to use copyrighted material, grateful acknowledgment is made to the copyright holders on pp. 645–647, which are hereby made part of this copyright page.

Essentials of Psychology: Concepts and Applications, Second Edition

Library of Congress Cataloging-in-Publication Data

Gerow, Joshua R.
    Essentials of psychology: concepts and applications / Josh R.
Gerow. —2nd ed.
        p.   cm.
    Includes bibliographical references and indexes.
    ISBN 0–673–99499–6
    1. Psychology.   2. Psychology, Applied.   I. Title.
BF121.G428   1996
150—dc20   95–18512

95 96 97 98   9 8 7 6 5 4 3 2 1

BRIEF CONTENTS

Detailed Contents vii

Preface xix

INTRODUCTION   **1**

1 WHAT PSYCHOLOGISTS DO   **13**

TOPIC 1A—A Working Definition of Psychology   14

TOPIC 1B—The Research Methods of Psychology   26

2 THE NERVOUS SYSTEM AND BEHAVIOR   **49**

TOPIC 2A—Neurons: Building Blocks of the Nervous System   50

TOPIC 2B—The Central Nervous System   58

3 HUMAN DEVELOPMENT   **79**

TOPIC 3A—Prenatal Development   80

TOPIC 3B—Development in Children   85

TOPIC 3C—Adolescence and Adulthood   101

4 SENSORY PROCESSES   **125**

TOPIC 4A—Sensation: A Few Basic Concepts   126

TOPIC 4B—Vision   130

TOPIC 4C—Hearing and the Other Senses   143

5 PERCEPTION AND CONSCIOUSNESS   **160**

TOPIC 5A—Perception   162

TOPIC 5B—Consciousness   178

6 LEARNING   **201**

TOPIC 6A—Classical Conditioning   203

TOPIC 6B—Operant Conditioning   216

TOPIC 6C—Cognitive Approaches to Learning   228

7 MEMORY   **239**

TOPIC 7A—How Can We Describe Human Memory?   240

TOPIC 7B—Why We Forget: Factors Affecting Retrieval   254

8 HIGHER COGNITIVE PROCESSES   **277**

TOPIC 8A—Problem Solving   278

TOPIC 8B—Language   288

TOPIC 8C—Intelligence   294

9 MOTIVATION AND EMOTION   **314**
TOPIC 9A—Issues of Motivation   315
TOPIC 9B—The Psychology of Emotion   338

10 PERSONALITY AND ITS ASSESSMENT   **350**
TOPIC 10A—Issues and Theories of Personality   351
TOPIC 10B—Personality Assessment   367

11 PSYCHOLOGY, STRESS, AND PHYSICAL HEALTH   **380**
TOPIC 11A—Stress, Stressors, and How to Cope   381
TOPIC 11B—Health Psychology   394

12 THE PSYCHOLOGICAL DISORDERS   **407**
TOPIC 12A—Defining and Classifying Psychological
Disorders   408
TOPIC 12B—A Sampling of Psychological Disorders   414

13 TREATMENT AND THERAPY   **444**
TOPIC 13A—History and Biomedical Treatments   445
TOPIC 13B—The Psychotherapies   455

14 SOCIAL PSYCHOLOGY   **475**
TOPIC 14A—Social Cognitions: Attitudes, Attributions,
and Attractions   477
TOPIC 14B—Social Influence   489

15 I/O, ENVIRONMENTAL, AND SPORTS PSYCHOLOGY   **511**
TOPIC 15A—Industrial/Organizational Psychology   512
TOPIC 15B—Environmental and Sports Psychology   524

STATISTICAL APPENDIX 541

Answers to Test Yourself Questions 555
Glossary 589
Bibliography 603
Credits 645
Author Index 648
Subject Index 657

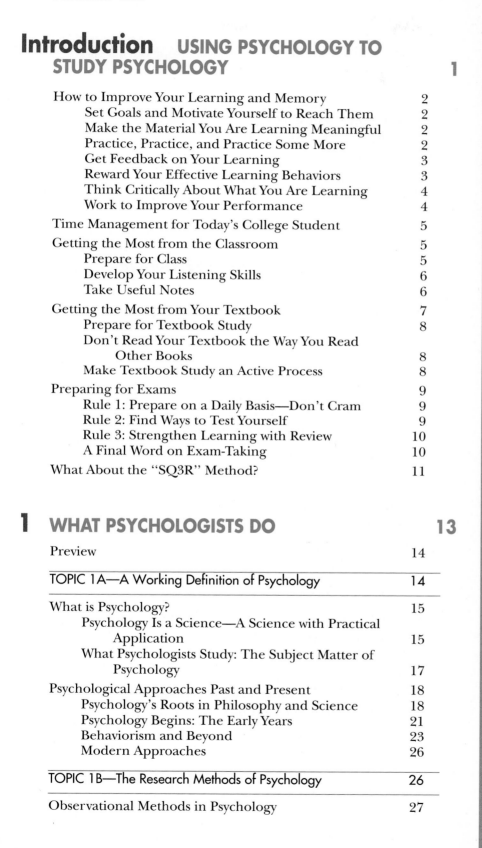

Introduction USING PSYCHOLOGY TO STUDY PSYCHOLOGY

1

How to Improve Your Learning and Memory | 2
Set Goals and Motivate Yourself to Reach Them | 2
Make the Material You Are Learning Meaningful | 2
Practice, Practice, and Practice Some More | 2
Get Feedback on Your Learning | 3
Reward Your Effective Learning Behaviors | 3
Think Critically About What You Are Learning | 4
Work to Improve Your Performance | 4
Time Management for Today's College Student | 5
Getting the Most from the Classroom | 5
Prepare for Class | 5
Develop Your Listening Skills | 6
Take Useful Notes | 6
Getting the Most from Your Textbook | 7
Prepare for Textbook Study | 8
Don't Read Your Textbook the Way You Read Other Books | 8
Make Textbook Study an Active Process | 8
Preparing for Exams | 9
Rule 1: Prepare on a Daily Basis—Don't Cram | 9
Rule 2: Find Ways to Test Yourself | 9
Rule 3: Strengthen Learning with Review | 10
A Final Word on Exam-Taking | 10
What About the "SQ3R" Method? | 11

1 WHAT PSYCHOLOGISTS DO

13

Preview | 14

TOPIC 1A—A Working Definition of Psychology | 14

What is Psychology? | 15
Psychology Is a Science—A Science with Practical Application | 15
What Psychologists Study: The Subject Matter of Psychology | 17
Psychological Approaches Past and Present | 18
Psychology's Roots in Philosophy and Science | 18
Psychology Begins: The Early Years | 21
Behaviorism and Beyond | 23
Modern Approaches | 26

TOPIC 1B—The Research Methods of Psychology | 26

Observational Methods in Psychology | 27

Naturalistic Observation 27

**PSYCHOLOGY IN THE REAL WORLD:
What Psychologists Do** **28**

Surveys 30
Case Histories 30

Correlational Methods in Psychology 31

Experimental Methods in Psychology 34
The Basic Procedures 34
Exercising Control 37

Ethics in Psychological Research 38

Important Themes and General Principles 40

Thinking Critically About What Psychologists Do 43

Summary 44

Test Yourself 47

2 **THE NERVOUS SYSTEM AND BEHAVIOR** **49**

Preview 50

TOPIC 2A—Neurons: Building Blocks of the Nervous System 50

The Neuron 50
The Structure of Neurons 51
The Function of Neurons 53

From One Cell to Another: The Synapse 55

TOPIC 2B—The Central Nervous System 58

Nervous Systems: The Big Picture 58

The Spinal Cord 60
The Structure of the Spinal Cord 60
The Functions of the Spinal Cord 61

The "Lower" Brain Centers 63
The Brain Stem 63
The Cerebellum 64
The Reticular Activating System (RAS) 66
The Limbic System 66
The Hypothalamus 67
The Thalamus 67

The Cerebral Cortex 68
Lobes and Localization 68

**PSYCHOLOGY IN THE REAL WORLD:
Who Left the Tack on the Hallway Floor?** **70**

The Two Cerebral Hemispheres—
Splitting the Brain 72

Thinking Critically About the Nervous System
and Behavior 74

Summary 75

Test Yourself 77

3 HUMAN DEVELOPMENT 79

Preview 80

TOPIC 3A—Prenatal Development 80

Physical Aspects of Prenatal Development 81
Environmental Influences on Prenatal Development 83
   Nourishment 83
   Smoking, Drinking, and Drugs 84
   Maternal Stress 85

TOPIC 3B—Development in Children 85

Motor Development—Getting from Here to There 85
Sensory and Perceptual Development 88
Cognitive and Social Development 89
   Cognitive Abilities of the Neonate: What Do
      Newborns Know? 89
   Piaget's Theory of Cognitive Development 90
   Reactions to Piaget 94
   Kohlberg's Theory of Moral Development 96
   Erikson's Theory of Psychosocial Development 98
   Developing Social Attachments 100

TOPIC 3C—Adolescence and Adulthood 101

What Are Adolescents Really Like? 101
Some Challenges of Adolescence 102
   The Challenge of Puberty 103
   The Challenge of Identity Formation 105
   The Challenge of Drug Use 105
   The Challenge of Sexuality 107
Early Adulthood 108
   Marriage and Family 109
   Career Choice 110

**PSYCHOLOGY IN THE REAL WORLD:
Divorce and Its Impact on Children 111**

Middle Adulthood 113
Late Adulthood 114
   What It Means to Be Old 115
   Death and Dying 116
Thinking Critically About Human Development 117
Summary 118
Test Yourself 122

4 SENSORY PROCESSES 125

Preview 126

TOPIC 4A—Sensation: A Few Basic Concepts 126

Sensory Thresholds 127
    Absolute Thresholds 127
    Difference Thresholds 128
    Signal Detection 129
Sensory Adaptation 129

TOPIC 4B—Vision 130

The Stimulus for Vision: Light 130
    Wave Amplitude (Intensity) 130
    Wavelength 131
    Wave Purity 132
The Eye 133
    Structures That Focus Visual Images 134
    The Retina 135
    More on Rods and Cones and What They Do 138
Color Vision and Color Blindness 140

TOPIC 4C—Hearing and the Other Senses 143

Hearing 143
    The Stimulus for Hearing: Sound 143
    The Receptor for Hearing: The Ear 146
The Chemical Senses 147
    Taste (Gustation) 148
    Smell (Olfaction) 149
The Skin, or Cutaneous, Senses 150
The Position Senses 152

**PSYCHOLOGY IN THE REAL WORLD:
Pain and Its Management** **153**

Thinking Critically About Sensory Processes 154
Summary 155
Test Yourself 158

5 PERCEPTION AND CONSCIOUSNESS 160

Preview 161

TOPIC 5A—Perception 162

Perceptual Selectivity: Paying Attention 162
    Stimulus Factors in Selectivity 162
    Personal Factors in Selectivity 163
Perceptual Organization: What Goes with What? 165
    Stimulus Factors in Organization 166
    Personal Factors in Organization 168
The Perception of Depth and Distance 169
    Ocular Cues 169
    Physical Cues 171
The Constancy of Visual Perception 174
    Perceptual Constancies 174
    Geometrical Illusions: When Constancy Fails? 175

TOPIC 5B—Consciousness 178

The Nature of Consciousness 178
    Normal, Waking Consciousness 178
    Levels of Consciousness 179
Sleeping and Dreaming 181
    Stages of a "Good Night's Sleep" 181
    REM and NREM Sleep 183

**PSYCHOLOGY IN THE REAL WORLD:
Sleep Disorders** **184**

Hypnosis 186
Altering Consciousness with Drugs 188
    Stimulants 189
    Depressants 191
    Hallucinogens 193
    Marijuana—A Rather Special Case 194
Thinking Critically About Perception and Consciousness 195
Summary 196
Test Yourself 199

6 LEARNING **201**

Preview 202

TOPIC 6A—Classical Conditioning 203

What Is Learning? 203
Pavlov and a Classic Demonstration 204
Classical Conditioning Phenomena 206
    Acquisition 207
    Extinction and Spontaneous Recovery 207
    Generalization and Discrimination 208
The Significance of Classical Conditioning 209
    Conditioned Emotional Responses 209
    The Case of "Little Albert" 210

**PSYCHOLOGY IN THE REAL WORLD:
Treating Fear with Classical Conditioning** **212**

Rethinking What Really Happens in Classical
Conditioning 212
    Can *Any* Stimulus Serve as a CS? 214
    Must the Time Interval Between the CS and
        the UCS Always Be Brief? 215

TOPIC 6B—Operant Conditioning 216

The Basics of Operant Conditioning 216
    Defining the Process 216
    Demonstrating Operant Conditioning 217
    The Course of Operant Conditioning 218
Reinforcement 220

Positive and Negative Reinforcers   220
Primary and Secondary Reinforcers   221
Scheduling Reinforcers   222
Punishment   225
Generalization and Discrimination   227

TOPIC 6C—Cognitive Approaches to Learning   **228**

Latent Learning and Cognitive Maps   229
Social Learning and Modeling   231
Thinking Critically About Learning   233
Summary   234
Test Yourself   237

7   MEMORY   **239**

Preview   240

TOPIC 7A—How Can We Describe Human Memory?   **240**

Memory as Information Processing   240
Sensory Memory   241
Short-Term Memory (STM)   242
The Duration of STM   244
The Capacity of STM   246
How Information Is Represented in STM   246
Long-Term Memory (LTM)   248
How Large is Long-Term Memory?   248
How Long Do Long-Term Memories Last?   249
How Do We Get Information into Long-Term Memory?   250
Are There Different Types of Long-Term Memories?   251

**PSYCHOLOGY IN THE REAL WORLD:
The Retrieval of Repressed Memories of
Childhood Trauma**   **253**

TOPIC 7B—Why We Forget: Factors Affecting Retrieval   **254**

How We Measure Retrieval   254
Direct, Explicit Measures   255
Indirect, Implicit Measures   255
How We Encode Information   257
The Power of Context   257
The Usefulness of Meaningfulness   259
The Value of Mnemonic Devices   261
The Role of Schemas   264
How We Schedule Practice   265
Overlearning   265
Distributing Practice   267
How We Overcome Interference   268
Retroactive Interference   268

Proactive Interference 270
A Reminder About Retrieval and Forgetting 271
Thinking Critically About Memory 272
Summary 272
Test Yourself 275

8 HIGHER COGNITIVE PROCESSES 277

Preview 278

TOPIC 8A—Problem Solving 278

What Is a Problem? 279
Problem Representation 280
Problem-Solving Strategies 282
    Algorithms 282
    Heuristics 282
Barriers to Effective Problem Solving 283
    Mental Set and Functional Fixedness 283
    Overcoming Barriers with Creative Problem Solving 285

TOPIC 8B—Language 288

Let's Talk: What Is Language? 288
Language Use as a Social Process 289
Language Acquisition 290
    What Happens in Language Acquisition 291
    Theories of Language Acquisition 292

TOPIC 8C—Intelligence 294

The Nature of Psychological Tests 295
Psychological Tests of Intelligence 296
    The Stanford-Binet Intelligence Scale 296
    The Wechsler Tests of Intelligence 299
Extremes of Intelligence 301
    The Mentally Gifted 301

PSYCHOLOGY IN THE REAL WORLD:
Blacks, Whites, IQ, and *The Bell Curve* 302
    The Mentally Retarded 305
Thinking Critically About Higher Cognitive Processes 307
Summary 308
Test Yourself 311

9 MOTIVATION AND EMOTION 314

Preview 315

TOPIC 9A—Issues of Motivation 315

How Shall We Characterize Motivation? 316
Instincts 316
Needs and Drives 316
Incentives 319
Balance or Equilibrium 320
Physiologically Based Drives 323
Temperature Regulation 323
Thirst and Drinking Behavior 325
Hunger and Eating Behavior 325

**PSYCHOLOGY IN THE REAL WORLD:
Eating Disorders** **328**
Sex and Sexual Behaviors 330
Psychologically Based Motives 334
Achievement Motivation 334
Power Motivation 336
Affiliation Motivation 337

TOPIC 9B—The Psychology of Emotion 338

Defining "Emotion" 338
Classifying Emotions 339
Physiological Aspects of Emotion 341
The Role of the Autonomic Nervous System 341
The Role of the Brain 342
Outward Expressions of Emotion 343
Thinking Critically About Motivation and Emotion 345
Summary 345
Test Yourself 348

10 PERSONALITY AND ITS ASSESSMENT **350**

Preview 351

TOPIC 10A—Issues and Theories of Personality 351

The Psychoanalytic Approach 352
Freud's Approach 352
The Psychoanalytic Approach after Freud 357
Evaluating the Psychoanalytic Approach 359
The Behavioral-Learning Approach 360
Evaluating the Behavioral-Learning Approach 361
The Humanistic-Phenomenological Approach 362
Evaluating the Humanistic-Phenomenological
Approach 363
The Trait Approach 364
Two Classic Examples 364
A Contemporary Perspective: The Big Five 365
Evaluating the Trait Approach 367

TOPIC 10B—Personality Assessment 367

Behavioral Observations 368

Interviews 370
Paper-and-Pencil Tests 371

PSYCHOLOGY IN THE REAL WORLD:
A Personality Test Just for You **372**

Projective Techniques 373
Thinking Critically About Personality and Its Assessment 375
Summary 376
Test Yourself 378

11 PSYCHOLOGY, STRESS, AND PHYSICAL HEALTH 380

Preview 381

TOPIC 11A—Stress, Stressors, and How to Cope 381

Stressors: The Causes of Stress 381
    Frustration-Induced Stress 382
    Conflict-Induced Stress 383
    Life-Induced Stress 385
Reacting to the Stressors in our Lives 387
    Individual Differences in Responding to Stressors 387
    Stress as a Physiological Reaction 388
    Effective Strategies for Coping with Stressors 390
    Ineffective Strategies for Coping with Stressors 393

TOPIC 11B—Health Psychology 394

Psychological Factors that Influence Physical Health 395
Promoting Healthy Behaviors 397
    Why Do People Die? 397
    Helping People to Stop Smoking 398
    Helping Patients "Follow Doctors' Orders" 399

PSYCHOLOGY IN THE REAL WORLD:
Having an Impact on AIDS, the Deadly STD **400**

Thinking Critically About Psychology, Stress, and
Physical Health 402
Summary 403
Test Yourself 405

12 THE PSYCHOLOGICAL DISORDERS 407

Preview 408

TOPIC 12A—Defining and Classifying
Psychological Disorders 408

Just What *Is* "Abnormal"? 409
The Classification of Abnormal Reactions 411

The DSM Series 411
Problems with Classification and Labeling 412
On "Insanity" 413

**PSYCHOLOGY IN THE REAL WORLD:
Attention-Deficit/Hyperactivity Disorder—
Not Just for Children Anymore** 414

TOPIC 12B—A Sampling of Psychological Disorders 414

Anxiety Disorders 415
Generalized Anxiety Disorder 416
Panic Disorder 416
Phobic Disorder 417
Obsessive-Compulsive Disorder (OCD) 419
Posttraumatic Stress Disorder (PTSD) 421
Somatoform Disorders 422
Hypochondriasis 422
Conversion Disorder 423
Dissociative Disorders 423
Dissociative Amnesia 424
Dissociative Fugue 424
Dissociative Identity Disorder 424
Personality Disorders 425
Delirium, Dementia, Amnestic, and Other Cognitive
Disorders—The Example of Alzheimer's 427
Mood Disorders 429
Types of Mood Disorder 430
Observations on the Causes of Depression 430
Schizophrenia 432
Incidence and Types of Schizophrenia 433
Observations on the Causes of Schizophrenia 436
Thinking Critically About the Psychological Disorders 438
Summary 439
Test Yourself 442

13 TREATMENT AND THERAPY 444

Preview 445

TOPIC 13A—History and Biomedical Treatments 445

A Historical Perspective 446
Who Provides Treatment and Therapy? 448
Biomedical Treatments of Psychological Disorders 450
Psychosurgery 450
Electroconvulsive Therapy 451
Drug Therapy 452

TOPIC 13B—The Psychotherapies 455

Psychoanalytic Techniques 455

PSYCHOLOGY IN THE REAL WORLD: What Shall We Do with the Most Seriously Disturbed?   **456**

    Freudian Psychoanalysis   457
    Post-Freudian Psychoanalysis   459

Humanistic Techniques   460

Behavioral Techniques   461

Cognitive Techniques   464
    Rational-Emotive Therapy   465
    Cognitive Restructuring Therapy   465

Group Approaches   467

Evaluating Psychotherapy   468

Thinking Critically About Treatment and Therapy   469

Summary   470

Test Yourself   473

14 SOCIAL PSYCHOLOGY   **475**

Preview   476

TOPIC 14A—Social Cognitions: Attitudes, Attributions, and Attractions   **476**

Attitudes   477
    The Components of Attitudes   478
    Attitude Formation   478
    Attitude Change and Persuasion   480

Attribution Theory   483

Interpersonal Attraction   485
    Theories of Interpersonal Attraction   485
    Factors Affecting Interpersonal Attraction   487

TOPIC 14B—Social Influence   **489**

Conformity   490

Obedience to Authority   491

Bystander Intervention   494

PSYCHOLOGY IN THE REAL WORLD: Violence   **496**

    A Cognitive Model of Bystander Intervention   496
    Audience Inhibition   498
    Pluralistic Ignorance   499
    Diffusion of Responsibility   500
    The Bystander Effect: A Conclusion   501

Social Loafing   501

Social Facilitation   502

Decision Making in Groups   503

Thinking Critically About Social Psychology   504

Summary   506

Test Yourself   509

15 I/O, ENVIRONMENTAL, AND SPORTS PSYCHOLOGY 511

Preview	512
TOPIC 15A—Industrial/Organizational Psychology	512
Fitting the Person to the Job	513
Defining "Good Work"—The Job Analysis	513
Selecting People Who Can Do Good Work	514
Training People to Do Good Work	516
Motivating People to Do Good Work	519
Fitting the Job to the Person	522
TOPIC 15B—Environmental and Sports Psychology	524
Psychology and the Environment	524
PSYCHOLOGY IN THE REAL WORLD: Safety in the Workplace	**525**
Space and Territory	526
Life in the City—An Example	529
Noise, Temperature, and Environmental Toxins	531
Psychology and Sports	534
The Psychological Characteristics of Athletes	534
Maximizing Athletic Performance	534
Thinking Critically About I/O, Environmental, and Sports Psychology	536
Summary	537
Test Yourself	539

STATISTICAL APPENDIX 541

Introduction and an Example	542
Organizing Data	543
Frequency Distributions	543
Graphic Representations	543
Descriptive Statistics	544
Measures of Central Tendency	545
Variability	547
Inferential Statistics	549
Some Normal Curve Statistics	552

ANSWERS TO TEST YOURSELF QUESTIONS 555

GLOSSARY 589

BIBLIOGRAPHY 603

CREDITS 645

AUTHOR INDEX 648

SUBJECT INDEX 657

I realize that my name is on the cover of this book, and I am quite willing to take responsibility for this text. I am also willing to acknowledge that writing a textbook is a very collaborative effort. It requires the loving support of family and friends. It requires the skilled craftsmanship of editors, designers, illustrators, and production people. It also requires the thoughtful guidance of colleagues willing to read early manuscript drafts and offer style and content suggestions.

For this text, input from colleagues has been critical. I am convinced that if anyone were to write an introductory psychology textbook that addressed all of the interests and desires of the psychologists who might use it, that text would be well over 2,000 pages long! As authors, we psychologists all seem to have our "favorite topics" that we feel should be included in an introductory text.

The basic idea behind this text was to prepare a brief, inexpensive text that presented the essential concepts of psychology, present them clearly and honestly, and show how these concepts can be applied in everyday life. Hence the title: *Essentials of Psychology: Concepts and Applications.* Another important goal was to build into the text as many features as possible to help the student appreciate and remember those concepts and applications. Although we wanted to build study-learning aids into the book, we wanted to do so in a way that would not interrupt the flow of the text itself. We wanted to avoid "clutter." In this regard, I believe we have succeeded.

Given the success of *Essentials of Psychology,* I am now willing to suggest that there are many fellow teachers of the introductory course in psychology who share our vision of what a truly student-oriented, supportive text can be. Still, there were some changes in the structure of the first edition that seemed called for.

What's New for the Second Edition?

If you are familiar with the first edition of this text, you will discover that at a glance almost everything is pretty much as it was in the first edition. We still have 15 chapters and—surprise, surprise—they're still in the same order! There are, of course, several changes that I think are reasonable and, in some cases, downright necessary. First let me mention a few "big" things, then I'll quickly review changes chapter-by-chapter.

The biggest organizational change that you'll notice (if you are familiar with the first edition) is the addition of *Topics* within chapters. I've liked the notion of Topics for a long time now. Mostly what the Topics do, is break down an otherwise lengthy chapter into meaningful segments. The application, of course, is to aid in distributed practice during study. Most chapters have two Topics, a few have three.

In terms of content, I would mention three additions: (1) Considerable updating of references. In fact, there are nearly 500 new reference citations in this edition, which is quite a few for an "Essentials" text. Of the new references, over half are citations from the 1990s. (2) Much more information on gender-related issues. These additions reflect the good work of a consultant, Dr. Carol Lawton of Indiana-Purdue at Fort Wayne. (3) Much more information on cross-cultural issues. These additions reflect the good work of another consultant, Dr. Richard Brislin, Director of Intercultural Programs, East-West Center, Honolulu. What pleases me about these additions is that they are subtle (I hope), and simply become part of the narrative. Note, for example, the inclusion of Mary Caulkins in the section on Psychology's history in Chapter 1, feminist criticism of Freudian theory in Chapter 10; new material in Chapter 3 on the role of the father in prenatal development; cross-cultural applications and criticisms of Kohlberg's theory in Chapter 3 and the discussion of social loafing in other cultures in Chapter 14. There are no new headings, chapters, or Topics devoted solely to these issues. I'll now list a change or two for each chapter that I think is significant. You may find other changes more significant than these.

Chapter 1—Added discussion of "scientist-practitioner," and added "No Two People Are Alike" to list of "Themes and Principles."

Chapter 2—Added to discussion of neural threshold, synapses, acetylcholine, and split brain.

Chapter 3—Expanded environmental influences on prenatal development; added a major section of attachment and day care, changed the thrust of section on middle adulthood and managed, somehow, to add 85 new references, 48 from the 1990s.

Chapter 4—Rewrote the opening on basic concepts, and moved pain and pain management to the "Psychology in the Real World" box.

Chapter 5—Addition of cross-cultural materials in sections on depth perception and alcohol use.

Chapter 6—Minor additions to sections on taste aversion, reinforcement in a cultural context, bribery vs. reinforcement, positive and negative punishers, and cognitive maps.

Chapter 7—Added section on eyewitness testimony, added box on repressed memories of child abuse, "equated" retrieval failure with forgetting.

Chapter 8—Added a section on language pragmatics; shortened discussion of psychological tests; expanded discussion on defining intelligence; added box on *The Bell Curve,* IQ, and race.

Chapter 9—Shortened section on sexuality; reworked discussion of relation between emotion and motivation.

Chapter 10—Expanded discussion of the nature of personality, introducing the "person-situation debate"; placed evaluations of theoretical approaches after each rather than together at end; added cultural usefulness of traits in different cultures.

Chapter 11—Shortened discussion of frustration; reworked section on physiological reactions to stress and Selye's GAS; totally reworked Health Psychology; new section on Why People Die; dropped most of STD discussion, but added to AIDS material and put in box; 54 new references, 36 from the 1990s.

Chapter 12—Changed everything to coincide with DSM-IV, instead of DSM-III-R; rearranged anxiety disorder coverage; added new box on ADHD.

Chapter 13—Reworked history section; adding a few major persons; updated drug therapy; added twenty-five 1990s references.

Chapter 14—Tightened section on attitudes; updated interpersonal attraction section; added new box on violence.

Chapter 15—Much updating in personnel selection section; changed examples in space and territory section; put worker safety issues in a box.

Features of This Text

Because we see the pedagogical learning aids as so important, we have built a large number into the text itself. They include:

- **"Introduction: Using Psychology to Study Psychology"** presents procedures for effective how-to-study techniques.
- **Chapter "Outlines"** provide a quick and easy overview of what is to come.
- **Chapter "Previews"** describe more fully the material to be covered in the chapter and demonstrate why psychologists care about this material, and why you as a student should care as well.
- **Boldface key terms** and **marginal glossary** highlight important terms and concepts; provide definitions in the text, in the margin (to aid review), and again in an end matter glossary.
- **"Before You Go On"** questions provide a "marker" for distributing one's practice or study time and an opportunity for interim summarizing. Answers are provided in each chapter summary.
- **"Psychology in the Real World"** boxes describe an application of material in the chapter in real-world situations.
- **"Thinking Critically About . . ."** sections encourage students to think critically about the information in the chapter and to relate that information to personal experiences.
- The chapter **summaries** restate the major ideas presented in each chapters in an abbreviated form and provide answers to the "Before You Go On" questions.
- **"Practice Tests"** and answers provide a final review of material from the chapter in an objective test format as well as examples of what to expect on exams. Answers are provided in annotated form, fostering the learning-review process.

Supplements to Accompany the Text

Instructor's Resource Kit
     by Judi M. Misale, Northeast Missouri State University
     ISBN 0673558983
     Three-Ring Binder
     ISBN 0673558991

This comprehensive manual comes bound in a three-ring binder and includes chapter outlines and learning objectives, lecture enhancements such as biographical profiles, demonstrations, and timelines, and critical thinking exercises for students. Also provided are a comprehensive media guide, APA publications, and additional readings.

     Test Bank
     by Gary Piggrem, DeVry Institute of Technology
     ISBN 0673558991

For each chapter, this resource contains more than 100 fully referenced multiple-choice items and five essay questions.

     TestMaster Computerized Test Bank
     (TestMaster DOS - ISBN 0673559017)
     (TestMaster Mac - ISBN 0673559041)
     by Gary Piggrem, DeVry Institute of Technology

Available in both IBM-PC and Mac versions, this computerized test generator allows the instructor to create and tailor tests, as well as edit existing items.

     Introductory Transparency Resource Package
     ISBN 0673558118

This package includes more than 100 4-color acetates.

Study Guide
by Glenda Streetman Smith, North Harris College
ISBN 0673999483

Packaged with the text, this invaluable educational aid provides students additional reinforcement of chapter learning objectives and vocabulary. Each chapter contains study tips and more than sixty self-test questions, including multiple-choice, true-false, matching, and fill-in-the-blank items.

Multimedia and Interactive Software
SuperShell Student Tutorial Software
ISBN 0673559009 (IBM)
ISBN 0673974855 (Macintosh)

This interactive program provides students with self-paced instruction, including chapter review material, practice exercises, self-tests with immediate correct responses, and individual diagnostic feedback. For IBM-PCs, compatibles, and Macintosh computers.

Journey II Interactive Software

This program involves students in a variety of simulations and experiments on a broad range of topics, including the nervous system and learning development. It is available for IBM and Macintosh users.

CD-ROM

Designed exclusively as presentation software and using state-of-the-art technology, this disk links the electronic text to interactive exercises, animations, and video clips. It covers the core concepts in the discipline by applying a game approach to the learning of psychology. James Hilton (University of Michigan) and Charles Perdue (West Virginia State College) were our consultants.

Also available for qualified adopters are a unique array of media items, including three laser discs, electronic transparencies, and videos. Please see your local sales representative for details.

Acknowledgments

As I said right at the very beginning, it took many many people to put this book together. Here, I get the opportunity to thank them all, but then to do little else but list their names and their professional affiliations. Before I start listing, however, there are three persons who really do deserve special mention. The first is my wife, Nancy, who not only read all of this manuscript (and more than once), and made many helpful suggestions, but who also served as research assistant and co-writer for the new "Psychology in the Real World" boxes—all of which helped enormously. I also need to acknowledge Catherine Woods, the HarperCollins psychology editor who got this project started and who has supported it through its production. My developmental editor for this edition, Ann Kirby, has also been very supportive and most helpful. Among other things, it was to Ann that fell the job of securing input from reviewers and helping me decide what needed to be changed and what could be left alone. Thanks also to Gloria Klaiman, Project Editor; Christine Pearson, Electronic Production Manager; Erica Smith, Editorial Assistant; Diane Wansing, Supplements Editor; and Mark Paluch, Marketing Manager.

Once again, feedback from my colleagues had a direct impact on this project. I would like to thank those instructors who served as reviewers on this project through the first and second editions: Allen R. Branum, South Dakota State University; Glenda Brewer, Rose State College; Dan W. Brunworth, Kishwaukee College; Roy Cohen, Mesa Community College; William

H. Curtis, Camden County College; Joseph R. Ferrari, Cazenovia College; Richard Florio, Passaic County Community College; Richard A. Girard, New Hampshire Technical College at Stratham; Phyllis Grilikhes-Maxwell, City College of San Francisco; Michael B. Guyer, John Carrol University; Jim Hail, McLennan Community College; James E. Hart, Edison State Community College; Jeanne Ivy, Tyler Junior College; Stan Kary, St. Louis Community College at Florissant Valley; Christopher Kilmartin, Mary Washington College; David Klein, Stark Technical College; Connie Lanier, Central Piedmont Community College; Denis Laplante, Lambton College; Vivian Leclaire, Community College of Rhode Island; Gloria M. Lewis, Tennessee State University; John F. Lindsay, Jr., Georgia College; Janet Lumpkin, Trinity Valley Community College; Kurt Mahoney, Mesa College; Terry Mason, Niagara College; Judi M. Misale, Northeast Missouri State University; David R. Murphy, Waubonsee Community College; Carrol Perrino, Morgan State University; Gary W. Piggrem, Devry Institute of Technology; Terri Sawyer, Carroll Community College; Jack P. Shilkret, Ann Arundel Community College; Sandra Stuebner, Chandler-Gilbert Community College; Ed Valsi, Oakland Community College; Anthony A. Walsh, Salve Regina University; Marcia Wehr, Santa Fe Community College; Fred W. Whitford, Montana State University; and Cecilia K. Yoder, Oklahoma City Community College.

Josh R. Gerow

A Visual Guide To:

ESSENTIALS OF PSYCHOLOGY
CONCEPTS AND APPLICATIONS
Second Edition

Josh R. Gerow
Indiana University/Purdue University at Fort Wayne

ISBN 0-673-99499-6

With an accessible writing style and an emphasis on developing strong study skills, Gerow's *Essentials of Psychology* presents a complete survey of introductory psychology for students of all abilities. Historical, cutting-edge, and cross-cultural examples are integrated throughout the text, and current issues and controversies are highlighted in a boxed feature in each chapter. The author presents information in a friendly tone that speaks directly to students, making difficult topics easy to understand. From the new breakdown of chapters into meaningful "topics" to Gerow's "Before You Go On" questions, text and information are organized into manageable chunks that are easier for students to review and retain. The pedagogical program reinforces the learning theme with marginal definitions, summaries tied to the interim questions, critical-thinking questions, and self-tests with answers provided. One of the briefest and most inexpensive texts available, every student copy of *Essentials of Psychology* comes shrinkwrapped with a free study guide.

GETTING THE MOST FROM YOUR TEXTBOOK ●

DON'T READ YOUR TEXTBOOK THE WAY YOU READ OTHER BOOKS

Perhaps the most significant insight about textbook study is that it is very different from casual reading. Reading a chapter is not studying a chapter. Studying is a process in which you must become actively and personally involved. Studying a text requires a great deal more concentration and mental effort than does reading for pleasure. What is the author trying to say? What are the major ideas? What evidence supports those ideas? What are the minor points? How can the material be related to what you already know from personal experience, previous reading, or classroom lectures? How will this information show up on a test?

There are times when you should look up from the book, pause, and think about what you have just read. You should be able to quickly summarize the material in your own words, which is why Before You Go On questions are included within each chapter of this book. If you cannot answer these questions, there is little point in going further. Go back over the section you've just read. Speed may be fine, but speed without comprehension is a waste of time.

Effective textbook study is a skill that can be learned by anyone, but it will not be learned automatically. It takes hard work and practice to develop textbook study skills. The rewards for your work, however, will be almost immediate.

MAKE TEXTBOOK STUDY AN ACTIVE PROCESS

There is no doubt that you must be mentally active and alert while studying so you can search, question, and think. This text and its accompanying Study Guide have been designed to facilitate active studying. If you have not done so yet, please go back now and read the section of the Preface titled "Features of this Text."

Underlining or highlighting in textbooks has become a common practice. Unfortunately, it often is misused. The purpose of underlining is to emphasize particular passages of the text so essential points can be reviewed by simply restudying underlined passages. The mistake that many students make is to underline too much: When 80 percent of a page is underlined for emphasis, the remaining 20 percent usually appears more striking.

You can increase the value of your textbook for studying by using the margins of the text for your personal notations. Make your text a storehouse of references. Cross-reference textbook material with information in your notes. If it's your book, use it—write in it.

PREPARING FOR EXAMS

Few occasions are quite as pleasant as the one you experience when you walk into class to take a big exam fully prepared, confident that you know the material and that you are going to do well. I also know from personal experience just how miserable it feels to face an exam unprepared, doomed before you begin—much less understand—much less answer—the first question. The key lies in being prepared. Proper preparation for exams helps to furnish the kind of positive reinforcement that education is meant to provide, but it isn't easy. You'll have to schedule your time, test your progress, and engage in continuous, active review.

STUDY TIPS PROVIDED IN SPECIAL INTRODUCTION TO THE TEXT

The text begins with a host of helpful tips to foster the development of students' study skills. Numerous strategies for success are introduced and supported consistently throughout the text to ensure proper comprehension and retention of the material.

MEMORY

7

PREVIEW

TOPIC 7A—How Can We
Describe Human Memory?

Memory as Information
Processing

Sensory Memory

Short-Term Memory (STM)

Long-Term Memory (LTM)

*PSYCHOLOGY IN THE
REAL WORLD*: The Retrieval
of Repressed Memories of
Childhood Trauma

TOPIC 7B—Why We
Forget: Factors Affecting
Retrieval

How We Measure Retrieval

How We Encode
Information

How We Schedule Practice

How We Overcome
Interference

A Reminder About Retrieval
and Forgetting

THINKING CRITICALLY
ABOUT MEMORY

CHAPTER SUMMARY

TEST YOURSELF

CHAPTER OUTLINES AND NEW "TOPICS" SECTIONS

These handy organizational tools provide a quick overview of the material discussed in each chapter and help students break down information into manageable "chunks." Following Gerow's "learning system" approach, each chapter is divided into two or more self-contained, highly manageable "topics," which make the material especially easy for students to study and review.

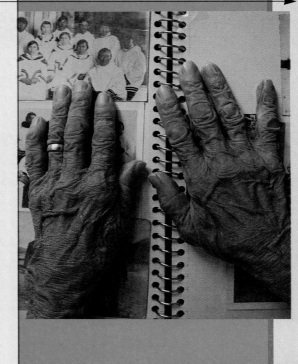

PREVIEW

perception
the cognitive process of selecting, organizing, and interpreting those stimuli provided to us by our senses

Now that we have a general idea of how our senses work, we can move on to consider what happens next as we process information about the world. As we have seen, the psychology of sensation is concerned with how our senses transduce physical energy from the environment into neural energy. **Perception** is concerned with the selection, organization, and interpretation of stimuli. Perception is a complex, active, cognitive process. You can think of these interrelated processes this way: Our senses present us with information about the world, while perception represents that information—often flavored by our motivational states, our emotions, our expectations, and our past experiences. That is, we create our perceptions of reality based on more than just the information provided by our senses.

Topic 5A begins with the consideration of a question: Given all of the stimuli presented to us by our senses, what factors determine which stimuli we pay attention to and which stimuli we ignore? Once stimuli are selected for further processing, they are organized into meaningful pieces of information. What factors influence the organization of our perceptions? Once we have these two basic issues resolved, we can move on to deal with two important perceptual matters: the perception of depth and distance, and the perceptual constancies.

Topic 5B takes us to a related set of issues, dealing with matters of human consciousness. **Consciousness** refers to our awareness, or our perception, of the environment and of our own mental processes. To be fully conscious is to be awake, aware, alert, and attentive. The extent to which we are conscious of ourselves and our environment will influence how—and the extent to which—we can process information. This is why I have chosen to put our discussion of consciousness in this chapter.

consciousness
the awareness or perception of the environment and of one's own mental processes

CHAPTER PREVIEWS

A helpful supplement to chapter outlines, these sections provide a more thorough description of all material to be addressed in the chapter and demonstrate the significance of these topics in psychology.

MARGINAL GLOSSARIES

The meanings of key terms are always close at hand thanks to these handy pedagogical aids.

major depression
an extreme of mood characterized by intense sadness, feelings of hopelessness, and a loss of pleasure and interest in normal activities

dysthymia
a reasonably mild, though chronic disorder of depression associated with low energy and low self-esteem

bipolar disorder
a severe mood disorder evidenced by unexplainable swings of mood between the more common depression and mania

mania
an extreme of mood characterized by euphoria, a sense of well-being, and an increase in activity level

Types of Mood Disorder

Mood disorders are defined in terms of extremes of mood, depression being the more common of the two extremes. Listed under the classification of mood disorder are several specific disorders, differentiated in terms of such criteria as length of episode, severity, and whether there is a known organic basis for the symptoms.

Major depression is a constellation of symptoms that includes feeling sad, low, and hopeless, coupled with a loss of pleasure or interest in one's usual activities. Associated with major depression are such factors as poor appetite, insomnia, loss of energy, decrease in sexual activity, and feelings of worthlessness. At the same time, there is no event or situation that can reasonably account for the extremeness of the observed depression.

This form of mood disorder is diagnosed about two times more in women than in men; during any 6-month period, approximately 6.6 percent of women and 3.5 percent of men will have an episode of major depression. This ratio of two women to every man developing major depression holds across nationalities and across ethnic groups (Cross-National Collaborative Group, 1992; McGrath et al., 1990). Worldwide, major depression is on the increase, with current incidence at more than 100 million persons (Gotlib, 1992; Weissman & Klerman, 1992). Unfortunately, research also tells us that relapse and reoccurrence are common for those who have had a depressive episode (Belsher & Costello, 1988; Klerman, 1990). Major depression seldom occurs in just one episode of illness, but rather is a chronic condition (Frank et al., 1990).

Dysthymia is the name of the disorder that is essentially a mild case of major depression. The disorder is chronic, with recurrent pessimism, low energy level, and low self-esteem. Whereas major depression tends to occur in a series of debilitating episodes, dysthymia is a more continuous sense of being depressed and sad.

As with major depression, there is no identifiable event that precipitates the depressed mood of dysthymia. In other words, to feel even overwhelmingly depressed upon hearing of the death of a friend is not enough to qualify as a disorder of any sort. From time to time we all feel depression, but there is usually some sensible reason for our depressed mood.

In **bipolar disorder**, episodes of depression are interspersed with episodes of mania. This disorder is often referred to as manic depression. **Mania** is characterized by an elevated mood with feelings of euphoria or irritability. In a manic state one shows an increase in activity, is more talkative than usual, and seems to be able to get by on a lot less sleep than usual. Mania is a condition of mood that cannot be maintained for long. It is just too tiring to stay manic for an extended time. Like depression, mania seldom occurs as an isolated episode. Follow-up studies show that recurrences of manic reactions are common. Relapse is found in approximately 40 percent of patients who have been diagnosed as having a manic episode (Harrow et al, 1990; Tohen et al., 1990). People are rarely ever manic without the interspersed periods of depression. Nearly 2 million Americans are presently diagnosed with bipolar disorder.

---

smooth one. At about the 7-minute mark, there is a change in the shape of the curve. This break in the curve is called the rod-cone break. At first—for 6 to 7 minutes—both rods and cones increase their sensitivity (represented by the first part of the curve). But our cones are basically daylight receptors. They are not cut out for seeing in the dark, and after those first few minutes, they have become as sensitive as they are going to get. Rods, on the other hand, keep lowering their threshold, or continue to increase their sensitivity (represented by the part of the curve after the "break").

Now that we've reviewed the nature of light and the eye, the stimulus and the receptor for vision, we'll end our discussion of vision by examining how our cones provide us with the experience of color.

● **Before You Go On**
Why can we claim that rods and cones provide us with two different kinds of visual experience?

Color Vision and Color Blindness

Explaining how the eye codes or responds to different intensities of light is not too difficult: High-intensity lights cause more rapid firing of neural impulses than do low-intensity lights. It is also sensible that high-intensity lights stimulate more cells to fire than do lights of low intensity. How the eye codes different wavelengths of light to produce different experiences of hue or color, however, is another story. Here things are not simple at all. There are many theories of color vision, two of which were proposed many years ago. As is often the case with competing theories that try to explain the same phenomenon, both are probably partially correct.

"BEFORE YOU GO ON" QUESTIONS

Strategically located throughout each chapter, these questions offer students a regular opportunity to assess their comprehension of the material. Doubling as interim summaries of the information covered thus far, these questions also serve as markers for distributing practice and study time. Answers to all questions are provided in chapter-ending summaries.

"PSYCHOLOGY IN THE REAL WORLD" BOXES

Featured in each chapter, these sections clearly illustrate the material at hand as it occurs in real-world situations. Topics illustrate a diverse range of timely, high-interest applications, such as the effects of divorce, daycare, lie-detection, ESP, consumer psychology, and many others.

PSYCHOLOGY IN THE REAL WORLD

Blacks, Whites, IQ, and the Bell Curve

That there are significant differences between the IQ test scores of black and white Americans is not a new discovery. It was one of the conclusions drawn from the testing program for Army recruits during the First World War. Since then, many studies have reconfirmed the fact that whites score as many as 15 points higher on tests of general intelligence (IQ) than do blacks. Blacks even earn lower scores on performance tests and on intelligence tests designed to minimize the influence of one's culture (so-called culture fair tests) (Helms, 1992; Jensen, 1980; Rushton, 1988). There also are data that tell us that Japanese children (between the ages of 6 and 16) score higher on IQ tests—about 11 points on the average—than do American children (Lynn, 1982; 1987). The nagging question, of course, is where do these test score differences come from?

The proposed answers have been very controversial and involve several possibilities we've touched on before in other contexts: (1) The tests are biased and unfair. IQ tests may reflect the experiences of white Americans to a greater extent than they reflect the lives and experiences of blacks. (2) Differences in IQ scores can be attributed to environmental factors, such as economic or educational opportunities, or the extent to which one is exposed to a wide range of stimuli. (3) Genetic factors are involved that place some groups at a disadvantage. (4) There are cultural differences in motivation and attitudes about performance on standardized tests.

Test bias may account for some of the observed differences in IQ scores, but assume for the moment that available techniques for assessing general intelligence are as valid as possible. (Remembering, of course, that even the best and fairest of tests only measures one, or a few, aspects of the various dimensions of intelligence.) What then? Let's concentrate on black-white differences in IQ.

In the 1950s and 1960s, psychologists were confident that most (if not all) of the difference in the average IQ scores of whites and blacks could be accounted for by environmental, sociocultural, and motivational factors. There wasn't much research to sup-

port the position, but the logic was compelling and it was consistent with prevailing attitudes. Blacks were at a disadvantage on standard IQ tests because they were often denied access to enriching educational opportunities. The lower socioeconomic status deprived many blacks of the sorts of experiences that could raise their IQ scores.

In 1969, Arthur Jensen shocked the scientific community with an article in the Harvard Educational Review. Jensen argued that there was insufficient evidence to justify the conclusion that the environment alone could produce the observed racial differences in IQ scores. The alternative was obvious to Jensen: the differences were attributable to genetic factors. Many readers took Jensen's claim to mean that blacks are genetically inferior to whites. Jensen said that his argument was meant only as a reasonable hypothesis, intended to provoke scientific efforts to explore the possibility (Jensen, 1981).

Perhaps you can imagine the furor created by Jensen's article. Researchers took up the challenge and tried to find convincing evidence that the environment is the cause of lower black IQ scores. After reviewing the body of evidence that resulted from these efforts, one scientist, Brian Mackenzie, wrote: "what is finally clear from such research, therefore, is that environmental factors have not been identified that are sufficient to account for all or even most of the 15-point mean difference in IQ between blacks and whites in the United States. Jensen's conclusion that half to two-thirds of the gap remains unaccounted for by any proposed combination of environmental influences is still unrefuted" (1984, p. 1217). What does that mean? Does that mean that racial differences in IQ are caused by genetic factors? Are blacks genetically less able than whites? Of course not. There is no evidence to support that conclusion either (Mackintosh, 1986).

Just as many were coming to believe that the debate over racial differences in IQ was settling down, the controversy was reignited late in 1994 with the publication of a book, titled *The Bell Curve*. (The bell curve refers to the symmetrical normal curve of IQ

THINKING CRITICALLY ABOUT PERSONALITY AND ITS ASSESSMENT

1. No matter what its proposals, hypotheses, or predictions, to what extent is it reasonable to assume that a theory of personality can emerge from the study and treatment of persons with psychological disorders?
2. Humankind is a unique species. For one thing, it is among the very few that regularly kill their own kind on purpose (in murder or war, for example). How can a personality theory take this aspect of human nature into account? (Freud was one of the few to try.)
3. Is it even possible to employ defense mechanisms consciously, or "on purpose"?
4. Freud proposed his theory of personality near the turn of the century. Now, nearly 100 years later, what might Freud think of his own theory's relevance in today's world?
5. Watson and Skinner never proposed a personality theory as such. How do you suppose either of them would have accounted for mental illness or psychological disorders?
6. Can you generate examples of how each of the "Big Five" traits of personality show up in behavior? Can you judge where you fall on each of the five proposed dimensions?
7. What are the major problems with the so-called "personality tests" that we find in magazines and newspapers? For that matter, what (if anything) is "wrong" with the little personality test included in the "Psychology in the Real World" box?
8. How can one determine the reliability of a test that measures anxiety if we know that anxiety is a characteristic that is itself very unreliable (i.e., sometimes we are more or less anxious than at other times)?
9. If you were to take the logic of projective techniques seriously, what could you conclude about someone who viewed all of the inkblots in the Rorschach series and said for each card, "It just looks like an inkblot to me."

"THINKING CRITICALLY ABOUT. . ." QUESTIONS

These insightful learning aids encourage students to contemplate each chapter's discussion further by relating the material to their own personal experiences.

CHAPTER SUMMARIES

These sections restate and reinforce each chapter's major ideas in abbreviated form and also provide answers to the "Before You Go On" questions located throughout each chapter.

SUMMARY

TOPIC 9A

ISSUES OF MOTIVATION

● How have the concepts of instinct, need, drive, and incentive been used to explain motivated behaviors?

Instincts are complex patterns of behavior that occur in the presence of certain stimuli. Instinct approaches take the position that some complex behavior patterns are unlearned or innate. The concept of instinct has not proven satisfactory in accounting for human behaviors. Needs are shortages of some biological necessity. Deprivation may lead to a need, which gives rise to a drive, which arouses and directs behavior. The relations among deprivation, need, drive, and behavior are often not very straightforward; drives can be more learned than biological. Maslow has proposed that human needs can be placed in a hierarchy, beginning with basic survival needs and ending with a need to self-actualize. Focusing on incentives explains behaviors in terms of goals and outcomes rather than on internal forces. In this sense, we are motivated to reach desired end states. These approaches are not mutually exclusive, and each may be used to explain some types of motivated behavior.

● How can the concept of balance or equilibrium be used to help us understand motivated behaviors?
In what way is cognitive dissonance theory based on equilibrium?

Organisms are motivated to reach and maintain a state of balance—a set point level of activity. With homeostasis, we have a general drive to maintain a state of equilibrium among internal physiological processes such as blood pressure, metabolism, and heart rate. Some psychologists argue for a general drive to maintain a balanced state of arousal, with different optimal levels of arousal being best suited for different tasks or situations. Festinger claims that we are motivated to maintain balance among cognitive states, and thereby to reduce cognitive states, and thereby to reduce cognitive dissonance.

● Given the concept of homeostasis, how might temperature regulation be thought of as a physiologically based drive?

Temperature regulation can be viewed as a physiological drive because we have a need (thus are driven) to maintain our body temperatures within homeostatic levels. Doing so may involve voluntary as well as involuntary responding.

● List some of the internal and external factors that influence drinking behavior.

We are motivated to drink for several reasons: to relieve dryness in our mouths and throats; to maintain a homeostatic level (monitored by the hypothalamus) of fluid within our bodies; and also as a response to external cues, such as taste, aroma, or appearance. What we drink is often influenced by our learning experiences.

● List the internal and external factors that influence eating.

Internal factors include cues mediated by the hypothalamus, which may be responding to stored fat levels, blood sugar levels, or some other indication that our normal homeostatic balance has been disrupted. Associated with this view is the position that body weight is maintained at a given set point by both intake and exercise levels. There is evidence that body size may be determined largely by genetic factors. External factors include the stimulus properties of foods, as well as habit patterns and social pressure.

● In what ways is the sex drive a unique physiologically based drive?

(1) Individual survival does not require its satisfaction. (2) The drive involves seeking or creating tension, not relieving tension. (3) It is not fully present at birth, but matures later. (4) The extent to which it is affected by learned or external influences varies from species to species. Like other physiologically-based drives, it does respond to both internal and external stimuli.

● What is homosexuality?
What causes homosexuality?

TEST YOURSELF

TOPIC 6A

CLASSICAL CONDITIONING

6.1 To say that learning is demonstrated by changes in behavior is to suggest that a) if we cannot remember something, we did not learn it in the first place. b) some changes in behavior do not last very long, or are cyclical. c) the only way we can be sure if someone learned something is to ask him or her. d) learning is an internal process that is inferred from performance.

6.2 Which of the following ideas is not found in our definition of learning? a) Changes in behavior due to learning must be relatively permanent. b) Learning involves making good and proper adjustments and adaptations to the environment. c) For changes to be classified as learned, they must result from practice or experience. d) Learning cannot be measured or observed directly.

6.3 As Pavlov noted, when we bring a dog to the laboratory, stand him on a table, and ring a bell the first thing we will notice is a) an orienting reflex. b) an unconditioned stimulus. c) habituation or acclimation. d) no response at all.

6.4 True or False? Ivan Pavlov won a Nobel Prize for psychology in 1902.

6.5 True or False? In a demonstration of classical conditioning, the unconditioned response occurs without any previous learning experience.

The next three items involve the following situation: A dog is exposed to the sound of a bell until it comes to ignore it. Now, soon after the bell is sounded, a shock is delivered to the front left paw of the dog. When it is shocked, the dog quickly lifts its foot. This procedure is repeated 12 times.

6.6 What is likely to be the response when the bell is sounded now? a) A UCS will occur. b) A UCR will occur. c) A CR will occur. d) Nothing will happen.

6.7 In this example of conditioning, the UCR is____ and the CR is _____. a) shock; foot withdrawal. b) shock; a bell. c) a bell; an orienting reflex. d) foot withdrawal; foot withdrawal.

6.8 If the bell were sounded alone (no more shock) for a few dozen presentations, what is likely to occur? a) extinction. b) generalization. c) acquisition. d) spontaneous recovery.

6.9 Which process is essentially the opposite of generalization? a) discrimination. b) reinforcement. c) acquisition. d) habituation.

6.10 Although each of these responses or behaviors is learned, which most clearly results from classical conditioning? a) typing or keyboard skills. b) feeling relief at realizing that a class period is about over. c) understanding the difference between a CS and a UCS. d) speaking the language you do rather than a different one.

6.11 With "Little Albert" as their subject, John Watson and Rosalie Rayner demonstrated each of the following except a) generalization. b) classical conditioning. c) extinction. d) a learned and unlearned stimulus for fear.

6.12 A stimulus will serve as a most effective CS if a) it is repeatedly presented after the presentation of the UCS. b) it naturally produces an orienting reflex. c) its presentation reliably predicts the UCS. d) it is repeatedly paired with an appropriate CR.

6.13 Taste aversion studies a) work with rats, but not with dogs or people. b) show us an application of classical conditioning. c) demonstrate that CS-UCS intervals may be quite long. d) explain why most children prefer sweet-tasting foods.

PRACTICE TESTS *WITHIN* THE BODY OF EACH CHAPTER

Designed as a review of each chapter's material, these sections feature objective, open-ended questions incorporated within the text. They enable students to quickly and easily test their comprehension and retention of the material *as they go through it* while also providing examples of what students can expect to find on exams.

EXPANDED COVERAGE OF MULTICULTURAL AND CROSS-CULTURAL ISSUES

Featured throughout the text, numerous research studies and references back-up the discussion of increasingly important cultural issues while illustrating the broadening scope of psychology's reach. Cultural bias is also specifically addressed.

another. On the other hand, as theories they offer little more than description. To say that someone acted in a certain way "because he is introverted" doesn't really explain his action. It functions merely as a label. Even with the Big Five traits, disagreement about how to specifically define the most basic traits that describe personality remains.

The basic relevance or value of personality traits varies across cultures. Traits are seen as reasonable and sensible to peoples of Western cultures, where people are viewed as individual actors and where knowing about the characteristics of those individual actors would be helpful. If people are viewed in terms of their long-term membership in a group or a collective (as they are in collectivistic cultures such as those found in Asia, Africa, and South America), then their individual characteristics will be of less interest than their roles, duties, responsibilities, and group loyalties, for example. (Miller, 1984; Shwedler & Sullivan, 1993).

So, as we might have predicted, when we try to evaluate the different theories of personality, there are no winners or losers. Each approach has its shortcomings, but each adds something to our appreciation of the concept of human personality.

animals to psychology—again reflecting the influence of Darwin. One of the most popular textbooks of this era was *The Animal Mind* by Margaret Floy Washburn (1871–1939), the first woman to be awarded a Ph.D. in psychology. Published in 1908, the book addressed animal consciousness and intelligence. In fact, one characteristic of functionalism was its willingness to be open to a wide range of topics—so long as they were in some way related to mental life, or adaptation, or had practical application. We can trace child, abnormal, educational, social, and industrial psychology to early functionalism.

In those early days of psychology, societal pressures were such that getting a graduate level education was exceedingly difficult for women, no matter how able or bright they were (Furumoto & Scarborough, 1986; Scarborough & Furumoto, 1987). Still, one woman, Mary Calkins (1863–1930), so impressed William James that he allowed her into his classes even though Harvard would not let her formally enroll. Nor would Harvard award her a Ph.D.—for which she had met all academic requirements. Mary Calkins went on to do significant experimental work on human learning and memory, and in 1905 was the first woman to be elected president of the American Psychological Association (Madigan & O'Hara, 1992).

INCREASED COVERAGE OF GENDER ISSUES

A host of highly relevant gender issues are incorporated within the chapters. Coverage includes historical contributions by women psychologists and the significance of maternal stress.

Experiments with split-brain patients confirm that speech production is a left hemisphere function in a great majority of people. Suppose you have your hands behind your back. I place a house key in your left hand, and ask you to tell me what it is. Your left hand feels the key. Impulses travel up your left arm, up your spinal cord, and cross over to your right cerebral hemisphere—remember cross-laterality. You can readily tell me that the object in your hand is a key because your brain is intact. Your right hemisphere passes the information about the key to your left hemisphere, and your left hemisphere directs you to say, "It's a key." Now suppose that your corpus callosum is severed (that you are a split-brain subject). Now you cannot answer my question, even though you understand it perfectly. Why not? Your right brain knows that the object in your left hand is a key, but without a corpus callosum, it has no way to inform the left hemisphere, where your speech center is located. You would be able to point out the key from among other objects placed before you, under the direction of the right cerebral hemisphere. Once your eyes saw you do so, they would communicate that information to your left hemisphere, and now it too would know, and tell us, what your right hemisphere knew all along!

A major task of the left hemisphere, then, is the production of speech. But before we go any further, we need to pause and caution against overinterpretation. When results from split-brain studies were first made known, many people—psychologists and nonpsychologists alike—rushed to premature conclusions. We now believe that virtually no behavior, virtually no mental process, is the simple and single product of just one hemisphere (e.g., Hellige, 1990). It is more reasonable to say that one hemisphere dominates the other, or is the primary processing area for certain actions. For example, the left hemisphere is dominant in the perception and interpretation of speech. But some language processing seems to be primarily the responsibility of the right hemisphere. The right hemisphere is more involved in the processing of common phrases and cliches such as "How do you do?" or "Have a nice day!" (Kempler & Van Lancker, 1987).

Being careful not to overinterpret, what are some of the activities processed primarily in one hemisphere or the other? We've seen that the left hemisphere can be given credit for most of our language skills, and given our reliance on language, that's no small matter. Simple arithmetic tasks of calculation also seem to be primarily a left brain function. Indeed, the left hemisphere is often credited with the processing of information in an analytical, one-piece-at-a-time sort of way, although the data here are a bit tenuous (Hellige, 1990, p. 59).

Although we must be careful not to overgeneralize, we may say that a major task of the left cerebral hemisphere is the use of language (as in working a crossword puzzle). A major task of the right cerebral hemisphere is the appreciation of spatial relations (as in working on a jigsaw puzzle).

PSYCHOLOGY IN THE REAL WORLD

Pain and Its Management

What is pain? What causes the experience of pain? Each of us knows what a pain pain can be, yet it is often difficult to find the exact words to adequately describe our pain to others (Verillo, 1975). Pain can be useful. It can alert us to problems occurring within our bodies so appropriate action can be taken. It is the experience of pain that prompts more than 80 percent of all visits to the doctor's office (Turk, 1994).

Many stimuli can cause pain. Too much light, strong pressures on the skin, loud sounds, and even very "hot" spices can result in our experiencing pain. But as we all know, the stimulus for pain need not be intense. In the right circumstances, even a light pinprick can be painful. Our skin has many receptors for pain, but pain receptors can also be found deep inside our bodies; consider stomachaches, back pain, and headaches. Pain is experienced in our brains, and the thalamus seems to play an important role, (Groves & Rebec, 1992, p. 265). On the other hand, pain is the only "sense" for which we can find no one specific center in the cerebral cortex.

One theory of pain claims that pain is experienced in the brain, not in the periphery, and that a gate-control mechanism (high in the spinal cord) acts to block pain messages by "closing the gate" so that pain messages never get to the brain for processing (Melzack & Wall, 1965; Melzack, 1973). A cognitive-behavioral theory of pain also suggests that central mechanisms are important, noting that the experience of pain is influenced by a person's attitudes, cognitions, and behaviors (Turk, 1994).

Even without a full understanding of how pain is sensed, there are techniques that can be used to minimize or manage the experience of pain. If pain is really experienced in the brain, what sorts of things can we do to keep pain messages from reaching those brain centers?

Drug therapy can be a choice for pain management. Opiates, such as morphine, when administered systemically, are believed to inhibit pain messages at the level of the spinal cord, as well as at the specific site, or source, of the pain (Basbaum & Levine, 1991; Clinton, 1992; Randall, 1993; Richmond et al., 1993).

Hypnosis and cognitive self-control (trying very hard to convince yourself that the pain you're experiencing is not really that bad and will go away) are effective in lessening the experience of pain (Litt, 1988; Melzack, 1973).

That psychological processes can inhibit pain is also reinforced by data on placebo effects. A placebo is a substance (often in pill form) a person believes will be useful in treating some symptom, such as pain. When people are given a placebo they believe will alleviate pain, painkilling endorphins are released in the brain and effectively keep pain-carrying impulses from reaching the brain (Levine, et al., 1979). This placebo effect is particularly strong when the health care provider is prestigious and demonstrates empathy and a positive attitude about the placebo (Turner et al., 1994).

Another process that works to ease the feeling of pain, particularly pain from or near the surface of the skin, is called counterirritation. The idea is to forcefully (but not painfully, of course) stimulate an area of the body near the location of the pain. Dentists have discovered that rubbing the gum near the spot of a novacaine injection significantly reduces the patient's experience of the pain of the needle.

The ancient Eastern practice of acupuncture can also be effective in the treatment of pain. We don't know yet why acupuncture works as well as it does. There are cases where it doesn't work well at all, but these usually involve patients who are skeptics, which suggests that one of the benefits of acupuncture is its placebo effect. As many as 12 million

USING PSYCHOLOGY TO STUDY PSYCHOLOGY

INTRODUCTION

Psychologists study many things, most of which are practical and relevant to our everyday lives. Among the issues that psychologists have investigated are the factors that influence efficient and effective studying behaviors. It is appropriate to introduce some of the advice that comes from this research now, as we get started. I firmly believe that if you put this advice into practice, your performance in this course will benefit directly. We'll return later to many of the points raised here—mostly in our discussion of learning and memory. As we go along, I'll point out how some of the features of this book can make your study of psychology easier.

How to Improve Your Learning and Memory

Time Management for Today's College Student

Getting the Most from the Classroom

Getting the Most from Your Textbook

Preparing for Exams

What About the "SQ3R" Method?

1

HOW TO IMPROVE YOUR LEARNING AND MEMORY

How people learn things, and how they might learn and remember more effectively, are concerns that predate psychology. They are concerns that can be traced to ancient times. What has always surprised me is that after all these hundreds of years, the list of factors known to have a direct and significant impact on learning and memory is really quite short.

Throughout this introduction, please keep in mind that effective study habits are not developed for their own sake, but in order to make learning more efficient. You don't go to college to study; you go to college to learn.

Set Goals and Motivate Yourself to Reach Them

We are all aware that we can learn some things "by accident," without intending to do so. Our most efficient learning, however, takes place when we intend to learn, when we make a conscious, concerted effort to acquire new information. In a way, this is saying that it helps to be motivated to learn. And we can motivate ourselves to learn. One thing that helps is to establish goals.

Difficulties in learning often arise when college students do not have clear goals. Some may not have the foggiest notion of why they are in college in the first place, and thus can find no particular reason for doing well in their classwork. So it is a good idea to clarify in your own mind just why you are in college, why you are taking an introductory course in psychology, and why it is important to you (not to someone else) to do well in the course.

Make the Material You Are Learning Meaningful

If you have never studied French, you would certainly find it easier to learn a list of 12 English words than to memorize a list of 12 French words. The reasons are clear: You know what the English words mean; they make you think of other words; you can associate them with other things; you know how they are used. The French words strike you as nonsense; you can't relate to them in a meaningful way.

This example can be generalized to other areas. The learning of any new information will be easier to the extent that that information can be made personal, meaningful, and useful. To a large degree, this means fitting the new information in with your past experiences and your plans for the future. To help you with this task, I've included many examples of the psychological concepts introduced in the text. The catch is that my examples are particularly meaningful to me. This may help you, but it would be much more useful for you to generate your own examples.

Practice, Practice, and Practice Some More

In Chapter 6 we will *define* learning to be the result of practice. Practice or rehearsal is an integral part of learning. Learning—academic learning in particular—is not something that happens automatically. Acquiring new information involves working with the material, studying it, practicing it. The more you practice any material, the better it will be retained. I'll have more to say about the quality of practice shortly, but for now: *With regard to practice, more is better than less.*

How you distribute practice time is extremely important. The research on this point is clear: Efficiency is improved when study time is interrupted with rest breaks. For most students and most courses, the recommended schedule is 45 minutes of study followed by a 15-minute rest break. So take short breaks. Get up and stretch, take a stroll, get a drink of water, and so on. But be careful—15 minutes of study followed by 45-minute breaks isn't going to be very efficient.

To encourage spaced or distributed study is one reason why I have divided each chapter into **Topics** and have inserted several **Before You Go On** sections within each Topic. They provide cues as to where a good place might be to take a break. To sit down and study a whole chapter straight through, without a break, is tough, and not a very efficient use of your time. Please notice that simply dividing a chapter into two, or three, or even four Topics doesn't make that chapter any longer or more difficult—in fact, dividing it into Topics will make it easier.

Get Feedback on Your Learning

A person with little or no knowledge of how his or her learning is progressing will be at a distinct disadvantage compared to a person who is informed. The process involved is what psychologists call "knowledge of results," or feedback. Imagine learning how to shoot basketball free throws while blindfolded. With no information about how you are doing or where the ball is going, there's little reason to suspect that you'll ever get to be very good. The same argument holds true for any kind of learning.

Some of the feedback that you get in college comes when your instructor evaluates your work. Use returned exams and papers as feedback. Review them, noting any errors you have made. Decide how your study habits can be changed to minimize errors in the future.

You can also provide yourself with important—and less costly—feedback by testing yourself on the material you are studying. Self-testing should be an ongoing process, but it is particularly useful as exams approach. For this course, you have three readily available means of providing yourself with feedback or knowledge of results: the **Before You Go On** questions within chapters, the **Test Yourself** questions at the end of each chapter, and the **Student Study Guide** that comes with the text.

Reward Your Effective Learning Behaviors

One of the most practical principles in psychology is that one's actions are often shaped by their consequences. Simply put, behaviors that are rewarded (later we will say *reinforced*) tend to get repeated whenever possible.

We all know the satisfaction that comes when our goals are met. That exhilarating feeling of doing well on a quiz, term paper, or lab report will go a long way to insure success in the future. As a college student, many of your rewards will probably come from instructors, friends, or family members. But you can't always depend on rewards from others to maintain your studying. Try to develop the habit of providing rewards for yourself for work well done. Study hard for 45 minutes, then reward yourself for putting in the honest effort (and by so doing, distribute your study time). Do something that will make you feel good. You'll be surprised at how something so simple can have such a significant impact on your behavior.

Think Critically About What You Are Learning

To be of any use, the learning that occurs in a college course should involve more than just the memorization of facts. It should enhance one's ability to think critically about the subject matter. This is particularly true of a psychology course.

Many of us have a tendency to accept without question what we are told by people we perceive to be experts. I am now challenging you to do otherwise. To be sure, I believe that the information I have included in this text is as accurate and honestly presented as such information can be. But do not accept what is said here (or any place else) without thinking—critically—about that information. To think critically doesn't mean just to be negative. More than anything else, it means to question, in your own mind, from your own point of view, in the context of your own experience, what is being presented. Thinking critically about what is presented here is an important way to make the information meaningful, and we know that that helps learning.

What sorts of questions should you ask about the ideas presented in your psychology class? There are many, but here are a few suggestions: Where did this information or conclusion come from? On what sort of research was it based? Are there any data at all to support what is being claimed? Are there any other ways in which these results can be explained? Does this information fit my own personal experience? How might this conclusion be biased? Given this information, what other possibilities come to mind?

In order to stimulate your thinking about the material in this text, there is a section at the end of each chapter called **Thinking Critically About. . . .** As the name suggests, these questions do not have one "best" answer. They simply raise issues worth thinking about and points to ponder.

Work to Improve Your Performance

Let's make an important distinction. Learning is a process that takes place *inside* an individual. We cannot see it as it occurs. We cannot measure it directly. We can only infer learning from performance. You may think that your little nephew can play a tune on the piano—indeed, he has told you that he has learned to do so. If you really needed to know if he had learned that tune, what would you do? You'd ask him to demonstrate what he has learned. You would ask him to perform. The same sort of situation exists in the college classroom.

Put simply, learning involves acquiring new information, while performance involves retrieving that information when it is needed. And justifiably or not, it is your performance—based on what you've learned—that is evaluated. Your performance, not your learning, earns your grades in the classroom, or your raise or promotion in the workplace. So to do well in a college class is a two-phase process. First you must learn the required material and then you must be able to retrieve it from memory when it is needed. In the next few pages, I'll elaborate on these general principles of learning by giving specific advice on how to get more out of class, how to use your textbook more effectively, and how to prepare for exams.

TIME MANAGEMENT FOR TODAY'S COLLEGE STUDENT

Here's a reality that causes problems for many of us: There are only 168 hours in each week. For many students, academic success is often a direct reflection of the extent to which these 168 hours are managed.

"Nontraditional" students were once thought of as students who were older, employed outside the home at least on a part-time basis, and living at home with household and family responsibilities. On many college campuses today, including my own, this description fits the majority of students. It is for this busy student, with many commitments outside the classroom, that time management is most critical.

A standard rule of thumb is the advice that one should spend three hours of study each week for every hour spent in class. Introductory psychology courses usually meet for about three hours a week, which means that the average student should begin a semester planning to *spend nine hours a week studying psychology*—in addition to going to class! Most of my students laugh when I tell them about this rule of thumb, but they also recognize that if they did study that much, they would have no trouble doing well in my class.

If you want to succeed as a college student, you have to schedule time (and a place) for studying as surely as you schedule time for sleep, meals, your job, taking out the trash, or driving the kids to their soccer games. In the process, don't forget what I've already said about distributing study time in small chunks rather than in large blocks.

One area of time management over which you have significant control is the number of classes in which you enroll each term. Here's what I tell my academic advisees: "Take your time. Enroll only in the number of classes you honestly feel that you can handle. Some day you will graduate, and no one—potential employer or graduate school committee, for example—is going to ask you how long it took for you to graduate. What they probably will ask you is how well you did—they'll ask about your grades. It seems to me much more reasonable to take 6 or 7 years to graduate with As and Bs than to rush through in 4 years with Cs."

GETTING THE MOST FROM THE CLASSROOM

"But I never missed a class!" is the claim instructors often hear from students who have not done well on an exam and who have not learned the difference between attending a class and taking an active part in class. The difference has a significant impact on how well students learn.

Prepare for Class

It is always easier to listen to and understand information you are familiar with than it is to listen to and try to understand totally unfamiliar information. To be sure, few lectures and class activities are designed to be about something you knew before you took the class. The material will have to be somewhat new; that is what you are paying for. But if you prepare and plan carefully, lectures and class discussions will not seem totally alien.

Once the term is under way, preparing for class will be relatively easy. You will have had time to "feel out" your instructor and develop a sense of what will be happening in class. At the very least you should have reviewed recent lecture notes and previewed the text for each meeting. Perhaps the most important thing to do is to familiarize yourself with the vocabulary that might come up in class. If you're familiar with vocabulary terms *before* you get to class, your listening for ideas and concepts will be easier because you will not have to think about new words. You will then have a chance to concentrate, to organize what is being said, and to summarize your thoughts in coherent notes.

Most good listening is a matter of attitude. To be an effective listener, you must be in the proper frame of mind. As you take your seat, you have to rid your mind of thoughts of the trivial activities of the day. You cannot do a good job of listening to a lecture if you are thinking about last night's date or this afternoon's lunch. You can't contribute to a discussion if all you want to talk about is last weekend's game. You must be thinking about psychology. Get your mind warmed up: What's the instructor going to talk about today? What contributions will you be expected to make? How will today's class fit in with what you've already learned? How can you relate this material to your own personal experience? When you find yourself totally surprised at what is being said in class, you have not prepared correctly.

Develop Your Listening Skills

Listening is an active process in which you relate what is being said to what you already have stored in your memory. It is a matter of taking in new information and organizing and storing it in such a way that it can be used again at some later time. Given the large amounts of information headed toward you in the classroom, active listening will require considerable concentration on your part.

We don't often think of it as such, but listening is a skill—one that can be developed just like bicycle riding, typing, or reading. Proficiency in listening can be increased through practice. Listening in class for new and useful information is different from listening to casual conversation or your favorite radio station. This is because a larger portion of the information will involve new or technical vocabulary, and because you will be expected to recall the information at some later time (on exams). Every time you listen in class you are practicing a basic learning skill.

In this regard, let me share with you my advice on the use of tape recorders in the classroom. I don't prohibit them in my classes, but I advise against their use. I'd rather have students force their attention and concentrate the first time around. Knowing that there's a "backup tape" can lead some students to take a lazy attitude toward listening in the first place.

Take Useful Notes

Class attendance and careful listening are important because lectures are presented to you only once. Therefore, you will need some written record of the information presented orally in class to study and review later. Good lecture notes written in your own words are as valuable as a summarized and organized compilation of classroom instruction.

There is a large body of research devoted to note-taking skills. For now, we will consider just two basic principles you can use—principles that will help you learn psychology or any other discipline.

Principle 1: Select and Organize the Material Presented to You. It will soon become apparent to you, if it isn't already, that there is no way that you can write down everything your instructor says in class. This can be an advantage. Note-taking should be an active process of selecting and organizing the information you write down. Although it generally is better to take too many notes than it is to take too few, you must be an active listener who participates in class—not just a mechanical writer.

The notes you take will be *your* notes, so put them in a form you can use. Except for technical terms and new vocabulary, use your own words. In this way, your notes will be more meaningful to you when you review them. Copying information is not learning it.

You should develop some shortcuts—alternatives to writing everything out in longhand. The key here is flexibility. Feel free to abbreviate, but only if you will be able to understand your own symbols and notes when you go back to study later. Illegible or incoherent notes are worse than useless: You have wasted valuable listening time writing them.

There will be times when it is best not to take any notes at all. Participating in a class discussion or asking questions may be most beneficial. Once again, one of the best ways to learn new material is to get involved, to work with it and make it personal.

Principle 2: Edit and Review Your Notes. Once class is over, only part of your work is done. During the class period you have been listening, selecting, organizing, participating, thinking, and writing. Now you should go back over your written record of the class. This is best accomplished in three stages.

1. Immediately after class, while the material is still fresh in your mind, review your notes, fill in gaps, underline for emphasis, note unclear sections that will require further work, and use the margins in your notebook to add information you simply did not have time to record.
2. Several times a week, as part of your study for each course, continue the editing process. Use your textbook, other notes, outside readings, or consult with your instructor for correct spellings, missing details, and the like.
3. An important stage in reviewing your notes should occur after each examination in a course. Go back and critically evaluate your own notes. To what extent did they help? How can they be improved? Did you write too much? Too little? Was the format the best one possible?

GETTING THE MOST FROM YOUR TEXTBOOK

For any class you take, you will find that there is more information stored in your textbook than could ever be presented in class. Since this is the case, learning how to get information from your text is one of the most important skills you can acquire in college. This is not to devalue the role of your instructor or class attendance. Instructors update text material, interject personal experience and points of view, and emphasize what they believe to be the most important sections of assigned readings. Here are a few general ideas to guide your study.

Prepare for Textbook Study

Because textbook study is so important, you should develop expectations about the material in each chapter by reading the chapter preview, skimming the summary, and glancing at the headings, subtitles, and illustrations. Before you actually begin reading/studying the text, you should have a series of questions in mind. If nothing else, you should begin each chapter by asking questions such as: "What in the world is *this* all about?" "How can this be of any use to me?" "How can I relate any of this to what I already know?" "Where is this material going to show up on our next classroom exam?" In order to help you frame such questions, we begin each chapter in this text with a complete, detailed **Chapter Outline** and a chapter **Preview**.

Don't Read Your Textbook the Way You Read Other Books

Perhaps the most significant insight about textbook study is that it is very different from casual reading. Reading a chapter is not studying a chapter. Studying is a process in which you must become actively and personally involved. Studying a text requires a great deal more concentration and mental effort than does reading for pleasure. What is the author trying to say? What are the major ideas? What evidence supports those ideas? What are the minor points? How can the material be related to what you already know from personal experience, previous reading, or classroom lectures? How will this information show up on a test?

There are times when you should look up from the book, pause, and think about what you have just read. You should be able to quickly summarize the material in your own words, which is why **Before You Go On** questions are included within each chapter of this book. If you cannot answer these questions, there is little point in going further. Go back over the section you've just read. Speed may be fine, but speed without comprehension is a waste of time.

Effective textbook study is a skill that can be learned by anyone, but it will not be learned automatically. It takes hard work and practice to develop textbook study skills. The rewards for your work, however, will be almost immediate.

Make Textbook Study an Active Process

There is no doubt that you must be mentally active and alert while studying so you can search, question, and think. This text and its accompanying Study Guide have been designed to facilitate active studying. *If you have not done so yet, please go back now and read the section of the Preface titled "Features of this Text."*

Underlining or highlighting in textbooks has become a common practice. Unfortunately, it often is misused. The purpose of underlining is to emphasize particular passages of the text so essential points can be reviewed by simply restudying underlined passages. The mistake that many students make is to underline too much: When 80 percent of a page is underlined for emphasis, the remaining 20 percent usually appears more striking.

You can increase the value of your textbook for studying by using the margins of the text for your personal notations. Make your text a storehouse of references. Cross-reference textbook material with information in your notes. If it's your book, use it—write in it.

PREPARING FOR EXAMS

Few occasions are quite as pleasant as the one you experience when you walk into class to take a big exam, fully prepared, confident that you know the material and that you are going to do well. I also know from personal experience just how miserable it feels to face an exam unprepared, doomed before you begin, unable to understand—much less answer—the first question. The key lies in being prepared. Proper preparation for exams helps to furnish the kind of positive reinforcement that education is meant to provide, but it isn't easy. You'll have to schedule your time, test your progress, and engage in continuous, active review.

Rule 1: Prepare on a Daily Basis—Don't Cram

This rule is a simple restatement of a point I made earlier about the value of spaced or distributed practice.

In almost every case, you will be notified of upcoming tests or examinations well in advance. Often, scheduled exams are noted on the course outlines handed out on the first day of class. Most of your exams should come as no surprise to you. The secret to good exam performance is that daily preparation is needed.

To be truthful, preparing daily isn't an easy task. It's difficult to sit down today to study for an exam that's three weeks away. With so much time before the exam, it seems that there will be plenty of opportunity for studying later.

On the other hand, daily preparation is not all that special. It involves the sort of things I mentioned above. Preparing for and carefully listening in class is daily preparation, as are taking good notes and editing and reviewing them soon after class. A crucial step in preparing for exams is to make a complete, realistic schedule. If you study your textbook on a regular basis, you won't even have to consider cramming for exams.

Rule 2: Find Ways to Test Yourself

As examination day approaches, you will want some indication of just how well your studying has been progressing. To be most effective, this self-testing should begin well in advance of any examination date. There are many techniques for evaluating your own achievement, all of which involve constructing, taking, and "grading" your own test on assigned material before your instructor does. For example, if you think that you may have to identify the important structures of the eye, try to draw a picture of one, labeling all of the structures you can think of, and then check your drawing with the one in your book. If you know that your next exam will ask for the definitions of new terms and concepts, see how many you can write out on your own.

Again, you should find two features of this text helpful: the **Before You Go On** questions, which follow every major section of every chapter, and the **Test Yourself** sections, which are found at the end of each chapter.

I am convinced that self-testing is the best thing you can do to prepare for classroom exams. Perhaps I'm soft-hearted, but I tend to believe those students who come to me after a test and say—with teary eyes and quivering lips—"But I read the book, over and over. I know the material." They probably did read the book over and over. They probably did learn a lot of psychology in the process, and that is certainly a good thing. But classroom tests do not measure what you have learned. They measure what you can remember. Students often spend too much time putting information into memory, and too little time getting information out of memory, which is what is being tested.

Imagine that you have just finished studying the section on the history of psychology in Chapter 1 of this book. I'd like to think that that material is presented clearly and in a form that is easy to understand. Let's say you agree. Having read this section, you can honestly say to yourself, "I understand all that. I appreciate some of psychology's history. I learned something." Now comes the crucial part in which you have to ask yourself, "How is this going to show up on the classroom exam?" You've got at least three things you can do: (1) You can check the **Test Yourself** sections at the end of each chapter; (2) you can check the **Student Study Guide** to see how it tests the material you've just read; or (3) you can pretend that you are the instructor and make up your own practice items. This last option actively involves you in the process of exam preparation, even though it takes time to develop the skill of writing test items.

Rule 3: Strengthen Learning with Review

If you have maintained a schedule of daily preparation and have consistently evaluated your own performance, you should be able to approach examination day with confidence. There is no way that everything you'll need to know for an exam can be assimilated the night before. You simply cannot understand and digest large amounts of material hours before an exam. However, it is well worth your time to review the material that is to be on the exam. To review means "to look at again." You should certainly review just before an exam. A more helpful procedure is to review on a regular basis throughout the term. You should be constantly reviewing what you've learned. Research evidence and common sense tell us that most forgetting occurs soon after learning. Frequent review, however, can improve retention significantly.

A Final Word on Exam-Taking

When you take an exam, you are being asked to perform on the basis of what you have learned. Although the effects of anxiety on learning are subtle, the effects of anxiety on performance are well known. Your performance will be poor if you become overly anxious, upset, and uptight—even if you have learned the material reasonably well. Just realizing that anxiety may reduce your efficiency does little to help. Anxiety is very difficult to eliminate by sheer force of willpower. The most effective way to reduce anxiety is to deal with its cause. If you have conscientiously applied yourself to the job of preparing for an exam, you should have reduced—if not eliminated—the most common cause of test anxiety. If being overly nervous about taking exams becomes a source of concern for you, consider talking to someone in the counseling center, learning lab, or psychology department who can help you with this problem. (We'll discuss related issues in Chapter 11 when we bring up strategies for dealing with stress.)

WHAT ABOUT THE "SQ3R" METHOD?

In this last section, I want to take the ideas we have been talking about and recast them in a slightly different way. Nearly half a century ago a teacher named Francis Robinson described a strategy for studying that he called the SQ3R Method. The method is highly recommended for two reasons: (1) It is simple; (2) it works. Although you are sure to recognize that there is nothing new here, thinking about your studying in this way may be helpful. SQ3R can be rewritten S-Q-R1-R2-R3. All we have to do is to see what these letters stand for.

S = Survey. The idea here is to anticipate what you are about to study by looking ahead, reading the chapter outline, the chapter Preview, skimming the Summary, and quickly glancing through the chapter. You should try to get an overview of what is going to come up during your reading and studying.

Q = Question. As you might have guessed, this is the one point of the five in the list that I feel is most important. The idea is to continually ask yourself questions about what you are reading. If nothing else, stop from time to time and ask what I call *The Universal Study Question:* "Whaaa?"—in the sense of: "What did I just read about?" As it happens, you get considerable help in this book because we're going to keep asking you questions in the **Before You Go On** sections.

R1 = Read. Once you've surveyed and questioned, the time has come to get to it and read the text. Remember: Don't try to sit down and read the entire chapter from beginning to end. Go for smaller sections and space or distribute your practice.

R2 = Recite. We usually think of reciting in terms of performing out loud, as in a "recital." In this instance, you needn't be so literal. The basic idea is to "talk to yourself" about what you're reading. Having surveyed the chapter, you've formed some questions and are now reading the chapter. By "recite" we mean that the time has come to answer those questions. Really. Go ahead and try to answer the **Before You Go On** questions, for example. Yes, in this book answers to **Before You Go On** questions are provided in the **Summary**. But don't just turn back there and read MY answer. Try to provide an answer on your own first.

R3 = Review. See, we *have* been through all this, haven't we? By review, Robinson meant what we meant when we talked about reviewing earlier. You should plan to schedule time to go back over your notes and the text, testing yourself anew each time. Just because you "knew" the answer to a question yesterday doesn't mean that you know it today. To find out: review.

WHAT PSYCHOLOGISTS DO

PREVIEW

TOPIC 1A—A Working
Definition Of Psychology

What is Psychology?

Psychological Approaches
Past and Present

*PSYCHOLOGY IN THE
REAL WORLD: What
Psychologists Do*

TOPIC 1B—The Research
Methods Of Psychology

Observational Methods in
Psychology

Correlational Methods in
Psychology

Experimental Methods in
Psychology

Ethics in Psychological
Research

Important Themes and
General Principles

THINKING CRITICALLY
ABOUT WHAT
PSYCHOLOGISTS DO

SUMMARY

TEST YOURSELF

"Why do I feel this way?" "Why did he do that?" "How can she possibly believe anything so strange?" Questions such as these occur to us regularly. Concerns about feelings, behaviors, and thoughts have challenged theologians and philosophers for thousands of years. Since the nineteenth century these issues have been at the center of the science of psychology. In Chapter 1, our aim is to describe the essential nature of this young science.

Topic 1A begins by generating a working definition of psychology. In this Topic, we'll take a brief look at some of the major events and contributors to its past, for psychology did not just spring forth, full-blown, a few years ago. By examining a bit of its history, we can better appreciate psychology as we know it today. Among other things, we'll note how the definition of psychology has changed over the past 100 years.

In many ways, Topic 1B also deals with our definition of psychology. In this Topic we'll take a closer look at the methods that psychologists use as they try to understand their subject matter. As we shall see, most of the questions of today's psychologists are ancient questions. What sets psychology apart from other approaches are the methods that psychologists use to answer those questions. To consider methodology is to get at the heart of what makes psychology psychology.

This chapter ends with a discussion of some of the abiding themes that have been central to psychology throughout the years. These themes are overarching areas of concern and interest in psychology and will be interwoven throughout the rest of our discussion.

TOPIC 1A

A WORKING DEFINITION OF PSYCHOLOGY

In the following chapters we'll explore in detail questions about our emotions, our motivations, our sexuality, and our development. We will consider the psychological disorders and see how they can be treated and we will see psychology applied in the classroom, business settings, athletics, and in social situations. We'll come to understand how we process information through the interrelated processes of sensation, perception, learning, and memory. But we should start at the beginning and generate a definition of psychology in general terms.

WHAT IS PSYCHOLOGY?

Psychology is the science of behavior and mental processes. This is a common definition—one that millions of psychology students before you have committed to memory. If there is a problem with this definition, it's that it is somewhat sterile; it doesn't tell us very much about what psychologists actually study or how they go about it. We'll need the rest of this book to fill in the details and make this definition more meaningful. Before we go on, let's see what it means to say that psychology is a science that studies behavior and mental processes.

psychology
the scientific study of behavior and mental processes

Psychology Is a Science—A Science with Practical Application

There are many ways to find out about ourselves and the world in which we live. Some of what we believe we have taken as a matter of faith ("There is a God"—or "There isn't."). Some understanding has come through tradition, passed on from previous generations, accepted simply because "they said it is so." Some of what we believe we credit to "common sense" ("You beat a dog often enough and sooner or later it will get mean."). Some of the insights that we have about ourselves and the human condition we have taken from art, literature, poetry, and drama. Psychologists, however, claim that there is a better way to understand its subject matter: by applying the values and methods of science.

We can define a **science** as an organized body of knowledge gained by the application of scientific methods. So to qualify as a science, a discipline has to demonstrate two things: (1) an organized body of knowledge and (2) the use of scientific methodology.

Over the years, psychologists have learned a great deal about their subject matter. To be sure, we can still ask interesting and important questions for which there are no good answers. Not having all the answers can be frustrating at times, but that is part of the excitement of psychology; there are still so many questions to be answered. The truth is, however, that psychologists do know a lot, and what is known is reasonably well organized. You have in your hands one version of the organized collection of knowledge that is psychology.

What we know in psychology we have learned through the application of **scientific methods**, a series of systematic approaches to problem solving that involve observation, description, control, and replication. To explain something scientifically is often a matter of ruling out alternative explanations. Science is a way of approaching problem solving. Science is "a process of inquiry, a particular way of thinking," not a carefully delineated set of specific procedures (Graziano & Raulin, 1993, p. 2).

The basic process goes something like this: The scientist (psychologist) makes observations about her or his subject matter. [Perhaps you notice that some students get better grades on psychology tests than do others and that there seems to be a relationship between where students sit and the grades they get.] On the basis of one's observations, a hypothesis is formed. A **hypothesis** is a tentative explanation of a phenomenon that can be tested and then supported or rejected. In a way, a hypothesis is an educated guess about one's subject matter. [You may hypothesize that intelligent, well-motivated students tend to sit as close to the front of a classroom as they can.]

science
an organized body of knowledge gained through application of scientific methods

scientific methods
a series of systematic approaches to problem solving, including observation, description, control, and replication

hypothesis
a tentative explanation of a phenomenon that can be tested and then either supported or rejected

"Well, you don't look like an experimental psychologist to me."

Drawing by Sam Gross; © 1994 The New Yorker Magazine, Inc.

The scientist observes relevant events again. These observations are then analyzed to see if the original hypothesis was well founded. Alternative hypotheses or explanations are also examined. [You might see if you can find IQ test scores (or SAT scores, or grade-point averages) for the students in your class, and then keep careful records of where students choose to sit. If students in the front of the room do earn high test grades, is there any other way to explain your observations?] The results of one's investigation are then shared with others who may test them further. [Do smart, well-motivated students tend to sit near the front in other classes, or at other campuses?]

A scientific hypothesis may be rejected or it may be supported, but it cannot be "proven" as true. This is because no matter how much support one finds for one's hypothesis, there may be other hypotheses (as yet unthought of) that will do a better job of explaining an observed phenomenon. "Scientists may have confidence in their explanations, but are nonetheless willing to entertain the possibility that their explanations are faulty" (Bordens & Abbott, 1991, p. 4).

Although all psychologists are scientists, most are what we call *scientist-practitioners*. This means that they are not as interested in formulating hypotheses and making new observations about behaviors and mental processes as they are in *applying* what is already known. Of those psychologists who are practitioners, most are clinical or counseling psychologists. Their goal is to apply what we know to help people deal with problems that are affecting their ability to adjust to the demands of their environments. Some scientist-practitioners apply psychological principles to issues that arise in the workplace; these are industrial/organizational (I/O) psychologists. Psychological practitioners can be found in many settings, dealing with a myriad of issues. Some attempt to improve the performance of athletes; some advise attorneys on how best to present arguments in the court room; some intervene to reduce prejudice; some establish programs to increase the use of automobile safety belts; some help people train their pets—the list goes on.

I hope that you recognize that the science and the practice of psychology are *not* mutually exclusive endeavors. For one thing, many psychologists who are practicing clinical, counseling, or industrial/organizational psychologists *are* active scientific researchers. Much of the scientific research in psychology gets its initial spark from problems that arise in real world applications of psychology (Hoshmand & Polkinghorne, 1992).

● **Before You Go On**

Why may we make the claim that psychology is a science?
What are scientist-practitioners in psychology?

What Psychologists Study: The Subject Matter of Psychology

Skimming through the pages of this book should convince you that trying to list everything that psychologists study would not be very instructive. Such a list would be much too long to be useful. However, it *is* fair to suggest, as our definition does, that the subject matter of psychology is behavior and mental processes. Let's explore a bit more fully just what that means.

Psychologists study **behavior**: what organisms do; their actions, reactions, and responses. The behaviors of organisms are observable and—potentially—can be measured. If I am concerned with whether a rat will press a lever under some circumstance, I can observe its behavior directly. If I wonder about Susan's ability to draw a circle, I can ask her to do so, and observe her efforts. Observable, measurable behaviors such as lever-pressing and circle-drawing have an advantage as the subject matter of a science because they are *publicly verifiable*. In other words, several observers (public) can agree on (verify) the behavior of the organism being studied. We can all agree that the rat did or did not press the lever or that Susan drew a circle, not a triangle.

When psychology first emerged as a separate discipline late in the nineteenth century, it was defined as the science of *mental processes*, or the science of consciousness. There are two types of mental processes: cognitions and affect. **Cognitions** are mental processes such as perceptions, beliefs, thoughts, ideas, and the like. Cognitive processes include activities such as perceiving, thinking, understanding, and remembering. **Affect** (aff'-ekt) refers to mental processes involving one's feelings, mood, or emotional state.

Here we have a scheme that we will encounter repeatedly: The *ABC*'s that comprise the subject matter of psychology. That is, psychology is the science of **A**ffect, **B**ehavior, and **C**ognition. To understand someone at any given time, or to predict what one will do next, we have to understand what he or she is feeling (A), doing (B), and thinking (C).

In general terms, we say that psychologists study what organisms (not just people, of course) do, how they feel, and what they think. Psychologists often find it useful, and occasionally find it necessary, to define their subject matter in terms of the operations they use to measure it. When they do

behavior
what an organism does; its actions, reactions, and responses

cognitions
the mental processes that include knowing, perceiving, thinking, and remembering

affect
mental processes involving one's feelings, mood, or emotional state

operational definition
a definition of a concept given in terms of the methods or procedures used to measure or create that concept

so, they are using operational definitions. **Operational definitions** define concepts in terms of the procedures used to measure or create them. Let's look at a few examples.

Let's say we are interested in the conditions under which a rat turns left, rather than right, in a maze (see Figure 1.1). It seems like a relatively simple matter to determine the direction that a rat turns in a maze. But exactly what will constitute a turn? Will sticking its nose around the corner be taken as a turn? What if it gets most of its body around the corner and then scoots back? Does the rat's tail have to make it all the way around? As silly as it sounds, you may have to operationally define a turn in the maze by specifying just how you intend to measure it.

What if we wanted to compare the behaviors of hungry and nonhungry rats in the same maze? How do we know when a rat is hungry? What do we mean by a "hungry rat"? We can offer an operational definition, specifying that—at least for the purposes of our study—a hungry rat is one that has been deprived of food for 24 hours. (We may also operationally define a hungry rat as one that has lost 15 or 20 percent of its normal body weight.)

Operational definitions do have their limits. They may oversimplify truly complex concepts. For example, we might operationally define intelligence in terms of how we are going to measure it—with some psychological test. Surely there is more to what we mean by intelligence than a score on a single test. On the other hand, operational definitions specify how we are going to measure the behavior or mental process we are studying, helping us communicate clearly with others. We will see many examples of operational definitions in this text.

● **Before You Go On**

What is the subject matter of psychology?
What are operational definitions?

PSYCHOLOGICAL APPROACHES PAST AND PRESENT

No two psychologists approach their subject matter in exactly the same way. They bring their own experiences, expertise, values, biases, and prejudices to the study of behavior and mental processes. This is true today, and it always has been the case. In this section we can add to our appreciation of what psychologists do by considering some of the major approaches that have evolved throughout its history.

Psychology's Roots in Philosophy and Science

Psychology did not suddenly appear full-blown as the productive enterprise that we know today. The roots of psychology can be found in both philosophy and science.

We credit philosophers for suggesting that it is reasonable and potentially profitable to seek explanations of human behaviors at a human level. Most of the earliest explanations of human behaviors tended to be at the level of God—or the gods. If someone were smarter than you, well, it was

FIGURE 1.1
A rat moves down a simple T-maze. Determining whether this rat turns left or right in the maze may necessitate operationally defining what we mean by turn.

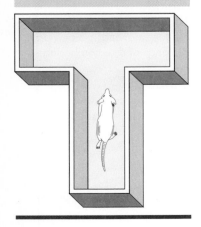

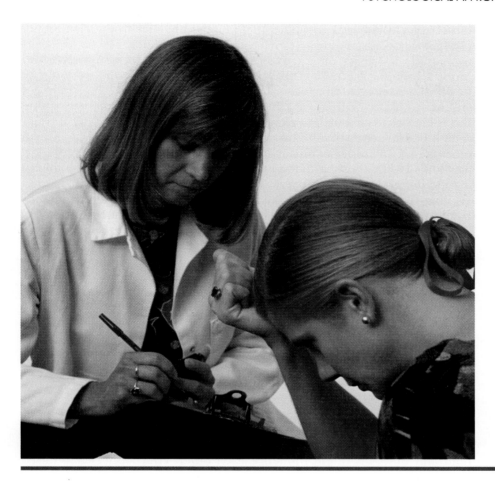

Because we cannot observe a person's intelligence directly, we may choose to define intelligence operationally as "that which an IQ test measures."

because God willed it that way. If someone suffered fits of terrible depression that could not be attributed to any obvious cause, it was because he or she had offended the gods. What a few philosophers did was to convince us that we might be able to explain why people felt, did, and thought as they did without reference to God's intentions in the matter.

The French philosopher René Descartes (1596–1650) provides a good example. Descartes liked to think about the nature of thinking. As he "lay abed of a morning thinking," he wondered how his body and mind functioned to produce the very process he was then engaged in—thinking. Descartes envisioned the human body to be rather like a piece of machinery—intricate and complicated, to be sure, but machinery nonetheless. If the body was composed essentially of tubes and gears and valves and fluids, then its operation must be subject to natural physical laws, and those laws could and should be discovered.

Descartes went further. Humans possess more than just a body; each has a mind. He thought it likely that the human mind functions in accord with the actions of knowable laws, but getting at *these* laws would be more difficult. Here's where Descartes had a truly important insight: we *can* learn about the mind, and the laws under which it operates, because the mind and the body *interact* with each other. We call Descartes's position **interactive dualism**: "dualism" because the mind and the body are separate entities, and "interactive" because each influences the other. Thus we have with

interactive dualism
Descartes's position that a separate body and mind influence each other and are thus knowable

René Descartes the real possibility that we might be able to understand the mind, how it works, and how it interacts with the body.

Nearly 100 years later, across the English Channel a group of British thinkers brought the part of philosophy concerned with the workings of the mind very close to what was soon to become psychology. This group got its start from the writings of John Locke (1632–1704). Locke was sitting with some friends after dinner one evening discussing philosophical issues when it became clear that no one in the group really knew how the human mind comes to understand anything, much less complex philosophical questions. Locke thought that by their next meeting he would be able to provide the group with a short description of the nature of human understanding. What was to have been a simple exercise took Locke many years to complete and gave philosophers a whole new set of ideas to ponder.

One of Locke's major concerns was how we come to represent the world "out there" in the internal world of the mind. Others (including Descartes) had also asked this question, and many assumed that we are born with certain (God-given) basic ideas—notions about ourselves, the world, and, of course, God. John Locke thought otherwise. He believed that we were born into the world with our minds quite empty, like blank slates. (The mind as a blank slate, or *tabula rasa,* was not new to Locke; it had been introduced as far back as Aristotle (384–322 B.C.).) So how *does* the mind come to be filled with all its ideas, thoughts, and memories? To this question Locke answered: "In one word, from *experience.*" Locke, and those who followed his initiative, are known as **British empiricists**, *empiricists* being those who credit experience and observation as the source of mental life.

British empiricists
philosophers (including Locke) who claimed, among other things, that the contents of the mind come from experience

Philosophers had gone nearly to the brink. Attention had been focused on the mind: how it worked, what contents it held, where those contents (ideas) came from, how ideas could be manipulated, and how the mind and the body might influence each other. Philosophers had raised some intriguing questions. Could the methods of science provide answers to the philosophers' questions?

During the nineteenth century, natural science was progressing on every frontier. By the middle of the century, Charles Darwin (1809–1882) had returned from his lengthy sea voyage on the *Beagle.* In 1859, he published *The Origin of Species,* which reported observations from his trip and spelled out the details of evolution. Few nonpsychologists would ever have as much influence on psychology. What Darwin did was to confirm that the human organism was part of the natural world of animals, special through no particular divine intervention. The methods of science could and should be turned to try to understand this creature of nature called human. Darwin also made it clear that the different species of this planet are related to one another in a nearly infinite number of ways. The impact of this observation, of course, is that what we discover about the tree sloth or the ground squirrel or the rhesus monkey may enlighten us about ourselves. Another relevant point that Darwin emphasized was that of *adaptation.* Species will survive and thrive only to the extent that they can adapt to their environments.

The mid-1800s found physiologists coming to a better understanding of how the human body functions. It was known that nerves carry electrical messages to and from different parts of the body, and that the nerves serving vision are different from those that serve hearing and the other senses, and different too from those that activate muscles and glands. Of the physiologists of the nineteenth century, the one whose work is most relevant to the beginning of psychology is Hermann von Helmholtz (1821–1894). Although a physician by trade, Helmholtz's true love was science, the labora-

Late in the nineteenth century, Wilhelm Wundt (center) and his students at the University of Leipzig used scientific methods in their attempts to understand human consciousness.

tory, and research. He developed an interest in matters that were clearly psychological and performed experiments and wrote theories on how long it takes nerves to respond to stimulation, how we process information through our senses, how we experience color and discriminate among the pitches of sound, and on similar issues of a psychological nature. But in the mid-1800s psychology did not exist, at least not the formal, recognized science we know today.

By the late nineteenth century, psychology's time had come. Philosophy had become intrigued with mental processes, the origin of ideas, and the contents of the mind. Physiologists had begun to focus on the nervous system, and on sensation and perception, and were doing so using scientific methodology. Biologists were raising questions about relationships between humans and other species, and how mental processes might help us to adapt and to survive. What was needed was someone with a vision to unite these interests and these methods and to establish a separate discipline. Such a person was Wilhelm Wundt.

● **Before You Go On**

   In what way did the philosophies of Descartes and Locke pave the way for psychology?

   In what way did the science of Darwin and von Helmholtz influence the emergence of psychology?

Psychology Begins: The Early Years

It is generally claimed that psychology began in 1879 when Wilhelm Wundt (1832–1920) officially opened his laboratory at the University of Leipzig. Wundt had been trained to practice medicine and had studied physiology. At Heidelberg University he was a laboratory assistant to Helmholtz, and he also held an academic position in philosophy. Wundt was a scientist/philosopher with an interest in such psychological processes as sensation, perception, word associations, attention, and emotions.

For Wundt, psychology was the science of the mind, or of consciousness. Wundt was a scientist who left nothing to chance. His hypotheses about conscious experience were tested and retested in his laboratory under carefully controlled conditions. Wundt wanted to find out how the mind worked. He wanted to carefully and systematically describe its contents. What *are* the basic elements of mental life? What is the nature of ideas, of images, of feelings, of sensations? Because of his focus on the structure of the human mind, Wundt's variety of psychology was called **structuralism**.

structuralism
the school of psychology (associated with Wundt) interested in the elements and structure of the human mind

About the same time that Wundt's laboratory was flourishing, William James (1842–1910), an American philosopher at Harvard University, began to take issue with the sort of psychology that was being practiced in Leipzig. James did not think of himself as a psychologist, although he taught classes on the subject and in 1890 published a two-volume textbook, *Principles of Psychology*. James did agree that psychology should study the mind and consciousness. He defined psychology as "the science of mental life," a definition very similar to Wundt's. On the other hand, he thought the German-trained psychologists were off-base trying to discover the contents and structure of the human mind. James said that consciousness could not be broken down or analyzed into elements. Consciousness is dynamic, a flowing stream, personal, changing, and continuous. Psychology should concern itself with the function of the mind, not with its structure. The focus of study should be on the practical uses of the mind and mental life. In this regard, James was responding to Darwin's lead. To survive requires that members of a species adapt to the environment. How does the mind function to help an organism adapt and survive in the world?

James's practical approach to psychology found favor in North America and a new approach emerged, initially at the University of Chicago. Psychologists still focused their scientific study on the mind, but now they emphasized its utilitarian, adaptive functions. We refer to this approach as **functionalism**. Functionalist psychologists relied on experimental methods, and they introduced the study of animals to psychology—again reflecting the influence of Darwin. One of the most popular textbooks of this era was *The Animal Mind* by Margaret Floy Washburn (1871–1939), the first woman to be awarded a Ph.D. in psychology. Published in 1908, the book addressed animal consciousness and intelligence. In fact, one characteristic of functionalism was its willingness to be open to a wide range of topics—so long as they were in some way related to mental life, or adaptation, or had practical application. We can trace child, abnormal, educational, social, and industrial psychology to early functionalism.

functionalism
an early approach to psychology emphasizing the scientific study of how the mind and consciousness help an organism adapt to its environment

In those early days of psychology, societal pressures were such that getting a graduate-level education was exceedingly difficult for women, no matter how able or bright they were (Furumoto & Scarborough, 1986; Scarborough & Furumoto, 1987). Still, one woman, Mary Calkins (1863–1930), so impressed William James that he allowed her into his classes even though Harvard would not let her formally enroll. Nor would Harvard award her a Ph.D.—for which she had met all academic requirements. Mary Calkins went on to do significant experimental work on human learning and memory, and in 1905 was the first woman to be elected president of the American Psychological Association (Madigan & O'Hara, 1992).

As more and more bright young scientists were drawn to psychology, new academic departments and laboratories began to prosper throughout the United States and Canada. Scientific psychology was well under way—as the scientific study of the mind, its structures, and its functions. Such was the case until John Watson, early in the twentieth century, turned psychology's attention to the study of behavior.

● **Before You Go On**

When and where did psychology "begin" and who do we credit with formally establishing the discipline?

Briefly describe the first approaches that psychologists took toward their subject matter.

Behaviorism and Beyond

John B. Watson (1878–1958) was born on a small farm in South Carolina. After graduating from nearby Furman University, Watson enrolled as a graduate student in psychology at the University of Chicago. He had read about the new science of psychology as an undergraduate and thought that Chicago—where many leading functionalists were—would be the best place to study. He was soon disappointed. It seems that he had little sympathy for and even less talent at attempts to study consciousness with scientific methods. Even so, he stayed on as a psychology major, studying the behavior of white rats.

With his Ph.D. in hand, at the age of 29 Watson moved to Johns Hopkins University in Baltimore, where he nearly single-handedly changed the focus and definition of psychology. Watson argued that if psychology were to become a mature, productive science, it had to give up its preoccupation with the mind, consciousness, and mental activity. Psychology should concentrate on events that can be observed and measured. It should give up the study of the mind and instead study behavior—hence the name of the new approach: **behaviorism.**

Neither Watson nor the behaviorists who followed him claimed that people do not think, have feelings, or form mental images. What he did say was that such processes were not the proper subjects of scientific inquiry. Science must focus on those events that observers can measure and agree upon, and behavior fits the bill. After all, no one else can share your thoughts or your feelings. Watson argued that psychology should be as rigorously scientific as possible. He referred to behaviorism as "common sense grown articulate. Behaviorism is a study of what people do" (Watson, 1926, p. 724).

No one has epitomized the behaviorist approach more than B. F. Skinner (1904–1990). Skinner took Watson at his word and spent a long, productive career in psychology trying to demonstrate that we can predict and control the behaviors of organisms by studying relationships between their observable responses and circumstances under which those responses occur (Lattal, 1992).

Skinner simply avoided any reference to the internal states of organisms, be they rats, pigeons, or people, and concentrated on how behaviors are modified by events in the environment. Behaviorists would not address the question of why a rat turns left in a maze by talking about what the rat wanted or what the rat was thinking at the time. Rather, they would try to specify the environmental conditions (the presence of food, perhaps) under which a rat is likely to make left turns. For more than 50 years, Skinner consistently held to the view that psychology should be defined as "the science of behavior" (Skinner, 1987, 1990).

behaviorism
an approach to psychology emphasizing the overt, observable, measurable behavior of organisms

Sigmund Freud brought the psychoanalytic approach to psychology. Among other things, the approach focused interest on human instincts and the unconscious.

Now we will take a very brief look at three other approaches to psychology that are still in evidence today. We'll be referring to these approaches again throughout the rest of the text.

Psychoanalytic Psychology. Sigmund Freud (1856–1939) was a practicing physician in Vienna who became intrigued with what were then called "nervous disorders." Freud was struck by how little was known about these disorders and, as a result, chose to specialize in psychiatry.

Freud was not a laboratory scientist. Most of his insights concerning the nature of the mind came from careful observations of his patients and of himself. Freud's works were particularly perplexing to the behaviorists. As the behaviorists were arguing that psychology should turn away from the study of consciousness, here was Freud declaring that we are subject to forces of which we are not aware. Our feelings, actions, and thoughts (A, B, and C) are often under the influence of the *unconscious mind*, wrote Freud. Our behaviors are expressions of instinctive drives or strivings, not pressures of the environment, he claimed. Freud's views were clearly at odds with Watson's. This variety of psychology, which traces its origin to Sigmund Freud and emphasizes innate strivings and the unconscious mind, is called **psychoanalysis.**

psychoanalysis
an approach associated with Freud, emphasizing instinctive strivings and an unconscious level of mind

● **Before You Go On**
Briefly summarize behaviorism and psychoanalysis as approaches to psychology.

Humanistic Psychology. In many respects, the humanistic approach in psychology arose as a reaction against behaviorism *and* psychoanalysis. Its

Abraham Maslow, shown here, and Carl Rogers are two psychologists associated with humanistic psychology.

original leaders were Carl Rogers (1902–1987) and Abraham Maslow (1908–1970). **Humanistic psychologists** take the position that the individual or the self should be the central concern of psychology. It is their argument that we need to focus on the "person" in psychology. If we only attend to stimuli in the environment and overt responses to those stimuli, we're leaving the person out of the middle, which is dehumanizing. Such matters as intention, caring, concern, will, love, and hate are real phenomena, and are worthy of scientific investigation whether they can be directly observed or not. Attempts to understand people without considering such processes will be doomed. Humanistic psychologists emphasize the possibility of personal growth and achievement. To humanists, Freudian reliance on instincts as even partially responsible for human action was too controlling. Our biology notwithstanding, we are—or can be—in control of our own destinies. This approach led Maslow to develop a theory of motivation (see Topic 9A) and Rogers to develop a system of psychotherapy (see Topic 13B).

humanistic psychology an approach to psychology emphasizing the person or self as a central matter of concern

Gestalt Psychology. In the first quarter of this century, a group of German scientists began a type of psychology that was different from that of Wundt, James, Watson, Freud, or Rogers. Under the leadership of Max

Gestalt psychology
the approach to psychology that emphasized perception, in particular how we select and organize information

Wertheimer (1880–1943), this approach became known as Gestalt Psychology. **Gestalt psychology** focuses on the process of perception, concerned in particular with how we select and organize information from the outside world. "Gestalt" is one of those words that is difficult to translate into English. Roughly, it means "whole" or "totality." If you can see the big picture, if you can focus on the forest and not the individual trees, you have formed a gestalt. It was the process of perception that most intrigued the Gestalt psychologists. They argued against trying to analyze perception, or consciousness, into bits and pieces. To do so would be to destroy the essence of what was being studied. "The whole is more than the sum of its parts," they said. When we look at a drawing of a cube, we don't see lines and angles and surfaces. We combine these elements to form a whole, a gestalt, which we recognize as a cube.

● **Before You Go On**

What is the major thrust of the humanistic approach in psychology?

What does "gestalt" mean?

What area of psychology was of major concern to the Gestalt psychologists?

Modern Approaches

We've noted that when scientists are faced with a concept that is difficult to define in abstract terms, they often rely on operational definitions. Here is something of an operational definition of psychology: Psychology is what psychologists do. I'm not proposing this as a serious definition of psychology, but there is something to be said for it. One of the things that you'll be learning about in this course is the wide range of things that psychologists do. In a sense, this course and this text provide a definition of psychology. If you were to ask me what psychology is I might answer, "Everything in this book—and more." For now, we'll summarize some of the activities of contemporary psychologists. This summary is found in the section "Psychology in the Real World: What Psychologists Do" (see page 28).

TOPIC 1B

THE RESEARCH METHODS OF PSYCHOLOGY

In Topic 1A we saw that psychology is a science because it has an organized body of knowledge and it uses scientific methods to understand its subject matter, the affects, behaviors, and cognitions of organisms. Scientific methods were defined as systematic procedures of observation, description, control, and replication. Now it is time to see what this general definition means in the context of psychology. To understand what psychology is, we need to understand its research methods.

OBSERVATIONAL METHODS IN PSYCHOLOGY

Before we can explain what people do, we must first make valid observations of what people do. As it happens, there are several ways in which psychologists make observations and several steps that they can take to ensure that their observations are valid.

Naturalistic Observation

Naturalistic observation involves carefully and systematically watching behaviors as they occur naturally—without any involvement from the observer. There is a logical appeal to the argument that if you are trying to understand what organisms do in real life, you should simply watch them while they are doing it, noting their behaviors and the conditions under which those behaviors occur.

As logical as naturalistic observation may sound, it does present a few difficulties that need to be acknowledged. For one thing, if we truly want to observe people (or any other organism for that matter) acting naturally, then we must make sure they do not realize that we're watching them. As you know from your own experience, people are likely to act differently from "normal" if they think they are being watched. You may do all sorts of things in the privacy of your home that you would never do if you thought that someone was watching you.

A second potential problem is observer bias. **Observer bias** occurs when one's motives, expectations, or experiences interfere with the objectivity of the observations being made. It might be very difficult for a researcher to be objective observing children in a playschool setting if she is aware of the hypothesis under study, say, that boys are verbally more aggressive than girls. Observer bias may be a subset of gender or cultural bias. For example, men often have different visions of what constitutes "sexual harassment" than do women (Fitzgerald, 1993). One person simply pushing another might be seen as an act of violence by a person from a culture in which the crime rate is very low (e.g., Japan) but barely aggressive by a person from a culture in which the crime rate is high. One remedy is to have observers note behaviors without knowledge of the hypothesis being investigated. Another protection is to check the reliability (dependability) of observations by using several observers and relying only on those observations that are verified by a number of observers.

A third potential problem with naturalistic observation is more difficult to deal with. The behaviors that you want to observe may not be there when you are. For example, if you are interested in conformity and want to observe people conforming naturally, where would you go? Where are you likely to observe conformity happening naturally? There may be some places where conformity behaviors are more likely to occur than others. But there is no guarantee that during any particular day, week, or month, the people you are watching will provide any evidence of conformity. If you manipulate a situation so people are more likely to conform, you are no longer doing *naturalistic* observation.

Even with these potential problems, naturalistic observation has proven to be useful for providing descriptions of actual behaviors in the real world. This method cannot *explain* the behaviors being observed, but it can describe what is happening. Adequate descriptions can then give rise to hypotheses that can be tested to see if we can explain what has been observed.

naturalistic observation
carefully and systematically watching the behaviors of organisms as they occur naturally—without involvement of the observer

observer bias
the problem that occurs when the researcher's own motives, expectations, and past experiences interfere with the objectivity of observations

When studying behavior and mental processes, psychologists often find it convenient, if not necessary, to use nonhuman animals in research.

What Psychologists Do

In the real world, psychologists work in many places: colleges and universities, hospitals, mental health centers, private practice, counseling centers, government agencies, schools, business and industry, and elsewhere (and in this order). The work that psychologists do in these settings varies considerably from psychologist to psychologist. Can we provide a reasonable overview of what psychologists do?

There are over 500,000 psychologists in the world, with about half of these in the United States (Rosenzweig, 1992). The largest professional organization of psychologists, the American Psychological Association (APA), claims nearly 120,000 members, and lists over 40 divisions to which members belong (Fowler, 1992). A list of "Psychological Specialty Areas" from the APA—to use in responding to a 1993 survey—lists 236 areas in which psychologists may be employed.

For now we need only sketch a few of the areas of concern in psychology, just to give you an idea of the variety of interests that fall under the label "psychologist." This short list combines many of the APA divisions into broader categories. A danger inherent in lists like this one is that someone may infer that it provides a ranking in some order of importance. Be assured: None is intended.

Physiological/biological psychology is concerned with the interactions among bodily activity, behavior, and mental processes. This subfield is concerned with structures and functions of the brain and the role it plays in our behavior. When we ask, "Why did I do (or feel or think)

that?" psychologists who take this approach will look to physiological, genetic, and biochemical explanations.

Developmental psychology is concerned with the physical and psychological development of the individual from conception to death. Most developmental psychologists focus on the childhood years, while others attend to adolescence, adulthood, old age, or take a broader life-span approach. Developmental psychologists share interests with those in many other areas because they deal with many psychological functions: cognitive, emotional, perceptual, social, and moral development, to name just a few.

Educational/instructional psychology is devoted to a study of learning and memory and the application of what we know about these processes in real-life situations. In academic and business settings, educational and instructional psychologists often serve as consultants to improve training and educational programs.

Clinical psychology includes those whose concern is with the psychological well-being of the individual. The training of clinical psychologists provides them with the means to diagnose and treat persons with psychological disorders. Clinical psychologists usually have a Ph.D. in psychology (or a Psy.D. degree). This distinguishes them from psychiatrists, who have a medical degree (M.D.). Clinical psychology is by far the largest subfield in psychology. When combined with counseling psychology it accounts for nearly 60 percent of all psychologists.

Counseling psychology is another applied area of psychology and is much like clinical psychology. Counseling psychologists, however, tend to serve persons with less severe and less chronic disorders. They are more likely to be involved in such processes as grief counseling for disaster victims, divorce counseling, or short-term work with college students who are having adjustment problems.

Health psychology is one of the newer—and fastest growing—fields in psychology. In general, health psychologists are committed to the notion that one's physical health is (or can be) affected by psychological variables and vice versa. Finding ways to minimize behaviors that have an adverse affect on one's health is typical of the activities of the health psychologist.

Cognitive psychology includes those psychologists who investigate the basic processes of the mind: perception, learning, memory, and thinking. There are several specialty areas within cognitive psychology, for example, psycholinguists, who focus on language—how it is acquired, produced, perceived, and interpreted.

Psychometrics involves the development and use of psychological tests and the statistical interpretation of data. Psychological testing is a big business in our society, particularly in educational and business settings.

Personality psychology is the subfield that most directly seeks to identify those traits or characteristics that unite us as a species and at the same time can be used to differentiate among us. The questions asked by these psychologists are among the most basic and most difficult: What *is* human nature? To what extent are our affects, behaviors, and cognitions a reflection of our personality and to what extent do they reflect the situation in which we find ourselves?

Social psychology reflects the observation that most organisms do not and cannot live without the company of others. How the behaviors of an individual affect others, and vice versa, is the general concern of social psychology. This area also has many subfields reflecting interests in sex roles, attitudes, prejudice, conformity, group conflict, and the like.

Cultural psychology goes further, recognizing that people live in a variety of cultures and ethnic environments. The aim of cultural psychology is to examine ethnic (e.g., Caucasian-American, African-American, Native American, Hispanic-American, and so on) and cultural sources of psychological diversity (Shweder & Sullivan, 1993).

Industrial-organizational (I/O) psychology is defined largely by the work setting of the psychologist. Some I/O psychologists are concerned with marketing and advertising, some with group productivity or consumer satisfaction, some with the design of equipment, and others with personnel decisions; still others focus on helping those who suffer from the stress of the workplace.

Many psychologists would claim that they do not fit any of these categories, while others might claim that they fit two or more. The very diversity of psychology is one of the things that makes it such an exciting field.

● **Before You Go On**

What is naturalistic observation?
List some of the potential problems that can
arise with this method.

Surveys

When we want to make observations about a large number of people, we may use a survey method. Doing a **survey** amounts to asking many people the same question or set of questions. The questions may be asked in person, in a telephone interview, or in the form of a written questionnaire. Survey studies yield data that would be difficult to gather otherwise.

If we wanted to know if there were a relationship between income level and the type of automobile one drives, or television programs that one watches regularly, we could ask about these issues in a survey of a large number of people. Surveys can tell us what large portions of the population think or feel and can provide insights about preferences for products or services or political candidates. If the staff of the cafeteria on your campus really wanted to know what students preferred to eat, they could conduct a survey of a sample of the student population. Textbook publishers often survey psychology instructors to see what they would like to have included in the books that they use.

Perhaps the most critical aspect of observations made from survey data is the size and representativeness of the sample that is surveyed. A **sample** is a subset or a portion of a larger population that has been chosen for study. Those publishers who survey only instructors at small liberal arts colleges, or cafeteria managers who survey only students attending morning classes, may very easily collect information (make observations) that does not generalize to the intended population—the larger set of persons from which the sample is drawn.

Case Histories

The case history method provides yet another sort of information. In the **case history** method, one person—or a small sample of persons—is studied in depth, often over a long period of time. Using this method usually involves an intense and detailed examination of a wide range of issues. The method is retrospective, which means that we start with some given situation that exists today and go back in time to see if there is any relationship between today's state of affairs and previous experiences or events. We may use interviews or psychological tests as a means of collecting our data.

As an example, say that we are interested in Mr. X, a known child abuser. Our suspicion (hypothesis) is that Mr. X's own childhood experiences might be related to his present status as a child abuser. We talk to Mr. X at length and interview his family and his friends, trying to form some retrospective picture of Mr. X's childhood. If we find some clues—for example, Mr. X was punished with severe spankings, or he missed class at school significantly more often than other children—we may then explore the early childhood experiences of other known child abusers, looking to find common experiences that might be related to the fact that they abuse children now that they are adults.

I have always been intrigued by the choices that college students make when they decide on a major course of study (maybe because when I

survey
a means of collecting observations from a large number of subjects, usually by interview or questionnaire

sample
the portion or subset of a larger population chosen for study

case history
an intensive, usually retrospective, detailed study of one (or a few) individual(s)

started college I was a chemistry major). Why do some students major in art, while others choose mathematics or psychology? Perhaps the case history method could provide some insights about the choice of a college major. How would we proceed? We'd choose a sample of students from each major, and ask them several penetrating questions about their experiences, listening for things that all students of one major had in common, but that were different from the experiences of those who opted for other majors.

As we shall see, Freud based his theory of personality on his intensive examination of the case histories of his patients (and himself). An advantage of the case history method is that it can provide us with a wealth of detailed information about a few cases. A disadvantage is that we have to be very careful when we try to generalize our findings beyond those individuals we have chosen to study.

● **Before You Go On**

How can surveys and case history studies be used to help us understand behavior and mental processes?

CORRELATIONAL METHODS IN PSYCHOLOGY

As you know from your own experience, observations are often quite useful in their own right. How many people in the United States and Canada smoke cigarettes? What do people think about abortions performed during the first trimester of pregnancy? How do people feel about a sequel to *Jurassic Park*? They can be interesting, informative, and insightful, but observations become scientific laws only when they are consistently related to other observations. **Correlation** is a statistical procedure that we can use to assess the nature and the degree to which sets of observations are lawfully related. To say that observations are correlated is to say that they are related to each other (co-related).

Let's work through an example to see how this method works. Imagine that we are interested in whether there is a relationship—a correlation—between reading ability and performance in introductory psychology. The only difficult part of this study is coming up with acceptable operational definitions for the responses in which we are interested. How will we measure *reading ability* and *performance in introductory psychology*?

Performance in introductory psychology is easy. We'll take that to mean the total number of points earned by a student on classroom exams over the course of the semester. *Reading ability* is a little more of a challenge. What do we mean by "reading ability"? We could design a test of our own to measure behaviors that we think reflect reading ability, but it turns out that we're in luck. There are several tests of reading ability already available. We decide to use the Nelson Denny Reading Test, or the NDRT (Brown, 1973).

Now we're ready to collect some data (make our observations). We'll give a large group of students our reading test (the NDRT). Once the tests are scored we have one large set of numbers. At the end of the semester, we add up all the points earned by each of our students and we have a second set of numbers. So for each student in our study we have a pair of numbers—one indicating reading ability and one indicating performance in the psychology course.

From here on, our method is more statistical than psychological. We enter our numbers into a calculator or a computer. A series of arithmetic

correlation
a statistical technique used to determine the nature and extent of the relationship between two measured responses

FIGURE 1.2

Positive, negative, and zero correlations. (A) A graph depicting the reading test scores and semester point totals earned by 40 students. These data indicate a positive (+) correlation between the two measured responses. As reading test scores increase, so do semester point totals. (B) A graph depicting the body size and gymnastic ability of 40 students. These data indicate a negative (-) correlation between the two measured responses. As body size increases, gymnastic ability decreases. (C) A graph depicting the head sizes and grade-point averages of 40 students. These data indicate a zero (0) correlation between the two measured responses. There is no relationship between head size and grade-point average.

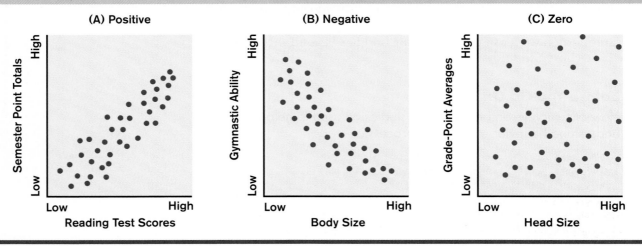

correlation coefficient
a number that indiciates the nature (+ or –) and the strength (0 to ±1) of the relationship between measured responses

procedures is applied (there are prescribed formulae for these calculations). The result of the calculations is a single number, the **correlation coefficient**—a number between –1.00 and +1.00 which tells us about the nature and the extent of the relationship between the responses we have measured. What does this number mean? How can one number be the basis for a scientific law? In truth, it takes some experience to be comfortable with the interpretation of correlation coefficients, but we can make some general observations.

First, let's deal with the sign of the correlation coefficient, which can be positive (+) or negative (–). A positive coefficient tells us that our two responses are related to each other and that high scores on one response are associated with high scores on the other. It also tells us that low scores on one measure are associated with low scores on the other. Most correlations are of this positive type—the correlation between SAT scores and grade-point averages, for example. In our example, a student who does well on the reading test will probably do well in an introductory psychology course. Those students who do poorly on the reading test are likely to earn lower grades in the psychology course. We can make these predictions if our measured responses are positively correlated and, as it happens, such is the case (Gerow & Murphy, 1980). Figure 1.2A shows what a graph of the scores from our example might look like, showing a positive correlation. This example demonstrates the major value of correlations: If we determine that two responses are correlated, we can use our observation of one response to make predictions about the other.

What if our calculations result in a correlation coefficient that is a negative (–) number? Here too we have a useful psychological law. We can still use scores of one response to predict scores of the other. But when the correlation coefficient is negative, we know that the relationship between our two measured responses is inverse, or upside down. With negative correlation coefficients, high scores on one response predict low scores on the other. If we measured body size to see if it were related to gymnastic ability, we might find a negative correlation: Large body size associated with poor gymnastic ability, and small body size (low scores) associated with good gymnastic ability (high scores). If these two sets of observations are negatively correlated, we can still use body size to predict gymnastic ability. Figure 1.2B shows data depicting the possible relationship between gymnastic ability and body size, a negative correlation.

What if our correlation coefficient turns out to be zero, or nearly so (say, .003)? In this case, we would have to conclude that the two sets of observations we have made are simply not related to each other in any consistent, lawful way. Let's say that I worked from the faulty notion that intelligence is a function of brain size, and that one's head size tells us how big a person's brain is. If I were to measure the head size of a large number of students and also measure grade point average (attempting to show a lawful relationship between grades and intelligence), I would find that the calculations for the correlation coefficient would result in a number very close to zero. As correlations approach zero, predictability decreases. Figure 1.2C completes our set of examples, showing what a graph of data from two sets of unrelated measures would look like.

So much for the sign of the correlation coefficient. What about its numerical value? Again, it takes some practice to get used to working with numbers such as −.46, +.55, and .002. For now, let us just say that the closer we get to the extremes of +1.00 or −1.00, the stronger the relationship between the responses we have measured. That is, as correlation coefficients approach +1.00 or −1.00 (say, +.84 or −.93), we have increased confidence in our ability to predict one response knowing the other. The closer our coefficient gets to zero (say, −0.12 or +0.04), the weaker the relationship and the less useful it is for making predictions. The confidence that we have in our correlations is in large part determined by how many observations are involved. In general, the larger the sample—the more observations we have made—the greater the confidence we can put in our correlation coefficient.

As you read through this text, you'll encounter many studies that use a correlational analysis of measured observations. As you do, you'll need to keep in mind two important points about correlations. (1) *Cause-and-effect conclusions are inappropriate for correlational studies.* Even if two responses are well correlated with each other, we cannot claim that one causes the other. For some reason, this point seems difficult to remember. Sometimes logic overwhelms us. It does make sense that an inability to read will actually cause some students to do poorly in an introductory psychology class, where reading is so important. Yes, it does make sense. But if all we have to guide us is the fact that reading ability and grades are correlated, we can make no statement at all about cause and effect—all we can say is that they are related. (2) *Even when two responses are well correlated with each other, we cannot make predictions for individual cases.* Again, reading ability and introductory psychology grades are positively correlated. By and large, students who read well do well in the course and students who do not read well tend to do poorly. So, in general, we can use reading test scores to predict grades, but we have to allow for exceptions. A few poor readers may do very well indeed, and a few excellent readers may still fail the course. Exceptions are to be expected. The further from +1.00 or −1.00 our correlation coefficient is, the more exceptions we can expect. Statements of correlation hold true only "generally," "in the long run," or "more often than not."

● **Before You Go On**

What data are needed to calculate a correlation coefficient?

What does a correlation coefficient tell us about the relationship between two measured responses?

EXPERIMENTAL METHODS IN PSYCHOLOGY

Most of what is known in psychology has been learned by doing experiments. **Experiments** are a set of operations used to investigate relationships between manipulated events and measured events, while extraneous events are controlled or eliminated. In the abstract that's quite a mouthful, but the actual procedures are not that difficult to understand. Like all other methods in psychology, experiments involve making observations.

The Basic Procedures

Experiments are intended to discover cause-and-effect relationships. When we do an experiment, we're no longer content to discover that two measured observations are simply related; now we want to be able to claim that—at least to some degree—one is caused by the other. To see if such a claim can be made, an experimenter manipulates one variable to see if that manipulation causes changes in another variable. A variable is simply something that can vary—a measurable event that can take on different values. Experimental methods are described in terms of variables.

The events or conditions that an experimenter manipulates are called **independent variables**. Events or conditions that the experimenter measures are **dependent variables**—their value should *depend* on the experimenter's manipulation of independent variables. The hope is that the manipulation of the independent variable will cause predictable changes in the dependent variable—changes predicted by one's hypothesis. Now, if there are changes in the measured dependent variable, the experimenter would like to claim that these changes are due solely to the influence of the manipulated independent variable. In order to make this claim, it must be shown that all other variables that could have influenced what is being measured have been controlled or eliminated. Those factors that need to be eliminated from an experimental situation so as not to influence the dependent variable are called **extraneous variables** (extraneous means "not essential" or "irrelevant"). So to do an experiment, one manipulates independent variables, measures dependent variables, and eliminates, or controls, the effects of extraneous variables. If you have not encountered this before, please don't be discouraged. It's not as confusing as it sounds—a couple of examples will help.

After a few quizzes in your biology class, you notice that the student sitting in front of you is consistently scoring higher than you are—not by much, but by enough to be aggravating. You ask this student how she does it, and she tells you that she has a system she learned in high school. To remember a series of otherwise unrelated concepts, she weaves the terms together to form some sort of story. Recalling the story is relatively easy, and can be used to help her recall terms for her quizzes. This sounds sensible to you, and you decide to do an experiment to see if there is a cause-and-effect relationship here (a decision made by Gordon Bower and M. C. Clark, who did such an experiment in 1969).

experiment
a series of operations used to investigate relationships between manipulated events (independent variables) and measured events (dependent variables), while other events (extraneous variables) are controlled or eliminated

independent variables
events in an experiment that are manipulated by the experimenter that are hypothesized to produce changes in responses

dependent variables
responses measured in an experiment whose values are hypothesized to depend upon manipulations of the independent variable

extraneous variables
factors in an experiment that need to be minimized or eliminated so as not to affect the relation between the independent and the dependent variable

You get some volunteers from your introductory psychology class and divide them into two groups. One group (A) is asked to memorize a list of ten unrelated nouns. They are left on their own to learn the list. The other group (B) is asked to memorize the very same list of nouns, but they are told about the scheme of tying the words together to form a meaningful story and are asked to try to use this strategy in learning the list.

Now let's get our terminology in here. Your hypothesis is that how people go about memorizing has an effect on how much they remember. You have manipulated this process, so using or not using a strategy in memorizing is your *independent variable*. You believe this variable will have an effect on memory. How will you measure this to see if it is so? What will be your *dependent variable*? You ask all students to return three weeks later. At that time you ask them to "write down as many of the words as you can recall from the list you learned here three weeks ago." Thus, you operationally define your dependent variable to be the average number of words recalled after a three-week interval. When you look at your data you discover that, on the average, group A recalls 3.5 of the original ten, and group B (those who made up a story) recalls 8.2 words correctly. It seems that a story-generating strategy is useful in memorizing words. That strategy seems to cause better recall.

Before we get too carried away, we had better consider the *extraneous variables* that might have been operating in this experiment. These are factors that might have affected the average recall of our two groups of students—over and above the memorization strategy (such factors should have been considered before the experiment actually began, of course). What extraneous variables might be involved in this experiment? For one thing, we need to be certain that the students in our two groups are of essentially the same ability to begin with. It would not do if the students in group A were below average, struggling students, while those in group B were honor students. Both groups of learners should be given the same materials to be learned, and the words should be presented in the same way to both groups.

The short of it is—and this is a very important point—when we are done with our experiment and find differences in our dependent variable, we want to be able to claim that these differences are due to our manipulation of the independent variable, and to nothing else. It is the extent to which extraneous variables are anticipated and eliminated that determines the quality of an experiment. Figure 1.3 reviews the steps in our example experiment.

Let's consider another potentially experimental question. Suppose you believe (hypothesize) that a stimulating environment in early childhood improves intellectual functioning at adolescence. You propose to do an experiment to test your hypothesis with two groups of young children. One group will be raised for three years in a very stimulating environment filled with toys and games, bright wallpaper and pictures in the nursery, and many adults around every day. The other group of children will be reared in isolation, in quiet, empty rooms, with only their basic biological needs attended to. Wait a minute! This sort of experimental manipulation is unethical and would be out of the question. You wouldn't isolate and deprive a group of children this way—particularly if your hypothesis is that doing so has negative consequences.

Although there are several alternatives, this problem provides a good example of an experiment that could be done with rats. Rats could be raised in cages that provide differing amounts of stimulation. When the

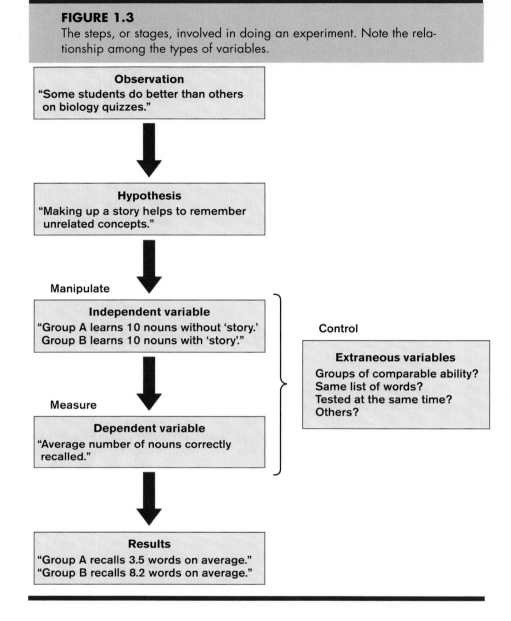

FIGURE 1.3
The steps, or stages, involved in doing an experiment. Note the relationship among the types of variables.

Observation
"Some students do better than others on biology quizzes."

↓

Hypothesis
"Making up a story helps to remember unrelated concepts."

↓

Manipulate

Independent variable
"Group A learns 10 nouns without 'story.' Group B learns 10 nouns with 'story'."

↓

Measure

Dependent variable
"Average number of nouns correctly recalled."

Control

Extraneous variables
Groups of comparable ability?
Same list of words?
Tested at the same time?
Others?

↓

Results
"Group A recalls 3.5 words on average."
"Group B recalls 8.2 words on average."

rats approach maturity, you could test their ability to negotiate mazes or learn a variety of responses. Early exposure to stimulation would be the independent variable, and scores on tests of learning ability would be the dependent variable.

One advantage of using rats in experiments is that extraneous variables are usually easy to deal with. You seldom have to be concerned with past experience, inherited differences, parental influences, and the like (all your rats have a known and very similar genetic history and have been raised under very similar conditions). The problem with using rats is obvious. Even if you do demonstrate your point with rats, you must then argue that the data you have collected for rats is applicable to humans. As we'll see, however, in many cases this argument is not difficult to make, and with the advantage of ease of control, we can see why the use of nonhuman organisms in psychology is commonplace.

Now that we've covered the basic procedures involved in experiments, we can examine in a little more detail some of the considerations that often determine the quality of an experimental method.

● **Before You Go On**

What is the essence of doing an experiment?

Define independent, dependent, and extraneous variables in the context of an experiment.

Exercising Control

The value of an experimental finding depends on the researcher's ability to eliminate or control the influence of extraneous variables. The most difficult extraneous variables to deal with are often those involving the past experience of the subjects. This was the case in our example experiment on a memorizing strategy. In designing an experiment, a common practice is to manipulate the independent variable by presenting one group of subjects with a treatment (such as a hint about how to memorize a list of words) while withholding that treatment from another group. Subjects in both groups are then tested for any effect. By definition, subjects who receive some treatment—the independent variable—make up the **experimental group**. An experiment may have several experimental groups; our example used just one. Subjects who do not receive an experimental treatment are in a **control group**. Experiments usually have one control group; in our example, this was Group A, the students who received no hint about how to memorize the words.

Controlling extraneous variables, then, is often a matter of making sure that control and experimental groups begin an experiment on an equal footing. How could you do that? You could try to match the groups on the variable of interest. In our example, you might have done this by giving all of your subjects a recall test before the experiment and then assigning them to Group A or Group B so that the average scores on this test were close to equal.

A more common technique would be to place subjects into groups by **random assignment**, which means that each participant in the research has an equal chance of being assigned to any one of the groups that you are using. If assignment is truly random, then honor students would be equally likely to be in either of the groups—the one that does or the one that does not get a hint about weaving the words into a story. But remember, matching or randomly assigning is something that must be considered before the experiment is actually begun.

Another method for controlling the differing past experiences of subjects is called a **baseline design**, which amounts to arranging your experiment so that all participants serve in both the control and the experimental conditions. Imagine, for example, that you wished to determine if a certain drug causes a decrease in the reaction time required for a subject to respond to a signal. Using a baseline design, you would first measure the reaction time of persons without giving them the drug (a baseline measure). Then you'd check the reaction times of the same persons after they were given the drug. Changes in reaction time (your dependent variable) could be attributed to the drug (your independent variable). You would then check the subjects' reaction times again, after the effects of the drug wear off, to see if the time it takes to respond to the signal behavior returns to its baseline.

experimental group
participants in an experiment who receive a treatment or manipulation—there may be more than one in an experiment

control group
participants in an experiment who do not receive any experimental treatment or manipulation

random assignment
the selection of members of a population in such a way that each has an equal opportunity to be assigned to any group

baseline design
a method in which participants' performance with an experimental treatment is compared with performance without that treatment (the baseline)

Naturalistic observation requires skill and great patience. The observer here is using a night vision lens to look for frogs as tape recorders play the frogs' mating call.

● **Before You Go On**

How do random assignment and baseline designs help minimize error in psychological experiments?

ETHICS IN PSYCHOLOGICAL RESEARCH

Ethical and moral concerns affect all the sciences. In most sciences, ethical issues center on the application of knowledge. We know how to split the atom; should we build a bomb? We can manufacture effective insecticides; should we use them? We have the means to render people infertile; should we? We can use machinery to keep people alive indefinitely; should we? We can bury toxic or radioactive waste; where should we?

Psychology has something of a unique problem with regard to ethics. To be sure, ethical considerations are important in the application of knowledge, be it in diagnosis, therapy, counseling, training, or whatever. (We'll deal with these in later chapters.) What is different about psychology is that ethics are often central in the *gathering* or accumulation of information. After all, the objects of study are living organisms. Their physical and psychological welfare must be protected as we investigate their behaviors and mental processes. Psychologists have recognized the ethical implications of their work for a long time. The American Psychological Association regularly revises its *Ethical Principles of Psychologists* for practitioners and researchers alike (the most recent version was published in 1992). We'll deal briefly with a few of the issues these guidelines address with regard to research.

As one plans his or her research, the degree to which subjects will be put at risk should be assessed. What are the potential physical or psychological dangers that might accompany participation? Even if potential risks are deemed slight, they need to be considered and balanced in light of what good might come from the experiment. Researcher Gregory Kimble put it this way: "Is it worth it? Do the potential benefits to science and eventually to animal and human lives justify the costs to be extracted here and now?" (1989, p. 499). Seldom will any one psychologist have to make the decisions about the potential benefits versus the risks of research. Advisory committees of researchers, familiar with the techniques and the problems of the proposed research, will have to approve it before the project begins.

What are some other ethical guidelines related to research in psychology?

1. The participant's confidentiality must be guaranteed. Often, the participant's name is not used; it is replaced instead with an identification number. No matter what a participant is asked to do or say, he or she should be confident that no one will have access to his or her responses but the researchers.
2. Participation in research should be voluntary. There are no circumstances in which one should feel that he or she must participate in psychological research. Participants should be allowed the option of dropping out of any research project, even after it has begun. For example, college students cannot be offered extra credit to participate in psychological research unless there are other options for earning the same amount of extra credit.
3. People should participate in experiments only after they have given their informed consent. Participants must be aware of the potential dangers of participation, why the project is being done, and what is expected of them. For example, no one can have access to a student's college records (GPA, exam scores, etc.) without his or her knowledge and approval. Clearly, some deception may be required in psychological research. Even so, the amount of deception needs to be balanced against the promise of the outcome of the research.
4. Subjects should be debriefed after the experiment has been completed. To be **debriefed** means that the true nature of the project and its basic intent should be explained fully to all who participated in it. Subjects should be informed of the results of the project when they become available.

debrief
to fully inform a subject about the intent and/or hypotheses of one's research once data have been collected.

Published ethical guidelines for the use of animals in research also are quite stringent. Only experts trained and experienced in proper and humane animal care and housing should have responsibility for laboratory animals. Those experts must then provide training to all others who work with the animals. Every effort must be made to minimize the discomfort, illness, and pain of animals. Putting animals in a situation where they might experience injury, pain, or stress is acceptable *only* if no other procedure is available, and when the goal is justified by its prospective scientific, applied, or educational value. As with human subjects, there are usually review committees that must approve the design of any research using nonhuman subjects, where the major concern is the ethical and humane protection of the animals.

● **Before You Go On**
Describe four ethical issues that must be considered when doing psychological research.

IMPORTANT THEMES AND GENERAL PRINCIPLES

Psychologists have learned a great deal about the behaviors and the mental processes of organisms. Some of the observations that psychologists have made seem so important, so general in their application, that they deserve special mention. The principles listed here are so well established that they are essentially part of our definition of psychology. In every chapter that follows you will recognize a reflection of these ideas.

1. Our biological nature and psychological nurture interact to make us who we are. How much of who we are—our affect, behavior, and cognition—is the result of our inheritance, or our biological *nature?* How much of who we are reflects the influence of our environment, or our *nurture?* Is intelli-gence inherited (nature) or due to experience (nurture)? Is aggressiveness inborn (part of our nature), or learned (reflecting our nurture)? Does al-coholism reflect innate nature, or is it an acquired reaction to events in the environment?

In fact, nearly all behaviors and mental processes result from the *inter-action* of inherited genetic influences and environmental, experiential in-fluences. In this concept, interaction is a difficult concept. We'll expand our understanding as we go along. For now, the logic is that any psycholog-ical characteristic is not going to be the result of *either* heredity *or* experi-ence, but will reflect the extent to which these two forces have influenced each other. "For all psychological characteristics, inheritance sets limits on, or creates a range of potentials for development. Environment determines how near the individual comes to developing these potentials" (Kimble, 1989).

2. No two persons are exactly alike. This observation may be psychology's most common and best documented. Given the diversity of genetic make-ups and the diversity of environments, including societal and cultural pres-sures, there are so many ways in which people can be different it is some-times a wonder that we can get along with each other at all. Not only is each individual unique, but no one person is exactly the same from one point in time to another. Depending on your experiences, your behaviors and men-tal processes are different today from what they were yesterday. Most likely you have not changed in any significant way, but some observations that may have been true of you yesterday may not be true of you today.

Imagine that a psychologist wants to study your behavior and mental activity and draw some conclusions that she can apply to people in general. Do you see the problem she is going to have? Because there is variability in you and because you are not exactly like everybody else, the best this psy-chologist will be able to do is make statements in general terms, in terms of probability. For example, we know that high school grades are reasonable predictors of success in college. But because of the fact that people differ, the best we can do is claim that students who do well in high school *probably* will do well in college. In fact, it is because no two people are alike that vir-tually all psychological laws are statements made "in general, in the long run, and by-and-large."

3. Our experience of the world may reflect something other than what is actually "out there." This classic notion has a name: phenomenology. **Phenomenology** has to do with the study of events as they are experienced by the individual (not as they occur "in reality"). As you might imagine, we could easily get involved in some fairly deep philosophical discussions here, but we need not. What we need to appreciate, and what we need to keep an eye out for as we go along, is the idea that we each attend to, interpret, and remember (i.e., experience) different aspects of the same world.

Here's a very simple, classic example of what I'm talking about, attributed to the philosopher John Locke. Imagine that you have before you three pails of water. The water in the pail on your left is really quite hot, the water in the pail on your right is nearly ice cold, and the water in the center pail is about body temperature. You put your left hand into the hot water and your right hand into the cold. Then, after a minute or two, you place both hands in the center pail of water. What is its temperature? How does the water feel? To your left hand (which had been in the hot water), the water seems quite cool, while to your right hand (which had been in the cold water) the very same water now feels warm. Well, what *is* the temperature of the water in the center pail? A physicist may come along and measure the temperature of the water in that center pail with astonishing accuracy. But we're not interested in the physics of the water. We're interested in the psychology of your *experience* of the water, and we may—with something of a smile—report that the water in the center pail is both warm and cool. What matters is not the physical temperature of the water in the center pail, but rather your experience of that water.

Here's another example (from Bruner & Goodman, 1947). Children are given the opportunity to manipulate the size of a small circle. They are asked to make the circle exactly the same size as a quarter. Most children overestimate the size of the coin. What is more interesting is that poor children overestimate the size of the quarter to a significantly greater degree. To the poorer children, quarters seem *much* larger than they actually are.

This theme has practical relevance in many areas of psychology. It will show up most clearly in our discussion of sensation and perception, where we will see that what we perceive often depends more on what we want to perceive or expect to perceive than on what is "really there." A quick study of Figure 1.4 will give you an idea of what I mean.

4. For many questions in psychology there are no simple answers. I alluded to this point earlier. For some of our questions, we have answers with which almost all psychologists agree. On the other hand, for other questions we don't even have reasonably acceptable hypotheses. What you are going to find in your study of psychology is that complex phenomena often have complex explanations.

As an example, let's briefly anticipate a discussion we'll have later when we cover psychological disorders. What causes schizophrenia? For now, let us simply acknowledge that schizophrenia is one of the most devastating and debilitating of all the psychological disorders, afflicting approximately 2.5 million people in the United States today. What causes the distortions in the way a person feels, thinks, and acts that define schizophrenia? The truth is that we just don't know. We have several hypotheses, and each holds some promise. Part of the answer is genetic; schizophrenia does tend to run in families. Part of the answer is biochemical; the brains of persons with schizophrenia do not function in the same way as the brains of those who do not have schizophrenia. Part of the answer is environmental, or situational; stress and experience can

phenomenology
the study of events as they are experienced by the individual; experience is reality

FIGURE 1.4
(A) This ambiguous drawing may be of an old hag with her chin tucked down into her coat collar or a young woman in Victorian clothing, depending on the context in which it is viewed. (B) Are the soldiers marching up or down the stairs?

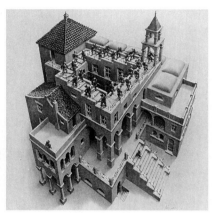

bring on symptoms or at least make symptoms worse than they would be otherwise. So what causes schizophrenia? Answer: a number of interacting factors, some genetic, some physiological, some environmental, perhaps all operating at the same time. And so it goes for virtually all of our behaviors and mental processes.

The main point of this theme in psychology is that if you are looking for simple answers to explain your own behavior or the behavior of others, you're bound to be disappointed. Disappointed you may be, but please do not be discouraged. Behaviors and mental processes are complex, and explaining them is going to take a certain degree of complexity. Complexity in itself should not be worrisome. Behaviors and mental processes generally have multiple causes. Our challenge is to discover them.

5. *Psychology is relevant to our daily lives.* We might get an argument from biologists, chemists, physicists, geologists, and even some astronomers, but I am willing to make the claim that no science has more practical application in the real world than does psychology. In everyday life, people *can* get by without thinking about physics or geology or biology; but they cannot get by without thinking psychologically. They must take into consideration a multitude of sensations, perceptions, memories, feelings, and consequences of their actions if they are going to survive, much less prosper. As you read about psychology on the following pages, you should always be on the lookout for how what you are reading about can be put to use in your own life.

Let's consider here just one area in which psychological principles can be usefully applied. Getting old and dying are natural processes, but the truth is that many people never get old, they just die—unnaturally. In many cases the cause of their death was preventable. It is possible to prevent some deadly diseases, such as polio, smallpox, or measles, simply by being vaccinated against them. What we have come to appreciate in the last twenty years or so is the extent to which illness and even death can be attributed to dangerous life-styles (Matarazzo, 1980; Miller, 1983). In fact, "7 of the 10 leading causes of death in the United States are in large part be-haviorally determined. We believe that these unhealthy behaviors can be significantly reduced with help from psychologists" (Heffernan & Albee, 1985, p. 202). We understand that it is not necessarily easy, but principles of psychology *can* be used to help people stop smoking, cut down on alcohol use, increase exercise, wear safety belts, cope with many of life's stresses, de-crease their overeating, engage in safe(r) sexual practices, and change many other behaviors with an end toward improving the physical health of the individual.

● Before You Go On

Describe five general principles that have emerged in psychol-ogy and that will appear repeatedly throughout our study.

THINKING CRITICALLY ABOUT WHAT PSYCHOLOGISTS DO

I claimed in the Introduction that one of your goals as a student of psychol-ogy should be to learn to think critically about psychological issues. This re-quires time and practice, and usually does not result in one sure, best an-swer. At the end of each chapter I will provide you with a short list of questions to ponder. Taking time to reflect on these questions will help you organize and remember the material presented in the chapter. It will also make you a better "consumer" of psychology.

1. Is psychology the only science that studies behavior and mental processes? Surely psychology is not the only science that cares about people and what they do or feel or think. In what ways are psychology the same as or different from anthropology, sociology, or economics?
2. We often say that if we understand something, we can make predic-tions about it. In fact, to demonstrate that we understand someone, we may be asked to predict what that person will do in certain situa-tions. If we understand someone and can make predictions about that person, does it follow that we can control that person?
3. If a magazine reports that Brand X is the most "trouble-free car in the world," how do you suppose "trouble-free" has been operationally de-fined?
4. Is it possible to be a religious person and a psychologist at the same time?
5. I often claim that "81.746 percent of what we know in psychology to-day, we have learned in the last 30 years." I'm not really serious when I say that, but how could we determine how much has been learned in psychology in the last 30 years, or 20 years, or 10 years?
6. Because all that I know about the relationship between reading ability and performance in introductory psychology reflects what I know from doing correlations, I cannot make any cause-and-effect state-ments about this relationship. If I hypothesized that students' reading levels actually caused them to get the grades that they do, how would I test my hypothesis?
7. You hear an ad on television that claims that in a "taste test," LOXO COLA was compared to two nationally known brands, and LOXO COLA was "preferred nearly 2 to 1." What extraneous variables might be having an influence on this result?

8. What experiments can you think of that would not be done with humans because of ethical concerns but could be ethically done with nonhuman animals?

SUMMARY

TOPIC 1A

A WORKING DEFINITION OF PSYCHOLOGY

● Why may we make the claim that psychology is a science?
● What are scientist-practitioners in psychology?

We claim scientific status for psychology because it meets two criteria: It has an organized body of knowledge and uses scientific methods. Within the discipline, scientist-practitioners are psychologists (mostly clinical and counseling psychologists) whose major concern is with the application of knowledge in the real world. *Pages 15–17.*

● What is the subject matter of psychology?
● What are operational definitions?

The subject matter of psychology is behavior and mental processes: affect, behavior, and cognition. Operational definitions define concepts in terms of the techniques, or operations, used to measure or create those concepts. *Pages 17–18.*

● In what way did the philosophies of Descartes and Locke pave the way for psychology?
● In what way did the science of Darwin and von Helmholtz influence the emergence of psychology?

Both René Descartes and John Locke directed the attention of philosophy to the study of the mind—how it interacts with the body and how it acquires information, and they did so without reference to religious issues. Charles Darwin (from biology) and

Hermann von Helmholtz (from physiology) brought scientific and experimental methods to bear on questions that were essentially psychological in nature. *Pages 18–21.*

● When and where did psychology "begin" and whom do we credit with formally establishing the discipline?
● Briefly describe the first approaches that psychologists took toward their subject matter.

We credit Wilhelm Wundt for having founded psychology at the University of Leipzig in 1879. Wundt used scientific methods to study the mind, or consciousness—particularly its contents and structure—hence his approach was called structuralism. Following the lead of William James, functionalists were also concerned with consciousness and mental activity, but focused on the adaptive usefulness or function of consciousness. *Pages 21–23.*

● Briefly summarize behaviorism and psychoanalysis as approaches to psychology.

Behaviorism (associated with Watson and Skinner) holds that the subject matter of the science of psychology should be measurable and observable, that is, behavior, rather than the mind. Psychoanalysis (associated with Freud and his followers) asserts that behaviors and mental processes are often under the influence of basic drives and unconscious forces. *Pages 23–24.*

● What is the major thrust of the humanistic approach in psychology?
● What does "gestalt" mean?
● What area of psychology was of major concern to the Gestalt psychologists?

Humanistic psychology (associated with Rogers and Maslow) focuses on the self or the person, emphasizing internal processes and the potential for growth and development. As such, this approach can be seen as a reaction against behaviorism and psychoanalysis. Gestalt means whole, totality, or configuration. Gestalt psychologists focus on factors that influence the selection and organization of perceptions. *Pages 24–26.*

T O P I C   1 B

THE RESEARCH METHODS OF PSYCHOLOGY

● What is naturalistic observation?
● List some of the potential problems that can arise with this method.

Naturalistic observation is the careful, systematic, reliable observation of behaviors as they occur naturally. Use of naturalistic observation requires that (1) the subjects not be aware of the fact that they are being observed; (2) the observers' biases not influence the observations; and (3) patience be exercised in the search for those behaviors that occur infrequently. *Page 27.*

● How can surveys and case history studies be used to help us understand behavior and mental processes?

Surveys provide a few responses (observations) from very large samples of respondents, whereas case history studies tend to provide detailed and specific information (observations) about just a few subjects. In either case, one may discover relationships among the responses observed. *Pages 30–31.*

● What data are needed to calculate a correlation coefficient?
● What does a correlation coefficient tell us about the relationship between two measured responses?

In order to calculate a correlation coefficient, one needs to measure two responses from the same group of subjects, yielding a set of paired observations or measurements. Positive correlation coefficients tell us that high scores on one response are associated with (and predict) high scores on the other response and that low scores on one response are associated with (and predict) low scores on the other. Negative correlations tell us that the two responses are inversely related, with high scores on one measure associated with low scores on the other. Correlation coefficients of or near zero tell us that our measured responses are not correlated in any way. The closer the coefficient is to the extremes of +1.00 or −1.00, the stronger the relationship between responses. In no case can one infer a cause-and-effect relationship from correlational data. *Pages 31–33.*

● What is the essence of doing an experiment?
● Define independent, dependent, and extraneous variables in the context of an experiment.

An experiment involves manipulating independent variables and measuring dependent variables while minimizing the effects of extraneous variables. Independent variables are hypothesized to have an effect on some mental process or behavior. To see if such is the case, one looks for changes in some measured dependent variable that are consistent with changes in the manipulated independent variable. Before we can claim a cause-and-effect relationship between the independent and dependent variables, all other events (extraneous variables) that could have affected the dependent variable must have been controlled or eliminated. *Pages 34–37.*

● How do random assignment and baseline designs help minimize error in psychological experiments?

Random assignment of subjects to experimental or control conditions of an experiment assures that each subject has an equal opportunity to be in any experimental treatment. Any pre-experimental differences among subjects should thus balance out over groups. With baseline designs, the same subjects serve in both experimental and control conditions, thus serving as their own controls. *Page 37.*

● Describe four ethical issues that must be considered when doing psychological research.

Subjects in psychological research must have their confidentiality maintained. They should give informed consent before voluntarily participating in the research and should be debriefed about the project when it is over. Above all, the investigator should consider whether potential risks in the research are offset by the present or future value of the results that may come from the research. Similar considerations are given to the use of animals in research. *Pages 38–39.*

● Describe five general principles that have emerged in psychology and that will appear repeatedly throughout our study.

(1) One's biological nature interacts with one's experiential nurture to create the psychological characteristics of the organism. (2) Because of differing genetic constitutions and experiences, no two organisms are alike, and organisms change from moment to moment. (3) What matters most to us is the world as we perceive it, or experience it, regardless of what may actually be going on. (4) Most psychological phenomena are complex, and simple answers to our questions are seldom available. (5) There are countless ways in which the issues, concerns, and techniques of psychology can find practical application in our everyday lives. *Pages 40–43.*

T O P I C 1 A
A WORKING DEFINITION OF PSYCHOLOGY

1.1 When a researcher develops a tentative explanation for some phenomenon that can be tested and then rejected or supported, that researcher has developed a) a scientific method. b) a theoretical case history. c) a hypothesis. d) an experimental method. *Pages 15–17.*

1.2 In the context of research studies, what can scientific methods do for us? a) They can lead us to reject hypotheses that are not true. b) They can tell us which results are likely to be popular. c) They can prove that one hypothesis is the best to explain a given phenomenon. d) They can help us decide which of a number of research issues ought to be investigated next. *Pages 15–17.*

1.3 True or False? Science is the only way for humans to gain insights about the nature of human behavior. *Pages 15–17.*

1.4 Which type of psychologist is likely to be most comfortable with the label "scientist-practitioner"? a) a clinical psychologist b) a physiological psychologist c) a developmental psychologist d) a social psychologist. *Pages 15–17.*

1.5 Which of the following provides the best statement of psychology's subject matter? a) what people do, both normally and abnormally b) the actions of organisms when they are stimulated c) the mental activity and behaviors of organisms d) what people think about the things that affect them. *Pages 17–18.*

1.6 To say that psychologists study affect is to say that part of the subject matter of psychology is a) thoughts, beliefs, and knowledge. b) underlying bi-

ological or physiological factors. c) behaviors, actions, and reactions. d) emotions, feelings, and moods. *Pages 17–18.*

1.7 Which of these is *least* publicly verifiable? a) how many times a pigeon pecks a disk b) the time it takes a rat to run through a maze c) the content of a person's dream d) a student's performance on an exam. *Pages 17–18.*

1.8 When psychology emerged as a separate discipline, it did so because it had combined a) energy and matter. b) scientific methods with philosophical questions. c) cognitive processes with affect. d) mental processes with behavior. *Pages 18–21.*

1.9 René Descartes and John Locke deserve mention in a discussion of the history of psychology because they both a) predicted that the science of psychology would be popular and successful. b) believed that human actions could be explained without relying on God or religion for explanations. c) realized the importance of the spinal cord for human behavior. d) applied scientific methods to issues of human nature and human understanding. *Pages 18–21.*

1.10 What did John Locke and Wilhelm Wundt share in common? a) a basic interest in the nature of consciousness and the contents of the mind b) a deep belief in the truth of Darwin's theory of evolution c) a reliance on the methods of science to support their claims and hypotheses d) all of the above. *Pages 21–23.*

1.11 True or False? The first psychology laboratory was opened in the late 1800s by Sigmund Freud in Vienna. *Pages 21–23.*

1.12 Of these, which type of psychologist was Margaret Floy Washburn? a) social b) feminist c) animal d) clinical. *Pages 21–23.*

1.13 About when in its history did psychology become known as "the science of behavior"? a) when Wundt opened his laboratory in Leipzig b) when Wertheimer founded Gestalt psychology c) when James was teaching psychology at Harvard d) when Watson was chair of the department at Johns Hopkins. *Pages 23–24.*

1.14 True or False? Sigmund Freud's laboratory began doing experiments on psychoanalysis in the 1920s. *Pages 23–24.*

1.15 Who is most likely to have made the statement, "Psychology should focus on the person, the self in all its aspects as it interacts with the fabric of experience"? a) a behaviorist psychologist b) a Freudian psychologist c) a Gestalt psychologist d) a humanistic psychologist. *Pages 24–26.*

TOPIC 1B
THE RESEARCH METHODS OF PSYCHOLOGY

1.16 Each of the following is true with regard to naturalistic observation *except* a) Organisms may not behave naturally if they believe they are being observed. b) The behaviors in which the observer is interested may occur infrequently. c) We can only observe the behaviors of organisms in social situations, when they interact with others. d) The expectations, motivation, and past experiences of the observer may bias his or her observations. *Page 27.*

1.17 Which of the following questions provides the best candidate for a study using naturalistic observation? a) Are nightmares more common after eating pizza? b) How do chess players develop their strategies? c) Do third-grade boys tend to play with girls or boys at recess? d) What are the effects of a tranquilizer on memory tasks? *Page 27.*

1.18 Most of Freud's theories and therapy derived from the use of the _____ method. a) case history b) correlational c) experimental d) survey. *Pages 30–31.*

1.19 True or False? Surveys involve more subjects than do case history studies. *Pages 30–31.*

1.20 Which of the following correlation coefficients indicates a relationship between two responses where we can most confidently predict one response knowing the other? a) +.56 b) +.0002 c) –.71 d) –2.34. *Pages 31–33.*

1.21 A correlation between which of these is most likely to be negative? a) high school GPAs and college GPAs b) scores on a typing test and typing skills c) number of cigarettes smoked and the likelihood of lung cancer d) amount of light in a restaurant and the price of a meal there. *Pages 31–33.*

1.22 True or False? Positive correlations are more useful than negative correlations. *Pages 31–33.*

1.23 The quality or value of an experiment depends mostly on a) the extent to which extraneous variables have been controlled or eliminated. b) the number of independent variables that have been manipulated. c) the extent to which the dependent variables are correlated with each other. d) whether humans or nonhumans have been used as experimental subjects. *Pages 34–37.*

1.24 If you want to experimentally test the usefulness of a new drug for the treatment of psychological disorders, the independent variable in your experiment will be a) the extent to which patients show improvement after using the drug. b) the amount of drug administered to the patients. c) the types of psychological disorders being treated. d) other forms of therapy or drugs the patients are receiving at the same time. *Pages 34–37.*

1.25 True or False? When we do an experiment, we wish to be able to claim that differences in our measured dependent variable depend on our manipulations of the independent variable and nothing else. *Pages 34–37.*

1.26 A major advantage of a baseline design is that a) all subjects serve in both control and experimental conditions. b) it takes much less time to do. c) they are more appropriate for human than for nonhuman subjects. d) subjects need not be debriefed when the experiment is over. *Page 37.*

1.27 True or False? Potentially harmful research in psychology typically has been approved by some committe or board of review. *Pages 38–39.*

1.28 "Phenomenology" has to do with a) the interaction of biological and environmental influences. b) the application of psychological principles in the real world. c) the differences between the way we perceive the world and the way it really is. d) the fact that no two organisms are alike and therefore psychological laws lack precision. *Pages 40–43.*

THE NERVOUS SYSTEM AND BEHAVIOR

2

PREVIEW

TOPIC 2A—Neurons: Building Blocks of the Nervous System

The Neuron

From One Cell to Another: The Synapse

TOPIC 2B—The Central Nervous System

Nervous Systems: The Big Picture

The Spinal Cord

The "Lower" Brain Centers

The Cerebral Cortex

PSYCHOLOGY IN THE REAL WORLD: Who Left the Tack on the Hallway Floor?

THINKING CRITICALLY ABOUT THE NERVOUS SYSTEM AND BEHAVIOR

CHAPTER SUMMARY

TEST YOURSELF

We have seen that psychology is a science that has many different subfields and that uses a variety of methods. This chapter reflects the reality that, regardless of one's approach to psychology, one must understand at least the basics of the biology and physiology of the organism being studied.

We will take a building-block approach, beginning with the individual nerve cell and ending with a discussion of the most complex of biological structures: the human brain. In Topic 2A we'll consider the nerve cell, called a neuron, and see how it works to transmit important messages from one part of the body to another. To do that, we'll have to deal with how the individual cells communicate with each other, a complex process which is now fairly well understood.

Our goal for Topic 2B is to examine some of the more important structures and functions of the human central nervous system. Starting with the spinal cord, we'll work our way up to the base of the brain, through its midsection, and on up to the outermost layers of the cerebral cortex. As we go along I'll describe anatomical features and point out how they are involved in our everyday lives.

Discussions of nervous systems, spinal cords, and brains can sound rather impersonal, as if we were talking about some strange mass of gooey tissue in a glass jar. What you'll need to do from time to time is remind yourself that we're talking about your neurons, your spinal cord, and your brain—and mine too. As you read these words, it is your spinal cord that carries impulses to the muscles in your arm to turn the page. It is your brain that directs your eyes to move across the page, seeks understanding, monitors your heart rate, and keeps you breathing as you read.

TOPIC 2A

NEURONS: BUILDING BLOCKS OF THE NERVOUS SYSTEM

THE NEURON

neuron
a nerve cell, the basic building block of the nervous system that transmits neural impulses

Our exploration of the nervous system begins with **neurons**, the microscopically small cells that exist throughout our nervous systems by the billions. Neurons were not even recognized as separate structures until about the

FIGURE 2.1
A typical neuron with its major features.

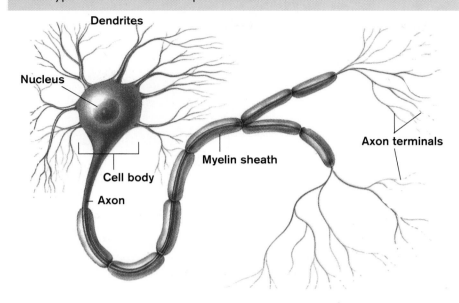

Dendrites

Nucleus

Cell body

Axon

Myelin sheath

Axon terminals

turn of the century. They are so tiny and complex that estimating their number is very difficult. To give you an idea of their size and number, there are about *125 million* specialized neurons on the back, inside surface of each human eye, and about *100 billion neurons* in the human brain (Hubel, 1979; Kolb, 1989).

The Structure of Neurons

We may not be sure about snowflakes, but it is a sure bet that no two neurons are identical. Even so, most neurons do have a few structures in common. Figure 2.1 illustrates these features, and Figure 2.2 illustrates what neurons actually look like.

One structure that all neurons are certain to have is a **cell body**, the largest concentration of mass of the neuron. It contains the nucleus of the cell, which, in turn, contains the genetic information that keeps the cell functioning. Extending away from the cell body are several tentacle-like structures called dendrites, and one particularly long structure called the axon. Our drawing in Figure 2.1 is very much simplified, showing only a few dendrites, when in a mature neuron there may be thousands. Typically, **dendrites** reach out to receive messages, called neural impulses, from other neurons. These impulses are then sent along to the cell body and down the **axon** toward other neurons, or to muscles or glands. Some axons are quite long—as much as two or three feet long in the spinal cord. It is generally true, then, that within a neuron impulses travel from dendrite to cell body to axon, and most of the trip will be made along the axon.

The neuron illustrated in Figure 2.1 has a feature not found on all neurons. The axon of this neuron has a cover or sheath of myelin. **Myelin** is a white fatty substance covering the axons of about half of the neurons in an adult's nervous system. It is myelin that allows us to tell the difference between the gray matter (dendrites, cell bodies, and unmyelinated axons)

cell body
the largest mass of a neuron, containing the cell's nucleus; may receive neural impulses

dendrites
branch-like extensions from a neuron's cell body where most neural impulses are received

axon
the long, tail-like extension of a neuron that carries an impulse away from the cell body toward the synapse

myelin
a white, fatty covering found on some axons that serves to insulate and protect them while increasing the speed of impulses

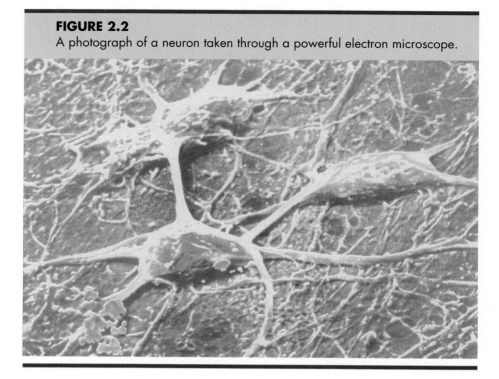

FIGURE 2.2
A photograph of a neuron taken through a powerful electron microscope.

and the white matter (myelinated axons) we see so clearly when we look at sections of nervous system tissue.

We tend to find myelin sheaths on axons that carry impulses relatively long distances. Fibers that carry messages up and down the spinal cord, for instance, are myelinated, while those that carry impulses back and forth across the spinal cord are not. Myelin serves several useful functions. It protects the long delicate axon and it acts as an insulator, keeping the activity of one neuron separate from those that are nearby. Myelin speeds impulses along the length of the axon: Axons covered with myelin carry impulses nearly 10 times faster than axons without myelin (up to 120 meters per second). Myelin sheaths are not fully developed at birth, but develop and adhere to axons as the nervous system matures (a process usually not complete until the age of 11 or 12 years). Whether they are myelinated or not, axons end in a branching series of bare end points called **axon terminals**, where one neuron communicates with others.

To quickly review: Within a neuron, impulses travel from the dendrites to the cell body to the axon (which may be myelinated) and then to the axon terminals.

Here's a far-reaching observation about neurons: Virtually no neurons are generated after we are born. We are born with more neurons than we'll ever have again—in fact, we are born with about twice as many neurons as we'll ever use. What happens to the rest? They just die—or are killed by physical trauma, or by the excess use of alcohol and other drugs. Bryan Kolb (1989), of the University of Lethbridge in Canada, gives us this analogy. During normal development, the brain is "constructed" in a manner rather like that in which a statue is chipped away from a block of granite. Instead of building up the finished product one piece at a time, more material than one needs is made available. Then what is needed, or used, is retained, and the rest dies away. Here's a related reality: In order to have those billions of neurons in our brains at the time of birth, brain cells must

axon terminals
the series of branching end points of an axon where one neuron communicates with the next in a series

be generating at a rate of approximately 250,000 per minute while the brain is being formed before birth (Cowan, 1979). There are implications about prenatal care here which we will explore in Chapter 3.

That dead neurons are not replaced with new ones makes neurons unique among cells. We're perpetually making new blood cells to replace lost ones. If we didn't, we could never donate a pint of blood. Skin cells are constantly replaced by new ones. You rinse away skin cells by the hundreds each time you wash your hands. Neurons are different; once they're gone, they're gone forever. We are often in luck, however, because *the functions* of lost neurons can be taken over by other, surviving neurons. I should add that recent evidence suggests that under just the right circumstances, new neurons and supporting cells from the brains of adult mice *can* be regenerated (Reynolds & Weiss, 1992). Whether this research can be generalized to other organisms or has any practical, real-life application remains to be seen.

Have you noticed that it is nearly impossible to talk about the structure of a neuron without referring to the function of the neuron: the transmission of neural impulses? We have seen that impulses typically are received by dendrites, passed on to cell bodies, and then to axons. We know that myelin speeds impulses along axons, but we haven't considered just what a neural impulse is. Let's do so now.

● **Before You Go On**

What are the major structures of a neuron?
What is myelin, and what is its function?

The Function of Neurons

The function of a neuron is to transmit neural impulses from one place to another within the nervous system. Let's start with a definition: A **neural impulse** is a sudden, reversible change in the electrical charges within and outside a neuron that travels from the dendrites to the axon terminals when the neuron fires. Now let's see what all that means.

Neurons exist in a complex biological environment. As living cells, they are filled with and surrounded by fluids. Only a thin membrane (like a skin) separates the fluids inside a neuron from the fluids outside it. These fluids contain tiny chemical ions. **Chemical ions** are particles that carry a very small electrical charge that is either positive (+) or negative (−). Ions float around in all the fluids of the body, but are heavily concentrated in the nervous system. Their source is no great mystery: Ions come from the chemicals in the foods and liquids we eat and drink that are dissolved by our digestive system.

Neurons that are just lying around not doing anything are said to be neurons at rest, although "at rest" may not be an accurate description. When it is at rest, the inside of the neuron has a negative (−) charge, compared to the positive (+) charge of the fluids on the outside of the neuron. The positive and negative ions are drawn to, or attracted toward each other, but they cannot become balanced because the neuron's membrane keeps them separate. As a result, a tension develops (which doesn't sound very restful, does it?). This tension is called a **resting potential**, and it makes each neuron like a tiny battery. The resting potential of a neuron is about −70 millivolts (mV). This number is negative because we measure the inside of the neuron relative to the outside, and the inside is where the negative ions are concentrated.

neural impulse
a sudden and reversible change in the electrical charges within and outside the membrane of a neuron which travels from the dendrite to the axon end of a neuron

chemical ions
electrically charged (either + or −) chemical particles

resting potential
the difference in electrical charge between the inside of a neuron and the outside when it is at rest (typically about −70mV)

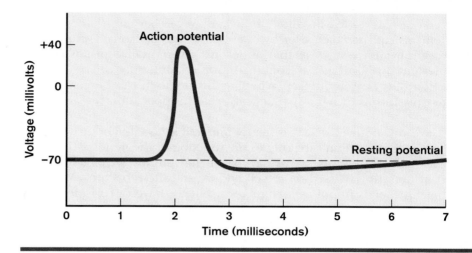

FIGURE 2.3

Changes in electrical potential that occur during the firing of a neuron. Note that the voltage is negative (−70 millivolts) when the neuron is "at rest," and positive (+ 40 millivolts) during the firing of the impulse. Note, too, that the entire process lasts but a few milliseconds.

action potential

the short-lived burst of a change in the difference in electrical charge between the inside and the outside of a neuron when it fires (typically about +40 mV)

If this sounds at all mysterious to you, think about a common D-cell battery of the sort you use in a flashlight. It too has two aspects (called poles), one positive, the other negative. The electrical charge that is possible with one of these batteries is usually about 1500 mV—much greater, of course, than that of a tiny neuron.

When a neuron is stimulated to fire, or to produce an impulse, the electrical tension of the resting potential is released. Suddenly and quickly, the polarity of the nerve cell changes. For a very brief instant (about 1/1000 of a second) at one point along the length of the neuron, the electrical charge within the cell becomes more *positive* than the area outside the cell. The "charge" of the neuron changes instantaneously. This new charge, where the inside of the cell is now positive compared to the outside, is called the **action potential** or neural impulse. The electric potential is now about +40 mV, the positive sign indicating that the inside of the neuron is now more positive than the outside. Then, in a few thousandths of a second, the neuron returns to its original state. The tension redevelops. It is ready to fire again.

To repeat: When a neuron is at rest, there is a difference between the electrical charges inside and outside its membrane (the inside is more negative). When the neuron fires, the difference suddenly reverses, so that the inside is slightly more positive. Then the tension of the resting potential returns again (see Figure 2.3).

When an impulse travels down a neuron, *nothing physically moves from one end of the neuron to the other*. The only movement of physical particles that takes place is that of ions moving in and out of the neuron through its membrane. What travels down a neuron is where this action potential takes place—where the release of tension of the resting potential occurs.

It is also true that neurons do not necessarily generate impulses every time they are stimulated. Each neuron has a level of stimulation that must be surpassed in order to get it to transmit an impulse. The minimum level of stimulation required to get a neuron to fire is called the **neural threshold**. The implication here is that there are neurons that often do not fire at all because they've not been adequately stimulated (at a level above threshold). This partially explains why a flashbulb going off in your face appears brighter than a candle flame viewed at a distance: Because of the high intensity of the flashbulb, more neurons are stimulated above threshold level and carry more impulses back to the brain.

neural threshold
the minimal level of stimulation needed to get a neuron to fire

● **Before You Go On**

What is the basic process involved when a neuron fires?

FROM ONE CELL TO ANOTHER: THE SYNAPSE

The general location where an impulse is relayed from one neuron to another is called the **synapse**. In the cerebral cortex of the human brain alone there are as many as 1 million billion synaptic interconnections among neurons (Edelman, 1992). Here's what happens at the synapse.

As we've seen, at the end of every axon are many branches called axon terminals (refer back to Fig. 2.1). Throughout a neuron, but concentrated in axon terminals, are small containers called **vesicles**, which hold neurotransmitters. **Neurotransmitters** are complex chemicals that will either excite or inhibit the transmission of neural impulses. When a neural impulse reaches the axon terminal, the vesicles near the membrane open and release the neurotransmitter they have been holding. Released from their vesicles, the neurotransmitter floods out into the **synaptic cleft**, a tiny space between two neurons. Note that the two neurons involved do not touch; they are separated by the synaptic cleft. Once in the synaptic cleft, some neurotransmitter molecules move to the membrane of the next neuron where they may fit into "receptor sites" and enter the membrane. See Figure 2.4.

Then what happens? The most likely scenario is that neurotransmitters float across the synaptic cleft, enter into receptor sites in the next neuron, and excite that neuron to release the tension of its resting potential and fire a new impulse down to its axon terminals. There, neurotransmitter chemicals are released from vesicles, cross the synaptic cleft, and stimulate the next neuron in the sequence to fire. In fact, this is the case when the neurotransmitter is an excitatory chemical. It simply stimulates the next neuron in a sequence to fire.

As it happens, there are many neurons throughout our nervous system that contain neurotransmitters that have the opposite effect. When they are released, they float across the synaptic cleft and actually work to prevent the next neuron from firing. We refer to these neurotransmitters as *inhibitory*. If you think back to our last section where we talked about neural thresholds, you might now have a better picture of just how that concept works. Imagine a neuron's dendrite sitting there "at rest," with many axon terminals (of many neurons) just across synaptic clefts. For this neuron to begin a new impulse, it may require more excitatory chemicals than just one axon terminal can provide, particularly if nearby terminals are releasing inhibitory neurotransmitters at about the same time.

The basic process I've just described also occurs at the synapse between neurons and nonneural cells. When a neuron forms a synapse with a muscle cell, for instance, the release of a neurotransmitter from the axon terminals may excite that muscle to contract momentarily. In the same

synapse
the location where an impulse is relayed from one neuron to another by means of neurotransmitters

vesicles
small containers, concentrated in axon terminals, that hold molecules of neurotransmitter chemicals

neurotransmitters
complex chemical molecules released at the synapse that either excite or inhibit neural impulse transmission

synaptic cleft
the space between the membrane of an axon terminal and the membrane of the next neuron in a sequence

FIGURE 2.4

A synapse, in which transmission is from upper left to lower right. As an impulse enters the axon terminal, vesicles release neurotransmitter chemicals into the synaptic space, or cleft. The neurotransmitter then either excites or inhibits an impulse in the next neuron.

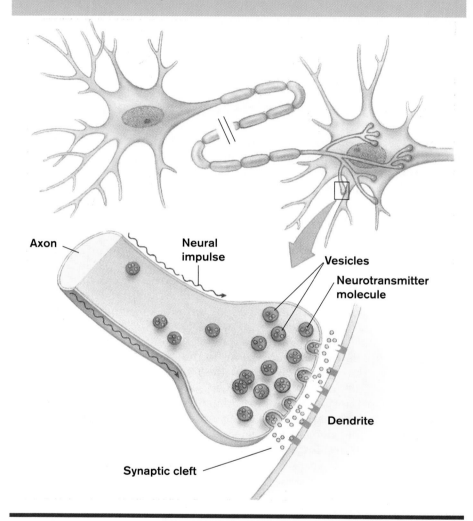

Axon

Neural impulse

Vesicles

Neurotransmitter molecule

Dendrite

Synaptic cleft

fashion, neurons that form synapses with a gland may cause that gland to secrete a hormone when stimulated by the appropriate neurotransmitter.

Not long ago, it was believed that neurons produce and release one of just two neurotransmitters: excitatory or inhibitory. We now realize that this view is much too simplistic. We now know of nearly 60 different neurotransmitters, and it is virtually certain that there are many others that have yet to be discovered. We'll be discussing them later in a variety of contexts, but for now we ought to at least briefly note a few of the better-known neurotransmitters.

Acetylcholine (usually pronounced uh-see'-til-koh"-leen), or ACh, can be found throughout the nervous system, where it acts as either an excitatory or inhibitory transmitter, depending upon where it is found. It is the most common of the neurotransmitters, and the first to be discovered (back in the 1920s). Not only is ACh found in the brain, but it commonly works in synapses between neurons and muscle tissue cells. A variety of food poisoning called *botulism* blocks the release of acetylcholine and thus causes paralysis (as does the drug curare). Some poisons (e.g., the venom of the Black Widow spider) have just the opposite effect, causing excess ACh to be released, which can result in muscle contractions or spasms so severe as to be deadly. Acetylcholine is also implicated in memory function and is thus a prime object for research on memory problems such as those associated with Alzheimer's disease. Nicotine is a chemical that, in small amounts, tends to increase the normal functioning of ACh, but in large doses, nicotine overrides the normal function of acetylcholine—a reaction that can lead to paralysis and even death. Smoking or chewing tobacco will not (usually) cause such a dramatic effect because large amounts of nicotine first stimulate a brain center that causes vomiting before too much nicotine can be absorbed into one's system (Palfai & Jankiewicz, 1991, p. 141).

Norepinephrine is a common and important neurotransmitter. Norepinephrine is normally involved in the physiological reactions associated with high levels of emotional arousal such as increased heart rate, increased perspiration, and heightened blood pressure (Groves & Rebec, 1992). When there is too much norepinephrine in a person's brain or spinal cord, the result is often a feeling of arousal, anxiety, or agitation. (One thing that cocaine does is increase the release of norepinephrine, leading to a state of agitation and a "high" mood state.) Too little norepinephrine in the brain has been linked to feelings of depression.

Dopamine is one of the neurotransmitters that most intrigues psychologists. It is involved in a very wide range of psychological functioning. Too much or too little dopamine within the nervous system seems to produce several different effects, depending primarily on which system of nerve fibers is involved. Dopamine has been associated with various thought and mood disturbances of some of the psychological disorders and with impairment of movement. When there is not enough dopamine, we find difficulty in making voluntary movements; too much and we find involuntary tremors.

Endorphins (plural because there are several of them) are our natural pain suppressors. By and large, what we call our pain threshold—our ability to tolerate different levels of pain—is a function of the production of endorphins (Watkins & Mayer, 1982). With excess endorphins, we feel little pain; a deficit in endorphins results in more experienced pain. When we are under extreme physical stress endorphin levels rise, as if to protect us against feelings of pain. Indeed, runners often report a near-euphoric "high" after they have run great distances, as if their endorphins had kicked in to protect them against the pain of physical exhaustion.

As you can imagine, we could continue this list, but for now it is the basic idea of what neurotransmitters do that matters: They are agents that excite or inhibit the transmission of neural impulses throughout the nervous system. That excitation or inhibition can have significant effects on our thoughts, feelings, and behaviors. Neural impulse transmission is seldom a matter of one neuron simply stimulating just one neuron that in turn stimulates yet one more. Any one neuron can have hundreds or thousands of axon terminals and synapses and thus has the potential for exciting or inhibiting many others.

● **Before You Go On**
Summarize neural impulse transmission at the synapse.
Name and briefly describe the actions of four neurotransmitters.

T O P I C 2 B

THE CENTRAL NERVOUS SYSTEM

Now that we have a sense of how neurons work, individually and in combination, let's step back for a moment to consider the broader context in which they function. First, let's quickly summarize how the different systems of neurons in the human body are organized. The major focus of this Topic is the central nervous system, or CNS, the network of nerve cells most intimately involved in our psychological functioning.

NERVOUS SYSTEMS: THE BIG PICTURE

Behavior and mental activity generally require large numbers of integrated neurons working together in complex organized systems. Figure 2.5 shows how these systems of nerve cells are related to each other.

The first major division of the nervous system is determined wholly on the basis of anatomy. The **central nervous system (CNS)** includes all of the neurons found in the spinal cord and brain. In many ways, this system of nerves is the most complex and the most intimately involved in the control of our behavior and mental processes. The **peripheral nervous system (PNS)** is composed of all the neurons in our body *not* in the CNS: the nerve fibers in our arms, face, fingers, intestines, and so forth. Neurons in the peripheral nervous system carry impulses either from the central nervous system to muscles and glands (on *motor neurons*), or they carry impulses to the CNS from receptor cells (on *sensory neurons*).

The peripheral nervous system is divided into two parts, based on the part of the body being served. The **somatic nervous system** includes those neurons outside the CNS that serve the muscles and that pick up impulses from the major sense receptors—the eyes and ears, for example. The other component of the PNS is the **autonomic nervous system (ANS)**, whose neurons and fibers of the ANS are involved in activating the smooth muscles (such as those of the stomach and intestines) and the glands. The ANS also provides feedback to the CNS on the activity of these internal processes.

Because the autonomic nervous system is so involved in our emotional responses, we'll return to it again in that context. For now, we will simply note that the autonomic nervous system is made up of two parts, the sympathetic division and the parasympathetic division. These two divisions work in opposition to each other. The **sympathetic division** is in control

central nervous system (CNS)
those neurons found in the brain and spinal cord

peripheral nervous system (PNS)
those neurons not found in the brain or spinal cord but in the peripheral organs of the body

somatic nervous system
sensory and motor neurons outside the CNS that serve the sense receptors and the skeletal muscles

autonomic nervous system (ANS)
those neurons of the PNS that activate the smooth muscles and glands

sympathetic division
those neurons of the ANS involved in states of emotionality

FIGURE 2.5
The various human nervous systems and how they are interrelated.

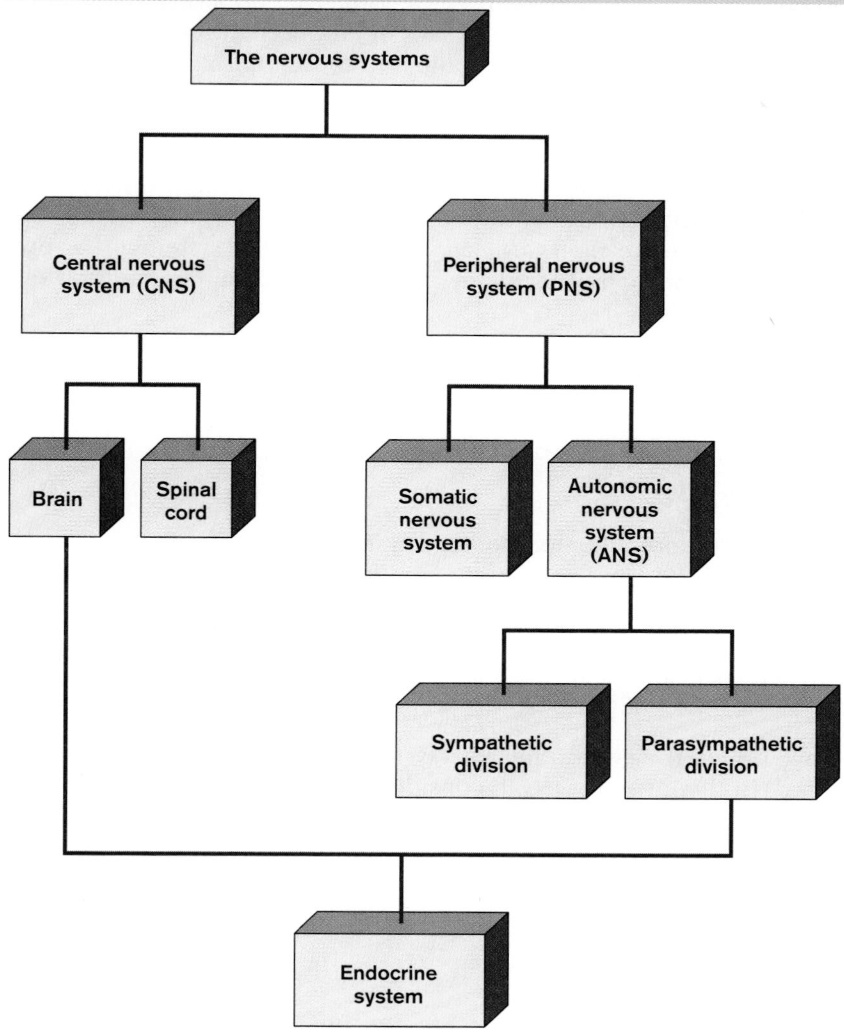

and active when we are feeling emotional, excited, or under stress—like riding up that first huge incline of a roller coaster at an amusement park. The **parasympathetic division** becomes active when we are relaxed and emotionally quiet—as we might be late at night, riding home from the amusement park with friends and family.

There is one other system shown in Figure 2.5—the endocrine system. The **endocrine system** is a network of glands that affects behavior through the secretion of chemicals, called hormones, into the bloodstream. Many of these hormones are chemically very similar to neurotransmitters and have a number of the same overall effects. The glands of the endocrine system are under the control of the brain and the autonomic nervous system, which is why it is drawn as it is in Figure 2.5. I've included the endocrine

parasympathetic division
those neurons of the ANS involved in the maintenance of states of calm and relaxation

endocrine system
a network of glands that secrete hormones directly into the bloodstream

system here because its function is similar to that of all the nervous systems: to transmit information from one part of the body to another. Nervous systems do so through neural impulses; the endocrine system uses hormones sent through the bloodstream. The endocrine system is slower to react, but many of its effects are longer lasting. Most of the endocrine system's involvement in our behavior occurs in states of emotion and motivation, and we'll discuss this system later in the context of these topics.

There is good reason to separate these different organizations of neurons—it's not just an academic exercise. It helps make very complex structures easier to deal with, and it reminds us that not all neurons in our body are doing the same thing for the same purpose at the same time. We do have to keep in mind that the outline of Figure 2.5 is very simplified to this extent: All of the nerve fibers in each of the different systems have profound influences on each other. They are not at all as independent as our diagram might imply.

Now we are ready to begin our discussion of the structures and functions of the human central nervous system. Given its relative simplicity, we'll begin with the spinal cord.

● **Before You Go On**
Name the different human nervous systems, and indicate how they are related to each other.

THE SPINAL CORD

As we have noted, the central nervous system consists of the brain and the spinal cord. In this section, we will consider the structure and the function of the spinal cord, reserving our discussion of the brain for later. As we look at the spinal cord, for the first time we clearly can see the role of the central nervous system in human behavior.

The Structure of the Spinal Cord

spinal cord
a massive collection of nerve fibers within the spinal column that carry impulses to and from the brain and that are involved in some reflex actions

sensory neurons
neurons that carry impulses toward the spinal cord or brain

motor neurons
neurons that carry impulses away from the spinal cord or brain

The **spinal cord** is a massive collection of neurons within the spinal column that looks like a section of rope or thick twine. It is surrounded and protected by the hard bone and cartilage of the vertebrae. Sometimes it is difficult to remember that the spinal cord itself is made up of delicate nerve fibers living just inside our backbone.

A cross-sectional view of the spinal cord is illustrated in Figure 2.6. There are only a few structural details that need mention now. Note that the spinal cord itself—the neurons of the CNS—is located in the middle of the spinal column that reaches from your lower back to high in your neck, just below your brain. Then note that the nerve fibers that enter and leave the spinal cord do so from the side, not the front or back. Neurons and nerve fibers that carry impulses to the brain or spinal cord are called **sensory neurons** or fibers. Sensory neurons and their impulses enter the spinal cord on dorsal roots (dorsal means "toward the back"). Neurons and nerve fibers that carry impulses from the brain or spinal cord to muscles and glands are called **motor neurons** or fibers. Impulses that leave the spinal

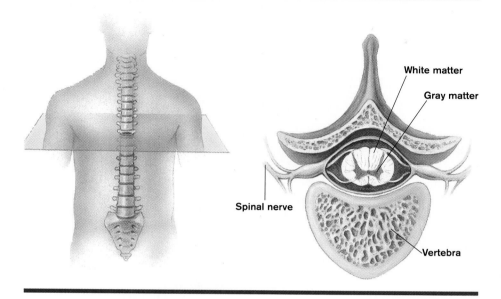

FIGURE 2.6
A cross-sectional view of the spinal column. Only the white matter and gray matter in the center represent actual spinal cord tissue.

White matter

Gray matter

Spinal nerve

Vertebra

cord on motor neurons do so on ventral roots (ventral means "toward the front"). Neurons within the central nervous system are called **interneurons**.

Also notice that the center area of the spinal cord is made up of dark gray matter, resembling the shape of a butterfly, while the outside area is light, white matter. Remember, this means that the center portion is filled with cell bodies, dendrites, and unmyelinated axons, while the outer section is filled with myelinated axons. Both of these observations about the structure of the spinal cord provide keys to understanding its function.

interneurons
neurons located within the spinal cord or brain

The Functions of the Spinal Cord

The spinal cord has two major functions, one of which is to transmit neural impulses rapidly to and from the brain. Whenever sensory impulses originate below the neck and make their way to the brain, they do so through the spinal cord. When the brain transmits motor impulses to parts of the body below the neck, those impulses first travel down the spinal cord.

Impulses to and from different parts of the body leave and enter the spinal cord at different levels (impulses to and from the legs, for example, enter and leave at the base of the spinal cord). If the spinal cord is damaged, the consequences can be disastrous, resulting in a loss of feeling from the part of the body served and a loss of voluntary movement (paralysis) of the muscles in the region. The higher in the spinal cord that damage takes place, the greater the resulting losses will be.

The second major function of the spinal cord is found in its role in **spinal reflexes**—very simple and automatic behaviors that occur without

spinal reflexes
involuntary responses that involve sensory neurons carrying impulses to the spinal cord, interneurons carrying them within the spinal cord, and motor neurons carrying them to muscles

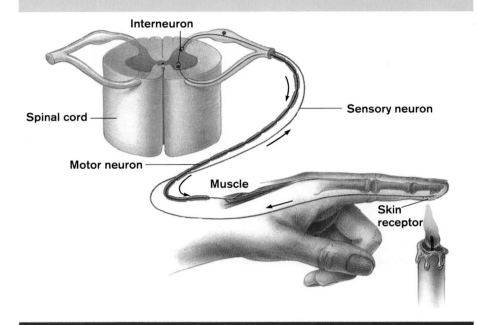

FIGURE 2.7
A spinal reflex. Stimulation of receptor cells in the skin, in turn, stimulates sensory neurons, interneurons, and motor neurons. Although a response is made without involvement of the brain, impulses also travel up fibers in the spinal cord's white matter to the brain.

the conscious, voluntary action of the brain. To understand how these reflexes work, follow along with the drawing in Figure 2.7. Here we have another drawing of the spinal cord to which we've added a few features.

Let's trace your reaction to having your fingertip placed over the flame of a candle (assuming you're blindfolded at the time). Receptor cells in your fingertip respond to the flame, sending neural impulses racing along sensory neurons, through a dorsal root into the spinal cord. Then two things happen at the same time. Impulses rush up the ascending pathways of the spinal cord's white matter to your brain. But impulses also travel to interneurons and go right back out of the spinal cord (through a ventral root) on motor neurons to your arm and hand, where muscles are stimulated to contract so your hand jerks back from the flame.

Here we have a simple reflex. Impulses travel *in* on sensory neurons, *within* on interneurons, and *out* on motor neurons. We are now involved with behavior. We have an environmental stimulus (here, a flame), activity in the central nervous system (the spinal cord), and an observable response (hand withdrawal).

There are a couple of observations I must make about reflexes of the type depicted in Figure 2.7 before we go on. First, the fact that neural impulses enter the spinal cord and immediately race to the brain is not indicated in the drawing. As you know, in a situation like the one depicted you may jerk your hand back "without thinking about it," but immediately thereafter you are aware of what has happened. That awareness occurs in the brain, not the spinal cord. It is also true that some reflexes are even more simple than the one in Figure 2.7 in that no interneurons are involved. That is, it is possible for sensory neurons to form synapses directly with motor neurons inside the spinal cord, which is what happens in the familiar knee-jerk reflex.

● **Before You Go On**
Why does spinal cord injury sometimes cause paralysis?
Describe the major features of a spinal reflex.

THE "LOWER" BRAIN CENTERS

There are several ways in which we could organize our discussion of the brain. We'll use a simple scheme and divide the brain into two parts: (1) the cerebral cortex and (2) everything else, which I'm calling lower brain centers. Because the cerebral cortex does so many important things, this division is a reasonable one.

The lower brain centers are "lower" in two ways. They are physically located below the cerebral cortex, and they are the brain structures to develop first, both in an evolutionary sense and within the developing human brain. They are the brain structures we most clearly share with other animals. You should not think of these lower centers as being unimportant. As we'll soon see, our very survival depends on them. You can use Figure 2.8 as a guide to locate the different structures as we discuss them.

The Brain Stem

As you look at the spinal cord and brain, you really cannot tell where one ends and the other begins. There is no abrupt division line separating these two parts of the central nervous system. Just above the spinal cord there is a slight widening of the cord that suggests that we're into brain tissue. Here are two important structures that together form the **brain stem**—the medulla and the pons.

The very lowest structure in the brain is the **medulla**, whose major functions involve involuntary reflexes. There are many small structures within the medulla that control such functions as reflexive eye and tongue movements. You don't have to think about blinking your eye as something rushes toward it, for example; your medulla will produce that eye blink reflexively.

The medulla also contains centers that control breathing reflexes and that monitor the muscles of the heart to keep it beating rhythmically. We *can* exercise some voluntary control over parts of the medulla, but only within certain limits. The medulla controls our respiration (breathing), but we can override the medulla and hold our breath. We cannot, however, hold our breath until we die (as children may threaten). We can hold our breath until we lose consciousness, which is to say until we give up higher-level voluntary control, at which point the medulla picks up where it left off and breathing continues.

At the medulla, nerve fibers to and from the brain cross over from left to right and vice versa. By and large, the left side of the brain receives impulses from and sends impulses to the right side of the body. Similarly, the left side of the body sends impulses to and receives messages from the right side of the brain. This process of crossing fibers from one side of the body

brain stem
the lowest part of the brain, just above the spinal cord, made up of the medulla and the pons

medulla
an area of the brain stem that monitors breathing and heart rate, and where most cross-laterality occurs

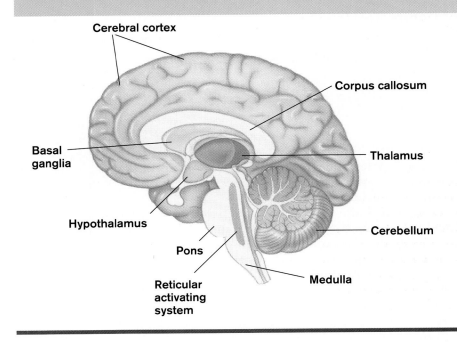

FIGURE 2.8
Some of the major structures of the human brain, of which the cerebral cortex is clearly the largest.

Cerebral cortex

Corpus callosum

Basal ganglia

Thalamus

Hypothalamus

Cerebellum

Pons

Medulla

Reticular activating system

cross-laterality
the process of nerve fibers crossing over the brain stem so that the left side of the body sends impulses to and receives impulses from the right side of the brain, and vice versa

pons
a brain stem structure forming a bridge between the brain and the spinal cord

to the opposite side of the brain is called **cross-laterality**, and it takes place in the brain stem.

Just above the medulla is the pons. (The pons is one structure—there is no such thing as a "pon.") Primarily, the **pons** serves as a bridge (which is what "pons" means in Latin) relaying sensory messages from the spinal cord up to higher brain centers and reversing the relay for motor impulses coming down. Cross-laterality also occus in the pons. Centers in the pons are responsible, at least in part, for the rapid movement of our eyes that occurs when we are asleep and dreaming (e.g., Sakai, 1985). Other pons centers are involved in determining our cycles of being awake and being asleep (Vertes, 1984).

● **Before You Go On**
Name the two brain stem structures, indicate where they are located, and describe what they do.

cerebellum
a spherical structure at the lower rear of the brain involved in the smoothing and coordination of bodily movements

The Cerebellum

The **cerebellum** is a brain stem structure whose major function is to smooth and coordinate rapid body movements. Your cerebellum (literally, "little brain") is about the size of your closed fist. It is more or less spherical

The ability of an athlete, such as this gymnast, to perform a complex coordinated movement over and over may involve training the cerebellum.

and is positioned behind the pons, tucked up under the base of the skull. Its outer region is very convoluted, meaning that the tissue there is folded in upon itself, creating many deep crevices and lumps.

Most voluntary movements originate in higher brain centers (usually the motor area of the cerebral cortex), and are only coordinated by the cerebellum. Because of the close relationship between body movement and vision many eye movements originate in the cerebellum.

Our ability to casually stoop, pick up a dime off the floor, and slip it into our pocket involves a complex series of movements made smooth and regular by our cerebellum. When athletes repeatedly practice a movement, such as a golf swing or a gymnastic routine, we sometimes say that they are trying to "get into a groove," so that their trained movement can be made simply and smoothly. In a sense, such an athlete is training the cerebellum.

Few of our behaviors are as well-coordinated as the movements of the muscles required to make speech sounds. The next time you talk to someone, try considering just how quickly and effortlessly your lips, mouth, and tongue are moving—thanks to your cerebellum. Damage to the cerebellum disrupts one's fine, coordinated movements. Speech becomes slurred; one may shake and stagger when walking. In fact, a person with cerebellum damage may appear to be quite drunk. (On what region of the brain do you suppose alcohol has a direct and noticeable effect? The cerebellum, of course.)

Damage to the cerebellum may disrupt motor activity in other ways. If the outer region of the cerebellum is damaged, a person may suffer jerky **tremors**, involuntary trembling movements, when he or she tries to move (called "intention tremors"). Damage to inner areas leads to "tremors at rest," where the limbs or head may shake or twitch even when the person tries to remain still.

tremors
involuntary trembling, jerky movements

● **Before You Go On**

Where is the cerebellum located, and what is its major function?

The Reticular Activating System (RAS)

reticular activating system (RAS)
a network of nerve fibers extending from the brain stem to the cerebrum that is involved in maintaining levels of arousal

The **reticular activating system (RAS)** is a complex network of nerve fibers that begins down in the brain stem and works its way up through and around other structures all the way to the top portions of the brain.

Exactly what the reticular activating system does and how it does so remains something of a mystery. As its name implies, the RAS is involved in determining our level of activation or arousal. It influences whether we're awake and attentive, sound asleep, or at some level in between. Electrical stimulation of the RAS can produce patterns of brain activity associated with being awake and alert. Severing the RAS causes a condition of constant sleep in laboratory animals (Lindsley et al., 1949; Moruzzi and Magoun, 1949). The reticular activating system acts something like a valve that either allows sensory messages to pass from lower centers up to the cerebral cortex or shuts them off, partially or totally. What we don't know yet is just how the RAS does what it does, and what stimulates it to produce the effects it does.

The Limbic System

limbic system
a collection of structures, including the amygdala and septum, (involved in emotionality) and the hippocampus (involved in forming long-term memories)

The **limbic system** is a collection of structures rather than a single unified one. It controls many complex behavioral patterns that we usually think of as instinctive. It is of the utmost importance in controlling the behaviors of nonhuman animals, which do not have as large or as well-developed cerebral cortexes as humans. The location of the limbic system and its constituent parts are presented in Figure 2.9.

FIGURE 2.9
A view of the brain showing structures deep within it. Among these, the septum, amygdala, hippocampus, constitute the limbic system.

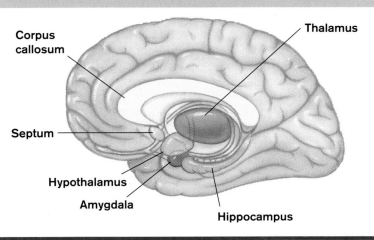

Within the human brain, parts of the limbic system are involved in the display of emotional reactions. One center, the *amygdala*, produces reactions of rage or aggression when stimulated, while the *septum* has the opposite effect, reducing the intensity of emotional responses when it is stimulated. The impact of the amygdala and septum on emotional reactions is quite immediate and direct in nonhumans. In humans it is more subtle, reflecting the influence of other brain centers.

Another center in the limbic system, the *hippocampus*, is less involved with emotion; it is involved in the formation of memories. People with a damaged hippocampus are often unable to "transfer" experiences into permanent memory storage. They may remember events for short periods of time. They also may be able to remember events from the distant past, but only if those events occurred before their hippocampus was damaged.

The Hypothalamus

The hypothalamus is often considered part of the limbic system. The **hypothalamus** is located near the limbic system and it too is involved in our motivational and emotional reactions. Among other things, it influences many of the functions of the endocrine system which, as we have seen, is involved in emotional responding.

The major responsibility of the hypothalamus seems to be to monitor critical internal bodily functions. It has centers that control eating behaviors and is sensitive to the amount of fluid in our bodies and indirectly gives rise to the feeling of being thirsty. The hypothalamus also acts as a thermostat, triggering several automatic reactions should we become too warm or too cold. Furthermore, this structure is involved in aggressive and sexual behaviors, and regulates many hormones. Recently, the hypothalamus has been implicated in the development of homosexual orientations (LeVay, 1991)—an implication we'll return to later. We'll discuss the hypothalamus again when we study needs, motives, and emotions in later chapters.

hypothalamus
a small structure near the limbic system in the center of the brain, associated with feeding, drinking, temperature regulation, sex, and aggression

The Thalamus

The last structure to discuss as a lower brain center is the thalamus. It is positioned right below the cerebral cortex and is intimately involved with its functioning. The major role of the **thalamus** involves the processing of information from the senses. Many impulses from the cerebral cortex to lower brain structures, the spinal cord, and out to the peripheral nervous system also pass through the thalamus.

In handling incoming sensory impulses, the thalamus collects and directs sensory messages to the appropriate areas of the cerebral cortex. Messages from our lower body, our eyes, ears, and other senses pass through the thalamus. For example, it is at the thalamus that nerve fibers from the eyes are sorted out and projected to the back of the cerebral cortex. Some evidence (e.g., Lugaresi et al., 1986) suggests that centers in the thalamus (as well as the pons) have a role in a person's normal pattern of wakefulness and sleep.

thalamus
the last sensory relay station; it sends impulses to the appropriate area of the cerebral cortex

●   **Before You Go On**

Indicate the locations and briefly describe the major function of the RAS, the limbic system, the hypothalamus, and the thalamus.

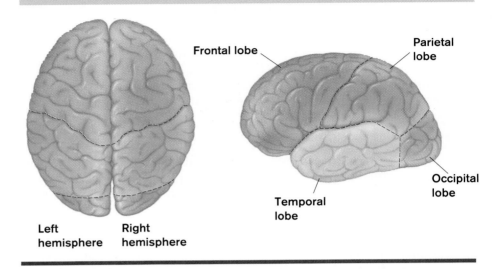

FIGURE 2.10

The human cerebral cortex is divided into left and right hemispheres, which in turn are divided into frontal, temporal, occipital, and parietal lobes.

THE CEREBRAL CORTEX

The human brain is a homely organ. There's just nothing very pretty about it. When we look at a human brain, the first thing we are likely to notice is the large, soft, lumpy, creviced outer covering of the cerebral cortex ("cortex" means outer bark, or covering). The **cerebral cortex** (sometimes called the cerebrum, or just the cortex) is our center for processing and storing information about the world in which we live and is also the starting place for virtually all of our voluntary action. The cerebral cortex is significantly larger than any other brain structure. It is the complex, delicate development of the cerebral cortex that makes us human.

Lobes and Localization

Figure 2.10 presents a top view and a side view of the cerebral cortex. You can see from these illustrations that deep folds of tissue of the human cerebral cortex provide us with markers for dividing it into major areas. The most noticeable division of the cortex can be seen in the top view, where we can see the very deep crevice that runs down the middle from front to back, dividing it into the left and right *cerebral hemispheres.*

A side view of a cerebral hemisphere (Fig. 2.10 shows us the left one) allows us to see the four major divisions of each hemisphere, called "lobes." The *frontal lobes,* located at the front of the brain, are the largest and are defined by two large crevices. The *temporal lobes* are located at the temples, with one on each side of the brain. The *occipital lobes,* at the very back of the brain, are defined arbitrarily, with no large crevices setting them off, and the *parietal lobes* are wedged in behind the frontal lobes and above the occipital and temporal lobes.

cerebral cortex

(or cerebrum) the large, convoluted outer covering of the brain that is the seat of cognitive functioning and voluntary action

FIGURE 2.11

A side view of the left cerebral hemisphere, showing the four lobes of the cerebral cortex and areas of localization of function.

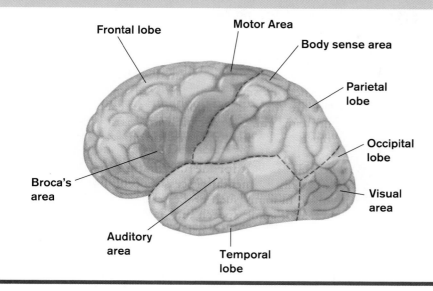

We have learned a lot about what happens in the different locations of the cortex, but many of the details of cerebral function have yet to be understood. There are three major areas that have been mapped: (1) *sensory areas*, where impulses from sense receptors are sent; (2) *motor areas*, where many voluntary movements originate; and (3) *association areas*, where higher mental processes occur. We'll now consider each of these areas in turn, referring to Figure 2.11, where general locations are indicated.

Sensory Areas. Let's review for just a minute. Receptor cells (specialized neurons) in our sense organs respond to stimuli in the environment. These cells pass neural impulses along sensory nerve fibers, eventually to the cerebral cortex. Senses in our body below our neck send impulses first to the spinal cord, then up the spinal cord, through the brain stem and thalamus, and beyond. After they leave the thalamus, impulses from our senses go to a particular **sensory area**—an area of the cerebral cortex that receives information from our senses. Which sensory area is involved depends on which sense is activated.

Reflecting their relative importance to us, large areas of the cerebral cortex are involved with vision and hearing. Virtually the entire occipital lobe processes visual information (the "visual area" in Fig. 2.11). Auditory (hearing) impulses end up in large centers ("auditory areas") in the temporal lobes.

Our body senses (touch, pressure, pain, and so on) from different parts of our body send impulses to a strip at the very front of the parietal lobe (the "body sense area" in Fig. 2.11). Within this area of the parietal lobe we can map out specific regions that correspond to different parts of the body. When we do so, we find that some body parts (e.g., the face, lips, and fingertips) are overrepresented in the body sense area of the cerebral

sensory areas
those areas of the cerebral cortex that receive impulses from our sense receptors

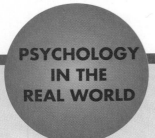
Who Left the Tack on the Hallway Floor?

You are walking down the hall late at night in your bare feet when—Ouch! You've stepped on a tack. Within seconds, you're hopping around on one foot, trying to grab the other, rapidly becoming angry at whomever it was who left the tack on the hallway floor. The whole scene lasts about two minutes. What role did your nervous system play in this scenario? Let's try to apply what we've learned in this chapter by formulating answers to a series of straightforward questions.

The point of the tack punctures the sole of your foot and stimulates a nerve cell. *What does it mean to say that a nerve cell is stimulated? What kind of nerve cell reacts to tacks? For that matter, what IS a nerve cell?*

Nerve cells, or neurons, are living cells that transmit impulses by releasing a tension that builds up between electrically charged chemical ions. When neurons are at rest (not stimulated), negatively charged ions are concentrated inside the neuron and positive ions are concentrated outside the neuron. Neurons can be stimulated to release their potential and transmit impulses in many different ways. Some specialized neurons respond directly to physical stimulation (like tacks). The neurons that carry impulses from our senses (such as pain) to our central nervous system are called sensory neurons.

The cell that is stimulated by the tack sends a message to other nerve cells. *Wait a minute! What do you mean "message?" How do messages get sent from one nerve cell to another?*

Saying that neurons send "messages" is a casual way of saying that they transmit impulses, changes in electrochemical potentials that travel from dendrite end to the axon end. Once at the end of the axon, impulses have reached the synapse, where the nature of transmission changes. At the synapse, chemical neurotransmitters are released from vesicles. The neurotransmitters travel across the synaptic cleft to the next neuron, stimulating it to fire.

Messages now race up your leg to the base of the spinal cord. *Why to the spinal cord? What does the spinal cord look like? What does it do?*

The spinal cord is one part of the central nervous system, a mass of neurons that looks like a piece of rope, and extends from your lower back up to the base of your brain (the other part of the CNS). One function of the spinal cord is to provide a quick route to and from

cortex, reflecting their high sensitivity. In other words, some parts of the body, even some very small ones, are processed in larger areas of the cortex than are other parts of the body.

This is a good place to remind ourselves of the concept of *cross-laterality*. Cross-laterality refers to the fact that information from senses on the left side of the body crosses over to the right side of the brain, and vice versa, with this crossing occurring in the brain stem. When someone touches your right arm, that touch is processed in your left parietal lobe. A tickle to your left foot is received by the right side of your cerebral cortex.

Motor Areas. We have seen that some of our actions—at least simple, involuntary, and reflexive ones—originate below the cerebral cortex. Although some lower brain centers may be involved, it is still fair to say that the brain, which is one reason why impulses enter there.

Once in the spinal cord, messages now go in two different directions: up to the brain and back down to the muscles in your leg. *How do the messages get to my brain? For that matter, how do they get to my leg? Do they go to my brain first?*

Impulses get to your brain by racing up nerve fibers in the white matter of your spinal cord. They pass through several structures, including the pons and the thalamus, on their way to your cerebral cortex. Neurons that carry these impulses are called interneurons because they are within the central nervous system. Once into the gray matter of the spinal cord, impulses also race back down to your leg to muscles there on motor neurons or motor fibers. These impulses do not go to the brain first—they are involved in a spinal reflex.

Messages from the spinal cord to your leg stimulate muscles to lift your leg quickly off the floor. At the same time, those messages to your brain are being interpreted. *Do you mean to say that my leg lifts up off the floor without my brain even thinking about it?*

That's right. This is a spinal reflex action for which your brain is quite unnecessary. *Doesn't my brain have to control that movement?* No, at least not the initial movement of jerking your foot up. True,

most movements—our voluntary, conscious movements in particular—do originate in the brain, usually at the very back of our frontal lobes of the cerebral cortex, in fact.

You identify the source of your pain as a tack. Still hopping on one foot, you wonder who left the tack on the hallway floor and start to get angry. *Ah, but to recognize a tack implies that I remember, or know, what a tack is. Where are memories stored in the brain? Are there separate parts of the brain involved in emotions like anger?*

Yes, recognizing that you've stepped on a tack does require memory, and we are quite sure that memories are stored in the brain—although we're not at all sure just how. More than that, it is most likely that memories are stored in those parts of the cerebral cortex we call association areas. There are many areas of the brain that become involved in emotionality. Perhaps of primary concern are the septum and the amygdala, two structures of the so-called limbic system.

And here's one more: *Suppose I stepped on that tack with my right foot instead of my left; to which side of the brain would impulses be sent?*

This is an easy one, isn't it? Given the cross-laterality that occurs in the brain stem, the left side of your cerebral cortex would be the first to know about the tack in this circumstance.

most *voluntary activity* originates in the **motor areas** of the cerebral cortex— in strips at the very back of our frontal lobes. The motor areas (there are two of them, left and right) are directly across the central fissure from the body sense areas in the parietal lobe (Fig. 2.11). I need to make the disclaimer that the actual, thoughtful decision-making process of whether or not one should move probably occurs elsewhere, almost certainly at the very front of the frontal lobes.

As is the case for sensory processing, some muscle groups (e.g., those that control movements of the hands and mouth) are processed by disproportionately larger areas of the cerebral cortex.

As you know, we also find cross-laterality with the motor area. It is your right hemisphere's motor area that controls the movements of the left side of your body. Someone who has had a cerebral stroke (a disruption of

motor areas
the strips at the back of the frontal lobes that control voluntary movement

association areas
the areas of the frontal, parietal, and temporal lobes in which higher mental processing occurs

blood flow in the brain resulting in the loss of neural tissue) in the *left side* of his or her brain will have impaired movement of the *right side* of his or her body.

Association Areas. Once we've located the cerebral areas that process sensory information and originate motor responses, we still have a lot of cortex left over. The remaining areas are called **association areas**—areas of the cerebral cortex in which sensory input is "associated" with motor responses—where cognitive functions such as problem solving, remembering, and thinking occur. There are three association areas in each hemisphere: frontal, parietal, and temporal. Just what happens in these association areas is not well understood.

There is considerable support for the idea that it is in our association areas that so-called higher mental processes occur. The frontal association areas are involved in many such processes. As Pierre-Paul Broca (1824–1880) discovered more than a century ago, most language and speech behaviors are localized in the frontal association area. Damage to the very front of the frontal lobes may interrupt or destroy the abilities to plan ahead, think quickly, or think things through.

We should remind ourselves not to get too carried away with localization of function in the cerebral cortex. Let's not fall into the trap of coming to believe that separate little parts of the cerebral cortex operate independently and have the sole responsibility for any one function. Neurologist Marcel Kinsbourne put it this way: "There are no discontinuities in the brain. No independent channels traverse it; nor is its territory divisible into areas that house autonomous processors" (1982, p. 412). This will be particularly important to keep in mind as we now look at the division of the cerebral cortex into right and left hemispheres.

● **Before You Go On**

Locate the four lobes of the cerebral cortex on a side view of the brain.

Locate the sensory, motor, and association areas of the cerebrum, and describe what happens there.

The Two Cerebral Hemispheres—Splitting the Brain

The ancient Greeks knew that the cerebral cortex was divided into hemispheres. That there should be a division of the cerebral cortex into two halves seemed quite natural. After all, we have two eyes, arms, legs, lungs, kidneys, and so forth—why not two divisions of the brain? Within the last 30 years, interest in this hemispheric division has heightened as researchers have accumulated evidence that each half of the cerebral cortex may have primary responsibility for different mental functions.

In most humans, the left hemisphere of the cerebral cortex is the larger of the two halves, contains a higher proportion of gray matter, and is thought to be the dominant hemisphere (more active in more tasks). We've already noted that the language center is housed in the left cerebral hemisphere. At least this is so for virtually all right-handed people. For *some* left-handed people, language may be processed primarily by the right hemisphere. Because humans are so language-oriented, not much attention was given to the "lowly" right hemisphere. Then a remarkable surgical procedure, first performed in the 1960s, provided us with new insights about the two cerebral hemispheres (Sperry, 1968; 1982; Springer & Deutsch, 1981).

Normally, the two hemispheres of the cerebral cortex are interconnected by a series of fibers called the **corpus callosum** (which can be seen in Figure 2.9). Through the corpus callosum, one side of our cortex remains in complete contact with the other. Separating the functions of the two hemispheres is possible through a surgical technique called a **split-brain procedure**, which destroys the corpus callosum's connections. The process is neither as complicated nor as dangerous as it sounds. The surgery was first tried on humans in 1961 by Joseph Brogan in an attempt to lessen the severity of the symptoms of epilepsy. As an irreversible treatment of last resort, the split-brain procedure has been very successful.

Most of what we know about the activities of the cerebral hemispheres we have learned from split-brain subjects, both human and animal. One of the things that makes this procedure remarkable is that under normal circumstances split-brain patients behave quite normally. Only in the laboratory can we see the results of having made the hemispheres of the cerebral cortex function independently (e.g., Gazzaniga & LeDoux, 1978; Hellige, 1983).

Experiments with split-brain patients confirm that speech production is a left hemisphere function in a great majority of people. Suppose you have your hands behind your back. I place a house key in your left hand, and ask you to tell me what it is. Your left hand feels the key. Impulses travel up your left arm, up your spinal cord, and cross over to your right cerebral hemisphere—remember cross-laterality. You can readily tell me that the object in your hand is a key because your brain is intact. Your right hemisphere passes the information about the key to your left hemisphere, and your left hemisphere directs you to say, "It's a key." Now suppose that your corpus callosum is severed (that you are a split-brain subject). Now you cannot answer my question, even though you understand it perfectly. Why not? Your right brain knows that the object in your left hand is a key, but without a corpus callosum, it has no way to inform the left hemisphere, where your speech center is located. You *would* be able to point out the key from among other objects placed before you, under the direction of the right cerebral hemisphere. Once your eyes saw you do so, they would communicate that information to your left hemisphere, and now it too would know, and tell us, what your right hemisphere knew all along!

A major task of the left hemisphere, then, is the production of speech. But before we go any further, we need to pause and caution against overinterpretation. When results from split-brain studies were first made known, many people—psychologists and nonpsychologists alike—rushed to premature conclusions. We now believe that virtually no behavior, virtually no mental process, is the simple and single product of just one hemisphere (e.g., Hellige, 1990). It is more reasonable to say that one hemisphere dominates the other, or is the primary processing area for certain actions. For example, the left hemisphere is dominant in the perception and interpretation of speech. But some language processing seems to be primarily the responsibility of the right hemisphere. The right hemisphere is more involved in the processing of common phrases and cliches such as "How do you do?" or "Have a nice day!" (Kempler & Van Lancker, 1987).

Being careful not to overinterpret, what are some of the activities processed *primarily* in one hemisphere or the other? We've seen that the left hemisphere can be given credit for most of our language skills, and given our reliance on language, that's no small matter. Simple arithmetic tasks of calculation also seem to be primarily a left brain function. Indeed, the left hemisphere is often credited with the processing of information in an analytical, one-piece-at-a-time sort of way, although the data here are a bit tenuous (Hellige, 1990, p. 59).

corpus callosum
a network of nerve fibers that interconnect the two hemispheres of the cerebrum

split-brain procedure
a surgical technique of severing the corpus callosum, causing the two hemispheres to operate independently

Although we must be careful not to overgeneralize, we may say that a major task of the left cerebral hemisphere is the use of language (as in working a crossword puzzle). A major task of the right cerebral hemisphere is the appreciation of spatial relations (as in working on a jigsaw puzzle).

What then of the right hemisphere? The right hemisphere of the cerebral cortex dominates the processing of visually presented information (Bradshaw & Nettleton, 1983; Kosslyn, 1987). Putting together a jigsaw puzzle, for instance, uses the right hemisphere more than the left. Skill in the visual arts (painting and drawing, for example) is associated with the right hemisphere more than the left. The right hemisphere is also credited with being more involved in emotionality—both interpreting emotional stimuli and expressing emotional reactions. Consistent with the hypothesis that the left hemisphere tends to be analytic and sequential in dealing with information, the right seems better able to grasp the big picture, see the overall view of things, and be somewhat more creative.

Even these few possibilities are intriguing. There do seem to be differences in how the two sides of the cerebral cortex process information. But the differences are slight, and many remain controversial. In fact, we are finding that the more we study hemispheric differences, the more we tend to find similarities. Any special programs or courses that claim to be designed to train or educate one side of your brain to the exclusion of the other are misguided, no matter how well-intentioned they may be.

● **Before You Go On**

What is a split-brain procedure, why has it been done on humans, and what have we learned from it?

Briefly summarize the different functions of the left and right cerebral hemispheres of the human brain.

THINKING CRITICALLY ABOUT THE NERVOUS SYSTEM AND BEHAVIOR

1. Why would a psychology student who wanted to be a clinical psychologist and help people deal with the problems of their lives need to know about the nervous systems, neurons, spinal cords, and brains?
2. How do you suppose that scientists have learned so much about the intricate workings of the neural impulse and impulse transmission at the synapse?

3. What would happen if someone were to take a drug that delivered extra amounts of an inhibitory neurotransmitter substance to the synapses of the nervous system? What if someone took a drug that stopped neurons from releasing excitatory neurotransmitters in the first place? Do such drugs exist?

4. What happens to neurotransmitter chemicals once they perform their function?

5. Can you review each of the structures of the spinal cord and brain that has been introduced in this chapter and indicate what would happen if that structure were either stimulated or destroyed?

6. If you wanted to begin an education or training program that "fully trained all aspects of the human brain," what sorts of training exercises would you include in your program? For example, how would you "train" the left and the right hemispheres of the cerebral cortex?

7. As it happens, the physical size of one's brain seems to have little to do with what we normally call "intelligence." Why is that? What aspect of the brain does?

SUMMARY

TOPIC 2A

NEURONS: BUILDING BLOCKS OF THE NERVOUS SYSTEM

● What are the major structures of a neuron?
● What is myelin, and what is its function?

There are three major structures of a neuron: the cell body, which houses the nucleus of the cell; a number of dendrites, which usually receive neural impulses; and an axon, which carries impulses away from the cell body. The axons of some neurons are covered by a white, fatty myelin sheath that insulates and protects the delicate axon and speeds impulses: along the axon. Even myelinated axons end with a set of bare axon terminals. *Pages 50–53.*

● What is the basic process involved when a neuron fires?

When a neuron fires, a tension created by an imbalance of electrically charged chemical ions is quickly released. When a neuron is *NOT* firing, or is at rest, the inside of the neuron is more negatively charged than is the outside (a resting potential of –70mv). Where the impulse occurs, this polarity changes, and the inside of the neuron momentarily becomes positive compared to the outside (an action potential of +40mv). *Pages 53–55.*

● Summarize neural impulse transmission at the synapse.
● Name and briefly describe the actions of four neurotransmitters.

At the synapse, an impulse triggers the release of neurotransmitter chemicals which flood across the synaptic cleft to the membranes of adjacent neurons. If sufficient quantities of neurotransmitter are released, either new impulses will be excited or the process will be inhibited. Acetylcholine is a common neurotransmitter involved in muscular activity and memory formation. Norepinephrine is involved in heightened states of emotionality. Dopamine affects a wide range of functioning, depending on which system of nerve fibers is involved. It is implicated in mood and thought disturbances. Endorphins are natural pain suppressors. *Pages 55–57.*

TOPIC 2B

THE CENTRAL NERVOUS SYSTEM

● Name the different human nervous systems, and indicate how they are related to each other.

See Figure 2.5. The major division is into CNS and PNS, where the CNS is divided into the brain and the spinal cord and the PNS is divided into the so-matic and autonomic (ANS) nervous systems. The ANS is further divided into the sympathetic and parasympathetic divisions. The endocrine system is a network of glands that, under the direction of the brain and the ANS, secretes hormones into the bloodstream which, in turn, influence behavior and mental processes. *Pages 58–60.*

● Why does spinal cord injury sometimes cause paralysis?
● Describe the major features of a spinal reflex.

If the spinal cord is damaged, impulses originating in the brain meant to move parts of the body cannot get past the damaged area to stimulate the appropriate muscles, resulting in paralysis. In a spinal reflex, impulses enter the spinal cord on sensory fibers, (may) synapse with interneurons, and then exit the spinal cord on motor fibers to activate a muscle response. At the same time, impulses are sent to the brain on fibers in the spinal cord's white matter. *Pages 60–63.*

● Name the two brain stem structures, indicate where they are located, and describe what they do.

The brain stem is made up of the medulla and the pons. The medulla, at the very base of the brain, controls several important reflexes, monitors heart rate and breathing, and is where most cross-laterality occurs. The pons, just above the medulla, acts like a bridge, passing impulses between the spinal cord and the brain. *Pages 63–64.*

● Where is the cerebellum located, and what is its major function?

The cerebellum is located at the posterior base of the brain and is most involved in the smoothing and coordinating of rapid muscular movements. *Pages 64–65.*

● Indicate the locations and briefly describe the major functions of the RAS, the limbic system, the hypothalamus, and the thalamus.

The RAS (reticular activating system) extends from the brain stem through the middle of the brain to the cerebral cortex and is involved in maintaining levels of arousal. The limbic system, just above the brain stem, is involved in emotional expression (the amygdala and septum in particular) and the transfer of information to long-term memory (the hippocampus). The hypothalamus, which is near the limbic system, is involved in reactions and responses such as feeding, drinking, sex, aggression, and temperature regulation. The thalamus, located just below the cerebral cortex, is a final relay station for sensory impulses that it projects up to the appropriate parts of the cerebrum. *Pages 66–67.*

● Locate the four lobes of the cerebral cortex on a side view of the brain.
● Locate the sensory, motor, and association areas of the cerebrum, and describe what happens there.

The location of the frontal, temporal, parietal, and occipital lobes can be reviewed in Figure 2.10. Figure 2.11 shows the location of the sensory, motor, and association areas. Sensory areas of the cerebral cortex (visual, auditory, and body sense) receive impulses (through the thalamus) from our senses. Voluntary motor activity is initiated in the motor areas, and cognitive processes, such as memory, thinking, and problem solving, are thought to occur in the so-called association areas. *Pages 68–72.*

● What is a split-brain procedure, why has it been done on humans, and what have we learned from it?
● Briefly summarize the different functions of the left and right cerebral hemispheres of the human brain.

The split-brain procedure severs the fibers of the corpus callosum, the structure that carries impulses back and forth between the two cerebral hemispheres. The procedure allows the hemispheres to function independently. It is used as a treatment of last resort for epilepsy. Although one hemisphere occasionally may dominate the other, seldom does one have total and complete control of any important brain function. It is safe to say that language and speech are usually processed in the left hemisphere, while visual, spatial information is usually processed in the right. Also possible, but less certain, is the left hemisphere's dominance in simple calculations, and the sequential, analytical processing of information. The right hemisphere is somewhat more involved with the "big picture," with the visual arts, and with emotionality. *Pages 72–74.*

TEST
YOURSELF

TOPIC 2A

NEURONS: BUILDING BLOCKS OF THE NERVOUS SYSTEM

2.1 Of the following structures, which is likely to occur in neurons in the greatest number? a) dendrites b) nuclei c) axons d) cell bodies. *Pages 50–53.*

2.2 Myelin sheaths serve a number of different functions. Which of these is *not* something that myelin does? a) It insulates axons from nearby neurons. b) It helps to speed up neural impulses. c) It contains the neuron's genes and chromosomes. d) It protects the delicate axon from physical damage. *Pages 50–53.*

2.3 If a neuron dies a) a new neuron will be created to take its place. b) the result will be paralysis. c) its function may be replaced by the action of other neurons. d) the psychological experience will be a slight sensation of pain. *Pages 50–53.*

2.4 True or False? Myelinated neurons carry impulses faster than unmyelinated neurons. *Pages 50–53.*

2.5 True or False? The number of neurons in our brains gradually increases from birth until they begin to die off in our old age. *Pages 50–53.*

2.6 When a neuron is "at rest" a) it has no electrical charge. b) the inside of the neuron has a negative charge compared to the outside. c) it is in the process of "firing" or transmitting an impulse. d) chemical ions are racing in and out of the neuron through its membrane. *Pages 53–55.*

2.7 When an impulse moves down, or along, a neuron, what physically moves from one end of the neuron to the other? a) the chemical ions b) the neural membrane c) the fluids within the neuron d) nothing. *Pages 53–55.*

2.8 Although there are many specific neurotransmitters, we can classify them in terms of their action as being either a) central or peripheral. b) sensory or motor. c) excitatory or inhibitory. d) axonic or dendritic. *Pages 55–57.*

2.9 The action of neurotransmitters at the synapse is basically a(n)_____ process. a) electrical b) mechanical c) chemical d) psychological. *Pages 55–57.*

TOPIC 2B

THE CENTRAL NERVOUS SYSTEM

2.10 Of the following, which nervous system is most intimately involved in our experience of emotionality? a) the peripheral nervous system b) the parasympathetic nervous system c) the automatic nervous system d) the sympathetic nervous system. *Pages 58–60.*

2.11 When we look at a cross-section of the spinal cord, we clearly see areas that are made up of white matter. In this white matter we have a) the location where reflexes occur. b) fibers going to and from the brain. c) dorsal roots, but few, if any, ventral roots. d) the part of the spinal cord that controls our emotions. *Pages 60–63.*

2.12 In a spinal reflex, neural impulses enter the spinal cord on a) motor neurons. b) ascending tracts or fibers. c) sensory neurons. d) descending tracts or fibers. *Pages 60–63.*

2.13 True or False? The correct sequence of events in a spinal reflex may be summarized as: In on sensory neurons, within on interneurons, and out on motor neurons. *Pages 60–63.*

2.14 As one travels up through the brain from the spinal cord, the first brain structure one encounters would be the a) corpus callosum. b) hypothalamus. c) medulla. d) thalamus. *Pages 63–64.*

2.15 Which of the following is best associated with the medulla? a) thinking or problem solving b) breathing reflexes c) sensory projections to the cerebral cortex d) muscle coordination. *Pages 63–64.*

2.16 Cross laterality occurs in the a) spinal cord. b) brain stem. c) limbic system. d) base of the cortex. *Pages 63–64.*

2.17 If someone were to cut your pons, the result would be that you would be a) blind. b) unable to control your emotions. c) unable to store information in memory. d) paralyzed from the neck down. *Pages 63–64.*

2.18 True or False? As the human organism develops, the first brain structure to develop is the most important: the cerebral cortex. *Pages 68–74.*

2.19 Speaking requires many different, interrelated areas of the brain. Which lower brain center is involved in coordinating the muscles that produce speech sounds? a) the right frontal lobe b) the limbic system c) the medulla d) the cerebellum. *Pages 63–69.*

2.20 If I were to electrically stimulate the reticular activating system of a sleeping cat, the result would be that the cat would a) no longer demonstrate normal emotional responses. b) die. c) begin to make small twitching movements, indicative of dreaming. d) wake up. *Pages 66–67.*

2.21 A railroad worker by the name of Phineas Gage survived an accident in which an iron bar was thrust through his head, destroying brain tissue. One result of the accident was that Gage had much less control of his emotional reactions, which suggests that the accident cut tissues between his cerebral cortex and his a) limbic system. b) corpus callosum. c) medulla. d) cerebellum. *Pages 63–69.*

2.22 Which lower brain center is most clearly involved in our experience of being thirsty? a) the hypothalamus b) the hippocampus c) the amygdala d) the septum. *Pages 66–67.*

2.23 The brain structure that sends, or projects, sensory impulses to the appropriate area of the cerebral cortex is the a) thalamus. b) projectotator. c) medulla nuclei. d) sense area of the parietal lobe. *Pages 66–67.*

2.24 Our body senses (touch, pressure, and so on) are largely processed in the front of the _____ lobe of the cerebral cortex. a) occipital b) parietal c) temporal d) frontal. *Pages 68–72.*

2.25 Most of the neurons located in the gray matter at the center of the spinal cord are a) myelinated neurons. b) sensory neurons. c) motor neurons. d) interneurons. *Pages 68–72.*

2.26 True or False? Visual information is processed in the occipital lobe of the cerebral cortex. *Pages 68–72.*

2.27 A person has had a split-brain operation to separate her left and right cerebral hemispheres. She is blindfolded. A paper clip is placed in her *left* hand and we ask her to tell us what we have placed there. She will a) tell us that the object is a paper clip and can point to it when it is placed on a table with other objects. b) have no idea what the object is. c) be unable to tell us what it is at first, but can point to it when it is placed on a table with other objects. d) respond just as if we had placed it in her right hand. *Pages 72–74.*

2.28 True or False? Someone whose corpus callosum has been severed in a split-brain operation probably will have to be hospitalized or closely supervised for the rest of his or her life. *Pages 72–74.*

HUMAN DEVELOPMENT

PREVIEW

TOPIC 3A—Prenatal Development

Physical Aspects of Prenatal Development

Environmental Influences on Prenatal Development

TOPIC 3B—Development in Children

Motor Development: Getting From Here to There

Sensory and Perceptual Development

Cognitive and Social Development

TOPIC 3C—Adolescence and Adulthood

What Are Adolescents Really Like?

Some Challenges of Adolescence

Early Adulthood

PSYCHOLOGY IN THE REAL WORLD: Divorce and Its Impact on Children

Middle Adulthood

Late Adulthood

THINKING CRITICALLY ABOUT HUMAN DEVELOPMENT

CHAPTER SUMMARY

TEST YOURSELF

From conception to death, human beings share certain developmental events that unite us as one species. As we have already noted, it is also true that each of us is unique—different from everyone else. Developmental psychologists are interested in the common patterns of our development and growth, *and* they care about the ways in which we differ throughout our lives.

There are several ways in which a discussion of human development can be organized. I've chosen to take a chronological approach and have divided this chapter into three Topics.

We tend to think that a person's development begins at birth. In fact, growth and development begin much earlier—at conception, and with the first division of one cell into two. Topic 3A focuses on factors that influence the development of the organism from conception to birth—the prenatal period of development. We'll turn our attention to the development of children in Topic 3B, considering some of the highlights in three areas of development: physical-motor, sensory-perceptual, and cognitive-social. In each case, we will first mention the capabilities of the newborn child, or neonate.

Topic 3C acknowledges the fact that growth and development do not end with childhood. Indeed, we continue to develop throughout adolescence and adulthood. Most of the changes that reflect our development during these periods are more gradual and subtle than those that occur in childhood.

Throughout this chapter we will be discussing human development in terms of developmental stages or periods and critical events. It is easy to be impressed with the apparent orderliness and predictability of human development. We must remember not to take all of this too literally. Orderly sequences of development emerge from examining averages and progressions *in general*. The individual differences we see around us constantly remind us that for any one person—child, adolescent, or adult—some of our generalizations may not hold true. Some of the apparent orderliness of human development may exist only in the eyes of the observer.

conception
the moment when the father's sperm cell unites with the mother's ovum to produce a zygote

zygote
the one-celled product of the union of the sperm and ovum at conception

T O P I C   3 A
PRENATAL DEVELOPMENT

Human development begins at **conception**, the moment when the father's sperm cell unites with the mother's ovum. At that time, 23 chromosomes from each parent pair off within a single cell, called a **zygote**. We have, at conception, the complete transmission of all inherited characteristics from our parents.

Within the next 30 hours or so, that one-cell zygote will divide and become two cells. In three days, there may be about a dozen cells; after five days, there will be slightly more than 100 (Moore, 1982; Torrey & Feduccia, 1979). No one knows how many cells the human organism has at birth, and few are willing to hazard a guess; "more than a trillion" is probably a conservative estimate (Moore, 1982).

As we review the physical stages of development, I hope you will keep in mind that our knowledge of these *physical processes* helps us to understand the ultimate development of *psychological processes*. If nothing else, if there are problems at any stage of physical development, there will also be problems in terms of psychological development.

Throughout our discussion, I will use the terms *growth* and *development* to mean slightly different things. Growth refers to simple physical enlargement—getting bigger. A child demonstrates growth just by becoming taller and heavier. Development, on the other hand, implies differentiation of structure or function. Something develops when it appears for the first time and remains; thus we say that the nervous system "develops" between week 2 and week 8 after conception.

PHYSICAL ASPECTS OF PRENATAL DEVELOPMENT

The period from conception to birth is called the **prenatal period** of development. Until recently, this period of human development received only minor attention from psychologists. We now recognize that events that can have lifelong consequences occur during this very sensitive period. Prenatal development is divided into three stages or periods: the stages of the zygote, embryo, and fetus.

The *stage of the zygote* is the shortest prenatal stage—from conception until approximately two weeks later, when the zygote becomes implanted in the wall of the uterus. The ovum usually is fertilized as it moves along the fallopian tubes from the ovaries, where ova (the plural of ovum) are stored and released, one at a time, at approximately 28-day intervals. It typically takes the zygote about seven days to travel down the fallopian tube to the uterus and another seven days to become firmly attached there (Figure 3.1). At this point, the zygote has grown to include hundreds of cells, and for the first time it is clear that not all the cells are exact replicas of one another. That is, there is now some differentiation among the cells of the zygote. Some cells, for example, develop to form the protective placenta, while others form the umbilical cord that ultimately will supply nourishment to the developing organism.

Once implantation is complete, the stage of the zygote is over, and the organism has entered the *stage of the embryo*. This stage lasts about six weeks, from week 2 to week 8. During this period, the embryo develops rapidly. At the beginning of this stage, we can identify three types of cells: those that will become the nervous system, the sense organs, and the skin; those that will form the internal organs; and those that will form the muscles, skeleton, and blood vessels. By the end of this stage, we can identify the face area, eyes, ears, fingers, toes, and male or female genitals. That is, not only does the number of cells increase, but the number of types of cells also increases.

prenatal period
the period of development from conception to birth

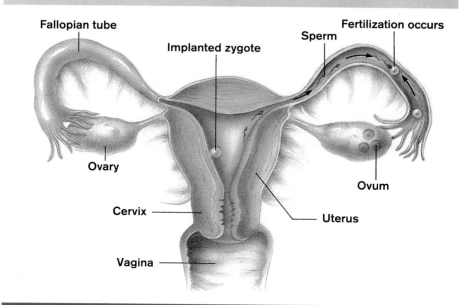

FIGURE 3.1
The female reproductive organs, indicating where fertilization and implantation normally take place.

During this stage—conservatively, within the first three months—the unborn is most sensitive to environmental influences. If there are going to be problems (e.g., birth defects), they are most likely to develop during this period. For example, if the heart, hands, eyes, or ears do not become differentiated and develop now, there will be no way to compensate later. The central nervous system is at risk throughout prenatal development, but particularly so in weeks 3 through 6.

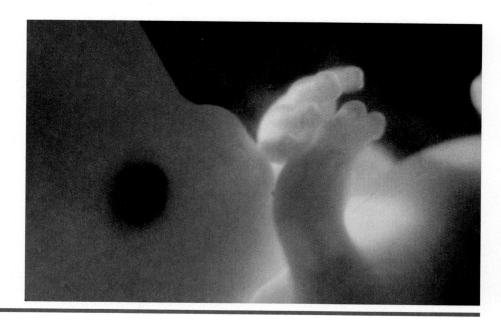

A human embryo at eight weeks, soon to enter the stage of the fetus. It is during the embryonic stage that environmental toxins are most likely to have an impact on the developing prenatal organism.

Two months after conception, the stage of the embryo draws to a close. The one-inch-long embryo now has enough of a primitive nervous system to respond to a light touch with a simple reflex movement.

The final period of prenatal development is also the longest, the *stage of the fetus,* which includes months 3 through 9. Not only do the organs of the body continue to increase in complexity and size, they begin to function. The arms and legs move spontaneously by the end of the third month. In two more months, these movements will be strong enough for the mother to feel them. At the end of the fifth month, the fetus is approximately 10 inches long. Internal organs have developed, but not to the point of sustaining life outside the uterus. The brain has developed, but neurons within it have not formed many synapses.

Development and growth continue through the last few months of pregnancy. The most noticeable change—certainly most noticeable to the mother—is the significant increase in weight and overall movement of the fetus. Sometime during the seventh month, most fetuses have reached the point of **viability**—the point at which, if forced to do so, an organism can survive and continue to develop without medical intervention if born prematurely. During its last few weeks in the uterus, the growth rate of the fetus slows. Its movements may be more powerful, but overall activity is also slowed due to the lack of room in which to move. After nearly 270 days, the fetus is ready to enter the world as a newborn.

viability
the ability to survive without interference or intervention

● **Before You Go On**

Briefly summarize the three stages of prenatal development.

ENVIROMENTAL INFLUENCES ON PRENATAL DEVELOPMENT

In most cases, development of the human organism from zygote to embryo to fetus progresses according to the blueprint laid down in the genes. Even in the prenatal period, however, the human organism is not immune to environmental influences.

"Until the early 1940s, it was generally accepted that human embryos were protected from environmental agents by their fetal membranes and their mother's abdominal walls and uterus" (Moore, 1982, p. 140). It was then discovered that birth defects often resulted when a pregnant woman contracted *rubella,* or German measles. By the 1960s, it was established that many drugs taken by a pregnant woman have measurable effects on the development of the embryo and fetus. It is now common knowledge that during the rapid stage of prenatal development even small environmental disturbances can have serious and lasting consequences. Most of the external influences on prenatal development that we know about are those that tend to have negative consequences.

Nourishment

Never meant to be taken literally, the old expression "You are what you eat" does have some truth to it. By the same token, before we are born we are what our mothers eat. When pregnant women eat poorly, the unborn may

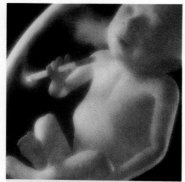

WOULD YOU GIVE A CIGARETTE TO YOUR UNBORN CHILD?

YOU DO EVERY TIME YOU SMOKE!

AMERICAN CANCER SOCIETY

Studies reveal that women who smoke during pregnancy significantly increase their chance of having miscarriages, stillbirths, low-weight babies, and babies who die shortly after birth.

fetal alcohol syndrome
a cluster of symptoms (e.g., low birth weight, poor muscle tone, intellectual retardation), associated with a child born to a mother who was a heavy drinker of alcohol during pregnancy

share in the consequences. Maternal malnutrition leads to increases in miscarriages, stillbirths, and premature births. At best, we can expect the newborn child of a malnourished mother to be similarly malnourished (Lozoff, 1989).

It is also the case that deficiencies in specific vitamins and minerals affect the prenatal organism (Bratic, 1982). For example, a mother's calcium deficiencies affect the development of bones and teeth in the fetus. As is the case for many nutrients, it may very well be the mother who suffers most. If there are inadequate supplies of calcium in the mother's system, "the fetal need for calcium will be met at the expense of the mother" (Hughes & Noppe, 1985, p. 140).

Smoking, Drinking, and Drugs

There is ample evidence that smoking has harmful effects on the smoker. Smoking by pregnant women has equally harmful effects on their unborn children (Frazier et al., 1961; Fribourg, 1982; Jacobson, 1984). Just *how* smoking affects the fetus is not known, but we know that cigarette smoking is a cause of retarded prenatal growth (Golbus, 1980). Children born to mothers who smoke during pregnancy are likely to be of lower weight at birth and to have hearing defects. Such children also have lower IQ scores, even at the age of only four (Fried, 1993). Smoking mothers have miscarriages, stillbirths, and babies who die soon after birth more frequently than do mothers who do not smoke (Frazier, et al., 1961; Golbus, 1980).

Alcohol is a commonly abused drug that can be injurious to unborn children. Alcohol is quickly passed through the umbilical cord from the mother to the fetus. Heavy drinking (3 drinks per day) significantly increases the chance of having smaller babies with retarded physical growth, poor coordination, poor muscle tone, intellectual retardation, and other problems, collectively called **fetal alcohol syndrome** (Jones et al., 1973; Mattson, Barron & Riley, 1988). In the United States, fetal alcohol syndrome is the leading preventable cause of birth defects that produce mental retardation (Streissguth et al., 1991). The Centers for Disease Control estimates that 8,000 babies with the syndrome are born in the United States every year. In the 1970s, it was thought that a social drink or two had no particular lasting effect on prenatal development. Now, the best advice is total abstinence (Abel, 1981, 1984; Barr et al., 1990).

Mothers who use or abuse drugs such as heroin, cocaine, or "crack" during pregnancy cause considerable complications for their unborn children. Such children enter the world with low birth weights, difficulty regulating sleep/wake cycles, and symptoms of fetal alcohol syndrome (Finnegan, 1982; Zuckerman & Bresnahan, 1991). They are born addicted themselves and must—within days of birth—suffer the pains of withdrawal, requiring a hospital stay averaging 42 days instead of the usual one to three days (Adler, 1989; Chasnoff, et al., 1989; Finnegan, 1982).

Some drugs (e.g., penicillin) taken by the mother during her pregnancy have few if any effects on the developing child (Golbus, 1980). Others have subtle or direct effects—some life-threatening, some not. The antibiotic tetracycline, for example, when passed to the developing fetus is deposited in the teeth and bones, coloring them yellow. Even common aspirin has become suspect as a potential cause of complications in pregnancy and labor (Govoni & Hayes, 1988; Sibai et al., 1993). The bottom-line advice is very clear: Pregnant women should use drugs of any sort only with great care, and only after consultation with their physicians.

Maternal Stress

There is a certain logic that tells us that a mother's emotional health can affect her unborn baby. There is even some physiological evidence to support the argument. As we shall see, emotionality is accompanied by many hormonal changes that may have some influence on the development of the embryo or fetus. Also, when a pregnant mother is under stress, the blood flow in her body is, at least for a while, diverted from the uterus to other organs, reducing the amount of oxygen available to the prenatal organism (Stechler & Halton, 1982). As logical and time-honored as the argument may be, research evidence is difficult to find (Istvan, 1986).

You've no doubt noted that most of our discussion so far has focused on the pregnant mother. What about Dad? We're only now coming to appreciate just how important the father is in setting the course of prenatal development. The issue, of course, revolves around the quality of the father's sperm at conception—and those factors that affect sperm quality. We know, for example, that about one-third of all cases of the form of retardation known as Down's Syndrome are due to difficulties with the father's sperm. (Among other things, the syndrome is significantly more likely in children whose fathers have jobs that involve the use of toxic chemicals.) Alcohol use by fathers has been implicated as a probable cause of prenatal and birth abnormalities, but most of this research has been done with rats and mice (Hood, 1990). It may be that many difficulties of pregnancy, birth, and development are due to the condition of the father—who may be undernourished, an alcohol abuser, a drug user, or under stress—near the time of conception (Brown, 1985; Soyka & Joffee, 1980).

● **Before You Go On**

Briefly review the impact of diet, drugs, and stress on prenatal development.

T O P I C   3 B

DEVELOPMENT IN CHILDREN

Now we turn our attention to development in **childhood**, the period between birth and adolescence. In this section, we'll focus on the physical growth of children and note the orderly sequence of the development of their motor responses—abilities to do things with their bodies. We'll begin by considering some of the abilities of the newborn infant.

childhood
the period of human development between birth and puberty (the onset of adolescence)

MOTOR DEVELOPMENT — GETTING FROM HERE TO THERE

As recently as 20 years ago, textbooks on child psychology seldom devoted more than a few paragraphs to the behaviors of the **neonate**—the newborn through the first two weeks of life. It was as if the neonate did not do much

neonate
the newborn, from birth to age two weeks

FIGURE 3.2
Reflexes of the Neonate

Name	Stimulus	Response	Age when disappears
Moro	Loud sound, or sudden loss of support	Arms and legs thrown outward; fingers spread; then, with fists clenched, arms and legs pulled back	4–6 months
Rooting	Light stroke on cheek	Head turns toward stimulus; mouth opens; sucking begins	3–4 months
Sucking	Object (e.g., nipple) inserted in mouth 3–4 cm.	Rhythmic sucking and mouth movements	variable
Grasping	Rod pressed in palm	Close fist and grasp firmly	3–5 months
Walking/ stepping	With feet just touching surface, baby moved forward	Coordinated rhythmic stepping movements	2–4 months
Babinski	Stroke sole of foot from heel to toes.	Small toes spread; big toe raised	9–12 months
Tonic neck	With baby on head to one side	Arm and leg thrust outward, while other arm and leg drawn in to body	3–4 months
Swimming	Place infant in water	Rhythmic swimming movements	4–6 months

worth writing about. Today, most child psychology texts devote considerable space to a discussion of the abilities of newborns. It is unlikely that over the past 20 years neonates have gotten smarter or more able. But psychologists have—they have devised better ways of assessing the abilities of neonates.

A careful examination of babies reveals that they are capable of a wide range of behaviors. Almost all of these behaviors are *reflexive*—simple, unlearned, involuntary reactions to specific stimuli. Many of the neonate's reflexive responses serve a useful purpose. Some do not seem to have any survival value, but even these are important because they can be used as diagnostic indicators of the quality of the neonate's development, particularly the development of the nervous system. There are more than a dozen reflexes that can be observed and measured (for strength and duration, for example) in the newborn child (see Figure 3.2).

Parents trying to keep their young children in properly fitting clothes know how quickly children grow. In their first three years, children's height and weight increase at a rate never again equaled. Although changes in size

FIGURE 3.3
The sequence of human motor development. Each bar represents the ages at which between 25 percent of children (left end) and 90 percent of children (right end) engage in a given behavior. The short vertical line indicates the age at which 50 percent of children exhibit that behavior. (After Frankenburg & Dodds, 1967.)

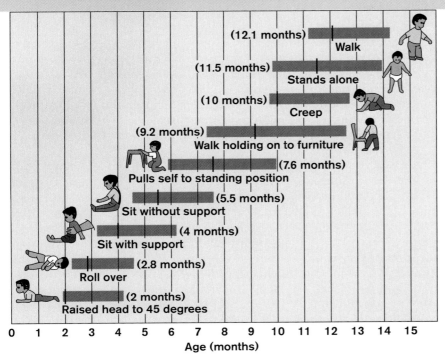

(12.1 months) **Walk**

(11.5 months) **Stands alone**

(10 months) **Creep**

(9.2 months) **Walk holding on to furniture**

(7.6 months) **Pulls self to standing position**

(5.5 months) **Sit without support**

(4 months) **Sit with support**

(2.8 months) **Roll over**

(2 months) **Raised head to 45 degrees**

Age (months)

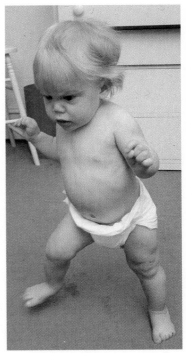

Whether a child begins to walk at 10 months or 13 months, he or she will still follow the same sequence of sitting, crawling, then walking. Here an 11-month-old works on mastering that first step.

and motor skills are rapid, they tend to be orderly and follow a prescribed pattern. It is with that pattern that we are concerned here.

No two children can be expected to grow at the same rate or develop control over their bodies at the same age. Joanne may walk at the age of 10 months. Bill may not venture forth on his own until he's 13 months old. Differences between children are often as great as their similarities.

Regardless of the *rate* of motor development, there are regularities in the *sequence* of motor development. The development of some common motor skills is summarized in Figure 3.3. There are two important things for you to notice here. The sequence of events is very regular, but *when* each behavior develops includes a range of ages that should be considered normal. The sequence and timing of the events in this figure hold equally for boys and girls. In these basic motor skills there are no sex differences.

● **Before You Go On**

Why do we care about neonatal reflexes?

What general observations can we make about physical growth and motor control in childhood?

FIGURE 3.4
The visual cliff was designed to determine if depth perception is innate or learned. By the time an infant can move about, most will avoid the deep side of the apparatus.

SENSORY AND PERCEPTUAL DEVELOPMENT

Psychologists used to think newborn children couldn't do much, following from their belief that newborns could not sense or perceive much. In fact, neonates respond to a range of stimuli. To some degree, all human senses function at birth, having developed in order: touch, body position, balance, taste, smell, hearing, and vision (Gibson, 1987; 1988; Hall & Oppenheim 1987).

The neonate's ability to sense even subtle changes is quite remarkable. However, there *are* limitations. The ability of the eyes to focus on an object, for example, does not develop fully until the child is about 4 months old. The neonate can focus well on objects held at a distance of one to two feet, but everything else appears blurred or out of focus. This means that even the newborn can adequately focus on the facial features of the person cradling or feeding him or her. Visual acuity—the ability to discern detail—shows at least a three-to fourfold improvement during the first year (Aslin & Smith, 1988).

An issue that has been of interest to psychologists for many years is when the perception of depth and distance develops. Even newborns have some simple reactions to depth—they will close their eyes and squirm away if you rush an object toward their face (Bower, Broughton & Moore, 1971).

In the late 1950s, two Cornell University psychologists, Eleanor Gibson and Richard Walk (1960), constructed an apparatus to test the depth perception of very young children. The *visual cliff*, as it is called, is a deep box covered by a sheet of thick, clear Plexiglas. It is divided into two sides, one shallow, one deep. The deep and shallow sides are separated by a center board (see Figure 3.4). Gibson and Walk found that 6-month-old children would not leave the center board to venture out over the deep side of the box, even to get to their mothers. By crawling age, the child is able to perceive depth *and* to make an appropriate response to it—scooting back to the "shallow side."

What about the other senses? Newborn infants can hear very well. They can direct their attention to the source of a sound, even a faint one. Wertheimer (1961) reports a study demonstrating sound localization in a newborn between three and ten minutes after birth! (The child moved her eyes to the left or right in response to a clicking sound.) Sounds may not mean much, but neonates can respond differently to sounds of different pitch and loudness. Even 3-day-old newborns are able to discriminate the sound of their mother's voice from other sounds (DeCasper & Fifer, 1980; Kolata, 1987; Martin and Clark, 1982).

Newborns also respond to differences in taste and smell. They discriminate among the four basic taste qualities of salt, sweet, bitter, and sour, displaying a distinct preference for sweet-tasting liquids. Though they are unable to use it then, the sense of smell seems to be established before birth. Right after birth, neonates respond predictably—drawing away and wrinkling their noses—to a variety of bad odors (e.g., Bartoshuk & Beauchamp, 1994).

In summary, a wide range of sensory and perceptual capabilities is available to the newborn child. The neonate may require some time to learn what to do with sensory information that it acquires from its environment, but many of its senses are operational. What the newborn makes of the sensations it receives will depend upon the development of its mental or cognitive abilities. This is the subject that we turn to now.

● **Before You Go On**

Summarize the basic sensory capacities of the neonate.

COGNITIVE AND SOCIAL DEVELOPMENT

Cognitive processes enable us to find out about and understand ourselves and the world around us. Let's now look at how these skills develop throughout childhood, beginning with the cognitive capacities of the newborn. Our major focus will be the theories of Jean Piaget. We'll also consider child development from a more social perspective, through the psychosocial theory of Erik Erikson and a theory of moral development proposed by Lawrence Kohlberg. We'll end this Topic with a brief section on the development of social attachments. (The development of another cognitive skill, language, will be addressed in Chapter 8.)

Cognitive Abilities of the Neonate: What Do Newborns Know?

Reflex reactions can help neonates survive. For long-term survival, neonates must learn to adapt to their environments and profit from their experiences. They have to begin forming memories of their experiences and learn to make discriminations among the many stimuli in their world. Are these cognitive processes possible in a baby just a couple of days or weeks old? In several ways, the answer is yes.

First, let's note that even newborns can demonstrate the ability to engage in simple learning tasks. A neonate (only 2 hours old!) is stroked on the forehead and seems not to respond. This stimulus is then paired with a sugar solution presented to the infant's lips. The sugar stimulus elicits the response of turning the head and making sucking movements. After several pairings of the stroking of the forehead and the sugar solution, the baby comes to make sucking and head movements simply when its forehead is touched (Blass, Ganchow & Steiner, 1984). This is an excellent example of simple learning.

Head turning and sucking movements can be brought under control learning as well. The rates of these responses will increase when they are followed (reinforced) by sugar solutions, the sound of the mother's voice, or the recorded sound of the mother's heartbeat (DeCasper & Sigafoos, 1983; Moon & Fifer, 1990; Sameroff & Cavanaugh, 1979).

Friedman (1972) reported a demonstration of what we might call memory in neonates only 1 to 4 days old. Babies were shown a picture of a simple figure, say, a checkerboard pattern, for 60 seconds. Experimenters recorded how long the baby looked at the pattern. After the same pattern was shown over and over again, the baby appeared bored and gave it less attention. When a new stimulus pattern was introduced, the baby stared at it for almost the full 60 seconds of its exposure. So what does this have to do with memory? The argument is that for the neonate to stare at the new stimulus, it must have formed some memory of the old one. How else would it recognize the new pattern as being new or different? In fact, if the new stimulus pattern was similar to the old one, the baby would not give it as much attention as it would if it were totally different. It is as if a cognitive judgment was being made about the distinctiveness of the new stimulus and remembered ones.

In this context, I should mention the research of Robert Fantz (1961, 1963). Fantz presented newborn children with pairs of visual stimuli. In most pairs, one stimulus was more complex than the other. As the babies lay on their backs, looking up at the stimuli, the experimenters could note which one of the two stimuli received the most attention from the child. In almost every case, a preference was shown for the more complex stimulus pattern.

This in itself is interesting and difficult to explain. The major finding is that babies could at least discriminate between the two stimuli. That attention equals "preference" is more of an assumption than a research finding. Fantz discovered that even newborn infants show a preference for (choose to attend to) drawings of a human face. They chose the face pattern as the focus of their attention no matter what it was paired with. These results have been confirmed by other researchers who have shown that infants will look more at a picture of their mother's face than any other face paired with it, and can even discriminate among facial expressions displaying different emotional states, looking more at facial expressions of joy than those of anger, for instance (Malatesta & Isard, 1984; Walton, Bower & Bower, 1992; Walton & Bower, 1993).

● **Before You Go On**

Cite an example of research evidence demonstrating a cognitive reaction in neonates.

Piaget's Theory of Cognitive Development

The increases in cognitive and intellectual abilities that occur during childhood are remarkable. By the time the human reaches adolescence, she or he has acquired an enormous stockpile of information. More than just learning facts, children come to appreciate *how* to learn. Strategies for survival and success begin to develop in childhood (Siegler, 1983).

Accounting for *how* children's intellectual skills change is a difficult business. It is important to be able to describe the changes that occur, but it is more important to be able to specify the principles that underlie cognitive development (Siegler, 1989). The theory that has attracted the most attention in this regard is that of the Swiss psychologist Jean Piaget (1896—1980). Although there are others, Piaget's theory has been so influential that it will be the focus of our discussion here (Piaget, 1948, 1954, 1967).

For Piaget, cognitive development centers on the formation of **schemas**, or organized mental representations of the world that have predictable behavioral consequences. For example, children develop a schema for "daddy," for "mommy," for "eating breakfast," and for "bedtime." Schemas aid the child in adapting to the demands and pressures of the environment and are formed by experience. Organizing the world into schemas is a process found in all children the world over.

Forming mental representations of the environment involves two processes, assimilation and accommodation. **Assimilation** involves taking new information and fitting it into an existing schema. Children develop a rather complex schema for mealtime, for instance. When they are taken to eat at a fast-food restaurant, new information will have to be added to the

schema
in Piaget's theory, a system of organized general knowledge, stored in memory, that guides the encoding and retrieval of information

assimilation
the process of adding new material or information to an existing schema

mealtime schema. As you learn about new and different things that psychologists do, we may say that information is being assimilated into your schema for "psychology."

Accommodation involves changing or revising existing schemas in the face of new experiences, not just adding to them. As children are shifted away from the bottle to strained foods then to regular food, they must accommodate their schemas for efficient feeding; what worked in the past doesn't work any longer. Learning that mommy and daddy won't necessarily come running when one cries may similarly require accommodation.

Piaget proposed that as children assimilate new ideas into existing schemas or make accommodations in old schemas, they progress through four stages of development: a sensorimotor stage, a preoperational stage, a concrete operations stage, and a formal operations stage. Determining precisely when each stage begins or ends is not always possible since two adjacent stages may overlap and blend for a while. Each stage is characterized by its own schemas, cognitive skills, methods, and insights.

Sensorimotor Stage   (Ages 0 to 2 years.) For children younger than two, language is not an effective means of finding out about the world. Children of this age are unable to discover much about their world by asking questions about it or by trying to understand long-winded explanations. Trying to explain to a 10-month-old baby *why* it shouldn't chew on an electrical extension cord is likely to be an unrewarding piece of parental behavior. In the **sensorimotor stage**, children discover by sensing (sensori-) and by doing (motor). A child may appreciate that a quick pull on a dog's tail (a motor activity) reliably produces a loud yelp (a sensory experience), perhaps followed in turn by parental attention.

One of the most useful schemas to develop in the sensorimotor stage is that of causality. Infants come to realize that events may have knowable causes and that some behaviors cause predictable reactions. Pushing a bowl of oatmeal off the high chair causes a mess and gets mommy's attention: If A, then B—a very practical insight. Another discovery that occurs during this developmental stage is that objects can exist even when they are not immediately in view. Early in the sensorimotor stage, an object that is out of sight is more than out of mind. It ceases to exist for the child. By the end of the period, children learn that objects can exist even if they are not present, and children can anticipate their reappearance. This awareness is called object permanence (see Figure 3.5).

Another useful skill that characterizes the sensorimotor stage is imitation. So long as it is within the baby's range of abilities, a baby will imitate almost any behavior it sees. A cognitive strategy has developed, one that will be used for a lifetime: trying to imitate the behaviors of a model.

● **Before You Go On**

How are schemas formed during the sensorimotor stage?
What characterizes this stage of development?

Preoperational Stage   (Ages 2 to 6 years.) By the end of the sensorimotor stage, a child recognizes that he or she is a separate, independent person in the world. Throughout most of the **preoperational stage**, a child's thinking is self-centered, or egocentric. According to Piaget, the child has

accommodation
in Piaget's theory, the process of altering or revising an existing schema in light of new information

sensorimotor stage
in Piaget's theory, from birth to age 2 years, when a child learns by sensing and doing

preoperational stage
in Piaget's theory, from age 2 years to 6 years, when a child begins to develop symbolic representations but cannot manipulate them; also characterized by egocentricity

FIGURE 3.5
By the end of the sensorimotor stage of development, a child comes to appreciate that simply because an object is no longer in view does not mean that object ceases to exist. Here, the infant sees a toy, and even when it is blocked from view, realizes that it is still there and crawls under the blanket to get at it.

difficulty understanding life from someone else's perspective. In this stage, the world is very much *me-*, *mine-*, and *I*-oriented.

In the preoperational stage, we see that children begin to develop symbols—usually in the form of words to represent concepts. At this stage, children do not appreciate how to manipulate those symbols in a consistent, rule-governed way, which is why it is referred to as preoperational. It's not until the end of this period that they can play "word games," or understand why riddles about rabbits throwing a clock out of a window in order to "see time fly" are funny. It is similarly true that children at this stage of development have great difficulty with abstract concepts, such as those involved with religious beliefs. Using concepts comes in the next stage of development.

● **Before You Go On**

In Piaget's theory, what characterizes the preoperational stage of development?

Concrete Operations Stage (Ages 7 to 12 years.) Children in the **concrete operations stage** develop many concepts *and* show that they can manipulate those concepts. For example, they can classify things: balls over here, blocks over there, plastic soldiers in a pile by the door, and so on. Each of these items is recognized as a toy, ultimately to be put away in the toy box and not stored in the closet, which is where clothes are supposed to go. It is in this period that we may say that rule-governed behavior begins. The concrete objects of the child's world can be classified, ranked, ordered, or separated into more than one category.

A sign of the beginning of the concrete operations stage is an ability to solve conservation problems. **Conservation**, in this context, is the cognitive awareness that changing the form or appearance of something does not necessarily change what it really is. Many experiments convinced Piaget that the ability to demonstrate conservation marked the end of the preoperational stage of development. Figure 3.6 shows a test for conservation of volume. We can demonstrate the conservation of size by showing two equal-sized balls of clay to a 4-year-old. When one is rolled into a long cigar shape, the child will now assert that it has more clay in it than the ball does. A 7-year-old will seldom hesitate to tell you that each form contains the same amount of clay. The 7-year-old has moved on to the next stage of cognitive development.

As its name suggests, in the concrete operations stage children begin to use and manipulate (operate on) concepts and ideas. Those manipulations are still very concrete, however, very much tied to real objects in the here and now. For example, an 8-year-old can be expected to find her way to and from school, even if she throws in a side trip or two along the way. On the other hand, she will have a difficult time describing just how she did so. Drawing a sensible map is difficult for her. If she actually stands on the corner of Maple Street and Oak Avenue, she knows where to go next. Dealing with the concrete reality, here and now, is fairly easy. Dealing with such knowledge in abstract terms is what is difficult.

● **Before You Go On**

What cognitive skills might we expect from a child in the concrete operations stage of development?

Formal Operations Stage (Ages over 12 years.) The manipulation of abstract, symbolic concepts does not appear until the last of Piaget's stages. The key to this **formal operations stage,** usually begun at adolescence, is abstract, symbolic reasoning. By the age of 12 years, most children can develop and then mentally test hypotheses—they can work through problems in their minds.

It is only at the stage of formal operations that youngsters are able to reason through hypothetical problems: "What if you were the only person in the world who liked rock music?" "If nobody had to go to school, what would happen?" Similarly, children are now able to deal with questions that

concrete operations stage
in Piaget's theory, from age 7 years to 12 years, when concepts can be manipulated, but not in an abstract fashion

conservation
in Piaget's theory, an appreciation that changing the physical properties of an object does not necessarily change its essence

formal operations stage
in Piaget's theory, ages older than 12 years, when one can generate and test abstract hypotheses, and think as an adult where thinking follows rules

FIGURE 3.6
In a demonstration of the concept of conservation of volume, a child in Piaget's preoperational stage of development will claim that there is more water in the tall beaker than in the shorter, wider one, even though the amounts of liquid are, in fact, equal.

are literally contrary to fact: "What if Ronald Reagan were still president of the United States?" The stages of Piaget's theory and the cognitive milestones associated with each are summarized in Figure 3.7.

● **Before You Go On**

What cognitive ability characterizes the stage of formal operations?

Reactions to Piaget

There can be no doubt of the importance of Piaget's influence. His observations, insights, and theories about intellectual development spanned decades. Finding evidence of Piaget's stages and the experiences that children need to demonstrate that they've reached a given stage is one of the success stories of cross-cultural research. The bulk of that research tells us that the stages we have just reviewed can be identified in children around the world (e.g., Brislin, 1993; Dasen & Heron, 1981; Segall et al., 1990).

On the other hand, some research questions a few of Piaget's basic ideas. The two major criticisms of Piaget's theory are that (1) the borderlines between his proposed stages are much less clear-cut than his theory suggests, and (2) Piaget significantly underestimated the cognitive talents of preschool children (Flavell, 1982, 1985; Gelman, 1978; Wellman & Gelman, 1992).

FIGURE 3.7
Piaget's Stages of Cognitive Development

1. **Sensorimotor stage (ages birth to 2 years)**
   Learns through active interaction with environment
   Becomes aware of cause-effect relationships
   Learns that objects exist even when not in view
   Imitates crudely the actions of others
2. **Preoperational stage (ages 2 to 6 years)**
   Begins by being very egocentric
   Language and mental representations develop
   Objects are classified on just one characteristic at a time
3. **Concrete operations stage (ages 7 to 12 years)**
   Develops conservation of volume, length, mass, etc.
   Organizes objects into ordered categories
   Understands relational terms (e.g., bigger than, above)
   Begins using simple logic
4. **Formal operations stage (ages over 12)**
   Thinking becomes abstract and symbolic
   Reasoning skills develop
   A sense of hypothetical concepts develops

For example, the egocentrism said to characterize the preoperational child may not be as obvious as Piaget would have us believe. In one study (Lempers et al., 1977), children were shown a picture that was pasted inside a box. They were asked to show the picture to someone else. Not only did they do so, but in showing the picture, they turned it so that it would be right-side up to the viewer. Every child over 2 years of age indicated such an appreciation of someone else's point of view. Similarly, object permanence may be neither universal nor consistently found in any one child—it depends on how you test for it (Harris, 1983).

Even Piaget's well-researched notion of conservation may not be such an obvious indicator of cognitive development as was once thought. When someone else pours liquid from a short beaker into a tall one, a 5-year-old probably will say that the taller beaker now holds more liquid—evidence of a failure to conserve in the preoperational stage. If the *child* does the pouring from one beaker to the other, as opposed to just watching, even 5-year-olds show conservation, recognizing that the amount of liquid is the same in both containers (Rose & Blank, 1974).

Another criticism is that Piaget's theory, focusing from the start on a stage approach, gives little attention to the impact of language development. Nor did Piaget have much to say about the smooth and gradual increases in the capacity of a child's memory.

So it seems that some of Piaget's observations and assumptions have come under attack. This is to be expected in science. In fact, one of the most important contributions of Jean Piaget is that he devised a theory of cognitive development that was so rich, so detailed, and so thought-provoking that it will continue to challenge researchers for years to come.

● **Before You Go On**

Cite two criticisms of Piaget's theory of cognitive development.

Kohlberg's Theory of Moral Development

How children acquire the capacity to reason about and make judgments about what is right and what is wrong is an issue that has received considerable attention (Darley & Shultz, 1990; Vitz, 1990). Piaget included moral development in his theory, arguing that morality is closely related to one's cognitive awareness and that children are unable to make moral judgments until they're at least 3 or 4 years old (Piaget, 1932).

Lawrence Kohlberg (1963, 1969, 1981, 1985) has proposed a theory that focuses on moral development. Like Piaget's approach, Kohlberg's is a theory of stages, of progressing from one stage to another in an orderly fashion. Kohlberg's data base comes from responses made by young boys who were asked questions about stories that involve a moral dilemma. A commonly cited example concerns whether or not a man should steal a drug in order to save his wife's life after the pharmacist who invented the drug refuses to sell it to him. Should the man steal the drug? Why or why not?

This method lead Kohlberg to propose that moral reasoning develops in three levels, with two stages (or "orientations") at each level. The result is six stages of moral development, which are briefly summarized in Figure 3.8. A child who says, for example, that the man should not steal the drug to save his wife's life because "he'll get caught and be put in jail," would be at the first, *preconventional* level of moral reasoning, where the sole focus of the child is the punishment that comes from breaking a rule. A child who says that the man should steal the drug because "it will make his wife happy, and most people would do it anyway," reflects reasoning at the second, *conventional*, level where the judgment is based on a blindly accepted social convention, and social approval matters as much or more than anything else. The argument that "he shouldn't steal the drug for a selfish reason, which in the long run would just promote more stealing in society," is an example of moral reasoning at Kohlberg's third, *postconventional*, level because it reflects complex, internalized standards.

Research tells us that the basic thrust of Kohlberg's theory has merit (Rest, 1983). It also has cross-cultural application. To varying degrees, Kohlberg's descriptions are valid for several cultures, including those in Israel, Turkey, India, and Nigeria (Edwards, 1977, 1981; Nisan & Kohlberg, 1982; Snarey, 1987; Snarey et al., 1985).

Problems with the theory also exist. For one thing, few people (including adults) operate at the higher stages of moral reasoning described by the theory (Colby & Kohlberg, 1984). This is particularly true in cultures that emphasize group or communal membership (such as the Israeli kibbutz or tribal groups in New Guinea) rather than individuality (Snarey, 1987). This observation gets us to a key concept in cross-cultural psychology: the dimension of individualism-collectivism (Bhawuk & Brislin, 1992; Erez & Early, 1993; Triandis, 1990, 1993). People in some cultures are socialized from early childhood to take others into account when setting goals and making decisions. Such a tendency toward **collectivism** is commonly found in Asia and South America. People in many other cultures are socialized to think mostly about themselves and the behaviors of individuals—a "pull yourself up by your own bootstraps and you'll get what you deserve" sort of mentality. This tendency toward **individualism** is more com-

collectivism
in cross-cultural psychology, the tendency to set goals and make decisions based on a concern for the group and the common good

individualism
in cross-cultural psychology, the tendency to set goals and make decisions based on a concern for one's self or the individual

FIGURE 3.8
Kohlberg's Stages of Moral Development

Level 1

Preconventional morality

1. Obedience and punishment orientation

2. Naive egotism and instrumental orientation

Rules are obeyed simply to avoid punishment; "If I take the cookies, I'll get spanked." Rules are obeyed simply to earn rewards; "If I wash my hands, will you let me have two desserts?"

Level 2

Conventional (conforming) morality

3. Good boy/girl orientation

4. Authority-maintaining orientation

Rules are conformed to in order to avoid disapproval and gain approval; "I'm a good boy 'cause I cleaned my room, aren't I?" Social conventions blindly accepted to avoid criticism from those in authority; "You shouldn't steal because it's against the law, and you'll go to jail if the police catch you."

Level 3

Postconventional morality

5. Contractual-legalistic orientation

6. Universal ethical principle orientation

Morality is based on agreement with others to serve the common good and protect the rights of individuals; "I don't like stopping at stop signs, but if we didn't all obey traffic signals, it would be difficult to get anywhere." Morality is a reflection of internalized standards; "I don't care what anybody says, what's right is right."

mon in North America and Western Europe. We are talking about a general dimension of comparison here; even within the same culture, individualism and collectivism exist to varying degrees.

This discussion relates to Kohlberg's theory because most of his ratings of moral reasoning put high values on the sort of thinking found in individualistic (largely Western) cultures. What this means is that what is true for one culture may not be for another, and neither is necessarily any "better" or more moral.

A similar argument has been raised about Kohlberg's theory as it applies to women (Ford & Lowery, 1986; Gilligan, 1982). All of Kohlberg's original data came from the responses of young boys, remember. Later, when young girls were tested, some studies suggested that girls showed slower moral development than boys. Carol Gilligan's argument is that the moral reasoning of females is neither slower nor faster but simply different from the reasoning of males. Males (at least males in Western cultures), are concerned with rules, justice, and individual rights. As a result, they approach moral dilemmas differently than do females, who are characteristically more concerned with caring, responsibility, and interpersonal relationships. Gilligan's book brought a new slant to research on morality and value development in general. The issue is not a judgmental one in the sense of determining if males are more or less moral in their thinking than are females. The question is whether or not females and males develop different styles of moral reasoning or different types of moral behaviors. In fact, most studies show that any differences between men and women in resolving moral conflicts is really quite small (Darley & Schultz, 1990; Donnenberg & Hoffman, 1988; Mednick, 1989; Walker, 1989).

● **Before You Go On**

Briefly summarize the stages of Koblberg's theory of moral development.

Erikson's Theory of Psychosocial Development

Erik Erikson (1902–1994) was a psychologist who, like Piaget, proposed a stage theory of human development (1963, 1965, 1968). Erikson's theory focuses on more than cognitive development, although this aspect is included. His theory is based on his observations of a wide range of people of different ages—as we will see, it extends from childhood through adolescence into adulthood. His ideas had more of a cross-cultural basis than did Piaget's. Erikson chose to focus on the social environment, which is why it is referred to as *psychosocial.*

Erikson lists eight stages of development through which a person passes. These stages are not so much periods of time as they are a series of conflicts, or crises, that need to be resolved. Each of the eight stages can be referenced by a pair of terms that indicates the nature of the conflict that needs to be resolved. As a stage theory, Erikson's implies that we naturally go through the resolution of each conflict or crisis in order and that any one type of crisis usually occurs at about the same age for all of us. Figure 3.9 is a summary of each of Erikson's eight stages of development. Included are brief descriptions of how each crisis might be resolved.

One of the strengths of Erikson's theory is that it covers the entire life span. While Piaget focused mainly on the stages of development of children, Erikson extended his views to late adulthood. For now, we'll only consider Erikson's first four crises, but we will return to his theory in Topic 3C.

During one's first year of life, according to Erikson, one's greatest struggle centers around the establishment of a sense of *trust or mistrust.* There's just not very much that a newborn can accomplish on its own. If its needs are met in a reasonable fashion, the child will develop a sense of safety and security, optimistic that the world is a predictable place. If the child's needs are not adequately met, what develops is a sense of mistrust— feelings of insecurity and frustration.

During the period of *autonomy vs. self-doubt,* what emerges most plainly is a sense of self-esteem. The child begins to act independently and to dress

FIGURE 3.9
Erikson's Eight Stages of Development

Approximate age	Crisis	Adequate resolution	Inadequate resolution
0–1 1/2	Trust vs. mistrust	Basic sense of safety	Insecurity, anxiety
1 1/2–3	Autonomy vs. self-doubt	Perception of self as agent capable of controlling own body and making things happen	Feelings of inadequacy to control events
3–6	Initiative vs. guilt	Confidence in oneself as initiator, creator	Feeling of lack of self-worth
6–puberty	Competence vs. inferiority	Adequacy in basic social and intellectual skills	Lack of self-confidence, feelings of failure
Adolescent	Identity vs. role confusion	Comfortable sense of self as a person	Sense of self as fragmented; shifting, unclear sense of self
Early adult	Intimacy vs. isolation	Capacity for closeness and commitment to another	Feeling of aloneness, separation; denial of need for closeness
Middle adult	Generativity vs. stagnation	Focus on concern beyond oneself to family, society, future generations	Self-indulgent concerns; lack of future orientation
Later adult	Ego-integrity vs. despair	Sense of wholeness, basic satisfaction with life	Feelings of futility, disappointment

and feed himself or herself. Physically more able, the child strikes off on its own, exploring ways of assuming personal responsibility. Frustration at this level of development leads to feelings of inadequacy and doubts of one's self-worth.

From ages 3 years to 6 years we have Erikson's period of *initiative vs. guilt*. Now the challenge is to develop as a functioning, contributing member of social groups, particularly the family. If the child is encouraged to do so, he or she should develop a sense of initiative, a joy of trying new things. You can just imagine, for instance, what it does for the self-image of a 5-year-old to be asked for an opinion on what the family should do this evening. Without encouragement, a child is likely to feel guilty, resentful, and lacking in self-esteem.

The final childhood period, *competence vs. inferiority*, lasts from about age 6 years to puberty. During this period of choices, the child is challenged to move beyond the safety and comfort of the immediate family unit. Now the major thrust of development is "out there" in the neighborhood and the school. Children have to at least begin to acquire those skills that will enable them to become fully functioning adults in society. If the child's efforts of industry are constantly belittled, criticized, or ignored, he or she may develop a sense of inadequacy and inferiority and remain dependent upon others even into adulthood.

● **Before You Go On**
Briefly describe the first four stages (crises) of development according to Erikson.

Developing Social Attachments

To a large degree, we adapt and thrive in this world to the extent that we profit from interpersonal relationships (Hartup, 1989; Goldsmith & Harman, 1994). The roots of social development can be found in early infancy—in the formation of attachment. **Attachment** is defined as a strong, two-way emotional bond, usually referring to the relationship between a child and his or her mother or primary caregiver (Bowlby, 1982). Attachment has survival value because it increases the chances of an infant being protected by those who are close by (Ainsworth, 1989). Well-formed attachment provides a child with freedom to explore the environment, satisfy his or her curiosity, learn adaptive problem solving, and develop competence when interacting with peers (Collins & Gunnar, 1990).

Forming an attachment between infant and mother (as an example) involves regular interaction and active give-and-take between the two. Strong attachments are most likely to be formed if the mother is sensitive to the needs of the child, picks up the baby when he or she cries, changes the diaper as soon as it is soiled, feeds on a regular basis, and so on. Attachment is promoted by hugging, smiling, eye contact, and vocalizing (Lamb et al., 1982; Stern, 1977). When the process is successful, we talk about children who are "securely attached." Forming an attachment is definitely a two-way street. Attachment will be most secure when the baby reciprocates by smiling, cooing, and clinging to mother when attended to (Ainsworth, 1979; Pederson et al., 1990). About 65 percent of American children become securely attached by the age of 1 year—a percentage close to that found in other countries (van Ijzendorn & Kroonenberg, 1988).

Are there long-term benefits of becoming securely attached in infancy? Yes. Secure attachment in infancy leads to (1) sociability (less fear with strangers, better relations with peers, more friends), (2) higher self-esteem, (3) better relationships with siblings, (4) fewer aggressive behaviors, (5) less concern by teachers about behaviors in the classroom, (6) greater concern for the feelings of others, (7) fewer behavior problems in later years, and (8) greater attention spans (from Bee, 1992, p. 433). Securely attached children also show greater persistence at problem solving, and are less likely to seek help from adults when injured or disappointed (Goldsmith & Harman, 1994).

I do need to mention that infants can and do form attachments with persons other than their mothers. Although fathers typically spend less time with young children than do mothers, father-child attachments are common and beneficial for the long-term development of the child (Lamb, 1977, 1979; Lynn, 1974). One researcher found that she could predict the extent to which a child showed attachment to its father simply by knowing how often Dad changes the baby's diaper (Ross et al., 1975).

attachment
a strong, two-way emotional bond, usually between a child and his or her parent or primary caregiver

Attachment between parents and children is a two-way street, where signs of mutual affection and interest are exchanged. Studies tell us that early father-child attachments are beneficial later in life.

Finally, let's review some data on attachment formation for those children who spend time—occasionally a lot of time—in day care facilities. After all, in the United States more than half of the mothers of children younger than three are employed outside the home. How do these children fare? It depends, mostly on the quality of the care the children are given—no matter where they get it. Children who are given warm, attentive, supportive care, adequate stimulation, and opportunities for exploration demonstrate secure attachment (Howes, 1990; Phillips et al., 1987). The impact of day care also depends on the likelihood that the child would have received good, warm, loving care at home (Scarr & Eisenberg, 1993). Evidence also suggests that the benefits of day care are directly related to the extent that the mother has a challenging job she enjoys and is excited about. Related to this observation is that fact that women now 60 years old or older who worked in challenging jobs outside the home while their children were young, now have higher self-esteem and suffered less depression than did those mothers who stayed home with their children (Woodruff, 1994).

The benefits or harm of nonparental child care may also depend on the age of the child. "There is little dispute about the conclusion that children who enter day care at 18 months, 2 years, or later show *no* consistent loss of security of attachment to their parents (Bee, 1992, p. 510). The main debate today centers on children less than 1 year old, and there is some evidence that secure attachment is less likely among those children who are not cared for at home during their first year (Belsky, 1990; Belsky & Rovine, 1988; Hennessy & Melhuish, 1991; Lamb & Sternberg, 1990).

● **Before You Go On**

In child development, what is meant by "attachment," and what are the benefits of developing secure attachments?

TOPIC 3C
ADOLESCENCE AND ADULTHOOD

In this Topic, we explore development in adolescence and adulthood. As I said in the chapter Preview, the changes that occur in these stages of our development can be a bit more subtle, but they are no less important than the changes that precede them. We'll begin with adolescence.

WHAT ARE ADOLESCENTS REALLY LIKE?

Adolescence is clearly a period of transition—from the dependence of childhood to the independence of adult life. In biological terms, one's adolescence begins with puberty and ends with the end of physical growth—usually late in the teen years. A more psychological perspective will emphasize the development of the cognitions, feelings, and behaviors that characterize adolescence. Psychological approaches emphasize the development of problem-solving skills and an increased reliance on the use of symbols, logic, and abstract thinking, as well as the importance of identity formation and a developing sense of self. From a more social perspective, we define adolescence in terms of being in between; not yet an adult, but no longer a child (Peterson & Ebata, 1987). In this context, adolescence usually lasts from the early teen years through one's highest educational level, when the individual is thought to enter the adult world.

Whether we take a biological, psychological, or social view of adolescence, we usually are talking about people who are between the ages of approximately 12 and 20. For the sake of our discussion, we will define **adolescence** as that period of development begun at puberty and lasting through the teen years.

One of the intriguing issues in the psychology of adolescence today is how to characterize the period in a general way. Is adolescence a period of personal growth, independence, and positive change? Or is adolescence a period of stress, turmoil, rebellion, and negativism?

The view that adolescence is characterized by turmoil, storm, and stress is the older of the two, attributed to G. Stanley Hall (who wrote the first textbook on adolescence in 1904) and to Anna Freud (who applied Freudian psychoanalytic theory to adolescents). This position claims that normal adolescence involves all sorts of adjustment problems. "To be normal during the adolescent period is by itself abnormal" wrote Anna Freud (1958, p. 275). Thus in this view, "Adolescents may be expected to be extremely moody and depressed one day and excitedly 'high' the next. Explosive conflict with family, friends, and authorities is thought of as commonplace" (Powers, Hauser & Kilner, 1989, p. 200).

Over the past 25 years, psychologists have come to appreciate that such a characterization of adolescents is probably inappropriate. Adolescence is not just a period of great emotional distress that, with time, one outgrows (e.g., Larson & Lampman-Petraitis, 1989). As we'll see, the teen years can present considerable pressure and conflict that require difficult choices. Sometimes teenagers do react to the pressures of their own adolescence in maladaptive ways (Larson & Ham, 1993; Quadrel et al., 1993; Takanishi, 1993). In 1992, in the Unites States, 1,738,180 juveniles under age 18 were arrested, and arrests for violent crimes increased by 82 percent over 1982. Yes, adolescence does require change and adjustment, *but* those changes and adjustments are usually made in healthy ways (Garbarino, 1985; Jessor, 1993; Manning, 1983; Offer & Offer, 1975; Peterson & Ebata, 1987). The picture of the troubled, rebellious, uncooperative adolescent is no doubt based on real experience, but is often just as much a reflection of a stereotype.

● **Before You Go On**

How might adolescence be defined, and how can the period be characterized?

SOME CHALLENGES OF ADOLESCENCE

Adolescence is marked by the stage of formal operations in Piaget's theory of cognitive development and by identity formation in Erikson's psychosocial theory. According to Piaget, an adolescent is now able to think abstractly and to imagine, to think about what *is*, and to ponder what *might be*. This higher level of cognition often gets turned toward self-analysis, toward

adolescence
the developmental period begun at puberty and lasting through the teen years

FIGURE 3.10

Females begin their growth spurt at about age 10, whereas the growth spurt in males does not begin until about age 12. In general, males will grow faster and for a longer period than females. (After Tanner et al., 1966.)

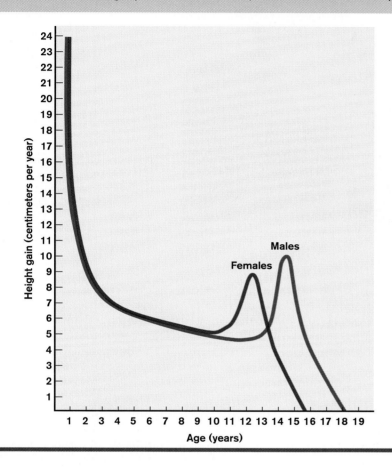

a contemplation of one's self in a social context (Keating, 1980). In this section, we will examine a few issues that present specific challenges to the adolescent: puberty, identity formation, drug use, and adolescent sexuality. We begin with the physical changes of puberty.

The Challenge of Puberty

The onset of adolescence generally is marked by two biological/physical changes. First there is a marked increase in height and weight, known as a growth spurt, and second there is sexual maturation.

The growth spurt of early adolescence usually occurs at an earlier age in girls than it does in boys. Girls begin their growth spurt as early as 9 or 10 years of age and then slow down at about age 15. Boys typically show their increased rate of growth between the ages of 12 and 17 years. Indeed, males usually don't reach their adult height until their early 20s, whereas girls generally attain their maximum height by their late teens (Roche & Davila, 1972; Tanner, 1981). Figure 3.10 shows one way to represent the adolescent growth spurt in graphic form.

Adolescence brings physical changes and psychological challenges, some major, some minor, including learning how to shave.

puberty
the stage of physical development at which one becomes capable of sexual reproduction

menarche
a female's first menstrual period, often taken as a sure sign of the beginning of adolescence

At least some of the challenge of early adolescence is a direct result of the growth spurt. It is not uncommon to find increases in weight and height occurring so rapidly that they are accompanied by real, physical growing pains, particularly in the arms and legs. Unfortunately, the spurt of adolescent growth seldom affects all parts of the body uniformly. Thirteen- and 14-year-old boys often appear incredibly clumsy and awkward as they try to coordinate their large hands and feet with the rest of their bodies. One of the most noticeable areas of growth in boys is that of the larynx and vocal cords. As the vocal cords lengthen, the pitch of the voice lowers. To the embarrassment of many a teenage boy, this transition is seldom a smooth one, and he may suffer through months of squeaking, crackling changes of pitch in the middle of serious conversations (Adams, 1977; Adams & Gullotta, 1983).

By definition, **puberty** occurs when one becomes physically capable of sexual reproduction. With the onset of puberty, there is a significant increase in the production of the sex hormones. Boys seldom know when their puberty begins. This is because boys experience penile erections and nocturnal emissions of seminal fluid for some time before sexual maturity. Biologically, puberty in males begins with the appearance of live sperm in their semen, and most males have no idea when *that* happens—such determinations require a laboratory test.

In females, puberty is noticeable. It is indicated by the first menstrual period, called **menarche**. The average age of menarche in the United States today is 12, but 150 years ago it was 16 (Hamburg & Takanishi, 1989). The age of menarche also varies around the world; African girls, for example, experience menarche at a significantly younger age than do European girls (Eveleth & Tanner, 1978).

With puberty, adolescents are ready, in a biological sense, to reproduce. Perhaps more important than the physical changes themselves are the psychological reactions of the adolescent and others to these physical changes (Peterson, 1988, p. 593).

● **Before You Go On**

Briefly describe the physical changes that accompany the beginning of adolescence.

The Challenge of Identity Formation

Adolescents around the world give the impression of being great experimenters. They experiment with hairstyles, music, religions, drugs, sexual outlets, fad diets, part-time jobs, part-time relationships, and part-time philosophies of life. It often appears that most of a teenager's commitments are made on a part-time basis. Teens are busily trying things out, doing things their own way, off on a grand search for Truth.

This perception of adolescents as experimenters is not without foundation. It is consistent with the view that a major task of adolescence is the resolution of an **identity crisis**—the struggle to define and integrate the sense of who one is, what one is to do in life, and what one's attitudes, beliefs, and values will be. "Who am I?" "What am I going to do with my life?" These are not trivial questions. A teen's search for his or her identity may lead to conflicts. Some of these conflicts may be resolved very easily, while others may continue into adulthood.

For Erik Erikson, the search for identity is the fifth stage of psychosocial development (see Figure 3.9). For many young people, adolescence brings little confusion or conflict in terms of attitudes, beliefs, or values. Many teenagers are willing to accept without question the values and sense of self that they began to develop in childhood.

For many teenagers, however, the conflict of identity is quite real. They have a sense of giving up the values of parents and teachers in favor of new ones—their own. Physical growth, increased sexuality, and perceived societal pressures to decide what they want to be when they "grow up" may lead to what Erikson calls *role confusion*. Wanting to be independent, to be one's own self, often does not fit in with the values of the past, of childhood. Hence, the teenager tries to experiment with different possibilities in an attempt to see what works best, occasionally to the dissatisfaction of bewildered parents.

identity crisis
the struggle to define and integrate one's sense of self and what one's attitudes, beliefs, and values should be

● **Before You Go On**

Summarize the adolescent's search for identity as described by Erikson.

The Challenge of Drug Use

There is simply no doubt that many adolescents experiment with drugs. Many use them on a regular basis, and many abuse them. Smoking (79%) and drinking alcohol (65%) lead the list of drug-related activities that teenagers have tried at least once by ninth grade (Gans & Blyth, 1990). About 30 percent have tried illegal drugs, usually marijuana, at least once (Millstein, 1989). As a general observation, drug use among teens rose steadily during the 1970s, began to drop slowly during the 1980s, and is on the increase again in the 1990s. A survey by the University of Michigan's Institute for Social Research showed a significant rise in drug use by secondary school students between 1993 and 1994. This study reports that over 45 percent of 12th graders (and over 25 percent of 8th graders) admitted to using illegal drugs—mostly marijuana. There are no racial differences in drug use or abuse among high school students, and there are *no*

Resisting the temptations of alcohol and drug use is a struggle for many adolescents.

differences in the rates of drug use between adolescents and adults (Oetting & Beauvais, 1990).

Jonathan Shedler and Jack Block, researchers at the University of California at Berkeley, recently reported on a study of adolescent drug use and psychological health that may affect the way we view drug use among teenagers (1990). The participants in this investigation were 18-year-olds who had been studied since they were 3 years old. The teens were divided into three groups: (1) *abstainers* ($N = 29$), who had never tried any drug; (2) *experimenters* ($N = 36$) who had used marijuana "once or twice, or a few times," and who tried no more than one other drug; and (3) *frequent users* ($N = 20$), who used marijuana frequently and tried at least one other drug. There were no socioeconomic or IQ differences among the groups.

The major findings of this study had to do with personality characteristics of the 18-year-olds in each group. *Frequent users* were found to be maladjusted, alienated, deficient in impulse control, and were "manifestly distressed." The *abstainers* were found to be overly anxious, "emotionally constricted," and lacking in social skills. These same results were apparent when the researchers examined records from when the same subjects were 7 and 11 years old. The surprise was that *experimenters* were generally better adjusted and psychologically "healthier" than either of the other two groups.

Shedler and Block are concerned that their data may be misinterpreted to indicate "that drug use might somehow improve an adolescent's psychological health" (p. 628). Clearly, this interpretation would be in error. You recognize these as correlational data for which no cause-and-effect conclusion is justified. All we know is that there is a relationship between a measure of drug use and specific measures of personality characteristics, or mental health.

While drug use among adolescents is a matter of great concern, there is evidence to suggest that we need not get hysterical about infrequent, occasional drug use among teenagers. In a review of substance use and abuse among teenagers, Newcomb and Bentler (1989) put it this way:

Not all drug use is bad and will fry one's brain (as the commercials imply). Such claims as reflected in the national hysteria and depicted in media advertisements for treatment programs, repeat the failed scare tactics of the past. All drug abuse is destructive and can have devastating consequences for individuals, their families, and society. The difference or distinction lies in the use versus abuse of drugs (p. 247).

To summarize: Some adolescents do use and do abuse drugs, but drug use is currently no greater for adolescents than for any other segment of the population. On the other hand, there are signs that drug use among teens is again on the rise.

● **Before You Go On**

Briefly summarize the data on drug use and abuse in adolescence.

The Challenge of Sexuality

For the adolescent, going through puberty is a personal, private, and potentially confusing process. Large doses of sex hormones stimulate the development of secondary sex characteristics: In males, the neck and shoulders expand, hips narrow, facial and body hair begins to sprout, the voice crackles and then lowers in pitch. In females, the breasts begin to develop, hips broaden and become more rounded, and the shoulders narrow. All of this takes time, but then puberty is more of a process than a single event. It is during this process that sex hormones give rise to sex drives, which are often expressed in sexual behaviors. With puberty, sexual behaviors can lead to pregnancy.

As personal and private as sexuality may be for the teenager, discussions of adolescent sexuality often revolve around statistics—impressive and occasionally depressing statistics. What do the statistics tell us?

A 1994 study from the Alan Guttmacher Institute tells us that about half of all women and about three-quarters of all men have had sexual intercourse by the time they reach their 18th birthday. A report from the Centers for Disease Control (CDC) released in early 1991 tells us that premarital sexual activity among adolescent females has risen in the last two decades—with a sharp increase since 1985. The CDC reports that nearly twice as many female teenagers (51.5%) had engaged in premarital sex by their late teens in 1988 as compared to 1970 (28.6%). The largest increase was among girls 15 years of age. Of the 12 million new cases of sexually transmitted diseases (from gonorrhea to chlamydia to AIDS) diagnosed each year, two-thirds occur among people under age 25.

The conflict for teenagers is that while biology says they are ready for sexual behaviors and pregnancy, our culture tells them they are not, even though that same culture promotes sexuality in advertising, clothing styles, and movies and television. Most teens do not "plan" to become sexually active; it "just happens" (Chilman, 1983). One study (Coles & Stokes, 1985), indicates that about 60 percent of the males, but only 23 percent of the females "felt glad" about their first intercourse (34% of the males and 61% of the females felt "ambivalent"). These data mirror those of Darling and Davidson (1986) who report that 67.4 percent of the males in their survey were "psychologically satisfied after their first sexual experience," while only 28.3 percent of the females shared that satisfaction.

With all this sexual activity, it is not surprising that teenage pregnancy is a major social problem. There are several ways of looking at the data. Each year, more than half a million babies are born to adolescent mothers. Nearly two-thirds of white adolescent mothers, and virtually all black adolescent mothers (97%) are single (Furstenberg et al., 1989). Girls in the United States younger than 15 are *five times more likely* to give birth than are girls from any other developed country for which data are available (Landers, 1987b). Between 1973 and 1987, pregnancy among youngsters between the ages of 10 and 14 increased 23 percent (Moore, 1992). These statistics reflect live births, not pregnancies: Hayes (1987) claims that an additional 400,000 teenage pregnancies end in abortion each year. Estimating pregnancies among adolescents at over a million a year is probably not far off (Auletta, 1984; Millstein, 1989; Zelnick & Kantner, 1980).

The physical, psychological, and financial costs of adolescent pregnancy to individuals, families, and society are very high. The child of a teenage mother is certainly a baby at risk. Teenage mothers face innumerable hurdles. They are much more likely to drop out of school, rely on welfare, and have poorer access to health care (Hayes, 1987; Hofferth & Hayes, 1987). But remember, most teens do not *plan* to become pregnant. More than anything else, teenage pregnancy may reflect a poor understanding of human sexuality. For example, a significant number of adolescents do not believe that they can become pregnant the first time they have intercourse, and teenagers hold negative attitudes about the use of contraceptives (Morrison, 1985).

What can we conclude about adolescents on the basis of the statistics we've reviewed? Sexually active adolescents number in the millions. Many adolescents are woefully ignorant of the consequences of their own sexual behaviors. Those for whom sexual activity results in pregnancy may exceed a million each year. But at the same time, let's not lose sight of the fact that most adolescents are *not* coping with unwanted pregnancies. Most adolescents know a lot about sex. Dealing with one's sexuality may not be easy, but it is one of the challenges that must be addressed as one passes through adolescence.

● **Before You Go On**

What evidence supports the notion that adolescents are a sexually active group?

Briefly summarize the data on teenage pregnancy.

EARLY ADULTHOOD

The changes that occur during our adult years do not seem as striking or dramatic as those that typify our childhood and adolescence. Many of the adjustments that we make as adults may go unnoticed as we accommodate physical changes and psychological pressures. An adult's health may become a concern for the first time. Psychological and social adjustments must be made to marriage, parenthood, career, the death of friends and family, retirement, and, ultimately, one's own death.

Psychologically, adulthood is marked by two phenomena that at first seem almost contradictory: (1) independence, in the sense of taking on responsibility for one's actions and no longer being tied to one's parents, and (2) interdependence, in the sense of building new commitments and intimacies in interpersonal relations.

Following Erikson (1968) and Levinson (1978, 1986), we will consider adulthood in terms of three overlapping periods, eras, or seasons: early adulthood (roughly ages 18 to 45), middle adulthood (approximately ages 45 to 65), and late adulthood (over 65). Presenting adult development in this way can be misleading, so we should be careful. Although there is support for the notion of developmental stages in adulthood, these stages may be better defined by the individual adult than by the developmental psychologist (Datan et al., 1987). Some psychologists find little evidence for orderly transitions in the life of adults (Costa & McCrea, 1980; McCrea & Costa, 1984), while others find sex differences in what determines the stage or status of one's adult life (Reinke et al., 1985).

If anything does mark the transition from adolescence to adulthood, it is choice and commitment independently made. The sense of identity fashioned in adolescence now needs to be put into action. In fact, the achievement of a strong sense of self by early adulthood is an important predictor of the success of intimate relationships later in adulthood (Kahn et al., 1985).

Levinson calls early adulthood the "era of greatest energy and abundance and of greatest contradiction and stress" (1986, p. 5). In terms of our physical development, we are at something of a peak during our 20s and 30s, and we're apparently willing to work hard to maintain that physical condition (McCann & Holmes, 1984; Shaffer, 1982). Young adulthood is a season for finding our niche, for working through the aspirations of our youth, for raising a family. On the other hand, it is a period of stress, taking on parenthood, finding and keeping the "right" job and keeping a balance among self, family, job, and society at large. Let's take a look at two decision-making processes of early adulthood: the choice of mate and family, and the choice of job or career.

Marriage and Family

It is Erikson's claim (1963) that early adulthood revolves around the basic choice of *intimacy versus isolation*. Failing to establish close, loving, intimate relationships may result in loneliness and long periods of social isolation. Marriage is not the only source of interpersonal intimacy, but it is the first choice for most Americans. More young adults than ever are postponing marriage plans, but fully 95 percent of us do marry (at least once). In fact, we're more likely to claim that happiness in adulthood depends more on a successful marriage than any other factor, including friendship, community activities, or hobbies (Glenn & Weaver, 1981).

Young adults may value marriage, but the choice of who to marry is a matter of no small consequence. Thirty years of research on this issue convinces us that mate selection is a complex process. Psychologist David Buss reviewed the data on mate selection with a focus on whether opposites attract and concluded that they do not. He found that "we are likely to marry someone who is similar to us in almost every variable" (Buss, 1985, p. 47). Similarities were found in (in order): age, education, race, religion, and ethnic background, followed by attitudes, mental abilities, socioeconomic status, height, weight, and even eye color. Buss and his colleagues also found that men and women are in nearly total agreement on the characteristics they seek in a mate (Buss & Barnes, 1986). When one studies the choice of marriage partners in different cultures, one finds that although there are many similarities, certain characteristics vary considerably. The trait that varies most across cultures is *chastity*.

> Samples from China, India, Indonesia, Iran, Taiwan, and Arab Palestine placed great importance on chastity in a potential mate. Samples from Ireland and Japan placed moderate importance on chastity. In contrast, samples from Sweden, Finland, Norway, the Netherlands, and West Germany generally judged chastity to be irrelevant or unimportant. (Buss et al., 1990, p. 16)

Choosing a marriage partner is not always a matter of making sound rational decisions based on personality traits, regardless of one's culture. Several factors, including romantic love or the realities of economic hardship, affect such choices. And sometimes original choices aren't necessarily the best. Nearly 50 percent of first marriages end in divorce (75 percent of second marriages suffer the same fate). In the United States, 9.4 years is the average span of a first marriage (U.S. Bureau of the Census, 1991). See "Psychology in the Real World."

Beyond establishing an intimate relationship, becoming a parent is often taken as a sign of adulthood. For many, parenthood has become more a matter of choice than ever before because of increased means of contraception and new treatments for infertility. Having one's own family helps foster the process of *generativity* that Erikson associates with middle adulthood. Generativity reflects a growing concern for family and for one's impact on future generations (Chilman, 1980). Though such concerns may not become central until one is over age 40, parenthood usually begins much sooner.

There is no doubt that having a baby around the house significantly changes established routines. Few couples have a realistic vision of what having children will do to their lives. The freedom for spontaneous trips, intimate outings, and privacy is often given up in trade for the joys of parenthood. As parents, men and women take on the responsibilities of new social roles: that of father and mother. These new roles in adulthood add to the already established roles of being a male or a female, a son or a daughter, a husband or a wife, and so on. Choosing to have children (or at least choosing to have a large number of children) is becoming less popular (Schaie & Willis, 1986). Although many people regard the decision not to have children as selfish, irresponsible, and immoral (Skolnick, 1979), there is little evidence that such a decision leads to a lessening in well-being or life satisfaction later in life (Beckman & Houser, 1982; Keith, 1983).

Career Choice

By the time a person has become a young adult, it is assumed that he or she has chosen a vocation or life's work. One's occupational choice and one's satisfaction with that choice go a long way toward determining self-esteem and identity. For women in early adulthood, employment outside the home is a major determinant of self-worth and satisfaction with one's self (Stein et al., 1990). These days, "dual-career" families, in which both the woman

Divorce and Its Impact on Children

How has divorce affected you? Even if you have never been married, it is very likely that divorce has touched your life in some way. Perhaps your parents have divorced. Maybe you have friends whose parents are divorced. Perhaps some of your friends or you yourself are divorced.

As noted in the text, slightly more than half of first marriages end in divorce. The rate of divorce among those in their second marriage is even higher (Gottman, 1994). Half of all divorces occur within the first seven years of marriage, and about one quarter occur when couples are over 40 years old. Divorce can be devastating for older adults, particularly for women, who often have fewer career options and less opportunity to remarry (Bee, 1994, p. 411; Chiriboga et al., 1991).

As is the case for many questions in psychology, we still do not know with any certainty why some marriages fail while others thrive. When couples who are happily married are asked what factors matter, they cite such aspects as liking one's spouse as a friend, agreeing on goals, and having a mutual concern for making the marriage work (Lauer & Lauer, 1985). One of the best predictors of a successful marriage is the extent to which the marriage partners maintained close relationships (as with parents) *before* they were married (Wamboldt & Reiss, 1989). "It isn't the lack of compatibility that predicts divorce, but the way couples handle their *incompatibilities*, not whether they fight all the time or never fight at all, but the way they resolve their conflicts and the overall quality of their emotional interactions" (Gottmann, 1994, p. 44). Curiously, seeking professional help in the form of therapy seems relatively ineffective for many couples. About 50 percent of couples who enter into marital therapy do not improve their marriages (Gottmann, 1994, p. 42).

The repercussions for children caught up in a divorce situation are significant. Nearly one in three American families with children under the age of 18 has only one parent. There were 10.9 million single parents rearing children in the United States in 1993, and 86 percent of those single-parent families were headed by mothers. For that matter, in 1993 over 4.7 million children lived with their grandparents, and not with either parent (U.S. Bureau of the Census, 1994).

Approximately 38 percent of divorced mothers move in the first year following a divorce, and frequently must change jobs or increase their working hours. "Children face increased school disruption and the loss of neighborhood friends—factors that many believe are more closely tied to childhood unhappiness than divorce itself" (Robinson, 1994, p. 29). Children whose parents have divorced may withdraw, become aggressive or depressed, or blame themselves for the divorce, depending on the child's age and sex. Boys seem to have a more difficult time adjusting than do girls (Hetherington, 1989). The most common reaction to divorce for "children of all ages is an obsessive desire to reunite the parents" (Conger, 1991, p. 181). Five years after the divorce of their parents, more than a third of the children in one study were still having significantly more problems than they had had before the divorce (Wallerstein, 1989).

Given today's rates of divorce, there is little doubt that learning how to help the children of divorce adjust and cope with what is happening is a research area of prime importance in psychology. Similarly, perhaps psychologists can find ways of helping individuals make more effective choices of marriage partners or find more effective ways of maintaining marital relationships.

and the man are pursuing a lifelong career, are becoming quite common (Gilbert, 1994; Wisensale, 1992). Women now constitute about 39 percent of the professional labor force in this country. Nearly 60 percent of women with children younger than 6 years and two-thirds of women with children younger than 18 years are employed outside the home.

With so many career options to choose from, the decision is often a difficult one. Selection of a career is driven by many factors; educational requirements, family influence, and potential for earnings are just three. In fact, many young adults are dissatisfied with their first choice (Rhodes, 1983; Shertzer, 1985).

Jeffrey Turner and Donald Helms (1987) claim that choosing a career path involves seven identifiable stages. Let's review their list:

1. *Exploration*: There is a concern that something needs to be done, a choice needs to be made, but alternatives are poorly defined, and plans for making a choice are not yet developed. This period is what Daniel Levinson (1978) calls "formulating a dream."
2. *Crystallization*: Some actual alternatives are being weighed, pluses and minuses are associated with each possibility, and although some are eliminated, a choice is not made.
3. *Choice*: For better or worse, a decision is made. There is a sense of relief that at least one knows what one wants, and an optimistic feeling develops that everything will work out.
4. *Career clarification*: The individual's self-image and career choice are meshed together. Adjustments and accommodations are made. This is largely a matter of fine-tuning one's initial choice: "I know I want to be a teacher; now what do I want to teach, and to whom?"
5. *Induction*: The career decision is implemented. This presents a series of potentially frightening challenges to one's own values and goals.
6. *Reformation*: One finds that changes need to be made if one is to fit in with fellow workers and do the job as expected.
7. *Integration*: The job and one's work become part of one's self, and one gives up part of self to the job. This is a period of considerable satisfaction.

By middle adulthood, most people have chosen career paths and have developed life-styles that allow for more leisure time.

From time to time, people make the wrong career decision. This is most likely to happen in the third stage of choosing a career path, but probably won't be recognized until the fourth or fifth stage. In such cases, there is little to do but begin again and work through the process, seeking the self-satisfaction that comes at the final stage.

● **Before You Go On**
What developments characterize early adulthood?

MIDDLE ADULTHOOD

As the middle years of adulthood approach, many aspects of one's life have been settled. By the time most people reach the age of 40, their place in the framework of society is fairly well set. They've chosen a life-style and have grown accustomed to it. They have children (or have decided not to). They have chosen what is to be their major life work or career. "Most of us during our 40s and 50s become 'senior members' in our own particular worlds, however grand or modest they may be" (Levinson, 1986, p. 6).

The shift to middle adulthood involves a transition filled with reexamination (Levinson et al., 1974; Sheehy, 1976). During the middle years, one is forced to contemplate one's own mortality. "Middle-age spread," loss of muscle tone, facial wrinkles, and graying hair are evident each day in the mirror. At about the age of 40, sensory capacities begin to slowly diminish. People in this stage now notice obituaries in the newspaper where more and more people of the same age—or younger—are listed every day.

For some people, perhaps for men more than for women, the realization that time is running out produces something of a crisis, even approaching panic. But by and large, the notion of a "midlife crisis" is mostly a myth (Costa & McCrea, 1980; Farrell & Rosenberg, 1981; Hunter & Sundel, 1989). For most adults, middle age is a time of great satisfaction and true opportunity (Rossi, 1980). The children are grown and gone, careers are in full bloom, time is available as never before for leisure and commitment to community, perhaps in the form of volunteer work.

There are several tasks that one must face in the middle years (Havighurst, 1972). For one thing, we must adjust to the physiological changes of middle age. Although there certainly are many physical activities that middle-aged persons can and do engage in, they sometimes must be selective or must modify the vigor with which they attack such activities. Heading out to the backyard for a basketball game with the neighborhood teenagers is something a 45-year-old may have to think twice about.

Career choices may have been made earlier, but in middle age one comes to expect satisfaction with one's job and the experience necessary to do that job well. If career satisfaction is not attained, there may be few opportunities left for change. Of course, there are situations in which changing jobs in middle age is more a matter of necessity than choice. In either case, the potential for growth and development or for crisis and conflict exists.

A major set of challenges that middle-aged persons face is dealing with other members of the family. At this stage of life, parents are often in the throes of helping their teenagers adjust and "leave the nest," while at the same time they are caring for their own aging parents. Adults in this situation are referred to as the "sandwich generation" (Brody, 1981; Neugarten & Neugarten, 1989). In spite of widespread opinions to the contrary, individual responsibility and concern for the care of the elderly has not deteriorated in recent years. In fact, 80 percent of all day-to-day health care for the elderly is provided by the family.

One task of middle adulthood is similar to what Erikson calls the crisis of *generativity versus stagnation*. People shift from thinking about all that they have done with their lives to considering what they will do with the time they have left and how they can leave a mark for future generations (Erikson, 1963; Harris, 1983).

All these "tasks" of middle adulthood are interdependent. This is particularly true of the processes of relating to one's spouse as a person and developing more leisure-time activities. As children leave home and financial concerns lessen, there may be more time for one's spouse and for leisure. Taking advantage of these opportunities in meaningful ways provides a new challenge for some adults whose lives have previously been devoted to children and career.

● **Before You Go On**

What are some of the issues typically faced during the middle years of adulthood?

LATE ADULTHOOD

The transition to late adulthood generally occurs in our early to mid–60s. Perhaps the first thing we need to acknowledge is that persons over the age of 65 comprise a sizable and growing proportion of the population in the United States. More than 30.4 million Americans were in this age bracket (by 1988), and the numbers are increasing by an average of 1,400 per day (Fowles, 1990). By the year 2020, Americans over 65 will make up nearly 20 percent of the population, compared to the current 12 percent (Cavanaugh & Park, 1993). Because of the coming of age of the "baby boom" generation, by the year 2030 there will be about 66 million older persons in the Unites States (Fowles, 1990), and by the year 2050 the number of persons of age 65-plus will be *78.9 million* (AARP, 1993). The data also tell us that aging is disproportionally a women's issue; the vast majority of those over age 80 are women (Cavanaugh & Park, 1993).

What It Means to Be Old

Ageism is the discriminatory practice or negative stereotyping that is formed solely on the basis of age. Ageism is particularly noticeable in attitudes about the elderly (Kimmel, 1988). One misconception about the aged is that they live in misery. We cannot ignore some of the difficulties that may accompany aging, but matters may also not be as bad as many people believe they are. For example, sensory capacities do diminish. But as Skinner (1983) suggested, "If you cannot read, listen to book recordings. If you do not hear well, turn up the volume of your phonograph (and wear headphones to protect your neighbors)." Some cognitive abilities suffer with age, but others are developed to compensate for most losses (Salthouse, 1989). Some memory loss may reflect more of a choice of what one chooses to remember rather than an actual loss. There is no doubt that mental speed is reduced, but the accumulated experience of years of living can, and often does, far outweigh any advantages of speed (Meer, 1986).

Children have long since "left the nest," but they're still in touch, and now there are grandchildren with whom to interact. Further, the children of the elderly have themselves now reached adulthood and are more able to provide support for aging parents. In fact, only about 5 percent of Americans over the age of 65 live in nursing homes (Fowles, 1990; Harris, 1975, 1983). Even among those elderly in the United States classified as "poor" or "near poor," almost two-thirds own and live in their own homes—a percentage significantly higher than for their children (USGAO, 1992).

Some individuals dread retirement, but most welcome it as a chance to do those things they have planned on for years (Haynes et al., 1978). Many people over 65 become *more* physically active after retiring from a job for which they sat at a desk all day long.

ageism
discrimination or negative stereotyping formed solely on the basis of age

Many people find late adulthood both enjoyable and productive. They look forward to good times with friends and also have time to do volunteer community service work.

We often assume that old age necessarily brings with it the curse of poor health, but only thirty-one percent of those over age 65 claim poor health to be a serious problem. That may sound like a high percentage, but it compares to 7 percent in the 18-to-54 age range and 18 percent in the 55-to-65 age range. Yes, health problems are more common, but they are not nearly as widespread or devastating as we might think.

Developmental psychologists are finding it useful to divide those over age 65 into two groups: the *young-old* and the *old-old*. This distinction is not made on the basis of one's actual age, but on the basis of psychological, social, and health characteristics (Committee on an Aging Society, 1986; Neugarten & Neugarten, 1986). This distinction reinforces the notion that aging is in itself not some sort of disease. The young-old group is the large majority of those over 65 years of age. They are "vigorous and competent men and women who have reduced their time investments in work or homemaking, are relatively comfortable financially and relatively well educated, and are well-integrated members of their families and communities" (Neugarten & Neugarten, 1989).

The concept of "successful aging" has been with us for some time, but has not received much attention. John Rowe and Robert Kahn (1987) would have us change the entire focus of our study of human aging, particularly aging late in life. Most research has focused on *average* age-related losses and deficits. Rowe and Kahn claim that "the role of aging per se in these losses has often been overstated and that a major component of many age-associated declines can be explained in terms of life style, habits, diet, and an array of psychosocial factors extrinsic to the aging process" (p. 143). The argument is that the deficits, or losses of the elderly, are not the result of age but of factors over which we can exercise some control (Schaie, 1993). The major contributors to decline in old age include such things as poor nutrition, smoking, alcohol use, inadequate calcium intake, not maintaining a sense of autonomy and control over one's life, and lack of social support. Attention to these factors may not significantly lengthen the life span, but should extend what Rowe and Kahn call the "health span, the maintenance of full function as nearly as possible to the end of life" (p. 149). Research tells us, for example, that maintaining close family relationships and regular physical exercise predict successful aging (Clarkson-Smith & Hartley, 1989; Krause, 1993; Valliant & Valliant, 1990).

Death and Dying

Of the two sure things in life, death and taxes, the former is the surer. There are no loopholes. Dealing with the reality of our own death is the last major crisis that we face in life. As it happens, many people never have to deal with their own death in psychological terms. These are the people who die young or suddenly, from natural or accidental causes. Many individuals *do* have the time to contemplate their own death, and this usually takes place in late adulthood.

Much attention was focused on the confrontation with death in the popular book *On Death and Dying* by Elisabeth Kübler-Ross (1969, 1981). Her description of the stages that one goes through when facing death was based on hundreds of interviews with terminally ill patients who were aware that they were dying. Kübler-Ross suggests that the process takes place in five stages: (1) *denial*—a firm, simple avoidance of the evidence; a reaction of, "No, this can't be happening to me." (2) *anger*—often accompanied by resentment and envy, along with a realization of what is truly happening; a sort of "Why me? Why not someone else?" (3) *bargaining*—a matter of dealing, or barter, usually with God; a search for more time; a sort of "If you'll just grant me a few more weeks, or months, I'll go to church every week; no, every day." (4) *depression*—a sense that bargaining won't work, that a great loss is imminent; a period of grief and sorrow both over past mistakes and what will be missed in the future. (5) *acceptance*—a quiet facing of the reality of death, with no great joy or sadness; simply a realization that the time has come.

It turns out that the Kübler-Ross description may be idealized. Many dying patients do not fit this pattern at all (Butler & Lewis, 1981; Kastenbaum & Costa, 1977). Some may show behaviors consistent with one or two of the stages, but seldom all five (Schultz & Alderman, 1974). There is some concern that this pattern of approaching death may be viewed as the "best" or the "right" way to go about it. The concern here is that caretakers may try to force dying people into and through these stages, instead of letting each face the inevitability of death in his or her own way (Kalish, 1976; 1985).

Although elderly people may have to deal with death, they are generally less morbid about it than are adolescents (Lanetto, 1980). In one study (Kalish, 1976), adults over 60 reported that they did think about and talk about death more often than did the younger adults surveyed. However, of all the adults in the study, the oldest group expressed the least fear of death, some even saying they were eager for it.

● **Before You Go On**
Briefly summarize some of what we know about the elderly.

THINKING CRITICALLY ABOUT HUMAN DEVELOPMENT

1. Without getting into whether you think it is "right" or "wrong," and given our discussion of prenatal development, what sort of information, if any, could psychologists provide that could help a person resolve conflicts about abortion? That is, is there anything that psychologists could or should add to the national policy debate on abortion?
2. Most of the data we have on the environment's impact on prenatal development comes from studies in the United States. What possibilities do you see for investigating prenatal development by examining the practices of other countries and other cultures?
3. How would you define "thinking" in a neonate, and what evidence would you have to generate to demonstrate whether neonates think?
4. To what extent should early childhood education programs be based on the results of research by developmental psychologists? For example, if we now know that even neonates can demonstrate basic learning and memory skills, should we start sending newborns to school?
5. What reasons might you provide for the "gap" that seems to exist between the world of the teenager and the world of parents? Why do adolescents seem to feel a need to reject the values—and the music—of the previous generations? Now the REAL question: *Do* adolescents reject the values and/or the music of the previous generation? Why are we so ready to believe they do?
6. What does your own experience as an adolescent tell you about that stage of development in terms of the abnormal being normal for adolescents?

7. If there is no such thing as a mid-life crisis, why do so many people seem to act as if there were?
8. As the population of the United States and Canada continues to grow older and older, what changes in policy, at a local and national level, do you see as being helpful?
9. How do different cultures view and treat the elderly in their societies?

SUMMARY

TOPIC 3A
PRENATAL DEVELOPMENT

● Briefly summarize the three stages of prenatal development.

Prenatal development begins at conception and ends at birth. This period is divided into three stages: the stage of the zygote (conception to week 2), at which time the zygote becomes implanted in the uterus; the stage of the embryo (week 2 to week 8), during which there is rapid growth and differentiation of developing cells; and the stage of the fetus (month 3 until birth), during which the organs begin to function *Pages 80–83*

● Briefly review the impact of diet, drugs, and stress on prenatal development.

A mother's diet and use of drugs can have profound effects on prenatal development. Malnutrition in the mother, or deficiencies of specific vitamins or minerals, are usually shared by the embryo or the fetus. Smoking and alcohol use during pregnancy have well-documented negative effects. A rule of thumb is to avoid all drugs unless prescribed by a physician. Research on the effects of stress has not produced clear-cut results, but we do know that the age, health, and behaviors of the father at the time of conception can have a significant impact on the developing child. *Pages 83–85*

TOPIC 3B
DEVELOPMENT IN CHILDREN

● Why do we care about neonatal reflexes?
● What general observations can we make about physical growth and motor control in children?

Most neonatal reflexes have survival value (e.g., the rooting, sucking, and grasping reflexes). Some other reflexes seem to have no particular survival value for the infant, but they do give us an idea of the adequacy of physical development.

The age at which motor abilities develop varies from child to child, but the sequence is quite regular and predictable. Review Figure 3.3 for the ages at which some motor behaviors tend to develop. *Pages 85–87*

● Summarize the basic sensory capacities of the neonate.

The neonate's senses function reasonably well right from birth. The eyes can focus well at arm's length, although they will require a few months to focus over a range of object distances. Rudimentary depth perception seems to be present even in the neonate, but improves considerably within the first year. Hearing is quite good, as are the senses of taste, smell, and touch. *Pages 88–89*.

● Cite an example of research evidence demonstrating a cognitive reaction in neonates.

Newborns just a few hours old give evidence of learning and memory. They will attend to a new visual pattern after coming to ignore a familiar one, showing an appreciation of the difference between familiar and new. They show definite preferences for complex visual patterns over simple ones, and seem to prefer (attend to) visual representations of the human face. *Pages 89–90*.

● How are schemas formed during the sensorimotor stage?
● What characterizes this stage of development?

During the sensorimotor stage of cognitive development, a child develops new schemas (assimilating new information and accommodating old concepts) through an active interaction with the environment—by sensing and doing. The baby begins to appreciate cause-and-effect relationships, imitates the actions of others, and develops a sense of object permanence. *Pages 90–91.*

● In Piaget's theory, what characterizes the preoperational stage of development?

Egocentrism is a cognitive reaction that occurs during the preoperational stage of development. The child becomes very me- and I-oriented, unable to appreciate the world from the perspective of others. Additionally, children develop and use symbols, in the form of words, to represent concepts. *Pages 91–93.*

● What cognitive skills might we expect from a child in the concrete operations stage of development?

In this stage of development, a child organizes concepts into categories and begins to use simple logic and understand relational terms. The cognitive skill of conservation is acquired at the end of the period. Conservation in this context involves understanding that the form of something (rolling out a ball of clay or pouring liquid from one container to another) does not change its essential nature or quantity. *Page 93.*

● What cognitive ability characterizes the stage of formal operations?

The essence of the formal operations stage is the ability to think, reason, and solve problems symbolically in abstract rather than concrete form. *Pages 93–94.*

● Cite two criticisms of Piaget's theory of cognitive development.

Piaget's theory has been very influential and has received support from cross-cultural studies, but has not escaped criticism. Two problems are: (1) There is little evidence that cognitive abilities develop in a series of well-defined, sequential stages. (2) Preschool children in particular seem to have more cognitive strengths than Piaget suggested. *Pages 94–95.*

● Briefly summarize the stages of Kohlberg's theory of moral development.

Kohlberg proposes that the sense of morality develops through three levels and six stages. First, one decides right from wrong on the basis of avoiding punishment and gaining rewards (preconventional morality), then on the basis of conforming to authority or social convention (conventional morality), and finally on the basis of one's understanding of the common good, individual rights, and internalized standards (postconventional morality). Although much of the theory has been supported, there is little evidence that many individuals reach the higher levels of moral reasoning. Also, there may be serious deficiencies in applying the theory equally to both sexes or to all cultures, since what is "moral" or "right" may vary. *Pages 96–98.*

● Describe the first four stages (crises) of development according to Erikson.

Of Erikson's eight stages of development, four occur in childhood. Stages are described in terms of crises that need resolution and include: (1) trust vs. mistrust (whether the child develops a sense of security or anxiety); (2) autonomy vs. self doubt (whether the child develops a sense of competence or doubt); (3) initiative vs. guilt (whether the child gains confidence in his or her own ability or develops a sense of inadequacy); and (4) competence vs. inferiority (whether the child develops a sense of confidence in intellectual and social skills or a sense of failure and a lack of confidence). *Pages 98–100.*

● In child development, what is meant by "attachment," and what are the benefits of developing secure attachments?

Attachment is a strong, two-way emotional bond formed early in childhood between the child and primary caregiver(s). It has survival value, keeping the child in proximity to those who can best care for him or her. Secure attachment in childhood has been associated with improved self-esteem and cognitive skills later in life. Fathers, as well as mothers, demonstrate appropriate attachment-related behaviors, and most data suggest that day care for young children (over the age of one year) does not generally have negative consequences, depending mostly on the quality of that day care. *Pages 100–101.*

TOPIC 3C

ADOLESCENCE AND ADULTHOOD

● How might adolescence be defined, and how can the period be characterized?

Physically, adolescence begins with puberty (reaching sexual maturity) and lasts until the end of one's physical growth. Psychologically, it is defined in terms of the cognitions that characterize the period, searching for identity and abstract reasoning. Socially, it is a period of transition between one's childhood and adulthood, and reflects how the adolescent is viewed by others. Historically, adolescence has been seen as a period of stress and abnormality. Contemporary views see adolescence as a period of challenge, but a period that most survive with no lasting negative consequences. *Pages 101–102.*

● Briefly describe the physical changes that accompany the beginning of adolescence.

Two significant physical developments mark adolescence: a spurt of growth, seen at an earlier age in girls (9 to 15) than in boys (12 to 17); and the beginning of sexual maturity, called *puberty.* As adolescents, individuals are for the first time physically prepared for sexual reproduction, and begin to develop secondary sex characteristics. *Pages 102–104.*

● Summarize the adolescent's search for identity as described by Erikson.

The search for one's identity—a sense of who one is and what one is to do with one's life—is, for Erikson, the major crisis of adolescence. Most do develop such a sense of identity, while some enter adulthood in a state that Erikson calls "role confusion." *Page 105.*

● Briefly summarize the data on drug use and abuse in adolescence.

Most teenagers have experimented with drugs (mostly alcohol, tried by 92 percent of high school seniors), and a disturbing number use drugs quite frequently. At the same time, there is no evidence that drug use among adolescents is any greater than among adults. One study demonstrated that among frequent users, experimenters, and abstainers, experimenters evidenced the fewest psychological problems as 18-year-olds. *Pages 105–107.*

● What evidence supports the notion that adolescents are a sexually active group?
● Briefly summarize the data on teenage pregnancy.

By the time they are 18 years old, more than half of all females and nearly three-quarters of all males report having had sexual intercourse. Sexual activity is increasing for both males and females. First sexual encounters most often "just happen" without planning or forethought. This may help explain why over 1 million teenagers will become pregnant this year. Slightly more than half these pregnancies will result in live births. About two-thirds of white teenage mothers are single, and nearly all black teenage mothers are unmarried. *Pages 107–108.*

● What developments characterize early adulthood?

Early adulthood (roughly ages 18 to 45) is a period characterized by choices and commitments independently made. One assumes new responsibilities and is faced with a series of difficult decisions concerning career, marriage, and family. For Erikson, the period is marked by the conflict between intimacy and social relationships on the one hand and social isolation on the other. Although many marriages fail, most young adults list a good marriage as a major source of happiness in their lives. Many factors determine one's selection of a mate, but there is little support for the notion that opposites attract. Traits sought in mates vary among cultures. Choosing one's career is another decision of early adulthood. It is a process that goes through several stages of and often involves initial failures. *Pages 108–113.*

● What are some of the issues typically faced during the middle years of adulthood?

Middle adulthood (roughly ages 45 to 65) is often a period of reexamination and then of settling down to one's life goals. Entering the period may be troublesome for some, but most find middle age a time of satisfaction and opportunity. The individual comes to accept his or her own mortality in a number of ways. The tasks or issues of middle age involve dealing with one's changing physiology, occupation, aging parents and growing children, social and civic responsibilities, one's spouse, and perhaps increased leisure time. *Pages 113–114.*

- ● Briefly summarize some of what we know about the elderly.

There are now more than 30 million Americans over the age of 65, and the number of elderly is growing steadily. Although there may be sensory, physical, and cognitive limitations forced by old age, only 31 percent of the elderly rate health problems as a major concern. Although some elderly are isolated and lonely, fewer than 5 percent live in nursing homes. Older people are naturally concerned about death, but they are neither consumed by nor morbid about it. With good nutrition, the development of a healthy life-style, proper social support, and the maintenance of some degree of autonomy and control over one's life, "successful aging" can become more common. *Pages 114–117.*

TOPIC 3A

PRENATAL DEVELOPMENT

3.1 How many cells does it take to form a zygote? a) 2 b) 23 c) 23 pairs, or 46 d) more than one trillion. *Pages 80–83.*

3.2 At which stage, or at what point is the developing human at greatest risk of physical defects? a) as a zygote b) during the stage of the embryo c) as a growing fetus d) during the birth process. *Pages 80–83.*

3.3 An organism is said to be viable when a) its brain is fully developed. b) it can survive without medical intervention. c) it is at least 270 days old. d) it can no longer be influenced by toxins or poisons from the environment. *Pages 80–83.*

3.4 Each of these can have a negative effect on the developing organism; which is generally the most negative? a) the mother's inability to gain weight during her pregnancy b) inadequate calcium intake during pregnancy c) taking antibiotics such as penicillin or tetracycline during pregnancy d) alcohol abuse during pregnancy. *Pages 83–85.*

3.5 True or False? Fetal alcohol syndrome includes the likelihood of mental or intellectual retardation. *Pages 83–85.*

3.6 In terms of prenatal development, what is of greatest concern with regard to the father? a) whether he lives at home b) socioeconomic status c) the quality of the sperm at conception d) the amount of stress he experiences. *Pages 83–85.*

TOPIC 3B

DEVELOPMENT IN CHILDREN

3.7 The behaviors of the neonate can be described as a) learned or acquired. b) essentially useless. c) difficult to observe. d) largely reflexive. *Pages 85–87.*

3.8 True or False? Most neonatal reflexes have no apparent survival value. *Pages 85–87.*

3.9 Which statement concerning physical or motor growth and development in young children (younger than age 5) is *true?* a) Physical growth in this period is slower than it has been earlier, or than it will be later. b) Growth and development occur at the same rate for all normal, healthy children. c) Development and control of the extremities of the body occur earlier in girls than in boys. d) Although rates of development vary, the sequence of development is very similar for all children. *Pages 85–87.*

3.10 Which sensory capacity or ability is probably the Weakest in a 6-month-old child? a) the perception of depth and distance b) the sense of balance and body position c) the ability to discriminate among sounds d) the visual perception of faces. *Pages 88.*

3.11 One way to show that a newborn has a cognitive ability is to show that a) it uses reflexes regularly. b) all newborns follow the same sequence of development. c) newborns respond differently to new and previously experienced stimuli. d) virtually all of its senses are functioning at birth. *Pages 89–90.*

3.12 On what basis are Piaget's stages of development determined? a) the actual age of the child b) whether the child uses assimilation or accommodation c) the extent to which the child is egocentric or social d) how schemas are formed or modified with experience. *Pages 90–95.*

3.13 Melanie is 9 years old. She easily can get to school and back, a distance of six city blocks. On the other hand, she has great difficulty telling you just how she manages to make the trip to school and back each day. Melonie is probably in Piaget's _____ stage of cognitive development. a) sensorimotor b) preoperational c) concrete operations d) formal operations. *Pages 90–95.*

3.14 True or False? In forming his theory of cognitive development, Piaget seems to have underestimated the cognitive skills of very young preschool children. *Pages 90–95.*

3.15 Kohlberg's theory of development focuses primarily on the development of a) cognitive representations, called schemas. b) strategies that children use to learn. c) morality and the sense of right and wrong. d) how children and adolescents interact with each other. *Pages 96–98.*

3.16 True or False? Although there is evidence supporting Kohlberg's theory in the United States, it has not been tested in other cultures. *Pages 96–98.*

3.17 True or False? Carol Gilligan has argued that with regard to moral development, there are sex differences in what is considered to be right or moral and what is considered to be wrong or immoral. *Pages 96–98.*

3.18 Which is the biggest difference between Piaget's and Erikson's theories of development? Erikson's theory a) relies less on the notion of stages. b) was based on experiments, not observations. c) is more relevant for boys than for girls. d) describes development throughout the lifespan. *Pages 98–100.*

3.19 What we call "self-esteem," or sense of self-worth, is most critically important in which of these stages of Erikson's theory? a) trust vs. mistrust b) autonomy vs. self doubt c) initiative vs. guilt d) competence vs. inferiority. *Pages 98–100.*

3.20 True or False? Although attachments are typically made between mother and child, children can form secure attachments with fathers or with day care providers. *Pages 100–101.*

TOPIC 3C

ADOLESCENCE AND ADULTHOOD

3.21 Which observation concerning adolescence is most valid? a) It is a stage or period through which many individuals never pass. b) It is a period defined in terms of stress, turmoil, and abnormality. c) It is a period through which most people pass in psychologically adaptive ways. d) It is virtually the only developmental period for which both the beginning and end are defined in biological terms. *Pages 101–104.*

3.22 True or False? Most adolescents are seriously troubled, rebellious, and uncooperative. *Pages 101–104.*

3.23 Which observation concerning menarche is *true*? a) It is found more commonly in boys than in girls. b) It occurs just before one's adolescence ends. c) It generally occurs two or three years after puberty begins. d) It is produced or triggered by the release of sex hormones. *Pages 101–104.*

3.24 The notion of teenagers facing an "identity crisis" is best associated with a) Freud. b) Erikson. c) Kohlberg. d) Piaget. *Page 105.*

3.25 Which observation concerning adolescent drug use is *true*? a) Adolescents experiment with and use drugs more than adults do. b) Adolescents are more likely to use illegal drugs than legal ones. c) Both the use and abuse of drugs by adolescents declined in the 1980s but is now rising again. d) Adolescents who have never used drugs experience fewer adjustment problems than those who have experimented with drugs. *Pages 105–107.*

3.26 True or False? Any sort of use or experimentation with drugs by adolescents is bound to have long-term negative effects. *Pages 105–107.*

3.27 The best estimate of the number of teenagers who will become pregnant this year is approximately a) 50,000. b) 100,000. c) 400,000. d) 1 million. *Pages 107–108.*

3.28 Which of the following "explanations" for teenage pregnancy is *least* acceptable or *least* reasonable? a) Teenagers are ignorant about their own sexuality.

b) Many teenagers want to start their own families. c) Teenagers have negative attitudes about contraceptive use. d) Pregnancies simply happen "by accident," without intention. *Pages 107–108.*

3.29 What two concepts, taken together, characterize the beginning of adulthood? a) independence and interdependence b) death and dying c) growth and development d) assimilation and accommodation. *Pages 108–113.*

3.30 For Erikson, early adulthood is best characterized in terms of a) competency vs. inferiority. b) ego-identity vs. despair. c) intimacy vs. isolation. d) generativity vs. stagnation. *Pages 108–113.*

3.31 True or False? Men and women are in agreement on those traits that make a good mate. *Pages 108–113.*

3.32 True or False? Most young adults are unhappy or dissatisfied with their first career choices. *Pages 108–113.*

3.33 True or False? Most Americans experience a real mid-life crisis accompanied by the realization that "time is running out" and they may not get to do all they want to do. *Pages 113–114.*

3.34 Which of the following best characterizes the elderly in the United States? a) Most (more than 50%) require supervision of the sort found in nursing homes. b) Most (more than 50%) are preoccupied with thoughts of their own death. c) Most (more than 75%) are vigorous and competent. d) Most (nearly 65%) list poor health as a serious problem. *Pages 114–117.*

SENSORY
PROCESSES

4

PREVIEW

TOPIC 4A—Sensation:
A Few Basic Concepts

Sensory Thresholds

Sensory Adaption

TOPIC 4B—Vision

The Stimulus for Vision:
Light

The Eye

Color Vision and Color
Blindness

TOPIC 4C—Hearing and
the Other Senses

Hearing

The Chemical Senses

The Skin, or Cutaneous,
Senses

The Position Senses

*PSYCHOLOGY IN THE
REAL WORLD: Pain and Its
Management*

THINKING CRITICALLY
ABOUT SENSORY
PROCESSES

SUMMARY

TEST YOURSELF

125

This chapter begins our discussion of memory. We are born into this world knowing very little. As newborns, we do have several important reflexes and we are able to start learning quickly, but our memories are pretty empty. By the time we are adults, our memories are packed with infomation, some of it critically important (what is edible and what isn't?), some of it fairly trivial (who played bass guitar for the Rolling Stones on their last concert tour?). A compelling and important question for many psychologists is *how* information gets processed into our memories. How do we find out about ourselves and the world in which we live? Answers to this question begin with a consideration of how our senses work.

Topic 4A considers some general observations about our senses. We begin with a definition of "sensation," and then discuss how we assess the sensitivity of our senses. We will also introduce the concept of sensory adaptation.

Topic 4B deals with vision. Indeed, most of our coverage of the senses will be on vision, in part because vision provides us with a great deal of information about the world, but also quite simply because we know more about vision than we do the other senses.

In Topic 4C we'll briefly review the other senses, examining the nature of the stimuli that excite them and discussing the relevant sense organ and sense receptors for each.

TOPIC 4A

SENSATION: A FEW BASIC CONCEPTS

Processing information from the environment begins with sensation. **Sensation** is the process that yields our immediate experience of stimuli in our environment. It is the process of receiving information from the environment and changing that input into nervous system activity. *Sense receptors* are the specialized neural cells in the *sense organs* (e.g., eyes, ears, nose, skin, etc.) that change physical energy into neural impulses. In other words, each of our senses is a **transducer**—a mechanism that converts energy from one form to another. A light bulb is a transducer—it converts electrical energy into light energy (and a little heat energy). Your eye is a sense organ that contains sense receptors that transduce light energy into neural energy. Your ears transduce the mechanical energy of sound wave vibrations into the energy of neural impulses.

sensation
the process of receiving information from the environment and changing that input into nervous system activity

transducer
a mechanism that converts energy from one form to another, as sense receptors do

126

Now, before we get into how our senses transduce physical energy from the environment into neural energy, we'll consider a few important concepts that apply to all our senses.

SENSORY THRESHOLDS

Psychophysics is the study of the relationships between the physical attributes of stimuli and the psychological experiences they produce. At a simple level, we can say that the techniques of psychophysics have been designed to assess the sensitivity of our senses. At a more theoretical level, we can think of psychophysics as providing a means of relating the outside physical world to the inner psychological world. In either case, the focus is on sensory thresholds.

Absolute Thresholds

Imagine the following experiment. You are seated in a dimly lighted room, staring at a small box. The side of the box facing you is covered by a sheet of plastic. Behind the plastic is a light bulb. I can decrease the physical intensity of the light bulb to the point where you cannot see it at all, and I can increase the light's intensity so that you can see it clearly. I also have the option of many settings between these extremes. My basic question is: At what point of physical intensity will the light first become visible to you?

Common sense tells us that there should be some level of intensity below which you cannot see the light and above which you can. That level of intensity would be your absolute threshold. The term *threshold* means the same thing here that it means in other contexts—a point of crossing over. Sensory thresholds are clearly related to sensitivity, but inversely. That is, as threshold levels decrease, sensitivity increases. The lower the threshold of a sense receptor, the greater its sensitivity.

Let's return to our imaginary experiment. I repeatedly vary the light's intensity and ask you to respond "Yes, I see the light," or "No, I don't see the light," depending on your experience. In this experiment, I won't allow you the luxury of saying that you don't know or aren't sure.

When this experiment is actually done, we discover something that at first seems strange. There are many intensities of the light for which your responses are inconsistent over several presentations of the very same light intensity. In other words, there are intensities of light to which you sometimes respond "yes" and sometimes respond "no," even though the actual, physical intensity of the light is unchanged.

In truth, there isn't very much that is absolute about absolute thresholds at all. They keep changing from moment to moment, reflecting small, subtle changes in the sensitivity of our senses. They also reflect such factors as momentary shifts in our ability to pay attention. Because there are no absolute measures of sensory sensitivity, psychologists resort to the following definition of **absolute threshold**: the physical intensity of a stimulus that a subject reports detecting 50 percent of the time. In other words, stimulus intensities below threshold are detected less than 50 percent of the time, while stimulus intensities above threshold are detected more than 50 percent of the time. This complication occurs for all our senses, not just for vision.

So what good is the notion of an absolute threshold? For one thing, absolute threshold levels can be used to discover if one's senses are operating properly and for detecting low levels of stimulation (as when you have

psychophysics
the study of the relationships between the physical attributes of stimuli and the psychological experiences they produce

absolute threshold
the physical intensity of a stimulus that one can detect 50 percent of the time

To be a professional wine taster requires that one's ability to detect just noticeable differences among various wines be extremely sensitive.

FIGURE 4.1
Examples of Absolute Threshold Values for Five Senses
(i.e., These Stimuli Will Be Detected 50 Percent of the Time)

Vision	A candle flame seen from a distance of 30 miles on a clear, dark night
Hearing	The ticking of a watch under quiet conditions from a distance of 20 feet
Taste	1 teaspoon of sugar dissolved in 2 gallons of water
Smell	One drop of perfume in a three-room apartment
Touch	The wing of a bee dropped on your cheek from a height of one centimeter

From Galanter, 1962.

your hearing tested). Engineers who design sound systems know about thresholds—speakers that do not reproduce sounds above threshold levels aren't of much use. Warning lights must be well above absolute threshold if they are to be of any use to us. How much perfume is required for it to be noticed? How low must you whisper so as not to be overheard in a classroom? Do I smell natural gas in the house, or is it my imagination? Unless stimulus intensity exceeds absolute threshold levels, they may not be experienced (sensed) at all. As it happens, our sense receptors are remarkably sensitive, as the oft-quoted examples in Figure 4.1 attest.

● **Before You Go On**

How is the process of sensation defined?

What is psychophysics?

What is an absolute threshold and how is it related to the sensitivity of our senses?

Difference Thresholds

We are much more often called upon to detect differences among stimuli than we are to detect very low-intensity stimuli. The issue is not if stimuli can be detected, but if they are in some way different from each other. A **difference threshold** is the smallest difference between stimulus attributes that can be detected. As you may have guessed, we encounter the same complication here that we find when we try to measure absolute thresholds. To slight degrees, one's difference threshold for any attribute tends to vary from moment to moment. So we say that to be above one's difference threshold, differences need to be detected more than 50 percent of the time.

Here is an example. I present you with two tones. You hear them both (they're above your absolute threshold), and report that they seem equally loud. If I gradually increase the intensity of one of the tones, I will eventually reach a point where you can just barely detect a difference in the loudness of the two tones. This **just noticeable difference (j.n.d.)** is defined as the smallest amount of change in a stimulus that sets it apart, or makes it just noticeably different from what it was.

The concept of just noticeable difference is relevant in many contexts. A parent tells a teenager to "turn down that stereo!" The teenager reduces

difference threshold
the minimal difference in some stimulus attribute, such as intensity, that one can detect 50 percent of the time

just noticeable difference (j.n.d.)
the smallest detectable change in some stimulus attribute, such as intensity

the volume, but not by a j.n.d. from the parent's perspective, and trouble may be brewing. Does the color of the belt match the color of the dress closely enough? Can anyone tell the difference between expensive ingredients in the stew and cheaper ones? Is this car so much cheaper than that one that the difference in price makes it worth buying?

Signal Detection

Sensory thresholds are not stable, fixed values. They vary from moment to moment and therefore are defined in terms of probability. The sensitivity of our senses changes for several reasons, including momentary shifts in our attention and the random activity of the nerve cells in our sensory systems.

When we are asked if a stimulus is present, we're really being asked to judge whether we can detect a signal against a background of other stimuli and randomly changing neural activity called *noise*. Thinking about threshold determination in this way involves the basics of **signal detection theory**. This theory takes the position that stimulus detection is a process of deciding if a signal exists against a background of noise (Green & Swets, 1966).

According to this theory, an absolute threshold is influenced by many factors in addition to the actual sensitivity of one's senses. Random nervous system activity needs to be accounted for. So do the individual's attention, expectations, and biases. In studies to determine absolute threshold, subjects are simply more likely to say that they detect a stimulus than they are to say that they don't (Block, 1965).

Remember the basics of the absolute threshold study with which we began our discussion of psychophysics? I had a light in a box, changed the intensity of the light, and asked whether you could see it. Your absolute threshold was the intensity of the light to which you responded "Yes" 50 percent of the time. Signal detection theory simply asks us to consider all of the factors that might have prompted you to say "Yes" at any exposure of the light. What might some of these factors be? One would be the amount of other light available in the room. Wouldn't you be more able to detect the signal of my light in a room that was totally dark than in a room in which all of the standard lights were on? What if I had offered you a reward, say $5, for each time you correctly detected the light. Wouldn't you tend to say "Yes" often, whether you were really sure of yourself or not? By the same token, if I were to fine you $1 each time you said "Yes" when the light was not really on, might you tend to become conservative, and say "Yes" only when you were very sure. Might we expect a difference in your pattern of saying "Yes" and "No" depending on whether we tested you in mid-morning or late in the day, when you were tired?

Signal detection procedures try to take into account such factors as background noise, level of attention, and subject bias in the determination of sensory thresholds. The result is a better, clearer picture of sensory sensitivity.

SENSORY ADAPTATION

Sensory adaptation is a process by which sensory experiences decrease with continued exposure to a stimulus. There are many examples of sensory adaptation. When we first jump into the pool or the lake, the water feels very cold, but after only a few minutes we adapt and are reassuring our friends, "Come on in; the water's fine." When we first walk into a house where cabbage is cooking, the odor is overwhelming, but soon we adapt

signal detection theory
the view that stimulus detection is a matter of decision making, of separating a signal from background noise

sensory adaptation
the process in which our sensory experience tends (in most cases) to decrease or diminish with continued exposure to a stimulus

and do not notice it. When the compressor motor of the refrigerator first turns on, it seems to make a very loud noise, one that we soon do not notice—until the motor stops and silence returns to the kitchen. Sensory adaptation again.

There is an important psychological point hidden in these examples. It is that the ability to detect the presence of a stimulus depends largely on the extent to which sense receptors are being newly stimulated or have to some degree already adapted. In other words, sense receptors respond best to *changes* in stimulation. The constant stimulation of a receptor leads to adaptation, and less of a chance that that stimulation will be detected.

There is an exception to this usage of the term "adaptation." Have you thought of it? What happens when you move from a brightly lit area to a dim place? Perhaps you enter a dark movie theater on a sunny afternoon. At first you can barely see anything at all, but in a few minutes you are seeing reasonably well. What happened? We say that you have "adapted to the dark." **Dark adaptation** refers to the fact that with time spent in the dark, our visual receptors actually become more sensitive to what little light is available.

dark adaptation
the process by which our eyes become more sensitive to light as we spend time in the dark

● **Before You Go On**
What is a difference threshold, or j.n.d.?
Briefly summarize the basic ideas of signal detection theory.
What is sensory adaptation?

TOPIC 4B

VISION

Discussing which of our senses is the most important is a pretty silly exercise. Each sense is of value in helping us process information about the environment. (I enjoy eating, and think highly of the sense of taste.) It remains the case, nonetheless, that vision *is* a very important sense for humans. Occasionally we even equate our visual experiences with truth, or reality, as in "Seeing is believing." Remember, too, that the entire occipital lobe is devoted to the processing of visual information. In this Topic we will first consider the stimulus for vision (light), then we'll deal with the sense organ (the eye).

THE STIMULUS FOR VISION: LIGHT

Light, the stimulus for vision, is a wave form of radiant energy. That is, light radiates from its source in waves (which we call light waves). Light waves have three major physical characteristics that are related to psychological experience: wave amplitude, wavelength, and wave purity.

Wave Amplitude (Intensity)

One of the ways in which light energy may vary is in its intensity. When we think about light traveling in the form of waves of energy, differences in intensity correspond to differences in the **wave amplitude** of light. The amplitude of a wave is represented by its height. Refer to Figure 4.2 and as-

light
a radiant energy that can be represented in wave form with wavelength between 380 and 760 nanometers

wave amplitude
a characteristic of wave forms (the height of the wave) that indicates intensity

FIGURE 4.2

Representations of light waves differing in wavelength and in wave amplitude. Wavelength gives rise to our experience of the hue of a light, whereas wave amplitude determines our experience of brightness.

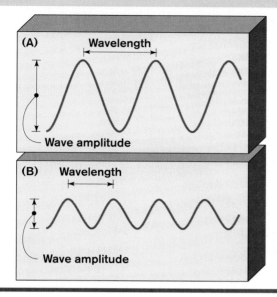

sume that the two waves there represent two different light waves. One of the physical differences between light (A) and light (B) is in the height of the waves, or wave amplitude.

Our psychological experience of wave amplitude, or intensity, is **brightness**. The difference between a dim light and a bright light is due to the difference in wave amplitude. Of the two lights in Figure 4.2, (A) has the higher amplitude and thus would be seen as the brighter light. Switches that control the brightness of light fixtures are in essence controlling the amplitude of light waves.

Wavelength

Wavelength is the distance between any point in a wave and the corresponding point on the next cycle—from peak to peak, for example. In Figure 4.2, one difference between waves (A) and (B) is their wavelength, where (A) has the longer wavelength. Although it is difficult to imagine distances so tiny, we *can* measure the length of a light wave. The unit of measurement is the *nanometer (nm),* which is equal to one billionth of a meter or one millionth of a millimeter!

The human eye responds only to radiant energy in wave form that has a wavelength between roughly 380 and 760 nanometers. This is the range of light waves that constitutes the visible spectrum. Wave forms of energy with wavelengths shorter than 380nm (e.g., X rays and ultraviolet rays) are too short to stimulate the receptors in our eyes, and they go unnoticed. Wave forms of energy with wavelengths in excess of 760nm (e.g., microwaves and radar) do not stimulate the receptor cells in our eyes either.

Wave amplitude gives rise to our experience of brightness. Wavelength is the attribute of light energy that determines the **hue**, or color, we

brightness
the psychological experience associated with light's intensity wave amplitude

wavelength
the distance between any point in a wave and the corresponding point on the next cycle

hue
the psychological experience associated with a light's wavelength

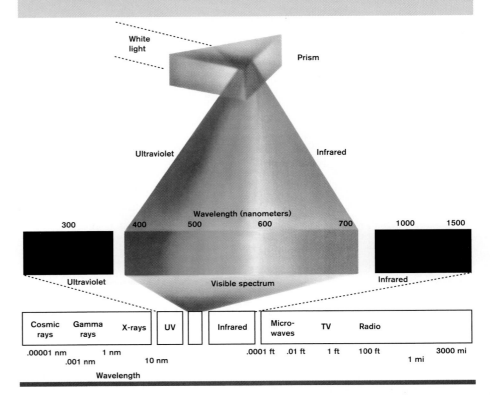

FIGURE 4.3
The spectrum of electromagnetic energy in wave form, of which light is but a small segment. Here we see that light is electromagnetic energy with a wavelength between 380 nm and 760 nm. As wavelength increases, our experience of light changes to produce a "rainbow."

perceive. As light waves increase in length from the short 380nm wavelengths to the long 760nm wavelengths, our experience of them changes—from violet to blue to green to yellow-green to yellow to orange to red along the color spectrum (see Figure 4.3, which also presents some of the invisible varieties of radiant energy in wave form).

A source of radiant energy with a 700-nanometer wavelength will be seen as a red light. In fact, that's what a red light *is*. (A bright red light has a high amplitude, and a dim red light has a low amplitude, but both have 700nm wavelengths.) As we can see from Figure 4.3, if a light had waves 550nm long, it would be seen as a yellow-green light, and so on. Note that yellow-green is a single hue produced by a given wavelength of light (550nm), and not some combination of yellow and green. We simply have no other name for this hue, so we call it yellow-green.

Wave Purity

Imagine a light of medium amplitude with all its wavelengths exactly 700 nanometers long. The light would appear to be of medium brightness. Because the wavelengths are all 700nm, it would appear red. More than that, it would appear as a pure, rich red. We call such a light **monochromatic** because it is made up of light waves all of one (mono) length or hue (chroma). We seldom see such lights outside the laboratory, because producing a pure, monochromatic light is expensive. The reddest lights that

monochromatic
literally one colored; a pure light made up of light waves all of the same wavelength

you and I see in our everyday experience still have other wavelengths of light mixed in along with the predominant 700nm red. (If the 700nm light wave did not predominate, the light wouldn't look red.) Even the red light on top of a police car has some violet and green and yellow wavelengths of light in it.

The physical purity of a light determines the psychological experience that we call **saturation**. Pure, monochromatic lights are the most highly saturated; their hue is rich and obvious. (You may think of highly saturated lights as being so filled—so saturated–with the one wavelength that there isn't room for any other.) As different wavelengths get mixed into a light, it becomes lower and lower in saturation, and it starts to look pale and washed out.

What do we call a light that is of the lowest possible saturation, a light that contains a random mixture of wavelengths? By definition, it is **white light**. It is something of a curiosity that white light is in fact as impure a light as possible. A pure light has but one wavelength; a white light contains many wavelengths. True white light is as difficult to produce as is a pure monochromatic light. Fluorescent light bulbs produce reasonable approximations, but their light contains too many wavelengths from the short (blue-violet) end of the spectrum. Light from regular incandescent light bulbs contains too many light waves from the orange and red end of the spectrum (even if we paint the inside of the bulb with white paint). A prism can take a beam of white light—sunlight is an approximation—and break it down into its various parts, giving us the experience of a rainbow of hues. Where did all those hues come from? They were there all along, mixed together as white light.

We have seen that three physical characteristics of light influence our visual experience. Wave amplitude determines brightness; wavelength determines hue; wave purity determines saturation. These relationships are summarized in Figure 4.4.

saturation
the psychological experience associated with the purity of a light wave, where the most saturated lights are monochromatic and the least saturated are white light

white light
a light of the lowest possible saturation, containing a mixture of visible wavelengths

● **Before You Go On**

In what ways do the major physical characteristics of light waves of energy (amplitude, length, and purity) affect our psychological experience of light?

THE EYE

Vision involves changing (transducing) light wave energy into neural impulses. This transduction does take place in the eye. But, as it happens, most of the structures of the eye have little to do with the actual process of

---

FIGURE 4.4
The Relationships Between the Physical Characteristics of Light and Our Psychological Experience of That Light

Physical characteristic	Psychological experience
Wave amplitude (intensity)	Brightness
Wavelength	Hue
Wave purity	Saturation

These two interact. (Brightness and Hue)

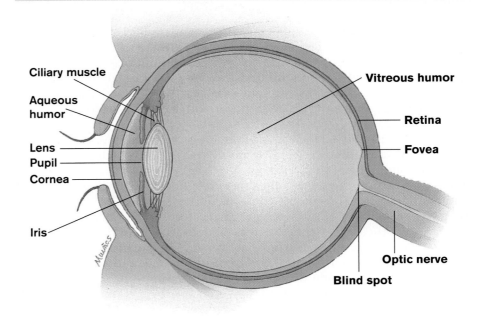

FIGURE 4.5
The major structures of the human eye.

energy transduction; the function of most structures is to focus the images that enter the eye onto the one layer of cells that does respond directly to light waves.

Structures That Focus Visual Images

Using Figure 4.5 as a guide, let's trace the path of light as it passes through the eye. Light enters through the cornea. The **cornea** is the tough, round, virtually transparent outer shell of the eye. Those of you who wear contact lenses float them on your corneas. The cornea protects the delicate structures behind it, and starts to bend the entering light waves in order to focus an image on the back surface of the eye.

Having passed through the cornea, light then travels through the **pupil**, an opening in the iris. The **iris** is pigmented, or colored. When we say that someone has blue, brown, or green eyes, we are referring to the color of their irises. The iris can expand or contract, which changes the size of the pupil. This is a reflex reaction, not something you can control by conscious effort. Contractions of the iris that change pupil size are made in response to the level of light present—opening the pupil wide when only small amounts of light are present and reducing its size (protectively) in response to high-intensity lights. Increasing pupil size is also one of the automatic responses that occurs with heightened levels of emotionality—an adaptive reaction to let in as much light as possible.

After the pupil, the next structure light encounters is the lens. As in a camera, the main function of the **lens** of the eye is to focus a visual image. The lens changes its shape to bring an image into focus—becoming flatter as we try to focus on an object in the distance and becoming rounder when we try to view something up close. This, too, is a reflex. Obviously, lenses

cornea
the outermost structure of the eye, which protects the eye and begins to focus light waves

pupil
the opening in the iris that changes size in relation to the amount of light available and emotional factors

iris
the colored structure of the eye that reflexively opens or constricts the pupil

lens
the structure behind the iris that changes shape to focus visual images in the eye

are not normally as hard as glass or they wouldn't be able to change their shape. With age, lenses tend to harden, making it difficult to focus and requiring the use of corrective lenses to help out.

Some very powerful little muscles called **ciliary muscles** push on the lens or relax in order to change the shape of the lens—a process called *accommodation*. It is often the case that an image does not focus as it should, because of either the shape of the lens or the eye itself or a failure of accommodation. Sometimes a healthy lens and functioning ciliary muscles still can't get an image to focus because of the shape of the eyeball itself. The result is nearsightedness or farsightedness. Figure 4.6 shows examples of what happens in these cases.

There is a space between the cornea and the lens filled with a clear fluid called **aqueous humor**. This humor (which means "fluid") provides nourishment to the cornea and the other structures at the front of the eye. If the fluid cannot easily pass back out of this space, pressure builds within the eye, causing distortions in vision or, in extreme cases, blindness. This disorder is known as *glaucoma*.

There is another, larger space behind the lens that is also filled with a fluid or humor. This fluid is called **vitreous humor**. It is not nearly as watery as aqueous humor. It is thick and filled with tiny structures that give it substance. Its major function is to keep the eyeball rounded.

The Retina

So far we have listed several structures of the eye, each important in its own way, but none of them doing much more than letting light waves back through the eye to other structures, usually in more focused form. It is at the **retina** that vision begins to take place. It is here that light energy is transduced into neural energy.

The retina is a series of layers of specialized nerve cells at the back surface of the eye. These cells are neurons, and in a sense should be thought of as part of the brain. The location of the retina and its major landmarks are shown in Figure 4.5, and Figure 4.7 shows the retina in more detail.

To describe the retina, let's move from the back of the eye out toward the front. The layer of cells at the very back of the retina are the receptor cells for vision, the transducers, or photoreceptors. It is here at this layer of cells that light wave energy is changed into neural impulses.

As it happens, there are two types of photoreceptor cells: **rods** and **cones**. They are aptly named, because they look like small rods and cones. Their ends or tips respond to light wave energy and begin neural impulses. The impulses travel down the rods and cones and pass on to other cells, also arranged in layers. Within these layers of nerve cells there is considerable combination and integration of impulses. The rods and cones do not have a single direct pathway to the cerebral cortex of the brain. Impulses from many rods and cones are combined in the eye (by *bipolar* and *ganglion cells*, among others). Fibers from ganglion cells gather together to form the **optic nerve**, which leaves the eye and starts back toward other parts of the brain.

Note the arrow in Figure 4.7 that indicates the direction of the light entering the retina. It is drawn correctly: Light waves pass through all those layers of nerve cells, to reach the tips of the rods and cones, where they initiate neural impulses. I have to admit that it would make more sense to me to point the light-sensitive tips of the rods and cones out toward the incoming light, yet all mammalian retinas are constructed in the manner shown in Figure 4.7.

ciliary muscles
small muscles attached to the lens that control its shape and focusing ability

aqueous humor
watery fluid found in the space between the cornea and the lens that nourishes the front of the eye

vitreous humor
the thick fluid behind the lens of the eye that helps keep the eyeball spherical

retina
layers of cells at the back of the eye that contain the photosensitive rod and cone cells

rods
photosensitive cells of the retina that are most active in low levels of illumination and do not respond differentially to different wavelengths of light

cones
photosensitive cells of the retina that operate best at high levels of illumination and are responsible for color vision

optic nerve
a fiber composed of many neurons, which leaves the eye and carries impulses to the occipital lobe of the brain

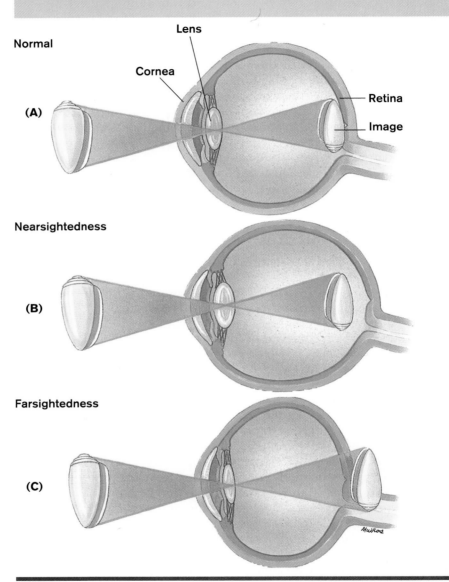

FIGURE 4.6
Sightedness. (A) Normal vision, where the inverted image is focused by the cornea and the lens to fall directly on the retina. (B) Nearsightedness, where the focused image falls short of the receptors in the retina. (C) Farsightedness, where a focused image falls beyond, or behind, the retina.

Normal

Lens

Cornea

Retina

Image

(A)

Nearsightedness

(B)

Farsightedness

(C)

fovea
the region at the center of the retina, comprised solely of cones, where acuity is best in daylight

blindspot
a small region of the retina, containing no photoreceptors, where the optic nerve leaves the eye

The two main features of the retina shown in Figure 4.5 are the fovea and the blindspot. There are no rods in the **fovea**, only cones tightly packed together. It is at the fovea that our ability to discern detail (acuity) is best—at least in reasonably high levels of illumination. When you try to thread a needle, you want to focus the image of the needle and thread directly on the fovea. The **blindspot** of the retina is where the nerve impulses from the rods and cones, having passed through all those other layers of

FIGURE 4.7
The major features of the human retina.

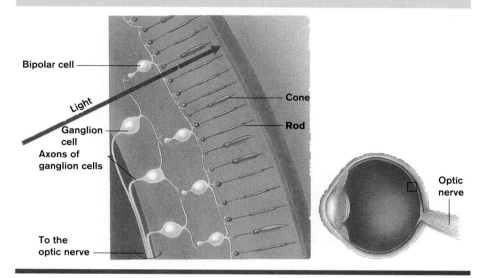

cells, exit the eye. At the blindspot, there are no rods and cones—there's nothing there but the optic nerve threading its way back deeper into the brain. Because there are no rods or cones, there is no vision here, hence the name. Figure 4.8 provides you with a way to locate your own blindspot.

● **Before You Go On**

List the major structures of the eye, and describe the function of each.

FIGURE 4.8
Two ways to find your blind spot. (A) Close your right eye and stare at the cross (+). Hold the page about a foot from your left eye and slowly move the page around until the star falls on your blind spot and disappears. (B) Close your right eye and stare at the cross. Hold the page about a foot from your left eye and slowly move the page around until the break in the line falls on your blind spot. The line will appear to be unbroken.

(A)

(B)

More on Rods and Cones and What They Do

Let's now deal with the fact that the human eye contains two distinctly different photoreceptor cells. Both rods and cones exist in our retinas, but they are not there in equal number. In one eye, there are approximately 120 million rods, but only 6 million cones; rods outnumber cones approximately 20 to 1. Not only are rods and cones found in unequal numbers, but they are not evenly distributed throughout the retina. Cones are concentrated in the center of the retina, at the fovea. Rods are concentrated in a band or ring surrounding the fovea, out toward the periphery of the retina. These observations have led psychologists to wonder if the rods and cones of our eyes have different functions.

In fact, cones function best in medium to high levels of illumination (as in daylight) and are primarily responsible for our experience of color. On the other hand, rods operate best under conditions of reduced illumination. They are more sensitive to low-intensity light. Rods do not discriminate among wavelengths of light, which means that rods do not contribute to our appreciation of color.

Some of the evidence supporting these observations can be verified by our own experiences. Don't you find it difficult to distinguish among colors at night, or in the dark? The next time you are at the movies eating some pieces of candy that are of different colors, see if you can tell them apart without holding them up to the light of the projector. You probably won't be able to tell a green piece from a red piece because they all appear black—a problem if you have a favorite flavor. You can't discriminate colors well in a dark movie theater because you are seeing them primarily with your rods which, again, are very good at seeing in the reduced illumination of the theater but don't differentiate among different wavelengths of light. Note that you have little difficulty making out the colors of the images being projected on the screen. This is simply because the light reflected from the screen is intense enough (bright enough) to stimulate the cones of your fovea, giving rise to the experience of different colors.

If you are looking for something small outside at night, you'll probably not see it if you look directly at it. Imagine that you're changing a tire along the roadside at night. You're replacing the wheel and can't find one of the lug nuts that you know is there in the gravel. If you look at it directly, the image of the nut falls on your fovea. Your fovea is made up almost entirely of cones. Cones do not operate well in relative darkness, and you won't see the nut. To have the best chance of finding it, you'll have to get the image of the nut to fall on the periphery of your eye, where your rods are concentrated.

One of the reasons why nocturnal animals (such as many varieties of owl) see well in low light is because their retinas are packed with rods. Such animals usually have no fovea, or have fewer cones and are demonstrably colorblind. (How you might test the color vision of an owl is discussed in Chapter 6, Topic 6B.)

Let's consider one other piece of evidence that supports the idea that our rods and our cones are providing us with two different types of vision. Let's take a closer look at what happens during dark adaptation, the process by which our eyes become more sensitive as we spend time in the dark (p. 130).

Figure 4.9 is a graphic representation of the dark adaptation process. It shows that with time spent in the dark, our sensitivity increases, or our threshold decreases. At first we see only very bright lights (say, the light re-

Nocturnal animals, such as this timber wolf, have a high concentration of rods in their retinas.

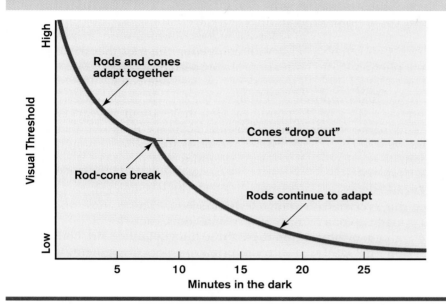

FIGURE 4.9

The dark-adaptation curve. At first, both rods and cones lower thresholds (increase their sensitivity). After 6 to 8 minutes, the cones have become as sensitive as possible, and drop out, leaving the rods alone to increase visual sensitivity.

flected from the movie screen); then we can see dimmer lights (those reflected from people in the theater), and then still dimmer ones (reflected from pieces of candy perhaps) as our threshold drops. As Figure 4.9 indicates, the whole process takes about 20 to 30 minutes.

But there is something strange going on. The dark adaptation curve is not a smooth one. At about the 7-minute mark, there is a change in the shape of the curve. This break in the curve is called *the rod-cone break*. At first—for 6 to 7 minutes—both rods and cones increase their sensitivity (represented by the first part of the curve). But our cones are basically daylight receptors. They are not cut out for seeing in the dark, and after those first few minutes, they have become as sensitive as they are going to get. Rods, on the other hand, keep lowering their threshold, or continue to increase their sensitivity (represented by the part of the curve after the "break").

Now that we've reviewed the nature of light and the eye, the stimulus and the receptor for vision, we'll end our discussion of vision by examining how our cones provide us with the experience of color.

● **Before You Go On**

Why can we claim that rods and cones provide us with two different kinds of visual experience?

COLOR VISION AND COLOR BLINDNESS

Explaining how the eye codes or responds to different intensities of light is not too difficult: High-intensity lights cause more rapid firing of neural impulses than do low-intensity lights. It is also sensible that high-intensity lights stimulate more cells to fire than do lights of low intensity. How the eye codes different wavelengths of light to produce different experiences of hue or color, however, is another story. Here things are not simple at all. There are many theories of color vision, two of which were proposed many years ago. As is often the case with competing theories that try to explain the same phenomenon, both are probably partially correct.

The older of the two theories of how we code color is the *trichromatic theory*. It was first proposed by Thomas Young early in the nineteenth century and was revised by Hermann von Helmholtz about 50 years later.

As its name implies, the *trichromatic theory* proposes that the eye contains *three* separate and distinct receptors for color. Although there is considerable overlap, each receptor responds best to one of three *primary hues* of light: red, green, and blue. These hues (or colors of light) are primary because by combining these three, all other colors can be produced. You see this everyday on your television screen. The picture on your TV screen is made up of a pattern of very small dots, each dot of light being either red, green, or blue. From these three hues, all others are constructed. (Please don't get confused with the primary colors of pigment, which are red, yellow, and blue—the three primary colors of paint, dye, pastel, and so forth, that can be mixed to form other colors of pigment. Our eyes respond to light, not to pigment.)

Because the sensitivities of the three receptors overlap, when our eyes are stimulated by a nonprimary color, say orange, the orange-hued light will stimulate each receptor to varying degrees to produce the sensation or experience of orange. What gives this theory credibility is that *there really are such receptor cells* in the human retina. Obviously, they are cones (which are responsible for color vision). The relative sensitivity of these three cone systems is shown in Figure 4.10.

Ewald Hering thought that the Young-Helmholtz theory left a bit to be desired, and in 1870 he proposed a theory of his own. This theory has come to be called the *opponent-process theory*. Hering's position is that there are three pairs of visual mechanisms that respond to different wavelengths of light. One is a blue-yellow processor, one a red-green processor, and the third deals with black-white differences.

Each mechanism is capable of responding to *either* of the two hues that give it its name, but not to both. That is, the blue-yellow processor responds to blue *or* yellow, but can't handle both at the same time. The second mechanism responds to red or green, but not both. The third codes brightness. Thus, the members of each pair work to oppose each other, giving the theory its name. If blue is excited, then yellow is inhibited. When red is excited, green is inhibited. A light may appear to be a mixture of red and yellow, but cannot be seen as a mixture of blue and yellow, because both blue and yellow cannot be excited at the same time. (It *is* difficult to imagine what a "reddish-green" or a "bluish-yellow" light would look like, isn't it? Can you picture a light that is bright and dim at the same time?)

The opponent-process theory may at first appear overly complicated, but there are some strong signs that Hering was on the right track. In the first place, excitatory-inhibitory mechanisms such as he proposed for red-

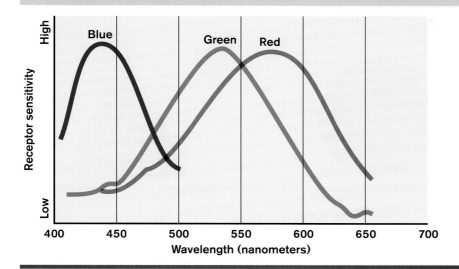

FIGURE 4.10
The relative sensitivities of three types of cones to lights of differing wavelengths. Although there is considerable overlap, each type is maximally sensitive to wavelengths corresponding to the primary hues of light: blue, green, and red.

green, blue-yellow, and black-white have been found. They are not at the level of rods and cones in the retina (as Hering thought), but at the layer of the ganglion cells (Figure 4.7) and also in an area of the thalamus.

Support for Hering's theory comes from our experiences with *negative afterimages*. If you stare at a bright green figure for a few minutes and then shift your gaze to a white surface, you'll notice an image of a red figure. Where did that come from? The explanation is that while you were staring at the green figure, the green component of the red-green process fatigued because of all the stimulation it was getting. When you stared at the white surface, both the red and green components of the process were equally stimulated, but because the green component was so fatigued, the red predominated, producing the experience of seeing a red figure. (Figure 4.11 provides an example for you to try.)

We have evidence to support both theories of normal vision that comes from the study of persons with color vision defects. Defective color vision of some sort occurs in about 8 percent of males and slightly less than 0.5 percent of females. Most cases are genetic in origin. It makes sense that if cones are our receptors for the discrimination of color, then people with a deficiency in color discrimination should have a problem with their cones. Such logic is consistent with the Young-Helmholtz theory of color vision. For the most common of the color vision deficiencies (dichromatism) there *is* a lack of a particular type of cone. For instance, people who are "red-green color-blind" have trouble telling the difference between red and green (a problem at stop lights, except that red is always on the top or on the left). People with this colorblindness also have trouble distinguishing yellow from either red or green. Notice that the deficiency is not in actually *seeing* reds or greens, it is in *distinguishing* reds and greens from other colors. Put another way, someone who is red-green colorblind can clearly see a

FIGURE 4.11

To illustrate the experience of color fatigue, or negative afterimages, stare at the blue circle for about 30 seconds; then quickly shift your gaze to a plain white surface. You should see the same figure, but it will appear yellow because the corresponding blue receptors are fatigued. Now try the same thing with the green triangle. What color did you see when you shifted your gaze?

bright red apple; it just looks no different from a bright green apple. See Figure 4.12.

Some color vision defects can be traced to the cones of the retina. But damage to cells higher in the visual pathway—more toward the cerebral cortex—are implicated in some rare cases of color vision problems. When such problems do occur, there are losses for both red and green or losses for both yellow and blue, color pairings predicted by the opponent process theory (e.g., Schiffman, 1990).

Because cone cells have been found in the retina that respond differentially to red, blue, and green light, we cannot dismiss the trichromatic theory. Because there are cells that operate the way the opponent-process theory predicts, we can't dismiss this theory either. Well, which one is right? Probably both. Our experience of color probably depends upon the interaction of different cone cells *and* different opponent-process cells within our visual pathway.

FIGURE 4.12

An illustration of the effect of red-green color-blindness. People with normal vision will be able to distinguish the images from the backgrounds, while people who are red-green color-blind will not.

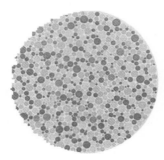
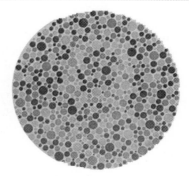

● **Before You Go On**

Summarize the trichromatic and the opponent-process theories of color vision.

T O P I C   4 C

HEARING AND THE OTHER SENSES

I've repeatedly made the point that vision is a very important sense. I'd like you to do a little experiment on your own some day. Try to bypass your heavy reliance on vision and spend the better part of a day doing without it—go about your everyday activities blindfolded. One thing you'll notice almost immediately is just how heavily you normally rely on vision. But consider for a moment the quantity and quality of the information you do receive from your *other* senses. You soon may come to a new appreciation of your nonvisual senses as they inform you of the wonder of your environment: the aroma and taste of a well-prepared barbecue, the sounds of birds and music, the feel of textures and surfaces, the sense of where your body is and what it's doing, the feedback from your muscles as you move.

HEARING

Hearing (more formally, *audition*) provides us with nearly as much useful information about our environment as vision does. One of its main roles is its involvement in our development of language and speech. Without hearing, these uniquely human skills are difficult to acquire.

The Stimulus for Hearing: Sound

The stimulus for vision is light; for hearing, the stimulus is sound. Sound is a series of pressures of air (or some other medium, such as water) that beat against our eardrums. We can represent these pressures as sound waves. As a source of sound vibrates, it pushes air against our eardrums. Figure 4.13 shows how we may depict sound as a wave form of energy. As there are for light waves, there are three major physical characteristics of sound waves—amplitude, frequency, and purity—and each is related to a different psychological experience. We'll briefly consider each in turn.

Wave Amplitude (Intensity). The amplitude of a sound wave depicts its intensity—the force with which the medium (air) strikes our eardrums. The physical intensity of a sound determines the experience of **loudness.** The higher its amplitude, the louder we perceive a sound to be. Soft, quiet sounds have low amplitudes.

Measurements of the physical intensity of sound are given in units of force per unit area (which is really pressure). Whereas intensity is a physical characteristic of sound, loudness is a psychological characteristic. The perceived loudness of a sound is indicated by its placement on a **decibel scale.** The zero point of the decibel is the lowest intensity of sound that can be detected, or the absolute threshold. Our ears are sensitive receptors and respond to very low levels of sound intensity. Sounds that are louder than

loudness
the psychological experience correlated with the intensity, or amplitude, of a sound wave

decibel scale
a scale of experience of loudness in which 0 represents the absolute threshold and 140 is sensed as pain

FIGURE 4.13
Sound waves are produced as air pressure is changed by the tine of the tuning fork vibrating to the right (A) and to the left (B). The point of greatest pressure is the high point or peak of the wave; least pressure is indicated by the low point of the wave.

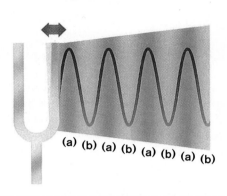

(a) (b) (a) (b) (a) (b) (a) (b)

hertz (Hz)
the standard measure of sound wave frequency, that is, the number of wave cycles per second

pitch
the psychological experience that corresponds to sound wave frequency and gives rise to high (treble) or low (bass) sounds

FIGURE 4.14
Loudness values in decibel units for various sounds.

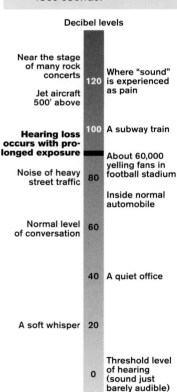

Decibel levels

Near the stage of many rock concerts	**120** Where "sound" is experienced as pain
Jet aircraft 500' above	
Hearing loss occurs with prolonged exposure	**100** A subway train
	About 60,000 yelling fans in football stadium
Noise of heavy street traffic	**80**
	Inside normal automobile
Normal level of conversation	**60**
	40 A quiet office
A soft whisper	**20**
	0 Threshold level of hearing (sound just barely audible)

those produced by jet aircraft engines (around 120 decibels) are usually experienced more as pain than as sound. Figure 4.14 shows decibel levels for some of the sounds we might find in our environment.

Wave Frequency. When we discussed light, we noted that wavelength was responsible for our perception of hue. With sound, we talk about wave frequency—the number of times a wave repeats itself within a period of time. Sound wave frequency is measured in terms of how many waves of pressure are exerted every second. The unit of sound frequency is the **hertz, (Hz)**. If a sound wave repeats itself 50 times in one second, it is a 50Hz sound; 500 repetitions is a 500Hz sound, and so on.

The psychological experience corresponding to sound wave frequency is pitch. **Pitch** is our experience of how high or low a tone is. The musical scale represents differences in pitch. Low frequencies correspond to low, bass sounds, such as those produced by foghorns or tubas. High-frequency vibrations give rise to the experience of high-pitched sounds, such as the musical tones produced by flutes or the squeals of smoke alarms.

Just as the human eye cannot respond to all wavelengths of radiant energy, the human ear cannot respond to all possible sound wave frequencies. A healthy human ear responds to sound wave frequencies between 20Hz and 20,000Hz. If air strikes our ears at a rate of less than 20 times per second, we don't hear it. Vibrations faster than 20,000 cycles per second cannot be heard either—at least by the human ear. Many animals, including dogs, *can* hear sounds with frequencies above 20,000Hz, such as those produced by dog whistles.

Wave Purity. A third characteristic of sound waves is *wave purity* (its opposite is called complexity). You'll recall that we seldom experience pure, monochromatic lights. Pure sounds are also uncommon in our everyday experience. A pure sound is one in which all the waves from the sound source are vibrating at exactly the same frequency. Such sounds can be generated electronically, and tuning forks produce reasonable approximations, but most of the sounds we hear every day are complex sounds, composed of many different sound wave frequencies.

A tone of middle C on the piano is a tone of 256Hz. (Again, this means that the source of the sound—here a piano wire—is vibrating 256 times per second). A pure 256Hz tone is composed of sound waves, or vibrations, of only that frequency. As it happens, a middle C played on a piano has other wave frequencies (called overtones) mixed in with the 256Hz wave frequency that predominates. (If the 256Hz wave did not predominate, the tone wouldn't sound like middle C.)

The psychological quality of a sound, reflecting its degree of purity, is called **timbre**. For example, each musical instrument produces a unique variety or mixture of overtones, so each type of musical instrument tends to sound a little different from all others. If a trumpet, a violin, and a piano were each to play the same note (say a C of 256Hz), we could still tell the instruments apart because of our experience of timbre. In fact, any one instrument can produce different timbres, depending on how it is played.

With light, we saw that the opposite of a pure light was white light—a light made up of all the wavelengths of the visible spectrum. Again, we have a parallel between vision and hearing. Suppose I have a sound source that produces all the possible sound wave frequencies. I produce a random mixture of these frequencies from 20Hz to 20,000Hz. What would that sound like? Actually, it would be a buzzing noise. The best example would be the sound that one hears when a radio is tuned in between stations (as it happens, it is easier to find this sound on FM than on AM). This sound, which contains a range of many audible sound frequencies, is useful in masking or covering other unwanted sounds. A random mixture of sound frequencies is called **white noise**, just as we called a random mixture of wavelengths of light white light.

The analogy between light and sound, between vision and hearing, is striking. Both types of stimulus energy can be represented as waves. In both cases, each of the *physical* characteristics of the waves (amplitude, length or frequency, and purity or complexity) is correlated with a *psychological* experience. All of these relationships are summarized in Figure 4.15.

timbre
the psychological experience related to wave purity by which we differentiate the quality of a tone

white noise
a sound composed of a random assortment of wave frequencies from the audible spectrum

FIGURE 4.15
A Summary of the Ways in Which the Physical Characteristics of Light and Sound Waves Affect Our Psychological Experiences of Vision and Hearing

Physical characteristic	Psychological experience for vision	Psychological experience for hearing
Wave amplitude	Brightness	Loudness
Wavelength or frequency	Hue	Pitch
Wave purity or mixture	Saturation	Timbre

FIGURE 4.16
The major structures of the human ear.

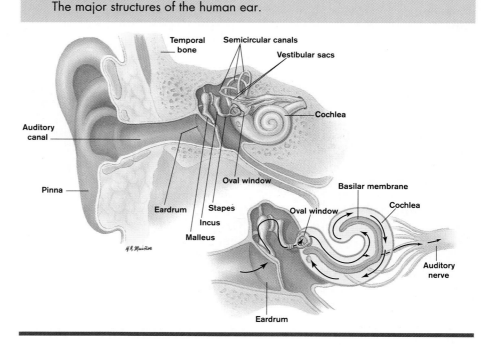

● **Before You Go On**

What are the three major physical characteristics of sound, and which psychological experiences do they produce?

pinna
the outer ear, which collects and funnels sound waves into the auditory canal toward the eardrum

eardrum
the outermost membrane of the ear; it is set in motion by the vibrations of a sound and transmits vibrations to the ossicles

malleus, incus, and stapes
(collectively, ossicles) three small bones that transmit and intensify sound vibrations from the eardrum to the oval window

cochlea
part of the inner ear where sound waves become neural impulses

The Receptor for Hearing: The Ear

Deep inside the ear, the energy of sound wave pressures is transduced into neural impulses. As with the eye, most of the structures of the ear simply transfer energy from without to within. Figure 4.16 is a drawing of the major structures of the human ear. We'll use it to follow the path of sound waves from the environment to the receptor cells for sound.

The outer ear is called the **pinna**. Its function is to collect sound waves and funnel them through the auditory canal toward the **eardrum**. Air waves beat against the eardrum, setting it in motion, so that it vibrates at the same rate as the sound source. The eardrum then transmits vibrations to three very small bones (collectively called *ossicles*) in the middle ear. In order, these bones are called the **malleus, incus,** and **stapes** (pronounced *stape-eez*). Because of their unique shapes, these bones are sometimes referred to as the hammer, anvil, and stirrup. The ossicles pass the vibrations of the eardrum along to the *oval window,* a membrane like the eardrum, only smaller. As the ossicles pass the sound vibrations along to the oval window, they also amplify them, increasing their force.

When sound waves pass beyond the oval window, they are in the *inner ear.* The main structure of the inner ear is the **cochlea**, a snaillike structure that contains the actual receptor cells for hearing. As the stapes vibrates

Sound is a series of pressures of air that produce vibrations of the eardrum.

against the oval window, a fluid inside the cochlea is set in motion at the same rate.

When the fluid within the cochlea moves, the **basilar membrane** bends up and down. Hearing occurs when very tiny **hair cells** are stimulated by the vibrations of the basilar membrane. Through a process not yet fully understood, the mechanical pressure of the basilar membrane on the hair cells starts a neural impulse that leaves the ear on the auditory nerve, traveling toward the temporal lobe.

● **Before You Go On**

Summarize how sound wave pressures pass through the different structures of the ear.

basilar membrane
a structure within the cochlea that vibrates and thus stimulates the hair cells of the inner ear

hair cells
the receptor cells for hearing, located in the cochlea, stimulated by the vibrating basilar membrane; they send neural impulses to the temporal lobe of the brain

THE CHEMICAL SENSES

Taste and smell are referred to as chemical senses because the stimuli for both of them are molecules of chemical compounds. For taste, the chemicals are dissolved in liquid (usually the saliva in our mouths). For smell, they are dissolved in the air that reaches the smell receptors high inside our noses. The technical term for taste is *gustation*; for smell, it is *olfaction*.

If you have ever eaten while suffering from a head cold that has blocked your nasal passages, you realize the extent to which our experiences of taste and smell are interrelated. Most foods appear to lose their taste when we cannot smell them. This is why we differentiate between the *flavor* of foods (which includes such qualities as odor and texture) and the *taste* of foods. A simple test can demonstrate this point. While blindfolded, eat a small piece of peeled apple and a small piece of peeled potato, and see if you can tell the difference between the two. You shouldn't have any trouble with this discrimination. Now hold your nose very tightly and try again. Without your sense of smell to help you, discrimination on the basis of taste alone is very difficult.

Taste (Gustation)

Our experience of the flavors of foods depends so heavily on our sense of smell, texture, and temperature that we sometimes wonder if there is any sense of taste alone. Well, there is. Even with odors and textures held constant, tastes vary. Taste has four basic psychological qualities: sweet, salt, sour, and bitter (Bartoshuk & Beauchamp, 1994). You should be able to generate a list of foods that produce each of these basic sensations. Most foods derive their special taste from a unique combination of the four basic tastes. Did you notice that it is more difficult to think of examples of sour- and bitter- tasting foods than it is to think of sweet and salty ones? This reflects the fact that we usually don't like bitter and sour tastes and have learned to avoid them.

The receptor cells for taste, located in the tongue, are called **taste buds**. We have about ten thousand taste buds, and each one is made up of a number of parts (see Figure 4.17). When parts of taste buds die (or are killed—by foods that are too hot, for example) new segments are regenerated. That in itself makes taste a unique sense—as receptor cells, taste buds are nerve cells, and we've already noted that nerve cells are usually not replaced when they die. At the same time, with age, fewer and fewer taste buds are replaced and one's sensitivity to taste decreases. This may explain why some older people seem to enjoy heavily seasoned or spicy foods which they did not enjoy when they were younger.

Different taste buds respond primarily to chemicals that produce one of the four basic taste qualities. That is, some receptor cells respond best to salts, while others respond primarily to sweet-producing chemicals, like sug-

taste buds
the receptors for taste located in the tongue

FIGURE 4.17
Enlarged view of a taste bud, the receptor for gustation.

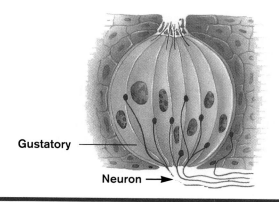

Gustatory

Neuron →

FIGURE 4.18

The olfactory system, showing its proximity to the brain and the transducers for smell—the hair cells.

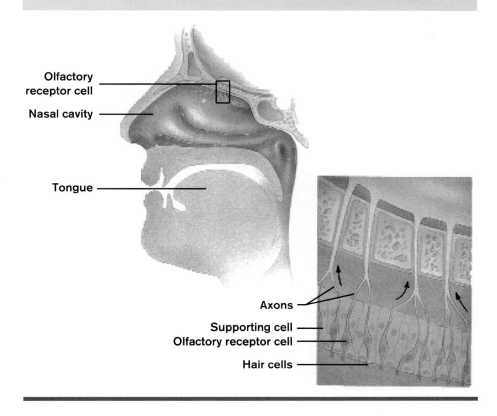

ars. For nearly fifty years it was believed that these specialized cells are not evenly distributed on the surface of the tongue; that receptors for sweet are only at the very tip of the tongue, for instance. We now know better. Although there is some truth in the idea that some areas of the tongue *are* a bit more sensitive to certain tastes than are other areas, all of the four basic qualities of taste can be perceived at all locations on the tongue (Bartoshuk & Beauchamp, 1994; Collings, 1974).

Smell (Olfaction)

Smell often gives us great pleasure—think of the aroma of bacon frying over a wood fire or of freshly picked flowers. It can also produce considerable displeasure—consider the smell of old garbage or rotten eggs.

The sense of smell originates in cells located high in the nasal cavity, very close to the brain. We know that the path from these receptors to the brain is the most direct and shortest of all the senses (see Figure 4.18). What we don't understand well is how molecules suspended in air (or some other gas) actually stimulate the small hair cells of the olfactory receptor to fire neural impulses. We know that it has been very difficult for researchers to come to any agreement on a list—much less a short list— of basic odors. It may be that there are different olfactory receptor cells for hundreds or even thousands of different chemical molecules (Bartoshuk & Beauchamp, 1994; Buck & Axel, 1991).

We know that the sense of smell is an important sense for many non-humans. The dog's sense of smell is legendary. Many organisms emit chemicals, called **pheromones**, which produce distinctive odors. Sometimes pheromones are secreted by cells in the skin, sometimes in the urine, and occasionally from other special glands (in some deer, for instance, this gland is located near the rear hoof). One purpose that pheromones serve is to mark or delineate one's territory. If you take a dog for a walk around the block and discover that the pooch wants to stop and deposit small amounts of urine on just about every front lawn, that dog is leaving behind a pheromone trail that essentially says, "I have been here; this is my odor; this is my turf."

Commonly, pheromones carry sexually related messages to members of the opposite sex of the same species. Most often that message is roughly translated into "I am available for sexual activities." The usual result is that the pheromones attract members of the opposite sex. Knowledge of this relationship can be useful. Japanese beetles are a common garden pest, difficult to kill safely with standard poisons. Traps are now available that contain a small amount of a pheromone attractive to the beetles, who smell the odor the trap gives off, come rushing to investigate, and slide off a slippery plastic platform to their doom in a disposable plastic bag. It is rather gruesome, but it works.

It is likely that pheromone production is related to the sex hormones, even in humans. For example, there is evidence that women who live in close quarters (e.g., in a college dormitory) for a long time soon synchronize their menstrual cycles. The same thing happens in rats when the only contact between them is that they share the same air supply, and thus the same odors (McClintock, 1971, 1979). It also may be possible that humans use pheromones to attract members of the opposite sex (Cutler et al., 1986; Wallace, 1977). If we do, the real effect is probably small, although people who advertise perfumes and colognes would like us to think otherwise (e.g., Doty, 1986).

pheromones
chemicals that produce an odor used as a method of communication between organisms

● **Before You Go On**

Discuss the chemical senses of taste and smell, noting the stimulus and sense receptor for each.

What are the primary qualities of taste?

THE SKIN, OR CUTANEOUS, SENSES

Most of us take our skin for granted—at least we seldom think about it. We often abuse our skin by overexposing it to the sun's rays in summer or to excess cold in winter. We scratch it, cut it, scrape it, and wash away thousands of its cells every time we bathe or shower.

Figure 4.19 is a diagram of some of the structures found in an area of skin from a hairy part of the human body. Each square inch of the layers of our skin contains nearly 20 million cells, including many sense receptors.

Some of the skin receptors have *free nerve endings*, while others have some sort of small covering over them. We call these latter cells *encapsulated nerve endings*, of which there are many different types. It is our skin that gives rise to our psychological experience of touch and pressure and of warmth and cold. It would be very convenient if each of the different types of receptor cells within the layers of our skin independently produced a different type of psychological sensation, but such is not the case.

Indeed, one of the problems in studying the skin senses, or cutaneous senses, is determining which cells in the skin give rise to the different sensations of pressure and temperature. We can discriminate between a light touch and a strong jab, and among vibrations, tickles, and itches. A simple proposal is that there are different receptors in the skin responsible for each different sensation, but this proposal is not supported by the facts. Although some types of receptor cells are more sensitive to some types of stimuli, current thinking is that our ability to discriminate among different cutaneous sensations is due to the combination of responses that the many receptor cells have to different types of stimuli.

By carefully stimulating very small areas of the skin, we can locate those that are particularly sensitive to temperature. We are convinced that warm and cold temperatures each stimulate different locations on the skin. Even so, there is no consistent pattern of receptor cells found at these locations, or temperature spots. That is, we have not yet located specific receptor cells for cold or hot. As a matter of fact, our experience of hot seems to come from the simultaneous stimulation of both warm and cold spots. A rather ingenious demonstration shows how this works. Cold water is run through one metal tube and warm water through another. The two tubes are coiled together (see Figure 4.20). If you were to grasp the coiled tubes, your experience would be one of heat—the tubes would feel hot even if you knew that they were not.

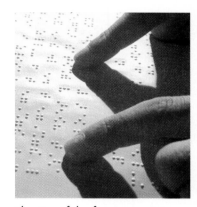

The tips of the fingers contain many receptors for touch and pressure.

FIGURE 4.19

A patch of hairy skin, showing the layers of skin and various nerve cells.

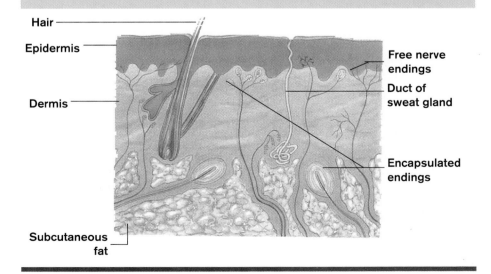

Hair

Epidermis

Dermis

Subcutaneous fat

Free nerve endings

Duct of sweat gland

Encapsulated endings

FIGURE 4.20
A demonstration that our sense of what is hot may be constructed from sensations of what is warm and cold. Even if you know that the coiled tubes contain only warm and cold water, when you grasp the tubes, they will feel hot.

Warm   Cold

● **Before You Go on**

What are the cutaneous senses, and what are the transducers for each?

THE POSITION SENSES

Another sensory capacity we often take for granted is our ability to detect how and where our bodies are positioned in space. Although we seldom worry about it, we can quickly become aware of how our bodies are positioned in regard to the pull of gravity. We also get sensory information about where different parts of our body are in relation to each other. We can tell if we are moving or standing still. Unless we are on a roller coaster, or racing across a field, we usually adapt to these sensory messages quickly and pay them little attention.

Pain and Its Management

What is pain? What causes the experience of pain? Each of us knows what a pain pain can be, yet it is often difficult to find the exact words to adequately describe our pain to others (Verillo, 1975). Pain can be useful: It can alert us to problems occurring within our bodies so appropriate action can be taken. It is the experience of pain that prompts more than 80 percent of all visits to the doctor's office (Turk, 1994).

Many stimuli can cause pain. Too much light, strong pressures on the skin, loud sounds, and even very "hot" spices can result in our experiencing pain. But as we all know, the stimulus for pain need not be intense. In the right circumstances, even a light pinprick can be painful. Our skin has many receptors for pain, but pain receptors can also be found deep inside our bodies; consider stomachaches, back pain, and headaches. Pain is experienced in our brains, and the thalamus seems to play an important role (Groves & Rebec, 1992, p. 265). On the other hand, pain is the only "sense" for which we can find no one specific center in the cerebral cortex.

One theory claims that pain is experienced in the brain, not in the periphery, and that a *gate-control mechanism* (high in the spinal cord) acts to allow pain messages up to the brain or blocks them by "opening or closing the gate" (Melzack & Wall, 1965; Melzack, 1973). A *cognitive-behavior theory* of pain also suggests that central mechanisms are important, noting that the experience of pain is influenced by a person's attitudes, cognitions, and behaviors (Turk, 1994).

Even without a full understanding of how pain is sensed, there *are* techniques that can be used to minimize or manage the experience of pain. If pain is really experienced in the brain, what sorts of things can we do to keep pain messages from reaching those brain centers?

Drug therapy can be a choice for pain management. Opiates, such as morphine, when administered systemically, are believed to inhibit pain messages at the level of the spinal cord, as well as at the specific site, or source, of the pain (Basbaum & Levine, 1991, Clinton, 1992; Randall, 1993; Richmond et al., 1993).

Hypnosis and cognitive self-control (trying very hard to convince yourself that the pain you're experiencing is not really that bad and will go away) *are* effective in lessening the experience of pain (Litt, 1988; Melzack, 1973).

That psychological processes can inhibit pain is also reinforced by data on *placebo effects*. A placebo is a substance (often in pill form) a person believes will be useful in treating some symptom, such as pain. When people are given a placebo they believe will alleviate pain, painkilling endorphins are released in the brain and effectively keep pain-carrying impulses from reaching the brain (Levine et al., 1979). This placebo effect is particularly strong when the health care provider is prestigious and demonstrates empathy and a positive attitude about the placebo (Turner et al., 1994).

Another process that works to ease the feeling of pain, particularly pain from or near the surface of the skin, is called *counterirritation*. The idea is to forcefully (but not painfully, of course) stimulate an area of the body *near* the location of the pain. Dentists have discovered that rubbing the gum near the spot of a novacaine injection significantly reduces the patient's experience of the pain of the needle.

The ancient Eastern practice of acupuncture can also be effective in the treatment of pain. We don't know yet why acupuncture works as well as it does. There are cases where it doesn't work well at all, but these usually involve patients who are skeptics, which suggests that one of the benefits of acupuncture is its placebo effect. As many as 12 million acupuncture therapies for pain management are performed in the United States each year (George, 1992; Parson, 1993).

Individual responses to pain are unique and are influenced by many factors that we have discussed before: prior experience, memory of those experiences, and feelings about pain, or one's cognitions, affect, and behavior (our A, B, C once again). It is clear that gender and cultural differences can be involved in the expression or display of pain. In Japan, for instance, individuals are socialized not to show pain—or any intense feeling, for that matter. In our Western culture, men are often similarly socialized not to show pain, to be "macho" and tough, no matter what. Among other things, this often creates problems in the diagnosis and treatment of illness or disease where pain is an informative symptom.

vestibular sense
the position sense that tells us about balance, where we are in relation to gravity, and acceleration or deceleration

kinesthetic sense
the position sense that tells us the position of different parts of our bodies and what our muscles and joints are doing

Most of the information about where we are in space comes through our sense of vision. If we want to know just how we are oriented in space, all we have to do is look around. But note that we *can* do the same sort of thing even with our eyes closed. We have two systems of position sense in addition to vision. One, the **vestibular sense**, tells us about balance, where we are in relation to gravity, and acceleration or deceleration. The other, the **kinesthetic sense**, tells us about the movement or the position of our muscles and joints.

The receptors for the vestibular sense are located on either side of the head, near the inner ear. Five chambers are located there: three semicircular canals and two vestibular sacs. (Their orientation was shown in Figure 4.16.) Each chamber is filled with fluid. When our head moves in any direction, the fluid in the semicircular canals moves, drawn by gravity or the force of our head accelerating in space. The vestibular sacs contain very small particles that float around in the fluid within the sacs. When these particles are forced against one side of the sacs, as happens when we move, they stimulate hair cells that start neural impulses. Overstimulation of the receptor cells in the vestibular sacs or semicircular canals can lead to feelings of dizziness or nausea, reasonably enough called *motion sickness.*

Most receptors for our kinesthetic sense are located in our joints, while some information also comes from muscles and tendons. Kinesthetic receptors sense the position and movements of parts of the body. Impulses from these receptors travel to our brain through pathways in our spinal cord. They provide excellent examples of reflex actions. As muscles in the front of your upper arm (your biceps) contract, the corresponding muscles in the back of your arm (your triceps) relax for you to bend your arm at the elbow. How fortunate it is that our kinesthetic receptors, operating reflexively through the spinal cord, take care of these details without our having to manipulate consciously all the appropriate muscular activity. In fact, about the only time we realize that our kinesthetic system is functioning is when it stops working well, as when our leg "falls asleep" and we have trouble walking.

Although the vestibular and kinesthetic senses are often thought of as "minor senses" (at least until they malfunction), for some individuals and in some cultures these two sensory processes, working together, are extremely important. What I have in mind here are those cultures that, for example, require individuals to get their food in ways that you and I seldom think much about. Racing through a forest after wild game or quickly scurrying up a palm tree after coconuts requires vestibular and kinesthetic skills that might challenge all but the most highly trained athletes of Western cultures. For that matter, we might even claim that those cultures that put a high value on athletic performance are cultures in which the kinesthetic sense is highly valued.

● **Before You Go On**
What are our position senses, and how do they operate?

THINKING CRITICALLY ABOUT SENSORY PROCESSES

1. One of the concerns of psychophysics is determining the sensitivity levels (we call them threshold values) for the various senses. In an experiment to determine your absolute threshold for brightness, I ask you to tell me if you can see a light located at the other end of a small room. You are to say simply "Yes" or "No." What factors other than the

A keen vestibular sense is a prime requirement for a tightrope walker.

actual intensity of the light itself may influence your responses? (These are the factors of concern in signal detection theory.)

2. Bob does very well on a surprise test in his physics class and claims that he "knew" the test was coming because he had dreamed about it the night before. Bob's now quite convinced that he has ESP, or extrasensory perception, which, among other things, involves the perception of information without that information passing through the senses (hence, "extra" sensory). How can we test whether Bob or anyone else has such powers of ESP? What other factors might have accounted for Bob's good fortune?

3. Here are a few questions to which psychologists do have answers, although they involve more information than we usually get into at the introductory level. What do you think: Why are some emergency vehicles (and tennis balls and golf balls) painted yellow-green? Why are the lights on top of police cars and along airport runways and taxiways blue? How could you determine if a dog is more or less colorblind than a cat?

4. Consider experiences of persons who have some sensory limitation. Can people who are blind from birth dream in pictures? If a person deaf from birth were to have his or her hearing restored, could he or she recognize the voice of a friend? What would it be like to have no sensation of pain at all?

SUMMARY

T O P I C   4 A

SENSATION: A FEW BASIC CONCEPTS

- How is the process of sensation defined?
- What is psychophysics?
- What is an absolute threshold and how is it related to the sensitivity of our senses?

Sensation is the first step in information processing. It involves converting, or transducing, physical energy from the environment into the energy of the nervous system. This conversion takes place at our senses. Psychophysics is the field of psychology that attempts to specify the nature of the relationships between physical stimuli and the psychological experience of those stimuli. Psychophysical methods can determine the sensitivity of one's senses. An absolute threshold is the intensity of a stimulus that can be detected 50 percent of the time. The lower one's threshold for any sense, the more sensitive that sense is; thus, sensitivity and threshold are inversely related. *Pages 126–128.*

- What is a difference threshold, or j.n.d.?

- Briefly summarize the basic ideas of signal detection theory.
- What is sensory adaptation?

A difference threshold is the value of the difference between stimuli that are detected to be just noticeably different (j.n.d.). Signal detection theory considers sensory thresholds as the detection of a signal against a background of noise; the subjects' biases, motivation, and attention are also considered. Sensory adaptation is the phenomenon in which our senses become less and less sensitive to stimuli that are constantly presented to us. An exception is dark adaptation, where our eyes actually become more sensitive to stimulation with increased time in the dark. *Pages 128–130*

T O P I C   4 B

VISION

- In what ways do the major physical characteristics of light waves of energy (amplitude, length, and purity) affect our psychological experience of light?

Wave amplitude determines our experience of the light's brightness; wavelength determines our experience of hue, or color; and wave purity determines a light's degree of saturation, from the extreme of a pure, monochromatic light to the lowest saturation of a white light. *Pages 130–133.*

● List the major structures of the eye, and describe the function of each.

Before light reaches the retina, it passes through several structures whose major function is to focus an image on the retina. In order, light passes through: the cornea, the pupil (an opening in the iris), aqueous humor, the lens (whose shape is controlled by the ciliary muscles), and vitreous humor. Then, at the retina, after passing through layers of neural fibers that combine and integrate visual information (e.g., ganglion and bipolar cells), light reaches the photosensitive rods and cones, which are the sense receptor cells for vision. Neural impulses that originate at the rods and cones, are collected at the optic nerve and exit the eyeball at the blindspot. *Pages 133–137.*

● Why can we claim that rods and cones provide us with two different kinds of visual experience?

Cones, which are concentrated in the fovea, respond best to medium-to-high levels of illumination (daylight) and also respond differentially to different wavelengths (producing our experience of hue or color). Rods, concentrated in the peripheral retina, do not discriminate among hues, but they do respond to relatively low levels of light. Evidence for this point of view comes from common experience, the examination of the retinas of nocturnal animals, and data on dark adaptation. *Pages 138–139*

● Summarize the trichromatic and the opponent-process theories of color vision.

These theories try to explain how the visual system codes different wavelengths of light, the process that gives rise to our experience of color. The trichromatic theory (associated with Young and von Helmholtz) claims that there are three different kinds of cones, each maximally sensitive to one of the three primary colors—red, green, or blue. Hering's opponent-process theory claims that there are three pairs of mechanisms involved in our experience of colors: a blue-yellow processor, a red-green processor, and a black-white processor. Each of these can respond to either of the characteristics that give it its name, but not to both. There is anatomical and physiological evidence that supports both of these theories, some of which comes from our understanding of why some people have defects in color vision. *Pages 140–143.*

TOPIC 4C

HEARING AND THE OTHER SENSES

● What are the three major physical characteristics of sound, and which psychological experiences do they produce?

Sound can be represented as a wave form of energy with three characteristics: wave amplitude, frequency, and purity (or complexity). These in turn give rise to the psychological experiences of loudness, pitch, and timbre. *Pages 143–146.*

● Summarize how sound wave pressures pass through the different structures of the ear.

Most of the structures of the ear (the pinna, auditory canal, eardrum, malleus, incus, stapes, and oval window) intensify and transmit sound wave pressures to the fluid in the cochlea. Motions of this fluid cause vibration of the basilar membrane, which in turn stimulates tiny hair cells to transmit neural impulses along the auditory nerve to the temporal lobes of the brain. *Pages 146–147.*

● Discuss the chemical senses of taste and smell, noting the stimulus and sense receptor for each.
● What are the primary qualities of taste?

The senses of taste (gustation) and smell (olfaction) are interrelated. They are referred to as the chemical senses because both respond to chemical molecules in solution. The receptors for smell are hair cells that line the upper regions of the nasal cavity. For taste, the receptors are cells in the taste buds located in the tongue. Taste appears to have four primary qualities: sweet, sour, bitter, and salt. *Pages 147–150.*

● What are the cutaneous senses, and what are the transducers for each?

The cutaneous senses are our skin senses: touch, pressure, warm, and cold. Specific receptor cells for each identifiable skin sense have not yet been localized, although they no doubt include free nerve endings and encapsulated nerve endings, which most likely work together in different combinations. *Pages 150–152.*

● What are our position senses, and how do they operate?

One of our position senses is the vestibular sense which, by responding to the movement of small particles suspended in a fluid within the vestibular sacs and semicircular canals near the inner ear, can inform us about orientation with regard to gravity or accelerated motion. Our other position sense is kinesthesis which, through receptors in our muscles and joints, informs us about the orientation of parts of our body. *Pages 152–154.*

TOPIC 4A

SENSATION: A FEW BASIC CONCEPTS

4.1 The major thrust of psychophysics is the search for a) relationships between events in the world and our experiences of those events. b) the basic or elemental particles of thought that make up human consciousness. c) ways to relate how we feel (affect) to the way we think (cognition) and the way we behave. d) the physiological or biological processes that allow us to sense the world as we do. *Pages 126–128.*

4.2 If a sound is determined to be below your absolute threshold, a) you will never hear that sound. b) that sound enters your unconscious mind only. c) you will hear that sound less than 50 percent of the time. d) you cannot tell if it is different from other sounds. *Pages 128–130.*

4.3 Signal detection theory suggests that determining sensory threshold values (for brightness, let us say) a) is virtually impossible. b) is a matter of recognizing detection to be a decision-making process. c) requires a subject to detect whether two signals are the same or different. d) can only be done in a very dark room. *Pages 128–130.*

4.4 The notion of sensory adaptation suggests that what we tend to experience most readily are a) lights and smells, not sounds and tastes. b) stimuli that have remained the same for a long time. c) objects and events that we are used to or have adapted to. d) changes in level and/or type of stimulation. *Pages 128–130.*

4.5 True or False? If a stimulus is above your absolute threshold, you will detect it every time it is presented. *Pages 128–130.*

TOPIC 4B

VISION

4.6 Wavelength is to hue as wave amplitude is to a) color. b) brightness. c) purity. d) saturation. *Pages 130–133.*

4.7 Which of the following is *not* technically possible? a) a bright, monochromatic light with 550nm wavelengths b) a light with 700nm and 400nm wavelengths mixed together c) a light that is both bright and of low saturation at the same time d) a highly saturated white light of medium brightness. *Pages 130–133.*

4.8 Where in the eye are light waves converted into neural impulses? a) the lens and ciliary muscles b) the blindspot and optic nerve c) the rods and cones d) the aqueous and vitreous humors. *Pages 133–135.*

4.9 The amount of light that strikes the eye will most noticeably affect the a) cornea. b) iris. c) lens. d) vitreous humor. *Pages 133–139.*

4.10 True or False? If someone is nearsighted or farsighted, he or she most obviously has a problem with his or her retina. *Pages 133–139.*

4.11 If we want to identify a small object at night, in low levels of illumination, the most sensible thing to do (other than making more light available) is to have the image of the object fall on the a) fovea. b) blindspot. c) periphery, away from the fovea. d) optic nerve. *Pages 133–139.*

4.12 When we plot a curve that shows how our eyes become more sensitive to the dark, the curve is not a smooth, regular one, but shows a "break" at about the 7-minute mark. This break occurs because a) the cones have now stopped adapting to the dark. b) the retina changes its orientation after 7 minutes in the dark. c) at that point, our ability to see color increases markedly. d) the rods have reached a point where they can no longer continue to increase their sensitivity. *Pages 133–139.*

4.13 True or False? Because they operate best at low levels of illumination, our rods give us the most information about the colors of objects in our environments. *Pages 133–139.*

4.14 True or False? In the human retina, there are many more cones than there are rods. *Pages 133–139.*

4.15 The Young-Helmholtz theory of color vision proposes that there are specially sensitive receptors for wavelengths of light that correspond to the primary colors of a) red, green, and yellow. b) black and white. c) red, orange, yellow, green, blue, and violet. d) blue, green, and red. *Pages 140–142.*

T O P I C   4 C

HEARING AND THE OTHER SENSES

4.16 The stimulus for audition is a) electromagnetic energy in wave form. b) pressures of a medium vibrating against the ear. c) chemicals that are dissolved in the air or in a liquid. d) the cochlea of the inner ear. *Pages 143–145.*

4.17 As sound waves increase in their frequency, our experience is that a) the sound gets louder. b) what used to be sound becomes painful. c) we hear more overtones. d) the pitch of the sound gets higher. *Pages 143–145.*

4.18 Wave amplitude of light is to brightness as wave amplitude of sound is to a) loudness. b) pitch. c) hue or color. d) timbre. *Pages 143–145.*

4.19 A sound made up of a random assortment of audible wave frequencies would sound like a) a pure, electronically produced sound. b) white noise. c) human speech. d) a musical chord, or harmony. *Pages 143–145.*

4.20 True or False? The human ear hears as sound the vibrations of a medium that cause the eardrum to vi-

brate at rates between 20Hz and 20,000 Hz. *Pages 143–145.*

4.21 True or False? The decibel scale provides a measure of the perceived loudness of sounds. *Pages 143–145.*

4.22 As sound waves approach the human ear, they are first collected by the a) pinna. b) cochlea. c) basilar membrane. d) oval window. *Pages 146–147.*

4.23 The transducers for sound are a) waves of air pressure. b) ossicles. c) cochlea. d) hair cells. *Pages 146–147.*

4.24 The technical name for one's sense of taste is a) flavor. b) gustation. c) biochemical transduction. d) olfaction. *Pages 147–150.*

4.25 True or False? Neural impulses from sense receptors in the nose do not go to the brain. *Pages 147–150.*

4.26 Pheromones are a) hormones that produce sexual behaviors in nonhumans. b) chemicals whose odors are related to territoriality and sex. c) neurotransmitters involved in the chemical senses. d) the actual sense receptors for both taste and smell. *Pages 147–150.*

4.27 What cutaneous stimulation leads to our experience of heat? a) the simultaneous stimulation of warm and cold receptors b) the continuous stimulation of free nerve endings c) above threshold stimulation of heat-receptor cells d) intermittent stimulation of encapsulated nerve endings. *Pages 150–152.*

4.28 Which sense informs us about the position of our bodies with respect to gravity? a) the vestibular sense b) the kinesthetic sense c) the cutaneous sense d) the gravitational sense *Pages 152–154.*

5

PERCEPTION AND CONSCIOUSNESS

PREVIEW

TOPIC 5A—Perception

Perceptual Selectivity: Paying Attention

Perceptual Organization: What Goes with What?

The Perception of Depth and Distance

The Constancy of Visual Perception

TOPIC 5B—Consciousness

The Nature of Consciousness

Sleeping and Dreaming

PSYCHOLOGY IN THE REAL WORLD: Sleep Disorders

Hypnosis

Altering Consciousness with Drugs

THINKING CRITICALLY ABOUT PERCEPTION AND CONSCIOUSNESS

SUMMARY

TEST YOURSELF

Now that we have a general idea of how our senses work, we can move on to consider what happens next as we process information about the world. As we have seen, the psychology of sensation is concerned with how our senses transduce physical energy from the environment into neural energy. **Perception** is concerned with the selection, organization, and interpretation of stimuli. Perception is a complex, active, cognitive process. You can think of these interrelated processes this way: Our senses present us with information about the world, while perception represents (re-presents) that information—often flavored by our motivational states, our emotions, our expectations, and our past experiences. That is, we create our perceptions of reality based on more than just the information provided by our senses.

Topic 5A begins with the consideration of a question: Given all of the stimuli presented to us by our senses, what factors determine which stimuli we pay attention to and which stimuli we ignore? Once stimuli are selected for further processing, they are organized into meaningful pieces of information. What factors influence the organization of our perceptions? Once we have these two basic issues resolved, we can move on to deal with two important perceptual matters: the perception of depth and distance, and the perceptual constancies.

Topic 5B takes us to a related set of issues, dealing with matters of human consciousness. **Consciousness** refers to our awareness, or our perception, of the environment and of our own mental processes. To be fully conscious is to be awake, aware, alert, and attentive. The extent to which we are conscious of ourselves and our environment will influence how—and the extent to which—we can process information. This is why I have chosen to put our discussion of consciousness in this chapter.

We begin Topic 5B with a characterization of our normal waking consciousness, which will get us involved with a brief discussion of the unconscious as well. Then we'll go on to look at three instances of "altered consciousness." The hope is that if we appreciate how consciousness is altered by sleeping and dreaming, hypnosis, and by drugs, we can better understand normal consciousness.

perception
the cognitive process of selecting, organizing, and interpreting those stimuli provided to us by our senses

consciousness
the awareness or perception of the environment and of one's own mental processes

TOPIC 5A

PERCEPTION

Learning about the factors that determine what we attend to is a major concern of the psychology of perception. Imagine that you are at a party, engaged in a dreadfully boring conversation with someone you've just met. It occurs to you that wearing your new shoes was not a good idea—your feet hurt. You're munching on an assortment of tasty appetizers. Music blares from a stereo. Aromas of foods and perfume fill the air. There must be at least 50 people at this party, and you don't know any of them. Your senses are being bombarded simultaneously by all sorts of information: sights, tastes, sounds, smells, even pain. Suddenly, you hear someone mention your name. You redirect your attention toward the person who mentioned your name, disregarding the person right in front of you.

PERCEPTUAL SELECTIVITY: PAYING ATTENTION

There are many variables that influence our selection of stimuli from the environment. They can be divided into two types: stimulus factors and personal factors. By stimulus factors I mean those characteristics of stimuli that make them more compelling, or attention-grabbing, than others, no matter *who* the perceiver is. By personal factors I am referring to those characteristics of the person, the perceiver, that influence which stimuli get attended to. We'll start by considering stimulus factors.

Stimulus Factors in Selectivity

contrast
the extent to which a stimulus is in some physical way different from other surrounding stimuli

The most common and important stimulus factor in perceptual selection is **contrast**, the extent to which a stimulus is physically different from other stimuli around it. One stimulus can contrast with other stimuli in a variety of ways. For example, we are more likely to attend to a stimulus if its *intensity* is different from the intensities of other stimuli. Generally, the more intense a stimulus, the more likely we are to select it for further processing. Simply put, a shout is more compelling than a whisper; a bright light is more attention-grabbing than a dim one.

Notice that this isn't always the case, however. The context in which a stimulus occurs makes a difference. A shout may be more compelling than a whisper—unless everyone is shouting; then it may very well be the soft, quiet, reasoned tone that gets our attention. When faced with a barrage of bright lights, a dim one may be the one we process most fully.

The same argument holds for the characteristic of physical *size*. Typically, the bigger the stimulus, the more likely we are to attend to it. There is little point in erecting a small billboard to advertise your new restaurant. You'll want to construct the biggest billboard you can afford in hopes of attracting attention. Although it may not hold true for billboards, contrast effects are such that when we are faced with many large stimuli, one that is smaller may be the one to which we attend. It seems to me that the easiest player to spot on a football field is the placekicker, who tends to be much smaller than the other players, and who usually does not wear as much protective padding.

A third physical dimension that may determine perceptual selectivity, and for which contrast is relevant, is *motion*. Motion is a powerful factor in determining visual attention. A bird in flight is much easier to see than a bird sitting in a bush. In the fall, walking through the woods, you may come close to stepping on a chipmunk before you notice it, so long as it stays still—an adaptive piece of camouflage that chipmunks do well. If that chipmunk makes a dash to escape, it is easily noticed scurrying across the leaves. Once again, the contrast created by movement is important.

Although intensity, size, and motion are three physical characteristics of stimuli that readily come to mind, there are many others. Indeed, any way in which stimuli contrast (are different) can determine which stimulus we attend to. (A very small spot can easily grab one's attention if it is right in the middle of a solid yellow tie.) This is why we have printed important terms in **boldface** type throughout this book—so you will notice them and attend to them as important stimuli.

There is another stimulus characteristic that can determine attention, but for which contrast is really not relevant, and that is *repetition*. Simply put, the more often a stimulus is presented, the more likely it will be attended to, everything else being equal, of course. Note that I have to say "everything else being equal," or I start to develop some contradictions. New and novel stimuli (because of contrast) attract our attention. But remember a point we made at the beginning of the last chapter: If stimuli are constantly available to us, we may *adapt* to them and no longer notice them. Even so, there are many examples that convince us of the value of repetition for getting someone to pay attention.

Instructors who want to get across an important point will seldom mention it just once, but will repeat it. (Most students recognize that there is a positive correlation between the importance of a piece of information and the frequency with which it is brought up in class.) This is why we have given definitions of important terms in the text and then repeated them in the margin, and again in the glossary at the end of the book. Think again of the billboard you're going to erect to advertise your restaurant. No matter how large or bright it is, you'll erect as many billboards as you can if you want to get the attention of as many people as possible. The people who write and schedule TV commercials want you to attend to their messages, and repetition is clearly one of their techniques.

There are many ways, then, in which stimuli can differ: brightness, size, motion, color, pitch, and loudness, for example. The greater the contrast between any one stimulus and the others around it, the greater the likelihood that that stimulus will capture or draw our attention. Everything else being equal, the more often a stimulus is presented (up to a point), the greater the likelihood that it will get our attention.

● **Before You Go On**

What stimulus factors determine the selection of perceptions?

Personal Factors in Selectivity

Sometimes attention is determined not by the physical characteristics of stimuli, but by the characteristics of the perceiver. Imagine that two students are watching a football game on TV. Both are presented with identical stimuli from the same television screen. One asks, "Wow, did you see that tackle?" The other responds, "No, I was watching the cheerleaders." The difference in perception here is not one that we can attribute to the nature of the stimuli, since both students received the very same sensory information. The difference is due to characteristics of the perceivers, or *personal factors,* which we can categorize as motivation, expectation, or past experience.

Imagine that the students watching the football game on TV are avid supporters of the two teams involved. One is a fan of the Chicago Bears and the other roots for the Cleveland Browns. These viewers have a wager on the outcome of this important game. Suppose that the Bears win the hard-fought game with a last-second field goal. Both students have watched exactly the same game on the same TV, but which of the two is more likely to have perceived the officiating of the game as fair, honest, and above reproach? Which student is more likely to have seen the game as "one of the poorest refereed games ever"? The perception of the officiating may depend on who won, who lost, and the *motivation* of the perceiver. The viewers tended to see what they wanted to see. You might not be surprised to learn that research confirms this very scenario (Hastorf & Cantril, 1954).

We often perceive what we want to perceive, and it is equally true that we often perceive what we *expect* to perceive—sometimes even when it's not there. Similarly, we often do not notice stimuli simply because we didn't expect them to be there. When we are psychologically prepared or predisposed to perceive something in a given way, we say that we have formed a **mental set**.

Take a second and quickly glance at the message in Figure 5.1. What did it say? [If you've seen this before, you'll have to try it with someone who hasn't.] Many people claim the message is PARIS IN THE SPRING. In fact, there are two THEs in the triangle—PARIS IN THE THE SPRING. People familiar with the English language (and with this phrase) do not expect there to be two *the*s right next to each other. Following their mental set, they report seeing only one. Others develop a different mental set. Their line of reasoning may be something like: "This is a psychology text, so there's probably a trick here someplace, and I'm going to find it." In this instance, skeptics are rewarded. There *is* a trick, and if their mental set was to find one, they probably did so. This example makes the point that if you don't expect something to happen—if you are not "looking for it"—you may miss it.

We will see later (Chapter 8, Topic 8B) that an inability to change a mentally set way of perceiving a problem may interfere with our finding a solution to that problem. What we call "creative" problem solving is often a matter of perceiving aspects of a problem in new, unique, or unexpected ways. Even as complex a cognitive process as problem solving often hinges on basic perceptual processes.

Have you noticed that when we say that paying attention is due to motivation and expectation, we are claiming that what we perceive is often influenced by our *past experiences*? Much of our motivation comes from our past experiences. The two watching the football game between Chicago and Cleveland were not born fans of those two teams. Their allegiances reflect their past experiences. Expectations also develop from past experiences. We expect to perceive, or are set to perceive, what we have perceived in the past in similar circumstances. Perhaps a personal example will make clear what I mean here.

I once took a course in comparative psychology that examined the behaviors of nonhuman organisms. One of the coteachers of the course was an ornithologist (a scientist who studies birds). A requirement of the course was to participate in an early morning bird-watching expedition. The memory is still vivid: Cold, tired, clutching my thermos of warm coffee, I slopped through the marshland looking for birds as the sun was just rising. After 20 minutes of this unpleasantness, our instructor had identified ten or eleven

mental set
a predisposed (set) way to perceive something: an expectation

FIGURE 5.1
How we perceive the world is determined at least in part by our mental set or our expectations about the world. How many THEs did you see when you first glanced at this simple figure? Why?

PARIS
IN THE
THE SPRING

different birds. I wasn't quite certain, but I thought I had spied a duck. I didn't know just what sort of duck it was, but I did think that I had seen a duck. Now the differences in perception between my instructor and me that cold, wet morning could be explained in terms of motivation (he did care more than I); but mostly, I suspect, his ability to spot birds so quickly reflected his experience. He knew where to look and what to look for.

● **Before You Go On**

What personal factors are involved in perceptual selectivity?

PERCEPTUAL ORGANIZATION: WHAT GOES WITH WHAT?

The bits and pieces of experience that are presented to our senses are organized by perception into meaningful, organized wholes. We don't really hear the individual sounds of speech; our brain organizes them and we perceive them as words and phrases and sentences. Our visual experience is not one of tiny bits of color and light and dark, as recorded at the retina, but of identifiable objects and events. We don't perceive a pat on the back as responses from hundreds of receptors in our skin.

Perceptual organization was of special interest to the Gestalt psychologists. As you recall from Chapter 1, **gestalt** is a German word that means "configuration" or "whole." One forms a gestalt when one sees the overall scheme of things. If you have a general idea of how something works, you have formed a gestalt.

One of the most basic principles of Gestalt psychology is the **figure-ground relationship**. Of all the stimuli in your environment, those that you attend to and group together are *figures*, while all the rest become the *ground*. As you focus your attention on the words on this page, they form figures against the ground (background, if you prefer) provided by the rest of the page. When you hear your instructor's voice during a lecture, that

gestalt
whole, totality, configuration; where the whole (gestalt) is seen as more than the sum of its parts

figure-ground relationship
the Gestalt psychology principle that stimuli are selected and perceived as figures against a ground or background

FIGURE 5.2
(A) A classic reversible figure-ground pattern. What do you see here? A white vase or two black profiles facing each other? Can you clearly see both figures at the same time? (B) After a few moments' inspection, a small square should emerge as a figure against a ground of diagonal lines.

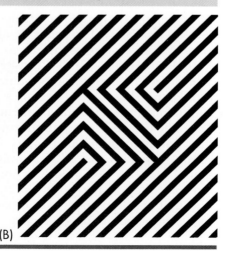

(A)   (B)

voice is the figure against the ground of all the other sounds in the room. Figure 5.2 provides a couple of examples of the figure-ground relationship.

The Gestalt psychologists were intrigued by the processes of perception that enabled us to group and organize stimuli to form meaningful gestalts. As was the case for perceptual selection, there are several factors that influence how we organize our perceptual worlds. Again, it will be useful to consider stimulus and personal factors.

Stimulus Factors in Organization

By stimulus factors, I am referring to characteristics of stimuli that help us perceive them as organized together in one figure or gestalt. We will consider five: proximity, similarity, continuity, common fate, and closure.

proximity
(also contiguity) the Gestalt principle of organization that stimuli will be perceived as belonging together if they occur together in space or time

1. *Proximity.* Glance quickly at Figure 5.3(A). Without giving it much thought, what did you see there? A bunch of Xs, yes; but more than that, there were two groups of Xs, weren't there? The group of eight Xs on the left seems somehow separate from the group on the right, while the Xs within each group seem to go together. This illustrates what the Gestalt psychologists called **proximity** or *contiguity.* What this means is that events that occur close together in space, or in time, are perceived as belonging together as part of the same figure. In Figure 5.3(A), it's difficult to see the Xs as falling into four rows or four columns. They just belong together as two groups of eight Xs.

Proximity operates on more than just visual stimuli. For example, sounds that occur together in speech are perceived as going together to form words or phrases. In written language there are physical spaces between words on the printed page; with spoken language there are very brief pauses between words. Thunder and lightning usually occur together, the sound of thunder following shortly after our experience of the lightning. And as a result of our experience of thunderstorms, it's rather difficult to even think about lightning without also thinking about thunder.

similarity
the Gestalt principle of organization that stimuli will be perceived together if they share some common characteristic(s)

2. *Similarity.* Now glance at Figure 5.3(B) and describe what you see there. We have a set of Xs and Os that clearly are organized into a pattern—two columns of Xs and two of Os. Perceiving rows of alternating Xs and Os is very difficult. This demonstrates the Gestalt principle of **similarity**. Stimulus events that are in some way alike or that have properties in common tend to be grouped together in our perception—a "birds of a feather are perceived together" sort of thing. Most of us perceive Australian koalas as "bears," because they look more like bears than anything else. Actually, they're not. They are related more to kangaroos and wallabies than to bears.

continuity
(also good continuation) the Gestalt principle of organization that a stimulus or a movement will be perceived as continuing in the same direction or fashion as it started

3. *Continuity.* The principle of **continuity** (or good continuation) suggests that we tend to see things as ending up consistent with the way they started off. Figure 5.3(C) illustrates this point with a simple line drawing. The clearest, easiest way to organize (to see or perceive) this drawing is as two separate but intersecting lines: one straight, the other curved. It's difficult to imagine seeing this figure any other way.

The principle of continuity may account for some of the ways we organize our perceptions of people. Aren't we particularly shocked when a young man who was an award-winning honor student throughout high school suddenly does poorly at college and flunks out? That's not how we interpret the way the world works. We wouldn't be nearly as surprised to find that another student, who barely made it through grade school and high school, fails to pass college.

FIGURE 5.3
(A) These Xs are organized as two groups, not as four rows or four columns because of *proximity*. (B) Here we see two columns of Os and two columns of Xs because of *similarity*. (C) We tend to see this figure as two intersecting lines—one straight, the other curved—because of continuity. (D) This figure is perceived as an R, not because it is a well-drawn representation, but because of *closure*.

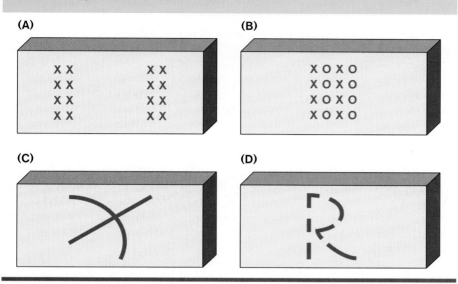

(A)

(B)

(C)

(D)

FIGURE 5.4
An example of subjective contours.

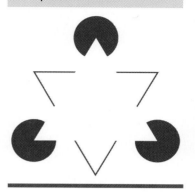

4. *Common Fate.* **Common fate** describes our tendency to group together in the same figure those elements of a scene that move together in the same direction and at the same speed. Common fate is like continuity, but for moving stimuli. Remember that chipmunk sitting motionless on the leaves in the woods? So long as both the chipmunk and the leaves stay still, the chipmunk won't be noticed. But when it moves, all parts of the chipmunk move together—sharing a common fate—and we see it clearly scurrying away.

5. *Closure.* A commonly encountered Gestalt principle of organization is **closure**. This is our tendency to fill in gaps in our perceptual world. Closure is a good example of what I mean when I say that perception is an *active* process. It underscores the notion that we constantly seek to make sense out of our environment—whether that environment presents us with sensible stimuli or not. Closure is illustrated by Figure 5.3(D). At a glance, anyone would tell you that this figure is the letter R, but of course it's not. That's not the way anybody makes an R. It may be the way we *perceive* an R, thanks to closure.

A phenomenon that many psychologists believe is a special case of closure is our perception of **subjective contours**, in which arrangements of lines and patterns enable us to see figures that are not actually there. Now if that sounds a bit spooky, look at Figure 5.4, where we have an example of subjective contour. In Fig. 5.4 you can "see" a solid triangle that is so clearly there it nearly jumps off the page. There is no accepted explanation for subjective contours (Bradley & Dumais, 1975; Coren, 1972; Kanizsa, 1976; Rock, 1986), but it does seem that they provide examples of our perceptual

common fate
the Gestalt principle of organization in which we group together all the elements of a scene that move together in the same direction at the same speed

closure
the Gestalt principle of organization of perceiving incomplete figures as whole and complete

subjective contours
the perception of a contour (a line or plane) that is not there, but is suggested by other (contextual) aspects of a scene

processes filling in gaps in our perceptual world in order to provide us with sensible information.

Personal Factors in Organization

We can cover the personal factors that influence perceptual organization quickly because they are the same as those that influence selection: motivation, expectation, and past experience. We perceive stimuli as going together, forming a gestalt or a figure, because we want to, because we expect to, and/or because we have perceived them together in the past. Consider this classroom demonstration, one I observed when I was a graduate student.

It was a grand old lecture hall. Nearly 600 students had settled down to listen to the lecture on perception. Suddenly a student burst through the doors at the rear of the room. I recognized the student as the lecturer's graduate student assistant, but no one else in the class knew who he was. The student stomped down the center aisle, screaming obscenities at the professor. "Dr. X, you failed me for the last time, you *&@#$ so-and-so. You're going to pay for this!" The class was stunned. No one moved as the student leaped over the lectern to grab the professor.

The two struggled briefly, then—in clear view of everyone—there was a chrome-plated revolver. Down behind the lectern they fell. **BANG!** The students sat frozen in their seats as the graduate student raced out the side door the professor had entered just minutes earlier. The professor lay sprawled on the floor, moaning loudly.

Six hundred students just sat there. At the right dramatic moment, the professor slowly drew himself up to the lectern and in a calm, soft voice said, "Now I want everyone to write down exactly what you saw here."

You can guess what happened. The "enraged" student was described as being from 5'4" to 6'3" tall, weighing between 155 and 235 pounds, and wearing either a blue blazer or a gray sweatshirt. The most remarkable misperception had to do with the gun. When the professor first reached the lectern, he reached into his suit coat pocket, removed the gun and placed it on top of his notes. When the student crashed into the room, the first thing the professor did was to reach down, grab the gun, and point it at the student. In fact, the student *never* had the gun. It was the professor who fired the shot that startled us all. *Fewer than 20 students of the 600 in class that day reported seeing these events as they actually occurred.* The overwhelming majority of "witnesses" claimed it was the crazy student who burst into the lecture hall with a gun in his hands.

First note that everyone did see the gun. The problem was not one of selection. The problem was one of organization—with whom did they associate the gun? No one was *mentally set* for, or expected, the professor to bring a gun to class. No one *wanted* to see the professor with a gun. And no one had ever *experienced* a professor with a gun in class. (Seeing crazed students with guns is not a common experience either, but with television and movies, it's certainly a more probable one.) This demonstration will come up again when we discuss ways in which our memories can be distorted, thus reinforcing our point that perception and memory are very much related.

How we perceive—select, organize, and interpret—a stimulus is often flavored by our perception of other stimuli presented at about the same time. That is, an important factor in how we organize our perceptions is the *context* in which they are perceived. We seldom make perceptual judgments in a vacuum. Figures usually occur in a given context. Context often affects what we expect to perceive or think we have perceived.

Figure 5.5 provides an example of the effect of context on visual perception. Is the highlighted stimulus letter an H or an A? In fact, by itself it isn't a good example of either. But in the proper context—given our past experience with the English language—that same stimulus may appear to be an A *or* an H.

How we organize our experience of the world depends on a number of factors. Our perception that some stimuli in our environments go together with other stimuli to form coherent figures is a process influenced by the proximity or similarity of the events themselves, by our interpretations of closure and continuity, by the context in which the stimuli appear, and by our own personal motives, expectations, and past experiences.

THE CAT SAT BY THE DOOR.

● **Before You Go On**

List stimulus and personal factors that determine how we organize stimuli in perception.

THE PERCEPTION OF DEPTH AND DISTANCE

We have noted that perception is a more complex cognitive process than the simple reception of information that we call sensation. Perception requires that we select and organize stimulus information. It also involves actively recognizing, identifying, and assigning meaning to stimuli. One of the ways in which we interpret a visual stimulus is to note not only *what* we are seeing, but *where* it happens to be. We perceive the world for what it is—three-dimensional. So long as we are paying attention (a required perceptual process), we don't run into buildings or fall off cliffs. We know with great accuracy just how far we are from objects in our environment. What is remarkable and strange about this ability is that the light reflected from objects in our environment falls on *two*-dimensional retinas. The depth and distance in our world is not something we directly *sense*, it is something we *perceive*.

The ability to judge depth and distance accurately is an adaptive skill that plays an important role in determining many of our actions. Our ability to make judgments about depth and distance reflects the fact that we are simultaneously responding to a large number of clues or cues to depth and distance. Some of these cues are built into the way our visual systems work and are referred to as *ocular cues*. What we call *physical cues* have more to do with our appreciation of the physical environment itself.

Ocular Cues

Cues for depth and distance involving both eyes are called *binocular cues* (*bi* means two). Binocular cues result from the fact that our eyes are separated. For example, when we look at a nearby three-dimensional object, each eye gets a slightly different view of it. Hold a pen with a clip on it about twelve inches away. Rotate the pen until the clip can be viewed by the right eye, but not the left. (You check that by closing one eye then the other as you rotate the pen.) Now each eye (retina) is getting a different (disparate) view of the same object. This phenomenon is called **retinal disparity**. It is a powerful cue that what we are looking at must be solid or three-dimensional. If it were not, each eye would see exactly the same image, not two disparate ones. See Figure 5.6.

retinal disparity
the phenomenon in which each retina receives a different (disparate) view of the same three-dimensional object

convergence
the eyes moving toward each other as we focus on objects up close

accommodation
in vision, the process in which the shape of the lens is changed by the ciliary muscles

Another binocular cue is **convergence**—the act of our eyes turning in toward each other when we view something up close. Convergence reflects the fact that we "know" how our eyes are aligned in our heads, even if we seldom pay much attention to it. As we gaze off into the distance, our eyes aim out in almost parallel fashion. As we focus our view on objects that are close to us, our eyes come together, or converge, and we interpret that convergence as an indication that what we are looking at is close to us. Convergence is also illustrated in Figure 5.6.

The rest of the cues we'll consider are monocular. Even the physical cues listed below are monocular cues because they can be appreciated by persons who see with only one eye. A unique monocular cue to distance—at least relatively short distances—is **accommodation**. This process, you may recall, is the changing of the shape of the lens by the ciliary muscles to focus images on the retina. When we focus on distant objects, accommodation flattens our lens, and when we focus on nearby objects, our lens gets rounder or fatter. Although the process is reflexive and automatic, our brain reacts to the activity of the ciliary muscles in terms of the distance of an object from our eyes. That is, our brain "knows" what our ciliary muscles are doing to focus an image and interprets these actions in terms of distance. Accommodation does not function as an effective cue for distances beyond arm's length because the changes in the activity of the ciliary muscles in such cases are too slight to be noticed. But after all, it is within arm's length that accurate decisions about distance are most critical.

FIGURE 5.6
When looking at one three-dimensional object, the right eye sees a slightly different image than does the left eye—a phenomenon called retinal disparity. This disparity gives us a cue that the object we are viewing is three-dimensional. Here we also note convergence—the fact that our eyes turn toward each other when we view an object close to us.

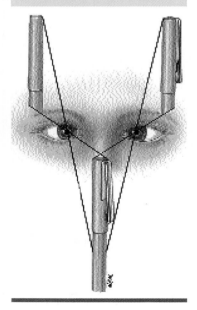

FIGURE 5.7
Although we know that the sides of the road are parallel, they appear to come together in the distance—an example of *linear perspective.*

Physical Cues

The physical cues to distance and depth are those that we get from the structure of our environment. These cues are sometimes called *pictorial cues* because they are used by artists to create the impression of three-dimensionality on two-dimensional canvas or paper. Here are some of the most important.

1. *Linear perspective* (see Figure 5.7). As you stand in the middle of a road, looking off into the distance, the sides of the road—which you know to be parallel—seem to come together in the distance. Using this pictorial cue in drawing obviously takes some time and experience to develop.
2. *Interposition* (see Figure 5.8). This cue to distance reflects our appreciation that objects in the foreground tend to cover, or partially hide, objects in the background, and not vice versa. One of the reasons I know that people sitting in the back of a room are farther away from me than people sitting in the front row is information that I get from interposition. People (and other objects) in the front partially block my view of the people sitting behind them.
3. *Relative size* (see Figure 5.9). This is a commonly used clue to our judgment of distance. As it happens, very few stimuli in this world change their size, but a lot of things get nearer or farther away from us. So,

FIGURE 5.8
Interposition occurs when objects in the foreground partially cover or obscure objects farther away.

FIGURE 5.9
Although all of these hot air balloons are about the same size, those in the distance project much smaller images on our retinas, demonstrating the importance of *relative size* as a cue to distance.

everything else being equal, we tend to judge an object that produces the larger retinal image as being closer to us.

4. *Texture gradients* (see Figure 5.10). Standing on a gravel road, looking down at your feet, you clearly can make out the details of the texture of the roadway. You can see individual pieces of gravel. But as you look on down the road, the texture gradually changes, details giving way to a smooth blending of a textureless surface. We interpret this gradual change (which is what *gradient* means) in texture as indicating a gradual change in distance.

5. *Patterns of shading* (see Figure 5.11). Drawings that do not use shading look flat and two-dimensional. Children eventually learn that if they want their pictures to look lifelike, they should shade in tree trunks and apples and show them as casting shadows. How objects create patterns of light and shade can tell us a great deal about their shape and solidity.

6. *Motion parallax.* This rather technical sounding label names something with which we are all familiar. The clearest example may occur when we are in a car, looking out a side window. Even if the car is going at a modest speed, nearby utility poles and fence posts seem to race by (in the opposite direction). Objects farther away seem to be moving more slowly, and mountains or trees way off in the distance

FIGURE 5.10
Gradients of texture provide cues to distance because we can more clearly see the details of objects close to us.

FIGURE 5.11
We see depth and distance in this image of sand dunes largely because patterns of light and shadow provide us with information about the three-dimensionality of objects in our environment.

seem not to be moving at all. This difference in apparent motion is known as motion parallax. Observations of this phenomenon during a train ride in 1910 was what first got Max Wertheimer interested in what evolved into Gestalt psychology.

It seems that even a process as "natural" as depth perception may be subject to the constraints of one's culture. Here are two examples. Turnbull (1961) reported that the Bambuti people live in the African Congo's Ituri forest, which is so dense that they seldom can see more than 100 feet in the distance. When Turnbull first took his Bambuti guide out of the forest to the open plains the guide, Kenge, was disoriented with regard to distance cues. Kenge thought that the buffalo grazing a few miles away were tiny insects, responding more to retinal size than to relative size as a cue.

Now take a look at Figure 5.12. If the man with the spear were trying to kill an animal, which animal would it be? Because you are responding to well-known depth cues such as relative size and interposition, the answer is obvious: the antelope. When pictures such as this one were shown to persons from remote areas of Africa, a surprising number failed to respond to these "standard" depth cues, and responded that the hunter was trying to

FIGURE 5.12

Which animal—the antelope or the elephant—is the hunter about to spear? One's response to this question depends on the interpretation of physical or pictorial cues to depth and distance. (Adapted from "Pictorial Perception and Culture," by Jan Deregowski. Copyright © 1972 by Scientific American, Inc. All rights reserved.)

kill the elephant (Deregowski, 1972, 1973; Hudson, 1960). In this example, the problem was not with judging distance or depth in the real world, but in the interpretation of physical cues represented in a picture or drawing (Serpell & Deregowski, 1980). With just a little bit of training on how the real world can be shown in drawings, most cultural differences of this sort disappear (Mshelia & Lapidus, 1990).

● **Before You Go On**

Name and describe some of the cues that provide us with information about depth and distance.

THE CONSTANCY OF VISUAL PERCEPTION

perceptual constancies
stable patterns of perceiving the world that help us organize and interpret stimulus inputs

There are a variety of **perceptual constancies**—stable patterns of perceiving the world—that help us organize and interpret the stimulus input we get from our senses. It is because of this stability that we can recognize a familiar object regardless of how far away it is, the angle from which we view it, or the nature of the light reflected from it. You can recognize your textbook whether you view it from a distance or close up, straight on or from an angle, in a dimly or brightly lit room, or in blue, red, or white light. If it were not for perceptual constancies, every sensation might be perceived as a new experience, and little, if anything, would appear familiar.

Perceptual Constancies

I have already mentioned the role of *size constancy* in helping us judge how far away we are from an object. A friend standing very close to us may fill our visual field. At a distance, the image of that same person may take up

FIGURE 5.13
Although we see (at the retina) four different images, we know that we are looking at the same door because of shape *constancy*.

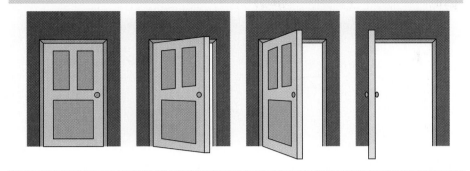

only a fraction of our visual field. The size of the image on our retina may be significantly smaller, but we know very well that our friend hasn't shrunk, but simply has moved farther away.

Shape constancy refers to our perception that solid objects maintain their shape even though they may produce different retinal images. Shape constancy can be simply demonstrated with any familiar object. As you look at a door from different places in a room, the shape of the image of the door on your retina changes radically (Figure 5.13). Closed, it appears rectangular; partially open, the image is that of a trapezoid; from the edge, the retinal image is that of a thin straight line. Regardless of the retinal image, because of shape constancy, your brain consults your memory and interprets the image as a door.

Due to *brightness constancy*, the apparent brightness of a familiar object is perceived as being the same regardless of the actual type or amount of light under which the object is viewed. The white shirt you put on this morning may be *sensed* as gray when you pass through a shadow, or as black as night falls, but it is still *perceived* as a white shirt, in no way darker than it was this morning. The same is true for color perception. If you know that you put on a white shirt this morning, you'd still perceive it as white even if I were to shine a red light on it. The light waves reflected from the shirt to your eyes would be associated with the experience of red, but you would still know the shirt was white and perceive it as white. Someone who didn't know any better might perceive your shirt as red, but you'd see it as a white shirt in a red light because of *color constancy*.

Geometrical Illusions: When Constancy Fails?

By now, you should appreciate that the relationship between the "real world" and our perception of it is tenuous at best. What we perceive often is flavored by many factors beyond the physical stimuli that impinge on our sense receptors. The interaction of physical reality and psychological experience can be seen clearly when we consider illusions. We define **illusions** as experiences in which our perceptions are at odds with what we know as physical reality.

Several very simple and compelling geometrical illusions are presented in Figure 5.14. Consider Figure 5.14(A). This is the vertical-horizon-

illusion

a perception that is at odds with (different from) what we know as physical reality

FIGURE 5.14

A few classic geometrical illusions. In each case you know the answer, but the relevant questions are: (A) Are the vertical and horizontal lines the same length? (B) Is the brim as wide as the hat is tall? (C) Are the two horizontal lines the same length? (D) Are the two horizontal lines the same length? (E) Are the two diagonals part of the same line? (F) Are the long diagonal lines parallel? (G) Are the two center circles the same size?

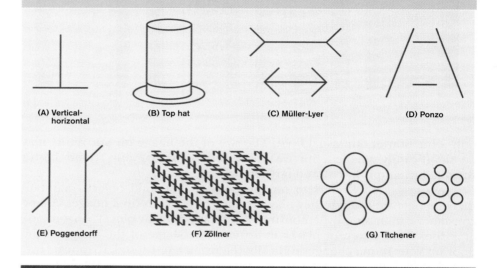

(A) Vertical-horizontal   (B) Top hat   (C) Müller-Lyer   (D) Ponzo

(E) Poggendorff   (F) Zöllner   (G) Titchener

tal illusion. Figure 5.14(B) is the same illusion but in more meaningful terms. Are the two lines in Figure 5.15(A) the same length? Yes, you know they are—we *are* talking about illusions here. But do they *appear* to be the same length? No, they do not. The vertical line seems significantly longer than the horizontal one. The hat in Figure 5.14(B) seems to be taller than it is wide. The illusion is inescapable. Notice that this illusion "works" even after you have measured the two lines to confirm that they are the same length. They still don't look equal. I've seen this illusion in many forms over the years, yet every time I see it, I'm taken in by it. This is one of three fundamental facts about illusions: They do not depend on our ignorance of the situation.

A second fact about illusions is that they do not happen at the retina. Figure 5.14(C) is the well-known Müller-Lyer illusion, named after the man who first drew it. The top line would continue to appear longer than the bottom one even if the two equal lines were presented to one eye, and the arrow-like vanes were simultaneously presented to the other. A third fact is that illusions do not depend on movements of the eye. Illusions appear vividly even when they are flashed before the eyes so quickly that there is no opportunity to scan the presented image (Gillam, 1980).

Illusions of the sort presented in Figure 5.14 are not new. Scientists have been searching for reasonable explanations for illusions for over a hundred years. How do geometrical illusions give rise to perceptions, to visual experiences, that are so much at odds with physical reality? Frankly, we can't say. Several factors seem to operate together to create illusions. Visual illusions depend largely on how we perceive clues about the size of objects in a three-dimensional world, and on inferences we make about the world

FIGURE 5.15
(A) One attempt to explain the Müller-Lyer illusion as the representation of edges and corners. (B) A variant of the Muller-Lyer illusion. The distance between circles A and B is equal to the distance between circles B and C. An explanation in trerms of edges and corners no longer seems reasonable

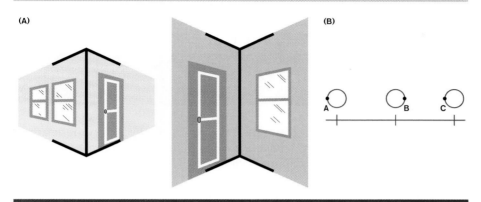

(A)   (B)

based on our experience with it (Coren & Girgus, 1978; Gillam, 1980; Gregory, 1977; Hoffman, 1983).

Here's an example. A reasonable-sounding explanation of the Müller-Lyer illusion is that the "vanes" of the arrows are taken to represent corners, as in a room. To see what I mean, refer to Figure 5.15(A). When corners are near us or far away, we are presented with perspective cues to their distance. Hence, we see the "arrows" of the illusion as edges and corners (Gregory, 1963). This point of view is referred to as the "carpentered world hypothesis" (e.g., Davidoff, 1975; Gregory, 1977). Indeed, in those cultures, such as the Zulus in Africa, where people have lived throughout history in circular houses with round doors and domed roofs—without all of our familiar edges and corners—the effects of the Müller-Lyer illusion are difficult to find (Segall et al., 1966).

The main instructional point of illusions is that they remind us that perception is a process at a higher level than simple sensation. Perception involves the selection, organization, and interpretation of the information we get from our senses, and things are not always as they seem. This point is made even more dramatically with what are called impossible figures (see Figure 5.16).

FIGURE 5.16
Impossible figures—examples of conflicting visual information.

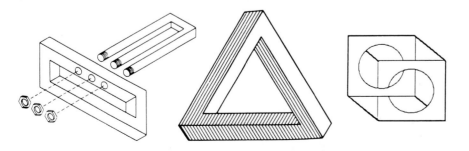

● **Before You Go On**

Name and discuss four types of perceptual constancy.
What do visual illusions teach us about the process of perception?

TOPIC 5B

CONSCIOUSNESS

Consciousness is such a central, integral part of our lives, we might argue that to be alive is to be conscious. You may remember that the early psychologists (e.g., Wundt and James) defined psychology as the science of consciousness, or mental activity. In the chapter preview I defined *consciousness* as the awareness, or perception, of the environment and of our own mental processes. After we briefly consider the nature of normal consciousness, we'll examine the changes that take place in consciousness, or perception, when it is altered by sleep, hypnosis, or drugs.

THE NATURE OF CONSCIOUSNESS

Consciousness is a state of mind—the awareness of our thoughts, feelings, memories, and perceptions. How then can we characterize human consciousness? What are its aspects or its dimensions?

Normal, Waking Consciousness

We probably have no better description of consciousness than that provided by William James nearly 100 years ago (1890, 1892, 1904). For James, there were four basic characteristics of normal waking consciousness.

1. Consciousness is always *changing*. Consciousness doesn't hold still. It cannot be held before the mind for study. "No state once gone can recur and be identical with what was before," James wrote (1892, p. 152).
2. Consciousness is a *personal* experience. Consciousness does not exist without an individual to have it. My consciousness and yours are separate and different. You may try to tell me about your state of mind, your consciousness, but I will never be able to appreciate it fully.
3. Consciousness is *continuous*. There are no gaps in our awareness. We really can't tell where one thought leaves off and another begins. James wrote, "Consciousness, then, does not appear to itself chopped up in bits. . . . A 'river' or 'stream' is most naturally described. In talking about it hereafter, let us call it the stream of thought, of consciousness" (James, 1890, p. 243).
4. Consciousness is *selective*. Awareness is often a matter of making choices, of selectively attending to or focusing on some aspect of experience while ignoring others. "We find it [consciousness] always doing one thing, choosing one out of several materials so presented to its no-

FIGURE 5.17
In the theories of Sigmund Freud, the mind is likened to an iceberg for which only a small part of one's mental life is available in normal waking consciousness; more is available, with some effort of retrieval, at a preconscious level; and most is stored away at an unconscious level from which retrieval occurs only with great difficulty.

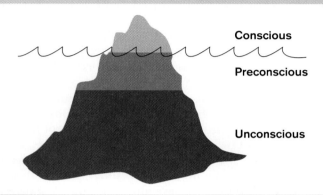

Conscious

Preconscious

Unconscious

tice, emphasizing and accentuating that and suppressing as far as possible all the rest" (James, 1890, p. 139). We spent quite a bit of time in the last Topic discussing the factors that affected such selectivity.

I trust you can appreciate that studying human consciousness scientifically or experimentally has been a challenge for psychologists over the years. An even more slippery notion is that consciousness functions to different degrees or levels of awareness. It is to this issue that we turn next.

● **Before You Go On**

Define perception and consciousness.

What, according to James, are the four major features of consciousness?

Levels of Consciousness

That levels of consciousness vary throughout the day seems intuitively obvious. There are times when we're wide awake, paying full attention to nearly everything going on around us. There are times when "our minds wander" and we don't seem to be paying much attention to anything. Then there are times when we're sound asleep, unaware of what is happening in the environment or in our own minds. Now we come to the interesting question: Is it possible to process information without being aware of it? Is it possible to process information *unconsciously*? The idea of an unconscious mind has a long history in philosophy and psychology (Epstein, 1994; Greenwald, 1992; Hilgard, 1992; Kihlstrom, 1987).

The unconscious mind was a central aspect of Sigmund Freud's theories about human nature. Freud's vision is often depicted as an iceberg—an analogy he used himself (Figure 5.17). The implication is that only a small portion of one's mental life is readily available to one's awareness at any given time. Ideas, memories, feelings, or motives that we are actively aware of are said to be *conscious*. Aspects of experience that are not conscious but that can easily be brought to our awareness are stored at a *preconscious* level. For example, right now you may not be thinking about what you had for dinner last night or will be having for dinner tonight, but with just a little effort, these matters can be brought to your conscious awareness.

Cognitions, feelings, or motives of which we are not aware, and cannot easily become aware, are said to be in the *unconscious*. This is a strange notion: that there are thoughts and feelings stored away in our minds of which we are totally unaware. Freud theorized that the unconscious level of the mind can and does influence us. A large part of the contents of the unconscious mind was put there because if we were to think about or dwell on these issues we would experience anxiety and distress. A husband, for instance, who completely forgets his wedding anniversary and occasionally cannot even remember his wife's name when he goes to introduce her may be experiencing some unconscious conflict about getting married in the first place (although there *are* other possible explanations). Unconscious mental content can show itself in dreams, humor, or slips of the tongue. It might be significant that following a discussion of some issue, Tom says to Heather, "Let's rape about this some more some time," when he *meant* to say, "Let's rap about this some more some time." As we'll see, many Freudian techniques of psychotherapy are aimed at helping a patient learn about the contents of his or her unconscious mind.

Demonstrating the reality of levels of consciousness as Freud proposed them has proven difficult in controlled laboratory research. Nonetheless, Freud's basic ideas about consciousness have gained wide acceptance in psychology, particularly among practicing clinical psychologists (Epstein, 1994; Erdelyi, 1985, 1992; Greenwald, 1992; Lockhard & Paulus, 1988).

Contemporary research is trying to bring the unconscious mind to the laboratory to see how (or if) information can be processed without our awareness. There are two ways in which psychologists characterize unconscious processing. In one sense, you have processed information unconsciously if you were not paying attention to it when it was presented. In another sense, you have processed information unconsciously if you cannot remember that it was presented, whether you were paying attention at the time or not. In either case, research indicates that we do process some things without awareness (Holyoak & Spellman, 1993; Loftus & Klinger, 1992).

We'll look at just one example. A person sits in front of a small screen. A word is flashed on the screen so dimly and so quickly that the person does not report seeing the word. Let's say the word is EASTER. Then two words are flashed on the screen so that the person *can* see them clearly. The task is to choose the word that is related in some way to the word that was not seen. Let's say that the words used in this example are BUNNY and PENCIL. Even when people claim that they are guessing, they choose BUNNY significantly more frequently than chance would predict. If the "unconscious prompt" word were PEN, not EASTER, then they would choose PENCIL. It is as if the initially presented word had influenced their choice (e.g., Cheeseman & Merikle, 1984; Dixon, 1981; Tulving & Schacter, 1990). For that matter, simply reading a list of words at one point in time increases the ability of people to read those words later when they are flashed very briefly on a computer screen, even though the people involved did not recognize that the words had been read earlier (Jacoby & Dallas, 1981).

So is there an unconscious mind, and if so, what is it like? At present, the data tell us that there is an unconscious level of awareness, but it is simple, primitive, and unsophisticated in terms of the amount or type of information it can handle.

A large body of research now suggests that the reality of unconscious processes is no longer questionable. Although there is not uniform agreement about how sophisticated these processes are, there seems to be a general consensus that the unconscious may not be as smart as previously believed. More important, there is absolute agreement that exciting times, both in research and theory are ahead for the unconscious (Loftus & Klinger, 1992, p. 764).

We will now consider consciousness when its nature is altered. By definition, when we are in an altered state of consciousness our perception of both ourselves and our environment will be changed. We'll first discuss an altered state of consciousness that is quite normal: sleep. (Altered states of consciousness need not be weird or bizarre.) Then we'll examine two means of altering consciousness that require some degree of voluntary, deliberate action: hypnosis and the use of drugs.

● **Before You Go On**

What are the three levels of consciousness proposed by Freud?

How may we characterize the unconscious processing of information?

SLEEPING AND DREAMING

Sleep alters our consciousness by reducing alertness and the perception of events occurring around us. Sleep is a normal process, yet it is one we do not understand well. We are seldom aware or conscious of our own sleeping, even though we may spend more than 200,000 hours of our lifetime asleep. Just as the level or degree of our awareness varies during the day, so does our sleep vary in its level or quality throughout the night and from night to night.

Stages of a "Good Night's Sleep"

How do we know when someone is asleep? Self-reports of sleeping are notoriously unreliable. A person who claims that he or she "didn't sleep a wink last night," may have slept soundly for several hours (Dement, 1974).

Our best indicators of sleep are measurements of brain activity and muscle tone. The **electroencephalograph (EEG)** is an instrument that records electrical activity in the brain. It does so through small electrodes that are pasted onto the scalp. The process is slightly messy, but it is not painful. An **electromyograph (EMG)** produces a record of a muscle's activity or relaxation.

When you are in a calm, relaxed state, with your eyes closed but not yet asleep, your EEG pattern shows a rhythmic cycle of brain waves called **alpha activity**. In this presleep stage, we find relatively smooth EEG waves cycling 8 to 12 times per second. If, as you sit or lie there, you start worrying about events of the day, or try to solve a problem, smooth alpha waves

electroencephalograph (EEG)
an instrument used to measure and record the overall electrical activity of the brain

electromyograph (EMG)
an instrument used to measure and record muscle tension or relaxation

alpha activity
an EEG pattern associated with quiet relaxation and characterized by slow wave cycles of 8 to 12 per second

FIGURE 5.18
EEG records showing the general electrical activity of the brain for a person at various levels of wakefulness and sleep.

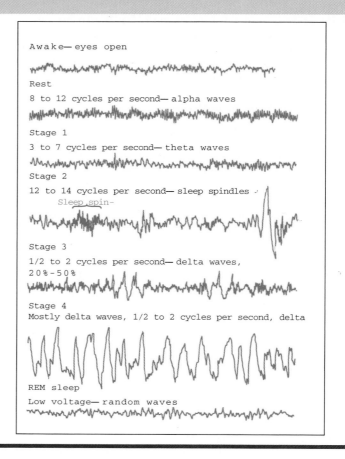

become disrupted and are replaced by an apparently random pattern of heightened electrical activity typical of what we find in wakefulness.

As you drift from relaxation into sleep, brain waves change, as alpha waves give way to the stages of sleep. The EEG tracings of sleeping subjects can be divided into four different stages (Borbely, 1986). As I review these four stages, you can refer to Figure 5.18, which shows the EEGs of a person in each stage. These tracings were chosen because they best illustrate each of the four stages. Actual EEG tracings are not always this clear.

Stage 1. This is a very light sleep from which you can be easily aroused. The smooth, cyclical alpha pattern disappears, replaced by the slower *theta waves* (3–7 cycles per second). The amplitude, or magnitude, of the electrical activity also lessens considerably. At the same time, your breathing is becoming more regular, and your heart rate is slowing and blood pressure is decreasing. This stage does not last very long—generally less than 10 minutes. Then, you start to slide into Stage 2 sleep.

Stage 2. In this stage, the EEG pattern is similar to Stage 1—low amplitude with no noticeable wavelike pattern. The difference is that we now see *sleep spindles* in the EEG record. These are brief, high-amplitude bursts of electrical activity that occur with regularity (about every 15 seconds or so). You're really getting off to sleep now, but still can be easily awakened.

Stage 3. Now you're getting into deep sleep. There is a reduction in the brain's electrical activity. We can clearly make out *delta wave* activity in your EEG. Delta waves are high, slow waves (from 0.5 to 3 cycles every second). In Stage 3, delta waves constitute between 20 and 50 percent of your EEG pattern. Your internal functions (temperature, heart rate, breathing) are lowering and slowing. It is difficult to wake you now.

Stage 4. You are in deep sleep. Your EEG record is virtually filled with slow delta waves, recurring over and over again (as opposed to Stage 3, where delta waves comprise only a portion of your brain wave activity). Readings from an electromyogram indicate that your muscles have become totally relaxed. About 15 percent of your night's sleep will be spent in this stage of deep sleep.

It usually takes about an hour to go from stage 1 to stage 4, depending on such things as how tired you are and the physical conditions surrounding you. After an hour's passage through these four stages, the sequence reverses itself. You go back through stage 3, then to stage 2, but before going through the cycle again, something remarkable happens. Your eyes start to move rapidly under closed eyelids.

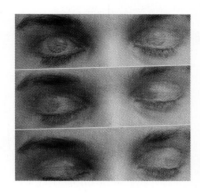

The rapid eye movements of REM sleep are captured in these double-exposure photographs.

● **Before You Go On**

What are the EEG and the EMG?

Briefly describe the four stages of sleep.

REM and NREM Sleep

In the early 1950s, Nathaniel Kleitman and Eugene Aserinsky made quite a discovery. They noticed that as sleeping subjects began their second cycle into deeper levels of sleep, their eyes began to dart back and forth under their closed eyelids (Aserinsky & Kleitman, 1953). This period of *rapid eye movement* is called **REM sleep**. When subjects are awakened during REM sleep, they usually (about 85% of the time) report that they are having a vivid, storylike dream. When awakened during sleep periods that are not accompanied by rapid eye movements—*NREM sleep*—people report fewer and much more fragmented dreams (Kleitman, 1963a; NCSDR, 1993). At first it was believed that eye movements during REM sleep were a result of the dreamer literally viewing, or scanning, images produced by the dream. It turns out that a dreamer's eye movements are unrelated to the content of his or her dream. Instead, eye movements are produced by a cluster of cells in the brain stem (Hobson, 1977; Kiester, 1980).

Periods of REM sleep occur throughout the night, normally lasting from a few minutes to half an hour. About 90 to 120 minutes each night is spent in REM sleep. As one goes through a night's sleep, REM periods tend to become longer and dreams more vivid (NCSDR, 1993).

Everyone REMs. Everyone dreams. Some of us have difficulty remembering what we have dreamed when we awake in the morning, but we can

REM sleep

rapid eye movement sleep during which vivid dreaming occurs, as do heightened levels of physiological functioning

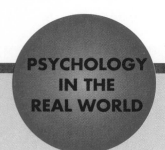

Sleep Disorders

A good night's sleep is a wonderful and apparently necessary thing. Some people have no difficulty sleeping and seem to be able to sleep through anything. Others experience problems, either in getting to sleep in the first place or during sleep itself. The National Commission on Sleep Disorder Research (NCSDR) released its report *Wake Up America: A National Sleep Alert* in January 1993. The commission found that approximately 40 million Americans suffer from chronic disorders of sleep and that another 20 to 30 million experience intermittent sleep-related problems. We will now briefly review three disorders of sleep.

Insomnia. At some time or another, each of us has suffered from a bout of insomnia—the inability to fall asleep and/or stay asleep when one wants to. We may be excited or worried about something that is going to happen the next day. We may have over-stimulated ourselves with drugs, such as caffeine. Most people who suffer from insomnia haven't the slightest idea why they have trouble sleeping. Chronic, debilitating insomnia afflicts nearly 30 million Americans, women more commonly than men, and the elderly about 1.5 times as often as younger adults (Fredrickson, 1987; NCSDR, 1993).

Using sleeping pills or over-the-counter medications to treat insomnia may cause more problems than it solves. The pills (usually sedatives or depressants) may have a positive effect for a while, but eventually dosages have to be increased as tolerance builds. When the drugs are discontinued, a rebound effect occurs, making it even more difficult to get to sleep than it was before (Kales et al., 1979; Kripke & Gillin, 1985; Palfai & Jankiewicz, 1991).

Narcolepsy. Narcolepsy involves going to sleep, even during the day, without intending to. Sleep occurs in "sleep attacks" of REM sleep as the person quickly falls asleep and then almost immediately begins dreaming. No one knows exactly what causes narcolepsy, and the disorder is resistant to treatment. Although only 50,000 cases of the disorder have been diagnosed, estimates are that nearly 350,000 Americans suffer from some degree of narcolepsy (NCSDR, 1993). The big problem with narcolepsy (in addition to any embarrassment) is that narcoleptic sleep attacks are sometimes accompanied by the total relaxation of muscle tone that is also associated with REM sleep (Dement, 1974; Lucas et al., 1979)—the danger in which is quite obvious. The following is a brief quote from someone who testified before the NCSDR:

> To help you understand narcolepsy, set your alarm for every 90 minutes, and stay awake for 10 minutes every time it goes off. Alternate that with periods of 48 hours without sleep. . . . Collapse on the floor every time you are angry, scared, surprised, laughing, or upset. Sleep for 1/2 hour before you drive anywhere; sleep again for 1/2 hour when you arrive. . . . Be late for everything. Fall asleep at every traffic light. . . . I figured out the difference between my life as a narcoleptic and dead people. The dead don't have to get up and go to work every day. (NCSDR, 1993, p. 35)

Sleep Apnea. Apnea means a sudden stop in breathing—literally, "without breath." If we stop breathing when we're awake and conscious, we can do something about it. We can exercise conscious, voluntary control over our breathing. We cannot do so, however, when we are asleep. Sleep apnea involves patterns of sleep during which breathing stops entirely. Episodes are usually short, and long-term dangers are few. When apnea episodes are longer—lasting a minute or two—carbon dioxide in the lungs builds to such a level that the sleeper is awakened, draws a few gasps of air, and returns to sleep, perhaps oblivious to what just happened.

Potential consequences of sleep apnea include hypertension, coronary heart disease, stroke, psychiatric problems, impotence, and memory loss. The Commission on Sleep Disorders Research estimates that 38,000 cardiovascular deaths each year are the result of sleep apnea (NCSDR, 1993, p. 33). For reasons that are not clear, sleep apnea appears most commonly in obese, middle-aged males. Sleep apnea is also a prime suspect in the search for a cause of Sudden Infant Death Syndrome (SIDS). In this syndrome, young infants with no other major illness, sometimes only with a slight cold or infection, suddenly die in their sleep. Such sudden death occurs in about two infants per thousand.

be sure that in the course of a normal night's sleep, we have dreamed several times. There is no great mystery why we don't remember our dreams any better than we do. Most dreams are quite ordinary, boring, and forgettable. Unless we make an effort to do so, we seldom try to store dream content in our memories so that they can be recalled later. That is, we are seldom motivated to remember our dreams.

Although we're sure that everyone does dream, we're less sure *why* everyone dreams. Some theories have their basis in the writings of Freud (1900), who believed that dreaming allows us the opportunity to engage in fantasy and wish fulfillment of a sort that would probably cause us discomfort or embarrassment if we entertained such thoughts while we were awake. Freud saw dreams as a pathway (a "royal road," as he called it) to the discovery of the content of our unconscious mind.

More modern theories of the function of REM sleep and dreaming emphasize the physiological activity that occurs during this phase of sleep. One hypothesis argues that REM sleep helps the brain consolidate memories of events that occurred during the day. In one study, for example, subjects were less able to recall stories they read before they went to bed if their REM sleep was interrupted during the night (Tilley & Empson, 1978). Another intriguing notion is that dreams (and our recall of them) are convenient cognitive "explanations" for what may be the random activity of our brains. For example, if the area of the brain associated with the movement of our legs is active while we are asleep, our brain will make up a reasonable story—a dream—that involves our running, or kicking, or in some way using our leg muscles (Hobson, 1988; Hobson & McCarley, 1977).

Dreaming isn't the only thing that happens during REM sleep. From the outside, a sleeper in REM sleep seems quiet and calm, but on the inside there is a different story. One noticeable change is muscular immobility—called **atonia**. The paralysis of atonia is not caused by a tensing of muscles, but because centers in the brain stem keep the muscles from acting (Chase & Morales, 1990). Sleep atonia has an adaptive function, keeping the body still so that the dreamer does not react physically to his or her dream. The immobilization of atonia may be interrupted occasionally by slight muscle "twitches" (which you may have observed if you've watched a sleeping dog that appears to be chasing some imaginary rabbit in its dream). Some people do not demonstrate normal atonia and thrash about wildly during REM sleep—a disorder reasonably called REM sleep disorder (Mahowald & Schenck, 1989).

In many ways, the REM sleeper is very active, even though he or she may be oblivious to, or not conscious of, most external stimulation. During REM sleep there is often an excitement of the sex organs, males having a penile erection, females having a discharge of vaginal fluids (although this latter finding is not as common). Breathing usually becomes shallow and rapid. Blood pressure levels can skyrocket, and heart rates increase, all while the person lies "peacefully" asleep. Indeed, there doesn't appear to be very much quiet and peaceful about it at all. These changes take place regardless of what the person is dreaming about: It matters little whether one is dreaming about lying on the beach getting a tan, enjoying a sexual encounter, or engaging in hand-to-hand combat; physiologically, the reactions are the same. This marked increase in physiological activity has long been suspected to be related to heart attacks, strokes, and other cardiovascular problems that can develop "even though the patient was asleep" (King et al., 1973; Kirby & Verrier, 1989; Somers et al., 1993).

atonia
muscular immobility associated with REM sleep, caused by the relaxation of the muscles

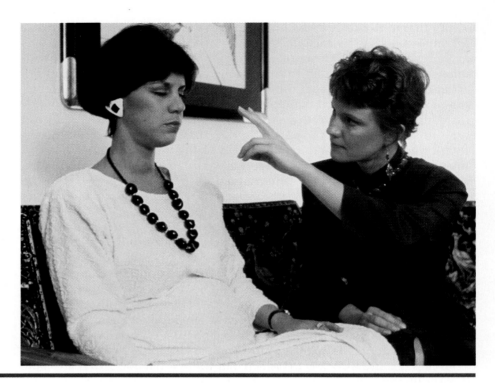

Hypnosis is an altered state of consciousness that one enters voluntarily. It has been used for a variety of purposes, including treatment of some psychological and physical disorders.

● **Before You Go On**
What are REM and NREM sleep?
What occurs during REM sleep?

HYPNOSIS

hypnosis
an altered state of consciousness characterized by an increase in suggestibility, attention, and imagination

Hypnosis is an altered state of consciousness that typically requires the co-operation of the person being hypnotized. Hypnosis is characterized by (1) a marked increase in suggestibility, (2) a focusing of attention, (3) exaggerated use of imagination, (4) inability or unwillingness to act on one's own, and (5) acceptance of distortions of reality without question (Hilgard & Hilgard, 1975). There is little truth to the belief that being hypnotized is like going to sleep. Few of the characteristics of sleep are found in the hypnotized subject. EEG patterns, for example, are significantly different.

Hypnosis has been used, with varying degrees of success, for several different purposes. As you know, it is used as entertainment, as a show business routine where members of an audience are hypnotized—usually to do silly things in public. Hypnosis has long been seen as a method of gaining access to memories of events that are not in immediate awareness and has been used as a treatment for a wide range of psychological and physical disorders. In this section, we'll address a few commonly asked questions about hypnosis.

1. *Can everyone be hypnotized?* No, probably not. Susceptibility to hypnosis varies rather widely from person to person. Contrary to popular belief, you cannot be hypnotized against your will, which is why I say that one enters a hypnotic state voluntarily. I do acknowledge that some

hypnotists claim that they can hypnotize anyone under the right conditions—which is why I hedged and said "probably" not (e.g., Lynn et al., 1990).

2. *What best predicts who can easily be hypnotized?* Although not everyone can easily be hypnotized, some people are excellent subjects who can readily be put into deep hypnotic states and easily learn to hypnotize themselves (Hilgard, 1975, 1978). A number of traits are correlated with hypnotizability. The most important factor seems to be the ability to engage easily in daydreaming and fantasy, to be able to "set ordinary reality aside for awhile" (Lynn & Rhue, 1986; Wilkes, 1986, p. 25). Other positively related traits include suggestibility and a certain degree of passivity or willingness to cooperate, at least during the session. Another intriguing notion is that persons who were punished often in childhood, or are avid readers, runners, or actors are good subjects. The logic is that these people have a history of self-induced trance-like states (to escape punishment, or to focus, and become absorbed in the task at hand), which makes them more likely to be easily hypnotized (Hilgard, 1970).

3. *Can I be made to do things under the influence of hypnosis that I would not do otherwise?* Next to being unknowingly hypnotized, this seems to be the greatest fear associated with hypnosis. Again, the answer is *probably* no. Under the influence of a skilled hypnotist, you may do some pretty silly things and do them publicly. Under the right circumstances, you might do those very same things without being hypnotized. It is unlikely that you would do under hypnosis anything that you would not do otherwise. It is also true that under certain (unusual) circumstances, people can do outrageous—and dangerous—things, which is why hypnosis should be used with caution.

4. *Are hypnotized subjects simply more open to suggestions, or is their consciousness really changed?* This issue is in dispute. Some believe that hypnosis is no more than a heightened level of suggestibility (Barber, 1972; Spanos & Barber, 1974). Others believe it to be a special state, separate from the compliance of a willing subject. When hypnotized subjects are left alone, they maintain the condition induced by their hypnosis. Those not hypnotized, but simply complying as best they can with an experimenter, revert quickly to normal behaviors when left alone (Hilgard, 1975; Orne, 1969).

5. *Can hypnosis be used to alleviate pain—real, physical pain?* Yes. It won't (can't) cure the underlying cause, but it can be used to control the feeling of pain. If a person is a good candidate for hypnosis in the first place, there is a good chance that at least a portion of perceived pain can be blocked from conscious awareness (Hilgard & Hilgard, 1975; Long, 1986).

6. *Is a person in a hypnotic state in any sense aware of what she or he is doing?* Yes, but in a strange way. It seems that within the hypnotized subject is what Hilgard calls a "hidden observer" who may be quite aware of what is going on. In one study (Hilgard & Hilgard, 1975), a subject was hypnotized and told that he would feel no pain as his hand was held in a container of ice water (usually very painful). When asked, the subject reported feeling very little pain, just as expected. The hypnotic suggestion was working. The Hilgards then asked the subject if "some part of him" was feeling any pain and to indicate the presence of such pain by using his free hand to press a lever (or even to write out a description of what he was feeling). Even though the subject

continued to report verbally no feeling of pain, the free hand (on the behalf of the "hidden observer") indicated that it "knew" there was considerable pain in the immersed hand.

7. *Can I remember things under hypnosis that I couldn't remember otherwise?* No, probably not, although there is no more hotly contested issue with regard to hypnosis than this. In the everyday sense of "Can you hypnotize me so that I'll remember my psychology material better for the test next Friday?" the answer is "Almost certainly not." (Sorry.) I might be able to convince you under hypnosis that you should remember your psychology and lead you to want to remember your psychology, but there is no evidence that hypnotic suggestion can directly improve your ability to learn and remember new material. In the more restrictive sense of "I don't recall the details of the accident and the trauma that followed. Can hypnosis help me recall those events more clearly?" the answer is less definite. When we get to our discussion of memory (Chapter 7), we'll see that distortions of memory in recollection easily occur in normal states. In hypnotic states, the subject is suggestible and susceptible to distortions in recall furnished by the hypnotist (even assuming that the hypnotist has no reason to cause distortions). To the extent that hypnosis can reduce feelings of anxiety and tension, it may help in the recollection of anxiety-producing memories. The evidence is neither clear nor convincing on this issue in either direction. What of the related question, "Can hypnosis make me go back in time (regress) and remember what it was like when I was only 3 or 4 years old?" Here, I'm afraid, we *do* have a clearcut answer, and the answer is no. So-called age-regression hypnotic sessions have simply not proven valid (e.g., Nash, 1987; Spanos et al., 1991).

Hypnosis does alter one's consciousness, does open one to suggestions of the hypnotist, can be used to treat symptoms (not their underlying causes), and can distort one's view of reality. However, we are learning that it is neither mystical nor magical; there are limits to what hypnosis can do.

● **Before You Go On**
What is hypnosis, and who can be hypnotized?

ALTERING CONSCIOUSNESS WITH DRUGS

In this final section, we'll discuss some of the chemicals that alter consciousness by inducing changes in our perception, mood, or behavior. Because they can alter basic psychological processes, these chemicals are referred to as **psychoactive drugs**.

Drugs have been used for centuries to alter consciousness. Drugs are taken—at least initially—to achieve a state of consciousness that the user considers to be good, positive, pleasant, even euphoric. No reasonable person would take a drug because he or she expected to have a bad, negative, unpleasant experience. As we all know, however, the use of psychoactive drugs often has seriously negative outcomes. In this regard, there are a few terms that will be relevant for our discussion. Although there is not complete agreement on how these terms are used, for our purposes, we'll use the following definitions.

psychoactive drug
a chemical that produces an affect on psychological processes and consciousness

1. *Dependence:* A state in which (a) use of a drug is required to maintain bodily functioning (physical dependence), or (b) when continued use of a drug is believed to be necessary to maintain psychological functioning at some level (psychological dependence). *"I just can't face the day without my three cups of coffee in the morning."*

2. *Tolerance:* A condition in which the use of a drug leads to a state in which more and more of it is needed to produce the same effect. *"I used to get high with just one of these; now I need three."*

3. *Withdrawal:* A strongly negative reaction, either physical or psychological (including reactions such as headaches, vomiting, and cramps), that results when one stops taking a drug. *"When I take these, I don't feel real good, but it sure does hurt when I stop."*

4. *Addiction:* An extreme dependency, physical or psychological, in which signs of tolerance and painful withdrawal are usually found (Schuckit, 1989). Addiction also implies seeking a short-term gain (say, a pleasurable feeling) at the expense of long-term negative consequences (Miller, 1992). *"No way I'm gonna give it up; no matter what. It feels too good, and it hurts too much without it."*

Another distinction we should make is that between drug use and **drug abuse**. Drug abuse involves (1) a lack of control, as evidenced by frequent intoxication and continued use, even given the knowledge that one's condition will deteriorate; (2) a disruption of interpersonal relationships or difficulties at work that can be traced to drug usage; and (3) signs that maladaptive drug use has continued for at least one month (American Psychiatric Association, 1987). In this distinction is the observation that drug use may not have negative consequences; drug abuse will. There is no clear dividing line between drug use and drug abuse. For that matter, there are no clear dividing lines between drug use, dependency on drugs, and drug addiction. There is, instead, a continuum from total abstinence through heavy social use to clear-cut addiction (Doweiko, 1993; Peele, et al., 1991).

There are many psychoactive drugs. We'll focus on four types: stimulants, depressants, hallucinogens, and (as a separate category) marijuana.

drug abuse
a condition defined by lack of control, disruption of interpersonal relationships, difficulties at work, and a history of maladaptive drug use for at least one month

Stimulants

Chemical **stimulants** do just that—they stimulate or activate the nervous system. They produce a heightened sense of arousal, creating an increase in general activity and an elevation of mood.

Caffeine is one of the most widely used of all stimulants. It is found in many foods and drinks (chocolate, coffee, and tea) as well as in many varieties of painkillers. It is also an ingredient in many soft drinks, notably colas. In moderate amounts, it has no life-threatening effects. At some point, a mild dependence may develop. Although it is not yet known precisely how caffeine does so, it temporarily increases metabolism (the process of converting food into energy), resulting in a burst of energy. It also blocks the effects of some inhibitory neurotransmitters in the brain (Julien, 1985).

There is usually a rebound sort of effect when caffeine intake is stopped. After lengthy use, giving up caffeine can result in the pain of withdrawal. If you drink a lot of coffee and cola drinks during the week but take a break from them on the weekend, you may experience the headaches of caffeine withdrawal. You may drink many cups of coffee to help stay awake

stimulants
drugs (e.g., caffeine, cocaine, and amphetamines) that increase nervous system activity

to withstand an all-night study session, but a few hours after you stop the caffeine you may rebound and experience a streak of mental and physical fatigue—perhaps right at exam time!

Nicotine is another popular stimulant, usually taken by smoking and absorption by the lungs. Nicotine is carried from the lungs to the brain very quickly—in a matter of seconds. Nicotine *is* a stimulant of central nervous system activity, but it also relaxes muscle tone slightly, which may partially explain the rationalization of smokers who claim they can relax by having a cup of coffee and a cigarette. Nicotine has its stimulant effect by activating excitatory synapses in both the central and peripheral nervous systems (McKim, 1986).

Many individuals develop a tolerance to nicotine, requiring more and more of it to reach the desired state of stimulation. Indeed, beginning smokers generally cannot smoke more than one or two cigarettes without becoming ill. The drug often leads to dependency. In 1989, Surgeon General C. Everett Koop declared cigarette smoking an addiction, the single most preventable cause of death in our society, accounting for more than one-sixth of all the deaths reported in 1985 (Shiffman et al., 1990). More recent reports blame tobacco use for nearly half the deaths annually in the United States, and a 1994 report from the World Health Organization claims that at current rates, by the year 2020 smoking will result in 10 million deaths a year worldwide. Just how addictive nicotine (or perhaps any other drug) becomes may depend primarily on how quickly it enters the brain. That is, people who take many quick deep puffs when smoking may become addicted more easily to nicotine than will people who take slow, shallow puffs (Bennett, 1980). We'll return to this discussion of smoking and nicotine in Topic 11B, health psychology.

Cocaine is a naturally occurring stimulant derived from leaves of the coca shrub (native to the Andes mountains in South America). The allure of cocaine and its derivative "crack" is the rush of pleasure and energy it produces when it first enters the bloodstream, either through the mucous membranes when inhaled as smoke ("freebasing"), through the nose as a powder ("snorting"), or directly, through injection as a liquid. A cocaine "high" doesn't last very long—15 to 20 minutes is typical.

There are many physiological reactions that result from cocaine use. It elevates blood pressure and heart rate. It blocks the reuptake of important neurotransmitters, which means that once these neurotransmitters have entered a synapse, cocaine will prohibit their being taken back into the neuron from which they have been released. The end result is that, for some period of time at least, excessive amounts of these neurotransmitters are available in the nervous system. The neurotransmitters involved are norepinephrine, which acts in both the central and peripheral nervous systems to provide arousal and the sense of extra energy, and dopamine, which acts in the brain to produce feelings of pleasure and euphoria.

Some of the physiological effects of cocaine use are very long-lasting, if not permanent, even though the psychological effects last but a few minutes. Not only is the rush of reactions to cocaine or "crack" short-lived, it is followed by a period of letdown approaching depression. As the user knows, one way to combat letdown and depression is to take more of the drug. This vicious cycle leads to dependency and addiction. Cocaine is such a powerfully addictive drug that many individuals become psychologically and physically dependent on its use after just one or two episodes. Determining the number of cocaine users or abusers is difficult (after all, the drug *is* illegal), but estimates range from slightly fewer than 2 million to over 6 million in the United States alone (Doweiko, 1993). Cocaine addiction runs in families to such an extent that current research is exploring the hypothesis that there is a genetic basis for cocaine addiction.

Amphetamines are synthetically manufactured chemical stimulants that usually come in the form of capsules or pills under many street names, such as bennies, uppers, wake-ups, cartwheels, dexies, or jellie babies. Amphetamines block reuptake and cause the release of excess dopamine and norepinephrine. However, their action is considerably slower and somewhat less widespread than that of cocaine. Once the amphetamine takes effect, users feel alert, awake, aroused, filled with energy, and ready to go. Whereas a reaction to cocaine fades after a few minutes, the impact of amphetamines can last for a few hours (Schuckit, 1989). Unfortunately, such results are short-lived and illusory. The drug does not create alertness so much as it masks fatigue, which ultimately will overcome the user when the drug wears off. These are not the only effects of amphetamine use; it has a direct effect on the cardiovascular system, causing an irregular heartbeat and increased blood pressure (McKim, 1986).

● **Before You Go On**

What are stimulant drugs, and what are their effects?

Depressants

In terms of their effect on consciousness, **depressants** are the opposite of stimulants. They reduce awareness of external stimuli, slow bodily functioning, and decrease levels of behavior. Predictably, one's reaction to depressants depends largely on how much is taken. In small doses, they can produce relaxation, a sense of freedom from anxiety, and a loss of inhibitions. In greater amounts, they can produce sedation, sleep, coma, or death.

Alcohol is the most commonly used of all depressants and has been in use for thousands of years—perhaps as far back as 8000 B.C. (Ray & Ksir, 1987). It is a dangerous drug because of its popularity and widespread use, if nothing else, but it can be a deadly drug. Over 100,000 deaths a year in the United States can be attributed directly to alcohol consumption. The devastating effects of alcohol consumption by pregnant women are also well documented (see Chapter 3, p. 84).

Perhaps the first thing to remember about alcohol is that it *is* a depressant. Some people may feel that they are entertaining and stimulating when drinking alcohol, but their nervous system is actually being depressed, or slowed. Alcohol increases urination, leading to an overall loss of fluids. It affects vision by making it more difficult to detect dim lights. There is no doubt that alcohol affects mood, leading to feelings of friendly elation as levels rise, and of anger, depression, and fatigue as alcohol levels drop (Babor et al., 1983).

The specific effects of alcohol on the drinker usually reflect several interacting factors. Primary among them (again) is the *amount* of alcohol that gets into a person's bloodstream. Blood alcohol level (BAL) is affected by how much one drinks and by how fast the alcohol can get into the bloodstream, which in turn is affected by what else is in the stomach. Drinking on an empty stomach is more dangerous than drinking while or after eating, because the alcohol will be more quickly absorbed. One-tenth of one percent BAL is enough to define someone as legally intoxicated in most states. At this level, brain activity is so depressed that decision making is distorted and motor coordination impaired (and both are skills required to drive

depressants
drugs (e.g., alcohol, opiates, heroin, and barbiturates) that slow or reduce nervous system activity

The behavioral consequences of drug use often depend on dosage. With too much alcohol, for example, a pleasant altered state of consciousness can become a total loss of consciousness.

safely). Drinking more than one mixed drink, one can of beer, or one glass of wine *per hour* will raise blood alcohol levels, but even lesser amounts impair judgments and increase reaction time (Maguire, 1990).

Alcohol use and abuse are particularly susceptible to sociocultural factors. For example, consider the social pressures on alcohol use that stem from religious beliefs. The use of alcohol is virtually nonexistent among Muslims and Mormons, and used sparingly—usually in religious rituals—by several Chinese religious sects and Orthodox Jews. Alcoholism rates are also low among these groups. In the United States, Irish Americans are six times more likely to suffer from alcoholism than are Greek Americans. Remember, these observations are "in general," and that there are many Irish Americans who do not use alcohol at all (Valliant, 1983). Adolescent Native Americans, especially those living on reservations, have much higher rates of alcohol use and abuse than any other American ethnic-racial population (Moncher et al., 1990; Swaim et al., 1993). Curiously, peer pressure, a major determining factor in drug and alcohol use for Anglo youths, is significantly less important in the culture of adolescent Native Americans (Oetting & Beauvais 1987). We also have to remember that economic issues are relevant—research clearly demonstrates a relationship between alcohol use and economic indicators such as poverty, unemployment, and lack of opportunity (Beauvais et al., 1989; Ley, 1985).

Opiates, such as morphine and codeine, are called "analgesics" because they can be used to reduce or eliminate sensations of pain. It was for this purpose that they were first commonly used. In small doses, they create feelings of well-being, ease, and a trancelike state. Unlike alcohol, they have little effect on motor behavior. The catch is that they produce strong dependence and addiction. Discontinuing the use of opiates results in extreme pain and depression.

Heroin is an opiate derived (in the 1890s) from morphine, but originally thought not to be as addictive—a notion soon proven wrong. Dependency and addiction grow rapidly. Estimates suggest that more than 500,000 persons in the United States are addicted to heroin —and nearly half of them live in New York City. As with other drugs, the addictive nature of heroin is related to its rapid entry into the brain. Methadone, used in some treatment programs for long-term heroin users, is a drug with many of the chemical properties of heroin and many of the same effects. A difference is that methadone is slow to reach the brain and tends not to produce heroin's predictable "rush," which makes it less addictive.

The psychological effects of heroin (in addition to whatever pain-killing use it may have) are mostly related to the user's emotional state and mood. Unlike alcohol or opiates, heroin seldom produces hallucinations or thought disturbances. But as increased amounts of heroin are needed to produce the desired euphoria, tolerance builds—and increased dosages of heroin can cause breathing to stop, often for long enough periods that death results.

Barbiturates are synthetically produced sedatives. There are many types and varieties. Well over 2,500 barbiturate chemicals have been isolated in laboratories (Doweiko, 1993). All barbiturates slow nervous system activity; in small amounts they produce a sense of calm and tranquility, and in higher doses they produce sleep or coma. Some barbiturates are addictive, producing strong withdrawal symptoms when their use is discontinued. All produce dependency if used with regularity. As is generally the case, once an addiction develops, conquering it is very difficult.

● Before You Go On

What are depressant drugs, and what are their effects?

Hallucinogens

The psychoactive drugs called **hallucinogens** have the most unpredictable effects on consciousness. One of the reactions is the formation of hallucinations, usually visual. That is, users report seeing things when there is nothing there to see, or seeing things in ways that others do not. Hallucinations of hearing, smell, touch, and taste are possible but are much less common.

There are nearly one hundred types of hallucinogenic substances around the world, and many have been in use for centuries. In many cultures the drugs are used in religious practices to induce trancelike states that may help the user communicate with the supernatural. The hallucinogenic drug is often used as part of a ceremony or ritual, and may be given to young people by their elders. In such cases, "unauthorized" use of the drug, or the abuse of the drug, is unheard of (e.g., Grob & Dobkin de Rois, 1992).

hallucinogens
drugs (e.g., LSD) whose major effect is the alteration of perceptual experience and mood

In some cultures, the use of hallucinogens is a sanctioned part of rites or ceremonies. Here, a Yanomamö Indian is receiving a wad of ebene—a powerful hallucinogen—blown up his nose.

LSD (lysergic acid diethylamide), a potent and popular hallucinogen in most Western cultures, was introduced to the United States in the 1940s. LSD raises levels of emotionality and can change perception profoundly, usually producing vivid visual hallucinations. One of the first steps in the discovery of how LSD works was finding that levels of the neurotransmitter serotonin increased when LSD was given to animals (Jacobs and Trulson, 1979; Jacobs, 1987). In itself, this was not surprising because LSD, and similar hallucinogens such as mescaline, have a chemical composition like that of serotonin. LSD acts on serotonin receptor sites, acting as if it were a neurotransmitter. And very small doses (measured in only millionths of a gram) can produce major behavioral effects.

The changes in mood that take place under LSD are commonly exaggerations of the user's present mood. From the start, this has been viewed as one of the dangers of LSD. Some people are drawn to drugs like LSD because things are not going well for them. Perhaps they are depressed and becoming hopeless. They think that LSD might help cheer them up. In fact, it may worsen their mood by exaggerating the feelings they had when they took the drug and resulting in a "bad trip."

● Before You Go On

What are hallucinogenic drugs, and what are their effects?

Marijuana—A Rather Special Case

Marijuana is a consciousness-altering drug that I'll consider a special case, because it doesn't fit neatly into any of the three previous categories. Marijuana can act as a depressant. In small dosages, its effects are similar to those of alcohol: decreased nervous system activity and depression of thought and action. In large doses, it can act as if it were a hallucinogen, producing hallucinations and alterations in mood.

Marijuana is produced from the hemp plant (Cannabis sativa), which was the source of most of the rope manufactured for sailing ships in the 18th century. It was an important crop in the American colonies, grown by George Washington, among other notables. As a source of raw materials for twine and rope, the plants were farmed in great numbers throughout the midwest during World War II. A hardy plant, many of the remnants of those cannabis farms of the early 1940s can still be found in Illinois and Indiana, where every summer adventurers come in search of another profitable—albeit illegal—harvest. More marijuana is grown in the United States than anywhere else in the world. Use of the drug is not uncommon, with estimates of Americans who have tried marijuana ranging from 40 to 60 million; as many as 3 to 6 million use the drug daily (Mirin et al., 1991).

The active ingredient in marijuana is the chemical tetrahydrocannabinol, or THC. Although marijuana, in large doses, has been found to increase overall levels of some neurotransmitters, it is not known just how it produces this effect. There do not seem to be any specific receptor sites at synapses for THC; at least, none have been found yet.

Marijuana is a difficult drug for society to deal with. In the United States, it is illegal to possess, use, or sell the drug, yet in some circumstances it can be prescribed to reduce the nausea associated with chemotherapy treatments for cancer. There is evidence that marijuana tolerance develops rapidly, but little evidence that by itself it is addictive. Is marijuana dangerous? Certainly, if for no other reason than that smoking is a danger. Smoking marijuana is more dangerous than cigarette smoking in terms of causing cancers, lung diseases, and respiratory problems. It is also dangerous in the sense that alcohol is dangerous: Continued use leads to impaired judgment, slowed reflexes, unrealistic moods, poor physical coordination, and hallucinations (Bennett, 1982; Weil et al., 1968).

The most debatable aspect of marijuana use involves the results of moderate to heavy long-term use. Long-term marijuana use has genetic implications (producing chromosomal abnormalities in nonhumans). It can adversely affect the body's immune system and white blood cells. It is partially responsible for lowering the sperm count of male users, and it can impair memory function, affecting memories of recent events in particular. Marijuana has predictably negative effects when taken during pregnancy, resulting in smaller babies, increased numbers of miscarriages, and other problems (Bloodworth, 1987; Doweiko, 1993; Grinspoon, 1977; Julien, 1985). An issue of great concern is the considerable variability in the potency and the quality, or purity, of marijuana available on the street today.

● **Before You Go On**

What is the active ingredient in marijuana, and what effects does it produce?

THINKING CRITICALLY ABOUT PERCEPTION AND CONSCIOUSNESS

1. How many different stimuli can you attend to at the same time? How many different stimuli can you attend to within a 10-second interval? What factors influence your answers to these questions?

2. If what we select to perceive (attend to) and how we organize what we perceive are influenced by so many factors over and above the stimuli themselves (factors such as motivation, mental set, and past experience, for example), why do we place so much weight on the value of eyewitness testimony in our court system?

3. To what extent (and how) does one's native language influence the way in which he or she perceives the world? Eskimos, for example, are said to have over forty different words for what we simply call "snow." Do you think Eskimos perceive snow differently from the way we do? To what extent and in what ways is one's perception of the world a reflection of one's culture?

4. List some of the things that might lead two different people to give totally different accounts of the same accident scene.

5. In Chapter 1, I made the point that "Things are not always as they seem." If things are not always as they seem, who or what are we to believe?

6. Can we determine why people dream what they dream? If so, how?

7. Different organisms have different sleep-wake cycles. (That is, within one day's time, people tend to sleep for about 8 hours and be awake for about 16 hours. Such is not the case for other animals. Rabbits and sheep, for example, sleep only for a few hours, while lions sleep much

longer than humans do.) What could account for the differences in sleep-wake cycles among different species?

8. Once people realize that drugs are no good for them, or could even kill them, why don't they just stop using them?

SUMMARY

T O P I C 5 A
PERCEPTION

● What stimulus factors determine the selection of perceptions?

Of all the information that stimulates our receptors, only a small portion is attended to or selected for further processing. One set of factors that affects which stimuli will be attended to concerns the characteristics of the stimuli themselves. We are more likely to attend to a stimulus if it *contrasts* with others around it (where contrast may be in terms of size, intensity, motion, or any other physical characteristic). Up to a point, the simple *repetition* of a stimulus also increases the likelihood that it will be attended to. *Pages 162–163.*

● What personal factors are involved in perceptual selectivity?

The selection of stimuli is partly based on characteristics of the perceiver. Relevant characteristics include such matters as motivation, expectation (mental set), and past experience. *Pages 163–165.*

● List stimulus and personal factors that determine how we organize stimuli in perception.

Perceptual organization depends in part on the characteristics of available stimuli, such as proximity, similarity, continuity, common fate, and closure. The personal factors that affect perceptual organization are the same as those that affect selection: motivation, mental set, and past experience. *Page 165–169.*

● Name and describe some of the cues that provide us with information about depth and distance.

We are able to perceive three-dimensionality and distance even though we sense the environment with a two-dimensional retina because of the many cues we are provided. Some have to do with the visual system itself and are called ocular cues, such as retinal disparity (each eye gets a different view of a three-dimensional object), convergence (when we look at something up close our eyes turn inward), and accommodation (our lenses change shape to focus images at different distances). Some cues come from the environment, including the physical cues of linear perspective (parallel lines appear to come together in the distance), interposition (near objects partially block our view of distant ones), relative size (everything else being equal, the smaller a stimulus, the farther away we judge it to be), texture gradients (details of texture can be seen clearly up close and gradually less clearly in the distance), patterns of light and shade, and motion parallax (as we move by stationary objects, those close to us seem to move past us more rapidly than do those objects in the distance). Even a process as basic as depth perception is subject to the influence of one's culture. *Pages 169–174.*

● Name and discuss four types of perceptual constancy.
● What do visual illusions teach us about the process of perception?

Perceptual constancy brings stability and order to our perceptual world. With size constancy, we perceive familiar objects as remaining the same size even when the size of their retinal images changes. Shape constancy refers to the stability of our perception of an object's shape regardless of the shape of its retinal image. With brightness and color constancy, we are able to perceive an object's true color or brightness regardless of the intensity or wavelength of the light actually reflected from it. Visual illusions and impossible figures demonstrate for us the difference between sensation and perception. Illusions give us a false impression (perception) of what is sensed at the receptor and really "there" in the environment. *Pages 174–177*

TOPIC 5B
CONSCIOUSNESS

● Define perception and consciousness. What, according to James, are the four major features of consciousness?

In processing information, perception is the cognitive process that intervenes between sensation and memory. *Perception* is the active process of selecting, organizing, and interpreting stimuli. Consciousness is more difficult to define. We say that *consciousness* is the awareness of the environment (which makes it related to perception) and the awareness of our own mental processes. According to William James, consciousness can be characterized as changing, personal, continuous, and selective. *Pages 178–179.*

● What are the three levels of consciousness proposed by Freud? How may we characterize the unconscious processing of information?

Sigmund Freud proposed that consciousness occurs at three levels. (1) That which is in your *conscious* mind is information of which you are aware, and is readily available. (2) Below the conscious level is the *preconscious*, memories, desires, feelings, ideas, and the like that are not immediately known to you but that can be brought to your awareness with relatively little effort. (3) Most of the contents of our minds, Freud said, are at an *unconscious* level. Feelings, information, and desires are stored there because becoming aware of these matters might lead to feelings of anxiety and distress. The contents of the unconscious may appear in humor, slips of the tongue, or our dreams, but can be purposively retrieved only with great effort. The idea of unconscious processing of information has recently returned to mainstream psychology. Unconscious processing occurs when information is stored without one's awareness of it. Current evidence suggests that such processing does occur, but that it is not very sophisticated processing, and that it need not be tied to any feelings of anxiety. *Pages 179–181*

● What are the EEG and the EMG? Briefly describe the four stages of sleep.

The EEG (electroencephalograph) is an instrument that measures the overall pattern of electrical activity in the brain and is the most common indicator of the stages of sleep. The EMG (electromyograph) measures muscle tension and is also used to indicate sleep. In addition to a state of relaxed wakefulness, characterized by EEG alpha waves, there are four stages of sleep: (1) light sleep with low-amplitude, slow theta waves; (2) sleep showing low-amplitude EEG waves with sleep spindles present; (3) a level where delta waves enter the EEG pattern; and (4) deep sleep, with more than 50 percent delta wave activity. *Pages 181–183.*

● What are REM and NREM sleep? What occurs during REM sleep?

REM sleep is rapid eye movement sleep, and it occurs four to seven times per night. NREM means sleep without rapid eye movements. Several events occur during REM sleep, most noticeably vivid, storylike dreams. During REM sleep we find loss of muscle tone (atonia), excitement of sexual organs, rapid breathing, and increased heart rate and blood pressure. NREM sleep is accompanied by little dream activity. *Pages 183–186.*

● What is hypnosis, and who can be hypnotized?

Hypnosis is an altered state of consciousness one enters voluntarily. It is characterized by an increase in suggestibility, a strict focusing of attention, an exaggeration of imagination, a reduction of spontaneous activity, and an unquestioning acceptance of distortions of reality. Not everyone can be hypnotized. Those who can be most readily hypnotized are persons who easily engage in fantasy and daydreaming and who show signs of suggestibility and a willingness to cooperate with the hypnotist. *Page 186–188.*

● What are stimulant drugs, and what are their effects?

Stimulants are psychoactive drugs such as caffeine, nicotine, cocaine, and amphetamines. Their basic effect is to increase the level of nervous system activity and to elevate mood, almost always by affecting the activity of the neural synapse, (usually) increasing levels of norepinephrine and dopamine. With heavy use, tolerance may develop, as may dependence and addiction. *Pages 188–191.*

● What are depressant drugs, and what are their effects?

The depressants include drugs such as alcohol, heroin, and many synthetic barbiturates. Depressants slow nervous system activity, reduce the awareness of external stimuli, and in small doses may alleviate feelings of nervousness or anxiety. In large doses, however, they produce sedation, sleep, coma, or death. Tolerance, dependence, or addiction may result from the use of these. The use of all psychoactive drugs—perhaps alcohol more than most, is sensitive to the pressures of one's society or culture. *Pages 191–193.*

● What are hallucinogenic drugs, and what are their effects?

Hallucinogens are drugs that alter mood and perception; LSD is an example. They get their name from their ability to induce hallucinations. *Pages 193–194.*

● What is the active ingredient in marijuana, and what effects does it produce?

The active ingredient in marijuana is the chemical compound THC. Listing its short- and long-term effects is difficult because of contradictory evidence. It is at least as dangerous as smoking cigarettes, and it is illegal. Of more concern is long-term, heavy use. Here marijuana use has many of the negative effects that we associate with long-term alcohol use: impaired judgment and reflexes, unrealistic moods, and poor coordination. Marijuana may have adverse effects on the body's immune system and has been implicated in a range of negative consequences when taken during pregnancy. *Pages 194–195.*

TOPIC 5A
PERCEPTION

5.1 Perception is a process that comes between _____ and _____. a) learning; memory b) sensation; memory c) memory; consciousness d) awareness; consciousness. *Pages 162–165.*

5.2 In the history of psychology, the psychologists most concerned with perception were the a) Gestalt psychologists. b) behaviorists. c) humanists. d) functionalists. *Pages 165–169.*

5.3 Of the following, it is most reasonable to classify perception as a _____ process. a) motivational b) learned c) cognitive d) sensory. *Pages 162–165.*

5.4 Of these factors that determine attention, which is most general in that it may include each of the others? a) size b) contrast c) motion d) intensity. *Pages 162–165.*

5.5 True or False? Perception is such a fundamental process that it is independent of—or not influenced by—"higher" processes, such as memory or motivation. *Pages 162–165.*

5.6 If you and I were standing next to each other at a party and someone behind us mentioned my name, I might turn around and attend to what was going on, while you might not even realize that my name had been mentioned. This would demonstrate the role of _____ in perceptual attention. a) repetition b) mental set c) contrast d) past experience. *Pages 162–165.*

5.7 When we say that someone is likely to perceive something that they *expect* to perceive, we are saying that a) figures and grounds are often confused. b) some stimuli are innately more attention-grabbing than others. c) motivational states often direct our attention. d) we can form a mental set that influences our attention. *Pages 165–169.*

5.8 We tend to hear the individual speech sounds of a word as organized together and separate from the sounds of other words largely because of the Gestalt organizational principle of a) proximity. b) novelty. c) continuity. d) similarity. *Pages 165–169.*

5.9 The appearance of subjective contours can be seen as a special case of the Gestalt principle of a) proximity. b) similarity. c) common fate. d) closure. *Pages 165–169.*

5.10 True or False? Common fate is an organizational principle that applies to objects in motion. *Pages 169–174.*

5.11 What makes our perception of the world as being three-dimensional remarkable is that a) it is a skill or ability found only in humans. b) it is a perception that has no particular survival value. c) images of the world are inverted by the lens of the eye to appear upside down. d) the retina records visual experiences in only two dimensions. *Pages 169–174.*

5.12 Which of the following cues to depth or distance is referred to as *binocular*? a) accommodation b) motion parallax c) linear perspective d) retinal disparity. *Pages 169–174.*

5.13 The physical cue to distance in which objects in the foreground partially cover or hide more distant objects, is called a) perspective. b) interposition. c) texture gradient. d) relative size. *Pages 169–174.*

5.14 True or False? Motion parallax is an example of a common illusion of motion—seeing motion where there is none to be perceived. *Pages 169–174.*

5.15 True or False? Depth perception is such a basic perceptual phenomenon that it is totally resistant to common pressures such as learning, experience, or culture. *Pages 169–174.*

5.16 Visual illusions a) involve the perception of objects or events that are not really there in the physical world, but are imagined. b) no longer have an effect once you know that you are dealing with an illusion. c) are not noticed if they are flashed before the eyes too quickly for the subject to scan the image. d) provide examples of perceptual experiences that are at odds with, or different from, physical reality. *Pages 174–177.*

TOPIC 5 B
CONCIOUSNESS

5.17 Which psychologist was *most* interested in matters relating to consciousness? a) B. F. Skinner b) William James c) John B. Watson d) Max Wertheimer. *Pages 178–179.*

5.18 James claimed that consciousness has four characteristics. Which of the following was *not* one of these? Consciousness is always a) selective. b) stable. c) continuous. d) personal. *Pages 178–179.*

5.19 To enter an altered state of consciousness a) is to change one's perception of one's self and the environment. b) is to have strange or bizarre experiences. c) is something that one cannot do voluntarily or on purpose. d) requires that the individual remain awake and aware. *Pages 179–181.*

5.20 According to Freud, the level of consciousness from which it is most difficult to retrieve information is a) one's preconscious. b) one's short-term memory. c) one's unconscious. d) one's long-term memory. *Pages 179–181.*

5.21 True or False? Although Freud had a lot to say about the notion of unconscious processing of information, today's psychologists have essentially abandoned the idea as untestable. *Pages 179–181.*

5.22 Delta waves are most common and most evident in an EEG record when a subject is a) relaxed, but not quite asleep. b) in the middle of a dream. c) thinking about something, perhaps a problem. d) in the deepest stage of sleep. *Pages 181–183.*

5.23 True or False? The most reliable indicator of sleep is one's self-report that he or she slept. *Pages 181–183.*

5.24 We know that by definition your eyes move when you are in REM sleep. What happens to your EEG record? a) It shows that your muscles are tense and immobile. b) It appears that you might be awake. c) It is filled with cyclical alpha wave patterns. d) It shows a preponderance of delta waves. *Pages 183–186.*

5.25 Which of the following is most likely to occur during REM sleep? a) Your muscles will become totally relaxed. b) You will be dreaming about some sexual fantasy. c) You will wake up as soon as the REM period is over. d) Your heart rate and blood pressure will decrease significantly. *Pages 183–186.*

5.26 With regard to hypnosis, which statement is most clearly *true*? a) There is no good way to predict who can be hypnotized. b) Under hypnosis anybody can be made to do anything. c) Hypnosis can ease the experience of real physical pain. d) When under hypnosis, a person has no idea what he or she is doing. *Pages 186–188.*

5.27 True or False? Hypnosis can help us remember details of traumatic or anxiety-producing events. *Pages 186–188.*

5.28 All drugs that alter one's state of consciousness are known as a) psychoactive. b) hallucinogenic. c) illicit (or illegal). d) uppers or downers. *Pages 188–195.*

5.29 What one word best differentiates drug abuse from drug use? a) legality b) maladaptive c) psychological d) amount. *Pages 188–195.*

5.30 Worldwide, the most common chemical stimulant is a) heroin. b) nicotine. c) alcohol. d) caffeine. *Pages 188–195.*

5.31 True or False? Stimulants, depressants, and hallucinogens influence cognition, but do not influence affects or behavior. *Pages 188–195.*

5.32 True or false? Alcohol, taken in the proper dosage, is a stimulant to thinking. *Pages 188–195.*

LEARNING

6

PREVIEW

TOPIC 6A—Classical Conditioning

What is Learning?

Pavlov and a Classic Demonstration

Classical Conditioning Phenomena

The Significance of Classical Conditioning

PSYCHOLOGY IN THE REAL WORLD: Treating Fear with Classical Conditioning

Rethinking What Really Happens in Classical Conditioning

TOPIC 6B—Operant Conditioning

The Basics of Operant Conditioning

Reinforcement

Punishment

Generalization and Discrimination

TOPIC 6C—Cognitive Approaches to Learning

Latent Learning and Cognitive Maps

Social Learning and Modeling

THINKING CRITICALLY ABOUT LEARNING

SUMMARY

TEST YOURSELF

201

PREVIEW

Directly or indirectly, learning has an impact on every aspect of our being. Learning affects how we perceive the world, how we interact with it as we grow and develop, how we form social relationships, and how we change during the course of psychotherapy. The human organism is poorly suited to survive in the world without learning. If we are to survive, much less prosper, we must profit from our experiences.

In this chapter, we'll begin Topic 6A by defining "learning". Then, we'll focus on a simple form of learning: classical conditioning. At first, most of our descriptions of classical conditioning will be based on Ivan Pavlov's work with salivating dogs. Once we have the basic principles in hand, we'll consider why classical conditioning is so important to all of us, and how the procedures of classical conditioning can be applied regularly in our daily lives. We'll also review how contemporary psychologists view classical conditioning, discovering that some of Pavlov's original assumptions may not have been correct.

In Topic 6B, we'll concentrate on operant conditioning. The basic premise of operant conditioning is that our behaviors are influenced by the consequences they produce. Learning is a matter of increasing the rate of responses that produce desirable consequences and decreasing responses that lead to undesirable consequences. In this Topic, we will discuss the nature of reinforcement and punishment.

We'll end the chapter with a short Topic that focuses on the role of the learner. Whereas both classical and operant conditioning emphasize observable stimuli and responses, what we call the "cognitive approaches" to learning tend to emphasize the mental processes (cognitions) of the organism involved in the learning task. Much of your own learning as a student can be thought of in this way.

T O P I C   6 A

CLASSICAL CONDITIONING

WHAT IS LEARNING?

We say that **learning** is demonstrated by a relatively permanent change in behavior that occurs as the result of practice or experience. This is a rather standard definition, and it raises a few important points that we should explore.

When we say that learning is *demonstrated* by changes in behavior, we are saying that learning (like many other psychological processes) cannot be observed directly. In a literal sense, there is no way that I can directly observe or measure what you have learned. All I can measure is your performance or behavior. To determine if you have learned something, I have to ask you to perform and then make inferences about your learning on the basis of your performance. Sometimes I may be wrong.

For example, you may learn everything there is to know about the psychology of learning for your next exam. But just days before the exam, someone you care about becomes seriously ill. As a result, you don't get much sleep. With your resistance weakened, you develop a sinus infection and catch the flu. When you come to class to take your exam, you feel miserable, have a high fever, and can't concentrate. You fail the exam. Your instructor may infer (incorrectly in this case) that you haven't learned very much about learning. On the other hand, there may be a student in class who hasn't studied at all and has learned very little. But the exam is of the multiple-choice type, and she correctly guesses the answers to 90 percent of the questions. Now your instructor infers (incorrectly again) that this student has learned a great deal.

Another way to make this point is to say that what is learned is a *potential*, or predisposition, to respond. Because what is learned is simply potential, we will not recognize that learning has taken place until that potential is realized in behavior.

Learned changes in behavior are characterized as *relatively permanent*. This means that they are not fleeting, short-lived, or cyclical changes, such as those due to fatigue or temporary shifts in motivation. Imagine, for example, the change in typing behavior that occurs—even for a skilled typist—between 8 AM and 10 AM on any given morning. There is likely to be an improvement in typing behavior that we really ought not attribute to learning, but to what is called *warm-up*. That skilled typist may not type quite so well toward the end of the day either—a change in behavior we might better attribute to *fatigue* than to forgetting. These are important changes in behavior, but they are not due to learning. Learned changes are relatively permanent.

We have another phrase in our definition to remind us that there are yet other, occasionally important, changes in behavior that do not result from learning. By definition we say that learned changes in behavior result from *practice* or *experience*. For one thing, this phrase reminds us that some changes may be due to maturation (i.e., heredity). That birds fly, that salamanders swim, or that humans walk has more to do with genes and physical development than with learning. This phrase also serves to remind us that

learning
demonstration of a relatively permanent change in behavior that occurs as the result of practice or experience

some changes in our behaviors are due to automatic physiological reactions, such as sensory adaptation. When we enter a darkened theater, we don't "learn" to see in the dark. Our vision improves and our behaviors change as our eyes adapt to the lighting—an unlearned reaction requiring neither practice nor experience.

One final point about learning: As students, parents, and teachers, we often fall into the habit of thinking that learning is necessarily a good thing. Clearly, it isn't. We learn bad, ineffective habits as readily as we learn good, adaptive ones. For example, no one I know ever claimed to enjoy the first cigarette that he or she smoked, yet many people have learned the habit, which is hardly an adaptive one. Learning is reflected in a change in behavior, be it for better or for worse.

If we put these ideas together, we come up with our definition: Learning is demonstrated by (or inferred from) a relatively permanent change in behavior that occurs as the result of practice or experience. We begin our discussion of learning by considering two varieties of learning called *conditioning*. Although conditioning and learning are not technically synonymous terms, they can be used interchangeably. We will follow common usage here and agree to call the most fundamental types of learning conditioning.

● **Before You Go On**
How do we define learning?

PAVLOV AND A CLASSIC DEMONSTRATION

When we think about learning, we generally think about such activities as memorizing the kings and queens of England, studying for an exam, or learning to *do* things, like ice skate. But our study of learning begins in the laboratory of a Russian physiologist who taught dogs to drool in response to tones.

Psychology was just beginning to emerge as a science late in the nineteenth century. At that time, Ivan Pavlov, a Russian physiologist, was studying the processes of digestion—work for which he would be awarded the Nobel Prize in 1904. Pavlov focused on the salivary reflex. He knew that he could get his dogs to salivate by forcing food powder into their mouths. A **reflex** is an unlearned, automatic response that occurs in the presence of a specific stimulus. Every time Pavlov presented his dogs with food, they salivated.

Pavlov earned his reputation in psychology by pursuing something not quite as simple as reflexive responses. He noticed that his dogs would occasionally salivate *before* the food powder was put in their mouths. They would salivate at the very sight of the food or even at the sight of the laboratory assistant who delivered the food. With this observation, Pavlov went off on a tangent that he pursued for the rest of his life (Pavlov, 1927; 1928). We call the phenomenon he studied **classical conditioning**—learning in which an originally neutral stimulus comes to elicit a response after having been associated with another stimulus that reflexively elicits that response. In the abstract, that may not make much sense, but as we go through the process step by step, I think you'll appreciate that the process is simple and straightforward.

To demonstrate classical conditioning, we first need a stimulus that consistently produces a predictable response. The relationship between

reflex
an unlearned automatic response that occurs in the presence of specific stimuli

classical conditioning
learning in which an originally neutral stimulus comes to elicit a new response after having been paired with a stimulus that reflexively elicits that same response

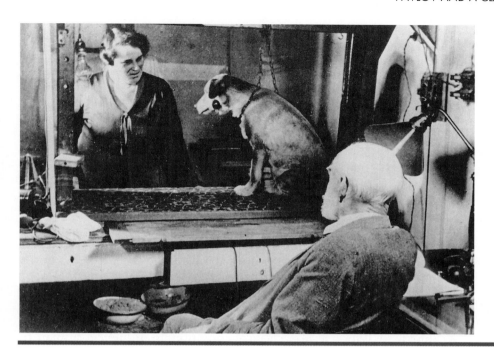

Ivan Pavlov (seated) watches a dog in one of his laboratory's testing chambers.

this stimulus and the response it elicits is usually an unlearned, reflexive one. Here is where Pavlov's food powder comes in. When the food powder is presented, the salivation reliably follows. There is no learning involved here, so this is an **unconditioned stimulus (UCS)** and the response that it elicits is an **unconditioned response (UCR)**. So we have a UCS (food powder) producing a UCR (salivation).

To get classical conditioning under way, we need a *neutral stimulus* that elicits a minimal response or a response of no interest. For this neutral stimulus, Pavlov chose a tone produced by a tuning fork.

At first, when a tone is sounded, a dog *will* respond. Among other things, it will perk up its ears and try to orient toward the source of the sound. We call this response an **orienting reflex**—a simple, unlearned response of attending to a new or unusual stimulus. After a while, however, the dog will get used to the tone and will ignore it. Technically, we call this process **habituation**—a simple form of learning in which an organism comes to ignore a stimulus of no consequence. Essentially, the dog learns to not orient toward the tone.

Now we are ready to go. We have two stimuli: (1) a tone (the neutral stimulus), which produces a minimal response, and (2) the food powder (the UCS), which reliably produces salivation (the UCR).

Once we get our stimuli and responses straight, the rest is easy. The two stimuli are paired. That is, they are presented at about the same time—the tone first, then the food powder. Salivation then occurs as a reflexive response to the food powder. We have a neutral stimulus, then a UCS, followed by a UCR.

Each pairing of the two stimuli constitutes a conditioning *trial*. If we repeat this procedure several times (for several trials) conditioning, or learning, takes place. We find a relatively permanent change in behavior as a result of this experience. After a number of trials, when we present the tone by itself, the dog salivates, something it did not do before. The dog now salivates not just in response to the food powder, but also in response

unconditioned stimulus (UCS)
in classical conditioning, a stimulus (e.g., food powder) that reflexively and reliably evokes a response (the UCR)

unconditioned response (UCR)
in classical conditioning, a response (e.g., salivation) reliably and reflexively evoked by a stimulus (the UCS)

orienting reflex
the simple, unlearned response of orienting toward, or attending to, a new or unusual stimulus

habituation
in classical conditioning, a simple form of learning in which an organism comes to ignore a stimulus of no consequence

conditioned stimulus (CS)
in classical conditioning, an originally neutral stimulus (e.g., a tone) that, when paired with a UCS, comes to evoke a new response (a CR)

conditioned response (CR)
in classical conditioning, the learned response (e.g., salivation) evoked by the CS after conditioning

to the tone. Clearly, the tone is no longer "neutral." Now it produces a response, so we now call the tone a **conditioned stimulus (CS)**. To keep the salivation response that it elicits separate from the salivation we get in response to the food powder, we call it a **conditioned response (CR)**, indicating that it has been conditioned, or learned.

Let's review this again: (1) We start with two stimuli—the neutral stimulus, which elicits no response, and the UCS, which elicits the UCR. (2) We repeatedly present the two stimuli together. (3) Finally, when we present the CS alone, it now elicits a CR.

Notice that the same stimulus—for example, a tone—can be a neutral stimulus (before learning occurs), or a conditioned stimulus (when it elicits a learned response). Similarly, the same type of response—salivation, for instance—can be an unconditioned response (if it is elicited without learning) or a conditioned response (if it is elicited as the result of learning).

If you have a pet at home, you've no doubt seen this process in action. If you keep your pet's food in the same cabinet all the time, you may note a range of excited, anticipatory behaviors by your pet every time you open that cabinet door. The open door (CS) has been repeatedly paired with the food within it (UCS), now producing the same sort of reaction (CR) that was originally reserved only for the food (UCR).

Shortly we'll look at how classical conditioning influences human reactions, but before we go on, let me make it clear that classical conditioning is not something that only occurs in dogs and cats. You demonstrate a classically conditioned salivation response (particularly when you're hungry) when you see pictures or smell the aromas of your favorite foods. If you respond with anxiety at the sight of an instructor coming into the classroom with a stack of exam papers, you are demonstrating a classically conditioned response.

There are two technical points I need to make. They remind us that even basic, fundamental psychological processes are not as simple as they first appear. First, the CR seldom reaches the strength of the UCR no matter how many times the CS and the UCS are paired. For example, in salivation conditioning, we rarely get as much saliva in response to the tone (salivation as a CR) as we originally got in response to the food powder (salivation as a UCR). Second, *how* the CS and the UCS are paired does matter. There are many ways in which two stimuli can be presented at about the same time (e.g., simultaneously, or UCS then CS, or CS then UCS). Only one method works best: The CS first, followed shortly (within a second or so) by the UCS—or, tone-food-salivation. (I tell my classes that classical conditioning is basically a matter of "ding-food-slobber.")

● **Before You Go On**
Summarize the essential procedures involved in classical conditioning.

CLASSICAL CONDITIONING PHENOMENA

Now that we've covered the basics of classical conditioning, we can consider some of the details that go along with it. We'll first go through the steps involved in an actual classical conditioning procedure. Just to keep

FIGURE 6.1

The stages of conditioning. (1) Acquisition is produced by the repeated pairing of a CS and a UCS. The strength of the CR increases rapidly at first, then slows, eventually leveling off. (2) Extinction is produced by presenting the CS without pairing it with the UCS. The strength of the CR then decreases. (3) After a rest interval (and following extinction), spontaneous recovery is demonstrated by a partial return of the CR.

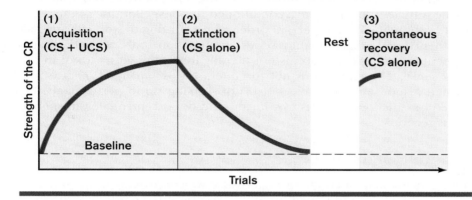

terminology firmly in mind, I'll continue to refer to the original Pavlovian example of salivating dogs.

Acquisition

The stage of classical conditioning during which the strength of the CR increases—the stage in which a dog acquires the conditioned response of salivating to a tone—is called **acquisition**. When conditioning begins, the neutral stimulus (NS) does not produce a conditioned response (CR), which is why the conditioned stimulus (CS) is referred to as a neutral stimulus at this point. After a few pairings of the CS and UCS together (conditioning trials), we can demonstrate the presence of a CR. To test for that, of course, we'll have to present the conditioned stimulus (CS) by itself. Now we find that there is some saliva produced in response to the tone presented alone. The more trials of the CS and UCS together, the more the dog will salivate in response to the tone presented alone. The increase in CR strength is rather rapid at first, but soon slows and eventually levels off. The first part of Figure 6.1 illustrates acquisition in classical conditioning.

acquisition
the process in classical conditioning by which the strength of the CR increases with repeated pairings of the CS and UCS

Extinction and Spontaneous Recovery

Assume that we now have a well-conditioned dog producing a good deal of saliva at the sound of a tone. Continuing to present the CS-UCS pair adds little to the amount of saliva we get when we present the tone alone. Suppose that we now go through a series of trials during which the CS (the tone) is presented but is *not* paired with the UCS (no more food powder). The result of this procedure is that the CR will weaken. As we continue to present the tone alone, the dog provides less and less saliva. If we keep it up, the dog will eventually stop salivating to the tone. This process is called **extinction**, and we say that the CR has extinguished.

extinction
the process in classical conditioning by which the strength of the CR decreases with repeated presentations of the CS alone (without the UCS)

It would appear that we are right back where we started. Because the CR has extinguished, our dog does nothing when we present the tone—at least it no longer salivates. Let's give our dog a rest in the kennel. Later, when the dog is returned to the laboratory and the tone is sounded, the dog salivates again! Not a lot, perhaps, but the salivation does return. Since it recovers automatically, or spontaneously, we call this phenomenon **spontaneous recovery**. Extinction and spontaneous recovery are also illustrated in Figure 6.1.

Spontaneous recovery takes place after extinction and following a rest interval, which indicates two things: First, one series of extinction trials may not be sufficient to eliminate a conditioned response. Because of the possibility of spontaneous recovery, in order to get our dog to stop salivating altogether, we may have to run a series of extinction trials. Second, what is happening during extinction is not literally forgetting, at least not in the usual sense. The response is not forgotten, but is *suppressed*. That is, the learned response is still there but is not showing up in performance because of extinction, which is why it can (and does) return later, in spontaneous recovery.

Generalization and Discrimination

During the course of conditioning, assume we consistently use a tone of a given pitch as the conditioned stimulus. After repeated pairings of this tone with food powder, a dog now salivates when that tone is presented alone.

What will happen if we present a different tone, one that the dog has not heard before? The dog will salivate in response to it also. The response won't be as strong as the original CR (there may not be as much saliva). How strong depends on how similar the new tone is to the original CS. The closer it is to the original, the more saliva will be produced. This process is called **generalization**, and we say that a conditioned response will generalize to other new, yet similar stimuli.

This is a powerful process. It means that an unconditioned stimulus need not be paired with all possible conditioned stimuli. If you choose an average, or midrange, CS, the conditioned response will automatically generalize to other similar stimuli. A graph of this process is shown in Figure 6.2.

Imagine that a young boy is bitten by a large black Labrador retriever. Originally, this dog was a neutral stimulus, but having been associated with the pain of a bite the dog (a CS) is now feared (a CR) by the boy. Is it not predictable that the boy's conditioned fear will generalize to other large, black dogs—and, to a lesser extent, to small gray ones?

So if a dog is conditioned to salivate to a tone of middle pitch, it will also salivate to higher and lower tones through generalization. What if we do not want it to? What if we want our dog to salivate to the CS alone and not to other tones? We would use a process called discrimination training, in which an organism learns to make a CR in response to only one CS, but not to others. In a sense, discrimination is the opposite of generalization. To demonstrate **discrimination** training, we would present a dog with many tones, and would pair the UCS food powder with only one of them—the CS we want the dog to salivate to. We might, for example, pair the food powder with a tone of middle *C*. A lower tone, say *A*, would also be presented to the dog, but *would not* be followed by food powder. At first, there probably would be some saliva produced in response to the *A* tone (generalization). Eventually, however, our subject would learn to discriminate and would no longer salivate to the *A* tone.

spontaneous recovery
the phenomenon in classical conditioning in which a previously extinquished CR returns after a rest interval

generalization
the phenomenon in classical conditioning in which a CR is elicited by stimuli different from, but similar to, the CS

discrimination
the process in classical conditioning in which one CS is paired with the UCS and other stimuli are not

FIGURE 6.2
Generalization. Presenting stimuli other than the CS may produce a CR. How much CR is produced depends on the similarity between the new stimulus and the original CS.

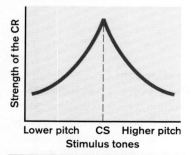

Strength of the CR

Lower pitch　CS　Higher pitch
Stimulus tones

Young children who have pleasant experiences with dogs probably will, when older, have pleasant thoughts and feelings about dogs.

● **Before You Go On**

In classical conditioning, what are acquisition, extinction, and spontaneous recovery?

What are generalization and discrimination?

THE SIGNIFICANCE OF CLASSICAL CONDITIONING

It is time to leave our discussion of dogs, tones, salivation, and Pavlov's lab. We need to turn our attention to the practical application of all of this. Once we start to look, we can find examples of classically conditioned human behaviors everywhere.

Conditioned Emotional Responses

One of the most significant aspects of classical conditioning is its role in the acquisition of emotional responses to stimuli in our environment. There are very few stimuli that naturally, or instinctively, elicit emotional responses. Yet think of all those things that *do* directly influence how we feel.

For example, very young children seldom seem afraid of spiders, plane rides, or snakes. Some children actually seem to enjoy them. Now consider how many people you know who *are* afraid of plane rides, spiders and snakes. There are many stimuli in our environments that cause us to be afraid. There also are stimuli that produce within us feelings of pleasure, calm, and ease. What scares you? What makes you feel at ease and relaxed? Why? Might you feel particularly upset or distressed in a certain store because you once had an unpleasant experience there? Might you happily anticipate a vacation at the beach because of a very enjoyable vacation you had there as a child? Do you shudder at the sight of a police car or a pile of exam papers? Do you smile at the thought of a payroll envelope? In each of these cases, we are talking about classical conditioning. (To be fair, I must say that not all our learned emotional reactions are acquired through classical conditioning alone. As we shall see, there are other possibilities.)

When I was a senior in high school, I had surgery on my nose. (A not-very-well-coordinated basketball player, I had broken it several times.) I won't bore you with all the gory details. Suffice it to say that the surgery was done under local anesthetic, and was painful and unpleasant. For nearly twenty years after that surgery whenever I visited a hospital I got a slight ache in my nose! Now, I knew better. I knew that the pain was just "in my head," but my nose hurt nonetheless. This is an example of some relatively permanent classical conditioning, isn't it? The CS of hospital sights, sounds, and odors was paired with the UCS of an operative procedure that caused a UCR of pain and discomfort. This pairing, which lasted for a few days, led to the establishment of a CR of discomfort associated with the CS of the hospital. Note too, that this conditioned response generalized to other hospitals, not just the one in which the surgery was performed, and the conditioned response took a very long time to extinguish.

Here's another example. I have before me two small boys, each 3 years old. I ask them to say quickly everything they think of when I say a word. I say "dog." Boy 1 smiles broadly and responds, "Oh, doggie; my doggie, Spot; my friend; good dog; go fetch; my dog; Spot." Boy 2 frowns and then says, "Oooo, dog; bite; bad dog; teeth; hurts me; bad dog." There's no doubt that both of these boys *know* what a dog is. How they feel about dogs, however, is quite another matter, and is probably a function of their experience with dogs—a classically conditioned reaction.

Advertising provides us with many examples of classical conditioning designed to change the way we feel about products or services. How many times have you seen TV ads showing healthy, good-looking young people having a great time—at the beach playing volleyball, riding bicycles down mountain trails, swinging on ropes over cool steams, and so on—while drinking large amounts of Brand X. All those attractive, "fun" stimuli are designed to make us "feel good." The intent of pairing "fun" stimuli (the UCS) with Brand X (the CS) is to have us acquire a "feel-good" response (CR) to the beverage being advertised. Yet another example is found in "Psychology in the Real World."

● Before You Go On

What sort of responses are most readily influenced by classical conditioning?

The Case of "Little Albert"

Let's take a detailed look at a famous example of the conditioning of an emotional response. In 1920, John Watson (yes, the founder of behaviorism) and his student assistant, Rosalie Rayner, published a summary article on experiments they performed with "Little Albert." Albert's experiences have become quite well known. Even though Watson and Rayner's report of their work tended to oversimplify matters (Samuelson, 1980), the story of Little Albert still provides a good model for the classical conditioning of emotional responses.

Eleven-month-old Albert was given many toys to play with. Among other things, he was allowed to play with a live white rat. Albert enjoyed the rat; at least he showed no signs of fearing it. Then conditioning began. One day, just as Albert reached for the rat, one of the experimenters (Rayner) made a sudden loud noise by striking a metal bar with a hammer. The loud noise was frightening—that much Watson and Rayner had established two

FIGURE 6.3

Conditioned fear in "Little Albert" as an example of classical conditioning.

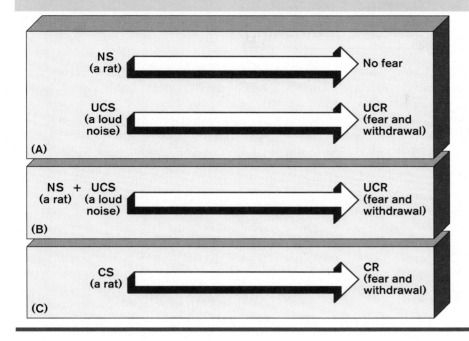

months earlier during initial observations of Albert in the laboratory. At least Albert made responses that Watson and Rayner felt indicated fear.

After repeated pairings of the rat and the loud noise, Albert's reaction to the rat underwent a relatively permanent change. Albert would at first reach out toward the rat, then he would recoil and cry, often trying to bury his head in his blanket. He was clearly making emotional responses to a stimulus that did not elicit those responses before it was paired with sudden loud noises. This sounds like classical conditioning: The rat is the CS, and the loud sudden noise is the UCS which elicits the UCR of fear. After repeated pairings of the rat and the noise (the CS and UCS), the rat elicits the same sort of fear response (or CR). Figure 6.3 presents a diagram of the procedures used to condition Little Albert to be afraid of a white rat.

Watson and Rayner then went on to demonstrate that Albert's fear of the white rat generalized to all sorts of other stimuli: a dog, a ball of cotton, and even a mask with a white beard and mustache. In some cases, however, Watson and Rayner did not test for generalization as they should have. They occasionally paired the loud noise with new stimuli before testing to see what the reaction might be (Harris, 1979).

Several issues have been raised concerning Watson and Rayner's research on learned fear—not the least of which is the unethical treatment of poor little Albert. It is unlikely that anyone would attempt such a project today. Watson had previously argued (1919) that emotional experiences of early childhood could affect an individual for a lifetime, yet here he was purposely frightening a young child (and without the advised consent of his mother). Although his acquired fears would have extinguished eventually, Albert's mother removed him from the hospital before Watson and Rayner had a chance to undo the conditioning. They were convinced that they could remove Albert's fear (by pairing the rat with pleasant stimuli) but as fate would have it, they never got the chance. Several researchers in

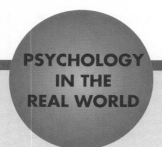
Treating Fear with Classical Conditioning

There are many things in this world that are life-threatening and downright frightening. Being afraid of certain stimuli is often a wise, rational, adaptive reaction. Occasionally, however, we find people who experience discomforting, distressing fears of stimuli that are not threatening in a real or rational sense.

Some people are intensely afraid of spiders, the dark, riding on elevators, being in small closed-in areas, or flying on airplanes. Psychologists say that these people are suffering from a *phobic disorder*—an intense, irrational fear of some object that leads a person to avoid contact with it. There are many possible explanations for how phobic disorders are formed, but one clear possibility is classical conditioning.

Sadly enough, phobic disorders are far from rare. Estimates place prevalence rates at between 7 and 20 percent of the population—that's tens of millions of people (Kessler et al., 1994; Marks, 1986; Robins et al., 1984). Phobic reactions seldom extinguish on their own. Why don't they? There are many reasons, but one is that someone with a phobia is usually successful at avoiding the conditioned stimulus that elicits the fear. Someone with a fear of flying may be able to manage simply by taking a bus or train or by driving.

Although there are a number of different techniques that can be used to treat phobic disorders (see Chapter 13), one of the most common is based on principles of Pavlovian classical conditioning. The procedure is called systematic desensitization, and was introduced by a psychoanalyst, Joseph Wolpe (1958, 1969, 1981). As an example, we'll consider a college student with an extreme fear of public speaking, now enrolled in a speech class.

In its standard form, there are three stages in systematic desensitization. First, the therapist instructs or trains the client to relax. There are many ways to go about such training. Some procedures use hypnosis, but most simply have the subject relax one foot, then both feet, then one leg, then both, and so on, until the whole body is relaxed. No matter what method is used, this stage generally doesn't take very long, and after a few hours of training, the client knows how to enter a relaxed state quickly.

The second step is to construct an "anxiety hierarchy"—a listing of stimuli that gradually decrease in their ability to elicit anxiety. The most feared stimulus is placed at the top of the list. Each item that follows elicits less and less fear until, at the bottom of the list, we place stimuli that elicit no fear at all (in our example, that might be "giving a formal speech to a large group," followed by "being called on in

the 1920s who tried to replicate Watson and Rayner's experiment, despite ethical considerations, were not terribly successful (Harris, 1979).

Even with these technical disclaimers, it is easy to see how the Little Albert project can be used as a model for the development of fear and other emotional responses. When they began, Albert did not respond fearfully to a rat, cotton, or a furry mask. After pairing a neutral stimulus (the rat) with an emotion-producing stimulus (the loud noise), Albert appeared afraid of all sorts of white, furry, fuzzy objects.

● **Before You Go On**
Briefly summarize the Little Albert demonstration.

RETHINKING WHAT REALLY HAPPENS IN CLASSICAL CONDITIONING

As you read about classical conditioning, you may very well get the idea that what we are describing here is only of historical interest. Most of our discus-

A phobic fear of heights, probably not a problem for this daring skier, may be a conditioned emotional response. It can be lessened with systematic desensitization.

class," "talking to a small group of strangers," "being introduced to two or more people," "talking with friends," and so on).

Now treatment is ready to begin. The student relaxes completely and thinks about the stimulus lowest on the anxiety hierarchy. The student is then instructed to think about the next highest stimulus, and the next, and so on, all the while remaining as relaxed as possible. As progress is made up the list toward the anxiety-producing stimuli at the top, the therapist constantly monitors the subject's level of tension-relaxation. When anxiety seems to overcome relaxation, the student is told to stop thinking about that item on the hierarchy and to think about an item lower on the list.

Systematic desensitization is more than the simple extinction of a previously conditioned fear response. The process is sometimes called *countercondi-tioning.* A new response (relaxation) is acquired to "replace" an old one (fear). A person cannot be relaxed and fearful at the same time—these responses are incompatible. So if I pair a stimulus (the CS) with the feeling of being relaxed (the UCS), through classical conditioning it will come to produce a reaction of calm (a new CR), not the incompatible response of fear and tension (the old CR). For many people, this technique can be effective (e.g., Wilson, 1982). It works best for those anxieties or fears that are associated with easily identifiable, specific environmental stimuli; it works least well for a diffuse, generalized fear (for which hierarchies are difficult to generate).

When we get to Chapter 13, we'll see that there are several techniques of psychotherapy that, like systematic desensitization, are derived directly from the learning laboratory.

sion has dealt with procedures associated with Pavlov's laboratory at the turn of the century. In fact, classical conditioning continues to be a very active area of research in experimental psychology (Adler & Cohen, 1993; Domjan, 1987; Lavond et al., 1993; Rescorla 1987, 1988; Spear et al., 1990). Psychologists today are interested in understanding exactly what happens in classical conditioning and what factors influence the effectiveness of the procedure.

Pavlov believed, as did generations of psychologists who followed him, that *any* stimulus paired with an unconditioned stimulus could serve as a conditioned stimulus. It's easy to see how psychologists came to this conclusion. A wide variety of stimuli *can* be paired with food powder, and as a result come to elicit a salivation response.

We now see conditioning in a much broader light—as the learning about relationships that exist among events in the world. Conditioning is seen as an active search for sensible ways to represent the environment, a search for information that one stimulus gives about another.

Pavlovian conditioning is not a stupid process by which the organism willy-nilly forms associations between any two stimuli that happen to co-occur. Rather, the organism is better seen as an information seeker using logical and perceptual relations among events, along with its own preconceptions, to form a sophisticated representation of its world. (Rescorla, 1988, p. 154)

Can *Any* Stimulus Serve as a CS?

At least two lines of research suggest that one cannot present just any stimulus with an unconditioned stimulus and expect classical conditioning to result. One research program is associated with Robert Rescorla, the other with Leon Kamin.

A rat can be conditioned to fear the sound of a tone by our presenting that tone and consistently following it with a mild electric shock. Assume that we present another rat with a tone, occasionally following it with a mild shock. But for this rat, we *also* simply present the shock from time to time *without the preceding tone.* This rat will end up receiving several shocks without a preceding tone, but it will have as many tone-shock pairings as our first rat. Will this second rat demonstrate a conditioned response to the tone when the tone is presented alone? No, it won't. Although this rat experienced the same number of tone-shock pairings, there will be no conditioning (Rescorla, 1968, 1987). Before I explain this failure of conditioning, let's consider Kamin's research.

In a demonstration of a phenomenon called *blocking,* rats are shocked (UCS) at the same time a noise (CS) is presented. Classically conditioned fear of the noise is readily established. The rats are then given a number of trials in which the noise *and* a light are paired with the UCS of a shock. Although the light (now presented with the noise) is paired with the shock many times, no conditioned fear of the light is found. That is, when the light is now presented by itself, no fear reaction is detected. The light continues to act as a neutral stimulus. The rats had already learned that noise is a good predictor of shock; the light is redundant or unnecessary (Kamin, 1968, 1969).

In both of these cases and others (e.g., Miller & Spear, 1985; Pearce & Hall, 1980; Rescorla & Wagner, 1972), what matters most in determining whether or not a stimulus will act as a CS is the extent to which the stimulus *provides useful information* signaling that another stimulus will soon occur. In the basic Pavlovian demonstration, the tone (CS) was highly informative: Every time the tone was presented, food powder followed, so the tone served as an effective CS. In Rescorla's research, we see that if a tone does not predict the onset of shock (if some shocks occur without a tone), then that tone will not serve as a CS no matter how many times it is paired with the UCS. In Kamin's experiments, we see that because the rats had already learned that the noise predicted the shocks, adding a light as a CS provided no additional useful information and hence was ineffective.

If we can talk about rats representing their environment by learning about which stimuli signal other stimuli, isn't it reasonable to think about classical conditioning in humans in the same way? We may experience a pleasant, warm feeling when we see a picture of a beach because it is the beach that is best associated with our favorite vacation—not because of the fact that we happened to have left for that vacation on a Wednesday. Beaches predict good times; Wednesdays don't. Little Albert's fear generalized to many stimuli, but Albert developed no particular fear of blankets, even though he was sitting on a blanket every time Rayner created the loud noise that Albert did come to associate with the rat.

- **Before You Go On**

  Under what circumstances are stimuli likely to serve effectively as CSs?

Must the Time Interval Between the CS and the UCS Always Be Brief?

Pavlov recognized that the time interval between the presentation of the CS and the UCS was a critical variable in classical conditioning. For nearly fifty years it was assumed that the most appropriate interval between these two stimuli was a brief one—a few seconds at most (Beecroft, 1966; Gormezano, 1972). The claim found in most textbooks on learning was that the shorter the interval between the CS and UCS, the faster conditioning would be. It now appears that there is at least one excellent example of classical conditioning in which the CS-UCS interval may be much longer than a few seconds—it may be hours long. This example also reinforces the point that some stimuli make more effective conditioned stimuli than others. The example is found in the research on the formation of aversions (very strong dislikes) to tastes.

Many experiments have confirmed that both rats and people (and several other organisms) can be classically conditioned to avoid particular foods (Garcia et al., 1966; Gemberling & Domjan, 1982; Revulky & Garcia, 1970). In experiments using rats, subjects eat or drink a food that has been given a distinctive taste. Then they are given a poison or are treated with X rays so they will become nauseous. The feeling of nausea, however, does not occur until hours after the food has been eaten. (In a few days the rats are perfectly normal and healthy again.) Even though there is a long delay between the flavored food (CS) and the feelings of nausea (UCS), the rats learn to associate the two and avoid the food—often in just one trial. Similarly patients treated for cancer may experience nausea as an unpleasant side effect of chemotherapy. Such patients will often show a strong taste aversion for whatever they ate hours before treatment—even if what they ate was something pleasant, such as ice cream (Bernstein, 1978).

The time delay between the CS and the UCS here is obviously at odds with the standard belief that to be effective the two stimuli need to be presented together. Yet another difficulty is why the *taste* of previously eaten food should so commonly serve as the CS for nausea that occurs hours later. Why is the nausea associated with the taste of food rather than some other stimulus event that could be paired with it? Think of this happening to you. At a restaurant, you order a piece of pumpkin pie. Hours later you suffer severe stomach cramps and nausea. Why should you associate these reactions with the pie rather than with the type of chair you sat on, or the car you drove to the restaurant, or the person you sat with? It seems that we have a predisposition, or bias, rooted in our biology for associating some things with others (Mackintosh, 1975, 1983; Revulsky, 1985). Food followed by nausea is an excellent example of just such a predisposition.

- **Before You Go On**

  What do taste-aversion studies tell us about the relationship between the CS and the UCS in classical conditioning?

TOPIC 6B

OPERANT CONDITIONING

The basic premise of operant conditioning is that behaviors are influenced by the consequences they produce. Learning is a matter of increasing the rate of responses that produce positive consequences and decreasing the rate of responses that produce negative consequences. We'll begin this Topic as we often do by defining some of the terminology involved. Because reinforcement is such a crucial concept in operant conditioning, it is important that you have a clear understanding of the varieties and principles of reinforcement.

THE BASICS OF OPERANT CONDITIONING

B. F. Skinner did most of the early research on operant conditioning, although he did not discover or invent it in any literal sense. The techniques of operant conditioning had been applied for hundreds of years before Skinner was born. What Skinner did was to bring the process and procedures into the psychology laboratory. There he studied operant conditioning with a unique vigor, and helped the rest of us realize the significance of the process.

Defining the Process

operant conditioning
the form of learning that involves changing the rate of a response on the basis of the consequences that result from that response

Operant conditioning changes the probability or rate of responses on the basis of the consequences that result from those responses. Responses that are followed by reinforcers tend to increase in rate; those not followed by reinforcers tend to decrease in rate. We are not claiming that the future governs what happens in the present, but we are claiming that past experiences influence present ones. As Skinner put it, "behavior is shaped by its

Operant conditioning techniques were used to train this whale to give his human friend a ride.

consequences, but only by consequences that lie in the past. We do what we do because of what *has* happened, not what *will* happen" (Skinner, 1989, p. 14).

The first clear statement of the essentials of operant conditioning came not from Skinner, but from E. L. Thorndike, a psychologist at Columbia University early in the twentieth century who worked to discover all of the "laws of learning." Thorndike's **law of effect** says that responses are learned ("stamped in," in his words) when they are followed by a "satisfying state of affairs" (Thorndike, 1911, p. 245). When an organism makes a response and then experiences a satisfying state of affairs (a reinforcement), the organism will tend to make that response again. If a response is not followed by a satisfying state of affairs (reinforcement does not occur), the organism will tend not to make that response again. This seemingly simple observation is also a profound one, because it is true. Our behaviors *are* shaped by their consequences.

Examples are all around us. You don't need a special apparatus or a laboratory to see operant conditioning at work. Imagine a father rushing through a supermarket with his toddler seated in a shopping cart. The child is screaming at the top of his lungs for a candy bar—over and over, echoing throughout the store, "I wanna candy bar! I wanna candy bar!" Father is doing a good (and appropriate) job of ignoring this behavior until he spies a neighbor coming down the next aisle. The neighbor has her three children with her, and all three are acting like quiet, perfect angels. What's a parent to do? Dad races by the checkout lanes, grabs a candy bar, and gives it to his child. One does not have to be an expert in child psychology (or operant conditioning) to predict what will happen on the next visit to the store. Screaming "worked" this time, so it will be tried again. Reinforced behaviors tend to recur.

As we did with classical conditioning, we'll use examples from the laboratory to describe the procedures and phenomena of operant conditioning. You should have little difficulty finding examples in your own experience.

law of effect
(Thorndike's) the observation that responses that lead to "satisfying states of affairs" tend to be repeated, while those that do not are not

Demonstrating Operant Conditioning

To demonstrate operant conditioning in the controlled environment of the laboratory, Skinner built a special apparatus called an operant chamber.

Although Skinner never used the term, and said he didn't like it (Skinner, 1984), we often call this device a "Skinner box." Figure 6.4 shows a standard operant chamber. The chamber pictured here is designed for rats. The box is empty except for a small lever that protrudes from one wall and a small cup to hold a piece of rat food. Pellets of food are automatically dispensed through a tube into the food cup. Pellets are released one at a time when the lever is depressed all the way down.

Now that we have our chamber, we need a subject. If we put a hungry rat into the chamber and do nothing else, the rat will occasionally press the lever. There is very little else for it to do in there. A rat naturally explores its environment and tends to manipulate objects in it. The rate at which the rat presses the lever is called its *base rate* of responding. Typically, a rat will press the lever 8–10 times over the course of an hour.

After a period of observation, we activate the food dispenser so that a pellet of food is delivered every time the lever is pressed. As predicted by Thorndike's law of effect, the rate of the lever-pressing response increases.

FIGURE 6.4

A drawing of an operant chamber, or Skinner box.

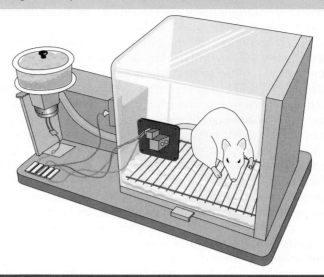

The rat may reach the point of pressing the lever at a rate of as many as 500 to 600 times per hour. Learning has taken place. There has been a relatively permanent change in behavior as a result of experience.

Here is a little subtlety: Has the rat learned to press the lever? In any sense can we say that we have taught the rat a lever-pressing response? No. The rat knew how to press the lever and did so long before we introduced the food pellets as a reward for its behavior. What it did learn—the change in behavior that took place—was a change in the *rate* of the response, not in the *nature* of the response per se.

● **Before You Go On**

What is the essence of operant conditioning?

The Course of Operant Conditioning

Now that we have the basic principles of operant conditioning in mind, let's review how the procedure is applied.

One reality of operant conditioning is that before you can reinforce a response, you have to get that response to occur in the first place. What if you place a rat in an operant chamber and find that, after grooming itself, it stops, stares off into space and settles down, facing away from the lever and the food cup? If your rat doesn't press the lever, it won't get a pellet. Your apparatus is prepared to deliver a food pellet as soon as your rat presses the lever, but it appears that you may have a long wait.

In such a circumstance, you could use a procedure called **shaping**, reinforcing *successive approximations* of the response you want to condition. You have a button that delivers a pellet to the food cup of the operant chamber even though the lever is not pressed. When your rat turns to face the lever you deliver a pellet, reinforcing that behavior. This is not exactly the response you want, but at least the rat is facing in the correct direction. You don't give your rat another pellet until it moves toward the lever. It gets another pellet for moving even closer to the lever. The next pellet doesn't come until the rat touches the lever. A reinforcer is delivered each time

shaping
a procedure of reinforcing successive approximations of a desired response until that desired response is made

your rat successively approximates the lever-press response.

Once an organism emits the responses you want to reinforce, the procedures of operant conditioning are simple. Immediately following the response, reinforcement is provided. As responses produce reinforcers, those responses become more likely to occur. The increase in response rate that follows reinforcement generally will be slow at first, then become more rapid, and eventually will level off. We call this stage of operant conditioning **acquisition**. Figure 6.5 depicts each of the stages of operant conditioning. It is important to note that the vertical, y-axis in this curve is a measure of rate of response, not response strength.

Once a rat is responding at a high rate, what will happen if reinforcers are now withheld? Say that a rat is pressing a lever at a rate of 550 presses per hour. From now on, however, it will receive no more food pellets for its efforts—no more reinforcers. What happens is very predictable: The rate of lever-pressing gradually decreases until it returns to the low base rate at which it began. Eventually the lever-pressing returns to base rate (not zero, because it didn't start at zero), and we can say that **extinction** has taken place.

Now assume that extinction has occurred, and that the rat has been removed from the operant chamber and returned to its cage for a few days. When we deprive it of food again, and return it to the chamber, what will it do? It will go over to the lever and begin to press it again. Athough the lever-pressing had gone through extinction—the last time we saw this rat in the operant chamber it was not pressing the lever—it will press the lever again after a rest interval. This return of an extinguished response after a rest interval is called **spontaneous recovery**. As in classical conditioning, the significance of spontaneous recovery is that once acquired, an operant response can seldom be eliminated in just one series of extinction trials. See Figure 6.5.

● **Before You Go On**

What is shaping, and how does it work?

Describe acquisition, extinction, and spontaneous recovery as they occur in operant conditioning.

acquisition
the process in operant conditioning in which the rate of a reinforced response increases

extinction
the process in operant conditioning in which the rate of a response decreases as reinforcers are withheld

spontaneous recovery
the phenomenon in operant conditioning in which a previously extinguished response returns after a rest interval

FIGURE 6.5
The stages of operant conditioning. (1) During acquisition, response rates increase as responses are reinforced. (2) In extinction, reinforcers are withheld and response rates return to their original baseline levels. (3) In spontaneous recovery, an increase in response rate is noted following a rest interval after extinction. Note that the vertical axis indicates a measure of the *rate* of a response, not its strength.

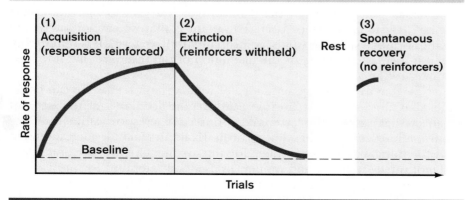

REINFORCEMENT

From what I've said so far, it should be obvious that reinforcement is a crucial concept in operant conditioning. **Reinforcement** is a process that increases the rate or the probability of the response it follows. It is a matter of administering a *reinforcer*. In this section we'll define reinforcer, and discuss a number of different types of them. We'll also examine the effects of scheduling reinforcers, and will then move on to consider punishment.

Positive and Negative Reinforcers

What qualifies as an effective reinforcer? What creates that satisfying state of affairs Thorndike claimed is necessary to increase response rate? For a hungry rat in an operant chamber, the answer seems deceptively simple. Here we can ensure that a rat is hungry, and we can confidently predict that the delivery of food will be reinforcing. For people, or for rats who are no longer hungry, the answer may not be so obvious.

Skinner and his students argue that we should define reinforcers only in terms of their effect on behavior. Reinforcers are stimuli. Stimuli that increase the rate or the probability of the response that they follow are **reinforcers**.

At first, this logic may sound a bit backward—or at least circular. A reinforcer is a stimulus that increases the rate of those responses that precede it. This reasoning suggests that nothing is *necessarily* going to be reinforcing. Reinforcers are defined only after we have noted their effect on behavior. We do not know ahead of time what will or will not produce an increased rate of response. We may have some suspicions, based on what has worked in the past, but we will not know for sure until we try.

For many people, money is a powerful reinforcer. What do you suppose would happen if your instructor offered $10 for every test item answered correctly? Such a scheme might increase the rate of students' studying behaviors. But, as difficult as this may be to believe, some students might not be interested. For them, the monetary award would not be at all reinforcing. In such a case, it would not lead to an increase in the studying behaviors of those students.

In many cultures (mostly Eastern and African), the group (e.g., family or tribe) is valued above the individual. In such cultures, reinforcing an individual's achievement will have less effect than in those cultures (mostly Western) in which individual effort and accomplishment are valued (e.g., Brislin, 1993; Triandis, 1990). In traditional Hawaiian culture, the sense of family is strong, and personal independence is not a sought-after goal. Thus, "the Hawaiian child may not be motivated by individual rewards (gold stars, grades) to the extent that his or her Caucasian counterpart may be" (Cushner, 1990, p. 107). The point is that we cannot always tell whether or not a stimulus will be reinforcing until we try it. It is reinforcing only if it increases the rate or the likelihood of the response that it follows (Kimble, 1981).

Now that we have a general idea of what a reinforcer is, we can begin to get a bit more specific. **A positive reinforcer** is a stimulus presented to an organism that increases (or maintains) the rate of a response that it follows. Positive reinforcers are often like rewards. Examples include such stimuli as food for hungry organisms, water for thirsty ones, high letter grades for well-motivated students, and money, praise, and attention for most of us. Remember, though: The intention of the person doing the reinforcing

---

reinforcement
a process that increases the rate or probability of the response that it follows

reinforcers
stimuli that increase the rate or probability of the response they follow

positive reinforcer
a stimulus that increases the rate of a response when it is presented after the response is made

does not matter at all. Reinforcers are defined solely on the basis of their effect on behavior.

A **negative reinforcer** is a stimulus that increases (or maintains) the rate of a response that precedes its removal. *Negative reinforcer* is a strange term. There is something contradictory about the very sound of it. If something is negative, how can it be a reinforcer? Part of the secret is to remember that the key word here is *reinforcer* and reinforcers increase the rate of responses. In terms of the law of effect, negative reinforcement must produce some sort of "satisfying state of affairs." It does. The reinforcement comes not from the delivery or presentation of negative reinforcers, but from their removal. (Another secret is to remember that reinforcement is a process. You may think of negative reinforcers as being generally unpleasant, aversive stimuli, while negative reinforcement is a pleasant outcome.)

So negative reinforcers are stimuli that increase the probability of a response when they are removed. They may include such stimuli as shocks, enforced isolation, and ridicule. They are exactly the sorts of things that an organism would like to *avoid* or *escape*. It may not sound like it, but "negative reinforcement is highly desirable. If offered negative reinforcement, one should accept the offer. It is always good to have bad things terminated or removed" (Michael, 1985, p. 107).

Let's consider a few examples. A rat in an operant chamber is given a constant shock (through the metallic floor of the chamber). As soon as the rat presses the lever, the shock is turned off. The lever-press has been reinforced and is likely to increase. Because a painful aversive stimulus was terminated, this is negative reinforcement—and the negative reinforcer is the shock.

You take an aspirin when you have a headache and are reinforced: The pain stops. You will be likely to try aspirin again the next time you have a headache. When Wayne says "uncle" to get Ken to stop twisting his arm, Ken does stop, thus reinforcing Wayne's saying "uncle." If this negative reinforcement is successful, Wayne will be more likely to say "uncle" in the future when Ken wants him to. When a prisoner is released from prison early "for good behavior" the good behavior is being reinforced. Imprisonment is terminated, and we have negative reinforcement.

Here's another hint that was provided by a few of my colleagues. Don't think of positive and negative reinforcement in terms of good and bad, but in terms of plus (+) and minus (−). When using positive reinforcement, one adds (+) a stimulus, and in negative reinforcement one takes away, or subtracts (−) a stimulus.

negative reinforcer
a stimulus that increases the rate of a response when that stimulus is removed after the response is made

● **Before You Go On**

What is reinforcement?

Distinguish between positive and negative reinforcers.

Primary and Secondary Reinforcers

Reinforcers are defined in terms of their effect on behavior. Both positive and negative reinforcers increase response rates. When we distinguish between primary and secondary reinforcers, the issue is the extent to which reinforcers are unlearned or acquire their reinforcing capability through learning or experience.

primary reinforcer
a stimulus (usually biologically or physiologically based) that increases the rate of a response with no previous experience required

secondary reinforcer
a stimulus that increases the rate of a response because of having been associated with other reinforcers; also called conditioned, or learned, reinforcer

Primary reinforcers do not require previous experience in order to be effective. They are in some way related to the organism's survival and are usually biological or physiological in nature. Food for a hungry organism or water for a thirsty one are common examples. Providing a warm place by the fire to a cold, wet stray dog involves primary reinforcement.

Secondary reinforcers are often referred to as learned, conditioned, or acquired reinforcers. Nothing about them suggests that they are inherently reinforcing or satisfying in any biological sense, yet they operate to strengthen responses. Most of the reinforcers that you and I work for are of this sort. Money, praise, high letter grades, and promotions are good examples. Money, in and of itself, is not worth much. But our previous learning experiences have convinced most of us of the reinforcing nature of money, and it can serve to increase the rate of a wide variety of responses. Among other things, we have learned that money can provide us with access to many other reinforcers, such as food and clothing.

The use of secondary reinforcers—and operant conditioning—can be illustrated by a type of psychotherapy called *contingency contracting* (see p. 464 in Topic 13B). Contingency contracting amounts to setting up a system—called a "token economy"—that provides secondary reinforcers for appropriate behaviors.

For example, a child earns a check mark on the calendar for each day he or she makes the bed (or takes out the trash, walks the dog, clears the table, or whatever). This economy hinges on the extent to which the check marks serve as secondary reinforcers. In other words, the child must first learn that a certain number of check marks can be exchanged for something that already reinforces the child's behaviors (e.g., an extra dessert, an hour of playing a video game, a new toy, etc.). Techniques such as this—when applied consistently—can be very effective in modifying behavior.

Some students and parents are disturbed by such examples. "Why, this isn't psychology," they claim, "You're just bribing the child to behave." I think there are two reasons why we need not be overly concerned. First, bribery involves contracting with someone to do something that *both parties view as inappropriate*. People are bribed to steal, lie, cheat, change votes, or otherwise engage in behaviors they know they should not. Token economies are designed to reinforce behaviors judged in the first place to be appropriate. Second, as Skinner argued for years, our only long-term hope is that children will reach a point where their behaviors are reinforced by intrinsic rewards rather than the extrinsic ones of a token economy. That is, the hope is that the child (as an example) will come to appreciate that having trash removed, or walking the dog, or having a clean room is a valued end in itself, one that results in the satisfying state of which Thorndike spoke.

● **Before You Go On**

Compare and contrast primary and secondary reinforcers, and give an example of each.

Scheduling Reinforcers

In all of our discussions and examples so far, I have implied that operant conditioning requires that a reinforcer be provided after every desired re-

FIGURE 6.6

The effects of a schedule of reinforcement on extinction. These are three hypothetical extinction curves following operant conditioning on (A) continuous reinforcement (CRF), (B) a fixed schedule (FR or FI), and (C) a variable schedule (VR or VI).

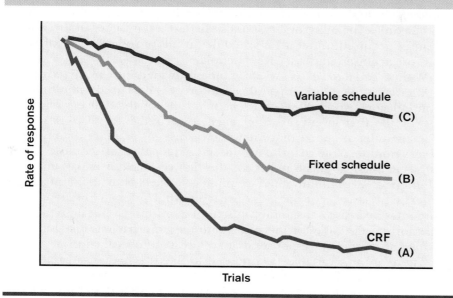

sponse. In fact, particularly at the start, it may be best to reinforce each response as it occurs. But once response rates begin to increase, there is good reason for reinforcing responses intermittently.

The procedure of reinforcing each and every response after it occurs is called a **continuous reinforcement (CRF)** schedule. A problem with CRF schedules is that earning a reinforcer after each response may soon reduce the effectiveness of that reinforcer. For example, once a rat has eaten its fill, food pellets will no longer serve to reinforce its behavior, and the rat will have to be removed from the operant chamber until it becomes hungry again (Skinner, 1956). Another problem is that responses acquired under a CRF schedule tend to extinguish very quickly. Once reinforcers are withheld, response rates decrease drastically.

Alternatives to reinforcing every response are **intermittent reinforcement schedules**. Simply put, these are strategies for reinforcing a desired behavior less frequently than every time it occurs. There are several ways to go about reinforcing responses according to an intermittent schedule. We'll review four: the fixed-ratio, fixed-interval, variable-ratio, and variable-interval schedules. These schedules were devised in the laboratory. In the world outside the laboratory, there are not many good examples of the literal application of intermittent schedules. There are, however, a few real-life examples that are fairly close and instructive. Although intermittent schedules do influence the manner in which responses are acquired, their major effects are on extinction. These effects are depicted in Figure 6.6.

continuous reinforcement schedule (CRF)
a reinforcement schedule in which each and every appropriate response is followed by a reinforcer

intermittent reinforcement schedules
reinforcement schedules in which appropriate responses are not reinforced every time they occur

With a *fixed-ratio (FR) schedule*, one establishes (fixes) a ratio of reinforcers to responses. In an FR 1: 5 schedule, for example, a reinforcer is delivered after every five responses. A 1:10 fixed-ratio schedule for a rat in an operant chamber means that the rat receives a pellet only after it presses the lever 10 times. Piecework is an example of a fixed-ratio schedule: "I'll pay you 25¢ for every 12 gizmos you assemble"; "You'll earn ten points of extra credit for every three book reports you hand in." As you might imagine, there is a high and steady rate of responding under an effective fixed ratio schedule. The more one responds, the more reinforcers there will be. Responses acquired under a FR schedule are more resistant to extinction than those acquired under a CRF schedule.

With a *fixed-interval (FI) schedule*, time is divided into set (fixed) intervals. After each fixed time interval, a reinforcer is delivered when the next response occurs. An FI 30-second schedule calls for the delivery of a food pellet for the first lever-press after each 30-second interval passes. With such a schedule, you know that you won't be dispensing more than two pellets every minute. Note that the rat doesn't get a pellet just because 30 seconds has elapsed; it gets a pellet for the first response it makes after the fixed interval. A commonly cited example is workers being paid on a regular interval of, say, every Friday, or once a month. Under an FI schedule, response rates decrease considerably just after a reinforcer, but then increase significantly as the time for the next reinforcer approaches. Fixed-interval schedules also produce responses that are resistant to extinction.

There are two variable (as opposed to fixed) schedules of reinforcement, the *variable-ratio (VR) schedule* and the *variable-interval (VI) schedule*. From the point of view of the learner, these schedules are very much alike. They differ mostly from the perspective of the dispenser of the reinforcers. For the VR schedule, one simply varies the ratio of reinforcers to responses. With a VR 1: 5 schedule, one reinforcer is delivered for every five responses *on the average*, but always in a different ratio. The first reinforcer may come after five responses, the next after six, the next after nine, the next after one, and so on. On the average, the ratio of reinforcers to responses is 1: 5, but the patterning of actual ratios is variable. From the learner's point of view, this is a random schedule. The most commonly cited example of VR reinforcement schedules is gambling devices, such as slot machines. They are programmed to pay off, or reinforce, on a variable ratio schedule where the ratios are usually quite large. The VR schedule produces a very high rate of responding, and produces responses that are very resistant to extinction.

Variable interval schedules follow the same logic as variable ratio schedules. The difference is that for these schedules, time intervals are established randomly. For a rat on a VI 30-second schedule in an operant chamber, a food pellet comes following the first lever-press response after a 30-second interval; the next follows the first response after a 50-second interval; then after a 10-second interval, and so on. The varied intervals *average* 30 seconds. An instructor who wants to keep a class on its toes, studying regularly, and attending class consistently, may schedule quizzes on a variable interval schedule. The students learn the quizzes are coming, but they never know when. What we find with VI schedules is a slower, but very steady pattern of performance. If you know when your exams are coming, you may hold off studying until just before they occur. If they are scheduled to occur randomly throughout the semester, you'll keep your studying rate up just in case there's a test scheduled for the next class.

The terminology we have used here is standard, but it is somewhat technical. The main point to remember is that operant conditioning does not require that each response be reinforced. The scheduling of reinforcers will influence the pattern of the learned responses and affects their resistance to extinction.

Another point should be made regarding the delivery of reinforcers. No matter how they are scheduled, reinforcers should come immediately after the desired response. Delayed reinforcement is usually ineffective. I'm not saying that delaying reinforcement destroys the possibility of learning; I'm simply suggesting that in most cases, the more immediate the reinforcer, the better the learning. For example, in one study, rats were reinforced for entering a black box instead of a white one. The task was learned readily when the reinforcers were given immediately. If the delivery of the reinforcers was delayed only a second or two, very little learning took place; with a 10-second delay, there was no learning at all (Grice, 1948). Several experiments have demonstrated the same phenomenon with humans (Hall, 1976). The point here is sensible. What if parents buy tickets to the circus to reinforce their son's behavior with the baby-sitter? But the circus is not until Saturday. When the family goes off to the circus Saturday afternoon, what is being reinforced may not be the child's appropriate behaviors of last Tuesday night, but all of his inappropriate behaviors on Wednesday, Thursday, Friday, and Saturday morning.

● **Before You Go On**
Define FR, FI, VR, and VI intermittent schedules of reinforcement.

PUNISHMENT

We've talked at length about reinforcement—positive and negative, primary and secondary—and how reinforcers can be scheduled. Let's now consider punishment. **Punishment** occurs when a stimulus delivered to an organism *decreases* the rate or the probability of occurrence of the response that preceded it. In common usage, punishment is in some way painful—either physically (e.g., a spanking) or psychologically (e.g., ridicule). It is a painful, unpleasant stimulus that is presented to an organism after some response is made. If the rate, or probability, of the organism's response then decreases, we may say that the response has been punished. It may have occurred to you that if punishers are *removed*, the result will be reinforcing—and we would have an example of negative reinforcement.

Determining ahead of time what stimulus will be punishing is as difficult to do as determining what stimulus will serve as a reinforcer. Once again, one's intentions are irrelevant. We know for sure that something is a punisher only in terms of its effect on behavior. For example, we may think we are punishing Richard by sending him to his room because he has begun to throw a temper tantrum. It may be that "in his room" is exactly where Richard would like to be; therefore, we may have reinforced Richard's temper tantrum behaviors simply by attending to them. Once again, the only way to know for sure is to note the effect on behavior. If Richard's tantrum-throwing behaviors become less frequent as a consequence of our actions, sending him to his room may indeed be a punishing thing to do.

We can think of punishers as being positive and negative in the same way we explained positive and negative reinforcers. Positive punishment means delivering or giving (adding, +) a painful, unpleasant stimulus (e.g.,

punishment
the administration of a punisher, which is a stimulus that decreases the rate or probability of a response that precedes it

a slap on the hand) following an inappropriate response, whereas negative punishment means removing (subtracting, –) a pleasant, valued stimulus, (e.g., "no more TV for a week") following an inappropriate response.

Is punishment an effective means of controlling behavior? Does punishment work? Yes—sometimes. Punishment can be an impressive modifier of one's behavior. A rat has learned to press a lever to get a food reinforcer. You now decide that you do not want the rat to press the lever. You pass an electric current through the lever so that each time it is touched, the rat receives a strong shock. What happens? As a matter of fact, several things may happen, but—if your shock is strong enough—there's one thing of which we can be sure: The rat will stop pressing the lever. If the use of punishment is all that effective, why do psychologists argue against its use, particularly the physical punishment of children for their misbehavior?

There are potential problems, or side effects, of the use of punishment, even when it is used correctly. Indeed, it is often used incorrectly. Let's review some of what we know about the effective use of punishment (e.g., Axelrod & Apsche, 1983; Azrin & Holz, 1966; Walters & Grusec, 1977).

1. To be effective, punishment should be delivered immediately after the response. The logic here is the same as for the immediacy of reinforcement. Priscilla is caught in mid-afternoon throwing flour all over the kitchen. Mother counts to ten (good), then says, "Just wait 'til your father gets home" (not so good). For the next three hours, Priscilla's behavior is perfect. When father gets home what is punished—Priscilla's flour-tossing or all of her appropriate behaviors that followed?

2. For punishment to be effective, it needs to be administered consistently. If one chooses to punish a certain behavior, it should be punished on every occasion—and often that is difficult to do.

3. Punishment may decrease (suppress) overall behavior levels. Although an effectively punished response may end, so may other responses. Not only will that rat who has been shocked for pressing the bar stop pressing the bar, but it will cower in the corner, doing very little of anything.

4. When responses are punished, alternatives should be introduced. Think about your rat for a minute. The poor thing knows what to do when it is hungry: Press the lever. Indeed, you taught it to do so. Now it gets shocked for doing that very thing. When the rat is given no alternative response to make in order to get food, it is in a conflict that has no solution. There is no way out. The result may be fear, anxiety, even aggressiveness. We say that punishment does not convey any information about what to do; it only communicates what *not* to do. Rubbing your puppy's nose in a "mess" it just made on the living room carpet doesn't give the dog much of an idea of what it is supposed to do when it feels a need to relieve itself.

5. Among other things, spanking or hitting provides a model for aggressive behaviors. It conveys the message that when one is frustrated, to hit or strike out is acceptable behavior. It particularly conveys the message that it's okay for "big" people to hit smaller people. As we shall see, such a message, provided by important people, can easily be taken as a model for what is appropriate.

● **Before You Go On**

What is a punisher?

How can punishers be used effectively?

GENERALIZATION AND DISCRIMINATION

In classical conditioning, we saw that a response conditioned to one stimulus could be elicited by similar stimuli. We have a comparable process in operant conditioning, and again we call it **generalization**—responses conditioned in the presence of a specific stimulus may appear in response to similar stimuli.

For example, Leslie may recieve a reinforcer for saying "doggie" as a neighbor's poodle wanders across the front yard. "Yes, Leslie, good girl. That's a doggie." Having learned that calling the neighbor's poodle a "doggie" earns parental approval, the response is tried again, this time with a German shepherd from down the street. Leslie's operantly conditioned response of "doggie" now generalizes to the German shepherd. The problem is that Leslie may overgeneralize "doggie" to virtually any small, furry, four-legged animal and she may call cats and raccoons "doggie" also. When a child turns to a total stranger and utters "Daddy," generalization can (usually) be blamed for the embarrassing mislabeling.

The process of generalization can be countered with **discrimination** training. Discrimination learning is basically a matter of differential reinforcement. What that means is that responses made to appropriate stimuli are reinforced, while responses made to inappropriate stimuli are ignored (but only by withholding reinforcers, not by punishing the response).

To demonstrate how discrimination training works, consider a strange question. Are pigeons colorblind? Disregarding for now why anyone would care, how might you go about testing the color vision of a pigeon? The standard tests we use for people surely won't work.

Pigeons can be trained to peck at a single lighted disk in order to earn a food reward. A pigeon in an operant chamber pecks at a lighted disk, and a grain of food is delivered. Soon the pigeon pecks the disk at a high rate. Let's now present the pigeon with two lighted disks, one red and one green. In all other ways the disks are identical: the same shape, brightness, size, and so on. Our basic question is whether the pigeon can tell the difference between red and green. We'll make the green disk the (positive) discriminative stimulus. Responses to the red disk will be extinguished or won't be reinforced. The position of the colored disks is randomly altered. We don't want to demonstrate that the pigeon can tell left from right.

The results of this sort of manipulation are depicted in Figure 6.7. At first, the red and green lighted disks are responded to at an approximately equal rate. But in short order, the pigeon ignores the red disk and pecks only at the green one, for which it receives its reinforcer.

In order to maintain this behavior, the pigeon must be able to tell the difference between the two colored disks. We don't know what red or green look like to a pigeon, but we can conclude that pigeons can discriminate between the two. This is sensible because the eyes of pigeons have cones in their retinas, and cones are the receptors for color. Some varieties of owls are virtually without cone cells in their retinas and thus are color-blind.

generalization

the process by which a response that was reinforced in the presence of one stimulus appears in response to similar stimuli

discrimination

the process of differential reinforcement in which one stimulus is reinforced while another stimulus is not

A pigeon in an operant chamber with a red disk and a green disk is able to distinguish one from the other.

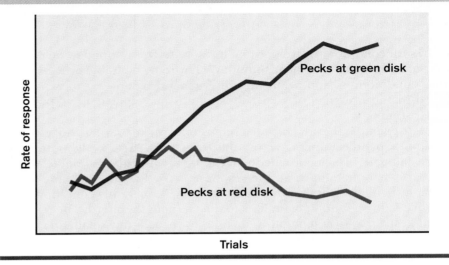

FIGURE 6.7
Discrimination training. Response rates for a pigeon presented with a green disk and a red disk. Pecks at the green disk are reinforced; those at the red disk are not.

Pecks at green disk

Pecks at red disk

Rate of response

Trials

They cannot discriminate between red and green and appear very frustrated in a discrimination learning task based on color.

Please don't think that generalization and discrimination learning in operant conditioning are processes relevant only to very young children and rats and pigeons. A lot of our own learning experience involves learning to discriminate when behaviors are appropriate and are likely to be reinforced, and when they are inappropriate and are likely to be ignored (at best) or punished. Many of the behaviors that may have been reinforced at a party you recognize as inappropriate responses in the classroom. You may have learned that it's okay to put your feet up on the coffee table at home, but not at your boss's house or at Grandma's.

● **Before You Go On**
In the context of operant conditioning, what are generalization and discrimination?

TOPIC 6C
COGNITIVE APPROACHES TO LEARNING

Cognitions, as you recall, are mental representations of our experiences, including knowledge, ideas, and beliefs. Cognitive approaches to learning emphasize changes that occur within an organism's system of cognitions.

Cognitive learning involves the acquisition of knowledge or understanding, and need not be reflected in behavior. We anticipated this approach when we covered the work of Rescorla and Kamin in Topic 6A. There we noted that a stimulus acts as an effective conditioned stimulus only when it informs the organism about something happening in its world, as in "when the tone sounds, food will soon follow." Extracting information from one's experiences is a cognitive experience. In this Topic, we'll review the work of two theorists who have stressed cognitive approaches to learning: Edward Tolman and Albert Bandura.

LATENT LEARNING AND COGNITIVE MAPS

Do rats have brains? Of course they do, though their brains aren't very large, and the cerebral cortex of a rat's brain is quite small indeed. A more intriguing question about rats is whether they can form and manipulate cognitions. Can they figure things out? Can they understand? Surely they can form simple associations. They can learn to associate a light with a shock. They can associate a lever-press with a reinforcer. Can they do more?

Consider a now-classic experiment performed over 60 years ago by Tolman and Honzik (1930). Even then, it was known that a rat could learn to run through a complicated maze of alleyways and dead ends to get to a goal box where it would receive a food reward. Tolman and Honzik wanted to understand just what the rats were learning when they learned to negotiate such a maze. They used three different groups of rats with the same maze.

One group of hungry rats was given a series of exposures to the maze (trials). Each time the rats ran from the starting point to the goal box, they were given a food reward for their efforts. Over the course of 16 days, the rats in this group showed a steady and predictable improvement in their maze-running. Their rate of errors dropped from approximately nine per trial to just two. Getting quickly and errorlessly from the start box to the goal box is what had earned them their reinforcers.

A second group of rats was also given an opportunity to explore the maze for 16 days of trials. These rats were not given a food reward for making it to the end of the maze; when they got to the goal box they were simply removed from the maze. The average number of errors made by the rats in this group also dropped over the course of the experiment (from about nine errors per trial down to about six). That the rats in this group did improve their maze-running skills suggests that simply being removed from the maze provided some measure of reinforcement. Even so, after 16 days this group was having much more difficulty in negotiating the maze than was the group being given a food reinforcer.

Now for the critical group of rats. A third group of rats was allowed to explore the maze on its own for ten days. The rats were not given a food reward upon reaching the goal box. But, beginning on day 11, a food reinforcer was delivered when they reached the end of the maze. The food was given as a reinforcer on days 11 through 16. The introduction of the food reward had a significant effect on the rats' behaviors. Throughout the first 10 days in the maze—without the food—performance showed only a slight improvement. As soon as the food was introduced, maze-running improved markedly. In fact, on days 13 through 16, they made even *fewer* errors than

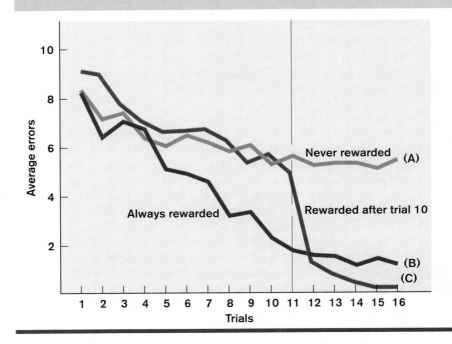

FIGURE 6.8
The performance of rats in a complicated maze where the rats were (A) never rewarded for reaching the maze's end, (B) rewarded every time they reached the maze's end, and (C) rewarded for reaching the end of the maze only on trials 11–16. (After Tolman & Honzik, 1930.)

did the rats who had received the food all along! Figure 6.8 shows the relative performance of these three groups of rats.

What do you make of this experiment? Why did that third group of rats perform so much better after the food reinforcer was introduced? Could the rats have learned something about that maze before they received reinforcement for getting to the goal box? Could they have figured out the maze early on, but failed to rush to the goal box until there was some good reason to do so?

Tolman thought that they had. He argued that the food only rewarded a change in the rats' performance, but that the actual learning had taken place earlier. This sort of learning is called **latent learning** because it is, in a sense, hidden and not shown in behavior at the time it occurs.

During those first 10 days in the maze, the rats developed what Tolman called a **cognitive map** of the maze; that is, they formed a mental picture, or representation, of what the maze was like. The rats knew about the maze, but until food was provided at the goal box, there was no reason, or purpose for getting there in any big hurry. This sort of logic led Tolman to refer to his approach as "purposive behaviorism" (Tolman, 1932). Introducing the notion of purpose and a distinction between performance and what was actually learned tended to focus attention on what was happening inside the learner during learning, which was one of Tolman's goals.

If the behaviors of Tolman's rats strike you as impressive, consider the cognitive maps formed by a variety of small birds that live in the Alps. These birds spend most of the summer and early fall hiding away seeds in

latent learning
hidden learning that is not demonstrated in performance until that performance is reinforced

cognitive map
a mental representation of the learning situation or physical environment

the ground (about four or five seeds at a time). During the harsh alpine winter, they find their buried seeds with remarkable accuracy. Have they formed cognitive maps of their seed placements? Apparently they have. Making their judgments on the basis of nearby landmarks, these small birds, called Clark's nutcrackers, can remember the location of at least 2,500 hiding places (Vander Wall, 1982)!

This may make some sense for rats, and even for nutcrackers, but what about for people? For one thing, there is the argument that if we can show that cognitive maps are formed or that cognitive restructuring takes place when rats and birds learn, it seems clear that such processes can also occur in humans.

You should be able to find examples from your own experiences that closely approximate latent learning and cognitive maps: You may take the very same route between home and campus every day. If one day an accident blocks your path, won't you use your knowledge of other routes (a cognitive map) to get where you are going? When you park your car in a new parking lot, what do you do as you walk away from your car? Don't you look around, trying to develop a mental image, or cognitive map, of the parking lot and some of its major features? Imagine that you are to meet a friend in a new classroom building on campus. You arrive early and stroll around for a few minutes. Isn't it likely that your unreinforced, apparently aimless behavior will be useful when you have to locate a room in that building for class the next semester?

Another setting in which we may find Tolman's purposive behaviorism is in athletics. Before the big game, the coaching staff may devise a perfect game plan—a set of ideas or cognitions dealing with what the team should do. In theory, the team knows what it is supposed to do to win (latent learning). But what will ultimately decide the contest is not the team members' understanding, but their performance. In sports this is called execution. Knowing what to do and doing it are often two different things.

● **Before You Go On**

What is learned when one forms a cognitive map?

What is latent learning?

SOCIAL LEARNING AND MODELING

Albert Bandura's approach to learning is also cognitive, but it adds a decidedly social flavor to the process and for that reason is referred to as **social learning theory** (Bandura, 1974, 1977, 1982). A central idea of this theory is that learning often takes place through the observation and imitation of models. What makes social learning theory *social* is the notion that we learn from others. What makes it *cognitive* is that what is learned through observation or modeling are changes in cognition that may neither be expressed as behavior nor be directly reinforced.

The classic study of observational learning was reported in 1963 by Bandura, Ross, and Ross. For this demonstration, 96 preschoolers were randomly assigned to one of four experimental conditions. One group of children observed an adult model act aggressively toward an inflated plastic "Bobo" doll (Figure 6.9). The adult model vigorously attacked the doll. Children in a second group watched the same behaviors directed toward the "Bobo" doll, but in a movie rather than live and in person. The third

social learning theory
the theory, associated with Bandura, that learning takes place through observation and imitation of others

FIGURE 6.9

In Albert Bandura's classic study, children who watched others (either in person, on film, or in a cartoon version) behave aggressively toward a "Bobo" doll displayed the same sort of behaviors themselves. Social learning theory claims that the children learned their aggressive behaviors through observation.

group watched a cartoon version of the same behaviors, this time performed by a cartoon cat. Children in the fourth group constituted the control group and did not watch anyone interact with "Bobo" dolls, either live or on film.

Then the test began. Each child, tested individually, was given new and interesting toys to play with, but only for a brief time. The child was then led to another room that contained fewer, older, and less interesting toys—including a small version of the inflated "Bobo" doll. Each child was left alone in the room while researchers watched the child's behavior. The children did not know they were being observed.

The children who had seen the aggressive behaviors of the model—whether live, on film, or in cartoon form—were themselves more aggressive in their play than were the children who did not have the observational experience. Children from each of the first three experimental conditions attacked the "Bobo" doll. What's more, they attacked it in the same vigorous, stereotyped sort of way the model had.

According to social learning theory, the children in the first three groups learned simply by observing. But as with latent learning, the learning was separated from performance. The children had no opportunity to imitate what they had learned until they had a "Bobo" doll of their own. The learning that took place during observation was symbolic, or cognitive. As Bandura explained it, "observational learning is primarily concerned with processes whereby observers organize response elements into new patterns of behavior at a symbolic level on the basis of information conveyed by modeling stimuli" (Bandura, 1976, p. 395).

Later studies have shown that reinforcement and punishment can play a major role in observational learning. For example, a new twist was added to an experiment that basically replicated the one just described. The difference was that after attacking the "Bobo" doll, adult models were either rewarded or punished for their behavior. As you might guess, children who saw the model being punished for attacking the doll engaged in little aggressive behavior toward their own dolls. Children who saw the model's behavior of attacking the doll get reinforced acted aggressively, imitating the model's behaviors in considerable detail (Bandura, 1965).

The application of this sort of research is straightforward. For example, most of Bandura's research suggests that children learn all sorts of potentially inappropriate behavior by watching television. Our real concern should be reserved for those occasions where inappropriate behaviors are left unpunished. As long as children are exposed to the consequences of the inappropriate behaviors, they will be less likely to imitate them. This logic suggests that it would be most unfortunate for a child's TV hero to get away with murder, much less be rewarded for doing so. It is also the case that reinforced behaviors of valued models are more likely to be imitated than are the punished behaviors of less valued models (Bandura, 1965).

Learning about the consequences of one's own behaviors by observing the consequences of someone else's behavior is called **vicarious reinforcement** or **vicarious punishment**. Our own experiences speak to the usefulness of these concepts. Aren't you much more likely to imitate the behaviors of a person who is rewarded for his or her efforts than you are to imitate the behaviors of someone who is punished? A child does not have to burn her fingers in a fire to learn to avoid the fireplace. Watching someone else get burned, or pretending to get burned, usually suffices (Domjan, 1987).

In fact, learning through observation and imitation is a common form of human learning. Your television on any Saturday provides many examples, particularly if you watch a PBS station. All day long there are people (models) trying to teach us how to paint landscapes, build solar energy devices, do aerobic exercises, reupholster a sofa, remodel the basement, replace a carburetor, or prepare a low-calorie meal. The basic message is: "Here, watch me; see how I do it. Then try it yourself."

vicarious reinforcement (or punishment)
increasing the rate (reinforcement) or decreasing the rate (punishment) of responses due to observing the consequences of someone else's behaviors

● **Before You Go On**

Summarize the basic concepts of social learning theory and modeling.

THINKING CRITICALLY ABOUT LEARNING

1. Psychologists say that few, if any, human behaviors are unlearned or instinctive. What would it take to demonstrate a human instinct? In other words, what criteria would we need to show that a human behavior was not learned?
2. Psychologists claim that the stimuli in our environment that produce fear reactions in us do so largely because of learning—classical conditioning in particular. What stimuli can you think of that elicit fear without the benefit of any previous learning?
3. We've spent a lot of time in this chapter talking about dogs and rats. To what extent are the learning experiences of dogs and rats relevant to the learning experiences of humans?
4. If, by some stroke of good fortune, "Little Albert" were still alive, do you suppose he would still be afraid of white rats and other white, furry things? Why or why not?
5. See if you can find ten examples of advertisers using classical conditioning to try to change your attitude about some product or service. I think you'll be surprised how easy it is.
6. Think about the issue of awareness and reinforcement. Can reinforcers "work" if you don't realize you're being reinforced? Will reinforcement work if you do realize that someone is purposively reinforcing you?

7. We say that gambling devices, such as slot machines, are scheduled to "pay off," or reinforce, the user's behavior on a variable ratio schedule. Can you imagine what it would be like to find a slot machine programmed to pay off on a fixed ratio schedule? a fixed interval schedule? a variable interval schedule?

8. Psychologists often make the argument that there is no justification for ever using physical punishment (slapping, spanking, etc.) with children. Why would they make such an argument, and if one doesn't use physical punishment, what alternatives are there?

9. How can you apply what you have learned in this chapter to help you study psychology—or any other class you may be taking?

Wait a minute! Here we are at the end of the chapter on learning and we haven't yet said anything about memorizing all of those definitions one needs to know when talking about classical conditioning. We haven't yet said anything about how we go about learning concepts, theories, and "academic" sorts of things. What happened to "human learning" as students generally think about human learning? Be assured I haven't forgotten about human learning. Here are two observations in that regard: (1) You should be convinced by now that classical conditioning, operant conditioning, and the cognitive approaches we've discussed so far *do* impact on everyday human learning. (2) Psychologists have moved much of their discussion of human learning to the treatment of human memory—and to the higher cognitive processes such as problem solving and concept formation. You will find most of the discussion of human learning that you're looking for in the next two chapters.

SUMMARY

TOPIC 6A

CLASSICAL CONDITIONING

● How do we define learning?

Learning is demonstrated by a relatively permanent change in behavior that occurs as the result of practice or experience. We define conditioning similarly, as it is a basic form of learning. *Pages 203–204.*

● Summarize the essential procedures involved in classical conditioning.

In classical, or Pavlovian, conditioning a neutral stimulus that originally does not elicit a response is paired with an unconditioned stimulus (UCS), one that reflexively and reliably produces an unconditioned response (UCR). As a result of this pairing, the once-neutral stimulus becomes a conditioned stimulus (CS) and elicits a conditioned response (CR) that is the same kind of response as the original UCR. *Pages 204–206.*

● In classical conditioning, what are acquisition, extinction, and spontaneous recovery?
● In classical conditioning, what are generalization and discrimination?

In classical conditioning, acquisition is an increase in the strength of the CR that occurs as the CS and the UCS continue to be presented together, whereas extinction is a decrease in the strength of the CR when the CS is repeatedly presented without being paired with the UCS. Spontaneous recovery is the return of the CR after extinction and then a rest interval. In generalization, we find that a response (CR) conditioned to a specific stimulus (CS) will also be elicited by similar stimuli. The more similar the new stimuli are to the CS, the greater the CR. Basically, discrimination is the opposite of generalization. It is a matter of learning to make a CR in response to a specific CS that is paired with the UCS, while learning not to make a CR in response to other stimuli not paired with the UCS. *Pages 206–209.*

● What sort of responses are most readily influenced by classical conditioning?

Classical conditioning has its most noticeable effect on emotion and mood, or affect. Most of the stimuli to which we respond emotionally probably have been classically conditioned to elicit those responses. *Pages 209–210.*

● Briefly summarize the Little Albert demonstration.

In the Watson and Rayner 1920 Little Albert study, a sudden loud noise (the UCS) was paired with the originally neutral stimulus of a white rat. As a result, Albert came to display a learned fear response (a CR) to the rat. The conditioned fear generalized to similar stimuli. This demonstration has been used to "explain" learned emotional reactions to events in our environment. *Pages 210–212.*

● Under what circumstances are stimuli likely to serve effectively as CSs?

Pavlov and many others believed that any stimulus could serve effectively as a conditioned stimulus if it were paired repeatedly with an unconditioned stimulus (UCS). We now believe this to be an oversimplification. Stimuli that are most effective as CSs are those that most reliably predict or signal the occurrence of the UCS. Stimuli are effective conditioned stimuli only if they provide useful information to the organism, for example, "a shock is going to follow this tone." *Pages 212–214.*

● What do taste-aversion studies tell us about the relationship between the CS and the UCS in classical conditioning?

Taste-aversion studies, in which subjects develop strong dislikes resulting in the avoidance of particular foods or tastes, tell us that the time interval between the CS and the UCS may be quite long, even hours long. This is in conflict with early conclusions that classical conditioning progressed best with very brief CS-UCS intervals (seconds long at most). These studies also provide evidence that some behaviors are more easily, more naturally, conditioned than others. *Page 215.*

TOPIC 6B

OPERANT CONDITIONING

● What is the essence of operant conditioning?

Operant conditioning is the type of learning in which the rate or probability of a response is changed as a result of its consequences. Reinforced responses increase in rate, while nonreinforced responses decrease in rate. *Pages 216–218.*

● What is shaping, and how does it work?
● Describe acquisition, extinction, and spontaneous recovery as they occur in operant conditioning.

Shaping is a procedure used in operant conditioning to establish a response that can then be reinforced; that is, to get the response we are interested in having occur in the first place. We shape a response by reinforcing successive approximations to that response. In operant conditioning, acquisition is produced by reinforcing a response so its rate will increase. Extinction is the process of decreasing the rate of a response (to return to baseline levels) by withholding reinforcement. After a rest interval, a previously extinguished response will return at a rate above baseline; that is, in the same situation, it will spontaneously return or recover. *Pages 218–219.*

● What is reinforcement?
● Distinguish between positive and negative reinforcers.

In general, reinforcement is a process that increases the rate or probability of the response that it follows. A positive reinforcer increases the rate of the response that precedes its presentation. A negative reinforcer increases the rate of the response that precedes its removal or termination. *Pages 220–221.*

● Compare and contrast primary and secondary reinforcers, and give an example of each.

Primary reinforcers are stimuli that are in some way biologically important or related to the organism's survival, such as food for a hungry organism or warm shelter for a cold organism. Secondary reinforcers increase the rate of a response because of the organism's previous learning history. Secondary reinforcers, such as praise, money, letter grades, or promotions, are acquired or conditioned reinforcers. *Pages 221–222.*

● Define FR, FI, VR, and VI intermittent schedules of reinforcement.

Intermittent schedules of reinforcement provide a reinforcer for less than every response. The FR (fixed-ratio) schedule calls for a reinforcer after a set number of responses (e.g., one reinforcer after every five responses). A VR (variable-ratio) schedule randomly changes the ratio of reinforcers to responses but maintains some given ratio as an average. The FI (fixed-interval) schedule calls for the administration of a reinforcer for the first response following a specified time interval. A VI (variable-interval) schedule calls for a reinforcer for the first response following a time interval whose length is varied. In general, responses reinforced by fixed schedules are more resistant to extinction than responses that have been reinforced every time (a CRF, or continuous reinforcement schedule). Responses acquired under variable schedules of reinforcement are even more resistant to extinction than those acquired under fixed schedules. *Pages 222–225.*

● What is a punisher?
● How can punishers be used effectively?

A punisher is a stimulus that decreases the rate or probability of a response that it follows. Punishers can be effective in suppressing a response when they are strong enough and delivered right after the response to be punished. Fear, anxiety, aggression, and an overall suppression of activity may accompany punishment, which in itself provides no information about what an organism should do in a given situation. Punishing one response should therefore be paired with the reinforcement of another, more appropriate response. *Pages 225–227.*

● In the context of operant conditioning, what are generalization and discrimination?

In operant conditioning, generalization occurs when a response reinforced in the presence of one stimulus also occurs in the presence of other, similar stimuli. Discrimination, on the other hand, is a matter of differential reinforcement—reinforcing responses to some stimuli while extinguishing responses to other (inappropriate) stimuli. *Pages 227–228.*

TOPIC 6C

COGNITIVE APPROACHES TO LEARNING

● What is learned when one forms a cognitive map?
● What is latent learning?

According to Tolman, when one forms a cognitive map, one develops a mental representation (or picture) of one's surroundings—an appreciation of general location and where significant objects are located. Forming cognitive maps can be seen as a type of latent learning, the acquisition of information (an internal, cognitive process) that may not be demonstrated in performance until later, if at all. *Pages 228–231.*

● Summarize the basic concepts of social learning theory and modeling.

Bandura's social learning theory emphasizes the role of observation of others and imitation in the acquisition of cognitions and behaviors. We often learn by imitating models and through vicarious reinforcement and punishment. *Pages 231–233*

TOPIC 6A
CLASSICAL CONDITIONING

6.1 To say that learning is demonstrated by changes in behavior is to suggest that a) if we cannot remember something, we did not learn it in the first place. b) some changes in behavior do not last very long, or are cyclical. c) the only way we can be sure if someone learned something is to ask him or her. d) learning is an internal process that is inferred from performance. *Pages 203–204.*

6.2 Which of the following ideas is *not* found in our definition of learning? a) Changes in behavior due to learning must be relatively permanent. b) Learning involves making good and proper adjustments and adaptations to the environment. c) For changes to be classified as learned, they must result from practice or experience. d) Learning cannot be measured or observed directly. *Pages 203–204.*

6.3 As Pavlov noted, when we bring a dog to the laboratory, stand him on a table, and ring a bell, the first thing we will notice is a) an orienting reflex. b) an unconditioned stimulus. c) habituation or acclimation. d) no response at all. *Pages 204–206.*

6.4 True or False? Ivan Pavlov won a Nobel Prize for psychology in 1902. *Pages 204–206.*

6.5 True or False? In a demonstration of classical conditioning, the unconditioned response occurs without any previous learning experience. *Pages 206–212.*

The next three items involve the following situation: A dog is exposed to the sound of a bell until it comes to ignore it. Now, soon after the bell is sounded, a shock is delivered to the front left paw of the dog. When it is shocked, the dog quickly lifts its foot. This procedure is repeated 12 times. *Pages 204–208.*

6.6 What is likely to be the response when the bell is sounded now? a) A UCS will occur. b) A UCR will occur. c) A CR will occur. d) Nothing will happen. *Pages 204–208.*

6.7 In this example of conditioning, the UCR is _____ and the CR is _____. a) shock; foot withdrawal b) shock; a bell c) a bell; an orienting reflex d) foot withdrawal; foot withdrawal. *Pages 204–208.*

6.8 If the bell were sounded alone (no more shock) for a few dozen presentations, what is likely to occur? a) extinction b) generalization c) acquisition d) spontaneous recovery. *Pages 204–208.*

6.9 Which process is essentially the opposite of generalization? a) discrimination b) reinforcement c) acquisition d) habituation. *Pages 204–208.*

6.10 Although each of these responses or behaviors is learned, which most clearly results from classical conditioning? a) typing or keyboard skills b) feeling relief at realizing that a class period is about over c) understanding the difference between a CS and a UCS d) speaking the language you do rather than a different one. *Pages 204–208.*

6.11 With "Little Albert" as their subject, John Watson and Rosalie Rayner demonstrated each of the following *except* a) generalization. b) classical conditioning. c) extinction. d) a learned and unlearned stimulus for fear. *Pages 209–212.*

6.12 A stimulus will serve as a most effective CS if a) it is repeatedly presented after the presentation of the UCS. b) it naturally produces an orienting reflex. c) its presentation reliably predicts the UCS. d) it is repeatedly paired with an appropriate CR. *Pages 212–215.*

6.13 Taste-aversion studies a) work with rats, but not with dogs or people. b) show us an application of classical conditioning. c) demonstrate that CS-UCS intervals may be quite long. d) explain why most children prefer sweet-tasting foods. *Pages 209–212.*

TOPIC 6B
OPERANT CONDITIONING

6.14 The basic thrust or premise of operant conditioning is that a) under the proper circumstances, any organism can learn to make any response. b) organisms learn to make responses that are only in their own best interest. c) behaviors are shaped or controlled by their consequences. d) people learn only if they want to learn. *Pages 216–219.*

6.15 If operant conditioning is successful, what is most likely to be changed? a) the rate or probability of a response b) cognitive representations of the organism c) the stimuli that produced the learned response d) the strength or nature of a response. *Pages 216–219.*

6.16 True or False? Skinner stated the law of effect after observing rats (and pigeons) in his operant chambers. *Pages 216–219.*

6.17 A rat in an operant chamber is given a pellet of food each time it depresses a lever. After 100 pellets have been provided for lever-pressing, the rat no longer gets a pellet when it depresses the lever. What is most likely to occur? a) The lever-pressing response will decrease. b) The rat will become frustrated, anxious, and aggressive. c) The rat will continue to press the lever at the same rate. d) The rat's operant rate will spontaneously recover. *Pages 216–219.*

6.18 You want to reinforce Mickey for hanging his coat in the closet, but he never does so—he simply drops his coat on the floor as he walks through the door. What procedure would be most effective? a) physical punishment b) discrimination learning c) stimulus generalization d) shaping. *Pages 220–225.*

6.19 True or False? Shaping is an operant conditioning technique accomplished by the method of successive approximations. *Pages 220–225.*

6.20 The major difference between positive and negative reinforcement is whether a) something is given or taken away. b) rates of responding go up or down. c) responses are rewarded or punished. d) reinforcers are innate or learned. *Pages 220–225.*

6.21 Which of the following provides the best example of negative reinforcement? a) paying Billy a dollar for every A or B on his report card b) having a root canal procedure to ease the pain of a severe toothache c) spanking Amy for playing with the water in the toilet bowl d) using play money to modify the behaviors of a retarded child. *Pages 220–225.*

6.22 True or False? Using a "token economy" means that one is using negative reinforcers. *Pages 220–225.*

6.23 Using each of the following reinforcement schedules, rats are trained to press levers at a high rate. The lever-pressing of rats trained on a_____schedule will now extinguish most quickly. a) continuous b) fixed-ratio c) fixed-interval d) variable-interval. *Pages 220–225.*

6.24 Which statement regarding punishment is most justified? a) Because it creates anxiety, it never should be used. b) Physical punishment is more effective than psychological. c) Punishment is only effective if it has been threatened repeatedly. d) Punishment decreases the rate of responses it follows. *Pages 225–228.*

6.25 True or False? You may punish responses even when you are trying to reinforce them. *Pages 225–228.*

6.26 In operant conditioning, discrimination training is mostly a matter of a) learning right from wrong. b) discovering the difference between reinforcement and punishment. c) differential reinforcement. d) extinction followed by spontaneous recovery. *Pages 225–228.*

TOPIC 6C
COGNITIVE APPROACHES TO LEARNING

6.27 In general, cognitive approaches to learning tend to emphasize a) the interaction of genetics and experience. b) knowing ahead of time what will serve as a reinforcer. c) changes inside the organism that may not result in changes in behavior. d) the role of learning in the acquisition of emotional responses. *Pages 228–231.*

6.28 If learning is latent it is by definition a) of no value to the learner. b) not (yet) reflected in behavior. c) learned, but not remembered. d) displayed only in social situations. *Pages 228–231.*

6.29 True or False? Because cognitive maps require a certain degree of intelligence, only humans are capable of forming them. *Pages 228–231.*

6.30 Of the following, what is it that makes Bandura's social learning theory social? a) the fact that it is a cognitive approach to learning b) it includes the concepts of vicarious reinforcement and punishment c) it requires that learning result from practice or experience. d) the fact that it can only be found in humans. *Pages 231–233.*

MEMORY

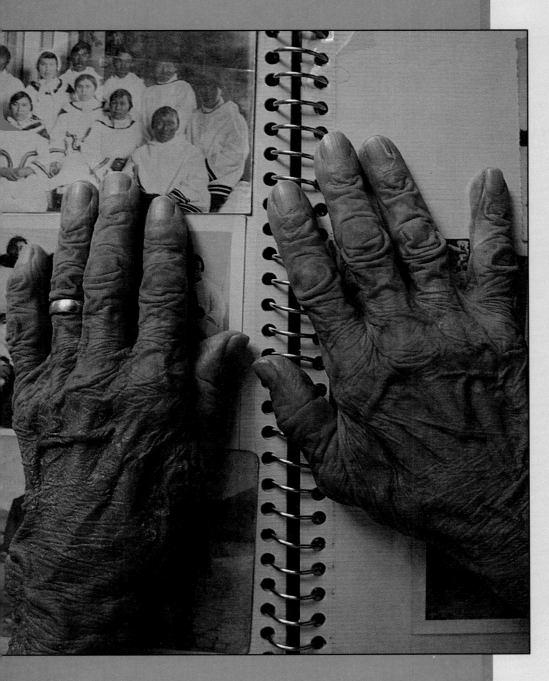

PREVIEW

TOPIC 7A—How Can We Describe Human Memory?

Memory as Information Processing

Sensory Memory

Short-Term Memory (STM)

Long-Term Memory (LTM)

PSYCHOLOGY IN THE REAL WORLD: The Retrieval of Repressed Memories of Childhood Trauma

TOPIC 7B—Why We Forget: Factors Affecting Retrieval

How We Measure Retrieval

How We Encode Information

How We Schedule Practice

How We Overcome Interference

A Reminder About Retrieval and Forgetting

THINKING CRITICALLY ABOUT MEMORY

SUMMARY

TEST YOURSELF

239

It is nearly impossible to imagine what life would be like without memory. For one thing, this sentence would make no sense. Without your memory, you would have no idea of what a textbook is or why you had it open in front of you. The black patterns of print that you now recognize as words would appear as no more than random marks. We care about memory in an academic, study—learn—test sense, but the importance of memory goes well beyond classroom exams. All of those things that define us as individuals are stored away somehow in our memories.

In Topic 7A, we begin our discussion by considering how information gets into our memories and is stored there. We'll begin by formulating a working definition of memory. Then we'll explore the possibility that there are several different types of memory. We'll see what these various memories might be, and how they function. In Topic 7B, we deal with the very practical matter of "retrieval," getting stored information out of our memories when we want to. We'll find that there are several things we can do to improve our ability to remember.

TOPIC 7A

HOW CAN WE DESCRIBE HUMAN MEMORY?

Over the past 30 years, there have been many changes in the ways psychologists think about memory. Psychologists now accept the notion that memory is not just one unified structure or process. There are several different types of memory processing. Psychologists no longer think of memory as just a passive storehouse of information and experiences. Remembering is seen as an active cognitive process. This Topic will explore these themes.

MEMORY AS INFORMATION PROCESSING

One contemporary way to think about human memory is to view it as the final step in a series of cognitive activities that process information. An information-processing view of memory takes the position that complex cognitive processes, such as remembering and forgetting, can be best understood as a series of simpler, associated functions. In this view, we come into this world knowing little about it. By the time we are adults, we have stored away an incredible number of things. Much of the information we have stored away may be trivial and irrelevant, but much of it is essential for survival. How do our memories come to be filled with so much information? As we noted in Chapter 3, the processing of information begins with sensation, when our sensory receptors are stimulated. Through perception, information from our senses is selected and organized. With memory, we form a record of the information we have processed.

Memory is the capacity to encode, store, and retrieve information. It is "the mental processes of acquiring and retaining information for later retrieval" (Ashcraft, 1994, p. 11). Using memory is a complex series of cognitive processes that involves three interrelated steps, or stages. The first puts information into memory, a process called **encoding**. To encode information, stimuli are represented in the nervous system. Encoding is the process of forming a cognitive representation of information. Once that representation is in memory, we then must keep it there. This process is called **storage**. To use stored information, we need to get it out again, the process of **retrieval**.

Modern theories view memory as being more than just one singular process. That is, not all of the information that gets into memory necessarily gets encoded or stored in the same way or in the same place (Baddeley, 1992; Loftus, 1991; Roediger, 1990; Schacter, 1992; Squire et al., 1993; Watkins, 1990). It is useful to think about three different types of memory: sensory memory, short-term memory (STM), and long-term memory (LTM). For each type of memory, we have the same questions: How does this memory receive information? What is its capacity, or how much information can be held there? What is its duration, or for how long will information be held there without further processing? In what form is information held in this memory?

● **Before You Go On**
How do we define memory?

SENSORY MEMORY

Sensory memory stores large amounts of information for very short periods of time (a few seconds or less). The concept of a very brief sensory memory is a strange one (we usually do not think about remembering something for only a few seconds), but it has a place in information-processing models. All of the information that gets stored in our memories first enters through our senses. Simply put, to be able to recall what a lecturer says, you first must be in class to hear that lecture. In order to remember a drawing from this book, the image of the drawing first must stimulate your visual system. You can't recognize the aroma of fried onions if you've never smelled them in the first place.

The basic idea of a sensory memory is that information does not pass directly through our sensory systems; instead, it is held in sensory memory for a brief period of time. After a stimulus has left the environment and it is no longer physically present, it has left its imprint, having formed a sensory memory.

The *capacity* of sensory memory is, at least in theory, very large indeed. At one time it was believed that we are able to keep as much in our sensory memory as our sense receptors can respond to at one time. Such

memory
the cognitive ability to encode, store, and retrieve information

encoding
the active process of representing information and putting it into memory

storage
the process of holding encoded information in memory

retrieval
the process of locating, removing, and using information that is stored in memory

sensory memory
the type of memory that holds large amounts of information from the senses for very brief periods of time

claims may give sensory memory more credit than it is due. Sensory memory can hold more information than we can attend to, but there are limits on its capacity.

The practical problem with sensory memory lies in its *duration*. We may be able to get vast amounts of information into our sensory memory, but we can't keep it there (storage) very long. What is the duration of sensory memory? It's difficult to say with precision, but memories stay in sensory storage only very briefly—about 0.5 second for visually presented materials (Sperling, 1960, 1963), perhaps for as long as 3 to 10 seconds for orally presented information (Cowen, 1984; Darwin et al., 1972; Massaro, 1975). It certainly won't be of much help for your next psychology exam if you process information to this memory and no further.

Sensory memory is viewed as a rather mechanical or physical type of storage. The information stored there cannot be acted upon. You can't *do* anything with it. Information is not encoded in sensory memory; you have to take information into your sensory memory as your receptors deliver it. It is as if stimuli from the environment make an impression on our sensory systems and then rapidly fade or are replaced by new stimuli.

Here are two examples that demonstrate sensory memory. In a dark area, stand about 20 feet away from a friend who is pointing a flashlight at you. Have your friend swing the flashlight around in a small circle, making about one revolution per second. What do you see? Your experience is that of a circle of light. At any one instant, you're seeing where the light is, *and* you are also experiencing, from your sensory memory, where the light has just been. If your friend moves the flashlight slowly, you see a "tail" of light following it, but you won't see a circle any more because some of the image of the light's position will have decayed from sensory memory.

Have you ever had this experience? Someone asks you a question to which your intelligent reply is something like, "Huh, what did you say?" Then, before the person gets a chance to repeat her question, you answer it. (Which in turn provokes a response such as "Why didn't you answer me in the first place?") Perhaps you didn't hear all of the question you were asked, but while it was still reverberating (echoing) in your sensory memory, you listened to it again and formed your answer.

As I said, the idea of a sensory memory as a very brief storage of large amounts of minimally processed information is an odd one. There is evidence that sensory memory is a real phenomenon—at least for vision and audition. We may not be aware of its usefulness in any practical sort of way, but perhaps that extra fraction of a second or two of storage in sensory memory provides us with the time we need to attend to information so we can then move it further along.

● **Before You Go On**

What is sensory memory?

What are its capacity and duration?

SHORT-TERM MEMORY (STM)

short-term memory (STM) a type of memory (also called working memory) with limited capacity (7±2 bits of information) and limited duration (15–20 seconds)

Once information gets to sensory memory, where does it go next? Most of it rapidly fades or is replaced by new stimuli. With a little effort, however, we can process material from our sensory memories more fully by moving it to short-term memory. **Short-term memory (STM)** is a level or storehouse

FIGURE 7.1

A simplified model of human memory.

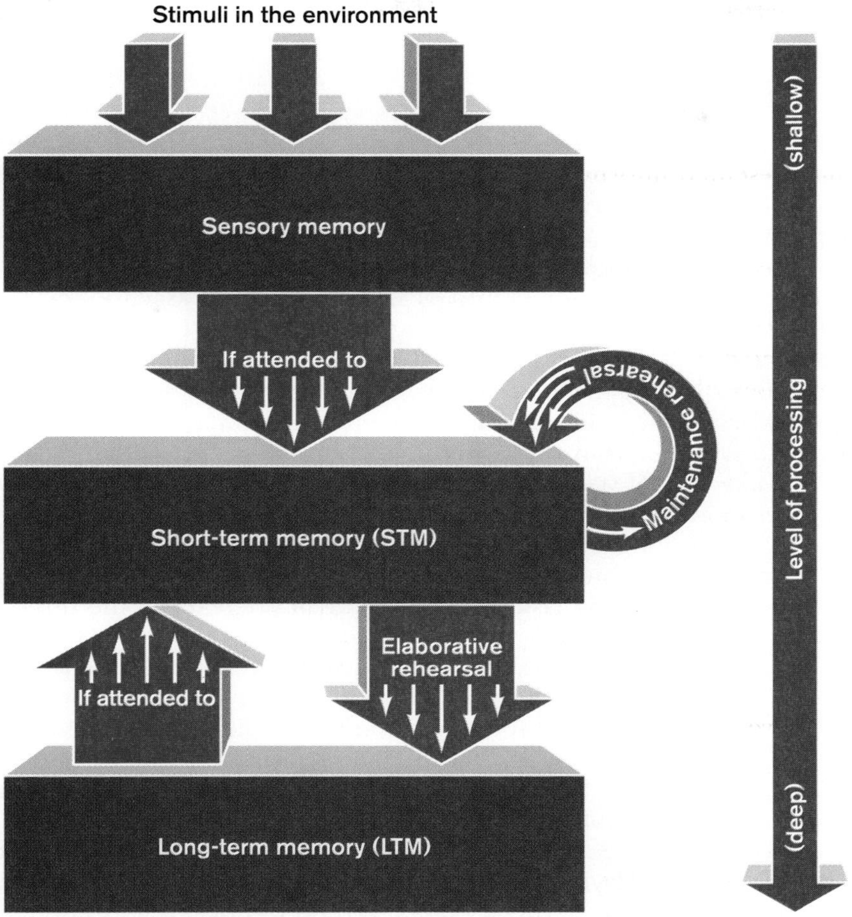

Stimuli in the environment

Sensory memory

If attended to

Maintenance rehearsal

Short-term memory (STM)

If attended to

Elaborative rehearsal

Long-term memory (LTM)

(shallow)

Level of processing

(deep)

of human memory with a limited capacity and, without the benefit of re-hearsal, a brief duration.

What I am here calling short-term memory is often referred to as working memory (Baddeley, 1982, 1990, 1992). It is viewed as something like a workbench or desk top on which we pull together, manipulate, and use the information to which we pay attention. To encode information into STM requires that we pay attention to it. Information can get into STM directly from sensory memory or it can be retrieved from long-term memory. The capacity of short-term memory is limited by our attention span. There are severe limits on the amount of information to which we can attend in a short period. In Chapter 5 we reviewed the factors that guide this process of selective attention.

Figure 7.1 presents a schematic diagram of the model of memory that we are constructing. At the top we have stimuli from the environment affecting our senses and moving directly into sensory memory. In the middle is short-term memory (STM). We see that information from sensory memory or from long-term memory can be moved into STM. It will be helpful to refer to this diagram as we expand our model. Because of its limited duration and capacity, STM sometimes acts like a bottleneck in the processing of information from our senses into long-term storage.

The Duration of STM

Interest in short-term memory processing can be traced to two experiments reported independently in the late 1950s (Brown, 1958; Peterson & Peterson, 1959). We'll review the Petersons' experiment.

In a typical trial, a student is shown three consonants, such as *KRW*, for 3 seconds. Presenting the letters for 3 seconds assures that they are attended to and hence encoded into STM. The student is asked to recall the three letters after time intervals ranging from 0 to 18 seconds. This doesn't sound like a very difficult task, and it isn't. Nearly anyone can remember three letters for 18 seconds. However, in this experiment, students are kept from rehearsing the letters during the retention interval. They are to count backward, by three, from an assigned three-digit number.

For example, if you were a participant in this sort of experiment, you would be shown a letter sequence, say *KRW*, and then immediately you would start counting backward from, say, 397 by threes: "397, 394, 391, 388," and so forth. You would count out loud as rapidly as possible. The idea is that the counting task prohibits you from rehearsing the three letters you were just shown.

Under these conditions, your correct recall of the letters depends on the length of the retention interval. If you are asked to name the letters after just a few seconds of counting, you won't do badly. If you have to count for 15 to 20 seconds, your recall of the letters drops to near zero (see Figure 7.2). Distracted by the counting, you cannot rehearse the letters, and they are soon unavailable to you.

This laboratory example is not as abstract as it may first appear. Consider this scenario. Having studied psychology for a few hours, you decide to reward yourself by ordering a pizza. Further, you decide to splurge and have the pizza delivered. Never having called Pizza City before, you find their phone number in the yellow pages: 555–5897. You repeat the number to yourself: 555–5897. You put away the phone book and dial the number without error. Buzz-buzz-buzz. Darn, the line's busy. Well, you'll call back in a minute.

Just as you hang up the phone, the doorbell rings. It's the paper boy. You owe him $11.60 for the past two weeks' deliveries. You don't have enough cash on hand to pay for the paper and a pizza, so you write a check. "Let's see, what is today's date? 10–16–96. How much do I owe you? Oh yeah, $11.60; plus a dollar tip comes to $12.60. This is check number 1177. I'd better write that down. Thanks a lot."

The paper boy leaves and you return to your studying. Then you remember that you were going to get a pizza. Only five or six minutes have passed since you got that busy signal from Pizza City. But now that you want to dial the number again, you can't recall any of it. You attended to the number, and thus entered it into short-term storage, where you could keep it until you were distracted.

We can extend the duration of short-term memory by rehearsing the information stored there. This kind of rehearsal is called **maintenance rehearsal**, and amounts to the simple rote repetition of information already

maintenance rehearsal
a process of rote repetition (re-attending) to keep information in STM

FIGURE 7.2
The recall of a stimulus of three letters as a function of retention interval when maintenance rehearsal is minimized. (After Peterson & Peterson, 1959).

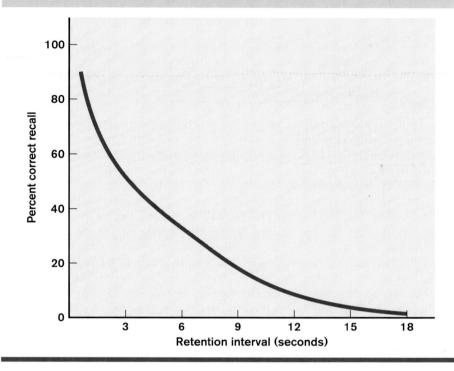

in STM. To get material into STM (encoding), we attend to it. By repeating that material over and over (as we might if we wanted to remember a telephone number until we could dial it), we are reattending to it with each repetition.

As a rule of thumb, we can say that unrehearsed material will stay in STM for 15 to 20 seconds. Experiments like that of the Petersons also tell us that once in short-term memory, some information becomes unavailable almost immediately. That's better than sensory memory, but short-term memory, by itself, still won't help when it comes to taking an exam next week.

The duration of storage in STM *is* long enough to allow us to use it in everyday activities. Usually we only want to remember a phone number long enough to dial it. Using STM in mathematical computations is another good example. Multiply 28 by 6 without paper and pencil. "Let's see. Eight times 6 is 48. Now I have to keep the 8 and carry the 4." Stop right there. Where do you "keep the 8" and where do you store the 4 until it is needed? Right. In your STM. And where did the notion that 8 x 6 = 48 come from? Where did the meaning of "multiply" come from? How did this information get into STM? Right again. This is an example of information entering STM, not from the outside through your senses, but from long-term storage (refer to Figure 7.1).

Having discussed the duration of short-term memory, let's deal with its capacity. Just how much information can we hold in STM for that 15 to 20 seconds?

● **Before You Go On**

How long is information stored in STM?

What is required to get material into STM and then keep it there?

The Capacity of STM

In 1956 George Miller wrote a charming paper on "the magical number seven, plus or minus two." He argued that the capacity of short-term memories is very small—limited to just five to nine (or 7±2) bits or "chunks" of information.

In the context of short-term memory, the concept of chunk is actually a technical term, although it is also an imprecise one (Anderson, 1980). A **chunk** may be defined as a representation in memory of a meaningful unit of information. The claim is that we can store approximately 7±2 meaningful pieces of information in STM.

We can easily attend to, encode, and store five or six letters in STM. Holding the letters YRDWIAADEFDNSYE in short-term memory would be quite a challenge. Fifteen randomly presented letters exceeds the capacity of STM for most of us. What if I asked you to remember the words FRIDAY and WEDNESDAY? Keeping these two simple *words* in STM is easy—even though they contain (the same) 15 letters. Here, you would be storing just two chunks of (meaningful) information, not fifteen. In fact, you easily could store 50 letters in short-term memory if you recoded them into one meaningful chunk: "days of the week."

As we all know, we can readily store a telephone number in short-term memory. Adding an area code makes the task somewhat more difficult because 10 digits now comes fairly close to the upper limit of our STM capacity. Notice, though, how we tend to cluster the digits of a telephone number into a pattern. The digit series 8694935661 is more difficult to deal with as a simple string than when it is seen and encoded as a phone number: (869) 493–5661 (Bower & Springston, 1970). Grouping the digits in this way lets us see them in a new, more meaningful way. So by chunking bits and pieces of information together, we can add meaningfulness and extend the apparent capacity of short-term memory.

At best, however, short-term memory works like a leaky bucket. From the vast storehouse of information available in our sensory memory, we scoop up some (and not much at that) by paying attention to it. We hold it for a while until we either use it, maintain it with maintenance rehearsal, move it to long-term storage, or lose it. Before we go on to our discussion of long-term memory, we'll consider how information is encoded and stored in STM.

● **Before You Go On**

How much information can be held in STM?

How can chunking affect the capacity of STM?

How Information Is Represented in STM

The material or information stored in our sensory memory is kept there in virtually the same form in which it was presented. Visually presented stimuli are held as visual impressions, auditory stimuli form auditory memories,

chunk
a somewhat imprecise concept referring to a meaningful unit of information as represented in memory

If we are not interrupted or distracted, we easily can hold a telephone number in STM long enough to dial it.

Many mathematical operations require the use of STM to hold information until we need it in our calculations.

and so on. Getting information into STM is not an automatic process. We first have to attend to the material to encode it into short-term memory. How, then, is information stored or represented in STM?

Conrad (1963, 1964) was one of the first to argue that information is stored in STM with an acoustic code. That means that material tends to be processed in terms of how it sounds. Conrad's conclusion was based on his interpretation of the errors that people make in short-term memory experiments.

In one experiment, Conrad presented a series of letters. The letters were presented visually, one at a time, and participants were asked to recall the letters they had just seen. It was not surprising that many errors were made over the course of the experiment. What was surprising was that when people responded with an incorrect letter, it was very frequently with a letter that sounded like the correct one. For example, if subjects were to recall the letter E and failed to do so, they would recall V, G, or T, or a letter that sounded like the E they were supposed to recall. They rarely responded with an F, which certainly looks more like the E they had just seen than does V, G, or T. This was true whether the subjects gave their recall orally or in writing.

It seems then that using short-term memory is a matter of talking to ourselves. No matter how it is presented, we tend to encode information acoustically, the way it sounds. At least that's what the early evidence suggested. Subsequent research has not changed the view that acoustic coding is the most important means of representing information in STM. However, some material may be encoded in STM in other ways—visually, or spatially, or semantically (Cooper & Shepard, 1973; Martindale, 1981; Shulman, 1971, 1972; Squire et al., 1993; Wickens, 1973). Perhaps the most we can say is that there is a tendency to rely heavily on the acoustic coding of information in short-term memory, but other codes also may be used.

● **Before You Go On**

How is information encoded (represented) in short-term memory?

LONG-TERM MEMORY (LTM)

long-term memory (LTM)
a type of memory with virtually unlimited capacity and very long, if not limitless, duration

Long-term memory (LTM) is memory as you and I usually think of it: memory for large amounts of information held for long periods of time. As we did for sensory and short-term memory, we'll begin by considering two basic issues: capacity and duration.

How Large is Long-Term Memory?

Our own experiences tell us that the capacity of long-term memory is huge—virtually limitless. At times we may even impress ourselves with the amount of material we have stashed away in LTM. Just how much can be stored in human memory may never be measured, but we can rest assured that we will never learn so much that there won't be room for more.

As an example of long-term memory's huge capacity, consider an experiment by Standing, Canezio, and Haber (1970). Over the course of five days, they presented 2500 different pictures to subjects and asked them to remember them all. Even a day or so later, subjects correctly identified, from a new collection of pictures, 90 percent of those they had seen before. Standing (1973) increased the number of pictures that subjects viewed to 10,000. (As you can imagine, it took a while just to view 10,000 pictures.) Again, subjects later correctly recognized more than 90 percent of them.

There seems to be no practical limit to the amount of information we can encode or process into long-term memory. Getting that information

The capacity of our long-term memories is so large that sometimes we surprise ourselves with how much information we have stored there.

out of our memories when we want it is another matter, which we'll get to in Topic 7B.

How Long Do Long-Term Memories Last?

On an experiential basis, we can again impress ourselves with the duration of some of our own memories. Assuming that you remain free from disease or injury, you're likely never to forget some things, such as your own name or the words to "Happy Birthday."

Determining the duration of LTM on a scientific basis is a different matter. At the moment, it is difficult to even imagine an experiment that could tell us how long memories remain stored in LTM. One thing we know is that we often cannot remember things we know we once knew. At issue is *why*. Do we forget because the information is no longer *available* to us in our long-term memories, just not there any more? Or do we forget because we are unable to retrieve the information from LTM, which implies that it is still available, but somehow not *accessible* (Watkins, 1990)?

Most psychologists believe that information in LTM stays there until we die. In fact, 84 percent of the psychologists who were asked agreed that "everything we learn is permanently stored in the mind, although sometimes particular details are not accessible" (Loftus & Loftus, 1980, p. 410). As intriguing as this view may be, there is reason to believe that it may not be all that accurate. A review article by Elizabeth and Geoffery Loftus (1980) questioned the permanence of long-term memories. When the Loftuses reviewed the data supporting the argument for permanence, they found that "the evidence in no way confirms the view that all memories are permanent and thus potentially recoverable" (p. 409). They claim that when we think we are remembering specific memories of the long-distant past, we are often reconstructing a reasonable facsimile of the original information from bits and pieces of our past. That is, when we remember something that happened to us a long time ago, we don't recall the events as they actually happened. Instead, we recall a specific detail or two and then *actively reconstruct* a reasonable story, a process which in itself creates new memories. Well if that's the case, how do we determine if our recall of events long past is accurate or an inaccurate, but reasonable, construction? This issue has led to research in two very practical areas: (1) memories of traumas experienced in childhood (dealt with in the "Psychology in the Real World" box, p. 253), and (2) the validity of eyewitness testimony.

If it is true that long-term memories may not be permanent, and that they can be distorted or replaced by events processed later, we may have to reconsider the weight given to eyewitness testimony (e.g., Clifford & Lloyd-Bostock, 1983; Egeth, 1983; Loftus, 1984; MacLeod & Ellis, 1986; Wells, 1993).

Let's review just one classic study in this area (Loftus & Zanni, 1975). Students viewed a short film showing the collision of two cars; later, the students were asked to estimate the speed of the cars as they collided. Actually, some students were asked about the cars "colliding," some were asked about the cars "hitting" each other, and others were asked about the cars "contacting," "bumping," or "smashing" each other. Estimates varied in accordance with the question. The cars were reported to be going nearly 41 mph when they "smashed" into each other, but only 31 mph when they "contacted" each other. Although this was a laboratory study—and there's always a danger in generalizing from the laboratory to the real world (Bekerian, 1993; Yuille, 1993)—the relevance for eyewitness testimony is fairly obvious.

FIGURE 7.3
Statements About Eyewitness Testimony with Which
"the Experts" Agree

1. An eyewitness's testimony about an event can be affected by how the questions put to the witness are worded.
2. Police instructions can affect an eyewitness's willingness to make an identification and/or the likelihood that he or she will identify a particular person.
3. Eyewitness' testimony about an event often reflects not only what they actually saw but information they obtained later on.
4. An eyewitness's confidence is not a good predictor of his or her identification accuracy.
5. An eyewitness's perception and memory for an event may be affected by his or her attitudes and expectations.
6. The less time an eyewitness has to observe an event, the less well he or she will remember it.
7. Eyewitnesses sometimes identify as a culprit someone they have seen in another situation or context.
8. The use of a one-person showup instead of a full lineup increases the risk of misidentification.
9. The rate of memory loss for an event is greatest right after the event, and then levels off with time.
10. White eyewitnesses are better at identifying other white people than they are at identifying black people.

From Kassin et al. 1989, pp. 1089–1098.

What do the "experts" say about eyewitness testimony? On what issues would psychologists be willing to go to court and claim that valid scientific evidence exists? Just this question was put to 113 researchers who had published data on eyewitness testimony (Kassin et al., 1989). Some of the results of this study are presented in Figure 7.3.

Now that we have a sense of LTM's capacity and duration of storage, we need to address how long-term memories are formed. We'll also see that there may be different types of LTM.

● **Before You Go On**

What can we say about the capacity, duration, and accuracy of long-term memory?

How Do We Get Information into Long-Term Memory?

We have seen how simple repetition (maintenance rehearsal) can be used to keep material active in short-term memory. This sort of rehearsal is also one way to move information from STM to LTM. Within limits, the more one repeats a bit of information, the more likely it is that it will be remembered beyond the limits of short-term memory. The truth of the matter, however, is that the simple repetition of information is an inefficient way to encode information in long-term memory.

To get information into long-term memory usually requires that we think about it, reorganize it, form images of it, make it meaningful, or relate it to something already in our long-term memories. In other words, to get information into LTM we need to use **elaborative rehearsal**, a term proposed by Craik and Lockhart (1972). Elaborative rehearsal is not an either-or sort of process. Information can be elaborated to greater or lesser degrees.

Consider a hypothetical experiment in which students are asked to respond to a list of words in a number of different ways. In one case they are asked to count the number of letters in each word. In another they are to generate a word that rhymes with the one they are reading. In a third case they are asked to use each word in a sentence. The logic is that in each instance the words were processed more fully, or more deeply, as subjects focused on (1) the simple, physical structure of the words, (2) the sounds of the words as they were said aloud, and (3) the meaning of the words, and their role in sentence structure. In such experiments, as processing increases, so does the recall of the words being processed (Cermack & Craik, 1979; Craik & Tulving, 1975).

elaborative rehearsal
a mechanism for processing information into LTM that involves the meaningful manipulation of the information to be remembered

● **Before You Go On**

Contrast elaborative rehearsal with maintenance rehearsal as a means of encoding information into long-term memory.

Are There Different Types of Long-Term Memories?

Our own experiences tell us that what we have stored in LTM can be retrieved in many different forms. We can remember the definitions of words. We can visualize people and events from the past. We can remember the melodies of songs. We can recall how our bodies moved when we first tried to roller skate. It may be that information in long-term memory is processed by different subsystems or types of LTM. This notion of different long-term memory systems is a relatively new one in psychology and, as you might expect, there is no general agreement on just what all of the systems within LTM might be (Johnson & Hasher, 1987). Here, we'll briefly review three possible LTM subsystems (Tulving, 1972, 1985, 1986). Although the three can and do interact with each other, they are basically different.

One type of long-term memory is called **procedural memory**. In this memory, we have stored our recollections of learned responses, or chains of responses. Also stored here is the collection of patterned responses that we have learned well, such as how to balance and ride a bicycle, how to write, how to type, how to shave, or how to apply makeup. Simply, what is stored in procedural memory are the basic procedures of our lives. What we have stored here is put into use with little or no effort. At one time in your life, for example, handwriting was difficult as you strained to form letters and words correctly. But by now your writing skills, or "procedures," are so ingrained in procedural memory that you retrieve the steps involved almost without thinking. John Anderson (1986, 1987) calls the information in this subsystem of LTM *procedural knowledge,* or "knowing how," while the other types of LTM hold *declarative knowledge, or "knowing that."*

In **semantic memory** we store simple concepts, vocabulary, and rules. Here is stored our (declarative) knowledge of ourselves and the world in which we live. Our semantic memories are crammed with facts, both important and trivial, such as:

procedural memory
in LTM, the storage of stimulus-response associations and skilled patterns of responses

semantic memory
in LTM, the storage of vocabulary, facts, simple concepts, rules, and the like

Who opened the first psychology laboratory in Leipzig in 1879?
How many stripes are there on the American flag?

Basic procedures, or movements, such as those acquired when one learns how to swim, are stored in procedural memory. The rules that govern the structure, or grammar, of one's language are stored in semantic memory. Life experiences, mundane and dramatic, are stored in episodic memory.

Is "Colorless green ideas sleep furiously" a grammatically correct sentence? What do dogs eat?

If we can answer these questions, we have found those answers in our long-term semantic memories.

It is also true that semantic memories are somewhat abstract. By that I mean that although we may know how many stripes there are on the American flag, and we have a general idea of what dogs eat, we would have difficulty remembering how, why, or even when we ever acquired such tidbits of information. Another way of saying the same thing is to suggest that the information in semantic memory is not tied in any real way to our memories of our own life experiences, which is what sets it apart from the third type of long-term memory.

The third variety of memory proposed by Tulving is **episodic memory**, where we store the memories of our life events and experiences. It is a time-related memory, with the experiences stored here laid down in chronological order. Episodic memory seems to operate something like a video camera that registers all of our life's events on one continuous videotape. The contents of episodic memories are memories for specific events, not abstract ideas. For example:

episodic memory
in LTM, the storage of life events and experiences

The Retrieval of Repressed Memories of Childhood Trauma

When we concern ourselves with the accuracy of long-term memories, we often think of situations where the accuracy or inaccuracy of recalled experiences is of little real consequence. Recently, considerable attention has been focused on the issue of the truth or validity of the "memories" of childhood trauma and abuse. In most cases, the focus has been on the recovery in adulthood of memories formed in early childhood that were then "repressed." Repression is a Freudian notion, said to have occurred when extremely unpleasant or traumatic events in one's life are pushed deep into the unconscious corners of one's memory from which retrieval is very difficult at best. That some process—call it repression—can help us to forget unpleasant events of the past is an idea that has gained wide acceptance in psychology (Baddeley, 1990; Byrd, 1994; Erdelyi, 1985; Erdelyi & Goldberg, 1979; Gold et al. 1994; Loftus, 1993a, 1994).

In recent years, thousands of people—mostly women in their 20s, 30s, and 40s—have come forward with accusations that they were sexually abused as children, usually by some member of their own family (Jaroff, 1993). Even the rich and famous have "gone public" with stories of the recovery of once-repressed memories of terrible child abuse: Roseanne and former Miss America Marilyn Van Derbur, to name just two (Garry & Loftus, 1994). The trauma of child abuse (sexual or not) seems to be a likely event to be repressed—to be put out of one's conscious awareness.

In 1993, Elizabeth Loftus challenged the authenticity of the reports of some adults who claimed that they had "remembered" events that may never have happened in the first place. Please understand: Loftus has never argued that child abuse is a fiction. No, the physical and sexual abuse of children by adults are certainly not rare phenomena. It may be,

however, that some people (genuinely) come to believe that they were abused as children in order to help make sense of some of the difficulties they are encountering as adults (Frankel, 1993; Gardner, 1993; Powell & Boer, 1994; Wakefield & Underwager, 1992; Yapko, 1993). In some cases, the idea that a person was molested or abused may come from a therapist who says something like, "You know, I have seen many cases like yours, and often find that the person was sexually abused as a child. Do you suppose anything like that could have happened to you?"

In May, 1994, a jury in Napa, California, awarded Gary Ramona $500,000 in a civil trial. Ramona's daughter, Holly, had entered psychotherapy in 1989 for treatment of bulimia, an eating disorder. Shortly thereafter, Holly began accusing her father of dozens of incidents of rape and abuse. The incidents reportedly happened when Holly was between five and eight years old, and had been repressed until they were uncovered in the course of therapy. We probably will never know what happened to Holly as a child, or what brought on the symptoms of her disorder, but at least this jury agreed with her father that her therapist had planted ideas of abuse in her "memory."

Whether repressed memories of child abuse and trauma are real, have been planted by someone else intentionally or not, or are fully imagined is not an academic question. The American Psychiatric Association, the American Medical Association, and the American Psychological Association have all formed study groups and committees to study the issue and bring it to some resolution. Interestingly enough, although there are opinions galore, the one thing on which all agree is that there is virtually no sound, scientific, empirical research that can resolve this question at this time (Byrd, 1994; Gleaves, 1994; Gold et al., 1994; Loftus, 1994; Olio, 1994).

What did you have for lunch yesterday?
Did you have a good night's sleep?
How did you spend your last summer vacation?
What did your dog eat yesterday?

The answers to these sorts of questions are stored in our episodic memories.

Some researchers claim there is a separate category of episodic memory they call *autobiographical memory* (Baddeley, 1990; Berscheid, 1994). Although episodic memory contains events that have happened to us, those autobiographical memories are particularly significant. What I had for lunch last Monday may be in my episodic memory, but teaching my first class in introductory psychology as a graduate student at the University of Tennessee is probably in my autobiographical memory as well. One's autobiographical memory does not seem to develop until about the age of 3–3 1/2 years, or until we are old enough to be able to talk to ourselves about the events of our lives (Nelson, 1993; Pillemer & White, 1989).

● **Before You Go On**

Name and briefly describe three possible subsystems, or types, of long-term memory.

T O P I C 7 B

WHY WE FORGET: FACTORS AFFECTING RETRIEVAL

In this Topic, we turn to the practical matter of accounting for why we forget things. In the terminology we've been developing in this chapter, forgetting is a matter of retrieval failure. Our focus, then, will be on factors that affect the retrieval of information from memory. Retrieval is an important memory process no matter what the information we have stored or where we have stored it. Whether we are talking about a simple, well-learned habit stored in procedural memory, a technical definition stored in semantic memory, or a personal experience stored in episodic memory, if retrieval fails at the critical time, that information will be of no use to us.

What sorts of things influence our ability to retrieve information from our long-term memories? In truth, the list is not a very long one. We'll organize our discussion around four different but interrelated factors: (1) how memory is measured, (2) how encoding strategies influence later retrieval, (3) how encoding is scheduled, and (4) how interference can affect retrieval. Throughout this discussion we will assume that the to-be-remembered information is actually stored in long-term memory. That is, we will focus on problems of retrieval, not retention. The truth is, of course, we may feel that we have "forgotten" something when it was never really stored in memory in the first place.

HOW WE MEASURE RETRIEVAL

One factor affecting the retrieval of information from memory is how one is asked to go about retrieving it. This is a factor over which you and I seldom have much control. For instance, unless you have an unusually demo-cratic instructor, you will not be allowed to vote on what kind of exams will be given in class.

Direct, Explicit Measures

Measures of retrieval are called direct, or explicit, when someone must con-sciously, or purposely, retrieve specified information from his or her memory (as on a classroom exam). Both *recall* and *recognition* qualify as direct measures.

Let's design an example to work with. We have students come to the laboratory on a given Tuesday to learn a list of 15 randomly chosen words. Some students take longer than others, but eventually all of them learn the list. The students then report to the laboratory two weeks later, when our basic question is: "How many of the words that you learned two weeks ago do you still remember?" How could we find out?

One thing we could do is ask for simple recall of the list of words. **Re-call** asks someone to produce information to which he or she has been pre-viously exposed. To use recall in our experiment, we need only provide our students with a blank sheet of paper and ask them to write, in any order, as many of the words from the learned list as they can. (Technically, this is *free recall*. If we asked them to recall the list in the order in which it was pre-sented, we'd be asking for *serial recall*.) For recall, we provide the fewest cues to aid the retrieval. We specify the information we want and essentially say, "Now go into your long-term memory, locate that information, get it out, and write it down." Let's assume that one student correctly recalls six words.

Now suppose that we furnish our student with a list of 50 words, in-cluding those on the previously learned list. We instruct her to "circle the words on this list that you recognize from the list you learned two weeks ago." Now we are not asking for recall, but for **recognition**, a task that re-quires someone to identify information learned previously. Isn't it likely that our student will do better on this task? She recalled 6 words, so let's say she recognizes 11 words. In a way, we have a slight dilemma. Do we say that our subject remembered 6 words or 11 words? The answer is, "Yes, either 6 or 11." Whether our subject remembered 6 words or 11 words depends on how we asked her to go about remembering.

In virtually every case, retrieval by recognition is superior to retrieval by recall (Bahrick, 1984; Brown, 1976; Schacter, 1987). Figure 7.4 provides some clear-cut data in support of this point. Recall and recognition are sim-ilar in that they both involve the retrieval of information stored in semantic memory (occasionally episodic memory) (Hayman & Tulving, 1989; Tulv-ing, 1983), and seem to involve the same physiological underpinnings in the brain (Haist et al., 1992; Squire, et al., 1993). The major difference is that with recall we provide minimal retrieval cues, whereas with recognition we provide maximum cues and ask the subject to identify a stimulus as be-ing one that she or he has seen before (Mandler, 1980).

Indirect, Implicit Measures

Measures of memory classified as indirect, or implicit, are more subtle than either recall or recognition. With indirect measures, someone demon-strates that information is stored in memory when he or she can take ad-vantage of previous experiences without consciously trying to do so.

recall
an explicit measure of retrieval in which an individual is given the fewest possible cues for retrieval

recognition
an explicit measure of retrieval in which an individual is re-quired to identify as familiar material previously learned

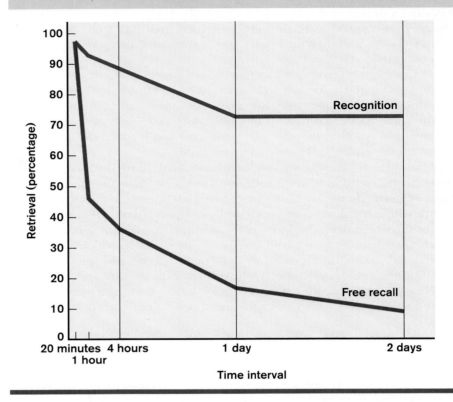

FIGURE 7.4

Differences in retrieval scores for the memory of nonsense syllables over a 2-day period. In one case, retrieval is measured with a test for recall, whereas in the other case, retrieval is measured by a recognition test. (From Luh, 1922.)

relearning

an implicit measure of memory in which one notes an improvement in performance when material is learned for a second time

What if one of the students in our example experiment returned to the laboratory two weeks after memorizing a list of words and then could neither recall nor recognize any of the items? We might be a bit surprised, but we'd be wrong if we assumed that our subject retained nothing. What if we ask the student to relearn the list of 15 words? Two weeks ago it took ten trials, or presentations, before she learned the list of words. Now, relearning the same list, it takes only seven trials. This is a common finding in memory research.

Relearning—the technique of noting changes in performance that occur when one is required to learn material for a second time—almost always takes less effort or fewer trials than did original learning. The difference is attributed to one's memory of the original learning. Because relearning does not require the direct, or conscious, retrieval of information from memory, it is referred to as an indirect, or implicit, test of memory retention (Graf & Schacter, 1985; Roediger, 1990; Schacter, 1987, 1992).

Among other things, research on implicit memory supports the hypothesis that information may be stored in various types of long-term memory. Although relearning a set of verbal materials, such as words, is an indirect measure of memory, most tests of implicit retention focus on *procedural memories*. Procedural memories include the storage of "knowing how to do things," such as tying a shoelace, typing, speaking, or riding a bicycle. Remembering how to accomplish these things is virtually automatic and unconscious. When we specifically try to recall how to do them, our performance may deteriorate. "In some sense, these performances reflect prior learning, but seem to resist conscious remembering" (Roediger, 1990, p. 1043).

Procedural memories may be very resistant to destruction. Patients who suffer from amnesia show significantly poorer performance on explicit tests of memory, such as recall or recognition tasks, but often perform as well as nonamnesic persons on implicit measures of memory (Warrington & Weiskrantz, 1968, 1970). This finding has been replicated many times (Bowers & Schacter, 1990; Shimamura, 1986). What this means is that even in the worst of amnesia cases, long-term procedural memories may be maintained. Remember the last time you heard about a victim of amnesia? Usually we hear about some adult found wandering, totally unaware of who he is, where he came from, or how he got there. There seems to be no *direct* recollection of long-term memories. But have you noticed that such amnesia patients do demonstrate all sorts of long-term memories? They remember how to talk, how to eat, and how to get dressed. They remember, in short, behaviors stored in procedural memory.

● **Before You Go On**

How do recall and recognition measures affect our assessment of retrieval?

What are implicit tests of retention, and what do they tell us about long-term memory?

HOW WE ENCODE INFORMATION

I have made the point before that encoding, storage, and retrieval are related memory processes. In this section, we'll explore the relationship between retrieval and encoding. At one level, the issue is simple: If you do not encode information appropriately, you will have difficulty retrieving it. We tend to forget those pieces of information that we did not adequately encode. You can't recall my mother's maiden name because you never encoded or stored it in the first place. You've never heard my mother's maiden name, but you have had countless encounters with pennies. Can you draw a picture of a penny, locating all of its features? Can you recognize from a set of drawings which one accurately depicts a penny (see Figure 7.5)? In fact, few of us can correctly recognize a drawing of a penny, and even fewer can recall all of its essential features, nearly 90 percent forgetting that the word "LIBERTY" appears right behind Lincoln's shoulder (Nickerson & Adams, 1979; Rubin & Kontis, 1983). These retrieval failures do not reflect a lack of experience, but a lack of adequate encoding. We'll cover four general encoding issues: context effects, meaningfulness, mnemonic devices, and schemas.

The Power of Context

Retrieval is best when the situation, or context, in which the retrieval occurs matches the context that was present at encoding. When cues present at encoding are also present during retrieval, retrieval is enhanced. The **encoding specificity principle** states that how we retrieve that information depends on how it was encoded in the first place (Flexser & Tulving, 1982; Newby, 1987; Tulving & Thompson, 1973). Not only do we encode and

encoding specificity principle
the hypothesis that how we retrieve information depends on how it was encoded, and that retrieval is enhanced to the extent retrieval cues match encoding cues

FIGURE 7.5
Fifteen drawings of the head of a penny. The fact that we cannot easily identify the correct rendition emphasizes that simple repetition of a stimulus does not guarantee that it will be stored usefully in long-term memory. (After Nickerson & Adams, 1979.)

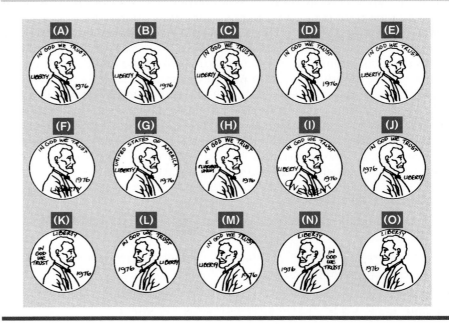

store particular items of information, but we also note and store the context in which those items occur. Recalling the months of the year in alphabetical order is very difficult because this is not the order in which they were processed into memory in the first place. The encoding specificity principle is as valid for animals as it is for humans. "Ease of retrieval is quite strongly influenced by the context in which the animal is asked to retrieve it. The closer the context is to training conditions and the more unique the context is for specific memories, the better the retrieval" (Spear et al., 1990, pp. 190–191).

Here's a hypothetical experiment (based on Tulving & Thompson, 1973) that demonstrates encoding specificity. Students are asked to learn a list of 24 common words. Half the students are given cue words to help them remember each item on the list. For the stimulus word *wood*, the cue word is *tree*, for *cheese*, the cue word is *green*, and so on for each of the 24 words. The other students receive no cue during their learning (i.e., while encoding). Later, the students are asked to recall as many words as they can. What we discover is that the cue helps those students who had seen it during learning, but it actually *decreases* the recall for those who had not seen it. If learning takes place without a cue, recall will be better without it.

How-to-study-in-college books often recommend that you choose one special place for studying. Your kitchen table is probably not a good choice, because that setting is already associated with eating experiences. The context of your kitchen is not a good one for encoding information unless you expect to be tested for retrieval in that same context—which seems highly unlikely. This advice was affirmed by a series of experiments by Smith (1979). For example, he had subjects learn material in one room, and then he tested their recall for that material in either the same room or a different one. When a different room—a new context, with different cues—was used for recall, retrieval performance dropped substantially. Simply instructing students to try to remember and think about the room in which learning took place helped recall. The best place to study for your next exam is in the room where the exam will be given.

Context effects are related to what is called **state-dependent memory**. The idea here is that to a degree, retrieval depends on the extent to which a person's *state of mind* at retrieval matches his or her state of mind at encoding (Leahey & Harris, 1989). If learning takes place while a subject is under the influence of a drug, for example, being under the influence of that drug at retrieval has beneficial effects (e.g., Eich et al., 1975; Goodwin et al., 1969; Parker et al., 1976). Research by Gordon Bower (Bower et al., 1978; Bower, 1981) and others suggests that one's mood can predict retrieval. Using moods (sad or happy) induced by hypnotic suggestion, Bower found that retrieval was best when mood at retrieval matched mood at learning, regardless of whether that mood was happy or sad. This effect seems particularly true for female subjects (Clark & Teasdale, 1985).

There also is evidence that our memories for emotionally arousing experiences are likely to be easier to recall than emotionally neutral events (Thompson, 1982). This may be because emotional arousal increases the levels of certain hormones that, in turn, help to form vivid memories associated with the emotional arousal (Gold, 1987; McGaugh, 1983). That emotional arousal may play a part in the formation of particularly vivid memories may help us understand what Brown and Kulik (1977) call **flashbulb memories**—memories of events that are unusually clear and vivid. You probably have flashbulb memories of several events: your high school graduation, the funeral of a friend, or how you learned about some significant news event. People of my father's generation still recall in considerable detail exactly what they were doing when they heard that Pearl Harbor had been bombed, while those in my generation similarly recall all the events that surround our learning of the assassination of President John Kennedy. Perhaps today's college students will form flashbulb memories of O. J. Simpson's white Ford Bronco being pursued down the Los Angeles freeway by squadrons of police cars. Although flashbulb memories *are* very clear and vivid, there is little reason to believe that they are any more complete or accurate than other memories (McCloskey et al, 1988; Neisser, 1982, 1991). They are typically memories of the sort that are stored in episodic LTM. It is also true that if the emotion that accompanies an event is personally experienced and one of extreme anxiety, the memory of the event may be *more* difficult to recall than normal (See the box "Psychology in the Real World," p. 253).

state-dependent memory
the notion that retrieval is enhanced to the extent that one's state of mind at retrieval matches one's state of mind at encoding

flashbulb memories
particularly clear and vivid memories—usually of emotional experiences—that are easily retrieved but not necessarily accurate in all details

● **Before You Go On**

How does the situation, or context, in which one encodes information affect retrieval of that information?

The Usefulness of Meaningfulness

I have a hypothesis: I believe I can determine the learning ability of students by noting where they sit in a classroom. The good, bright students tend to choose seats farthest from the door. Poorer students sit by the door, only interested in easily getting in and out of the room. (Although there may be some truth to this, I'm not serious.) To make my point, I propose an experiment. Students seated away from the door are asked to learn a list

Flashbulb memories often reflect one's age or generation. For many Americans, receiving word of President John Kennedy's assassination has become a clear and vivid memory. Perhaps the television image of O. J. Simpson's white Bronco being pursued by Los Angeles police on the L.A. freeway system will, similarly, become a flashbulb memory.

meaningfulness
the extent to which information evokes associations with information already in memory

of words that I read aloud only once. I need a second list of words for those students seated by the door because they've already heard my first list. The list that my "smart students" hear is: *university, registrar, automobile, environmental, computer, white,* and so forth. As I predicted, they have no problem recalling this list after just one or two presentations. The students huddled by the door get my second list: *insidious, tachistoscope, sophistry, flotsam, episcotister,* and so forth. Needless to say, my hypothesis will be confirmed.

This obviously is not a fair experiment. Students sitting by the door will yell foul. My second list of words is clearly more difficult to learn and recall than the first. The words on the first list are more familiar, they occur more frequently, and are easier to pronounce. However, the major difference between the words on these two lists is the **meaningfulness** of the items—the extent to which they elicit existing associations in one's memory. The *university, registrar, automobile* list is relatively easy to remember because each word is meaningful. Each word makes us think of many other things, or produces many associations, that is, they are easy to elaborate. Words like *tachistoscope* and *episcotister* are more difficult because they evoke few if any associations.

A very important point is that meaningfulness is not a characteristic or a feature built into material to be learned. *Meaningfulness resides in the memory of the learner. Tachistoscope* may be a meaningless collection of letters for some people, but for others, it is rich in meaning, a word with which they can form many associations. What is meaningful and what is not is a function of our individual experiences.

It follows, then, that one of your tasks as a learner is to do whatever you can to make the material you are learning as meaningful as possible. You need to seek out or establish associations between what you are learning and what you already know. You need to elaboratively rehearse what you are encoding so you can retrieve it later, asking yourself a series of questions about what you are studying. What does this mean? What does it make me think of? Does it remind me of anything I already know? Can I make this material meaningful? If you cannot, there is little point in going on to more. Perhaps you now see a major reason for including "Before You Go On" questions within each chapter.

● **Before You Go On**

What is meaningfulness?

How does meaningfulness relate to retrieval?

The Value of Mnemonic Devices

Retrieval is enhanced when we elaborate on the material we are learning—when we organize it or make it meaningful during the encoding process. Now we'll look at a few specific encoding strategies, **mnemonic devices**, that we can use to aid our retrieval by helping us organize and add meaningfulness to new material.

Research by Bower and Clark (1969) shows that we can improve the retrieval of unorganized material if we can weave it into a meaningful story—a technique called **narrative chaining**. One group of college students was asked to learn a list of 10 nouns in order. It is not a difficult task, and students had little trouble with it. Then they were given another list of 10 nouns to learn, then another—12 lists in all. The students were given no instructions other than to remember each list of words in order.

A second group of students was given the same 12 lists of 10 nouns each to learn. They were asked to make up little stories that used each of the words on the list in turn. After each list was presented, both groups were asked to recall the words they had just heard. At this point, there was no difference in recall for the two groups. Then came a surprise. After all 12 lists had been studied and recalled, students were tested again on their recall for each list. The students were given a word from one of the 12 lists, and were asked to recall the other 9 words on that list. The difference in recall between the two groups of students in this instance was striking (see Figure 7.6). The students who used a narrative chaining technique recalled 93 percent of the words, whereas those who did not use narrative chaining to organize the random list of words recalled only 13 percent. The message is clear: Organizing unrelated words into stories helps us remember them.

Forming *mental images*, or pictures in our minds, also can improve memory. Using imagery at encoding to improve retrieval is helpful in many different situations (Begg & Paivio, 1969; Marschark et al., 1987; Paivio, 1971, 1986). Mental imagery is what helps us to retrieve words such as *horse*, *rainbow*, and *typewriter* more readily than words such as *treason*, *session*, and *effort*—even when factors such as frequency of occurrence and meaningfulness are equated.

Assume, for example, that you have to learn the meanings of a large number of Spanish words. You could use simple rote repetition, but this technique is tedious and not very efficient. Atkinson (1975) claims that to improve memory for foreign language vocabulary, it is useful to imagine some connection that visually unites the English and Spanish words. He calls this the *key word* method of study. For example, the Spanish word for "horse" is *caballo*, pronounced *cab-eye-yo*. To remember this association, you might choose *eye* as the key word and picture a horse kicking someone in the eye. If you are not prepared to be that gruesome, you might imagine a horse with a very large eye. The Spanish word for "duck" is *pato*. Here your key word might be *pot*, and you could picture a duck wearing a pot on its

mnemonic devices
strategies for improving retrieval that take advantage of existing memories in order to organize information and make new material meaningful

narrative chaining
the mnemonic device of relating words together in a story, thus organizing them in a meaningful way

FIGURE 7.6

Percent correct recall for words from 12 lists learned under two study, or encoding, conditions. In the narrative condition, subjects made up short stories to relate words meaningfully, whereas in the control condition, simple memorization without any specified mnemonic device was used. (After Bower & Clark, 1969.)

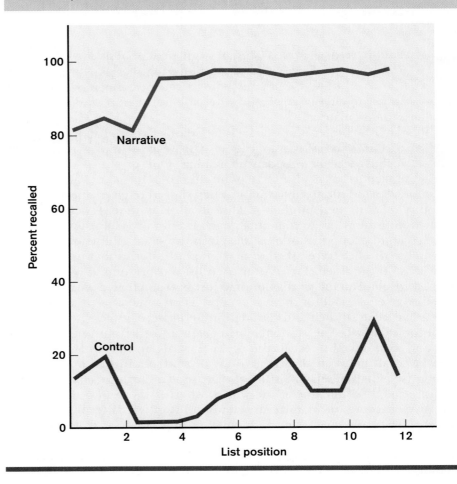

FIGURE 7.7

An illustration of how the key word method can be used to help foreign language retrieval. (After Atkinson, 1975.)

head (Figure 7.7) or sitting in a pot on the stove. This may sound strange, but research suggests that it actually works very well (Pressley et al., 1982).

The same basic technique works whenever you need to remember any paired information. Bower (1972) had students learn lists of English word pairs. Some were instructed to form a mental image that showed an interaction between the two words. One pair was *piano-cigar*. There are many ways to form an image of a piano and a cigar: The cigar could be balanced on the edge of the piano, for instance. Recall for word pairs was much better for those students who formed mental images than it was for those who did not. As it happens, interactive, commonplace images are *more useful* than strange and bizarre ones (Bower, 1970; Wollen et al., 1972). That is, to remember the piano-cigar pair, it is better to pic-

The method of loci is an ancient mnemonic device. This illustration is by a Dominican monk in the sixteenth century. On the left are the abbey and the surrounding buildings through which the speaker will mentally walk, placing the ideas (illustrated on the right) that he or she needs to recall.

ture a cigar balanced on a piano than it is to picture a piano actually smoking a cigar (see Figure 7.8). To remember that it was Bower and Clark who did the experiment on narrative chaining, try to picture two storytellers chained together, each holding a Clark Bar as they take a bow on a stage.

The last imagery-related mnemonic device I'll mention may be the oldest. It is the **method of loci**, attributed to the Greek poet Simonides (Yates, 1966). The idea here is to get in your mind a well-known location (*loci* are locations) such as the floor plan of your house or apartment. Visually place the material you are to recall in various locations throughout your house in a sensible order. When the time comes to retrieve the material, mentally walk through your chosen locations, retrieving the information you have stored at each different place.

Some time ago, I was asked to give a short talk. There were several points I wanted to make, and I didn't want to use written notes as a memory aid. I also didn't want to appear nervous, so I decided to try the method of loci. I divided my talk into six or seven major ideas, imagined my house, and walked through it in my mind. I stored my introduction at the front door, point 1 got me to the living room, point 2 to the dining room, and so on through the house until I got to my conclusion at the back door. Even though I have been telling others about the method of loci for many years, this was the first time that I had used it, and I was very impressed with how easy it was to remember my little speech.

Mnemonic devices don't have to be formal techniques with special names. You used a mnemonic trick to learn which months of the year have 30 days and which have 31 when you learned the ditty, "Thirty days hath September, April, June, and November. All the rest have. . . ." Some students originally learned the colors of the rainbow (we called it the visible spectrum) in order by remembering the name "Roy G. Biv," which I grant you

method of loci
the mnemonic device that mentally places information to be retrieved at a series of familiar locations (loci)

FIGURE 7.8
The key word method can also be used to help us remember pairs of English words. (After Wollen et al., 1972.)

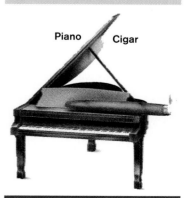
Piano   Cigar

FIGURE 7.9
The Balloons Passage

If the balloons popped, the sound would not be able to carry since everything would be too far away from the correct floor. A closed window would also prevent the sound from carrying since most buildings tend to be well insulated. Since the whole operation depends on a steady flow of electricity, a break in the middle of the wire would also cause problems. Of course the fellow could shout, but the human voice is not loud enough to carry that far. An additional problem is that a string could break on the instrument. Then there could be no accompaniment to the message. It is clear that the best situation would involve less distance. Then there would be fewer potential problems. With face-to-face contact, the least number of things could go wrong.

From Bransford & Johnson, 1972

isn't terribly meaningful. But it does help us remember "red, orange, yellow, green, blue, indigo, violet." My guess is that you can think of other mnemonic devices you have used to organize material and make it meaningful.

● **Before You Go On**

Describe narrative chaining, mental imagery, and the method of loci as mnemonic devices.

The Role of Schemas

schema
a system of organized general knowledge, stored in long-term memory, that may guide the encoding and retrieval of information

The encoding specificity hypothesis tells us that how we retrieve information is affected by how we have encoded it. One of the processes that influences how we encode and retrieve information is our use of schemas (sometimes called scripts). A **schema** is an organized, general knowledge structure stored in long-term memory (Mayer, 1983). Schemas provide a framework that we can use to understand new information and also to retrieve that information later (Alba & Hasher, 1983; Lord, 1980).

Let's look at a few examples of research that involve the use of schemas as encoding strategies. Before you go any further, stop and read the short passage in Figure 7.9. As it stands, the paragraph doesn't make much sense, does it? All the words are sensible. Even individual sentences seem reasonable. But as a story, it seems virtually meaningless because you have no schema available to comprehend its meaning (Bransford & Johnson, 1972). Now look at the drawing in Figure 7.14 at the very end of this chapter. This drawing provides a schema that gives meaning to the paragraph. Students who were shown this picture *before* they read the passage recalled more than twice as much about it than did students who didn't see the picture at all or who were shown the picture after they read the paragraph. The message here is that schemas help retrieval only if the same schemas were available at encoding.

I've never learned how to play chess. I know what a chessboard looks like and I can probably name most of the pieces. I realize that there are rules about how pieces can be moved in a chess game, but I don't know what those rules are. In other words, I have a very sketchy schema for chess. If you showed me a chessboard with pieces positioned as if in the midst of a game and then later asked me to reconstruct what I had seen, I'm afraid that I would do very poorly. When chess experts are asked to reconstruct the positions of pieces from memory, they do very well (DeGroot, 1965, 1966). Part of the explanation for their success is that they have complete, detailed schemas for chess games, which helps them encode and later retrieve the positions on the board. In fact, when chess pieces are positioned randomly on a chessboard, the memory of chess experts is no better than mine or that of any other novice (Chase & Simon, 1973). This is because the randomly positioned pieces don't fit the experts' schemas for chess, taking away their advantage.

So what's the bottom line? When to-be-remembered information is consistent with prior, existing information (such as schemas) retrieval will be enhanced. If to-be-remembered material is at odds with existing schema, those schemas may actually inhibit retrieval.

● **Before You Go On**
What are schemas, and how do they affect retrieval?

HOW WE SCHEDULE PRACTICE

A point I have made repeatedly is that retrieval, no matter how it is measured, depends largely on how one goes about encoding, rehearsing, or practicing information in the first place. Retrieval also depends on the amount of practice and how that practice is scheduled. One reason why some students do not do as well on exams as they would like is that they simply do not have (or make) enough time to study or practice material covered on the exams. A related reason is that some students do not schedule wisely what time they do have.

Overlearning

What you and I often do once we decide to learn something is to read, practice, and study the material until we just know it. We practice until we are satisfied that we have encoded and stored the required information in our memories, and then we quit. In other words, we often fail to engage in **overlearning**—the process of practicing or rehearsing material over and above what is needed to learn it. Consider this fictitious example and see if you can extend this evidence to your study habits.

A student comes to the laboratory to learn a list of syllables such as: *dax, wuj, pib, zuw,* and so on. There are 15 such items on the list, and the list has to be presented repeatedly before our student can recall all the items correctly. Having recalled the items once, our student is dismissed with in-

overlearning
the practice or rehearsal of material over and above what is needed to learn it

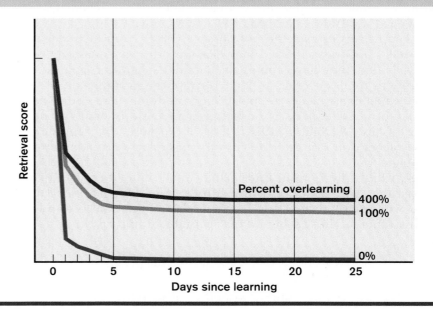

FIGURE 7.10
Idealized data showing the short- and long-term advantage of over-learning. Note the diminished returns with additional overlearning. (From Krueger, 1929.)

structions to return two weeks later for a test of his recall of the syllables. Not surprisingly, the student doesn't fare very well on the retrieval task.

What do you think would have happened if we had continued to present our student with the list of syllables at the time of learning, well beyond the point where he first learned them? Say the list was learned in 12 trials. We have the student practice the list for six more presentations (50 percent overlearning—practice that is 50 percent over that required for learning). Or let's require an additional 12 trials of practice (100 percent overlearning), or an additional 48 trials of practice (400 percent overlearning).

The effects of overlearning practice are well documented and very predictable. The recall data for this imaginary experiment might look like those presented in Figure 7.10. Note three things about these data: (1) If we measure retrieval at different times after learning, forgetting is impressive and rather sudden. (This is one of the results of the work on memory that Hermann Ebbinghaus reported back in 1885, and that many other researchers have confirmed since then.) (2) Overlearning improves retrieval, having its greatest effects with longer retention intervals. (3) There is a "diminishing returns" phenomenon present; that is, 50 percent overlearning is much more useful than no overlearning; 100 percent overlearning is better than 50 percent; and 400 percent is a bit better than 100 percent, but not by very much. For any learning task or individual there is probably an optimum amount of overlearning.

In summary, with everything else being equal, the more we practice what we are learning, the easier it will be to retrieve it. How one *schedules* practice or learning time is also important, and it is to this issue that we turn next.

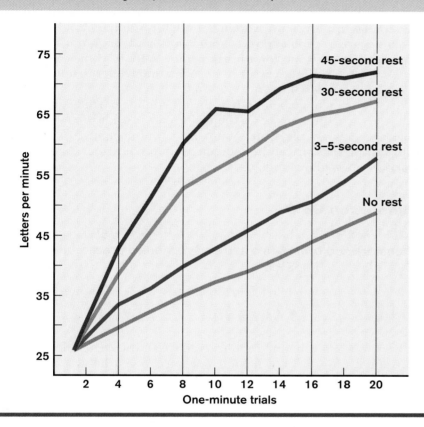

FIGURE 7.11

Improvement in performance as a function of distribution of practice time. The task involved was printing the letters of the alphabet upside-down and backward with twenty 1-minute trials separated by rest intervals of various lengths. (After Kientzle, 1946.)

Distributing Practice

Some of the oldest data in psychology tell us that retrieval can be improved if practice (encoding) is spread out over time with rest intervals spaced in between. The data in Figure 7.11 are fairly standard. In fact, this 1946 experiment provides such reliable results it is commonly used in psychology laboratory classes. The task is to write the letters of the alphabet, but upside down and from right to left. (If you think that sounds easy, you should give it a try.)

Subjects are given the opportunity to practice this task under four conditions. The *massed practice* group works on the task with no break between trials. The three *distributed practice* groups receive the same amount of actual practice, but get rest intervals interspersed between each 1-minute practice trial. One group gets a 3- to 5-second break between trials, a second group receives a 30-second rest, and a third group gets a 45-second break between practice trials.

As we can see in Figure 7.11, subjects in all four groups begin at the same (poor) level of performance. After 20 minutes of practice, the performance of all the groups shows improvement. By far, however, the massed practice (no rest) group does the poorest, and the 45-second-rest group does the best.

The conclusion to be drawn from years of research is that, almost without exception, distributed practice is superior to massed practice. There are exceptions, however. Some tasks might suffer from having rest intervals inserted in practice time. In general, when you must keep track of many things at the same time, you should continue practice until you have finished whatever it is you are working on. If, for example, you are working on a complex math problem, you should work it through until you find a solution, whether it's time for a break or not. And, of course, you should not break up, or distribute, practice in such a way as to disrupt the meaningfulness of the material you are studying.

What we're talking about here is the scheduling of study time. Discussions of study schedules make up the major part of all how-to-study books. The message is always the same: Many short (but meaningful) study periods with rest periods spaced in between are more efficient than are a few study periods massed together.

● **Before You Go On**

What is overlearning, and how does it affect retrieval?

Compare and contrast massed and distributed practice, noting their effects on retrieval.

HOW WE OVERCOME INTERFERENCE

Think back to when you were in third grade. Can you remember the name of the student who sat right behind you at school? I know I can't. I can guess who it might have been, but there seems to be no way that I can directly access and retrieve that information from my long-term memory. One possibility is that that information is no longer there. It may be, in some literal sense, lost forever. Perhaps I never encoded that information in a way that would allow me to retrieve it effectively. Yet another possibility is that the name of that student is, in fact, available in my memory, but it is inaccessible at the moment simply because I have had so many classes since third grade. So much has happened and entered my memory since third grade that the name I am looking for is "covered up" and being *interfered with* by information that entered later.

How about your most recent class? Can you recall who sat behind you in your last class? That might be a little easier, but remembering that name with confidence is still not easy. Again, our basic problem with retrieval may be one of interference. If we assume that the name we are searching for is still there (which *is* an assumption), we may not be able to retrieve it (we may have forgotten it) because so many *previous* experiences (classes attended earlier) are getting in the way, interfering with retrieval.

Retroactive Interference

The idea that interference can account for forgetting, or retrieval failure, is an old one in psychology. Early experiments showed that subjects who are active for a period of time after learning remember what they learned less well than do subjects who use the intervening time for sleep (Jenkins & Dallenbach, 1924). Figure 7.12 shows data from two reasonably comparable

FIGURE 7.12

These graphs illustrate how activity following learning can interfere with the retrieval of the learned material. In both cases, normal waking activity caused more interference than did forced inactivity (for cockroaches) or sleeping (for college students). (After Minami & Dallenbach, 1946.)

(A) Retention in the immobilized cockroach

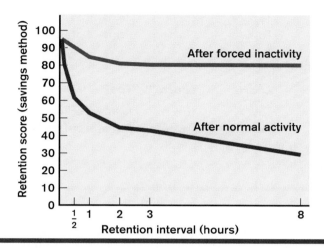

(B) Retention in the sleeping college student

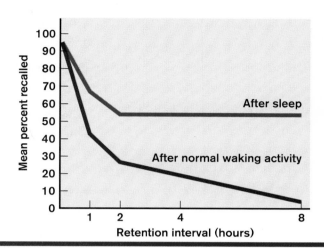

experiments—one with college students who had learned a list of nonsense syllables, and the other with cockroaches that had learned to avoid an area of their cage. In both cases, subjects who engaged in normal waking activity did less well on tests of retrieval over different retention intervals.

When interfering activities come *after* the learning of material to be retrieved, we are dealing with **retroactive interference**. Let's go back into the laboratory. We'll need two groups of subjects randomly assigned to either an experimental group or a control group. (You can follow along with the summary diagram in Figure 7.13). The subjects in both groups are asked to learn something (almost anything will do; we'll say it's a list of nonsense syllables). Having learned their lists, the groups are treated differently. Subjects in the experimental group are now asked to learn something else, perhaps a new list of nonsense syllables. At the same time, control group subjects are asked to do nothing (which is impossible, of course, in a literal sense). These subjects might be asked to rest quietly or to play some simple game.

Now for the test. Both groups are asked to remember whatever was presented in the first learning task. Control group subjects will show a higher retrieval score than experimental group subjects. For the latter group, the second set of learned material interferes with the retrieval of the material learned first. And, so long as it is the same for both groups, the method used to measure retrieval is irrelevant.

Most of us are familiar with retroactive interference from our own educational experiences. A student who studied French in high school takes a few courses in Spanish at college and now can't remember very much French. The Spanish keeps getting in the way. I have two students who are scheduled to take a psychology exam tomorrow morning at 9:00. Both are equally able and well-motivated. One student is taking only one class—mine. She studies psychology for two hours, watches TV for two hours, and goes to bed. The second student also studies psychology for two hours, but then reads a chapter and a half in her sociology textbook, just in case she is

retroactive interference
the inhibition of retrieval of previously learned material caused by material learned later

---

FIGURE 7.13

Designs of Experiments to Demonstrate Retroactive Interference and Proactive Interference

(A) Retroactive interference

	Learn	**Learn**	**Test**
Experimental group	Task A	Task B	Retrieval of Task A
Control group	Task A	Nothing	Retrieval of Task A

(B) Proactive interference

	Learn	**Learn**	**Task**
Experimental group	Task A	Task B	Retrieval of Task B
Control group	Nothing	Task B	Retrieval of Task B

Note: If interference is operating, the control group will demonstrate better retrieval than will the experimental group.

---

called on in class. After reading the sociology, she goes to bed. Everything else being equal, this second student will be at a disadvantage at exam time. The sociology that she studied will retroactively interfere with her retrieval of the psychology she learned previously. What is this student to do? Perhaps all she can do is set herself up for proactive interference.

Proactive Interference

proactive interference
the inhibition of retrieval of recently learned material caused by material learned earlier

Proactive interference occurs when *previously* learned material interferes with the retrieval of material learned later. First follow along in Figure 7.13(B), then we'll get back to our student and her studying problem. Again we have two groups of subjects, experimental and control. The experimental group starts off by learning something—that same list of syllables, perhaps. This time the control group subjects begin by resting quietly while the experimental group goes through the learning task. Both groups learn a second list of syllables. We now test for retrieval, but this time we test for the retrieval of the more recently learned material. Once again, the control group will be at an advantage. They have none of that first list in their memories to interfere with retrieval. The advantage is less than it was for retroactive interference. Proactive interference is seldom as detrimental as retroactive interference, which is why I would advise my student to study what she thinks is her most important assignment last.

Although retroactive and proactive interference effects are well documented, there are several factors that influence the extent of such interference (Underwood, 1957). Very meaningful, well-organized material is less susceptible to interference than is less meaningful material, such as nonsense syllables. It should also strike you as reasonable that *the nature of the interfering task* matters. As a rule of thumb, the more similar the interfering material is to the material being retrieved, the greater will be the interference (e.g., McGeoch & McDonald, 1931). My student who had to study for her psychology exam and read a sociology text will experience more interference (retroactive *or* proactive) than will a student who has to study for the psychology

FIGURE 7.14
A picture providing a possible schema for the story about balloons presented in Figure 7.9. (From Bransford & Johnson, 1972.)

exam and work on calculus problems. This is because there is little about calculus problems to get in the way, or interfere, with the psychology lesson.

● **Before You Go On**
Briefly describe retroactive and proactive interference.

A REMINDER ABOUT RETRIEVAL AND FORGETTING

Virtually all of our discussion in Topic 7B has been presented in terms of *retrieving information from long-term memory.* Before we leave this chapter, I simply want to remind you that this discussion has also been about what we usually call "forgetting." You should be able to recast this Topic in terms of an answer to the question, "Why do we forget things?" What would be some of your answers? Because those things were never learned or encoded into long-term memory in the first place. Because the cues available now are different from what they were when they were learned. Because we did not adequately elaborate them. Because they failed to fit any of our existing schemas. Because we spent an inadequate amount of time practicing or encoding those things. Because other things are interfering with our ability to remember them. And so on.

THINKING CRITICALLY ABOUT MEMORY

1. The ancient Greek view of human memory likened it to a block of wax in one's head onto which impressions, both deep and vivid or shallow and blurred, were made. Although this metaphor is no longer thought to be valid, it does present an intriguing picture. Can you think of any other metaphors for human memory that work as well or better?

2. Is there any way in which an individual can be conscious of the differences among the three major processes of memory: encoding, storage, and retrieval? That is, can you tell when one ends and the next begins?

3. How do we retrieve information from sensory memory?

4. Can you imagine how you could do an experiment to test the capacity or the duration of sensory memory for each of the senses?

5. When we hear that "So-and-so doesn't have any problems studying because he has a photographic memory," what do people mean when they use the term "photographic memory" in this context? How could we demonstrate whether such a thing exists?

6. How is short-term memory useful in the processing of spoken language? That is, could we talk to each other sensibly if we did not have short-term memories?

7. In what way does your experience confirm the research finding that information in short-term memory is processed acoustically, or in terms of how it sounds?

8. How do all of the different types of classroom exams that you have taken compare in terms of the exam question providing useful retrieval cues? (Multiple-choice and fill-in-the-blank are easy. What about other types of exams?)

9. What mnemonic devices can you think of other than the ones listed in the text?

10. Is there such a thing as "test anxiety"? What might be done about it?

11. How would you know if you had a "repressed memory"?

SUMMARY

TOPIC 7A

HOW CAN WE DESCRIBE HUMAN MEMORY?

● How do we define memory?

Memory is the cognitive process of actively representing information in memory (encoding), keeping it there (storage), and later bringing it out again (retrieval). *Pages 240–241.*

● What is sensory memory? What are its capacity and duration?

Sensory memory gives us the ability to store large amounts of information for very brief periods of time. We cannot encode or manipulate this information, so it is stored in the form in which it was presented to the senses. The capacity of sensory memory may approximate the capacity of our senses, but its duration is very limited. Visually presented stimuli last in sensory memory for only a fraction of a second; orally presented material may last for a few seconds. *Pages 241–242.*

● How long is information stored in STM?
● What is required to get information into STM and then keep it there?

Once entered into short-term memory, information can be held there for approximately 15–20 seconds before it fades or is replaced by new information. Some information will be inaccessible soon after encoding. Processing information into this memory requires that we attend to it. Information can enter into short-term memory from either sensory memory or long-term memory. We can keep information in STM by reattending to it, a process called "maintenance rehearsal." *Pages 242–245.*

● How much information can be held in STM? How can chunking affect the capacity of STM?

The capacity of STM is limited to approximately 7±2 bits of information. By "chunking" information together into meaningful clusters or units, more can be processed in STM, but the limit remains at about 7±2 chunks. *Page 246.*

● How is information encoded (represented) in short-term memory?

Information in our short-term memories may be encoded in several different forms, but acoustic encoding seems to be the most common. *Pages 246–247.*

● What can we say about the capacity, duration, and accuracy of long-term memory?

LTM can hold a virtually limitless amount of information for a very long time. A problem is that there is presently no scientific means of determining whether information that cannot be retrieved from LTM is unavailable or inaccessible. We do know that information in long-term memory is subject to distortion or replacement. *Pages 248–250.*

● Contrast elaborative rehearsal with maintenance rehearsal as a means of encoding information into long-term memory.

Although maintenance rehearsal may sometimes be sufficient to encode or move material from STM into LTM, there seems to be little doubt that the best mechanism for placing information into LTM is elaborative rehearsal—that is, to think about the material, forming associations or images of the material, and relating it to something already stored in LTM. The more elaboration, or the "deeper" the elaboration, the better retrieval will be. *Pages 250–251.*

● Name and briefly describe three possible subsystems, or types, of long-term memory.

Information may be stored in different ways in a variety of LTM systems. One is procedural memory, in which we retain learned connections between stimuli and responses—in essence, how we perform simple, well-learned behaviors. Semantic memories store facts, knowledge, rules, and vocabularies. Episodic memories are autobiographical; they provide a record of one's life experiences and events. *Pages 251–254.*

TOPIC 7B

WHY WE FORGET: FACTORS AFFECTING RETRIEVAL

● How do recall and recognition measures affect our assessment of retrieval?
● What are implicit tests of retention, and what do they tell us about long-term memory?

Our retrieval of information from memory is often a function of how we ask for retrieval. When we ask for retrieval by recall, we provide the fewest possible retrieval cues. For recognition, we provide the information to be retrieved and ask that it be identified as familiar. Both are direct, or explicit measures of retrieval. Retrieval by recognition is generally superior to retrieval by recall. As opposed to explicit tests of retrieval, implicit tests assess the extent to which previously experienced material is helpful in subsequent tasks. They do not require the conscious retrieval of specific information. For example, relearning shows us that even when once-learned material can be neither recalled nor recognized, that material will be easier to relearn than it was in the first place. Implicit tests of memory show us that even information that cannot be consciously or voluntarily retrieved from memory still can be influential. *Pages 254–257.*

● How does the situation, or context, in which one encodes information affect retrieval of that information?

The greater the extent to which the cues or context available at encoding match the cues or context available at retrieval, the better retrieval will be. The encoding specificity hypothesis asserts that how we retrieve information depends on how it was encoded. Psychologists have found that even matching an individual's state of mind at encoding and at retrieval is helpful. Heightened emotionality at encoding may produce (flashbulb) memories that are more vivid even if they are not more accurate. *Pages 257–259.*

● What is meaningfulness?
● How does meaningfulness relate to retrieval?

Meaningfulness is the extent to which material is related to, or associated with, information already stored in memory. In general, meaningful material (or material that is made meaningful) is easier to retrieve than meaningless material. Meaningfulness resides in the individual, not in the material to be learned, however. *Pages 259–261.*

● Describe narrative chaining, mental imagery, and the method of loci as mnemonic devices.

Mnemonic devices are strategies used to organize and add meaningfulness to material that is to be retrieved. Narrative chaining involves making up a story that meaningfully connects a list of otherwise unrelated items that need to be remembered. Several mnemonic devices suggest forming visual images of the material to be learned, which may provide an additional code for that material. Images that show commonplace interactions among stimuli are more useful than bizarre images. The method of loci also uses mental imagery and involves mentally placing items to be retrieved in a sequence of familiar locations (loci). *Pages 261–264.*

● What are schemas, and how do they affect retrieval?

Schemas are organized general knowledge systems stored in long-term memory. Based on one's past experiences, schemas summarize the essential features of common events or situations. They are used as a means of guiding the organization and meaning of new information. The more complete one's schema for information, the better will be the encoding and retrieval. *Pages 264–265.*

● What is overlearning, and how does it affect retrieval?
● Compare and contrast massed and distributed practice, noting their effects on retrieval.

Overlearning is the rehearsal over and above that needed for immediate recall of a specific bit of information. Within limits, the more one overlearns, the greater the likelihood of accurate retrieval. In massed practice, one's study or rehearsal occurs without intervening rest intervals. Distributed practice uses shorter segments of rehearsal, interspersed with rest intervals. In almost all cases, distributed practice leads to better retrieval than does massed practice. *Pages 265–268.*

● Briefly describe retroactive and proactive interference.

Retroactive interference (RI) occurs when previously learned material cannot be retrieved because it is inhibited or blocked by material or information that is learned later. Proactive interference (PI) occurs when information cannot be retrieved because it is inhibited or blocked by material that was learned earlier. Retroactive interference is usually more detrimental to retrieval than proactive interference. *Pages 268–271.*

TOPIC 7A

HOW CAN WE DESCRIBE HUMAN MEMORY?

7.1 If retrieval from memory is thought of as the final stage of information processing, what would be the first? a) learning b) perception c) thinking d) sensation. *Pages 240–241.*

7.2 Psychologists talk about passing information through three different types of memory called a) encoding, storage, and retrieval. b) primary, secondary, and tertiary. c) central, peripheral, and somatic. d) sensory, short-term, and long-term. *Pages 240–241.*

7.3 Which of the following best describes how information is represented, or coded, in sensory memory? We can say that the code for information in sensory memory is essentially a) physical. b) semantic. c) acoustic. d) symbolic. *Pages 241–242.*

7.4 True or False? For information to be processed into memory, the first thing that we do to or with that information is to learn it. *Pages 241–242.*

7.5 The minimal requirement for keeping information in short-term memory with maintenance rehearsal is that we a) elaborate on it in some way. b) make it meaningful. c) organize it. d) re-attend to it. *Pages 242–247.*

7.6 The amount of information held in STM (i.e., its capacity) can be extended if we can _____ that information. a) rehearse b) attend to c) chunk d) elaborate. *Pages 242–247.*

7.7 The best way to encode information in long-term memory is by a) rote repetition. b) taking extensive notes. c) maintenance rehearsal. d) elaborating it. *Pages 248–251.*

7.8 Elaboratively rehearsing information is mostly a process of organizing it and a) making it meaningful. b) re-attending to it. c) retrieving it. d) repeating it. *Pages 248–251.*

7.9 Imagine a 42-year-old man who has not ice skated since he was 12 years old. Even though it has been 30 years, he finds that he still can skate quite well. His ability to ice skate has been stored in his _____ memory. a) physical b) procedural c) episodic d) semantic. *Pages 248–251.*

7.10 The answer to which question is most likely to be found in episodic memory? a) When and where did you learn to ride a bicycle? b) When and where did Wundt open his laboratory? c) What sorts of information are stored in episodic memory? d) What is the result of dividing 134 by 12? *Pages 248–251.*

TOPIC 7B

WHY WE FORGET: FACTORS AFFECTING RETRIEVAL

7.11 True or False? Information in semantic memory is probably stored in chronological order; that is, in the order in which it was experienced. *Pages 254–257.*

7.12 When psychologists talk about "retrieval failure," what assumption do they make? a) We are dealing with short-term memory. b) Information is available, but not accessible. c) There must be some sort of brain damage involved. d) The material was never stored in the first place. *Pages 254–257.*

7.13 True or False? Retrieval measured by recall is usually superior to retrieval measured by recognition. *Pages 254–257.*

7.14 Research that involves _____ is dealing with implicit measures of memory. a) recognition b) free recall c) serial recall d) relearning. *Pages 254–257.*

7.15 Even in the worst cases of amnesia, many memories stored in _____ can be retrieved with relative ease. a) procedural memory b) semantic memory c) the hippocampus d) the cerebral cortex. *Pages 254–257.*

7.16 True or False? We may think of explicit memory retrieval as an unconscious process. *Pages 254–257.*

7.17 Most people cannot remember all the features on a dollar bill. Which one of the following phrases best describes the problem in such instances? a) lack of availability b) poorly worded questioning c) improper encoding d) proactivity. *Pages 257–261.*

7.18 What does the "encoding specificity hypothesis" tell us? a) Retrieval is enhanced to the extent that retrieval cues match encoding cues. b) We tend to remember pleasant experiences more readily than we remember unpleasant experiences. c) Retrieval is enhanced to the extent that we use explicit measures rather than implicit measures. d) The effects of interference are most noticeable at encoding, not retrieval. *Pages 257–261.*

7.19 Studies of state dependent memory provide support for a) recognition being superior to recall. b) retrograde amnesia. c) the encoding specificity hypothesis. d) the value of studying for exams. *Pages 257–261.*

7.20 True or False? Flashbulb memories are usually stored in procedural LTM. *Pages 257–261.*

7.21 Mnemonic devices enhance or improve retrieval because they a) involve the continued repetition of information. b) make material more meaningful. c) involve the right brain as well as the left brain. d) lengthen the storage in LTM. *Pages 261–264.*

7.22 Making up a little story that contains all of the words in a list to be recalled is a mnemonic technique called a) the pegword method. b) the method of loci. c) mental imagery. d) narrative chaining. *Pages 261–264.*

7.23 True or False? Mnemonic devices are useful at retrieval, but are unrelated to encoding information. *Pages 261–264.*

7.24 Organized, but general, representations of knowledge stored in long-term memory are called a) mnemonic devices. b) schemas. c) episodes. d) retrieval strategies. *Pages 261–265.*

7.25 After a list of words has been presented to Bob eight times, we have evidence that he has learned the list. If we want Bob to engage in 200 percent overlearning, how many additional presentations of this list would be required? a) 0 b) 8 c) 16 d) 20. *Pages 265–268.*

7.26 Which is true most often? a) Retroactive interference is less disrupting than proactive interference. b) Overlearning increases the capacity and duration of STM. c) Overwhelming anxiety explains most retrieval failures on classroom exams. d) Distributed practice is superior to massed practice. *Pages 265–268.*

7.27 If, during the course of a semester, you have nine classroom exams, for which exam will proactive interference be the greatest? a) the first b) the fifth [the one in the middle] c) the ninth d) Proactive interference will be the same for all nine exams. *Pages 265–268.*

7.28 You are in an experiment to demonstrate retroactive interference that may occur between two learning tasks, A and B, and are assigned to the experimental group. The first thing that you will be asked to do is to a) take a test on your retrieval of Task A. b) learn Task A. c) learn Task B. d) rest while the control group learns Task A. *Pages 268–271.*

HIGHER COGNITIVE PROCESSES

8

PREVIEW

TOPIC 8A—Problem Solving

What is A Problem?

Problem Representation

Problem-Solving Strategies

Barriers to Effective Problem Solving

TOPIC 8B—Language

Let's Talk: What is Language?

Language Use as a Social Process

Language Acquisition

TOPIC 8C—Intelligence

The Nature of Psychological Tests

Psychological Tests of Intelligence

Extremes of Intelligence

PSYCHOLOGY IN THE REAL WORLD: Blacks, Whites, IQ and The Bell Curve

THINKING CRITICALLY ABOUT HIGHER COGNITIVE PROCESSES

SUMMARY

TEST YOURSELF

Cognitions include ideas, beliefs, memories, thoughts, and images. When we know, understand, or remember something, we use cognitions to do so. Thus, cognitive processes involve the formation, manipulation, and use of cognitions. We discussed cognitive processes when we covered the selective and organizing processes of *perception*, the relatively permanent changes in mental processes that take place with *learning*, and the encoding, storing, and retrieving of information that are *memory*.

In this chapter, we will consider three complex cognitive processes: problem solving, language use, and intelligence. Because they rely so heavily on the basic processes of perception, learning, and memory, I refer to them as "higher" cognitive processes. I trust that you recognize that the manipulation of cognitions (memories, ideas, images, etc.) we are talking about here amounts to what most of us mean when we refer to *thinking*. Indeed, thinking involves the complex manipulation of cognitions in the sorts of ways we'll be discussing in this chapter.

Topic 8A deals with problem solving. Our daily lives are filled with all sorts of problems. Some are straightforward, or trivial; others are complex and important to us. We'll focus on problems that require the manipulation of cognitions for their solution and see how problem solving proceeds.

The second cognitive process we'll examine, in Topic 8B, is language. Using language involves a remarkable set of cognitive processes. Again, our first step will be to define language; then we'll deal with language as a social issue, as a means of communication. We'll also take a brief look at language acquisition.

Finally, we'll consider intelligence in Topic 8C. The use of one's intelligence can be considered the most complex of all cognitive processes, involving perception, learning, memory, problem solving, and language. We'll see how psychologists have characterized and measured intelligence (which will introduce us to psychological testing), and we'll look at differences in that aspect of intelligence that is determined by IQ tests.

TOPIC 8A

PROBLEM SOLVING

Solving problems requires several interrelated processes. First, we need to recognize that a problem exists. Then we have to decide how to represent the problem in such a way that we have a chance of solving it. We then have to devise a strategy to help us reach a solution. Finally, we need to determine whether our solution will actually work.

WHAT IS A PROBLEM?

Sometimes our goals are obvious, our present situation is clear, and how to get from where we are to where we want to be is also obvious. In these cases, we really don't have a problem. Say you want a nice breakfast. You have butter, eggs, bacon, and bread. You also have the implements needed to prepare these foods, and you know how to use them. For you, a nice breakfast would be two eggs over easy, three strips of fried bacon, and a piece of buttered toast. With little hesitation, you can engage in the appropriate behaviors to reach your goal.

A **problem** exists when there is a discrepancy between one's present state and one's perceived goal, *and* there is no readily apparent way to get from one to the other. In situations where the path to one's goal is not clear or obvious, one needs to engage in problem-solving behaviors.

A problem has three major components: (1) an *initial state*—the situation as it is perceived to exist at the moment; (2) a *goal state*—the situation as the problem solver would like it to be; and (3) *possible routes or strategies* for getting from the initial state to the goal state.

Psychologists also distinguish between well-defined and ill-defined problems. *Well-defined problems* are those in which both the initial state and the goal state are clearly defined. "What English word can be made from the letters *teralbay*?" We know that this question presents a problem. We understand the question, have some ideas about how we might go about answering it, and we'll know when we have succeeded. "How do you get home from campus if you discover that your car won't start?" Again, we know our initial state (on campus with a car that won't start), we'll know when we have reached our goal (when we are at home), but we have to find a new or different way to get there.

Many of the problems that we face every day are of the *ill-defined* variety. We do not have a clear idea of what we are starting with, nor are we able to clearly identify an ideal solution. "What should my college major be?" Many high school seniors (and some college seniors) do not even know what their options are. They have few ideas about how to find out about possible college majors. And once they have selected a major, they are not at all sure that their choice was the best one—which may be why so many college students change their majors so often.

Because ill-defined problems usually involve many variables that are difficult to define, much less control, psychologists tend to study problems that are reasonably well-defined.

problem
a situation in which there is a discrepancy between one's current state and one's desired or goal state, with no clear way of getting from one to the other

● **Before You Go On**
What are the three components of a problem?
Contrast well-defined and ill-defined problems. Give an example of each.

Some problems are ill defined, such as the problem of where to go to college and which classes to take.

FIGURE 8.1
A problem in which representation is critical. The diameter of this circle is exactly 10 inches long. What is the length of line "L" (From Köhler, 1969.)

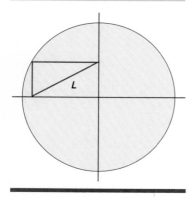

PROBLEM REPRESENTATION

Once we realize that we're faced with a problem, the first thing we should do is put it in a form that allows us to think about it in familiar terms. We should *represent* the problem in our own minds, interpreting it so that the initial state and the goal state are clear. We should note whether there are restrictions on how to go about seeking solutions. In short, we should try to understand the nature of the problem and make it meaningful by relating it to information we have available in our memories.

By examining a few problems of the sort that have been used in the psychology laboratory, we can see that how we choose to represent a problem can be critical. Refer to the problem in Figure 8.1. You're told that the diameter of this circle is exactly 10 inches long. The problem is to determine the length of line L (Köhler, 1969). On first inspection you may decide that this problem is just too difficult to attempt, requiring an in-depth knowledge of trigonometry or geometry. If you work with this problem for a moment, however, a few relevant insights may emerge. You realize that if the diameter of the circle is 10 inches, then any radius must be 5 inches long. Okay, but that in itself doesn't help much until you see that line L is a diagonal of the rectangle and that the other diagonal is also a radius of the circle. It then becomes obvious that if the radius is 5 inches long, then line L must also be 5 inches long (see Figure 8.10, p. 307).

Ultimately, the problem in Figure 8.1 could be solved by representing it in a new or different way. Visually representing the problem in Figure 8.2 would not be wise. You can imagine someone working on this problem by drawing little train stations with trains moving toward each other, tracing the path of a little bird racing back and forth between the trains. If you tried this, you discovered that it didn't help much.

FIGURE 8.2
Another Problem Whose Solution May Depend on How It Is Represented by the Problem Solver

Two train stations are fifty miles apart. At 2:00 P.M. one Saturday afternoon two trains start toward each other, one from each station. Just as the trains pull out of the stations, a bird springs into the air in front of the first train and flies ahead to the front of the second train. When the bird reaches the second train it turns back and flies toward the first train. The bird continues to do this, flying back and forth between the two trains until the trains meet.

If both trains travel at the rate of twenty-five miles per hour and the bird flies at one hundred miles per hour, how many miles will the bird have flown before the two trains meet?

From Posner, 1973.

Instead of visualizing this problem, think about the logic involved. The stations are 50 miles apart, and the trains travel at 25 miles per hour. At that rate, how long will it take for the trains to meet? Exactly one hour. You know that the bird flies at a rate of 100 miles per hour. Now if the bird flies for one hour (back and forth—or any place else for that matter), how far will it fly? Right! 100 miles. This solution becomes obvious as soon as the problem is stripped to its essentials and is represented in such a way that a solution is possible.

As a final example of the importance of problem representation consider this (from Adams, 1974):

Imagine you have a very large sheet of paper, 1/100 of an inch thick. Imagine folding it over onto itself so that now you have two layers of paper. Fold it again so that there are four layers. It is impossible to actually fold a sheet of paper 50 times, but imagine that you could. About how thick would the paper be if it were folded 50 times?

Picturing what a piece of paper folded 50 times would look like is very difficult. Some people guess a few inches, whereas some imagine that the folded paper would be several feet thick. Many have no idea at all. Representing this problem in visual terms is of little help. If one sees this as a problem of mathematics, and exponents, then a correct solution is more likely. Actually, 50 folds would increase the paper's thickness by a factor of 2^{50}. That comes to 1,100,000,000,000,000 folds, and the resulting paper would be so thick as to nearly reach from the earth to the sun! For those who find this impossible (or difficult) to believe, I can only say, "Try it and see how far you get."

Finding the best way to represent a problem isn't a simple task. Often, problem representation is *the* stumbling block to finding a solution (Bourne et al., 1983). Once you realize that you are faced with a problem, your first step should be to represent it in a variety of ways. Eliminate any inessential information. Relate your problem to other problems of a similar type that you have solved before. Having done so, if the solution is still not obvious, you may have to develop some strategy to find a solution. We now turn to how one might go about generating possible solutions.

● **Before You Go On**

In the context of problem solving, what is meant by problem representation?

PROBLEM-SOLVING STRATEGIES

Once you have represented the initial state of a problem and have a clear idea of what an acceptable goal might be, you still have to figure out how to get to your goal. Even after you have adequately represented a problem, how to go about solving it may not be readily apparent. You might spend a few minutes guessing wildly at a solution, but soon you'll have to settle on some strategy. In this context, a **strategy** is a systematic plan for generating possible solutions that can be tested to see if they are correct. The main advantage of cognitive strategies is that they give the problem solver a degree of control over the task at hand. They allow people to choose the skills and knowledge they will bring to bear on any problem (Gagne, 1984). There are many strategies that one could use. We'll cover two different types of strategies: algorithms and heuristics.

Algorithms

An **algorithm** is a problem-solving strategy that guarantees you will arrive at a solution. Algorithms systematically explore and evaluate all possible solutions until a correct one is found. This approach is referred to as a *generate-test* strategy because one generates hypotheses about potential solutions and tests each one in turn. Given their speed, most computer programs solve problems using algorithmic strategies.

Simple anagram problems (letters of a word presented in a scrambled fashion) can be solved using an algorithm. "What English word has been scrambled to make *uleb*?" With sufficient patience, you systematically can rearrange these four letters until you hit on a correct solution: *leub, lueb, elub, uleb, buel, beul, blue!* There it is, *blue*. With only four letters to deal with, finding a solution generally doesn't take long—there are only 24 possible arrangements of four letters (4 x 3 x 2 x 1= 24).

Now, consider the anagram composed of eight letters that I mentioned earlier: *teralbay*. There are 40,320 possible combinations of these eight letters—8 x 7 x 6 x 5 x 4 x 3 x 2 x 1 = 40,320 (Reynolds & Flagg, 1983). Unless your system for moving letters around happens to start in a good place, you could spend a lot of time before finding a combination that produces an English word. If we were dealing with a 10-letter word, there would be 3,628,800 possible combinations to check.

Imagine that you go to the supermarket just to find a small jar of horseradish. You're sure the store has horseradish, but you have no idea where to find it. One plan would be to systematically go up and down every aisle of the store, checking first the top shelf, then the second, then the third, until you spied the horseradish. This strategy will work *if* the store does carry horseradish and *if* you search carefully. There must be a better way to solve such problems. Here's where heuristic strategies come in.

Heuristics

A **heuristic** strategy is an informal, rule-of-thumb method for generating and testing problem solutions. Heuristics are more economical strategies than algorithms. When one uses a heuristic (and there are several heuristic

---

strategy
in problem solving, a systematic plan for generating possible solutions that can be tested to see if they are correct

algorithm
a problem-solving strategy in which all possible solutions are generated and tested and an acceptable solution is guaranteed

heuristic
a problem-solving strategy in which hypotheses about problem solutions are generated and tested in a time-saving and systematic way but which does not guarantee an acceptable solution

strategies that have been studied in the psychology laboratory), there is no guarantee of success. On the other hand, heuristics are usually less time-consuming than algorithm strategies and lead toward goals in a logical, sensible way.

A heuristic strategy for finding horseradish in a supermarket might take you to various sections in the store in an order you believe to be reasonable. You might start with spices, and you'd be disappointed. You might look among the fresh vegetables. Then, recalling that horseradish needs to be refrigerated, you would go to the dairy case, and there you'd find the horseradish. You would not have wasted your time searching the cereal aisle or the frozen food section—which you might have if you tried an algorithmic search. Another, even more reasonable, heuristic would be to ask an employee where the horseradish is kept.

If you tried the *teralbay* anagram, you probably used a heuristic strategy. To do so, you rely on your knowledge of English. You seriously consider only those letter combinations that you know occur frequently. You generate and test the most common combinations first. You don't worry about the possibility that the solution may contain a combination like *brty*. Nor do you search for a word with an *aae* string. You explore words that end in *able*, because you know these to be fairly common. But that doesn't work. What about *br* words? No, that doesn't work either. How about words with the combination *tray* in them? *Traybeal*? No. *Baletray*? No. "Oh! Now I see it: *betrayal*."

● **Before You Go On**

How are algorithmic and heuristic strategies used to solve problems?

BARRIERS TO EFFECTIVE PROBLEM SOLVING

It is difficult, sometimes impossible, to solve problems without relying heavily on one's memory. If you failed to remember that the radius of a circle is exactly half its diameter, you couldn't solve the problem in Figure 8.1. If you forgot how fast the bird was flying, you couldn't deal with the problem in Figure 8.2. If you can't remember the recipe for something you want for supper, you'll have a difficult time buying the right ingredients when you're at the store. There *are* times, however, when our previous experiences (and our memories of them) create difficulties in problem solving.

Mental Set and Functional Fixedness

In Chapter 5, p. 164, we saw that perceptions can be influenced by our expectations or mental set. The concept of mental set is also relevant in problem solving. A **mental set** is a tendency to perceive, or think about, or respond to something in a given (set) way. It is a cognitive predisposition. We may develop expectations that interfere with effective problem solving.

Figure 8.3 provides a classic example of how an inappropriate mental set can interfere with problem solving. Most people, when first presented with this problem, make an assumption (form a mental set). They assume the nine dots form a square and that their lines somehow must stay within that square. Only when this mental set is "broken" can the problem be solved. See Figure 8.11 (p. 308) for one solution to this "nine-dot problem."

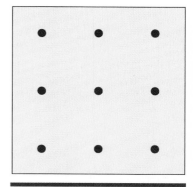

FIGURE 8.3
The classic "nine-dot problem." The task is to connect all nine dots with just four straight lines, without removing your pen or pencil from the paper. (From Scheerer, 1963.)

mental set
a predisposed (set) way to perceive something; an expectation

FIGURE 8.4
Maier's two-string problem. The subject is to manage to get both strings in his grasp. They are separated so that when one string is held, the other cannot be reached. See text for solution. (After Maier, 1931.)

I should point out that mental sets do not necessarily hinder problem solving. A proper or appropriate mental set can be facilitating. For example, if I were to have told you to look beyond the confines of any imagined square when attempting the problem in Figure 8.3, *that* mental set—which seems strange out of context—would have made the problem easier to solve.

Functional fixedness is a type of mental set that was defined by Duncker (1945) as the inability to find an appropriate new use for an object because of one's experience using the object in some other function. The problem solver fails to see a solution to a problem because he or she has already "fixed" some "function" to an object, which makes it difficult to see how it could help with the problem at hand.

A standard example is from Maier (1931). Two strings hang from the ceiling. The problem is that they are so far apart that a person cannot reach both of them at the same time. The goal is to do just that: to hold on to both strings at once. If there were nothing else in the room, this problem might never get solved. However, there are other objects in the room that the person can use, including a pair of pliers (see Figure 8.4). One solution is to tie the pliers to one string and swing them like a pendulum. As the person holds the other string, the string with the pliers attached can be grasped as it swings nearby. Because many people fail to see pliers as useful for anything but turning nuts and bolts, they fail to see them as a pendulum weight and fail to solve the problem. They have "fixed" the "function" of the pliers in their mind.

Another famous example that demonstrates functional fixedness is one reported by Duncker (1945). Here, subjects are given a box of tacks, a candle, and matches. The task is to use these materials to mount the candle on the wall and light it. Clearly, one cannot just tack a candle to the wall.

functional fixedness
the phenomenon in which one is unable to see a new use or function for an object because of experience using the object in some other function

FIGURE 8.5
The materials provided in the candle problem—and one possible solution. (After Duncker, 1945.)

The solution requires breaking the mental set of functional fixedness for the box holding the tacks, seeing it as a candleholder, tacking *it* to the wall, and mounting the candle on it (see Figure 8.5).

● **Before You Go On**

What is a mental set, and how might a mental set hinder problem solving?

What is functional fixedness, and how might it hinder problem solving?

Overcoming Barriers with Creative Problem Solving

Creative solutions to problems are innovative and useful. It is very important to note that in the context of problem solving, "creative" means much more than unusual, rare, or different. Someone may generate a very original plan to solve a given problem, but unless that plan is likely to work, we shouldn't view it as creative (Newell et al., 1962; Vinacke, 1974). Creative solutions should be put to the same test as more ordinary solutions: Do they solve the problem at hand?

Creative solutions generally involve new and different organizations of problem elements. As I mentioned earlier, it is often at the stage of problem representation that creativity is most noticeable. Seeing a problem in a new light, or combining elements in a new and different way, may lead to creative solutions.

One observation has been made many times: There is virtually no correlation between creative problem solving and what is usually referred to as "intelligence" (Barron & Harrington, 1981; Horn, 1976; Kershner & Ledger, 1985). At least there are virtually no significant correlations between tests for creativity and tests for intelligence.

We say that creative problem solving often involves **divergent thinking**, that is, starting with one idea and generating from it several alternative possibilities and new ideas (Dirkes, 1978; Guilford, 1959b). One simple test for divergent thinking skills requires one to generate as many uses as possible for simple objects such as a brick or a paper clip. When we engage in **convergent thinking**, we take many different ideas and try to reduce them to

divergent thinking
the creation of many ideas or potential problem solutions from one idea

convergent thinking
the reduction or focusing of many different ideas into one possible problem solution

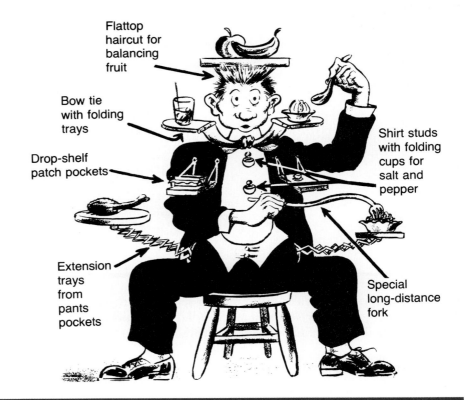

Flattop haircut for balancing fruit

Bow tie with folding trays

Drop-shelf patch pockets

Shirt studs with folding cups for salt and pepper

Extension trays from pants pockets

Special long-distance fork

Creative problem solutions must be more than unusual or different—they must provide a workable solution to the problem at hand. (Rube Goldberg/Reprinted with special permission of King Features Syndicate.)

just one possible solution (Figure 8.6). An example of convergent thinking would be trying to come up with just one or two courses of action (from dozens of possibilities that have been offered) to reduce the dropout rate of high school students. Obviously, convergent thinking has its place, but for creative problem solving, divergent thinking is generally more useful, because many new and different possibilities are explored. We must remember, however, that these new and different possibilities for a problem's solution need to be judged ultimately in terms of whether they really work.

Creative problem solving can be divided into four interrelated stages. This view of problem solving is an old one in psychology (Wallas, 1926), although it has held up well over the years.

1. *Preparation:* This is not unlike problem representation. The basic elements of the problem are considered. Past experience is relevant, but should not become restrictive. Various ways of expressing the problem are considered, but a solution is not found. Determining which elements of the problem are most relevant, and combining those elements in new ways, fosters creative problem solving (Sternberg & Lubert, 1993).

2. *Incubation:* In this stage, the problem is "put away" and not thought about. Perhaps fatigue has developed during failed efforts and can now dissipate. Perhaps inappropriate strategies can be forgotten. Perhaps unconscious processes can be brought to bear on the problem. Why setting aside a problem for a while can lead to its solution we

FIGURE 8.6

A schematic representation of convergent and divergent thinking in the context of problem solving.

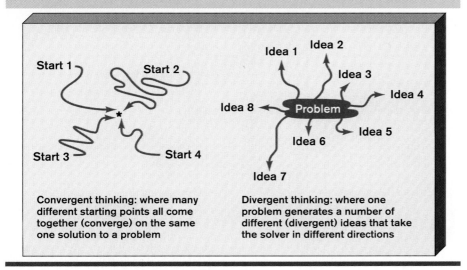

Convergent thinking: where many different starting points all come together (converge) on the same one solution to a problem

Divergent thinking: where one problem generates a number of different (divergent) ideas that take the solver in different directions

cannot say for sure. We do know, however, that is often very useful (Koestler, 1964; Yaniv & Meyer, 1987).

3. *Illumination:* This is the most mysterious stage of the process. Like insight, a potential solution to the problem seems to materialize as if from nowhere. Some critical analogy becomes apparent, as does a new path to the problem's solution (Glass et al., 1979; Metcalf & Wiebe, 1987).

4. *Verification:* Now the proposed solution must be tested, or verified, to see if it does, in fact, provide an answer to the question posed by the problem.

You've probably noted that there is really nothing extraordinary about Wallas's description of the creative problem-solving process. It sounds like the sort of thing that anyone should do when faced with a problem to solve. The truth is, however, that we often fail to go through these stages in a systematic fashion. Doing so often helps with problem solving. It has long been recognized that good problem solvers show more conscious awareness of what they are doing during the course of problem solving than do poor problem solvers (Glaser, 1984).

● **Before You Go On**

What is the difference between divergent and convergent thinking?

What are the four stages of creative problem solving according to Wallas?

Language is a vehicle for communicating our understanding of events to others.

TOPIC 8 B

LANGUAGE

Language allows us to communicate to others how we feel and what we think. Using language is a social process that reflects a marvelously complex set of cognitive processes. The philosopher Suzanne Langer put it this way:

> Language is, without a doubt, the most momentous and at the same time the most mysterious product of the human mind. Between the clearest animal call of love or warning or anger, and a man's least, trivial *word*, there lies a whole day of Creation—or in a modern phrase, a whole chapter of evolution. (1951, p. 94)

In this Topic, we'll review a few issues involved in the subfield of psychology called psycholinguistics. **Psycholinguistics** is a discipline of scientists trained in both psychology and in linguistics. Psycholinguists "are interested in the underlying knowledge and abilities which people must have in order to use language and learn language in childhood" (Slobin, 1979, p. 2). First, let's define the concept of language.

psycholinguistics
a hybrid scientific discipline of psychologists and linguists who study all aspects of language

language
a collection of arbitrary symbols that follow certain rules of combination and that have significance for the language-using community

LET'S TALK: WHAT IS LANGUAGE?

Language is a large collection of arbitrary symbols that have significance for a language-using community and that follow certain rules of combination (after Morris, 1946). Now, let's pull apart this definition of language and examine the points it raises.

First, language consists of a large number of *symbols*. The symbols that make up a language are commonly referred to as *words*. They are the labels that we have assigned to the mental representation of our experiences. When we use the word *chair* as a symbol, we don't use it to label any one specific instance of a chair. We use it to represent our concept of what a chair is. Note that, as symbols, words do not have to stand for real things in the real world. With language, we can communicate about owls and pussycats in teacups; four-dimensional, time-warped hyperspace; and a cartoon beagle that flies his doghouse into battle against the Red Baron. Words are used to stand for our cognitions, our concepts, and we have a great number of them.

It is important that we define the symbols of language as *arbitrary*. You call what you are reading a *book*. We have all agreed (in English) that book is the appropriate symbol for what you are reading. We don't have to. We could agree to call it a *fard*, or a *relm*, if we liked. On the other hand, once a word is established by common use or tradition, it becomes part of a language and must be learned and used by each new language user.

To be part of a language, language symbols need to have *significance for some language-using community*. That is, people need to agree on the symbols used in their language, and agree on what those symbols mean. This is another way of saying that language use is a social enterprise. You and I might decide to call every *book* a *fard*, but then you and I would be in a terribly small language-using community.

The final part of our definition tells us that the symbols of a language must *follow certain rules of combination*. What this means is that language is structured, or rule-governed. There are rules about how we can and cannot string symbols together in a language. In English, we say "The small boy slept late." We do not say "Slept boy late small the." Well, we could say it, but no one would know for sure what we meant by it, and everyone would recognize that the utterance violates the rules of English.

Even with this complex definition of language, there are a few points I've left out. For one, using language is a remarkably *creative, generative* process. Virtually every time we use our language, we use it in new and creative ways, a fact that emphasizes the importance of the underlying rules of language. Another point: Language allows for *displacement*, the ability to communicate about the "not here and the not now." We can use language to discuss yesterday's lunch and tomorrow's class schedule. We can talk about things that are not here, never were, and never will be. Language is the only form of communication that allows us to do so.

A final observation: Language and speech are not synonymous terms. Speech is only one way in which language is expressed as behavior. There are others, such as writing, coding (as in Morse code), or signing (as in American Sign Language).

● **Before You Go On**

What are some of the defining characteristics of language?

LANGUAGE USE AS A SOCIAL PROCESS

The main purpose to which language is put is communication. Language allows us to share our thoughts, feelings, intentions, and experiences with others. Language use is social behavior. **Pragmatics** is the study of how lin-

pragmatics
the study of how linguistic events and their interpretation are related to the context in which they occur

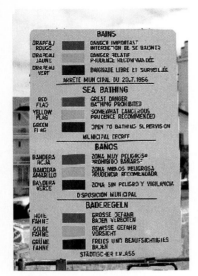

Although the symbols of a language are arbitrary, many people have to agree on what the symbols are, what they mean, and how they will be used.

guistic events are related to the social context in which they occur. Our understanding of sarcasm (as in, "Well, it sure is a beautiful day!" when in fact it is rainy, cold, and miserable), or simile (as in "Life is like a sewer, the more you put into it. . . ."), or metaphor (as in "His slam dunk with two minutes left in the game delivered the knockout blow."), or cliché (as in "It rained cats and dogs.") depend on many things, including our appreciation of the context in which the utterance occurred.

Pragmatics involves decisions based on the perception of the social situation at the moment. Think how you modify your language when you talk to your best friend, a preschool child, a professor in her office, or a driver who cut you off at an intersection. Contemporary concerns about "political correctness" seem relevant here, don't they? In some contexts, words such as *pig, Uncle Tom, boy,* and *girl* can be reasonable and proper, while in other contexts they may evoke angry responses. In many Native American Indian cultures, periods of lengthy silence during conversation are quite acceptable and common. Someone not familiar with this pragmatic reality could become anxious and upset about long pauses in the midst of a conversation (e.g. Basso, 1970; Brislin, 1993, pp. 217–221). As you can imagine, translations from one language to another can cause huge changes in meaning as contexts change. Two of my favorites (from Berkowitz, 1994) are the translation of the Kentucky Fried Chicken slogan "Finger Lickin' Good" into Chinese, yielding "Eat Your Fingers Off"; and in Taiwan, the slogan "Come Alive with the Pepsi Generation" becomes "Pepsi will bring your ancestors back from the dead."

There are only a few, very slight, differences in language use based on gender, and these differences are generally related to pragmatics—the context and purpose of the conversation (Pearson et al., 1991). For example, men are more talkative than women and tend to interrupt more often (Key, 1975). Women have a tendency to use more qualifiers such as "It seems to me . . ." or "In my opinion . . ." (Quina et al., 1987). In some situations, women are a bit more likely to express ideas and feelings about themselves than are men (Cozby, 1973).

Now let's consider how this "mysterious product of the human mind" called language develops.

● **Before You Go On**

What is the study of pragmatics, and what does it tell us about language use?

LANGUAGE ACQUISITION

One of the most significant achievements of childhood is the acquisition of language. There are few cognitive skills that compare to language in complexity and utility. How children acquire language has long been a concern of psycholinguists. The process seems nearly magical: cooing and babbling one day, then a word or two, then "Why is the sky blue, Daddy, why is the sky blue?"—and all in the span of just a few months' time. Steven Pinker, director of the Center for Cognitive Science at M.I.T., calls language acquisition "the jewel in the crown of cognition—it is what everyone wants to explain" (deCuevas, 1990, p. 63). At best, we have theories and hypotheses. We are getting close to adequately describing *what* happens. Understanding exactly *how* it happens will take longer.

What Happens in Language Acquisition

Infants create speech sounds spontaneously. They come into the world with a cry, and make noise with regularity forever after. At about the age of 6 months, random cries and noises are replaced by the more regular sounds of babbling. **Babbling** is the production of speech sounds, often in repetitive, rhythmic patterns, such as "ma-ma" or "lu-lu-lu." A curiosity is that when children babble, they do so by producing virtually all the known sounds of all languages. Sounds that are not part of a child's language eventually drop out of its repertoire. All babies babble in the same way (Nakazima, 1962; Oller, 1981). An adult cannot distinguish the babbling of a Chinese infant from that of a Greek or an American infant. Even deaf infants produce babbling sounds that cannot be distinguished from those of hearing children (Lenneberg et al., 1965). Deaf babies also "babble" with their fingers and hands. These motions are meaningless—nonsense syllables, really, but the basis for what will later become (for many of them) their native (sign) language.

babbling
speech sounds produced in rhythmic, repetitive patterns

The acquisition of vocabulary follows soon after babbling begins. In all cases, comprehension comes before production. That is, children understand and respond appropriately to the meaning of utterances long before they are able to produce those utterances themselves. We usually notice the appearance of a child's first word or two at about the age of 1 year (parents often argue that the onset of speech comes sooner, but independent observers often fail to confirm what may be parental wishful thinking). Once it begins, word acquisition is truly remarkable. A 1-year-old may produce only two or three words (remember, he or she may very well understand dozens of words, but can produce only a few). By the age of 2 years, word production is up to about 50. In terms of comprehension, by age 2 1/2, a child understands 200–300 words; by age 3, over 1,000; by age 6, somewhere between 8,000 and 14,000 words (Benedict, 1979; Brown, 1973; Carey, 1978).

Describing the development of syntactic rules, or grammar, in children has been quite difficult. As linguists began to understand the rules that govern adult language, it seemed reasonable to look for these same rules in the language of children. What became apparent was that the grammar of adult forms of language does not emerge until long after children have begun stringing words together in utterances. Although we do not find adult structure in the language use of children, children *do* use language in a rule-governed way. In other words, young children do not speak adult language badly; instead, their language follows its own rules (Radford, 1990).

The first use of speech as language is holophrastic speech. **Holophrastic speech** is the use of one word to communicate a range of intentions and meanings—dependent upon context, gestures, intonation, and so on. Before this stage, a child may produce a number of words, but will do so only as a naming exercise. Words are used as labels for concepts and nothing else. With holophrastic speech, individual words are used to communicate a range of possibilities. Picture a young child sitting in a highchair. Can't you just see how the one-word utterance "milk" could be used to communicate such things as "*I want my milk!*" or "Uh-oh, I dropped my milk" or "Yea! here's my milk" or "Yuck, not milk again."

holophrastic speech
the use of one word to communicate a number of different meanings

At about the age of 2 years, we note the appearance of two-word utterances. When carefully analyzed, these two-word utterances are very regular—as if they were being put together according to some fairly strict rules.

Given an understanding of the words *big* and *little* and many nouns, a child may say, "big ball," "big plane," "big doggie," "little stick," "little cup," and so on. What is curious is that this child will not reverse this word order. He or she will *not* say, for instance, "ball big" or "doggie little" (Braine, 1976).

From the point of the two-word utterance on, language development is so rapid that it is difficult to note any stages through which the process may pass. Following the two-word utterance stage there is a period typified by **telegraphic speech**—spoken language consisting of nouns, verbs, and adjectives, but hardly any "function words" such as articles or prepositions. We hear children say things such as: "Daddy go store now" or "Billy draw pictures." Then, at about age 2 1/2 years, language use expands at an explosive rate. There really is no three-word or four-word stage of development. Phrases are lengthened, noun phrases first, so that "Billy's ball" becomes "Billy's red ball," which then becomes "Billy's red ball that Mommy got at the store." When children are ready to begin school—about age 5— they demonstrate the understanding and the production of virtually every type of sentence structure in their language.

Now that we have a very basic idea of what happens when children acquire language, we'll consider how we can account for the process.

telegraphic speech
spoken language consisting of nouns, verbs, adjectives and adverbs, but few "function words"

● **Before You Go On**
What are some of the landmark events that occur during language acquisition?

Theories of Language Acquisition

How is one's language acquired? If you've ever studied a foreign language, did it occur to you that there were little children somewhere in the world who were acquiring the same language that you were struggling with? They were not having any problems with it at all. Acquiring one's language is a cognitive feat at which all (normal) humans succeed.

Have you noticed that I have avoided the phrase "language learning," referring instead to language "acquisition" or "development?" This was intentional, because I do not want to suggest that acquiring language is only a matter of learning. On the other hand, language use is not instinctive in the usual sense, or everyone would speak the same language. Some of language acquisition can be accounted for by learning (in the ways we discussed in Chapter 6), but most aspects of language acquisition defy explanation in terms of learning and suggest a biological basis for the process.

Theories of language development as learning (e.g., Skinner, 1957; Whitehurst, 1982) have their place. No one will claim that language emerges free of the influence of learning, experience, reinforcement, and the like. We can be most comfortable with learning approaches when we try to account for the acquisition of speech sounds and word meanings. Part of what words mean comes from classical conditioning (Chapter 6, p. 204–208). The use of some words is reinforced and the use of others is not—as predicted by operant conditioning. Some vocabulary growth results from observational learning—using words that others use. Some words develop through direct instruction. By and large, learning seems to handle the acquisition of vocabulary rather nicely, but there *are* a few problems.

For one thing, as children begin to acquire the rules that change the meaning of a word, they do so with disturbing regularity. For no good reason that learning theory can account for, children learn to add *-ing* to words before they form possessives (by adding *-'s*), which they learn before learning to form the past tense of verbs (by adding -*ed*). That is, when asked what he is doing, a child may be expected first to respond "I draw." Later will come "I drawing." Only later may we expect "That Billy's picture." Still later we will hear something like "I drawed it yesterday." That is, there is a predictable order in which many word sequences are acquired.

Another problem for learning theory is **overregularization**—the continued application of an acquired language rule (e.g., for forming plurals or past tense) in a situation where it is not appropriate. A child might say, "I have two foots," "four mans," or "I goed to the store," even after correctly using the words *feet, men,* and *went* in similar contexts. What accounts for overregularization? Biologically oriented theories (e.g., Chomsky, 1965, 1975; Lenneberg, 1967; McNeil, 1970) say that there is some innate, "prewired" biological mechanism that the child uses to seek out and apply rules during a "critical period" of language acquisition. The mechanism is called a *language acquisition device,* or LAD, and becomes active and useful when we are about 1 year old and turns off by the time we are 5 or 6 years old. In this scenario, the child is so predisposed to find and use rules that she or he will do so with great consistency, even when a particular application of that rule is wrong. Actually, "two foots" is much more reasonable than "two feet," even though "two foots" is not likely to be heard in adult speech (Anisfeld, 1984).

Reliance on some LAD is even more sensible when we consider the acquisition of rules reflected in the generation of sentences and comes mostly from observing the orderliness of language development. The ages of the children are not always the same, but with uncanny regularity, children everywhere acquire their language in virtually the same pattern. Holophrastic speech, the stability of the two-word utterance, the expansion of noun phrases, and the ordered acquisition of word endings has been noted over and over as a consistent pattern—a pattern more consistent than we could ever expect from the learning histories of the children being observed (Slobin, 1979).

Another point often raised against the learning approach is that when it comes to the rules of grammar, or sentence construction, most adults cannot tell us what the rules of their language *are*. The argument then follows: How can you begin to teach something to someone else if you haven't got the slightest idea yourself what it is that you're teaching? The argument is sensible. Yet there is the logic that as adults we do have certain linguistic intuitions. We can tell when an utterance is correctly formed, even if we can't specify why. Perhaps we use this intuition to reinforce proper use and to correct improper use. The problem is that when we watch adults interacting with young children, we find that they are much more likely to correct the *content* of what the child says than the *form* in which it is said. For example, if a child says, "Me no like oatmeal," a parent is likely to respond with a statement such as, "Sure you do; you eat it all the time" (Brown, 1973; Brown et al., 1969). "Explicit language teaching from adults is not necessary. In fact, if adults try to structure and direct a child's language learning, the outcome may be interference . . ." (Rice, 1989).

So, when it comes to explaining language acquisition, just where are we? We are a long way from any final answers, but a reasonable, if conservative, position is an interactionist one: Humans have an innate biological predisposition to acquire a language. The language they ultimately do acquire reflects their experiences in their language-using community, where they learn appropriate speech sounds, word meanings, and pragmatic realities.

overregularization
the excessive application of an acquired language rule (e.g., for plurals or past tense) in a situation where it is not appropriate

● **Before You Go On**

Briefly summarize the learning-oriented and biology-oriented theories of language acquisition.

TOPIC 8C

INTELLIGENCE

In a chapter on higher cognitive processes, it makes sense to consider what is, perhaps, the ultimate reflection of human cognitive processing: intelligence. Intelligence is a another one of those troublesome concepts in psychology. We know what we mean when we use the term, but we have a terrible time trying to define it concisely. We've gotten into the habit of using "intelligence" as a label for so many cognitive abilities that it seems to defy specific definition.

Nonetheless, we need to settle on some definition to guide us throughout this Topic. I propose we accept two definitions, one academic and theoretical, the other operational and practical. For our theoretical definition, let us say that **intelligence** is the capacity of a person to understand the world and the resourcefulness to cope with its challenges (Wechsler, 1975, p. 139). This definition, and others like it, does present us with ambiguities. Just what does "capacity" mean? What is meant by "understand the world"? What if the world never really challenges one's "resourcefulness"? Would such people be unintelligent? What at first may seem like a sensible and all-inclusive definition of intelligence may, upon reflection, pose even more definitional problems. Once we start asking questions such as these, many others follow quickly: Is intelligence a unitary characteristic, or are there several different varieties of intelligence? To what extent is intelligence situational? That is, can behaviors be intelligent in one context, or in one culture, and unintelligent in another context or culture? Are men and women "intelligent" in the same way(s)? To what extent is one's intelligence a reflection of inherited traits, and to what extent does it reflect one's ability to profit from experience?

Without going into any details here, let me simply suggest that ever since the turn of the twentieth century and the theory of British psychologist Charles Spearman (1904), psychology has considered and struggled with dozens of theories or models of "intelligence." To this day, psychologists get very excited and quite emotional debating the issue of whether the concept of a single general intelligence is an all-important, sometimes-important, or never-important component of what we call "intelligence" (Ackerman & Kanfer, 1993; Barrett & Depinett, 1991; Helms, 1992; McClelland, 1973, 1993; Ree & Earles, 1992; Sternberg & Wagner, 1993).

Perhaps we ought to follow our advice from Chapter 1, where we saw that using operational definitions can help with such theoretical problems. We have to be careful here but, as many psychologists do, we may operationally define intelligence as "that which intelligence tests measure." Note that using this definition simply sidesteps the thorny problem of coming to grips with the "true" nature of intelligence. It does what operational definitions are meant to do—it gives us a definition we can work with for a while. To use this definition, we need to understand how tests measure intelligence.

intelligence
the capacity to understand the world and the resourcefulness to cope with its challenges; that which an intelligence test measures

● **Before You Go On**

Provide a theoretical and an operational definition of intelligence.

THE NATURE OF PSYCHOLOGICAL TESTS

Just as there are several ways to define intelligence, there are also several different ways of measuring it. Although the focus of our discussion here is intelligence, we must recognize that psychological tests have been devised to measure the full range of human abilities and characteristics. For that reason, I'll begin this section with a few words about psychological tests in general.

A **psychological test** is an objective, standardized measure of a sample of behavior (Anastasi, 1988; Dahlstrom, 1993). A psychological test measures *behavior*. It measures behavior because that is all we can measure. We cannot measure those concepts that we call feelings, aptitudes, or abilities. Based on what we learn from our measurement of behavior, we may be willing to make assumptions or inferences about underlying mental processes.

A psychological test can only measure a *sample* of one's behavior. Let's say that I want to know about your tendency to be aggressive. I cannot very well ask you everything that relates to aggression in your life (e.g., "List all of the situations in which you have ever acted aggressively"). What I have to do is sample (identify a portion of) the behaviors in which I am interested. I then assume that responses to my sample can be used to predict responses to questions I have not asked. Even a classroom exam only asks you about a sample of the material you have learned.

There are two other definitional points to consider. If a test is to have any value, its administration must be *standardized* and its scoring must be *objective*. Imagine a placement test that will be used to determine which courses in English composition you will be required to take. You are given 45 minutes to answer 50 multiple-choice questions and write a short essay on a prescribed topic. Later, you discover that some students were given the same examination, but with instructions to "take as long as you like to finish the test." You also discover that those students could write their essay on any one of three suggested topics. This testing system lacks standardization.

A psychological test should be objective. Objectivity in this context refers to the evaluation of the behaviors being measured. Several examiners (at least those of the same level of expertise) should give the same interpretation and evaluation to a test response. If the same responses to a psychological test lead one psychologist to say a person is perfectly normal, a second to consider the person a mass of inner conflict, and a third to wonder why this person is not now in a psychiatric institution, we have a problem, and it may be with the objectivity of our test.

As both a consumer and a student of psychology, you should be able to assess the value or quality of psychological tests. The quality of a psychological test depends on the extent to which it has three characteristics: reliability, validity, and adequate norms.

In the context of psychological testing, **reliability** means what it means in other contexts: consistency or dependability. Suppose someone gives you a psychological test and, on the basis of your responses, claims that you have an IQ just slightly below average—94, let's say. Three weeks later, you take the same test and are told that your IQ is now 127—nearly in the top 3 percent of the population! Something is wrong. We have not yet discussed

psychological test
an objective, standardized measure of a sample of behavior

reliability
consistency or dependability; in testing, consistency of test scores

validity

in testing, the extent to which a test measures what it claims to measure

norms

in the context of psychological testing, results of a test taken by a large group of persons whose scores can be used to make comparisons or give meaning to new scores

IQ scores, but surely we recognize that one's IQ—as a measure of intelligence—does not change by 33 points within three weeks.

When people worry about the usefulness of a test, their concern is usually with **validity**. Measures of validity tell us the extent to which a test actually measures what it claims to measure. It is the extent to which there is agreement between a test score and the quality or trait the test is believed to measure (Kaplan & Saccuzzo, 1989).

Let's add just one more important issue: adequacy of test norms. Say that you have filled out a long, paper-and-pencil questionnaire designed to measure the extent to which you are extroverted. You know that the test is a reliable and valid instrument. You are told that you scored a 50 on the test. So what? What does *that* mean? It does not mean that you answered 50 percent of the items correctly—on this test there are no correct or incorrect answers. If you don't have a basis of comparison, one test score by itself is meaningless. You need to compare your score with the scores of other people like yourself who have already taken the test. Results of a test taken by a large group of people whose scores are used to make comparisons are called **norms**. You may discover by checking the norms that a score of 50 is average and indicative of neither extreme extroversion nor extreme introversion. On the other hand, a 50 might be a very high or a very low score. You just can't tell without adequate norms.

Now that we have an idea of some of the matters to be considered when one constructs a psychological test, we can examine attempts to measure intelligence. Given the difficulty we've had coming to any agreement on the nature of intelligence, you won't be surprised to find that not all psychologists are pleased with the currently available intelligence tests.

● **Before You Go On**

What is a psychological test?

In the context of psychological testing, what are reliability, validity, and test norms?

PSYCHOLOGICAL TESTS OF INTELLIGENCE

As we briefly review some psychological tests used to measure intelligence you will need to remember that test scores provide only one measure of intelligence, and no one measure is going to provide a universally satisfactory description or assessment of a concept as complex as intelligence.

The Stanford-Binet Intelligence Scale

Alfred Binet (1857–1911) was the leading psychologist in France at the turn of the century. Of great concern at that time were those children in the Paris school system who seemed unable to profit from the educational experiences they were being given. Binet set out to construct a test to measure the intellectual abilities of children. Binet and his most important collaborator, Théodore Simon, wanted to identify students who should be placed in special (remedial) classes, where their education could proceed more efficiently than in the standard classroom.

FIGURE 8.7
The intellectual factors tested by the Stanford-Binet Intelligence Scale, Fourth Edition, arranged in three levels below "g," or general intellectual ability. Each subtest is noted at the lowest level. (After Thorndike et al., 1986.)

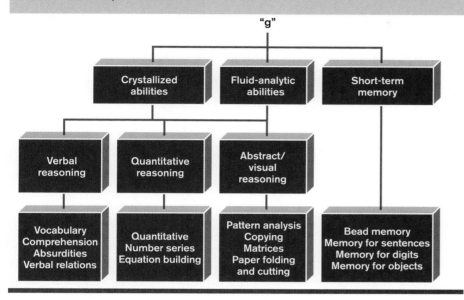

Binet's first test appeared in 1905 and was an immediate success. It caught the attention of Stanford University Professor Lewis M. Terman, who supervised a translation and revision of the test in 1916. Since then, the test has been referred to as the *Stanford-Binet* and has undergone subsequent revisions, the most recent published in 1986. This edition, the fourth, made several significant changes in the test and in its scoring. So what is this test like?

The test now follows what its authors call a "three-level hierarchical model" of cognitive ability (Thorndike et al., 1986). As in Binet's original test, the current edition yields an overall test score that reflects **g**, or general intellectual ability, which the test's authors describe as "what an individual uses when faced with a problem that he or she has not been taught to solve" (1986, p. 3). Underlying **g** are three second-level factors (Figure 8.7). *Crystallized abilities* represent skills required for acquiring and using information about verbal and quantitative concepts. They are influenced by schooling and could be called an academic ability factor. *Fluid-analytic abilities* are skills needed to solve problems that involve figural or nonverbal types of information. The bases of these skills are less tied to formal schooling. Essentially, they involve the ability to see things in new and different ways. The third factor is *short-term memory*. Items that test one's ability to hold information in memory for short periods of time can be found on Binet's original test.

The next level of abilities tested by the *Stanford-Binet* provides more specific, content-oriented definitions of the factors from level two. As you can see from Figure 8.7, crystallized abilities are divided into verbal and quantitative reasoning, fluid-analytic abilities are seen as abstract/visual

g
on an intelligence test, a measure of one's overall, general intellectual abilities, commonly thought of as IQ

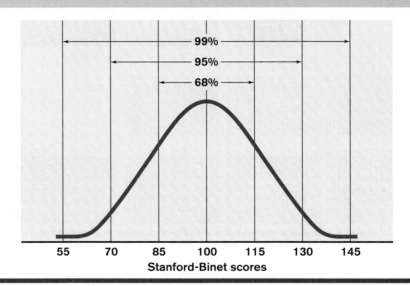

FIGURE 8.8
An idealized curve that shows the distribution of scores on the Stanford-Binet Intelligence Scale if the test were taken by a large sample of the general population. The numbers at the top of the curve indicate the percentage of the population expected to score within the indicated range of scores; that is, 68% earn scores between 85 and 115, 95% score between 70 and 130, and 99% earn scores between 55 and 145.

IQ

literally, intelligence quotient: the result of dividing one's mental age by one's chronological age, and multiplying the dividend by 100

reasoning, and there is no ability at this level that corresponds to short-term memory. At the very base of the hierarchy are the 15 subtests that constitute the actual *Stanford-Binet* test.

What all of this means is that the authors of the *Stanford-Binet* acknowledge that a person's measured intelligence should be reflected in more than just one test score. Now, not only can we determine an overall **g** score, we can also calculate scores for each factor at each of three levels. In addition, there are scores for the 15 subtests by themselves. Figure 8.8 shows how **g** scores on the *Stanford-Binet* are distributed in the general population.

Before we go on, let's take a minute to discuss what has become of the concept of IQ. **IQ** is an abbreviation for the term *intelligence quotient*. As you know, a quotient is the result you get when you divide one number by another. For the early versions of the *Stanford-Binet*, the examiner's job was to determine a person's *mental age* (MA), the age at which the person was functioning in terms of intellectual abilities. IQ was found by dividing the person's mental age by his or her actual age (*chronological age*, or CA). This quotient was then multiplied by 100 to determine IQ, or IQ = MA/CA x 100. If an 8-year-old girl has a mental age of 8, that girl would be average, and her IQ would equal 100 (8/8 x 100 = 1x100 = 100). If the 8-year-old were above average, with the intellectual abilities of an average 10-year-old, her IQ would be 125 (that's 10/8 x 100, or 1.25 x 100). If she were below average, say, with the mental abilities of an average 6-year-old, then her IQ

The Wechsler Tests provide verbal and performance scores that are compared to scores earned by subjects of the same age in the norm group. The Wechsler Intelligence Scale for Children (WISC-R) is a general intelligence test for children between the ages of 6 and 17.

would be 75. Because it is so engrained in our vocabularies, we will continue to use the term "IQ," even though we now compare an individual's test scores with test scores earned by large norm groups, and no longer compute MAs or calculate quotients.

● **Before You Go On**
Briefly describe the Stanford-Binet Intelligence Scale.

The Wechsler Tests of Intelligence

David Wechsler published his first intelligence test in 1939. Unlike the *Stanford-Binet* that existed at that time, it was designed for use with adult populations and was meant to reduce the heavy reliance on verbal skills that characterized Binet's tests. With a major revision in 1955, the test became the *Wechsler Adult Intelligence Scale (WAIS)*. The latest revision (the *WAIS-R*) was published in 1981. It is appropriate for people between 16 and 74 years of age, and is one of the most commonly used psychological tests (Lubin et al., 1984).

A natural extension was the *Wechsler Intelligence Scale for Children (WISC)*, originally published 11 years after the *WAIS*. After a major revision in 1974, it became known as the *WISC-R*. With updated norms and several new items (designed to minimize bias against any ethnic group or gender), the *WISC-III* appeared in 1991. It is appropriate for testing children between the ages of 6 and 16 (there is some overlap with the *WAIS-R*). A third test in the Wechsler series is for younger children (between the ages of 4 and 6 1/2). It is called the *Wechsler Preschool and Primary Scale of Intelligence (WPPSI)*. It was first published in 1967 and was revised in 1989 and is now the *WPPSI-R*. There are some subtle differences among the three Wechsler

FIGURE 8.9
The Subtests of the Wechsler Adult Intelligence Scale, Revised (WAIS-R)

Verbal Scales

Information	(29 items) Questions designed to tap one's general knowledge about a variety of topics dealing with one's culture; for example, "Who wrote *Huckleberry Finn*?" or "How many nickels in a quarter?"
Digit span	(7 series) Subject is read a series of three to nine digits and is asked to repeat them; then a different series is to be repeated in reverse order.
Comprehension	(16 items) A test of judgment, common sense, and practical knowledge; for example. "Why is it good to have prisons?"
Similarities	(14 pairs) Subject must indicate the way(s) in which two things are alike; for example, "In what way are an apple and a potato alike?"
Vocabulary	(35 words) Subject must provide an acceptable definition for a series of words.
Arithmetic	(14 problems) Math problems must be solved without the use of paper and pencil; for example, "How far will a bird travel in 90 minutes if it flies at the rate of 10 miles per hour?"

Performance Scales

Picture completion	(20 pictures) Subject must identify or name the missing part or object in a drawing; for example, a truck with only three wheels.
Picture arrangement	(10 series) A series of cartoonlike pictures must be arranged in an order that tells a story.
Block design	(9 items) Using blocks whose sides are either all red, all white, or diagonally red and white, subject must copy a designed picture or pattern shown on a card.
Object assembly	(4 objects) Free-form jigsaw puzzles must be put together to form familiar objects.
Digit symbol	In a key, each of nine digits is paired with a simple symbol. Given a random series of digits, the subject must provide the paired symbols within a time limit.

tests, but each is based on the same logic. Therefore, we'll consider only one, the *WAIS-R.*

The *WAIS-R* consists of 11 subtests that are organized into two categories. Six subtests define the *verbal scale,* and five constitute a *performance scale.* Figure 8.9 lists the different subtests of the *WAIS-R* and describes some of the items found on each. With the Wechsler tests, we can compute three scores: a verbal score, a performance score, and a total score. As with the *Stanford-Binet*, the total score is typically interpreted as an approximation of **g,** or general intellectual ability. In addition to one overall score, the Wechsler tests provide verbal and performance scores, which can tell us about a person's particular strengths and weaknesses.

For many years, there has been controversy about the quality of individually administered intelligence tests, such as the Wechsler tests and the Stanford-Binet. The extent to which the tests are culturally biased, favoring one group over another; whether they truly measure intelligence or just academic success; and whether test results can be used for political purposes, are just a few of the questions that keep finding their way into the popular press. A survey of over 600 experts in psychological testing, from several disciplines, indicates considerable agreement about the basic value of intelligence tests (Snyderman & Rothman, 1987). Although experts do allow that the tests may be slightly biased on racial or socioeconomic grounds, they "believe that such tests adequately measure more important elements of intelligence" (p. 143). The important point to remember is that, at best, psychological testing provides us with only one measure (an approximation) of a characteristic called intelligence that is itself multidimensional and very difficult to define. Scores on standard tests of intelligence (such as the two described here) do correlate well with success in school, or with academic achievement, but is that all there is to what we mean by "intelligence?"

● **Before You Go On**

What are the major features of the Wechsler intelligence scales?

EXTREMES OF INTELLIGENCE

When we look at the IQ scores earned by large random samples of individuals, we find that they are distributed in a predictable pattern. The most frequently occurring score is the average IQ of 100. Most other scores are close to this average—in fact, about 95 percent of all IQ scores fall between scores of 70 and 130 (See Fig. 8.8). In this final section, we will consider those people whose IQ scores place them beyond these normal limits. First, we'll consider the upper extreme, then we'll look at the lower extreme.

The Mentally Gifted

There are several ways in which a person can be gifted. The United States Office of Education (1972) defines giftedness as *a demonstrated achievement or aptitude for excellence* in any one of six areas:

1. *Psychomotor ability.* This is one of the most overlooked areas in which some individuals clearly can excel. We are dealing here with people of outstanding abilities in behaviors or skills that require agility, strength, speed, quickness, coordination, and the like.
2. *Visual and performing arts.* Some people, even as children, demonstrate an unusual talent for art, music, drama, and writing.
3. *Leadership ability.* Leadership skills are valued in most societies, and there seem to be individuals who are particularly gifted in this area. This often is true even in very young children. Youngsters with good

Blacks, Whites, IQ, and *The Bell Curve*

That there are significant differences between the IQ test scores of black and white Americans is not a new discovery. It was one of the conclusions drawn from the testing program for Army recruits during the First World War. Since then, many studies have reconfirmed the fact that whites score as many as 15 points higher on tests of general intelligence (IQ) than do blacks. Blacks even earn lower scores on performance tests and on intelligence tests designed to minimize the influence of one's culture (so-called culture fair tests) (Helms, 1992; Jensen, 1980; Rushton, 1988). There also are data that tell us that Japanese children (between the ages of 6 and 16) score higher on IQ tests—about 11 points on the average— than do American children (Lynn, 1982, 1987). The nagging question, of course, is where do these test score differences come from?

The proposed answers have been very controversial and involve several possibilities we've touched on before in other contexts: (1) The *tests are biased* and unfair. IQ tests may reflect the experiences of white Americans to a greater extent than they reflect the lives and experiences of blacks. (2) Differences in IQ scores can be attributed to *environmental factors*, such as economic or educational opportunities, or the extent to which one is exposed to a wide range of stimuli. (3) *Genetic factors* are involved that place some groups at a disadvantage. (4) There are *cultural differences in motivation* and attitudes about performance on standardized tests.

Test bias may account for some of the observed differences in IQ scores, but assume for the moment that available techniques for assessing general intelligence are as valid as possible. (Remembering, of course, that even the best and fairest of tests only measures one, or a few, aspects of the various dimensions of intelligence.) What then? Let's concentrate on black-white differences in IQ.

In the 1950s and 1960s, psychologists were confident that most (if not all) of the difference in the average IQ scores of whites and blacks could be accounted for by environmental, sociocultural, and motivational factors. There wasn't much research to support the position, but the logic was compelling and it was consistent with prevailing attitudes. Blacks were at a disadvantage on standard IQ tests because they were often denied access to enriching educational opportunities. Their lower socioeconomic status deprived many blacks of the sorts of experiences that could raise their IQ scores.

In 1969, Arthur Jensen shocked the scientific community with an article in the *Harvard Educational Review* in which he argued that there was insufficient evidence to justify the conclusion that the environment alone could produce the observed racial differences in IQ scores. The alternative was obvious to Jensen: The differences were attributable to genetic factors. Many readers took Jensen's claim to mean that blacks are genetically inferior to whites. Jensen said that his argument was meant only as a reasonable hypothesis, intended to provoke scientific efforts to explore the possibility (Jensen, 1981).

Perhaps you can imagine the furor created by Jensen's article. Researchers took up the challenge and tried to find convincing evidence that the environment *is* the cause of lower black IQ scores. After reviewing the body of evidence that resulted from these efforts, Brian Mackenzie, a scientist, wrote: "what is finally clear from such research, therefore, is that environmental factors have not been identified that are sufficient to account for all or even most of the 15-point mean difference in IQ between blacks and whites in the United States. Jensen's conclusion that half to two-thirds of the gap remains unaccounted for by any proposed combination of environmental influences is still unrefuted" (1984, p.

leadership skills tend to be intellectually bright, but they are not necessarily the smartest of the group.

4. *Creative or productive thinking.* This aspect of giftedness has received much attention over the past 25 years. Here we are talking about

1217). What does *that* mean? Does that mean that racial differences in IQ *are* caused by genetic factors? *Are* blacks genetically less able than whites? Of course not. There is no evidence to support that conclusion either (Mackintosh, 1986).

Just as many were coming to believe that the debate over racial differences in IQ was settling down, the controversy was reignited late in 1994 with the publication of *The Bell Curve.* (The bell curve refers to the symmetrical normal curve of IQ scores we saw in Figure 8.8.) The book, by psychologist Richard Herrnstein and political analyst Charles Murray, makes several points about the nature of intelligence and intelligence testing. Relevant to our discussion are their assertions that intelligence (1) is largely inherited (up to 60 percent inherited—they claim), (2) is virtually unchangeable from very early childhood on, (3) accounts for the "winners and losers" in today's society, and (4) *is possessed in varying degrees by different races.* Murray and Herrnstein go on to predict one class of the "cognitive elite" and an impoverished, low-IQ underclass, the former being largely white, the latter mostly black. Objections to the book were immediate, loud, widely publicized, and from experts in psychology, biology, genetics, education, and anthropology.

To understand why this issue of the inheritance of IQ and race has not yet been resolved requires that we understand three points: (1) Evidence that genetic factors accounts for some differences in intelligence *within* races cannot be used as evidence of genetic factors affecting differences in intelligence *between* races. (2) It is incorrect to assume that the failure to identify specific environmental causes of racial differences in IQ is sufficient reason to drop the argument that environmental factors are important. (3) Even if specific environmental factors that cause racial differences in IQ are not identified, that doesn't mean that we have to accept genetic explanations.

An interesting twist to the debate over racial differences in intelligence has recently been introduced by several geneticists and anthropologists. Their argument is that when one looks at genetic evidence and other biological evidence, there really is no such thing as "race" in the first place (e.g., Molnar, 1992; Shipman, 1994). What we refer to as a "racial group" is a fiction, created by us to help explain some of the differences we see among people in the world. The truth is, however, that *biologically* (and genetically) there is more variation within any "race" than there is between any "races." For example, if you are a white American of European ancestry and need a blood transfusion, you are just as likely to find a good match of blood type from an African American or a Hispanic as you are from another Caucasian. Exactly the same argument holds for organ transplants. If you were in need of a heart, liver, or kidney, finding a perfect match for transplantation would have nothing at all to do with what we commonly call "race." Perhaps the very same thing is true for intelligence.

So where do we stand on the issue of racial differences in IQ? We stand in a position of considerable uncertainty. For one thing, the concept of race itself is under challenge as a meaningful descriptor of persons. There *are* data to support the impact of *both* genetic and environmental influences on what we call intelligence. Whether any of these data can be used to settle the issue of perceived racial differences in IQ scores is unlikely. We would do well to keep in mind the following position: "Whether intelligence is largely genetically or largely environmentally determined is actually irrelevant in the context of group differences. The real issue is whether intelligence can be changed, an issue that does not at all go hand in hand with the issue of heritability" (Angoff, 1988, p. 713).

those who may be intellectually or academically above average, but not necessarily so. Indeed, there is ample evidence that scores on measures of creativity are unrelated to measures of general intelligence (e.g., Horn, 1976; Kershner & Ledger, 1985). People with this type of giftedness are able to generate unique and different, but still useful, solutions to problems. Persons who have exceptional creative talents in one area (e.g., art, math, or language) usually show no particular creativity in other areas (Amabile, 1985; Weisberg, 1986).

5. *Specific academic aptitude.* In this case, we are talking about people who have a special ability in a particular subject or two. Someone who is a whiz in math, history, or laboratory science, without necessarily being outstanding in other academic areas, would fit this category.

6. *Intellectually gifted.* Inclusion in this group is based on scores earned on a test of general intelligence, usually a Wechsler test or the Stanford-Binet. It is most likely that when people use the term "mentally gifted," they are referring to someone who fits this category—people of exceptionally high IQ. (IQ scores of 130 or above usually qualify for inclusion in this category, although some prefer to reserve the label for those with lQs above 135. In either case, we are dealing with a very small portion of the population—fewer than 3 percent.)

How can we describe intellectually gifted individuals? The truth is, there have been few large-scale attempts to understand mental giftedness (Horowitz & O'Brien, 1985; Reiss, 1989). Much of what we know about the mentally gifted comes from a classic study begun by Lewis Terman in the early 1920s (yes, the same Terman who revised Binet's IQ test in 1916). Terman supervised the testing of more than 250,000 children throughout California. His research group at Stanford University focused on those childen who earned the highest scores, about 1500 in all, each with an IQ above 135.

Lewis Terman died in 1956, but the study of those mentally gifted individuals, who were between the ages of 8 and 12 in 1922, continues. Ever since their inclusion in the original study, and at regular intervals, they have been retested and interviewed by psychologists from Stanford (Goleman, 1980; Oden, 1968; Sears & Barbee, 1977).

The Terman study has drawbacks. Choosing a narrow definition of "gifted" in terms of IQ alone is an obvious one. Failing to control for factors such as the education or socioeconomic level of the parents is another. There is evidence that researchers may have excluded some children who showed signs of psychological disorders or other adjustment problems, whether their IQ scores were high or not. Nonetheless, the study is an impressive one for having been continued for 60 years, if nothing else.

What can this long-term analysis tell us about people with very high lQs? Most of Terman's results fly in the face of the common stereotype of the bright child as being skinny, anxious, clumsy, sickly, and wearing thick glasses (Sears & Barbee, 1977). In fact, if there is any overall conclusion to be drawn from the Terman-Stanford study, it is that gifted children experience advantages in virtually everything. They are taller, faster, stronger, better coordinated, have better eyesight, fewer emotional problems, and tend to stay married longer than average. These findings have been confirmed by others with different samples of subjects (Holden, 1980). Many obvious things are also true of Terman's sample of children, now senior citizens. They received much more education, found better, higher-paying jobs, and had brighter children than did people of average intelligence. By now, we know better than to overgeneralize. Not every one of the children in Terman's study (sometimes referred to as "Termites") grew up to be rich and famous and live happily ever after. Many did, but not all. The conclusions of this study, like so many others, are valid only "in general, on the average."

● **Before You Go On**

List six ways in which individuals can be considered gifted.

Summarize the basic findings of the Terman-Stanford study of the intellectually gifted.

The Mentally Retarded

Our understanding of mental retardation has changed considerably over the past 25 years. We have seen changes in treatment and care, and great strides in prevention. There have been substantial changes in how psychology defines mental retardation (Baumeister, 1987; Landesman & Ramey, 1989).

Intelligence as measured by IQ tests is often used to confirm suspected cases of mental retardation. As is the case for the mentally gifted, there is more to retardation than IQ alone. The American Association of Mental Deficiency (AAMD) cites three factors in its definition of **mental retardation**: "subaverage general intellectual functioning which originated during the developmental period and is associated with impairment in adaptive behavior" (Grossman, 1973).

The IQ cutoff for mental retardation is usually 70, with the following subcategories (Zigler & Hodapp, 1991):

IQ 70–85: *borderline or slow*
IQ 55–69: *mildly mentally retarded*
IQ 40–54: *moderately mentally retarded*
IQ 25–39: *severely mentally retarded*
IQ less than 25: *profoundly mentally retarded.*

As you review this list, you need to keep two things in mind. First, these IQ test scores are *suggested* limits. Given what we know about IQ tests and their reliability, it would be ridiculous to claim after one administration of a test that a person with an IQ of 69 is mentally retarded, while someone else with an IQ of 71 is not. Second, a diagnosis of mental retardation is not (should not be) made on the basis of IQ score alone.

To fit the AAMD definition of mental retardation, the cause or the symptoms of the below-average intellectual functioning must appear during the usual period of intellectual development (up to age 18). In many circles, the term *developmentally delayed* is coming to replace the narrower term *mentally retarded*. Diagnosis may come only after administering an IQ test, but initial suspicions come from perceived delays in an individual's normal developmental or adjustive patterns of behavior.

By making "impairment in adaptive behavior" a part of its definition of mental retardation, the AAMD acknowledges that there is more to getting along in this world than the intellectual and academic skills that IQ tests emphasize. Being mentally retarded does not mean being totally helpless, particularly for those in the mild to moderate levels of retardation. Of major consideration is an individual's ability to adapt to his or her environment. In this regard, such skills as the abilities to dress oneself, follow directions, make change, find one's way home from a distance, and so on are relevant (Coulter & Morrow, 1978).

Even without a simple, one-dimensional definition, it is clear that the population of retarded citizens is a large one. It is difficult to obtain exact

mental retardation
below-average general intellectual functioning which began before the age of 18 and is associated with maladaptive behaviors

figures, because many individuals who might fit the criteria and be classified as mildly retarded have never been diagnosed as such. Even so, standard estimates indicate that approximately 3 percent of the population (at least 6 million people) at any one time falls within the IQ range for retardation. Two other relevant estimates are that approximately 900,000 children with mental retardation between the ages of 3 and 21 years are being served in the public schools (Schroeder et al., 1987) and that 200,000 mentally retarded individuals are to be found in community residential facilities, state and county mental hospitals, and nursing homes (Landesman & Butterfield, 1987). Let's now turn to a brief discussion of the causes, treatment, and prevention of mental retardation.

We cannot begin to explain the causes of all types of mental retardation, but we have some good ideas. Psychologists suspect that there are hundreds of causes; the list of known and highly suspected causes exceeds 200 (Grossman, 1983). The more we learn about the sources of mental retardation, the better able we will be to treat it or prevent it altogether.

Approximately one-fourth of the mental retardation cases reflect some problem that developed before, during, or just after birth. Between 15 and 20 percent of persons referred to as mentally retarded were born prematurely, where prematurity is defined as being born at least 3 weeks before the due date *or* weighing below 5 pounds, 8 ounces.

We appreciate that the health of the mother during pregnancy—and the health of the father at conception—can affect the health of the child. Many prenatal conditions are thought to cause developmental delays, including hypertension, exposure to X rays, lowered oxygen intake, rubella (German measles), maternal syphilis, and the mother's use of drugs—from narcotics to aspirin, alcohol, and nicotine. To greater or lesser degrees, all of these have been linked to retardation. In addition, some cases stem from difficulties or injuries during the birth process itself.

As we've noted, the extent to which normal levels of intelligence are inherited is open to debate. Some varieties of mental retardation, however, are clearly genetic in origin. One of the clearest examples of such a case is the intellectual retardation that accompanies **Down syndrome**, first described in 1866. For reasons not understood, occasionally a fetus develops with 47 chromosomes instead of the usual 23 pairs. We do know that Down syndrome is more likely as the age of either parent increases. The signs of Down syndrome are well known: small, round skull; flattened face; large tongue; short, broad nose; broad hands; and short, stubby fingers. During childhood, behavioral development is delayed. Down syndrome children may fall into any of the levels of retardation listed above. Many are educable and lead lives of considerable independence, although it remains true that even as adults, many require supervision at least some of the time.

Fragile X syndrome is a variety of mental retardation with a genetic basis that was discovered more recently—in the late 1960s (Bregman et al., 1987). Although it does occur in females, it is found primarily in males, who characteristically have long faces, big ears, and, as adults, large testes (Zigler & Hodapp, 1991). Individuals with this form of mental retardation have difficulty processing sequences of events, or events in a series, which means that they have problems with language skills. One curiosity is that whereas males with Down syndrome show a gradual, steady decrease in IQ scores with age, males with Fragile X syndrome show more noticeable declines during puberty.

Most cases of mental retardation do not have obvious causes. About one-half to three-quarters of cases of mental retardation do not seem to have biological or organic causes (Zigler & Hodapp, 1991).

Down syndrome
a condition of many symptoms, including mental retardation, caused by an extra (47th) chromosome

To some degree, our ability to treat mental retardation depends on our ability to specify its causes. Special education programs have helped, but not all have been equally successful (Gallagher, 1994; Zigler & Hodapp, 1991). Preparing teachers and mental health professionals to be sensitive to the wide range of behaviors and feelings that mentally retarded persons are capable of has helped. Impressive changes *can* be made in the IQs of some mildly and a few moderately retarded children (Landesman & Ramey, 1989). For severely and profoundly retarded persons, the outlook is not bright—at least not in terms of raising IQ points (Spitz, 1986). But we always need to remind ourselves that quality of life is not necessarily a function of IQ. The emphasis in recent years has been to focus less on intellectual growth in general and more on the specific skills and abilities—social as well as intellectual—that can be improved.

There is greater hope in the area of prevention. As we continue to appreciate the influences of the prenatal environment on the development of cognitive abilities, we can educate mothers and fathers about how their behaviors can affect their children even before they are born. We have already noted that intellectual retardation is one of the symptoms associated with fetal alcohol syndrome (Chapter 3, p. 84). An excellent example of how mental retardation can be prevented concerns **phenylketonuria,** (feenel'-keet-o-nureea), or **PKU.** This disorder is genetic in origin, and over 50 years ago it was discovered to be a cause of mental retardation. PKU results when a child inherits genes that fail to produce an enzyme that breaks down chemicals found in many foods. Although a newborn with PKU appears quite normal, a simple blood test has been developed that can detect the disorder soon after birth. Upon detection, a prescribed diet can reduce or eliminate the symptoms of the disorder. Unfortunately, most cases (about 70 percent) of mental retardation cannot be detected at birth, which means that preventive or therapeutic intervention also has to wait until the child is older (Scott & Carran, 1987).

phenylketonuria (PKU) a genetically caused disorder that produces mental retardation and that is now detectable and preventable

● **Before You Go On**

How might we best define mental retardation?

List some of the possible causes of mental retardation.

THINKING CRITICALLY ABOUT HIGHER COGNITIVE PROCESSES

1. Given the definition that we used in this chapter, how many specific tasks can you characterize as "higher cognitive processes?"
2. What problems did you encounter yesterday? Which were ill-defined and which were well-defined?
3. Imagine a group of scientists trying to build and program an enormous computer to think as a human does. How would we know if the scientists were successful? That is, how could you test a computer to see if it thinks as people think?
4. What sort of curriculum would you establish if you were in charge of a class that was to teach problem-solving skills to fourth graders?
5. If it is true that most language users acquire the rules of their language before they are 6 years old, what do we really teach when we offer classes in English?

FIGURE 8.10
An example of a problem in which representation is critical. The diagonal of this circle is exactly 10 inches long. What is the length of line "L"? (From Köhler, 1989.)

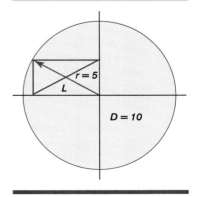

FIGURE 8.11
A solution to the "nine-dot problem."

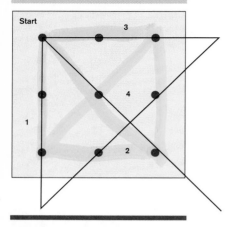

6. Why do some students seem to have a much easier time than others learning a second or a third "foreign" language?
7. What is wrong and what is right about the heavy reliance we put on intelligence testing in American culture? What might be some alternatives? If IQ does not equal intelligence, then what is it?
8. What are the short- and long-term advantages and disadvantages of placing children with intellectual disadvantages in regular classrooms?

SUMMARY

TOPIC 8A

PROBLEM SOLVING

● What are the three components of a problem?
● Contrast well-defined and ill-defined problems.
● Give an example of each.

A problem has three components: (1) an initial state—the situation as it exists at the moment; (2) a goal state—the situation as the problem solver would like it to be; and (3) routes or strategies for getting from the initial state to the goal state. Whether a problem is ill-defined or well-defined is a matter of the extent to which the initial state and the goal state are delineated and understood by the problem solver. An example of a well-defined problem might be that which you face when a familiar route home from campus is blocked. An example of an ill-defined problem might be that which you face when you are required to write a term paper on a topic of your choice. *Pages 278–279.*

● In the context of problem solving, what is meant by problem representation?

Problem representation involves the mental activity of thinking about a problem, focusing on relevant ele-

ments, and putting it in a form we can deal with effectively. In essence, problem representation means reducing a problem into familiar terms. *Pages 280–281*

● How are algorithmic and heuristic strategies used to solve problems?

Algorithms and heuristics are strategies or systematic plans we can use for seeking problem solutions. Algorithms employ a systematic examination of all possible solutions until the goal is reached. With algorithms, a solution, if there is one, is guaranteed to be found. A heuristic strategy—of which there are many—is a more informal, rule-of-thumb approach that involves generating and testing hypotheses that may lead to a problem solution in an organized way. *Pages 282–283.*

● What is a mental set, and how might a mental set hinder problem solving?
● What is functional fixedness, and how might it hinder problem solving?

A mental set is a tendency or a predisposition to perceive or to respond to something in a particular way. Mental sets generally develop from past experience and involve the continued use of strategies that were successful in the past, but may no longer be relevant. Functional fixedness is a variety of mental set in which an object is seen as serving only a few fixed functions. Because we may not see an object as being able to serve new and different functions, fixedness can interfere with effective problem solving. *Pages 283–285*

● What is the difference between divergent and convergent thinking?
● What are the four stages of creative problem solving according to Wallas?

Divergent thinking is a technique in which several problem solutions are generated and tested later for usefulness. Convergent thinking involves selecting a large number of ideas or possibilities for problem solution and reducing them to one or a few. A scheme developed by Wallas in 1926 suggests four stages for creative problem solving: (1) preparation, (2) incubation, (3) illumination, and (4) verification. *Pages 285–287.*

TOPIC 8B
LANGUAGE

● What are some of the defining characteristics of language?

Language use is a creative cognitive process used for communication. A language is made up of a large number of arbitrary symbols (e.g., words) that stand for our conceptualization of objects and events, which have meaning for users of the language and which are combined in accordance with rules. The use of language is a generative process that, among other things, allows us to communicate about the not-here and the not-now. *Pages 288–289.*

● What is the study of pragmatics, and what does it tell us about language use?

Pragmatics is the study of how the social situation, or context, influences the meaning of language utterances. An appreciation of context allows us to recognize the use of sarcasm, simile, metaphors, and the like. *Pages 289–290.*

● What are some of the landmark events that occur during language acquisition?

Although infants cry and babble, the first truly linguistic utterances are called holophrastic speech, which occurs when one word is used to communi-

cate a range of feelings, intentions, and meanings. A two-word stage of development shows the presence of structure in word-ordering—a grammar that is not just a simple reflection of adult language. From the two-word utterance on, language development is extremely rapid. By the time a child is 5 years old he or she will know thousands of words, will understand more than he or she will produce, and be able to combine those words in virtually every acceptable sentence structure allowed by the language. *Pages 290–292.*

● Briefly summarize the learning-oriented and biology-oriented theories of language acquisition.

Neither learning/experiential nor instinctual/biological theories can totally account for language acquisition. Learning history has an impact on the acquisition of speech sounds, words, and word meanings. At the same time, learning theory is challenged by the cross-cultural regularities that occur in language acquisition—that all children of all languages seem to develop their language in the same general, patterned way. The complex process is too rapid and too regular not to have some strong biological basis. *Pages 292–293.*

TOPIC 8C
INTELLIGENCE

● Provide a theoretical and an operational definition of intelligence.

In theory, we may define intelligence as the capacity of an individual to understand the world about him or her and the resourcefulness to cope with its challenges. An operational definition of intelligence would be "that which intelligence tests measure." *Page 294.*

● What is a psychological test?
● In the context of psychological testing, what are reliability, validity, and test norms?

A psychological test is an objective (not open to multiple interpretation), standardized (administered and scored in the same way for everyone) measure of a sample (we cannot measure all we are interested in) of behavior (because behavior is all we can measure). Reliability means consistency or dependability. Validity is the extent to which a test measures what it claims to measure. Test norms are the scores of large numbers of subjects, similar to those for whom the test has been designed. It is against the standard of these scores that an individual's test score can be compared. *Pages 295–296.*

● Briefly describe the Stanford-Binet Intelligence Scale.

The Stanford-Binet is the oldest of the tests of general intelligence (commonly called IQ tests). Its most recent (1986) revision provides an overall score as well as subscores for several abilities that underlie general intelligence. The test is comprised of 15 subtests, each assessing a specific cognitive task, where items are arranged in order of difficulty. Scores on the test, standardized by age, reflect the subject's performance as compared to others of the same age level. *Pages 296–299.*

● What are the major features of the Wechsler intelligence scales?

The Wechsler scales are individually administered tests of general intelligence. There are three of them and each appropriate for a different age group, ranging from ages 4 to 74. Each test is made up of several subtests of different content. The subtests are grouped as either verbal or performance. Hence, three scores can be determined: an overall score (usually taken as IQ), a score on verbal subtests, and a score on performance subtests. Scores on the Wechsler tests are standard scores that compare one's abilities to those of others of the same age. *Pages 299–301.*

● List six ways in which individuals can be considered gifted.
● Summarize the basic findings of the Terman-Stanford study of the intellectually gifted.

Giftedness can refer to several things, including (1) overall intellectual ability as measured by IQ tests (usually taken to be an IQ over 130 points), (2) talent in the visual and performing arts, (3) psychomotor skills, (4) leadership, (5) creativity, and (6) abilities in specific academic areas. Most simply, individuals who were tested to have very high IQs were also found to do well in almost everything else measured by the researchers. *Pages 301–304.*

● How might we best define mental retardation?
● List some of the possible causes of mental retardation.

Mental retardation should be thought of as reflecting subaverage intellectual functioning (usually indicated by IQ test scores below 70), originating during the developmental period (within one's first 18 years), and associated with impairment in adaptive behavior (as well as academic behaviors). In addition to genetic causes, most known causes of mental retardation (there may be over 200) revolve around the health and care of the mother and the fetus during pregnancy, where drugs, lack of oxygen, poor nutrition, and the like have been implicated in mental retardation. The condition of the father at the time of conception is also relevant. In other words, many of the biologically based causes of mental retardation seem to be preventable. *Pages 305–307.*

TOPIC 8A
PROBLEM SOLVING

8.1 More than anything else, what makes a problem "well defined" as opposed to "ill defined"? a) knowing with certainty when a solution is found b) the extent to which we realize that we are faced with a problem c) the adequacy of problem representation d) the choice of an adequate strategy for problem solving. *Pages 278–279.*

8.2 Which provides the best example of a well-defined problem? a) How can Israeli-Palestinian differences be peacefully resolved? b) Which country in North America has the longest coastline? c) What would be required to establish a psychology laboratory in a new college? d) What is the best way to organize a surprise birthday party for a co-worker? *Pages 278–279.*

8.3 When we say that problem solving begins with problem representation, we are suggesting that one needs to a) put the problem in numerical or mathematical form. b) examine all possible solutions before one begins. c) decide if the problem has a solution. d) make the problem meaningful. *Pages 280–281.*

8.4 Problem representation typically is easiest when a) the problem deals with familiar information. b) the problem is well-defined. c) there is only one way in which a solution can be found. d) the problem is ill-defined. *Pages 280–281.*

8.5 As more and more solutions and routes to problem solution become available, the more sensible it is to use a) a comprehensive, systematic search of all possibilities. b) a heuristic strategy. c) fewer and fewer hypotheses. d) an algorithmic approach. *Pages 282–283*

8.6 The major advantage of a heuristic rather than an algorithmic strategy for problem solving is that heuristics a) guarantee that eventually you'll reach your goal. b) are systematic. c) tend to save time and effort. d) produce solutions that can be tested and confirmed. *Pages 282–283.*

8.7 True or False? Computers cannot use algorithms to solve problems effectively—only people can. *Pages 282–283.*

8.8 Which statement concerning mental sets and problem solving is *false*? a) Mental sets influence how we represent problems. b) Mental sets always interfere with problem solving. c) Mental sets generally evolve from past experiences. d) Mental sets are mental predispositions. *Pages 282–283.*

8.9 Functional fixedness is essentially a type of a) problem representation. b) heuristic strategy. c) creativity. d) mental set. *Pages 283–287.*

8.10 The ultimate test of a creative solution to a problem is whether a) anyone else has ever thought of it before. b) it is artistic, balanced, or beautiful. c) it works to solve the problem at hand. d) it is convergent or divergent. *Pages 283–287.*

8.11 True or False? Divergent thinking involves generating as many potential solutions as possible, while convergent thinking involves reducing the number of possibilities in problem solving. *Pages 283–287.*

TOPIC 8B
LANGUAGE

8.12 Which of these is *least* descriptive of language? Language is a) rule governed. b) either correct or incorrect. c) both creative or generative. d) both cognitive and social. *Pages 288–289.*

311

8.13 Which term is most general and includes the other three? a) communication b) language c) speech d) word. *Pages 288–289.*

8.14 When we say that language allows us to communicate about things that are not present, neither here nor now, we are saying that language demonstrates a) displacement. b) a behavior that follows rules. c) a cognitive process. d) arbitrariness. *Pages 289–290.*

8.15 In the study of language, pragmatics involves a) the social context in which language occurs. b) the meaning of utterances within a language. c) how words of a language are ordered or structured. d) whether language is used for communication or for some other purpose. *Pages 289–290.*

8.16 True or False? Research has confirmed many times that women are more talkative than men. *Pages 289–290.*

8.17 True or False? Children do not show an appreciation of language as a form of communication until they are producing 3- or 4- word utterances. *Pages 290–293.*

8.18 A child says, "I got two hands, and I got two foots," providing us with an example of a) displacement. b) holophrastic speech. c) the emergence of a two-word grammar. d) overregularization. *Pages 290–293.*

8.19 In accounting for language acquisition, learning accounts best for a) the acquisition of the syntactic rules of one's language. b) how and why babbling begins and ends. c) the understanding of the meaning of the words of one's language. d) the observed similarities that occur in language acquisition across cultures. *Pages 290–293.*

T O P I C   8 C

INTELLIGENCE

8.20 Which of the following provides an operational definition of intelligence? Intelligence is a) the sum of those cognitive abilities that allow us to adapt to the environment. b) that which is measured by an IQ test. c) the accumulation of information over a life-

time. d) the ultimate problem-solving skill. *Pages 294.*

8.21 When we talk about a psychological test being objective, what is our major concern? a) that test performance be evaluated fairly b) that subjects understand what they are to do c) that it is not possible to measure everything d) that each question have only one correct answer. *Pages 295–296.*

8.22 Dr. Woods has written a test. She gives the test to one of her classes, and then gives the same test to the same class two weeks later. Dr. Woods's concern is with a) assessing the reliability of her test. b) collecting scores for a norm group. c) the validity of her test. d) establishing the test's objectivity. *Pages 295–296.*

8.23 True or False? Psychological tests provide measures of samples of behaviors. *Pages 295–296.*

8.24 True or False? A test can be valid without being reliable. *Pages 295–296.*

8.25 When Binet and Simon wrote their test of intelligence, their major concern or intent was to a) study the long-term consequences of being judged mentally gifted as a child. b) determine how much of one's intelligence is inherited and how much is due to the influence of the environment. c) identify those children who needed to be placed in remedial or special education classes. d) discover if intelligence is one unitary **g** factor, or several specific **s** factors. *Pages 296–299.*

8.26 The current version of the Stanford Binet provides estimates of intellectual skills at several different levels. Which of these is the highest level? a) short-term memory b) **g** c) crystallized abilities d) vocabulary. *Pages 296–299.*

8.27 Using the classic approach to IQ as an intelligence quotient, if 10-year-old Sally demonstrates intellectual functioning typical of an average 8-year-old, Sally's IQ is a) 70. b) 80. c) 100. d) 125. *Pages 296–299.*

8.28 True or False? The current revision of the Stanford-Binet test yields just one score—a measure of general intelligence, **g**. *Pages 296–299.*

8.29 When David Wechsler first introduced his tests, what did he introduce to IQ testing? a) individually administered tests b) tests that were more valid for children than for adults c) nonverbal items on which one's performance was scored d) the number of items they are correct minus the number of items that are incorrect. *Pages 299–301.*

8.30 Down syndrome a) can be treated by changes in diet if diagnosed at birth. b) children are invariably either severely or profoundly retarded intellectually.

c) develops as a result of a chromosomal abnormality. d) is usually caused by alcohol or drug use during pregnancy. *Pages 301–307.*

8.31 True or False? We stand a better chance of preventing mental retardation than we do of treating it effectively. *Pages 301–307.*

9

MOTIVATION AND EMOTION

PREVIEW

TOPIC 9A—Issues of Motivation

How Shall We Characterize Motivation?

Physiologically Based Drives

PSYCHOLOGY IN THE REAL WORLD: Eating Disorders

Psychologically Based Motives

TOPIC 9B—The Psychology of Emotion

Defining "Emotion"

Classifying Emotions

Physiological Aspects of Emotion

Outward Expressions of Emotion

THINKING CRITICALLY ABOUT MOTIVATION AND EMOTION

SUMMARY

TEST YOURSELF

In this chapter we address some important practical issues. For the first time, our focus will be on questions that begin with the word "why." "Why did she *do* that (as opposed to doing nothing)?" "Why did she do *that* (as opposed to doing something else)?" "Why does she *keep* doing that (as opposed to stopping)?" As you can see, the study of motivation gets us involved with attempts to explain the causes of one's behaviors.

We will begin our discussion in Topic 9A by considering some ways that psychologists have approached the study of motivation. The theoretical approaches presented here are not always in conflict. They have much in common, and we should be able to find useful ideas within each approach. The remainder of Topic 9A will focus on two types of motivating forces: (1) those rooted in biology and related to survival (physiological drives), and (2) those more clearly learned or social in nature (psychological motives).

Topic 9B deals with emotions and emotionality—issues that are very related to motivation. Both involve arousal—becoming excited, activated, and prepared to act—as well as underlying physiological reactions that often are quite similar. In fact, motivation and emotion are usually so much related that it is a bit artificial to separate our treatment of them. We'll begin by seeing that defining and classifying emotions has proven to be a difficult task. We will focus on two areas of research that have been very promising: discovering the underlying physiological reactions that correspond to emotional states and finding how emotions are reflected or expressed in behavior.

TOPIC 9A

ISSUES OF MOTIVATION

Motivation involves two subprocesses. First, it involves *arousal*—one's overall level of activation or excitement. Here we are using the term *motivation* as a force that initiates or activates behaviors, that gets an organism going, energized to do something and to keep doing it. The second process provides *direction*, or focus, to one's behaviors. In addition to simply being aroused and active, a motivated organism's behavior is goal-directed, or in some way purposeful. Thus, **motivation** is the process that arouses, directs, and maintains behavior.

motivation
the process of arousing, maintaining, and directing behavior

315

HOW SHALL WE CHARACTERIZE MOTIVATION?

From its earliest days, psychology has tried to find some systematic theory to organize and summarize what various motivational states have in common. Psychologists have struggled to develop one general pattern or scheme that could be used to account for *why* organisms do what they do. In this section, we'll review some of these theories in a somewhat chronological order. As you know, no one approach to motivation is going to answer all our questions. Although each of the approaches summarized below may have its drawbacks, we should focus our attention on how each makes a contribution to our understanding of behavior and mental processes.

Instincts

instincts
unlearned, complex patterns of behavior that occur in the presence of particular stimuli

In the psychology of the 1800s, behavior was often explained in terms of **instincts**—unlearned, complex patterns of behavior that occur in the presence of certain stimuli. Why do birds build nests? It's because of a nest-building instinct. When conditions are right, birds build nests. Why do salmon swim upstream to mate? Instinct. Its simply a part of what it means to be a salmon. Yes, these behaviors can be modified by the organisms' experiences, but the basic driving force behind them is unlearned or instinctive.

Instinct may explain some of the behavior of birds and salmon, but what about people? William James (1890) reasoned that humans, being more complex, had to have many more instincts than did the "lower" animals. William McDougall (1908) championed the instinctual explanation of human behaviors as forcefully as anyone. He claimed that human behaviors were motivated by 11 basic instincts: repulsion, curiosity, flight, parental, reproduction, gregariousness, acquisitiveness, construction, self-assertion, self-abasement, and pugnacity. Soon McDougall extended his list to include 18 instincts. As new and different behaviors required explanation, new and different instincts were devised to explain them.

As lists of human instincts got longer and longer, the problem with this approach became obvious. Particularly for humans, "explaining" behavior patterns by alluding to instinct simply renamed or relabeled them and didn't explain anything at all. Even so, psychologists who argued for instincts did draw attention to an idea that is still with us: We engage in some behaviors for reasons that are basically physiological, and more inherited than learned.

Needs and Drives

One approach that provided an alternative to explaining behavior in terms of instincts was one that attempted to explain behavior in terms of needs and drives. We'll look at two theories that incorporate these concepts.

need
a lack or shortage of some biological essential resulting from deprivation

drive
a state of tension resulting from a need that arouses and directs an organism's behavior

Clark Hull. Clark Hull's ideas about motivation were dominant in the 1940s and 1950s (e.g., Hull, 1943). In Hull's system, a **need** is a shortage or lack of some biological essential required for survival. Needs may arise from deprivation: When an organism is kept from food, it develops a need for food. A need gives rise to a drive. A **drive** is a state of tension, arousal, or activation. When an organism is in a *drive state*, it is motivated. It is aroused and directed to do something to satisfy the drive by reducing or eliminating the

Why do salmon swim upstream at mating season? Why do birds, such as this osprey, build nests? We may explain these behaviors by referring to instincts, but such explanation has not proven to be useful for explaining most human behavior.

underlying need. Needs produce tensions (drives) that the organism seeks to reduce, so this approach is referred to in terms of drive reduction.

Hull's approach is less circular than an appeal to instincts. Instincts are tied to a specific pattern of behavior, but needs and drives are not. They are concepts that can be used to explain why we do what we do while clearly allowing for the influence of experience and the environment. Going without food gives rise to a need, which in turn gives rise to a drive, but how that drive is expressed in behavior is influenced by one's experience and learning history.

One problem with a drive-reduction approach centers on the biological nature of needs. To claim that needs result only from biological deprivations seems unduly restrictive. Surely not all of the drives that activate a person's behavior are based on biological needs. Humans often engage in behaviors to satisfy *learned* drives. Drives based on one's learning experiences are called **secondary drives**, as opposed to *primary drives*, which are based on unlearned, physiological needs. In fact, most of the drives that arouse and direct our behavior have little to do with physiology. You may feel that you need a new car this year. I may convince myself that *I need* a new set of golf clubs, and we both will work very hard to save the money to buy what we need. We may say that we are "driven" to work for money, but it's difficult to imagine how your car or my golf clubs are satisfying a biological need. A lot of advertising is directed at trying to convince us that we "need" many products and services that will have very little impact on our survival.

In summary, we often do behave in order to reduce drives and, thereby, satisfy needs. How either primary or secondary drives are satisfied will reflect the learning history of the organism. The concept of drive reduction is a useful one and is still with us in psychology, but it cannot be accepted as a complete explanation for motivated behaviors.

Abraham Maslow. Abraham Maslow is a psychologist we associate with the humanistic movement in psychology. Humanistic psychologists have emphasized the person and his or her psychological growth. Maslow combined his concern for the person with Hull's drive reduction theory and

secondary drive
arousers and directors of behavior that stem from learned, or acquired, needs that are not tied to one's biological survival

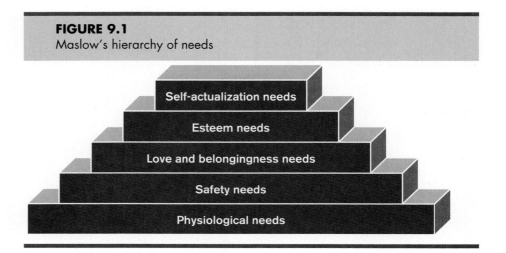

FIGURE 9.1
Maslow's hierarchy of needs

Self-actualization needs

Esteem needs

Love and belongingness needs

Safety needs

Physiological needs

proposed that human behavior does, in fact, respond to needs. Not all of those needs are physiological. Maslow believed that the needs that motivate human action are few and are arranged in a hierarchy (Maslow, 1943, 1970). Figure 9.1 summarizes this hierarchy of needs in pictorial form.

Maslow's is basically a stage theory. It proposes that what motivates us first are *physiological needs*. These include the basic needs that are related to survival—food, water, shelter, and so on. Until these needs are met, there is no reason to suspect that a person will be concerned with anything else. Once one's physiological needs have been met, a person is still motivated, but now by *safety needs*—the need to feel secure, protected from dangers that might arise in the future. We are now motivated to see to it that the cupboard has food for later, that we won't freeze this winter, and that there is enough money saved to protect against sudden calamity. The hierarchical nature of this scheme is already clear. We're not going to worry about what to eat tomorrow if there's not enough to eat today; but if today's needs *are* taken care of, we can focus on the future.

Once safety needs are met, concern shifts to needs for *love and belongingness*—the need for someone else to care about us, to love us. If these needs are satisfied, our concern is for *esteem*. Our aim is to be recognized for our achievements and our efforts. These needs are not physiological, but social; they imply that our behaviors are motivated by our awareness of others and our concern for their approval. One moves higher in the hierarchy only if lower needs are met. Ultimately, we may reach the highest stage in Maslow's hierarchy: *self-actualization needs*. We self-actualize when we become the best that we can be, taking the fullest advantage of our potential as human beings. We are self-actualizing when we strive to be as productive or creative as possible.

In many ways, Maslow's arrangement of needs in a hierarchy does conform to common sense, at least in Western cultures. We do not expect people to be motivated to grow and achieve "success" when they are worried about their very survival on a day-to-day basis. Even when a person's needs for safety, belonging, and esteem are reasonably met, they don't just die, unmotivated to do anything else. Maslow believed that most people never achieve the self-actualization stage in this hierarchy of needs. There are millions of people who have great difficulty with the very lowest stages and never have the time, energy, or inclination to be concerned about issues of self-esteem and belongingness, much less self-actualization.

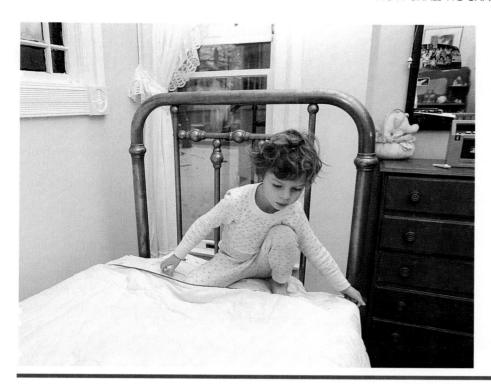

Motivating a child to clean his room and make his bed can be viewed as attempting to get the child to share some of the incentives of his parents.

As a comprehensive theory of human motivation, Maslow's hierarchy has some difficulties. Perhaps the biggest stumbling block is the idea that one can assign ranks to needs and put them in a neat order, whatever that order may be. Some persons are motivated in ways that violate the stage approach of this theory. Some individuals will, for example, give up satisfying basic survival needs for the sake of "higher" principles (as in hunger strikes). For the sake of love, people may abandon their own needs for safety and security. It remains the case, however, that because of its intuitive appeal, Maslow's theory of human motivation has found favor both within and outside of psychology.

Incentives

One alternative to a drive-reduction approach to motivation focuses on the *end state,* or goal, of behavior, not needs or drives within the organism. According to this view, external stimuli serve as motivating agents or **incentives** for behavior. Incentives are external events that act to *pull* our behavior, as opposed to drives, which are internal and *push* our behavior.

When a mountain climber says that she climbs a mountain "because it is there," the climber is indicating a type of motivation through incentive. After a large meal we may order a piece of cheesecake, not because we need it in any physiological sense, but because it's there on the dessert cart and looks so good—and because experience tells us that it is likely to taste very good.

Some parents want to know how to motivate their child to clean up his room. We can interpret this example in terms of establishing goals or incentives. What these parents *really* want to know is how they can get their child to value, work for, and be reinforced by a clean room. What they want is a clean room, and they want the child to clean it. If they want the child "to be motivated" to clean his room, the child needs to learn the value or incentive of having a clean room. How to teach a child that a clean room is

incentives
external stimuli that an organism may be motivated to approach or avoid

a thing to be valued is another story, probably involving other incentives that the child does value. For now, let's acknowledge that establishing a clean room as a valued goal is the task at hand, and that having a clean room is not an inborn need.

If this discussion of incentives sounds like our treatment of operant conditioning (Topic 6B), you're right. Remember, the basic tenet of operant conditioning is that behaviors are controlled by their consequences. We are motivated to do what leads to reinforcers (positive incentives), and not to do whatever leads to punishment or failure of reinforcement (negative incentives).

● **Before You Go On**

How have the concepts of instinct, need, drive, and incentive been used to explain motivated behaviors?

Balance, or Equilibrium

A concept that has proven useful in discussions of motivated behavior is that of balance, or equilibrium. The basic idea is that we are motivated or driven to maintain a state of balance. What are we are motivated to balance? We may be motivated to maintain equilibrium among (1) internal, physiological processes, (2) our overall level of excitement, or (3) our thoughts or cognitions.

homeostasis
a state of balance or equilibrium among internal, physiological conditions

Homeostasis. One of the first references to a need for equilibrium is found in the work of Walter Cannon (1932). Cannon was concerned with internal physiological reactions, and the term he used to describe a state of balance among those reactions was **homeostasis**. Each of our physiological processes has a balanced, *set point* of operation. One's set point is a level of activity that can be considered "normal," or most suitable. Whenever anything happens to upset this balance, we become motivated. We are driven to return to our set point, our optimum, homeostatic level. If we drift just slightly out of homeostasis, our physiological mechanisms act to return us to balance without our intention or our awareness. If these automatic, involuntary processes are unsuccessful, we may have to take action to maintain equilibrium.

For example, everyone has a normal, set level of body temperature, heart rate, blood pressure, basal metabolism (the rate at which energy is used by the body), and so on. When any of these levels deviates from its set point, we become motivated to do something that will return us to balance. Cannon's concept of homeostasis was devised to explain physiological processes. As we shall soon see, however, the basic ideas of balance and optimum level of operation have been applied to psychological processes as well.

arousal
one's level of activation or excitement

Arousal. **Arousal** is defined in terms of level of activation or excitement. A person's level of arousal may change from day to day and throughout the same day. After a good night's sleep, a cup of coffee, and a morning shower, your level of arousal may be quite high. (It also may be high as your instructor moves through your class handing out exams.) Late at night, after a busy day, your level of arousal may be low. Your arousal is at its lowest when you are in the deepest stages of sleep.

Arousal theories of motivation (e.g., Berlyne, 1960, 1971; Duffy, 1962; Hebb, 1955), claim that there is an optimal level (set point again) of arousal that organisms are motivated to maintain. Drive reduction approaches, re-

For many of us, jumping off a high platform attached only by a bungee cord on our ankles, or climbing upside-down, held only by spikes driven into the rock, would be overly arousing. But for "sensation seekers," bungee jumping and rock climbing may provide optimum levels of arousal.

member, argue that we are motivated to *reduce* tension or arousal by satisfying needs. Arousal theories argue that sometimes we actually seek out arousing, tension-producing activities, motivated to maintain our optimal arousal level. If we find ourselves bored and in a rut, the idea of going to an action-adventure movie may seem like a good one. If we've had a very busy, hectic day, just staying at home doing nothing may sound appealing.

This approach is, of course, like Cannon's idea of homeostasis, but in more general terms than specific physiological processes. It claims that for any activity or situation, there is a "best," or most efficient, level of arousal. To do well on an exam, for example, requires that a student have a certain overall level of arousal. If a student is tired, bored, or just doesn't care about the exam, we can expect a poor performance. If, on the other hand, a student is *so* worried or anxious that he or she can hardly think straight, we can also predict a poor score. The relationship between arousal and the efficiency of performance is depicted in Figure 9.2.

An interesting twist on the theory of arousal is the observation that, for unknown reasons, optimum levels of arousal vary considerably from person to person. Some people apparently need and seek high levels of arousal and excitement in their lives. They are what Marvin Zuckerman (1978; Zuckerman et al. 1980) calls "sensation seekers." They enjoy skydiving or mountain climbing and actually look forward to the challenge of driving in heavy city traffic, for example.

Cognitive Dissonance. There is also a point of view that we are motivated to maintain a balance among our ideas or beliefs—our cognitions—as well as our physiological processes and our levels of arousal. This approach claims that we are motivated to preserve what Leon Festinger (1957) calls a *state of consonance* among our cognitions.

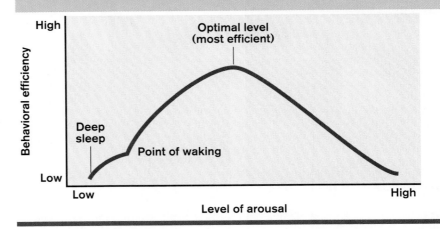

FIGURE 9.2
For each task we attempt, there is an optimal level of arousal. What that level is depends on several factors, including the difficulty of the task. In other words, it is possible to be too aroused (motivated), just as it is possible to be underaroused. (Hebb, 1955.)

cognitive dissonance
a discomforting, motivating state that occurs when one's ideas or beliefs are not in balance or equilibrium

Suppose you believe yourself to be a good student. You study hard for a test in biology—you think that you're prepared. You judge the test to be a fairly easy one. But when you get your test paper back, you discover that you failed! That's hard to accept, since you are confident you studied adequately. You believe the test wasn't difficult, but you also know that you failed the test. Here are cognitions that don't fit together. They are not balanced. You are experiencing what Festinger calls **cognitive dissonance**, a state of tension or discomfort that exists when one holds, and is aware of, inconsistent cognitions. When this occurs, Festinger argues, we become motivated to change our system of cognitions. In our example, you may come to believe that you are not such a good student after all. Or you may come to believe that your test was graded unfairly. Or you may come to believe that you are a poor judge of a test's difficulty. This theory doesn't predict specifically *what* will happen, but it predicts that cognitive dissonance does motivate one to return to a balanced state of cognitive consonance.

These days, almost all smokers experience cognitive dissonance. They know that smoking is a deadly habit, and yet they continue to smoke. Smokers often reduce dissonance by convincing themselves that although smoking is bad for one's health, it really isn't bad for *them*—at least when compared to perceived "benefits." We'll return to Festinger and cognitive dissonance when we discuss attitude change (Topic 14A).

● **Before You Go On**

How can the concept of balance or equilibrium be used to help us understand motivated behaviors?

In what way is cognitive dissonance theory based on equilibrium?

PHYSIOLOGICALLY BASED DRIVES

Now that we have reviewed some theoretical approaches to the motives that activate and direct our behaviors, we can turn our attention to a few specific examples. As you can imagine, this discussion could be organized in several ways. As I suggested earlier, we'll use a system that refers to just two types of motivators: those that have a biological basis, which we will call *physiologically based,* and those that are more clearly learned or social in nature, which we'll call *psychologically based.*

There are two points to keep in mind throughout this discussion. First, we will follow convention and use the term *drive* for activators and directors of behavior that have a known biological or physiological basis (e.g., "hunger drive") and the term *motive* for those that do not (e.g., "power motive"). Second, even drives rooted in an organism's physiology are often influenced by psychological processes. Hunger, for example, is clearly a physiologically based drive, but what we eat, when we eat, and how much we eat often are influenced by psychological and social factors.

Temperature Regulation

Most of us seldom give our own body temperature much thought. We all have a fuzzy notion that 98.6°F is a normal, homeostatic body temperature. That body temperature has anything to do with motivation becomes sensible in terms of homeostasis. When anything happens to change our body temperature from its homeostatic, set point range, we become motivated to return our body temperature to normal. (In passing, I should mention that research confirms that one's body temperature tends to fluctuate throughout the day, and that, actually, 98.2°F is a better estimate of "normal," or average temperature than is 98.6°F. [Mackowiak, Wasserman, & Levine, 1992]).

Let's say you are outside on a very cold day, and are improperly dressed for the low temperature and high wind. Your body temperature begins to drop. Automatically, your body responds to do what it can to bring your temperature back to its normal level: Blood vessels in your hands and feet constrict, forcing blood to the center of your body to conserve heat (as a result, your lips turn blue), you shiver (the involuntary movements of

We are driven to maintain our body temperatures within rather strict limits. When our autonomic nervous system cannot deal adequately with temperature changes, we may be driven to do something that will raise or lower our body temperatures.

FIGURE 9.3
A section of the human brain, showing the location of the hypothalamus.

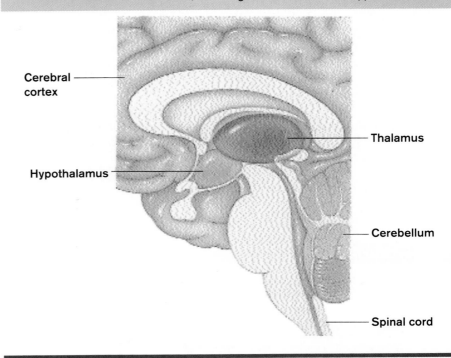

Cerebral cortex

Hypothalamus

Thalamus

Cerebellum

Spinal cord

your muscles creating small amounts of heat energy), and you get "goose bumps" (as your skin thickens to insulate against the cold). These are exactly the sorts of reactions that Cannon had in mind when he wrote about physiological homeostasis.

As another example, imagine that you are walking across a desert at noon on a day in August. Your temperature begins to rise. Automatically, blood is forced toward your body's surface, and your face becomes flushed. You perspire, and as the moisture on the surface of the skin evaporates, the skin is cooled, as is the blood, now near the surface—all in an attempt to return your body's temperature to its homeostatic level.

There are two centers that together act as a thermostat and start these attempts at temperature regulation. Both are in the **hypothalamus** deep inside the brain (see Figure 9.3). One is particularly sensitive to elevated body temperatures, the other to lowered temperatures.

If these automatic reactions are not successful, you may be motivated to take some voluntary action. You may have to get inside, out of the cold or heat. You may need to turn on a furnace or air conditioner. In fact, you may *anticipate* the lowering or raising of your body temperature and act accordingly—by putting on your coat before going out on a blustery day, for example. Over and above what your body can do, you may have to engage in learned behaviors in order to maintain homeostasis.

hypothalamus
a small midbrain structure near the limbic system associated with feeding, drinking, temperature regulation, sex, and aggression

● **Before You Go On**

Given the concept of homeostasis, how might temperature regulation be thought of as a physiologically based drive?

Thirst and Drinking Behavior

We need water for survival. If we don't drink, we die. As the need for water increases, it gives rise to a thirst drive. The intriguing issue is not that we need to drink, but how we *know* that we're thirsty. What actually causes us to seek liquid and drink it?

For a very long time, it was thought that we drink simply to relieve the discomfort caused by the dryness of our mouths and throats. No doubt, the unpleasantness of a dry mouth and throat *can* motivate us to drink, but there must be more to drinking than this. Animals with no salivary glands—whose mouths and throats are always dry—drink no more than normal animals (they do drink more frequently, but do not drink more in terms of quantity). Normal bodily processes (like urination, exhaling, and perspiration) cause us to lose about 2 1/2 liters of water a day (Levinthal, 1983). That water needs to be replaced, but what motivates us to do so?

About two-thirds of the fluid in our bodies is contained *within* our body's cells (intercellular), and about one-third is held in the spaces *between* cells (extracellular). There seem to be two separate mechanisms sensitive to losses of fluid. Intercellular loss of fluid is monitored by the hypothalamus. One small center acts to "turn on" the thirst drive when fluid levels are low, and another center "turns off" the thirst drive when fluid levels are adequate. Extracellular fluid loss is also monitored in the brain, through a complex chain of events involving the kidneys, which stimulate the production of a hormone that leads to a thirst drive.

Sometimes drinking arises from our physiological need for water. Sometimes, however, drinking behavior may be influenced by external factors, or incentives. For example, the aroma of freshly brewed coffee may stimulate us to have a second cup, which is in no way "needed." A frosty glass of iced tea may look too good to refuse. We may drink a cold beer or a soda simply because it tastes good, whether we *need* the fluid they contain or not.

Notice also that once our thirst drive has been aroused, *what* we drink will be strongly influenced by our previous learning experiences. Choices and preferences for what we drink are shaped by availability (people in Canada do not regularly drink coconut milk) and by past experience. Even with so obvious a physiological drive as thirst, and so obvious a physiological need as our need for water, psychological factors can be very relevant.

● **Before You Go On**

List some of the internal and external factors that influence drinking behavior.

Hunger and Eating Behavior

Our need for food is as obvious as our need for water. If we don't eat, we die. Again, the interesting question is, what gives rise to the hunger drive? As it happens, there are many factors that motivate a person to eat. Some of

We eat for many reasons, not just simply in response to a physiological need for food. For some of us, sporting events are more enjoyable when accompanied by a hot dog and snack foods.

them are physiological. Some are psychological, reflecting learning experiences. Others involve social pressures.

People and animals with no stomachs still eat amounts of food similar to those eaten by people with their stomachs intact. Cues from our stomachs, then, don't seem to be very important in producing a hunger drive. The two structures most involved in the hunger drive are the hypothalamus (again) and the liver, which is involved in the production and breakdown of fat.

Theories of hunger that focus on the hypothalamus are referred to as *dual-center* theories, because they suggest that there are *two* regions in the hypothalamus that regulate food intake. One is an "eat center" that gives rise to feelings of hunger, whereas the other is a "no-eat center" that lets us know when we have had enough.

Removing the "eat center" leads to starvation, as does an electrical stimulation to the "no-eat center." Removing the "no-eat center" leads to extreme overeating—a condition called *hyperphagia* (Friedman & Stricker, 1976; Keesey & Powley, 1975).

The hypothalamus may be involved in experiencing hunger, but normal eating patterns are not caused by electrical stimulation or lesioning. What does activate the brain's hunger-regulating centers in a normal organism? Here, we are still at the level of hypothesis and conjecture, not yet fact (Martin et al., 1991). One proposal is that our bodies respond to levels of blood sugar, or the amount of glucose in our blood that can be metabolized. When glucose levels are low, which they are when we haven't eaten for a while, we are stimulated to eat. When blood sugar levels are adequate, we will stop eating. Our *liver* most closely monitors such blood chemistry for us.

Another position holds that we respond, through a complex chain of events, to levels of fat stored in our bodies. When fat stores are adequately filled, we do not feel hungry. When fat supplies are depleted, a hunger drive arises. Once again, the *liver* is thought to monitor the cycle of storing and depleting fat supplies.

Yet another view that emphasizes the role of internal physiological cues relies on the concept of homeostasis, or set point. This position claims that *body weight*, like blood pressure, is physiologically regulated (Bouchard et al., 1990; Brownell & Rodin, 1994; Nisbett, 1972). "Being so regulated, weight is normally maintained at a particular level or set-point, not only by the control of food intake, as is often assumed, but also by complementary adjustments in energy utilization and expenditure" (Keesey & Powley, 1986). The idea is that as body weight decreases significantly, either through dieting, exercise, or both, the organism becomes motivated to return to the set-point level. The result may be to abandon the diet, cut down on exercise, or both. Still to be determined are the mechanisms involved in establishing the set points of body weight and energy utilization levels to begin with.

There is evidence that suggests there are genetic forces at work that determine body size *and* the distribution of fat throughout the body (Stunkard, 1988; Stunkard et al. 1986, 1990). One experiment (Bouchard et al., 1990) looked at the effects of overeating on 12 pairs of adult (ages 19 to 27) male identical twins. After eating normally for two weeks, the men consumed 1000 excess calories of food each day for 6 days a week over a 100-day period. Weight gains among twin pairs varied considerably by the end of the study. But, *there were virtually no differences in weight gain within each pair of twins!* In addition, *where* the excess weight was stored in the body (waist or hips, for example) during the overeating similarly varied among the pairs of twins, but not within twin pairs. The researchers concluded that, "the most likely explanation for the intrapair similarity . . . is that genetic factors are involved" (p. 1477).

A related study looked at the body weights of sets of twins reared together and apart and found that regardless of where or how the twins were reared, there was a significant relationship between genetic similarity and body mass (Stunkard et al., 1990). Even early childhood environments had little or no effect. Such data tell us that genetic factors are important in the ultimate determination of body weight and size and the distribution of fat within the body. They do not suggest that the only factors involved are genetic (Brownell & Rodin, 1994; Sobal & Stunkard, 1989).

As we all know, eating behaviors are influenced by factors beyond those from our physiology. Sometimes just the stimulus properties of foods—aroma, appearance, or taste—may be enough to get us to eat. You may not want any dessert after a large meal until the waitress shows you a piece of chocolate cake. Eating that cake has nothing to do with your internal physiological conditions.

Sometimes people eat more from *habit* than from need (Schachter & Gross, 1968). "It's twelve o'clock. It's lunch time; so let's eat." We may fall into habits of eating at certain times, tied more to the clock than to internal cues from our bodies. Some people seem virtually unable to watch television without poking food into their mouths—a behavioral pattern motivated more by learning than by physiology.

Occasionally we find that we eat simply because others around us are eating. Such socially facilitated eating has been noted in many species (e.g., Harlow, 1932; Tolman, 1969). For example, if a chicken is allowed to eat its fill of grain, it eventually stops eating. When other hungry chickens are placed in the cage and begin to eat, the "full" chicken starts right in eating

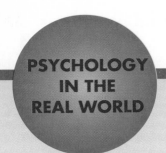
Eating Disorders

Eating well is something that few of us do all the time. Some of us simply eat too much—too much saturated fat in particular. In the real world, there are those whose problems with eating go beyond eating too much, or eating the wrong foods. These are people who suffer from two disorders of eating: anorexia nervosa and bulimia.

Anorexia nervosa is characterized by an inability (or refusal) to maintain body weight. It is essentially a condition of self-starvation, accompanied by a fear of being fat, and feeling that one is overweight despite the fact that the person is considerably *underweight* (usually less than 85 percent of normal weight) (APA, 1987; Yates, 1989). The person with anorexia nervosa maintains reduced body weight by severely cutting down on food intake, by increasing levels of physical activity, or both. The disorder is surprisingly common, particularly among females. Nearly 1 percent of adolescent girls and females of college age suffer from anorexia (Edmands, 1993). Incidence rates are increasing in this country and in diverse cultural settings around the world (Pate et al., 1992). Only about 10–15 percent of anorexic patients are males (Yates, 1990).

Bulimia is a disorder characterized by episodes of binge eating followed by purging—usually self-induced vomiting or the use of laxatives to rapidly rid the body of just-eaten food (APA, 1987; Yates, 1989). The binge eating episodes are often well planned, anticipated with a great deal of pleasure, and involve rapidly eating large amounts of high-calorie, sweet-tasting food. Like the anorexic patient, the person with bulimia shows great concern about body weight, but unlike someone with anorexia nervosa, a bulimic patient is typically of normal to slightly below normal weight. Again, most bulimic patients are female, and often from upper socioeconomic classes. Nearly 4 percent of college freshman females suffer from the disorder, compared to only 0.4 percent of male freshmen. An estimated fifteen percent of female medical students develop an eating disorder sometime in their lives (Yates, 1989).

What causes eating disorders, and what can be done to treat them effectively? Eating disorders probably have a number of interacting causes. The high value that Western culture places on thinness is one. We are constantly being bombarded with messages with the same theme: "To be thin is good; to be fat is bad." Role models for many girls include superthin fashion models, dancers, gymnasts, and entertainers. More than half of all women and more than 75 percent of all adolescent girls would like to weigh less than they do (Brownell & Rodin, 1994; Yates, 1989). The cultural emphasis on feminine thinness probably contributes to the greater dissatisfaction among women than among men about body size and shape (Rolls et al., 1991). One study found that women eat less when they are in the company of a desirable male partner than when they are with a less desirable partner (Mori & Pliner, 1987).

When we look for specific behavioral or personality traits that might predict the development of eating disorders, we find very little. There is a tendency for adolescent girls with eating disorders to have high needs for achievement and approval. Patients with eating disorders show relatively high rates of depression. But the depression may be a response to an eating disorder rather than a cause (Garner et al., 1990).

Some psychologists have looked at parenting and family style as contributors to eating disorders. Anorexia nervosa patients *do* tend to come from

again. Its behaviors are not noticeably different from those of the chickens just added to the cage.

For those people who are overweight, it would be nice if there were a simple, foolproof way to lose weight. Indeed, 31 percent of all men and 24 percent of women in this country are overweight (National Academy of Sci-

Many patients with eating disorders see themselves as overweight, even obese, when in fact their body weights are below normal.

rather rigid, rule-governed, over-protecting families. And bulimic patients often experienced inordinate blame and rejection in childhood (Bruch, 1980; Yates, 1990). You know by now not to overinterpret general findings like these; there are many exceptions.

Obviously, researchers have considered physiological processes as causes of eating disorders. One

significant line of scientific detective work stems from the often-confirmed observation that bulimic patients do not "feel full" after they eat—even after they binge (Pyle et al., 1981; Walsh et al., 1989). This may be due to the fact that the hormone *cholecystokinin* (or CCK) is produced in very low levels in bulimic patients. This is significant because CCK is a hormone normally produced in the small intestine that may signal that one is full and need eat no more. When drug treatment elevates CCK levels in bulimic patients, they often show fewer symptoms of the disorder.

In terms of treatment, the prognosis (the future course of a disorder) for anorexia nervosa is particularly poor. Nearly 50 percent of patients released from treatment relapse within one year (Yates, 1990). About 5 percent of patients with anorexia actually die from excessive weight loss (Hsu, 1986). At first, treatment will be medical in response to nourishment needs. Hospitalization may be required. Virtually all forms of psychotherapy have been tried, but with little consistent success. No one form of therapy seems significantly more effective than any other. The best predictor of the success of psychotherapy is the extent to which the family gets involved—which supports the idea that parental and family pressures may be part of the cause of eating disorders.

The outlook for bulimia is usually much better. If nothing else, bulimic patients are seldom malnourished and do not require hospitalization. The prognosis is much better with family-oriented therapy programs than with individual treatment (e.g., Fairburn et al., 1993). With bulimic patients there has been some sort-lived success with anti-depressant medications (Geracioti & Liddle, 1988; Pope et al., 1985; Pope & Hudson, 1986), but when one looks at long-term success, the data are not as encouraging (Pyle et al., 1990; Walsh et al., 1991).

ences National Research Council, 1989). More than one-third of all men and more than one-half of all women *feel* that they are overweight, and most of them support a $30 *billion* a year weight-loss industry (Brownell & Rodin, 1994; Horn & Anderson, 1993). According to a 1994 report from the Centers for Disease Control, approximately 15 percent of teenagers were deemed to be overweight throughout the 1970s, but that percentage jumped to 21 percent in the period from 1988 to 1991. There's no doubt that obesity is unhealthy, even deadly (Colditz, 1992; Lee et al., 1993). On the other hand, there are indications that dieting is not necessarily in the best interest of someone who is only slightly overweight, and that, occasionally, dieting can be dangerous in itself (e.g., Brownell, 1993; Brownell & Rodin, 1994). We also find considerable disagreement among experts over whether dieting can ever be effective. "Fully 95 percent of those starting a weight-loss program will return to their original weight within five years" (Martin et al., 1991, p. 528). Our society's preoccupation with weight and body size may help to explain the increasing rates of eating disorders that have occurred in the last decade (e.g., Fairburn & Wilson, 1993). (See Box on "Psychology in the Real World: Eating Disorders," pp. 328–329).

● **Before You Go On**

List the internal and external factors that influence eating.

Sex and Sexual Behaviors

Sex can be an important motivator for humans and nonhumans alike. What is quite remarkable is how sexual motivation varies, not only among individuals, but also among species.

As a physiologically based drive, the sex drive is unique in several ways. First, the survival of the individual does not depend on its satisfaction. If we don't drink, we die; if we don't regulate our temperature, we die; if we don't have sex—well, we don't die. The survival of the species may require that an adequate number of its members respond to a sex drive, but an individual member can get along without doing so.

Second, most physiologically based drives, such as hunger and thirst, provide mechanisms that replenish or maintain the body's energy. When it is satisfied, the sex drive depletes bodily energy. In fact, the sex drive actually motivates the organism to seek tension, as opposed to drives that seek to reduce tension in order to return to the balanced state of homeostasis.

A third point that makes the sex drive different is that it is not present at birth, but requires a certain level of maturation (puberty) before it is apparent. The other drives are present, and even most critical, early in life.

A fourth unique quality of the sex drive is the extent to which the importance of internal and external influences differ depending on the species involved. The role of internal physiological states is much greater in "lower" species than it is in primates and humans. For humans, sex hormones may be necessary, but they are seldom sufficient to maintain sexual response; and for an experienced human, they may not even be necessary.

Internal and External Cues for the Sex Drive. For rats, matters of sex are very simple and straightforward. If adequate supplies of testosterone (the male sex hormone) are present, and if there is the opportunity, a male rat will respond to its hormone-induced sex drive and will engage in sexual behaviors. If adequate supplies of estrogen and progesterone (the female sex hormones) are present, the female rat will also engage in appropriate sexual behaviors. For rats, learning and experience have little to do with sexual behaviors—they are tied closely to physiology, to hormonal levels.

There is little difference between the mating behaviors of sexually experienced rats, rats that have mated once or twice, and virgin rats. Removing the sex hormones of a female rat will cause a complete and immediate loss of sexual receptivity. If these sex hormones are replaced by injection, sexual behaviors quickly return to normal (Davidson et al., 1968). Removing the sex hormone from male rats yields a slightly different story. Sexual behaviors diminish and may disappear, but they take longer to do so. Injections of testosterone return the male rat to normal sexual functioning.

Removal of the sex hormones from male dogs or cats ("higher" species than rats) also produces a reduction in sexual behaviors, but more gradually. Experienced male primates ("higher" still) persist in sexual behaviors for the rest of their lives, even after sex hormones have been removed. (The same also seems true of human males, although the data here are sketchy.)

So we find that the sex drive in "lower" species is tied to a physiological, hormonal base. As the complexity of the organism increases, from rats, to dogs, to primates, to humans, the role of internal cues becomes less certain.

No one would get far arguing that sex is not an important human drive. On the other hand, one can lose sight of the fact that it is a *physiological* drive. Researchers at the University of Chicago also tell us that sex may not be as all-consuming as many believe. As an example: One-third of Americans have sex twice a week or more, one-third have sex "a few times a month," and one-third only a few times a year, if at all (Laumann et al., 1994). In societies like ours, where so much learning is involved, one could come to believe that sex drives are learned through experience and practice alone. Hormones may provide humans with an arousing force to do something, but *what* to do, and *how* to do it, and *when* to do it seem to require training and practice. Sex manuals of a "how to" nature sell well, and sex therapy is a full-time practice for many psychologists trying to help people cope with the pressures that external factors put on their sexual motivation.

In addition to the forces produced by the hormones, sex drives in humans can be stimulated by a wide range of stimuli. Some people engage in sexual behaviors simply to reproduce; some do so for the physical pleasure they experience; some feel it demonstrates a romantic "love"; others want to display their femininity or masculinity. Sex drives in humans are seldom satisfied with just anybody. Social (external) and cognitive constraints often are placed on one's choice of a sexual partner. Any of the senses—touch, smell (particularly important in lower mammals and primates), sight, and sound—can stimulate sexual arousal, and there are large individual differences in terms of what will be effective. It seems that American sexual tastes are not nearly as "kinky" as some would have us believe—the activity that brings the greatest sexual pleasure (ranked second after vaginal sex) is simply watching one's partner undress (Laumann et al., 1994).

● **Before You Go On**

In what ways is the sex drive a unique physiologically based drive?

Homosexuality. The complexities of human sexual behaviors are no more apparent than when we consider **homosexuals**—persons sexually attracted to and aroused by members of their own sex, as opposed to het-

homosexuals
persons who are attracted to and sexually aroused by members of their own sex

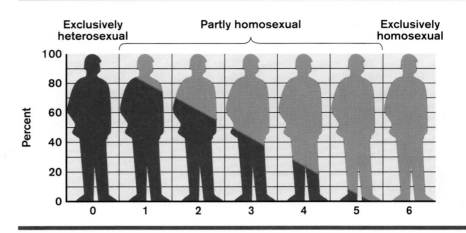

FIGURE 9.4
Kinsey's scale of sexual orientation.

erosexuals, who seek outlets for their sexual drives among members of the opposite sex. Psychologists argue that homosexuality should be referred to as an orientation, not as a matter of preference. Like handedness, for example, it is not chosen voluntarily (Committee on Lesbian and Gay Concerns, 1991; Money, 1987).

Homosexuality and heterosexuality are not mutually exclusive categories, but are end points of a dimension of sexual orientation. Alfred Kinsey and his colleagues (1948, 1953) devised a seven-point scale (0 to 6) of sexual orientation with those who are exclusively heterosexual at one end and persons who are exclusively homosexual at the other extreme (see Figure 9.4). Kinsey found that about half the males who responded to his surveys fell somewhere between these two endpoints. Even though homosexuality is now more openly discussed than it was in the 1940s and 1950s, it is still difficult to get accurate estimates of the numbers of persons who are exclusively or predominantly homosexual. Conservative estimates suggest that about 2 percent of North American males are exclusively homosexual, and that 8 to 10 percent have had more than just an occasional homosexual encounter. The recent survey from the University of Chicago tells us that when asked if they are sexually attracted to persons of the same gender, 6.2 percent of the men and 4.4 percent of the women responded affirmatively. When asked about having an actual sexual encounter with someone of the same gender *in the past year*, 2.7 percent of the men and 1.3 percent of the women responded "yes." When the question was phrased *since puberty*, comparable figures were 7.1 percent and 3.8 percent, respectively (Laumann et al., 1994).

There is little difference between homosexuals and heterosexuals in the pattern of their sexual responsiveness. Most homosexuals have experienced heterosexual sex. They just find same-sex relationships more satisfying. Homosexual couples are often more at ease and comfortable with their sexual relationship than are most heterosexual couples (Masters & Johnson, 1979). Contrary to popular opinion, most homosexuals are indistinguishable from heterosexuals in appearance or mannerisms.

As yet, we have no generally accepted theory of the causes of homosexuality. What we do know is that the matter is not simple and probably in-

Although homosexuals are now able to be more open about their sexual orientation, homosexuality is still a controversial issue. This is a photo of the wedding announcement of a lesbian couple.

volves an interaction of genetic, hormonal, and environmental factors (Money, 1987). For example, there is now ample evidence that homosexuality tends to "run in families" (Bailey & Pillard, 1991; Diamond & Karlen, 1980; Pool, 1993). In 1993, a team of researchers claimed that they had located a segment of the X chromosome that seems certain to be the site for genes that influence the development of homosexual orientations in men (Hamer et al., 1993). This is only a beginning, and the results need to be confirmed by other researchers. There are several hundred genes in the identified area, but "once a specific gene has been identified, we can find out where and when it is expressed and how it ultimately contributes to the development of both homosexual and heterosexual orientation" (Hamer et al., 1993, p. 326).

There is no evidence of any significant differences in the hormone levels of heterosexuals and homosexuals at adulthood. Providing gay males and lesbians with extra amounts of sex hormones may increase overall sex drive and the incidence of sexual behaviors, but it has virtually no effect on sexual orientation. One hypothesis with research support is that *prenatal* hormonal imbalances may affect one's sexual orientation in adulthood (Money, 1987). Embryos (genetically male or female) that are exposed to above average levels of female hormones will develop into adults attracted to persons having masculine characteristics (Ellis & Ames, 1987).

In 1991, Dr. Simon LeVay of the Salk Institute in San Diego published an article on his research that immediately became headline news (LeVay, 1991). LeVay had performed postmortem examinations on the brains of 19 gay males and 16 men and 6 women with heterosexual orientation. He found a small area in the hypothalamus that was significantly smaller in the gay men. In gay men this area was precisely the same size as in the hypothalamuses of the women LeVay examined. Here was evidence of a biological correlate of homosexuality. Notice that LeVay has not claimed that he located a *cause* of homosexual orientation. His observations lead us only to a correlation, from which cause-and-effect conclusions would be unwarranted. Still, as one scientist (Dennis Landis of Case Western Reserve University) said about LeVay's work, "It would begin to suggest why male homosexuality is present in most human populations, despite cultural constraints. It suggests it's a biological phenomenon" (Barinaga, 1991).

Even as biological evidence accumulates, some psychologists remain unwilling to disregard hypotheses that emphasize environmental influences. It is clear, however, that sexual orientation cannot be attributed to any one early childhood experience. A reasonable position at the moment would be to hypothesize that genetic and hormonal predispositions may interact with subtle environmental influences in complex ways to form one's adult sexual orientation.

● **Before You Go On**

What is homosexuality?

What causes homosexuality?

PSYCHOLOGICALLY BASED MOTIVES

Occasionally you may be able to analyze your behaviors in terms of physiologically based needs and drives. That you had breakfast this morning soon after you got up might have reflected your response to a hunger drive. That you got dressed might have been your attempt to do what you could to control your body temperature, which may have influenced your choice of clothes. Perhaps some sexual motivation further affected what you chose to wear.

Many of our behaviors seem to be aroused and directed (motivated) by forces that are subtle and less clearly biological in origin. In this section, we'll review a few of the motivators that reflect learned or social influences on behavior. We will refer to these psychologically based drives as *motives*. Although there is potentially a large number of such motives, we'll review just three that have proven useful for "explaining" human behavior: achievement, power, and affiliation motivation.

Achievement Motivation

need to achieve (nAch)
the learned need to meet or exceed some standard of excellence in performance

The hypothesis that people are motivated, to varying degrees, by a need to achieve was introduced to psychology in 1938 by Henry Murray. The **need to achieve (nAch)** is the acquired need to meet or exceed some standard of excellence in one's behaviors. Measuring nAch and determining its sources and implications have been the major work of David McClelland and his associates (e.g., McClelland et al., 1953; McClelland, 1958, 1985; Smith, 1992).

Thematic Apperception Test (TAT)
a projective personality test requiring a person to tell a series of short stories about a set of ambiguous pictures

Although there are short paper-and-pencil tests for the same purpose, nAch is usually assessed by means of the **Thematic Apperception Test (TAT)**, a *projective test*. People are asked to tell short stories about a series of ambiguous pictures depicting people in various settings (see Figure 9.5). Stories are interpreted and scored according to objective criteria that note references to attempting difficult tasks, succeeding, being rewarded for one's efforts, setting short- and long-term goals, and so on. There are no right or wrong responses to the TAT pictures, so judgments are made about the references to achievement that a person "projects" into the picture.

FIGURE 9.5
The administration of the TAT. The subject is shown an ambiguous picture and asked such questions as, "What is going on here? What led to this situation? What is likely to happen now?"

One of the first things that McClelland and his coworkers discovered was that there *were* consistent differences in measured levels of nAch among the males they tested. One finding concerned people with high needs for achievement and the nature of tasks they choose to attempt. When given a choice, they generally will try tasks in which success is not guaranteed (otherwise, there is no challenge), but in which there is a reasonable chance of success. Both young children (McClelland, 1958) and college students (Atkinson & Litwin, 1960) high in nAch were observed playing a ring-toss game, where the object was to score points by tossing a small ring over a peg from a distance. The farther away from the peg one stood, the more points could be earned with success. Subjects with high achievement needs in both studies chose to stand at a moderate distance from the peg. They didn't stand very close to guarantee success, but they didn't stand so far away that they would almost certainly fail. People with low nAch scores tended to go to either extreme—very close, where they earned few points for their successes, or so far away they rarely succeeded.

McClelland would argue that you are reading this text at this moment because you are motivated by a need to achieve. You want to get a good grade in this course, and you have decided that to do so you need to study the assigned text. Some students read assignments not because they are motivated by a need to achieve, but because they are motivated by a *fear of failure* (Atkinson & Feather, 1966). In such a case, the incentive that is relevant is a negative one (avoid an F), which is a different matter than working toward a positive incentive (earn an A). Individuals motivated by a fear of failure tend to take very few risks. They either choose tasks that they are bound to do well or attempt tasks that are virtually impossible (if the task is impossible, they needn't blame themselves for their failures). There *are* explanations for why people choose tasks of the difficulty they do that do not rely on the notions of achievement or failure. One (e.g., Dweck, 1986) is that persons choose tasks of moderate difficulty if they are motivated to learn from their experience and improve themselves, whereas they choose easy tasks if they are motivated to "show off" or demonstrate superior performance.

In this regard, I should mention the notion of *fear of success*. This concept was introduced by Martina Horner in 1969, and was used to account for the motivation of many women who were said to "back off" from competition for fear of succeeding and thereby losing popularity and femininity. Although there may be some merit in the concept of fear of success, it has not fared well in experimental tests (e.g., Jackaway & Teevan, 1976; Mednick, 1979). Upon close inspection, to the extent that there is such a thing, men are as likely to demonstrate a fear of success as are women.

It seems that the need to achieve is learned, usually in childhood. Children who show high levels of achievement motivation are those who have been encouraged in a positive way to excel ("Leslie, that grade of B is very good. You must be proud of yourself." as opposed to "What! Only a B?"). High nAch children are encouraged to work things out for themselves, independently, perhaps with parental encouragement or support ("Here, Leslie, you see if you can do this," as opposed to, "Here, Dummy, let me do it. You'll never get it right!"). Further, McClelland is convinced that achievement motivation can be taught to and acquired by almost anyone, of any age, and he has developed training programs designed to increase achievement motivation levels (e.g., McClelland & Winter, 1969).

We should not get the impression that people with high achievement needs are always interested in their own successes at the expense of others. Particularly in collective societies, people will work very hard to reach goals that are available only to the group of which they are a part (e.g., Brislin, 1993).

● **Before You Go On**

What is achievement motivation, and how is it usually measured?

Power Motivation

need for power
the learned need to be in control of events or persons, usually at another's expense

Some people are motivated not only to excel, but to be in control—to be in charge both of the situation and of others (McClelland, 1982; Winter & Stewart, 1978). In these cases, we speak of a **need for power**. Power needs

Some people are strongly influenced by a need for affiliation: to be with others, socializing, perhaps working together for common goals.

generally are measured in the same way as achievement needs, through the interpretations of stories generated with the Thematic Apperception Test. Notice that a high need for power is, in itself, neither good nor bad. What matters is the end to which one's power is put.

People with high power needs like to be admired. They prefer situations where they can control the fate of others, usually by manipulating access to information. They present an attitude of, "If you want to get this job done, you'll have to come to me to find out how to do it." People with low power needs try to avoid situations in which others have to depend on them and also tend to be submissive in interpersonal relationships. In Western cultures, men are still more commonly found in positions of power than are women (Darley & Fazio, 1980; Falbo & Peplau, 1980; Mulac, Incontro & James, 1985). At the same time, there are no reliable differences between men and women in measured *needs* for power (Winter, 1988).

Affiliation Motivation

Another psychologically based motivator that has been helpful in explaining the behaviors of some people is the **need for affiliation**. This motive involves a need to be with others, to work with others toward some end, and to form friendships and associations.

One interesting implication of having a high need for affiliation is that it is often at odds with a need for power. If you are simultaneously motivated to be in control and to be with others in a truly supportive way, conflicts may arise. It is more difficult to exercise power over people whose friendship you value than it is to exercise control over people whose friendship is of little concern to you. There are circumstances in which we find persons who are high on both power and affiliation needs, however. Politicians, for example, certainly enjoy the exercise of power, but also value being public figures and being surrounded by aides and advisors (Winter, 1987). Affiliation and achievement needs are reasonably independent.

need for affiliation
the need to be with others and to form relationships and associations

Achievement and success can be earned with others (high affiliation) or on one's own (low affiliation).

Although we are confident that achievement and power motives are learned, we are less sure about the sources of affiliation motivation. There is an argument that the need to affiliate and be with others is at least partly biologically based. We are social animals for whom complete social isolation is quite difficult (particularly when we are young). On the other hand, it is clear that the extent to which we value relationships can be attributed to our learning experiences.

● **Before You Go On**
Define the needs for power and affiliation.

TOPIC 9B

THE PSYCHOLOGY OF EMOTION

Since its emergence in the late 1800s, psychology has included the study of emotion as part of its subject matter. Psychologists have learned a great deal about emotional reactions, but answers to some critical questions have remained elusive. We wish that psychologists could tell us exactly what emotions are and where they come from. We want to know how to increase pleasant emotions and how to avoid unpleasant ones. It is in regard to our emotional reactions that we most want simple and direct answers.

DEFINING "EMOTION"

Try to recall the last time you experienced an emotional reaction of some significance—perhaps the fear of going to the dentist, the joy of receiving an A on a classroom exam, the sadness at the death of a friend, or the anger at being unable to register for a class you really wanted to take. You may be able to identify as many as four components of an emotional reaction. (1) You experience a *subjective feeling*, or *affect*, which you may label fear, joy, sadness, or anger. (2) You have a *cognitive reaction;* you "know," or recognize, what has just happened to you. (3) You have an internal, *physiological reaction* which is largely visceral, involving glands, hormones, and internal organs. (4) You (probably) engage in an overt, observable, *behavioral reaction.* You tremble as you approach the dentist's office. You run down the hall, a broad smile on your face, waving your exam paper over your head. You cry at the news of your friend's death. You shake your fist and yell at the registrar when you cannot enroll in the class of your choice.

When we add a behavioral component to emotion, we see how emotion and motivation are related. Emotions are often viewed as being motivational (Greenberg & Safran, 1989; Lang, 1985; Lazarus, 1991a, 1991b, 1993). As we saw earlier, to be motivated is to be aroused and directed to action. Emotional experiences often arouse behaviors, although their direction of behaviors is less clear. Theorist Richard Lazarus puts it this way, "Without some version of a motivational principle, emotion makes little sense, inasmuch as what is important or unimportant to us determines what we define as harmful or beneficial, hence emotional" (1991c, p. 352).

There has been considerable debate in psychology concerning how best to define emotion. "There is no consensus about the definition of emotion; one may quarrel endlessly about the word" (Frijda, 1988). Rather than joining the quarrel, I'll take a rather classic view and define an **emotion** as an experience that includes a subjective feeling, a cognitive interpretation, a physiological reaction, and a behavioral expression. With this definition in mind, we turn to the related issue of how to classify emotions, and whether there are, in fact, any fundamental emotions.

emotion
a reaction involving subjective feeling, physiological response, cognitive interpretation, and behavioral expression

● **Before You Go On**

What are the four components that define an emotional experience?

CLASSIFYING EMOTIONS

Although cognitions, physiology, and overt behaviors are involved in an emotional reaction, the critical aspect seems to be that "subjective feeling" component. Perhaps it would help if we had a scheme or a plan that described and classified various affects or feeling in a systematic way.

In fact, there are several ways to classify emotional responses. Wilhelm Wundt, in that first psychology laboratory in Leipzig, was concerned with emotional reactions. He wrote that emotions could be described in terms of three intersecting dimensions: pleasantness-unpleasantness; relaxation-tension; and calm-excitement. Let's look at a few somewhat more recent attempts to classify emotions.

Carroll Izard (1972, 1977, 1993) has proposed a system calling for nine primary emotions. From these, all others follow. Izard's nine primary emotions are fear, anger, shame, contempt, disgust, distress, interest, surprise, and joy. (Isn't it sad that all but the last three are negative, unpleasant emotions?) Izard calls these emotions primary because they cannot be dissected into simpler, more basic ones, *and* because each is thought to have its own unique underlying physiological basis.

Robert Plutchik (1980a, 1980b) argues for eight basic emotions. What makes these emotions primary, Plutchik claims, is that each can be directly tied to an adaptive pattern of behavior; they are emotions that can be related to one's survival. Plutchik's primary emotions, and their adaptive significance, are listed in Figure 9.6.

Richard Lazarus (1991c, 1991d, 1993) is in the process of developing a new theory that stresses the motivational role of emotions. He claims that emotion is the result of specific relationships or interactions between people and their environments. Some relations are perceived as (potentially) harmful to one's well-being and yield negative emotions, such as anger, anxiety, fear, shame, sadness, and guilt. These are the emotions we are motivated to avoid. Some relations are (potentially) beneficial and give rise to positive emotions, such as joy, pride, gratitude, and love. These are the emotions we are motivated to seek, or approach. Following this logic, Lazarus has proposed 15 primary emotions.

I'm sure you won't be surprised to learn that none of the attempts to classify emotions has proven completely satisfactory. Psychologists continue to propose theories to account for the nature of emotional reactions (Berkowitz, 1990; Buck, 1985; Ekman, 1993; Frijda, 1988; Greenberg &

FIGURE 9.6
Plutchik's Eight Primary Emotions and How They Relate to Adaptive Behaviors

Emotion or feeling	Common stimulus	Typical behavior
1. Anger	Blocking of goal-directed behavior	Destruction of obstacle
2. Fear	A threat or danger	Protection
3. Sadness	Loss of something valued	Search for help and comfort
4. Disgust	Something gruesome or loathsome	Rejection; pushing away
5. Surprise	A sudden, novel stimulus	Orientation; turning toward
6. Curiosity	A new place or environment	Explore and search
7. Acceptance	A member of own group; something of value	Sharing; taking in; incorporating
8. Joy	Potential mate	Reproduction; courting; mating

Safran, 1989; Mathews & MacLeod, 1994; Oatley & Jenkins, 1992; Ortony et al., 1988; Ortony & Turner, 1990; Weiner, 1985).

Whether there are eight or nine (or more or fewer) primary emotions and how they combine to form other emotions will depend on one's theoretical perspective. A review by Ortony and Turner (1990) lists more than a dozen theoretical versions of basic or primary emotions. A similar review by Plutchik (1994) lists sixteen, and *none of these versions is in agreement with the others.* ("Fear" and "anger," for example, do appear on all the lists.) The only issue on which there seems to be consensus among the theoreticians is that emotions are valanced states—meaning that emotions can be classified as either positive (relief, joy, happiness, and the like) or negative (fear, anger, shame, and the like). Unfortunately, there isn't much agreement on how to distinguish between positive and negative emotions. Fear, for example, seems like a reasonable candidate for a list of negative emotions. Yet, it is clear that fear can be *useful* and can serve to guide one's behaviors in positive, or adaptive, ways.

So, where does all this leave us? As sensible as it may sound to try to construct a system of basic, primary emotions—particularly if such a system had a physiological or evolutionary foundation—such an attempt will prove difficult at best. Perhaps part of the problem here is coming to grips with just what we mean by *basic* or *primary.* Ortony and Turner put it this way: "Thus, the question 'Which are the basic emotions?' is not only one that probably cannot be answered, it is a misdirected question, as though we asked, 'Which are the basic people?' and hoped to get a reply that would explain human diversity" (1990).

If there is one conclusion regarding emotion with which all theorists agree, it is that part of being emotional is a physiological, visceral response. Being emotional is a gut-level reaction. To be emotional involves more than our cool, thinking, reasoning, cerebral cortex. We turn next to discuss the physiological aspects of emotion.

● **Before You Go On**
Can emotions be classified?

PHYSIOLOGICAL ASPECTS OF EMOTION

Let's generate a useful—if somewhat unusual—example to work with for a while. You are on a camping trip with some friends. Having just eaten a large meal, you decide to take a short, solitary stroll down a nearby path through the woods. Totally relaxed, you are about 200 yards away from your friends, who are still sitting around the campfire. Just as you start to head back, a huge, growling black bear suddenly appears without warning from behind a dense thicket. It takes a look at you, bares its teeth, and roars! What will you do now?

To say that your reaction would be an emotional one seems an understatement. You will experience affect (call it fear, if not panic). You will have a cognitive reaction (realizing you've just encountered a bear and that you'd rather you hadn't). You will engage in some overt behavior (either freezing in your tracks or racing back to camp). A major part of your reaction will be internal, physiological, and gut-level. Reacting to a bear in the wild is not something that most people would do in a purely intellectual, cognitive sort of way. When we are emotional, our viscera get involved.

The Role of the Autonomic Nervous System

As you will recall, the *autonomic nervous system,* or ANS, consists of two parts that serve the same organs, but that have nearly the opposite effect on those organs. *The parasympathetic division* is involved in maintaining a relaxed, calm, unemotional state. As you strolled down the path into the woods, the parasympathetic division of your ANS actively directed your digestive processes to do the best they could with the meal you'd just eaten. Saliva flowed freely. Blood was diverted from your extremities to your stomach and intestines. With your stomach full, and with blood diverted to it, you felt a bit sleepy as your brain responded to the lower levels of blood supply. Your breathing was slow, deep, and steady, as was your heart rate. Again, all of these activities were under the control of the parasympathetic division of your autonomic nervous system.

Suddenly, there's that bear! Now the sympathetic division of your ANS takes over. Automatically, many physiological changes take place—changes that are usually quite adaptive.

1. The pupils of your eyes dilate, letting in as much light as is available—you need to see what's going on.
2. Your heart rate and blood pressure are elevated—energy needs to be mobilized as fast as possible.
3. Blood is diverted away from the digestive tract to the limbs and brain, and digestion stops—you've got a bear to deal with; dinner can wait. Let's get the blood out to the arms and legs where it can do some good (with what is called the "fight or flight" response).
4. Respiration increases, becoming deeper and more rapid—you'll need all the oxygen you can get.
5. Moisture is brought to the surface of the skin in the form of perspiration—as it evaporates, the body is cooled, thus conserving energy.

6. Blood sugar levels increase—again, you'll need the extra energy available.
7. You may lose control of your bladder and bowels—messy, perhaps, but there are more important things to worry about now.
8. Blood will clot more readily than usual—for obvious, hopefully unnecessary reasons.

The sympathetic system makes some of these changes directly (e.g., stopping salivation and stimulating the cardiac muscle). The others are made indirectly through the release of hormones into the bloodstream, and it takes a few seconds for many hormones to have their effect. As a result, we may sense a delayed reaction. If you were confronted by a bear in the woods, you probably would not have the presence of mind to notice, but the physiological reactions of sweaty palms, gasping breaths, and "butterflies in your stomach" take a few seconds to develop.

Is the autonomic and endocrine system reaction the same for every emotional reaction we experience? There may be a few slight differences. There appears to be a small difference in the hormones produced during rage and fear reactions. There may be differences in the biological bases of emotional reactions that prepare us for defense—fight—or retreat—flight—(Blanchard & Blanchard, 1988). Other differences in physiological reaction for emotions have not been found consistently. This remains a controversial and actively researched issue in psychology (Blanchard & Blanchard, 1988; Levinthal, 1983; Plutchik, 1994; Selye, 1976).

The Role of the Brain

When we become emotional, our sympathetic nervous system does not spring into action all by itself. Autonomic nervous system activity is related to, and coordinated by, central nervous system activity.

The two brain structures most intimately involved in emotionality are the *limbic system* and the *hypothalamus,* that small structure in the middle of the brain that is so involved with physiological drives. The limbic system is a "lower" center in the brain consisting of several small structures (the amygdala may be the most important for emotionality). The limbic system is most involved in emotional responses that call for either defensive or attacking responses—emotions stimulated by threat. Electrical stimulation or the destruction of portions of the limbic system produces predictable changes in emotional reactions.

It is to be expected that the hypothalamus has a role to play in emotionality. It is involved in many motivational states. Strong emotional reactions can be produced by hypothalamic stimulation—including reactions that lead to attacking and killing any nearby prey—at least in some nonhumans (Flynn et al., 1970). Just how the limbic system and hypothalamus are coordinated in the normal experience and expression of emotion is not understood.

The role of the cerebral cortex in emotionality is also poorly understood, but we know it is mostly inhibitory. The limbic system and hypothalamus act as (primary) sources for extreme and rather poorly directed emotional reactions. The cerebral cortex interprets impulses from these lower centers along with other information available to it and then modifies and directs the emotional reaction accordingly.

The clearest involvement of the cerebral cortex in emotionality is in the *cognitive* aspect of emotion. The cerebral cortex is involved in the interpretation and memory of emotional events. When you get back to the campfire, having just been frightened by a bear, you will use your cerebral cortex to tell all the emotional details of your story. There is evidence that emotional reactions tend to be processed more in the right hemisphere of the human brain than in the left (Sperry, 1982; Tucker, 1981).

To review, along with the autonomic nervous system two lower brain centers, the limbic system and the hypothalamus, are involved in emotional reactions. These centers are coordinated, and often controlled by, higher centers in the cerebral cortex which, among other things, provide the cognitive interpretation of emotional responses.

Another aspect of emotional reactions that has long intrigued psychologists is how one's inner emotional states are expressed or communicated to others. Charles Darwin was one of the first to popularize the idea that facial expressions can provide a meaningful indicator of emotional state. Now, more than 100 years later, psychologists are discovering new evidence that Darwin was correct.

● **Before You Go On**

Summarize the activities of the sympathetic division of the autonomic nervous sytem during emotional states.

What brain centers are involved in emotionality?

OUTWARD EXPRESSIONS OF EMOTION

It is extremely useful for one organism to be able to let another know how it is feeling. As one wild animal approaches a second, the second better have a good idea of the emotional state of the first. Is it angry? Does it come in peace? Is it just curious, or is it looking for dinner? Is it sad, looking for comfort, or is it sexually aroused, looking for a mating partner? Being unable to make such determinations—quickly—can be disastrous.

Nonhuman animals have many ritualistic, instinctive patterns of behavior to communicate interest in courtship, aggressiveness, submission, and other emotional states. Humans can express their emotional states in a variety of ways, including verbal report. If I am happy, sad, angry, or jealous, I can try to *tell* you how I feel. The human ability to communicate with language often puts us at a great advantage. Even without verbal language, there is a school of thought that suggests that the human animal, like the nonhuman, uses *body language* to communicate its emotional state (Birdwhistell, 1952; Fast, 1970). Someone sitting quietly, slumped slightly forward, with head down, may be viewed as feeling sad, even from a distance. We may interpret postural cues and gestures as associated with fear, anger, happiness, and so on. Such expressions often result from learning and may be modified by one's culture.

Darwin recognized facial expression as a cue to emotion in animals, especially mammals. Might facial expression provide the key to underlying emotions in humans too? Are there facial expressions of emotional states that are universal in the human species, as there appear to be among non-humans (Andrews, 1963)? A growing body of evidence suggests that facial expressions of at least a few basic emotional states is an innate response, only slightly sensitive to cultural influence (Adelmann & Zajonc, 1989; Buck, 1980; Gellhorn, 1964; Oatley & Jenkins, 1992; Tomkins, 1962).

Paul Ekman and his colleagues have conducted several studies to try to find a reliable relationship between emotional state and facial expression that can be found across cultures (Ekman, 1972, 1992, 1993; Ekman,

As animals approach each other it is important that they convey an expression of their emotional state. Is he hungry? Is he sexually aroused? Does he come in peace?

FIGURE 9.7
Photos displaying facial expressions like these were shown to subjects from the United States, Brazil, Chile, Argentina, and Japan. (The subjects were asked to identify the emotions being displayed. The percentage of subjects who identified the photos with emotion labels is indicated.)

   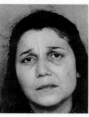  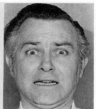

	Happiness	Disgust	Surprise	Sadness	Anger	Fear
United States (N=99)	97%	92%	95%	84%	67%	85%
Brazil (N=40)	95%	97%	87%	59%	90%	67%
Chile (N=119)	95%	92%	93%	88%	94%	68%
Argentina (N=168)	98%	92%	95%	78%	90%	54%
Japan	100%	90%	100%	62%	90%	66%

et al., 1987). In one study, Ekman and his associates (1973) showed college students six pictures of people's faces. In each picture, a different emotion was displayed: happiness, disgust, surprise, anger, sadness, and fear. When students from the United States, Argentina, Japan, Brazil, and Chile were asked to name the emotion being felt by the people in the photos, their agreement was remarkable (see Figure 9.7).

Another study of facial expression (Ekman et al., 1983) has shown that simply moving one's facial muscles into the positions that are associated with emotional expression actually can cause distinctive physiological changes associated with an emotional state (see also Adelmann & Zajonc, 1989; Laird, 1984; Matsumoto, 1987; Schiff & Lamon, 1989). As bizarre as that may sound, the idea is that if you raise your eyebrows, open your eyes very widely, and raise the corners of your mouth, you will produce an internal physiological change very much like that which occurs when you are happy.

● **Before You Go On**
 What is the relationship, if any, between facial expression and emotion?

THINKING CRITICALLY ABOUT MOTIVATION AND EMOTION

1. This chapter used a somewhat dramatic example of meeting a bear in the woods to discuss physiological reactions to emotion-producing

stimuli. Can you recast the same discussions with more likely examples, for instance, a big exam coming up tomorrow, or being fired from a job for no apparent reason?

2. With the same meeting-a-bear story in mind, can you "explain" the behaviors of the camper taking a walk in terms of the different models, theories, or approaches to motivation that we covered in the first section of Topic 9A?

3. Have you determined in your own mind the difference (and it is subtle) between an instinctive behavior and a reflexive behavior?

4. What am I trying to do when I try to "motivate" students in my classes to do as well as they can?

5. What motivated you to take this class in psychology? How do you feel about it now?

6. Can you examine your own life in terms of how it fits Maslow's hierarchy of needs?

7. How is it that music and art can influence our emotions? How much of that influence is innate; how much is learned?

8. To what extent do you believe that homosexuality or heterosexuality is a matter of choice freely made, or that orientations are rooted in biology?

9. Do you think that the sorts of things that motivate women are the same as or different from the sorts of things that motivate men?

10. If you were asked to list the primary human emotions, which would we find on your list?

SUMMARY

TOPIC 9A

ISSUES OF MOTIVATION

● How have the concepts of instinct, need, drive, and incentive been used to explain motivated behaviors?

Instincts are complex patterns of behavior that occur in the presence of certain stimuli. Instinct approaches take the position that some complex behavior patterns are unlearned or innate. The concept of instinct has not proven satisfactory in accounting for human behaviors. Needs are shortages of some biological necessity. Deprivation may lead to a need, which gives rise to a drive, which arouses and directs behavior. The relations among deprivation, need, drive, and behavior are often not very straightforward; drives can be more learned than biological. Maslow has proposed that

human needs can be placed in a hierarchy, beginning with basic survival needs and ending with a need to self-actualize. Focusing on incentives explains behaviors in terms of goals and outcomes rather than on internal forces. In this sense, we are motivated to reach desired end states. These approaches are not mutually exclusive, and each may be used to explain some types of motivated behavior. *Pages 315–320.*

● How can the concept of balance or equilibrium be used to help us understand motivated behaviors?
● In what way is cognitive dissonance theory based on equilibrium?

Organisms are motivated to reach and maintain a state of balance—a set point level of activity. With homeostasis, we have a general drive to maintain a state of equilibrium among internal physiological processes such as blood pressure, metabolism, and heart rate. Some psychologists argue for a general drive to maintain a balanced state of arousal, with different optimal levels of arousal being best suited for different tasks or situations. Festinger claims that we are motivated to maintain balance among cognitive states, and thereby to reduce cognitive dissonance. *Pages 320–322*

● Given the concept of homeostasis, how might temperature regulation be thought of as a physiologically based drive?

Temperature regulation can be viewed as a physiological drive because we have a need (thus are driven) to maintain our body temperatures within homeostatic levels. Doing so may involve voluntary as well as involuntary responding. *Pages 322–324.*

● List some of the internal and external factors that influence drinking behavior.

We are motivated to drink for several reasons: to relieve dryness in our mouths and throats; to maintain a homeostatic level (monitored by the hypothalamus) of fluid within our bodies; and also as a response to external cues, such as taste, aroma, or appearance. What we drink is often influenced by our learning experiences. *Page 325.*

● List the internal and external factors that influence eating.

Internal factors include cues mediated by the hypothalamus, which may be responding to stored fat levels, blood sugar levels, or some other indication that our normal homeostatic balance has been disrupted. Associated with this view is the position that body weight is maintained at a given set point by both intake and exercise levels. There is evidence that body size may be determined largely by genetic factors. External factors include the stimulus properties of foods, as well as habit patterns and social pressure. *Pages 325–330.*

● In what ways is the sex drive a unique physiologically based drive?

(1) Individual survival does not require its satisfaction. (2) The drive involves seeking or creating tension, not relieving tension. (3) It is not fully present at birth, but matures later. (4) The extent to which it is affected by learned or external influences varies from species to species. Like other physiologically based drives, it does respond to both internal and external stimuli. *Pages 330–331.*

● What is homosexuality?
● What causes homosexuality?

Homosexuals are persons who are attracted to and sexually aroused by members of their own sex. There is thought to be a continuum, or gradual dimension, that extends from exclusive homosexuality on the one extreme to exclusive heterosexuality on the other. Kinsey found that more than half the males in his sample fell somewhere between these two endpoints. A recent survey suggests that about 6.2 percent of men and about 4.4 percent of women are homosexual in orientation. We do not know what causes homosexuality, but strongly suspect genetic predispositions and hormonal influences during prenatal development. Some psychologists claim that we cannot rule out the impact of early childhood experiences. *Pages 331–334.*

● What is achievement motivation, and how is it usually measured?

Achievement motivation (nAch) is defined as one's need to attempt and succeed at tasks in such a way as to meet or exceed some standard of excellence. nAch is usually assessed through the interpretation of stories generated in response to the Thematic Apperception Test, or TAT, in which one looks for themes of striving and achievement. *Pages 334–336.*

● Define the needs for power and affiliation.

The need for power is defined as the need to be in charge, to be in control of the situation and of others, often at the expense of others. Affiliation needs involve being motivated to be with others, to form friendships, and maintain interpersonal relationships. *Pages 336–338.*

T O P I C   9 B
THE PSYCHOLOGY OF EMOTION

● What are the four components that define an emotional experience?

There are four components of an emotional reaction: (1) a subjective feeling, or affective component; (2) a cognitive appraisal or interpretation; (3) an internal, visceral physiological reaction; and (4) an overt behavioral response. *Pages 338–339.*

● Can emotions be classified?

There have been several attempts to categorize emotional reactions, dating back to Wundt in the late 1800s. Izard has a scheme that calls for nine primary emotions. Plutchik argues that there are eight basic emotions and many degrees and combinations of them. Other theorists have proposed as few as two or as many as dozens of primary emotions. The inconsistency among theories has led some psychologists to wonder if the attempt to classify basic emotions is misguided. *Pages 339–340.*

● Summarize the activities of the sympathetic division of the autonomic nervous system during emotional states.

● What brain centers are involved in emotionality?

Among the many changes that take place when we become emotional are those produced by the sympathetic division of the ANS. Occurring to varying degrees are such reactions as dilation of the pupils, increased heart rate and blood pressure, cessation of digestion, deeper and more rapid breathing, increased perspiration, the elevation of blood sugar levels, and easier clotting of the blood. The cerebral cortex is involved in the cognitive interpretation of emotional events and also acts as an inhibitory mechanism, exerting control over the lower brain centers for emotionality, the hypothalamus and the limbic system (largely the amygdala). Basically, the brain coordinates physiological aspects of emotionality. *Pages 341–343*

● What is the relationship, if any, between facial expression and emotion?

Facial expressions indicate the internal emotional state of an individual. What leads us to believe that facial expressions of emotions are unlearned is that there is such universal reliability in the interpretation of facial expressions across widely different cultures. *Pages 343–344.*

TEST YOURSELF

TOPIC 9A
ISSUES OF MOTIVATION

9.1 Which of these is *least* involved in motivational states? a) the arousal of behavior b) the memory of behavior c) the directing of behavior d) the maintenance of behavior. *Pages 315–320.*

9.2 The major difference between what your text calls "drives" and what your text calls "motives" is whether or not the motivator a) involves the ANS or the CNS. b) is physiologically or psychologically based. c) is intrinsic or extrinsic. d) is essentially positive or essentially negative. *Pages 315–320.*

9.3 What is the major problem with using the concept of instinct to explain human behaviors? a) There are just too many human instincts to keep track of. b) There are too few human behaviors that have a biological basis. c) Referring to instincts may describe or name behaviors, but doesn't explain them. d) Too many human instincts have opposites, such as needs to socialize and needs to be alone. *Pages 315–320.*

9.4 Which of these does *not* go with the others? a) acquired drives b) learned drives c) primary drives d) conditioned drives. *Pages 315–320.*

9.5 In Hull's theory (as an example), what gives rise to a drive? a) a need b) a motive c) a behavior d) a goal or incentive. *Pages 315–320.*

9.6 Of these needs from Maslow's hierarchy, which is likely to be satisfied last, after the others? a) physiological needs b) esteem needs c) needs for love and belongingness d) safety needs. *Pages 315–320.*

9.7 Approaches to motivation that focus on stimuli or events *outside the organism* are approaches that focus on a) incentives b) drives c) arousal d) needs. *Pages 315–320.*

9.8 Which term or concept is most like Cannon's concept of homeostasis? a) drive b) sensation-seeking c) fulfillment d) balance. *Pages 320–322.*

9.9 Which approach to motivation would be most appreciated by those psychologists who value the concepts of operant conditioning? Approaches based on a) instincts. b) drives. c) incentives. d) balance or equilibrium. *Pages 320–322.*

9.10 We are motivated to change the way we think about things when we experience a) homeostasis. b) a mental set point. c) cognitive dissonance. d) arousal. *Pages 320–322.*

9.11 True or False? Arousal theory tells us that one's performance on a task will continue to improve so long as one's level of arousal continues to increase. *Pages 320–322.*

9.12 More than anything else, what "informs us" that our body temperatures have become too high or too low? a) our limbic system b) our skin c) our hypothalamus d) our autonomic nervous system. *Pages 322–324.*

9.13 Most of the water in our bodies is contained a) in our bloodstream. b) within the cells of our body. c) in our sweat glands. d) in spaces between the cells of our body. *Page 325.*

9.14 Which of these is *least* directly involved in motivating us to eat or not eat? a) the physical appearance of food b) our hypothalamus c) how empty our stomachs are d) reactions of our liver. *Pages 325–330.*

9.15 True or False? Although our hypothalamus may inform us that we are thirsty or hungry, learning and experience inform us about what to drink or eat. *Pages 325–330.*

9.16 How much you weigh is determined by a) how much you eat. b) genetic factors. c) early childhood experiences. d) all of these. *Pages 325–330.*

9.17 In what way is the sex drive in humans most different from the sex drive in rats? a) It does not appear until after puberty. b) Its satisfaction does not determine the survival of the individual. c) It is strongly influenced by learning and experience. d) Its physiological basis is largely hormonal. *Pages 330–331.*

9.18 With regard to homosexuality, which observation is most true? a) Sexual preference is a matter of choice freely made. b) Adult male homosexuals have excess female hormones in their systems. c) Homosexuality is a dimension, a matter of degree, not either/or. d) Most homosexuals (male or female) have never tried heterosexual sex. *Pages 331–334.*

9.19 At the moment, which of these is taken as the most reasonable hypothesis for the development of homosexuality? a) genetic differences in the X and Y chromosomes b) lack of a father-figure in single-parent homes c) unsatisfying or frustrating sexual encounters in adolescence d) hormonal imbalances that occur during prenatal development. *Pages 331–334.*

9.20 If given a choice, a person with a high need to achieve (nAch) probably would choose a job in which he or she a) could succeed with little effort. b) would be in a position to control the fate of others. c) would be working with as many people as possible. d) could do well, but only with effort and hard work. *Pages 334–338.*

TOPIC 9B
THE PSYCHOLOGY OF EMOTION

9.21 Attempts to classify the basic human emotions a) have yielded inconsistent results. b) find that there are fewer than there are in nonhumans. c) result in a pyramid of emotions with love on the top and hate on the bottom. d) have failed to improve on Wundt's scheme from the 1880s. *Pages 338–340.*

9.22 Which change is *least* likely during an emotional reaction? a) Heart rate decreases. b) Digestion stops. c) Blood flow is diverted to the limbs. d) Pupils dilate. *Pages 341–343.*

9.23 Which structure of the brain is most involved in emotion? a) the thalamus b) the limbic system c) the brain stem d) the cerebellum. *Pages 341–343.*

9.24 Which expression of emotional state is uniquely human? a) verbal descriptions b) facial expressions c) body language d) posture and gestures. *Pages 343–344.*

10

PERSONALITY AND ITS ASSESSMENT

PREVIEW

TOPIC 10A — Issues and Theories of Personality

The Psychoanalytic Approach

The Behavioral-Learning Approach

The Humanistic-Phenomenological Approach

The Trait Approach

TOPIC 10B — Personality Assessment

Behavioral Observations

Interviews

Paper-and-Pencil Tests

PSYCHOLOGY IN THE REAL WORLD: A Personality Test Just for You

Projective Techniques

THINKING CRITICALLY ABOUT PERSONALITY AND ITS ASSESSMENT

SUMMARY

TEST YOURSELF

Most of us think that we understand ourselves fairly well. We believe that we have a pretty good sense of who we are, how we tend to think and feel, and what we are likely to do in most situations. To a somewhat lesser extent, we also feel that we understand a few other people, such as very close friends and family members. We believe that knowing about someone's personality is required to truly understand that person. We also have come to appreciate that knowing someone's personality is not easily done—that what constitutes someone's personality are internal and private experiences, often difficult to determine from the outside.

Psychology has valued the concept of personality throughout its history. Over the years, many theories have emerged that have sought to describe the nature of personality. In Topic 10A, we'll examine some of them. In truth, we can only skim the surface of these complex theories, but perhaps we can see how each in its own way has contributed to our contemporary understanding of personality. Topic 10B reviews some of the techniques that psychologists have devised to measure this set of internal dispositions we refer to as personality.

T O P I C   1 0 A
ISSUES AND THEORIES OF PERSONALITY

The task of this Topic is to briefly describe a few of the major theories of personality. We'll organize our discussion of specific theories into four basic approaches. Before we do so, let's see what we mean by *theory* and *personality* in this context.

A theory is a series of assumptions. In our present context, the assumptions are about people and their personalities. The ideas or assumptions that constitute a theory are based on the theorist's observations, and are reasonably and logically related to each other. The ideas and assumptions of a theory should lead, through reason, to specific, testable hypotheses. Thus, a **theory** is an organized collection of testable ideas used to explain a particular subject matter.

Now then, what is personality? Few terms in psychology have been as difficult to define. In many ways, each of the approaches we will study in this Topic generates its own definition. For our purposes, **personality** includes the *a*ffects, *b*ehaviors, and *c*ognitions of people that characterize them in many situations over time. (Here, again, is our ABC from Topic

theory
an organized collection of ultimately testable ideas used to explain a particular subject matter

personality
those affects, cognitions, and behaviors that can be said to characterize an individual in several situations and over time

351

1A.) Personality includes dimensions that we can use to judge how people are different from one another. With *personality theories*, we're looking for ways to describe both how individuals remain the same over time and circumstances and differences that we know exist among people (Baumeister, 1987). Note that personality somehow resides *inside* the person; it is something that a person brings to his or her interaction with the environment.

One of the major debates among personality psychologists has been the extent to which one's personality leads one to behave *consistently* in a variety of situations. Think about your own behaviors and your own personality for a moment. Suppose you think of yourself as an easygoing person. Are you *always* easygoing, easy to get along with? Are there some situations in which you would be easygoing and others in which you would fight to have your way? Are there some circumstances in which you tend to be sociable and outgoing, and other situations in which you prefer to be alone and not mix in? Questioning the consistency of personality dates back to a challenge issued by theorist Walter Mischel in 1968. Others joined in, and agreed: Perhaps the apparent consistency in some people's behaviors is simply a convenience that reflects the fact that we usually only observe people in a restricted range of situations, where their behaviors would likely be consistent (Council, 1993; Epstein, 1979; Mischel & Peake, 1982).

Challenging the consistency of internal personality variables was essentially a challenge to the concept of personality and, as you can imagine, such a challenge created quite a stir. As it happens, behaviors may not be as unstable or situation-bound as Mischel originally suggested. In fact, most of the variabilities we see in the behaviors of people reflects individual differences (in personality) even more than the pressures of the situation (Digman, 1990; Rowe, 1987; Wiggins & Pincus, 1992). By and large, current research supports the notion that there are personality-related characteristics that show remarkable stability over a wide range of situations. At the same time, it is folly not to take into account the situations in which behaviors occur. That is, how anyone behaves reflects an interaction of personality characteristics (inside the person) and the situation (the external environment).

THE PSYCHOANALYTIC APPROACH

We begin our discussion of personality by considering the psychoanalytic approach, which is associated with Sigmund Freud and his students. We begin with Freud because he was one of the first to present a truly unified theory of personality; his theory has been one of the most influential and, at the same time, most controversial in all of science. There are many facets of Freud's theory (and the theories of his students), but two fundamental points characterize the **psychoanalytic approach**: (1) a reliance on innate, inborn drives as explanatory concepts for human behavior, and (2) an acceptance of the power and influence of unconscious forces to mold and shape behavior.

Freud's Approach

Freud's ideas about personality arose largely from his reading of the works of many philosophers, observations of his patients, and intense self-examination. He was also influenced by the writings of Darwin which, among other things, emphasized biological instincts for survival and the impor-

psychoanalytic approach
the approach to personality associated with Freud and his followers that relies on instincts and the unconscious as explanatory concepts

tance of emotions—not just conscious intellect—in molding behavior. The context of his private practice provided Freud with experiences that formed the basis of a theory of personality and a technique of therapy called *psychoanalysis*. Freud's variety of psychotherapy is covered in Chapter 13. Here we will review some of Freud's ideas about the structure and dynamics of human personality.

Levels of Consciousness. Central to Freudian theory is the notion that information, feelings, wants, drives, desires, and the like can be found at various levels of consciousness, or awareness. You'll recall that Topic 5B centered on a discussion of consciousness—and Freud's views on the matter. Let's quickly review.

Freud thought that only a small portion of one's mental life was readily available to a person's awareness at any one time. Thoughts, feelings, or motives of which we are actively aware at the moment are said to be *conscious*. Aspects of one's mental life that are not conscious, but that can easily be brought to awareness, are stored at a *preconscious* level. When you shift your awareness to think about something you may do this evening, those plans probably were already there, in your preconscious mind.

Cognitions, feelings, or motives not available at the conscious or preconscious level are said to be in the *unconscious*. At this level we keep many ideas, memories, or desires of which we are not aware and cannot easily become aware. Remember the significance of the unconscious level of the mind: Although thoughts, desires, and feelings are stored there so that we are completely unaware of them, the contents of the unconscious mind can still influence us. Unconscious content passing through the preconscious may show itself in slips of the tongue, humor, and, of course, dreams. There was no doubt in Freud's mind, at least, that unconscious forces could be used to explain many behaviors that otherwise seemed irrational and beyond description.

● **Before You Go On**
What are the three levels of consciousness proposed by Freud?

Basic Instincts, or Impulses. According to Freud, behaviors, thoughts, and feelings are largely governed by biological drives, or instincts. These are inborn impulses or forces that rule our personalities. There may be many individual impulses, but they can be grouped into two categories (Fadiman & Frager, 1994).

On the one hand are **life instincts (eros)**, impulses for survival; in particular, those that motivate sex, hunger, and thirst. Each has its own energy that compels us into action (drives us). Freud called the energy through which sexual instincts operate **libido**. Opposed to the life instincts are the **death instincts (thanatos)**. These are largely impulses of destruction. Directed inward, they lead to depression or suicide; directed outward, they result in aggression. In large measure, according to Freud, life is an attempt to resolve conflicts between these two natural but diametrically opposed instincts or impulses.

The Structure of Personality. We've seen that Freud believed that the mind operates on three interacting levels of awareness: conscious, preconscious, and unconscious. He also proposed that human personality consists of three separate, but interacting, structures or subsystems: the id, ego, and

life instincts (eros)
inborn impulses, proposed by Freud, that compel one toward survival, including hunger, thirst, and sex

libido
the energy that activates the sexual instincts

death instincts
(thanatos) inborn impulses, proposed by Freud, that compel one toward destruction, including aggression and hostility

id
the instinctive aspect of personality that seeks immediate gratification of impulses; operates on the pleasure principle

pleasure principle
the impulse of the id to seek immediate gratification to reduce tensions

ego
the aspect of personality that encompasses the sense of "self"—in contact with the real world; operates on the reality principle

reality principle
the force that governs the ego, arbitrating between the demands of the id, the superego, and the real world

superego
the aspect of personality that refers to ethical or moral considerations; operates on the idealistic principle

idealistic principle
the force that governs the superego—opposed to the id, it seeks adherence to standards of ethics and morality

superego. Each subsystem has its own job to do and its own principles to follow.

The **id** is the totally inborn or inherited portion of personality. The id resides in the unconscious level of the mind, and it is through the id that basic instincts develop. The driving force of the id is libido, or sexual energy, although it may be more fair to Freud to say "sensual" rather than "sexual" so as not to leave the impression that he was always referring to sexual intercourse. The id operates on what Freud labeled the **pleasure principle**, indicating that the major function of the id is to find immediate satisfaction for basic pleasurable impulses. Although other parts of personality develop later, our id remains with us, essentially unchanged, as the basic energy source in our lives.

The **ego** is the part of the personality that develops through one's experience with reality. In many ways, it is our self, the rational, reasoning part of our personality. The ego operates on the **reality principle**. One of the ego's main jobs is to try to find satisfaction for the id, but in ways that are reasonable and rational. The ego may have to delay gratification of some libidinal impulse or may need to find an acceptable outlet for some need. Freud said that "the ego stands for reason and good sense while the id stands for the untamed passions" (Freud, 1933).

The last of the three structures to develop is the **superego**, which we can liken to a sense of morality or conscience. It reflects one's internalization of society's rules. The superego operates on the **idealistic principle**. A problem with superegos is that they—like the id—have no contact with reality, and therefore often place unrealistic demands on the individual. The superego demands that one does what *it* says is right and proper, no matter what the circumstances. Failure to do so can lead to shame and guilt. Again, it falls to the ego to try to maintain a balance between the conscience of the superego and the libido of the id.

This isn't as complicated as it may sound. Suppose a bank teller discovers an extra $20 in her cash drawer at the end of the day. She really could use an extra $20. "Go ahead. Nobody will miss it. The bank can afford a few dollars. Think of the fun you can have with an extra $20," is the message from her id. "You shouldn't even think about taking that money! Shame on you! It's not yours. It belongs to someone else and should be returned," the superego protests. "The odds are that you'll get caught if you take this money. If you are caught, you might lose your job, then you'll have to find another one," reasons her ego. Obviously, the interaction of the components of one's personality is not always this straightforward, but this example illustrates the general idea.

● **Before You Go On**

According to Freud, what are the three structures of personality, and by what principle does each operate?

defense mechanisms
unconsciously applied techniques that protect the self (ego) from feelings of anxiety

The Defense Mechanisms When the ego cannot find acceptable ways to satisfy the impulses of the id, or when it cannot deal with the demands of the superego, conflict and anxiety result. Then, ways must be found to combat the resulting anxiety. It was for this purpose that Freud proposed the existence of **defense mechanisms**—*unconsciously* applied techniques that protect the self (ego) against strong feelings of anxiety. Figure 10.1 is a list

FIGURE 10.1
Freudian Ego Defense Mechanisms

Repression: (motivated forgetting)—"forgetting" about some anxiety-producing event or experience by forcing the memory of the event into one's unconscious. Ex: Paul had a teacher with whom he did not get along at all. After trying his best for the entire semester, Paul failed the course. The following summer, while walking with his girlfriend, Paul encountered this teacher. When he went to introduce him to his girlfriend, Paul could not remember his teacher's name. He had repressed it.

Denial: a mechanism in which a person simply refuses to acknowledge or accept the realities of an anxiety-producing situation. Ex: When a physician first tells a patient that he or she has a serious or terminal illness, a common reaction is denial; a refusal to believe that the diagnosis is correct.

Rationalization: making up excuses for one's behaviors rather than facing the (anxiety-producing) real reasons for them. Ex: Kevin failed his psychology midterm because he didn't study and missed several classes. He hates to think that he could have failed an important exam because of his own actions (or inactions), so he rationalizes: "It really wasn't my fault. I had a terrible professor. The test was grossly unfair. We used a lousy textbook. And I've been fighting the flu all semester."

Fantasy: engaging in escape from anxiety through imagination and daydreaming. Ex: After a week of exams and term paper deadlines, lying on the sofa, eyes closed, thinking about going through graduation exercises and being honored for having such high grades.

Projection: seeing in others the same motives or traits that would make one anxious if seen in oneself. Ex: Under enormous pressure to do well on a test, Kirsten plans to cheat. By test time, she is unable to cheat herself, but sees many other students cheating openly.

Regression: a return to earlier, more primitive, even childish levels of behavior that were once effective. Ex: A 4-year-old first child now has a new baby sister who seems to be getting all of their parents' attention. The 4-year-old reverts to earlier behaviors, starts to wet the bed, scream for a bottle of his own, and goes back to crawling on all fours.

Displacement: directing one's motives or behaviors (usually aggressive) at a substitute person or object rather than expressing them directly. Ex: When Dorothy does not get an expected promotion at work, she's angry and upset at her boss, but she displaces her aggression by yelling at her husband, children, and the family cat.

of some of the more common ego defense mechanisms, with an example of each.

The list of defense mechanisms presented in Figure 10.1 is not an exhaustive one. These are among the most common, and should give you an idea of what Freud had in mind. Of all the aspects of Freud's theory of personality, it is safe to say that the notion of defense mechanisms, such as those listed in Figure 10.1, is one of the most widely accepted.

There are a couple of points about defense mechanisms that deserve mention: (1) Using defense mechanisms is a reasonably normal reaction.

Please do not be alarmed if you find that some of these defense mechanisms sound like reactions you have used. In moderation, they can help us cope with the anxieties and conflicts of everyday life. (2) Although they are normal, and even common, they can become maladaptive. So long as defense mechanisms are successful in alleviating the unpleasant feelings of anxiety, one may no longer feel a need to search for the true sources of felt anxiety, and thus will be less likely to resolve the conflicts that produced the anxiety in the first place. We'll have more to say about this point when we discuss effective and ineffective strategies for dealing with stress in Chapter 11.

● **Before You Go On**

List and define seven defense mechanisms.

The Psychosexual Stages of Personality Development. Freud put a lot of stock in the biological bases of personality, relying as he did on concepts such as drive and instinct. This same orientation flavored his view of personality development. According to Freud, personality develops naturally, in a series of overlapping stages. The events that occur in early stages have the potential to produce profound effects on later development.

One of Freud's most controversial assumptions about human behavior was that even infants and young children were under the influence of the sexual impulses of the id and its libidinal energy. The outlet for the sexual impulses (again, "sensual" may be a better term) of children is not the reproductive sex act. Nonetheless, Freud said that much of the pleasure derived by children is essentially sexual in nature; hence we refer to Freud's stages of development as *psychosexual.* Freud claimed that there are five such stages:

1. *Oral Stage* (birth to 1 year). Pleasure and satisfaction come from oral activities: feeding, sucking, and making noises. The mouth continues to be a source of pleasure for many people into adulthood as demonstrated by overeating, fingernail biting, smoking, or talkativeness.
2. *Anal stage* (ages 1 to 3 years). Sometime in their second year, children develop the ability to control bowel and bladder habits. At this time, the anus becomes the focus of pleasure. Satisfaction is gained through bowel control. Aggressiveness (the id again) can be displayed (particularly against parents) by either having bowel movements at inappropriate times or by refusing "to go" when placed on the potty chair. Here we clearly can see the thoughtful, reasoning ego emerging and exercising some control. After all, the parents can't *make* their child do what they want it to do. The child is in control, and that control can lead to great satisfaction.
3. *Phallic Stage* (ages 3 to 5 years). Here there is an awareness of one's sexuality. The genitals replace the mouth and anus as the source of pleasure, and masturbation or fondling of the genitals may become a common practice. Freud himself admitted that he never felt that he understood women or the psychology of women (Fadiman & Frager, 1994, p. 18). He often offended the feminists of his day; one of the things that got him in trouble was suggesting that, in the phallic stage, girls come to realize that they do not have a penis, and feel inferior, "lacking," and jealous as a result (Freud, 1933, p. 126). Freud said that such "penis envy" led mature women to desire children—a male child

in particular, who will bring the "longed-for penis with him." It is during this stage of development that children tend to form close (sexually based) attachments to the parent of the opposite sex, and feelings of jealousy and/or fear of the same-sex parent may arise. This pattern of reaction is called the *Oedipus complex* in boys and the *Electra complex* in girls. It is in the phallic stage that the superego begins to develop.

4. *Latency Stage* (ages 6 years until puberty). At this stage in life, sexual development gets put on hold. Now the ego is developing very rapidly. There is much to be learned about the world and how it operates. Sexual development can wait. Sexuality is suppressed. Friends tend to be of the same sex. You have no doubt heard the protestations of a 9-year-old boy, "Oh yuck; kiss a girl? Never! Yuck!" And you counsel, "Just wait; soon girls won't seem so 'yucky.'"

5. *Genital Stage* (after puberty). With puberty, there is a renewal of the sexual impulse, a reawakening of desire, and an interest in matters sexual, sensual, and erotic.

● Before You Go On
Briefly review Freud's five psychosexual stages of development.

The Psychoanalytic Approach after Freud

Sigmund Freud was a persuasive communicator: He was a powerful speaker, and in his writings, he was without peer. His ideas were challenging and new, and they attracted many students. Freud founded a psychoanalytic society in Vienna. He had an "inner circle" of friends and colleagues who shared his ideas, although some did not entirely agree with his theory. Among other things, they were bothered by his reliance on biological drives and libido and on what they perceived as a lack of concern for social influences. Some of these psychoanalysts left Freud and proposed theories of their own. They became known as **neo-Freudians**. Because they had their own ideas, they had to part from Freud; he would not tolerate disagreement with his theory. One had to accept all of psychoanalysis or leave Freud's inner circle.

Remembering that a theory consists of a set of logically interrelated, testable assumptions, it is obvious that we cannot do justice to someone's theory of personality in a short paragraph or two. What we can do, perhaps, is sketch the basic idea behind the theories of a few neo-Freudians.

neo-Freudians
personality theorists (including Adler, Jung, and Horney) who kept many basic psychoanalytic principles, but differed from a strict Freudian view, adding new concepts of their own

Alfred Adler (1870–1937).
As the psychoanalytic movement was first taking shape, Adler was one of Freud's closest friends. Nonetheless, Adler left Freud and, in 1911, founded his own version of a psychoanalytic approach to personality. Two things seemed to offend Adler: the negativity of Freud's views (including a death instinct) and the idea of sexual libido as the prime impulse in life.

Adler proposed that we are a product of the social influences on our personality. We're motivated not so much by drives and instincts, but by goals and incentives. The future and one's hope for what it holds can be more important than the past. Our major goal is the achievement of success or superiority. This goal is fashioned in childhood when, because we are weak and vulnerable, we develop an *inferiority complex*—the feeling that we are less able than others to solve life's problems and get along in the world. We may seem inferior as children, but with the help of social influences and our own creativity, we can overcome and succeed.

Carl Jung (1875–1961). Another student and colleague, Carl Jung was chosen by Freud to be his successor, but disagreements developed, mostly about the role of sexuality and the nature of the unconscious. Jung was more mystical in his approach to personality and, like Adler, was certainly more positive about one's ability to control one's own destiny. He believed that our major goal in life was to unify all aspects of our personality, conscious and unconscious, introverted (inwardly directed) and extroverted (outwardly directed). Libido was energy, but not sexual energy; it was energy for personal growth and development.

Jung accepted the idea of an unconscious mind and expanded on it, claiming that there are two types of unconscious: the *personal unconscious*, which is much like Freud's view of the unconscious, and the *collective unconscious*, which contains very basic ideas that go beyond an individual's own personal experiences. The ideas and notions of the collective unconscious are common to all of humanity and are inherited from all past generations. The contents of our collective unconscious include what Jung called *archetypes*—universal forms and patterns of thought. These are very basic "ideas" that transcend generations and even all history. They include themes that show up in myths: motherhood, opposites, good, evil, masculinity, femininity, and the circle as a symbol representing travel from a beginning back to where one started, or the complete, whole self.

Karen Horney (1885–1952). Trained as a psychoanalyst in Germany, Horney came to the United States in 1934. She kept some Freudian concepts in her approach, but changed most of them significantly. Horney believed that the idea of levels of consciousness made sense, as did anxiety and repression. But she theorized that the prime impulses that motivate behavior are not biological and inborn or sexual and aggressive.

A major concept for Horney was *basic anxiety*, which arises in childhood when a child feels alone and isolated in a hostile environment. If proper parental nurturance is forthcoming, basic anxiety can be overcome. If parents are punishing, inconsistent, or indifferent, children may develop *basic hostility* and feel aggressive toward their parents. Young children cannot express hostility toward their parents openly, so the hostility gets repressed (to the unconscious), building even more anxiety.

Horney placed great emphasis on social interaction and personal growth in early childhood experience. She claimed that there are three ways in which people learn to interact with each other. In some cases, people *move away from others*, seeking self-sufficiency and independence. The idea here is something like, "If I'm on my own and uninvolved, you won't be able to hurt me." On the other hand, some may *move toward others*, tending to be compliant and dependent. This style of interaction protects against anxiety in the sense of "If I always do what you want me to do, you won't be upset with me." Horney's third interpersonal style is *moving against others*, where the effort is to be in control, to gain power and dominate: "If I'm in control, you'll have to do what I want you to." The ideal, of course, is to maintain a balance among these three styles of interpersonal relationships, but Horney argued that many people tend to have one of these three predominate in their dealings with others. Horney also disagreed with

Karen Horney based some of her personality theory on how individuals learn to interact with others.

Freud's position regarding the biological basis of differences between men and women. While Freud's theories have been taken to task a number of times for their male bias (Fisher & Greenberg, 1977; Jordan et al., 1991), Horney was one of the first to do so.

● **Before You Go On**

Briefly summarize the contributions of Adler, Jung, and Horney to the psychoanalytic approach to personality.

Evaluating the Psychoanalytic Approach

There is little doubt that the psychoanalytic approach, particularly as modified by the neo-Freudians, is the most comprehensive and complex of the theories we'll review. Psychologists have debated the relative merits of Freud's works for decades, and the debate continues. On the positive side, Freud and other psychoanalytically oriented theorists must be credited with focusing our attention on the importance of the childhood years and for suggesting that some (even biologically determined) impulses may affect our behaviors even though they are beyond our immediate awareness. Although Freud may have overstated the matter, drawing our attention to the impact of sexuality and sexual impulses as influences on personality and human behavior is also a significant contribution.

On the other hand, many psychologists have been critical of psychoanalytic theory. We have seen how the neo-Freudians tended to minimize innate biological drives and take a more social approach to personality development than did Freud. One of the major criticisms of the psychoanalytic approach is that so many of its insights are untestable. Freud thought of himself as a scientist, but he tested none of his ideas about human nature experimentally. Some seem beyond testing. Just what *is* libidinal energy? How can it be measured? How would we recognize it if we saw it? Concepts such as id, ego, and superego may sound sensible, but how can we prove or disprove their existence? It also seems that a heavy reliance on instincts, especially with sexual and aggressive overtones, as explanatory concepts goes beyond where most psychologists are willing to venture.

THE BEHAVIORAL-LEARNING APPROACH

Many American psychologists in the early twentieth century did not think much of the psychoanalytic approach, regardless of its form or who happened to propose it. From the beginning, American psychology was oriented toward the laboratory and theories of learning. Explaining personality in terms of learning and focusing on observable behaviors seemed to be a reasonable course of action.

John B. Watson (1878–1958). Psychology should turn away from the study of consciousness and the mind because they are unverifiable and ultimately unscientific argued Watson and his followers in behaviorism. Psychology should study observable behavior. Yet here were the psychoanalysts arguing that *un*conscious or *pre*conscious forces are determiners of behavior. "Nonsense," the behaviorist would say. "We don't even know what we mean by consciousness, and here you want to talk about levels of unconscious influence!"

Watson and his followers emphasized the role of the environment in shaping one's behaviors. Behaviorists could not accept the Freudian notion of inborn traits or impulses, whether called id or libido or anything else. What matters is *learning*, not a personality theory. A theory of learning would include all the details about so-called personality one would ever need.

Who we are is determined by our learning experiences, and early childhood experiences count heavily—on that Watson and Freud would have agreed. Even our fears are conditioned (remember Watson's "Little Albert" study?). So convinced was Watson that instincts and innate impulses had little to do with the development of behavior that he wrote, albeit somewhat tongue-in-cheek: "Give me a dozen healthy infants, well-formed, and my own specified world to bring them up in and I'll guarantee to take any one at random and train him to become any type of specialist I might select—doctor, lawyer, artist, merchant, chief, and yes, even beggarman and thief, regardless of his talents, penchants, tendencies, abilities, vocations, and race of his ancestors" (Watson, 1925).

B. F. Skinner (1904–1990). What others were calling personality, Skinner claimed was no more than a collection of patterned behaviors shaped by one's genetics and experiences. Skinner's behaviorism refused to refer to any sort of internal variables to explain behavior—which is just what personality theories try to do. Look at observable stimuli, observable responses, and the relationships among them; do not go meddling around in the "mind" of the organism, Skinnerians argue. Behavior is shaped by its consequences. Some behaviors result in reinforcement and tend to be repeated. Some behaviors are not reinforced, and thus tend not to be repeated. Consistency in behavior reflects the consistency of one's reinforcement history. The real question is, how shall external conditions in the environment be manipulated to produce the consequences we want?

John Dollard (1900–1980) and Neal Miller (b. 1909). As behaviorists and learning theorists, Dollard and Miller wanted to see if they could use the basic principles of learning to explain personality and how it developed. What matters for personality, Dollard and Miller argued, was the system of habits one developed in response to cues in the environment. Behavior was motivated by primary drives, which needed to be satisfied if the organism were to survive, and on learned drives, which developed through experience. Motivated by drives, habits that are reinforced are those that tend to be repeated and eventually become part of the stable collection of habits that make up personality.

Repression into the unconscious, for example, is simply learned forgetfulness—forgetting about some anxiety-producing experience is reinforcing and thus tends to be repeated. It was Miller (1944) who proposed that conflict can be explained in terms of tendencies (habits) to approach or avoid goals and has little to do with the id, ego, and superego, or with unconscious impulses of any sort.

Albert Bandura (b. 1925). A learning theorist, Badura is more than willing to consider the internal, cognitive processes of the learner. He also claims that many aspects of our behavior and our personality *are* learned, but often they are learned through observation and social influence. For Bandura, learning involves more than the formation of connections between stimuli and responses or between responses and resulting reinforcers; it involves a cognitive representation and rearrangement of those representations. In simpler terms, this approach argues that you may very well learn to behave honestly, for example, through the observation of others. If you view your parents as being honest and see their behaviors being reinforced (vicarious reinforcement), you may acquire similar responses.

● **Before You Go On**

Specify a contribution to the concept of personality contributed, repectively, by Watson, Skinner, Dollard and Miller, and Bandura.

Evaluating the Behavioral-Learning Approach

Many critics of the behavioral-learning approach argue that Watson, Dollard, Miller, and Skinner dehumanize personality, and that even the social learning theory of Bandura is too deterministic. The impression is that virtually everything a person does, thinks, or feels is in some way determined by his or her environment or learning history. This leaves nothing for the person, for personality, to contribute. Behavioral-learning approaches to personality often are not theories at all—at least not very comprehensive theories. To their credit, they demand that theoretical terms be carefully defined and that hypotheses be verified experimentally. It is also undeniable that many of the concepts of the behavioral psychologist have found application in the many forms of behavior therapy, which we will discuss in Chapter 13.

THE HUMANISTIC-PHENOMENOLOGICAL APPROACH

To some degree, the humanistic-phenomenological approach to personality contrasts with both the psychoanalytic and behavioral approaches. For one thing, it claims that people *can* shape their own destiny, chart and follow their own course of action, and that biological, instinctive, or environmental influences can be overcome or minimized. The humanistic view may be thought of as more optimistic than the Freudian view (with its death instincts and innate impulses) or learning theories (with their emphasis on control exerted by the environment). It tends to focus more on the here-and-now than on early childhood experiences as important molders of personality. The humanistic approach also emphasizes the wholeness or completeness of personality, rather than focusing on its structural parts. What matters most is *how people view themselves and others*, which is essentially what *phenomenological* means.

Carl Rogers (1902–1986). He suggested an approach to personality that is a person-centered or self theory. Like Freud, Rogers developed his views of human nature by observing his clients in a clinical, therapeutic setting. Rogers believed that the most powerful human drive is to become fully functioning.

To be *fully functioning* implies that a person has become all that he or she can be. To be fully functioning is to experience "optimal psychological adjustment, optimal psychological maturity, complete congruence, complete openness to experience" (Rogers, 1959, p. 235). People who realize this drive can also be described as living in the present, getting the most from each experience, not moping over opportunities past or anticipating events to come. As long as we act only to please others, we are not fully functioning. To be fully functioning involves an openness to one's feelings and desires, an awareness of one's inner self, and a positive self-regard. Helping children become fully functioning requires that we offer more of what Rogers calls *unconditional positive regard*. When we are children, some of what we do brings rewards, but some of what we do does not. How we are regarded by those we care about is often conditional on how we behave. We tend to receive conditional positive regard. If we do what is expected or desired, then we get rewarded. As a result, we try to act in ways that bring rewards and avoid punishment; we try to act in ways that satisfy others. Feelings of self and self-worth then, depend on the actions of others who either reward us, don't reward us, or punish us. Rogers also argued that we should separate the child's behaviors from the child's self. That means that we may punish a child for doing a bad thing, but never for being a bad child ("I love you very much, but what you've done is inappropriate and, therefore, will be punished"). Helping people to achieve positive self-regard is one of the major goals of person-centered therapy.

Note that what matters here is not so much what *is*, but what is *felt* or *perceived*. One's true self (whatever it may be) is less important than one's *image* of one's self. How the world is experienced is what matters—a clearly phenomenological point of view. You may be an excellent piano player (better, perhaps, than 98 percent of all of us), but if you feel that you are a poor piano player, that perception is what matters.

Abraham Maslow (1908–1970). He criticized the psychology he had studied as being altogether too pessimistic and negative. The individual

FIGURE 10.2
Some of the Characteristics or Attributes of Self-Actualizers

1. They tend to be realistic in their orientation.
2. They accept themselves, others, and the world for what they are, not for what they should be.
3. They have a great deal of spontaneity.
4. They tend to be problem-centered rather than self-centered.
5. They have a need for privacy and a sense of detachment.
6. They are autonomous, independent, and self-sufficient.
7. Their appreciation of others (and of things of the world) is fresh, free, and not stereotyped.
8. Many have spiritual or mystical (although not necessarily religious) experiences.
9. They can identify with humankind as a whole and share a concern for humanity.
10. They have a number of interpersonal relationships, some of them very deep and profound.
11. They tend to have democratic views in the sense that all are created equal and should be treated equally.
12. They have a sense of humor that tends more to the philosophical than the hostile.
13. They tend to be creative in their approach.
14. They are hard working.
15. They resist pressures to conform to society.

After Maslow, 1954.

person was seen as battered about by either a hostile environment or depraved instincts, many of which propelled the person on a course of self-destruction.

There must be more to living than this, thought Maslow. He preferred to attend to the positive side of human nature. Maslow felt that people's basic needs are not ugly, base, and mean but are positive or, at worst, neutral (Maslow, 1954). Our major goal in life is to realize and put into practice those needs, or to *self-actualize*. (You recall that Maslow's views were presented in Topic 9A in our discussion of motivation.)

Maslow argued that we should look at the very best among us, focusing attention on the characteristics of those who have realized their fullest potential and have become self-actualized (see Figure 10.2). In his search for self-actualizers, Maslow didn't find many. Most of his examples were historical figures, including Thomas Jefferson and Eleanor Roosevelt.

● **Before You Go On**

Briefly summarize the humanistic-phenomenological approach to personality as epitomized by Rogers and Maslow.

Evaluating the Humanistic-Phenomenological Approach

Like the others, the humanistic-phenomenological approach has several strengths. For one, it reminds us of the wholeness of personality and of the danger in analyzing something so complex into artificial segments. That the approach, stressing as it does personal growth and development, is positive and upbeat in its flavor serves to inform us that at least such views are possible. As we'll see in our Topic on psychotherapy (Topic 13B), the humanistic-phenomenological approach has had a major impact on many therapists and counselors. A problem with this approach is not unlike the basic problem with Freud's theory. It may make sense, but how does one go about testing any of the observations and statements made by proponents of the approach? Many of the key terms are defined in general, fuzzy ways. What really is self-image? How do we know when someone is "growing"? How can one test the effects of unconditional positive regard? In many ways, what we have here is a blueprint, a vision for the nature of personality and not a scientific theory. There are also those critics who argue that the vision of striving for self-actualization and a basic drive to be fully-functioning is terribly naive, and far from universal.

THE TRAIT APPROACH

Trait theories of personality have a markedly different flavor from the approaches we have looked at so far. Trait theories are more concerned with the adequate *description* of personality than with the *explanation* of personality. We may define a **trait** as "any distinguishable, relatively enduring way in which one individual differs from others" (Guilford, 1959a, p. 5).

trait
any distinguishable, relatively enduring way in which one individual differs from others

Traits are descriptive *dimensions*. That is, any trait (e.g., friendliness) is not a simple either-or proposition. Friendliness falls along a continuum, from extremely unfriendly to extremely friendly, with many possibilities in between. To be useful, personality traits need to be measurable so that we can assess the extent to which people differ on those traits (Hogan & Nicholson, 1988; Kagan, 1988; Ozer & Reise, 1994; Wiggins & Pincus, 1992).

The issues for psychologists who take this approach include such matters as: Which traits are the important ones? Which dimensions best characterize a person and how she or he is different from everyone else? How can personality traits be organized? The answers to these and similar questions have given rise to several trait theories. We'll briefly summarize two classic trait theories (Allport's and Cattell's), and then look at a contemporary trait theory.

Two Classic Examples

For Gordon Allport (1897–1967), personality traits exist within a person and explain the consistency in that person's behavior. In different situations, for example, a personality trait of friendliness might produce a range of specific responses, but those responses would be, in their essence, very much alike.

Allport proposed two types of personality traits: *common traits* and *personal traits*. Common traits are aspects of personality shared by almost everyone (to greater or lesser degrees perhaps, but shared with everyone else). Aggressiveness is an example of a common trait, and so is intelligence. These are traits that we can use to make comparisons among people. Personal traits, on the other hand, are unique to a person. How one displays a sense of humor (sharp wit, sarcasm, dirty jokes, long stories, philosophical puns, and so on) is thought of as a unique disposition or trait.

Allport went on to claim that personal traits are of three different subtypes. He wrote of cardinal, central, and secondary personal traits. A *cardi-*

nal trait is one that is so overwhelming that it influences nearly everything a person does. The personalities of very few of us are ruled by cardinal traits. Allport could think of only a few (Don Quixote, the Marquis de Sade, and Don Juan among them). No, what predominates in influencing our behaviors are not likely to be cardinal traits, but *central traits,* or central dispositions. These traits usually can be described in just one word, and they are the 5–10 traits that best characterize someone (e.g., honest, friendly, outgoing, fair, kind, etc.). Finally, each of us is occasionally influenced by *secondary traits.* These are traits (dispositions) that seldom govern many of our reactions and may be applied only in specific circumstances. For example, someone may be very calm and easygoing, even when threatened (reflecting central traits), but when threatened in his or her own home (by intruders, let's say) can be very aggressive and not calm at all.

Raymond Cattell's (b. 1905) approach to personality is an empirical one, relying on psychological tests, questionnaires, and surveys. Talking about personality traits without talking about how they are to be measured makes little sense to Cattell. Cattell used a statistical technique called *factor analysis*—a correlational procedure that identifies groups of highly interrelated variables that may be assumed to measure the same underlying factor (here, a personality trait). The logic is that if you know that someone is outgoing, you really don't need to test them to see if they are sociable or extroverted—such information would be redundant.

On the basis of his research, Cattell (1973, 1979) argues that there are two major types of personality traits. *Surface traits* are the clusters of behaviors that go together, like those that make up curiosity, trustworthiness, or kindliness. These traits are easily observed and can be found in many settings. More important than surface traits are the fewer number of underlying traits from which surface traits develop, which he called source traits. It is one's pattern of source traits that determines which surface traits will get expressed in behavior. Source traits are not as easily measured as surface traits because they are not directly observable. Catell's source traits are listed in Figure 10.3.

● **Before You Go On**

What is a personality trait?

What are the major traits that influence personality, according to Allport and Cattell?

A Contemporary Perspective: The Big Five

We've taken a brief look at only two theories that have tried to identify distinguishable, relatively enduring personality traits, and we've generated quite a list. Allport named common traits and personal traits (and three varieties of the latter). Cattell found many surface traits and a smaller number of source traits. Which set of traits is the most reasonable? Is there a set of traits anyplace that is acceptable?

It may surprise you to learn that personality theorists have come to something of a consensus concerning which traits best qualify as descriptors of personality. This approach is called the *Five-Factor Model* (Digman, 1990; McCrae & Costa, 1986, 1987; McCrae & John, 1992; Ozer & Reise, 1994; Wiggins & Pincus, 1992). Which dimensions of personality are now referred to as "The Big Five?"

FIGURE 10.3
Sixteen Source Traits as Identified by Cattell
(Remember that each trait is a dimension.)

Reserved ↔ Outgoing		Trusting ↔ Suspicious	
(detached, aloof)	(participating)	(accepting)	(circumspect)
Less intelligent ↔ More intelligent		**Practical ↔ Imaginative**	
(dull)	(bright)	(down-to-earth)	(absentminded)
Affected by feelings ↔ Emotionally stable		**Forthright ↔ Shrewd**	
(easily upset)	(calm)	(unpretentious)	(astute, wordly)
Submissive ↔ Dominant		**Self-assured ↔ Apprehensive**	
(obedient, easily led)	(assertive)	(secure, complacent)	(insecure, troubled)
Serious ↔ Happy-go-lucky		**Conservative ↔ Experimenting**	
(sober, taciturn)	(enthusiastic)	(disinclined to change)	(experimenting)
Expedient ↔ Conscientious		**Group-dependent ↔ Self-sufficient**	
(disregards rules)	(moralistic, staid)	(a joiner)	(resourceful)
Timid ↔ Venturesome		**Uncontrolled ↔ Controlled**	
(shy, restrained)	(socially bold)	(follows own urges)	(shows will power)
Tough-minded ↔ Sensitive		**Relaxed ↔ Tense**	
(rejects illusions)	(tender-minded)	(tranquil, composed)	(frustrated, driven)

From Cattell, 1973, 1979.

Although there may be some agreement that five major dimensions will suffice to characterize human personality, there is disagreement on exactly how to describe these five. The following is from Digman (1990) and Goldberg (1993):

Dimension I is usually called "Extroversion/Introversion" and embodies such things as assurance, talkativeness, openness, self-confidence, and assertiveness on the one hand, and silence and passivity on the other.

Dimension II is "Agreeableness" or "Friendliness" with altruism, caring, and emotional support at one end; hostility, indifference, selfishness, and distrust at the other.

Dimension III is called "Conscientiousness," and amounts to a "will to achieve" (or simply "will"). It includes matters such as self-control, persistence, planning, thoroughness, and dependability paired with carelessness, negligence, and unreliability. It is well correlated with educational achievement.

Dimension IV is an "Emotionality" dimension. In many ways, this is the extent to which one is emotionally stable or in some way psychologically disordered. It includes such things as nervousness and moodiness.

Dimension V is "Intellect," "Intelligence," or "Openness to Experience and Culture." I should say that in this context, "culture" is referring to aspects of experience such as an interest in a variety of forms of art, dance, music, literature, etc., and not in the sense that cross-cultural psychologists use the term.

The recurrent finding that all personality traits can be reduced to just five, with these names (or names like these), is remarkable. What we have to remember is that each of these five traits represents a dimension of possible habits and individual responses that a person may bring to bear in any given situation. There is still much work to be done.

These five traits have resulted from nearly 50 years of research. We find these five traits emerging from research in many cultures (Paunonen et al., 1992; Stumpf, 1993; Wiggins & Pincus, 1992). They have emerged repeatedly, regardless of the individuals being assessed, and "the Big Five have appeared now in at least five languages, leading one to suspect that something quite fundamental is involved here" (Digman, 1990, p. 433). On the other hand, Revelle (1987, p. 437) notes that "the agreement among these descriptive dimensions is impressive, [but] there is a lack of theoretical explanation for the *how* and the *why* of these dimensions" (see McAdams, 1992; Wiggins, 1992).

● **Before You Go On**

What are the Big Five personality dimensions?

Evaluating the Trait Approach

As I've already mentioned, trait approaches to personality are different from the others, even in their basic intent. Trait theories have a few obvious advantages: They provide us with descriptive terms, and with means of measuring dimensions of personality. They also give us a sense of how measured traits are related to one another. On the other hand, as theories they offer little more than description. To say that someone acted in a certain way "because he is introverted" doesn't really explain his action. It functions merely as a label. Even with the Big Five traits, disagreement remains about how to specifically define the most basic traits that describe personality.

The basic relevance or value of personality traits varies across cultures. Traits are seen as reasonable and sensible to peoples of Western cultures, where people are viewed as individual actors and where knowing about the characteristics of those individual actors would be helpful. If people are viewed in terms of their long-term membership in a group or a collective (as they are in collectivistic cultures such those found in Asia, Africa, and South America), then their individual characteristics will be of less interest than their roles, duties, responsibilities, and group loyalties, for example. (Miller, 1984; Shwedler & Sullivan, 1993).

So, as we might have predicted, when we try to evaluate the different theories of personality, there are no winners or losers. Each approach has its shortcomings, but each adds something to our appreciation of the concept of human personality.

TOPIC 10B

PERSONALITY ASSESSMENT

As we know, personality is a difficult concept to define. Common to most definitions is the idea that there are characteristics of an individual that remain fairly consistent over time and over many (if not all) situations. It is further reasoned that if we know which traits are typical of a person, we can use that knowledge to make predictions about his or her behaviors or mental processes. The key, then, is to reliably and validly measure personal characteristics.

Why do psychologists engage in personality assessment in the first place? There are three goals that lie behind the measurement of personality. One is related to mental illness and psychological disorders. A question that a psychologist may ask in a clinical setting is, "What is wrong with this person?" In fact, the first question is often, "Is there anything wrong with this person?" (Burisch, 1984). Adequate diagnosis is a common aim of personality measurement.

A second use for personality assessment is in theory building, where there are a number of interrelated questions (Ozer & Reise, 1994): Which personality traits can be measured? How may traits be organized within the person? Which traits are most important for describing a personality? For trait theorists, this is obviously the major purpose for constructing personality tests.

The third goal involves the question of whether a personality characteristic can be used to predict some other behavior. This concern is a practical one—particularly in vocational placement. For example, if we know that Joe is dominant and extroverted, what does that knowledge tell us about his leadership potential? What characteristics are associated with success as a sales clerk? What personality traits best describe a successful astronaut, police officer, or secretary?

In brief, personality assessment has three goals: diagnosis, theory building, and behavioral prediction. These goals often interact. A clinical diagnosis made in the context of some theoretical approach is often used to predict possible outcomes, such as which therapy is most appropriate for a given diagnosis.

In this Topic, we will look at some of the assessment techniques that are used to discover the nature of someone's "personality."

BEHAVIORAL OBSERVATIONS

behavioral observation
the personality assessment technique of drawing conclusions about one's personality based on observations of one's behaviors

As you and I develop our own impressions of the personalities of our friends and acquaintances, we do so largely by relying on **behavioral observation**. As its name suggests, this technique involves drawing conclusions about an individual's personality on the basis of observations of his or her behaviors. We judge Dan to be bright because he was the only one who knew the answer to a question in class. We feel that Maria is submissive because she always seems to do whatever her husband demands.

As helpful as our observations may be, there may be problems with the casual, unstructured observations that you and I normally make. When we have observed only a small range of behaviors in a small range of settings, we may overgeneralize when we assume that those same behaviors will show up in new, different situations. Dan may never again know the answer to a question in class. Maria may give in to her husband only because she knows that we are there. That is, the behaviors we happen to observe may not be typical or characteristic at all.

Nonetheless, behavioral observations can be an excellent source of useful information, particularly when the observations being made are purposeful, careful, and structured—as opposed to the casual observations that you and I usually make. Among other things, the accuracy of one's ob-

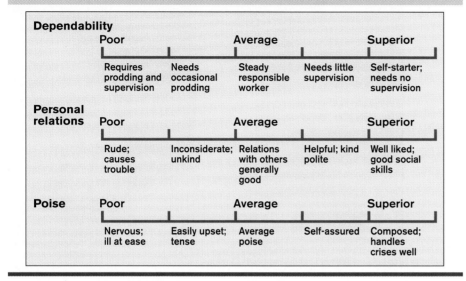

FIGURE 10.4

A graphic rating scale such as this might be used by an employer in evaluating employees or potential employees.

Dependability					
	Poor		Average		Superior
	Requires prodding and supervision	Needs occasional prodding	Steady responsible worker	Needs little supervision	Self-starter; needs no supervision
Personal relations	Poor		Average		Superior
	Rude; causes trouble	Inconsiderate; unkind	Relations with others generally good	Helpful; kind polite	Well liked; good social skills
Poise	Poor		Average		Superior
	Nervous; ill at ease	Easily upset; tense	Average poise	Self-assured	Composed; handles crises well

servations are related to the degree of acquaintance between the observer and the person being observed (Paulus & Bruce, 1992). Behavioral observations are commonly a part of any clinical assessment. The clinical psychologist may note several behaviors of a client as potentially significant—style of dress, manner of speaking, gestures, postures, and so on.

Let's consider an example. A child is reportedly having trouble at school, behaving aggressively and being generally disruptive. One thing a psychologist may do is visit the school and observe the child's behaviors in the natural setting of the classroom. It may be that the child does behave aggressively and engage in fighting behavior, but only when the teacher is in the room. Otherwise, the child is pleasant and quite passive. Perhaps the child's aggressive behaviors reflect a ploy to get the teacher's attention.

In an attempt to add to her original observations, a psychologist may use *role-playing* as a means of collecting more information. Role-playing is a matter of acting out a given life situation. "Let's say that I'm a student and you're the teacher, and it's recess time," the psychologist says to the child. "Let's pretend that someone takes a toy away from me, and I hit him on the arm. What will you do?"

Observational techniques can be supplemented with some sort of rating scale (Figure 10.4). Rating scales provide many advantages over casual observation. For one thing, they focus the attention of the observer on a set of specified behaviors to be observed. Rating scales also yield a more objective measure of a sample of behavior. With rating scales, one can have behaviors observed by many raters. If several raters are involved in the observation of the same behaviors (say, children at play at recess), you can check on the reliability of the observations. That is, if all five of your observers agree that Timothy engaged in "hitting behavior" an average of five times per hour, the consistency (or reliability) of that assessment adds to its usefulness.

Behavioral observation involves drawing conclusions about an individual's personality on the basis of his or her behaviors. Role playing is one technique that psychologists use to gain insights about a child's behaviors. This child may make disclosures while "talking on the telephone" that she would not make otherwise.

Although the data derived from casual, unstructured interviews are seldom reliable or valid, psychologists can gain useful insights about personality using formal, structured interviews.

● **Before You Go On**

What are the basic goals of personality assessment?

How are behavioral observations used to assess personality?

INTERVIEWS

We can learn some things about people simply by watching them. We also can gain insight about some aspects of their personality by asking them about themselves. In fact, the **interview** "remains the most important instrument of clinical assessment" (Korchin & Scheldberg, 1981). It is "one of the oldest and most widely used, although not always the most accurate, of the methods of personality assessment" (Aiken, 1984, p. 296). Its popularity is due largely to its simplicity and flexibility.

The basic data of the interview are what people say about themselves, rather than what they do. At the same time, the interviewer is well aware of the behaviors such as facial expressions and gestures that accompany what is being said. The interview is not, strictly speaking, a measurement technique, because results are relatively impressionistic and are not easily quantifiable (although some interview techniques are clearly more structured and objective than others). Interviews are techniques of discovering generalities rather than specifics.

An advantage of the interview is its flexibility. The interviewer can drop a line of questioning if it is producing no useful information and pursue some other area of interest. Unfortunately, there is little evidence that unstructured interviews have very much reliability or validity (Tenopyr, 1981).

As is the case for observational techniques, there is variation in the degree to which interviews are unstructured or structured. In the latter type of interview, there is a specific set of questions to be asked in a prescribed

interview

the personality assessment technique involving an interchange between an interviewer and a subject to gain personal information about the subject order. The structured interview is more like a psychological test to the extent that it is objective, standardized, and asks about a particular sample of behavior. Recent analyses of structured interviews show that their validity can be high (Landy et al., 1994).

● **Before You Go On**

Cite one advantage and one disadvantage of the interview as a technique of personality assessment.

PAPER-AND-PENCIL TESTS

Observational and interview techniques barely qualify as psychological tests. They are seldom as standardized or as objective as we would like them to be. (At this point, you might want to review our discussion of psychological tests in Chapter 8.) In this section, we'll focus on one of the most often used paper-and-pencil personality tests, the **Minnesota Multiphasic Personality Inventory,** or **MMPI.** The test is referred to as "multiphasic" because it measures several personality dimensions with the same set of items.

The MMPI was designed to aid in the diagnosis of mental disorders and hence is not a personality test in the sense of identifying personality traits. The test is the most researched test in all of psychology, and remains one of the most commonly used (Lubin et al., 1984). In 1989, a revision of the MMPI (the MMPI-2) became available. The revision made two major changes, and a number of lesser ones. Antiquated and offensive items (mostly having to do with religion or sexual practices) were replaced and the norm group was expanded from about 770 to more than 2600 persons. The intent of the authors of the MMPI-2 was to update and improve, but *not* to change, the basic design of the test or the meaning of test scores. The extent to which the revision has succeeded remains to be seen (Adler, 1990a; Edwards & Edwards, 1991). Many psychologists had grown comfortable with the original MMPI and some were against changing such a well-researched test.

The MMPI-2 consists of 567 true-false questions about feelings, attitudes, past experiences, and physical symptoms. The MMPI-2 is a *criterion-referenced test*, which means that items on the test are associated with one of the criterion groups—either normal persons or patients with a specific diagnosis. Some of the items appear very sensible. "I feel like people are plotting against me," seems like the sort of item that a person with paranoia would call "true," while others would respond "false." Many items, however, are not so obvious. "I like to visit zoos," is not an MMPI–2 item, but it might have been if persons of one diagnostic group responded to the item differently from the way others did. What the item *appears* to be measuring is irrelevant. The only thing that matters is if people of different groups respond differently to the item. I need also mention that no one will make even a tentative diagnosis of a psychological disorder on the basis of a person's responses to just a few items. What matters is the pattern of responses to many items. What also matters is not just the simple scores or pattern of scores on any set of items, but the *interpretation* of those scores by a trained, experienced psychologist.

The MMPI-2 also has *validity scales* made up of items from among the 567 that assess the extent to which the subject is attending to the task at hand, or is trying to present herself or himself in a favorable light instead of responding truthfully to the items. For example, responding "true" to

Minnesota Multiplastic Personality Inventory (MMPI-2)

a paper-and-pencil inventory of 567 true-false questions used to assess a number of personality dimensions, some of which may indicate the presence of a psychological disorder

A Personality Test Just for You

I have been teaching introductory psychology for more than 25 years. During that time, I have been observing the personality characteristics of thousands of students and by now, I feel that I understand the basic personalities of most introductory psychology students quite well. Some of my observations are listed below, presented in the form of a short personality test. To check the validity of my test, simply go through the list and indicate the extent to which each of these statements applies to you. If you think that the statement is a true, accurate appraisal, mark it with a 1. If you think that it is true of you only sometimes, give it a 2. If you think that the statement does not apply to you at all, give it a 3.

_____ You have a rather strong need for other people to like you and admire you.

_____ You have a tendency to be critical of yourself.

_____ You feel somewhat uncomfortable when called on in class, even if you know the answer to the instructor's question.

_____ While you have some personality weaknesses, you generally are able to compensate for them.

_____ Disciplined and controlled on the outside, you tend to be a bit insecure inside.

_____ You prefer a certain amount of change and variety, and become dissatisfied when hemmed in by restrictions and limitations.

_____ You have found it unwise to be too frank in revealing yourself to others.

_____ At times you are extroverted, easy-going, and sociable, while at other times you are introverted, wary, and reserved.

_____ Some of your hopes and aspirations tend to be pretty unrealistic.

_____ You occasionally have difficulty relating what you are reading in your psychology class to your own experiences.

_____ Your sexual adjustments have presented some problems for you.

_____ At times you have serious doubts as to whether you have made the right decision or done the right thing.

Now that you have a score (1, or 2, or 3) for each item, add them up so we can see how well I have been able to assess your personality. A low score would mean that I did pretty well and I was accurate with every item. How did I do?

When I do this exercise in class, I find that nearly 90 percent of my students get a score of 18 or less. That's pretty good, isn't it?

But, wait a minute! How could I possibly have any insight about the personality of students in my classes, most of whom I hardly know at all? How could I manage to describe your personality, when we've never even met? Something is wrong here.

This little "personality test" is a variation of a demonstration that dates back at least to 1956 (Munn, 1956). Ten of these items come from the *General Personality Test (or GPT)* described in an article by Ulrich, Stachnick, and Stainton in 1963. I do not claim to have any special wisdom or insight about the personalities of introductory psychology students—or anyone else, for matter. The truth is that these statements are so general that they are virtually meaningless and can apply to nearly everyone. Did you also notice that they are very similar to the sorts of statements one commonly finds in horoscopes?

several statements such as "I always smile at everyone" would lead an examiner to doubt the validity of the subject's responses.

Although the MMPI is the most commonly used personality inventory, it certainly is not the only paper-and-pencil personality test. There are dozens of such tests. The *California Personality Inventory (CPI)*, for example, is a criterion-referenced test written using only normal persons, not those diagnosed as having a psychological disorder. It assesses 18 personality traits, including self-acceptance, dominance, sociability, and responsibility. Because it is designed to measure several different traits, it can also be referred to as a multiphasic test.

Some multiphasic tests have been designed in conjunction with a particular personality theory. For example, Cattell's trait theory approach investigates a number of potential personality traits. These traits are measured with the *16 PF Questionnaire* (PF stands for "personality factors"). Analyses of responses on this test result in a personality profile which can be compared with one gathered from a large norm group.

Finally, there are many personality tests or questionnaires designed to measure just one trait and are, therefore, not multiphasic. The number of these specific tests is increasing dramatically (Ozer & Reise, 1994). A classic example is the *Taylor Manifest Anxiety Scale*. Taylor began with a very large pool of items—many of them from the MMPI—and asked psychologists to choose items that they thought would best measure anxiety. The 50 items most commonly chosen constitute this test, which has gained wide acceptance as an indicator of anxiety. A more recent test, the *Endler Multidimensional Anxiety Scale*, not only assesses anxiety levels, but claims to distinguish between anxiety and experienced depression (Endler et al., 1992).

● **Before You Go On**
What does "multiphasic" mean?
How was the MMPI constructed?

PROJECTIVE TECHNIQUES

A **projective technique** involves asking a subject to respond to ambiguous stimuli. The stimuli can be any number of things, and there are no clearly correct or incorrect answers. The procedure is reasonably unstructured and open-ended. The idea is that because there is, in fact, so little content in the stimulus being presented, the person will project some of his or her own self into a response. Projective techniques are actually more of an aid to interviewing than they are psychological tests (Korchin & Schuldberg, 1981).

Some projective techniques are very simple. The word association technique, introduced by Galton in 1879 and commonly used in psychoanalysis, is a projective technique. "I will say a word, and I want you to say the first thing that pops into your head. Do not think about your response; just say the first thing that comes to mind." There certainly are no right answers in this type of procedure. The idea is that the psychologist can perhaps gain some insight into the problems of a patient, by using this technique.

A similar technique is the *unfinished sentences* or *sentence completion test*. For example, a sentence is begun, "My greatest fear is . . ." The subject is asked to complete the sentence. Although there are several published tests available (e.g., the *Rotter Incomplete Sentences Blank*), many clinicians prefer to make up their own forms. Again, there are no right or wrong responses, and interpreting responses is a bit subjective, but a skilled examiner can

projective technique
a personality assessment technique requiring a subject to respond to ambiguous stimuli, thus projecting his or her self into the responses

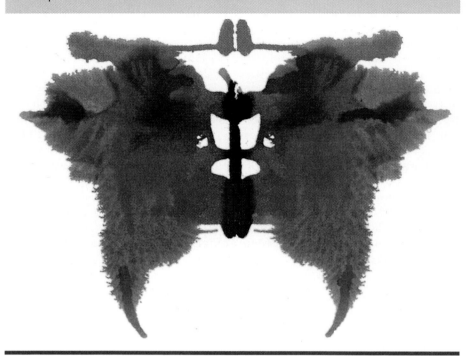

FIGURE 10.5
A sample Rorschach-like inkblot. The subject is asked what the inkblot represents and what she or he sees in it.

Rorschach inkblot test
a projective technique in which the subject is asked to say what he or she sees in a series of inkblots

use these procedures to gain insights about a subject's personality.

Of the projective techniques, none is as well known as the **Rorschach inkblot test**. This device was introduced in 1921 by Hermann Rorschach, who believed that people with different personalities respond differently to inkblot patterns (Figure 10.5). There are ten cards in the test—five are black on white, two are red and gray, and three are multicolored. People are asked to tell what they see in the cards or what the inkblot represents.

Scoring of Rorschach test responses has become quite controversial. Standard scoring procedures require attending to many factors: what the person says (content), where the subject focuses attention (location), mention of detail versus global features, reacting to color or open spaces, and how many distinct responses there are per card. Many psychologists have questioned the efficiency of the Rorschach as a diagnostic instrument. Much of what it can tell an examiner may be gained directly. For example, Rorschach responses that include many references to death, sadness, and dying are said to be indicative of a depressed subject. One has to wonder if inkblots are really needed to discover such depression. As a psychological test, the Rorschach seems neither very reliable nor particularly valid, yet it remains a very popular instrument. It is used primarily as an aid to assessment and the development of impressions.

Thematic Apperception Test (TAT)
a projective personality test requiring a subject to tell a series of short stories about a set of ambiguous pictures

A projective device we've discussed before (in Chapter 9, in the context of achievement motivation), is the **Thematic Apperception Test**, or **TAT**, devised by Henry Murray in 1938. This test consists of a series of ambiguous pictures about which a person is asked to tell a story. The person is asked to describe what is going on, what led up to this situation, and what the outcome is likely to be.

The test is designed to provide a mechanism to discover the subjects' hidden needs, desires, and emotions—which will be projected into their stories. The test is called *thematic* because scoring depends largely on the interpretation of the themes of the stories that are told. Although some formal scoring schemes are available, scoring and interpretation are usually quite subjective and impressionistic. It is likely that the TAT remains popular for the same reason as the Rorschach: Psychologists are used to it, comfortable with the insights it provides, and are willing to accept any source of additional information they can use to make a reasonable assessment or diagnosis.

● **Before You Go On**

What is the essence of a projective technique, the Rorschach and TAT in particular?

THINKING CRITICALLY ABOUT PERSONALITY AND ITS ASSESSMENT

1. No matter what its proposals, hypotheses, or predictions, to what extent is it reasonable to assume that a theory of personality can emerge from the study and treatment of persons with psychological disorders?
2. Humankind is a unique species. For one thing, it is among the very few that regularly kill their own kind on purpose (in murder or war, for example). How can a personality theory take this aspect of human nature into account? (Freud was one of the few to try.)
3. Is it even possible to employ defense mechanisms consciously, or "on purpose"?
4. Freud proposed his theory of personality near the turn of the century. Now, nearly 100 years later, what might Freud think of his own theory's relevance in today's world?
5. Watson and Skinner never proposed a personality theory as such. How do you suppose either of them would have accounted for mental illness or psychological disorders?
6. Can you generate examples of how each of the "Big Five" traits of personality show up in behavior? Can you judge where you fall on each of the five proposed dimensions?
7. What are the major problems with the so-called "personality tests" that we find in magazines and newspapers? For that matter, what (if anything) is "wrong" with the little personality test included in the "Psychology in the Real World" box?
8. How can one determine the reliability of a test that measures anxiety if we know that anxiety is a characteristic that is itself very unreliable (i.e., sometimes we are more or less anxious than at other times)?
9. If you were to take the logic of projective techniques seriously, what could you conclude about someone who viewed all of the inkblots in the Rorschach series and said for each card, "It just looks like an inkblot to me."

SUMMARY

TOPIC 10A
ISSUES AND THEORIES OF PERSONALITY

● **What are the three levels of consciousness proposed by Freud?**

Freud claimed that at any one time, we were only fully aware or conscious of a few things. With a little effort, some ideas or memories can be accessed from our preconscious, while others—those in our unconscious mind—can only be accessed with great effort. *Pages 351–353.*

● **According to Freud, what are the three structures of personality, and by what principle does each operate?**

The structures of personality according to Freud are the inborn, instinctive id, operating on the pleasure principle and seeking immediate gratification; the ego, or sense of self, which operates on the reality principle, mediating needs in the context of the real world; and the superego, one's sense of morality or conscience, which operates on the idealistic principle, attempting to direct one to do what is right and proper. *Pages 353–354.*

● **List and define seven defense mechanisms.**

When aspects of the personality are in conflict, anxiety may result. To fend off feelings of anxiety, the ego may unconsciously employ one of the many defense mechanisms. *Repression* is motivated forgetting—forcing into the unconscious those ideas, beliefs, or desires that cause us anxiety. *Denial* involves the simple refusal to acknowledge the realities of an anxiety-producing situation. *Rationalization* is the process of making up excuses for our anxiety-producing behaviors rather than facing their real causes. *Fantasy* is a matter of escaping from anxiety and reality through daydreaming or imagination. *Projection* is seeing in others those characteristics that would cause us anxiety if we were to acknowledge them in ourselves. *Regression* is acting in a primitive, childish way—taking on old behaviors that at one time were reinforcing. *Displacement* is a matter of di-

recting one's motives or behaviors, usually aggressive, at some "safe" substitute person or object. *Pages 354–356.*

● **Briefly review Freud's five psychosexual stages of development.**

Freud believed that one's personality developed through five stages, each with a different sexual/sensual focus: the oral stage (birth to 1 year), the anal stage (ages 1–3), the phallic stage (ages 3–5), the latency stage (age 6–puberty), and the genital stage (from puberty on). *Pages 356–357.*

● **Briefly summarize the contributions of Adler, Jung, and Horney to the psychoanalytic approach to personality.**

Adler, Jung, and Horney each parted with Freud on theoretical grounds while remaining basically psychoanalytic in orientation. For Adler, social influences and inferiority complexes mattered much more than Freud's innate drives. Jung was less biological, more positive, and expanded on Freud's view of the unconscious mind, adding the idea of the collective unconscious. Horney rejected the stress on instinctual impulses and discussed instead the notion of basic anxiety and how one reacts to it as the sculptor of one's personality. *Pages 357–359.*

● **Specify a contribution to the concept of personality contributed respectively by Watson, Skinner, Dollard and Miller, and Bandura.**

Many psychologists have argued that personality can be approached using learning principles and observable behaviors—without reference to "internal" dispositions. Watson first emphasized focusing on behavior and abandoning mental concepts. Dollard and Miller tried to explain personality in terms of learning theory and habit development. Skinner emphasized the notion of the consequences of one's behaviors as molding what one does. Bandura stressed the role of observation and social learning in the formation of personality. *Pages 359–361.*

● **Briefly summarize the humanistic-phenomenological approach to personality as epitomized by Rogers and Maslow.**

The theories of Rogers and Maslow are alike in several ways, emphasizing the integrity of the self and the power of personal growth and development. Both deny the negativity and biological bias of psychoanalytic theory and the environmental determinism of behaviorism. *Pages 361–363.*

● What is a personality trait? What are the major traits that influence personality according to Allport and Cattell?

A personality trait is a characteristic and distinctive way in which one person may differ from others. According to Allport, there are two kinds of traits, common traits and personal traits—the former found to varying degrees in virtually everyone, the latter specific to some individuals. Cattell also feels that there are two kinds of traits: surface traits, which are readily observable, and source traits, from which surface traits develop. *Pages 363–365.*

● What are the Big Five personality dimensions?

Recent research in personality trait theory suggests that from all the traits that have been proposed over the years, five emerge most regularly, although there is as yet no total agreement on how to characterize these dimensions. We agreed to call them (1) extroversion-introversion, (2) agreeableness or friendliness, (3) conscientiousness, (4) emotionality, and (5) intelligence. *Pages 365–367.*

TOPIC 10B
PERSONALITY ASSESSMENT

● What are the basic goals of personality assessment?
● How are behavioral observations used to assess personality?

Personality assessment (including testing) is used to make a clinical diagnosis about the presence or nature of a psychological disorder, help build theories of personality based on which traits are important and how they are interrelated, and predict what someone may do in the future. Conclusions about one's personality can be inferred from the observation of that individual's behaviors. Behaviors should be observed in a large number of settings. Observations should be as objective as possible, and may involve the use of behavioral rating scales to check on observer reliability. *Pages 367–369.*

● Cite one advantage and one disadvantage of the interview as a technique of personality assessment.

The major advantage of the interview is its flexibility, allowing an interviewer to pursue avenues of interest and to abandon lines of questioning that are not informative. Unfortunately, there is little evidence that interviewing is a valid technique for many of the purposes to which it is put. The more structured the interview, the more valid it is. *Pages 370–371.*

● What does "multiphasic" mean?
● How was the MMPI constructed?

In the context of psychological testing, multiphasic instruments attempt to measure a number of different characteristics or traits with the same set of items. The MMPI was designed (in the early 1940s and revised as the MMPI-2 in 1989) as an aid to psychological diagnosis. The test includes items that discriminate between subjects of different diagnostic categories (including "normal"). The test also includes items to assess the extent to which the subject is doing a thorough and honest job of answering the 567 true-false questions of the test. Such paper-and-pencil tests can serve as screening devices to indicate which traits or patterns of traits are likely to be found within an individual. *Pages 371–373.*

● What is the essence of a projective technique, the Rorschach and TAT in particular?

With a projective technique, the assumption is that in responding to an ambiguous stimulus (describing a series of inkblots for the Rorschach or telling short stories about a set of pictures for the TAT), a person will project conscious and unconscious aspects of his or her self into his or her responses. *Pages 373–375.*

TOPIC 10A

ISSUES AND THEORIES OF PERSONALITY

10.1 Ideas, thoughts, or memories of which we are not immediately aware, but which we can think about with reasonably little effort are said by Freudians to be stored in our _____ level of awareness. a) immediate b) unconscious c) preconscious d) subconscious. *Pages 351–353.*

10.2 Freud would tend to "explain" war and mankind's inhumanity to man in terms of a) thanatos. b) libido. c) wish-fulfillment. d) eros. *Pages 353–354.*

10.3 Which aspect of one's personality—according to Freudian theory—operates on a "reality principle?" a) the id b) the ego c) the superego d) All of these operate on a reality principle. *Pages 353–354.*

10.4 The aspect or structure of personality that is responsible for feelings of guilt or blame is the a) id. b) superego. c) libido. d) ego. *Pages 353–354.*

10.5 Seeing in others those motives that would make us anxious if we were to see them in ourselves involves the use of the defense mechanism of a) denial. b) suppression. c) projection. d) displacement. *Pages 354–356.*

10.6 Otis doesn't get invited to a party that he really hoped to attend. He soon convinces himself that he "really didn't want to go to that dumb party in the first place." It sounds like Otis is engaging in a) repression. b) fantasy. c) projection. d) rationalization. *Pages 354–356.*

10.7 The stage of Freudian psychosexual development in which sexuality is suppressed or "put on hold" is called the _____ period. a) anal b) latency c) genital d) phallic. *Pages 356–357.*

10.8 The neo-Freudians left Freud and devised their own personality theories because they objected—more than anything else—to Freud's heavy emphasis on a) instincts and biological concepts. b) the importance of early childhood. c) parent-child social interactions. d) the notion of levels of consciousness. *Pages 357–359.*

10.9 The notion of "moving away" or "moving toward" or "moving against" others is best associated with a) Freud. b) Jung. c) Adler. d) Horney. *Pages 357–359.*

10.10 With which personality theorist do we best associate the concept of "inferiority complex?" a) Charles Spearman b) Carl Jung c) Alfred Adler d) Karen Horney. *Pages 357–359.*

10.11 More so than other theorists, psychologists such as Watson, Dollard, Miller, and Skinner tended to talk about personality in terms of a) conscious choices made by people with difficult decisions to make. b) how a person's behaviors could be explained by referring to external, environmental factors. c) personality traits that remained reasonably stable once they were formed. d) cognitive representations of the environment that guide one's behaviors. *Pages 359–361.*

10.12 To say that a personality theory takes a phenomenological approach is to say that it tends to emphasize a) instinctive, biological mechanisms. b) how people see themselves and their environments. c) unconscious, unknowable influences. d) learning and conditioning. *Pages 361–363.*

10.13 Which term, from Carl Rogers's approach to personality, is most similar to Maslow's concept of self-actualization? a) archetype b) unconditioned positive regard c) self-fulfilling prophecy d) to be fully functioning. *Pages 361–363.*

10.14 True or False? Unlike Freud, Carl Rogers never engaged in psychotherapy of any sort. *Pages 361–363.*

10.15 Personality traits most commonly have been defined a) in terms of how personality is related to survival. b) by how someone scores on a personality test. c) to explain individual differences among people. d) in the context of life-span development. *Pages 363–365.*

10.16 Factor analysis is largely a _____ technique. a) correlational b) experimental c) common sense d) subjective. *Pages 363–365.*

10.17 Perhaps the greatest advantage of the trait theories of personality is that they a) give us operational definitions of the terms they use. b) emphasize the importance of early childhood experiences. c) tend to be social or interpersonal in nature. d) are directly related to concepts from the learning laboratory. *Pages 363–365.*

10.18 In the context of personality theory, what makes the Big Five so remarkable? a) Five major theorists have agreed on what personality is. b) We can show when one's personality is important and when the situation is important. c) There seems to be a consensus on how to describe personality. d) There are actually five levels of consciousness, not just the three that Freud described. *Pages 365–367.*

10.19 True or False? Most trait theories, including the so-called Big Five, do not include intelligence as a personality trait. *Pages 365–367.*

TOPIC 10B

PERSONALITY ASSESSMENT

10.20 When assessing personality, interviews are most useful when they are a) spontaneous and free-flowing. b) highly structured. c) as unlike psychological tests as possible. d) conducted by someone who does not know the individual being interviewed. *Pages 367–371.*

10.21 To say that a test such as the MMPI-2 is "criterion referenced" implies that a) questions do not have right or wrong answers. b) people from different groups respond to items differently. c) the test has been designed to predict who is likely to suffer mental illness in the future. d) test scores have been factor analyzed. *Pages 371–373.*

10.22 As opposed to intellectual assessment, personality assessment a) seldom uses psychological tests. b) attempts to measure you at your best. c) is used to predict behavior. d) measures one's usual, or typical, behaviors. *Pages 371–375.*

10.23 True or False? Both the Rorschach and the TAT are projective tests. *Pages 373–375.*

11

PSYCHOLOGY, STRESS, AND PHYSICAL HEALTH

PREVIEW

TOPIC 11A—Stress, Stressors, and How to Cope

Stressors: The Causes of Stress

Reacting to the Stressors in Our Lives

TOPIC 11B—Health Psychology

Psychological Factors that Influence Physical Health

Promoting Healthy Behaviors

PSYCHOLOGY IN THE REAL WORLD: Having an Impact on AIDS, the Deadly STD

THINKING CRITICALLY ABOUT PSYCHOLOGY, STRESS, AND PHYSICAL HEALTH

SUMMARY

TEST YOURSELF

The focus of this chapter is the role of psychological factors as they affect our physical health and well-being. We have encountered the basic theme before: biological and psychological processes interact; body and mind are interrelated.

Topic 11A deals with stress, its causes and its ramifications. Stress is much like an emotion—it involves both physiological reactions and unpleasant feelings, or affect. Stress is also a motivator. People experiencing stress are motivated to do something to get rid of it, or at least to minimize the negative affect that often accompanies it. Stress is so common, so pervasive, we may argue that it is simply part of being alive.

An issue of considerable interest in psychology is the extent to which stress produces negative consequences for one's physical health. Exploring this issue, in Topic 11B, will provide us with an opportunity to look at the very rapidly growing field of health psychology. Health psychologists are trying to understand the relationships among psychological variables and physical health. We'll explore two major issues: (1) What is the relationship between our behaviors, thoughts, and feelings and the state of our physical health? (2) What role can psychologists play in improving our physical health?

TOPIC 11A

STRESS, STRESSORS, AND HOW TO COPE

Our study of stress is divided into two main sections. First we'll see, at least in general terms, where stress comes from. What are common stressors in our lives? Second, we'll examine the patterns of responses we make when we experience stress. One reality we'll encounter here is that stress is unavoidable. Another is that there are both maladaptive, unproductive reactions to stress and adaptive, mentally healthy reactions.

STRESSORS: THE CAUSES OF STRESS

As we have so often in previous chapters, let's begin with some definitions. Although we all are intimately familiar with stress, psychologists have struggled with the concept for nearly 60 years—and the issue is far from settled (Hobfoll, 1989). We will define **stress** as a complex set of reactions made by

stress
a complex pattern of reactions to real or perceived threats to one's sense of well-being that motivates adjustment

381

a person under pressure to adapt. In other words, stress is a response made to a perceived threat to one's well-being. There are physiological reactions and unpleasant feelings (distress or anxiety) associated with stress.

There are many circumstances or events that can produce stress. *The sources of stress are called* **stressors**. In this section, we'll consider three types of stressors: frustration, conflict, and life events. In each case I'll provide examples, some of which you may view as trivial. I have chosen to include such examples as a reminder that stress is not necessarily a response to some overwhelming catastrophic event, such as the death of a loved one or a natural disaster. We all have experienced stress in our lives, albeit to varying degrees. Once we've seen where stress comes from, we can consider different techniques and mechanisms that people use to cope with it.

Frustration-Induced Stress

As we saw in Topic 9A, we can characterize motivated behaviors as *"goal-directed."* Whether by internal processes (needs and drives) or by external stimuli (incentives), we are pushed or pulled toward positive goals and away from negative goals.

Now let me introduce an assumption: *Organisms don't always reach all of their goals.* Have you always gotten everything you've ever wanted? Have you always been able to avoid unpleasantness, pain, or sorrow? Do you know anyone who has?

Sometimes we are totally prohibited from ever reaching a particular goal. At other times our progress may be slower or more difficult than we would like. In either case, we are being frustrated. **Frustration** is the blocking of goal-directed behavior—blocking that may be total and permanent or partial and temporary (see Figure 11.1).

Seen in this way, stress resulting from frustration is a normal, commonplace reaction. Frustration is a stressor, and the stress it produces is a fact of life. The stress that results from frustration does not imply weakness, pathology, or illness. What does matter is how individuals react to the stressors in their lives. Before we consider how one might react to frustration, let's look at some of the varieties of frustration.

To someone who feels the stress that results from frustration, the actual source of that stress may be of little consequence. However, in order to respond adaptively to frustration-induced stress, it can be helpful to recognize the source of the blocking—the specific stressor—keeping us from our goals. There are two basic types of frustration: environmental and personal.

Environmental frustration implies that the blocking or thwarting of goal-directed behavior is caused by something or someone in the environment. (Note that we talk about the source of frustration, not *fault* or *blame*, which are evaluative terms.) I'm really thirsty, so I put 60¢ in a vending machine to get a soft drink. The machine takes my money and gives me nothing in return. It even fails to return my 60¢. Now that's frustrating! My goal-directed behaviors were thwarted by the vending machine. My experience is one of stress. Kristy is about two-thirds of the way through typing a term paper on her word processor when suddenly the power goes out. Having failed to save her work as she went along, she'll have to redo it all. Here is another example of environmental frustration as a stressor.

Occasionally, we are frustrated not because something in our environment is blocking progress toward our goals, but because of some internal or personal reason. This is *personal frustration*. Doug fails to make the basketball team simply because he is too short. Someone wanting to be a con-

stressors
real or perceived threats to one's sense of well-being; sources of stress

frustration
a stressor; the blocking or thwarting of goal-directed behavior

FIGURE 11.1
A depiction of frustration, the blocking or thwarting of goal-directed behavior.

cert pianist may be frustrated in her attempt to do so because she happens to have short, stubby fingers and can reach only half an octave on the keyboard. She may learn to be a good pianist, but she probably will not make it in the world of classical piano. Her frustration and resulting stress are not the fault of people who write piano music or build piano keyboards. Her failure to play some piano music is not *her fault,* but if she persists in this goal-directed behavior, she will be frustrated. Some of us are learning that getting older can be stressful. I know that I am frustrated when I have difficulty doing things that at one time I was able to do with ease. The stress we experience in such situations is frustration-induced, and the type of frustration is personal.

● **Before You Go On**

What is meant by frustration-induced stress?
Define environmental and personal frustration.

Conflict-Induced Stress

Sometimes we are unable to satisfy a drive or motive because it is in **conflict** with other motives that are influencing us at the same time. Thus, stress may result not from frustration caused by the blocking of our goal-directed behaviors, but because of conflicts within our own motivational system.

With motivational conflicts, there is the implication of a decision or a choice that has to be made. Sometimes the decision is easy to make, and the resulting stress will be slight; sometimes decision making is very difficult, and the resulting stress will be greater. When discussing conflict, it is useful to talk about positive goals or incentives we wish to approach and negative goals or incentives we wish to avoid. Let's look at some stress-inducing motivational conflicts.

1. *Approach-Approach Conflicts* Conflicts are necessarily unpleasant and produce stress; they will be so even when the goals involved are positive, or desired. In an approach-approach conflict, one is caught between two (or more) alternatives, each of which is positive (Figure 11.2). If the person chooses alternative A, he or she will reach a desired goal. If B is chosen, a different desirable goal will be attained. What makes this a conflict is that not both alternatives are an option—it has to be one or the other. A choice has to be made.

Once an approach-approach conflict is resolved, the subject ends up with some desired goal no matter which alternative is chosen. For example, if Carla enters an ice cream shop with only enough money to buy one scoop of ice cream, she may experience a conflict when faced with all of the flavors from which to choose. Typical of a conflict situation, we'll probably see some vacillation in Carla's behavior, some swaying back and forth between alternatives. But we can assume that this conflict will be resolved, and Carla will at least walk out of the store with an ice cream cone of some flavor she likes. Her life might have been easier (less stressful) if the store provided just one flavor and she didn't have to make such choices, but she'll contemplate that possibility with an ice cream cone in hand.

Sometimes the choices we are called upon to make are much more serious than those involving ice cream flavors. What will be your college major? On the one hand, you'd like to go to medical school and be a surgeon

Stress resulting from frustration occurs when our goal-directed behaviors are blocked or thwarted. On some days, being stuck in a traffic jam can be very frustrating.

conflict
a stressor in which some goals can be satisfied only at the expense of other goals

FIGURE 11.2
A diagram of an approach-approach conflict. In such a conflict, a person is faced with two (or more) attractive, positive goals, and must choose from among them.

FIGURE 11.3
A diagram of an avoidance-avoidance conflict. In such a conflict, a person is faced with two (or more) unattractive, negative goals, and must choose from among them. This is a no win situation.

FIGURE 11.4
A diagram of an approach-avoidance conflict. Here, a person is faced with but one goal. What makes this a conflict is that the goal has both positive and negative aspects or features.

(that's a positive incentive, or goal). On the other hand, you'd like to cultivate your aptitude for music and study composition and conducting at a school of music (also a positive incentive). At the moment, you can't do both. The courses that you would take as a pre-med student are quite different from those you'd take if you were to follow music as a career path. Both avenues are constructive, desirable alternatives; but now, at registration, you have to make a choice, one that may have long-lasting repercussions. The nature of such a conflict qualifies it as a stressor.

2. *Avoidance-Avoidance Conflicts.* Perhaps the most stress-inducing of all conflicts are the avoidance-avoidance conflicts (Figure 11.3). In this type of conflict, a person is faced with a number of alternatives, and each is negative. To be in an avoidance-avoidance conflict is, in a way, to be boxed in so that no matter what you do, the result will be punishing or unpleasant.

This sort of conflict is not at all unusual in the workplace. Imagine you are a supervisor in charge of a successful, profitable division of a large corporation. Word comes down from management that you must cut your operating budget by 20 percent by next month. There *are* ways that you can reduce expenses—limit travel, cut down on supplies, reduce pay, eliminate a few positions, eliminate expense accounts—but each involves an action you'd rather not take. The result is stress, and the stressor is an avoidance-avoidance conflict.

3. *Approach-Avoidance Conflicts.* With approach-avoidance conflicts, a person is in the position of considering only one goal, or one option (Figure 11.4). What makes this situation a conflict is that the person would very much like to reach that goal, but, at the same time, would very much like not to. It's a matter of "Yes, I'd love to . . . Well, actually, I'd rather not . . . Well, maybe I would . . . No, I wouldn't . . . yes . . . no." Consider the possibility of entering into a relationship with someone you think of as special. On the one hand, such a relationship might turn out to be wonderful and rewarding. On the other hand, the relationship might put you in the position of being hurt and rejected. Typical of motivational conflicts, we see vacillation, swinging back and forth between options—motivated to approach and at the same time motivated to avoid.

4. *Multiple Approach-Avoidance Conflicts.* Multiple approach-avoidance conflicts may be the most common of the motivational conflicts experienced by adults (Figure 11.5). This type of conflict arises when an individual is faced with several alternatives, each one of which is in some way positive and in some way negative at the same time.

Perhaps you and some friends are out shopping on a Saturday morning. You discover that it's getting late and that you're all hungry. Where will you go to lunch? You may have a multiple approach-avoidance conflict here. "We could go to Bob's Diner, where the food is cheap and the service is fast, but the food is terrible. Or we could go to Cafe Olé, where the food is better, but more expensive, and the service is a little slow. Or we could go to The Grill, where the service is elegant and food superb, but the price is very high." Granted this is not an earth-shaking dilemma, but in each case there are pluses and minuses to be considered. The more difficult the choice, and the more important or valued the goal, the greater the induced stress.

Life is filled with such conflicts, and some can be severe and very stressful. They may encompass questions of the "What shall I do with the rest of my life?" sort. "Should I stay at home with the children (+ and –), or should I have a career (+ and –)?" "Should I attend University X (+ and –), or should I go to College Y (+ and –)?" "Should I get married or stay single, or is there another way (again, + and – in each case)?" "Should I work for Company A, or should I work for Company B?" You might want to reflect on the conflicts you have faced during the past few weeks. You should be able to categorize each of them into one of the four types I have listed here.

● **Before You Go On**

Name and describe four types of motivational conflict.

Life-Induced Stress

It is clear that frustration and conflict can be potent sources of stress in our lives and are often unavoidable consequences of being a motivated organism. Psychologists have also considered sources of stress that do not fit neatly into our descriptions of either frustration or conflict. One useful approach has been to look at certain events and changes that occur in one's life as potential sources of stress.

In 1967, Thomas Holmes and Richard Rahe published their first version of the *Social Readjustment Rating Scale*, or *SRRS* (Holmes & Holmes, 1970). The basic idea behind this scale is that stress results whenever life situations change. The scale provides a list of life events that potentially can be stressful. The original list came from the reports of patients suffering from moderate to high levels of stress. Marriage was (arbitrarily) assigned a value of 50 stress points, or *life change units*. With "marriage = 50" as their guide, people rated other more-or-less typical life changes in terms of the amount of stress they might provide. The death of a spouse got the highest rating (100 units), followed by divorce (with 73 units). Pregnancy (40 units), trouble with the boss (23 units), changing to a new school (20 units), and minor violations of the law (11 units) are some other stress-inducing life change events on the scale. So, in a rather direct way, the SRRS gives us a way to measure the stress in our lives.

There *is* a positive correlation between scores on the SRRS and the incidence of physical illness and disease (Adler et al., 1994; Brett et al., 1990; Herbert & Cohen, 1993; Rahe & Arthur, 1978; Weiss, 1992). People with scores between 200 and 299 have a 50–50 chance of developing symptoms of physical illness within the next two years. Eighty percent of those with scores above 300 develop physical symptoms within the same time period. The logic is that stress predisposes one to physical illness, particularly cardiovascular disorders. But we must remember what we said in Chapter 1 about correlations: They do not tell us about cause and effect. Some of the SRRS items are related to physical illness or are health-related (e.g., pregnancy, personal injury). It may not be much of a surprise, then, to find scores on this scale correlated to levels of physical illness. It may be that what matters most is how one internalizes or reacts to life experiences rather than the experiences themselves, a point we'll return to in Topic 11B.

Socioeconomic status, or **SES,** is a measure that reflects one's income, educational level, and occupation. Not surprisingly, there is a correlation between socioeconomic status and experienced stress. SES is related to stress in at least two ways. (1) Persons of high socioeconomic status are less

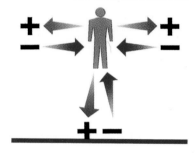

FIGURE 11.5
A diagram of a multiple approach-avoidance conflict. In such a conflict, a person is faced with two (or more) alternatives, each of which has both positive and negative aspects or features, and a choice must be made from among the alternatives.

socioeconomic status (SES)
a measure that reflects one's income, educational level, and occupation

FIGURE 11.6
Ten Common Stressors in the Lives of Middle-aged Adults and College Students

For middle-aged adults:

1. Concerns about weight
2. Health of a family member
3. Rising prices of common goods
4. Home maintenance (interior)
5. Too many things to do
6. Misplacing or losing things
7. Yard work or outside home maintenance
8. Property, investments, or taxes
9. Crime
10. Physical appearance

For college students:

1. Troubling thoughts about the future
2. Not getting enough sleep
3. Wasting time
4. Inconsiderate smokers
5. Physical appearance
6. Too many things to do
7. Misplacing or losing things
8. Not enough time to do the things you need to do
9. Concerns about meeting high standards
10. Being lonely

From Kanner, Coyne, Schaefer, & Lazarus, 1981.

likely than persons of low SES to encounter *negative* life events (unemployment, less access to adequate health care, poor housing, and so on [McLeod & Kessler, 1990]). (2) Persons of low SES have fewer resources available to deal with stressful life events when they do occur (Adler et al., 1994).

Richard Lazarus (1981, 1991c, 1993) argues that psychologists ought to focus more attention on those causes of stress that are less dramatic than major life changes such as the death of a family member. What often matters most are life's little hassles—the traffic that moves too slowly, the toothpaste tube that splits, the ants at a picnic, the cost of a pizza compared to what it was just a few years ago, and so on. Part of this argument is that big crises or major life change events are too large to affect us directly. What may cause us to feel stressed are the ways in which big events produce little, irritating, changes in our lives (hassles). Being retired may mean a lack of access to friendly conversation at coffee break time. A spouse's starting to work may make life a little more difficult; the other spouse may have to cook dinner for the first time. Thus, stress results not so much from the event itself, but from the hassles it creates. The ten most commonly cited daily hassles for college students and for middle-aged adults are listed in Figure 11.6. These items come from the *Hassles Scale*, a test devised by Lazarus and his colleagues. This scale turns out to be an even better predictor of physical health and psychological symptoms such as anxiety and depression than is the Holmes and Rahe Social Readjustment Scale (DeLongis et al., 1988).

Notice that to be stressful, events in our lives do not have to be in themselves negative. Many things that we look forward to, that we judge to be changes for the better can bring with them the hassles associated with stress. For example, everybody is happy about Cindy and Jerry getting married, a pleasant, positive life event. But at the same time—anyone who has

Sometimes life events such as weddings, which are evaluated as positive events, can be stressors.

ever gone through the process will attest—weddings can be stressors. If they invite Aunt Sarah, do they have to invite Aunt Louise? Cindy and Jerry are planning an outdoor reception. What if it rains? Or Wayne has been a salesman for 11 years, and he's used to the freedom of setting his own hours. What will the promotion to district sales manager—an office job—mean in terms of his daily routine?

● **Before You Go On**

In what ways might simply being alive in the world produce stress?

REACTING TO THE STRESSORS IN OUR LIVES

So far we've defined stress and reviewed a number of potential stressors—frustration, conflict, and life events that involve making changes. Now we need to consider what someone might do when he or she experiences stress. We often hear about people trying to "cope with the stress in their lives." Consistent with the terminology we're using in this Topic, it would be more correct to speak of "coping with, or dealing with, the *stressors* in one's life." Remember, stress is a reaction to stressors. Stress may motivate us, but it motivates us to do something about the perceived threats to our well-being that we are calling stressors.

Individual Differences in Responding to Stressors

Before we go any further, an important point needs to be made. As with many other things, there are large individual differences in response to stressors. What constitutes a stressor, and what someone may do when he or she experiences stress, can vary considerably from person to person. Some people fall apart at weddings; others don't find them stressful at all. For some people, even simple choices are difficult to make; for others, choices are not enough, they seek challenges.

Indeed, some people seem so generally resistant to the negative aspects of stress that they have been labeled as having *hardy personalities* (Kobasa, 1979, 1982, 1987; Maddi & Kobasa, 1984; Neubauer, 1992). Hardiness in this context is related to three things: (1) *challenge* (being able to see difficulties in one's life as an opportunity for change and growth, not as threats to one's status); (2) *control* (being in charge of what's happening in one's life and believing that one is the master of one's fate); (3) *commitment* (being engaged and involved with one's life and circumstances, not just "watching life from the sidelines").

Here's another point about how we deal with stressors: Some responses are more effective or adaptive than others. An adaptive, effective response will ultimately reduce the experience of stress. To think that one can *avoid* stress altogether is not realistic. A certain amount of stress in our lives is natural and to be expected. Stress often follows as a natural consequence of being alive and motivated in the real world. What is unfortunate is that we occasionally develop ineffective, maladaptive strategies for dealing with the stress we experience. By ineffective or maladaptive responses to stressors I mean that one's reaction will not, in the long run, be successful in reducing stress. Before we consider adaptive and maladaptive responses, however, let's first acknowledge that one universal reaction to stress is physiological.

Stress as a Physiological Reaction

No matter how we ultimately cope with stress, stressors stimulate physiological reactions within us. Remember, this is one of the ways in which stress is like an emotional response; it has a physiological component.

general adaptation syndrome (GAS)
Selye's description of the physiological reactions to stressors which includes the three stages of alarm, resistance, and exhaustion

The most widely accepted description of the physiological reactions to stressors is found in Hans Selye's **general adaptation syndrome**, or **GAS.** According to Selye (1956, 1974), the pattern of reactions to stressors occurs in three stages: alarm, resistance, and exhaustion (see Figure 11.7).

The first response to the perception of a stressor is *alarm*. A perceived threat produces rapid and noticeable changes in the sympathetic division of the autonomic nervous system, causing an increase in heart rate and blood pressure, dilation of the pupils, rerouting of the blood supply, etc. The adrenal glands secrete norepinephrine into the bloodstream and mobilize the body's resources, providing increased levels of blood sugar.

This strong, even dramatic reaction cannot last very long. We usually can maintain high levels of sympathetic activity for no more than several minutes, a few hours at the most.

In *resistance*, the second stage of the general adaptation syndrome, the cause of stress remains present, and one's body continues to fight off the challenge of the stressor. Resources are mobilized in the alarm stage, and in resistance, sympathetic nervous system reactions continue, increasing the drain on the body's resources. In this stage one becomes vulnerable to physical illness and infections to a greater degree than if the stressor were removed. High blood pressure, ulcers, skin rashes, or respiratory difficulties may develop. Indeed, in the resistance stage of the GAS a person is more susceptible to all sorts of physical ailments from the common cold to cancer.

FIGURE 11.7

The general adaptation syndrome (GAS), as proposed by Hans Selye, calls for three identifiable, largely physiological, reactions to stressors. In the first stage (alarm reaction), resources are quickly mobilized as the sympathetic division of the ANS springs into action. If the stressor persists, the organism shows a defensive reaction (resistance stage) in an attempt to react to the continuing stress. Following prolonged exposure to stress, the energy necessary for adaptation may become depleted (exhaustion stage).

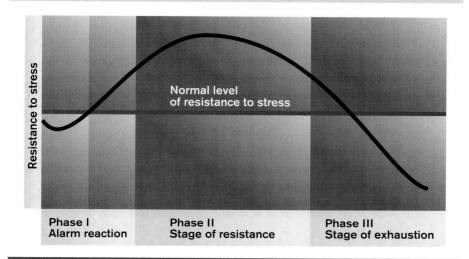

If some useful way of dealing with the experienced stress cannot be found, the third physical reaction to the still-present stressor may be *exhaustion*. In this stage, bodily resources become nearly depleted. Although the resistance stage can last for as long as several months, eventually one's resources become expended. In extreme cases, the exhaustion stage of the GAS can result in death.

For Selye, then, stress is a three-stage mobilization of the body's resources to combat real or perceived threats to one's well-being. We have a limited supply of such resources. Repeated exposure to stressors tends to have cumulative effects. Selye's model focuses only on the physiological aspects of responding to stressors. It does not take into account just how a person can respond to stressors in more cognitive and behavioral ways. Let's first consider effective strategies for dealing with stress and stressors, and then look at some common ineffective strategies.

● **Before You Go On**

What does it mean to say that there are individual differences in reacting to stressors?

Name and describe the three stages of Selye's general adaptation syndrome.

Effective Strategies for Coping with Stressors

In the long run, the most effective way of dealing with stress is to make relatively permanent changes in our behaviors as a result of the experience of stress. You'll recall that we defined learning as a relatively permanent change in behavior that occurs as the result of practice or experience. To respond to a stressor with learning makes particularly good sense for frustration-induced stress. Here, our path to a goal is being blocked or thwarted. An adaptive way to handle such a stressor is to find a new way to reach our goal or to learn to modify our goal (see Figure 11.8).

In fact, much of our everyday learning is motivated by frustration-induced stress. We've had to learn many new responses as a means of coping with frustration. Let's look at a few imaginary examples. Having been frustrated once (or twice) by locking yourself out of your house or car, you've learned to hide a second set of keys where you can easily find them. Having been denied promotion because you didn't have a college degree, you are learning about general psychology on the way toward earning such a degree. Having been caught at home in a snowstorm with no cookies in the house, you've learned to bake them yourself. Having discovered that you're too short to make the basketball team, you've learned to play tennis. As a child, you may have learned to get what you wanted from your parents by smiling and asking politely. In each of these cases, what prompted or motivated the learning of new responses or the establishment of new goals was stress resulting from frustration.

Learning motivated by stress also may have taught you the value of escape and avoidance. You know how to avoid getting into many motivational conflicts. You try to plan things to keep your options open, so as not to get trapped in conflicts in the first place. You may have learned that the only thing to do once you are in an avoidance-avoidance conflict is to escape or make major changes in what is motivating you. This is one way in which stress can be seen as a positive force in our lives. If we were never challenged, if we never set difficult goals, if we never faced stressful situations, we would miss out on many opportunities for personal growth. Stress can be very unpleasant at the time it occurs, but it may produce positive consequences.

To say that we should respond to stressors by learning new, effective behaviors is sensible enough in general, but are there any specific measures we can take to help alleviate the unpleasantness of stress in our lives? Yes, there are many. Here, we'll review eight such strategies.

(1) Identify the stressor. Remember that stress is a reaction to any one of several types of stressors. If you are experiencing stress in your life, perhaps the first thing you should ask is, "Where is it coming from?" Are you having difficulty resolving a motivational conflict? What positive or negative goals are involved? Is your goal-directed behavior being blocked? If so, what is the source of your frustration? What recent changes or events in your life are particularly upsetting or problematic? Any successful strategy for coping with stress will require change—and effort—on your part. The first thing to do is to make sure that your efforts are well directed.

In this regard, part of what I am talking about is directing your focus on efforts that are either *problem focused* or *emotion focused* (Lazarus & Folkman, 1984). The difference is rather self-evident. Strategies that are emotion focused deal with how you feel, and with finding ways to feel better. This is often one's first reaction to stressors. Real progress usually requires that you look beyond how you feel at the moment to discover the under-

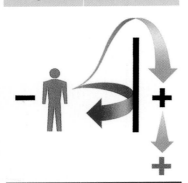

FIGURE 11.8
Reacting to frustration with learning is the most effective long-term reaction to stressors. That is, when one's goal-directed behaviors are continually blocked or thwarted, one should consider bringing about a relatively permanent change in those behaviors, or consider changing one's goals.

lying situation that has caused the present feelings—a problem-focused strategy.

(2) Remove or negate the stressor. Once a stressor has been identified, the next logical question is, "Can anything be done about it?" Do I *have* to stay in this situation, or can I institute a change? If an interpersonal relationship has become a constant, nagging source of stress, might this be the time to think about breaking it off? If the stress you experience at work has become overwhelming, might this be a good time to consider looking for a different job? The issue is one of taking control, of trying to turn a challenge into an opportunity. Remember: The tendency to take control of potentially stressful situations is one of the characteristics of persons with the so-called "hardy personality." Even people with a terminal illness fare much better if they take control, find out everything there is to know about their illness, seek second and third opinions, make the most of what time they have left, and so on (Folkman, 1984).

(3) Reappraise the situation. We should assess whether the stressors in our lives are real or (even partially) imagined threats to our well-being. Doing so is part of what is called a *cognitive reappraisal* of one's situation (e.g., Schultz & Decker, 1985). In the context of stress management, cognitive reappraisal means rethinking a situation to put it in the best possible light. Is that co-worker *really* trying to do you out of a promotion? Do you *really* care if you're invited to that party? *Must* you earn an A on the next test to pass the course? Are things *really* as bad as they seem? Lazarus (1993, p. 9) sees this as realizing that "people should try to change the noxious things that can be changed, accept those that cannot, and have the wisdom to know the difference"—a paraphrase of an ancient Hebrew prayer.

Meichenbaum (1977) argues that we can deal with lots of stress simply by talking to ourselves, replacing negative statements such as, "Oh boy, I'm really in trouble now. I'm sure I'll be called on and I'll embarrass myself in front of the whole class" with coping statements such as, "I'll just do the best I can. I bet I'm as prepared as anybody here; and in a little while this will all be over." This cognitive approach does take a bit of practice, but it can be very effective.

(4) Inoculate against future stressors. Among other things, this strategy involves accepting and internalizing much of what we have been saying about the universality of stress and stressors. It's a matter of convincing yourself that stress has occurred before, will occur again, and that this too will pass. It involves anticipation and preparation—truly coming to accept the reality that "worrying about this won't make it any better." We know, for example, that surgery patients recover faster and with fewer postsurgical complications if they are fully informed *before their surgery* what they can expect, how they are likely to feel, and (importantly) what they can do to aid in their own recovery (MacDonald & Kuiper, 1983).

Inoculating oneself against future stressors is also a matter of trying to develop a sense of optimism, where optimism may be defined as the belief that good things, as opposed to bad things, will generally happen in one's life. People with this sort of outlook "routinely maintain higher levels of subjective well-being during times of stress than do people who are less optimistic" (Scheier & Carver, 1993, p. 27). Optimism also predicts such things as better adjustments in one's first year away at college, less felt depression in mothers following childbirth, and quicker rate of recovery from

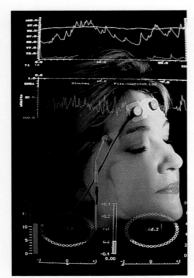

Biofeedback is an emotion-focused strategy for dealing with stressors. Even when effective, it won't remove the source of one's stress, but it can help one feel better.

heart surgery (Aspinwall & Taylor, 1992; Carver & Gaines, 1987; Scheier & Carver, 1992, 1993; Scheier et al., 1989).

(5) Take your time with important decisions. Stress often accompanies the process of making tough decisions. You're frustrated. A goal-directed behavior is being blocked. You have to decide if you will pursue a different course of action. Which course of action? Would it be wiser to change your goal? Remember we defined conflict in terms of making difficult decisions. Do you want to do this (+ and −), or do you want to do that (+ and −)? All I am implying in this strategy is that we make matters worse by rushing into a decision "just to have it over with." Occasionally we are faced with deadlines by which final decisions must be made. But in many cases, we add to an already stressful situation by racing to conclusions before we have all the facts, before we have explored the costs and benefits of our options (e.g., Hogan, 1989). For example, if you really can't make up your mind about a new car you're thinking about buying, why not rent one for a few days to see if you'll be happy with it?

So far, the strategies I've listed are designed to deal with stressors. They are "problem-focused" strategies and are, in the long run, effective ways of dealing with stress. In the meantime, however, there a few things that you can do to deal with the unpleasant affect or feelings that accompany stress (the "emotion-focused" strategies). We'll look at three.

(6) Learn techniques of relaxation. Learning effective ways to relax may not be as easy as it sounds, but the logic is simple: Feeling stressed and being relaxed are incompatible responses. If you can become relaxed, the experience (at least the feelings) of stress will be diminished (e.g., Lehrer & Woolfolk, 1984). Hypnosis may help. Meditation may help. So may relaxation training.

A variety of operant conditioning called biofeedback can provide relief from the tension associated with stress (Kamiya et al., 1977; Shirley et al., 1992; Yates, 1980). Biofeedback is "the process of providing information to an individual about his [or her] bodily processes in some form which he [or she] might be able to use to modify those processes" (Hill, 1985, p. 201). One's heart rate, let us say, is constantly monitored, and the rate is fed back to the person, perhaps in the form of an audible tone. As heart rate increases, the pitch of the tone becomes higher. As heart rate decreases, the tone gets lower. Once the learner knows (through the feedback) what his or her heart rate (or blood pressure, or muscle tension, and so on) is doing, a certain amount of control over that response is possible. The reinforcement involved is simply the newly gained knowledge that a desired change is being made. As a result of being reinforced, the stress-fighting responses increase in their frequency (Kaplan, 1991; Kimmel, 1974; Miller, 1978; Thackwray-Emerson, 1989).

(7) Engage in physical exercise. There is a body of evidence that claims that physical exercise can be a useful agent in the battle against stress (Brown, 1991; Crews & Landers, 1987; McCann & Holmes, 1984; Wheeler & Frank, 1988). Exercise may be helpful indirectly, improving physical health, stamina, self-esteem, and self-confidence. But of course, one must be careful. Deciding that tomorrow you'll start running five miles a day, rain or shine, may be a decision that may cause more stress than it reduces. It's important to choose an exercise program that is enjoyable, not overly strenuous, and that helps one feel better about oneself.

(8) Seek social support. Finally, I should mention the advantage of social support. Stress is a common experience. Perhaps no one else knows precisely how you feel, or has experienced exactly the same situation in which you find yourself, but all of us have known stress, and we are all aware of the sorts of situations that give rise to it. Social support from friends and relatives, or from physicians, clergy, therapists, or counselors, can be very helpful (Adler & Matthews, 1994; Coyne & Downey, 1991; Gottlieb, 1981; Hobfoll, 1986; Janis, 1983b; Jennison, 1992; Lieberman, 1983; Rook, 1987). If at all possible, one should not face stress alone.

Now that we've reviewed some of the steps one can take to help alleviate the unpleasantness of stress, let's consider some reactions stressors may produce that are not so adaptive.

● **Before You Go On**

What are some adaptive ways of dealing with stress?

Ineffective Strategies for Coping with Stressors

Simplistically speaking, if one experiences stress and does *not* do any of the things listed above, then that person is not dealing effectively with the stressors in his or her life. More than anything else, coping effectively with stress implies change. Not to change is to *fixate*, accepting the same stress from the same stressor. Fixation is seldom an adequate reaction to stress. Don't get me wrong here. "If at first you don't succeed, try, try, again." Of course; this is sound advice. But again, and again, and again? At some point one must be able to give up a particular course of action to try something else. In addition to not changing one's behaviors or goals, there are two other common reactions to stressors that are maladaptive: aggression and anxiety.

It is clear that there are many causes of aggression and that one thing that does motivate aggressive behavior is stress, particularly stress resulting from frustration. At one time, it was proposed that frustration was the only cause of aggression, an idea called the **frustration-aggression hypothesis** (Dollard et al., 1939). This point of view claimed that frustration produced several reactions, including aggression, but that aggression is always caused by frustration. We now believe that there many sources of aggression (some view it as an innate reaction, while others see it as a response learned through reinforcement or modeling). It is true, however, that frustration *is* a prime candidate as the cause of a great deal of aggression. It doesn't do much good in the long run, but a flash of aggressive behavior often does follow stress (Berkowitz, 1978, 1982, 1989, 1990).

There you are in the parking lot, trying to get home from class, and your car won't start. Over and over you crank the ignition. Now, totally frustrated, you swing open your door, get out, kick the front left fender, throw up the hood, and glower at the engine. You're mad! Having released a bit of tension, you might feel better for a few seconds, but being angry and kicking at the car, or yelling at someone who offers to assist won't help you solve your problem.

Another unfortunate consequence of stress is **anxiety**—a general feeling of tension, apprehension, and dread that involves predictable physiological changes. Anxiety is a very difficult concept to define precisely, but everyone "knows" what you're talking about when you refer to anxiety. It is a reaction that we all have experienced. Often, it is a reaction that follows or accompanies stress. In many ways we can think of anxiety as an unpleas-

frustration-aggression hypothesis
the view (now discredited) that all aggression stems from frustration

anxiety
a general feeling of tension, apprehension or dread that involves predictable physiological changes

Aggression that often follows frustration is an ineffective response because it does nothing to remove the stressor that caused the stress in the first place.

ant emotional component of the response to stressors. As much as anything else, we want to rid ourselves of stress in order to minimize our anxiety.

Sometimes the amount of stress and anxiety in one's life becomes more than one can cope with effectively. Feelings of anxiety start to interfere with natural, normal adaptation to the environment and to other people and can become the prime focus of one's attention. More anxiety follows, and more distress, and more discomfort, and more pain. For many people—tens of millions of people in the United States and Canada—the anxiety that results from the stress is so discomforting and so maladaptive that we may say they are suffering from a psychological disorder. In our next chapter we begin our discussion of psychological disorders, and we'll begin with the anxiety disorders. Please try to keep in mind when you get to that discussion just how commonplace stress and anxiety are—and where most anxiety comes from.

● **Before You Go On**

What are some maladaptive reactions to stressors?
What is the frustration-aggression hypothesis?

TOPIC 11B

HEALTH PSYCHOLOGY

Health psychology is a subfield of psychology just over 25 years old, although the issues involved have been of general concern for a very long time. Health Psychology became a division of the American Psychological

Association in 1978, and now has approximately 3,000 members—nearly a 200 percent increase over 1980 membership. **Health psychology** is the study of psychological or behavioral factors that affect physical health and illness. The involvement of psychologists in the medical realm of physical health and well-being is based on at least four assumptions:

1. Certain behaviors increase the risk of certain chronic diseases.
2. Changes in behaviors can reduce the risk of certain diseases.
3. Changing behaviors is often easier and safer than treating many diseases.
4. Behavioral interventions are comparatively cost-effective (Kaplan, 1984).

In this Topic, we'll look at two major thrusts of health psychology. We'll examine the relationship between psychological variables and physical health, an issue we anticipated in our last Topic when we saw that stress—a psychological reaction—can have serious physical consequences. Then we'll consider how psychologists are joining the fight against illness and disease.

health psychology
the field of applied psychology that studies psychological factors affecting physical health and illness

PSYCHOLOGICAL FACTORS THAT INFLUENCE PHYSICAL HEALTH

Is there a relationship between aspects of personality and a person's state of physical health? Can psychological evaluations of an individual be used to predict physical as well as psychological disorders? Is there a "disease-prone personality?" "Why do some people get sick and some stay well?" (Adler & Matthews, 1994, p. 229). Our responses are very tentative, and the data are not all supportive, but for now we can say, "Yes, there is a correlation between some personality characteristics and physical health."

One analysis of 101 published research articles looked for relationships between personality and physical disease (including coronary heart disease, asthma, ulcers, arthritis, headaches). The strongest associations were those that predicted coronary heart disease (CHD), although depression, anxiety, and anger or hostility were each associated to a degree with all of the physical disorders studied (Friedman & Booth-Kewley, 1987).

When we talk about relating personality variables to physical diseases, what commonly comes to mind is the **Type A behavior pattern (TABP)** and its relation to coronary heart disease. As it was originally defined, TABP referred to a competitive, achievement-oriented, impatient individual who generally is working at many tasks at the same time, is easily aroused, and is often hostile or angry (Friedman & Rosenman, 1959; Rosenman et al., 1964). Coronary heart disease is a general label given to a number of physical symptoms, including chest pains and heart attacks, caused by a build-up of substances (e.g., cholesterol) that block the supply of blood to the heart.

For nearly twenty years—from the early 1960s to the early 1980s—study after study found a clear, positive correlation between CHD and behaviors typical of the Type A personality (Jenkins, 1976; Rosenman et al., 1975; Wood, 1986). A panel of the National Institutes of Health declared the Type A behavior pattern an independent risk factor for heart disease (NIH Panel, 1981). It all seemed quite clear: Find people with the Type A

Type A behavior pattern (TABP)
a collection of behaviors or traits (competitive, achievement-oriented, impatient, easily aroused, often hostile or angry) often associated with coronary heart disease

behavior pattern, intervene to change their behaviors, and just watch how coronary heart disease rates decline. By now you know to be suspicious when complex problems seem to have such simple solutions.

Beginning in the early 1980s, data began to surface that failed to show a clear relationship between TABP and coronary heart disease (Fishman, 1987; Hollis et al., 1990; Krantz & Glass, 1984; Matthews, 1982, 1988; Shekelle et al., 1985; Wright, 1988). Perhaps people with Type A personalities were no more at risk for heart disease than anyone else. Perhaps studies that failed to find a relationship between TABP and CHD were seriously flawed. In fact, both these hypotheses have evidence to support them. For one thing, the Type A behavioral pattern *is* complex and difficult to diagnose. It is likely that simple paper-and-pencil inventories—of the sort used in many studies—fail to identify a large number of people with the TABP.

It also may be that the TABP is too global, or general, a pattern of behaviors (Adler & Matthews, 1994; Dembroski & Costa, 1987). Perhaps there is a subset of behaviors within the constellation of Type A behaviors that *does* predict coronary disease. This hypothesis is being investigated by many psychologists, including Logan Wright, a self-confessed Type A personality who had bypass surgery to relieve blockage of a coronary artery. As Wright put it, "if certain so-called active ingredients, or subcomponents of the TABP are what is really responsible for coronary-prone risk, one would expect to find them to correlate more highly with CHD than does the global Type A pattern itself" (1988, p. 3).

What are Wright's candidates for the most likely active ingredients of the Type A personality?

1. *Time urgency*—concern over wasting small bits of time; shifting lanes while in traffic to gain a car length
2. *Chronic activation*—the tendency to stay alert, aroused, and ready nearly all the time; being "fired up" for everything, no matter how silly or mundane
3. *Multiphasia*—the tendency to have a number of projects all going at once; having many irons in the fire; doing homework and eating while watching TV.

Some research indicates that these components do predict coronary heart disease, but the evidence isn't conclusive. Other research tells us that the most potent ingredients of a Type A personality are *anger* and *hostility* (Barefoot et al., 1983; Dembroski et al., 1985; Friedman et al., 1994; Houston & Vavak, 1991; Smith, 1992).

An analysis by Scott Lyness concluded that there is a correlation between the Type A behavior pattern and both heart rate and blood pressure levels (Lyness, 1993). What may be most significant about these findings is that there were no differences between Type A persons and Type B persons (people with none of the characteristics of Type A and who are relatively relaxed and easy going) *on baseline measures*. Differences appeared when people of these "personality types" were exposed to stressful situations. When responding to stressors, the Type A individuals showed significant increases in blood pressure and heart rate.

Lyness found no sex differences in Type A and Type B patterns. This finding is consistent with data from others who have found that women with Type A or Type B patterns are equally at risk for nonfatal heart attacks (Shekelle & Gale, 1985). On the other hand, Lynda Powell and her associates have found sex differences, but in a curious way (Powell et al., 1993).

These researchers found that after one has had an initial heart attack, women with a *Type B* behavior pattern are more likely than other women to have a subsequent heart attack. That is, there is a survival advantage for women with Type A behavior patterns following a heart attack (see Eaker et al., 1988, 1992).

More work needs to be done. We need research on adequately diagnosing Type A behavior patterns and on the mechanisms that underlie whatever relationships there may be between TABP and CHD. We also need research on how to bring about psychological changes in people to reduce the likelihood of their contracting any physical disease. The ingredients of the Type A personality are precisely the characteristics that many people in our society learn to value and imitate in their quest to "get ahead." How can psychologists best intervene to help people change behaviors that affect their health? It is to matters of intervention that we now turn.

● **Before You Go On**

Briefly summarize the relationship between the Type A behavioral pattern and coronary heart disease.

PROMOTING HEALTHY BEHAVIORS

At the very least, it is possible that some personality characteristics have an impact on one's physical health. The specific traits involved and the nature of that impact are the subject of debate and research. There is no debate and no doubt, however, that some behaviors put people at risk for certain physical disease and death. One role of the health psychologist is to help change potentially dangerous behaviors (Kirscht, 1983; Levine et al., 1993; Matarazzo, 1980; Miller, 1983).

Why Do People Die?

Obviously, people die for an almost infinite number of reasons. Ultimately, death is unavoidable. On the other hand, many deaths are "premature" and preventable.

Let's review a few gruesome statistics. The leading causes of death in the United States are cardiovascular disorders and cancers, diseases caused by the interaction of several factors, biological, social, environmental, and behavioral. Of the latter, such variables as cigarette smoking, nutrition, obesity, and stress have been identified as important risk factors (Krantz et al., 1985). This means that millions of people engage in what may be referred to as a deadly life-style. Here are some more numbers from a recent article in the *Journal of the American Medical Association*:

> In 1990 there were 2,148,000 deaths in the United States. Of these, 400,000 deaths could be traced to tobacco use; diet and activity patterns accounted for 300,000 deaths, alcohol use accounted for 100,000 deaths, microbial agents (bacteria and viruses) 90,000 deaths, toxic agents 60,000 deaths, firearms 35,000 deaths, sexual behaviors 30,000 deaths, motor vehicles 25,000 deaths, and illegal drug use 20,000 deaths (McGinnis & Foege, 1993, p. 2207).

Antismoking ads, such as this one from the American Cancer Society, are aimed at getting people to stop smoking—or not to start in the first place. Psychologists can have a powerful impact on physical health in that they can help reduce cigarette smoking.

In many of these cases, there was probably little or nothing that could be done to delay or prevent death. But in many cases, bringing about changes in behavior in a timely fashion might have reduced these numbers.

Notice that a deadly life-style may involve behaviors that directly lead to death, such as failure to wear safety belts, or knowingly engaging in unsafe behaviors at work or play. The Centers for Disease Control tell us that deaths by gunfire have surpassed deaths by traffic accidents. Nearly 50,000 children and teenagers were killed by firearms between 1979 and 1991—a number nearly equal to the American casualties in the Vietnam War. By early 1995, the leading cause of death among Americans ages 25–44 was AIDS.

Interventions designed to prevent health problems have been applied to a range of behaviors and situations, including smoking and the misuse of alcohol. Programs have been develped to try to change nutrition, physical fitness and exercise, diet, stress control, immunization, and unsafe sexual practices (Jeffery, 1989; McGinnis, 1985; Rodin & Salovey, 1989). Psychologists also use behavioral techniques in attempts to promote healthy and safe behaviors, such as the wearing of safety belts (Geller et al., 1987). Many psychologists argue that we should be doing all we can to help promote healthy environments (such as smoke-free areas, safe workplaces, air bags in cars), as well as working to change individual behaviors (Aldwin & Stokals, 1988; Fielding & Phenow, 1988; Geller et al., 1982; Stokals, 1992).

As an example of programs that seem to be having the desired effect—on behaviors, and ultimately on death rates—consider the organized attempts to get drinking drivers off the road. Students Against Drunk Driving (SADD) and Mothers Against Drunk Driving (MADD), among other action groups, have had an impact on politicians, who have changed state laws to reduce the legal limits for intoxication, raise minimum drinking ages, and increase the penalties for drinking and driving. In late 1994, the Centers for Disease Control reported that the number of intoxicated drivers involved in fatal accidents dropped 33 percent, from 21,780 in 1982 to 14,589 in 1993. Clearly, there is a long way to go, but at least the trend is in the right direction.

For the remainder of this Topic, we'll examine three areas in which psychologists have been particularly active: helping people to stop smoking, helping patients follow their doctors' orders, and—in a "Psychology in the Real World"—helping people deal with the reality of HIV and AIDS.

Helping People to Stop Smoking

Although efforts to effect attitudinal and behavioral change have been moving forward on all these fronts, few have received as much attention as efforts to discourage young people from smoking. One reason for the special efforts in this area is that smoking is so deadly, accounting for about one-third of all cancer deaths (Doll & Peto, 1981), and nearly 400,000 of all deaths each year (Jeffery, 1989). According to a 1994 estimate of the World Health Organization, smoking is the leading cause of premature death in the industrialized world, killing one person in the world every 10 seconds! The former Surgeon General of the United States, C. Everett Koop, has called cigarette smoking *the* most preventable cause of death in America. Cigarettes are viewed as one of the most addictive substances (Fiore et al., 1989; Schelling, 1992; Surgeon General, 1988). In the 1990s, concern includes the impact of "secondhand smoke," as we see emerging evidence that the children of parents who smoke are significantly at risk for lung cancer even if they, as adults, have never smoked. A 1994 analysis of data collected in 1985 claimed that secondhand smoke caused enough heart disease in nonsmokers to kill 62,000 Americans that year and cause 200,000 nonfatal heart attacks. Of particular concern is the fact that nearly *2.2 million* adolescents between the ages of 12 and 17 smoke cigarettes, and *9 million* children under the age of 5 years live with smokers. Each day, an estimated 3,000 children begin smoking, claims James Moller, president of the American Heart Association.

Yet another reason for concern among health psychologists is that the success rates of programs to persuade smokers to quit smoking have not been encouraging: nearly 80 percent of "quitters" relapse within a year (Cohen et al., 1989; Glasgow & Lichtenstein, 1987; Leventhal & Cleary, 1980). This statistic isn't quite as depressing as it sounds at first when we consider that a person who finally does give up smoking permanently has quit before—an average of five times. Quitters who can deal with other stressors in their lives effectively are significantly more likely to stay off cigarettes than are those quitters who experience additional stress (Cohen & Lichtenstein, 1990). One of the best predictors of whether an attempt to stop smoking will be successful is the absence of what Thomas Brandon (1994) calls "negative affect"—an aversive and unpleasant emotional state, related to anxiety and depression. Most smokers who quit permanently do so without any special program or intervention. And, in fact, the total number of smokers in the United States and Canada *is* decreasing, albeit at a rather slow rate (Hugick & Leonard, 1991).

Although there's obviously a very long way to go, psychologists have been reasonably successful designing programs aimed at getting people— teenagers in particular—to refrain from smoking in the first place. Given the pressures of national advertising by the tobacco industry, which some argue targets younger audiences, the effort has not been an easy one. Informational campaigns aimed at high school students *can* be effective (Evans et al., 1981). Approaches that use role models and peers to teach skills for resisting the pressure to begin smoking have been successful. These approaches emphasize short-term benefits, such as freedom from coughing and bad breath, and positive factors, such as improved appearance, while they downplay long-term benefits such as "living longer" (Murray et al., 1984).

● **Before You Go On**

Why do psychologists care about smoking behaviors, and what can be done about them?

Helping Patients "Follow Doctors' Orders"

In addition to designing and implementing programs aimed at preventing disease, health psychologists also intervene to help in the actual treatment of physical illness and disease (Meichenbaum & Turk, 1987; Rodin & Salovey, 1989). As an example of this sort of work, consider efforts to help patients comply with their physicians' orders. Even the best medical advice will be useless if it is not followed. I was surprised to learn that as many as 50 percent of patients fail to follow doctors' orders with regard to taking prescribed medicines (Adler & Stone, 1984; Andersen et al., 1994; DiMatteo & Friedman, 1988; Ley, 1977). This is particularly true when the illness produces no immediate discomfort or apparent risk (Rodin & Salovey, 1989). And most physicians fail to notice that their patients are not following orders (Witenberg et al., 1983).

Having an Impact on AIDS, the Deadly STD

Sexually transmitted diseases (STDs) are contagious diseases, usually passed on through sexual contact. They are common diseases, with very unpleasant and serious symptoms and consequences. The bacterial infection *chlamydia* affects nearly 4 million Americans every year. Approximately 2 million cases of *gonorrhea* and 100,000 cases of *syphilis* will be diagnosed this year alone. Estimates of the incidence of *genital herpes* claim that as many as 40 million Americans have this STD. These sexually transmitted diseases are common, but they are also very treatable. Drugs can alleviate symptoms (for genital herpes) and even cure the disease (for the others). What makes *acquired immune deficiency syndrome*, or *AIDS*, most worrisome is that it is one STD with no cure and no effective treatment. People with AIDS die. For the present, the only hope is behavioral intervention and prevention.

AIDS was virtually unknown in the United States before 1981. Just 12 years later, over 250,000 cases and 160,000 deaths had been reported. It is the fifth most common killer of women in the United States. Estimates of the World Health Organization are that, globally, nearly 20 million men and women will be infected by the year 2000. AIDS is caused by the *human immunodeficiency virus*, or *HIV*. The HIV almost always enters the body through sexual contact, or though the use of contaminated needles in intravenous (IV) drug use. About 1 child in 3 born to an HIV-positive mother will also be infected. An infected person may experience few symptoms at first, other than those associated with the common cold. Then the person enters a *carrier state*, when he or she may pass the virus on to others, yet remain symptom free. What is not yet clear is just how many persons infected with the HIV will develop AIDS, or how long the process takes. Of those whose HIV infection leads to full-blown AIDS, virtually all will die within four years.

"Behavior change remains the only means for primary prevention of HIV disease. Psychology should take a leading role in efforts to curtail this epidemic . . ." (Kelly et al., 1993, p. 1023). Attempts to prevent AIDS, or at the very least to reduce its spread, have met with mixed results. Successful interventions have been multifaceted, involving education, the changing of attitudes, increasing motivation to engage in safe (or safer) sexual practices, and providing

There are many reasons why patients fail to comply with the treatment plan prescribed by their doctors, including lack of communication between patient and doctor, the financial burden imposed by expensive medications, the disruption of daily routine required to follow the regimen of daily medication, and the lack of a clear vision of the advantage of doing so (e.g., Richardson et al., 1988).

Psychologists can assist in improving patient-physician communication with regard to medication and can assist patients in monitoring their daily medications. At the very least, it seems to help to give patients written instructions rather than oral instructions, although these benefits appear to be short-lived (Morris & Halperin, 1979). Consistent with the argument we made in the last Topic, providing social support for a patient will increase compliance with doctors' orders (Dunbar-Jacob et al., 1991). And consistent with what we said in Topic 6B, on operant conditioning, providing specific reinforcers for compliance is also effective (Epstein & Cluss, 1982).

people with the "negotiating skills (e.g., to say 'no' or 'please wear a condom')" to avoid high-risk situations (Brigham, 1992, p. 617).

Attempts to inform and educate have been reasonably successful. In 1987, the Surgeon General's office mailed a pamphlet about AIDS, and suggesting what could be done to avoid HIV infection, to every household in the United States. The effort was well received and has been credited for increasing the sales of condoms (Gerbert & Maguire, 1989; Moran et al., 1990). By and large, most Americans *are* aware of AIDS, do have a reasonable idea of what causes the disease, and are aware of what can be done to avoid it (Levine et al., 1993; Sheridan et al., 1990). What is discouraging is that even with considerable knowledge about HIV and AIDS, few people (teenagers in particular) seem willing to change their sexual practices (e.g., Hansen et al., 1990; Klepinger et al., 1993).

Programs that go beyond just providing information and actively seek to change behaviors *have* been effective—particularly when they are aimed at members of "high risk" populations such as gay men or IV drug users (DeJarlais & Friedman, 1988; Kelly et al., 1993; Stall et al., 1988). What works best are long-term, small-group sessions that present informa-

tion and then provide social support for changing high-risk behaviors (Kelly et al., 1989; Sorensen et al., 1991).

AIDS *is* a physical disease, but it is one with unprecedented psychological implications. Patients diagnosed with HIV, but who have not yet developed AIDS, are more depressed and disturbed than those who have developed the full-blown and fatal symptoms of the disease (Chuang et al., 1989). As you might expect, people with AIDS experience significant levels of stress, depression, anger, anxiety, and denial—reactions that need to be tended to (Herek & Glunt, 1988; Kelly & St. Lawrence, 1988; Namir et al., 1987). Males with AIDS are *7.5 times* more likely to commit suicide than are men in the general population (Coté et al., 1992). Because AIDS can be such a devastating disease, AIDS patients are often shunned—by loved ones and even health care professionals. In 1987, the American Medical Association felt it necessary to issue a statement declaring that it is unethical for a physician to refuse treatment to an AIDS patient. The fear, alienation, and stress experienced by HIV-positive and AIDS patients (and often by their friends and families) are in many ways as painful as the disease itself and often require psychological treatment (e.g., Knapp & VandeCreek, 1989).

As an example, many diabetics find it difficult to maintain their daily treatment regimens. Several strategies have proven useful for this purpose including:

1. *Specific assignments* that unambiguously define what is to be done
2. *Skill training* to develop new behaviors relevant to treatment
3. *Cueing* specific behaviors with salient stimuli; that is, telling the patient exactly what is to be done under specified conditions
4. *Tailoring* the regimen to meet the schedule and particular needs of the patient
5. *Contracts* between patient, therapist, and significant others for prescribed behavior change
6. *Shaping* of successive approximations of the desired treatment regimen

7. *Self-monitoring* of behaviors relevant to treatment
8. *Reinforcement* of new behaviors (Surwit et al., 1983, p. 260)

● **Before You Go On**

What are some of the ways health psychologists intervene to promote physical health?

THINKING CRITICALLY ABOUT PSYCHOLOGY, STRESS, AND PHYSICAL HEALTH

1. In Topic 11A, I mentioned for the second time that psychologists assume that one's behaviors are motivated or goal-directed (the first mention was in Topic 9A). Can you think of any behaviors for which this statement might not be true?
2. Is stress an emotion? Why or why not?
3. What is the relationship, if any, between a society's degree of "technology" or "civilization" and the likelihood of encountering environmental frustration? Do you suppose that frustration, stress, or anxiety were as common at the turn of the 20th century as they are now, at the turn of the 21st century?
4. Describe how each of the types of motivational conflicts could be demonstrated with rats. How relevant (or similar) are the behaviors of rats in these situations to the behaviors of people in similar situations?
5. How is it possible to reflect on all of the stressors in life and remain optimistic?
6. Recall the discussion of Freud's defense mechanisms in Topic 10A. Just where do these fit into our discussion of stressors, stress, and reactions to them?
7. Do you see any general sex differences in the manner in which people you know tend to deal with the stressors in their lives?
8. Freud "explained" war in terms of a death instinct (to oversimplify). How can the frustration-aggression hypothesis and our discussion of stress be used to "explain" war—or violence of any sort?
9. If stress can have an impact on one's physical health, how does one's physical health affect one's experience of stress?
10. Is a "workaholic" the same as a person with a Type A behavior pattern? Is being a "workaholic" necessarily a bad thing?
11. Imagine that you had to address a 7th grade class about the dangers of AIDS, and what they could do about it. What sorts of things would you tell the class?
12. Have you always followed your doctor's orders? Why or why not?

SUMMARY

TOPIC 11A
STRESS, STRESSORS, AND HOW TO COPE

- What is meant by frustration-induced stress?
- Define environmental and personal frustration.

Stress is a reaction to stressors in our lives, that is, reactions to real or perceived threats to one's sense of well-being. One source of stress is frustration—the blocking or thwarting of goal-directed behaviors. When something or someone in our environment blocks our goal-directed behaviors, we say that we are experiencing *environmental frustration*. When our goal-directed behaviors are thwarted by our own shortcomings, the frustration is referred to as *personal frustration*. The amount of stress we experience depends on both the importance of the goal we are seeking and the completeness or totality of the blocking or thwarting. *Pages 381–383.*

- Name and describe four types of motivational conflict.

Motivational conflicts are stressors. They are situations in which we find that we cannot achieve all of our goals because our own motives are in conflict. In an *approach-approach motivational conflict*, one is faced with two (or more) positive goals and must choose from among them. In an *avoidance-avoidance conflict*, a choice must be made among unpleasant, potentially punishing alternatives. In an *approach-avoidance conflict*, there is only one goal under consideration; in some ways that goal is attractive, while in other ways it is not—it both attracts and repels at the same time. Perhaps the most common conflict for humans is the *multiple approach-avoidance conflict* in which one faces a number of alternatives, each with its strengths and weaknesses. *Pages 383–385.*

- In what ways might simply being alive in the world produce stress?

Many psychologists argue that life events, particularly changes in one's life situation, act as stressors. The Social Readjustment Rating Scale (SRRS), for

example, is an attempt to measure the severity of life stress by having a person note recent life change events. Some events are rated as more stress-inducing than others. High scores on the SRRS have been correlated with increased incidence of physical illness. Some psychologists argue that little "hassles" in life are often more stress-producing than big, catastrophic events. The events of one's life that act as stressors need not, in themselves, be rated as negative or unpleasant events—they just bring unpleasant consequences. *Pages 385–387.*

- What does it mean to say that there are individual differences in reacting to stressors?
- Name and describe the three stages of Selye's general adaptation syndrome.

People often respond differently when presented with the same stressor. What some people find challenging, others find overwhelming. One's reaction to stressors also varies over time; what seemed stressful yesterday may not seem so tomorrow. Some individuals are particularly resistant to stressors and have what is called a "hardy personality." Such people tend to see challenges as opportunities, have a sense of being in control of their lives, and are fully engaged and committed to life. According to Hans Selye, a prolonged stress reaction progresses through three stages, collectively referred to as the general adaptation syndrome. At first there is mobilization of the sympathetic division of the ANS in an *alarm stage* as the body prepares to cope with the stressor. If the stressor is not removed, the body goes into a *resistance stage* in which resources continue to be mobilized but where new stressors are difficult to deal with and in which physical illness becomes more likely. If the stressor remains, one may finally enter the *exhaustion stage* in which the body's resources become depleted, adaptation breaks down, and serious illness or death may result. *Pages 387–389.*

- What are some adaptive ways of dealing with stress?

The only way to deal with stress effectively in the long run is to bring about a relatively permanent change in the situation or in one's self. That is, one must learn to change one's goal-directed behaviors or learn to modify one's goals. To think that one can deal with stress by avoiding stressors is unrealistic. In many cases, stress provides experiences that motivate new learning. Specific strategies for dealing with stressors include problem-focused and emotion-focused techniques. Among the former are: (1) identifying the stressor, (2) removing or negating the stressor, (3) cognitive reappraisal of the situation, (4) inoculating against future stressors, and (5) taking one's time with difficult decisions. Emotion-focused techniques include: (1) learning methods of relaxation, (2) engaging in physical exercise, and (3) seeking social support. *Pages 390–393.*

● What are some maladaptive reactions to stressors?
● What is the frustration-aggression hypothesis?

Unfortunately, many reactions to stressors are maladaptive or unhealthy, in both a physical and a psychological sense. They are maladaptive because they do nothing to remove the ultimate source of our stress. Maladaptive reactions to the experience of stress include *fixation* (trying the same unsuccessful behavior over and over), *aggression* (which may release tension momentarily but will not remove the stressor itself), and *anxiety*. The frustration-aggression hypothesis holds that frustration may produce several reactions, but that aggression is always caused by frustration. This view is now seen as overly simplistic, but there is no doubt that much aggression does, in fact, stem from frustration. *Pages 393–394.*

TOPIC 11B
HEALTHY PSYCHOLOGY

● Briefly summarize the relationship between the Type A behavioral pattern and coronary heart disease.

Many health psychologists believe there is a positive correlation between personality variables and physical health—that some psychological traits put one at risk for disease. Beginning in the late 1950s, evidence accumulated that showed a strong positive relationship between the Type A behavioral pattern (TABP) (typified by a competitive, achievement-oriented, im-

patient, easily aroused, often angry or hostile person, who tends to have many projects going at once) and coronary heart disease (blockage of major arteries). More recent evidence suggests that perhaps only some of the characteristics of TABP are predictors of coronary heart disease. The prime candidates for the moment are chronic hostility and anger. For women, a Type B behavior pattern may be a significant predictor of cardiovascular problems—particularly after an initial heart attack. *Pages 394–397.*

● Why do psychologists care about smoking behaviors, and what can be done about them?

Of the leading causes of death in the United States, most could be reduced by behavioral change. There are few behaviors that impact as directly on the state of one's health to a greater degree than smoking. It is a central part of what has been called a "deadly lifestyle." Smoking may account for as many as 400,000 deaths each year. Health psychologists continue to search for effective means of helping people to stop smoking. By and large, efforts have not met with much success. Most smokers that do quit permanently do so "on their own." Overall, the number of smokers *is* decreasing, and some efforts to get children and teenagers to avoid smoking in the first place have met with some success. *Pages 397–399.*

● What are some of the ways health psychologists intervene to promote physical health?

Reacting to the observation that approximately 70 percent of the causes of death in the United States are in large part determined by life-style behaviors that put an individual at risk, many health psychologists try to bring about changes in self-destructive behaviors such as smoking, the abuse of alcohol, overeating, and not exercising. Two recent areas of focus have been trying to keep adolescents from taking up smoking and educating people about safe sexual practices to reduce the epidemic of AIDS. Health psychologists assist in the actual treatment of physical disease as well; for example, helping patients to understand and to comply with physicians' orders. Health psychologists are also actively involved in efforts to deal directly with the emotional distress that accompanies the awareness that one has a serious or life-threatening physical disease. *Pages 399–402.*

TOPIC 11A

STRESS, STRESSORS, AND HOW TO COPE

11.1 A real or perceived threat to one's sense of well-being defines a) stress. b) anxiety. c) a psychological disorder. d) a stressor. *Pages 381–383.*

11.2 The concept of frustration is based on which basic assumption? a) People are basically good and well-meaning. b) Motivation and emotion both involve physiological reactions. c) All behavior is motivated, or goal-directed. d) Stress results from negative experiences. *Pages 381–383.*

11.3 Which of these is the best example of frustration? a) You get a flat tire on the way to an important meeting. b) You can't decide which courses to take next semester. c) Your best friend is going to get married. d) You win a lottery and now everybody wants to be your best friend. *Pages 381–383.*

11.4 Which of these provides the clearest example of personal frustration? a) Bob is unable to qualify for the city golf tournament. b) Yolanda has the stereo stolen from her new car. c) Tim gets a letter telling him the I.R.S. will be auditing his 1992 tax returns. d) The power goes out, erasing a term paper Louise was writing on her computer. *Pages 381–383.*

11.5 As adults, which conflict situation are we *least* likely to encounter? a) approach-approach b) avoidance-avoidance c) approach-avoidance d) multiple approach-avoidance. *Pages 383–385.*

11.6 Scott is going to get a new car, but can't decide if he wants a red one or a white one. Scott may be experiencing a(n)_____ conflict. a) approach-approach b) avoidance-avoidance c) approach-avoidance d) multiple approach avoidance. *Pages 383–385.*

11.7 True or False? Motivational conflicts are stressful only some of the time. *Pages 383–385.*

11.8 Which one word best describes the essential nature of motivational conflicts? a) blocking b) fatigue c) choice d) disappointment. *Pages 383–385.*

11.9 It is the position of Richard Lazarus that the real stressors we face in life are a) necessarily negative, unpleasant events that we try to avoid. b) those of which we are typically unaware. c) the little hassles of life, not big catastrophes. d) rated on a scale from 1 to 100. *Pages 385–387.*

11.10 Josh used to be able to play 36 holes of golf in a day with little apparent effort. Now, given his age and general physical condition, he finds it too tiring to play that much, a situation he finds stressful. We would best describe Josh's stress as induced by a) environmental frustration. b) personal frustration. c) motivational conflict. d) a perceived threat to resources. *Pages 385–387.*

11.11 True or False? To be alive in the world is to experience stress in some form or another. *Pages 387–389.*

11.12 Of these, which is the most effective or adaptive reaction to stress? a) learning b) frustration c) aggression d) simply giving up. *Pages 390–393.*

11.13 True or False? Stress is so unpleasant and so negative a reaction that we can say that the only way to be truly happy in life is to avoid stress altogether. *Pages 390–393.*

11.14 Of these mechanisms for coping with stress and stressors, which is the most inefficient or ineffective? a) engaging in cognitive reappraisal b) gathering social support c) fixating d) relaxation training. *Pages 393–394.*

11.15 True or False? The "frustration-aggression hypothesis" claims that all aggression results from frustration. *Pages 393–394.*

405

11.16 Which of these is most clearly a problem-focused, as opposed to an emotion-focused, strategy for coping with stress? a) seeking social support b) identifying the stressor c) engaging in a physical exercise program d) using biofeedback. *Pages 390–393.*

11.17 True or False? Stressors and stress affect nearly everyone in about the same way. *Pages 387–389.*

11.18 Biofeedback is essentially an application of a) common sense. b) the medical model of stress reduction. c) operant conditioning. d) Freudian psychotherapy. *Pages 390–393.*

11.19 True or False? When faced with difficult, stress-inducing decisions, the best thing to do is simply to decide quickly and get the decision over with. *Pages 393–394.*

TOPIC 11B

HEALTH PSYCHOLOGY

11.20 Whereas clinical psychology is concerned with psychological disorders, the field of health psychology is concerned with a) persons who do not have and have never had psychological disorders. b) personality disorders. c) physical health and well-being. d) only psychological disorders that have physical symptoms. *Pages 394–397.*

11.21 Positive correlations between personality variables and physical health are generally for associations that predict a) stomach problems, such as ulcers. b) skin rashes and disorders. c) coronary heart disease. d) many varieties of cancer. *Pages 394–397.*

11.22 Which characteristic or description is *not* included in the Type A behavior pattern, or TABP? a) high cholesterol levels b) lack of patience c) achievement orientation d) general hostility. *Pages 394–397.*

11.23 Logan Wright suggests that there are three "active ingredients" of the Type A behavior pattern. Which of the following is *not* one of these three? a) time urgency b) perfectionism c) chronic activation d) multiphasia. *Pages 394–397.*

11.24 What one behavior change would have the greatest impact on physical health of those living in the United States? a) stopping smoking b) eating less saturated fat c) drinking less caffeine d) using condoms. *Pages 397–399.*

11.25 Psychologists estimate that of the 10 leading causes of death in the United States, _____ are in large part behaviorally determined. a) 1 b) 3 c) 5 d) 7. *Pages 397–399.*

11.26 With regard to cigarette smoking, which statement is *false*? a) There would be 100,000 fewer deaths in the United States if no one smoked. b) Secondhand smoke is unrelated to lung cancer. c) About 80 percent of those who quit smoking start up again within a year. d) We're better at getting people not to start smoking than we are at getting smokers to stop. *Pages 397–399.*

11.27 True or False? As many as 50 percent of patients fail to follow their doctor's orders with regard to taking prescribed medications. *Pages 399–402.*

THE PSYCHOLOGICAL DISORDERS

12

PREVIEW

TOPIC 12A—Defining and Classifying Psychological Disorders

Just What *Is* "Abnormal"?

The Classification of Abnormal Reactions

PSYCHOLOGY IN THE REAL WORLD: Attention-Deficit, Hyperactivity Disorder—Not Just for Children Anymore

TOPIC 12B—A Sampling of Psychological Disorders

Anxiety Disorders

Somatoform Disorders

Dissociative Disorders

Personality Disorders

Delirium, Dementia, Amnestic, and Other Cognitive Disorders—The Example of Alzheimer's

Mood Disorders

Schizophrenia

THINKING CRITICALLY ABOUT THE PSYCHOLOGICAL DISORDERS

SUMMARY

TEST YOURSELF

PREVIEW

This chapter begins our discussion of psychological disorders, a discussion that we'll continue in Chapter 13. If we can say nothing else about psychological disorders, we can acknowledge that they are unpleasant, distressful, painful, and often devastating in their effects. We can also acknowledge that psychological disorders have an impact on us all. I will spare you a lengthy recitation of statistics on incidence and prevalence here—we'll talk about these data as we cover specific disorders. For now, we note that the best estimates tell us that as you read this sentence, approximately 28 percent of adults in the United States—nearly 50 million men and women—are suffering from a psychological disorder, and fewer than one-third of those are seeking help for their problems (National Institute of Mental Health, 1984, 1993; Offord et al., 1987). Another claim is that at any point in time, "one in five Americans has mental illness" (Anderson et al., 1987; Baker & Richardson, 1989). A recent study tells us that in their lifetimes, nearly half of all Americans will suffer from a psychological disorder (Kessler et al., 1994). In many respects, statistics such as these are both astounding and frightening; they are also impersonal. It is difficult to conceptualize what it means to say that tens of millions of persons are suffering from a psychological disorder. What we can say is that it is unlikely that any of us can be exempt from personally experiencing, or having someone close to us experience, the pain and suffering of psychological disorders.

Topic 12A covers matters of definition, classification, and labeling. Once we have an idea of what it means to use the term "abnormal" in a psychological context, we'll review, in Topic 12B, several of the more common and the more bizarre psychological disorders

TOPIC 12A

DEFINING AND CLASSIFYING PSYCHOLOGICAL DISORDERS

We all have a basic idea of what is meant by such terms as *abnormal, mental illness,* and *psychological disorder.* The more we think about psychological abnormality, however, the more difficult it becomes to define. In this Topic, we'll do two things: We'll generate a working definition of abnormal from a psychological perspective, and we'll consider some of the implications of classifying and labeling psychological disorders.

What is considered abnormal or deviant in one culture may be quite normal in another. Cultures vary in many respects, including styles of dress. This Arab woman's layered clothing (right) is in sharp contrast to the way these Bororo people of West Africa are dressed (left).

JUST WHAT *IS* "ABNORMAL"?

The concept of abnormal as it is used in psychology is a complex one. We'll use this definition: **Abnormal** means maladaptive cognitions, affect, and/or behaviors that are at odds with social or cultural expectations and that result in distress and discomfort. That's a lengthy definition, but to be complete our definition needs to include each of these crucial points.

Literally, abnormal means "not of the norm" or "not average." Thus, behaviors or mental processes that are rare should be considered abnormal, and *in a literal sense*, of course, they are. The problem is that this statistical approach would identify the behaviors of Michael Jordan, Jane Pauley, Robert Frost, Mother Theresa, and David Letterman as abnormal. Statistically, they *are* rare or abnormal; there are few others who do what these people do (or did). But, as far as we know, none of these people has (or had) a psychological disorder.

The reactions of people with a psychological disorder are *maladaptive.* This is a critical part of our definition. Thoughts, feelings, and behaviors are such that the person with a disorder does not function as well as he or she could without it. To be different or to be strange does not in itself mean that someone has a psychological disorder. There must be some degree of impairment, some interference with growth and functioning (Carson & Butcher, 1992, p. 8).

An observation reflected in our definition is that abnormality may show itself in a number of different ways. A person with a disorder may experience abnormal *affect*, engage in abnormal *behaviors*, have abnormal *cognitions*, or a combination of these. Once again we see our ABCs from Chapter 1.

abnormal

maladaptive cognitions, affect, and/or behaviors that are at odds with social or cultural expectations and that result in distress or discomfort

FIGURE 12.1
Culture-Specific Syndromes

Syndrome	Culture	Symptoms
amok	Maylay	acute indiscriminate homicidal mania
koro	Chinese, S.E. Asia	fear of retraction of penis into abdomen with the belief that this will lead to death
latah	S.E. Asia	startle-induced disorganization, hyper-suggestibility, automatic obedience
piblokto	Eskimo	attacks of screaming, crying, and running naked through the snow
windigo	Canadian Indians	delusions of being possessed by a cannabalistic monster (Windigo), attacks of agitated depression, oral sadistic fears and impulses

From The American Psychiatric Association's *Psychiatric Glossary*, 1984, p. 25 [Published and distributed by the American Psychiatric Press, Inc., 1400 K Street, Washington, DC 20005].

Any definition of psychological abnormality has to acknowledge *social and/or cultural* expectations. What may be clearly abnormal and disordered in one culture may be viewed as quite normal or commonplace in another. In some cultures, loud crying and wailing at the funeral of a total stranger is thought to be strange or deviant; in others, it is common and expected. To claim that you've been communicating with dead ancestors would be taken as a sign of severe disturbance in some cultures; in others, it would be treated as a great gift (see Figure 12.1). Even in our own culture, behaviors that are appropriate—or at least tolerated—in one situation, say a party, may be judged quite inappropriate in another context, such as a religious service.

One additional issue needs to be addressed: Psychological disorders involve *distress* or *discomfort*. People we consider abnormal are suffering, or are the source of suffering in others. Psychological disorders cause emotional distress, and people with psychological disorders are often the source of distress and discomfort to others—friends and family who care and worry about them.

As complex as it is, I hope you can see that there is a reason for each point in our definition of abnormal: behaviors or mental processes that are maladaptive, at odds with social/cultural expectations, and result in distress or discomfort.

● **Before You Go On**

How do we define psychological abnormality?

THE CLASSIFICATION OF ABNORMAL REACTIONS

One way of dealing with the broad concept of psychological abnormality is to consider each psychological disorder separately, in terms of how it is diagnosed. **Diagnosis** is the act of recognizing a disorder on the basis of specified symptoms. Then, once we have described individual disorders, it would help if we could organize them in some systematic way.

Systems of classification are common in science and not new to psychology. In 1883, Emil Kraepelin published the first significant classification scheme for what he called "mental disturbances." It was based on the premise that each disorder had its own identifying symptoms and a specific biological cause.

The DSM Series

In 1952, the American Psychiatric Association first published its system for classifying psychological disorders, a book called the *Diagnostic and Statistical Manual of Mental Disorders*, which became known as the *DSM*. In 1987, a revised version of the third edition, the *DSM-III-R* was published. Even before the *DSM-III-R* was available, work had begun on its revision, the **DSM-IV**, which was published in 1994.

The *DSM* series is the system of classification most widely used in all mental health fields. We'll follow the general outline of the *DSM-IV* in Topic 12B. Figure 12.2 presents a partial listing of the disorders listed in the *DSM-IV* and shows a few of the subtypes for each major category of disorder.

In fact, the *DSM-IV* is more than just an organized list of disorders in terms of symptoms. The *DSM-IV* recommends that a diagnosis of any disorder be sensitive to: (1) any physical illnesses or ailments present, (2) the amount of stress the person has experienced recently, and (3) the level of adaptive functioning the person has managed over the past three years. Except for cases for which there are known biological causes, the manual attempts to avoid any reference to the **etiology**, or causes, of disorders. It is meant to be objective, to be based on research evidence, to describe as completely as possible, and to theorize as little as possible. The *DSM-IV* also contains much more material and references to ethnic and cultural issues than did its predecessor, thanks largely to a three-year effort of the "Group on Culture and Diagnosis," sponsored by the National Institute of Mental Health (DeAngelis, 1994).

There are many advantages to having a classification scheme for psychological disorders. The major advantage, of course, is ease of communication. If I mean one thing when I use the term *phobia*, and you mean something quite different, we cannot hold a very reasonable conversation about your patient's problem. If we both agreed on the *DSM-IV*'s definition, we would at least be using the term in the same way. A related advantage is that a reliable way of classifying disorders allows psychologists to think in terms of how best to prescribe appropriate treatment or therapy. I cannot leave the impression that there is but one appropriate treatment for each of the categories in the *DSM-IV*. As we'll see in Chapter 13, on treatment and therapy, that is far from the case, but it certainly makes sense that we be able to classify disorders before we treat them. At the same time, classification can cause difficulties.

diagnosis
the act of recognizing a disorder on the basis of the presence of particular symptoms

DSM-IV
a publication of the American Psychiatric Association that lists, organizes, and describes psychological disorders

etiology
the source or cause; in this context, of psychological disorders

FIGURE 12.2
A Sample of Psychological Disorders Listed in the DSM-IV

Type of disorder	Subtypes (examples)
Disorders usually first diagnosed in infancy, childhood, or adolescence	a. Mental retardation b. Learning disorders c. Autistic disorder
Delirium, dementia, amnestic, and other cognitive disorders	a. Dementia of the Alzheimer's type
Substance-related disorders	a. Alcohol use disorders b. Amphetamine use disorders c. Cocaine use disorders d. Hallucinogen disorders
Schizophrenia and other psychotic disorders	a. Schizophrenia
Mood disorders	a. Depressive disorders b. Dysthymic disorder c. Bipolar disorder
Anxiety disorders	a. Panic disorder b. Specific phobia c. Obsessive-compulsive disorder d. Posttraumatic stress disorder e. Generalized anxiety disorder
Somatoform disorders	a. Conversion disorder b. Hypochondriasis
Dissociative disorders	a. Dissociative amnesia b. Dissociative fugue c. Dissociative identity disorder
Eating disorders	a. Anorexia nervosa b. Bulimia
Personality disorders	a. Paranoid personality disorder b. Schizoid personality disorder c. Antisocial personality disorder d. Histrionic personality disorder e. Narcissistic personality disorder

Problems with Classification and Labeling

Assigning labels to people may be useful for communication purposes, but it can be dehumanizing. It is occasionally difficult to remember that Sally Jane is a complex and complicated human being with a range of feelings, thoughts, and behaviors, not just a "paranoid schizophrenic." In response to this concern, the *DSM-IV* refers only to disordered behaviors and patterns of behaviors, not to disordered people. That is, it refers to paranoid reactions, not to people who are paranoid; to persons with anxiety, not anxious persons.

A second problem inherent in classification and labeling is that it is so easy to fall into the habit of believing that labels *explain*, when clearly they don't. Accurately diagnosing and labeling a pattern of behaviors does not explain those behaviors. It does not tell us why such a pattern of behaviors developed or what we can or should do about them now.

Third, labels often create unfortunate and lasting stigmas of negative attitudes about people. To learn that someone is "mentally ill" or has a "psychological disorder" often carries with it a wide range of negative reactions, and the labels may stick long after the disorder has been treated and the symptoms are gone.

One final consequence of diagnostic labeling is that the brunt of the problem tends to fall on the individual person. It is a person who has a psychological disorder; not the group, the family, or the society of which the person is a part. Classification schemes focus on the person and not on the context in which people live (Gorenstein, 1984; Szasz, 1960, 1982). This issue is quite complex and has been debated within psychology for years. Here's an example of this difficulty: Mary Beth, a third-grader, is referred to the school psychologist because she is withdrawn, often seems to be on the verge of tears, will not talk about her home life, and is doing poorly in her academic work. Without going into the particulars, doesn't it seem misguided to focus all of our attention on Mary Beth, disregarding her family or the demands of the school, as we try to diagnose her problems? Is it proper to diagnose and label the individual without attending to the larger social networks of which that person is a part?

So far I have used terms such as *mental illness, psychological disorder,* and *mental disorder* interchangeably. I'll continue to do so because the differences among such terms are of no real consequence. There is a term, however, with which we need to exercise particular care, and that is *insanity.*

On "Insanity"

Insanity is not a psychological term. It is a legal term. It is related to problems with psychological functioning, but in a rather restricted sense. Definitions of **insanity** vary from state to state, but to be judged insane usually requires evidence that a person did not know or fully understand the consequences of his or her actions at a given time, could not discern the difference between right and wrong, and was unable to exercise control over his or her actions.

A related issue has to do with whether a person is in enough control of his or her mental and intellectual functions to understand courtroom procedures and aid in his or her own defense. If one is not, one may be ruled "not competent" to stand trial for his or her actions, whatever those actions may have been.

We now turn our attention to specific psychological disorders. I won't bring up all of the disorders discussed in the *DSM-IV.* Instead, I'll choose some of the more common disorders. To do much more than describe some of these disorders is beyond the scope of this introductory text. The intent is simply to give you an idea of what psychological disorders are like.

insanity
a legal term involving judgments of diminished capacity and the inability to tell right from wrong

● **Before You Go On**

What is the *DSM-IV*?

What are some of the advantages and disadvantages of classifying psychological disorders?

Attention-Deficit/Hyperactivity Disorder — Not Just for Children Anymore

The *DSM-IV* lists nearly a dozen "Disorders First Diagnosed in Infancy, Childhood, or Adolescence." One of the most common is *attention-deficit/hyperactivity disorder (ADHD)*. Actually, we've got three disorders here under this one label. There is attention deficit disorder (ADD), characterized by a failure to attend to details; messy, careless work; difficulty persisting with a task; failure to listen when spoken to; distractibility; and the like. There is also hyperactivity, characterized by fidgeting and squirming when seated, leaving one's seat to run about, difficulty in playing quietly, incessant talking, and difficulty waiting for one's turn. And, of course, there is the—more common—combination of the two. Diagnosis of this set of disorders requires that symptoms have been present before age 7. It is estimated that ADHD is an appropriate diagnosis for as many as 10 percent of school-age children (Ciaranello, 1993). ADHD occurs in several cultures, and is 4 to 8 *times* more likely to be found in boys than in girls (e.g., Friedman & Doyal, 1987).

These disorders were first described in 1902 by Dr. George Still, a British pediatrician who, even then, theorized that the behaviors of his patients were due to an interference with proper brain functioning rather than inappropriate parenting. The disorder has also been called "minimal brain dysfunction" and "hyperactive child syndrome." There still is little doubt that the behavioral problems of a child with ADHD involve an interference with normal brain functioning, perhaps related to thyroid gland activity (e.g. Ciaranello, 1993). Stimulant drugs such as Ritalin, Dexedrine, and Cylert are often prescribed for the disorder, and at least three-

quarters of patients respond favorably to such drug treatment. The theory is that the drugs help the brain filter out distracting or irrelevant stimuli, thus increasing the ability to attend and concentrate—and we've already seen how important attention is in information processing, learning, and memory.

Only a decade ago, most physicians believed that children would simply outgrow attention-deficit/hyperactivity disorder, usually by the time they reached puberty. We now know that this syndrome can continue into adulthood. Estimates are that as few as 30 percent to as many as 80 percent of children with ADHD will continue to show symptoms of the disorder through adolescence and into adulthood. Think about it. Do you know anyone who seems constantly restless, can't "sit still," has held numerous jobs, has difficulty following through with nearly any task, and whose mind seems to "wander" from time to time? You may know an adult with ADHD. The disorder in adults need not be as disruptive as it usually is in children—if some of that "hyper" energy can be channeled in the right direction. Some believe that Ben Franklin, Winston Churchill, and Albert Einstein had ADHD as adults. There is a down side to adult attention-deficit disorder, of course. Adults with ADHD do show signs of other psychological disorders (comorbidity, yet again), have a high rate of drug abuse and demonstrate more antisocial behaviors. With adults, then, therapy often comes down to finding acceptable ways to manage and focus their extra energy into productive daily activities. Medication may also be warranted when the diagnosis of ADHD is properly made.

TOPIC 12B

A SAMPLING OF PSYCHOLOGICAL DISORDERS

As we quickly go through the listing of psychological disorders in this Topic, there are a few important points I'd like you to keep in mind.

1. Abnormal and normal are not two distinct categories. They may be thought of as endpoints on some dimension we can use to describe people, but there is a large gray area between the two where distinctions get fuzzy.

2. Abnormal does not mean dangerous. True, some people diagnosed as having a mental disorder *may* do great violence to themselves or to others, but most people with psychological disorders are not dangerous at all. Even among persons who have been in jail for violent crimes, those with psychiatric disorders have no more subsequent arrests than do persons without disorders (Teplin et al., 1994).

3. Abnormal does not mean bad. People diagnosed with a psychological disorder are not "bad people," or "weak people," or people with "no will power," in any evaluative sense. They may have done bad things, and bad things may have happened to them, but it is not in psychology's tradition to make moral judgments about people.

4. Most of our depictions of psychological disorders will be made in terms of extreme and obvious cases. Psychological disorders, like physical disorders, can occur in mild or moderate forms. As we have seen repeatedly, no two people are exactly alike; there are individual differences in psychological functioning. Such is also the case here. No two people, even with the same diagnosis of a psychological disorder, will be exactly alike in all regards.

Unless I specify otherwise, diagnostic criteria for psychological disorders are taken from the *DSM-IV*, and the statistics on the prevalence of the disorders are from the *DSM-IV*, the National Institute of Mental Health (Freedman, 1984), or the National Comorbidity Survey (Kessler et al., 1994).

ANXIETY DISORDERS

In Topic 11A, we defined **anxiety** as a feeling of apprehension or dread accompanied by such physiological changes as increased muscle tension, shallow, rapid breathing, cessation of digestion, increased perspiration, and drying of the mouth. Thus anxiety involves two levels of reaction: subjective feelings (dread or fear) and physiological responses (e.g., rapid breathing). The major symptom of the *anxiety disorders* is felt anxiety, often coupled with "avoidance behaviors," or attempts to resist or get away from any situation that seems to produce anxiety.

Anxiety disorders are the most common of all the psychological disorders. The National Institute of Mental Health reports high rates: within any 6-month period, from 7 to 15 percent of the population can be diagnosed with one or more of the several anxiety diagnoses. The National Comorbidity Survey claims that 17 percent of those surveyed had some anxiety disorder in the year before the survey was taken, and 24.5 percent had an anxiety disorder at some time in their lives. Others have reported similar estimates (Reich, 1986; Weissman, 1988). Anxiety disorders are two to three times more common in women than in men (Kessler et al., 1994; Roth & Argyle, 1988). Percentages of this sort do not begin to convey the magnitude of the problem. We're talking about real people here—people like you and me. In this section, we'll consider five types of anxiety disorders: generalized anxiety disorder, panic disorder, phobic disorder, obsessive-compulsive disorder, and posttraumatic stress disorder.

anxiety
a general feeling of apprehension or dread accompanied by predictable physiological changes

Generalized Anxiety Disorder

The major symptom of the **generalized anxiety disorder** is distressing, felt anxiety. Here we have unrealistic, excessive, and persistent worry. People with generalized anxiety disorder report "substantial interference with their life . . . and a high use of medication" because of their symptoms (Wittchen et al., 1994). The *DSM-IV* added the criterion that people with this disorder find it difficult to control their anxiety or worry. The anxiety they experience may be very intense, but it is also quite diffuse, meaning that it does not seem to be brought on by anything specific in the person's environment. The anxiety just seems to come and go (or stay) without reason or warning. People with this disorder are almost always in some state of uneasiness, and seldom have a clear idea of what is causing the anxiety they are experiencing. The self-reports of persons with generalized anxiety disorder show that their major concerns are with (in order): an inability to relax, tenseness, difficulty concentrating, feeling frightened, being afraid of losing control, and so on (Beck & Emery, 1985).

Although people with this disorder can usually continue to function in social situations and on the job, they may be particularly prone to drug and alcohol abuse (Wittchen et al., 1994). This point is an important one. **Comorbidity** refers to having two or more diseases or illnesses at the same time. The 1994 National Comorbidity Survey found that the prevalence of psychological disorders was even greater than had been suspected. It also demonstrated that of people who experience a disorder in their lifetime, most (79 percent) will experience two or more different disorders. Where 52 percent of those surveyed never had any psychological disorder, 14 percent had a history of three or more disorders (Kessler et al., 1994).

● **Before You Go On**
Describe the symptoms of generalized anxiety disorder.
What is comorbidity, and what is its significance?

Panic Disorder

In the generalized anxiety disorder, the experience of felt anxiety may be characterized as *chronic*, implying that the anxiety is nearly always present, albeit sometimes more than at other times. For a person suffering from **panic disorder**, the major symptom is more acute—a recurrent, unpredictable, unprovoked onset of sudden, intense anxiety, or a "panic attack." Attacks may last for a few seconds or for hours. Significantly, there is no particular stimulus to bring it on. The panic attack is unexpected. It just happens. Because of that, a complication of this disorder is that a person with panic disorder soon begins to fear the next attack and the loss of control that it will bring. The *DSM-IV* is quite clear on the point that panic attacks can occur in conjunction with other disorders. They're not restricted to panic disorder. With panic disorder, however, it is the recurrent pattern of attacks and a building worry about future attacks that are significant.

At some point in their lives, between 1.5 and 3.5 percent of the adult population will experience panic disorder. (That doesn't sound very significant until we realize that that's 4 to 9 million people!) The age of onset for panic disorder is commonly the mid-twenties (Hayward et al., 1992; Markowitz et al., 1989). Initial panic episodes are commonly associated with stress, particularly from the loss of an important relationship (Ballenger, 1989). A complication of panic disorder is that it is often accompanied by feelings of depression (Noyes et al., 1990). This may be why the rate of suicide and suicide attempts is so high for persons with this diagnosis (20 percent), a rate higher than for those diagnosed with depression alone (15 percent) (Johnson et al., 1990; Weissman et al., 1989).

● **Before You Go On**

What is a panic disorder?

Contrast panic disorder with generalized anxiety disorder.

Phobic Disorder

The essential feature of a **phobic disorder** (or phobia) is a persistent fear of some object, activity, or situation that consistently leads a person to avoid that object, activity, or situation. Implied in this definition is the notion that the fear is intense enough to be disruptive or debilitating. The definition also implies that there is no real or significant threat involved in the stimulus that gives rise to a phobia; the fear is unreasonable, exaggerated, or inappropriate.

There are many things in this world that are life-threatening and downright frightening. If, for example, you were driving down a rather steep hill and suddenly realized that the brakes on your car were not working, you would be likely to feel an intense reaction of anxiety. Such a reaction would not be phobic, because it is not *irrational*. Similarly, there are few of us who enjoy the company of large numbers of bees. Just because we don't like bees and would rather they weren't around does not qualify us as having a phobic disorder. What's missing is the *intensity* of the response. People who have a phobic reaction to bees (called mellissaphobia) often will refuse to leave the house in the summer for fear of encountering a bee, and become genuinely upset and anxious at the buzzing sound of any insect, fearing it to be a bee. People with this disorder may be uncomfortable simply reading a paragraph such as this one about bees.

There are many different types of phobias, and the incidence of the disorder is quite high. Within one year, nearly 15 percent of the population

phobic disorder
an intense, irrational fear that leads a person to avoid the feared object, activity, or situation

Working as a steel worker, laboring high above the city, would be out of the question for someone suffering from acrophobia, the fear of high places. Similarly, someone with agoraphobia would find sitting in a crowd unbearably anxiety producing.

FIGURE 12.3
A Sample of Phobic Reactions

Phobia	Is a fear of
Acrophobia	High places
Agoraphobia	Open places
Algophobia	Pain
Astraphobia	Lightning and thunder
Autophobia	One's self
Claustrophobia	Small, closed places
Hematophobia	Blood
Monophobia	Being alone
Mysophobia	Dirt or contamination
Nyctophobia	The dark
Pathophobia	Illness or disease
Pyrophobia	Fire
Thanatophobia	Death and dying
Zoophobia	Animals

prognosis
the prediction of the future course of an illness or disorder

agoraphobia
a phobic fear of open places, of being alone, or of being in public places from which escape might be difficult

experiences a phobic disorder. Most phobias are named after the feared object or activity. Figure 12.3 lists a few phobic reactions. Most involve a fear of animals—although these phobias are not the ones for which people most commonly seek treatment (Costello, 1982). Many college students experience an intense and irrational fear of public speaking. In some cases, the person with a phobic disorder can successfully avoid the source of fear, and as a result never seek treatment. Sometimes avoiding the source of one's phobia is impossible. Fortunately, the **prognosis** (the prediction of the course of a disorder) is good for phobic disorders. That is, therapy for persons with phobic disorder is likely to be successful. You might want to review our earlier discussion of phobias (in Topic 6B) where we examined possible causes and treatments for simple phobias.

One of the most commonly *treated* phobic disorders is **agoraphobia**, which literally means "fear of open places." This fear is not reserved for those occasions in which one stands in the middle of a large open field, however. The diagnosis is for people who have an exaggerated fear of being alone, or venturing forth into the world where they may be trapped in an unpleasant or embarrassing situation. People with agoraphobia avoid crowds, streets, stores, and the like. They establish a safe home base for themselves and, in extreme cases, refuse to leave it altogether. It is common to find agoraphobia as an associated complication of panic disorder (comorbidity again). After experiencing several panic attacks—brought on by no particular stimulus, remember—one finds it more and more difficult to venture out in the world, for fear of having yet another panic attack in some public place.

● **Before You Go On**
What are the essential characteristics of a phobic disorder?

Obsessive-Compulsive Disorder (OCD)

The **obsessive-compulsive disorder (OCD)** is an anxiety disorder characterized by a pattern of recurrent obsessions and compulsions. **Obsessions** are ideas or thoughts that involuntarily and constantly intrude into awareness. Generally speaking, obsessions are pointless, groundless thoughts, most commonly of violence, disease, danger, or doubt (Swedo et al., 1989). Many of us have experienced obsessive-like thoughts. Worrying throughout the first few days of a vacation if you really did turn off the stove would be an example. Have you ever awakened to a radio that was playing some particular song? As you take your morning shower, the lyrics keep coming to mind. Even as you get dressed, you hear yourself humming the same song. Driving to work, you still think about it. You have the feeling that "I can't get that song out of my head!" Imagine having an idea like that constantly interrupting, constantly coming to mind, day after day, whenever you were not consciously focusing your attention on something else. To qualify as a symptom of OCD, obsessions must be disruptive; they must interfere with normal functioning. They are also time consuming and the source of anxiety and distress.

Compulsions are constantly intruding repetitive acts or behaviors. The most commonly reported compulsions involve hand washing, grooming, and counting or checking behaviors, such as checking over and over again to be sure that the door is really locked (Swedo et al., 1989a). Again, from your own experience, have you ever found yourself walking along on a sidewalk, avoiding the cracks in the pavement? Have you ever checked your answer sheet to see that you've *really* answered all of the questions and then checked it again, and again, and again? To do so is a compulsive sort of response. It serves no real purpose, and provides no real sense of satisfaction, although it is done very conscientiously. The person with OCD recognizes that these behaviors serve no useful purpose, but cannot stop them. It is as if she or he engages in these behaviors in order to prevent some other (more anxiety-producing) behaviors from taking place.

In extreme cases, a particular obsession or compulsion may come to exert an enormous influence on a person's life. For example, consider the case of a happily married accountant, the father of three. For reasons he can't explain, he has become obsessed with the fear of contracting AIDS. There is no reason for him to be worried: his sexual activities have been entirely monogamous; he has never used drugs; he has never had a blood transfusion. Nonetheless, he is overwhelmed with the idea that he will contract this deadly disease. We find several ritualized, compulsive behaviors associated with his obsessive thoughts: He washes his hands vigorously at every opportunity and becomes very anxious if he cannot change his clothes completely at least three times a day (all in his effort to avoid contact with the dreaded AIDS virus). You can imagine how distressing this must be, and you also can appreciate that OCD involves much more than avoiding cracks in the sidewalk and tunes we keep humming to ourselves. Figure 12.4 lists some of the more common obsessions and ritualized compulsions found in persons with OCD.

Notice that we are using *compulsive* in an altogether different way when we refer to someone being a compulsive gambler, a compulsive eater, or a compulsive practical joker. What is different about the use of the term *compulsive* in such cases is that although the individual engages in habitual patterns of behavior, he or she gains pleasure from doing so. The compul-

obsessive-compulsive disorder (OCD)
an anxiety disorder characterized by a pattern of recurrent obsessions and compulsions

obsessions
ideas or thoughts that involuntarily and persistently intrude into one's awareness

compulsions
constantly intruding, stereotyped, and essentially involuntary acts or behaviors

FIGURE 12.4
Common Obsessions and Compulsions in OCD

Common obsessions

Fear of getting dirty, contaminated, or infected by people or things in the environment

Fear of AIDS

Disgust over body wastes or secretions

Concern that a task or assignment has been done poorly or incorrectly, even when the person knows this is not the case

Extreme concern with order, symmetry, or exactness

Fear of thinking evil or sinful thoughts that go against one's religion

Fear of losing important things that will be needed later

Recurring thoughts about harming or killing others or oneself

Fear of committing a crime, such as theft

Recurring thoughts or images of a sexual nature

Extreme concern with certain sounds, images, words, or numbers

Fear of blurting out obscenities or insulting others

Fear that some disaster will occur

Common compulsive rituals

Cleaning and grooming behaviors such as washing hands, showering, and brushing teeth in particular ways

Touching certain objects in a specific way

Repeatedly cleaning items in the house

Ordering or arranging things in a certain way

Checking locks, electrical outlets, light switches, and the like repeatedly

Repeatedly putting clothes on, then taking them off

Repeating certain actions, such as going through a doorway

Counting over and over again to a certain number

Hoarding items such as old newspapers, mail, and containers

Checking to see that no one has been hurt or killed, or no other disaster has occurred because of something the person with OCD has done

Constantly seeking approval (especially children)

From CIBA-GEIGY, 1991, pp. 6–7.

sive gambler enjoys gambling; the compulsive eater loves to eat. Such people may not enjoy the ultimate, long-term consequences of their actions, but they feel little discomfort about the behaviors themselves. To have a compulsive anxiety disorder requires that the behavior be recognized as senseless and not be the source of pleasure.

Obsessive-compulsive disorder is much more common than once believed. It affects nearly 1 of every 200 teenagers, and a total of as many as 5 million Americans (CIBA-GEIGY, 1991; Flament et al., 1988). Commonly, obsessive-compulsive disorder is first diagnosed in childhood or adolescence. Unfortunately, the prognosis for OCD is not very good. One study found that after as many as seven years of treatment, only 6 percent of the sample of patients could be considered totally symptom-free, and 43 percent still met the diagnostic criteria for the disorder (Leonard et al., 1993).

Research suggests that obsessive-compulsive disorder has a biological basis. The most likely candidate for the source of the problem is the frontal lobe, particularly the pathways used for communication between the frontal lobe and the basal ganglia (Hollander et al., 1992; Swedo et al., 1989b). Partial support for the biological basis of OCD comes from the observation that drug treatment (antidepressant medications) can be successful in eliminating the symptoms of OCD (Flament et al., 1985).

● **Before You Go On**

What characterizes the obsessive-compulsive disorder?

Posttraumatic Stress Disorder (PTSD)

An anxiety disorder that has been the subject of much public discussion over the past decade is **posttraumatic stress disorder (PTSD)**. This disorder involves several symptoms that arise at a time *after* (at least 6 months) experiencing a traumatic, highly stressful event that resulted in intense fear, helplessness, or horror at the time. The traumatic events that trigger PTSD are many, from natural disasters, to life-threatening situations (e.g., kidnapping, rape, assault, or combat), to the sudden loss of property (e.g., the house burned down). Posttraumatic stress syndrome is often associated with veterans of military conflict, the Vietnam War in particular. It is estimated that nearly 1.7 million veterans—nearly half of all who served in Southeast Asia—have suffered from partial or full PTSD at some time since discharge from the military (True et al., 1993).

No psychologist will diagnose someone who just experienced an horrendous event—such as the loss of a friend who died in the patient's arms in a furious battle—as having a disorder simply because he or she becomes very emotional and anxious. What makes the anxiety of PTSD qualify as a symptom of disorder is that it occurs persistently, in distressing dreams, in recurrent, disruptive recollections of the event, or in sudden feelings that the traumatic event is occurring again (flashbacks) well after the event itself. Persons with posttraumatic stress disorder try to avoid anything that could remind them of the trauma they have experienced; some Vietnam veterans refuse to visit the Vietnam Memorial in Washington, for example. People with PTSD see themselves as special, detached from others who cannot "share their experience."

Not recognized as a separate diagnostic category of anxiety disorder until 1980, posttraumatic stress disorder is not uncommon. About 1 percent of the population can be expected to experience the disorder in their lifetime. Of those who experience a severe trauma, nearly 15 percent will experience at least some of the symptoms of PTSD (Helzer et al., 1987; MacFarlane, 1988). A national survey found that of women who report being raped or physically assaulted, 26 percent experienced PTSD. This same survey found that nearly 70 percent of their sample of women had experienced at least one significant traumatic event in their lifetime (Resnick et al., 1993).

We often find comorbidity with PTSD. It is commonly associated with alcohol and substance abuse or depression. The prognosis for posttraumatic stress syndrome is related to the extent to which there are comorbid factors (such as alcoholism), the extent to which the person experienced psychological problems before the trauma that precipitated the disorder, and the extent to which social support is available (Jordan et al., 1992). Some research claims that there may be genetic factors that predispose someone to develop the symptoms of PTSD (Charney et al., 1993; True et al., 1993).

posttraumatic stress disorder (PTSD)
an anxiety disorder in which disruptive recollections, distressing dreams, flashbacks, and felt anxiety occur well after the experience of a traumatic event

Posttraumatic stress disorder (PTSD) may be one of the long-term effects of experiencing traumatic, life-threatening situations such as those that occur in military combat.

● **Before You Go On**
Describe the symptoms of posttraumatic stress disorder.

SOMATOFORM DISORDERS

somatoform disorders
psychological disorders that reflect imagined physical or bodily symptoms or complaints

Soma means "body." Hence, all of the **somatoform disorders** in some way involve physical symptoms or complaints. What makes these *psychological* disorders is that there is no known medical or biological cause for the symptoms. We'll consider just two somatoform disorders: one common—hypochondriasis—the other rare, but very dramatic—conversion disorder.

Hypochondriasis

hypochondriasis
a mental disorder involving the unrealistic fear of developing a serious disease or illness

Hypochondriasis is the appropriate diagnosis for individuals preoccupied with the fear that they have or will soon develop a serious disease. Persons with this disorder are unusually aware of every ache and pain. They read popular magazines devoted to health issues, and feel free to diagnose their own ailments. The catch is that they *have* no medical illness or disease. Nonetheless, they seek medical attention all the time, and will not be convinced of their good health despite the best medical opinion and reassurance.

A man with occasional chest pains, for example, diagnoses his own condition as lung cancer. Even after many physicians reassure him that his lungs are perfectly fine and that he has no signs of cancer, the patient's fears are not put to rest. "They're just trying to make me feel better by not telling me, because they know, as I do, that I have lung cancer and I'm going to die soon."

If a person believes that he or she (hypochrondiasis is found equally in men and women) has contracted some serious disease, three problems might be solved. (1) The person now has a way to explain otherwise unexplainable anxiety: "Well, my goodness, if you had lung cancer, you'd be anxious too." (2) The illness may be used to excuse the person from those activities that he or she finds anxiety producing: "As sick as I am, you don't possibly expect me to go to work today, do you?" (3) The illness or disease may be used as a way to gain attention or sympathy: "Don't you feel sorry for me, knowing that I have such a terrible disease?"

Conversion Disorder

Although **conversion disorder** is now rare (accounting for fewer than 5 percent of anxiety disorders), its symptoms are striking. Here we find an individual with a loss or alteration in physical functioning that suggests a physical disorder, but which is really an expression of a psychological conflict or need. The symptoms are not intentionally produced, and cannot be explained by any physical disorder. The loss in physical functioning is typically of great significance: paralysis, blindness, and deafness are classic examples. The symptoms are not fully imaginary; they are real in the sense that the person cannot feel, see, or hear.

What makes the disorder psychological is that there is no medical reason for the symptoms. In some cases, medical explanations run contrary to the symptoms. One type of conversion disorder is *glove anesthesia*, in which the hands lose feeling and become paralyzed from the wrist down. As it happens, it is physically impossible to have paralysis and loss of feeling in the hands alone; normally there would be some paralysis in the forearm, upper arm, and shoulder as well. Actual physical paralysis, of course, must follow neural pathways.

One of the most remarkable secondary symptoms of this disorder (which occurs only in some patients) is known as *la belle indifference*—a seemingly inappropriate lack of concern over one's condition. Persons with conversion disorder seem quite comfortable with and accepting of their infirmity. Here are people who are blind, deaf, or paralyzed, and who show very little concern over their condition.

This particular disorder holds an important position in psychology's history. This was the disorder that most intrigued Sigmund Freud and ultimately led him to develop a new form of therapy (see Topic 13B). The disorder was known to the ancient Greeks, who named it *hysteria*, a label still used occasionally, as in "hysterical blindness." The Greeks believed the disorder was found only in women and reflected a disorder of the uterus, or *hysterium*, hence the name. The logic was that the disease would leave the uterus, float through the body, and settle in the eyes, hands, or whatever part of the body was affected. Of course, this idea is no longer valid, although the potential sexual basis for the disorder was one of the aspects that caught Freud's attention.

conversion disorder
the display of a severe physical disorder for which there is no medical explanation; often accompanied by an apparent lack of concern on the part of the patient

● **Before You Go On**
Describe hypochondriasis and conversion disorder.

DISSOCIATIVE DISORDERS

To *dissociate* means to become separate from or to escape. The underlying theme of the **dissociative disorders** is that in some way a person escapes from an aspect of life or personality that is seen as the source of distress or

dissociative disorders
disorders in which the person tries in some way to flee or escape from an aspect of personality or experience that is the source of distress

anxiety. These disorders are statistically uncommon, but they are also dramatic and are often the subject of novels, movies, and television shows.

Dissociative Amnesia

dissociative amnesia
a psychologically caused inability to recall important personal information

Dissociative amnesia is defined as an inability to remember important personal information—a memory loss too extensive to be explained by ordinary forgetfulness. Before the publication of the *DSM-IV* in 1994, this disorder was known as psychogenic amnesia; *psychogenic* means "psychological in origin," and *amnesia* refers to a loss of memory. Usually what is forgotten is a traumatic incident and some or all of the experiences that led up to it or followed it. As you might suspect, there is no medical reason for the loss of memory. As you also might suspect, there is a large range of the extent of psychogenic amnesia. In some cases, a person may "lose" entire days and weeks at a time; in other cases, only specific details cannot be recalled. Predictably, cases of this disorder tend to be more common in wartime, when traumatic experiences are more common.

Dissociative Fugue

dissociative fugue
a condition of amnesia accompanied by unexplained travel or change of location

Occasionally, amnesic forgetfulness is accompanied by seemingly pointless travel. That is, the person finds himself or herself in a strange and different place, with no reasonable explanation for how he or she got there. When this dimension is added, we have a disorder known as **dissociative fugue**. For example, we may find a man wandering around a Florida beach dressed in a three-piece business suit. He has no idea how or why he got there or even where he is.

Both dissociative amnesia and dissociative fugue are, in their own way, like the somatoform disorders in that they involve an escape from stressful situations. With a conversion disorder, a person may escape from stress by taking on the symptoms of a major physical disorder. With amnesia and fugue, escape is more literal. People escape by simply forgetting, or they avoid conflict and stress by psychologically and physically running away.

Dissociative Identity Disorder

dissociative identity disorder
the existence within one individual of two or more personalities, each of which is dominant at a particular time

This disorder is still commonly known as *multiple personality disorder*, and perhaps the most important fact to recognize about dissociative identity disorder is that it is listed here, as a dissociative disorder, and not as schizophrenia. I say that because the popular media consistently give the impression that these are one and the same. They are not. Schizophrenia is a psychotic disorder that we will discuss shortly.

The major symptom of **dissociative identity disorder** is the existence within the same person of two or more distinct personalities or personality states. It is an extremely rare disorder, although for unknown reasons its incidence—at least in the United States—is increasing dramatically (Carson & Butcher, 1992).

The very idea of two or more personalities inhabiting the same person is difficult for most of us to imagine. Perhaps it would help to contrast this disorder with a pattern of behavior that is typical of all of us. We all change our behaviors and, in some small way, our personalities change every day, depending on the situation in which we find ourselves. We do not act, think, or feel exactly the same way at school as we do at work, at a party, or at church. We modify our behaviors to fit the circumstance in which we find ourselves. At a party, you may be carefree, uninhibited, and happy. At work, you may be a different person: reserved, quiet, serious, and concentrating on the task at hand. These changes do not qualify as an identity disorder. What is the difference?

The main differences are of degree and quality. For a person with a dissociative identity disorder, the change in personality is usually dramatic, extreme, and complete. We are not dealing with a person who alters his or her behaviors slightly. We are dealing with two or more *distinct* personalities, which implies a change in underlying consciousness, not just a change in behaviors. About half the reported cases show more than 10 distinct personalities. Another difference is that when you and I change our behaviors, we do so as a response to cues from the situation in which we find ourselves. Such is not the case for a person with this dissociative disorder, whose changes in personality can take place without warning or provocation. Another major difference concerns control. When we change our behaviors, we do so consciously or intentionally. People with dissociative identity disorder can neither control nor predict which of their personalities will be dominant at any one time. Persons diagnosed with this disorder often have been victims of child abuse, sexual abuse, and/or drug abuse. Women are more often the victims of such abuses, which perhaps helps explain why the disorder is significantly more common in women than it is in men (Putnam et al., 1986; Ross et al., 1989). Women also demonstrate more identities than do males, averaging 15, while makes average about 8 identities.

● **Before You Go On**

What are the defining symptoms of the dissociative disorders?

PERSONALITY DISORDERS

The psychological disorders we have reviewed so far, and those we will consider later, seem to afflict people who previously were quite normal and undisturbed. In most cases, we can remember a time when the person did not show any symptoms of his or her disorder. This is more difficult with the personality disorders because persons with these disorders have a long-standing history of symptoms. **Personality disorders** are long-lasting patterns of perceiving, relating to, and thinking about the environment and oneself that are inflexible and maladaptive and that cause impaired functioning or distress. The problems associated with personality disorders are usually identifiable by the time one is an adolescent.

The *DSM-IV* lists several personality disorders organized in three clusters or groups. Group 1 includes disorders in which the person can be characterized as odd or eccentric. People with these disorders are often difficult to get along with. Group 2 includes disorders in which the person is overly dramatic, emotional, or erratic, and where behaviors tend to be impulsive. Group 3 includes disorders that add anxiety, fearfulness, or depression to the standard criteria for personality disorder.

Rather than trying to deal with all the personality disorders (PDs) in detail, I'll simply list and describe some of the more common disorders below. Keep in mind as you review this list that to be classified as a PD, these behaviors must be relatively long-standing, usually beginning in childhood or adolescence.

personality disorders
enduring patterns of perceiving, relating to, and thinking about the environment and one's self that are inflexible and maladaptive

Cluster I: *Disorders of odd or eccentric reactions*

Paranoid personality disorder: Extreme sensitivity, suspiciousness, envy, and mistrust of others; the actions of other people are seen as deliberately demeaning or threatening. This attitude of suspicion is not justified. A person with this disorder shows a restricted range of emotional reactivity, is humorless, and seldom seeks help. Example: A person who continuously, and without justification, accuses a spouse of infidelity, and believes that every wrong number was a call from the spouse's lover.

Schizoid personality disorder: A lack of, and indifference to, interpersonal relationships. A person with this disorder appears "cold and aloof," and often engages in excessive daydreaming. Example: A person who lives, as she has for years, alone in a one-room flat in a poor part of town, venturing out only to pick up a social security check and a few necessities at the corner store.

Cluster II: *Disorders of dramatic, emotional, or erratic reactions*

Histrionic personality disorder: Overly dramatic, reactive, and intensely expressed behaviors. A person with this disorder is very lively, tending to draw attention to himself or herself, overreacting to matters of small consequence, seeking excitement while avoiding the routine. Example: A woman who spends an inordinate amount of time on her appearance, calls everyone "Darling," seems to be constantly asking for feedback on how she looks, and describes most of her experiences as "wonderful!" and "vastly outstanding!" even when such an experience was finding that detergent is on sale at the grocery.

Narcissistic personality disorder: A grandiose exaggeration of self-importance, a need for attention and admiration, and a tendency to set unrealistic goals. Someone with this disorder maintains few lasting relationships and in many ways engages in a "childish" level of behavior. Example: A person who always wants to be the topic of every conversation, and shows a lack of interest in saying anything positive about anyone else. Someone who believes that no one else has ever taken a vacation as stupendous as his or hers, and who will do whatever it takes to be complimented.

Antisocial personality disorder: An exceptional lack of regard for the rights and property of others; engaging in impulsive behaviors with little or no regard for the consequences of those behaviors. Someone with this disorder shows early signs of lying, truancy, stealing, fighting, resisting authority, and general irresponsibility, and has difficulty keeping a job. Example: A young man who first steals a car, then drives it down an alley, knocking over garbage cans, "just for the fun of it" before abandoning the car in a deserted part of town.

Cluster III: *Disorders involving anxiety and fearfulness*

Avoidant personality disorder: An oversensitivity to the possibility of being rejected by others and an unwillingness to enter into relationships for fear of being rejected. A person with this disorder is devastated by disapproval, but holds out the desire for some social relationship. Example: A man with few close friends who almost never dates and only talks to women who are older and less attractive than he. A man who has worked at the same job for years, never seeking a job change or promotion, who rarely speaks in public, and who may attend meetings and public gatherings, but does not participate.

Dependent personality disorder: Allowing and seeking others to dominate and assume responsibility for one's actions; poor self-image and lack of confidence. A person with this disorder sees himself or herself as stupid and helpless, thus deferring to others. Example: A woman whose husband commonly abuses her. Although she has from time to time reported the abuse, she refuses to take an active role in finding treatment for her husband, arguing that it is "her place" to do as he says, and that if she does not please him, it is her fault.

Because personality disorders are difficult to diagnose accurately, estimates of prevalence tend to be inexact. Most cases of PD first come to the attention of mental health professionals on referral from the courts or from family members, or because of related problems such as child abuse or alcoholism. We find that the overall rate of PD is between 10 percent and 20 percent, but the rates of specific disorders are very low. About one-fourth of those with a personality disorder fit more than one diagnostic category—another example of comorbidity (Blashfield & Breen, 1989; Zimmerman & Coryell, 1989).

The prognosis usually is quite poor for personality disorders. The maladaptive patterns of behavior often have taken a lifetime to develop. Changing them won't be easy. This makes prevention—and understanding the causes of these disorders—all the more important. What hypotheses are being considered? There are several: (1) There is a biologically based lack of adequate emotional arousal (Eysenck, 1960; Lykken, 1957, 1982; Raine et al., 1990). (2) There is an unusually high need to seek stimulation (Quay, 1965; Zuckerman, 1978). (3) There is a genetic basis for some of the personality disorders. For example, although antisocial personality disorder is not inherited directly, it tends to "run in families" (Kendler & Gruenberg, 1982; MacMillan & Kofoed, 1984; Mednick et al., 1987; Nigg & Goldsmith, 1994). (4) There is a high incidence of parental loss. Many adults with PDs were abandoned in childhood by at least one parent, usually the father (Greer, 1964; Hare, 1970). (5) There is a high level of abuse in childhood (Ogata et al., 1990). (6) There was an inappropriate, or lack of, emotional "bonding" or attachment in childhood (Buss, 1966; Magid, 1988). As we've noted before and will see again, no one of these hypotheses is wholly adequate to explain why a particular individual will develop a personality disorder. The key is probably in the interaction of two or more of these factors in the life of an individual.

● **Before You Go On**

What are the defining characteristics of the personality disorders?

DELIRIUM, DEMENTIA, AMNESTIC, AND OTHER COGNITIVE DISORDERS— THE EXAMPLE OF ALZHEIMER'S

Disorders classified as delirium, dementia, amnestic, and other cognitive disorders used to be called *organic mental disorders*. The implication was that what these disorders have in common is a behavioral or mental problem caused by some known organic brain dysfunction. The label was changed with the *DSM-IV* because of the implication that other disorders could somehow be independent of brain function. The new label tells us that the

FIGURE 12.5
The Ten Warning Signs of Alzheimer's Disease

Normal	Possible Alzheimer's
1. Temporarily forgetting a colleague's name	Not being able to remember the name later
2. Forgetting the carrots on the stove until the meal is over	Forgetting that a meal was ever prepared
3. Unable to find the right word, but using a fit substitute	Uttering incomprehensible sentences
4. Forgetting for a moment where you're going	Getting lost on your own street
5. Talking on the phone, temporarily forgetting to watch a child	Forgetting there is a child there
6. Having trouble balancing a checkbook	Not knowing what the numbers mean
7. Misplacing a wristwatch until steps are retraced	Putting a wristwatch in the sugarbowl
8. Having a bad day	Having rapid mood shifts
9. Gradual changes in personality with age	Drastic changes in personality
10. Tiring of housework, but getting back to it	Not knowing or caring that housework needs to be done

From: *Is It Alzheimer's? Warning Signs You Should Know*, a pamphlet form the Alzheimer's Association, 919 North Michigan Avenue, Suite 1000, Chicago, IL 60611-1676.

delirium
a clouded state of consciousness with a lessening of cognitive awareness and attention

dementia
a loss of intellectual abilities; memory is poor and deteriorates; impulse control and judgment adversely affected

amnestic disorders
showing an impairment of memory while other cognitive functions remain intact

main issue with these disorders is a disruption of cognitive function. The key revolves around the definitions of three terms: (1) **Delirium** is a clouded state of consciousness, involving a lessening of awareness and difficulty paying attention. There may be confusion and disorientation. Someone who is delirious cannot relate to what is happening now or to what has happened earlier. (2) **Dementia** is characterized by a loss of intellectual abilities. Attention may be intact, but use of memory is poor and deteriorates. Impulse control and judgment may also be adversely affected. (3) **Amnestic disorders** involve an impairment of memory functioning while all other cognitive skills or abilities remain intact. Often the problem is with processing information from short-term to long-term memory. For each disorder in this category, there is a known, or suspected, underlying medical condition. The most common is dementia of the Alzheimer's type.

A slow deterioration of intellectual functioning is the most common symptom associated with Alzheimer's disease (Katzman, 1987). Problems of recent memory mark the early stages, such as, "Did I take my pills this morning?" Figure 12.5 is from a summary table recently prepared by the Alzheimer's Association.

This dementia was first described in 1907 by Alois Alzheimer, and was thought to be an inevitable consequence of aging (incorrectly referred to as *senile psychosis*). Symptoms associated with dementia of the Alzheimer's type are *not* normal, natural, or a necessary part of growing old, but a general acceptance of this reality did not occur until the early 1970s. Alzheimer's disease has been diagnosed in persons younger than age 65. In such cases, we often hear of an "early onset" form of the disease, but researchers are coming to the conclusion that age of onset does not define different forms of the disease (Bondareff et al., 1993).

Estimates are that 3 to 4 million Americans are afflicted with Alzheimer's dementia, and over 11,000 patients die each year (Fackelman, 1992; Hostetler, 1987; Wurtman, 1985). The rates of death attributed to Alzheimer's disease have increased nearly *1,000 percent* since the late 1970s, an increase attributed to several factors, including greater awareness and willingness to diagnose the disease and a greater number of persons living to advanced ages, when Alzheimer's is more likely to occur. It is therefore estimated that 14 million Americans will have the disease by the year 2050.

Although the major symptoms of Alzheimer's dementia are psychological, it *is* a physical disease caused by changes in brain tissue. Reliable diagnostic tests may be on the near horizon, but at the moment, the only sure diagnosis comes at autopsy with an examination of the brain. There are four signs of Alzheimer's: (1) a mass of tangles ("a spaghetti-like jumble of abnormal protein fibers" [Butler & Emr, 1982]); (2) plaques—waste material, degenerated nerve fibers wrapped around a core of protein; (3) several small cavities filled with fluid and debris; and (4) atrophy—some structures of the brain are reduced in size. Two problems with these observations are that these signs can be found in a normal brain, and we don't know what causes them in the first place.

Scientists are getting closer, but we still don't know what causes dementia of the Alzheimer's type. There surely is a genetic predisposition for the disease, although no one yet is claiming that it is directly inherited (Marx, 1990). Researchers now know the nature of the protein molecule that forms the plaques in the brains of patients with Alzheimer's, but they don't know where that protein comes from (Marx, 1990; Selkoe, 1990). There are several other possibilities, of course. Patients with dementia of the Alzheimer's type often show a decrease in levels of acetylcholine, a neurotransmitter that is involved in the formation of memories (e.g., Coyle et al., 1983). There is the possibility that the disease is the result of low levels of a poison, or toxin (aluminum salts have been shown to produce Alzheimer's-like symptoms). As is often the case, it is likely that each of these hypotheses will be part of the final picture.

● **Before You Go On**
   What is Alzheimer's disease, and what causes it?

MOOD DISORDERS

The **mood disorders** (called *affective disorders* until the publication of the *DSM-III-R*) clearly involve a disturbance in one's emotional reactions or feelings. We have to be careful here. Almost all psychological disorders have an impact on mood or affect, but with mood disorders, the intensity or extremeness of mood is the primary symptom.

mood disorders
disorders of affect or feeling; usually depression; less frequently mania and depression occurring in cycles

Types of Mood Disorder

Mood disorders are defined in terms of extremes of mood, depression being the more common of the two extremes. Listed under the classification of mood disorder are several specific disorders, differentiated in terms of such criteria as length of episode, severity, and whether there is a known organic basis for the symptoms.

major depression
an extreme of mood characterized by intense sadness, feelings of hopelessness, and a loss of pleasure and interest in normal activities

Major depression is a constellation of symptoms that includes feeling sad, low, and hopeless, coupled with a loss of pleasure or interest in one's usual activities. Associated with major depression are such factors as poor appetite, insomnia, loss of energy, decrease in sexual activity, and feelings of worthlessness. At the same time, there is no event or situation that can reasonably account for the extremeness of the observed depression.

This form of mood disorder is diagnosed about two times more in women than in men; during any 6-month period, approximately 6.6 percent of women and 3.5 percent of men will have an episode of major depression. This ratio of two women to every man developing major depression holds across nationalities and across ethnic groups (Cross-National Collaborative Group, 1992; McGrath et al., 1990). Worldwide, major depression is on the increase, with current incidence at more than 100 million persons (Gotlib, 1992; Weissman & Klerman, 1992). Unfortunately, research also tells us that relapse and reoccurrence are common for those who have had a depressive episode (Belsher & Costello, 1988; Klerman, 1990). Major depression seldom occurs in just one episode of illness, but rather is a chronic condition (Frank et al., 1990).

dysthymia
a reasonably mild, though chronic disorder of depression associated with low energy and low self-esteem

Dysthymia is the name of the disorder that is essentially a mild case of major depression. The disorder is chronic, with recurrent pessimism, low energy level, and low self-esteem. Whereas major depression tends to occur in a series of debilitating episodes, dysthymia is a more continuous sense of being depressed and sad.

As with major depression, there is no identifiable event that precipitates the depressed mood of dysthymia. In other words, to feel even overwhelmingly depressed upon hearing of the death of a friend is not enough to qualify as a disorder of any sort. From time to time we all feel depression, but there is usually some sensible reason for our depressed mood.

bipolar disorder
a severe mood disorder evidenced by unexplainable swings of mood between the more common depression and mania

mania
an extreme of mood characterized by euphoria, a sense of well-being, and an increase in activity level

In **bipolar disorder**, episodes of depression are interspersed with episodes of mania. This disorder is often referred to as *manic depression*. **Mania** is characterized by an elevated mood with feelings of euphoria or irritability. In a manic state one shows an increase in activity, is more talkative than usual, and seems to be able to get by on a lot less sleep than usual. Mania is a condition of mood that cannot be maintained for long. It is just too tiring to stay manic for an extended time. Like depression, mania seldom occurs as an isolated episode. Follow-up studies show that recurrences of manic reactions are common. Relapse is found in approximately 40 percent of patients who have been diagnosed as having a manic episode (Harrow et al. 1990; Tohen et al., 1990). People are rarely ever manic without the interspersed periods of depression. Nearly 2 million Americans are presently diagnosed with bipolar disorder.

Observations on the Causes of Depression

The answers we find to the question "What causes depression?" depend largely on where and how we look. It seems most likely that depression is caused by a number of different but interrelated causes. Some of them are biological, others psychological.

Biological Factors. Bipolar mood disorder is not very common. Anyone chosen at random has less than a one-half of one percent chance of developing the symptoms of the disorder. The chances of developing the symptoms rise to 15 percent if a brother, sister, or either parent ever had the disorder. This 15 percent figure seems to be true for fraternal twins, too. If, however, one member of a pair of identical twins has bipolar mood disorder, the chance that the other twin will be diagnosed as having the disorder jumps to more than 70 percent (Allen, 1976). What that means, of course, is that there is good evidence of a genetic predisposition for bipolar mood disorder. The data are not as striking for depression alone, where the similar data for identical twins is 40 percent and 11 percent for fraternal twins. We still suspect that there is some genetic basis for major depression (Hammen et al., 1990; Kendler et al., 1993).

Even if we did know the site of a specific gene, or two, or three that provided the basis for a mood disorder, researchers would still face the challenge of specifying the biological mechanisms that then produce the symptoms of that disorder. In the case of the mood disorders, attention has been focused on neurotransmitters that appear to influence mood directly. Collectively they are referred to as *biogenic amines* and include such neurotransmitters as serotonin, dopamine, and norepinephrine. The major breakthrough in this research came when it was discovered that a drug used to treat high blood pressure (reserpine) produced depression. It was then discovered that reserpine lowered the brain's normal level of norepinephrine, and the search for neurotransmitter involvement in mood disorders was on (Bennett, 1982).

One theory holds that depression is caused by a shortage of biogenic amines, and that mania is caused by an overabundance of these chemicals. It remains to be seen why these imbalances occur in some people and not in others. Perhaps they reflect an inherited predisposition. Another argument follows from the observation that stress causes changes in the neurotransmitters in the brain—including an increase in biogenic amines (Anisman & Zacharko, 1982). If these substances are overstimulated by prolonged stress, perhaps their supply becomes depleted in the long run, leading to symptoms of depression. In cases of depression that occur without any unusual stressors, we suspect that a genetic predisposition makes some people susceptible to the biochemical changes that accompany stress in any degree. The theory seems logical, but as yet there is insufficient evidence for us to draw any firm conclusions.

Psychological Factors. Learning theorists have attributed depression to experiential phenomena, including a lack of effective reinforcers. Given a history of responding without earning reinforcement, an individual may just stop responding and become quiet, withdrawn, passive, and, in many ways, depressed (Seligman, 1975). Some people, lacking ability to gain (or earn) reinforcers, simply respond less often to environmental cues. They enter into a long, generalized period of extinction, which ultimately leads to depression. On the other hand, we must consider the research that suggests that the ineffectiveness of reinforcers in some people's lives is more a result of their depression than a cause of it. That is, *because* they are depressed, people find less reinforcement in the world about them (Carson & Carson, 1984).

Other theorists (most notably psychiatrist Aaron Beck [1967, 1976]), argue that although depression is viewed as a disorder of affect, its causes are largely cognitive. Some people, the argument goes, tend to think of themselves in a poor light. They believe that they are, in many ways, ineffective people. They blame themselves for a great many of their failures, whether deservedly so or not. Facing life every day with negative attitudes about oneself tends to foster even more failures and self-doubt, and such cycles then lead to feelings of depression.

To be sure, there are other views about the causes of depression, including the psychoanalytic view that depression reflects early childhood experiences that lead to anger that is directed inward. In brief, we do not yet understand the causes of mood disorders. Depression probably stems from a combination of genetic predispositions, biochemical factors, learning experiences, situational stress, and cognitive factors.

● **Before You Go On**

How are the mood disorders defined?

What do we know about their prevalence and their causes?

SCHIZOPHRENIA

schizophrenia
complex psychotic disorders characterized by impairment of cognitive functioning, delusions and hallucinations, social withdrawal, and inappropriate affect

Schizophrenia is "the most devastating, puzzling, and frustrating of all mental illnesses" (Bloom et al., 1985). **Schizophrenia** is the label given to several specific disorders, all of which have in common a distortion of reality and a retreat from others, accompanied by disturbances in affect, behavior, and cognition (our ABC again). One of the things that qualifies schizophrenia as the ultimate psychological disorder is that it can impair virtually every aspect of living. The range of symptoms is so great that it is difficult to specify which symptoms are fundamental and which are secondary.

Let's begin by summarizing some of the symptoms commonly associated with schizophrenia. First, there is usually a disturbance of thinking. In fact, schizophrenia nearly always involves delusions and hallucinations in some phase of the illness. **Delusions** are false beliefs, ideas that are firmly held regardless of what others may say or do. **Hallucinations** are false perceptions; perceiving that which is not there or failing to perceive that which is clearly there. As reflected in their delusions, people with schizophrenia come to believe strange and unusual things that are simply not true. The delusions of someone with schizophrenia tend to be inconsistent, and are clearly unsupportable. Most hallucinations of persons with schizophrenia are auditory (hearing things, usually voices). Distortions of time are not uncommon. Sometimes a minute seems to last for hours or hours seem to race by in seconds. A person with schizophrenia may also engage in unusual behaviors, typically ritualized, stereotyped, and meaningless.

delusions
false beliefs; ideas that are firmly held regardless of what others say or do

hallucinations
false perceptions; perceiving that which is not there

Persons with schizophrenia are unusually withdrawn, seldom interacting with others. It is also common to find affect disordered. Most commonly, we find *flattened affect,* meaning that the person shows little or no emotional response. Occasionally, there is inappropriate affect: giggling in the midst of serious conversation or crying and sobbing for no apparent reason at all.

Two things need to be made clear. First, as unsettling as these symptoms may be, the average patient with schizophrenia *does not* present the picture of the crazed, wild, lunatic that is often depicted in movies and on television. Day in and day out, the average schizophrenic patient is quite colorless, socially withdrawn, and of very little danger. Although there are exceptions to this rule of thumb, it is particularly true when the patient with schizophrenia is medicated or under treatment.

Second, when literally translated, schizophrenia means "splitting of the mind." The term was first used by a Swiss psychiatrist, Eugen Bleuler, in 1911. The split that Bleuler was addressing was a split of the mind of the patient from the real world and the social relationships that the rest of us enjoy. Never has the term been used to describe a multiple or split personality of the Dr. Jekyll and Mr. Hyde variety. Such disorders do occur, but they are rare, and as we've already seen, they are called dissociative identity disorders.

● **Before You Go On**

What are the major symptoms of schizophrenia?

Incidence and Types of Schizophrenia

Schizophrenia occurs around the world at approximately the same rate: 1 percent of the population at any point in time. This figure has been stable for many years. It is a common claim that patients with schizophrenia fill more than half the hospital beds in mental or psychiatric hospitals in this country (Bloom et al., 1985). Again, however, the statistics are difficult to deal with on a personal level. No matter how you state the statistics, we certainly are talking about very large numbers of persons—persons who are usually diagnosed in their late teens or early twenties.

The prognosis is not very encouraging. About 25 percent recover fully from their first episode of the disorder and have no recurrences; in about 50 percent of the cases, we have a recurrent illness with periods of remission in between, and about 25 percent of the time, we have no signs of recovery and a long-term deterioration in functioning. In one study, only 10 to 17 percent of patients with schizophrenia were symptom-free in a follow-up five years after initial diagnosis (Carone et al., 1991). Prognosis is related to when treatment begins. If treatment begins right after an initial episode, the prognosis is fairly good, with as many as 83 percent recovering (Lieberman et al., 1993). Here's a picture we see with many physical ailments: The sooner therapy begins, the better the likelihood of recovery.

I have already indicated that schizophrenia is a label that applies to several different specific disorders. In this way, the term *schizophrenia* is not unlike the term *cancer*. To say that one has cancer communicates only a general diagnosis. We then want to know, "What sort of cancer?" Let's now consider some of the ways in which the collection of disorders called schizophrenia can be divided into subtypes or varieties. Although the categories I'm using here are common ones, you should know at the outset that the goal of defining separate categories of schizophrenia has not been met. "Schizophrenia is a heterogeneous illness that, paradoxically, resists subdivision" (Heinrichs, 1993, p. 221).

DSM Subtypes. *The DSM-IV* lists five categories of schizophrenia, all of which share many of the same symptoms of disorganized cognition, inappropriate affect, and strange behavior, but each subtype has a symptom or cluster of symptoms that makes it different. (The following descriptions are from Carson & Butcher, 1992.)

The *paranoid type* diagnosis reflects a collection of symptoms dominated by absurd, illogical, and changeable delusions, often accompanied by hallucinations, resulting in a severe impairment of judgment. Someone with paranoid schizophrenia may come to believe that others are out to do him great harm and will hear voices that tell him so, and may also direct him to harm others.

Patients with the *disorganized type* of schizophrenia usually suffer a more severe disintegration of personality than most other patients. Emotional distortion is shown in inappropriate laughter and silliness, peculiar mannerisms, and bizarre, often obscene, behavior. The *catatonic type* is characterized by alternating periods of extreme withdrawal and extreme excitement. In withdrawal, the patient may become totally motionless for hours, even days (a condition called "catatonia"). As a stage of excitement comes on, the person may talk or shout incoherently, pace rapidly, and engage in uninhibited, frenzied behaviors.

As its name suggests, the diagnosis of the *undifferentiated type* is used for those patients that show many of the symptoms of schizophrenia, but who do not meet the criteria of being paranoid, disorganized, or catatonic. In many cases, the term is used for patients in early stages of the disorder for whom a more specific diagnosis is not yet possible. The label *residual type* is reserved for persons with an indication of mild symptoms who are in the process of recovering from a clearly schizophrenic episode.

process schizophrenia
schizophrenia in which the onset of the symptoms is comparatively slow and gradual

reactive schizophrenia
schizophrenia in which the onset of the symptoms is comparatively sudden

Process and Reactive. So far, we have classified psychological disorders in terms of specific defining symptoms. With schizophrenia, there is a distinction that is not made on the basis of the nature of symptoms, but on the basis of their *onset*. We use the term **process schizophrenia** to describe schizophrenic symptoms that have developed gradually, usually over a period of years. **Reactive schizophrenia**, on the other hand, is the term used for the sudden onset of schizophrenic symptoms. As you know, these are extremes, with many possibilities in between.

The significance of this distinction is that there is some reason to believe that the prognosis for schizophrenia can be, at least to a degree, based on the nature of its onset—the more toward the *process* variety, the worse the prognosis; the more toward the *reactive* type, the better. We need to be careful not to overinterpret what is at best a rule of thumb. Some data suggest that outcome, or recovery, from schizophrenia, is not as related to type of onset as once believed (e.g., Harding, 1988).

Positive and Negative Symptoms. As early as 1919, Kraepelin claimed that schizophrenia could be divided into two types depending on the symptoms found at diagnosis. In one type, the major symptoms are hallucinations, delusions, muscular rigidity, and/or bizarre behaviors. In the other type, symptoms include emotional and social withdrawal, reduced energy and motivation, apathy, and poor attention (Kay & Singh, 1989; Lenzenweger et al., 1989). These two varieties have come to be known as *positive* and *negative schizophrenia*, respectively (Andreasen, 1982; Andreasen et al., 1990b; Crow, 1980). It is a bit of an oversimplification, but it is as if in the case of positive symptoms we notice reactions of a person that have been added to his or her normal functioning, and in the case of negative symp-

These drawings show the varying levels of progress of a patient—an artist—with paranoid schizophrenia. The first image was chosen from a magazine for the patient to copy. The second image shows the patient's attempt at copying the picture when fully symptomatic, before therapy began, while the third image shows a picture created by the same patient after therapy.

toms we notice a lack of or the disappearance of behaviors that once were present. Obviously, these two varieties are not mutually exclusive.

Again, the usefulness of the negative-positive distinction is that there may be differences in both the causes and most effective treatment plans for the two types. To summarize a large body of evidence, we find the correlates of negative symptoms to include more structural abnormalities in the brain, several deficiencies on tests that measure frontal and parietal lobe functions, a clearer genetic basis, more severe complications at birth, a lower educational level, poorer adjustment patterns before onset, and a poorer prognosis, mostly because of the relative ineffectiveness of medications. Correlated with positive symptoms are factors such as an excess of the neurotransmitter dopamine, relatively normal brain configuration, severe disruptions in early family life, overactivity and aggressiveness in adolescence, and a relatively good response to treatment (Andreason, et al., 1990b; Breier et al., 1991; Buchanan et al., 1994; Cannon et al., 1990; Kay & Singh, 1989; Lenzenweger et al., 1989; McGlashan & Fenton, 1992; Tandon & Greden, 1989). On the other hand, any distinction based on negative and positive symptoms, like the one based on nature of onset, may be of less predictive value than was once hoped (Kay, 1990; Pogue-Geile & Zubin, 1988).

● **Before You Go On**

What characterizes the following varieties of schizophrenia: paranoid, disorganized, catatonic, undifferentiated, residual, process vs. reactive, and positive vs. negative?

Can you tell that this woman was diagnosed as having acute schizophrenia? There is no "typical" behavior or "look" that you can expect to find in persons with schizophrenia.

Observations on the Causes of Schizophrenia

Schizophrenia is obviously a complex set of disorders. As you might suspect, our bottom-line conclusion on the cause of schizophrenia is going to be tentative and multidimensional. Although we don't know what causes the disorder, we do have a number of interesting leads to follow.

Hereditary Factors.   There is little doubt that schizophrenia runs in families (Gottesman & Bertelsen, 1989; Kessler, 1980; Rosenthal, 1970). The data are not as striking as they are for the mood disorders, but it is clear that one is at a higher risk of being diagnosed as schizophrenic if there is a history of the disorder in one's family. If one parent has schizophrenia, his or her child is 10 to 15 *times* more likely to develop the disorder as an adult; when both parents are schizophrenic, their children are 40 times more likely to develop the illness (Cornblatt & Erlenmeyer-Kimmling, 1985; Kety et al., 1994; Kendler et al., 1994). The risk of developing schizophrenia is 4 to 5 times greater for an identical twin than it is for a fraternal twin if the other member of the twin pair has the disorder. Recall that the odds of having schizophrenia are, in the general population, about 1 in 100. We also need to remember that data such as these do not mean that schizophrenia is directly inherited. After all, nearly half the identical twins of persons with schizophrenia never do develop the disorder, and "89 percent of diagnosed schizophrenics have no known relative who is schizophrenic" (Cromwell, 1993; Plomin, 1988). It is more reasonable to say that one may inherit a predisposition to develop schizophrenia.

Biochemical Factors: The Dopamine Hypothesis.

The neurotransmitter dopamine is found in every human brain. The role of dopamine in schizophrenia has come to light from several different lines of research.

For one thing, we know that the abuse of amphetamines can lead to many of the symptoms found in schizophrenia. We also know that amphetamines are chemically very similar to dopamine and may cause an increase in dopamine levels in the brain. Logic then leads us to wonder if schizophrenic symptoms (particularly those we call positive symptoms) are caused by excess amounts of dopamine.

Support for this view, called the **dopamine hypothesis,** comes from examining the action of drugs that actually reduce schizophrenic symptoms. Some drugs that ease schizophrenic symptoms block receptor sites for dopamine in the brain (Snyder, 1980). If reducing the effectiveness of dopamine by blocking its activity at the synapse can control schizophrenic symptoms, might we assume that these symptoms are caused by dopamine in the first place (Tandon & Greden, 1989)?

The arguments for this hypothesis appear compelling, but are far from certain. For one thing, there is little evidence that persons with schizophrenia have elevated levels of dopamine in their brains (Karoum et al., 1987). Even so, there may be a heightened sensitivity in the brains of schizophrenics to whatever levels of dopamine are present (e.g., perhaps there are more receptor sites for dopamine). Again, this may sound reasonable, but there is little direct evidence to support such a conclusion. For another thing, not all medications used to treat schizophrenia have their effects by blocking dopamine receptor sites. It is also troublesome that when drugs are effective, their effects usually take weeks to show up. If the effect of the drugs on receptor sites is immediate, why isn't the effect on symptoms immediate also?

We also have a "chicken-and-egg" problem here. If dopamine were related to schizophrenia, we would still have to ask if the relationship was causal. Do high levels of dopamine cause schizophrenic symptoms, or does the disorder cause elevated dopamine levels? Does some other factor, such as stress cause elevated dopamine levels *and* schizophrenic symptoms? We have the same chicken-and-egg problem with other findings concerning brain structure and schizophrenia. The brains of many patients with schizophrenia, most commonly those with positive symptoms, have abnormally large ventricles (cavities or openings that contain cerebrospinal fluid) (Andreasen et al., 1982, 1990a), and evidence suggests a lack of balance between the two hemispheres of the brain (Gur et al., 1987; Reveley et al., 1987). Even if these differences in the brain are confirmed, we still don't know if we're dealing with causes or effects.

Psychological and Social Factors.

Perhaps genetic and/or biochemical factors predispose a person to develop the symptoms of schizophrenia. What sorts of events or situations tend to turn such predispositions into reality for the schizophrenic? To this question, our answers are very sketchy.

One of the standard views is that schizophrenia develops as a response to early experiences within the family unit (e.g., Lidz, 1973). The early experiences of persons who later develop schizophrenic symptoms sometimes seem different from those who do not develop schizophrenia. In truth, however, very few mental health professionals put much stock in the notion that family life style has much to do with the development of schizophrenia.

dopamine hypothesis
the point of view that schizophrenia results from unusually high levels of the neurotransmitter dopamine in the brain

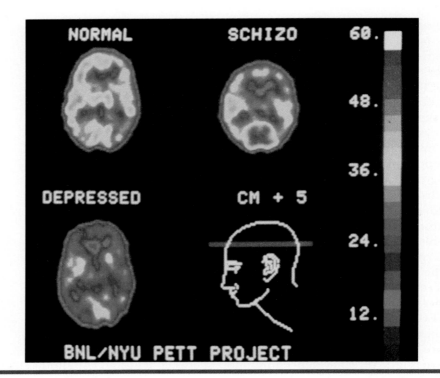

Demonstrating the involvement of the brain in psychological disorders, these PET scans show brain images of someone diagnosed with schizophrenia and of someone in a depressed state. A normal brain image is shown for comparison.

There is evidence that the symptoms of schizophrenia in some people remain dormant, or unexpressed, unless or until the individual is subjected to environmental stressors (Gottesman & Bertelsen, 1989; Johnson, 1989; Ventura et al., 1989). The idea here is that some people are genetically prone to develop schizophrenia when they are exposed to stressors, while other people, faced with the same stressors, might develop ulcers, or become excessively anxious, or show no symptoms at all. So it is possible that some life experiences bring on the symptoms of schizophrenia or make those symptoms worse than they would be otherwise. The consensus, however, is that with schizophrenia we are dealing with a disease of the brain that presents itself with psychological symptoms, and not a "disorder of living" (Johnson, 1989). "How the environment interacts with genetic risk to trigger the development of schizophrenia remains unknown" (Iacono & Grove, 1993).

● **Before You Go On**

Describe some of the factors that have been implicated as possible causes of schizophrenic symptoms.

THINKING CRITICALLY ABOUT THE PSYCHOLOGICAL DISORDERS

1. Given that the differences between normality and abnormality are often difficult to determine precisely, under what circumstances is it justifiable to declare that someone has a psychological disorder?
2. Why is it that someone who might be willing to tell us about his or her physical illnesses (e.g., all the gory details of a recent surgery), will

probably be unwilling to openly talk about any personal experiences with mental illness?

3. Did you notice that throughout all of Chapter 12 there was no mention of anyone having a "nervous breakdown?" This is because, technically, there is no such psychological disorder, even though the term is used frequently outside of psychology. What do you think would be the appropriate diagnosis (or diagnoses) for someone said to have had a nervous breakdown?

4. Phobias are characterized by an intense, irrational fear. What is the difference, if any, between "fear" and "anxiety?"

5. What is the source of most of the anxiety associated with the anxiety disorders? (Hint: Think back to the last chapter.)

6. Women are diagnosed as suffering from major depression much more commonly than are men. This could be because the disorder simply occurs more frequently in women. If this is the case, why does it? What other reasons might there be for the diagnosis being more common for women than for men?

7. What does the fact that schizophrenia occurs at about the same rate worldwide suggest about its cause or its source?

SUMMARY

TOPIC 12A
DEFINING AND CLASSIFYING PSYCHOLOGICAL DISORDERS

● How do we define psychological abnormality?

In the context of psychological disorders, abnormal means maladaptive behaviors, cognitions, and/or affect that are at odds with social or cultural expectations, and that result in distress or discomfort. *Pages 408–410.*

● What is the *DSM-IV*?
● What are some of the advantages and disadvantages of classifying psychological disorders?

The *DSM-IV* is the fourth edition of the *Diagnostic and Statistical Manual of Mental Disorders*, the accepted standard classification system for psychological disorders as determined by a committee of psychologists and psychiatrists. The major advantage of the system is that it provides an agreed-upon label and symptoms for each disorder that all mental health professionals can use; it is an aid to communication. It has its limitations, however. Labels tend to dehumanize. They put the brunt of a disorder on the person, not the group to which the individual belongs. Also, classification systems and labels only describe; they do not explain. *Pages 411–413.*

TOPIC 12B
A SAMPLING OF PSYCHOLOGICAL DISORDERS

● Describe the symptoms of generalized anxiety disorder.
● What is comorbidity, and what is its significance?

The major defining symptom of generalized anxiety disorder is a high level of felt anxiety that cannot be attributed to any particular source. In this disorder, the anxiety is chronic, persistent, and diffuse. Comorbidity refers to a situation in which one person is diagnosed with two or more different disorders at the same time. It is a significant concept in psychology because so many disorders do occur along with others—more than three-quarters of those who have a psychological disorder in their lifetime will have two or more different disorders. *Pages 414–416.*

● What is a panic disorder?
● Contrast panic disorder with generalized anxiety disorder.

The defining symptom of a panic disorder is a sudden, often unpredictable attack of extreme anxiety, called a panic attack. These attacks may last for seconds or hours. There is no particular stimulus to prompt the attack. Where the anxiety of generalized anxiety disorder may be characterized as chronic, with panic disorder, it is acute. *Pages 416–417.*

● What are the essential characteristics of a phobic disorder?

By definition, a phobic disorder is typified by an intense, persistent fear of some object, activity, or situation that is in no real sense a threat to the individual's well-being; in brief, an intense, irrational fear. The disorder also prompts attempts to avoid the feared stimulus. *Pages 417–418.*

● What characterizes the obsessive-compulsive disorder?

Obsessions and compulsions are the main presenting complaint in obsessive-compulsive disorder (OCD). An obsession is an idea or thought that constantly intrudes on awareness. A compulsion, on the other hand, is a repeated and stereotyped act that intrudes on one's behavior. The person gains no pleasure from these repeated thoughts or actions, but cannot stop them. *Pages 419–421.*

● Describe the symptoms of posttraumatic stress disorder.

Posttraumatic stress disorder, or PTSD, is an anxiety disorder in which the symptoms of high levels of anxiety, recurrent and disruptive dreams, and recollections of a highly traumatic event (e.g., rape, combat, natural disaster) occur well after the danger of the event has passed. *Pages 421–422.*

● Describe hypochondriasis and conversion disorder.

These are two of the somatoform disorders—psychological disorders reflected by a physical or bodily symptom or complaint. In each case, however, there is no known biological cause for the complaint. In hypochondriasis, a person lives in fear and dread of contracting some serious illness or disease, when there is no medical evidence to justify such a fear. In conversion disorder, there is an actual loss or alteration in physical functioning—often dramatic—not under voluntary control, which suggests a physical disorder, but with no physical basis for the loss or alteration. *Pages 422–423.*

● What are the defining symptoms of the dissociative disorders?

Dissociative disorders are marked by a retreat or escape (dissociation) from an aspect of one's personality. It may be a matter of an inability to recall some life event (dissociative amnesia), sometimes accompanied by unexplained travel (dissociative fugue). In some rare cases, certain aspects of one's personality become so dissociated that we say that the person suffers from dissociative identity disorder (multiple personality), where two or more personalities are found within the same person. *Pages 423–425.*

● What are the defining characteristics of the personality disorders?

Personality disorders (PDs) are enduring patterns of perceiving, relating to, and thinking about the environment and oneself that are both inflexible and maladaptive. These are essentially life-long patterns of maladjustment and are classified as belonging to one of three clusters, or groups. Group 1 includes PDs involving odd or eccentric reactions, such as the paranoid or schizoid personality disorders. Group 2 includes disorders of dramatic, emotional, or erratic reactions, such as the antisocial or histrionic personality disorders. Group 3 includes disorders involving fear or anxiety, such as the avoidant or dependent personality disorder. *Pages 425–427.*

● What is Alzheimer's disease, and what causes it?

Alzheimer's disease is a form of degenerative dementia associated with known abnormalities of the brain—among other things, the formation of tangles and plaques. There is a gradual but steady loss of intellectual abilities, notably a loss of memory functions. There is a strong likelihood of a genetic basis for the disease. Research is also focusing on the formation of certain brain proteins and the neurotransmitter acetylcholine. *Pages 427–429.*

- How are the mood disorders defined?
- What do we know about their prevalence and their causes?

Although many psychological disorders involve disturbances of affect, in the mood disorders, a disturbance in mood or feeling is the prime, perhaps only, major symptom. Most commonly we find depression alone (major depression). Less commonly we find depression and mania occurring in cycles (in bipolar mood disorder). In milder, but chronic forms of experienced depression coupled with anxiety, we have the disorder dysthymia. In any case, whether the major symptom is depression, mania, or a combination, there is no acceptable reason for the extent or duration of one's mood. Depression is a common disorder, affecting as many as 20 percent of all women and 10 percent of all men at some time in their lives. The disorder has a strong hereditary basis. Neurotransmitters (biogenic amines) such as serotonin and dopamine have been implicated in depression. Psychological explanations tend to focus on the learned ineffectiveness of reinforcers, and cognitive factors such as poor self-image, as explanations of the causes of depression. *Pages 429–432.*

- What are the major symptoms of schizophrenia?

Schizophrenia is a label applied to several disorders that all involve varying degrees of cognitive impairment (delusions, hallucinations, disturbances of thought), social isolation, and disturbances of affect and behavior. *Pages 432–433.*

- What characterizes the following varieties of schizophrenia: paranoid, disorganized, catatonic, undifferentiated, residual, process vs. reactive, and positive vs. negative?

Paranoid schizophrenia involves delusions and hallucinations that often support these delusions. Disorganized schizophrenia involves a severe disintegration of personality with emotional distortions, inappropriate laughter, and bizarre behaviors. Catatonic schizophrenia is characterized by catatonia (physical immobility) or extreme excitement. Undifferentiated schizophrenia involves several symptoms of the disease, none of which dominates, and residual schizophrenia indicates a mild form of the disorder following a schizophrenic episode. Process schizophrenia is the term used when symptoms develop gradually. When symptoms develop quickly, it is called reactive schizophrenia. The latter has a somewhat better prognosis than the former. Positive symptoms of schizophrenia include the addition of delusions, hallucinations, or bizarreness to one's behaviors, whereas negative symptoms refer to losses: social withdrawal, loss of appropriate affect, apathy, and loss of ability to pay attention. *Pages 433–435.*

- Describe some of the factors that have been implicated as possible causes of schizophrenic symptoms.

Although we certainly do not know the causes of schizophrenia, three lines of investigation have produced helpful leads: (1) There is little doubt of a genetic predisposition for the disorder. Schizophrenia is not directly inherited, but it does tend to run in families. (2) Research on biochemical correlates have localized the neurotransmitter dopamine as being involved in the production of schizophrenic symptoms, although dopamine's role in the disorder is now being questioned. (3) It also seems reasonable to hypothesize that early childhood experiences, particularly those involving parent-child interactions, may predispose one to the disease, but such influences are small. Schizophrenia is, after all, a disease of the brain with psychological symptoms. A reasonable position at the moment is that for some persons, environmental events, such as extreme stressors, trigger biochemical and structural changes in the brain that result in the symptoms of schizophrenia. *Pages 435–438.*

TOPIC 12A

DEFINING AND CLASSIFYING PSYCHOLOGICAL DISORDERS

12.1 As you read this item, which provides the best estimate of the percentage of Americans who are suffering from a psychological disorder? a) 10 percent b) 20 percent c) 40 percent d) There is no way to make such an estimate. *Pages 408–410.*

12.2 Which of these is *not* included in our definition of psychological abnormality? a) maladaptive b) bizarre or strange c) distress or discomfort d) affect, behavior, and/or cognition. *Pages 408–410.*

12.3 Which of the following is *true* concerning people with psychological disorders? a) They tend to be more dangerous than others. b) They usually realize that they have some sort of problem. c) They are distinctly different from people who are normal. d) They are people who have poor self-control or will power. *Pages 411–413.*

12.4 Classification schemes and labels for psychological disorders, such as those found in the *DSM-IV*, have some potential problems. Which of these is *not* one of those problems? a) Labels tend to dehumanize real human suffering. b) There is no logical or sensible rationale behind such schemes. c) They usually focus on the individual and the groups to which the individual belongs. d) Schemes and labels may define and describe, but they do not explain. *Pages 411–413.*

12.5 True or False? Insanity is a term that comes from the legal profession, not from psychology or psychiatry. *Pages 411–413.*

TOPIC 12B

A SAMPLING OF PSYCHOLOGICAL DISORDERS

12.6 Everything else being equal, which disorder has the best prognosis? a) schizophrenia b) multiple personality c) phobic disorder d) antisocial personality disorder. *Pages 414–416.*

12.7 True or False? The most common phobia is a fear of the dark. *Pages 417–418.*

12.8 What two words or terms best differentiate between panic disorder and generalized anxiety disorder? a) acute and chronic b) stimulus and response c) rational and irrational d) distress and discomfort. *Pages 414–417.*

12.9 Constantly checking to confirm that the front door is really locked may be a sign of a(n) a) fugue state. b) phobia. c) conversion disorder. d) obsessive-compulsive disorder. *Pages 419–421.*

12.10 By definition, what do the somatoform disorders have in common? a) either hallucinations or delusions b) bodily symptoms or complaints c) exaggerated fears and anxieties d) feelings of profound depression. *Pages 422–423.*

12.11 True or False? Persons with hypochondriasis typically show symptoms of blindness, deafness, or paralysis. *Pages 422–423.*

12.12 The disorder that used to be called "multiple personality" is a) significantly less common than it was 50 years ago. b) a common form of schizophrenic disorder. c) classified as a dissociative disorder.

d) characterized by a sense of "la belle indifference." *Pages 423–425.*

12.13 True or False? Fugue states are typically accompanied by amnesia. *Pages 423–425.*

12.14 Which is characterized in terms of being overly dramatic, with intensely expressed behaviors? a) histrionic personality disorder b) avoidant personality disorder c) antisocial personality disorder d) paranoid personality disorder. *Pages 423–425.*

12.15 Tracy reports feeling anxious, nervous, and "on edge" all day long. She is tired, but cannot sleep well, and sometimes feels like crying for no apparent reason. If Tracy has a disorder, the best diagnosis is that Tracy is experiencing a(n) _____ disorder. a) psychogenic fugue b) obsessive-compulsive c) generalized anxiety d) panic. *Pages 423–425.*

12.16 True or False? The personality disorders are classified as anxiety disorders. *Pages 425–427.*

12.17 The collection of disorders called mood disorders has as its major symptom a) disorganized thinking and confusion. b) strange, unexplainable behaviors. c) disturbances of affect. d) cognitive disorientation. *Pages 429–432.*

12.18 By far, the most common form of mood disorder is a) depression. b) bipolar. c) paranoia. d) mania. *Pages 429–432.*

12.19 Concerning the mood disorders, each of the following is true *except* a) Depression is more common in women than in men. b) It is more common to find depression alone than mania alone. c) Depression generally occurs in a series of episodes. d) The symptoms of mania rarely reoccur or relapse. *Pages 429–432.*

12.20 Of these factors, which seems to be the *least* involved as a cause of depression? a) early childhood experiences b) genetic predispositions c) neurotransmitters d) biogenic amines. *Pages 429–432.*

12.21 True or False? By definition, patients cannot be depressed and anxious at the same time. *Pages 429–432.*

12.22 In what way can we refer to schizophrenia as the text does—as the "ultimate" psychological disorder? a) It is the most prevalent or common disorder. b) It impairs affect, behavior, and cognitions. c) It is a disorder from which virtually no one recovers. d) It produces symptoms that are wild and bizarre. *Pages 432–433.*

12.23 Which of these symptoms is *not* associated with schizophrenia? a) high levels of felt anxiety b) social withdrawal or retreat from others c) flattened or inappropriate affect d) disturbed cognitions, including delusions. *Pages 432–433.*

12.24 True or False? Schizophrenia means "split mind" —literally splitting the mind into two (or more) different and distinct personalities. *Pages 432–433.*

12.25 When the symptoms of the disorder develop gradually, even over a period of years, we are seeing an example of _____ schizophrenia. a) positive b) process c) undifferentiated d) negative. *Pages 433–435.*

12.26 Each of these is a symptom of schizophrenia. Which is a positive symptom? a) social withdrawal b) poor attention c) hallucinations d) gradual onset. *Pages 432–433.*

12.27 About which statement concerning the causes of schizophrenia may we feel most certain? a) Excessive levels of dopamine cause schizophrenia. b) Schizophrenia results from child abuse. c) Schizophrenia runs in families. d) Parents of schizophrenics are cold and aloof. *Pages 436–438.*

12.28 True or False? About one-quarter of those diagnosed as having schizophrenia recover from the disorder and remain symptom free for at least five years. *Pages 436–438.*

13

TREATMENT
AND THERAPY

PREVIEW

TOPIC 13A—History and
Biomedical Treatments

A Historical Perspective

Who Provides Treatment
and Therapy?

Biomedical Treatments of
Psychological Disorders

TOPIC 13B—The
Psychotherapies

Psychoanalytic Techniques

PSYCHOLOGY IN THE
REAL WORLD: What Shall
We Do with the Most
Seriously Disturbed?

Humanistic Techniques

Behavioral Techniques

Cognitive Techniques

Group Approaches

Evaluating Psychotherapy

THINKING CRITICALLY
ABOUT TREATMENT AND
THERAPY

SUMMARY

TEST YOURSELF

In Chapter 12 we discussed psychological disorders and noted that such disorders are far from rare. Tens of millions of Americans are afflicted with psychological problems—from minor difficulties in adjusting to stress to the disruption of functioning of schizophrenia. In this chapter, we turn our attention to what can be done to help those people suffering from psychological disorders.

To begin, we'll take a very brief look at the history of treatment for psychological disorders. This history provides us with some insight as to why, even today, so many people have such strong negative attitudes about people with psychological disorders. We'll review a list of the types of professionals who provide treatment or therapy for psychological disorders, and we'll end Topic 13A by considering methods of treatment that generally fall outside the realm of psychology: treatments that are medical in nature. We'll consider psychosurgery and shock therapies but will concentrate on the use of drugs to control and treat the symptoms of mental illness.

Topic 13B is devoted to varieties of psychotherapy—techniques "designed to influence the patient's behavior by psychological means, that is, they seek to persuade the patient to think, feel, or act differently" (Strupp, 1986, p. 128). We'll discuss five types of therapy: psychoanalytic (or Freudian), humanistic, behavioral, cognitive, and group techniques. Having reviewed some of the major methods, we will try to evaluate psychotherapy as a whole. Does it work? If so, under what circumstances?

TOPIC 13A

HISTORY AND BIOMEDICAL TREATMENTS

Mental illness is not a new phenomenon. Among the earliest written records from the Babylonians, Egyptians, and ancient Hebrews we find descriptions of what we now recognize as psychological disorders (Murray, 1983). How individuals were treated was consistent with the prevailing view of what caused their disorders. Let's take a brief look at some of that history.

This painting by Hieronymus Bosch depicts one of the procedures used on the psychologically disordered in the Middle Ages. Based on the belief that evil stones in the head were the cause of a patient's problems, attempts to remove them involved boring a hole in the skull—without the benefit of anesthetic.

A HISTORICAL PERSPECTIVE

The history of the treatment of psychological disorders in the Western world is not a pleasant one. By today's standards, therapy—in the sense of an active, humane intervention to improve the condition of persons in psychological distress—does not even seem like an appropriate term to describe the way in which most disordered persons were dealt with in the past.

The ancient Greeks and Romans believed that people who were depressed, manic, irrational, intellectually retarded, or who had hallucinations and delusions had in some way offended the gods. In some cases, persons were seen as temporarily out of favor with the gods, and it followed that their condition could be improved by prayer and religious ritual. More severely disturbed persons were seen as being physically possessed by evil spirits. These cases were more difficult, often impossible to cure. The goal of the ancients was to exorcise the evil spirits and demons inhabiting the minds and souls of the mentally deranged. Many unfortunates died as a direct result of their treatment, or were killed outright when treatment failed. Treatment was left to the priests who were, after all, thought to be skilled in the means of spirit manipulation.

There were those in ancient times who had a more enlightened or reasonable view of psychological disorders. Among them was Hippocrates (460–377 B.C.), who believed that mental disorders had physical causes, not spiritual ones. He identified epilepsy as being a disorder of the brain, for example. Some of his views were wrong (e.g., that hysteria is a disorder of the uterus), but at least he tried to demystify mental illness.

During the Middle Ages (A.D. 1000–1500) the oppression and persecution of the disordered were at their peak. During this period, the prevailing view continued to be that psychologically disordered people were "bad people," under the spell of devils and evil spirits. They had brought on their own grief, and there was no hope for them, except that they confess their evil ways and save their immortal souls.

For hundreds of years, well into the eighteenth century, the attitude toward the mentally ill continued to be that they were in league with the devil or that they were being punished by God for sinful thoughts and deeds. They were witches who could not be cured except through confession. When confessions were not forthcoming, the prescribed treatment was torture. If torture failed to evoke a confession, death was the only recourse; often it was death by being burned at the stake. Between the fourteenth and mid-seventeenth centuries roughly 200,000 to 500,000 "witches" were put to death (Ben-Yehuda, 1980).

When the disordered (or severely retarded) were not tortured or immediately put to death, they were placed in asylums. The first insane asylum, established in 1547, was St. Mary of Bethlehem Hospital in London, which housed "fools" and "lunatics." The institution became known as Bedlam (a cockney pronunciation of Bethlehem). It was a terrible place. Inmates were tortured, poorly fed, or starved to death. To remove the "bad blood" from their systems, thought to be a cause of their symptoms, patients were led to bleeding chambers, where a small incision was made in a vein in the calf of their legs so their blood would ooze into leather buckets. There was no professional staff at Bedlam. The keepers, as they were called, could make extra money by putting their charges on view for the general public. Viewing the lunatics of Bedlam became an established entertainment for the nobility. Inmates who were able were sent into the streets to beg, wearing a sign identifying them as "fools of Bedlam." Even today we use the word *bedlam* to describe a condition or scene of wild uproar and confusion.

It would be comforting to think that Bedlam was an exception. It was not. In the eighteenth and nineteenth centuries asylums like Bedlam were commonplace. Against this backdrop of misery and despair, the names of a few enlightened individuals deserve mention. One is *Philippe Pinel* (1745–1826), a French physician who in the midst of the French Revolution was named director of an asylum for the insane in Paris. We know of Pinel today largely because of an act of compassion and courage. The law of the day required that inmates be chained and confined. On September 2, 1793, Pinel ordered the chains and shackles removed from about fifty of the inmates of his "hospital." He allowed them to move freely about the institution and grounds. This humane gesture had surprising effects. In many cases, symptoms were relieved. A few patients were even released from the asylum. Unfortunately, Pinel's "humane therapy," as he called it, did not spread to other institutions, but his successes were recorded for future generations.

Benjamin Rush (1745–1813) was the founder of American psychiatry. He published the first text on mental disorders in the United States in 1812. Although some of the treatments suggested by Rush seem barbaric by today's standards (he was a believer in bleeding, for example), his general attitudes were very humane. He argued vehemently and successfully, for example, that the mentally ill should not be placed on display to satisfy the curiosity of onlookers. *Dorothea Dix* (1802–1887) was a nurse. In 1841 she took a position in a women's prison and was appalled at what she saw there. Included among the prisoners were hundreds of women who clearly were mentally retarded or psychologically disordered. Despite her slight stature and her own ill health, Dix entered upon a crusade of singular vigor. She went from state to state, campaigning for reform in prisons, mental hospitals, and asylums.

Clifford Beers, a graduate of Yale University, had been institutionalized in a series of hospitals and asylums. It seems likely that he was suffering from what we now call a bipolar mood disorder. Probably in spite of his treatment rather than because of it, Beers recovered and was released—in itself an unusual occurrence. In 1908, he wrote a book about his experience, *A Mind That Found Itself*. The book became a bestseller—Theodore Roosevelt and William James were said to be very impressed with Beers and his story—and is often cited as providing a stimulus for the reform we now identify as the "mental health movement."

Thus, history tells us that until recently, the prevailing view of the psychologically disturbed was that they were bad people, possessed by demons and devils, unable to control their behaviors and thoughts and unable to be cured. The only recourse was to separate them from everyone else—to "put them away." Since the early 1900s, progress in providing help for the mentally ill has been both slow and unsteady. World War I and the Depression reduced the funds available to support state institutions for mental patients. Within the past 50 years, conditions have improved greatly, but there is still a long way to go. We continue to fight a prejudice against people suffering from psychological disorders.

Associating psychological disorders with witches and witchcraft was an attitude that flourished during the fifteenth and sixteenth centuries. Goay's painting, entitled *The Witches Sabbath*, reflects this popular preoccupation of the times.

Regardless of the specifics involved, all forms of psychotherapy are designed to persuade a person to think, feel, and act differently.

● **Before You Go On**
Briefly trace the history of the treatment of people with psychological disorders.

WHO PROVIDES TREATMENT AND THERAPY?

Many professionals are equipped to provide treatment or therapy for psychological disorders. Below is a list of the most common types of mental health providers, as they are sometimes called. Please keep in mind that what follows is a list of generalities; my descriptions will not hold true for everyone within a given category. Remember also that because of their experience or training, professionals develop specialties within their fields. That is, some therapists specialize in the disorders of children and adolescents; some work primarily with adults; some prefer to work with families; some devote their efforts to people with substance and alcohol abuse problems. Some have special training in dealing with clients from various cultures or ethnic groups (Koslow & Salett, 1989; Sue & Sue, 1990). Finally, a psychotherapist can and will use several of the techniques of therapy outlined in this chapter. In other words, few therapists take just one approach to treatment. As many as 40 percent of therapists claim to have no particularly dominant approach to their psychotherapy (Norcross, 1986). The following types of professionals may be described as psychotherapists:

1. The *clinical psychologist* usually has earned a Ph.D. in psychology from a program that provides practical, applied experience, as well as an emphasis on research. The Ph.D. clinician spends a year on internship, usually at a mental health center or psychiatric hospital. The

clinical psychologist has extensive training in psychological testing (in general, *psychodiagnostics*). Some clinical psychologists have a Psy.D. (pronounced "sigh-dee") which is a Doctor of Psychology, rather than the Doctor of Philosophy degree. Psy.D. programs generally take as long to complete as Ph.D. programs, but emphasize more practical, clinical work and place less emphasis on research.

2. Psychiatry is a specialty area in medicine. In addition to the course work required for an M.D., the *psychiatrist* spends an internship (usually one year) and a residency (usually 3 years) in a mental hospital, specializing in the care of psychologically disturbed patients. At least at the moment, the psychiatrist is the only kind of psychotherapist permitted to use the biomedical treatments we will be discussing. [There is now a campaign underway to get some medical privileges for Ph.D. psychologists.]

3. The *counseling psychologist* usually has a Ph.D. in psychology. The focus of study (and the required one-year internship), however, is generally on patients with less severe psychological problems. Rather than spending an internship in a psychiatric hospital, a counseling psychologist would more likely spend time at a university counseling center.

4. A *licensed professional counselor* will have a degree in counselor education and will have met state requirements for a license to do psychotherapy. Counselors can be found in school settings, but also work in mental health settings, specializing in family counseling and drug abuse.

5. *Psychoanalyst* is a special label given either to a clinical psychologist or a psychiatrist who also has received intensive training and certification in the methods of Freudian psychoanalysis.

6. The terminal degree for *clinical social workers* is generally the master's degree, although P.h.Ds in social work are becoming more common. Social workers engage in a variety of psychotherapies, but their traditional role has been involvement in family and group therapy.

Psychotherapy may be offered by other professionals and paraprofessionals. Some people practice therapy or counseling with a master's degree in psychology (although because of licensing or certification laws in many states, they usually cannot advertise themselves as "psychologists"). *Occupational therapists* typically have a master's degree in occupational therapy and internship training in aiding the psychologically and physically handicapped. *Psychiatric nurses* often work in mental hospitals and clinics. In addition to their R.N. degrees, psychiatric nurses have special training in the care of mentally ill patients. *Pastoral counseling* is a specialty of many with a religious background and a masters degree in either psychology or educational counseling. A *mental health technician* generally has an associate's degree in mental health technology (MHT). MHT graduates seldom are allowed to provide unsupervised psychotherapy, although they may be involved in the delivery of many mental health services.

● **Before You Go On**

Who may offer psychotherapy?

What is the major difference between psychologists and psychiatrists?

BIOMEDICAL TREATMENTS OF PSYCHOLOGICAL DISORDERS

As I just noted, treatments that are medical in nature are not used by psychologists. Currently, performing surgery, administering shock treatments, or prescribing drugs requires a medical degree. Psychologists often are involved in biomedical treatments, however. Psychologists may recommend medical treatment and refer a client to the care of a physician or psychiatrist.

Here we'll review three biomedical interventions: psychosurgery, which was quite common just 50 years ago, but is now quite rare; shock treatment, which is far from uncommon; and drug therapy, which is the newest and one of the most promising developments in the treatment of mental illness.

Psychosurgery

psychosurgery
a surgical procedure designed to affect one's psychological or behavioral reactions

Psychosurgery is the name we give to surgical procedures (usually directed at the brain) designed to affect psychological reactions. Psychosurgical techniques in use today are largely experimental. They are aimed at making minimal lesions in the brain (to treat chronic pain, epilepsy, or depression, for example). Small surgical lesions in the limbic system have been found to be effective in reducing some violent behaviors. Surgical techniques also have been used, although infrequently, to reduce extreme anxiety and the symptoms of obsessive-compulsive disorder.

lobotomy
a psychosurgical technique in which the prefrontal lobes of the cerebral cortex are severed from lower brain centers

Of all the varieties of psychosurgery, none has ever been used as commonly as a procedure called a prefrontal **lobotomy** (Valenstein, 1980, 1986). This procedure severs the major neural connections between the prefrontal lobes (the area at the very front of the cerebral cortex) and lower brain centers.

A lobotomy was first performed in 1935 by Portuguese psychiatrist Egas Moniz. For developing the procedure, Moniz was awarded the Nobel Prize in 1949. (The next year, in an ironic twist of fate, Moniz was shot by one of his lobotomized patients. He was rendered a paraplegic and confined to a wheelchair for the rest of his life.) The logic behind a lobotomy was that the frontal lobes influence the emotional centers of the brain and that psychotic patients had difficulty in coordinating these lower brain centers. It was reasoned that if they were separated surgically, the more depressed, agitated, or violent patients could be brought under control.

Treating severely disturbed, depressed, and schizophrenic patients had always been difficult. Perhaps we shouldn't be surprised that this relatively simple surgical technique was accepted so widely and uncritically at first. The procedure often was done under local anesthetic in the doctor's office, lasting only ten minutes. An instrument that looks very much like an ice pick was inserted through the eye socket, on the nasal side, and was pushed up into the brain. A few simple movements of the instrument and the job was done—the lobes were severed. Within hours, the patient was ready to return to his or her room.

It always was appreciated that the procedure was irreversible. What took longer to realize was that it often carried with it terrible side effects. Between 1 and 4 percent of patients receiving lobotomies died (Carson & Butcher, 1992, p. 610). Many of those who survived suffered seizures, memory loss, an inability to plan ahead, listlessness and loss of affect. Many

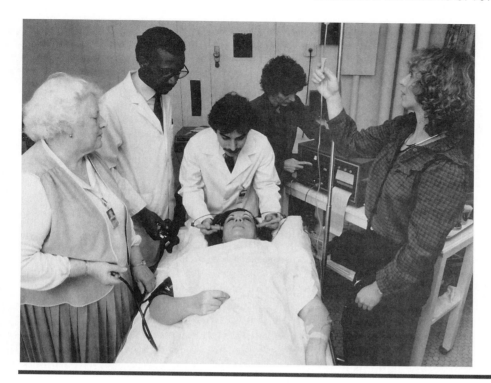

Electroconvulsive shock therapy is not pleasant to watch, and there is concern that we do not yet fully understand why the procedure often seems to be an effective treatment for extreme cases of major depression.

acted childishly and were difficult to manage. By the late 1950s, lobotomies had become rare. Contrary to common belief, it is not an illegal procedure, although the conditions under which it might even be considered are very restrictive. Prefrontal lobotomies are not done anymore for the simple reason that they are no longer needed. There are other means, with fewer side effects, that produce similar beneficial results more safely and reliably.

● Before You Go On

What is a prefrontal lobotomy?

Why was it ever used, and why is it not used today?

Electroconvulsive Therapy

As gruesome as the procedures of psychosurgery can be, many people find the very notion of **electroconvulsive therapy (ECT)** even more difficult to appreciate. This technique, first introduced in 1937, involves passing an electric current of between 70 and 150 volts across a patient's head for a fraction of a second. The patient has been given a fast-acting general anesthetic and is unconscious when the shock is delivered. As soon as the anesthetic is administered, the patient also receives a muscle relaxant to minimize muscular contractions, which were quite common—and dangerous—in the early days of ECT. The electric shock induces a reaction in the brain that is similar to an epileptic seizure. The whole procedure takes about five minutes. One of the side effects of ECT is a memory loss for events just preceding the shock and for the shock itself.

At first, the treatment was used to help calm agitated schizophrenics, but it soon became clear that its most beneficial results were for patients suffering from major depression. It often alleviates depression and, in

electroconvulsive therapy (ECT)

a treatment, usually for the symptoms of severe depression, in which an electric current passed through a patient's head causes a seizure and loss of consciousness some cases, has beneficial effects on other symptoms as well. In fact, the group of patients that seem best suited to the ECT procedure are those for whom depression is a major symptom, and for whom other symptoms (hallucinations or delusions) are present also (Joyce & Paykel, 1989).

Virtually all patients (97 percent) consent to the procedure, and negative side effects are rare. The most commonly reported side effect is memory loss and general mental confusion. In nearly all cases, these effects disappear in a few days or weeks. Once they have experienced the procedure, most ECT patients are far from terrorized by the notion of having an electric shock sent through their brain. In one study, 82 percent of the 166 patients surveyed rated ECT as no more upsetting than a visit to the dentist (Sackeim, 1985). The beneficial effects of ECT are reasonably long-lasting. After only 10 to 12 treatments, many patients remain free of symptoms for months.

On the other hand, the poor reputation that ECT has among the general population and among some psychologists and psychiatrists did not develop without foundation. There *are* horror stories of the negative side effects that can follow abuse of the procedure. At first, the seizures of the shock treatment were induced by drugs, not electricity. It was from these treatments that we have the stories of convulsions so massive as to result in broken bones. It is now recommended that no more than a dozen treatments be given, and that they be administered over an extended period of time. Some patients in the past have received hundreds of ECT treatments. In such cases, there may have been brain damage and permanent memory loss.

We do not understand why ECT produces the benefits that it does. Research efforts today are focusing on the action of neurotransmitters in the brain for possible explanations. Even though we do not understand how ECT works and even though it must be used with extreme care, ECT is still very much in practice today. Although the numbers declined during the late 1970s, nearly 100,000 patients receive shock treatments each year, and numbers again are on the rise (Thompson & Blaine, 1987).

The introduction of psychoactive medications has reduced the need to use ECT. But drug treatment is not always successful, and even when it is, it often takes six to eight weeks for the drugs to produce beneficial results. In many cases ECT is a more effective treatment than are antidepressant medications (Small et al., 1988). Some researchers argue that administering a shock to just one side of the brain, called *a unilateral ECT,* is a safer, equally effective procedure with fewer side effects. More success has been found by creating seizures in the right hemisphere of the cerebral cortex (thought to be more associated with emotional reactions) than in the left (Squire & Slater, 1978).

● **Before You Go On**

What is ECT?

Why is it still being used?

Drug Therapy

Chemicals that alter a person's cognitions, affect, or behavior are called *psychoactive drugs.* As we've already seen, there are many of them, and most are used to produce an altered state of consciousness. Using chemicals to improve the condition of the mentally disordered has been a much more recent development and has been hailed as one of the most significant scientific achievements of the last half of the twentieth century (Snyder, 1984).

Antipsychotic Drugs. As their name suggests, **antipsychotic drugs** have the effect of alleviating the major symptoms of psychoses—those severe disorders, such as schizophrenia, that involve gross impairment in functioning and a loss of contact with reality—delusions and hallucinations in particular. The real breakthrough in the use of antipsychotic drugs came with the introduction of *chlorpromazine*. In 1950, a French neurosurgeon, Henri Laborit, was looking for a drug to calm his patients just before surgery. Laborit wanted to help his patients relax because he knew that if they did, their postsurgical recovery would be improved. A drug company gave Laborit chlorpromazine to try. It worked better than anyone had expected, producing calm and relaxation in his patients. Laborit convinced some of his colleagues to try the drug on their more agitated patients who had psychological disorders. The experiments met with great success, and by the late 1950s the drug was widely used both in North America and in Europe. By 1956 more than half a dozen antipsychotic medications were available in the United States.

Chlorpromazine is just one of many drugs currently being used with success to treat psychotic symptoms. Most antipsychotic drugs are of the same general type, and most work in essentially the same way—by blocking receptor sites for dopamine in the brain (see p. 57). Antipsychotic drugs are most effective in treating the positive symptoms of psychosis—delusions, hallucinations, and bizarre behaviors. Clozapine (trade name *Clozaril*) appears to be an exception, because it seems to be effective in reducing negative symptoms as well as positive ones. Unfortunately, clozapine carries with it the risk of some very serious side effects, some of which can be fatal. As a result the use of this drug is very carefully monitored.

The effects of the antipsychotic drugs are remarkable and impressive, and they have revolutionized the care of psychotic patients. Nonetheless, they are not the ultimate solution for disorders such as schizophrenia. About 30 percent of patients with schizophrenia do not respond to antipsychotic drugs (Kane, 1989). The drugs are most effective when they are used early on, with patients who have recently been diagnosed (Lieberman et al., 1993). With high dosages or prolonged use a variety of side effects emerge that are very unpleasant at best, including dry mouth and throat, sore muscles and joints, heavy sedation, sexual impotence, and tremors. Sometimes side effects are even more significant, including seizures and cardiovascular damage. Although the most effective antipsychotic drugs do control symptoms, the question is: Are they in any sense curing the disorder? Symptom-free patients, who are released from institutional care to the outside world, often stop using their medication only to find that their psychotic symptoms return.

● **Before You Go On**

What are antipsychotic drugs, and what are their effects?

Antidepressant Drugs. **Antidepressant drugs** elevate the mood of persons who are feeling depressed. An antidepressant that has no measurable effect on one person may produce severe unpleasant side effects in another person and yet may have remarkably beneficial effects for a third person (Joyce & Paykel, 1989). Some antidepressant medications are useful in

antipsychotic drugs
chemicals, such as chlorpromazine, that are effective in reducing psychotic symptoms

antidepressant drugs
chemicals that reduce or eliminate the symptoms of depression

treating disorders other than depression, such as panic disorder and generalized anxiety disorder (Rickels et al., 1993).

These medications generally take 10 to 14 days to show any effect. The maximum effects often take six weeks to develop, and the medications need to be taken on a long-term basis to prevent a recurrence of the depression (Maxman, 1991). Antidepressant drugs can elevate the mood of many truly depressed people, but they have virtually no effect on people who are not depressed. That is, they do not make people who already feel good feel even better.

As you might have guessed, these drugs can produce unfortunate side effects, including intellectual confusion, increased perspiration, and weight gain. A problem with some types of antidepressant drugs is that they require adherence to a strict diet and carefully monitored dosages to have their best effect. They also produce a wide range of serious side effects, such as dizziness, sexual impotence, elevated blood pressure, and liver damage.

Fluoxetine (trade name *Prozac*) was introduced in 1987. It is the single most prescribed antidepressant; about 650,000 new or renewed prescriptions are written each month. By 1996, sales of *Prozac* are projected to exceed $5 billion. Chemically, it is unrelated to any other antidepressant. Often a very effective medication, its major advantage is that it produces fewer negative side effects. Nonetheless, these side effects (e.g., skin rashes, agitation, and weight loss) can be so unpleasant that patients stop using it. Before it was marketed, 15 percent of the patients receiving *Prozac* on a trial basis discontinued treatment because of adverse side effects. Since it has been available for a relatively short time, long-term effects of its use are as yet unknown. An even newer drug, *Effexor*, was approved by the Food and Drug Administration in 1993. So far, the drug shows great promise, and with few side effects. Like *Prozac*, *Effexor* targets levels of the neurotransmitter serotonin in the brain, but it does so with slightly more precision and also regulates norepinephrine levels.

This is an appropriate context in which to mention *lithium*, or lithium salts, such as lithium carbonate. Lithium salts are referred to as "mood stabilizers" (Maxman, 1991). They have been used with success in treating major depression, but are most useful in controlling the manic stage of bipolar disorders. A major benefit of lithium treatments is that they are often effective in preventing or reducing the occurrence of future episodes of mood disorder. Predictably, there are those for whom the drug has no beneficial effects, and its prolonged use can cause convulsions, kidney failure, and other serious reactions.

Unlike antipsychotic drugs, there is evidence that when antidepressant drugs *are* effective, they may actually bring about a long-term cure rather than just symptom suppression. In other words, the changes in mood caused by the drugs may outlast use of the drug itself. The hope and plan, in fact, is to gradually reduce the dosage of the drug over time. For persons with mood disorders who do not respond to the drugs now available, other varieties are being tested, and electroconvulsive therapy may be indicated.

● **Before You Go On**

What are antidepressant drugs, and what are they meant to do?

antianxiety drugs
(tranquilizers) chemicals that are effective in reducing the experience of anxiety

Antianxiety Drugs. **Antianxiety drugs** (or tranquilizers) help reduce the felt aspect of anxiety. They are the most commonly prescribed of all drugs. Some antianxiety drugs, the meprobamates (e.g., *Miltown* or *Equanil*), are basically muscle relaxants. When muscle tension is reduced, the patient often reports feeling calm and at ease. The other major variety of antianxiety drug is the group of chemicals called benzodiazepines (e.g., *Librium* and *Valium*). These drugs act directly on the central nervous system, and their impact is obvious and significant. They help anxious people feel less anxious. At first, the only side effects appear to be drowsiness, blurred vision, and a slight impairment of coordination.

Unfortunately, the tranquilizing effects of the drugs are not long lasting. Patients can fall into a pattern of relying on the drugs to alleviate even the slightest of fears and worries. A dependency and addiction can develop from which withdrawal can be very difficult. In fact, a danger of the antianxiety medications is the very fact that they *are* so effective. So long as one can avoid the unpleasant feelings of anxiety simply by taking a pill, there is little to motivate that person to seek and deal with the actual cause of his or her anxiety.

An interesting curiosity is that these drugs are significantly more likely to be prescribed for women, especially women over age 45, than they are for men (Travis, 1988). This may well be the result of a tendency on the part of physicians to see women as more likely to be anxious in the first place (Unger & Crawford, 1992).

● **Before You Go On**

What are antianxiety drugs, and what are the dangers inherent in their use?

TOPIC 13B

THE PSYCHOTHERAPIES

Because there are so many types of psychotherapy—literally hundreds—this Topic is called the psychotherap*ies*. We'll examine some of the major forms of psychotherapy. The overriding goal of all psychotherapy is to persuade a person to think, feel, or act differently. Additionally, various types of therapy have different specific goals, and they have different means or techniques for bringing about change.

PSYCHOANALYTIC TECHNIQUES

Psychoanalysis began with Sigmund Freud at the end of the nineteenth century. As a technique of therapy, it really did not evolve from Freud's personality theory (Chapter 10). If anything, the reverse is true. Freud was a therapist first, a personality theorist second. But his therapy and his theory sprang forth from the same mind, and are thus interrelated.

Psychoanalysis is based on a number of assumptions, most of them having to do with the nature of conflict and the unconscious mind. For Freud, one's life is often a struggle to resolve conflicts between naturally opposing forces. The biological, sexual, aggressive strivings of the id are often in conflict with the superego, associated with overcautiousness and guilt. The strivings of the id also can be in conflict with the rational, reality-based ego, which is often called on to mediate between the id and the

psychoanalysis
the form of psychotherapy associated with Freud, aimed at helping the patient gain insight into unconscious conflicts

What Shall We Do with the Most Seriously Disturbed?

As I mentioned earlier, the first institution for the mentally ill was St. Mary of Bethlehem Hospital, so designated in 1547. Despite many well-intentioned efforts to promote mental health and provide humane treatment, not much changed for the nearly 400 years after "Bedlam" was opened. By the middle of the 20th century, large government-supported institutions had become the common residences of the mentally retarded and the psychologically disordered. The institutions were overcrowded and nearly unmanageable. Lack of public support and a lack of adequate funding resulted in what amounted to a national disgrace.

Within the last 40 years, there has been a revolutionary shift in mental health care. For several seemingly sound and sensible reasons, many patients with mental disorders have experienced *deinstitutionalization*. They have been released from the large mental institutions to return to family and community. The drop in institutional patient population has been dramatic. Compared to 1955, the number of patients in state and county mental hospitals has fallen nearly 80 percent—from a high of 560,000 to 113,000 in 1988. What has brought about this change, and has it been a change for better or worse?

There are several reasons for deinstitutionalization. Let's consider three of the most important. (1) *A concern for the rights of the patient:* The overcrowded and virtually inhumane conditions in many institutions simply became more than society was willing to bear. The courts entered the picture and in 1971 ruled that either patients receive adequate and proper treatment or be released. (2) *Symptoms can be managed with drugs:* We've already touched on this matter. The introduction of effective drugs in the mid-1950s that suppressed psychotic symptoms made it seem reasonable that patients no longer displaying unusual or bizarre behaviors could be released from institutional care. (3) *Community mental health centers were to be established.* In 1963 Congress passed the Community Mental Health Act. This law included a provision for the establishment of a large number of mental health centers to be located in local communities rather than centralized in one or two state institutions. The plan was for there to be one easily accessible mental health center for every 50,000 people in the country. These centers would accommodate people on an outpatient basis and were to provide other services, including consultation, education, and prevention programs.

superego. Anxiety-producing conflicts that are not resolved are repressed; that is, they are forced out of awareness to the unconscious levels of the mind. Conflicts and anxiety-producing traumas of childhood can be expected to produce symptoms of psychological disturbance later on in life.

According to Freud, the way to rid oneself of anxiety is to enter the unconscious mind, identify the nature of repressed, anxiety-producing conflicts, bring them out into the open, and resolve them as best as possible. The first step is to gain insight into the nature of one's problems; only then can problem solving begin. Thus, the major goals of Freudian psychoanalysis are insight and resolution of repressed conflict. The entire process should be very gradual as old, repressed experiences are well integrated in one's current life situation (Kaplan & Sadock, 1991).

Sigmund Freud died in 1939, but his approach to psychotherapy did not die with him. It has been modified by others (as Freud himself modified it over the years), but it remains true to the basic thrust of Freudian psychoanalysis. Before we consider how it has changed, let's look at Freudian analysis as Freud practiced it.

Has deinstitutionalization worked? On this issue the house is divided. There are those who applaud the change (Braun et al., 1981) and argue that, within limits, "continued optimism about community care seems warranted" (Shadish, 1984).

On the other hand, many see deinstitutionalization as trading one set of problems for a host of others. Many of the patients released from mental hospitals are, quite literally, "dumped" back into their home communities, where resources to assist them often are minimal. Many require the support of the welfare system. There is seldom adequate housing for those who have been released. Patients end up in nursing homes, boarding houses, and other settings, ill-prepared to care for their needs (Bellack & Mueser, 1986; Smith et al., 1993). Frequently, negative attitudes are involved, as in, "We don't want housing for those people in our neighborhood." Many released patients become homeless, "street people," particularly in large cities. The National Institute of Mental Health estimates the percentage of homeless persons with psychological disorders at 30 to 35 percent; others place the percentage at closer to 50 percent (Bellack, 1986; Levine et al., 1993; Toro et al., 1991).

No matter how capable a community mental health center and its staff may be (assuming there *is* one nearby), if patients do not seek its support, it will do them little good. Inadequate funding for community mental health centers has become a chronic condition. As we have noted, most of the antipsychotic medication that patients need does not have lasting effects. When patients stop taking their medication (perhaps because of expense or side effects), symptoms reappear and they will likely need to return once again to the institution. And, as many as one-half to two-thirds of released patients *do stop* taking their medication (e.g., McGrath et al., 1990). In fact, since deinstitutionalization has become a matter of policy, admissions to mental hospitals have actually increased, although the average length of stay has decreased. Those who work in community mental health centers often refer to this phenomenon as the "revolving door" of deinstitutionalization.

It appears that the trend to reduce the population of patients in institutions is likely to continue. Effective community programs and more resources are needed to assist those released from these institutions to ensure that discharge is appropriate for them and for the community to which they return. Mental health professionals view the care and treatment of the chronically mentally disordered as a national health concern of high priority (e.g., Levine et al., 1993; Smith et al., 1993; Youngstrom, 1991).

Freudian Psychoanalysis

Psychoanalysis with Sigmund Freud was a time-consuming (up to five days per week for six to ten years), often tedious process of self-examination and introspection. The task for the patient was to talk openly and honestly about all aspects of his or her life, from early childhood memories to the dreams of the present. The task of the therapist, or analyst, was to interpret what was being expressed by the patient, always on the lookout for clues to possible repressed conflict. Once identified, patient and analyst could try to resolve the conflict(s) that brought the patient to analysis in the first place. Several procedures were used to search for repressed conflicts.

Free Association. In 1881, Freud graduated from the University of Vienna Medical School. From the start, he was interested in the treatment of what were then called nervous disorders. He went to France to study the technique of hypnosis, which many were claiming to be a worthwhile treatment. Freud wasn't totally convinced, but when he returned to Vienna, he and a colleague, Josef Breuer, tried hypnosis to treat nervous disorders,

Classic Freudian psychoanalysis required the use of a couch, where the patient would lie down, relax, and try to uncover unconscious conflicts, under the direction of the analyst.

free association
the procedure in psychoanalysis in which the patient is to express whatever comes to mind without editing responses

resistance
in psychoanalysis, the inability or unwillingness to freely discuss some aspect of one's life

conversion disorder (then called "hysteria") in particular. They both became convinced that hypnosis itself was of little benefit. What mattered was to have the patient talk—about anything and everything. In fact, Freud and Breuer's method became known as the "talking cure."

The method of **free association** became a technique of psychoanalysis. Patients were told to say out loud whatever came into their minds. Sometimes the analyst would provide a stimulus word to get a chain of freely flowing associations under way. To free associate the way Freud would have wanted is not an easy task. Patients often required many sessions to learn the technique. Patients were not to edit their associations. They were to say whatever they thought of, and that is not always an easy thing to do. Many people are uncomfortable (at least initially) sharing their private, innermost thoughts and desires with anyone, much less a stranger. Here is where the "Freudian couch" came in. To help his patients relax, Freud would have them lie down, be comfortable, and avoid eye contact with him. The job of the analyst through all this was to try to interpret the apparently free-flowing and random verbal responses, always looking for expressions of unconscious desires and conflicts.

Resistance. During the course of psychoanalysis, the analyst listens carefully to what the patient is saying. The analyst also carefully listens for what the patient is *not* saying. Freud believed **resistance**—the unwillingness or inability to discuss freely some aspect of one's life—was a significant process in analysis. Resistance can show itself in many ways, from simply avoiding the mention of some topic, to joking about matters as being inconsequential, to disrupting a session when a particular topic came up for discussion, to missing appointments altogether.

Let's say, for example, that over the last six months in psychoanalysis a patient has talked freely about a wide variety of subjects, including early childhood memories and all the members of her family—all, that is, except for her

going to judge you. If that's the way you feel, that's the way you feel. Whatever you have to say in here is okay." This contrasts considerably with the situations in which one usually gains positive regard. In most cases, positive regard is conditional. "*If* you do so-and-so, *then* I will think highly of you." Positive regard is typically conditional upon an action or behavior of the person, but not so in client-centered therapy.

The exchange presented in Figure 13.1 is rather typical. This is an idealized example. Things seldom go as smoothly as depicted here, but this dialogue does reflect several of the principles of humanistic approaches to psychotherapy.

Gestalt therapy is associated with Fritz Perls (1893–1970) and shares many of the same goals as Rogers's approach (Perls, 1967, 1971; Perls et al., 1951). You'll remember that we've used the term *gestalt* several times before (in Chapters 1 and 4), and that it means (roughly) "whole" or "totality." Thus it follows that the goal of gestalt therapy is to assist a person in integrating his or her thoughts, feelings, and actions—to assist in increasing the person's self-awareness, self-acceptance, and growth. The therapy is aimed at helping a person become aware of his or her whole self—including conflicts and problems—and begin working on ways to deal with them.

What makes Perls's therapy significantly different from Rogers's is that it is very directive. The therapist becomes actively involved, challenging the client. Whereas a client-centered technique is accepting, a gestalt technique is questioning. If a patient were to say, "But I never feel very anxious," the therapist would immediately challenge that assertion, "Oh come on, be serious. Do you really want me to believe that you never feel very anxious? Being anxious from time to time is a part of being alive! Deal with it. Admit it." Indeed, what we have here is a matter of "getting in touch with one's feelings," acknowledging them as valid, and moving on with one's life. Although the focus of gestalt therapy is the individual, sessions are often convened in small group settings. Clients may be given role-playing exercises in which they have to play several parts. They may be asked to act out both how they feel about a given situation and how they wish they could respond in that situation.

● **Before You Go On**
What are the characteristics of client-centered and gestalt therapy?

BEHAVIORAL TECHNIQUES

There is no one behavior therapy. **Behavior therapy** is a collection of many specific techniques. What unites them is that they are "methods of psychotherapeutic change founded on principles of learning established in the psychological laboratory" (Wolpe, 1981, p. 159). There are many different principles of learning, and many disorders to which such methods and principles can be applied. In fact, we've already discussed two varieties of behavior therapy in our learning chapter (see pp. 212–213 and 222). In this section, I will list some of the more prominent applications that have become part of behavior therapy.

Systematic desensitization, applying of classical conditioning procedures to alleviate feelings of anxiety, particularly those associated with phobias, is one of the first applications of learning principles to have been used

behavior therapy
techniques of psychotherapy founded on principles of learning established in the psychological laboratory

systematic desensitization
the application of classical conditioning procedures to alleviate anxiety in which anxiety-producing stimuli are paired with a state of relaxation

FIGURE 13.1

Barbara is an 18-year-old freshman at City College. Living at home with her parents and two younger brothers, she is having difficulty dealing with demands on her time. She has a job at a restaurant and is trying to manage four classes at CC. Pressures of home, school, and work are making Barbara uncharacteristically anxious and depressed. She is falling behind in her school work, doing poorly at her job, and finding life at home almost unbearable. Barbara has been seeing a counselor at the Student Services Center.

Psychotherapist: Good morning, Barbara; how do you feel today?

Barbara: [snapping back] Good lord, can't you ever say anything but "how do you feel today?" I feel fine, just fine.

P.: You sound angry.

B.: [in a sarcastically mocking tone] "You sound angry."

P.: [silence]

B.: Well, I'm not angry, so there.

P.: Um. Hmm.

B.: Yeah, so I'm angry. So big deal! So what of it? Is there something wrong with being angry?

P.: Of course not.

B.: You'd be angry too.

P.: Oh?

B.: My father threatened to throw me out of the house last night.

P.: He threatened you?

B.: He said that if I didn't get my act together and shape up, he'd send me packing. I don't know where I'd go, but if he pulls that crap on me one more time I'll show him. I will leave.

P.: Would you like to leave?

B.: Yes! No! No! I don't really want to. It's just that nobody cares about me around there. They don't know how hard it is trying to work and go to school and everything, ya' know?

P.: [nods]

B.: *They* never went to college. What do *they* know? They don't know what it's like.

P.: You feel that your parents can't appreciate your problems?

B.: Damn right! What do they know? They never tried to work and go to college at the same time.

P.: They don't know what it's like.

B.: No, they don't. Of course, I suppose it's not all their fault. They've never been in this situation. I suppose I could try to explain it to them better.

P.: So it would be helpful to share with them how you feel, and maybe they'll understand?

B.: Yeah. Maybe that's a good idea; I'll do that. At least I'll try. I don't want to just whine and complain all the time, but maybe I can get them to understand what it's like. Boy that would help—to have somebody besides you understand and maybe be on my side once in awhile instead of on my case all the time.

successfully. It was formally introduced by Joseph Wolpe in the late 1950s (Wolpe, 1958, 1982), although others had used similar procedures earlier. The therapy is designed to alleviate extreme anxieties, particularly of the sort we find in phobic disorders. You'll recall from Topic 6A that systematic desensitization is basically a matter of teaching a patient to relax totally and then to remain relaxed as he or she thinks about or is exposed to a range of stimuli that produce anxiety at ever-increasing levels. If the patient remains calm and relaxed, that response becomes a conditioned response to replace the fearful or anxious response that previously was associated with a particular stimulus.

Flooding is another behavioral procedure aimed at eliminating anxieties or fear associated with specific stimuli. **Flooding** is an *in vivo,* or real-life, procedure in which the client, accompanied by the therapist, is actually placed in his or her most fear-arousing situation and is prohibited from escaping. For example, someone afraid of heights may be taken to the top of a tall building or to a very high bridge. Someone afraid of water might be taken out on a large lake or to a swimming pool. There, with the therapist close at hand providing encouragement and support, the person comes face to face with his or her fear, survives the situation (although the session may be terrifying), and thus comes to learn that the fear is irrational. Although flooding sounds a bit bizarre and is not for everyone, it is often effective and it does require less time than systematic desensitization.

You should recognize **aversion therapy** as another example of classical conditioning applied to psychological problems. In aversion therapy, a stimulus that may be harmful, but that produces a pleasant response, is paired with an aversive, painful stimulus until the original stimulus is avoided. Every time you put a cigarette in your mouth, I deliver a painful shock to your lip. Every time you take a drink of alcohol, you get violently sick to your stomach. Every time a child molester is shown a picture of a young child, he receives a shock.

None of these situations sounds like the sort of thing that anyone would agree to voluntarily. Many people do, however, for two reasons: (1) Aversion therapy is very effective at suppressing a specific behavior, at least for a while; and (2) it is seen as the lesser of two evils—shocks and nausea-producing drugs are not fun, but clients see the continuation of their inappropriate behaviors as even more dangerous in the long run.

There are a couple of things that we need to recognize. One is that aversion therapy, in any form, is not commonly practiced. A second reality is that, at best, it suppresses behaviors for a relatively short time. During that time, other techniques may be used in an attempt to bring about a more lasting change in behavior. That is, the techniques of aversion therapy seldom are effective when used alone; they should be used in conjunction with some other form(s) of therapy.

Contingency management and contingency contracting borrow heavily from the learning principles of operant conditioning. The basic idea is to have a person come to appreciate the consequences of his or her behaviors. Appropriate behaviors lead to rewards and opportunities to do valued things; inappropriate behaviors do not lead to reinforcement and provide fewer opportunities to engage in valued activities.

In many cases, these basic procedures work very well. Their effectiveness often reflects the extent to which the therapist has control over the situation. If the therapist can control rewards and punishments, called **contingency management**, he or she stands a good chance of modifying a client's behaviors. For example, *if* a patient (say, a severely disturbed, hospitalized person with schizophrenia) engages in appropriate behavior (say, leaving

flooding
an in vivo technique of behavior therapy in which the client is placed in the situation that most arouses a phobic reaction and is prohibited from escaping

aversion therapy
a technique of behavior therapy in which an aversive stimulus, such as a shock, is paired with an undesired behavior

contingency management
bringing about changes in one's behaviors by controlling rewards and punishments

contingency contracting
establishing a token economy of secondary reinforcers to reward appropriate behaviors

modeling
the acquisition of new responses through the imitation of another who responds appropriately

her room to go to dinner), *then* she will get something she really wants (say, a chance to watch TV for an extra hour that evening).

Contingency contracting often amounts to establishing a token economy of secondary reinforcers (see Chapter 6). What that means is that a patient is first taught that some token—a checker, a poker chip, or a mark on a pad—can be saved. When enough tokens are saved, they can be cashed in for something of value to the patient. With contracting, the value of a token for a specific behavior is spelled out ahead of time. That is, the therapist and patient enter into a "contract" that indicates exactly how certain appropriate behaviors will be reinforced. Because control over the environment is most complete in such circumstances, this technique is particularly effective in institutions and with young children.

Realizing that not all learning can be explained in terms of classical or operant conditioning, you should not be surprised that some types of behavior therapy use learning principles other than simple conditioning. **Modeling**, a term introduced by Albert Bandura, involves the acquisition of a new, appropriate response through the imitation of a model. As we saw in Topic 6C, modeling can be an effective means of learning. In a therapy situation, modeling amounts to having patients watch someone else perform a certain appropriate behavior, perhaps earning a reward for it (called vicarious reinforcement). Some phobias, particularly those in children, can be overcome through modeling. A child who is afraid of dogs, for example, may profit from watching another child (which would be more effective than using an adult) playing with a dog. Assertiveness training involves helping individuals stand up for their rights and come to the realization that their feelings and opinions matter and should be expressed. Such training involves many processes (including direct instruction, group discussion, role-playing, and contingency management) and often relies on modeling to help someone learn appropriate ways to express how they feel and what they think in social situations.

● **Before You Go On**

Briefly describe some of the techniques used in behavior therapy, including systematic desensitization, flooding, aversion therapy, contingency management and contracting, and modeling.

COGNITIVE TECHNIQUES

Psychotherapists who use cognitive techniques do not deny the importance of a person's behaviors (these therapies are often called *cognitive-behavioral*). However, they believe that what matters *most* in the therapeutic session are the client's beliefs, thoughts, perceptions, and attitudes about himself or herself and the environment. The major principle here is that to change how one feels and acts, therapy should first change how one thinks. As we have seen with other approaches to psychotherapy, there is not just one version of cognitive-behavioral therapy; there are many. We'll examine two: rational-emotive therapy and cognitive restructuring therapy.

Rational-Emotive Therapy

Rational-emotive therapy (RET) is associated with Albert Ellis (1970, 1973, 1991). Its basic premise is that psychological problems arise when a person tries to interpret what happens in the world (a cognitive activity) on the basis of irrational beliefs. Ellis puts it this way, "Rational-emotive therapy hypothesizes that people largely disturb themselves by thinking in a self-defeating, illogical, and unrealistic manner—especially by escalating their natural preferences and desires into absolutistic, dogmatic musts and commands on themselves, others, and their environmental conditions" (Ellis, 1987, p. 364).

Compared to client-centered techniques, RET is quite directive. In fact, Ellis takes exception with techniques of psychotherapy that are designed to help a person *feel* better without providing useful strategies by which the person can *get* better (Ellis, 1991). In rational-emotive therapy, the therapist takes an active role in interpreting the rationality of a client's system of beliefs and encourages active change. Therapists often act as role models and make homework assignments for clients that help them bring their expectations and perceptions in line with reality.

To give a very simplified example, refer back to the dialogue between Barbara and her client-centered therapist in Figure 13.1. A cognitive therapist might see several irrational beliefs operating in this scene, including two that Ellis (1970) claims are very common ones: (1) A person should always be loved for everything they do, and (2) it's better to avoid problems than to face them. These are exactly the sort of cognitions that create difficulties (others are listed in Figure 13.2). Rather than waiting for self-discovery, which might never come, a rational-emotive therapist would point out to Barbara that the fact that her parents never went to college and don't understand what it is like to work and go to school at the same time is *their* problem, not hers. Rather than agonizing over the fact that her parents don't seem to appreciate her efforts, she needs to set them straight (pleasantly, of course, which might constitute a homework assignment for Barbara) or move out (there *are* other possibilities).

rational-emotive therapy (RET)
a form of cognitive therapy, associated with Ellis, aimed at changing the subject's irrational beliefs or maladaptive cognitions

Cognitive Restructuring Therapy

Similar to rational-emotive therapy is **cognitive restructuring therapy**, associated with Aaron Beck (1976, 1991). Although the basic goals are similar, restructuring therapy is much less confrontational.

Beck's assumption is that considerable psychological distress stems from a few simple but misguided beliefs (cognitions, again). According to Beck, people with psychological disorders (particularly those related to depression, for which cognitive restructuring was first designed) share certain characteristics. For example:

1. They tend to have very negative self-images. They do not value themselves or what they do.
2. They tend to take a very negative view of life experiences.
3. They overgeneralize. For example, having failed one test, a person comes to believe that there is no way he can do college work and withdraws from school and looks for work, even though he believes there's

cognitive restructuring therapy
a form of cognitive therapy, associated with Beck, in which patients are led to overcome negative self-images and pessimistic views of the future

FIGURE 13.2
Some Irrational Beliefs that Lead to Maladjustment and Disorder. The More Rational Alternative to These Beliefs Should Be Obvious.

1. One should be loved by everyone for everything one does.
2. Because I strongly desire to perform important tasks competently and successfully, I absolutely must perform them well at all times.
3. Because I strongly desire to be approved of by people I find significant, I absolutely must always have their approval.
4. Certain acts are wicked and people who perform them should be severely punished no matter what.
5. It is horrible when things are not the way we want them to be.
6. It is better to avoid life's problems, if possible, than to face them.
7. One needs something stronger or more powerful than oneself to rely on.
8. One must have perfect and certain self-control.
9. Because I very strongly desire people to treat me considerately and fairly, they must absolutely do so.
10. Because something once affected one's life, it will always affect it.

From Ellis, 1970, 1987.

little chance that anyone would offer a job to someone who is such a failure and a college dropout.
4. They actually seek out experiences that reinforce their negative expectations. The student in the above example may apply for a job as a law clerk or a stockbroker. Lacking even minimal experience, he will not be offered either job, thereby confirming his own worthlessness.
5. They tend to hold a rather dismal outlook for the future.
6. They tend to avoid seeing the bright side of any experience.

In cognitive restructuring therapy, the patient is given opportunities to test or demonstrate her or his beliefs. The patient and therapist make up a list of hypotheses based on the patient's assumptions and beliefs and then actually go out and test these hypotheses. Obviously, the therapist tries to exercise enough control over the situation so that the experiments do not confirm the patient's beliefs about himself or herself but lead instead to positive outcomes. For example, given the hypothesis, "Nobody cares about me," the therapist need only find one person who does to refute it. This approach, of leading a person to the self-discovery that negative attitudes about oneself are inappropriate, has proven very successful in the treatment of depression, although it has been extended to cover a wide range of psychological disorders (Beck, 1985, 1991; Beck & Freeman, 1990; Zinbarg et al., 1992).

● **Before You Go On**

Briefly summarize the logic behind rational-emotive therapy and cognitive restructuring therapy.

GROUP APPROACHES

Many patients profit from some type of *group therapy*. Group therapy is a label applied to a variety of situations in which several people are involved in a therapeutic setting at the same time. If nothing else, group therapy provides an economic advantage over individual psychotherapy—one therapist can interact with a number of people at once.

In standard forms of group therapy, clients are brought together at the same time under the guidance of a therapist to share their experiences and feelings. Groups are quite informal, and no particular form of psychotherapy is dominant. In other words, meeting with people in groups is something that a psychotherapist with any sort of training or background might do from time to time.

There are several possible benefits that can be derived from this procedure, including an awareness that "I'm not the only one with problems." The sense of support that one can get from someone else with problems occasionally may be greater than that afforded by a therapist alone—a sort of "she really knows from her own experience the hell that I'm going through" logic. And there is truth in the idea that helping someone else with a problem is in itself therapeutic. Yet another advantage of group therapy is that a person may learn new and more effective ways of "presenting" herself or himself to others.

A group approach that has become quite popular is **family therapy**, which focuses on the roles, interdependence, and communication skills of family members. Family therapy is often begun after one member of a family enters psychotherapy. After discussing that person's problems for a while, other members of the family are invited to join in therapy sessions. Getting the family unit involved in therapy benefits patients with a wide range of disorders (Bloch & Simon, 1982; Feist, 1993; Goldfried et al., 1990).

Two related assumptions underlie a family therapy approach. One is that each family member is a part of a *system* (the family unit), and his or her feelings, thoughts, and behaviors necessarily impact on other family members (e.g., Minuchin & Fishman, 1981; Thomas, 1992). Bringing about a change (even a therapeutic change) in one member of the family system without involving the other members of the system will not last for long without the support of the others. This is particularly true when the initial problem appears to be with a child or adolescent. I say "appears to be" because we can be confident that other family members have at least contributed to the symptoms of the child's or adolescent's behavior. A therapist is going to have a very difficult time bringing about significant and lasting change in a child whose parents refuse to become involved in therapy.

A second assumption that is often relevant in family therapy sessions is that difficulties arise from improper methods of family *communication* (Satir, 1967). Quite often, individuals develop false beliefs about the feelings or needs of family members. The goal of therapy in such situations is to meet with the family in a group setting to foster and encourage open expressions of feelings and desires. It may be very helpful for an adolescent to learn that her parents are upset and anxious about work-related stress and

family therapy
a variety of group therapy focusing on the roles, interdependence, and communication skills of family members

financial affairs. The adolescent has assumed all along that her parents yelled at her and each other because of something *she* was doing. And the parents didn't want to share their concerns over finances with their daughter for fear that it would upset her.

Evaluating group therapy techniques is particularly difficult, and few good outcome studies are available. In general, there seems to be support for the sorts of group approaches we have outlined here, and there is some indication that family therapy is a better approach for many problems than is individual treatment (Gurman, et al., 1986; Opalic, 1989; Yalom, 1985). One large study recently found significant beneficial effects of marital and family therapies (Shadish et al., 1993).

● **Before You Go On**

What are some advantages of group therapy?

Describe two assumptions underlying family therapy.

EVALUATING PSYCHOTHERAPY

Evaluating psychotherapy has proven to be a difficult task. Is psychotherapy effective? Compared to what? Is any type of psychotherapy better than any other? These are obviously important questions, but the best we can do, I'm afraid, is offer tentative and partial answers. Yes, psychotherapy is effective. Compared to what? Certainly when compared to doing nothing. "By about 1980 a consensus of sorts was reached that psychotherapy, as a generic treatment process, was demonstrably more effective than no treatment" (VandenBos, 1986, p. 111; see also Gelso & Fassinger, 1990; Goldfried et al., 1990).

More treatment appears to be better than less treatment, with most improvement made early on (Howard et al., 1986). More recent studies indicate that there are limits to this observation, however. In one study, time-limited therapy that actively involved the family in dealing with problems of children was as effective as therapy that used an unlimited number of sessions (Smyrnios & Kirkby, 1993). Whether short- or long-term intervention will be best is often a function of known variables, such as the client's awareness of his or her problems, a willingness to change, and the extent to which the client lives in a supportive environment (Steenbarger, 1994). Research confirms the logical assertion that the sooner one begins therapy, the better the prognosis (Kupfer et al., 1989). There is evidence that some therapists are simply more effective than others, regardless of what type of therapy they use (Beutler et al., 1986; Lafferty et al., 1989).

I should mention just a few of the problems involved in doing research on the effectiveness of psychotherapy. First, we have little good quality data on how people might have responded without treatment. In other words, we often do not have a good baseline for comparison. We know that sometimes there is a spontaneous remission of symptoms. Sometimes people get better without the intervention of a therapist. But to say that people get better on their own is not literally accurate. There are many factors that can contribute to the improvement of one's mental health, even for one not officially in psychotherapy (Erwin, 1980). You can imagine several such factors—in an experiment we call them extraneous variables. Perhaps the source of one's stress is removed; a nagging parent moves out of state; an aggravating boss gets transferred. Perhaps an interpersonal relationship is begun that provides needed support.

Second, we can't seem to agree on what we mean by recovery, or cure. For some, it is simply the absence of observable symptoms for a specified period of time. For others, however, the goal of therapy is something different—a self-report of "feeling better," personal growth, a relatively permanent change in behavior, a restructuring of cognitions, or insight into deep-seated motivational conflicts.

Finally, even when we can agree on criteria for recovery, there is often concern about how to measure or assess therapy outcomes. It hardly seems realistic to expect unbiased responses from therapists or their patients if we were to ask them to report if therapy had been a helpful experience.

These are three of the most commonly cited problems with studies designed to evaluate the outcome of psychotherapy. Even so, many quality studies have been done. Most have focused on just one technique at a time, and generally the results have been positive (Erwin, 1980; Eysenck, 1952; Greenberg & Safran, 1987; Kazdin et al., 1987; Lipsey & Wilson, 1993; Marziali, 1984; Miller & Berman, 1983; Scogin & McElreath, 1994; Wolpe, 1981). A review by Mark Lipsey and David Wilson looked at 302 studies of psychotherapy outcomes and came to the same conclusion: what psychotherapy provides is beneficial. Moreover, "the magnitude of the effects for a substantial portion of those treatments is in a range of practical significance by almost any reasonable criterion" (Lipsey & Wilson, 1993). Several studies also have indicated that even when the the primary treatment is medical (say, an antidepressant drug), psychotherapy and medication together provide the best prognosis (Frank et al., 1990; Free & Oei, 1989; Klerman, 1990).

What about comparing psychotherapy methods? Here the answer is also clear: *In general*, there are no differences. There is virtually no evidence that any one type of therapy is significantly better than any other (Stiles et al., 1986). This conclusion is based on a broad generality. There is evidence that some types of therapy are better suited for some types of psychological problems than are other treatments. Behavioral methods, such as systematic desensitization, are useful for phobic disorders, whereas cognitive therapies seem best suited to patients with depression.

Which therapy is best suited for which particular disorder is one of the questions to which we do not have a definitive answer, and is the most active area of research in psychotherapy (Deffenbacher, 1988; Goldfried et al., 1990; Lipsey & Wilson, 1993).

● **Before You Go On**

Is there any evidence that psychotherapy is effective?

Is any one type of psychotherapy better than the others?

THINKING CRITICALLY ABOUT TREATMENT AND THERAPY

1. In this chapter we have reviewed several techniques for dealing with psychological disorders. How do these processes get started? That is, how does a person "get into" therapy in the first place?
2. If you felt that you had problems and could profit from some form of therapy, how would you go about getting in contact with a therapist?
3. Without going into detail, I slipped in the notion that regardless of one's approach to therapy, some therapists seem to be more effective

than others. What sorts of characteristics do you think would be found among effective therapists?

4. Think about what is meant by the concept of "asylum." In what way did insane asylums ever grant asylum to the insane?

5. What ethical considerations are involved in asking a person with a severe psychological disorder (perhaps depression or schizophrenia) to give his or her informed consent to a procedure like ECT or psychosurgery?

6. Is it reasonable for a patient or client to ask a therapist what approach to psychotherapy he or she uses? What do you suspect the answer to such a question to be?

7. Assume that you are asked to treat a child with a psychological disorder. Why do I make the claim that it is crucially important to get the child's parents involved in the therapy?

8. Although treating people with psychological disorders is often very effective, what steps can be taken to try to prevent or reduce the prevalence of psychological disorders in the first place?

9. Psychotherapists often claim that it is inadvisable, even dangerous, for persons without formal training in psychology and therapy (like you and me) to engage in "amateur psychotherapy." Why do they make this claim?

SUMMARY

TOPIC 13A

HISTORY AND BIOMEDICAL TREATMENTS

● Briefly trace the history of the treatment of people with psychological disorders.

In ancient times, and throughout the Middle Ages, the prevailing view of the mentally ill was that they were possessed by evil spirits. As a result, treatment was often harsh, involving torture and placement in dungeon-like asylums. Throughout history there have been attempts to provide humane treatment, but it wasn't until the twentieth century that the treatment of the mentally ill could be classified as humane or therapeutic. *Pages 445–447.*

● Who may offer psychotherapy?
● What is the major difference between psychologists and psychiatrists?

Many types of mental health professionals provide psychotherapy, including clinical psychologists, Ph.D.s or Psy.D.s in psychology who have had a one-year clinical internship; psychiatrists, M.D.s who have had an internship and residency in a mental hospital; counseling psychologists, Ph.D.s in psychology specializing in less severe disorders; licensed counselors, who have degrees in education or psychology; psychoanalysts, who specialize in Freudian therapy; clinical social workers, who usually have a master's degree; and others, such as psychiatric nurses, pastoral counselors and mental health technicians. *Pages 448–449.*

● What is a prefrontal lobotomy?
● Why was it ever used, and why is it not used today?

A prefrontal lobotomy is a psychosurgical technique that severs connections between the prefrontal lobes and lower brain centers. It was a common treatment in the 1940s and 1950s because it was often successful in alleviating the worst of psychotic symptoms. It is no longer used because more effective, safer, and reversible treatments are now available. *Pages 450–451*

● What is ECT? Why is it still being used?

ECT stands for electroconvulsive therapy. In this procedure, a brain seizure is produced by passing an electric current across a patient's head. Although there may be a few negative side effects, ECT is often used as a fast and effective means of reducing or eliminating severe depression. *Pages 451–452.*

● What are antipsychotic drugs, and what are their effects?

Antipsychotic drugs reduce the severity of, or remove, psychotic symptoms such as hallucinations, delusions, disordered thoughts, and the like. They function by altering the action of neurotransmitters in the brain. Unfortunately, the symptoms of psychotic disorders often return when the drugs are discontinued. *Pages 452–453.*

● What are antidepressant drugs, and what are they meant to do?

Unlike the antipsychotic drugs, antidepressants often have long-term beneficial effects (alleviating feelings of depression) even after the patient stops taking them. They often require weeks to become effective, do not work for everyone, and often have harmful or unpleasant side effects. *Pages 453–454.*

● What are the antianxiety drugs, and what are the dangers inherent in their use?

The most common antianxiety drugs (tranquilizers), including meprobamates and benzodiazepines, are effective in reducing felt aspects of anxiety. Some patients who use the drugs develop an addiction to them. The drugs suppress symptoms; they do not cure the underlying causes of the anxiety the patient is experiencing. *Pages 454–455.*

TOPIC 13B
THE PSYCHOTHERAPIES

● Describe the essential nature of Freudian psychoanalysis and some of its major features.
● How is psychoanalysis different today from when it was practiced by Freud?

Psychoanalysis aims to uncover repressed conflicts (perhaps developed in early childhood) so that they can be resolved. The process may involve: (1) free association, in which the patient is to say whatever comes to mind; (2) resistance, in which patients seem unable or unwilling to discuss some aspect of their lives; (3) dream interpretation, in which latent and manifest content are analyzed for insights about the patient's unconscious; and (4) transference, in which feelings that were once directed toward someone significant are now directed toward the analyst. Today's psychoanalysis is likely to be shorter, spend less emphasis on early childhood, and be more directive than when it was practiced by Freud. *Pages 455–460.*

● What are the characteristics of client-centered and gestalt therapy?

Client-centered therapy (associated with Carl Rogers) is based on the belief that people can control their lives and solve their own problems if they can be helped to understand the true nature of their feelings. It promotes self-discovery and personal growth. Gestalt therapy (associated with Fritz Perls) is also aimed at achieving insight, getting in touch with one's feelings, personal growth, and experiencing "wholeness." It is more directive than client-centered therapy. *Pages 460–461.*

● Briefly describe some of the techniques used in behavior therapy, including systematic desensitization, flooding, aversion therapy, contingency management and contracting, and modeling.

Behavior therapies are techniques of treatment that have their basis in the work of the learning laboratory. Systematic desensitization is well suited for the treatment of phobic disorders. The subject is taught how to relax. An anxiety hierarchy is constructed, listing stimuli in order of their capacity to elicit anxiety. Desensitization is accomplished by presenting more anxiety-producing stimuli while the subject remains relaxed. Flooding is a more dramatic form of behavior therapy in which the subject is confronted with the object of his or her fear while accompanied by the therapist. Aversion therapy pairs an unwanted behavior with a strongly negative stimulus, such as a shock or a nausea-producing drug. Contingency management amounts to exercising control over the rewards that an individual receives for appropriate behaviors. Contracting usually involves a token economy system in which a subject agrees to engage in certain appropriate behaviors in order to earn specified rewards. Modeling implies that persons can acquire appropriate behaviors by imitating the behaviors of models. *Pages 461–464.*

● Briefly summarize the logic behind rational-emotive therapy and cognitive restructuring therapy.

Cognitive therapies are designed to alter the ways in which one thinks about oneself and the environment. Rational-emotive therapy (RET) operates from the premise that people often form irrational assumptions about themselves and the world. Cognitive restructuring is somewhat less directive but is also based on the premise that some people have formed negative self-images and negative views about the future that are not founded in reality. *Pages 464–466.*

● What are some advantages of group therapy?
● Describe two assumptions underlying family therapy.

The advantages of group approaches include: (1) One's basic problem may be largely interpersonal and understood best in an interpersonal situation. (2) There is value in realizing that one is not the only person with a problem. (3) There is value in providing support for someone else. (4) The dynamics of communication can be analyzed and changed in a group setting. Family therapy is based on the assumptions that family members are part of a system in which one member affects all others, and that many problems arise from faulty styles of communication within the family. *Pages 467–468.*

● Is there any evidence that psychotherapy is effective?
● Is any one type of psychotherapy better than the others?

There is ample evidence to take the position that psychotherapy is effective. Some therapies may be better suited to some persons and to some disorders than other therapies, but there is no evidence that any one technique is generally better than any other. *Pages 468–469.*

TOPIC 13A

HISTORY AND BIOMEDICAL TREATMENTS

13.1 We can claim that the treatment of persons with psychological disorders in humane, systematic ways was generally accepted a) during the Greek and Roman empires. b) early in the Middle Ages (about 1200 A.D.). c) late in the seventeenth century. d) at the beginning of the twentieth century. *Pages 445–447.*

13.2 Throughout history, the treatment of the mentally ill has been guided mostly by a) those politicians in power wanting to remain in power. b) whatever religion happened to dominate the period. c) the profit motive—the desire to profit from the grief of others. d) the contemporary understanding of what caused the disordered symptoms. *Pages 445–447.*

13.3 True or False? Hippocrates believed that what we now call hallucinations and delusions arose when an individual had offended the Greek gods. *Pages 445–447.*

13.4 Which of these psychotherapists can prescribe drugs or medication for psychological problems? a) psychiatric nurses b) clinical psychologists c) psychiatrists d) Any of these can prescribe medications. *Pages 448–449.*

13.5 A prefrontal lobotomy a) severs connections between the cerebral cortex and lower brain centers. b) lesions or removes the corpus callosum, thus separating the two hemispheres of the brain. c) destroys the amygdala of the limbic system. d) involves gradually removing more and more brain tissue until symptoms disappear. *Pages 450–451.*

13.6 Prefrontal lobotomies a) were very dangerous; nearly one-quarter of patients died as a result. b) were discovered by accident when a psychotic patient was shot in the head and his symptoms disappeared. c) are now outlawed in the United States. d) were done on tens of thousands of persons in the 1940s and 1950s. *Pages 450–451.*

13.7 True or False? "Psychosurgery" means "lobotomy." *Pages 450–451.*

13.8 Why does electroconvulsive therapy produce the effects that it does? a) Levels of the neurotransmitter dopamine are increased. b) Pleasure centers of the brain are stimulated. c) Unpleasant, depressing memories are destroyed. d) No one really knows why it works. *Pages 451–452.*

13.9 ECT is most commonly used to treat a) schizophrenia. b) persons with aggressive or violent tendencies. c) depression. d) many (but not all) anxiety disorders. *Pages 451–452.*

13.10 True or False? ECT produces a seizure in the brain very much like an epileptic seizure. *Pages 451–452.*

13.11 The general name for chemicals that affect one's psychological functioning is a) hallucinogenic. b) psychoactive. c) narcotic. d) analgesic. *Pages 452–453.*

13.12 The first antipsychotic drug used effectively was a) chlorpromazine. b) valium. c) lithium salt. d) Prozac. *Pages 452–453.*

13.13 True or False? Antipsychotic medications suppress symptoms, but rarely can they be said to cure a disorder. *Pages 452–453.*

13.14 True or False? The main advantage of antidepressant medications over ECT is that, when the medications work, they work more quickly than does ECT. *Pages 453–454.*

13.15 Antianxiety drugs a) have long-lasting effects. b) are classified as either tricyclics or MAO inhibitors. c) cure the symptoms of hallucinations and delusions. d) ease or alleviate the feelings of anxiety. *Pages 454–455.*

TOPIC 13B

THE PSYCHOTHERAPIES

13.16 Freudian psychoanalysis is based on many assumptions, including each of the following *except* a) The patient genuinely may be unable to tell the analyst why he or she is experiencing anxiety. b) Early childhood experiences can have an impact on how one feels as an adult. c) Once the analyst gets the patient to act better, he or she will also feel better and think better. d) The true nature of the patient's problems may be revealed in the content of his or her dreams. *Pages 455–460.*

13.17 In Freudian psychoanalysis, the process of coming to feel about the analyst as one used to feel about an important or significant other person is a process called a) transference. b) free association. c) latent analysis. d) resistance. *Pages 455–460.*

13.18 One thing that psychoanalysts after Freud still hold to as a basic assumption is that a) there is no good reason for anxiety to feel so unpleasant. b) hypnosis can be a useful way of establishing transference. c) anxiety stems from some sort of repressed conflict. d) analysis is to be a time-consuming process, usually lasting for years. *Pages 455–460.*

13.19 True or False? As opposed to latent content, the manifest content of a dream is the content as expressed and reported by the patient. *Pages 455–460.*

13.20 What do client-centered therapy and psychoanalysis have in common? a) the assumption of an active role by the therapist to interpret and evaluate what the client has to say b) an assumption that, at least at the beginning of therapy, the client may not understand the source of his/her distress c) the assumption that the focus of therapy should be on what the person feels, not what the person thinks d) the assumption that earlier, childhood experiences are more significant than how one feels currently. *Pages 460–461.*

13.21 To be an active listener and to be able to share and understand the feelings of another is to a) offer unconditional positive regard. b) be existential. c) self-actualize. d) be empathic. *Pages 460–461.*

13.22 Most of the techniques used in behavior therapies come from a) suggestions made by previous patients. b) Freud's theories. c) the learning laboratory. d) research in education. *Pages 461–464.*

13.23 Which of these is *most* appropriate (or most likely) for treating phobic disorders? a) electroconvulsive shock therapy b) systematic desensitization c) psychoanalysis d) contingency contracting. *Pages 461–464.*

13.24 Which behavioral therapy technique derives most directly from the work of Albert Bandura? a) aversion therapy b) contingency contracting c) gestalt therapy d) modeling. *Pages 461–464.*

13.25 True or False? By definition, contingency management is essentially the opposite of unconditional positive regard. *Pages 461–464.*

13.26 A basic premise of cognitive therapies is that people a) don't realize how they feel. b) develop irrational beliefs about themselves and the world. c) do strange things in order to be reinforced by attention. d) act out childhood fantasies when they become adults. *Pages 464–466.*

13.27 One type of disorder for which cognitive therapy seems particularly well suited is a) schizophrenia. b) personality disorders. c) depression. d) phobias. *Pages 464–466.*

13.28 True or False? All psychotherapies are equally effective for any particular psychological disorder. *Pages 468–469.*

SOCIAL PSYCHOLOGY

14

PREVIEW

TOPIC 14A—Social Cognitions: Attitudes, Attributions, and Attractions

Attitudes

Attribution Theory

Interpersonal Attraction

TOPIC 14B—Social Influence

Conformity

Obedience to Authority

Bystander Intervention

PSYCHOLOGY IN THE REAL WORLD: Violence

Social Loafing

Social Facilitation

Decision Making in Groups

THINKING CRITICALLY ABOUT SOCIAL PSYCHOLOGY

SUMMARY

TEST YOURSELF

Social psychology deals with people as they live: in a social world, influencing, and being influenced by others. We'll spend the bulk of Topic 14A on matters of social cognition. "Discovering how people mentally organize and represent information about themselves and about others has been a central task of social cognition research" (Berscheid, 1994). We'll see how social psychologists define attitudes, how attitudes are formed, and how they can be changed. We'll review how we explain or "attribute" our behaviors and the behaviors of others. We'll end this Topic with a discussion of interpersonal (or social) attraction and consider some of the factors that determine why some people are attracted to others.

The focus of Topic 14B is on social influence. The major research areas here are conformity and obedience, but a related issue is when an individual will come to the aid of another in distress, an issue which is referred to in social psychology as "bystander intervention." We'll end with a few questions related to the influence of group membership: Does the presence of others enhance or inhibit the behavior of the individual? Do people tend to make better judgments when in a group or when they are alone? In terms of practical, day-to-day application, there may be no more relevant chapter than this one.

TOPIC 14A

SOCIAL COGNITIONS: ATTITUDES, ATTRIBUTIONS, AND ATTRACTIONS

social psychology
the scientific study of how others influence the thoughts, feelings, and behaviors of the individual

Social psychology is the field of psychology concerned with how others influence the thoughts, feelings, and behaviors of the individual. Social psychologists focus their attention on the person and not the group *per se* (which is more likely to be the focus of sociology). Since we are social organisms, each of us is familiar in our own way with many of the concerns of social psychology.

To claim that we are familiar with the concerns of social psychology has certain implications. On the one hand, it means that social psychology is perceived as being interesting and relevant because it deals with everyday situations that affect us all. On the other hand, it means that we may be willing to accept common sense and personal experience as the basis for our assumptions about social behavior. Although common sense occasionally may be valid, it is not an acceptable basis for a science of social behavior. Social psychology relies on experimentation and other scientific methods as sources of knowledge, even if the results of applying these methods are contrary to our intuition.

During the last 25 years, much of social psychology has taken on a cognitive flavor. Social psychologists are trying to understand social behaviors by looking at the mental processes and mental structures that are reflected in those behaviors. A basic premise of this approach (and this Topic) is that we do not view our environment solely on the basis of the stimulus information that it presents us (Baldwin, 1992; Berscheid, 1994; Higgins & Bargh, 1987). Instead, the argument goes, we've developed several cognitive structures and processes (attitudes, schemas, prejudices, stereotypes, and the like) that influence our interpretation of the world around us. Social cognition then, involves two related questions (Sherman et al., 1989). What information about the social world do we have stored in our memories? How does that information influence social judgments, choices, attractions, and behaviors? We will see these questions underlying each of the three major sections of Topic 14A. We begin with attitudes.

● **Before You Go On**
What is social psychology, and what are social cognitions?

ATTITUDES

Since the 1920s, a central concern to social psychologists has been the nature of attitudes (McGuire, 1985). We'll define **attitude** as a relatively stable disposition to evaluate some object or event. An attitude has consequences for influencing one's beliefs, feelings, and behaviors toward the object or event (Olson & Zanna, 1993).

The concept of *evaluation* in this definition refers to an aspect of attitudes that includes being for or against, pro or con, positive or negative (Eagly & Chaiken, 1992). By *disposition* I mean a tendency or a preparedness to respond to the object of the attitude, and that actual responding is not necessary. Attitudes are stored in one's memory which, if nothing else, makes them cognitions (Fazio, 1990). Notice that, by definition, attitudes have an object. We have attitudes toward or about something. I realize that the word *attitude* is occasionally used differently in common speech. We hear that someone has a "bad attitude," or "an attitude" in general, as in "Boy, does he have an attitude!" In psychology, an attitude—as a technical term—requires an object.

Anything can be the object of an attitude, whether it be a person, an object, or an idea (Petty & Cacioppo, 1986). You may have attitudes about this course, the car you drive, your father, the president, or the corner fast-food restaurant where you eat lunch. Some of our attitudes are more important than others, of course, but the fact that we have attitudes toward so many things is precisely the reason why the study of attitudes is so central to social psychology.

attitude
a relatively stable and general evaluative disposition directed toward some object, consisting of feelings, behaviors, and beliefs

The Components of Attitudes

Although many definitions of attitude have been proposed over the years, most of them suggest that an attitude has three components (Chaiken & Stangor, 1987). When we use the term *attitude* in our everyday conversation, we most likely are referring to the *affective component*, which consists of our feelings about the attitudinal object (Zanna & Rempel, 1988). The *behavioral component* consists of our tendencies to respond to the object of our attitude. This component includes our actual behaviors and our intentions to act should the opportunity arise. The *cognitive component* includes our beliefs or thoughts about the attitudinal object. Any of these three may be primary. We may form a positive attitude about a particular beverage because we know it is good for us (cognitive), because it is very convenient to buy (behavioral), or because we like the way it tastes (affective). By now, these three components of affect, behavior, and cognition, or ABC, ought to sound very familiar.

In many cases, the cognitive, affective, and behavioral components of our attitudes are consistent. We think that classical music is relaxing and like to listen to it, so we buy classical music recordings. You believe that knowledge of psychology will be an asset in your career, you are enjoying your psychology class, and you plan to take more psychology classes in the future. However, there are occasions when our behaviors are not consistent with or do not reflect our true beliefs and feelings (Ajzen & Fishbein, 1980). For example, we may have very strong unfavorable beliefs and very negative feelings about someone, yet when we encounter that person at a social gathering, we smile, extend our hand, and say something pleasant. The situation may "overpower" the cognitive and affective components of our attitudes. This is another way of saying that the components of an attitude *may* lack consistency, and it is the behavioral component that is most often inconsistent with the other two.

Because our actual behaviors may not reflect our true feelings or beliefs, some psychologists (Fazio, 1989; Fishbein & Ajzen, 1975) prefer to exclude the behavioral component from their definition; they reserve the term *attitude* to refer to a fundamental liking or disliking for the attitudinal object. Other psychologists argue that an attitude is a two-dimensional concept, involving affect and cognition, but not behavior (Bagozzi & Burnkrant, 1979; Zajonc & Markus, 1982).

● **Before You Go On**

What is an attitude and what are its three components?

Attitude Formation

As it happens, we have all formed many attitudes about a wide range of objects and events. Let us now briefly consider where they came from. Most experts agree that attitudes are learned and that simple conditioning processes go a long way toward explaining attitude formation.

Some attitudes are no doubt acquired through the simple associative process of *classical conditioning*. As shown in Figure 14.1, pleasant events (the unconditioned stimuli) may be paired with an attitudinal object (the conditioned stimulus). As a result of this association, the attitudinal object

FIGURE 14.1
How attitudes may be classically conditioned.

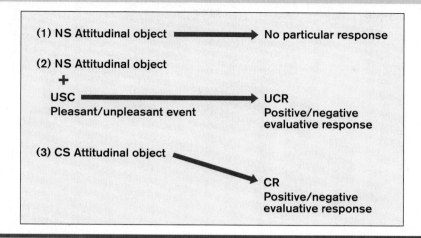

comes to elicit the same good feeling that was produced by the uncondi-tioned stimulus. The good feeling, which originally was an unconditioned response elicited by a pleasant event, is now a conditioned response elicited by the attitudinal object. Of course, negative attitudes can be ac-quired in the same way (e.g., Cacioppo et al., 1992).

Some advertising attempts to work in this way by taking an originally neutral object (the product) and trying to create positive associations to it. For instance, a soft drink advertisement may depict young, attractive peo-ple having a great time playing volleyball, dancing, or enjoying a concert while drinking a particular soft drink. The intent is that you and I will asso-ciate the product with good times and having fun. That sports figures often wear brand name logos and trademarks on their uniforms also suggests that manufacturers might like us to learn to associate their product with the skills of the athlete we're watching.

Attitudes can also be formed as a result of the direct reinforcement of behaviors consistent with some attitudinal position, a matter of *operant con-ditioning*. Several studies have shown that verbal reinforcement (saying "good," "fine," or "right") when people agree with attitudinal statements leads those people to develop attitudes that are consistent with the position expressed (Insko, 1965).

As we discussed in Topic 6C, people tend to imitate behaviors they have seen reinforced in others (called vicarious reinforcement). To the ex-tent that we perceive that others are gaining reinforcers for having and ex-pressing some attitude, we are likely to adopt that attitude ourselves. Adver-tising that relies on testimonials from "satisfied customers" is appealing to this sort of *observational learning*. The potential consumer is shown someone who has used a product with success (received reinforcement), and the ad-vertiser hopes that this exposure will lead the observer to develop a favor-able evaluation of the product. The advertiser is going to show us only peo-ple who are happy with their product or service. We seldom stop to think about how many people may have used the product or service and are un-happy with it.

Cognitive dissonance occurs when you find yourself test-driving and considering buying a new car that you previously have been reluctant to buy.

● **Before You Go On**

Briefly describe three ways in which attitudes might be acquired.

Attitude Change and Persuasion

Much of the research on attitudes has been concerned with the practical question of how attitudes change. This research deals largely with planned attempts to change attitudes by exposing them to information—a process called *persuasion* (Olson & Zanna, 1993). In this section, we'll examine a few factors involved in attitude change.

Cognitive Dissonance. It seems reasonable to suggest that one's attitudes will mold one's behaviors, and that attitude change will lead to behavior change. In 1957, Leon Festinger proposed the reverse: that attitudes can be shaped by behavior. Festinger's proposal referred to a concept called **cognitive dissonance**. Cognitions are beliefs, thoughts, perceptions, and so on. Dissonance means discord, discomfort, or distress due to things being out of balance or inconsistent. Cognitive dissonance often arises when we realize (a cognition) that we have behaved in a way that is not consistent (dissonant) with other cognitions.

One of the best examples of how this might work is found in one of the original demonstrations of the phenomenon (Festinger & Carlsmith, 1959). Participants in the research were asked to perform an extremely boring task that required them to rotate row after row of small wooden knobs. Following a lengthy knob-turning session, the experimenter explained that the research really had to do with the effects of motivation on such a task. The subject was told that the person sitting in the waiting area just outside the laboratory was to be the next subject in the project. This

cognitive dissonance
a motivating discomfort or tension caused by a lack of balance or consonance among one's cognitions

next subject was led to believe that the task was fun, interesting, and educational. Explaining that his assistant, who told these "lies" to the waiting subject was absent, the experimenter asked the subject to do this selling job, and offered to pay for the help. Subjects invariably agreed and actually worked very hard at trying to convince the next subject that the project was fun and educational. Weeks later, at the end of the semester, all subjects filled out a questionnaire that asked about their reactions to the knob-turning experiment in which they had participated.

The only experimental manipulation was a simple one: Some of the subjects were paid $20 for trying to convince the waiting person (who was not really a subject, but was in on the experiment) that the obviously boring task was fun and interesting, while others were paid only $1. Keep in mind that this was the late 1950s and for college students living in a dormitory, $20 was a lot of money. In all other respects, every subject had the same experience in the laboratory.

At the end of the semester, which subjects do you suppose expressed more positive attitudes about the project, those paid $20 or those paid $1? Doesn't it seem logical that those paid $20 would remember the task as fun and enjoyable and indicate a willingness to participate in other, similar projects? Festinger and Carlsmith predicted just the opposite. They reasoned that subjects paid only $1 would feel that their behavior had not been sufficiently justified. They had told a "lie" and had been given only a trivial amount of money for doing so. These subjects would experience a great deal of discomfort about this inconsistency—cognitive dissonance would have been created. "I lied for a lousy dollar." One way to resolve their dissonance would be to modify their attitude about the project so that it fit better with their behavior, or was more consonant. The prediction was that these subjects would convince themselves that they had not lied at all; the experiment had been fun and interesting—a sort of, "Well, I didn't really lie. The experiment wasn't all that bad. They didn't shock me or anything. They didn't ask me a bunch of questions I couldn't answer. In fact, it was kinda fun at that."

The subjects paid $20, on the other hand, had plenty of justification for their actions. Sure, they had lied, but they had "good reason" to do so. These students would experience little cognitive dissonance and should not be expected to change their attitude about the experiment. "Yeah, I lied, but I got paid 20 bucks to do so." The results of this project are presented in Figure 14.2. Seldom do we find differences in an experiment as clear-cut as these.

The results of this experiment (and by now numerous others) suggest that one good way to change people's attitudes is to get them to change their behaviors first. Not only that, but there is a clear advantage in offering as little incentive as possible to bring about that change in behavior. Simply "buying someone off" to change his or her behavior may get you compliance, but it won't produce the cognitive dissonance required to bring about lasting attitude change.

You should be able to generate many other examples of cognitive dissonance influencing attitude change. A student who supports a military intervention in a Middle East conflict is invited by a good friend to attend a peace rally. Accepting the invitation might produce dissonance: "I favor military involvement, but here I am at a peace rally." These two cognitions are dissonant. What will happen next? We can't say, but we can predict that *something* is likely to change in order to reduce dissonance; perhaps it will be the student's initial attitude. Consider the number of students who have

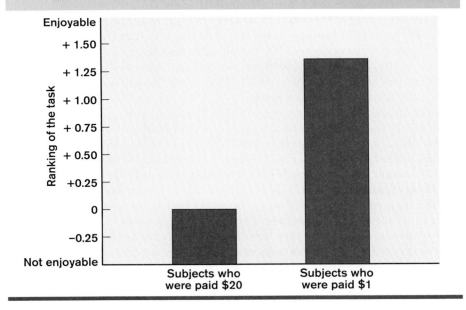

FIGURE 14.2
After being paid either $1 or $20 to "lie" about their participation in a boring task, subjects were later asked to rate that task in terms of enjoyment, interest, and educational value. As can be seen in this figure, those paid $1 (those with cognitive dissonance) gave the task much higher ratings than did subjects paid $20. (From Festinger & Carlsmith, 1959.)

changed their attitude about a course or a discipline, because they were required to take a course in that discipline. As an undergraduate chemistry major, my (rather negative) attitudes about psychology changed because of the dissonance created when I was required to take a (very enjoyable and informative) class in introductory psychology.

Extensions of Festinger's original work tell us that what may matter most in producing attitude change is the perception of responsibility for unfortunate or unpleasant outcomes—whether those outcomes are consistent with other cognitions or not (Cooper & Sher, 1992; Sher & Cooper, 1989). In other words, when we feel that our behaviors have led to some unfortunate consequence, we are more likely to end up convincing ourselves that the consequence wasn't really all that bad after all. For example, I once bought a car that I thought I really wanted, even though friends and relatives strongly advised me not to. In fact, the car was a lemon, rarely ran properly, and spent most of its life in the shop being repaired. Nonetheless, I was continually heard to claim that "when this car is running, it's the best darn car I ever had." I was responsible for an "unpleasant outcome," and I tried to resolve my dissonance by convincing myself that I had not really made a mistake.

● **Before You Go On**

What is cognitive dissonance, and how does it operate?

The Source of Persuasive Communication. There may be two different pathways, or routes, involved in changing someone's attitudes (Petty &

Cacioppo, 1986; Tressor & Shaffer, 1990). One pathway, the *central route*, involves the nature and quality of the message itself—what is being communicated. The other pathway is the *peripheral route*, and involves issues beyond the content of the message itself, such as when and how it is presented. This peripheral route is of more importance when one has a relatively weak message to convey. What the research tells us is that a highly credible (believable) source will be more persuasive than will a less credible source (Petty & Cacioppo, 1986). There are several factors involved in credibility, including vocal pleasantness and facial expression, but two that seem especially important are perceived *expertise* and *trustworthiness*.

Several studies (Aronson et al., 1963; Hovland & Weiss, 1951) indicate that the greater the perceived expertise of the communicator, the greater the persuasion that occurs. People who are convinced they are listening to an expert are more likely to be persuaded than they would be if they thought that the speaker knew little about the subject matter—even if the message was exactly the same. For example, I am more likely to be persuaded by Garth Brooks if he were trying to change my attitudes about a guitar than I would be if he were trying to sell me a toaster oven or spaghetti sauce. Celebrities *are* used to promote or sell products even without any apparent expertise, on the basis of the following logic: First, you'll recognize them and attend to what they say. Second, their credibility and expertise in some other area, which has brought about their celebrity or fame, will transfer to the product they are selling.

Another factor likely to enhance a communicator's credibility is a high degree of trustworthiness (Cooper & Croyle, 1984). Studies by Walster and Festinger (1962) showed that more attitude change resulted when people *overheard* a persuasive communication than when they believed that the communication was directed at them. Trustworthiness and credibility apparently were enhanced by the perceived lack of intent to persuade ("Why should they lie? They don't even know we can hear them.").

● **Before You Go On**

What communicator characteristics are known to have an impact on attitude change?

ATTRIBUTION THEORY

Another facet of the cognitive orientation that we find in social psychology is the study of attribution theory. Social psychologists working with attribution theory are interested in understanding the cognitions we use in trying to explain the sources of behavior, both our own and that of others. One question is, "Do we tend to attribute behaviors we observe to internal, personal dispositions, or to external, environmental situations?" This question is related to issues we raised in the chapter on personality, when we discussed the extent to which behaviors reflect internal, personality factors or external, environmental factors.

Internal attributions explain the source of a person's behaviors in terms of a characteristic of the person, often a personality trait or disposition, and for this reason are sometimes called dispositional attributions. **External attributions**, on the other hand, explain the source of a person's behaviors in terms of the situation or context in which the person finds himself or herself; they are referred to as situational attributions.

internal attribution
an explanation of behavior in terms of something (a trait) within the person; a dispositional attribution

external attribution
an explanation of behavior in terms of something outside the person; a situational attribution

We tend to rely on different types of information when making judgments about the sources of behavior. Imagine, for example, that your best friend shows his temper only when he is with his girlfriend. That information is useful because it is *distinctive* (his bad temper only shows up when he's with his girlfriend). As a result, you may take it as a signal of a troubled relationship.

Imagine that you've just received an A on a test in your history class. In this case, you would use information about how well everyone else did on the test before you decided about your own superiority. That is, you would seek out information about *consensus*. If you found that everyone else also received an A, your explanation of your behavior (and theirs) might be different from a situation in which yours is the only A in the class. Before you got too excited about your accomplishment, you might also wait for some sign of *consistency* lest this one exam be just a fluke. Information about distinctiveness, consensus, and consistency is important in determining the kinds of attributions we make about our own behaviors and the behaviors of others (Kelley, 1967, 1973, 1992; Kelley & Michela, 1980).

An active area of research in social cognition deals with errors we tend to make in our social thinking. In general terms, we tend to make attribution errors because of preexisting cognitive biases that influence our judgments of causality. One example of such a bias is the **fundamental attribution error**—the tendency to favor internal, or personal, attributions rather than external, situational explanations (Jones, 1979; Ross, 1977). We see a man pick up a wallet that has been dropped on the street and race half a block to return it to its true owner. We say to ourselves, "Now there's an honest man." The truth may be, however, that the fellow returned the wallet only because he knew that we (and many others) saw him pick it up in the first place. It may be that if no one else were around, the wallet would not have been returned. The fundamental attribution error then, is the tendency to disregard or overly discount situational factors in favor of internal, dispositional factors when we make inferences about the causes of behaviors. There is evidence that biases such as the fundamental attribution error are more common in Western cultures. People from India, for example, particularly adults, make many fewer dispositional attributions than do Americans (Miller, 1984). They are much more likely than Americans to explain behavior in terms of the situation than in terms of personality characteristics.

As you might imagine, there are other biases that can lead us to make incorrect attributions about our behaviors or the behaviors of others. One is the **just world hypothesis**, in which people take on the belief that we live in a just world where good things happen only to good people and bad things happen only to bad people (Lerner, 1965, 1980). It's a sort of "everybody ultimately gets what they deserve" mentality. We see this bias (fallacy might be better) when we hear people claim that victims of rape often "ask for it by the way they dress and act." In fact, rape victims sometimes even engage in self-blame in an attempt to explain why in the world they were singled out for what was in fact a crime in which they were the true victim (Janoff-Bulman, 1979).

Another bias that affects attributions is the **self-serving bias** (Harvey & Weary, 1984; Miller & Ross, 1975). It occurs when we attribute our positive or successful outcomes to personal, internal sources and our failures or negative outcomes to situational, external sources. We tend to think that when we do something well it is because we're talented and work hard, whereas when we do poorly it's the fault of someone or something else.

fundamental attribution error
the tendency to overuse internal attributions when explaining behavior

just world hypothesis
the belief that the world is just and that people get what they deserve

self-serving bias
the tendency to attribute our successes to our own effort and ability and our failures to external, situational factors

"Boy, didn't I do a great job of painting that room?" versus "The room looks so shoddy because the paint was cheap and the brush was old" are examples. (Perhaps you'll recall from our discussion of depression in Chapter 12 that some cognitive theorists argue that some depression can be explained as a reversal of the self-serving bias. That is, some people get into the habit of blaming themselves for failures and negative outcomes regardless of where the real blame [if any] resides.)

An extension of the self-serving bias is the **actor-observer bias** (Jones & Nisbett, 1971; Monson & Snyder, 1977). When influenced by this bias we tend to use external attributions for our behaviors (as actors) more than we do for others (where we are observers): "I took this class because the instructor is entertaining" versus "He took this class because he's so lazy." "I went to that hotel because the rates were low" versus "He went to that hotel to show off." That we tend to explain our behaviors in ways that are different from the ways in which we account for the behaviors of others is not surprising. For one thing, we have more information about ourselves and our own past experiences than we do about anyone else. That is, our schemas of self are more complete. In fact, the more information we have about someone else, the less likely we are to use internal attributions to explain their behaviors. Also, in any situation the actor gets a different view of what is happening than does the observer.

actor-observer bias
the overuse of internal attributions to explain the behaviors of others and external attributions to explain our own behaviors

● **Before You Go On**

What are the two basic types of attribution?

Explain the ways in which attributions can be distorted or biased.

INTERPERSONAL ATTRACTION

Interpersonal attraction can be seen as a favorable, powerful attitude toward another person. It reflects the extent to which a person has formed positive feelings and beliefs about another and is prepared to act on those affects and cognitions.

Theories of Interpersonal Attraction

Social psychologists have put forth several models or theories to explain the bases of interpersonal attraction. We'll briefly review just four.

Probably the simplest theory is the *reinforcement model,* which claims that we are attracted to people we associate with rewards (Clore & Byrne, 1974; Lott & Lott, 1974). We learn to like people and are attracted to them through conditioning, by associating them with rewards or reinforcers. It follows that we tend not to be attracted to those we associate with punishment. An implication of this model is that you will like your instructor more, and seek him or her out for other classes in the future, if you get (earn) a high grade in his or her class than you will if you get a low grade.

Another popular theory of interpersonal attraction is not as direct. It Is called the *social exchange model* (Kelley & Thibault, 1978; Thibault & Kelley, 1959). According to this model, what matters most is a comparison of the costs as well as the benefits of establishing or maintaining a relationship. For example, Leslie may judge that John is physically attractive, but that entering into an intimate relationship with him is not worth the grief she would get from friends and family, who believe John to be lazy and untrustworthy. On the other hand, if Leslie has recently gone through a series of failed relationships with men who were not physically attractive, she might take a chance on John, judging (in her frustration) that he was "worth it." This theory takes into account a series of comparative judgments that people make in social situations. Being attracted to someone else is not just a matter of "Is this a good thing?" It's more a matter of "Is the reward that I might get from this relationship worth the cost, given the alternatives that exist at the moment?"

A third theoretical approach to interpersonal attraction is the *equity model*, and it is more an extension of social exchange theory than a departure from it (Greenberg & Cohen, 1982; Walster et al., 1978). Social exchange theory added the notion of cost to that of reward. Equity theory adds the appraisal of rewards and costs for *both* parties of a social relationship. That is, you may feel that a certain relationship is worth the effort you've been putting into it, but if your partner in that relationship does not feel likewise, the relationship is in danger. What matters, then, is that both (or all) members of a relationship feel that they are getting a fair deal (equity). Notice two things about this model: (1) Both members of a relationship do not have to share rewards equally. What matters is that the ratio of costs to rewards be equitable for both members. (2) If one person were to feel that he or she was getting more from a relationship than was deserved, the relationship would not be equitable and would be in danger. The best relationships are those in which everyone receives an equal ratio of rewards to costs.

A more recent approach to understanding interpersonal relationships is based more on feelings or affect than on cognitions. This model is referred to as *attachment theory* (Bersheid, 1994; Feeney & Noller, 1990; Hazan & Shaver, 1987). It suggests that interpersonal relationships can be classified into one of three types depending on the attitudes that one has about them (from Shaver, Hazan & Bradshaw, 1988, p. 80):

Secure: "I find it relatively easy to get close to others and am comfortable depending on them and having them depend on me. I don't often worry about being abandoned or about someone getting too close to me."

Avoidant: "I am somewhat uncomfortable being close to others; I find it difficult to trust them completely, difficult to allow myself to depend on them. I'm nervous when anyone gets too close, and often, love partners want me to be more intimate than I feel comfortable being."

Anxious-ambivalent: "I find that others are reluctant to get as close as I would like. I often worry that my partner doesn't really love me or won't stay with me. I want to merge completely with another person, and this desire sometimes scares people away."

One of the things that makes attachment theory appealing is the evidence that one's "style" of forming attachments is remarkably stable throughout the life span. It may be that the kind of interpersonal relationships we form as adults are influenced by the kind of attachments we developed as very young children.

Finally, I should point out that few people enter into interpersonal relationships having carefully considered all the factors that these models imply. Assessments of reinforcement, exchange, or equity value are seldom made consciously; nor do we purposely seek out relationships that mirror those we had in childhood (Bargh, 1993).

● **Before You Go On**

Briefly summarize four theoretical models that account for inter-personal attractions.

Factors Affecting Interpersonal Attraction

Let's now look at some empirical evidence related to attraction. What determines who you will be attracted to? What factors provide the rewards, or the reward/cost ratios, that serve as the basis for strong relationships? We'll consider four determinants of interpersonal attraction.

Reciprocity, our first factor, is perhaps the most obvious. Not surprisingly, we tend to value and like people who like and value us (Backman & Secord, 1959; Curtis & Miller, 1986). We've already noted, in our discussion of operant conditioning, that the attention of others can be a powerful reinforcer. This is particularly true if that attention is positive, supportive, or affectionate. The value of someone else caring for us is particularly powerful when that someone initially seemed to have neutral or even negative attitudes toward us (Aronson & Linder, 1965). That is, we are most attracted to people who like us now, but who once didn't. The logic here is related to attribution. If someone we meet for the first time expresses nothing but positive feelings toward us, we are likely to attribute their reaction to the way the person is—rather shallow and the sort who likes everybody. But if someone at first were to express neutral, or slightly negative, feelings toward us and then were to become more positive, we might have a different, more positive view of their ability to judge others.

Proximity leads to liking and attraction, which is why teenagers who go to the same school and live in the same neighborhood are likely to form friendships.

mere exposure phenomenon
the tendency to increase our liking of people and things the more we see of them

Our second principle, *proximity*, claims that physical closeness tends to produce attraction. Sociologists, as well as your own experience, will tell you that people tend to establish friendships (and romances) with others with whom they have grown up, worked, or gone to school. Similarly, studies consistently have found that residents of apartments or dormitories tend to become friends with other residents living closest to them (Festinger et al., 1950). Being around others gives us the opportunity to discover just who can provide those rewards we seek in a friendship.

There may be another social-psychological phenomenon at work here: the **mere exposure phenomenon**. Research pioneered by Robert Zajonc (1968) has shown with a variety of stimuli that liking tends to increase with repeated exposure. Examples of this phenomenon are abundant in everyday life. Have you ever bought a CD that you haven't heard before, assuming that you will like it because you have liked other CDs by this performer? The first time you listen to your new CD, however, your reaction may be lukewarm at best, and you may be disappointed. Not wanting to feel that you've wasted your money, you play the CD a few more times. What often happens is that you soon realize that you like this CD after all. The mere exposure effect has occurred, and this commonly happens in our formation of attitudes about other people as well. Familiarity is apt to breed attraction, not contempt. There seems to be ample evidence that the mere exposure phenomenon is real, but there is still a lot of disagreement about *why* familiarity and repeated interactions breed attraction (e.g., Birnbaum & Mellers, 1979; Kunst-Wilson & Zajonc, 1980). I also have to add that there *are* limits. Too much exposure may lead to boredom and ultimately to devaluation (Bornstein, 1989; Bornstein et al., 1990).

Physical attractiveness is our third determinant of interpersonal attraction. Most people are aware of the role of appearance in interpersonal communication and may spend many hours each week doing whatever they can to improve the way they look. The power of physical attractiveness in the context of dating has been demonstrated in a classic experiment directed by Elaine Walster (Walster et al., 1966). University of Minnesota freshmen completed several psychological tests as part of an orientation program. The students were then randomly matched for dates to an orientation dance, during which they took a break and evaluated their assigned partners. Researchers hoped to uncover intricate, complex, and subtle facts about interpersonal attraction, such as which personality traits might mesh in such a way as to produce attraction. As it turned out, none of these complex factors, so carefully controlled for, was important. The impact of physical attractiveness was so powerful that it wiped out all other effects. For both men and women, the more physically attractive their date, the more they liked the person, and the more they wanted to date him or her again. Numerous studies of physical attractiveness followed. Some of these studies simply gave people a chance to pick a date from a group of several potential partners (usually using descriptions and pictures). Almost invariably, subjects selected the most attractive person available to be their date (Reis et al., 1980).

It may have occurred to you that in real life we seldom have the luxury of asking for a date without at least the possibility of being turned down. When experiments built in the possibility of rejection, an interesting effect emerged: Subjects no longer picked the most attractive candidate but selected partners whose level of attractiveness was closer to their own. This is called the **matching phenomenon**, and has been verified repeatedly (Walster & Walster, 1969). Even when we consider relationships among

matching phenomenon
the tendency to select partners whose level of physical attractiveness matches our own

The more similar another person is to you, the more you will tend to like that person. Our friends tend to be people who share our attitudes and who like to do the things we like to do.

friends of the same sex, we find that such friends tend to be very similar when rated for physical attractiveness (Cash & Derlega, 1978).

Our fourth determinant is *similarity*. There is a large body of research on similarity and attraction, but the findings are quite consistent, so we can summarize them briefly. Much of this research has been done by Donn Byrne and his colleagues (Byrne, 1971; Smeaton et al., 1989). There is a strong positive correlation between attraction and number of attitudes held in common. Simply, the more similar another person is to you, the more you will tend to like that person (Buss, 1985; Davis, 1985; Rubin, 1973). Sensibly, we tend to be repelled by persons we believe to be dissimilar to us (Rosenbaum, 1986). Opposites may occasionally attract, but similarity is probably the glue that holds romances and friendships together.

● **Before You Go On**

What are four determinants of interpersonal attraction?

TOPIC 14B

SOCIAL INFLUENCE

So far we've reviewed some of the ways in which our social nature has an impact on our cognitions about ourselves and others. Now it is time to consider more direct influences of the social world on our everyday behaviors.

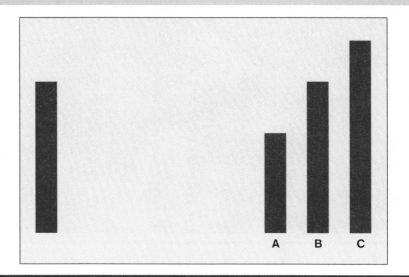

FIGURE 14.3
The type of stimuli used in Asch's conformity experiments. Subjects are to say which of the three lines on the right (A, B, or C) equals the line on the left. Associates of the experimenter will occasionally make incorrect choices.

CONFORMITY

conformity
the changing of one's behavior under perceived pressure, so that it is consistent with the behavior of others

One of the most direct forms of social influence occurs when we modify our behavior, under perceived pressure to do so, so that it is consistent with the behavior of others, a process referred to as **conformity**. Although we often think of conformity in a negative way, to conform is a natural and often desirable process. Conformity helps make social behaviors efficient and, at least to some degree, predictable.

When he began his research, Solomon Asch believed that people are not very susceptible to social pressure when the social situation is clear-cut and unambiguous. Asch hypothesized that subjects would behave independently of group pressure when there was little question that their own judgments were accurate, and he developed an interesting technique for testing his hypothesis (Asch, 1951, 1956).

A subject in Asch's procedure would join a group seated around a table. In the original study the group consisted of seven people. Unknown to the subject, the six others were confederates of the experimenter; that is, they were "in on" the experiment. The subjects were led to believe that the study dealt with the ability to make perceptual judgments. A participant had to do nothing more than decide which of three lines was the same length as a standard line (Figure 14.3). The experimenter showed each set of lines to the group and then collected responses, one by one, from each member of the group. There were 18 sets of lines to judge, and the real subject was always the last one to respond.

It is important to note that each of the 18 judgments the subjects made involved unambiguous stimuli. The correct answer was always obvious. However, on 12 of the 18 trials, the confederates gave a unanimous, but *incorrect* answer. What would the subjects do now? How would they resolve this conflict? Their perceptual experience was telling them what the correct answer was, but the group was saying something else. Should they trust the judgments of the others, or should they trust their own?

The results of his initial study surprised Asch, because they did not confirm his original hypothesis. Across the critical trials (when the confederates gave "wrong" answers), conformity occurred 37 percent of the time. That is, subjects responded with an incorrect answer that agreed with the majority on more than one-third of the critical trials. Moreover, three-quarters of Asch's subjects conformed to the group pressure at least once.

In subsequent studies, Asch tried several variations of his original procedure. In one experiment, he varied the size of the unanimous, incorrect majority. As you might expect, the level of conformity increased as the size of the majority increased, leveling off at about three or four people (Asch, 1956; Knowles, 1983). Subjects gave an erroneous judgment only 4 percent of the time if only one incorrect judgment preceded their own. In another study, subjects gave an erroneous judgment only 10 percent of the time when there was just one dissenter among the six confederates who voiced an accurate judgment before the subjects gave theirs. In other words, when the subjects had any social support for what their eyes had told them, they tended to trust their own judgment. Other experiments have shown that a minority opinion (say, one dissenter) can have significant effects on conformity if that position is maintained consistently (e.g., Moscovici et al., 1969, 1985; Nemeth, 1986).

Conformity involves yielding to the perceived pressure of a group. In most circumstances, it is assumed that group members are peers, or at least similar to the conformer. When one yields to the pressure of a perceived authority, the result is obedience. It is to *obedience* that we turn next.

● **Before You Go On**

Briefly describe the methodology and the basic findings of the Asch conformity studies.

OBEDIENCE TO AUTHORITY

The participants in Asch's studies took the procedure seriously, but the consequences of either conforming or maintaining independence were rather trivial. At worst, Asch's subjects might have experienced some discomfort as a result of sticking to their independent judgments. There were no rewards or punishments for their behavior, and there was no one telling them how to respond. Stanley Milgram (1933–1984), a social psychologist at Yale University, went beyond Asch's procedure. Milgram's experiments pressured subjects to comply with the demand of an authority figure—a demand that was both unreasonable and troubling (Milgram, 1963, 1965, 1974).

All of Milgram's studies involved the same basic procedure. Subjects arrived at the laboratory to discover that they would be participating with another person (again, a confederate of the experimenter). The experimenter explained that the research dealt with the effects of punishment on learning, and that one subject would serve as a teacher while the other would act as learner. The two roles were assigned by a rigged drawing in which the actual subject was always assigned the role of teacher, while the confederate was always the learner. The subject watched as the learner was

After consistently disagreeing with other subjects in Asch's study, the lone dissenter (here, on the right) begins to doubt his judgment and looks again at the card, even though the correct answer is obvious.

taken to the next room and wired to electrodes that would be used for delivering punishment in the form of electric shocks.

The teacher then received his instructions. First, he was to read to the learner a list of four pairs of words. The teacher was then to read the first word of one of the pairs, and the learner was to supply the second word. The teacher sat in front of a rather imposing electric "shock generator" that had 30 switches, each with its voltage level labeled (Figure 14.4). From left to right, the switches increased by increments of 15 volts, ranging from 15 volts to 450 volts. Labels were printed under the switches on the generator. These ranged from "Slight" to "Moderate" to "Extreme Intensity" to "Danger: Severe Shock." The label at the 450-volt end simply read "XXX."

As the task proceeded, the learner periodically made errors according to a prearranged schedule. The teacher had been instructed to deliver an electric shock for each incorrect answer. With each error, the teacher was to move up the scale of shocks, giving the learner a more potent shock with each new mistake. (The learner, remember, was part of the act, and no one was actually receiving any shocks.)

Whenever the teacher (subject) hesitated or questioned if he should continue, the experimenter was ready with a verbal prod, such as "Please continue," or "The experiment requires that you continue." If the subject protested, the experimenter would become more assertive and offer an alternative prod: "You have no choice; you must go on," he might say. The degree of obedience was determined by the level of shock at which the teacher refused to go further.

Milgram was astonished by the results of his study, and the results continue to amaze us 30 years later. Twenty-six of Milgram's 40 subjects—65 percent—obeyed the experimenter and went all the way to the highest shock and closed all the switches. In fact, no one stopped prior to the 300-volt level, the point at which the learner pounded on the wall in protest. One later variation of this study added vocal responses from the learner, who delivered an increasingly stronger series of demands to be let out of the experiment. The level of obedience in this study still was unbelievably high, as 25 of 40 subjects, or 62.5 percent, continued to administer shocks to the 450-volt level.

It is important to note that all of the subjects (teachers) experienced genuine and extreme stress in this situation. Some fidgeted, some trembled, many perspired profusely. Several subjects giggled nervously. In short,

FIGURE 14.4
A shock generator apparatus of the sort the "teacher" would use to punish the "learner" in Stanley Milgram's research on obedience. In the bottom photo, the "learner" is given a sample shock.

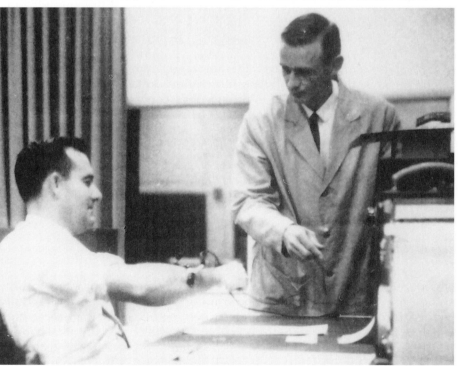

the people caught up in this unusual situation showed obvious signs of conflict and anxiety. Nevertheless, they continued to obey the orders of the authoritative experimenter even though they had good reason to believe that they might well be harming the learner.

Milgram's first study used only male subjects ranging in age from 20 to 50. A replication with adult women produced precisely the same results: 65 percent obeyed fully. Other variations uncovered several factors that could reduce the extent of obedience. Putting the learner and teacher in the same room, or having the experimenter deliver his orders over the telephone, for example, reduced obedience markedly. When the shocks were delivered by a team consisting of the subject and two disobedient confederates, full-scale obedience dropped to only 10 percent.

Upon first hearing about these rather distressing results, there is a tendency for many people to think that Milgram's obedient subjects were cold, callous, unfeeling, or downright cruel and sadistic people (Safer, 1980). Nothing could be further from the truth. The participants in this research were truly troubled by what was happening. If you thought that Milgram's subjects must be strange or different, perhaps you were a victim of what we identified in our last Topic as an *attribution error.* That is, you were willing to attribute the subjects' behavior to (internal) personal characteristics instead of recognizing the powerful situational forces at work.

In reading about Milgram's research, it should have occurred to you that putting people in such a stressful experience could be considered ethically objectionable. Milgram himself was concerned with the welfare of his subjects. He took great care to debrief them fully after each session had been completed. He told them that they had not really administered any shocks and explained why deception had been necessary. Milgram reported that the people in his studies were not upset over having been deceived and that their principal reaction was one of relief when they learned that no electric shock had in fact been used. Milgram also indicated that a follow-up study performed a year later with some of the same subjects showed that no long-term adverse effects had been created by his procedure.

Despite these precautions, Milgram was severely criticized for placing people in such an extremely stressful situation. Indeed, one of the effects of his research was to establish in the scientific community a higher level of awareness of the need to protect the well-being of human research subjects. It is probably safe to say that because of Milgram's experience, no one would be allowed to perform such experiments today.

● **Before You Go On**

Briefly describe Stanley Milgram's experimental demonstrations of obedience.

BYSTANDER INTERVENTION

It was roughly thirty years ago that a New York City cocktail waitress, Kitty Genovese, was brutally murdered in front of her apartment building as she returned from work about 3:30 A.M. Murders, and violence in general, have today become nearly commonplace (see "Psychology in the Real World" box). Nonetheless, there were some unusual and particularly disturbing circumstances surrounding Genovese's death. Here is the account of the incident as reported in the *New York Times:*

> For more than half an hour, thirty-eight respectable law-abiding citizens in Queens watched a killer stalk and stab a woman in three separate attacks in Kew Gardens.
>
> Twice the sound of their voices and the sudden glow of their bedroom lights interrupted him and frightened him off. Each time he returned, sought her out and stabbed her again. Not one person telephoned the police during the assault; one witness called after the woman was dead. (March 27, 1964)

This story has become a classic example in the social psychology of bystander behaviors. Still, I was concerned that because the incident took place so many years ago, it might have lost some of its relevance. As I pondered whether to tell the story of Kitty Genovese, I read another newspaper story:

> **Cheering bystanders spur on woman's killer.** Oakland, Calif. (AP)—
>
> A dozen people who chanted "Kill her, kill her," as a 32-year-old woman was stabbed to death could face murder charges, authorities say.
>
> Police said Friday they were looking for members of the crowd who egged on the woman's attacker. The people could be charged with aiding and abetting a killing. (*Toronto Times*, August 15, 1993)

Then, even more recently,

> **Tourists watched woman drown** Mont Saint-Michel, France—Dozens of tourists at the medieval Mont Saint-Michel abbey impassively watched and even videotaped a woman drown as she tried to save her child.
>
> Victoria Guillernée, 6, and her mother, Marie–Noëlle, 42, were walking along the base of the hill when the girl fell into a water hole. As the mother tried to save her, tourists apparently watched without trying to intervene.
>
> Residents reported hearing one tourist say, "I got the whole thing on tape."
>
> (*The Journal Gazette*, Fort Wayne, IN, August 29, 1994)

Yes, the murder of Kitty Genovese occurred over thirty years ago. No, sadly, the story is not dated; nor is it irrelevant. Here was a young woman brutally slain in full view of (at least) 38 witnesses, none of whom came to her aid. The event stimulated a great deal of public concern. People wondered how the witnesses could have shown such a lack of concern for a neighbor. *Alienation* and *apathy* were terms often used to describe what had happened.

Bibb Latané and John Darley, two social psychologists who at the time were at universities in New York City, were not satisfied that terms such as *bystander apathy* or *alienation* adequately explained what happened in the Genovese case. They were not willing to attribute people's failure to help to internal or personality characteristics. They were convinced that situational factors make such events possible.

Latané and Darley (1970) pointed out that there *are* logical reasons why people should not be expected to offer help in an emergency. Emergencies tend to happen quickly and without advance warning. Except for medical technicians, firefighters, and a few other select groups, people generally are not prepared to deal with emergencies when they do arise. In fact, one good predictor of who will intervene in an emergency turns out to be previous experience with similar emergency situations (Cramer et al., 1988; Huston et al., 1981).

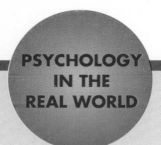
Violence

Violence is a form of aggression in which one purposively inflicts physical injury or pain on another. Each of us is affected by what seems to be a daily escalation of violent behaviors. Every time we read a newspaper, watch television, or venture out into the world, we are likely to be confronted with issues of violence. The news of the 90s seems filled with allegations concerning the likes of the Menendez brothers, Susan Smith, O. J. Simpson, Lorena Bobbitt, and Robert "Yummy" Sandifer, an 11-year-old Chicago boy who allegedly killed a 14-year-old girl, and in return was killed by members of his own gang.

What has led to the increase in violence in our lives? This is another question for which there are no simple answers. The following statistics do suggest some areas to explore (from Adler, *Newsweek*, Jan. 10, 1994, p. 44).

Changes in the Family

Single-Parent Homes
There has been a 200 percent growth in single-parent households since 1970, from 4 million to 8 million homes.

Working Mothers
The number of married moms leaving home for work each morning rose 65 percent from 10.2 million in 1970 to 16.8 million in 1990.

Married with Children
Married couples with children now make up only 26 percent of U.S. households, down from 40 percent in 1970.

Chores
36 percent of children said their chores included making their own meals in 1993. Only 18 percent said the same in 1987.

Crime Begins at Home
An estimated 70 percent of juvenile offenders come from single-parent families.

Outside Influences

Television Violence
The average child has watched 8,000 televised murders and 100,000 acts of violence before finishing elementary school.

Real Violence
One in six youths between the ages of 10 and 17 has seen or knows someone who has been shot.

Child Abuse
The estimated number of child abuse victims increased 40% between 1985 and 1991.

Sex
In 1988, 26 percent of girls age 15 reported being sexually active, compared to only 5 percent in 1970.

Violent Crime
Children under 18 are 244 percent more likely to be killed by guns than they were in 1986.

The National Education Association reports that 50,000 children were killed by firearms between 1979 and 1991, a figure equal to the number of American casualties in the Vietnam War. Guns

A Cognitive Model of Bystander Intervention

Latané and Darley (1968) suggest that a series of cognitive events must occur before a bystander can intervene in an emergency (Figure 14.5). First, the bystander must *notice* what is going on. A person who is windowshopping and thus fails to see a man collapse on the other side of the street cannot be expected to rush over and offer help. If the bystander does notice something happen, he or she still must *interpret* the situation as an emergency—perhaps the person who has collapsed is simply drunk or tired. The third step involves the decision that it is the bystander's (and not someone else's) *responsibility* to do something.

are the number one cause of death among 10- to 24-year-old black males (NEA, 1994). The homicide rate for black males ages 15–19 doubled between 1984 and 1988 (Glazer, 1992). In 1991 alone, 130,000 youths (ages 10–17) were arrested for rape, robbery, homicide, and aggravated assault (Giuliano, 1994). One in five high school students carries a weapon at least once a month, with knives or razors being the most popular weapons (Glazer, 1992).

It is estimated that the population of the United States will rise about 12 percent by 2005, but the number of teens, aged 15 through 19, will increase 21 percent. "Young Black and Hispanic men—those with the highest violent crime rates—will increase 24 percent and 47 percent, respectively" (Gest & Friedman, 1994). John Richters, the head of the Conduct Disorder Program at the National Institute of Mental Health recently claimed that: "Americans are by far the most violent people in the world." When asked about prevention, Richters called the situation "a pretty bleak one: We don't know what works" but he did say that early pervention was crucial (Goldberg, 1994).

Violence in the workplace also has been on the increase. A study from 1992–1993 reported that 2.2 million workers were victims of physical attack, 6.3 million were threatened, and 16.1 million were harassed (Martin, 1994).

In 1986, an international committee of 20 scholars met in Seville, Spain, to discuss violence and aggression. The committee issued a statement, *The Seville Statement on Violence*, whose purpose was to dispel the belief that humans are necessarily or inevitably predisposed to war and violence because of some innate, biologically determined trait or traits. The five points made by the Seville Statement are: (1) that humans have not inherited a tendency to make war; (2) they are not genetically programmed to be violent; (3) that aggressive behavior has not selectively evolved more than other kinds of behavior; (4) that humans do not have a "violent brain"; and (5) that war is not caused by "instinct" (APA, 1994). The American Psychological Association endorsed this statement in 1987. Some psychologists have criticized the Seville Statement, arguing that it makes claims that are not scientifically valid, at least at this time (e.g., Beroldi, 1994), while others support the statement, at least as a "work in progress" (e.g., Scott & Ginsburg, 1994).

While psychologists will not be able to solve all of the problems related to violence, more discussions, research, and the development and implementation of effective programs will assist in addressing this critically important problem of society (Eron et al., 1995).

Even if the bystander has noticed something happening, has interpreted the situation as one calling for action, and has assumed responsibility for helping, he or she still faces the decision of what form of assistance to offer. Should he or she try to administer first aid? Should he or she try to find the nearest telephone, or simply start shouting for help? As a final step in the process, the bystander must decide how to *implement* his or her decision to act. What is the best form of first aid? Just where can a phone be found? Thus we can see that intervening on behalf of someone else in a social situation involves a series of cognitive choices.

Crossing the village, Mowaka is overpowered by army ants. (Later, bystanders were all quoted as saying they were horrified, but "didn't want to get involved.")

A negative outcome at any of these cognitive steps of decision making will lead a bystander to decide to not offer assistance. When one considers the cognitive chain of events necessary for actually helping, it becomes apparent that the deck is stacked against the victim in an emergency. As Latané and Darley have suggested, perhaps we should be surprised that bystanders ever *do* offer to help (Cunningham, 1984; Shotland, 1985). There may be many psychological processes that account for what is called the *social inhibition of helping*, or *bystander effect*. We'll review three such processes (Latané & Darley, 1970; Latané & Nida, 1981).

Audience Inhibition

audience inhibition
reluctance to intervene and offer assistance in front of others

Audience inhibition is the tendency to be hesitant to do things in front of others, especially when the others happen to be strangers. We tend to be concerned about how others will evaluate us. In public, no one wants to do anything that appears to be silly, incompetent, or improper. The bystander who intervenes risks embarrassment (at the very least) if he or she blun-

FIGURE 14.5

Some of the decisions and outcomes involved as a bystander considers intervening in a perceived emergency situation. (After Latané & Darley, 1968.)

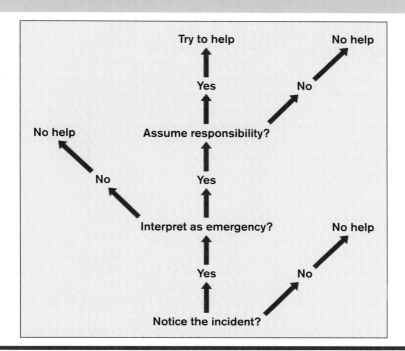

ders. That risk increases as the number of people present increases. Predictably, people who are generally more sensitive to, or afraid of, being embarrassed are least likely to help in a social situation (Tice & Baumeister, 1985).

Pluralistic Ignorance

Emergencies tend to be ambiguous: Is the man who has collapsed on the street ill or drunk? Is the commotion in a neighboring apartment an assault or a family quarrel that's just a little out of hand? When social reality is unclear, we often turn to others for clues. While someone is in the process of getting information from others, he or she will try to remain calm and collected, behaving as if there is no emergency. Everyone else, of course, is doing exactly the same thing, showing no outward sign of concern. The result is that each person is led by the others to think that the situation is really not an emergency after all, a psychological state called **pluralistic ignorance** (Miller & McFarland, 1987). Pluralistic ignorance amounts to an individual's belief that only he or she is confused and doesn't know what to do, while everyone else is standing about doing nothing for some good reason. The group becomes paralyzed by a sort of conformity—conformity to the inaction of others.

pluralistic ignorance
a condition in which the inaction of others leads each individual in a group to interpret a situation as a nonemergency, thus leading to general inactivity

Researchers have found several reasons why people should not be expected to get involved in a perceived emergency situation. Nonetheless, some bystanders will choose to intervene, as was the case with the heart attack victim pictured here.

diffusion of responsibility the tendency to allow others to share in the obligation to intervene

This process was demonstrated clearly in a classic experiment by Latané and Darley (1968, 1970). Columbia University students reported to a campus building to participate in an interview. They were sent to a waiting room and asked to fill out some preliminary forms. While they did so, smoke began to billow through a vent in the wall. After six minutes (at which time the study was terminated if the "emergency" had not been reported), there was enough smoke in the room to cause difficulty breathing and prevent seeing across the room.

When subjects were alone in the waiting room, 75 percent of them emerged to report the smoke. However, when two passive confederates were in the room with the subject, only 10 percent responded. Those people who reported the smoke did so quickly. Those from the groups who failed to do so generated all sorts of explanations for the smoke: steam, vapors from the air conditioner, smog introduced to simulate an urban environment, even "truth gas." In short, subjects who remained unresponsive had been led by the inaction of others to conclude just about anything other than the obvious—that something was wrong.

Diffusion of Responsibility

In the Kitty Genovese murder, it was terribly clear that an emergency was in progress. There was little ambiguity about what was happening. Furthermore, the 38 witnesses were not in a face-to-face group that would allow social influence processes such as pluralistic ignorance to operate. Latané and Darley suggested that a third important process is necessary to understand bystander behavior.

A single bystander in an emergency situation must bear the full responsibility for offering assistance, but the witness who is part of a group shares that responsibility with other onlookers. The greater the number of other people present, the smaller is each individual's perceived obligation to intervene, a process referred to as **diffusion of responsibility**.

Latané and Darley devised a clever demonstration of this phenomenon. In this study, college students arrived at a laboratory to take part in a group discussion of some of the personal problems they experienced as college students in an urban environment. To reduce the embarrassment of talking about such matters in public, each group member was isolated in his or her own cubicle and communicated with the others through an intercom system. Actually, there were no other group members, only tape-recorded voices. There was only one subject in each group, and the perceived size of the group could be easily manipulated to see whether diffusion of responsibility would occur.

The first person to speak mentioned that he was prone to seizures when under pressure, such as when studying for a test. The others, including the actual subject, then took turns talking for about 10 minutes about their problems. A second round of discussion then began with the seizure-prone student who, shortly after he started talking, began to suffer a seizure. It was very obvious that something was wrong. As the "victim" stammered, choked, and pleaded for help, the typical subject became quite nervous—some trembled, some had sweaty palms. Remember: Subjects could not be sure if any other "participants" had taken any action.

As expected, the likelihood of helping decreased as the perceived size of the group increased. Eighty-five percent of those in two-person groups (just the subject and victim) left the cubicle to report the emergency. When the subject thought that he or she was in a three-person group, 62 percent responded. Only 31 percent of those who believed that they were in a six-person group took any step to intervene. The responsibility for reporting the seizure was clearly diffused among those thought to be present.

Incidentally, diffusion of responsibility does come in forms that are less serious in their implications. Those of you with a few siblings can probably recall times at home when the telephone rang five or six times before anyone made a move to answer it, even though the entire family was home at the time. Some of you probably have been at parties where the doorbell went unanswered while everyone thought "someone else will get it."

The Bystander Effect: A Conclusion

The situational determinants of helping behaviors continued to be a popular research topic for social psychologists throughout the 1970s. Many of these studies included a manipulation of the size of the group witnessing the event that created the need for help in the first place. Latané and Nida (1981) reviewed some 50 studies involving nearly 100 different helping-or-not-helping situations. Although these experiments involved a wide range of settings, procedures, and participants, the social inhibition of helping (the bystander effect) occurred in almost every instance. The researchers concluded that there is little doubt that a person is more likely to help when he or she is alone rather than in a group. The bystander effect is a remarkably consistent phenomenon, perhaps as predictable as any phenomenon in social psychology.

● **Before You Go On**

What effect does the presence of others have on a person's willingness to help in an emergency?

How do audience inhibition, pluralistic ignorance, and diffusion of responsibility account for the lack of bystander intervention?

SOCIAL LOAFING

Social loafing is the tendency to work less (decrease one's individual effort) as the size of the group in which one is working becomes larger (Latané et al., 1979). Initial studies of social loafing required subjects to shout or clap as loudly as possible, either in groups or alone. If individuals were led to believe that their performance could not be identified, they invested less and less effort in the task as group size increased. Other studies (Petty et al., 1977; Weldon & Gargano, 1988) have used more cognitive tasks, such as evaluating poetry. The results tend to be consistent: When people can hide in the crowd, their effort (and hence their productivity) declines.

Although social loafing is a widespread phenomenon, it does not *always* follow when one works in a group situation. Remember our earlier discussions of cultures that can be described in terms of collectivist or individualist characteristics? As you might predict, social loafing is significantly less likely in those collectivist societies—such as in Japan, China, and other Asian countries—that place a high value on participation in group activities (e.g., Early, 1989; Gabrena et al., 1985). In individualist cultures, such as in the United States and most Western countries, social loafing can be virtually eliminated if group members believe their effort is special and required for the group's success, or if group members believe their performance can be identified or evaluated individually (Harkins, 1987; Harkins

social loafing
the tendency for a person to work less hard when part of a group in which everyone's efforts are pooled

Because of social facilitation, we tend to perform better when we are in the presence of others—at least when we are engaged in simple or well-rehearsed behaviors. Bicycle riders, for example, ride faster when racing against other riders than when racing against the clock.

& Petty, 1982; Harkins & Syzmanski, 1989; Williams et al., 1981, 1989). This is not unlike the behavior of a student in a very large lecture class, virtually assured that he won't be called on, as opposed to his behavior in a small discussion class. Indeed, there are situations in which the social influence of group participation facilitates behavior.

SOCIAL FACILITATION

Almost a century ago, a psychologist named Norman Triplett observed that bicycle riders competing against other cyclists outperformed those racing against a clock. He then did what is considered to be the first laboratory experiment in social psychology (Triplett, 1898). Triplett had children wind a fishing reel as rapidly as they could. They engaged in this task either alone or with another child alongside doing the same thing. Just as he had noticed in his records of bicycle races, Triplett found that the children worked faster when another child was present. We now know that such an effect can occur not only with co-actors (others engaged in the same task), but also if a person simply performs in front of an audience. For example, joggers, both male and female, pick up their pace and run faster when running past women sitting on a park bench (Worringham & Messick, 1983). When the presence of others improves an individual's performance on some task, we have evidence of what is called **social facilitation.**

Numerous studies on social facilitation were performed early in this century, but with a puzzling inconsistency in their results. Sometimes social facilitation would be found, but on some occasions, the opposite effect would occur. At times people actually performed more poorly in the presence of others than they did alone, an effect social psychologists

social facilitation
improved performance due to the presence of others

called **social interference**. The inconsistencies in the research findings were so bewildering that most psychologists eventually gave up investigating social facilitation.

social interference
impaired performance due to the presence of others

In 1965, Robert Zajonc resurrected the topic of social facilitation by providing a plausible interpretation for the lack of consistency in social facilitation effects. In his examination of the research, Zajonc noticed that social facilitation occurred whenever the behavior being studied was simple, routine, or very well learned (such as bicycle riding or winding a fishing reel). Social interference tended to occur whenever the behavior involved was complex or not well practiced. Zajonc's insight was that the presence of others creates increased arousal, which in turn energizes the dominant (most likely) response. When the dominant response is correct, as with a simple, well-practiced task, facilitation occurs. When the dominant response is incorrect, as with a complex task or one with which we have had little practice, the result is interference (Levine et al., 1993).

You may have experienced this effect yourself if you have ever tried to acquire a skill at a sport that is totally new to you. Whereas skilled athletes tend to perform better in front of audiences, the novice tends to do better when alone. (Even skilled athletes don't always perform better in front of audiences, sometimes "choking" in front of home crowds during important games [Baumeister, 1985].) You may have experienced—as a novice, that is—the frustration of finding it difficult to even make contact with a golf ball or tennis ball when there are others standing nearby watching you.

● **Before You Go On**

What can we conclude concerning the effects of social influence on the quality of an individual's performance?

DECISION MAKING IN GROUPS

Many of the decisions that we make in our daily lives are the sort that are made in a group setting. Committees, boards, family groups, and group projects for a class are only a few examples. There is logic in the belief that group efforts to solve problems should be superior to the efforts of individuals. One might reason that problem solving ought to be more effective in a group because individuals can pool resources. Having more people available should necessarily mean having more talent and knowledge available. It also seems logical that the cohesiveness of the group should contribute to a more productive effort (and for some groups and problems, this is the case). But by now we know better than to assume that simply because a conclusion is logical it is necessarily true. Consider two curious phenomena that can occur in group decision making.

When he was an MIT graduate student in industrial management, James Stoner gave subjects in his research a series of dilemmas to grapple with (Stoner, 1961). The result of each decision was to be a statement of how much risk a fictitious character in the dilemma should take. To his surprise, Stoner found that the decisions rendered by groups generally were much riskier than those that the individual group members had made prior to the group decision. Stoner called this move away from conservative solutions a *risky shift*. For example, doctors, if they were asked individually, might express the opinion that a patient's present problem could be handled with medication and a change in diet. If these very same doctors were to get together to discuss the patient's situation, they might very well end up concluding that what was called for was a new and potentially dangerous (risky) surgical procedure.

Several hundred experimental studies later, we now know that this effect can occur in the opposite direction as well (Levine & Moreland, 1990; Moscovici et al., 1985). In other words, the risky shift is simply a specific case of a more general **group polarization** effect—the effect of making an individual's reactions or decisions more extreme (or polarized) as a function of group decision making. Group discussion usually leads to an enhancement of the beliefs of the group members that existed before the discussion began. The group process tends to push members further in the direction in which they leaned initially. One explanation for group polarization is that open discussion gives group members a chance to hear persuasive arguments they have not previously considered, leading to a strengthening of their original attitudes (Isenberg, 1986). Another possibility is that after comparing positions with each other, some group members feel pressure to catch up with other group members who have more extreme positions (Hinsz & Davis, 1984).

Irving Janis (1972; 1983a) described a related phenomenon of social influence that he calls **groupthink**—an excessive concern for reaching a consensus in group decision making to the extent that critical evaluations are withheld. Groupthink is especially likely to occur in cohesive groups. Alternative courses of action are not considered realistically and the frequent result is a poor decision. Janis has analyzed several key historical events—including responding to the Pearl Harbor invasion, planning the Bay of Pigs invasion, and escalating the Vietnam War—in terms of the operation of groupthink. He argues that each of these situations involved a cohesive decision-making group that was relatively isolated from outside judgments, a directive leader who pressured others to conform to his position, and an illusion of unanimity (see also McCauley, 1989). When for example, decisions about minorities or women are made by a group of white males (no matter how well intentioned) we might at least suspect that groupthink could be at work.

Before you conclude that decision making in groups always leads to negative consequences, let me point out that there are circumstances in which groups are more efficient than individuals working alone. As I implied above, groups are useful when problems are complex and require skills and abilities that are more likely to be found in a number of different individuals working together. Group decision making also can serve to identify errors that individuals might not identify.

group polarization
the tendency for members of a group to give more extreme judgments following a discussion than they gave initially

groupthink
a style of thinking of cohesive groups concerned with maintaining agreement to the extent that independent ideas are discouraged

● **Before You Go On**
How does social influence affect decision making in groups?

THINKING CRITICALLY ABOUT SOCIAL PSYCHOLOGY

1. We often hear the claim that humans are social animals. What would be the long-term consequences of social isolation? How do you sup-

Many of the decisions we face every day are the sort that are best made in groups, whether they be committees, boards, or family groups.

pose that you would react to being literally stranded alone on a remote island? How can social isolation be used in brainwashing?

2. Are there some periods in human history in which we might expect to find more or less conformity, both in society and in the laboratory? Can you cite examples?

3. Many early social psychological and sociological studies tell us that, in general again, the political and social attitudes of students become more liberal as they pass through college. Why do you think this is so? Do you think that this is true for you?

4. Imagine that you want to change a friend's attitude about abortion (in either direction). How would you do so?

5. Why is the fundamental attribution error so common, particularly in Western cultures?

6. Can you explain your interpersonal attraction to any of your friends in terms of the theories presented in this chapter?

7. Which statement is true: "Out of sight, out of mind" or "Absence makes the heart grow fonder"? How would you design an experiment or research study to support your point of view on this issue?

8. Now that you know all about the results of his project, how do you think that you would have reacted if you were one of Milgram's "teachers?"

9. To what extent can you observe "bystander apathy" occurring on your campus? When there is a student government election, what percentage of the student body votes?

10. What sorts of problems are likely to get better quality solutions from groups than from individuals?

SUMMARY

TOPIC 14A

SOCIAL COGNITIONS: ATTITUDES, ATTRIBUTIONS, AND ATTRACTIONS

● What is social psychology, and what are social cognitions?

Social psychology is that subfield of psychology that deals primarily with how others influence the thoughts, feelings, and behaviors of the individual. Social cognitions are ideas, beliefs, thoughts, and the like, stored in memory, that guide our interactions in the social environment. *Pages 476–477.*

● What is an attitude and what are its three components?

An attitude is an evaluative disposition (positive or negative) directed toward some object or event. An attitude usually has three components: feelings (affects), behaviors, and beliefs (cognitions). Although the affective and cognitive components are usually consistent with each other, behavior—influenced by so many other variables—may be inconsistent with the other two components of an attitude. *Pages 477–478.*

● Briefly describe three ways in which attitudes might be acquired.

Attitudes are most certainly learned. They may be acquired through classical conditioning: After positive or negative experiences are associated with an attitudinal object, the object itself comes to produce a positive or negative evaluation. Attitudinal behaviors also may be directly reinforced (operant conditioning) or they may be reinforced vicariously (observational learning). *Pages 478–480.*

● What is cognitive dissonance, and how does it operate?

Cognitive dissonance is an unpleasant state of tension that may occur when our attitudes or cognitions are inconsistent or when we behave in a manner that is inconsistent with our attitudes. Because we are motivated to reduce dissonance, we may do so by changing our attitudes so they become consistent with the way we behave. *Pages 480–482.*

● What communicator characteristics are known to have an impact on attitude change?

Concern with communicator characteristics and other situational variables reflects a focus on peripheral routes to attitude change. Those communicators perceived as being expert or trustworthy are seen as credible sources, and hence are more persuasive. *Pages 482–483.*

● What are the two basic types of attribution?
● Explain the ways in which attributions can be distorted or biased.

Attributions are cognitions we use to explain the sources of the behaviors we see in our social worlds. The two basic types of attribution are internal and external. An *internal attribution* identifies the source of behavior as within the person and is sometimes called a dispositional attribution. An *external attribution* finds the source of behavior to be outside the person and may be called a situational attribution. The *fundamental attribution error* leads us to overuse internal, personal, attributions when explaining behaviors. Persons who hold to the *just world hypothesis* are likely to believe that good things happen only to good people and bad things happen only to bad people, who in some way deserve their misfortune. The *self-serving bias* has us attribute successes to our own efforts and actions and our failures to other, external factors. The *actor-observer bias* refers to the tendency to use external attributions to explain our own behaviors (as actor), while using internal attributions to explain the behaviors of others (as observer). *Pages 483–485.*

● Briefly summarize four theoretical models that account for interpersonal attractions.

The *reinforcement model* claims that we tend to be attracted to those persons we associate with rewards or reinforcers. The *social exchange model* adds the notion of cost to the equation, claiming that what matters in interpersonal relationships is the ratio of the benefits received to the costs invested in that relationship. The *equity model* suggests that all members of a relationship assess a benefit/cost ratio and the best, most stable relationships are those in which the ratio is nearly the same (equitable) for all parties, no matter what the value of the benefits for any one member of the relationship. *Attachment theory* tells us that there are only a few relationship styles, and that people are consistent over their lifetime in the style they use when relating to others. *Pages 485–487.*

● What are four determinants of interpersonal attraction?

The principle of *reciprocity* states that we tend to like people who like us back. This is the most straightforward example of interpersonal attraction being based on a system of rewards. *Proximity* promotes attraction by means of the mere exposure phenomenon: Being near another person on a frequent basis gives us the opportunity to see what that other person has to offer. We also tend to be attracted to people whom we judge to be *physically attractive*. The principle of *similarity* suggests that we tend to be attracted to those we believe are similar to ourselves. *Pages 487–489.*

TOPIC 14B
SOCIAL INFLUENCE

● Briefly describe the methodology and the basic findings of the Asch conformity studies.

In the Asch studies, people made judgments about unambiguous perceptual stimuli—the length of lines. On some trials, confederates gave clearly incorrect judgments before the actual subject had a chance to respond. Although there were situations in which yielding to the perceived group pressure could be lessened, many of Asch's subjects followed suit and yielded, or conformed. *Pages 489–491.*

● Briefly describe Stanley Milgram's experimental demonstrations of obedience.

Subjects in Milgram's research were led to believe that they were administering more and more potent shocks to another subject in a learning task. Whenever they hesitated to deliver the shocks, an authority figure, the experimenter, prodded them to continue. All subjects obeyed to some degree, and nearly two-thirds delivered what they thought was the most intense shock, even over the protests of the learner. Those who obeyed in Milgram's experiments were neither cruel nor inhumane. Rather, the experimenter created a powerful social situation that made it very difficult to refuse the authority figure's orders. *Pages 491–494.*

● What effect does the presence of others have on a person's willingness to help in an emergency?
● How do audience inhibition, pluralistic ignorance, and diffusion of responsibility account for the lack of bystander intervention?

The likelihood that someone will intervene on behalf of another decreases as the number of others (bystanders) present at the time increases. Several factors may account for this phenomenon. *Audience inhibition* is the term used to describe the hesitancy to intervene in front of others, perhaps for fear of embarrassing oneself. *Pluralistic ignorance* occurs when other bystanders lead one to think (by their inactivity) that nothing is wrong in an ambiguous emergency situation. *Diffusion of responsibility* causes a member of a group to feel less obligated to intervene (less responsible) than if he or she were alone. *Pages 494–501.*

● What can we conclude concerning the effects of social influence on the quality of an individual's performance?

As group size increases, social loafing increases, that is, one is less likely to invest full effort and energy in a task as a member of a group than he or she would if working alone. The quality of one's performance also tends to suffer when one works in a group, a phenomenon called *social interference*. On the other hand, when tasks are simple or well rehearsed, performance may be enhanced, a process called *social facilitation*. *Pages 501–503.*

● How does social influence affect decision making in groups?

There are some advantages to problem solving in a group setting. With proper leadership and communication, the combined expertise present in a group may provide better solutions and a better check on errors than we might find if individuals worked independently. On the other hand, group polarization—the tendency of group discussion to solidify and enhance preexisting attitudes—and groupthink—the unwillingness to promote an unpopular view in front of others in a group—operate to detract from group decision making. *Pages 503–504.*

TOPIC 14A

SOCIAL COGNITIONS: ATTITUDES, ATTRIBUTIONS, AND ATTRACTIONS

14.1 Which of these provides the poorest, or weakest, example of a social cognition? a) having a negative attitude about sociologists b) attributing the behavior of a stranger to some internal personality trait c) feeling depressed at final exam time d) being attracted to the good-looking laboratory assistant in the physics lab. *Pages 476–477.*

14.2 True or False? Attitudes require an object; that is, one must have an attitude "about" something, not just "have an attitude." *Pages 477–478.*

14.3 Most psychologists believe that attitudes are made up of different components or aspects. The one aspect that seems most central or critical to an attitude is a) the attitudinal object. b) a belief or cognition. c) a tendency to behave in a certain way. d) an evaluative (+ or -) feeling. *Pages 477–478.*

14.4 True or False? Attitudes have three components: personal, social, and environmental. *Pages 478–480.*

14.5 When an advertiser tries to change your attitude about a product, in which component of your attitude is the advertiser most interested? a) cognitive b) evaluative c) affective d) behavioral. *Pages 480–483.*

14.6 If I can get you to do something that is contrary to an attitude you currently hold, you may change your attitude. If I am successful, I have changed your attitude using a) cognitive dissonance. b) classical conditioning. c) coercive persuasion. d) cognitive response theory. *Pages 480–483.*

14.7 A communicator is trying to persuade others to change their attitudes. Which characteristic of the communicator is *least* important in predicting whether the communication will be successful? a) credibility b) celebrity c) expertise d) trustworthiness. *Pages 480–483.*

14.8 Attributions typically are made in terms of each of the following *except* a) internal vs. external factors. b) dispositional vs. situational factors. c) learned vs. inherited factors. d) intrinsic vs. extrinsic factors. *Pages 483–485.*

14.9 When we tend to overemphasize personal reasons in our explanations of another's behaviors and overlook the forces of the situation or the environment, we are a) making a fundamental attribution error. b) demonstrating our belief in the just world hypothesis. c) employing a self-serving bias in our judgment. d) failing to take into account the actor-observer bias. *Pages 483–485.*

14.10 Basically, attributions deal with a) different techniques for changing the attitudes of others. b) how we tend to explain the behaviors of ourselves and others in social situations. c) factors and processes that lead to interpersonal attraction. d) forming expectations about how we should act in a variety of social situations. *Pages 483–485.*

14.11 True or False? Most people attribute their own successes to dispositional factors and their own failures to situational factors. *Pages 483–485.*

14.12 With regard to interpersonal attraction, attachment theory suggests that a) Everyone relates to others in essentially the same way. b) How one forms relationships as a child predicts how one will form relationships as an adult. c) Women tend to form interpersonal attachments that are different from those of men. d) How one forms attachments depends more on the situation than it does on the persons involved. *Pages 485–487.*

14.13 With regard to interpersonal attraction, which is *false*? a) The "mere exposure phenomenon" tells us that familiarity breeds contempt. b) We tend to like and value those who like and value us. c) Physical attractiveness is positively correlated with attraction. d) People tend to be attracted to those who have similar attitudes. *Pages 487–489.*

14.14 Which of these is likely to have the *least* impact on interpersonal attraction? a) physical closeness b) physical attractiveness c) attitudinal similarity d) perceived sexuality. *Pages 487–489.*

14.15 True or False? Even if someone likes us now, if they did not like us originally, we probably will not value them as a friend. *Pages 487–489.*

T O P I C   1 4 B

SOCIAL INFLUENCE

14.16 When Solomon Asch studied conformity, he found each of the following *except* that a) even subjects' perceptual judgments could be influenced by group pressure. b) most of his subjects (more than 75%) conformed at least once. c) the least amount of social support was sufficient to help a subject resist group pressure. d) most of the subjects continued to conform even after they learned that others in the group were confederates of the experimenter. *Pages 489–491.*

14.17 True or False? Up to a point, the more people who express the same judgment, the more likely it is that an individual will yield or conform to that judgment. *Pages 489–491.*

14.18 The major difference between conformity and obedience is a) peer pressure. b) the presence of an authority figure. c) the nature of the task involved. d) the subject's perception of social influence. *Pages 491–494.*

14.19 Which conclusion from Milgram's research on obedience is justified? a) Persons of some nationalities are more likely to obey than are others. b) When told to harm others, few subjects felt guilty about it. c) The perception of authority is a strong force in conformity. d) Women are more likely to obey than are men. *Pages 491–494.*

14.20 True or False? Even Milgram was surprised by the results of his experiment. *Pages 491–494.*

14.21 Which of the following is *not* taken to be a necessary step in considering whether or not to intervene in an emergency? a) One must notice or perceive the emergency. b) One must interpret the situation as an emergency. c) One must know or care about the victim. d) One must decide to take responsibility to do something. *Pages 494–501.*

14.22 Which of these best characterizes pluralistic ignorance? a) the feeling that one doesn't know what to do in an emergency b) the perception that there is a good reason why others are not acting c) the decision that there is nothing that could be done to help d) the belief that intervention will cause more harm than good. *Pages 494–501.*

14.23 The concept of "diffusion of responsibility" tells us that if you were in need of assistance, you most likely would receive such assistance if a) there were only a few people around at the time. b) the persons who see you are women not men. c) you happen to be in a small town, not a large city. d) there happens to be a large crowd present. *Pages 494–501.*

14.24 Based on his observation of bicycle riders in competition, Norman Triplett performed one of the first experiments in social psychology on the phenomenon he called a) bystander apathy. b) cognitive dissonance. c) audience inhibition. d) social facilitation. *Pages 501–503.*

14.25 Zajonc and others suggest that the presence of others is likely to improve the quality of one's performance if a) the task is easy and/or well learned. b) those others act in a supportive, approving fashion. c) the task is difficult or complex. d) those others act in a hostile, disapproving fashion. *Pages 501–503.*

14.26 True or False? Social interference and social loafing are more common phenomena than is social facilitation. *Pages 501–503.*

14.27 In the context of group decision making, "polarization" refers to the observation that a) groups are consistently better at making decisions than are individuals. b) being in a group is likely to enhance and solidify initially held attitudes. c) the more groups discuss an issue, the riskier their decision will be. d) throughout the discussion, one person will emerge as actual group leader. *Pages 503–504.*

14.28 Janis's concept of "groupthink" tells us that a) groups strive to reach consensus, right or wrong. b) people are more likely to express divergent opinions in a group than when they are alone. c) members of a group prefer that other members do most of the work. d) group decisions tend to be conservative and unoriginal. *Pages 503–504.*

I/O, ENVIRONMENTAL, AND SPORTS PSYCHOLOGY

15

PREVIEW

TOPIC 15A—Industrial/ Organizational Psychology

Fitting the Person to the Job
Fitting the Job to the Person

TOPIC 15B—Environmental and Sports Psychology

Psychology and the Environment

PSYCHOLOGY IN THE REAL WORLD: Safety in the Workplace

Psychology and Sports

THINKING CRITICALLY ABOUT I/O, ENVIRONMENTAL, AND SPORTS PSYCHOLOGY

SUMMARY

TEST YOURSELF

By now you have come to realize that psychology has many practical applications in everyday life. Indeed, this is one of the themes I introduced back in Chapter 1. The principles of psychology are relevant for many of the problems we face from day to day. In this last chapter, we will focus on three subfields of psychology that have a strong orientation toward application in the real world.

We begin with a brief examination of industrial/organizational (I/O) psychology. Industrial/organizational psychologists specialize in the study of affect, behavior, and cognition in work settings. They are concerned with using evidence from psychology to improve the effectiveness and efficiency of business or industrial organizations. That does not mean that I/O psychologists are "company people," concerned only with the best interests of management. I/O psychologists care about the workplace in general, and that includes a consideration of workers' needs as well as management's needs.

In Topic 15B, we'll take a brief look at two other subfields of applied psychology. First, we'll sample some of the work of psychologists concerned about interactions between the physical environment and one's psychological state of well-being. We'll examine the notions of space and territory, using life in a big city as an example. We'll review some of the evidence concerning the psychological reactions to environmental pollutants such as noise, temperature, and toxins. Finally, we'll look at a few ways in which psychology can be applied in the world of sports and athletics.

TOPIC 15A
INDUSTRIAL/ORGANIZATIONAL PSYCHOLOGY

Industrial/organizational (I/O) psychology is one of the fastest growing areas of specialization in psychology. In this Topic, we'll examine two major thrusts of I/O psychology. First we'll discuss how best to fit the right person to a given job. This will entail a brief discussion of what is meant by "doing a good job," followed by a consideration of how we can select, train, and motivate someone to do that job well. Then we'll look at how to best fit the job to the person, which will involve examining such matters as job satisfaction, quality of work life, and worker safety. Each of these issues is relevant and meaningful to anyone who enters the world of work.

FITTING THE PERSON TO THE JOB

It is to everyone's advantage to have the best available person assigned to any job. Employers benefit from having workers who are well qualified and motivated to do their work. Employees benefit from being assigned tasks that they enjoy and that are within the scope of their abilities. On these points I have some personal experience. For example, when I was a college student, I had a summer job which required that I fill in for another employee and drive a large truck loaded with milk from a dairy in upstate New York to various locations in New York City. That I ever got that milk where it was to go had more to do with good luck and youthful enthusiasm than anything else. It took me twice as long as the regular driver to make the deliveries and, to say the least, I did not enjoy spending most of a summer's day lost in New York City with a truck filled with milk. I clearly was not the best worker for the task.

What is involved in getting the best person to do a job? The main issues from the perspective of the industrial/organizational psychologist are personnel selection, training, and motivation. That is, one way to get a person to do good work is to *select* and hire a person who already has the ability and the motivation to do that work. On the other hand, we may choose to *train* people to do good work. We also may have to face the task of *motivating* people with ability to do good work. Before we can begin selecting, training, or motivating someone for a job, we need to understand the nature of the job itself.

Defining "Good Work"—The Job Analysis

Assume that you are an industrial organizational psychologist hired to help a company select a manager for one of its retail stores in a local shopping mall. You could not begin to tell your employers which person to hire until you had a full description of the job this new manager was to do. In general terms, you would have to know the duties and responsibilities of a store manager in this company. Then you could translate that job description into a set of measurable characteristics that a successful store manager should possess. In other words, you would begin by doing a **job analysis**, "the systematic study of the tasks, duties, and responsibilities of a job and the knowledge, skills, and abilities needed to perform it" (Riggio, 1990, p. 59).

A job analysis may be written by someone who currently holds the job in question or a supervisor of that job position. What matters is that the person doing the job analysis have full knowledge of what the job entails (Fleishman & Mumford, 1991; Landy et al., 1994). Typically, writing a job analysis is a two-step process. The first step is to compile a complete description of what a person in that job is to do. There are several sources of information that could be used to generate this description. Most companies have job descriptions for their employees, but these usually are stated in general terms, such as "supervise workers in the store; maintain acceptable levels of sales; prepare payrolls; monitor inventory; schedule work periods," and the like. To be useful, a job analysis must be specific and describe the actual *behaviors* engaged in by someone in a given position. Does a store manager have to know how to operate the cash register or inventory control devices? Does the manager deal with the sales staff on a one-to-one basis or in groups? Are interactions with employees informal, or are there regularly scheduled formal meetings that need to be organized? To what

job analysis
a complete and specific description of a job including the qualities required to do it well

extent is the store manager responsible for employee training and development? Will he or she be involved in labor negotiations? Clearly, this list of questions can be a long one. The underlying concern at this level is "On a daily basis, just what does a store manager do?"

Once duties and responsibilities have been specified, the second step requires that these be translated into terms of measurable personal characteristics. That is, one determines the **performance criteria** required to do a job well. The goal is to list the characteristics that a person in the position should have in order to do that job as well as possible.

There are several areas that might be explored at this point. Smith (1976), for example, distinguishes between what she calls "hard" (or objective) criteria and "soft" (or subjective) criteria. The former come from available data—salary, number of units sold, number of days absent, and the like. Soft criteria require a degree of judgment—sense of humor, creativity, congeniality, and so forth. Let's use an academic example. Suppose your psychology department wants to give an award to its "outstanding senior." Some of the criteria that determine which student is worthy of the award may be objective—senior class standing, a certain grade point average, a minimum number of courses, and so on. Other criteria may be subjective. The department may want to honor a student only if she or he is well-known to many members of the faculty, has impressive communication skills, or has been active in the Psychology Club. These criteria require the judgment of those making the award. Indeed, most job analyses involve consideration of both hard, objective and soft, subjective criteria.

Remember that the basic task is to find the best available person to do a job as well as possible. If we are not fully aware of the demands of a job and have not translated those demands into specific performance criteria, we'll have difficulty determining if we have found the right person. In other words, we need to build in procedures by which our selection program can be evaluated (Dunnette & Borman, 1979). Once a job analysis is ready—once we know what an applicant is expected to do on the job and we have translated those tasks into measurable criteria—we're ready to begin designing an assessment procedure.

performance criteria
specific behaviors or characteristics that a person should have in order to do a job as well as possible

● **Before You Go On**
What is involved in doing a job analysis?

Selecting People Who Can Do Good Work

Personnel selection involves not only devising procedures to help one decide which of many applicants to hire but also making decisions relating to retention, promotion, and termination (Guion & Gibson, 1988). If the job analysis has been done properly, the I/O psychologist has a complete list of the duties and traits in which the employer is interested. The task now is to find the person who has those traits.

Useful information can be gleaned from a well-constructed *job application form*. An application form can serve three functions: (1) It can be used as a rough screening device—some applicants may be denied simply because they do not meet some basic requirement for the job, such as a minimal educational level or job experience. (2) It can supplement or provide cues for interviewing—data from application forms can be pursued later during in-depth interviews. (3) It provides biographical data, called *biodata*, including educational and work history, that may be useful in making di-

The interview remains an integral part of the employee selection process, although research has shown that unstructured interviews may be subject to bias and misinterpretation.

rect predictions about a candidate's potential for success. Some I/O psychologists list the information that can be found on job application forms as the best source of data for predicting success on the job (Baley, 1985; Drakely et al., 1988; Muchinsky, 1987; Mumford et al., 1992; Reilly & Chao, 1982; Rothstein et al., 1992). Although one cannot rule out the possibility of faking responses, people generally give honest answers when completing biodata forms (Shaffer et al., 1986).

An integral part of many selection procedures is the *employment interview*. I've already commented (pp. 370–371) on the dangers of relying too heavily on information gained through interviews. Unstructured interviews in particular are subject to error. For one thing, interviews, by their very nature, involve the interaction of two people: the interviewer and the person being interviewed, and the biases of the interviewer, conscious or unconscious, may influence the results of an interview (Cash & Kilcullen, 1985). Nonetheless, the interview remains widely used in the United States (Arvey & Campion, 1982; Thayer, 1983). There are individual differences in the skills of interviewers. Some consistently obtain more useful (or valid) information than do others (Thayer, 1983; Zedeck et al., 1983). Training interviewers to be sensitive to bias can improve the validity of the technique.

Over the last few years, the outlook for the interview has become more positive and optimistic. In large measure, this is because of the increased use of the *structured interview* (Harris, 1989; Wiesner & Cronshaw, 1988). As the name implies, structured interviews use a carefully prescribed set of questions that is asked of all applicants in the same order. Structured interviews may take away some of an interviewer's latitude and freedom to explore different issues, but they are demonstrably more valid than are unstructured interviews (Arvey et al., 1987; Landy et al., 1994; Schmitt & Robertson, 1990; Wiesner & Cronshaw, 1988).

Beyond the job application and interview, personnel selection often involves administering and interpreting *psychological tests* (see Chapter 8). Many tests are designed to assess only one specific characteristic (e.g., finger dexterity, which a job analysis may indicate to be very relevant for an assembly-line worker in an electronics plant). Other tests are more general, assessing several different skills and abilities. Tests of intelligence or personality traits may be called for, particularly when evaluating candidates for managerial or supervisory positions. There are literally hundreds of psychological tests designed to measure traits, from typing skills, to critical thinking skills, to mechanical aptitude, to leadership style, to motivation for sales work. Some popular tests of general traits are being modified to focus more on work-related tasks (Gough, 1985).

In general, the most useful of all psychological tests are those that assess some sort of cognitive function, such as ability or achievement tests (Guion & Gibson, 1988). One of the most controversial questions in all of psychology (not just I/O) is whether tests of general intelligence are better predictors of job performance than are tests of specific cognitive abilities or aptitudes (Ackerman, 1992; Ackerman & Kanfer, 1993; Landy et al., 1994; McClelland, 1993; Ree & Earles, 1992, 1993; Schmidt & Hunter, 1993; Sternberg & Wagner, 1993). At this point in the controversy, the best answer now seems to be "it depends"—mostly on which tests of which behaviors are involved.

From time to time, it may be necessary to construct one's own test to assess some unique or special ability not measured by standard instruments. A form of testing found in employment settings is called *situational testing*, in which the applicants are given the opportunity to role-play some of the tasks they may be hired to do (Lin et al., 1992; Weekly & Gier, 1987). If you were to hire someone to work at the counter of your dry cleaning business, for instance, you might ask an applicant how he or she would respond to an irate customer whose suit was damaged in cleaning. Actually role-playing the part of the angry customer while the applicant plays the part of the employee might provide very useful information.

An important issue when psychological tests are used for personnel decisions is the demonstrated validity of such tests. What is crucial in employee testing is that the employer be able to demonstrate that performance on a test is actually related to performance on the job (Landy et al., 1994; Schmidt et al., 1992).

It may not always be practical or possible to find people who have the abilities or characteristics to do a particular job the way the employer wants it done. It may be that the major personnel issue facing the organization is training or motivating present workers to do good (or better) work. Let's first look at training.

● **Before You Go On**

What are some of the sources of information that can be used in making personnel decisions?

Training People to Do Good Work

The training of employees is one of the major concerns of business, industry, and government. The cost of such training runs into billions of dollars every year. Training or retraining will be even more critical in the years ahead as the number of people who enter the workforce decreases (Offer-

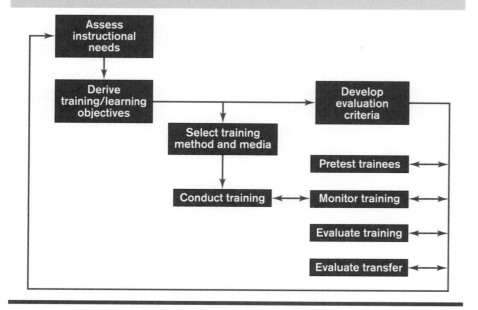

FIGURE 15.1
The steps involved in planning and conducting a training program.
(From Goldstein, 1986.)

mann & Gowing, 1990; Tannenbaum & Yukl, 1992). Additional training needs stem from the move of many businesses to open operations overseas. Training concerning cultural issues in foreign countries is seen as essential for such businesses (Brislin, 1990, 1993; Erez & Early, 1993; Tung, 1988).

In the context of industrial/organizational psychology, training means "a systematic intentional process of altering behavior of organizational members in a direction which contributes to organizational effectiveness" (Hinrichs, 1976). Training is meant to increase the skills or abilities of employees to do their jobs. Training also implies a systematic intervention, as opposed to hit-or-miss instruction. Training programs have been found to be successful in a wide range of settings, with various types of personnel, as indicated by several criteria, including quantity and quality of work, cost reduction, turnover, accident reduction, and absenteeism (Katzell & Guzzo, 1983).

Developing a successful training program is a complex, multifaceted enterprise. Let's review some of the steps involved in the design and implementation of a training program. Our discussion is based on a system proposed by Goldstein (1980, 1986, 1989) and is summarized in Figure 15.1. Assume for the moment that you are a psychologist in charge of training and development for Acme Flange.

Assessing Training Needs Training programs are designed to address some need within the organization. So one of the first things you will have to do is a complete assessment of instructional needs. In many ways, this assessment is like a job analysis in personnel selection. There are several questions that must be raised and answered at this critical stage. Just what is the problem that training is supposed to solve? Is production down? Is there a new product that salespeople need to know about? Is the accident

Training—and retraining—employees to learn new skills and procedures helps keep worker motivation high and helps companies stay abreast of new technologies.

rate getting too high? At this point, a very difficult question is whether a training program is the best solution for a given problem. Often, the most crucial decision about training is if it is needed at all (Latham, 1988).

The second step requires translating one's general goals into actual training objectives—general statements will no longer suffice. Now you need specific statements of what you expect the training program to accomplish. Precisely what do you want trainees to know (or be able to do) at the end of the training session that they do not know (or cannot do) now? Your training program will be evaluated in terms of these specific objectives. Indeed, it is now, before training actually begins, that the criteria for evaluating the effectiveness of your program should be devised.

Training Techniques. After you've determined the criteria for assessing outcomes, you have to decide how you will go about the actual training. Given what you know about your objectives and what you know about your employees, what will be the most efficient type of training mechanism you can use to reach your goals?

There are many methods that might be used in a training program. In some cases, bringing workers together for classroom instruction works well. On the other hand, there are situations in which assembling large numbers of workers would be unrealistic. Automobile manufacturers, for example, can hardly be expected to have all their salespeople report to the home office for instruction on improvements in the new models they will be selling. Occasionally, training has to go to the worker—in the form of printed material, audio cassettes, videotaped programs, or presentations by a trainer—rather than having the worker go to the training.

As designer of a training program, you will have many decisions to make about the methods you will use. Should you use "live" instructors, or should information be presented in the form of media: print, audiotapes, videotapes, videodisks, or the like? Should the training be formalized and time-limited, or can trainees be allowed to work alone, at their own pace?

Will there need to be hands-on experience? Will training be in groups or will it be individually oriented? Will on-the-job training be efficient or disruptive? Can the job be simulated for the purposes of training? As you can see, your options are many, and some are more effective than others for certain kinds of training. Too many trainers get into the habit of using only one or two techniques for a variety of different needs and objectives. For example, televised instruction may be very useful to point out a few new features of an automobile to a salesperson, but quite ineffective as a means of describing a new health insurance program. By and large, presenting information is less effective than demonstrating it, and involving one's audience as participants (a hands-on, or simulation, approach) is the most effective method. But that's only by-and-large. What is needed is the best "fit" between training needs and available training techniques (Campbell, 1988; Tannenbaum & Yukl, 1992; Thornton & Cleveland, 1990).

Having decided on a training technique, you are ready to begin. You will have to monitor the effectiveness of the training program as it runs its course (review Figure 15.1). Even the best of plans may need to be adjusted during actual training.

Measuring Training Effectiveness. When you have finished your training program, you're ready to consider (again) what may be the most difficult part of training and development. You must evaluate the success of your intervention. You now need some measure of the extent to which your training transfers to the actual job in the workplace, thus meeting the organizational needs that prompted the training in the first place.

There are many difficulties involved in the evaluation of training programs, and we need not review them all here. I will make only these three observations:

1. Training programs can be evaluated at various levels. You may ask participants to evaluate or rate *how they feel about* the program. You may assess the extent to which the training has produced *behavioral changes.* You may try to measure *how much has been learned,* perhaps with a formal testing before and after training. Or you may go right to the bottom line and ask about *increases in productivity or profit* (Kirkpatrick, 1976).

2. Training programs that do not include ways of evaluating short-term and long-term effectiveness generally will be of little value. Sadly, few training programs are well evaluated. Many are taken simply on faith or face value because of their logical appeal (Brinkerhoff, 1989; Saari et al., 1988; Schultz & Schultz, 1990).

3. The greater the effort put into the assessment of organizational needs, job analysis, performance criteria, and the establishment of training objectives at the beginning of a training project, the easier it will be to evaluate the program when it is over.

● **Before You Go On**

List some of the factors that need to be considered in the design, implementation, and evaluation of a training program.

Motivating People to Do Good Work

Let's review for a moment. Our concern in this section is fitting the person to the job—finding someone to do good work. The first step in that process involves carefully delineating just what is meant by a *good job*. To this end,

People who do good work should be reinforced for their good work. Something as simple as a special parking place in the company parking lot can suffice.

expectancy theory
the view that workers make logical choices to do what they believe will result in their attaining outcomes of highest value

equity theory
the view that workers are motivated to match their inputs and outcomes with those of fellow workers in similar positions

one does a job analysis and lists specific performance criteria for the job. An employer then can go through the process of selection to locate the best person—someone who already has all the skills to do the job well. Another possibility is to train a present employee to do good work. There remains an important consideration. Something may still be missing: the motivation to do good work. Being able to do a job well and wanting to do a job well are two different matters. Notice, too, that issues of training and motivation are both continuous, ongoing concerns. People change and jobs change. Seldom will one training program or one attempt to motivate employees be sufficient over the long term.

As you can imagine, I/O psychologists have been interested in how to motivate employees for a long time. When we talk about work motivation, we are referring to three interrelated processes: *arousing* (getting the worker to do a task), *directing* (getting the worker to do what we want done), and *sustaining* (keeping the worker at the task). As you can also imagine, there is no one simple answer to questions about what motivates workers to do a particular job well and stick with it. We'll briefly review a few popular approaches.

Values and Expectations. The expectancy theory of work motivation has been around for many years and has been modified by many theorists, but it is best associated with Victor Vroom (1964). It is cognitive in its orientation. **Expectancy theory** claims that workers behave rationally and logically, and that they make work-related decisions based on their beliefs, judgments, and expectations.

Vroom's theory is quite complex, but what it amounts to is that we are motivated to work if: (1) We expect to be rewarded on the basis of the level of our performance, and (2) we value the rewards that are being offered to us. We also must believe that rewards are attainable, that we actually can do the work to a level of performance that will earn those rewards.

There are several implications here for employers concerned about motivating employees to do good work. For one thing, employers should see to it that outcomes that follow good work are truly valued by the workers. For example, in one company, doing good work is rewarded by recognition with a plaque and a free trip awarded at the annual company dinner. (The dinner is viewed by management as a reward for a profitable year.) What if most of the workers found company dinners to be a huge bore, plaques to be an embarrassment, and free trips a nuisance? What if the employees would much rather have a cash bonus? That is, what if the employees believed that there was little or no value in what the company defined as rewards?

Another implication of expectancy theory is that workers must understand the relationship between their behaviors and outcomes (Ilgen & Klein, 1989). Simply put, workers need to know what to expect if they behave in a certain way. Which behaviors lead to positive outcomes, and which lead to negative outcomes? Why should any employee work hard, put in overtime, and take work home on the weekend if he or she has little reason to believe that such behaviors will lead to real rewards? In fact, fewer than one-third of workers believe that their compensation is actually based on their work performance (Plawin & Suied, 1988).

Fair Rewards. Another approach to motivation that has received support is called **equity theory**, associated with J. Stacy Adams (1965). Equity theory is also cognitive, claiming that what matters most to workers is their perception of the extent to which they are being treated fairly compared to fellow workers in similar work situations.

In Adams's view, workers make a number of social comparisons (or cognitive judgments). They judge how much they are getting from the organization compared to what they are putting into it. That is, the worker judges the extent to which effort, skill, education, and experience (inputs) are rewarded by salary, fringe benefits, praise, awards, and the like (outcomes). Then this ratio of inputs and outcomes is compared with ratios earned by some other, similarly placed employees. If the relationship is seen as approximately the same, or equitable, the worker will not be motivated to change. If there is a perceived inequity when compared to the inputs and outcomes of a fellow worker, then changes can be predicted. The worker may increase or decrease inputs (work longer or shorter hours; take fewer or more breaks) or try to effect a change in outcomes. What matters most here is not the real value of what a worker gains for his or her efforts. What matters is the *perception* of equity—what he or she perceives in comparison to others. A worker will be much more willing to maintain effort (input) and take a cut in pay (outcome) if that worker believes that everyone else is taking a similar cut in pay (Locke, 1976; Middlemist & Peterson, 1976; Mowday, 1983).

Goal-setting. Attention to establishing goals has been the centerpiece of several approaches to worker motivation, particularly that of Edwin Locke (1968; Locke & Latham, 1984). This approach also has a cognitive base, and assumes that workers are motivated to perform a task for which goals are clearly and specifically delineated. For goal-setting to have a positive influence on a worker's behavior, two things are necessary. First, the employee must be clearly *aware* of just what he or she is working for. Second, the employee must *accept* that goal as worth the effort.

Goal-setting is the approach to motivating workers that is presently generating the most research interest (Smither, 1994). The following are some general conclusions.

1. Difficult but achievable goals increase productivity more than easy goals. The issue here seems to hinge on the acceptance of goals as being worthwhile. Goals that are too easy to reach may not require any change in performance. At the same time, goals that are perceived as being too difficult and beyond the abilities of workers are not likely to be very useful (Erez & Zidon, 1984).
2. Specific goals are better than general ones. Simply telling workers to "do better" or "do your best" provides little information about what behaviors are expected.
3. Feedback that informs workers of their progress toward established goals is important in maintaining motivated behaviors. Feedback delivered soon after an appropriate response is made is more effective than delayed feedback (e.g., Geller et al., 1985; Geller et al., 1987).
4. Although it may seem reasonable to predict that goals set by employers and employees working together are more effective than goals established by employers alone, this is not necessarily the case. What matters most is that the employee simply be aware of specific goals and accept those goals as reasonable (Locke et al., 1981).
5. Cultural concerns are also relevant here. The more one is used to working together (as in collectivist cultures), the more important it is to be involved in goal setting. In most Western cultures, involvement is less critical (Early, 1986; Erez & Early, 1987).

As you can well imagine, there are other approaches to work motivation. Some refer to motivational concepts introduced in Chapter 9, where we discussed motivation in general. That is, some approaches stress the importance of workers' needs (as in Maslow's hierarchy from basic physiological needs to needs to self-actualize). Some approaches stress the importance of behavior change through operant conditioning and attention to the consequences of behavior (often called "organizational behavior management" when applied in work environments).

Here's a brief summary of our discussion. Workers will be motivated to do a job well if:

1. Clear and specific goals are established and accepted.
2. The goals that employers set match workers' expectations and needs.
3. Workers clearly see the relationship between their work performance and accepted outcomes.
4. Workers judge the outcomes that follow from their efforts as being in line with those earned by fellow workers making similar efforts.
5. Workers are given feedback about the nature of their work (Katzell & Thompson, 1990).

Now let's shift our emphasis slightly from a concern about finding and fitting the person to the job to the issue of fitting the job to the person. Largely, our interest here is with what we call *job satisfaction*. What can be done to make jobs more satisfying? What is the result of doing so?

● **Before You Go On**

Briefly summarize some of the factors that affect the motivation of workers to do a good job.

FITTING THE JOB TO THE PERSON

job satisfaction
an attitude; a collection of positive feelings about one's job or job experiences

Job satisfaction refers to the attitude that one holds toward work—"a pleasurable or positive emotional state resulting from the appraisal of one's job or job experiences" (Locke, 1976). It amounts to how one feels about his or her job (Hui, 1990). Although we often talk about job satisfaction in general terms (a "global approach"), a worker's satisfaction can vary considerably for different aspects of the job (a "facet approach") (Riggio, 1990). As you know from your own work experience, you can be reasonably happy with your physical working conditions, very unhappy with base salary, pleased with your fringe benefits, satisfied with the level of challenge provided by the job, very dissatisfied with relationships with co-workers, and so on. There may be as many facets of job satisfaction or dissatisfaction as there are aspects to the job.

A great deal of research has looked for relationships between job satisfaction and personal characteristics of workers. We can summarize that research briefly.

1. There is a positive correlation between global, overall job satisfaction and age. Younger workers tend to be most dissatisfied with their jobs (Rhodes, 1983), but there is evidence that older employees develop dissatisfaction with their jobs toward the end of their careers (Kacmar & Ferris, 1989).

2. Data on sex differences in job satisfaction are inconsistent. By and large, sex differences are quite small (Sauser & York, 1978) and virtually nonexistent when pay, tenure, and education are controlled.

3. Racial differences in job satisfaction in the United States have consistently been shown to be small, with whites having slightly more positive attitudes about their jobs than blacks (Weaver, 1980), and Mexican Americans showing slightly more job satisfaction than anglos.

4. Satisfaction is positively related to the perceived level or status of one's job, where those positions of lowest rank tend to be filled by least-satisfied workers (King et al., 1982).

5. The data are few, but there appear to be some cultural differences in job satisfaction. In one survey of ten countries, Sweden had the largest proportion of satisfied workers (63%), whereas Japan had the lowest (20%) (de Boer, 1978). The low level of job satisfaction in Japan has been reported by others (e.g., Azumi & McMillan, 1976; Lincoln & Kalleberg, 1985). Researchers cite strong commitment and motivation for success coupled with unrealistically high expectations as reasons for the low ratings in Japan (Cole, 1979).

Of course, the real issue for I/O psychologists is to determine *why* differences in job satisfaction occur (or why they do not).

It may seem reasonable to assert that "a happy worker is a productive worker"—that increased satisfaction will be reflected in increased worker productivity. For the last 50 years, many executives have assumed without question a causal relationship between satisfaction and productivity. In many ways, satisfaction and productivity *are* related, but the relationship is not a simple one and is at best a weak one (Iaffaldano & Muchinsky, 1985). In fact, some research refutes the claim that better performance necessarily results from increased worker satisfaction (Howell & Dipboye, 1982; Staw, 1984). Over and over, we find contradictory evidence. The only conclusion we can draw about satisfaction and productivity is that in some instances they are correlated. Cause-and-effect statements are out of the question.

The lack of a consistent relationship between satisfaction and productivity may not be that difficult to explain. Some workers may hate their present jobs but work very hard at them so that they can be promoted to some other position they expect they will prefer. Some workers may be satisfied with their present positions simply because expectations for productivity are low; if demands for productivity increase, satisfaction may decrease. *Increasing productivity may increase satisfaction*, rather than vice versa. A well-motivated employee, who wants to do her best at her job, will be pleased to enter a training program to improve her on-the-job efficiency. Doing the job well leads to pride and an increase in satisfaction for this worker. For another employee, the same training program may be viewed as a ploy on management's part to make life miserable.

I should not give the impression that job satisfaction is unrelated to all work behaviors. There is evidence that job satisfaction measures can be used to predict which workers are likely to be absent from work or are likely to quit; what Saal and Knight (1988) call "withdrawal behaviors." As it happens, job satisfaction is not the best predictor of absenteeism (marital status, age, and size of one's work group are better [Watson, 1981]), but the correlations are at least reasonably consistent (Porter & Steers, 1973). The relationship between dissatisfaction with one's job and turnover seems to be even stronger, although even this relationship may not be direct. That is, dissatisfaction may be an important contributing factor, but it is only one of several variables that can be used to explain why one leaves a job. (Many

Although it seems logical that job satisfaction will be a predictor of job productivity, the relationship between satisfaction and productivity is tenuous.

times people are forced to quit for reasons that have nothing to do with their job satisfaction or their employer—illness and family concerns, for example.) Nonetheless, the logic that those who are most unhappy with their work are the ones most likely to leave it does have research support (Mobley, 1977; Muchinsky & Tuttle, 1979).

● **Before You Go On**

Briefly summarize the relationship between job satisfaction and job productivity.

TOPIC 15B

ENVIRONMENTAL AND SPORTS PSYCHOLOGY

PSYCHOLOGY AND THE ENVIRONMENT

environmental psychology
the field of applied psychology that studies the effect of the general environment on organisms within it

Environmental psychology is the subfield of psychology that studies how the general environment (as opposed to specific stimuli) affects the behavior and mental processes of organisms living in it, and how people, in turn, affect their environments (Saegert & Winkel, 1990). Environmental psychologists work with people from many disciplines, including urban planners, economists, clinical psychologists, sociologists, architects, landscape designers, builders, and others.

The range of specific interest areas within environmental psychology is large. Some psychologists are interested in such issues as how color and

Safety in the Workplace

In 1994, as he released statistics for 1993, Labor Secretary Robert B. Reich observed that, "the workplace is still a dangerous environment." The Labor Department reported 6,271 job-related deaths, up from 6,217 in 1992. During the peak years of the Vietnam War (1966–1970), more Americans were killed in industrial accidents than were killed in combat (Schultz & Schultz, 1990, p. 445). From a different perspective, accidents in the workplace cost the United States over $100 billion a year in lost wages, insurance, medical expenses, and property loss (Riggio, 1990). The challenge is clear: increase the safety of the workplace. But how?

One of the oldest approaches to worker safety is based on the popular notion that some people are simply more "accident prone" than others, or that at least there are some personality traits that should be related to accident levels. The problem with this popular notion is that it simply is not true. At least so far, no one has been able to identify any personality characteristics that are reliably related to the incidence of accidents. Still, there is some obvious sense to this approach. The less well qualified a person is for a job, the less well trained, or the less well motivated, the more likely that person will have an accident—particularly if the job is a dangerous one. Workers younger than 25 or over 55 do have more accidents than do workers whose ages are between the mid–20s and mid–50s (Smither, 1994).

A position consistent with our discussion of worker motivation suggests that sometimes workers need to be motivated to work safely. At first you might think that anyone in his or her right mind would want to work safely and avoid accidents. You might be right. But does the worker *know specifically* what constitutes safe behaviors? Does the worker know that the employer *values* safe work, and that safe work will be rewarded? If such is not the case, workers may cut corners, working too quickly and too dangerously, if they believe that rewards are only

for amount of work and output. This approach suggests that employers must make sure that workers are trained in safe ways to do their jobs (Levine, 1983) and that they understand that safe behaviors are valued (Zohar, 1980). As we have seen before, what matters is clearly establishing safety goals, providing feedback to workers, and reinforcing behaviors that lead to the stated goals.

What Landy (1989) calls the "engineering approach" to worker safety tries to reduce accidents by designing safer equipment and implementing safer procedures. Over the years this approach has proven the most successful in a wide range of applications. Examples abound: Automobiles now sold in this country are required to have a third brake light positioned at eye level. This requirement evolved from a study done with taxis in San Francisco in a successful attempt to reduce rear-end collisions (Voevodsky, 1974). Reflecting the reality that highway accidents caused 20 percent of the job-related deaths in 1993, we soon will see all cars equipped with dual air bags and running lights. Complex control panels are engineered with safety in mind so that the most critically important dials, meters, switches, and buttons are in clear view and easy to read and interpret (e.g., Wickens, 1992). Work areas are designed so there is adequate illumination and sufficient space to move about, and so scrap materials and trash can be readily removed. Computer screens have shields to protect against glare and radiation, and keyboards are now engineered to reduce the physical damage to the wrist that may result from spending hours at the keyboard.

Engineering approaches to accident prevention may also involve matters such as the scheduling of work time and rest periods. There is ample evidence of a positive relationship between fatigue and accidents. Scheduling work time to minimize fatigue (by reducing overtime, for example) improves safety records (e.g., Dunham, 1979).

lighting affect workers' productivity, students' learning, or hospital patients' mental and physical health. Some are concerned with behavioral reactions to poisons or toxins in our environments. Some are interested in the design and construction of physical space that maximizes the functions for which that space is constructed. Some seek efficient ways of changing personal behaviors in order to influence the natural environment in positive ways, perhaps through anti-littering campaigns. Others focus on crowding, territoriality, or adjustment to the demands of city living.

Environmental psychologists recognize that what may influence behavior most is one's *perception* of the physical environment. A room with ten persons in it can appear to be terribly small and crowded if it is perceived as an office. The same room can seem large and uncrowded if the room is perceived as a waiting area. In fact, two rooms of exactly the same area, one square, the other rectangular, will be perceived as being of different size; the square room will appear smaller than the rectangular room (Sadalla & Oxley, 1984). Let's begin our introduction to environmental psychology by considering the perception of space and distance.

● **Before You Go On**
Define environmental psychology, and list some of the issues that environmental psychologists study.

Space and Territory

Imagine that you are seated in the library, studying alone at a large table. Another student enters and sits right next to you. There are seven other chairs available, but this student opts to sit in the one just to your left. Imagine that you are buying a used car. While you are examining one of the cars on the lot, a salesperson approaches, stands right in front of you (not more than 8 inches away) and begins to tell you about the features of the car you are looking at. Imagine that you always sit in the same seat in your psychology class. The semester is about over, and you have gotten to know some of the people who sit near you. Then, the next time you go to class, you find that there is someone else in "your" seat. Imagine that you are a suburban homeowner. You've spent years getting your backyard to look just the way you want it to. Then neighborhood children discover that going through your rose garden makes a great shortcut for them on their way to school.

In each of these scenarios, and in hundreds of others, you probably would feel a sense of discomfort. Your personal space, or territory, has been invaded without invitation. The study of the effects of invading personal space and territory has been an active research area for environmental psychologists.

personal space
the mobile "bubble" of space around you reserved for intimate relationships into which others may enter only by invitation

Personal space is mobile. It goes with you wherever you go. It is an imaginary "bubble" of space that surrounds you and into which others may enter by invitation only. The extent of your personal space depends on the situation, as well as other factors, including your age (Aiello & Aiello, 1974), gender (Evans & Howard, 1973), cultural background (Pandey, 1990), and who the "intruder" happens to be. You will be much more likely to allow an invasion of your personal space by someone you know well, someone your own age, or an attractive member of the opposite sex (Hayduk, 1983). The anthropologist Edward Hall (1966) claimed that the extent of one's personal space is also determined in part by one's culture. Westerners, for example, are said to require a larger personal space than either Arabs or Japanese (Sommer, 1969). This cultural stereotype may be somewhat overgeneralized. The evidence supporting cultural differences in personal space is not that compelling; too many situational factors are more so (Hayduk, 1983).

Hall (1966) also claimed that personal space can be divided into four different distances, each relevant for different types of social interaction.

1. *Intimate distance* is defined as being between actual contact and about 18 inches. This space is reserved for very special, intimate communications: displays of affection by lovers, offerings of comfort, and the like. This space usually is reserved only for people whom you know very well and care about, and you will feel uncomfortable if anyone else is in it.

2. *Personal distance* is reserved for day-to-day interactions with acquaintances and friends. It extends from about 18 inches to approximately 4 feet, or just beyond arm's length. This space can be seen clearly in social gatherings, where small clusters of people gather to share in conversation. Physical contact in this sort of situation is unusual and unwelcomed. We typically keep our bubble of personal space adjusted to this size.

3. Hall refers to the distance of 4 to 12 feet as *social distance*. This distance is used for social interactions with persons we do not know well. It commonly includes some sort of physical barrier, such as a desk or table, between us and others around us. Within this space, two-way communication can continue, but there is an implied lack of intimacy. This is the distance used when conducting business or at formal meetings.

4. Finally, there is *public distance*, in which personal contact is kept to a minimum, although communication remains possible. This distance is defined as between 12 and 25 feet. Formal lectures in large classrooms, performances from a stage, and after-dinner talks presented from behind the head table are examples. Because of the distances involved, communication in these settings tends to flow in only one direction.

The main point here is that we tend to feel pressured, stressed, or discomforted whenever these distances are violated. When that stranger sits right next to you in the library, he or she is violating your personal space. The salesman with his nose almost touching yours is violating your intimate space. When a lecturer leaves the podium to wander through the audience, we feel strange because our public space is being invaded.

Territoriality is also related to an individual's use of space in the environment. It involves the setting off and marking of a piece of a geographical area as one's own. It is the tendency to declare that "this space is mine, and someone else can enter here only with permission."

Territoriality was first studied extensively in nonhumans (e.g., Lorenz, 1969). Many species of animals establish, mark, and defend geographical areas that they use for hunting, for mating, or for rearing their young. These territories are often defended vigorously—most commonly with ritualistic posturing and threats of aggression, but occasionally with actual combat (Leger, 1992).

It seems clear that people also establish territories, not to be entered without invitation. Altman (1975) noted that, like personal space, our territories vary in their value to us. Some are *primary* territories, defined by us as ours and no one else's. "This is my room, and you'd better stay out of it." We often invest heavily in our primary territories. We decorate our homes, yards, dormitory rooms, or apartments to put our mark on our space. By controlling our primary territory, we maintain a sense of privacy and identity.

Altman claims that we are sensitive to two other types of territory: *secondary* and *public*. Secondary territories are more flexible and less well-defined than are primary territories. They are areas we set aside for social

territoriality
the setting off and marking of a piece of territory (an area) as one's own

Intimate distance is reserved for interactions with good friends, as illustrated in the picture above right. Personal distance is reserved for day-to-day interactions with acquaintances (above left). Social distance is appropriate for persons we do not know well (middle right). Public distance minimizes personal contact, although communication is still possible (bottom right).

gatherings, not so much for personal privacy. Members of the faculty may stake out a room in a college building for a faculty lounge and may be quite unnerved to discover students using it, even if they are using it to study. Secondary territories are not "owned" by those who use them and tend not to be used for expressing personal identity. There may be a sign on the door that says "Faculty Lounge," but the area *can* be used for other functions, and occasional intrusions by others may be tolerated.

Public territories are those we usually occupy for only a short time. They are not ours in any literal sense, and we will not feel much distress if they are violated. While waiting for your plane, you take a seat in the airport terminal and place your luggage at your feet. You get up for a minute to buy a newspaper, and when you return, you find that someone has taken your seat. You may be momentarily annoyed, but you will probably just find another seat, rather than starting a major confrontation.

Personal space and territories that we claim as our own serve many functions. They provide a sense of structure and continuity in what otherwise may seem to be a complex and ever-changing environment. They help us claim some sense of identity. They help us set ourselves apart from others and regulate and reinforce needs for privacy. Although expressed differently from culture to culture, these needs appear to be universal (Lonner, 1980). When space and territory are violated, we can predict negative outcomes: anxiety, distress, and even aggressive attempts of reclamation.

● **Before You Go On**

Define the concepts of personal space and territoriality.

Life in the City—An Example

In the fall of 1994, the World Bank held a meeting of about 900 urban leaders from around the world. Some of the statistics from that session underscore the importance of our understanding the dynamics of people living in large urban areas. Each week, the combined population of the world's largest cities increases by about 1 million people. These cities will be home to more than half the planet's population soon after the turn of the twenty-first century. By the year 2000, there will be 391 cities with more than 1 million residents, and of these, 26 will be "mega-cities," home to over 10 million people each. A concern for issues of city living, overcrowding, and the consequences of urbanization has been a part of environmental psychology for over thirty years. Curiously, it was a series of experiments involving rats that sparked most of that concern.

In 1962, John B. Calhoun published a paper on the consequencess of crowding on rats. The data were impressive and intriguing. Calhoun raised colonies of rats in a number of environments. In some, population density was allowed, even encouraged, to increase to the point where the overcrowding began to affect the behavior of the rats within the colony. Male rats became aggressive. Newborn rats were cannibalized or ignored and left to die. Female rats became unreceptive to sexual advances from male rats. When mating did occur, litter size decreased—apparently in response to the pressures of colony overpopulation. As you might imagine, it didn't take long for some psychologists to look for parallels between Calhoun's rat studies and life in the city.

Early research found several correlations between population density and negative behavioral consequences, such as mental illness, crime, and delinquency (Altman, 1975; Freedman, 1975). As psychologists began to look more closely at the lives of people in urban environments, it became

One's territory can take on different dimensions. We have primary territories (above left) that we think of as ours alone. We also have secondary territories (above right) that we see as primarily ours, and may mark as ours, but that are used by others. And we have a certain claim on public territories (bottom right) that we occupy for only a short period of time and then relinquish to others.

population density
a quantitative measure of the number of persons (or animals) per unit of area

crowding
the subjective feeling of discomfort caused by a sense of lack of space

clear that the data from Calhoun's rats did not translate directly to residents of metropolitan centers.

The first thing we need to do is distinguish between two easily confused terms (Stokols, 1972). The first is **population density**—the number of persons (or animals) inhabiting one unit of area. Density is an objective, descriptive measure. **Crowding**, on the other hand, is a psychological concept. It is a *subjective feeling* of discomfort or distress produced by a perceived lack of space. Crowding may be independent of the number of persons involved. You might feel crowded and very uncomfortable if you had to sit in the back seat of a small car with just two other people, but not crowded at all when you get to the football stadium and are jammed together with 60,000 others to watch a game (Freedman, 1975).

Crowding is a negative condition that leads to negative consequences. But it is not correct to conclude that living in a densely populated city necessarily produces negative consequences. Potential stressors—such as noise, pollution, and the threat of crime—that we commonly associate with big-city life may be more than offset by better medical care, better sanitation, and better systems for handling emergencies of all types (Creekmore, 1985). One's perception of control matters (Rodin, 1976). When Ruback and Pandey (1988) looked at the role of perceived control for married couples in the United States and in India, they found striking similarities. Among other things, those people who believed that they could leave the city whenever they so chose had more positive attitudes about living in the city than did people who felt "trapped" there.

There is evidence to support the claim that living in the city *can* be healthier, in a variety of physical and psychological ways, than living in the country (Creekmore, 1985; Krupat, 1985; Milgram, 1970, 1977). Many of the advantages of city living are unavailable to residents of smaller communities. Not many cities with populations of fewer than 50,000 can support large symphony orchestras, opera companies, museums, or art galleries (for residents who can afford them), parks and playgrounds (for those who want them), or fully staffed emergency rooms or trauma centers (for those who need them) such as those found in larger, urban areas. Nor can small communities generally afford stadiums and arenas for professional sports (Barker, 1968). The challenge for environmental psychologists is to help urban planners and architects design living spaces in areas of high population density that minimize the subjective experience of crowding, that maintain privacy, and that allow for expressions of personal territoriality.

● Before You Go On

What is the difference between population density and crowding?
What are some of the positive and negative aspects of city living?

Noise, Temperature, and Environmental Toxins

In this section, we'll review some of the evidence that suggests that three aspects of the physical environment can have a profound effect on behavior. We'll consider noise, temperature, and environmental toxins (poisons) and how they affect human performance.

Noise is defined as any intrusive, unwanted, or excessive experience of sound. Almost any environment provides some level of background noise, and noise per se need not be disruptive or stressful. In fact, the complete absence of sound can induce stress. Noise becomes most stressful when it is loud, high-pitched, and unpredictable (Glass & Singer, 1972). Continued exposure to high-intensity sound can produce lasting deafness (Scharf, 1978; Taylor et al., 1965), although prolonged exposure to noise produces few other serious *physical* problems directly (Matlin, 1983). However, there is ample evidence that prolonged exposure to noise increases levels of stress, anxiety, and aggressive behaviors (Bell et al., 1978; Smith & Stansfield, 1986).

Noise levels have predictable effects on the performance of cognitive tasks, such as problem solving and school work. Cohen and his associates (1980, 1986), for example, have shown that children who attended schools near the busy Los Angeles airport tended to have higher blood pressure

noise
any intrusive, unwanted, or excessive experience of sound

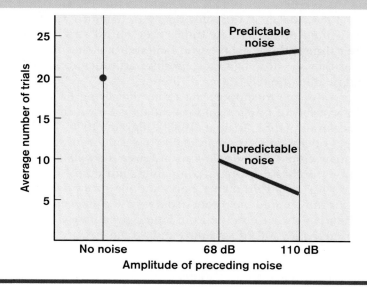

FIGURE 15.2
The effects of the predictability of noise as a distractor during a cognitive task. When noise occurred unpredictably, subjects spent fewer trials attempting to solve unsolvable puzzles. (From Glass, Singer, & Friedman, 1969).

and were more easily distracted from their work than children who attended schools in quieter neighborhoods. Persistently high levels of noise can have a negative impact on all sorts of behaviors (e.g., Smith & Stansfield, 1986). Glass and Singer (1972) claim that absolute levels of background noise are not the major determinant of behavioral disruption. What matters more in the disruption of performance is the *predictability* of and the degree of *control* over noise. The results of one experiment that demonstrated this phenomenon are presented in Figure 15.2 (Glass et al., 1969).

Students were given the task of solving problems that, in fact, had no solution. Students worked on these puzzles under three levels of background noise. In one condition, there was no unusual noise; in a second, a relatively soft (68 decibel) noise was present; in the third, a loud (110 decibel) noise was introduced. In the conditions using background noise, the predictability of the noise was also manipulated. That is, in one condition, the onset of the noise was regular and predictable; in the other, the noise was introduced on a random schedule. The introduction of predictable noise—either soft or loud—did not significantly alter the students' persistence in working on the problems. Unpredictable noise, however, reduced the number of trials the students were willing to invest in the problem-solving task. Glass and Singer (1972) also report that when students are able to control the occurrence of noise, performance on their problem-solving tasks was unaffected. When noise was uncontrollable, performance levels dropped, and often remained poor even after the noise had been removed.

Extremes of temperature can also have adverse effects on behavior. Probably any task can be accomplished most effectively within a range of moderate environmental temperatures (Baron, 1977). It is important, for example, to try to keep the temperature of a workplace within reasonable

Environmental pollutants pose a serious threat not only to people's health but also to their entire way of life. Imagine this scene (left) as a site of illegal dumping, or an oil spill (right), and you can imagine how quality of life would be changed for persons who lived nearby.

limits. If temperatures become excessively high or low, performance will deteriorate, although the specific effects of temperature depend in large measure on the type of task being performed.

Environmental psychologists have been concerned with the effects of extremely high temperatures on social interactions, aggression in particular. There is a common perception that riots and other displays of violent behaviors are more frequent during the long, hot days of summer. This observation is supported by research evidence (Anderson, 1989; Anderson & Anderson, 1984; Rotton & Frey, 1985). C. A. Anderson (1987, 1989), for example, reported on a series of studies that show that violent crimes are more prevalent in hotter months and in hotter years, although nonviolent crimes were less affected. Anderson also concluded that differences in crime rates are better predicted by temperature than by demographic (age, race, education) or economic variables. Baron and Ransberger (1978) point out that riots are most likely to occur when the outside temperature is only moderately high, between about 75° and 90° Fahrenheit. When temperatures get much above 90°, energy (even for aggression) becomes rapidly depleted, and rioting is less likely.

As societies become more heavily invested in technological advancement, an accompanying side effect is that increased levels of environmental toxins or pollutants find their way into the environment. Psychologists concerned with issues of the quality of life are becoming increasingly involved in issues related to the quality of the natural environment (Daniel, 1990; Fischhoff, 1990; Kaplan, 1987; Stokols, 1990). Of the nearly 100,000 chemicals in use in this country's industries, more than 600 have been declared dangerous by the federal government (Anderson, 1982). Many of the chemicals that poison the natural environment are called **neurotoxins** because they have poisonous, toxic effects on the human nervous system. Even in small doses, they can cause detectable behavioral and emotional changes in individuals.

Environmental psychologists are involved in research on neurotoxins at several levels. Education is a high priority—workers and consumers need to know about the short- and long-term effects of contact with chemical toxins and how to deal with them. Because many of the effects of pollutants are psychological in nature, it is becoming more common to find psychologists involved in the diagnosis of reactions to toxins (Fein et al., 1983). Exposure to neurotoxins may be more readily diagnosed through behavioral or psychological means than through medical diagnosis.

neurotoxins
chemicals (poisons) that affect psychological processes through the nervous system

● **Before You Go On**

What are some of the effects that noise, temperature extremes, and neurotoxins have on behavior?

PSYCHOLOGY AND SPORTS

sports psychology
the subfield that attempts to apply principles of psychology to sport and physical activity at all levels of skill development

Sports psychology is another new and exciting area of applied psychology. Although it has had a long history in Europe, sports psychology has become an organized field in the United States only within the last 20 to 25 years. **Sports psychology** is "the application of psychological principles to sport and physical activity at all levels of skill development" (Browne and Mahoney, 1984, p. 605). There are many applications of psychology to sports and athletes, but we'll review just two: analyzing the psychological characteristics of athletes and maximizing athletic performance.

The Psychological Characteristics of Athletes

Psychology's history is filled with research on the assessment of individual differences. Wouldn't it be useful to be able to predict who might become a world-class athlete on the basis of psychological testing? It is certainly the case that there are physiological differences between athletes and nonathletes—amount and type of muscle, height, weight, lung capacity, and so on. Are there any differences between athletes and nonathletes on psychological, or personality, measures?

Generally, research in this area has been less than rewarding, and results often tend to confirm the obvious. Differences are generally small, but athletes do score higher than nonathletes on measures of assertion, dominance, aggression, and need for achievement; they score lower on measures of anxiety level, depression, and fatigue (Browne & Mahoney, 1984; Cox, 1990; Morgan, 1980). This is particularly true when the athletes are at a high skill level. Athletes in some sports, such as football and hockey, are more tolerant of pain than are athletes in other sports, such as golf and bowling (Ryan & Kovacic, 1966). Tolerance of pain, however, may be more of an outcome (result of their activity) for some athletes than a determinant of success. And this last point raises a problem that has long plagued research on the personality of athletes: How shall we define *athlete*? Given the differences among hockey players, long-distance runners, golfers, billiards players, cowboys, rock climbers, fencers, bowlers, and gymnasts, it's surprising that research can find any differences between athletes and nonathletes. In fact, when general trends are sought, they often are not found (e.g., Fisher, 1977).

Maximizing Athletic Performance

One issue of practical importance to coaches and athletes (and psychologists) is the performance of the athlete in competition, and what can be done to maximize that performance.

One area of interest focuses on manipulating the athlete's arousal level. The athlete in competition needs to be fully aroused and motivated to perform—"psyched up." Psychologists know that too much arousal can interfere with performance. They also know that optimum levels of arousal vary as a function of the task at hand. Making a long putt in golf requires a relatively low level of arousal, blocking a shot in volleyball requires a slightly higher level, making a tackle in football an even higher level, and bench pressing in weight lifting requires a very high level of arousal (e.g., Cox, 1990, p. 98). (If this argument sounds familiar, it's because we addressed issues of arousal in general terms back in Chapter 9.) Psychologists can help athletes become sensitive to maintaining high levels of arousal while still keeping appropriate levels of concentration on the task at hand. This often involves training athletes to monitor and control arousal levels by learning to attend to such indicators as their own heart rate, blood pressure, respiration rate, and muscle tension (Harris, 1973; Landers, 1982).

Sport psychologists have tried to find scientific evidence for a performance phenomenon that many athletes and nonathletes take for granted: the notion of getting a "hot hand," or being "in a groove," or "in the zone." The concept is not terribly well defined, but is usually assumed to be demonstrated by a string or cluster of successful performances (e.g., made shots) greater than chance or past history would predict (Vallerand et al., 1988). Evidence for a "hot hand" in sports is very weak at best. It doesn't occur at all in team sports such as basketball (Adams, 1992; Gilovich et al., 1985), and occurs only minimally in individual sports such as tennis or raquetball (Iso-Ahola & Blanchard, 1986; Silva et al., 1988).

Bob Adams, of Eastern Kentucky University, may have found an exception in professional pocket billiards (Adams, 1993). In nine-ball tournaments, there *was* evidence that a player could get on a "hot streak," make significantly more shots, and win more games than usual. Adams claims that there are two reasons why pocket billiards is different from most other sports, and more susceptible to streaks and "hot hands": (1) There is not much time between opportunities to shoot (as opposed to basketball, for instance), and (2) once a player starts shooting, the opponent can do nothing to affect outcomes (as opposed to tennis, for instance).

In a similar vein, sports psychologists now claim that the so-called "home field advantage" (Varca, 1980) is exaggerated, particularly in important games (Baumeister, 1985; Baumeister & Steinhilber, 1984). The argument is that the frenzied, yelling, screaming hometown fans raise arousal levels of the home team beyond the point of maximum efficiency. The negative effect of fans' reactions seems more potent when teams are on offense than when they are playing defense, and is clearly more potent in end-of-season playoff and championship games.

One sports psychologist, Michael Mahoney, commenting on Olympic athletes, has said, "At this level of competition, the difference between two athletes is 20 percent physical and 80 percent mental" (quoted in Kiester, 1984a, pp. 20–21). To the extent that this view is accurate, psychologists have tried to help athletes to do their best—to give what is called a *peak performance*. Mental practice or "imagery" combined with physical practice has proven to be quite beneficial (e.g., Smith, 1987). In addition to manipulating acceptable levels of arousal, mental practice is useful in the following:

1. Mentally rehearsing a particular behavioral pattern. (Think about and mentally picture that golf swing and the flight of the ball before you step up to the tee.)

2. Reducing negative thoughts that may interfere with performance. (Forget about earlier errors and focus on positive experiences, perhaps past victories.)
3. Rehearsing one's role in a team sport. (Mentally practice what you are supposed to do and when you are supposed to do it in various game situations.)
4. Setting realistic goals. (Don't get tense worrying about a competitor in this race; simply try to better your last performance.) (Creekmore, 1984; Fenker & Lambiotte, 1987; Kiester, 1984a, 1984b; Ogilvie & Howe, 1984; Scott & Pelliccioni, 1982; Smith, 1987; Suinn, 1980)

Obviously, using mental imagery is not the only way in which athletes can improve performance. It's just one technique with which sports psychologists can help.

● **Before You Go On**

What are some of the ways in which psychologists may become involved in sports and athletics?

THINKING CRITICALLY ABOUT I/O, ENVIRONMENTAL, AND SPORTS PSYCHOLOGY

1. In Chapter 1 I stated as a general principle that "psychology has practical application in the real world." This is clearly true in this chapter. Can you now go back through the chapters in the text and cite an example where psychological principles from each have had an impact on your life?
2. Imagine that you are an employer trying to hire someone who, among other things, will be responsible for handling large amounts of money. Do you think that you should have the right to access information about the criminal records of applicants? What information about applicants (if any) do you think you should *not* have access to?
3. Consider your most recent job. Could you write a complete job analysis for that position? What would it include?
4. Consider jobs that you have had. What motivated you to do your best at those jobs? What could have been done to motivate you to work harder? Can you describe any of these factors in terms of the theories of work motivation summarized in this chapter?
5. List examples from your own experience of occasions when your personal space or territoriality has been invaded. How did you feel about such invasions?
6. Upon graduation you are offered a position with a large company that gives you a choice of location. You could work in a large metropolitan area or a small farm community. What are the advantages and disadvantages that you see associated with each location?
7. One slogan of the environmental movement is "Think globally and act locally." What are the psychological implications of such a challenge?
8. Many professional sports teams now employ full-time psychologists. What are some of their duties and responsibilities?

SUMMARY

INDUSTRIAL/ ORGANIZATIONAL PSYCHOLOGY

● What is involved in doing a job analysis?

Doing a proper job analysis involves two stages: (1) constructing a complete and specific description of the activities performed by someone in a given position; that is, a listing of those characteristics required to do the job; and (2) developing a means of evaluating the performance (behaviors) of a person in that job (performance criteria). This information is gathered through an inspection of official documents, interviews, questionnaires, and the direct observation of job activities. *Pages 512–514.*

● What are some of the sources of information that can be used in making personnel decisions?

Once a job analysis has been completed, personnel selection involves using assessment tools to measure the relevant characteristics of applicants. Many tools are available, including application forms, structured and unstructured interviews, and psychological tests. Of these, unstructured interviews seem to be of the least value, or validity. *Pages 514–516.*

● List some of the factors that need to be considered in the design, implementation, and evaluation of a training program.

Several factors need to be considered in the design and implementation of an employee training program, including an assessment of the organization's instructional needs (what training, if any, is required?), the development of specific training objectives, the means by which training will be evaluated, and the selection of appropriate methods and media for the actual training. Once training has begun, it should be constantly monitored to see if objectives are being met. After training has been completed, the program itself should be evaluated in the short and long term, as should the transfer of information and skills from training to actual on-the-job performance. *Pages 516–519.*

● Briefly summarize some of the factors that affect the motivation of workers to do a good job.

Even workers with ability may not do a good job unless they are motivated to do so. There are many theories to describe what motivates workers. We looked at three. Vroom's expectancy theory says that workers develop expectations about the relationship between their work behaviors and the likelihood of certain outcomes. They also assign values to different outcomes. They will be most highly motivated to behave in ways that earn valued rewards. Adams's equity theory says that what matters most is the perception of fairness or equal reward for equal effort when one's work behaviors are gauged against those of a comparable other. Locke's goal-setting approach says that what matters most is that workers be clearly aware of just what they are working for and that they accept that goal as worth the effort. *Pages 519–522.*

● Briefly summarize the relationship between job satisfaction and job productivity.

Job satisfaction is an attitude, a measure of an employee's evaluation of his or her position in an organization. Although job satisfaction and productivity may be related, there is little evidence to suggest that the relationship is a strong one and no evidence to suggest that one causes the other. Interventions designed to increase job satisfaction sometimes have a positive impact on productivity, but interventions designed to improve production may also increase job satisfaction. Job satisfaction is more closely related to employee turnover and somewhat related to absenteeism. *Pages 522–524.*

ENVIRONMENTAL AND SPORT PSYCHOLOGY

● Define environmental psychology, and list some of the issues that environmental psychologists study.

Environmental psychology is the study of how the physical environment affects the behavior and mental processes of its inhabitants, and vice versa. Environmental psychologists study various issues, including personal space, crowding, privacy, interior design, territoriality, environmental pollutants and neurotoxins, and the psychological effects of weather and noise. *Pages 524–526.*

● Define the concepts of personal space and territoriality.

Personal space is the imaginary bubble of area around a person into which others enter only by invitation or in specified situations. It is mobile and goes with the person. There may be different types of personal space—acceptable distances—defined for different situations. Territoriality, on the other hand, is one's claim to certain areas (territories) in the environment. Territories may be defended against intrusion and are often used as statements of self-expression. Intrusion into one's personal space or territory can lead to tension, stress, and even aggression. *Pages 526–529.*

● What is the difference between population density and crowding? What are some of the positive and negative aspects of city living?

Population density is simply a quantitative measure of the number of units (people, for example) occupying a given geographic area. Crowding, on the other hand, involves a psychological reaction of distress that occurs when a person feels that his or her space or privacy has been invaded. City living does increase the probability of living with crowding, noise, and other pollutants, but these stressors may be offset by the advantages of a wide range of opportunities not found outside large population centers, such as modern health care, police protection, and access to the arts. *Pages 529–531.*

● What are some of the effects that noise, temperature extremes, and neurotoxins have on behavior?

Noise, temperature extremes, and neurotoxins are viewed as environmental pollutants and potentially stressful, even when not directly harmful to physical and psychological well-being. Noise is more stressful if it is unexpected, unpredictable, or uncontrollable. High temperatures may lead to aggressive, violent reactions, but extremely high (and low) temperatures tend to decrease all levels of behavior. Many chemicals commonly found in the environment have negative consequences for behavior and mental activities; those that directly affect the nervous system are called neurotoxins. *Pages 531–533.*

● What are some of the ways in which psychologists may become involved in sports and athletics?

Psychologists have become involved in sports and athletics in a variety of ways, including trying to find how athletes are different from nonathletes, attempting to improve an athlete's peak performance, studying the effects of audience reactions on athletic performance, and investigating the effects of participation on the athlete. *Pages 534–536.*

TOPIC 15A

INDUSTRIAL ORGANIZATIONAL PSYCHOLOGY

15.1 Which of these is *best* associated with industrial/organizational psychology? a) experimental psychology b) applied psychology c) clinical psychology d) developmental psychology. *Pages 512–514.*

15.2 Typically, an employee selection program begins with a) a listing of required or desired characteristics provided by management. b) an inventory of available tests and assessment techniques. c) an appraisal of skills of current employees. d) a complete job analysis. *Pages 512–514.*

15.3 In a job analysis, when Smith differentiates between "hard" and "soft" criteria, she is really differentiating between a) physical labor and mental labor careers. b) objective data and subjective judgments. c) blue-collar and white-collar positions. d) criteria that require professional psychological measurement and criteria that can be assessed by almost anyone. *Pages 512–514.*

15.4 Preparing "soft" criteria—as opposed to "hard" criteria, in a job analysis involves a) objective data. b) behaviors, but not affect or cognitions. c) subjective judgments. d) results from psychological tests. *Pages 512–514.*

15.5 Of the following techniques for gathering information about prospective employees, which tends to provide the *least* useful information? a) psychological tests of specific skills b) unstructured interviews c) application forms d) tests of general intelligence. *Pages 512–514.*

15.6 True or False? Application forms provide a good source of biodata. *Pages 514–516.*

15.7 True or False? Structured interviews are more valid than unstructured interviews. *Pages 514–516.*

15.8 In devising a training program for employees, what is the first question that an I/O psychologist should ask? a) Who is going to receive this training? b) What techniques will be used to get the information across to the trainees? c) How will the outcome of this training be evaluated? d) Is this training really necessary? *Pages 514–516.*

15.9 The evaluation of a training program should be done a) as soon as training begins. b) as soon as training is completed. c) at points in time well after training is completed. d) at each of these stages. *Pages 516–519.*

15.10 In general, most training programs are evaluated in terms of a) job analyses. b) training objectives. c) employees' needs. d) trainee satisfaction. *Pages 516–519.*

15.11 Although there are exceptions, which approach to employee training is generally the most effective? a) one that involves hands-on experience b) one that uses classroom instruction by an expert c) one that uses as many media as possible d) one that involves repeated demonstrations. *Pages 516–519.*

15.12 Expectancy theory is mostly _____ in its orientation. a) affective b) cognitive c) evaluative d) behavioral. *Pages 519–522.*

15.13 Equity theory claims that what matters most to employees is the extent to which they a) are making more money than employees in similar positions. b) understand the goals they are trying to reach. c) perceive that they are being treated fairly compared to others. d) expect to be rewarded for what they value. *Pages 519–522.*

539

15.14 True or False? Setting goals for employees is significantly more effective when those goals are set by the employees themselves. *Pages 519–522.*

15.15 True or False? Vroom's 1964 expectancy theory is mostly cognitive in orientation. *Pages 519–522.*

15.16 Which of the following is best correlated with most measures of job satisfaction? a) the race of employees b) overall productivity c) whether workers are male or female d) the age of employees. *Pages 522–524.*

TOPIC 15B

ENVIRONMENTAL AND SPORTS PSYCHOLOGY

15.17 Environmental psychologists have defined many types of space or territories. Of these, the one with the smallest area is called _____ space. a) intimate b) personal c) social d) public. *Pages 524–526.*

15.18 True or False? Primary territories are those spaces we think of as ours and no one else's. *Pages 526–529.*

15.19 The difference between population density and overcrowding is mostly a difference in a) one's previous experience. b) the types of organisms involved. c) feelings of distress or discomfort. d) the number of organisms per unit of area. *Pages 529–531.*

15.20 Which of the following is *not* likely to be a stressor associated with life in a big city? a) airborne toxins b) available resources c) noise pollution d) crime rates. *Pages 529–531.*

15.21 What aspect of noise can make it particularly stressful to one attempting a cognitive task? a) its unpredictability b) its tone or pitch c) its loudness d) its melody. *Pages 531–533.*

15.22 Chemicals in the environment that poison the nervous system are called a) psychoactive drugs. b) neurotoxins. c) hallucinogenic chemicals. d) neurotransmitters. *Pages 531–533.*

15.23 At which of these temperatures are riots most likely to occur? a) 36°F b) 66°F c) 86°F d) 106°F. *Pages 531–533.*

15.24 True or False? By definition, neurotoxins are chemicals that harm the environment but that need not have any discernible behavioral or emotional effects on people. *Pages 531–533.*

15.25 When is frenzied, excessive fan support most likely to have a negative or adverse effect on the home team's performance? a) early in the season when the team is on defense. b) early in the season when the team is on offense. c) in a championship game when the team is on defense. d) in a championship game when the team is on offense. *Pages 534–536.*

15.26 An athlete is most likely to "get a hot hand" and have a streak in which he or she does better than usual in which sport? a) basketball b) tennis c) pocket billiards d) bowling. *Pages 534–536.*

15.27 True or False? Mental imagery or mental practice can help an athlete reach his or her peak performance. *Pages 534–536.*

STATISTICAL APPENDIX

INTRODUCTION AND AN EXAMPLE

ORGANIZING DATA

DESCRIPTIVE STATISTICS

INFERENTIAL STATISTICS

SOME NORMAL CURVE STATISTICS

INTRODUCTION AND AN EXAMPLE

When we do research in psychology, or apply psychology in the real world, part of our task often involves measuring some mental process or some aspect of behavior. The result of our measurement is a set of numbers, which we now have to deal with. That's where statistics come in.

> Before we go on, I would like to insert a word of caution. In this appendix, we are going to be working with numbers and a few simple formulas. Please don't let the numbers make you anxious. Some students find dealing with numbers difficult and think that statistics are not relevant for psychology students. Keep in mind that statistics are tools, necessary ones, to help us understand our subject matter. You don't need to be mathematically sophisticated to appreciate statistics. What are required are a positive attitude and a few arithmetic skills, such as addition, subtraction, multiplication, and division. If you haven't had much math background, just go slowly and think about the issues involved.

When we measure something, we assign it a numerical value, and statistics help us to analyze and understand measurements once we have made them. So that we'll have some numbers to work with, let's consider the following problem.

You and your best friend are both enrolled in the same introductory psychology class. You have just taken your first 50-item multiple-choice test. Your instructor used two forms of the test, form A and form B. They both covered the same material, but the questions were different on the two forms. By chance, you took form A of the test and your friend took form B. You had studied together, and you thought that you both knew the material equally well. But your score on the test was eight points lower than your friend's. You suspect that perhaps the two forms of your test were not equally difficult. You believe that *your* test (form A) was more difficult than your friend's (form B). You ask your instructor for all the grades on the test. Because of confidentiality, he cannot provide you with names, but he does supply you with all the grades from the test. There are 100 students in your class who took the first test. Fifty had form A and fifty had form B. When you get the scores from your instructor, you find them arranged as follows:

FORM A						FORM B:				
98	86	100	60	94		82	100	90	80	60
72	80	78	66	86		72	86	82	88	80
92	62	86	96	62		82	76	84	74	84
82	86	78	88	84		86	74	78	78	78
64	86	68	76	80		78	74	84	80	80
86	96	76	72	80		90	84	68	78	86
80	82	82	64	78		80	80	80	84	80
68	74	98	98	84		76	76	80	82	82
66	64	70	90	86		86	74	70	78	76
96	92	82	68	92		82	82	80	76	80

What a mess. Just looking at all these numbers doesn't tell you much at all. Arranged as they are, it's difficult to see if either form of the test yielded higher or lower scores. To answer your original question (was there a difference in performance on the two forms of the test?), you're going to have to do something with these numbers. As we'll see throughout this appendix, statistics are tools that we use to help us make sense out of data we have collected. They will be helpful in analyzing these data. Statistical manipulations are more useful (even necessary) when we have collected many more than 100 numbers.

ORGANIZING DATA

Let's assume that we have collected measurements (data) in which we are interested. Now the task before us is to draw conclusions based on those data. The first thing we need to do is to assemble our data in a sensible way so that we can quickly and easily get some idea of what they mean. At the very least, we should put our data into the form of a frequency distribution.

Frequency Distributions

Once we have a large number of numbers, we seek to organize and summarize them in order to make them useful and meaningful. One of the easiest things to do with our numbers is to arrange them in a **frequency distribution.** As its name suggests, a frequency distribution lists, in order, all of the numbers or scores that we have collected and indicates the frequency with which each occurs.

Figure A.1 shows two types of frequency distributions for the scores earned on form A and form B of the test I introduced as our example. One frequency distribution indicates the frequency of each score with a hash mark (/), while the other type simply indicates the frequency of each score with a number. In this figure, I've placed the two frequency distributions side by side. You can easily see, just by inspection of these distributions, that there *is* a difference between the scores earned on forms A and B of our imaginary exam.

frequency distribution
an ordered listing of all X-values, indicating the frequency with which each occurs

Graphic Representations

It is often helpful to go one step beyond the simple frequency distribution and draw a graph of our data. A number of different graphs have been used throughout this text. Graphs of frequencies of scores are among the most common graphs in psychology. For such a graph, our scores (in general referred to as *X-scores*) are plotted on the horizontal (*x*) axis, and frequencies (*f*) are plotted on the vertical (*y*) axis of our graph.

Figure A.2 shows one way to graph frequencies. This sort of bar graph is called a **histogram.** The frequency of each *X*-score is indicated by the height of the bar just above that score. When we have only few *X*-scores, and when frequencies are not too large, histograms provide clear depictions of our data. The differences between form A and form B of

histogram
a bar graph; a graphical representation of a frequency distribution

FIGURE A.1
Frequency Distributions for Our Sample Data of Two Forms (A and B) of a Classroom Exam

Scores, or Measurements, are Listed in Order in the Left Column, and the Frequency with Which Each Occurs Is Indicated with Either a Hash Mark (/) or a Number

Score	Form A Frequency		Form B Frequency	
100	/	1	/	1
98	//	2		0
96	///	3		0
94	/	1		0
92	///	3		0
90	/	1	//	2
88	/	1	/	1
86	///// //	7	////	4
84	//	2	/////	5
82	////	4	///// //	7
80	////	4	///// ///// /	11
78	///	3	///// /	6
76	//	2	/////	5
74	/	1	////	4
72	//	2	/	1
70	/	1	/	1
68	///	3	/	1
66	//	2		0
64	////	4		0
62	//	2		0
60	/	1	/	1
		$N = 50$		$N = 50$

the classroom exam are more clearly seen in the two histograms of Figure A.2 than in a simple frequency distribution.

Figure A.3 shows the same data in a line graph. The advantage of this sort of graph is obvious: We can show both distributions of test scores on the same axes. As is the case with histograms, scores are plotted on the x-axis and frequencies on the y-axis. With line graphs, it is important to provide a key indicating which line represents each group of scores.

DESCRIPTIVE STATISTICS

Let's continue working with our opening problem. We began with two sets of 50 numbers, scores earned on form A and form B of a classroom test. Our basic question was whether these two forms were really equally difficult. To get started, we put the scores in frequency distributions and then

FIGURE A.2

Histograms showing the frequency with which scores were earned on form A and B of a classroom exam.

(A)

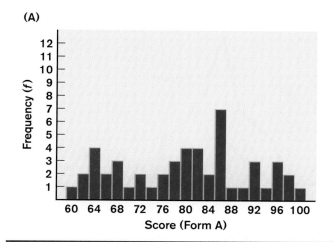

(B)

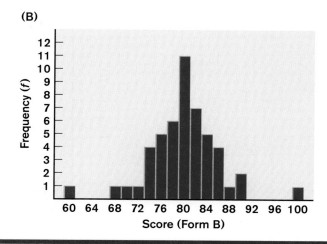

constructed graphs that represented our data. That helped, but there is much more that we can do.

When describing collections or distributions of data, our two major concerns are with measures of central tendency and variability. Measures of **central tendency** are statistics that tell us where our scores tend to center. In general terms, measures of central tendency are called *averages*. If we want to know if performance on form A was better or worse *on the average* than performance on form B, we would have to compute a measure of central tendency for both distributions of scores. Measures of **variability** are statistics that tell us about the extent of dispersion, or the spread of scores within a distribution. Are scores clustered closely around the average, or are they more variable, deviating considerably from the average? First we'll deal with central tendency.

central tendency
a measure of the middle, or average, score in a set of data

variability
the extent of spread or dispersion in a set or distribution of scores

Measures of Central Tendency

There are three statistics used to represent the central tendency of a distribution of numbers. The most commonly used is the mean. The median and mode are also measures of central tendency, but they are used less frequently.

The Mean. When we compute "the average" of a set of scores we usually compute the mean. The **mean** of a set of scores is their total divided by the number of scores in the set. For example, if Max is 6 feet tall and Ruth is 4 feet tall, their mean height is 5 feet. Four inches of snow yesterday and 2 inches today yields a mean snowfall of 3 inches for the two days (4" + 2" = 6" ÷ 2 = 3").

mean
a measure of central tendency computed by dividing the sum of all scores by the number of observations; sometimes called the average

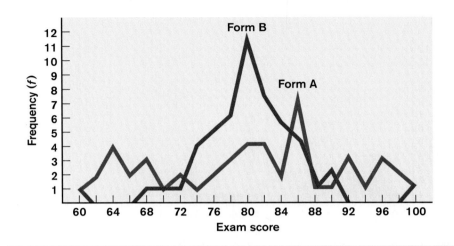

FIGURE A.3

A line graph showing the frequency of scores earned on classroom exams for both form A and form B.

So to compute the mean scores for form A of our example we add up all the scores and divide by 50, because there are 50 scores in the set. We'd do the very same thing for the scores earned on form B—add them up and divide by 50.

The mean of a set of numbers is symbolized by $\bar{X}$, read *X bar*. The uppercase Greek letter sigma, Σ, stands for "take the sum of whatever follows." We use the symbol X to represent an individual score from a set of scores and N for the number of scores in the set. So the formula for computing a mean looks like this:

$$\bar{X} = \Sigma X/N$$

This is just a fancy shorthand way of expressing what you already know: To find the mean of a set of scores ($\bar{X}$), add the scores (ΣX) together and then divide by the number of scores (N). When we do this for form A and form B of our classroom exam example, we find that the mean for both sets of scores is 80. That is, $\Sigma X = 4000$ and $N = 50$ in each case, so $\Sigma X \div N = 80$ for both forms of the exam. In terms of the mean score, there is clearly no difference between the two forms of the test.

The Median. Although the mean is generally the central-tendency measure of choice, there are occasions when it may not be appropriate. These occasions occur when a distribution includes a few extreme scores. For a simple example, the mean of the numbers, 2, 3, 3, 5, 7 is 4 ($\Sigma X = 20$; $N = 5$; so $\bar{X} = 4$). Even on inspection, 4 looks right; it is a value near the middle or center of the set. Now consider the numbers 2, 3, 3,

5, 37. What is their mean? The sum of these 5 numbers is 50, so their mean equals 10. Here, it seems by inspection that the extreme score of 37 is adding too much weight to our measure of central tendency—it's really not near the center. For example, imagine computing the average income of a small working-class community that happens to include two millionaires. The mean income of this community would be unduly influenced by just two persons with unusually high incomes.

In such cases, we might prefer to use the median as our measure of central tendency. The **median** is the value of a set of numbers that divides it exactly in half. There are as many scores above the median as below it. Perhaps you recognize that the median is the same as the fiftieth percentage of a distribution—50 percent of the scores are higher; 50 percent are lower.

Don't fall for this trick: "What is the median of these test scores: 42, 58, 37, 62, 55?" There is a tendency to want to say "37" because it is in the middle of the list with two scores to the left and two scores to the right. But "37" certainly isn't at the center of these scores; it's the lowest! Before you choose the median, the scores must first be placed in order: 37, 42, 55, 58, 62. *Now* the score in the middle, 55, is the median, the one that divides the set in half. Whenever we have an even number of scores, there will be no one number in the middle, will there? What is the median of these numbers: 3, 6, 8, 10, 14, 18? What we do here is calculate the mean of the two numbers in the middle (here 8 and 10). So, the median of these six numbers is 9. When we have a large number of scores to deal with, the computation of the median becomes slightly more complicated. We can't always just put our scores in order and identify the median by inspection. But in such cases, the logic is the same, and we have formulas that tell what steps to take to calculate the median. For the two distributions of our example, the median for form A of the test is 80; for form B it is 79.

median
the score above which and below which half the scores in an ordered set fall

The Mode. No doubt the easiest measure of central tendency to calculate is the mode. The **mode** is the most frequently occurring value in a set or distribution of scores. If you have already constructed a frequency distribution, finding the mode is particularly easy. Just locate the X-value with the greatest frequency and you've found the mode. For many psychological characteristics measured for very large numbers of subjects, the mode does tend to fall near the center of the distribution of scores. For our example problem, the mode of scores earned on form A is 86 and on form B the mode is 80.

mode
the most frequently occurring X-values in a set

As it happens, the mode is seldom used as a measure of central tendency. For one thing, computing the mode disregards all of the other values in the distribution. For another, there is no guarantee that the most frequently occurring number will be at (or even near) the middle. Notice also that it is quite possible for a collection of numbers to have two modes (be "bimodal") or three modes, or more.

Variability

If we know how two sets of scores differ "on the average," we know a lot. We know, for instance, that there is no apparent difference in central tendency for the two sets of scores we have been using as an example. There is, however, a second descriptive characteristic of distributions of numbers that may be of interest: their dispersion, spread, or variability.

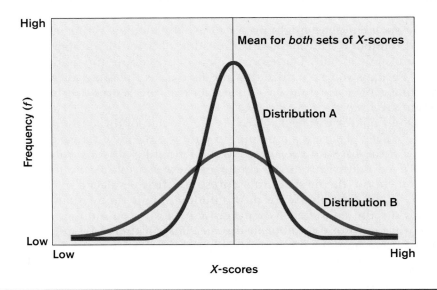

FIGURE A.4
Two distributions of X-scores (A and B) that have identical means, but clearly different variabilities.

It is quite possible to have two sets of scores that have identical means but that, at the same time, are clearly different from each other. This sort of difference can be seen in Figure A.3 and is even more clearly obvious in Figure A.4. In this figure, we can see that most of the scores of distribution A are clustered around the mean of the distribution. The scores of distribution B are much more spread out, or variable, even though the mean of this set of scores equals the mean of distribution A.

Imagine for a moment that the two graphs in Figure A.4 represent grades earned by two very large classes. Further imagine that the mean grade for each class is a C. If this is the case, then these graphs tell us that almost everyone in class A received a C, a C+, or a C-. Some may have received a B or a D, but most grades were near the average C. In class B, on the other hand, there were obviously many more As, Bs, Ds, and Fs than were earned by the other class, even though the mean grade for the two classes was a C. So knowing about a distribution's variability is to have some useful information. How shall we represent variability statistically?

One way to measure the spread of scores in a distribution is to use a statistic called the range. **Range** is found by subtracting the lowest score from the highest. Unfortunately, range (as a measure of variability) simply disregards all the other scores between the highest and lowest. Even when most scores are bunched tightly around the mean, if there are just a couple of extreme scores, the range will be large. The range would be an inappropriate measure of variability for our example. Scores on both form A and form B of the classroom test range from a high score of 100 to a low score of 60. Thus, the range for both sets of scores is 40 points. An inspection of our Figure A.3, however, indicates that scores on form A are generally more variable than scores on form B.

range
the difference between the highest and lowest scores in a distribution

A measure of variability that takes into account all the scores of a distribution is **standard deviation.** Standard deviation is usually abbreviated SD. It is a kind of average of the extent to which all the scores in a distribution are different from (deviate from) their mean. Let's go through the procedures of computing a standard deviation.

The first thing that we need is the mean of our distribution ($\overline{X}$). Then we find the difference between each score (X, remember) and the mean ($\overline{X}$). This is a simple process of subtraction, yielding a collection of ($X - \overline{X}$) scores. Because means are, by definition, in the middle of distributions, some X-scores will be above the mean (so $X - \overline{X}$ will be a positive number), and some X-scores will be below the mean (so $X - \overline{X}$ will be a negative number). If we then simply add up all of our deviations, $\Sigma(X - \overline{X})$, we will always have a sum of zero. What we do to deal with this complication is simply square each deviation score, so that we have a set of ($X - \overline{X})^2$ scores. Any number—even a negative one—that is squared (multiplied by itself) yields a positive number. Now, we add together our squared deviations, $\Sigma(X - \overline{X})^2$. We then find an average by dividing this total by N, the number of scores we are dealing with. In formula form, what we have so far is: $\Sigma(X - \overline{X})^2/N$. This statistic is called **variance.**

In our calculations, we introduced a squaring operation simply to get rid of negative numbers. We now reverse that operation by taking the square root of our result (variance). What we end up with then is our formula for standard deviation, and it looks like this:

$$SD = \sqrt{\Sigma(X - \overline{X})^2/N}$$

You may never be called upon to compute a standard deviation using this formula. For one thing, even simple hand-held calculators often come with a button that yields a standard deviation value once you've punched in all the X-scores. For another, there are simpler computational formulas that provide the same result in fewer, easier steps. But you should appreciate what standard deviations do. They tell us the extent to which scores in a distribution deviate from the distribution's mean. We use them often in psychology.

To reinforce our discussion, Figure A.5 depicts the computation of a standard deviation for some simple data. When the procedure is applied to our example data we find that the standard deviation for form A of the test is 11.29; for form B, SD = 6.18. This result conforms to our observation that the scores on form A of the test are more variable than those earned on form B.

INFERENTIAL STATISTICS

We've already seen that statistics can be used to summarize and describe some of the essential characteristics of large collections of data. They also can be used to guide our decision making concerning the data we have collected. That is, statistics can allow us to make inferences about our data. **Inferential statistics** tell us about the significance of the results of our experimental or correlational studies. In general, they tell us the likelihood that the data we have collected might have occurred by chance. Let's use another example, again dealing with means.

standard deviation
the average difference between the scores in a distribution and their mean

variance
the square of the standard deviation

inferential statistics
statistical tests of the significance of the results from experimental or correlational studies

FIGURE A.5
An Example of the Computation of the Standard Deviation for a Small Distribution of X-Scores

X-scores	$X - \bar{X}$	$(X - \bar{X})^2$
12	6.5	42.25
10	4.5	20.25
7	1.5	2.25
6	.5	.25
5	−.5	.25
5	−.5	.25
4	−1.5	2.25
4	−1.5	2.25
1	−4.5	20.25
1	−4.5	20.25

$$110.50 = \Sigma(X - \bar{X})^2$$

$$\Sigma X = 55$$
$$N = 10$$
$$\bar{X} = \Sigma X \div N = 5.5$$
$$SD = \sqrt{\Sigma(X - \bar{X})^2/n} = \sqrt{110.50/10} = \sqrt{11.05} = \underline{3.32}$$

Let's say that our concern is with the effects of background music on studying. You want to do an experiment to determine if background music affects study skills. To keep matters simple, let's also assume that you have two groups of volunteer students. Each group is to try to learn 50 words in a five-minute study session. One group will practice in silence (your control group); the other will have classical music playing in the background (the experimental group). We'll call the first group, group S and the second, group C. Let's say there are 40 students in each group, or $N = 40$. After each group studies the word list for five minutes, you test to see how many words have been learned. Then you construct a frequency distribution of your data and compute the means and standard deviations for each set of data. What you discover is that group S has a mean number of words learned equal to 26.0 and group C's mean is 28.5. Now what? There's no doubt that 28.5 is larger than 26.0, but the difference is not very large. Is the difference large enough for you to claim that the background music had an effect? We need to backtrack just a little.

Imagine that we had two groups of students in a similar experiment, but that both groups received exactly the same treatment. That is, both groups performed the same task under the same conditions. Some dependent variable is measured for both groups (perhaps the number of words that were learned in a 5-minute study session). Even though both groups were treated exactly the same, would we expect the mean scores for the two groups to be *exactly* equal? Wouldn't we expect some variation in scores between the two groups? If we did this same experiment again tomorrow, or next week, would we expect to get exactly the same mean scores again, even though experimental conditions remain the same? No. We generally anticipate that simply because of chance factors alone there will be some difference between the scores earned by two different groups of subjects—even if they are doing the same thing under the same conditions. So if mean scores for our two groups turn out to be a bit different, we aren't surprised; we can attribute the difference to chance. But what if the groups *are* treated differently? What if the differences in measured responses are large? Can these differences also be attributed to chance? Or do they reflect real, significant differences between the two groups? This is where inferential statistics come in.

Inferential statistics allow us to make probability statements. They help us to determine the likelihood that observed differences in our descriptive statistics (such as means) are differences due to chance and random factors or some true difference between the groups we have measured. Differences that are not likely to have occurred by chance are called **statistically significant differences.** If the difference between two calculated means is found to be statistically significant, that difference may or may not be important or meaningful, but we can claim that the difference is not likely to be due to chance.

One way to think about statistical significance is in terms of replication. If two means are found to be significantly different, it is likely that if the measurements were taken over and over again, the same difference in the same direction would show up most of the time. Inferential statistics can be used to judge the statistical significance of any statistic. They can be used to tell us the probability with which means, medians, standard deviations, proportions, or correlation coefficients are truly different or else are different by chance alone.

Significance is usually stated as a proportion. We talk about means being different at the "0.05 level," for instance. What this means is that the likelihood of our finding a mean difference as large as we did by chance alone is less than 5 in 100. The "0.01 level of significance" is even more conservative. It implies that the difference we have observed would have occurred by chance—if in fact no real differences exist—less than 1 time in 100.

Let's return now to the example with which we are working in this section and add a small insight. We've reported that the results of an experiment provide us with two mean scores: 26.0 for the group that studied in silence and 28.5 for students who studied with classical music in the background. Our interest now is in determining the extent to which these means are statistically different or due to chance factors. As we have implied, there is a statistical test of significance that can be applied to our data to this very question. The statistical test is called a *t-test.*

There are three factors that influence a test of significance such as the one that would be applied to our data for this example. One, of course, is the size of the mean difference itself. Everything else being equal, the larger the measured difference, the more likely that the difference reflects a real difference and not chance factors. A second factor is the size of the samples, or the number of measurements being tested. Everything else being equal, differences based on large numbers of observations are more likely to be significant than the same differences based on fewer observations. The third factor that influences a measure of statistical significance is the variability of the data.

To see why variability (usually standard deviation) matters in determining the significance of difference between means, refer to Figure A.6.

statistically significant differences
differences in measurements that cannot be explained by the chance or random factors

FIGURE A.6

The possible outcomes of two experiments. In both cases the mean differences $(\bar{B} - \bar{A})$ and $(\bar{D} - \bar{C})$ are the same, and the Ns are also the same for each distribution. Because the variabilities in the left distributions are smaller than the ones in the right, the difference between $\bar{B} - \bar{A}$ is more likely to be significant than is the difference between $\bar{D} - \bar{C}$.

(A)

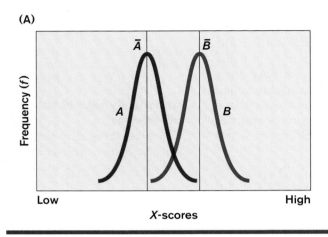

(B)

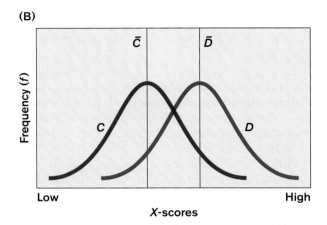

On the left of Figure A.6 we see two distributions of X-scores that have different means ($\bar{X}_A$ and $\bar{X}_B$). The right side of the figure shows two distributions that have the very same mean difference ($\bar{X}_C$ and $\bar{X}_D$). Because the variability (standard deviations) of distributions A and B are small, it is more likely that their means reflect significant differences than is the case for distributions C and D—even though the actual mean difference is the same in either case. In fact, the formula for the t-test of the significance of the difference between two means includes: (1) the mean difference itself, (2) the size of the groups involved, and (3) the standard deviations of the scores from each group.

SOME NORMAL CURVE STATISTICS

As we have seen in our discussions of personality assessment and intelligence, many of the measurements we make in psychology fall into a similar pattern. Particularly when measurements are made on large numbers of subjects, we commonly find that they fall into a distribution we call the **normal curve** (see Figure A.7). The normal curve is a frequency distribution that is symmetrical and bell-shaped. As you can see, scores that are normally distributed tend to bunch around the mean and become infrequent at the extreme values of X (whatever the X-scores may be). Because this normal curve of scores does occur so often, we tend to know a lot about the nature of this distribution.

The normal curve is simply a graphical representation of a large set of numbers. Thus we can compute the mean and the standard deviation of the scores that make up the distribution. Because the normal distribution is symmetrical, the mean always falls precisely in the middle of the distribu-

normal curve

a commonly found symmetrical, bell-shaped frequency distribution

FIGURE A.7

The percentage of cases in a normal distribution falling between ±1 SD around the mean (68 percent), ±2 SD (95 percent), and ±3 SD (99 percent). The curve is symmetrical, and the mean divides it exactly in half. Also note that virtually all scores fall between 3 standard deviations below the mean and 3 standard deviations above the mean.

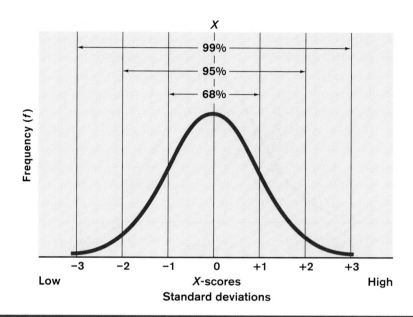

tion and is coincident with the median and the mode. That is, there are just as many scores above the mean as there are below it. We also know how many scores (or what proportion of scores) fall within standard deviation units around the mean. For example, we know that 68 percent of all scores fall between 1 standard deviation below the mean and 1 standard deviation above the mean (see Figure A.7). It is also true that 95 percent of the cases fall between ±2 standard deviations around the mean. Almost all the cases (about 99 percent) in a normal distribution fall between −3 and +3 standard deviations around the mean. What good is this sort of information? Let's look at an example problem.

When many people are measured, IQ scores tend to fall in distributions that we may consider to be normal distributions. Figure A.8 depicts a theoretical IQ distribution where, by definition, the mean equals 100 and the standard deviation is equal to 15 IQ points. We might want to know, for instance, what percentage of the population has an IQ score above 100. Well, that's an easy one. Because the mean equals 100, and the mean divides the distribution exactly in half, 50 percent of the cases fall above 100 and 50 percent fall below an IQ of 100, so the answer is 50 percent.

What percentage of the population has an IQ score above 115? This takes a little more effort, and following along with Figure A.8 will help. We might work backward. If we know the percentage of cases in the shaded

FIGURE A.8

A theoretical normal curve of IQ scores. Here we can see, with the mean = 100, and SD = 15, that 84 percent of the population has an IQ of 115 or less (50 percent to the mean and 34 percent from the mean to +1 SD above the mean). Thus, only 16 percent have IQs above 115.

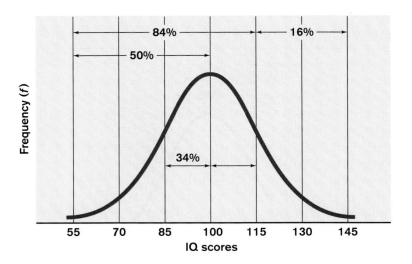

portion of the curve (up to IQ = 115), then the difference between that percentage and 100 will be the percentage who have IQs above 115. We can't determine the shaded percentage by inspection, but we can do so in a few easy steps. Up to the mean fall one-half, or 50 percent, of the cases (this we've already established). Now what about that segment between 100 and 115? What we do know (check on Figure A.7 again) is that 68 percent of the cases fall between −1 standard deviation and +1 standard deviation. In a normal distribution, the mean divides this segment exactly in half, so that between the mean and 1 standard deviation above the mean are included 34 percent of the cases. (Note that IQ =115 is 1 SD above the mean.) So now we have 50 percent to the mean of 100, and 34 percent from the mean to 115. We add the two together and determine that 84 percent of the cases fall below an IQ of 115, so 16 percent must fall above it. Using the same logic, we can convert any score to a percentage if we are dealing with a normal curve. To do so for scores that do not fall precisely on standard deviation units above or below the mean involves a slight complication, but the general method is the same as we have indicated here. What percentage of the population (from Figures A.7 and A.8) have IQ scores above 130? The answer is 2.5 percent. Can you see where that comes from?

CHAPTER 1
Topic 1A A Working Definition of Psychology

1.1 All you need to do here is recognize the definition of the term "hypothesis." Hypotheses are part of doing science, case histories, and experiments, but the answer here is *c. Page 47.*

1.2 Science cannot lead us to decide which issues to pursue, nor can it tell us which hypothesis is the correct one, but it can tell us which hypotheses to reject as unfounded. *Page 47.*

1.3 This statement is false. There are many ways of gaining insight about human nature. As it happens, psychology values scientific methods. *Page 47.*

1.4 As psychologists, they are all scientists, but it is the clinical psychologist who is most likely to also be a practitioner. *Page 47.*

1.5 Psychologists study all of these things, but the only alternative that is general enough not to exclude a part of psychology's subject matter is *c. Page 47.*

1.6 This item assesses whether you know that "affect" refers to one's emotions, feelings, and moods. Alternatives *a, b,* and *c* are relevant to psychology's subject matter; affect deals only with *d. Page 47.*

1.7 Someone may tell us about a dream they had, but there is no way that we—or anyone else—can verify the contents of a dream. *Page 47.*

1.8 Alternatives *c* and *d* tell us about psychology's subject matter, but when psychology began, the focus was on applying scientific methods to old philosophical questions about the nature of the mind; hence the best answer is *b. Page 47.*

1.9 Neither of these men made scientific contributions that warrant mention, and neither had much to say about the spinal cord. What both did, as philosophers, was seek explanations of human activity in human terms, which is what alternative *b* claims. *Page 47.*

1.10 In fact, neither Locke nor Wundt would have known anything about Darwin's theories, which were published after each had made his mark on psychology. Although Wundt relied on scientific methods, they were not the methods of the philosopher Locke. What they had in common was their interest in the structure and contents of the human mind. *Page 47.*

1.11 No, the first psychology laboratory was Wundt's. Freud, as it happens, never had a laboratory. *Page 47.*

1.12 Washburn was an experimental psychologist who studied and compared the behaviors and mental processes of various species of animals, so. . . . *c. Page 47.*

1.13 Psychology became known as the science of behavior when John Watson chaired the Psychology Department at Johns Hopkins University, right after World War I. Wundt, Wertheimer, and James were more interested in other matters. *Page 47.*

1.14 This is a bit sneaky. Freud did much of his significant writing in this time period and we do call his approach "psychoanalytic," but it arose from his practice of therapy, not a laboratory or experiments, so as it stands, this statement is false. *Page 48.*

1.15 Although no psychologist would violently disagree with such a statement, it is most likely to have been made by a humanistic psychologist. *Page 48.*

Topic 1B The Research Methods of Psychology

1.16 Alternatives *a, b,* and *d* are all true. Naturalistic observation need not be reserved for organisms in social situations. *Page 48.*

1.17 Each of these questions is one in which psychologists might be interested; however, naturalistic observation will only be useful in trying to answer the question about children during recess. *Page 48.*

1.18 Most of Freud's work was based on his in-depth study of many of his patients, using the case history method. *Page 48.*

1.19 Almost certainly. Indeed, the advantage of surveys is that they can reach many subjects easily. *Page 48.*

1.20 This is a rather "standard" item. Alternative *d* is wrong because correlation coefficients cannot exceed −1.00 or +1.00. Useful prediction depends on the strength of a relationship, whether it is positive or negative, so a −.71 is more useful than a +.56 (−.71 is closer to the extreme of −1.00 than +.56 is to +1.00). *Page 48.*

1.21 The first three pairs are clearly positively related. At least it is my experience that the less light there is in a restaurant, the more expensive the food, or as the light goes down, the price goes up, which is a negative correlation. *Page 48.*

1.22 Remember: Usefulness depends on the size of the number, not its sign (whether it is positive or negative). *Page 48.*

1.23 Doing an experiment involves manipulating independent variables and measuring dependent variables, but the quality of that experiment hinges on the extent to which extraneous variables have been controlled or eliminated. *Page 48.*

1.24 The independent variable is the one you manipulate; here the amount or dosage of the drug. Alternative a might be your dependent variable, and alternatives *c* and *d* are possible extraneous variables. *Page 48.*

1.25 This statement is about as good a summary statement of the nature of an experiment that I can come up with. It is true. *Page 48.*

1.26 Baseline designs use subjects as their own controls, where each subject gets both the experimental treatment and the control condition. None of the statements in alternatives *b, c,* or *d* is correct. *Page 48.*

1.27 In virtually all research settings this statement is true. *Page 48.*

1.28 Phenomenology deals with the reality that what matters most to an individual is not what happened, but what that individual perceived happened. *Page 48.*

CHAPTER 2
Topic 2A Neurons: Building Blocks of the Nervous System

2.1 A neuron will have only one cell body and only one nucleus. As it happens, some neurons do have two axons, but the structures most likely to occur in large numbers are dendrites. *Page 77.*

2.2 Myelin serves each of the functions named in alternatives *a, b,* and *d.* Be careful to note the *not* in this item. *Page 77.*

2.3 Unlike many other cells, neurons are not replaced when they die, but their functions can be taken over by other neurons, particularly in younger organisms. *Page 77.*

2.4 Indeed, one of the functions of myelin is to speed impulses along. *Page 77.*

2.5 As logical as the statement may sound, it is simply not true. We are born with more neurons than we'll ever have again. *Page 77.*

2.6 At rest, a neuron is in a position to fire, with many more negative ions inside the cell and positive ions outside the cell, which makes alternative *b* correct. *Page 77.*

2.7 Nothing physically moves down a neuron when it fires. Physical movement is that of ions going in and out through the neural membrane. What moves down the neuron is *where* this ion movement takes place. *Page 77.*

2.8 Watch out here! An important term in the stem is "in terms of their action," which means we're looking for what they do, which is either to excite or inhibit neural impulse transmission. *Page 77.*

2.9 Within a neuron, impulse transmission is electrochemical, but at the synapse, it is basically a chemical process, involving neurotransmitters. *Page 77.*

Topic 2B The Central Nervous System

2.10 It is important to know how the various nervous systems are interrelated, and to know the major functions of each. While the parasympathetic division is active when we are relaxed, the sympathetic is involved in emotionality. Note the spelling of alternative *c*—there is no such system as an automatic nervous system. *Page 77.*

2.11 The white matter looks white because of the myelin that surrounds the axons of fibers going up and down the spinal cord, to and from the brain. *Page 77.*

2.12 This is a straightforward terminology item. For the spinal reflex, it is: in on sensory neurons, within on interneurons, and out on motor neurons. *Page 77.*

2.13 This is basically the same question in true-false form as item 2.12 was in multiple-choice form. This sequence of events is true. By now do you get the idea that this is an important concept? *Page 77.*

2.14 Although it is difficult to say just where it begins, the first structure to be encountered would be the medulla. *Page 78.*

2.15 The medulla contains centers that control several important reflexes, including those that control respiration, or breathing. *Page 78.*

2.16 Cross laterality occurs in the medulla and in the pons. Because these two structures taken together comprise what we call the brain stem, this is the best answer. *Page 78.*

2.17 The pons provides a sensory and motor bridge between the brain and the lower body. Not only would you be paralyzed, you would also be without feeling below your neck. *Page 78.*

2.18 Quite the contrary. Lower brain centers develop first, and the cerebral cortex is the last to fully develop. In fact, we may argue that one's cerebral cortex continues to develop throughout most of one's lifetime. *Page 78.*

2.19 Yes, speech and language centers are located in the left hemisphere of the cerebral cortex, but notice that this is not one of your choices. The issue in this item has to do with muscular coordination, which is a function of the cerebellum. *Page 78.*

2.20 The reticular activating system, as its name implies, controls one's level of arousal. All that would happen in this scenario is that the cat would awaken. *Page 78.*

2.21 Don't get distracted by the story of Phineas Gage and the iron bar that got blasted through his head. The basic issue here is that the limbic system is the seat of most primitive emotionality and when connections between it and the cerebral cortex are cut, control of emotionality is more difficult. *Page 78.*

2.22 The hypothalamus is not only involved in the thirst drive, it is also implicated in the hunger drive, temperature regulation drive, sex drive, and others. *Page 78.*

2.23 This item describes very succinctly the function of the thalamus. *Page 78.*

2.24 This does get a bit technical, but you should know the major features of cerebral localization, vision, hearing, movement, etc., and you should know that the body senses are processed at the front of the parietal lobe. *Page 78.*

2.25 Notice what I did here—I inserted an item that is "out of order." This "goes back" to the spinal cord. You must be ready to deal with test items one at a time, not necessarily in the order in which they are presented in the text. Like all neurons within the CNS, these are called interneurons. *Page 78.*

2.26 Again, you should know the localization of major functions in the cerebral cortex, including the fact that vision is processed in the occipital lobe. *Page 78.*

2.27 Don't panic just because this item is wordy. Remember the basics of the split brain procedure and remember that speech is a left hemisphere process, and that information from the left hand would be processed in the right hemisphere. Given these few details, alternative *c* is the only correct one. *Page 78.*

2.28 No, as a matter of fact, it is often difficult to tell that someone has had the procedure, except when certain behavioral functions are tested. Split-brain subjects can and do lead relatively normal lives. *Page 78.*

CHAPTER 3
Topic 3A Prenatal Development

3.1 A zygote is formed by just two cells, one from each parent. *Page 122.*

3.2 Be careful here. During the periods of the zygote, embryo, and fetus, a developing organism is at risk. That risk is greatest during the period of the embryo. *Page 122.*

3.3 To be viable is to be able to survive in the world without (heroic or extreme) medical intervention. *Page 122.*

3.4 Alcohol abuse is certainly the most devastating factor (of these listed), leading to birth defects, but even moderate alcohol use is generally to be discouraged. *Page 122.*

3.5   There are many signs and symptoms associated with the fetal alcohol syndrome (retarded physical growth, poor coordination, poor muscle tone, etc.). By definition, one of those is intellectual retardation. *Page 122.*

3.6   The father's role in the physical, prenatal development of the organism is fairly restricted to the moment of conception. *Page 122.*

Topic 3B Development in Children

3.7   As is usually the case with multiple-choice items, there may be some truth to each of these alternatives, but that last one is most generally, universally true. *Page 122.*

3.8   Sure they do. Without its reflexes, a neonate probably would not survive at all. As it happens, some reflexes seem to be without specific purpose, but as it is worded, this statement is false. *Page 122.*

3.9   Not only is the last statement the best of these choices, but in this item, the first three make claims that are essentially the opposite of a true claim. *Page 122.*

3.10   We need to get at this one by inference and elimination. Because we know that the sense of depth, motion and sound discrimination are so well developed even at birth, we can conclude that the sense of balance is the poorest of these. *Page 122.*

3.11   There is really nothing wrong with alternatives *a, b,* and *d,* except that they have very little to do with the question at hand, which makes the third alternative the best one. *Page 122.*

3.12   The stages are determined in terms of how the child goes about forming or modifying schemas on the basis of his or her interaction with the environment. *Page 123.*

3.13   Melanie is probably in Piaget's stage of concrete operations, which would be reasonable for a 9-year-old. *Page 123.*

3.14   Yes, this is one of the most common criticisms of Piaget's theory. *Page 123.*

3.15   Kohlberg's is referred to as a theory of moral development. *Page 123.*

3.16   Actually, one of the strengths of Kohlberg's ideas is their application cross-culturally. *Page 123.*

3.17   Most of Kohlberg's theory of moral development was based on the study of males. Carol Gilligan suggests that females may have a different system of morality than do males. *Page 123.*

3.18   Erikson's stages of development are equally relevant for girls and boys and were based on observation. What makes his stages different is that they extend through adolescence into adulthood, whereas Piaget's do not. *Page 123.*

3.19 This one is fairly technical, and the answer is initiative vs. guilt. *Page 123.*

3.20 This statement is most certainly true. *Page 123.*

Topic 3C Adolescence and Adulthood

3.21 Although some (including G. Stanley Hall and Anna Freud) would claim that alternative *b* is correct, current thinking would make alternative *c* your best choice. *Page 123.*

3.22 To some of us, this observation may seem to be true, but it is not. It reflects more of an incorrect stereotype than reality. *Page 123.*

3.23 Menarche is the defining characteristic for puberty in girls, so *d* is correct. *Page 123.*

3.24 Resolving this crisis is one of the main tasks of adolescence, according to Erik Erikson. *Page 123.*

3.25 Alternatives a and *b* are clearly false. Alternative *d* is also false, but newly controversial. Alternative *c* is most clearly true. *Page 123.*

3.26 It's a matter of degree, of course, but this statement is, in fact, false. *Page 123.*

3.27 I hate to ask picky questions about details and numbers, but the fact is that teenage pregnancies probably exceed one million each year, a detail I find awesome. *Page 123.*

3.28 Alternatives *a, c,* and *d* are all reasonable and commonly offered explanations for the high rate of teenage pregnancy. *Page 123.*

3.29 Although they appear to be contradictory, independence and interdependence characterize early adulthood. *Page 124.*

3.30 Here again, this item hinges on your knowledge of Erikson's stages. Early adulthood is associated with conflicts between intimacy and isolation. *Page 124.*

3.31 This true statement is lifted virtually verbatim from the text. *Page 124.*

3.32 Sadly enough, this is quite true. *Page 124.*

3.33 We often hear this used as an "excuse" for some pretty silly behaviors by middle-aged adults, but there is little hard evidence for a general stage or period of development that we can characterize as a midlife crisis. *Page 124.*

3.34 Alternative *c* is the only one even close to being true. *Page 124.*

CHAPTER 4
Topic 4A Sensation: A Few Basic Concepts

4.1 The first alternative gives about as simple a statement of psychophysics as I can manage. *Page 158.*

4.2 By definition, stimuli that are found to be below one's absolute threshold will be detected less than 50 percent of the time. *Page 158.*

4.3 The complete statement that signal detection is essentially a decision-making process is almost a direct quote from the text. *Page 158.*

4.4 You might get this one simply by elimination. The first alternative is downright silly. The second and third alternatives say virtually the same thing, which makes alternative *d* the correct choice. *Page 158.*

4.5 Not in actuality—only in theory. If it is above threshold, all we can say is that it will be detected more than 50 percent of the time. *Page 158.*

Topic 4B Vision

4.6 Here's another analogy item, and a simple one at that. What is the issue here? Wavelength determines hue; wave amplitude determines what? Brightness. *Page 158.*

4.7 You ought to be able to imagine what each of the lights described in the first three alternatives would look like. What makes the last alternative the correct choice is that white light is of the lowest possible saturation and thus one cannot have a white light of high saturation. *Page 158.*

4.8 The cells that convert the physical energy of light into neural impulses are the rods and cones of the retina. *Page 158.*

4.9 Indeed, what the iris does is move to change the size of the pupil in response to the amount of light presented to the eye. *Page 158.*

4.10 Sightedness has to do with whether or not images are clearly focused on the retina. There are any number of problems that can cause this to happen (poorly shaped lens, or cornea, or eyeball for that matter) but hardly any have to do with the retina itself. *Page 158.*

4.11 Because of the location of our rods, and because they function best "in the dark" or in low levels of illumination, we would want to focus the object on the periphery of the retina. *Page 158.*

4.12 The dark adaptation curve has a "break" in it because at about the 7-minute mark, the cones no longer become more sensitive, while the rods continue to adapt, which makes the first statement the correct choice. *Page 158.*

4.13 In fact, our rods are colorblind. Don't let the fact that this statement starts off with a correct assertion (rods operate best at low levels of illumination) confuse you. *Page 159.*

4.14 This item is quite false in that there are about 20 times as many rods as cones in the human retina. *Page 159.*

4.15 The major issue here is remembering that although red, blue, and yellow are the primary colors for paint, the primaries for light are red, green, and blue. *Page 159.*

Topic 4C Hearing and the Other Senses

4.16 The stimulus for audition is sound, of course, and alternative *b* gives a reasonable definition or description of sound. *Page 159.*

4.17 Amplitude determines loudness, mixture determines timbre, and— as this item asks—frequency determines pitch. *Page 159.*

4.18 Another analogy. Wave amplitude of sound determines loudness. *Page 159.*

4.19 This is simply by definition white noise. *Page 159.*

4.20 This wordy statement contains a lot of information, but it is a fairly good description of what hearing is. *Page 159.*

4.21 This one ought to sound familiar. It's the correct repeat of the definition of the decibel scale. *Page 159.*

4.22 Sound waves are first collected by those flaps on the side of our head called pinnas (or pinnae); they are then passed on to the eardrum. *Page 159.*

4.23 Located within the cochlea, the actual receptor cells for sound are hair cells. *Page 159.*

4.24 I think that it is important for college students to know the actual ("technical") names for the various senses. Smell is olfaction. Taste is gustation. *Page 159.*

4.25 This one is so silly you almost have to think about it for a minute. Of course impulses for the sense of smell go to the brain, and rather directly at that. *Page 159.*

4.26 You probably got this correct. Pheromones are natural chemicals that are used to attract members of the opposite sex or mark off territory. *Page 159.*

4.27 Our experience of hot can be the result of simultaneously stimulating both warm and cold receptors. There seem to be no specific receptors for "hot" alone. *Page 159.*

4.28 Again, this is a matter of definition. Vestibular senses tell us about position relative to gravity; cutaneous senses about touch and pressure; and kinesthetic senses tell us about the movement of muscles and joints. There is no such thing as a "gravitational" sense. *Page 159.*

CHAPTER 5
Topic 5A Perception

5.1 We say that information processing begins with sensation, ends with retrieval from memory, and has perception in between. *Page 199.*

5.2 Although they were interested in other matters, the study of perception almost defines the Gestalt psychologists. *Page 199.*

5.3 Although perception may involve our motivations, learning, and sensory input, it is best classified as a cognitive process. *Page 199.*

5.4 Intensity, size, and motion are best considered to be dimensions on which stimuli may contrast with other stimuli, making contrast the most general of these factors. *Page 199.*

5.5 Yes, perception is a basic, fundamental cognitive process, but it is still very much dependent on such "higher level" processes as one's memory of past experience and motivational state. *Page 199.*

5.6 My name would attract my attention and not yours because of my past experience with that name, a personal factor. *Page 199.*

5.7 To say that some stimuli are attended to because of an expectation to perceive them is to say that one has developed a mental set. *Page 199.*

5.8 Speech sounds within a word are perceived and organized together because they are close together, separated by small spaces, which reflects the Gestalt factor of proximity—which means "nearness" or "togetherness." *Page 199.*

5.9 Subjective contours provide compelling examples of closure. *Page 199.*

5.10 This is true by definition. If you're in doubt, go back and check the definition. *Page 199.*

5.11 Alternatives a and *b* are really quite absurd. Alternative *c* is a correct statement, but is unrelated to three-dimensionality. That makes *d* the best choice. *Page 199.*

5.12 Retinal disparity—where disparity means differentness—requires that we have two retinas that receive different images of the same object. *Page 199.*

5.13 This is a straightforward definition of interposition. *Page 199.*

5.14 This one is almost tricky. The name is deceiving. In fact, motion parallax has little to do with our perception of motion. It is a cue to depth and distance. *Page 199.*

5.15 Hardly anything, even a process as basic as depth perception, is immune to the influence of learning, experience, or culture. This is false. *Page 199.*

5.16 Alternative *a* defines hallucinations, not illusions. Alternatives *b* and *c* are both incorrect statements (in fact, the opposite is true), while alternative *d* provides a reasonable definition of visual illusions. *Page 199.*

Topic 5B Consciousness

5.17 I hope I didn't catch you on this one, which actually goes back to Chapter 1. John Watson, remember, began behaviorism which denied the usefulness of consciousness in scientific psychology. *Page 200.*

5.18 James claimed that our consciousness is selective, continuous, personal, and changing, not stable. *Page 200.*

5.19 Altered states of consciousness need not be bizarre or strange and include sleeping. They are simply changes in the way we perceive ourselves and the environment. *Page 200.*

5.20 Indeed, one of the defining characteristics of the unconscious level of mental events is that it is so difficult to retrieve information from it. *Page 200.*

5.21 To the contrary, there has been more research and excitement about the unconscious lately than there has been for years. *Page 200.*

5.22 Although the first three statements *may* be true, only the fourth is most generally true. Remember, in multiple-choice items, the task is to find the best alternative. *Page 200.*

5.23 Self-report is probably the most unreliable source. The best way to know if someone is sleeping is by examination of EEG recordings. *Page 200.*

5.24 EEG records tells us nothing about muscle activity, have virtually no alpha waves during REM sleep, and do not show theta waves. They appear almost like waking states. *Page 200.*

5.25 During REM sleep one is likely to become paralyzed, not because of muscle tension but because of total relaxation, called "atonia." Alternatives *b* and *c* are possible; *d* is the opposite of what actually happens. *Page 200.*

5.26 All four statements sound reasonable (as they should in a good multiple-choice item), but here only alternative *c* is actually true. *Page 200.*

5.27 Hypnosis can do little to help us learn and remember information we have not yet encountered, but can help reduce anxiety and thus enable us to remember details of anxiety-producing events we might not otherwise be able to recall. *Page 200.*

5.28 Alternatives *b, c,* and *d* may be true of some drugs, but mind-altering agents are collectively referred to as *psychoactive. Page 200.*

5.29 This one requires some thought. By definition, we find that drug abuse in some way interferes with normal functioning to the extent that it is maladaptive, getting in the way of one's proper adaptation to the environment and to others. *Page 200.*

5.30 Here we have a trivia detail item. Caffeine is the most common stimulant. *Page 200.*

5.31 Nonsense. Of course all these drugs can and often do affect the way one feels and behaves as well as how one thinks. *Page 200.*

5.32 Sorry. No matter the dosage in which it is taken, alcohol is a depressant drug. *Page 200.*

CHAPTER 6
Topic 6A Classical Conditioning

6.1 Alternative *a* is simply not true. Alternatives *b* and *c* may be true, but not related to the word "demonstrated," which makes *d* correct. *Page 237.*

6.2 By definition, learning implies no value judgment. Alternatives *a, c,* and *d* are all part of the definition. *Page 237.*

6.3 The first thing that will happen when the bell is sounded is that the dog will orient reflexively to it. *Page 237.*

6.4 This statement is false for two reasons: Pavlov won his Nobel Prize in 1904, not 1902 (but that's picky), and there is no such thing as a Nobel Prize for psychology. *Page 237.*

6.5 Yes, this is exactly what it means to say that the response is unconditioned. *Page 237.*

6.6 This one is straightforward, but you must have your stimuli and responses sorted out. Responding to the bell is a conditioned response. *Page 237.*

6.7 The shock and the bell are both stimuli, so all alternatives including these are wrong. Withdrawal is both the CR and the UCR. *Page 237.*

6.8 By definition, the strength of the CR will diminish, which is a demonstration of extinction. *Page 237.*

6.9 Discrimination training is usually used to offset the effects of the opposite process of generalization. *Page 237.*

6.10 Classical conditioning affects emotional responses, such as relief at class end. *Page 237.*

6.11 Although they may have wanted to, Watson and Rayner never got the chance to see if Little Albert's fear would extinguish. *Page 237.*

6.12 Pavlov did not recognize this reality, but we now know that a stimulus will serve as an effective CS only if it signals or predicts the occurrence of a UCS that follows it. *Page 237.*

6.13 I doubt that many psychologists would agree with the statements made in alternatives *a*, *b*, and *d*, which makes the third choice correct. *Page 237.*

Topic 6B Operant Conditioning

6.14 It might be fun to debate the other alternatives, but it is alternative *c* that defines operant conditioning. *Page 238.*

6.15 The relatively permanent change in behavior that occurs as the result of operant conditioning is a change in the rate or probability of a response. *Page 238.*

6.16 Actually, Thorndike stated the law of effect. *Page 238.*

6.17 This is a wordy item, but the most likely thing to happen is that the rat's rate of response will decrease, which is extinction. *Page 238.*

6.18 If Mickey never does what you want him to do, there will be nothing for you to reinforce, so in this situation you'll have to try shaping his behaviors. *Page 238.*

6.19 This statement is true by definition; "shaping" and "successive approximations" are nearly synonymous terms. *Page 238.*

6.20 Positive reinforcers are given to organisms after an appropriate response, while negative reinforcement involves taking away something (something that is usually aversive or painful). *Page 238.*

6.21 Because the root canal procedure takes away the pain of the toothache, the end result is very reinforcing (how reinforcing depends on how painful the toothache was). The reinforcement here is negative reinforcement. *Page 238.*

6.22 I'd call this statement false because it is not necessarily so. Token economics involve secondary reinforcers, which may be (usually are) positive. *Page 238.*

6.23 Responses learned under a continuous reinforcement schedule will extinguish more quickly than those learned under any other schedule. *Page 238.*

6.24 Actually, the first three statements are quite false. The only thing that we can say for sure is that punishment decreases response rates. *Page 238.*

6.25 Remember that the intention of the person doing the reinforcing is quite irrelevant, which makes this statement true. *Page 238.*

6.26 Because we reinforce some stimuli and not others, we say that discrimination training is a matter of differential reinforcement. *Page 238.*

Topic 6C Cognitive Approaches to Learning

6.27 Cognitive approaches emphasize the development of cognitions (cleverly enough), which means that they focus on changes inside the organism that may or may not be evidenced in behavior. *Page 238.*

6.28 Latent means hidden from view, or not presently observable; hence the second alternative is the best choice. *Page 238.*

6.29 I hope you didn't fall for this one. Remember, Tolman demonstrated cognitive maps in rats. As it happens, it is very easy to find human examples, but the point is that the phenomenon is not restricted to humans. *Page 238.*

6.30 Vicarious reinforcement and vicarious punishment deal with the consequences of observing someone else being reinforced or punished and are, therefore, social concepts. *Page 238.*

CHAPTER 7
Topic 7A How Can We Describe Human Memory?

7.1 As we've said before, information processing that ends with memory begins with sensation. *Page 275.*

7.2 The first alternative looks pretty good until you realize that this item is asking about types of memory, which makes the last alternative the best one. *Page 275.*

7.3 Information appears to be stored in sensory memory in the same way in which it is presented—technically, it is not encoded in any way. Thus we say that the code is physical in nature. *Page 275.*

7.4 No. Actually, before we learn it we must first sense the information, then attend to and perceive it. *Page 275.*

7.5   Again, be careful. The word "minimal" is very important here. Any one of these three alternatives will do the job, but the minimum necessary is simply paying attention to it again. *Page 275*.

7.6   The best term here (and there are arguments that could be made for some of the others) is the technical term "chunk," largely because the others are more related to duration than to capacity. *Page 275*.

7.7   The best way is to work with it, using elaborative rehearsal. *Page 275*.

7.8   We say that elaborative rehearsal gets information into LTM, so "retrieving it" won't do. And alternatives *b* and *d* say the same thing and are related to STM, so the answer involves making the material meaningful. *Page 275*.

7.9   These procedures are most likely in procedural memory. *Page 275*.

7.10   Mostly because it is personal and autobiographical, the answer to the question about learning to ride a bicycle is probably in episodic memory. (Note that actually remembering what it takes to ride the bike would be in procedural memory.) *Page 275*.

Topic 7B Why We Forget: Factors Affecting Retrieval

7.11   Information in semantic memory is no doubt well organized, and one of the ways in which it may be organized is chronologically. Having said that, I am still going to claim that the answer here is "False" because there are better, more common ways of organizing information in semantic memory and because chronological organization better fits episodic memory. *Page 275*.

7.12   When we talk about retrieval failure, we're probably going to assume that the information that cannot be remembered is in memory, but cannot be gotten out for some reason, which is essentially what the second alternative is saying. *Page 275*.

7.13   No, in fact quite the opposite is true. *Page 275*.

7.14   The process of relearning is an implicit way of demonstrating the presence of information in memory that cannot be consciously retrieved. *Page 276*.

7.15   Even in the worst cases of memory loss, skills stored in procedural memory (talking, feeding, etc.) seem to be preserved. *Page 276*.

7.16   Probably. At least assessing memory through implicit means does not involve voluntary, conscious attempts to recall or recognize. *Page 276*.

7.17   The simple thing to say is that we cannot remember these features because we have never tried to, which is a way of saying that the information was not properly encoded. *Page 276*.

7.18   The first sentence here is a good, concise statement of the encoding specificity hypothesis. Note that although alternatives *b* and *d* are essentially true statements, they are not related to this question. *Page 276.*

7.19   State dependent memory studies have to do with the subject's "state of mind" at encoding and at retrieval and verify what we suspect concerning the encoding specificity hypothesis. *Page 276.*

7.20   This is terribly unlikely—so much so, I'd call it false. What we call flashbulb memories are usually stored in episodic memory. *Page 276.*

7.21   More than anything else they may do, mnemonic devices enhance meaningfulness. *Page 276.*

7.22   This item provides a pretty good description of what is involved in narrative chaining. *Page 276.*

7.23   Yes, mnemonic devices affect retrieval, but they do so by having their real impact on encoding, putting information into memory in a more meaningful way. *Page 276.*

7.24   This item provides a good definition for what schemas are. *Page 276.*

7.25   If Bob does no more trials, overlearning = 0%; 8 trials = 100%; 16 trials = 200%; and 20 trials = 250% overlearning. *Page 276.*

7.26   Alternative *a* is virtually never true; alternative *b* incorrectly talks about STM instead of LTM; alternative *c* sounds good, but is untrue; while alternative *d* is almost always true. *Page 276.*

7.27   The very last test will always suffer the most proactive interference—interference from material learned earlier. *Page 276.*

7.28   You may want to go back and examine the design for both retroactive and proactive interference. The correct choice here is that, as an experimental subject, you would begin by learning Task A. *Page 276.*

CHAPTER 8
Topic 8A Problem Solving

8.1   With a well-defined problem, the goal state is clear, so we know when we are there, and we know it with some certainty. We can say, "There, this problem is solved." *Page 311.*

8.2   Given our answer to the last question, the only acceptable choice here is alternative *b*. *Page 311.*

8.3   Once we realize that we have a problem, the first—and most difficult—step is to put that problem into terms that are meaningful to us. *Page 311.*

8.4   Given the answer to the last item, it follows that if a problem already exists in a form with which we are familiar, representation will be relatively easy. *Page 311.*

8.5   Heuristics (in general) allow us to reduce the number of choices we may pursue in problem solving. The more possibilities there are, the more important it is to develop a heuristic strategy. *Page 311.*

8.6   Heuristics may lead us down the wrong path now and then, but the ultimate advantage of heuristic strategies is that they save time. *Page 311.*

8.7   In fact, computers can solve problems with heuristic strategies, but they are best and fastest at using algorithmic strategies—checking out all the alternatives. *Page 311.*

8.8   Alternatives *a, c,* and *d* are all quite true. The proper mental set may actually facilitate problem solving, which makes *b* false. *Page 311.*

8.9   By definition, functional fixedness is a variety of mental set. *Page 311.*

8.10   No matter how original, no matter how convergent or divergent, no matter how artistic or beautiful, the ultimate test of a creative solution is whether or not it actually works to solve the problem. *Page 311.*

8.11   Not only is this statement true, it also provides a pretty good definition of both convergent and divergent thinking. *Page 311.*

Topic 8B Language

8.12   Language *is* rule-governed; it *is* creative or generative, and it *is* both social and cognitive. I'm not sure I know what it means to say that language is either correct or incorrect. *Page 311.*

8.13   Word is a part of speech, speech is a form of language, and language is a form of communication, which makes communication the most general term. *Page 311.*

8.14   Although language is an arbitrary cognitive process that follows rules, communicating about the not-here and not-now reflects displacement. *Page 312.*

8.15   If you chose the first alternative you've got a nice definition of pragmatics. *Page 312.*

8.16   There are stereotypes and then there are stereotypes. Actually, the opposite is true. *Page 312.*

8.17 This is quite false; they've shown appreciation for some time before. *Page 312.*

8.18 This child probably has already indicated knowledge of the word "feet," but is here demonstrating overregularization. *Page 312.*

8.19 Actually, about the only thing that learning theory is relevant for in language acquisition is picking up the meanings of words in one's language. *Page 312.*

Topic 8C Intelligence

8.20 Each of these defines intelligence, and reasonably so at that, but only the second alternative is an operational definition, specifying the operations used to measure intelligence. *Page 312.*

8.21 Objectivity in the context of psychological testing usually has to do with performance—how test responses are evaluated. *Page 312.*

8.22 She is interested in reliability: Will these results hold up two weeks later? *Page 312.*

8.23 This one is deceptively simple. The statement is true. *Page 312.*

8.24 Think about this one. To calculate reliability, we correlate a test with itself at a later date. To calculate validity, we correlate a test with some other criterion. Doesn't it make sense that a test is bound to correlate better with itself than it will with anything else, making this statement false? *Page 312.*

8.25 Their basic job was to identify children in the French school system who needed a different style of education because of some intellectual deficit. *Page 312.*

8.26 This one is almost a giveaway. Alternatives *a, c,* and *d* are each included under the most general level of a **g** factor. *Page 312.*

8.27 What we're looking for here is MA divided by CA, times 100, or 8 divided by 10, times 100, which is 80. *Page 312.*

8.28 No, what makes this revision different from previous ones is that it can provide several specific scores in addition to the one general IQ score. *Page 312.*

8.29 One of Wechsler's major complaints about IQ tests was that they were so heavily verbal and vocabulary oriented. He included many performance items on his tests, and allowed for the calculation of a performance IQ. *Page 312.*

8.30 Down syndrome appears when a zygote picks up an extra chromosome, yielding 47 chromosomes rather than the normal 23 pairs. *Page 312.*

8.31 We do. *Page 312.*

CHAPTER 9
Topic 9A Issues of Motivation

9.1 We say that motivation arouses, directs, and maintains behavior. Memory is surely involved in motivation—it's involved in virtually everything—but it's less critical than the other three. *Page 348.*

9.2 The difference is quite arbitrary, but standard: Drive is used for physiologically based motivators of behavior and motive is used for psychologically based motivators. *Page 348.*

9.3 There is value in the concept of instinct, of course, but with regard to human behaviors, instinct tends to rename and describe rather than explain. *Page 348.*

9.4 To say acquired, learned, or conditioned is to say the same thing, so "primary" is the odd term of these four. *Page 348.*

9.5 In virtually anyone's system, including Hull's, a need gives rise to a drive. *Page 348.*

9.6 I do think that it's important to know Maslow's hierarchy. If you think about it, the order is very sensible. Of those listed, the highest in the hierarchy are esteem needs. *Page 348.*

9.7 Drives, arousal, and needs all refer to conditions or states within the organism, while incentives are thought of as "out there" in the environment. *Page 348.*

9.8 By definition, homeostasis is a state of balance. *Page 348.*

9.9 In actual practice, there is scant difference between the motivational concept of incentive and the operant conditioning concept of positive reinforcer. *Page 348.*

9.10 I argue that cognitive dissonance is very much like the concept of homeostasis; whenever our thoughts (cognitions) are out of balance (dissonant), we will be motivated to change the way we think about things. *Page 348.*

9.11 Well, at first, maybe, but what makes this statement false is that if arousal continues to rise, eventually it will be so high as to be debilitating. *Page 348.*

9.12 Although all of these may be involved to some extent, the fact that sometimes we feel too hot or too cold is mostly a function of the hypothalamus. *Page 348.*

9.13 Most of the water in our bodies is contained within the structure of individual cells. *Page 348.*

9.14 Clearly it has some impact, but of these choices, the stomach is the least important. *Page 348.*

9.15   If the truth of this statement is not obvious, you need to think about it a bit longer. *Page 348.*

9.16   This one is almost a giveaway. All of these factors, and more, contribute to one's body weight. *Page 348.*

9.17   Alternatives *a, b,* and *d* are true of the sex drive for both humans and rats. The sex drive and sexual behaviors in rats do not seem to be affected by learning or experience. *Page 349.*

9.18   Only the third alternative is true; the others are very false indeed. *Page 349.*

9.19   The total picture is far from clear. We're quite sure that none of the observations made in the first three alternatives is even relevant, and are becoming convinced that the fourth alternative is the best statement we can make at the moment. *Page 349.*

9.20   The best alternative here is the last one—not the first, where there would be too little challenge to really experience a sense of achievement. *Page 349.*

Topic 9B The Psychology of Emotion

9.21   Whenever we read someone's system for classifying emotions, it seems to make great sense—until we read someone else's system. The first alternative here is the best. *Page 349.*

9.22   Heart rate increases, it doesn't decrease—in fact, think in terms of "what would happen if you were to meet a bear in the woods." *Page 349.*

9.23   As we've seen, the brain tends to work together, with all its aspects involved in everything, including emotionality, but—having said that—it is the limbic system that is most involved in emotions. *Page 349.*

9.24   This item has to do with the difference between humans and other organisms. Only humans can talk (verbalize) about how they feel. *Page 349.*

CHAPTER 10
Topic 10A Issues and Theories of Personality

10.1   The key here is "reasonably little effort." This indicates that the information is stored at a preconscious level. *Page 378.*

10.2   In fact, Freud had quite a bit to say about war and unpleasantness that he saw about him. He suggested that humans must have some sort of drive for destruction, which he called "thanatos," to match their drive for life and survival, which he called "eros." *Page 378.*

10.3 It is the ego that operates under what is called the reality principle. *Page 378.*

10.4 It is our superego that informs us of moral issues and keeps us in touch with "right and wrong." *Page 378.*

10.5 Although this may *seem* like displacement, this item provides a good definition for the defense mechanism called projection. *Page 378.*

10.6 It sounds to me like Otis is rationalizing. *Page 378.*

10.7 It is during the Freudian stage of latency that one's sexuality is essentially put on hold. *Page 378.*

10.8 There were many grounds on which people broke away from Freud. Of these, the first statement summarizes a problem that many of them had. *Page 378.*

10.9 These concepts are best associated with Karen Horney. *Page 378.*

10.10 This may appear to be a picky, detailed item, but it seems to me that you ought to be able to form at least one good association with each of the theorists in this chapter (and note that Spearman is not even in this chapter). The best association here is Adler. *Page 378.*

10.11 The psychologists listed here would say that forces outside the organism—in the environment, not in the person—should be used to explain behaviors. *Page 378.*

10.12 Phenomenology has to do with perception. Here the issue is the perception of one's self and the perception of others. Here again we have the point that what is perceived is what matters. *Page 378.*

10.13 To be fully functioning is to strive, at least, to reach what Maslow called self-actualization—as in the cliché: To be the best that one can be. *Page 378.*

10.14 Rogers's form of psychotherapy was quite different, of course, but Rogers developed a very popular form of psychotherapy. *Page 378.*

10.15 Personality traits are dimensions of description and have most often been determined or identified by factor analyzing test scores of many subjects to see which characteristics are intercorrelated. *Page 379.*

10.16 Doing a factor analysis is largely a matter of computing several correlations, looking for traits that cluster together to form a "factor." *Page 379.*

10.17 By definition, personality trait theories are going to tell us how to measure the trait that is being described, perhaps even providing the test that operationally defines each trait. This is a major advantage, which makes the first alternative the best choice here. *Page 379.*

10.18 The Big Five are five personality traits (or clusters of traits, perhaps). What makes these five remarkable is the extent of consensus about their universality. *Page 379.*

10.19 Virtually all personality theories, including the Big Five, include intelligence (or something very much like it) as an important aspect of one's personality. *Page 379.*

Topic 10B Personality Assessment

10.20 Actually, most interviews are quite unreliable unless they are conducted by trained interviewers who use highly structured interviews. *Page 379.*

10.21 What makes the MMPI–2, for example, a criterion-referenced test is that each item tends to be answered differently by people from different (criterion) groups. *Page 379.*

10.22 On an intelligence test I want you to try to do your best, to put your best foot forward, while on a personality assessment technique, I want you to act normally and give me your most characteristic responses. *Page 379.*

10.23 They are both commonly used projective techniques. *Page 379.*

CHAPTER 11
Topic 11A Stress, Stressors, and How to Cope

11.1 This is a good definition of a stressor—not stress, please note. *Page 405.*

11.2 By definition, frustration is the blocking or thwarting of goal-directed behaviors, the assumption being that all behavior is goal-directed. *Page 405.*

11.3 The first alternative is a good example of frustration—environmental frustration at that. *Page 405.*

11.4 I think we can assume that Bob's inability to qualify for the tournament is a reflection of his own poor golf game, which makes this an example of personal frustration. *Page 405.*

11.5 I suppose we could argue about this one because I do not have any quality data to support my contention that, as adults, we tend to "keep our options open," and thus less frequently get trapped in simple approach-avoidance conflicts. *Page 405.*

11.6 I think that most of us will agree that we're not going to feel too sorry for Scott, momentarily stuck with an approach-approach conflict. *Page 405.*

11.7 It is true that some motivational conflicts cause much less stress than do others, but by definition, conflicts are stressors and are stressful all of the time (i.e., if there's no stress, there's no conflict). *Page 405.*

11.8 The basic issue with motivational conflicts is the difficulty of choices or decisions that have to be made. *Page 405.*

11.9 Lazarus is one who would have us focus our attention on the small, nagging hassles of life as the real sources of our stress. *Page 405.*

11.10 This is a long one (and somewhat self-disclosing), but what we have here is someone who is experiencing frustration because of some personal reason, hence, personal frustration. *Page 405.*

11.11 This sounds awfully depressing, but needn't be—even though it is essentially true. *Page 405.*

11.12 Learning—bringing about a relatively permanent change—is an adaptive response to the stressors in our lives. *Page 405.*

11.13 Here's an attitude destined to get one in trouble. A person is setting himself or herself up for considerable grief if he or she believes that it is possible to avoid stress altogether. *Page 405.*

11.14 Each of these may—in some circumstances—be a bit helpful, but fixating, just doing the same thing over and over again, obviously doesn't work and is inefficient. *Page 405.*

11.15 Yes, it does. It's wrong, but that's what it claims. *Page 405.*

11.16 All of these are recommended procedures for someone experiencing stress, but only the first can be categorized as a problem-focused strategy. *Page 406.*

11.17 Hardly. There are enormous individual differences here. *Page 406.*

11.18 Biofeedback is a mechanism of learning to control physiological processes through processes derived from basic operant conditioning. *Page 406.*

11.19 Not only is this false, we might argue that the opposite is true. *Page 406.*

Topic 11B Health Psychology

11.20 By definition, health psychologists are involved in the management and prevention of physical illness and disease—whether psychological disorders are involved or not. *Page 406.*

11.21 Perhaps because it is so deadly, there is a lot of concern about coronary heart disease (CHD), and it is one set of physical disorders that is reasonably well correlated with personality variables. *Page 406.*

11.22 High cholesterol is a physical measure, not a psychological one as required to be part of TABP. *Page 406.*

11.23 Type A personality is often (incorrectly) associated with someone who strives for perfection in all he or she does, but this is *not* one of the active ingredients of the pattern. *Page 406.*

11.24 Surely each of these would be helpful, but none would be as significant as to get everyone to stop smoking. *Page 406.*

11.25 Here we have some trivial statistics again, but these are so impressive! The best answer is that nearly three quarters (about 70%) of the most common causes of death in the United States are determined largely by behavioral causes. *Page 406.*

11.26 The statement about secondhand smoke, we know now, is absolutely false. *Page 406.*

11.27 This statement is, sadly, true. *Page 406.*

CHAPTER 12
Topic 12A Defining and Classifying Psychological Disorders

12.1 Granted, it's only an estimate, and granted it is probably a bit too conservative, but of these choices, the best would be to say that approximately 20 percent of the population has a psychological disorder. *Page 442.*

12.2 Yes, some of the reactions of persons with psychological disorders may be thought of as strange and bizarre, but these terms are not in the definition of abnormality. *Page 442.*

12.3 One of the sad realities of mental disorders is that in virtually every case the person with a disorder is (or at one time was) aware of the fact that something is not right. The other alternatives are clearly false. *Page 442.*

12.4 There are several problems with schemes of labeling and classifying disorders, but each of those schemes is certainly based on some logical and sensible rationale for doing so. *Page 442.*

12.5 Insanity is a term that has been around for a very long time in many different contexts. As it is used today, however, it is a legal term, not a psychological one. *Page 442.*

Topic 12B A Sampling of Psychological Disorders

12.6 By definition all disorders are unpleasant and distressing, but in most cases phobias are easily treated and have a positive prognosis. *Page 442.*

12.7 The most common phobias include some irrational fear of some sort of animal. The most commonly *treated* phobia is agoraphobia. *Page 442.*

12.8 The anxiety in panic disorder is acute—of short duration, but intense. The anxiety of generalized anxiety disorder is chronic—of long duration. *Page 442.*

12.9 This would be a definitional symptom of obsessive-compulsive disorder. *Page 442.*

12.10 Soma means "body"; hence, somatoform disorders involve some sort of bodily symptom or complaint. *Page 442.*

12.11 No, these symptoms are better associated with conversion disorder, although it is true that hypochondriasis involves bodily complaints. *Page 442.*

12.12 Multiple personality disorder (now dissociative identity disorder) is, in fact, an anxiety disorder, and alternatives *a, b,* and *d* are clearly false statements. *Page 442.*

12.13 Fugue states usually are associated with amnesia, generally psychogenic amnesia. *Page 443.*

12.14 This one is a bit picky, but I think it would be useful to have at least one good solid association for each of the personality disorders. These symptoms are typical of the histrionic personality. *Page 443.*

12.15 This example provides a good description of the symptoms of generalized anxiety disorder. *Page 443.*

12.16 No, they're not. They're classified as personality disorders, an altogether different category. *Page 443.*

12.17 This item goes back to Chapter 1, where we first identified affect as dealing with mood and emotion. *Page 443.*

12.18 This one isn't even close, and the answer is depression. Do note that paranoia isn't even a mood disorder. *Page 443.*

12.19 As is the case for depression, episodes of mania tend to reoccur. That is, we seldom find an isolated case of mania. *Page 443.*

12.20 There is likely a genetic predisposition for depression, and depression (somehow) involves the collection of neurotransmitters called biogenic amines. *Page 443.*

12.21 Sure they can. *Page 443.*

12.22 Actually, alternatives *a, c,* and *d* aren't even true! What makes schizophrenia so disruptive is that it tends to have its impact on all levels of psychological functioning: affect, behavior, and cognition. *Page 443.*

12.23 There may be some anxiety associated with schizophrenia, but the other listed symptoms virtually define the disorder. *Page 443.*

12.24 Schizophrenia does mean "splitting of the mind," but not into separate personalities. The split referred to is a split from reality as the rest of us experience it. *Page 443.*

12.25 The gradual development of symptoms defines the variety of schizophrenia we call process schizophrenia. *Page 443.*

12.26 A negative symptom is a deficit—something missing that used to be there. A positive symptom is something new, such as delusions or hallucinations, added to the person's response repertoire. *Page 443.*

12.27 That schizophrenia runs in families is an assertion with which most psychologists would agree. *Page 443.*

12.28 Here's a fact we often overlook as we focus so on the negativity of this disorder. In fact, about half of those with the diagnosis recover for periods of time when they are relatively symptom-free, although the symptoms often do return. Only about one quarter of them are chronic and essentially beyond cure by current means. *Page 443.*

CHAPTER 13
Topic 13A History and Biomedical Treatments

13.1 Although there certainly were those through history who took a humane approach to the mentally ill, a general acceptance of such treatment is really a twentieth-century phenomenon. *Page 473.*

13.2 How one goes about treating psychological disorders is driven— more than anything else—by how one understands the nature and causes of those disorders, which makes the last statement the best of these choices. *Page 473.*

13.3 Hippocrates believed quite the opposite. His beliefs did not have much of a lasting impact, but he believed psychological disorders had a physical or biological cause. *Page 473.*

13.4 The time is approaching when clinical psychologists may have the "right" to prescribe medication, under certain circumstances—but even then the best choice to answer this question is psychiatrists, who have an M.D. *Page 473.*

13.5 Regardless of the specific procedure involved, all lobotomies sever connections between the controlling cerebral cortex and lower brain centers. *Page 473.*

13.6 None of the first three statements is true. It is true, however, that tens of thousands of these operations were performed in the mid-twentieth century. *Page 473.*

13.7 Lobotomy is a type of psychosurgery, but it is not correct to equate the two as synonyms. There are other types of psychosurgery besides lobotomies. *Page 473.*

13.8 We do have some fairly reasonable hypotheses, but the truth is we still don't know why ECT has the beneficial effects that it does. *Page 473.*

13.9 ECT has been used, and with some success, on virtually all psychological disorders, but it works best, and is most commonly used, as a treatment for depression. *Page 473.*

13.10 Just why this has the effects that it does is not known, but as stated, this statement is true. *Page 473.*

13.11 All chemicals that have an impact on psychological functioning are referred to as psychoactive drugs. *Page 473.*

13.12 I typically don't like to ask questions about specific drugs because there are so many of them and because new drugs are being introduced continuously. However, I do think that it is noteworthy that chlorpromazine was the very first. *Page 473.*

13.13 On an individual basis we may find exceptions, but by and large, antipsychotic medications are more likely to suppress symptoms than cure disorders. *Page 473.*

13.14 In fact, quite the opposite is true, which is one of the benefits of ECT. *Page 473.*

13.15 Antianxiety drugs do just what their name suggests: They alleviate feelings of anxiety. *Page 474.*

Topic 13B The Psychotherapies

13.16 Alternative *c* is a much better statement for a goal of behavioral therapy than for Freudian therapy. *Page 474.*

13.17 This statement provides a reasonable definition for the Freudian concept of transference. *Page 474.*

13.18 Psychoanalysis today has changed significantly from the way Freud practiced it, but what makes it psychoanalysis is the basic assumption that disordered symptoms reflect repressed conflict of some sort. *Page 474.*

13.19 Latent content is the "hidden," symbolic content of dreams, while manifest content is the content as the person describes it. *Page 474.*

13.20 Both types of therapist would agree that patients or clients may not be aware of the true source of their distress, at least at the onset of therapy. *Page 474.*

13.21 Here we have a straightforward definition of empathy. *Page 474.*

13.22 Behavior therapies—in general, again—are aimed at bringing about relatively permanent changes in one's behaviors following principles derived from the learning laboratory. *Page 474.*

13.23 You may argue that any of these techniques *could* be used to treat phobias, but systematic desensitization was designed for that purpose and is the most appropriate. *Page 474.*

13.24 You should know this one without even having read this chapter, if you remember our discussion of Bandura and his theories about modeling from Chapter 6. *Page 474.*

13.25 This one takes a bit of thought. (I like it.) Unconditional positive regard provides reinforcement for virtually everything the client says (or does). Contingency management gives conditional positive regard: One earns reinforcers only for doing what is appropriate. Hence, they are in this way opposite. *Page 474.*

13.26 Cognitive therapy deals with cognitions, in particular, irrational cognitions or thoughts about oneself and the world. *Page 474.*

13.27 Yes, cognitive therapy can be—and has been—used for virtually all disorders, but of these choices, it is most suited for treating depression, often in conjunction with ECT or drug therapy. *Page 474.*

13.28 The key here, of course, is the notion of "for any particular disorder." Although it is true that, in general, psychotherapy techniques are all about equally useful, for particular disorders, some have been found to be more effective than others. *Page 474.*

CHAPTER 14
Topic 14A Social Cognitions: Attitudes, Attributions, and Attractions

14.1 *Feeling* depressed, or feeling anything is more a matter of affect than cognition, while alternatives *a, b,* and *d* all deal with cognitions. *Page 509.*

14.2 This is exactly one of the ways in which attitudes are different from feelings or moods; attitudes require an attitudinal object. *Page 509.*

14.3 As you know, there is some considerable disagreement on how to best characterize the nature of attitudes, but the one thing that all characterizations agree on is that attitudes involve some degree of evaluation. *Page 509.*

14.4 Yes, attitudes often are said to have three components, but those components are the familiar affect, behavior, and cognition. The statement is therefore false. *Page 509.*

14.5 What matters most to an advertiser is the behavioral component. The advertiser wants you to do something, that is, purchase the advertised product or service. *Page 509.*

14.6 If you act contrary to your attitude, I will have established cognitive dissonance. This will motivate you to do something, perhaps change your attitude. *Page 509.*

14.7 It may be helpful to have a communicator who is a celebrity delivering your message, just to get people's attention, but if that celebrity is not perceived as credible, expert, and trustworthy, it will do little good. *Page 509.*

14.8 Actually, alternatives *a, b,* and *d* are just different ways of saying the same thing. I can't imagine how learned vs. inherited factors would fit into a discussion of attribution. *Page 509.*

14.9 These actions provide a good definition of the fundamental attribution error. *Page 509.*

14.10 Social psychologists are interested in each of these, of course, but attribution theory specifically concerns how one goes about explaining the behaviors of oneself and others. *Page 509.*

14.11 Here's a true piece of social psychology that conforms to common sense. *Page 509.*

14.12 One of the appealing aspects of attachment theory is that it views the formation of interpersonal relationships as a lifelong process and suggests that there is evidence that styles remain quite consistent. Statement *b* is the best one. *Page 509.*

14.13 The first statement is, in fact, quite the opposite of reality. If anything, familiarity breeds attraction. (And don't forget: We're talking "in general." Yes, there may be exceptions.) *Page 510.*

14.14 Sexuality is an important component of attraction for some, but compared to the others it would be rated last, or least important. *Page 510.*

14.15 Actually, we probably are going to like someone who likes us now, but didn't originally. *Page 510.*

Topic 14B Social Influence

14.16 The last alternative is the best choice here, because if Asch's subjects knew that the others in the group were confederates of Asch, the project wouldn't have worked at all. *Page 510.*

14.17 This is precisely what Asch found in his experiments. *Page 510.*

14.18 What makes obedience obedience is that it is conformity to the demands or wishes of an authority figure, real or perceived. *Page 510.*

14.19 Of these choices, the only justified conclusion is that the perception of authority is a strong situational force in obedience. *Page 510.*

14.20 He sure was. *Page 510.*

14.21 We must notice, interpret, and take responsibility. It matters little whether the victim knows us or not. *Page 510.*

14.22 Actually, the second statement (alternative *b*) provides a good statement of pluralistic ignorance. *Page 510.*

14.23 Alternatives *b* and *c* are basically irrelevant. Diffusion of responsibility tells us that you are less likely to be helped if you are in a large crowd. *Page 510.*

14.24 Triplett was interested in social facilitation and he demonstrated it by having children reel in a fishing line, either alone or in groups. *Page 510.*

14.25 When we are performing "in public," the main thing that happens is that arousal levels go up, which is okay as long as what we are doing is something simple or well-rehearsed. *Page 510.*

14.26 There is an unsettling, unpleasant side of this statement, which as stated is true. The quality of our performance is—in general—more likely to be hindered by group membership than facilitated by it. *Page 510.*

14.27 Group polarization refers to the phenomenon that the individual attitudes of group members will tend to be strengthened (i.e., polarized) during the course of decision making. *Page 510.*

14.28 The problem with groupthink is not that it is pressure to reach consensus, but that it is pressure to reach consensus, right or wrong. *Page 510.*

CHAPTER 15
Topic 15A Industrial/Organizational Psychology

15.1 I/O psychology may be associated with all of these, but it is *best* thought of as a field of applied psychology. *Page 539.*

15.2 Any one of the first three statements might describe actions you would like to take, but to get things going, one first does a complete job analysis. *Page 539.*

15.3 Hard criteria are objective and can be measured, while soft criteria are more subjective and call for opinions or judgments of others. *Page 539.*

15.4 By definition, "soft criteria" involve making subjective judgments. *Page 539.*

15.5 Unstructured interviews are notoriously poor in terms of validity as an assessment technique (which is not to say that interviews have no place in the process, particularly if they are structured interviews). *Page 539.*

15.6 Biodata are personal biographical information—exactly the sort of thing asked for on application forms. *Page 539.*

15.7 Definitely. In fact, structured devices of any sort are usually more valid than unstructured ones. *Page 539.*

15.8 The very first thing that must be asked is whether or not any sort of training program is needed in the first place. *Page 539.*

15.9 This is one of those "all of the above" items. Evaluation should be a constant, on-going matter during, after, and well after a training program. *Page 539.*

15.10 Training programs usually are evaluated in terms of specific behavioral goals, which are specified in the program's training objectives. *Page 539.*

15.11 As is the case in virtually all types of training or education, the more the learner, or trainee, is actually involved in hands-on experience, the more effective training will be. *Page 539.*

15.12 More than anything else, this theory is cognitive in its approach. *Page 539.*

15.13 By definition, equity theory deals with the worker's perception of fair treatment compared to other workers at the same level within the organization. *Page 539.*

15.14 This may sound reasonable, but it is, in fact, false. *Page 540.*

15.15 Vroom believed that workers behaved rationally and logically and on that basis constructed a very cognitive model of worker motivation. *Page 540.*

15.16 The only one of these that is correlated (and positively so) is worker age. *Page 540.*

Topic 15B Environmental and Sports Psychology

15.17 These labels for psychological space judgments are listed in order, from smallest to largest. *Page 540.*

15.18 This is a pretty good definition of a primary territory. *Page 540.*

15.19 The main issue here is one of perception—feelings of distress and discomfort that accompany overcrowding—may occur in a small town as easily as in a large city. *Page 540.*

15.20 Indeed, one of the advantages of city life, not one of its stressors, is that there generally tend to be many more resources available to its residents. *Page 540.*

15.21 I'm not quite sure I know what the "melody" of a noise would be, and loudness does matter, but what matters most is the predictability of noise. *Page 540.*

15.22 By definition, they are called neurotoxins. *Page 540.*

15.23 This may appear to be a picky item, but I don't think that it is. The answer is 86°F, not 106°F, where the temperature is so high as to debilitate nearly everyone—it's too hot to riot. *Page 540.*

15.24 No, by definition neurotoxins will indeed have a negative, poisonous effect on behavior and/or emotion. *Page 540.*

15.25 This is a two-parter. First, it's clear that fan support will have more of an effect (either way) in a championship game. Then, the negative effect occurs when the team is on offense, trying to execute a variety of maneuvers that are difficult with high levels of arousal. This is true, by the way, for virtually any team sport. *Page 540.*

15.26 For good reason, the only sport in which a hot hand has been demonstrated (so far) is professional pocket billiards. *Page 540.*

15.27 There is considerable evidence that mental practice and imaging can be beneficial in athletic training. *Page 540.*

GLOSSARY

abnormal maladaptive cognitions, affect, and/or behaviors that are at odds with social or cultural expectations and that result in distress or discomfort (p. 409)

absolute threshold the physical intensity of a stimulus that one can detect 50 percent of the time (p. 127)

accommodation in Piaget's theory, the process of altering or revising an existing schema in light of new information (p. 91)

accommodation in vision, the process in which the shape of the lens is changed by the ciliary muscles (p. 171)

acquisition the process in classical conditioning by which the strength of the CR increases with repeated pairings of the CS and UCS (p. 207)

acquisition the process in operant conditioning in which the rate of a reinforced response increases (p. 219)

action potential the short-lived burst of a change in the difference in electrical charge between the inside and the outside of a neuron when it fires (typically about +40 mV) (p. 54)

actor-observer bias the overuse of internal attributions to explain the behaviors of others and external attributions to explain our own behaviors (p. 485)

adolescence the developmental period begun at puberty and lasting through the teen years (p. 102)

affect mental processes involving one's feelings, mood, or emotional state (p. 17)

ageism discrimination or negative stereotyping formed solely on the basis of age (p. 115)

agoraphobia a phobic fear of open places, of being alone, or of being in public places from which escape might be difficult (p. 418)

algorithm a problem-solving strategy in which all possible solutions are generated and tested and an acceptable solution is guaranteed (p. 282)

alpha activity an EEG pattern associated with quiet relaxation and characterized by slow wave cycles of 8 to 12 per second (p. 181)

amnestic disorders showing an impairment of memory while other cognitive functions remain intact (p. 428)

antianxiety drugs (tranquilizers) chemicals that are effective in reducing the experience of anxiety (p. 454)

antidepressant drugs chemicals that reduce or eliminate the symptoms of depression (p. 453)

antipsychotic drugs chemicals, such as chlorpromazine, that are effective in reducing psychotic symptoms (p. 453)

anxiety a general feeling of tension, apprehension, or dread accompanied by predictable physiological changes (p. 393, p. 415)

aqueous humor watery fluid found in the space between the cornea and the lens that nourishes the front of the eye (p. 135)

arousal one's level of activation or excitement (p. 320)

assimilation the process of adding new material or information to an existing schema (p. 90)

association areas the areas of the frontal, parietal, and temporal lobes in which higher mental processing occurs (p. 72)

atonia muscular immobility, associated with REM sleep, caused by the relaxation of the muscles (p. 185)

attachment a strong, two-way emotional bond, usually between a child and his or her parent or primary caregiver (p. 100)

attitude a relatively stable and general evaluative disposition directed toward some object, consisting of feelings, behaviors, and beliefs (p. 477)

audience inhibition reluctance to intervene and offer assistance in front of others (p. 498)

autonomic nervous system (ANS) those neurons of the PNS that activate the smooth muscles and glands (p. 58)

aversion therapy a technique of behavior therapy in which an aversive stimulus, such as a shock, is paired with an undesired behavior (p. 463)

axon the long, tail-like extension of a neuron that carries an impulse away from the cell body toward the synapse (p. 51)

axon terminals the series of branching end points of an axon where one neuron communicates with the next in a series (p. 52)

babbling speech sounds produced in rhythmic, repetitive patterns (p. 291)

baseline design a method in which participants' performance with an experimental treatment is compared with performance without that treatment (the baseline) (p. 35)

basilar membrane a structure within the cochlea that vibrates and thus stimulates the hair cells of the inner ear (p. 147)

behavior what an organism does; its actions, reaction, and responses (p. 17)

behavior therapy techniques of psychotherapy founded on principles of learning established in the psychological laboratory (p. 461)

behavioral observation the personality assessment technique of drawing conclusions about one's personality based on observations of one's behaviors (p. 368)

behaviorism an approach to psychology emphasizing the overt, observable, measurable behavior of organisms (p. 23)

bipolar disorder a severe mood disorder evidenced by unexplainable swings of mood between the more common depression and mania (p. 430)

blindspot a small region of the retina, containing no photoreceptors, where the optic nerve leaves the eye (p. 136)

brain stem the lowest part of the brain, just above the spinal cord, made up of the medulla and the pons (p. 63)

brightness the psychological experience associated with light's intensity of wave amplitude (p. 131)

British empiricists philosophers (including Locke) who claimed, among other things, that the contents of the mind come from experience (p. 20)

case history an intensive, usually retrospective, detailed study of one (or a few) individual(s) (p. 30)

cell body the largest mass of a neuron, containing the cell's nucleus and may receive neural impulses (p. 51)

central nervous system (CNS) those neurons found in the brain and spinal cord (p. 58)

central tendency a measure of the middle, or average, score in a set of data (p. 545)

cerebellum a spherical structure at the lower rear of the brain involved in the smoothing and coordination of bodily movements (p. 64)

cerebral cortex (or cerebrum) the large, convoluted outer covering of the brain that is the seat of cognitive functioning and voluntary action (p. 68)

chemical ions electrically charged (either + or −) chemical particles (p. 53)

childhood the period of human development between birth and puberty (the onset of adolescence) (p. 85)

chunk a somewhat imprecise concept referring to a meaningful unit of information as represented in memory (p. 246)

ciliary muscles small muscles attached to the lens that control its shape and focusing ability (p. 135)

classical conditioning learning in which an originally neutral stimulus comes to elicit a new response after having been paired with a stimulus that reflexively elicits that same response (p. 204)

client-centered therapy the humanistic psychotherapy associated with Rogers, aimed at helping the client grow and change from within (p. 460)

closure the Gestalt principle of organization of perceiving incomplete figures as whole and complete (p. 167)

cochlea part of the inner ear where sound waves become neural impulses (p. 146)

cognitions the mental processes that include knowing, perceiving, thinking, and remembering (p. 17)

cognitive dissonance a motivating discomfort or tension caused by a lack of balance or consonance among one's cognitions (p. 480)

cognitive map a mental representation of the learning situation or physical environment (p. 230)

cognitive restructuring therapy a form of cognitive therapy, associated with Beck, in which patients are led to overcome negative self-images and pessimistic views of the future (p. 466)

collectivism in cross-cultural psychology, the tendency to set goals and make decisions based on a concern for the group and the common good (p. 96)

common fate the Gestalt principle of organization in which we group together all the elements of a scene that move together in the same direction at the same speed (p. 167)

comorbidity the extent to which persons evidence symptoms of two or more disorders at the same time (p. 416)

compulsions constantly intruding, stereotyped, and essentially involuntary acts or behaviors (p. 419)

conception the moment when the father's sperm cell unites with the mother's ovum to produce a zygote (p. 80)

concrete operations stage in Piaget's theory, from age 7 years to 12 years, when concepts can be manipulated, but not in an abstract fashion (p. 93)

conditioned response (CR) in classical conditioning, the learned response (e.g., salivation) evoked by the CS after conditioning (p. 206)

conditioned stimulus (CS) in classical conditioning, an originally neutral stimulus (e.g., a tone) that, when paired with a UCS, comes to evoke a new response (a CR) (p. 206)

cones photosensitive cells of the retina that operate best at high levels of illumination and are responsible for color vision (p. 135)

conflict a stressor in which some goals can be satisfied only at the expense of other goals (p. 383)

conformity the changing of one's behavior under perceived pressure, so that it is consistent with the behavior of others (p. 490)

consciousness the awareness or perception of the environment and of one's own mental processes (p. 161)

conservation in Piaget's theory, an appreciation that changing the physical properties of an object does not necessarily change its essence (p. 93)

contingency contracting establishing a token economy of secondary reinforcers to reward appropriate behaviors (p. 464)

contingency management bringing about changes in one's behaviors by controlling rewards and punishments (p. 463)

continuity (also good continuation) the Gestalt principle of organization that a stimulus or a movement will be perceived as continuing in the same direction or fashion as it started (p. 166)

continuous reinforcement schedule (CRF) a reinforcement schedule in which each and every appropriate response is followed by a reinforcer (p. 222)

contrast the extent to which a stimulus is in some physical way different from other surrounding stimuli (p. 162)

control group participants in an experiment who do not receive any experimental treatment or manipulation (p. 37)

convergence the eyes moving toward each other as we focus on objects up close (p. 170)

convergent thinking the reduction or focusing of many different ideas into one possible problem solution (p. 285)

conversion disorder the display of a severe physical disorder for which there is no medical explanation; often accompanied by an apparent lack of concern on the part of the patient (p. 423)

cornea the outermost structure of the eye, which protects the eye and begins to focus light waves (p. 134)

corpus callosum a network of nerve fibers that interconnect the two hemispheres of the cerebrum (p. 73)

correlation a statistical technique used to determine the nature and extent of the relationship between two measured responses (p. 31)

correlation coefficient a number that indiciates the nature (+ or −) and the strength (0 to 1) of the relationship between measured responses (p. 32)

cross-laterality the process of nerve fibers crossing over the brain stem so that the left side of the body sends impulses to and receives impulses from the right side of the brain, and vice versa (p. 64)

crowding the subjective feeling of discomfort caused by a sense of lack of space (p. 530)

dark adaptation the process by which our eyes become more sensitive to light as we spend time in the dark (p. 130)

death instincts (thanatos) inborn impulses, proposed by Freud, that compel one toward destruction, including aggression and hostility (p. 353)

debrief to fully inform a subject about the intent and/or hypotheses of one's research once data have been collected. (p. 39)

decibel scale a scale of experience of loudness in which 0 represents the absolute threshold and 140 is sensed as pain (p. 143)

defense mechanisms unconsciously applied techniques that protect the self (ego) from feelings of anxiety (p. 354)

delirium a clouded state of consciousness with a lessening of cognitive awareness and attention (p. 428)

delusions false beliefs; ideas that are firmly held regardless of what others say or do (p. 432)

dementia a loss of intellectual abilities; memory is poor and deteriorates; impulse control and judgment adversely affected (p. 428)

dendrites branch-like extensions from a neuron's cell body where most neural impulses are received (p. 51)

denial a mechanism in which a person simply refuses to acknowledge or accept the realities of an anxiety-producing situation (p. 355)

dependent variables responses measured in an experiment whose values are hypothesized to depend upon manipulations of the independent variable (p. 34)

depressants drugs (e.g., alcohol, opiates, heroin, and barbiturates) that slow or reduce nervous system activity (p. 191)

diagnosis the act of recognizing a disorder on the basis of the presence of particular symptoms (p. 410)

difference threshold the minimal difference in some stimulus attribute, such as intensity, that one can detect 50 percent of the time (p. 128)

diffusion of responsibility the tendency to allow others to share in the obligation to intervene (p. 500)

discrimination the process in classical conditioning in which one CS is paired with the UCS and other stimuli are not (p. 208)

displacement directing one's motives or behaviors (usually aggressive) at a substitute person or object rather than expressing them directly. (p. 355)

dissociative amnesia a psychologically caused inability to recall important personal information (p. 424)

dissociative disorders disorders in which the person tries in some way to flee or escape from an aspect of personality or experience that is the source of distress (p. 423)

dissociative fugue a condition of amnesia accompanied by unexplained travel or change of location (p. 424)

dissociative identity disorder the existence within one individual of two or more personalities, each of which is dominant at a particular time (p. 424)

divergent thinking the creation of many ideas or potential problem solutions from one idea (p. 285)

dopamine hypothesis the point of view that schizophrenia results from unusually high levels of the neurotransmitter dopamine in the brain (p. 437)

Down syndrome a condition of many symptoms, including mental retardation, caused by an extra (47th) chromosome (p. 306)

drive a state of tension resulting from a need that arouses and directs an organism's behavior (p. 316)

drug abuse a condition defined by lack of control, disruption of interpersonal relationships, difficulties at work, and a history of maladaptive drug use for at least one month (p. 189)

DSM-IV a publication of the American Psychiatric Association that lists, organizes, and describes psychological disorders (p. 411)

dysthymia a reasonably mild, though chronic disorder of depression associated with low energy and low self-esteem (p. 430)

eardrum the outermost membrane of the ear; it is set in motion by the vibrations of a sound and transmits vibrations to the ossicles (p. 146)

ego the aspect of personality that encompasses the sense of "self"—in contact with the real world; operates on the reality principle (p. 354)

elaborative rehearsal a mechanism for processing information into LTM that involves the meaningful manipulation of the information to be remembered (p. 251)

electroconvulsive therapy (ECT) a treatment, usually for the symptoms of severe depression, in which an electric current passed through a patient's head causes a seizure and loss of consciousness (p. 451)

electroencephalograph (EEG) an instrument used to measure and record the overall electrical activity of the brain (p. 181)

electromyograph (EMG) an instrument used to measure and record muscle tension or relaxation (p. 181)

emotion a reaction involving subjective feeling, physiological response, cognitive interpretation, and behavioral expression (p. 339)

empathic able to understand and share the essence of another's feelings, or to view from another's perspective (p. 460)

encoding the active process of representing information and putting it into memory (p. 241)

encoding specificity principle the hypothesis that how we retrieve information depends on how it was encoded, and that retrieval is enhanced to the extent retrieval cues match encoding cues (p. 257)

endocrine system a network of glands that secrete hormones directly into the bloodstream (p. 59)

environmental psychology the field of applied psychology that studies the effect of the general environment on organisms within it (p. 524)

episodic memory in LTM, the storage of life events and experiences (p. 252)

equity theory the view that workers are motivated to match their inputs and outcomes with those of fellow workers in similar positions (p. 520)

etiology the source or cause; in this context, of psychological disorders (p. 411)

expectancy theory the view that workers make logical choices to do what they believe will result in their attaining outcomes of highest value (p. 520)

experiment a series of operations used to investigate relationships between manipulated events (independent variables) and measured events (dependent variables), while other events (extraneous variables) are controlled or eliminated (p. 34)

experimental group participants in an experiment who receive a treatment or manipulation—there may be more than one in an experiment (p. 37)

external attribution an explanation of behavior in terms of something outside the person; a situational attribution (p. 483)

extinction the process in classical conditioning by which the strength of the CR decreases with repeated presentations of the CS alone (without the UCS) (p. 207)

extinction the process in operant conditioning in which the rate of a response decreases as reinforcers are withheld (p. 219)

extraneous variables factors in an experiment that need to be minimized or eliminated so as not to affect the relation between the independent and the dependent variable (p. 34)

family therapy a variety of group therapy focusing on the roles, interdependence, and communication skills of family members (p. 467)

fantasy engaging in escape from anxiety through imagination and daydreaming (p. 355)

fetal alcohol syndrome a cluster of symptoms (e.g., low birth weight, poor muscle tone, intellectual retardation), associated with a child born to a mother who was a heavy drinker of alcohol during pregnancy (p. 84)

figure-ground relationship the Gestalt psychology principle that stimuli are selected and perceived as figures against a ground or background (p. 165)

flashbulb memories particularly clear and vivid memories—usually of emotional experiences—that are easily retrieved but not necessarily accurate in all details (p. 259)

flooding an in vivo technique of behavior therapy in which the client is placed in the situation that most arouses a phobic reaction and is prohibited from escaping (p. 463)

formal operations stage in Piaget's theory, ages older than 12 years, when one can generate and test abstract hypotheses, and think as an adult where thinking follows rules (p. 93)

fovea the region at the center of the retina, comprised solely of cones, where acuity is best in daylight (p. 163)

free association the procedure in psychoanalysis in which the patient is to express whatever comes to mind without editing responses (p. 458)

frequency distribution an ordered listing of all *X*-values, indicating the frequency with which each occurs (p. 543)

frustration a stressor; the blocking or thwarting of goal-directed behavior (p. 382)

frustration-aggression hypothesis the view (now discredited) that all aggression stems from frustration (p. 393)

functional fixedness the phenomenon in which one is unable to see a new use or function for an object because of experience using the object in some other function (p. 284)

functionalism an early approach to psychology emphasizing the scientific study of how the mind and consciousness help an organism adapt to its environment (p. 22)

fundamental attribution error the tendency to overuse internal attributions when explaining behavior (p. 484)

g on an intelligence test, a measure of one's overall, general intellectual abilities, commonly thought of as IQ (p. 297)

general adaptation syndrome (GAS) Selye's description of the physiological reactions to stressors which includes the three stages of alarm, resistance, and exhaustion (p. 388)

generalization the phenomenon in operant conditioning in which a response that was reinforced in the presence of one stimulus appears in response to other similar stimuli (p. 208)

generalized anxiety disorder persistent, chronic, and distressingly high levels of unattributable anxiety (p. 416)

gestalt whole, totality, configuration; where the whole (gestalt) is seen as more than the sum of its parts (p. 165)

Gestalt psychology an approach to psychology that focuses on perception, particularly how we select and organize information from the environment (p. 26)

group polarization the tendency for members of a group to give more extreme judgments following a discussion than they gave initially (p. 504)

groupthink a style of thinking of cohesive groups concerned with maintaining agreement to the extent that independent ideas are discouraged (p. 504)

habituation in classical conditioning, a simple form of learning in which an organism comes to ignore a stimulus of no consequence (p. 205)

hair cells the receptor cells for hearing, located in the cochlea, stimulated by the vibrating basilar membrane; they send neural impulses to the temporal lobe of the brain (p. 147)

hallucinations false perceptions; perceiving that which is not there (p. 432)

hallucinogens drugs (e.g., LSD) whose major effect is the alteration of perceptual experience and mood (p. 193)

health psychology the field of applied psychology that studies psychological factors affecting physical health and illness (p. 395)

hertz (Hz) the standard measure of sound wave frequency that is the number of wave cycles per second (p. 144)

heuristic a problem solving strategy in which hypotheses about problem solutions are generated and tested in a time-saving and systematic way but which does not guarantee an acceptable solution (p. 282)

histogram a bar graph; a graphical representation of a frequency distribution (p. 544)

holophrastic speech the use of one word to communicate a number of different meanings (p. 291)

homeostasis a state of balance or equilibrium among internal, physiological conditions (p. 320)

homosexuals persons who are attracted to and sexually aroused by members of their own sex (p. 331)

hue the psychological experience associated with a light's wavelength (p. 131)

humanistic psychology an approach to psychology emphasizing the person or self as a central matter of concern (p. 25)

hypnosis an altered state of consciousness characterized by an increase in suggestibility, attention, and imagination (p. 186)

hypochondriasis a mental disorder involving the unrealistic fear of developing a serious disease or illness (p. 422)

hypothalamus a small structure near the limbic system in the center of the brain, associated with feeding, drinking, temperature regulation, sex, and aggression (p. 67 p. 324,)

hypothesis a tentative explanation of a phenomenon that can be tested and then either supported or rejected (p. 15)

id the instinctive aspect of personality that seeks immediate gratification of impulses; operates on the pleasure principle (p. 354)

idealistic principle the force that governs the superego—opposed to the id, it seeks adherence to standards of ethics and morality (p. 354)

identity crisis the struggle to define and integrate one's sense of self and what one's attitudes, beliefs, and values should be ageism discrimination or negative stereotyping formed solely on the basis of age (p. 105)

illusion a perception that is at odds with (different from) what we know as physical reality (p. 175)

incentives external stimuli that an organism may be motivated to approach or avoid (p. 319)

independent variables events in an experiment that are manipulated by the experimenter that are hypothesized to produce changes in responses (p. 34)

individualism in cross-cultural psychology, the tendency to set goals and make decisions based on a concern for one's self or the individual (p. 96)

inferential statistics statistical tests of the significance of the results from experimental or correlational studies (p. 550)

insanity a legal term involving judgments of diminished capacity and the inability to tell right from wrong (p. 413)

instincts unlearned, complex patterns of behavior that occur in the presence of particular stimuli (p. 316)

intelligence the capacity to understand the world and the resourcefulness to cope with its challenges; that which an intelligence test measures (p. 294)

interactive dualism Descartes's position that a separate body and mind influence each other and are thus knowable (p. 19)

intermittent reinforcement schedules reinforcement schedules in which appropriate responses are not reinforced every time they occur (p. 223)

internal attribution an explanation of behavior in terms of something (a trait) within the person; a dispositional attribution (p. 483)

interneurons neurons located within the spinal cord or brain (p. 61)

interview the personality assessment technique involving an interchange between an interviewer and a subject to gain personal information about the subject (p. 370)

IQ literally, intelligence quotient: the result of dividing one's mental age by one's chronological age, and multiplying the dividend by 100 (p. 298)

iris the colored structure of the eye that reflexively opens or constricts the pupil (p. 134)

job analysis a complete and specific description of a job including the qualities required to do it well (p. 513)

job satisfaction an attitude; a collection of positive feelings about one's job or job experiences (p. 522)

just noticeable difference (j.n.d.) the smallest detectable change in some stimulus attribute, such as intensity (p. 128)

just world hypothesis the belief that the world is just and that people get what they deserve (p. 484)

kinesthetic sense the position sense that tells us the position of different parts of our bodies and what our muscles and joints are doing (p. 154)

language a collection of arbitrary symbols that follow certain rules of combination and that have significance for the language-using community (p. 288)

latent learning hidden learning that is not demonstrated in performance until that performance is reinforced (p. 230)

law of effect (Thorndike's) the observation that responses that lead to "satisfying states of affairs" tend to be repeated, while those that do not are not (p. 217)

learning demonstration of a relatively permanent change in behavior that occurs as the result of practice or experience (p. 203)

lens the structure behind the iris that changes shape to focus visual images in the eye (p. 134)

libido the energy that activates the sexual instincts (p. 353)

life instincts (eros) inborn impulses, proposed by Freud, that compel one toward survival, including hunger, thirst, and sex (p. 353)

light a radiant energy that can be represented in wave form with wavelength between 380 and 760 nanometers (p. 130)

limbic system a collection of structures, including the amygdala and septum (involved in emotionality) and the hippocampus (involved in forming long-term memories) (p. 66)

lobotomy a psychosurgical technique in which the prefrontal lobes of the cerebral cortex are severed from lower brain centers (p. 450)

long-term memory (LTM) a type of memory with virtually unlimited capacity and very long, if not limitless, duration (p. 248)

loudness the psychological experience correlated with the intensity, or amplitude, of a sound wave (p. 143)

maintenance rehearsal a process of rote repetition (re-attending) to keep information in STM (p. 244)

major depression an extreme of mood characterized by intense sadness, feelings of hopelessness, and a loss of pleasure and interest in normal activities (p. 430)

malleus, incus, and stapes (collectively, ossicles) three small bones that transmit and intensify sound vibrations from the eardrum to the oval window (p. 146)

mania an extreme of mood characterized by euphoria, a sense of well-being, and an increase in activity level (p. 430)

matching phenomenon the tendency to select partners whose level of physical attractiveness matches our own (p. 488)

mean a measure of central tendency computed by dividing the sum of all scores by the number of observations; sometimes called the average (p. 546)

meaningfulness the extent to which information evokes associations with information already in memory (p. 260)

median the score above which and below which half the scores in an ordered set fall (p. 547)

medulla an area of the brain stem that monitors breathing and heart rate, and where most cross-laterality occurs (p. 63)

memory the cognitive ability to encode, store, and retrieve information (p. 241)

menarche a female's first menstrual period, often taken as a sure sign of the beginning of adolescence (p. 104)

mental retardation below-average general intellectual functioning which began before the age of 18 and is associated with maladaptive behaviors (p. 305)

mental set a predisposed (set) way to perceive something: an expectation (p. 164)

mere exposure phenomenon the tendency to increase our liking of people and things the more we see of them (p. 488)

method of loci the mnemonic device that mentally places information to be retrieved at a series of familiar locations (loci) (p. 263)

Minnesota Multiplastic Personality Inventory (MMPI–2) a paper-and-pencil inventory of 567 true-false questions used to assess a number of personality dimensions, some of which may indicate the presence of a psychological disorder (p. 371)

mnemonic devices strategies for improving retrieval that take advantage of existing memories in order to organize information and make new material meaningful (p. 261)

mode the most frequently occurring X-values in a set (p. 547)

modeling the acquisition of new responses through the imitation of another who responds appropriately (p. 464)

monochromatic literally one colored; a pure light made up of light waves all of the same wavelength (p. 132)

mood disorders disorders of affect or feeling; usually depression; less frequently mania and depression occurring in cycles (p. 429)

motivation the process of arousing, maintaining, and directing behavior (p. 315)

motor areas the strips at the back of the frontal lobes that control voluntary movement (p. 71)

motor neurons neurons that carry impulses away from the spinal cord or brain (p. 60)

myelin a white, fatty covering found on some axons that serves to insulate and protect them while increasing the speed of impulses (p. 51)

narrative chaining the mnemonic device of relating words together in a story, thus organizing them in a meaningful way (p. 262)

naturalistic observation carefully and systematically watching the behaviors of organisms as they occur naturally—without involvement of the observer (p. 27)

need a lack or shortage of some biological essential resulting from deprivation (p. 316)

need for affiliation the need to be with others and to form relationships and associations (p. 337)

need for power the learned need to be in control of events or persons, usually at another's expense (p. 336)

need to achieve (nAch) the learned need to meet or exceed some standard of excellence in performance (p. 334)

negative reinforcer a stimulus that increases the rate of a response when that stimulus is removed after the response is made (p. 221)

neo-Freudians personality theorists (including Adler, Jung, and Horney) who kept many basic psychoanalytic principles, but differed from a strict Freudian view, adding new concepts of their own (p. 357)

neonate the newborn, from birth to age 2 weeks (p. 85)

neural impulse a sudden and reversible change in the electrical charges within and outside the membrane of a neuron which travels from the dendrite to the axon end of a neuron (p. 53)

neural threshold the minimal level of stimulation needed to get a neuron to fire (p. 55)

neuron a nerve cell, the basic building block of the nervous system that transmits neural impulses (p. 50)

neurotoxins chemicals (poisons) that affect psychological processes through the nervous system (p. 533)

neurotransmitters complex chemical molecules released at the synapse that either excite or inhibit neural impulse transmission (p. 55)

noise any intrusive, unwanted, or excessive experience of sound (p. 531)

normal curve a commonly found symmetrical, bell-shaped frequency distribution (p. 552)

norms in the context of psychological testing, results of a test taken by a large group of persons whose scores can be used to make comparisons or give meaning to new scores (p. 296)

observer bias the problem that occurs when the researcher's own motives, expectations, and past experiences interfere with the objectivity of observations (p. 27)

obsessions ideas or thoughts that involuntarily and persistently intrude into one's awareness (p. 419)

obsessive-compulsive disorder (OCD) an anxiety disorder characterized by a pattern of recurrent obsessions and compulsions (p. 419)

operant conditioning the form of learning that involves changing the rate of a response on the basis of the consequences that result from that response (p. 216)

operational definition a definition of a concept given in terms of the methods or procedures used to measure or create that concept (p. 18)

optic nerve a fiber composed of many neurons, which leaves the eye and carries impulses to the occipital lobe of the brain (p. 135)

orienting reflex the simple, unlearned response of orienting toward, or attending to, a new or unusual stimulus (p. 205)

overlearning the practice or rehearsal of material over and above what is needed to learn it (p. 265)

overregularization the excessive application of an acquired language rule (e.g., for plurals or past tense) in a situation where it is not appropriate (p. 293)

panic disorder a disorder in which anxiety attacks occur suddenly and unpredictably; there may be periods free from anxiety (p. 416)

parasympathetic division those neurons of the ANS involved in the maintenance of states of calm and relaxation (p. 59)

perception the cognitive process of selecting, organizing, and interpreting those stimuli provided to us by our senses (p. 161)

perceptual constancies stable patterns of perceiving the world that help us organize and interpret stimulus inputs (p. 174)

performance criteria specific behaviors or characteristics that a person should have in order to do a job as well as possible (p. 514)

peripheral nervous system (PNS) those neurons not found in the brain or spinal cord but in the peripheral organs of the body (p. 58)

personal space the mobile "bubble" of space around you reserved for intimate relationships into which others may enter only by invitation (p. 526)

personality those affects, cognitions, and behaviors that can be said to characterize an individual in several situations and over time (p. 351)

personality disorders enduring patterns of perceiving, relating to, and thinking about the environment and one's self that are inflexible and maladaptive (p. 425)

phenomenology the study of events as they are experienced (p. 41)

phenylketonuria (PKU) a genetically caused disorder that produces mental retardation and that is now detectable and preventable (p. 307)

pheromones chemicals that produce an odor used as a method of communication between organisms (p. 150)

phobic disorder an intense, irrational fear that leads a person to avoid the feared object, activity, or situation (p. 416)

pinna the outer ear, which collects and funnels sound waves into the auditory canal toward the eardrum (p. 146)

pitch the psychological experience that corresponds to sound wave frequency and gives rise to high (treble) or low (bass) sounds (p. 144)

pleasure principle the impulse of the id to seek immediate gratification to reduce tensions (p. 354)

pluralistic ignorance a condition in which the inaction of others leads each individual in a group to interpret a situation as a nonemergency, thus leading to general inactivity (p. 499)

pons a brain stem structure forming a bridge between the brain and the spinal cord (p. 64)

population density a quantitative measure of the number of persons (or animals) per unit of area (p. 530)

positive reinforcer a stimulus that increases the rate of a response when it is presented after the response is made (p. 220)

posttraumatic stress disorder (PTSD) an anxiety disorder in which disruptive recollections, distressing dreams, flashbacks, and felt anxiety occur well after the experience of a traumatic event (p. 421)

pragmatics the study of how linguistic events and their interpretation are related to the context in which they occur (p. 289)

prenatal period the period of development from conception to birth (p. 81)

preoperational stage in Piaget's theory, from age 2 years to 6 years, when a child begins to develop symbolic representations but cannot manipulate them; also characterized by egocentricity (p. 91)

primary reinforcer a stimulus (usually biologically or physiologically based) that increases the rate of a response with no previous experience required (p. 221)

proactive interference the inhibition of retrieval of recently learned material caused by material learned earlier (p. 270)

problem a situation in which there is a discrepancy between one's current state and one's desired or goal state, with no clear way of getting from one to the other (p. 279)

procedural memory in LTM, the storage of stimulus-response associations and skilled patterns of responses (p. 251)

process schizophrenia schizophrenia in which the onset of the symptoms is comparatively slow and gradual (p. 434)

prognosis the prediction of the future course of an illness or disorder (p. 418)

projection seeing in others the same motives or traits that would make one anxious if seen in oneself (p. 355)

projective technique a personality assessment technique requiring a subject to respond to ambiguous stimuli, thus projecting his or her self into the responses (p. 373)

proximity (also contiguity) the Gestalt principle of organization that stimuli will be perceived as belonging together if they occur together in space or time (p. 166)

psychoactive drug a chemical that produces an affect on psychological processes and consciousness (p. 188)

psychoanalysis the form of psychotherapy associated with Freud, aimed at helping the patient gain insight into unconscious conflicts (p. 445)

psychoanalytic approach the approach to personality associated with Freud and his followers that relies on instincts and the unconscious as explanatory concepts (p. 352)

psycholinguistics a hybrid scientific discipline of psychologists and linguists who study all aspects of language (p. 288)

psychological test an objective, standardized measure of a sample of behavior (p. 295)

psychology the scientific study of behavior and mental processes science an organized body of knowledge gained through application of scientific methods (p. 15)

psychophysics the study of the relationship between the physical attributes of stimuli and the phychological experiences they produce (p. 127)

psychosurgery a surgical procedure designed to affect one's psychological or behavioral reactions (p. 450)

puberty the stage of physical development at which one becomes capable of sexual reproduction (p. 104)

punishment the administration of a punisher, which is a stimulus that decreases the rate or probability of a response that precedes it (p. 225)

pupil the opening in the iris that changes size in relation to the amount of light available and emotional factors (p. 134)

random assignment the selection of members of a population in such away that each has an equal opportunity to be assigned to any group (p. 37)

range the difference between the highest and lowest scores in a distribution (p. 548)

rational-emotive therapy (RET) a form of cognitive therapy, associated with Ellis, aimed at changing the subject's irrational beliefs or maladaptive cognitions (p. 465)

rationalization making up excuses for one's behaviors rather than facing the (anxiety-producing) real reasons for them (p. 355)

reactive schizophrenia schizophrenia in which the onset of the symptoms is comparatively sudden (p. 434)

reality principle the force that governs the ego, arbitrating between the demands of the id, the superego, and the real world (p. 354)

recall an explicit measure of retrieval in which an individual is given the fewest possible cues to retrieval (p. 255)

recognition an explicit measure of retrieval in which an individual is required to identify as familiar material previously learned (p. 255)

reflex an unlearned automatic response that occurs in the presence of specific stimuli (p. 204)

regression a return to earlier, more primitive, even childish levels of behavior that were once effective (p. 355)

reinforcement a process that increases the rate or probability of the response that it follows (p. 220)

reinforcers stimuli that increase the rate or probability of the response they follow (p. 220)

relearning an implicit measure of memory in which one notes an improvement in performance when material is learned for a second time (p. 256)

reliability consistency or dependability; in testing, consistency of test scores (p. 295)

REM sleep rapid eye movement sleep during which vivid dreaming occurs, as do heightened levels of physiological functioning (p. 183)

repression (motivated forgetting)—"forgetting" about some anxiety-producing event or experience by forcing the memory of the event into one's unconscious (p. 355)

resistance in psychoanalysis, the inability or unwillingness to freely discuss some aspect of one's life (p. 458)

resting potential the difference in electrical charge between the inside of a neuron and the outside when it is at rest (typically about –70mV) (p. 53)

reticular activating system (RAS) a network of nerve fibers extending from the brain stem to the cerebrum that is involved in maintaining levels of arousal (p. 66)

retina layers of cells at the back of the eye that contain the photosensitive rod and cone cells (p. 135)

retinal disparity the phenomenon in which each retina receives a different (disparate) view of the same three-dimensional object (p. 169)

retrieval the process of locating, removing, and using information that is stored in memory (p. 241)

retroactive interference the inhibition of retrieval of previously learned material caused by material learned later (p. 269)

rods photosensitive cells of the retina that are most active in low levels of illumination and do not respond differentially to different wavelengths of light (p. 135)

Rorschach inkblot test a projective technique in which the subject is asked to say what he or she sees in a series of inkblots (p. 374)

sample the portion or subset of a larger population chosen for study (p. 30)

saturation the psychological experience associated with the purity of a light wave, where the most saturated lights are monochromatic and the least saturated are white light (p. 133)

schema in Piaget's theory, a system of organized general knowledge, stored in memory, that guides the encoding and retrieval of information (p. 90)

schizophrenia complex psychotic disorders characterized by impairment of cognitive functioning, delusions and hallucinations, social withdrawal, and inappropriate affect (p. 432)

scientific methods a series of systematic approaches to problem solving, including observation, description, control, and replication (p. 15)

secondary drive arousers and directors of behavior that stem from learned, or acquired, needs that are not tied to one's biological survival (p. 317)

secondary reinforcer a stimulus that increases the rate of a response because of having been associated with other reinforcers; also called conditioned, or learned, reinforcer (p. 222)

self-serving bias the tendency to attribute our successes to our own effort and ability and our failures to external, situational factors (p. 484)

semantic memory in LTM, the storage of vocabulary, facts, simple concepts, rules, and the like (p. 251)

sensation the process of receiving information from the environment and changing that input into nervous system activity (p. 126)

sensorimotor stage in Piaget's theory, from birth to age 2 years, when a child learns by sensing and doing (p. 91)

sensory adaptation the process in which our sensory experience tends (in most cases) to decrease or diminish with continued exposure to a stimulus (p. 129)

sensory areas those areas of the cerebral cortex that receive impulses from our sense receptors (p. 69)

sensory memory the type of memory that holds large amounts of information from the senses for very brief periods of time (p. 241)

sensory neurons neurons that carry impulses toward the spinal cord or brain (p. 60)

shaping a procedure of reinforcing successive approximations of a desired response until that desired response is made (p. 218)

short-term memory (STM) a type of memory (also called working memory) with limited capacity (7±2 bits of information) and limited duration (15–20 seconds) (p. 242)

signal detection theory the view that stimulus detection is a matter of decision making, of separating a signal from background noise (p. 129)

similarity the Gestalt principle of organization that stimuli will be perceived together if they share some common characteristic(s) (p. 166)

social facilitation improved performance due to the presence of others (p. 502)

social interference impaired performance due to the presence of others (p. 503)

social learning theory the theory, associated with Bandura, that learning takes place through observation and imitation of others (p. 231)

social loafing the tendency for a person to work less hard when part of a group in which everyone's efforts are pooled (p. 501)

social psychology the scientific study of how others influence the thoughts, feelings, and behaviors of the individual (p. 476)

socioeconomic status (SES) a measure that reflects one's income, educational level, and occupation (p. 385)

somatic nervous system sensory and motor neurons outside the CNS that serve the sense receptors and the skeletal muscles (p. 58)

somatoform disorders psychological disorders that reflect imagined physical or bodily symptoms or complaints (p. 422)

spinal cord a massive collection of nerve fibers within the spinal column that carry impulses to and from the brain and that are involved in some reflex actions (p. 60)

spinal reflexes involuntary responses that involve sensory neurons carrying impulses to the spinal cord, interneurons carrying them within the spinal cord, and motor neurons carrying them to muscles (p. 61)

split-brain procedure a surgical technique of severing the corpus callosum, causing the two hemispheres to operate independently been approved by some committee or board of review. (p. 73)

spontaneous recovery the phenomenon in classical conditioning in which a previously extinquished CR returns after a rest interval (p. 208)

spontaneous recovery the phenomenon in operant conditioning in which a previously extinguished response returns after a rest interval (p. 219)

sports psychology the subfield that attempts to apply principles of psychology to sport and physical activity at all levels of skill development (p. 534)

standard deviation the average difference between the scores in a distribution and their mean (p. 549)

state-dependent memory the notion that retrieval is enhanced to the extent that one's state of mind at retrieval matches one's state of mind at encoding (p. 259)

statistically significant differences differences in measurements that cannot be explained by chance or random factors (p. 551)

stimulants drugs (e.g., caffeine, cocaine, and amphetamines) that increase nervous system activity (p. 189)

storage the process of holding encoded information in memory (p. 241)

strategy in problem solving, a systematic plan for generating possible solutions that can be tested to see if they are correct (p. 282)

stress a complex pattern of reactions to real or perceived threats to one's sense of well-being that motivates adjustment (p. 381)

stressors real or perceived threats to one's sense of well-being; sources of stress (p. 382)

structuralism the school of psychology (associated with Wundt) interested in the elements and structure of the human mind (p. 22)

subjective contours the perception of a contour (a line or plane) that is not there, but is suggested by other (contextual) aspects of a scene (p. 167)

superego the aspect of personality that refers to ethical or moral considerations; operates on the idealistic principle (p. 354)

survey a means of collecting observations from a large number of subjects, usually by interview or questionnaire (p. 30)

sympathetic division those neurons of the ANS involved in states of emotionality (p. 58)

synapse the location where an impulse is relayed from one neuron to another by means of neurotransmitters (p. 55)

synaptic cleft the space between the membrane of an axon terminal and the membrane of the next neuron in a sequence (p. 55)

systematic desensitization the application of classical conditioning procedures to alleviate anxiety in which anxiety-producing stimuli are paired with a state of relaxation (p. 461)

taste buds the receptors for taste located in the tongue (p. 148)

telegraphic speech spoken language consisting of nouns, verbs, adjectives and adverbs, but few "function words" (p. 292)

territoriality the setting off and marking of a piece of territory (an area) as one's own (p. 527)

thalamus the last sensory relay station; it sends impulses to the appropriate area of the cerebral cortex (p. 67)

Thematic Apperception Test (TAT) a projective personality test requiring a person to tell a series of short stories about a set of ambiguous pictures (p. 334, p. 374)

theory an organized collection of ultimately testable ideas used to explain a particular subject matter (p. 351)

timbre the psychological experience related to wave purity by which we differentiate quality of a tone (p. 145)

trait any distinguishable, relatively enduring way in which one individual differs from others (p. 364)

transducer a mechanism that converts energy from one form to another, as sense receptors do (p. 126)

transference in psychoanalysis, the situation in which the patient comes to feel about the analyst in the same way he or she once felt about some other important person (p. 459)

tremors involuntary trembling, jerky movements (p. 65)

type A behavior pattern (TABP) a collection of behaviors or traits (competitive, achievement-oriented, impatient, easily aroused, often hostile or angry) often associated with coronary heart disease (p. 395)

unconditioned response (UCR) in classical conditioning, a response (e.g., salivation) reliably and reflexively evoked by a stimulus (the UCS) (p. 205)

unconditioned stimulus (UCS) in classical conditioning, a stimulus (e.g., food powder) that reflexively and reliably evokes a response (the UCR) (p. 205)

validity in testing, the extent to which a test measures what it claims to measure (p. 296)

variability the extent of spread or dispersion in a set or distribution of scores (p. 545)

variance the square of the standard deviation (p. 549)

vesicles small containers, concentrated in axon terminals, that hold molecules of neurotransmitter chemicals (p. 55)

vestibular sense the position sense that tells us about balance, where we are in relation to gravity, and acceleration or deceleration (p. 154)

viability the ability to survive without interference or intervention (p. 83)

vicarious reinforcement (or punishment) increasing the rate (reinforcement) or decreasing the rate (punishment) of responses due to observing the consequences of someone else's behaviors (p. 233)

vitreous humor the thick fluid behind the lens of the eye that helps keep the eyeball spherical (p. 135)

wave amplitude a characteristic of wave forms (the height of the wave) that indicates intensity (p. 130)

wavelength the distance between any point in a wave and the corresponding point on th next cycle (p. 131)

white light a light of the lowest possible saturation, containing a mixture of visible wavelengths (p. 133)

white noise a sound composed of a random assortment of wave frequencies from the audible spectrum (p. 145)

zygote the one-celled product of the union of the sperm and ovum at conception (p. 80)

BIBLIOGRAPHY

AARP. (1993). Census Bureau ups 65+ population estimates. *AARP Bulletin, 34,* 2.

Abel, E. L. (1981). Behavioral teratology. *Psychological Bulletin, 90,* 564–581.

Abel, E. L. (1984). *Fetal alcohol syndrome and fetal alcohol effects.* New York: Plenum.

Ackerman, P. L. (1992). Predicting individual differences in complex skill acquisition: Dynamics of ability determinants. *Journal of Applied Psychology, 77,* 598–614.

Ackerman, P. L., & Kanfer, R. (1993). Integrating laboratory and field study for improving selection: Development of a battery for predicting air traffic controller success. *Journal of Applied Psychology, 78,* 413–432.

Adams, G. R. (1977). Physical attractiveness, personality, and social reactions to peer pressure. *Journal of Psychology, 96,* 287–296.

Adams, G. R., & Gullotta, T. (1983). *Adolescent life experiences.* Monterey, CA: Brooks/Cole.

Adams, J. L. (1974). *Conceptual blockbusting.* Stanford, CA: Stanford Alumni Association. Cited in A. L. Glass, K. J. Holyoak, & J. L. Santa (1979). *Cognition.* Reading, MA: Addison-Wesley.

Adams, J. S. (1965). *Inequity in social exchange.* In L. Berkowitz (Ed.), *Advances in experimental social psychology.* New York: Academic Press.

Adams, R. M. (1992). The "hot hand" revisited: Successful basketball shooting as a function of intershot interval. *Perceptual and Motor Skills, 74,* 934.

Adams, R. M. (1993). Momentum in the performance of professional tournament pocket billiards players. *International Journal of Sport Psychology,* in press.

Adelmann, P. K., & Zajonc, R. B. (1989). Facial efference and the experience of emotion. *Annual Review of Psychology, 40,* 249–280.

Adler, J. (1994). Kids Growing Up Scared. *Newsweek,* January 10, pp. 43–49.

Adler, N. E., Boyce, T., Chesney, M. A., Cohen, S., Folkman, S., Kahn, R. L., & Syme, S. L. (1994). Socioeconomic status and health: The challenge of the gradient. *American Psychologist, 49,* 15–24.

Adler, N., & Matthews, K. (1994). Health psychology: Why do some people get sick and some stay well? *Annual Review of Psychology, 45,* 229–259.

Adler, R., & Cohen, N. (1993). Psychoneuroimmunology: Conditioning and stress. *Annual Review of Psychology, 44,* 23–51.

Adler, T. (1989). Cocaine babies face behavior deficits. *APA Monitor, 20,* 14.

Adler, T. (1990a). Does the "new" MMPI beat the "classic"? *APA Monitor, 21,* 18–19.

Aiello, J. R., & Aiello, T. D. (1974). The development of personal space: Proxemic behavior of children 6 through 16. *Human Ecology, 2,* 177–189.

Aiken, L. R. (1984). *Psychological testing and assessment* (4th ed.). Boston: Allyn & Bacon.

Ainsworth, M. D. S. (1979). Infant-mother attachment. *American Psychologist, 34,* 932–937.

Ainsworth, M. D. S. (1989). Attachments beyond infancy. *American Psychologist, 44,* 709–716.

Ajzen, I., & Fishbein, M. (1980). *Understanding attitudes and predicting social behavior.* Englewood Cliffs, NJ: Prentice-Hall.

Alba, J. W., & Hasher, L. (1983). Is memory schematic? *Psychological Bulletin, 93,* 201–231.

Aldwin, C., & Stokals, D. (1988). The effects of environmental change on individuals and groups: Some neglected issues in stress research. *Journal of Environmental Psychology, 8,* 57–75.

Allen, M. G. (1976). Twin studies of affective illness. *Archives of General Psychiatry, 33,* 1476–1478.

Altman, I. (1975). *The environment and social behavior.* Monterey, CA: Brooks/Cole.

Amabile, T. M. (1985). Motivation and creativity. *Journal of Personality and Social Psychology, 48,* 393–399.

American Psychiatric Association. (1987). *Diagnostic and statistical manual of mental disorders* (3rd rev. ed.). Washington, DC: American Psychiatric Association.

American Psychological Association. (1994). The Seville Statement on Violence. *American Psychologist, 49,* 845–846.

Anastasi, A. (1988). *Psychological testing* (6th ed.). New York: Macmillan.

Andersen, B. L., Kiecolt-Glaser, J. K., & Glaser, R. (1994). A biobehavioral model of cancer stress and disease course. *American Psychologist, 49,* 389–404.

Anderson, A. (1982). Neurotoxic follies. *Psychology Today, 16,* 30–42.

Anderson, C. A. (1987). Temperature and aggression: Effects on quarterly, yearly, and city rates of violent and nonviolent crime. *Journal of Personality and Social Psychology, 52,* 1161–1173.

Anderson, C. A. (1989). Temperature and aggression: Ubiquitous effects of heat on occurrence of human violence. *Psychological Bulletin, 106,* 74–96.

Anderson, C. A., & Anderson, D. C. (1984). Ambient temperature and violent crime: Tests of the linear and curvilinear hypotheses. *Journal of Personality and Social Psychology, 46,* 91–97.

Anderson, J. C., Williams, S., McGee, R., & Silva, P. A.

(1987). DSM-III disorders in preadolescent children. *Archives of General Psychiatry, 44,* 69–76.

Anderson, J. R. (1980). *Cognitive psychology and its implications.* San Francisco: Freeman.

Anderson, J. R. (1986). *Knowledge compilation: The general learning mechanism.* In R. Michalski, J. Carbonnell, & T. Mitchell (Eds.), *Machine Learning II.* Palo Alto, CA: Tioga Press.

Anderson, J. R. (1987). Skill acquisition: Compilation of weak-method problem solutions. *Psychological Review, 94,* 192–210.

Andreasen, N. C. (1982). Negative versus positive schizophrenia: Definition and validation. *Archives of General Psychiatry, 39,* 789–794.

Andreasen, N. C., Ehrhardt, J. C., Swayze, V. W., Alliger, R. J., Yuh, W. T. C., Cohen, G., & Ziebell, S. (1990). Magnetic resonance imaging of the brain in schizophrenia. *Archives of General Psychiatry, 47,* 35–44.

Andreasen, N. C., Flaum, M., Swayze, V. W., Tyrrell, G., & Arndt, S. (1990). Positive and negative symptoms in schizophrenia. *Archives of General Psychiatry, 47,* 615–621.

Angoff, W. H. (1988). The nature-nurture debate, aptitudes, and group differences. *American Psychologist, 43,* 713–720.

Anisfeld, M. (1984). *Language development from birth to three.* Hillsdale, NJ: Erlbaum.

Anisman, H., & Zacharko, R. M. (1982). Depression: The predisposing influence of stress. *The Behavioral and Brain Sciences, 5,* 89–137.

APA (1994). *Diagnostic and statistical manual of mental disorders.* (4th ed.). Washington, DC: American Psychiatric Association.

Aronson, E., & Linder, D. (1965). Gain and loss of esteem as determinants of interpersonal attractiveness. *Journal of Personality and Social Psychology, 1,* 156–171.

Aronson, E., Turner, J. A., & Carlsmith, J. M. (1963). Communicator credibility and communication discrepancy as a determinant of opinion change. *Journal of Abnormal and Social Psychology, 67,* 31–36.

Arvey, R. D., & Campion, J. E. (1982). The employee interview: A summary and review of recent research. *Personnel Psychology, 35,* 281–322.

Asch, S. E. (1951). *The effects of group pressure upon the modification and distortion of judgment.* In H. Guetzkow (Ed.), *Groups, leadership, and men.* Pittsburgh: Carnegie Press.

Asch, S. E. (1956). Studies of independence and conformity: I. A minority of one against a unanimous majority. *Psychological Monographs: General and Applied,* 70 (Whole No. 416), 1–70.

Aserinsky, E., & Kleitman, N. (1953). Regularly occurring periods of eye mobility and concomitant phenomena during sleep. *Science,* 118, 273–274.

Ashcraft, M. H. (1994). *Human memory and cognition* (2nd ed.). New York: HarperCollins.

Aslin, R. N., & Smith, L. B. (1988). Perceptual development. *Annual Review of Psychology,* 39, 435–473.

Aspinwall, L. G., & Taylor, S. E. (1992). Modeling cognitive adaptation: A longitudinal investigation of the impact of individual differences and coping on college adjustment and performance. *Journal of Personality and Social Psychology, 63,* 989–1003.

Atkinson, J. W., & Feather, N. T. (1966). *A theory of achievement motivation.* New York: Wiley.

Atkinson, J. W., & Litwin, G. H. (1960). Achievement motive and test anxiety conceived as motive to approach success and motive to avoid failure. *Journal of Abnormal and Social Psychology, 60,* 27–36.

Atkinson, R. C. (1975). Mnemotechnics in second-language learning. *American Psychologist,* 30, 821–828.

Auletta, K. (1984). Children of children. *Parade Magazine,* 17, 4–7.

Axelrod, S., & Apsche, J. (1983). *The effects of punishment on human behavior.* New York: Academic Press.

Azrin, N. H., & Holz, W. C. (1966). *Punishment.* In W. K. Honig (Ed.), *Operant behavior: Areas of research and application.* Englewood Cliffs, NJ: Prentice-Hall.

Azumi, K. & McMillan, C. J. (1976). *Worker sentiment in the Japanese factory: Its organizational determinants.* In L. Austin (Ed.), *Japan: The paradox of progress.* New Haven, CT: Yale University Press.

Babor, T. F., Berglas, S., Mendelson, J. H., Ellingboe, J. & Miller, K. (1983). Alcohol, affect and the disinhibition of behavior. *Psychopharmacology,* 80, 53–60.

Backman, C. W., & Secord, P. F. (1959). The effect of perceived liking on interpersonal attraction. *Human Relations,* 12, 379–384.

Baddeley, A. (1990). *Human memory: Theory and practice.* Boston: Allyn and Bacon.

Baddeley, A. (1992). Working memory. *Science,* 225, 556–559.

Baddeley, A. D. (1982). Domains of recollection. *Psychological Review, 89,* 708–729.

Bagozzi, R. P., & Burnkrant, R. E. (1979). Attitude organization and the attitude-behavior relationship. *Journal of Personality and Social Psychology*, 37, 913–929.

Bahrick, H. P. (1984). Semantic memory content in permastore. *Journal of Experimental Psychology: General*, 113, 1–29.

Bailey, J. M., & Pillard, R. C. (1991). A genetic study of male sexual orientation. *Archives of General Psychiatry*, 48, 1089–1096.

Baldwin, M. W. (1992). Relational schemas and the processing of social information. *Psychological Bulletin*, 112, 461–484.

Baley, S. (1985). The legalities of hiring in the 80s. *Personnel Journal*, 64, 112–115.

Ballenger, J. C. (1989). Toward an integrated model of panic disorder. *American Journal of Orthopsychiatry*, 59, 284–293.

Bandura, A. (1965). Influence of models' reinforcement contingencies on the acquisition of imitative responses. *Journal of Personality and Social Psychology*, 1, 589–595.

Bandura, A. (1974). Behavior theory and the models of man. *American Psychologist*, 29, 859–869.

Bandura, A. (1976). *Modeling theory: Some traditions, trends and disputes*. In W. S. Sahakian (Ed.), *Learning: Systems models, and theories*. Skokie, IL: Rand McNally.

Bandura, A. (1977). *Social learning theory*. Englewood Cliffs, NJ: Prentice-Hall.

Bandura, A. (1982). Self-efficacy mechanism in human agency. *American Psychologist*, 37, 122–147.

Bandura, A., Ross, D., & Ross, S. A. (1963). Imitation of film-mediated aggressive models. *Journal of Abnormal and Social Psychology*, 66, 3–11.

Barber, T. F. X. (1972). *Suggested (hypnotic) behavior: The trace paradigm vs. an alternative paradigm*. In E. Fromm & R. E. Shorr (Eds.), *Hypnosis: Research developments and perspectives*. Chicago: Aldine-Atherton.

Barefoot, J. C., Dahlstrom, W. D., & Williams, R. B. (1983). Hostility, CHD incidence, and total mortality: A 25-year follow-up study of 255 physicians. *Psychosomatic Medicine*, 45, 59–63.

Barinaga, M. (1991). *Is homosexuality biological?* Science, 253, 956–957.

Barker, R. (1968). *Ecological psychology*. Stanford, CA: Stanford University Press.

Baron, R. A. (1977). *Human aggression*. New York: Plenum Press.

Baron, R. A., & Ransberger, V. M. (1978). Ambient temperature and the occurrence of collective violence: The "long hot summer" revisited. *Journal of Personality and Social Psychology*, 36, 351–360.

Barr, H. M., Streissguth, A. P., Darby, B. L., & Sampson, P. D. (1990). Prenatal exposure to alcohol, caffeine, tobacco, and aspirin: Effects on fine and gross motor performance in 4-year-old children. *Developmental Psychology*, 26, 339–348.

Barrett, G. V., & Depinet, R. L. (1991). A reconsideration of testing for competence rather than for intelligence. *American Psychologist*, 46, 1012–1024.

Barron, F., & Harrington, D. M. (1981). Creativity, intelligence, and personality. *Annual Review of Psychology*, 32, 439–476.

Bartoshuk, L. M., & Beauchamp, G. K. (1994). Chemical senses. *Annual Review of Psychology*, 45, 419–449.

Basbaum, A. I., & Leine, J. D. (1991). Opiate analgesia: How central is a peripheral target? *New England Journal of Medicine*, 325, 1168-1169.

Basso, K. (1970). "To give up words:" Silence in Western Apache culture. *Southwestern Journal of Anthropology*, 26, 213–230.

Baumeister, A. A. (1987). Mental retardation: Some conceptions and dilemmas. *American Psychologist*, 42, 796–800.

Baumeister, R. F. (1985). The championship choke. *Psychology Today*, 19, 48–52.

Baumeister, R. F. (1987). How the self became a problem: A psychological review of historical research. *Journal of Personality and Social Psychology*, 52, 163–176.

Baumeister, R. F., & Steinhilber, A. (1984). Paradoxical effects of supportive audiences on performance under pressure: The home field disadvantage in sports championships. *Journal of Personality and Social Psychology*, 47, 85–93.

Beauvais, F., Oetting, E. R., Wolf, W., & Edwards, R. W. (1989). American Indian youth and drugs: 1975–1987, a continuing problem. *American Journal of Public Health*, 79, 634–636.

Beck, A. T. (1991). Cognitive therapy: A 30-year retrospective. *American Psychologist*, 46, 368–375.

Beck, A. T. (1967). *Depression: Clinical, experimental, and theoretical aspects*. New York: Harper Collins.

Beck, A. T. (1976). *Cognitive therapy and the emotional disorders*. New York: International University Press.

Beck, A. T. (1985). *Theoretical perspectives in clinical anxiety*. In A. H. Tuma & J. D. Master (Eds.), *Anxiety and the anxiety disorders*. Hillsdale, NJ: Erlbaum.

Beck, A. T., & Emery, G. (1985). *Anxiety disorders and phobias: A cognitive perspective*. New York: Basic Books.

Beck, A. T., & Freeman, A. (1990). *Cognitive therapy of personality disorders*. New York: Guilford.

Beckman, L. J., & Houser, B. B. (1982). The consequences of childlessness on the social-psychological well-being of older women. *Journal of Gerontology,* 37, 243–250.

Bee, H. (1992). *The developing child* (6th ed.). New York: HarperCollins.

Bee, H. (1994). *Lifespan development.* New York: HarperCollins.

Beecroft, R. (1966). *Classical conditioning.* Goleta, CA: Psychonomic Press.

Begg, I., & Paivio, A. (1969). Concreteness and imagery in sentence meaning. *Journal of Verbal Learning and Verbal Behavior,* 8, 817–821.

Bekerian, D. A. (1993). In search of the typical eyewitness. *American Psychologist,* 48, 574–576.

Bell, P. A., Fisher, J. D., & Loomis, R. J. (1978). *Environmental psychology.* Philadelphia: Saunders.

Bellack, A. S. (1986). Schizophrenia: Behavior therapy's forgotten child. *Behavior Therapy,* 17, 199–214.

Bellack, A. S., & Mueser, K. T. (1986). A comprehensive treatment program for schizophrenia and chronic mental illness. *Community Mental Health Journal,* 22, 175–189.

Belsher, G., & Costello, C. G. (1988). Relapse after recovery from unipolar depression: A critical review. *Psychological Bulletin,* 104, 84–96.

Belsky, J. (1990). *The "effects" of infant day care reconsidered.* In N. Fox & G. G. Fein (Eds.), *Infant day care: The current debate.* Norwood, NJ: Ablex.

Belsky, J., & Rovine, M. (1988). Nonmaternal care in the first year of life and the security of infant-parent attachment. *Child Development,* 59, 157–167.

Ben-Yehuda, N. (1980). The European witch craze. *American Journal of Sociology,* 86, 1–31.

Benedict, H. (1979). Early lexical development: Comprehension and production. *Journal of Child Language,* 6, 183–200.

Bennett, T. L. (1982). *Introduction to physiological psychology.* Monterey, CA: Brooks/Cole.

Bennett, W. (1980). The cigarette century. *Science,* 80, 36–43.

Berkowitz, H. (1994). U.S. firms trip over their tongues in wooing the world. *The Journal Gazette,* June 21, Fort Wayne, IN.

Berkowitz, L. (1978). What ever happened to the frustration-aggression hypothesis? *American Behavioral Scientist,* 21, 691–708.

Berkowitz, L. (1982). Aversive conditions as stimuli to aggression. *Advances in Experimental Social Psychology,* 15, 249–288.

Berkowitz, L. (1989). Frustration-aggression hypothesis: Examination and reformulation. *Psychological Bulletin,* 106, 59–73.

Berkowitz, L. (1990). On the formation and regulation of anger and aggression. *American Psychologist,* 45, 494–503.

Berlyne, D. E. (1960). *Conflict, arousal, and curiosity.* New York: McGraw-Hill.

Berlyne, D. E. (1971). *Aesthetics and psychobiology.* Englewood Cliffs, NJ: Prentice-Hall.

Bernstein, I. (1978). Learned taste aversion in children receiving chemotherapy. *Science,* 200, 1302–1303.

Beroldi, G. (1994). Critique of the Seville Statement on Violence. *American Psychologist,* 49, 847–848.

Berscheid, E. (1994). Interpersonal relationships. *Annual Review of Psychology,* 45, 79–129.

Beutler, L. E., Crago, M., & Arizmendi, T. G. (1986). *Therapist variables in psychotherapy process and outcome.* In S. L. Garfield & A. E. Bergin (Eds.), *Handbook of psychotherapy and behavior change* (3rd ed.), New York: Wiley.

Bhawuk, D. P. S., & Brislin, R. (1992). The measurement of intercultural sensitivity using the concepts of individualism and collectivism. *International Journal of Intercultural Relations,* 16, 413–436.

Binder, J. L. (1993). Research findings on short-term psychodynamic therapy techniques. *Directions in Clinical Psychology,* 3, 10.3-10.13.

Birdwhistell, R. L. (1952). *Introduction to kinesics.* Louisville, KY: University of Louisville Press.

Birnbaum, M. H., & Mellers, B. A. (1979). Stimulus recognition may mediate exposure effects. *Journal of Personality and Social Psychology,* 37, 391–394.

Blanchard, D. C., & Blanchard, R. J. (1988). Ethoexperimental approaches to the biology of emotion. *Annual Review of Psychology,* 39, 43–68.

Blashfield, R. K., & Breen, M. J. (1989). Face validity of the DSM-III-R personality disorders. *American Journal of Psychiatry,* 146, 1575-1579.

Blass, E. M., Ganchow, J. R., & Steiner, J. E. (1984). Classical conditioning in newborn human infants 2–48 hours of age. *Infant Behavior and Development,* 7, 223–235.

Bloch, D., & Simon, R. (Eds.). (1982). *The strength of family therapy: Selected papers of Nathan Ackerman.* New York: Brunner/Mazel.

Block, J. (1965). *The challenge of response sets.* Englewood Cliffs, NJ: Prentice-Hall.

Bloodworth, R. C. (1987). Major problems associated with marijuana abuse. *Psychiatric Medicine,* 3, 173–184.

Bloom, F. E., Lazerson, A., & Hotstadter, L. (1985). *Brain, mind, and behavior.* San Francisco: Freeman.

Bondareff, W., Mountjoy, C. Q., Wischik, C. M., Hauser, D. L., LaBree, L. D., & Roth, M. (1993). Evidence of subtypes of Alzheimer's Disease and implications for etiology. *Archives of General Psychiatry, 50*, 350–356.

Borbely, A. (1986). *Secrets of sleep.* New York: Basic Books.

Bordens, K. S., & Abbott, B. B. (1991). *Research design and methods: A process approach.* Mountain View, CA: Mayfield.

Bornstein, R. F. (1989). Exposure and affect: Overview and meta-analysis of research 1968–1987. *Psychological Bulletin, 106*, 265–289.

Bornstein, R. F., Kale, A. R., & Cornell, K. R. (1990). Boredom as a limiting condition of the mere exposure effect. *Journal of Personality and Social Psychology, 58*, 791–800.

Bouchard, C., Tremblay, A., Després, J., et al. (1990). The response to long-term overfeeding in identical twins. *The New England Journal of Medicine, 322*, 1477–1482.

Bourne, L. E., Dominowski, R. L., & Loftus, E. F. (1983). *Cognitive process.* Englewood Cliffs, NJ: Prentice-Hall.

Bower, G. H. (1970). Imagery as a relational organizer in associative learning. *Journal of Verbal Learning and Verbal Behavior, 9*, 529–533.

Bower, G. H. (1972). Mental imagery and associative learning. In L. W. Gregg (Ed.), *Cognition in learning and memory.* New York: Wiley.

Bower, G. H. (1981). Mood and memory. *American Psychologist, 36*, 129–148.

Bower, G. H., & Clark, M. C. (1969). Narrative stories as mediators for serial learning. *Psychonomic Science, 14*, 181–182.

Bower, G. H., Monteiro, K. P., & Gilligan, S. G. (1978). Emotional mood as a context for learning and recall. *Journal of Verbal Learning and Verbal Behavior, 17*, 573–587.

Bower, G. H., & Springston, F. (1970). Pauses as recoding points in letter series. *Journal of Experimental Psychology, 83*, 421–430.

Bower, T. G. R., Broughton, J. M., & Moore, M. K. (1971). Infant responses to approaching objects: An indicator of response to distal variables. *Perception and Psychophysics, 9*, 193–196.

Bowlby, J. (1982). *Attachment and Loss: Vol. 1, Attachment* (2nd ed.). New York: Basic Books.

Bradley, D. R., & Dumais, S. T. (1975). Ambiguous cognitive contours. *Nature, 257*, 582–584.

Bradshaw, J. L., & Nettleton, N. C. (1983). *Human cerebral asymmetry.* Englewood Cliffs, NJ: Prentice-Hall.

Braine, M. D. S. (1976). Children's first word combinations. *Monographs for the Society for Research in Child Development, 41*, (Serial No. 164).

Brandon, T. H. (1994). Negative affect as motivation to smoke. *Current Directions in Psychological Sciences, 3*, 33–37.

Bransford, J. D., & Johnson, M. K. (1972). Contextual prerequisites for understanding: some investigations of comprehension and recall. *Journal of Verbal Learning and Verbal Behavior, 11*, 717–720.

Bratic, E. B. (1982). Healthy mothers, healthy babies coalition. *Prevention, 97*, 503–509.

Braun, P., Kochansky, G., Shapiro, R., Greenberg, S., Gudeman, J. E., Johnson, S., & Shore, M. (1981). Overview: Deinstitutionalization of psychiatric patients, a critical review of outcome studies. *American Journal of Psychiatry, 138*, 736–749.

Bregman, J., Dykens, E., Watson, M., & Leckman, J. (1987). Fragile X syndrome: Variability in phenotype expression. Journal of the *American Academy of Child and Adolescent Psychiatry, 26*, 463–471.

Breier, A., Schreiber, J. L., Dyer, J., & Pickar, D. (1991). National Institute of Mental Health longitudinal study of chronic schizophrenia: Prognosis and predictors of outcome. *Archives of General Psychiatry, 48*, 239–246.

Brett, J. F., Brief, A. P., Burke, M. J., George, J. M., & Webster, J. (1990). Negative affectivity and the reporting of stressful events. *Health Psychology, 9*, 57–68.

Brigham, J. C. (1992). *Social psychology* (2nd ed.). New York: HarperCollins.

Brinkerhoff, R. O. (1989). *Evaluating training programs in business and industry.* San Fransisco: Jossey-Bass.

Brislin, R. (1993). *Understanding culture's influence on behavior.* Fort Worth, TX: Harcourt Brace.

Brislin, R. W. (1993). *Understanding culture's influence on behavior.* Fort Worth, TX: Harcourt Brace.

Brody, E. M. (1981). Women in the middle and family help to older people. *Gerontologist, 21*, 471–480.

Brown, J. (1958). Some tests of the decay theory of immediate memory. *Quarterly Journal of Experimental Psychology, 10*, 12–21.

Brown, J. (1976). *An analysis of recognition and recall and of problems in their comparison.* In J. Brown (Ed.), *Recall and recognition.* New York: Wiley.

Brown, J. D. (1991). Staying fit and staying well. *Journal of Personality and Social Psychology, 60*, 555–561.

Brown, J. I. (1973). *The Nelson-Denny Reading Test.* Boston: Houghton-Mifflin.

Brown, N. A. (1985). Are offspring at risk from their father's exposure to toxins? *Nature,* 316, 110.

Brown, R. (1973). *A first language: The early stages.* Cambridge, MA: Harvard University Press.

Brown, R., Cazden, C. B., & Bellugi, U. (1969). The child's grammar from 1 to 3. *Symposia on child language* (Vol. 2). Minneapolis: University of Minnesota Press.

Brown, R., & Kulik, J. (1977). Flashbulb memories. *Cognition,* 5, 73–99.

Browne, M. A., & Mahoney, M. J. (1984). Sport psychology. *Annual Review of Psychology,* 35, 605–626.

Brownell, K. D. (1993). Whether obesity should be treated. *Health Psychology,* 12, 339–341.

Brownell, K. D., & Rodin, J. (1994). The dieting maelstrom: Is it possible and advisable to lose weight? *American Psychologist,* 49, 781–791.

Bruch, H. (1980). Preconditions for the development of anorexia nervosa. *American Journal of Psychoanalysis,* 40, 169–172.

Bruner, J. S., & Goodman, C. C. (1947). Value and need as organizing factors in perception. *Journal of Abnormal and Social Psychology,* 42, 33–44.

Buchanan, R. W., Strauss, M. E., Kirkpatrick, B., Holstein, C., Brier, A., & Carpenter, W. T., Jr. (1994). Neuropsychological impairments in deficit vs. nondeficit forms of schizophrenia. *Archives of General Psychiatry,* 51, 804–811.

Buck, L., & Axel, R. (1991). A novel multi-gene family may encode odorant receptors: A molecular basis for odor recognition. *Cell,* 65, 165–187.

Buck, R. (1980). Nonverbal behavior and the theory of emotion: The facial feedback hypothesis. *Journal of Personality and Social Psychology,* 38, 811–824.

Buck, R. (1985). Prime theory: An integrated view of motivation and emotion. *Psychological Review,* 92, 389–413.

Burisch, M. (1984). Approaches to personality inventory construction. *American Psychologist,* 39, 214–227.

Buss, A. H. (1966). *Psychopathology.* New York: Wiley.

Buss, A. H. (1989). Personality as traits. *American Psychologist,* 44, 1378–1388.

Buss, D., & Barnes, M. (1986). Preferences in human mate selection. *Journal of Personality and Social Psychology,* 50, 559–570.

Buss, D. M. (1984). Evolutionary biology and personality psychology. *American Psychologist,* 39, 1135–1147.

Buss, D. M. (1985). Human mate selection. *American Scientist,* 73, 47–51.

Buss, D. M., Abbott, M., Angleitner, A., Asherian, A., Biaggio, A., Blanco-Villasenor, A., et al. (1990). International preferences in mate selection: A study of 37 cultures. *Journal of Cross-Cultural Psychology,* 21, 5–47.

Butler, R., & Lewis, M. (1981). *Aging and mental health.* St. Louis: Mosby.

Butler, R. N., & Emr, M. (1982). SDAT research: Current trends. *Generations,* 7, 14–18.

Byrd, K. R. (1994). The narrative reconstruction of incest survivors. *American Psychologist,* 49, 439–440.

Byrne, D. (1971). *The attraction paradigm.* New York: Academic Press.

Cacioppo, J. T., Marshall-Goodell, B. S., Tassinary, L. G., & Petty, R. E. (1992). Rudimentary determinants of attitudes: Classical conditioning is more effective when prior knowledge about the attitude stimulus is low than high. *Journal of Experimental Social Psychology,* 28, 207–233.

Calhoun, J. B. (1962). Population density and social pathology. *Scientific American,* 206, 139–148.

Campbell, J. P. (1988). *Training design for performance improvement.* In J. P. Campbell & R. J. Campbell (Eds.), *Productivity in organizations.* San Francisco: Jossey-Bass.

Cannon, T. D., Mednick, S. A., & Parnas, J. (1990). Antecedents of predominantly negative- and predominantly positive-symptom schizophrenia in a high-risk population. *Archives of General Psychiatry,* 47, 622–632.

Cannon, W. B. (1932). *The wisdom of the body.* New York: Norton.

Carey, S. (1978). *The child as word learner.* In M. Halle, J. Bresnan, & G. A. Miller (Eds.), *Linguistic theory and psychological reality.* Cambridge, MA: MIT Press.

Carone, B. J., Harrow, M., & Westermeyer, J. F. (1991). Post-hospital course and outcome in schizophrenia. *Archives of General Psychiatry,* 48, 247–253.

Carson, R. C., & Butcher, J. N. (1992). *Abnormal psychology and modern life* (9th ed.). New York: HarperCollins.

Carson, R. L. (1962). *Silent Spring.* Boston: Houghton Mifflin.

Carson, T. P., & Carson, R. C. (1984). *The affective disorders.* In H. E. Adams & P. B. Sutker (Eds.),

Comprehensive handbook of psychopathology. New York: Plenum.

Carver, C. S., & Gaines, J. G. (1987). Optimism, pessimism, and postpartum depression. *Cognitive Therapy and Research,* 11, 449–462.

Cash, T. F., & Derlega, V. J. (1978). The matching hypothesis: Physical attractiveness among same-sexed friends. *Personality and Social Psychology Bulletin,* 4, 240–243.

Cash, T. F., & Kilcullen, R. N. (1985). The eye of the beholder: Susceptibility to sexism and beautyism in the evaluation of managerial applicants. *Journal of Applied Social Psychology,* 15, 591–605.

Cavanaugh, J. C., & Park, D. C. (1993). Vitality for life: Psychological research for productive aging. *APS Observer,* special issue: December.

Cermack, L. S., & Craik, F. I. M. (Eds.). (1979). *Levels of processing in human memory.* Hillsdale, NJ: Erlbaum.

Chaiken, S., & Stangor, C. (1987). Attitudes and attitude change. *Annual Review of Psychology,* 38, 575–630.

Charney, D. S., Deutch, A. Y., Krystal, J. H., Southwick, S. M., & Davis, M. (1993). Psychobiological mechanisms of posttraumatic stress disorder. *Archives of General Psychiatry,* 50, 294–305.

Chase, M. H., & Morales, F. R. (1990). The atonia and myoclonia of active (REM) sleep. *Annual Review of Psychology,* 41, 557–584.

Chase, W. G., & Simon, H. A. (1973). *The mind's eye in chess.* In W. G. Chase (Ed.), *Visual information processing.* New York: Academic Press.

Chasnoff, I. J., Griffith, D. R., MacGregor, S., Dirkes, K., & Burns, K. (1989). Temporal patterns of cocaine use in pregnancy. *Journal of the American Medical Association,* 261, 1741–1744.

Cheesman, J., & Merikle, P. M. (1984). Priming with and without awareness. *Perception and Psychophysics,* 36, 387–395.

Chilman, C. S. (1980). Parent satisfactions, concerns, and goals for their children. *Family Relations,* 29, 339–346.

Chilman, C. S. (1983). *Adolescent sexuality in a changing American society: Social and psychological perspectives for the human services profession* (2nd ed.). New York: Wiley.

Chiriboga, D. A., Catron, L. S., & Associates (1991). *Divorce: Crisis, challenge, or relief?* New York: New York University Press.

Chomsky, N. (1965). *Aspects of a theory of syntax.* Cambridge, MA: Harvard University Press.

Chomsky, N. (1975). *Reflections of language.* New York: Pantheon Books.

Chuang, H. T., Devins, G. M., Hunsley, J., & Gill, M. J. (1989). Psychosocial distress and well-being among gay and bisexual men with immunodeficiency virus infection. *American Journal of Psychiatry,* 146, 876–880.

Ciaranello, R. D. (1993). Attention deficit-hyperactivity disorder and resistance to thyroid hormone—A new idea? *New England Journal of Medicine,* 238, 1038–1039.

CIBA-GEIGY (1991). *OCD: When a habit isn't just a habit.* Pine Brook, NJ: CIBA-GEIGY Corporation.

Clark, D. M., & Teasdale, J. D. (1985). Constraints on the effects of mood on memory. *Journal of Personality and Social Psychology,* 48, 1595–1608.

Clarkson-Smith, L., & Hartley, A. A. (1989). Relationships between physical exercise and cognitive abilities in older adults. *Psychology and Aging,* 4, 183–189.

Clifford, B. R., & Lloyd-Bostock, S. (Eds.), (1983). *Evaluating witness evidence: Recent psychological research and new perspectives.* Norwood, NJ: Ablex.

Clinton, J. J. (1992). Acute pain management can be improved. *The Journal of the American Medical Association,* 267, 2580.

Clore, G. L., & Byrne, D. (1974). *A reinforcement-affect model of attraction.* In T. L. Huston (Ed.), *Foundations of interpersonal attraction.* New York: Academic Press.

Cohen, S., Evans, G. W., Krantz, D. S., Stokols, D., & Kelly, S. (1980). Aircraft noise and children: Longitudinal and cross-sectional evidence on the adaptation to noise and the effectiveness of noise abatement. *Journal of Personality and Social Psychology,* 40, 331–345.

Cohen, S., Evans, G. W., Stokols, D., & Krantz, D. S. (1986). *Behavior, health, and environmental stress.* New York: Plenum.

Cohen, S., & Lichtenstein, E. (1990). Perceived stress, quitting smoking, and smoking relapse. *Health Psychology,* 9, 466–478.

Cohen, S., Lichtenstein, E., Prochaska, J. O., Rossi, J. S., Gritz, E. R., Carr, C. R., et al. (1989). Debunking myths about self-quitting: Evidence from 10 prospective studies of persons who attempt to quit smoking by themselves. *American Psychologist,* 44, 1355–1365.

Colby, A., & Kohlberg, L. (1984). *Invariant sequence and internal consistency in moral judgment stages.* In W. M. Kurtines & J. L. Gewitz (Eds.), *Morality, moral behavior, and moral development.* New York: Wiley.

Colditz, G. A. (1992). Economic costs of obesity. *American Journal of Clinical Nutrition,* 55, 5035–5075.

Coles, R., & Stokes, G. (1985). *Sex and the American teenager.* New York: HarperCollins.

Cole, R. E. (1979). *Work, mobility, and participation.* Berkeley, CA: University of California Press.

College Board. (1989). *College-bound seniors: 1989 SAT profile.* New York: College Entrance Examination Board.

Collings, V. B. (1974). Human taste response as a function of locus of stimulation on the tongue and soft palate. *Perception and Psychophysics, 16,* 169–174.

Collins, W. A., & Gunnar, M. R. (1990). Social and personality development. *Annual Review of Psychology, 41,* 387–416.

Committee on Aging Society (1986). *America's aging: Productive roles in an older society.* Washington, DC: National Academy Press.

Committee on Lesbian and Gay Concerns (1991). Avoiding heterosexual bias in language. *American Psychologist, 46,* 973–974.

Conger, J. J. (1991). *Adolescence and youth: Psychological development in a changing world.* New York: HarperCollins.

Conrad, R. (1963). Acoustic confusions and memory span for words. *Nature, 197,* 1029–1030.

Conrad, R. (1964). Acoustic confusions in immediate memory. *British Journal of Psychology, 55,* 75–84.

Cooper, J., & Croyle, R. T. (1984). Attitudes and attitude change. *Annual Review of Psychology, 35,* 395–426.

Cooper, L. A., & Shepard, R. N. (1973). *Chronometric studies of the rotation of mental images.* In W. G. Chase (Ed.), *Visual information processing.* New York: Academic Press.

Coren, S. (1972). Subjective contours and apparent depth. *Psychological Review, 79,* 359–367.

Coren, S., & Girgus, J. S. (1978). *Seeing is deceiving: The psychology of visual illusions.* Hillsdale, NJ: Erlbaum.

Cornblatt, B. A., & Erelenmeyer-Kimling, L. (1985). Global attention deviance as a marker of risk for schizophrenia: Specificity and predictive validity. *Journal of Abnormal Psychology, 94,* 470–486.

Costa, P. T., & McCrea, R. R. (1980). *Still stable after all these years: Personality as a key to some issues in adulthood and old age.* In P. B. Baltes & O. G. Brim, Jr. (Eds.), *Life-span development and behavior.* New York: Academic Press.

Costello, C. G. (1982). Fears and phobias in women: A community study. *Journal of Abnormal Psychology, 91,* 280–286.

Coté, T. R., Biggar, R. J., & Dannenberg, A. L. (1992). Risk of suicide among persons with AIDS: A national assessment. *Journal of the American Medical Association, 268,* 2066–2068.

Coulter, W. A., & Morrow, H. W. (Eds.). (1978). *Adaptive behavior: Concepts and measurements.* New York: Grune & Stratton.

Council, J. R. (1993). Context effects in personality research. *Current Directions in Psychological Research, 2,* 31–34.

Cowan, W. M. (1979). *The development of the brain.* In *The brain* (pp. 56–69). San Francisco: Freeman.

Cowen, N. (1984). On short and long auditory stores. *Psychological Bulletin, 96,* 341–370.

Cox, R. H. (1990). *Sport psychology: Concepts and applications.* Dubuque, IA: Brown.

Coyle, J. T., Price, D. L., & DeLong, M. H. (1983). Alzheimer's disease: A disorder of central cholinergic innervation. *Science, 219,* 1184–1189.

Coyne, J. C., & Downey, G. (1991). Social factors and psychopathology: Stress, social support, and coping processes. *Annual Review of Psychology, 42,* 401–425.

Cozby, P. C. (1973). Self-disclosure: A literature review. *Psychological Bulletin, 79,* 73–91.

Craik, F. I. M., & Lockhart, R. S. (1972). Levels of processing: A framework for memory research. *Journal of Verbal Learning and Verbal Behavior, 11,* 671–684.

Craik, F. I. M., & Tulving, E. (1975). Depth of processing and the retention of words in episodic memory. *Journal of Experimental Psychology: General, 104,* 268–294.

Cramer, R. E., McMaster, M. R., Bartell, P. A., & Dragna, M. (1988). Subject competence and minimization of the bystander effect. *Journal of Applied Social Psychology, 18,* 1133–1148.

Creekmore, C. R. (1984). Games athletes play. *Psychology Today, 19,* 40–44.

Creekmore, C. R. (1985). Cities won't drive you crazy. *Psychology Today, 19,* 46–53.

Crews, D. J., & Landers, D. M. (1987). A meta-analytic review of aerobic fitness and reactivity to psychosocial stressors. *Medicine and Science in Sport and Exercise, 19,* 114–120.

Cromwell, R. L. (1993). Searching for the origins of schizophrenia. *Psychological Science, 4,* 276–279.

Cross-National Collaborative Group. (1992). The changing rate of major depression: Cross-national comparisons. *Journal of the American Medical Association, 268,* 3098–3105.

Crow, T. J. (1980). Molecular pathology of schizophrenia: More than one disease process? *The British Medical Journal, 280,* 66–68.

Cunningham, S. (1984). Genovese: 20 years later, few heed stranger's cries. *APA Monitor, 15,* 30.

Curtis, R. C., & Miller, K. (1986). Believing another likes or dislikes you: Behaviors making the beliefs come true. *Journal of Personality and Social Psychology, 51*, 284–290.

Cushner, K. (1990). Cross-cultural psychology and the formal classroom. In R. W. Brislin (Ed.), *Applied cross-cultural psychology.* Newbury Park, CA: Sage.

Cutler, W. B., Preti, G., Krieger, A., Huggins, G. R., Ramon Garcia, C., & Lawley, HJ. J. (1986). Human axillary secretions influence women's menstrual cycles: The role of donor extract from men. *Hormones and Behavior, 20*, 463–473.

Dahlstrom, W. G. (1993). Tests: Small samples, large consequences. *American Psychologist, 48*, 393–399.

Daniel, T. C. (1990). Measuring the quality of the natural environment: A psychophysical approach. *American Psychologist, 45*, 633–637.

Darley, J. M., & Fazio, R. H. (1980). Expectancy confirmation processes arising in the interaction sequence. *American Psychologist, 35*, 861–866.

Darley, J. M., & Schultz, T. R. (1990). Moral rules: Their content and acquisition. *Annual Review of Psychology, 41*, 525–556.

Darling, C. A., & Davidson, J. K. (1986). Coitally active university students: Sexual behaviors, concerns, and challenges. *Adolescence, 21*, 403–419.

Darwin, C. T., Turvey, M. T., & Crowder, R. G. (1972). An auditory analogue of the Sperling partial report procedure: Evidence for brief auditory storage. *Cognitive Psychology, 3*, 255–267.

Dasen, P., & Heron, A. (1981). *Cross-cultural tests of Piaget's theory.* In H. C. Triandis & A. Heron (Eds.), *Handbook of cross-cultural psychology.* Vol. 4, *Developmental psychology.* Boston: Allyn & Bacon.

Datan, N. Rodeheaver, D., & Hughes, F. (1987). Adult development and aging. *Annual Review of Psychology, 38*, 153–180.

Davidoff, J. B. (1975). *Differences in visual perception: The individual eye.* New York: Academic Press.

Davidson, J. M., Smith, E. R., Rodgers, C. H., & Bloch, G. J. (1968). Relative thresholds of behavioral and somatic responses to estrogen. *Physiology and Behavior, 3*, 227–229.

Davis, K. (1985). Near and dear: Friendship and love compared. *Psychology Today, 19*, 22–30.

de Boer, C. (1978). The polls: Attitudes toward work. *Public Opinion Quarterly, 42*, 414–423.

DeAngelis, T. (1994). Ethnic-minority issues recognized in DSM-IV. *Monitor,* November, p. 36.

DeCasper, A. J., & Fifer, W. P. (1980). Of human bonding: Newborns prefer their mother's voice. *Science, 208*, 1174–1176.

DeCasper, A. J., & Sigafoos, A. D. (1983). The interuterine heartbeat: A potent reinforcer for newborns. *Infant Behavior and Development, 6*, 19–25.

deCuevas, J. (1990, September/October). "No, she holded them loosely." *Harvard Magazine,* pp. 60–67.

Deffenbacher, J. L. (1988). Some recommendations and directions. *Counseling Psychology, 35*, 234–236.

DeGroot, A. D. (1965). *Thought and chance in chess.* The Hague: Mouton Press.

DeGroot, A. D. (1966). *Perception and memory versus thought: Some old ideas and recent findings.* In B. Kleainmuntz (Ed.), *Problem solving,* New York: Wiley.

DeJarlais, D. C., & Friedman, S. R. (1988). The psychology of preventing AIDS among intravenous drug users: A social learning conceptualization. *American Psychologist, 43*, 865–870.

Delongis, A., Folkman, S., & Lazarus, R. S. (1988). The impact of daily stress on health and mood: Psychological and social resources as mediators. *Journal of Personality and Social Psychology, 54*, 486–495.

Dembroski, T. M., MacDougall, J. M., Williams, R. B., Haney, T. I., & Blumenthal, J. A. (1985). Components of Type A, hostility, and anger in relationship to angiographic findings. *Psychosomatic Medicine, 47*, 219–233.

Dembroski, T. M., & Costa, P. T., Jr. (1987). Coronary prone behavior: Components of the Type A pattern and hostility. *Journal of Personality, 55*, 211–235.

Dement, W. C. (1974). *Some must watch while some must sleep.* San Francisco: Freeman.

Deregowski, J. B. (1972). Pictorial perception and culture. *Scientific American,* November 1972, 83.

Deregowski, J. B. (1973). *Illusion and culture.* In R. L. Gregory & G. H. Gombrich (Eds.), *Illusion in nature and art.* New York: Scribner's., pp. 161–192.

Digman, J. M. (1990). Personality structure: Emergence of the five-factor model. *Annual Review of Psychology, 41*, 417–440.

Dirkes, M. A. (1978). The role of divergent production in the learning process. *American Psychologist, 33*, 815–820.

Dixon, N. F. (1981). *Preconscious processing.* New York: Wiley.

Doll, R., & Peto, R. (1981). *The causes of cancer.* New York: Oxford University Press.

Dollard, J., Doob, L., Miller, N., Mowrer, O. H., & Sears, R. R. (1939). *Frustration and aggression.* New Haven, CT: Yale University Press.

Domjan, M. (1987). Animal learning comes of age. *American Psychologist, 42,* 556–564.

Donnenberg, G. R., & Hoffman, L. W. (1988). Gender differences in moral development. *Sex Roles, 18,* 701–717.

Doty, R. Y. (1986). *Gender and endocrine-related influences on human olefactory perception.* In H. Meiselman & R. S. Rivlin (Eds.), *Clinical measurement of taste and smell.* New York: Macmillan.

Dove, A. (1968). Taking the Chitling Test. *Newsweek,* July.

Doweiko, H. E. (1993). *Concepts of chemical dependency* (2nd. ed.). Pacific Grove, CA: Brooks/Cole.

Drakeley, R. J., Herriot, P., & Jones, A. (1988). Biographical data, training success and turnover. *Journal of Occupational Psychology, 61,* 145–152.

Duffy, E. (1962). *Activation and behavior.* New York: Wiley.

Dunbar-Jacob, J., Dwyer, K., & Dunning, E. J. (1991). Compliance with antihypertensive regimen: A review of the research in the 1980s. *Annals of Behavioral Medicine, 13,* 31–39.

Duncan, J. (1985). Two techniques for investigating perception without awareness. *Perception and Psychophysics, 38,* 296–298.

Duncker, K. (1945). On problem solving. *Psychological Monographs, 58* (Whole No. 270).

Dunham, R. B. (1979). *Job design and redesign.* In S. Kerr (Ed.), *Organizational behavior.* Columbus, OH: Grid.

Dunnette, M. D., & Borman, W. C. (1979). Personnel selection and classification systems. *Annual Review of Psychology, 30,* 477–525.

Dweck, C. S. (1986). Motivational processes affecting learning. *American Psychologist, 41,* 1040–1048.

Eagly, A. H., & Chaiken, S. (1992). *The psychology of attitudes.* San Diego: Harcourt Brace Jovanovich.

Eaker, E. D., Packard, B., Wenger, N. K., et al. (1988). Coronary heart disease in women. *American Journal of Cardiology, 61,* 641–644.

Eaker, E. D., Pinsky, J., & Castelli, W. P. (1992). Myocardial infarction and coronary death among women: Psychosocial predictors from a 20-year follow-up on women in the Framingham study. *American Journal of Epidemiology, 135,* 854–864.

Early, C. (1989). Social loafing and collectivism: A comparison of the United States and the People's Republic of China. *Administrative Science Quarterly, 34,* 555–581.

Early, P. C. (1986). Supervisors and shop stewards as sources of contextual information in goal-setting: A comparison of the U.S. with England. *Journal of Applied Psychology, 71,* 111–118.

Edelman, G. (1992). *Bright air, bright fire: On the matter of mind.* New York: Basic Books.

Edmands, M. S. (1993). Caring for students with eating disorders on college and university campuses. *Advances in Medical Psychotherapy, 6,* 59-75.

Edwards, C. P. (1977). *The comparative study of the development of moral judgment and reasoning.* In R. L. Munroe, R. Munroe, & B. B. Whiting (Eds.), *Handbook of cross-cultural human development.a* New York: Garland.

Edwards, C. P. (1981). *The development of moral reasoning in cross-cultural perspective.* In R. H. Munroe, R. L. Munroe, & B. B. Whiting (Eds.), *Handbook of cross-cultural human development.* New York: Garland Press.

Edwards, L. K., & Edwards, A. L. (1991). A principal components analysis of the Minnesota Multiphasic Personality Inventory Factor Scales. *Journal of Personality and Social Psychology, 60,* 766–772.

Egeth, H. E. (1993). What do we *not* know about eyewitness identification? *American Psychologist, 48,* 577–580.

Eich, J. E., Weingartner, H., Stillman, R. C., & Gillan, J. C. (1975). State-dependent accessibility of retrieval cues in the retention of a categorized list. *Journal of Verbal Learning and Verbal Behavior, 14,* 408–417.

Ekamn, P., Friesen, W. V., O'Sullivan, M., Diacoyanni-Tarlatzis, I., Krause, R., et al. (1987). Universals and cultural differences in the judgment of facial expressions of emotion. *Journal of Personality and Social Psychology, 53,* 712–717.

Ekman, P. (1972). *Universals and cultural differences in facial expression of emotion.* In J. K. Cole (Ed.), *Nebraska symposium on motivation.* Lincoln: University of Nebraska Press.

Ekman, P. (1973). *Cross-cultural studies in facial expression.* In P. Ekman (Ed.), *Darwin and facial expressions: A century of research in review.* New York: Academic Press.

Ekman, P. (1992). Facial expression and emotion: New findings, new questions. *Psychological Science, 3,* 34–38.

Ekman, P. (1993). Facial expression and emotion. *American Psychologist, 48,* 384–392.

Ekman, P., Levenson, R. W., & Friesen, W. V. (1983). Autonomic nervous system activity distinguishes among emotions. *Science, 221,* 1208–1210.

Ellis, A. (1970). *Reason and emotion in psychotherapy.* Secaucus, NJ: Stuart.

Ellis, A. (1973). *Humanistic psychotherapy: The rational-emotive approach.* New York: McGraw-Hill.

Ellis, A. (1987). The impossibility of achieving consistently good mental health. *American Psychologist, 42,* 364–375.

Ellis, A. (1991). *How can psychological treatment aim to be briefer and better?* The rational-emotive approach to brief therapy. In K. N. Anchor (Ed.), *Handbook of medical psychotherapy.* Toronto: Hogrefe & Huber.

Ellis, L., & Ames, M. A. (1987). Neurohormonal functioning and sexual orientation: A theory of homosexuality-heterosexuality. *Psychological Bulletin,* 101, 233–258.

Endler, N. S., Cox, B. J., Parker, J. D. A., & Bagby, R. M. (1992). Self-reports of depression and state-trait-anxiety: Evidence for differential assessment. *Journal of Personality and Social Psychology,* 63, 832-838.

Epstein, S. (1979). The stability of behvaior: On predicting most of the people much of the time. *Journal of Personality and Social Psychology,* 37, 1097–1126.

Epstein, S. (1994). Integration of the cognitive and the psychodynamic unconscious. *American Psychologist,* 49, 709–724.

Epstein, L. H., & Cluss, P. A. (1982). A behavioral medicine perspective on adherence to long-term medical regimes. *Journal of Consulting and Clinical Psychology,* 50, 950–971.

Erdelyi, M. H. (1985). *Psychoanalysis: Freud's cognitive psychology.* New York: Freeman.

Erdelyi, M. H. (1992). Psychodynamics and the unconscious. *American Psychologist,* 47, 784–787.

Erdelyi, M. H. & Goldberg, B. (1979). *Let's not sweep repression under the rug: Toward a cognitive psychology of repression.* In J. F. Kihlstrom & F. J. Evans (Eds.), *Functional disorders of memory.* Hillsdale, NJ: Erlbaum.

Erez, M., & Early, P. C. (1987). Comparative analysis of goal-setting strategies across cultures. *Journal of Applied Psychology,* 72, 658-665.

Erez, M., & Early, P. C. (1993). *Culture, self-identity, and work.* New York: Oxford University Press.

Erez, M., & Zidon, I. (1984). Effect of goal acceptance on the relationship of goal difficulty to performance. *Journal of Applied Psychology,* 69, 69–78.

Erikson, E. H. (1963). *Childhood and society.* New York: Norton.

Erikson, E. H. (1965). *The challenge of youth.* Garden City, NY: Doubleday (Anchor Books).

Erikson, E. H. (1968). *Identity: Youth and crisis.* New York: Norton.

Eron, L., Gentry, J., & Schlegel, P. (Eds.). *Reason to hope: A psychosocial perspective on violence and youth.* Washington, DC: American Psychological Association.

Erwin, E. (1980). Psychoanalytic therapy: The Eysenck argument. *American Psychologist,* 35, 435–443.

Evans, G. W., & Howard, R. B. (1973). Personal space. *Psychological Bulletin,* 80, 334–344.

Eveleth, P., & Tanner, J. (1978). *Worldwide variations in human growth.* Cambridge, UK: Cambridge University Press.

Eysenck, H. J. (1952). The effects of psychotherapy: An evaluation. *Journal of Consulting Psychology,* 16, 319–324.

Eysenck, H. J. (1960). *Behavior Therapy and the Neuroses.* London: Pergamon Press.

Fackelman, K. A. (1992). Anatomy of Alzheimer's: Do immune proteins help destroy brain cells? *Science News,* 142, 394–396.

Fadiman, J. & Frager, R. (1994). *Personality and personal growth.* (3rd ed.). New York: HarperCollins.

Fairburn, C. G. & Wilson, G. T. (Eds.). (1993). *Binge eating: Nature, assessment and treatment.* New York: Guilford.

Fairburn, C. G., Jones, R., Peveler, R. C., Hope, R. A., & O'Conner, M. (1993). Psychotherapy and bulimia nervosa. *Archives of General Psychiatry,* 50, 419–428.

Falbo, T., & Peplau L. A. (1980). Power strategies in intimate relationships. *Journal of Personality and Social Psychology,* 38, 618–628.

Fantz, R. L. (1961). The origin of form perception. *Scientific American,* 204, 66–72.

Fantz, R. L. (1963). Pattern vision in newborn infants, *Science,* 140, 296–297.

Farrell, M. P., & Rosenberg, S. D. (1981). *Men at midlife.* Boston: Auburn House.

Fast, J. (1970). *Body language.* New York: M. Evans.

Fazio, R. H. (1989). *On the power and functionality of attitudes: the role of attitude accessibility.* In A. R. Pratkanis, S. J. Breckler, & A. G. Greenwald (Eds.), *Attitude structure and function.* Hillsdale, NJ: Erlbaum.

Fazio, R. H. (1990). Multiple processes by which attitudes guide behavior: The MODE model as an integrative framework. *Advances in Experimental Social Psychology,* 23, 75–109.

Feeney, J. A., & Noller, P. (1990). Attachment style as a predictor of adult romantic relationships. *Journal of Personality and Social Psychology,* 58, 281–291.

Fein, G. G., Schwartz, P. M., Jacobson, S. W., & Jacobson, J. L. (1983). Environmental toxins and behavior development. *American Psychologist,* 38, 1188–1197.

Feist, S. C. (1993). Marriage and family therapy:

Theories and applications. *Directions in Clinical Psychology*, 3, 4.3–4.24.

Fenker, R. M., & Lambiotte, J. G. (1987). A performance enhancement program for a college football team: One incredible season. *The Sport Psychologist*, 1, 224–236.

Festinger, L. (1957). *A theory of cognitive dissonance.* Stanford, CA: Stanford University Press.

Festinger, L., & Carlsmith, J. M. (1959). Cognitive consequences of forced compliance. *Journal of Abnormal and Social Psychology*, 58, 203–210.

Festinger, L., Schachter, S., & Back, K. (1950). *Social processes in informal groups: A study of human factors in housing.* New York: HarperCollins.

Fielding, J. E., & Phenow, K. J. (1988). Health effects of involuntary smoking. *The New England Journal of Medicine*, 319, 1452–1460.

Finnegan, L. P. (1982). *Outcome of children born to women dependent upon narcotics.* In B. Stimmel (Ed.), *The effects of maternal alcohol and drug abuse on the newborn.* New York: Haworth.

Fiore, M. C., Novotny, T. E., Pierce, J. P., Hatzlandreu, E. J., Patel, K. M., & Davis, R. M. (1989). Trends in cigarette smoking in the United States: The changing influence of gender and race. *Journal of the American Medical Association*, 261, 49–55.

Fischoff, B. (1990). Psychology and public policy: Tool or toolmaker? *American Psychologist*, 45, 647–653.

Fishbein, M., & Ajzen, I. (1975). *Belief, attitude, intention, and behavior: An introduction to theory and research.* Reading, MA: Addison-Wesley.

Fisher, A. C. (1977). Sport personality assessment: Facts, fallacies, and perspectives. *Motor Skills: Theory into Practice*, 1, 87–97.

Fisher, S., & Greenberg, R. P. (1977). *The scientific credibility of Freud's theories and therapy.* New York: Basic Books.

Fishman, J. (1987). Type A on trial. *Psychology Today*, 21, 42–50.

Fitzgerald, L. (1993). Sexual harassment: Violence against women in the workplace. *American Psychologist*, 48, 1070–1076.

Flament, M. F., Rapoport, J. L., Berg, C. J., Sceery, W., Kilts, C., Mellstrom, B., & Linnoila, M. (1985). Clomipramine treatment of childhood obsessive-compulsive disorder: A double-blind study. *Archives of General Psychiatry*, 42, 977–983.

Flament, M. F., Whitaker, A., Rapoport, J. L., Davies, M., Berg, C. Z., Kalikow, K., Sceery, W., & Shaffer, D. (1988). Obsessive-compulsive disorder in adolescence: An epidemiologic study. *Journal of the American Academy of Child and Adolescent Psychiatry*, 27, 289–296.

Flavell, J. H. (1982). On cognitive development. *Child Development*, 53, 1–10.

Flavell, J. H. (1985). *Cognitive development* (2nd ed.). Englewood Cliffs, NJ: Prentice-Hall.

Fleishman, E. A., & Mumford, M. D. (1991). Evaluating classifications of job behavior: A construct validation of the ability requirement scales. *Personnel Psychology*, 44, 523–575.

Flexser, A. J., & Tulving, E. (1982). Priming and recognition failure. *Journal of Verbal Learning and Verbal Behavior*, 21, 237–248.

Folkman, S. (1984). Personal control and stress and coping processes: A theoretical analysis. *Journal of Personality and Social Psychology*, 46, 839–852.

Ford, M. R., & Lowery, C. R. (1986). Gender differences in moral reasoning: A comparison of justice and care orientations. *Journal of Personality and Social Psychology*, 4, 777–783.

Fowler, R. D. (1992). Report of the chief executive officer: A year of building for the future. *American Psychologist*, 47, 876–883.

Fowles, D. G. (1990). *A profile of older Americans: 1989.* Washington, DC: American Association of Retired Persons.

Frank, E., Kupfer, D. J., Perel, J. M., Cornes, C., Jarret, D. B., et al. (1990). Three-year outcomes for maintenance therapies in recurrent depression. *Archives of General Psychiatry*, 47, 1093–1099.

Frankel, F. H. (1993). Adult reconstruction of childhood events in the multiple personality literature. *American Journal of Psychiatry*, 150, 954–958.

Frazier, T. M., David, G. H., Goldstein, H., & Goldberg, I. D. (1961). Cigarette smoking and prematurity. *American Journal of Obstetrics and Gynecology*, 81, 988–996.

Fredrickson, P. A. (1987). The relevance of sleep disorders medicine to psychiatric practice. *Psychiatric Annals*, 17, 91–100.

Free, M. L., & Oei, T. P. S. (1989). Biological and psychological processes in the treatment and maintenance of depression. *Clinical Psychology Review*, 9, 653–688.

Freedman, D. X. (1984). Psychiatric epidemiology counts. *Archives of General Psychiatry*, 41, 931–934.

Freedman, J. L. (1975). *Crowding and behavior.* New York: Viking Press.

Freud, A. (1958) *Adolescence: Psychoanalytic study of the child.* New York: Academic Press.

Freud, S. (1900). The interpretation of dreams. In J. Strachey (Ed.), *The complete psychological works of Sigmund Freud.* London: Hogarth Press.

Freud, S. (1933). *New introductory lectures on psychoanalysis: Standard edition.* New York: Norton.

Fribourg, S. (1982). Cigarette smoking and sudden infant death syndrome. *Journal of Obstetrics and Gynecology,* 142, 934–941.

Fried, P. A. (1993). Prenatal exposure to tobacco and marijuana: Effects during pregnancy, infancy, and early childhood. *Clinical Obstetrics and Gynecology,* 36, 319–337.

Friedman, H. H., Hawley, P. H., & Tucker, J. S. (1994). Personality, health and longevity. *Current Directions in Psychological Science,* 3, 37–41.

Friedman, H. S., & Booth-Kewley, S. (1987). The "disease-prone personality": A meta-analytic review of the construct. *American Psychologist,* 42, 539–555.

Friedman, M., & Rosenman, R. (1959). Association of specific overt behavior patterns with blood and cardiovascular findings. *Journal of the American Medical Association,* 169, 1286.

Friedman, M. I., & Stricker, E. M. (1976). The physiological psychology of hunger: A physiological perspective. *Psychological Review,* 83, 409–431.

Friedman, R. J., & Doyal, G. T. (1987). *Attention deficit disorder and hyperactivity* (2nd ed.). Danville, IL: The Interstate.

Friedman, S. (1972). Habituation and recovery of visual response in the alert human newborn. *Journal of Experimental Child Psychology,* 13, 339–349.

Frijda, N. H. (1988). The laws of emotion. *American Psychologist,* 43, 349–358.

Furstenberg, F. F., Brooks-Gunn, J., & Chase-Lansdale, L. (1989). Teenaged pregnancy and childbearing. *American Psychologist,* 44, 313–320.

Furumoto, L., & Scarborough, E. (1986). Placing women in the history of psychology: The first American women psychologists. *American Psychologist,* 41, 35–42.

Gabrena, W., Wang, Y., Latané, B. (1985). Social loafing on an optimizing task: Cross-cultural differences among Chinese and Americans. *Journal of Cross-cultural Psychology,* 16, 223–242.

Gagné, R. M. (1984). Learning outcomes and their effects: Useful categories of human performance. *American Psychologist,* 39, 377–385.

Galanter, E. (1962). *Contemporary psychophysics.* In R. Brown et al. (Eds.), *New directions in psychology.* New York: Holt, Rinehart and Winston.

Gallagher, J. J. (1994). Teaching and learning: New models. *Annual Review of Psychology,* 45, 171–195.

Galss, D. C., Singer, J. E., & Friedman, L. N. (1969). Psychic cost of adaptation to an environmental stressor. *Journal of Personality and Social Psychology,* 12, 200–210.

Gans, J. E., & Blyth, D. A. (1990). *American adolescents: How healthy are they?* AMA Profiles of Adolescent Health series. Chicago: American Medical Association.

Garbarino, J. (1985). *Adolescent development: An ecological perspective.* Columbus, OH: Merrill.

Garcia, J., Ervin, F. R., & Koelling, R. A. (1966). Learning with prolonged delay of reinforcement. *Psychonomic Science,* 5, 121–122.

Gardner, M. (1993). The false memory syndrome. *Skeptical Inquirer,* 17, 370–375.

Garfield, S. L. (1981). Psychotherapy: A 40-year appraisal. *American Psychologist,* 36, 174–183.

Garner, D. M., Olmstead, M. P., Davis, R., Rockert, W., Goldbloom, D., & Eagle, M. (1990). The association between bulimic symptoms and reported psychopathology. *International Journal of Eating Disorders,* 9, 1–15.

Garry, M. & Loftus, E. F. (1994). Repressed memories of childhood trauma: Could some of them be suggested? *USA Today,* January, 82–84.

Gazzaniga, M. S., & LeDoux, J. E. (1978). *The integrated mind.* New York: Plenum.

Geller, E. S., Bruff, C. D., & Nimmer, J. G. (1985). "Flash for life": Community-based prompting for safety belt promotion. *Journal of Applied Behavioral Analysis,* 18, 309–314.

Geller, E. S., Winett, R. A., & Everett, P. B. (1982). *Preserving the environment: new strategies for behavior change.* New York: Pergamon.

Geller, E. S., Rudd, J. R., Kalsher, M. J., Sreff, F. M., & Lehman, G. R. (1987). Employer-based programs to motivate safety belt use: A review of short-term and long-term effects. *Journal of Safety Research,* 18, 1–17.

Gellhorn, E. (1964). Motion and emotion: The role of proprioception in the physiology and path-ology of the emotions. *Psychological Review,* 71, 457–472.

Gelman, R. (1978). Cognitive development. *Annual Review of Psychology,* 29, 297–332.

Gelso, C. J., & Fassinger, R. E. (1990). Counseling psychology: Theory and research on interventions. *Annual Review of Psychology,* 41, 355–386.

Gemberling, G. A., & Domjan, M. (1982). Selective associations in one-day-old rats: Taste toxicosis and texture-shock aversion learning. *Journal of Comparative and Physiological Psychology,* 96, 105–113.

George, L. (1992). Acupuncture: Drug free pain relief. *American Health,* 11, 45.

Geracioti, T. D., & Liddle, R. A. (1988). Impaired cholecystokinin secretion of bulimia nervosa. *New England Journal of Medicine,* 319, 683–688.

Gerbert, B., & Maguire, B. (1989). Public acceptance of the Surgeon General's brochure on AIDS. *Public Health Report,* 104, 130–133.

Gerow, J. R., & Murphy, D. P. (1980). The validity of the Nelson-Denny Reading Test as a predictor of performance in introductory psychology. *Educational and Psychological Measurement, 40,* 553–556.

Gest, T. & Friedman, D. (1994, August/September). The New Crime Wave. *U. S. News and World Report,* pp. 26–28.

Gibson, E. J. (1987). Introductory essay: What does infant perception tell us about theories of perception? *Journal of Experimental Psychology: Perception and Performance, 13,* 515–523.

Gibson, E. J. (1988). Exploratory behavior in the development of perceiving, acting, and the acquiring of knowledge. *Annual Review of Psychology, 39,* 1–41.

Gibson, E. J., & Walk, R. D. (1960). The visual cliff. *Scientific American, 202,* 64–71.

Gilbert, L. A. (1994). Current perspectives on dual-career families. *Current Directions in Psychological Science, 3,* 101–104.

Gillam, B. (1980). Geometrical illusions. *Scientific American, 242,* 102–111.

Gilligan, C. (1982). *In a different voice.* Cambridge, MA: Harvard University Press.

Gilovich, T., Vallone, R., & Tversky, A. (1985). The hot hand in basketball: On the misperception of random sequences. *Cognitive Psychology, 17,* 295–314.

Giuliano, J. D. (1994). A peer education program to provide the use of conflict resolution skills among at-risk school age males. *Public Health Reports, 109,* 158–161.

Glaser, R. (1984). Education and thinking. *American Psychologist, 39,* 93-104.

Glasgow, R. E., & Lichtenstein, E. (1987). Long term effects of behavioral smoking cessation interventions. *Behavior Therapy, 18,* 297–324.

Glass, A. L., Holyoak, K. J., & Santa, J. L. (1979). *Cognition.* Reading, MA: Addison-Wesley.

Glass, D. C., & Singer, J. E. (1972). *Urban stress.* Hillsdale, NJ: Erlbaum.

Glazer, S. (1992). Violence in schools. *C Q Researcher, 2,* 787–795.

Gleaves, D. H. (1994). On "The reality of repressed memories." *American Psychologist, 49,* 440–441.

Glenn, N. D., & Weaver, C. N. (1981). The contribution of marital happiness to global happiness. *Journal of Marriage and the Family, 43,* 161–168.

Golbus, M. S. (1980). Teratology for the obstetrician: Current status. *American Journal of Obstetrics and Gynecology, 55,* 269.

Gold, P. E. (1987). Sweet memories. *American Scientist, 75,* 151–155.

Gold, S. N., Hughes, D., & Hohnecker, L. (1994). Degrees of repression of sexual abuse memories. *American Psychologist, 49,* 441–442.

Goldberg, J. R. (1994). AAMFT annual conference focuses on violence. *Family Therapy News,* December, pp. 1, 16.

Goldfried, M. R., Greenberg, L. S., & Marmar, C. (1990). Individual psychotherapy: Process and outcome. *Annual Review of Psychology, 41,* 659–688.

Goldsmith, H. H., & Harman, C. (1994). Temperament and attachment; individuals and relationships. *Current Directions in Psychological Science, 3,* 53–57.

Goldstein, I. L. (1980). Training in work organizations. *Annual Review of Psychology, 31,* 229–272.

Goldstein, I. L. (1989). *Training and Development in Organizations.* San Francisco: Jossey-Bass.

Goldstein, I. L. (1986). *Training in organizations.* Monterey, CA: Brooks/Cole.

Goleman, O. (1980). 1,528 little geniuses and how they grew. *Psychology Today, 14,* 28–53.

Goodwin, D. W., Powell, B., Bremer, D., Hoine, H., & Stein, J. (1969). Alcohol and recall: State-dependent effects in man. *Science, 163,* 1358–1360.

Gorenstein, E. E. (1984). Debating mental illness. *American Psychologist, 39,* 50–56.

Gormezano, I. (1972). *Investigations of defense and reward conditioning in the rabbit.* In A. H. Black & W. F. Prokasky (Eds.). *Classical conditioning II: Current theory and research.* Englewood Cliffs, NJ: Prentice-Hall.

Gotlib, I. H. (1992). Interpersonal and cognitive aspects of depression. *Current Directions in Psychological Science, 1,* 149–156.

Gottesman, I. I., & Bertelsen, A. (1989). Confirming unexpressed genotypes for schizophrenia. *Archives of General Psychiatry, 46,* 867–872.

Gottlieb, B. H. (1981). *Social networks and social support.* Beverly Hills, CA: Sage.

Gottman, J. (1994). Why marriages fail. *Networker, 18,* 41–48.

Gough, H. G. (1985). A work orientation scale for the California Psychological Inventory. *Journal of Applied Psychology, 70,* 505–513.

Govoni, L. E., & Hayes, J. E. (1988). *Drugs and nursing implications* (6th ed.). Norwalk, CT: Appleton & Lange.

Graf, P., & Schacter, D. A. (1985). Implicit and explicit memory for new associations in normal and amnesic subjects. *Journal of Experimental Psychology: Learning, Memory, and Cognition, 11,* 501–518.

Graziano, A. M., & Raulin, M. L. (1993). *Research*

methods: A process of inquiry. New York: Harper-Collins.

Green, D. M., & Swets, J. A. (1966). *Signal detection theory and psychophysics.* New York: Wiley.

Greenberg, J., & Cohen, R. L. (1982). *Equity and justice in social behavior.* New York: Academic Press.

Greenberg, L. S., & Safran, J. D. (1987). *Emotion in psychotherapy.* New York: Guilford.

Greenberg, L. S., & Safran, J. D. (1989). Emotion in psychotherapy. *American Psychologist, 44,* 19–29.

Greenwald, A. G. (1992). New look 3: Unconsciousness reclaimed. *American Psychologist, 47,* 776–779.

Greer, S. (1964). Study of parental loss in neurotics and sociopaths. *Archives of General Psychiatry, 11,* 177–180.

Gregory, R. L. (1963). Distortion of visual space as inappropriate constancy scaling. *Nature, 199,* 678–679.

Gregory, R. L. (1977). *Eye and brain: The psychology of seeing* (3rd ed.). New York: New World Library.

Grice, G. R. (1948). The relation of secondary reinforcement to delayed reward in visual discrimination learning. *Journal of Experimental Psychology, 38,* 1–16.

Grinspoon, L. (1977). *Marihuana reconsidered (2nd ed.).* Cambridge, MA: Harvard University Press.

Grob, C., & Dobkin de Rois, M. (1992). Adolescent drug use in cross-cultural perspective. *Journal of Drug Issues, 22,* 121–138.

Grossman, H. (Ed.). (1983). *Classification in Mental Retardation (3rd ed.).* Washington, DC: American Association of Mental Deficiency.

Grossman, H. J. (Ed.). (1973). *Manual on terminology and classification in mental retardation.* Washington, DC: American Association on Mental Deficiency.

Groves, P. M. & Rebec, G. V. (1992). *Introduction to biological psychology* (4th ed.). Dubuque, IA: Wm. C. Brown.

Guilford, J. P. (1959a). *Personality.* New York: McGraw-Hill.

Guilford, J. P. (1959b). *Traits of creativity.* In H. H. Anderson(Ed.), *Creativity and its cultivation.* New York: HarperCollins.

Guion, R. M., & Gibson, W. M. (1988). Personnel selection and placement. *Annual Review of Psychology, 39,* 349–374.

Gur, R. E., Resnick, S. M., Alavi, A., Gur, R. C., Caroff, S., Dann, R., et al. (1987). Regional brain function in schizophrenia. *Archives of General Psychiatry, 44,* 119–125.

Gurman, A. S., Kniskern, D. P., & Pinsof, W. M. (1986). *Research on the process and outcome of marital and family therapy.* In S. L. Garfield & A. E. Bergin (Eds.), *Handbook of psychotherapy and behavior change (3rd ed.).* New York: Wiley.

Haist, F., Shimamura, A. P., & Squire, L. R. (1992). On the relationship between recall and recognition memory. *Journal of Experimental Psychology: Learning, Memory, and Cognition, 18,* 691–702.

Hall, J. F. (1976). *Classical conditioning and instrumental conditioning: A contemporary approach.* Philadelphia: Lippincott.

Hall, E. T. (1966). *The hidden dimension.* Garden City, NY: Doubleday.

Hall, W. G., & Oppenheim, R. W. (1987). Developmental psychology. *Annual Review of Psychology, 38,* 91–128.

Hamburg, D. A., & Takanishi, R. (1989). Preparing for life: The critical transition of adolescence. *American Psychologist, 44,* 825–827.

Hamer, D. H., Hu, S., Magnuson, V. L., Hu, N., & Pattatucci, A. M. L. (1993). A linkage between DNA markers on the X chromosome and male sexual orientation. *Science, 261,* 321–327.

Hammen, C., Burge, D., Burney, E., & Adrian, C. (1990). Longitudinal study of diagnoses in children of women with unipolar and bipolar affective disorder. *Archives of General Psychiatry, 47,* 1112–1117.

Hansen, W. B., Hahn, G. L., & Wolkenstein, J. (1990). Perceived personal immunity: Beliefs about susceptibility to AIDS. *Journal of Sex Research, 27,* 622–628.

Harding, C. M. (1988). Course types in schizophrenia: An analysis of European and American studies. *Schizophrenia Bulletin, 14,* 663–642.

Hare, R. D. (1970). *Psychopathology: Theory and Research.* New York: Wiley.

Harkins, S. (1987). Social loafing and social facilitation. *Journal of Experimental Social Psychology, 23,* 1–18.

Harkins, S. G. & Petty, R. E. (1982). Effects of task difficulty and task uniqueness on social loafing. *Journal of Personality and Social Psychology, 43,* 1214–1229.

Harkins, S. G., & Syzmanski, K. (1989). Social loafing and group evaluation. *Journal of Personality and Social Psychology, 56,* 934–941.

Harlow, H. F. (1932). Social facilitation of feeding in the albino rat. *Journal of Genetic Psychology, 41,* 211–221.

Harris, B. (1979). What ever happened to Little Albert? *American Psychologist, 34,* 151–160.

Harris, D. V. (1973). *Involvement in sport: A somatopsychic rationale for physical activity.* Philadelphia: Lea & Febiger.

Harris, L. & Associates. (1975, 1981, 1983). *The myth and reality of aging in America.* Washington, DC: The National Council on Aging.

Harris, P. L. (1983). *Infant cognition.* In P. H. Mussen (Ed.), Handbook of child psychology (Vol. 2). New York: Wiley.

Harris, M. M. (1989). Reconsidering the employment interview: A review of recent literature and suggestions for future research. *Personnel Psychology*, 42, 691–726.

Harrow, M., Goldberg, J. F., Grossman, L. S., & Meltzer, H. Y. (1990). Outcome in manic disorders. *Archives of General Psychiatry*, 47, 665–671.

Hartup, W. W. (1989). Social relationships and their developmental significance. *American Psychologist*, 44, 120–126.

Harvey, J. H., & Weary, G. (1984). Current issues in attribution theory. *Annual Review of Psychology*, 35, 427j–459.

Hastorf, A. H., & Cantril, H. (1954). They saw a game: A case study. *Journal of Abnormal and Social Psychology*, 49, 129–134.

Havighurst, R. J. (1972). *Developmental tasks and education (3rd ed.).* New York: McKay.

Hayduk, L. A. (1983). Personal space: Where we now stand. *Psychological Bulletin*, 94, 293–335.

Hayes, C. D. (Ed.). (1987). *Risking the future (Vol. 1).* Washington, DC: National Academy Press.

Hayman, C. A. G., & Tulving, E. (1989). Contingent dissociation between recognition and fragment completion: The method of triangulation. *Journal of Experimental Psychology: Learning, Memory, and Cognition*, 15, 220–224.

Haynes, S. G., McMichael, A. J., & Tyroler, H. A. (1978). Survival after early and normal retirement. *Journal of Gerontology*, 33, 872–883.

Hayward, C., Killan, J. D., Hammer, L. D., Litt, I. F., Wilson, D. M, Simmonds, B., & Taylor, C. B. (1992). Pubertal stage and panic attack history in sixth- and seventh-grade girls. *American Journal of Psychiatry*, 149, 1239–1243.

Hazan, C., & Shaver, P. (1987). Romantic love conceptualized as an attachment process. *Journal of Personality and Social Psychology*, 52, 511–524.

Hebb, D. O. (1955). Drives and the C.N.S. (conceptual nervous system). *Psychological Review*, 62, 243–254.

Heffernan, J. A., & Albee, G. W. (1985). Prevention perspectives. *American Psychologist*, 40, 202–204.

Heinrichs, R. W. (1993). Schizophrenia and the brain: Conditions for a neuropsychology of madness. *American Psychologist*, 48, 221–233.

Hellige, J. B. (Ed.). (1983). *Cerebral hemisphere asymmetry: Method, theory, and application.* New York: Praeger.

Hellige, J. B. (1990). Hemispheric asymmetry. *Annual Review of Psychology*, 41, 55–80.

Helms, J. E. (1992). Why is there no study of cultural equivalence in standardized cognitive ability testing? *American Psychologist*, 47, 1083– 1101.

Helzer, J. E., Robins, L. N., & McEnvoy, L. (1987). Post-traumatic stress disorder in the general population. *New England Journal of Medicine*, 317, 1630–1634.

Hennessy, J., & Melhuish, E. C. (1991). Early day care and the development of school-age children. *Journal of Reproduction and Infant Psychology*, 9, 117–136.

Herbert, T. B., & Cohen, S. (1993). Depression and immunity: A meta-analytic review. *Psychological Bulletin*, 113, 472–486.

Herek, G. M., & Glunt, E. K. (1988). An epidemic of stigma: Public reactions to AIDS. *American Psychologist*, 43, 886–891.

Hetherington, E. M. (1989). Coping with family transitions: Winners, losers, and survivors. *Child Development*, 60, 1–14.

Higgins, E. T., & Bargh, J. A. (1987). Social cognition and social perception. *Annual Review of Psychology*, 38, 369–426.

Hilgard, E. R. (1992). Divided consciousness and dissociation. *Consciousness and Cognition*, 1, 16–31.

Hilgard, E. R. (1975). Hypnosis. *Annual Review of Psychology*, 26, 19–44.

Hilgard, E. R. (1978, January). Hypnosis and consciousness. *Human Nature*, pp. 42–49.

Hilgard, E. R., & Hilgard, J. R. (1975). *Hypnosis in the relief of pain.* Los Altos, CA: W. Kaufman.

Hilgard, J. R. (1970). *Personality and hypnosis: A study of imaginative involvement.* Chicago: University of Chicago Press.

Hill, W. F. (1985). *Learning: A Survey of Psychological Interpretations (4th ed.).* New York: Harper & Row.

Hinrichs, J. R. (1976). *Personnel training.* In M. Dunnette (Ed.), *Handbook of industrial and organizational psychology*, Skokie, IL: Rand McNally.

Hinsz, V. B., & Davis, J. H. (1984). Persuasive arguments theory, group polarization, and choice shifts. *Personality and Social Psychology Bulletin*, 10, 260–268.

Hobfoll, S. E. (1986). *Stress, social support, and women.* Washington, DC: Hemisphere.

Hobfoll, S. E. (1989). Conservation of resources: A new attempt at conceptualizing stress. *American Psychologist, 44,* 513–524.

Hobson, J. A. (1988). *The dreaming brain.* New York: Basic Books.

Hobson, J. A. (1977). *The reciprocal interaction model of sleep cycle control: Implications for PGO wave generation and dream amnesia.* In R. R. Drucker-Colin & J. L. McGaugh (Eds.), *Neurobiology of sleep and memory.* New York: Academic Press.

Hobson, J. A., & McCarley, R. W. (1977). The brain as a dream state generator: An activation-synthesis hypothesis of the dream process. *American Journal of Psychiatry, 134,* 1335–1348.

Hofferth, S. L., & Hayes, C. D. (eds.). (1987). *Risking the future: Adolescent sexuality, pregnancy, and childbearing.* Washington, DC: National Academy Press.

Hoffman, D. D. (1983). The interpretation of visual illusions. *Scientific American, 245,* 154–162.

Hogan, J. (1989). Personality correlates of physical fitness. *Journal of Personality and Social Psychology, 56,* 284–288.

Hogan, R., & Nicholson, R. A. (1988). The meaning of personality test scores. *American Psychologist, 43,* 621–626.

Holden, C. (1980). A new visibility for gifted children. *Science, 210,* 879–882.

Hollander, E., DeCaria, C. M., Nitescu, A., Gully, R., Suckow, R. F., et al. (1992). Serotonergic function in obsessive-compulsive disorder. *Archives of General Psychiatry, 49,* 21–28.

Hollis, J. F., Connett, J. E., Stevens, V. J., & Greenlick, M. R. (1990). Stressful life events, Type A behavior, and the prediction of cardiovascular and total mortality over six years. *Journal of Behavioral Medicine, 13,* 263–281.

Holmes, T. H., & Rahe, R. H. (1967). The social readjustment rating scale. *Journal of Psychosomatic Research, 11,* 213–218.

Holmes, T. S., & Holmes, T. H. (1970). Short-term intrusions into the life-style routine. *Journal of Psychosomatic Research, 14,* 121–132.

Holyoak, K. J., & Spellman, B. A. (1993). Thinking. *Annual Review of Psychology, 44,* 265–315.

Hood, R. D. (1990). *Paternally mediated effects.* In R. D. Hood (Ed.), *Developmental toxicology: Risk assessment and the future.* New York: Van Nostrand Reinhold.

Horn, J., & Anderson, K. (1993). Who in America is trying to lose weight? *Annals of Internal Medicine, 119,* 672–676.

Horn, J. L. (1976). Human abilities: A review of research and theories in the early 1970s. *Annual Review of Psychology, 27,* 437–485.

Horowitz, F. D., & O'Brien, M. (Eds.). (1985). The gifted and talented: Developmental perspectives. Washington, DC: *American Psychological Association.*

Hoshmand, T. L., & Polkinghorne, D. E. (1992). Redefining the science-practice relationship and professional training. *American Psychologist, 47,* 55–66.

Hostetler, A. J. (1987). Alzheimer's trials hinge on early diagnosis. *APA Monitor, 18,* 14–15.

Houston, B. K., & Vavak, C. R. (1991). Cynical hostility: Developmental factors, psycho-social correlates, and health behaviors. *Health Psychology, 10,* 9–17.

Hovland, C. I., & Weiss, W. (1951). The influence of source credibility on communication effectiveness. *Public Opinion Quarterly, 15,* 635–650.

Howard, K. I., Kopata, S. M., Krause, M. S., & Orlinsky, D. E. (1986). The dose-effect r relationship in psychotherapy. *American Psychologist, 41,* 159–164.

Howell, W. C., & Dipboye, R. L. (1982). *Essentials of industrial and organizational psychology.* Homewood, IL: Dorsey Press.

Howes, C. (1990). Can the age of entry into child care and the quality of child care predict adjustment in kindergarten? *Developmental Psychology, 26,* 292–303.

Hubel, D. H. (1979). The brain. *Scientific American, 241,* 45–53.

Hudson, W. (1960). Pictorial depth perception in subcultural groups in Africa. *Journal of Social Psychology, 52,* 183–208.

Hughes, F. P., & Noppe, L. D. (1985). *Human development.* St. Paul, MN: West.

Hui, C. H. (1990). *Work attitudes, leadership styles, and managerial behaviors in different cultures.* In R. W. Brislin (Ed.), *Applied cross-cultural psychology.* Newbury Park, CA: Sage.

Hull, C. L. (1943). *Principles of behavior.* Englewood Cliffs, NJ: Prentice-Hall.

Hunter, S., & Sundel, M. (Eds.). (1989). *Midlife myths.* Newbury Park, CA: Sage.

Huston, T. L., Ruggiero, M., Conner, R., & Geis, G. (1981). Bystander intervention into crime: A study based on naturally occurring episodes. *Social Psychology Quarterly, 44,* 14–23.

Iacono, W. G., & Grove, W. M. (1993). Schizophrenia reviewed: Toward an integrative genetic model. *Psychological Science, 4,* 273–276.

Ilgen, D. R., & Klein, H. J. (1989). Organizational behavior. *Annual Review of Psychology, 40,* 327–351.

Insko, C. A. (1965). Verbal reinforcement of attitude. *Journal of Personality and Social Psychology*, 2, 621–623.

Isenberg, D. J. (1986). Group polarization: A critical review and meta-analysis. *Journal of Personality and Social Psychology*, 50, 1141–1151.

Iso-Ahola, S. E., & Blanchard, W. J. (1986). Psychological momentum and competitive sport performance: A field study. *Perceptual and Motor Skills*, 62, 763–768.

Istvan, J. (1986). Stress, anxiety, and birth outcomes: A critical review of the evidence. *Psychological Bulletin*, 100, 331–348.

Izard, C. E. (1972). *Patterns of emotion: A new analysis of anxiety and aggression.* New York: Academic Press.

Izard, C. E. (1977). *Human emotions.* New York: Plenum.

Izard, C. E. (1993). Four systems for emotion activation: Cognitive and metacognitive processes. *Psychological Review*, 100, 68–90.

Jackaway, R., & Teevan, R. (1976). Fear of failure and fear of success: Two dimensions of the same motive. *Sex Roles*, 2, 283–294.

Jacobs, B. L. (1987). How hallucinogenic drugs work. *American Scientist*, 75, 386–392.

Jacobs, B. L., & Trulson, M. E. (1979). Mechanisms of action of LSD. *American Scientist*, 67, 396–404.

Jacobson, D. S. (1984). Neonatal correlates of prenatal exposure to smoking, caffeine, and alcohol. *Infant Behavior and Development*, 7, 253–265.

Jacoby, L. L., & Dallas, M. (1981). On the relationship between autobiographical memory and perceptual learning. *Journal of Experimental Psychology: General*, 3, 306–340.

James, W. (1890). *Principles of psychology.* New York: Holt, Rinehart and Winston.

James, W. (1892). *Psychology: Briefer course.* New York: Holt, Reinhart and Winston.

James, W. (1904). Does consciousness exist? *Journal of Philosophy*, 1, 477–491.

Janis, I. L. (1972). *Victims of groupthink.* Boston: Houghton Mifflin.

Janis, I. L. (1983a). *Groupthink: Psychological studies of policy decisions and fiascoes (2nd ed.).* Boston: Houghton Mifflin.

Janis, I. L. (1983b). The role of social support in adherence to stressful decisions. *American Psychologist*, 38, 143–160.

Janoff-Bulman, R. (1979). Characterological versus behavioral self-blame: Inquiries into depression and rape. *Journal of Personality and Social Psychology*, 37, 1798–1809.

Jaroff, L. (1993). Lies of the mind. *Time*, November 29, 52–59.

Jeffery, R. W. (1989). Risk behaviors and health: Contrasting individual and population perspectives. *American Psychologist*, 44, 1194–1202.

Jenkins, C. D. (1976). Recent evidence supporting psychological and social risk factors for coronary disease. *New England Journal of Medicine*, 294, 1033–1038.

Jenkins, J. G. & Dallenbach, K. M. (1924). Oblivescence during sleep and waking. *American Journal of Psychology*, 35, 605–612.

Jensen, A. R. (1980). *Bias in mental testing.* New York: Free Press.

Jensen, A. R. (1981). *Straight talk about mental tests.* London: Methuen.

Jessor, R. (1993). Successful adolescent development among youth in high-risk settings. *American Psychologist*, 48, 117–126.

Johnson, D. L. (1989). Schizophrenia as a brain disease. *American Psychologist*, 44, 553–555.

Johnson, J., Weissman, M. M., & Klerman, G. L. (1990) Panic disorder, comorbidity, and suicide attempts. *Archives of General Psychiatry*, 47, 805–808.

Johnson, M. K., & Hasher, L. (1987). Human learning and memory. *Annual Review of Psychology*, 38, 631–638.

Jones, E. E. (1979). The rocky road from acts to dispositions. *American Psychologist*, 34, 107–117.

Jones, E. E., & Nisbett, R. E. (1971). *The actor and the observer: Divergent perceptions of behavior.* Morristown, NJ: General Learning Press.

Jones, K. L., Smith, D. W., Ulleland, C. N., & Streissgoth, A. P. (1973). Patterns of malformation in offspring of chronic alcoholic mothers. *Lancet*, 3, 1267–1271.

Jordan, B. K., Marmar, C. R., Fairbank, J. A., Schlenger, W. E., Kulka, R. A., Hough, R. L., & Weiss, D. S. (1992). Problems in families of male Vietnam veterans with posttraumatic stress disorder. *Journal of Consulting and Clinical Psychology*, 60, 916–926.

Jordan, J., Kaplan, A., Miller, J., Striver, I., & Surrey, J. (1991). *Women's growth in connection.* New York: Guilford.

Joyce, P. R., & Paykel, E. S. (1989). Predictors of drug response in depression. *Archives of General Psychiatry*, 46, 89–99.

Julien, R. M. (1985). *A primer of drug action (4th ed.).* San Francisco: Freeman.

Kacmar, K. M., & Ferris, G. R. (1989). Theoretical and methodological considerations in the age-job satisfaction relationship. *Journal of Applied Psychology*, 74, 201–207.

Kagan, J. (1988). The meanings of personality predicates. *American Psychologist, 43,* 614–620.

Kahn, S., Zimmerman, G., Csikzentmihalyi, M., & Getzels, J. W. (1985). Relations between identity in young adulthood and intimacy at midlife. *Journal of Personality and Social Psychology, 49,* 1316–1322.

Kales, A., Scharf, M. B., Kales, J. D., & Soldatos, C. R. (1979). Rebound insomnia: A potential hazard following withdrawal of certain benzodiazepines. *Journal of the American Medical Association, 241,* 1692–1695.

Kalish, R. A. (1976). *Death and dying in a social context.* In R. H. Binstock & E. Shanas (Eds.), *Handbook of aging and the social sciences.* New York: Van Nostrand Reinhold.

Kalish, R. A. (1985). *Death, grief, and caring relationships.* Monterey, CA: Brooks/Cole.

Kamin, L. (1968). "Attention-like processes in classical conditioning." In M. Jones (Ed.), *Miami symposium on the prediction of behavior: Aversive stimulation.* Miami: University of Miami Press.

Kamin, L. (1969). *Predictability, surprise, attention, and conditioning,* In R. Church & B. Campbell (Eds.), *Punishment and aversive behaviors.* Englewood Cliffs, NJ: Prentice-Hall.

Kamiya, J., Barber, T. X., Miller, N. E., Shapiro, D., & Stoyva, J. (1977). Biofeedback and Self-control. Chicago: Aldine.

Kane, J. (1989). The current status of neuroleptics. *Journal of Clinical Psychiatry, 50,* 322–328.

Kanizsa, G. (1976). Subjective contours. *Scientific American, 234,* 48–52.

Kanner, A. D., Coyne, J. C., Schaefer, C., & Lazarus, R. S. (1981). Comparison of two modes of stress measurement: Daily hassles and uplifts versus major life events. *Journal of Behavioral Medicine, 4,* 1–39.

Kaplan, H. I., & Sadock, B. J. (1991). *Synopsis of psychiatry.* Baltimore: Williams & Wilkins.

Kaplan, G. M. (1991). The use of biofeedback in the treatment of chronic facial tics: A case study. *Medical psychotherapy, 4,* 71–84.

Kaplan, R. M. (1984). The connection between clinical health promotion and health status. *American Psychologist, 39,* 755–765.

Kaplan, S. (1987). Aesthetics, affect and cognition: Environmental preference from an evolutionary perspective. *Environment and Behavior, 19,* 3–32.

Karoum, F., Karson, C. N., Bigelow, L. B., Lawson, W. B., & Wyatt, R. J. (1987). Preliminary evidence of reduced combined output of dopamine and its metabolites in chronic schizophrenia. *Archives of General Psychiatry, 44,* 604–607.

Kassin, S. M., Ellsworth, P. C., & Smith, V. L. (1989). The "general acceptance" of psychological research on eyewitness testimony: A survey of experts. *American Psychologist, 44,* 1089–1098.

Kastenbaum, R., & Costa, P. (1977). Psychological perspectives on death. *Annual Review of Psychology, 28,* 225–249.

Katzell, R. A., & Guzzo, R. A. (1983). Psychological approaches to productivity improvement. *American Psychologist, 38,* 468–472.

Katzell, R. A., & Thompson, D. E. (1990). Work motivation: Theory and practice. *American Psychologist, 45,* 144–153.

Katzman, R. (1987). Alzheimer's disease. *New England Journal of Medicine, 314,* 964–973.

Kay, S. R. (1990). Significance of the positive-negative distinction in schizophrenia. *Schizophrenia Bulletin, 16,* 635–652.

Kay, S. R., & Singh, M. M. (1989). The positive-negative distinction in drug-free schizophrenic patients. *Archives of General Psychiatry, 46,* 711–717.

Kazdin, A. E., Esveldt-Dawson, K., French, N. H., & Unis, A. S. (1987). Problem-solving skills training and relationship therapy in the treatment of antisocial child behavior. *Journal of Consulting and Clinical Psychology, 55,* 76–85.

Keating, D. P. (1980). Thinking processes in adolescents. In J. Adelson (ed.) *Handbook of adolescent psychology.* New York: Wiley.

Keesey, R. E., & Powley, T. L. (1975). Hypothalamic regulation of body weight. *American Scientist, 63,* 558–565.

Keesey, R. E., & Powley, T. L. (1986). The regulation of body weight. *Annual Review of Psychology, 37,* 109–133.

Keith, P. M. (1983). A comparison of the resources of parents and childless men and women in very old age. *Family Relations, 32,* 403–409.

Kelley, H. H. (1973). The process of causal attribution. *American Psychologist, 28,* 107–128.

Kelley, H. H., & Michela, J. L. (1980). Attribution theory and research. *Annual Review of Psychology, 31,* 457–501.

Kelley, H. H., & Thibault, J. W. (1978). *Interpersonal relations: A theory of interdependence.* New York: Wiley.

Kelly, H. H. (1967). Attribution theory in social psychology. In D. Levine (Ed.), *Nebraska symposium on motivation.* Lincoln: University of Nebraska Press.

Kelly, J. A., Murphy, D. A., Sikkema, K. J., & Kalichman, S. C. (1993). Psychological interventions to prevent HIV infection are urgently needed. *American Psychologist, 48,* 1023–1034.

Kelly, J. A., & St. Lawrence, J. S. (1988). *The AIDS health crisis.* New York: Plenum.

Kelly, J. A., St. Lawrence, J. S., Hood, H. V., & Brasfield, T. L. (1989). Behavior intervention to reduce AIDS risk activities. *Journal of Consulting and Clinical Psychology, 57,* 60–67.

Kempler, D., & Van Lanker, D. (1987). The right turn of phrase. *Psychology Today, 21,* 20–22.

Kendler, K. S., & Gruenberg, A. M. (1982). Genetic relationship between paranoid personality disorder and the "schizophrenic" spectrum disorders. *American Journal of Psychiatry, 139,* 1185–1186.

Kendler, K. S., Gruenberg, A. M., & Kinney, D. K. (1994). Independent diagnoses of adoptees and relatives as defined by the DSM-III-R in the Provincial and National Samples of the Danish Adoption Study of Schizophrenia. *Archives of General Psychiatry, 51,* 456–468.

Kendler, K. S., Neale, M. C., Kessler, R. C., Heath, A. C., & Eaves, L. J. (1993). A longitudinal twin study of 1-year prevalence of major depression in women. *Archives of General Psychiatry, 50,* 843–852.

Kershner, J. R., & Ledger, G. (1985). Effect of sex, intelligence, and style of thinking on creativity: A comparison of gifted and average IQ children. *Journal of Personality and Social Psychology, 48,* 1033–1040.

Kessler, R. C., McGonagle, K. A., Zhao, S., Nelson, C. P., et al. (1994). Lifetime and 12-month prevalence of DSM-III-R psychiatric disorders in the United States: Results from the National Comorbidity Survey. *Archives of General Psychiatry, 51,* 8–19.

Kessler, S. (1980). *The genetics of schizophrenia: A review.* In S. J. Keith & L. R. Mosher (Eds.), *Special report: Schizophrenia.* Washington, DC: U.S. Government Printing Office.

Kety, S. S., Wender, P. H., Jacobsen, B., Ingraham, L. J., Jansson, L., Faber, B., & Kinney, D. K. (1994). Mental illness in the biological and adoptive relatives of schizophrenic adoptees. *Archives of General Psychiatry, 51,* 442–455.

Key, M. R. (1975). *Male/female language.* Metuchen, NJ: Scarecrow Press.

Kholberg, L. (1963). Moral development and identification. In H. W. Stevenson (Ed.), *Child Psychology.* Chicago: University of Chicago Press.

Kientzle, M. J. (1946). Properties of learning curves under varied distributions of practice. *Journal of Experimental Psychology, 36,* 187–211.

Kiester, E. (1984a). The playing fields of the mind. *Psychology Today, 18,* 18–24.

Kiester, E. (1984b). The uses of anger. *Psychology Today, 18,* 26.

Kiester, E., Jr. (1980). Images of the night: The physiological roots of dreaming. *Science 80, 1,* 36–43.

Kihlstrom, J. F. (1987). The cognitive unconscious. *Science, 237,* 1445-1452.

Kimble, G. A. (1981). *Biological and cognitive constraints on learning.* In L. Benjamin (Ed.), *The G. Stanley Hall Lecture Series* (Vol. 1). Washington, DC: American Psychological Association.

Kimble, G. A. (1989). Psychology from the standpoint of a generalist. *American Psychologist, 44,* 493–499.

Kimmel, D. C. (1988). Ageism, psychology, and public policy. *American Psychologist, 43,* 175–178.

Kimmel, H. D. (1974). Instrumental conditioning of autonomically-medicated responses in human beings. *American Psychologist, 29,* 325–335.

King, M. J., Zir, L. M., Kaltman, A. J., & Fox, A. C. (1973). Variant angina associated with angiographically demonstrated coronary artery system spasm and REM sleep. *American Journal of Medical Science, 265,* 419–422.

King, M., Murray, M. A., & Atkinson, T. (1982). Background, personality, job characteristics, and satisfaction with work in a national sample. *Human Relations, 35,* 119–133.

Kinsbourne, M. (1982). Hemispheric specialization and the growth of human understanding. *American Psychologist, 37,* 411–420.

Kinsey, A. C., Pomeroy, W. B., & Martin, C. E. (1948). *Sexual behavior in the human male.* Philadelphia: Saunders.

Kinsey, A. C., Pomeroy, W. B., Martin, C. E., & Gebhard, P. H. (1953). *Sexual behavior in the human female.* Philadelphia: Saunders.

Kirby, D. A., & Verrier, R. L. (1989). Differential effects of sleep stage on coronary hemodynamic function during stenosis. *Physiology and Behavior, 45,* 1017–1020.

Kirkpatrick, D. L. (1976). *Evaluation of training.* In R. L. Craig (Ed.), *Training and development handbook* (2nd ed.). New York: McGraw-Hill.

Kirscht, J. P. (1983). Preventive health behavior: A review of research and issues. *Health Psychology, 2,* 277–301.

Kleitman, N. (1963a). Patterns of dreaming. *Scientific American, 203,* 82–88.

Kleitman, N. (1963b). *Sleep and wakefulness.* Chicago: University of Chicago Press.

Klepinger, D. H., Billy, J. O. G., Tanfer, K., & Grady, W. R. (1993). Perceptions of AIDS risk and severity and their association with risk-related behavior among U. S. men. *Family Planning Perspectives*, 25, 74–82.

Klerman, G. L. (1990). Treatment of recurrent unipolar major depressive disorder. *Archives of General Psychiatry*, 47, 1158–1162.

Knapp, S., & VandeCreek, L. (1989). What psychologists need to know about AIDS. *The Journal of Training and Practice in Professional Psychology*, 3, 3–16.

Knowles, E. S. (1983). Social physics and the effects of others: Tests of the effects of audience size and distance on social judgments and behavior. *Journal of Personality and Social Psychology*, 45, 1263–1279.

Kobasa, S. C. (1987). *Stress responses and personality*. In R. C. Barnette, L. Beiner, & G. K. Baruch (Eds.), *Gender and stress*. New York: Free Press.

Kobasa, S. C. (1979). Stressful life events, personality, and health: An inquiry into hardiness. *Journal of Personality and Social Psychology*, 37, 1–11.

Kobasa, S. C. (1982). *The hardy personality: Toward a social psychology of stress and health*. In G. S. Sanders & J. Suls (Eds.), *Social Psychology of Health and Illness*. Hillsdale, NJ: Erlbaum.

Koestler, A. (1964). *The act of creation*. New York: Macmillan.

Kohlberg, L. (1969). *Stages in the development of moral thought and action*. New York: Holt, Rinehart and Winston.

Kohlberg, L. (1969). *The task of Gestalt psychology*. Princeton, NJ: Princeton University Press.

Kohlberg, L. (1981). *Philosophy of moral development*. New York: HarperCollins.

Kolata, G. (1987). What babies know, and noises parents make. *Science*, 237, 726.

Kolb, B. (1989). Brain development, plasticity, and behavior. *American Psychologist*, 44, 1203–1212.

Korchin, S. J., & Scheldberg, D. (1981). The future of clinical assessment. *American Psychologist*, 36, 1147–1158.

Koslow, D. R., & Salett, E. P. (1989). *Crossing cultures in mental health*. Washington, DC: SIETAR International.

Koss, M. P., & Butcher, J. N. (1986). *Research on brief psychotherapy*. In S. L. Garfield & A. E. Bergin (Eds.), *Handbook of psychotherapy and behavior change (3rd ed.)*. New York: Wiley.

Kosslyn, S. M. (1987). Seeing and imagining in the cerebral hemispheres: A computational approach. *Psychological Review*, 94, 148–175.

Krantz, D. S., & Glass, D. C. (1984). *Personality, behavior patterns, and physical illness: Conceptual and methodological issues*. In W. D. Gentry (Ed.), *Handbook of behavioral medicine*. New York: Guilford.

Krantz, D. S., Grunberg, N. E., & Braum, A. (1985). Health psychology. *Annual Review of Psychology*, 36, 349–383.

Krause, N. (1993). Early parental loss and personal control in later life. *Journal of Gerontology: Psychological Sciences*, 48, 117–126.

Kripke, D. F., & Gillin, J. C. (1985). *Sleep disorders*. In J. O. Cavenar (Ed.), *Psychiatry*. Philadelphia: Lippincott.

Krueger, W. C. F. (1929). The effect of overlearning on retention. *Journal of Experimental Psychology*, 12, 71–78.

Krupat, E. (1985). *People in cities: The urban environment and its effects*. New York: Cambridge University Press.

Kübler-Ross, E. (1969). *On death and dying*. New York: Macmillan.

Kübler-Ross, E. (1981). *Living with death and dying*. New York: Macmillan.

Kunst-Wilson, W. R., & Zajonc, R. B. (1980). Affective discrimination that cannot be recognized. *Science*, 207, 557–558.

Kupfer, D. J., Frank, E., & Perel, J. M. (1989). The advantage of early treatment intervention in recurrent depression. *Archives of General Psychiatry*, 46, 771–775.

Lafferty, P., Beutler, L. E., & Crago, M. (1989). Differences between more and less effective psychotherapists: A study of select therapist variables. *Journal of Consulting and Clinical Psychology*, 57, 76–80.

Laird, J. (1984). The real role of facial response in the experience of emotion: A reply to Tourangeau and Ellsworth, and others. *Journal of Personality and Social Psychology*, 47, 909–917.

Lamb, M. E. (1977). Father-infant and mother-infant interaction in the first year of life. *Child Development*, 48, 167–181.

Lamb, M. E. (1979). Paternal influences and the father's role: A personal perspective. *American Psychologist*, 34, 938–943.

Lamb, M. E., Hwang, C. P., Frodi, A. M., & Frodi, M. (1982). Security of mother and father infant attachment and its relation to sociability with strangers in traditional and nontraditional Swedish families. *Infant Behavior and Development*, 5, 355–368.

Lamb, M. E., & Sternberg, K. J. (1990). Do we really

know how day care affects children? *Journal of Applied Developmental Psychology*, 11, 499.

Landers, D. M. (1982). Arousal, attention, and skilled performance: Further considerations. *Quest*, 33, 271–283.

Landers, S. (1987a). AIDS: Behavior change yes, test no. *APA Monitor*, 18, 28–29.

Landers, S. (1987b). Panel urges teen contraception. *APA Monitor*, 18, 6.

Landesman, S., & Butterfield, E. C. (1987). Normalization and deinstitutionalization of mentally retarded individuals. *American Psychologist*, 42, 809–816.

Landesman, S., & Ramey, C. (1989). Developmental psychology and mental retardation: Integrating scientific principles with treatment practices. *American Psychologist*, 44, 409–415.

Landy, F. J. (1989). *Psychology of work behavior* (2nd ed.). Homewood, IL: Dorsey Press.

Landy, F. J., Shankster, L. J., & Kohler, S. S. (1994). Personnel selection and placement. *Annual Review of Psychology*, 45, 261–296.

Lanetto, R. (1980). *Children's conceptions of death*. New York: Springer.

Lang, P. J. (1985). *The cognitive psychophysiology of emotion: Fear and anxiety*. In A. H. Tuma & J. D. Maser (Eds.), *Anxiety and the anxiety disorders*. Hillsdale, NJ: Erlbaum.

Langer, S. (1951). *Philosophy in a new key*. New York: New American Library.

Larson, R., & Ham, M. (1993). Stress and "storm and stress" in early adolescence: The relationship of negative events with dysphoric affect. *Developmental Psychology*, 29, 130–140.

Larson, R., & Lampman-Petraitis, R. (1989). Daily emotional states as reported by children and adolescents. *Child Development*, 60, 1250-1260.

Latané, B., & Darley, J. M. (1968). Group inhibition of bystander intervention in emergencies. *Journal of Personality and Social Psychology*, 10, 215–221.

Latané, B., & Darley, J. M. (1970). *The unresponsive bystander: Why doesn't he help?* Englewood Cliffs, NJ: Prentice-Hall.

Latané, B., & Nilda, S. (1981). Ten years of research on group size and helping. *Psychological Bulletin*, 89, 308–324.

Latané, B., Williams, K., & Harkins, S. (1979). Many hands make light work: The causes and consequences of social loafing. *Journal of Personality and Social Psychology*, 37, 822–832.

Latham, G. P. (1988). Human resource training and development. *Annual Review of Psychology*, 39, 545–582.

Lattal, K. A. (1992). B. F. Skinner and psychology: Introduction to the special issue. *American Psychologist*, 47, 1269–1272.

Lauer, J., & Lauer, R. (1985). Marriages made to last. *Psychology Today*, 19, 22–26.

Laumann, E. O., Michael, R., Michael, S., & Gagnon, J. (1994). *The social organization of sexuality*. Chicago: University of Chicago Press.

Lavond, D. G., Kim, J. J., & Thompson, R. F. (1993). Mammalian brain substrates of aversive classical conditioning. *Annual Review of Psychology*, 44, 317–342.

Lazarus, R. S. (1981). Little hassles can be hazardous to your health. *Psychology Today*, 15, 58–62.

Lazarus, R. S. (1991a). Cognition and motivation in emotion. *American Psychologist*, 46, 352–367.

Lazarus, R. S. (1991b). Progress on a cognitive-motivational-relational theory of emotion. *American Psychologist*, 46, 819–834.

Lazarus, R. S. (1991c). *Emotion and adaptation*. New York: Oxford University Press.

Lazarus, R. S. (1993). From psychological stress to the emotions: A history of changing outlooks. *Annual Review of Psychology*, 44, 1–21.

Lazarus, R. S., & Folkman, S. (1984). *Stress, appraisal, and coping*. New York: Springer.

Leahey, T. H., & Harris, R. J. (1989). *Human learning (2nd ed.)*. Englewood Cliffs, NJ: Prentice-Hall.

Lee, I. M., Manson, J. E., Hennekens, C. H., & Paffenbarger, R. S. (1993). Body weight and mortality: A 27-year follow-up of middle-aged men. *Journal of the American Medical Association*, 270, 2823–2828.

Leger, D. W. (1992). *Biological foundations of behavior: An integrative approach*. New York: HarperCollins.

Lehrer, P. M., & Woolfolk, R. L. (1984). *Are stress reduction techniques interchangeable, or do they have specific effects? A review of the comparative empirical literature*. In L. Woolfolk & P. M. Leher (Eds.), *Principles and practice of stress management*. New York: Guilford.

Leiberman, J., Jody, D., Geisler, S., Alvir, J., Loebel, A., et al. (1993). Time course and biological correlates of treatment response in first-episode schizophrenia. *Archives of General Psychiatry*, 50, 369-376.

Lempers, J. D. Flavell, E. R., & Flavell, J. H. (1977) The development in very young children of tactile knowledge concerning visual perception. *Genetic Psychology Monographs*, 95, 3–53.

Lenneberg, E. H. (1967). *Biological foundations of language*. New York: Wiley.

Lenneberg, E. H., Rebelsky, F. G., & Nichols, I. A. (1965).

The vocalizations of infants born to deaf and hearing parents. *Human Development, 8*, 23–27.

Lenzenweger, M. F., Dworkin, R. H., & Wethington, E. (1989). Models of positive and negative symptoms in schizophrenia: An empirical evaluation of latent structures. *Journal of Abnormal Psychology, 98*, 62–70.

Leonard, H. L., Swedo, S. E., Lenane, M. C., Rettew, D. C., Hamburger, S. D., et al. (1993). A 2- to 7-year follow-up study of 54 obsessive-compulsive children and adolescents. *Archives of General Psychiatry, 50*, 429–439.

Lerner, M. J. (1965). The effect of responsibility and choice on a partner's attractiveness following failure. *Journal of Personality, 33*, 178–187.

Lerner, M. J. (1980). *The belief in a just world.* New York: Plenum.

LeVay, S. (1991). A difference in hypothalamic structure between heterosexual and homosexual men. *Science, 253*, 1034–1037.

Leventhal, H., & Cleary, P. D. (1980). The smoking problem: A review of the research and theory in behavioral risk modification. *Psychological Bulletin, 88*, 370–405.

Levine, H. Z. (1983). Safety and health programs. *Personnel, 3*, 4–9.

Levine, J. D., Gordon, N. C., & Fields, H. L. (1979). Naloxone dose dependently produces analgesia and hyperanalgesia in post-operative pain. *Nature, 278*, 740–741.

Levine, J. M., & Moreland, R. L. (1990). Progress in small group research. *Annual Review of Psychology, 41*, 583–634.

Levine, J. M., Resnick, L. B., & Higgins, E. T. (1993). Social foundations of cognition. *Annual Review of Psychology, 44*, 585–612.

Levine, M., Toro, P. A., & Perkins, D. V. (1993). Social and community interventions. *Annual Review of Psychology, 44*, 525–558.

Levinson, D. J. (1978). *The seasons of a man's life.* New York: Ballantine Books.

Levinson, D. J. (1986). A conception of adult development. *American Psychologist, 41*, 3–13.

Levinson, D. J., Darrow, C. M., Klein, E. B., Levinson, M. H., & McKee, B. (1974). *The seasons of a man's life.* New York: Knopf.

Levinthal, C. F. (1983). *Introduction to physiological psychology (2nd ed.).* Englewood Cliffs, NJ: Prentice-Hall.

Ley, B. W. (1985). *Alcohol problems in special populations.* In J. H. Mendelson & N. K. Mello (Eds.), *The diagnosis and treatment of alcoholism (2nd ed.).* New York: McGraw-Hill.

Ley, P. (1977). Psychological studies of doctor-patient communication. In S. Rachman (Ed.), *Contributions to medical psychology (Vol. 1).* Elmsford, NY: Pergamon Press.

Lidz, T. (1973). *The origin and treatment of schizophrenic disorders.* New York: Basic Books.

Lieberman, J., Jody, D., Geisler, S., Alvir, J., Loebel, A., Szymanski, S., Woener, M., & Borenstein, M. (1993). Time course and biological correlates of treatment response in first-episode schizophrenia. *Archives of General Psychiatry, 50*, 369–376.

Lieberman, M. A. (1983). The effects of social support on response to stress. In L. Goldbert & D. S. Breznitz (eds.), *Handbook of stress management.* New York: Free Press.

Lin, T. R., Dobbins, G. H., & Farh, J. L. (1992). A field study of race and age similarity effects on interview ratings in conventional and situational interviews. *Journal of Applied Psychology, 77*, 363–371.

Lincoln, J. R., & Kalleberg, A. L. (1985). Work organization and workforce commitment: A study of plants and employees in the U. S. and Japan. *American Sociological Review, 50*, 738–760.

Lindsley, D. B., Bowden, J., & Magoun, H. W. (1949). Effect upon EEG of acute injury to the brain stem activating system. *Electroencephalography and Clinical Neurophysiology, 1*, 475–486.

Lipsey, M. W., & Wilson, D. B. (1993). The efficacy of psychological, educational, and behavioral treatment: Confirmation from meta-analysis. *American Psychologist, 48*, 1181–1209.

Litt, M. D. (1988). Self-efficacy and perceived control: Cognitive mediators of pain tolerance. *Journal of Personality and Social Psychology, 54*, 149–160.

Locke, E. A. (1968). Toward a theory of task motivation and incentives. *Organizational Behavior and Human Performance, 3*, 157–189.

Locke, E. A. (1976). The nature and causes of job satisfaction. In M. D. Dunnette (Ed.), *Handbook of industrial and organizational psychology.* Skokie, IL: Rand McNally.

Locke, E. A., Shaw, K. N., Saari, L. M., & Latham, G. (1981). Goal-setting and task performance: 1969–1980. *Psychological Bulletin, 90*, 124–152.

Lockhard, J. S., & Paulus, D. L. (Eds.). (1988). *Self-deception: An adaptive mechanism?* Englewood Cliffs, NJ: Prentice-Hall.

Loftus, E. F. (1991). The glitter of everyday memory . . . and the gold. *American Psychologist, 46*, 16–18.

Loftus, E. F. (1993a). The reality of repressed memories. *American Psychologist, 48*, 518–537.

Loftus, E. F. (1993b). "Therapeutic Memories of

Early Childhood Abuse: Fact or Fiction." Paper presented at the Annual Meeting of the American Psychological Association, Toronto, Canada.

Loftus, E. F. (1994). The repressed memory controversy. *American Psychologist*, 49, 443–445.

Loftus, E. F. (1984). *The eyewitness on trial*. In B. D. Sales & A. Alwork (Eds.), *With liberty and justice for all*. Englewood Cliffs, NJ: Prentice-Hall.

Loftus, E. F., & Klinger, M. R. (1992). Is the unconscious smart or dumb? *American Psychologist*, 47, 761–765.

Loftus, E. F., & Loftus, G. R. (1980). On the permanence of stored information in the human brain. *American Psychologist*, 35, 409–420.

Loftus, E. F., & Zanni, G. (1975). Eyewitness testimony: The influence of wording on a question. *Bulletin of the Psychonomic Society*, 5, 86–88.

Long, P. (1986). Medical mesmerism. *Psychology Today*, 20(1), 28–29.

Lonner, W. J. (1980). *The search for psychological universals*. In H. C. Triandis & W. W. Lambert (Eds.), *Handbook of cross-cultural psychology*. Vol. I. Boston: Allyn & Bacon.

Lord, C. G. (1980). Schemas and images as memory aids. *Journal of Personality and Social Psychology*, 38, 257–269.

Lorenz, K. (1969). On aggression. New York: Bantam Books.

Lott, A. J., & Lott, B. E. (1974). *The role of reward in the formation of positive interpersonal attitudes*. In T. L. Huston (Ed.), *Foundations of interpersonal attraction*. New York: Academic Press.

Lozoff, B. (1989). Nutrition and behavior. *American Psychologist*, 44, 231–236.

Lubin, B., Larsen, R. M., & Matarazzo, J. D. (1984). Patterns of psychological test usage in the United States: 1935–1982. *American Psychologist*, 39, 451–454.

Luborsky, I., Barber, J. P., & Beutler, L. (Eds.). (1993). Curative factors in dynamic psychotherapy. *Journal of Consulting and Clinical Psychology*, 61, 539–610.

Lucas, E. A., Foutz, A. S., Dement, W. C., & Mittler, M. M. (1979). Sleep cycle organization in nacorelptic and normal dogs. *Physiology and Behavior*, 23, 325–331.

Lugaresi, E., Medori, R., Montagna, P., Baruzzi, A., Cortelli, P., Lugaesi, A., et al. (1986). Fatal familial insomnia and dyautonomia with selective degeneration of the thalamic nuclei. *New England Journal of Medicine*, 315, 997–1003.

Luh, C. W. (1922). The conditions of retention. *Psychological Monographs*, Whole No. 142.

Lykken, D. T. (1957). A study of anxiety in the sociopathic personality. *Journal of Abnormal and Social Psychology*, 55, 6–10.

Lykken, D. T. (1982). Fearlessness: Its carefree charm and deadly risks. *Psychology Today*, 16, 20–28.

Lyness, S. A. (1993). Predictors of differences between Type A and B individuals in heart rate and blood pressure reactivity. *Psychological Bulletin*, 114, 266–295.

Lynn, D. (1974). *The father: His role in child development*. Monterey, CA: Brooks/Cole.

Lynn, R. (1982). IQ in Japan and the United States shows a greater disparity. *Nature*, 297, 222–223.

Lynn, R. (1987). The intelligence of the Mongoloids: A psychometric, evolutionary and neurological theory. *Personality and Individual Differences*, 8, 813–844.

Lynn, S. J., & Rhue, J. W. (1986). The fantasy-prone person: Hypnosis, imagination, and creativity. *Journal of Personality and Social Psychology*, 51, 404–408.

Lynn, S. J., Rhue, J. W., & Weekes, J. R. (1990). Hypnotic involuntariness: A social cognitive analysis. *Psychological Review*, 97, 69–184.

MacDonald, M. R., & Kuiper, N. A. (1983). Cognitive-behavioral preparations for surgery: Some theoretical and methodological concerns. *Clinical Psychology Review*, 3, 27–39.

MacFarlane, A. C. (1988). The longitudinal course of posttraumatic morbidity. *Journal of Nervous Disorders*, 176, 30–39.

Mackenzie, B. (1984). Explaining race differences in IQ: The logic, the methodology, and the evidence. *American Psychologist*, 39, 1214–1233.

Mackintosh, N. J. (1975). A theory of attention: Variations in the associability of stimuli with reinforcement. *Psychological Review*, 82, 276–298.

Mackintosh, N. J. (1983). *Conditioning and associative learning*. New York: Oxford University Press.

Mackintosh, N. J. (1986). The biology of intelligence? *British Journal of Psychology*, 77, 1–18.

Mackowiak, P. A., Wasserman, S. S., & Levine, M. M. (1992). A critical appraisal of 98.6°F, the upper limit of the normal body temperature, and other legacies of Carl Reinhold August Wunderlich. *Journal of the American Medical Association*, 268, 1578–1580.

MacLeod, M. D., & Ellis, H. D. (1986). Modes of presentation in eyewitness testimony research. *Human Learning Journal of Practical Research and Applications*, 5, 39–44.

MacMillan, J., & Kofoed, L. (1984). Sociobiology and antisocial personality: An alternative perspective. *Journal of Mental Disorders*, 172, 701–706.

Maddi, S. R., & Kobasa, S. C. (1984). *The Hardy Executive: Health and Stress*. Homewood, IL: Dorsey Press.

Madigan, S., & O'Hara, R. (1992). Short-term memory at the turn of the century: Mary Whiton Calkin's memory research. *American Psychologist*, 47, 170–174.

Magid, K. (1988). *High Risk: Children Without a Conscience*. New York: Bantam.

Maguire, J. (1990). *Care and feeding of the brain*. New York: Doubleday.

Mahowald, M. W., & Schenck, C. H. (1989). *REM sleep behavior disorder*. In M. H. Krygr, T. Roth, & W. C. Dement (Eds.), *Principles and practice of sleep medicine*. Philadelphia: Saunders.

Maier, N. R. F. (1931). Reasoning in humans II: The solution of a problem and its appearance in consciousness. *Journal of Experimental Psychology*, 105, 181–194.

Malatesta, C. A., & Isard, C. E. (1984). *The ontogenesis of human social signals: From biological imperative to symbol utilization*. In N. A. Fox & R. J. Davidson (Eds.), *The psychobiology of affective development*. Hillsdale, NJ: Erlbaum.

Mandler, G. (1980). Recognizing: The judgment of previous occurrence. *Psychological Review*, 87, 252–271.

Manning, M. L. (1983). Three myths concerning adolescence. *Adolescence*, 18, 823–829.

Markowitz, J. S., Weissman, M. M., Quellete, R., Lish, J. D., & Klerman, G. L. (1989). Quality of life in panic disorder. *Archives of General Psychiatry*, 46, 984–992.

Marks, I. M. (1986). Epidemiology of anxiety. *Social Psychiatry*, 21, 167–171.

Marshark, M., Richmond, C. L., Yuille, J. C., & Hunt, R. R. (1987). The role of imagery in memory: On shared and distinctive information. *Psychological Bulletin*, 102, 28–41.

Martin, G. B., & Clark, R. D. (1982). Distress crying in neonates: Species and peer specificity. *Developmental Psychology*, 18, 3–9.

Martin, R. J., White, B. D., & Hulsey, M. G. (1991). The regulation of body weight. *American Scientist*, 79, 528–541.

Martin, S. (1994). Workplace is no Longer a Haven from Violence. *APA Monitor*, October, p. 29.

Martindale, C. (1981). *Cognition and consciousness*. Homewood, IL: Dorsey Press.

Marx, J. (1990). Alzheimer's pathology explored. *Science*, 249, 984–986.

Marziali, E. (1984). Prediction of outcome of brief psychotherapy from therapist interpretive interactions. *Archives of General Psychiatry*, 41, 301–304.

Maslow, A. H. (1943). A theory of human motivation. *Psychological Review*, 50, 370–396.

Maslow, A. (1954). *Motivation and personality*. New York: Harper.

Maslow, A. H. (1970). *Motivation and personality (2nd ed.)*. New York: HarperCollins.

Massaro, D. W. (1975). *Experimental psychology and information processing*, Skokie, IL: Rand McNally.

Masters, W., & Johnson, V. (1979). *Homosexuality in perspective*. Boston: Little, Brown.

Matarazzo, J. D. (1980). Behavioral health and behavioral medicine: Frontiers for a new health psychology. *American Psychologist*, 35, 807–817.

Mathews, A., & MacLeod, C. (1994). Cognitive approaches to emotion and emotional disorders. *Annual Review of Psychology*, 45, 25–50.

Matlin, M. W. (1983). *Perception*. Boston: Allyn & Bacon.

Matsumoto, D. (1987). The role of facial response in the experience of emotion: More methodological problems and a meta-analysis. *Journal of Personality and Social Psychology*, 52, 769–774.

Matthews, K. A. (1982). Psychological perspectives on the Type A behavior pattern. *Psychological Bulletin*, 91, 293–323.

Matthews, K. A. (1988). Coronary heart disease and Type A behavior: Update on an alternative to the Booth-Kewley and Friedman (1987) quantitative review. *Psychological Bulletin*, 104, 373–380.

Mattson, S. N., Barron, S., & Riley, E. P. (1988). *The behavioral effects of prenatal alcohol exposure*. In K. Kuriyama, A. Takada, & H. Ishii (Eds.), *Biomedical and social aspects of alcohol and alcoholism*. Tokyo: Elsevier.

Maxman, J. S. (1991). *Psychotropic drugs: Fast facts*. New York: W. W. Norton.

Mayer, R. E. (1983). *Thinking, problem solving, cognition*. San Francisco: Freeman.

McCann, I. L., & Holmes, D. S. (1984). Influence of aerobic exercise on depression. *Journal of Personality and Social Psychology*, 46, 1142–1147.

McCauley, C. (1989). The nature of social influence in groupthink: Compliance and internalization. *Journal of Personality and Social Psychology*, 57, 250–260.

McClelland, D. C. (1958). *Risk-taking in children with high and low need for achievement*. In J. W. Atkinson (Ed.), *Motives in fantasy, action, and society*. New York: Van Nostrand Reinhold.

McClelland, D. C. (1973). Testing for competence rather than for "intelligence." *American Psychologist*, 28, 1–14.

McClelland, D. C. (1982). The need for power, sympathetic activation, and illness. *Motivation and Emotion, 6,* 31–41.

McClelland, D. C. (1985). *Human motivation.* Glenview, IL: Scott, Foresman.

McClelland, D. C. (1993). Intelligence is not the best predictor of job performance. *Current Directions in Psychological Science, 2,* 5–6.

McClelland, D. C., Atkinson, J. W., Clark, R. A., & Lowell, E. L. (1953). *The achievement motive.* Englewood Cliffs, NJ: Prentice-Hall.

McClelland, D. C., & Winter, D. G. (1969). *Motivating economic development.* New York: Free Press.

McClintock, M. K. (1971). Menstrual synchrony and suppression. *Nature, 229,* 244–245.

McClintock, M. K. (1979). Estrous synchrony and its mediation by airborne chemical communication. *Hormones and Behavior, 10,* 264.

McCloskey, M., Wible, C., & Cohen, N. J. (1988). Is there a special flashbulb-memory mechanism? *Journal of Experimental Psychology:* General, 117, 171–181.

McCrae, R. R. & John, O. P. (1992). An introduction to the five-factor model and its applications. *Journal of Personality, 60,* 175–215.

McCrea, R. R., & Costa, P. T. (1984). *Emerging lives, enduring dispositions: Personality in adulthood.* Boston: Little, Brown.

McCrea, R. R., & Costa, P. T. (1986). Clinical assessment can benefit from recent advances in personality psychology. *American Psychologist, 41,* 1001–1002.

McCrea, R. R., & Costa, P. T. (1987). Validation of the five-factor model of personality across instruments and observers. *Journal of Personality and Social Psychology, 52,* 81–90.

McDougall, W. (1908). *An introduction to social psychology.* London: Methuen.

McGaugh, J. L. (1983). Hormonal influences on memory. *Annual Review of Psychology, 34,* 297–323.

McGeoch, J. A., & McDonald, W. T. (1931). Meaningful relation and retroactive inhibition. *American Journal of Psychology, 43,* 579–588.

McGinnis, J. M. (1985). Recent history of federal initiatives in prevention policy. *American Psychologist, 40,* 205–212.

McGinnis, J. M., & Foege, W. H. (1993). Actual causes of death in the United States. *Journal of the American Medical Association, 270,* 2207–2212.

McGlashan, T. H., & Fenton, W. S. (1992). The positive-negative distinction in schizophrenia: Review of natural history indicators. *Archives of General Psychiatry, 49,* 63–72.

McGrath, E., Keita, G. P., Strickland, B., & Russo, N. F. (Eds.) (1990). *Women and depression: Risk factors and treatment issues.* Washington, DC: American Psychological Association.

McGuire, W. J. (1985). *Attitudes and attitude change.* In G. Lindzey & E. Aronson (Eds.), *Handbook of social psychology.* New York: Random House.

McKim, W. A. (1986). *Drugs and behavior.* Englewood Cliffs, NJ: Prentice-Hall.

McLeod, J. D., & Kessler, R. C. (1990). Socioeconomic status and differences in vulnerability to undesirable life events. *Journal of Health and Social Behavior, 31,* 162–172.

McNeil, D. (1970). *The acquisition of language: The study of developmental psycholinguistics.* New York: HarperCollins.

Mednick, M. T. (1989). On the politics constructs: Stop the bandwagon, I want to get off. *American Psychologist, 44,* 1118–1123.

Mednick, M. T. S. (1979). *The new psychology of women: A feminist analysis.* In J. E. Gullahorn (Ed.), *Psychology and women: In transition.* New York: Wiley.

Mednick, S. A., Moffitt, T. E., & Stack, S. (1987). *The Causes of Crime: New Biological Approaches.* New York: Cambridge University Press.

Meer, J. (1986). The reason of age. *Psychology Today, 20,* 60–64.

Meichenbaum, D. (1977). *Cognitive-behavior modification: An integrative approach.* New York: Plenum.

Meichenbaum, D., & Turk, D. C. (1987) *Facilitating treatment adherence.* New York: Plenum.

Melzack, R. (1973). *The puzzle of pain.* Baltimore: Penguin Books.

Melzack, R., & Wall, P. D. (1965). Pain mechanisms: A new theory. *Science, 150,* 971–979.

Metcalfe, J., & Wiebe, D. (1987). Intuition and insight and noninsight problem solving. *Memory and Cognition, 15,* 238–246.

Michael, J. L. (1985) *Behavior analysis: A radical perspective.* In B. L. Hammonds, (Ed.), *Psychology and learning.* Washington, DC: American Psychological Association.

Middlemist, R. D., & Peterson, R. B. (1976). Test of equity theory by controlling for comparison of workers' efforts. *Organizational Behavior and Human Performance, 15,* 335–354.

Milgram, S. (1963). Behavioral studies of obedience. *Journal of Abnormal and Social Psychology, 67,* 371–378.

Milgram, S. (1965). Some conditions of obedience and disobedience to authority. *Human Relations, 18,* 57–76.

Milgram, S. (1970). The experience of living in cities. *Science, 167,* 1461–1468.

Milgram, S. (1974). *Obedience to authority.* New York: HarperCollins.

Milgram, S. (1977). *The individual in a social world.* Reading, MA: Addison-Wesley.

Miller, D. T., & McFarland, C. (1987). Pluralistic ignorance: When similarity is interpreted as dissimilarity. *Journal of Personality and Social Psychology*, 53, 298–305.

Miller, D. T., & Ross, M. (1975). Self-serving biases in the attribution of causality: Fact or fiction? *Psychological Bulletin*, 82, 213–225.

Miller, J. (1984). Culture and the development of everyday social explanation. *Journal of Personality and Social Psychology*, 46, 961-978.

Miller, J. G. (1984). Culture and the development of everyday social explanation. *Journal of Personality and Social Psychology*, 46, 961–978.

Miller, N. E. (1944). Experimental studies of conflict. In J. M. Hunt (Ed.), *Personality and the behavior disorders.* New York: Ronald Press.

Miller, N. E. (1978). Biofeedback and visceral learning. *Annual Review of Psychology*, 29, 373–404.

Miller, N. E. (1983). Behavioral medicine: Symbiosis between laboratory and clinic. *Annual Review of Psychology*, 34, 1–31.

Miller, R. C., & Berman, J. S. (1983). The efficacy of cognitive behavior therapies: A quantitative review of the research evidence. *Psychological Bulletin*, 94, 39–53.

Miller, R. R., & Spear, N. E. (Eds.), (1985). *Information processing in animals: Conditioned inhibition.* Hillsdale, NJ: Erlbaum.

Miller, W. R. (1992). Client/treatment matching in addictive behaviors. *The Behavior Therapist*, 15, 7–8.

Millstein, S. G. (1989). Adolescent health: Challenges for behavioral scientists. *American Psychologist*, 44, 837–842.

Minami, H. J., & Dallenbach, K. M. (1946). The effect of activity upon learning and retention in the cockroach. *American Journal of Psychology*, 59, 682–697.

Minuchin, S., & Fishman, H. C. (1981). *Family therapy techniques.* Cambridge, MA: Harvard University Press.

Mirin, S. M., Weiss, R. D., & Greenfield, S. F. (1991). *Psychoactive substance abuse disorders.* In A. J. Galenberg, E. L. Bassuk, & S. C. Schoonover (Eds.), *The practitioner's guide to psychoactive drugs.* New York: Plenum.

Mischel, W. (1968). *Personality and assessment.* New York: Wiley.

Mischel, W., & Peake, P. K. (1982). Beyond déja vu in the search for cross-situational consistency. *Psychological Review*, 89, 730–755.

Mobley, W. H. (1977). Intermediate linkages in the relationship between job satisfaction and employee turnover. *Journal of Applied Psychology*, 62, 237–240.

Molnar, S. (1992). *Human variation: Races, types and ethnic group* (3rd ed.). Englewood Cliffs, NJ: Prentice-Hall.

Moncher, M. S., Holden, G. W., & Trimble, J. E. (1990). Substance abuse among Native American youth. *Journal of Consulting and Clinical Psychology*, 58, 408–415.

Money, J. (1987). Sin, sickness, or status? Homosexual gender identity and psychoneuroendocrinology. *American Psychologist*, 42, 384–399.

Monson, T. C., & Snyder, M. (1977). Actors, observers, and the attribution process. *Journal of Experimental Social Psychology*, 13, 89–111.

Moon, C., & Fifer, W. P. (1990). Syllables as signals for 2-day old infants. *Infant Behavior and Development*, 13, 377–390.

Moore, K. (1992). *Facts at a glance.* Washington, DC: Childtrends.

Moore, K. L. (1982). *The developing human (3rd ed.).* Philadelphia: Saunders.

Moran, J. S., Janes, H. R., Peterman, T. A., & Stone, K. M. (1990). Increase in condom sales following AIDS education and publicity, United States. *American Journal of Public Health*, 80, 607–608.

Morgan, W. P. (1980). The trait psychology controversy. *Research Quarterly for Exercise and Sport*, 51, 50–76.

Mori, D., & Pliner, P. L. (1987). "Eating lightly" and the self-presentation of femininity. *Journal of Social and Personality Psychology*, 53, 693–702.

Morris, C. W. (1946). *Signs, language, and behavior.* Englewood Cliffs, NJ: Prentice-Hall.

Morris, L. A., & Halperin, J. (1979). Effects of written drug information on patient knowledge and compliance: A literature review. *American Journal of Public Health*, 69, 47–52.

Morrison, D. M. (1985). Adolescent contraceptive behavior: A review. *Psychological Bulletin*, 98, 538–568.

Moruzzi, G., & Magoun, H. W. (1949). Brain stem reticular formation and activation of the EEG. *Electroencephalography and Clinical Neurophysiology*, 1, 455–473.

Moscovici, S., Lage, E., & Naffrechoux, M. (1969). Influences of a consistent minority on the response of a majority in a color perception task. *Sociometry*, 32, 365–380.

Moscovici, S., Mugny, G., & Van Avermaet, E. (1985). *Persepctives on minority influence.* New York: Cambridge University Press.

Mowday, R. T. (1983). *Equity theory prediction of behavior in organizations.* In R. M. Steers & L. W.

Porter (Eds.), *Motivation and work behavior* (3rd ed.). New York: McGraw-Hill.

Mshelia, A. Y. & Lapidus, L. B. (1990). Depth picture perception in relation to cognitive style and training in non-western children. *Journal of Cross-cultural Psychology*, 21, 414–433.

Muchinsky, P. M. (1987). *Psychology applied to work* (2nd ed.). Homewood, IL: Dorsey Press.

Muchinsky, P. M., & Tuttle, M. L. (1979). Employee turnover: An empirical and methodological assessment. *Journal of Vocational Behavior*, 14, 43–77.

Mulác, A., Incontro, C. R., & James, M. R. (1985). Comparison of gender-linked language effect and sex role stereotypes. *Journal of Personality and Social Psychology*, 49, 1098–1109.

Mumford, M. D., Uhlman, C. E., & Kilcullen, R. N. (1992). The structure of life history: Implications for the construct validity of background data scales. *Human Performance*, 5, 109–137.

Munn, N. L. (1956). *Introduction to psychology*. Boston: Houghton Mifflin.

Murray, C. & Herrnstein, R. (1994). *The bell curve: Intelligence and class structure*. New York: The Free Press.

Murray, D. J. (1983). *A history of western psychology*. Englewood Cliffs, NJ: Prentice-Hall.

Murray, D. M., Johnson, C.A., Leupker, R. F., & Mittlemark, M. B. (1984). The prevention of cigarette smoking in children: A comparison of four strategies. *Journal of Applied Social Psychology*, 14, 274–288.

Nakazima, S. (1962). A comparative study of the speech developments of Japanese and American English in children. *Studies in Phonology*, 2, 27–39.

Namir, S., Wolcott, D. L., Fawzy, F. I., & Alumbaugh, M. J. (1987). Coping with AIDS: Psychological and health implications. *Journal of Applied Social Psychology*, 17, 309–328.

Nash, M. (1987). What, if anything, is regressed about hypnotic age regression? *Psychological Bulletin*, 102, 42–52.

National Academy of Sciences National Research Council. (1989). *Diet and health: Implications for reducing chronic disease risk*. Washington, DC: National Academy Press.

National Commission on Sleep Disorders Research [NCSDR] (1993). *Wake up America: A national sleep alert*. Washington, DC: Department of Human Services.

National Education Association. (1994, March). Fighting school violence means taking on guns. *NEA Today*, pp. 4–5.

National Institute of Mental Health (NIMH) (1984). The NIMH epidemiological catchment area program. *Archives of General Psychiatry*, 41, 93–1011.

National Institutes of Health, *Review Panel on Coronary Prone Behavior and Coronary Heart Disease*. (1981). *Coronary-prone behavior and coronary heart disease: A critical review*. Circulation, 63, 1199–1215.

Neisser, U. (1982). *Memory observed*. San Francisco: Freeman.

Neisser, U. (1991). A case of misplaced nostalgia. *American Psychologist*, 46, 34–36.

Nelson, K. (1993). The psychological and social origins of autobiographical memory. *Psychological Science*, 4, 7–14.

Nemeth, C. (1986). Differential contributions of majority and minority influence. *Psychological Review*, 93, 23–32.

Neugarten, B. L., & Neugarten, D. A. (1986). *Changing meaning of age in the aging society*. In A. Piter & L. Bronte (Eds.), *Our aging society: Paradox and promise*. New York: Norton.

Neugarten, B. L., & Neugarten, D. A. (1989) *Policy issues in an aging society*. In M. Storandt & G. R. VandenBos (Eds.), *The adult years: Continuity and change*. Washington, DC: American Psychological Association.

Newby, R. W. (1987). Contextual areas in item recognition following verbal discrimination learning. *Journal of General Psychology*, 114, 281–287.

Newcomb, M. D., & Bentler, P. M. (1989) Substance abuse among children and teenagers. *American Psychologist*, 44, 242–248.

Newell, A., Shaw, J. C., & Simon, H. A. (1962). *The process of creative thinking*. In H. E. Gruber, G. Terrell, & M. Wertheimer (Eds.), *Contemporary approaches to creative thinking*. New York: Atherton Press.

Nickerson, R. S., & Adams, M. J. (1979). Long-term memory for a common object. *Cognitive Psychology*, 11, 287–307.

Nigg, J. T., & Goldsmith, H. H. (1994). Genetics of personality disorders: Perspectives from personality and psychopathology research. *Psychological Bulletin*, 115, 346–380.

Nisan, M., & Kohlberg, L. (1982). Universality and variation in moral judgment: A longitudinal and cross-sectional study in Turkey. *Child Development*, 53, 865–876.

Nisbett, R. E. (1972). Hunger, obesity, and the ventromedial hypothalamus. *Psychological Review*. 79, 433–453.

Norcross, J. C. (1986). *Handbook of eclectic psychotherapy*. New York: Brunner/Mazel.

Oatley, K., & Jenkins, J. M. (1992). Human emotions: Function and dysfunction. *Annual Review of Psychology, 43,* 55–85.

Oden, M. H. (1968). The fulfillment of promise: 40-year follow-up of the Terman gifted group. *Genetic Psychology Monographs, 77*(1), 3–93.

Oetting, E. R., & Beauvais, F. (1987). Peer cluster theory, socialization characteristics and adolescent drug use: A path analysis. *Journal of Counseling Psychology, 34,* 205–213.

Oetting, E. R., & Beauvais, F. (1990). Adolescent drug use: Findings of national and local surveys. *Journal of Consulting and Clinical Psychology, 58,* 385–394.

Offer, D., & Offer, J. (1975) *From teenage to young manhood: A psychological study.* New York: Basic Books.

Offerman, L. R., & Gowing, M. K. (1990). Organizations of the future: Changes and challenges. *American Psychologist, 45,* 95–108.

Offord, D. R., Boyle, M. H., Szatmari, P., Rae-Grant, N. I., Links, P. S., et al. (1987). Ontario child heath study. *Archives of General Psychiatry, 44,* 832–836.

Ogata, S. N., Silk, K. R., Goodrich, S., Lohr, N. E., & Hill, E. M. (1990). Childhood sexual and physical abuse in patients with borderline personality. *American Journal of Psychiatry, 147,* 1008–1013.

Ogilvie, B. C., & Howe, M. A. (1984). Beating slumps at their game. *Psychology Today, 18,* 28–32.

Olio, K. A. (1994). Truth in memory. *American Psychologist, 49,* 442–443.

Oller, D. K. (1981). *Infant vocalization.* In R. E. Stark (Ed.), *Language behavior in infancy and early childhood.* New York: Elsevier.

Olson, J. M., & Zanna, M. P. (1993). Attitudes and attitude change. *Annual Review of Psychology, 44,* 117–154.

Opalic, P. (1989). Existential and psychopathological evaluation of group psychotherapy of neurotic and psychotic patients. *International Journal of Group Psychotherapy, 39,* 389–422.

Orne, M. (1969). *Demand characteristics and the concept of quasi-controls.* In R. Rosenthal & R. Rosnow (Eds.), *Artifact in behavioral research.* New York: Academic Press.

Ortony, A., Clore, G. L., & Collins, A. (1988). *The cognitive structure of emotions.* New York: Cambridge University Press.

Ortony, A., & Turner, T. J. (1990). What's basic about basic emotions? *Psychological Review, 97,* 315–331.

Ozer, D. J., & Reise, S. P. (1994). Personality assessment. *Annual Review of Psychology, 45,* 357–388.

Paivio, A. (1971). *Imagery and verbal processes.* New York: Holt, Rinehart and Winston.

Paivio, A. (1986). *Mental representations: A dual coding approach.* New York: Oxford University Press.

Palfai, T., & Jankiewicz, H. (1991). *Drugs and human behavior.* Dubuque, IA: Wm. C. Brown.

Pandey, J. (1990). *The environment, culture, and behavior.* In R. W. Brislin (Ed.), *Applied cross-cultural psychology.* Newbury Park, CA: Sage.

Parker, E. S., Birnbaum, I. M., & Noble, E. P. (1976). Alcohol and memory: Storage and state dependency. *Journal of Verbal Learning and Verbal Behavior, 15,* 691–702.

Parson, A. (1993). Getting the point. *Harvard Health Letter, 18,* 6–9.

Pate, J. E., Pumariega, A. J., Hester, C., & Garner, D. M. (1992). Cross-cultural patterns in eating disorders: A review. *Journal of the American Academy of Child and Adolescent Psychiatry, 31,* 802–809.

Paulus, D. L., & Bruce, M. N. (1992). The effect of acquaintanceship on the validity of personality impressions: A longitudinal study. *Journal of Personality and Social Psychology, 63,* 816–824.

Paunonen, S. P., Jackson, D. N., Trzebinski, J., & Fosterling, F. (1992). Personality structures across cultures: A multimethod evaluation. *Journal of Personality and Social Psychology, 62,* 447–456.

Pavlov, I. (1927). *Conditioned reflexes.* New York: Oxford University Press.

Pavlov, I. (1928). *Lectures on conditioned reflexes: The higher nervous activity of animals* (Vol. 1) (H. Gantt, Trans.). London: Lawrence and Wishart.

Pearce, J. M., & Hall, G. (1980). A model for Pavlovian conditioning: Variations in the effectiveness of conditioned but not of unconditioned stimuli. *Psychological Review, 87,* 532–552.

Pearson, J. C., Turner, L. H., & Todd-Mancillas, W. (1991). *Gender and communication* (2nd. ed.). Dubuque, IA: Wm. C. Brown.

Peck, M. (1982). Youth suicide. Death Education, 6, 29–47.

Pederson, D. R., Morgan, G., Sitko, C., Campbell, K., Ghesquire, K., & Acton, H. (1990). Maternal sensitivity and the security of infant-mother attachment: A Q-sort study. *Child Development, 61,* 1974–1983.

Peele, S., Brodsky, A., & Arnold, M. (1991). *The truth about addiction and recovery.* New York: Simon and Schuster.

Perls, F. S. (1967). Group vs. individual psychotherapy. *ETC: A Review of General Semantics, 34,* 306–312.

Perls, F. S. (1971). *Gestalt Therapy Verbatim.* New York: Bantam Books.

Perls, F. S., Hefferline, R. F., & Goodman, P. (1951). *Gestalt Therapy.* New York: Julian Press.

Peterson, A. C. (1988). Adolescent development. *Annual Review of Psychology, 39,* 583–607.

Peterson, A. C., & Ebata, A. T. (1987). *Developmental transitions and adolescent problem behavior: Implications for prevention and intervention.* In K. Hurrelmann (Ed.), *Social prevention and intervention,* New York: de Gruyter.

Peterson, L. R., & Peterson, M. J. (1959). Short-term retention of individual verbal items. *Journal of Experimental Psychology, 58,* 193–198.

Petty, R. E., & Cacioppo, J. T. (1986). The elaboration likelihood model of persuasion. *Advances in Experimental Social Psychology, 19,* 123–205.

Petty, R. E., Harkins, S. G., Williams, K. D., & Latané, B. (1977). The effects of group size on cognitive effort and evaluation. *Personality and Social Psychology Bulletin, 3,* 579–582.

Phillips, D., McCartney, K., & Scarr, S. (1987). Childcare quality and children's social development. *Developmental Psychology, 23,* 537-543.

Piaget, J. (1932/1948). *The moral judgment of the child.* New York: Free Press.

Piaget, J. (1954). *The construction of reality in the child.* New York: Basic Books.

Piaget, J. (1967). *Six psychological studies.* New York: Random House.

Pillemer, D. B., & White, S. H. (1989). *Childhood events recalled by children and adults.* IN H. W. Reese (Ed.), *Advances in child development and behavior,* Vol. 21. New York: Academic Press.

Plawin, P., & Suied, M. (1988, December). Can't get no satisfaction. *Changing Times,* p. 106.

Plomin, R. (1988). *The nature and nurture of cognitive abilities.* In J. Sternberg (Ed.), *Advances in the psychology of human intelligence.* Vol. 4. Hillsdale, NJ: Erlbaum.

Plutchik, R. (1980a). *Emotion: A psychoevolutionary synthesis.* New York: HarperCollins.

Plutchik, R. (1980b, February). A language for the emotions. *Psychology Today,* 68–78.

Plutchik, R. (1994). *The psychology and biology of emotion.* New York: HarperCollins.

Pogue-Geile, M. F., & Zubin, J. (1988). Negative symptomatology and schizophrenia: A conceptual and empirical review. *International Journal of Mental Health, 16,* 3–45.

Pool, R. (1993). Evidence for homosexuality gene. *Science, 261,* 291–292.

Pope, H. G., & Hudson, J. I. (1986) Antidepressant therapy for bulimia: Current status. *Journal of Clinical Psychiatry, 47,* 339–345.

Pope, H. G., Hudson, J. I., Jonas, J. M., & Yurgelun-Todd, D. (1985). Antidepressant treatment of bulimia: A two-year follow-up study. *Journal of Clinical Psychopharmacology, 5,* 320–327.

Porter, L. W., & Steers, R. M. (1973). Organizational, work, and personal factors in employee turnover and absenteeism. *Psychological Bulletin, 80,* 151–176.

Powell, L. H., Shaker, L. A., Jones, B. A., Vaccarino, L. V., et al., (1993). Psychosocial predictors of mortality in 83 women with premature acute myocardial infarction. *Psychosomatic Medicine, 55,* 221–225.

Powell, R. A., & Boer, D. P. (1994). Did Freud mislead patients to confabulate memories of abuse? *Psychological Reports, 74,* 1283-1298.

Powers, S. I., Hauser, S. T., & Kilner, L. A. (1989). Adolescent mental health. *American Psychologist, 44,* 200–208.

Pressley, M., Levin, J. R., & Delaney, H. D. (1982). the mnemonic keyword method. *Review of Educational Research, 52,* 61–91.

Pyle, R. L., Mitchell, J. E., & Eckert, E. D. (1981). Bulimia: Report of 34 cases. *Journal of Clinical Psychiatry, 42,* 60–64.

Pyle, R. L., Mitchell, J. E., Eckert, E. D., Hatsukami, D. K., Pomeroy, C., & Zimmerman, R. (1990). Maintenance treatment and 6-month outcome for bulimic patients who respond to initial treatment. *American Journal of Psychiatry, 147,* 871–875.

Quadrel, M. J., Fishhoff, B., & Davis, W. (1993). Adolescent (in)vulnerability. *American Psychologist, 48,* 102–116.

Quay, H. C. (1965) Psychopathic personality as pathological stimulation seeking. *American Journal of Psychiatry, 122,* 180–183.

Quina, K., Wingard, J. A., & Bates, H. G. (1987). Language style and gender stereotypes in person perception. *Psychology of Women Quarterly, 11,* 111–222.

Radford, A. (1990). *Syntactic theory and the acquisition of English syntax: The nature of early child grammars of English.* Oxford: Blackwell.

Rahe, R. H., & Arthur, R. J. (1978). *Life changes and illness reports.* In K. E. Gunderson & R. H. Rahe (Eds.), *Life stress and illness.* Springfield, IL: Thomas.

Raine, A., Venables, P. H., & Williams, M. (1990). Relationship between central and autonomic measures of arousal at age 15 years and criminality at age 24 years. *Archives of General Psychiatry*, 46, 1003–1007.

Randall, T. (1993). Morphine receptor cloned—improved analgesics, addiction therapy expected. *The Journal of the American Medical Association*, 270, 1165–1166.

Ray, O. S. & Ksir, C. (1987). *Drugs, society, and human behavior*. St. Louis: C. V. Mosby.

Ree, M. J., & Earles, J. A. (1992). Intelligence is the best predictor of job performance. *Current Directions in Psychological Science*, 1, 86–89.

Ree, M. J., & Earles, J. A. (1993). g is to psychology what carbon is to chemistry: A reply to Sternberg and Wagner, McClelland, and Calfee. *Current Directions in Psychological Science*, 2, 11–12.

Reich, J. (1986). The epidemiology of anxiety. *The Journal of Nervous and Mental Disease*, 174, 129–136.

Reilly, R. R., & Chao, G. T. (1982). Validity and fairness of some alternative employee selection procedures. *Personnel Psychology*, 35, 1–62.

Reinke, B. J., Ellicott, A. M., Harris, R. L., & Hancock, E. (1985). Timing of psychological changes in women's lives. *Human Development*, 28, 259–280.

Reis, H. T., Nezlek, J., & Wheeler, L. (1980). Physical attractiveness in social interaction. *Journal of Personality and Social Psychology*, 38, 604–617.

Reis, S. M. (1989). Reflections on policy affecting the education of gifted and talented students: Past and future perspectives. *American Psychologist*, 44, 399–408.

Rescorla, R. A. (1968). Probability of shock in the presence and absence of CS in fear conditioning. *Journal of Comparative and Physiological Psychology*, 66, 1–5.

Rescorla, R. A. (1987). A Pavlovian analysis of goal-directed behavior. *American Psychologist*, 42, 119–129.

Rescorla, R. A. (1988). Pavlovian conditioning: It's not what you think it is. *American Psychologist*, 43, 151–160.

Rescorla, R. A., & Wagner, A. R. (1972). *A theory of Pavlovian conditioning: Variations in the effectiveness of reinforcement and nonreinforcement*. In A. H. Black & W. F. Prokasy (Eds.), *Classical conditioning II: Current research and theory*. Englewood Cliffs, NJ: Prentice-Hall.

Resnick, H. D., Kilpatrick, D. G., Dansky, B. S., Saunders, B. E., & Best, C. L. (1993). Prevalence of civilian trauma and posttraumatic stress disorder in a representative national sample of women. *Journal of Consulting and Clinical Psychology*, 61, 984–991.

Rest, J. R. (1983). *Morality*. In J. Flavell & E. Markman (Eds.), *Handbook of child development: Cognitive development*. New York: Wiley.

Reveley, M. A., Reveley, A. M., & Baldy, R. (1987). Left cerebral hemisphere hypodensity in discordant schizophrenic twins. *Archives of General Psychiatry*, 44, 624–632.

Revelle, W. (1987). Personality and motivation: Sources of inefficiency in cognitive performance. *Journal of Research in Personality*, 21, 436-452.

Revulsky, S. H. (1985). *The general process approach to animal learning*. In T. D. Johnson & A. T. Petrewicz (Eds.), *Issues in the ecological study of learning*. Hillsdale, NJ: Erlbaum.

Revulsky, S. H. & Garcia, J. (1970). *Learned associations over long delays*. In G. H. Bower & J. T. Spence (Eds.), *The psychology of learning and motivation*. (Vol. 4). New York: Academic Press.

Reynolds, A. G., & Flagg, P. W. (1983). *Cognitive psychology*. Boston: Little, Brown.

Reynolds, B. A., & Weiss, S. (1992). Generation of neurons and astrocytes from isolated cells of the adult mammalian nervous system. *Science*, 225, 1707–1710.

Rhodes, S. R. (1983). Age-related differences in work attitudes and behaviors: A review and conceptual analysis. *Psychological Bulletin*, 93, 328–367.

Rice, M. L. (1989). Children's language acquisition. *American Psychologist*, 44, 149–156.

Richardson, J. L., Marks, G., Levine, A. (1988). The influence of symptoms of disease and side effects of treatment on compliance with cancer therapy. *Journal of Clinical Oncology*, 6, 1746–1752.

Richardson-Klavehn, A., & Bjork, R. A. (1988). Measures of memory. *Annual Review of Psychology*, 39, 475–543.

Richmond, C. E., Bromley, L. M., & Woolf, C. J. (1993). Preoperative morphine pre-empts postoperative pain. *The Lancet*, 342, 73–75.

Rickels, K., Downing, R., Schweizer, E., & Hassman, H. (1993). Antidepressants for the treatment of generalized anxiety disorder. *Archives of General Psychiatry*, 50, 884–895.

Riggio, R. E. (1990). *Introduction to industrial/organizational psychology*. Glenview, IL: Scott, Foresman.

Robins, L. N., Helzer, J. E., Weissman, M. M., Orvaschel, H., Guenberg, E., Burke, J. D., & Regier, D. A. (1984). Lifetime prevalence of specific psychiatric disorders in three sites. *Archives of General Psychiatry*, 41, 949–958.

Robinson, K. (1994). Which side are you on? *Networker*, 18, 18–30.

Roche, A. F., & Davila, G. H. (1972). Late adolescent growth in stature. *Pediatrics, 50,* 874–880.

Rock, I (1986). *The description and analysis of object and event perception.* In K. R. Boff, L. Kaufman, & J. P. Thomas (Eds.), *Handbook of perception and human performance:* Vol. 2. Cognitive processes and performance. New York: Wiley.

Rodin, J. (1976). Crowding, perceived choice and response to controllable and uncontrollable outcomes. *Journal of Experimental Social Psychology, 12,* 564–578.

Rodin, J., & Salovey, P. (1989). Health psychology. *Annual Review of Psychology, 40,* 533–579.

Roediger, H. L. (1990). Implicit memory: Retention without remembering. *American Psychologist, 45,* 1043–1056.

Rolls, B. J., Federoff, I. C., & Guthrie, J. F. (1991). Gender differences in eating behavior and body weight regulation. *Health Psychology, 10,* 133–142.

Rook, K. S. (1987). Social support versus companionship: Effects of life stress, loneliness, and evaluation by others. *Journal of Personality and Social Psychology, 52,* 1132–1147.

Rose, A. S., & Blank, M. (1974). The potency of context in children's cognition: An illustration through conversation. *Child Development, 45,* 499–502.

Rosenbaum, M. E. (1986). The repulsion hypothesis: On the nondevelopment of relationships. *Journal of Personality and Social Psychology, 51,* 1156–1166.

Rosenman, R. H., Brand, R. J., Jenkins, C. D., Friedman, M., Strauss, R., & Wurm, M. (1975). Coronary heart disease in the Western Collaborative Group Study: Final follow-up experience of 8 years. *Journal of the American Medical Association, 233,* 872–877.

Rosenman, R. H., Friedman, M., Strauss, R., Wurm, M., Kositcheck, R., Hahn, W., & Werthessen, N. T. (1964). A predictive study of coronary heart disease. *Journal of the American Medical Association, 189,* 15–22.

Rosenthal, D. (1970). *Genetics of psychopathology.* New York: McGraw-Hill.

Rosenzweig, M. R. (1992). Psychological science around the world. *American Psychologist, 47,* 718–722.

Ross, C. A., Heber, S., Norton, G. R., & Anderson, G. (1989). Differences between multiple personality disorder and other diagnostic groups on structured interview. *Journal of Nervous and Mental Disorders, 177,* 487–491.

Ross, G., Kagan, J., Zelazo, P. & Kotelchuck, M. (1975). Separation protest in infants in home and laboratory. *Developmental Psychology, 11,* 256–257.

Ross, L. D. (1977). *The intuitive psychologist and his shortcomings: Distortions in the attributional process.* In L. Berkowitz (Ed.), *Advances in experimental social psychology (Vol. 10).* New York: Academic Press.

Rossi, A. S. (1980). *Aging and parenthood in the middle years.* In P. B. Baltes & O. G. Brim, Jr. (Eds.), *Lifespan development and behavior* Vol. III). New York: Academic Press.

Roth M., & Argyle, N. (1988). Anxiety, panic and phobic disorders: An overview, *Journal of Psychiatric Research, 22* (Suppl. 1). 33–54.

Rothstein, H. R., Schmidt, F. L., Erwin, F. W., Owens, W. A., & Sparks, C. P. (1990). Biographical data in employment selection: Can validities be made generalizable? *Journal of Applied Psychology, 75,* 175–184.

Rotton, J., & Frey, J. (1985). Air pollution, weather, and violent crimes: Concomitant analysis of archival data. *Journal of Personality and Social Psychology, 49.*

Rowe, D. C. (1987). Resolving the person-situation debate. *American Psychologist, 42,* 218–227.

Rowe, J. W., & Kahn, R. L. (1987). Human aging: Usual and successful. *Science, 237,* 143–149.

Ruback, R. B., & Pandey, J. (1988). Crowding and perceived control in India. Unpublished manuscript, cited in Pandey, J. (1990).

Rubin, Z. (1973). *Liking and loving: An invitation to social psychology.* New York: Holt, Rinehart and Winston.

Rushton, J. P. (1988). Race differences in behavior: A review and evolutionary analysis. *Personality and Individual Differences, 9,* 1009–1024.

Ryan, E. D., & Kovacic, C. R. (1966). Pain tolerance and athletic participation. *Journal of Personality and Social Psychology, 22,* 383–390.

Saal, F. E., & Knight, P. A. (1988). *Industrial/organizational psychology.* Monterey, CA: Brooks/Cole.

Saari, L. M., Johnson, T. R., Mclaughlin, S. D., & Zimerle, D. M. (1988). A survey of management training and education practices in U. S. companies. *Personnel Psychology, 41,* 731–743.

Sackheim, H. A. (1985). The case for ECT. *Psychology Today, 19,* 36–40.

Sadalla, E. K., & Oxley, D. (1984). The perception of room size: The rectangularity illusion. *Environment and Behavior, 16,* 394–405.

Saegert, S., & Winkel, G. H. (1990). Environmental

psychology. *Annual Review of Psychology, 41,* 441–477.

Sakai, K. (1985). *Neurons responsible for paradoxical sleep.* In A. Wauquier (Ed.), *Sleep: Neurotransmitters and neuromodulators.* New York: Raven Press.

Salthouse, T. A. (1989). *Age-related changes in basic cognitive processes.* In M. Storandt & G. R. VandenBos (Eds.), *The adult years: Continuity and change.* Washington, DC: American Psychological Association.

Sameroff, A. J. & Cavanaugh, P. J. (1979). *Learning in infancy: A developmental perspective.* In J. D. Osofsky (Ed.), *Handbook of infant development.* New York: Wiley.

Samuelson, F. J. B. (1980). Watson's Little Albert, Cyril Burt's twins, and the need for a critical science. *American Psychologist, 35,* 619–625.

Sandler, J., Dare, C., & Holder, A. (1992). *The patient and the analyst: The basis of the psychoanalytic process* (2nd ed.). Madison, CT: International University Press.

Satir, V. (1967). *Conjoint family therapy.* Palo Alto, CA: Science and Behavior Books.

Sauser, W. J., & York, C. M. (1978). Sex differences in job satisfaction: A reexamination. *Personnel Psychology, 31,* 537–547.

Scarborough, E., & Furumoto, L. (1987). *Untold lives: The first generation of American women psychologists.* New York: Columbia University Press.

Scarr, S., & Eisenberg, M. (1993). Child care research: Issues, perspectives, and results. *Annual Review of Psychology, 44,* 613–644.

Schacter, D. L. (1992). Understanding implicit memory: A cognitive neuroscience approach. *American Psychologist, 47,* 559–569.

Schacter, D. L. (1987). Implicit memory: History and current status. *Journal of Experimental Psychology: Learning, Memory, and Cognition. 13,* 501–518.

Schacter, S., & Gross, L. P. (1968). Manipulated time and eating behavior. *Journal of Personality and Social Psychology, 10,* 98–106.

Schaie, K. W. (1993). The Seattle Longitudinal Studies of Adult Intelligence. *Current Directions in Psychological Science, 2,* 171–175.

Schaie, K. W., & Willis, S. L. (1986). *Adult development and aging* (2nd ed.). Boston: Little, Brown.

Scharf, B. (1978). *Loudness,* In E. C. Carterette & M. P. Friedman (Eds.), *Handbook of perception.* New York: Academic Press.

Scheerer, M. (1963). Problem solving. *Scientific American, 208,* 118–128.

Scheier, M. F., & Carver, C. S. (1992). Effects of optimism on psychological and physical well-being: Theoretical overview and empirical update. *Cognitive Therapy and Research, 16,* 201–228.

Scheier, M. F., & Carver, C. S. (1993). On the power of positive thinking: The benefits of being optimistic. *Current Directions in Psychological Science, 2,* 26–30.

Scheier, M. F., Matthews, K. A., Owens, J. F., Magovern, G. J., Lefebvre, R., Abbott, R. C., & Carver, C. S. (1989). Dispositional optimism and recovery from coronary artery bypass surgery: The beneficial effects of optimism on physical and psychological well-being. *Journal of Personality and Social Psychology, 57,* 1024–1040.

Schelling, T. C. (1992). Addictive drugs: The cigarette experience. *Science, 255,* 430–433.

Schiff, B. B., & Lamon, M. (1989). Inducing emotion by unilateral contraction of facial muscles: A new look at hemispheric specialization and the experience of emotion. *Neuropsychologia, 27,* 923–925.

Schiffman, H. R. (1990). *Sensation and perception: An integrated approach.* New York: Wiley.

Schmidt, F. L., & Hunter, J. E. (1993). Tacit knowledge, practical intelligence, general mental ability, and job knowledge. *Current Directions in Psychological Science, 2,* 8–9.

Schmidt, F. L., Ones, D. S., & Hunter, J. E. (1992). Personnel selection. *Annual Review of Psychology, 43,* 627–670.

Schmitt, N., & Robertson, I. (1990). Personnel selection. *Annual Review of Psychology, 41,* 289–319.

Schroeder, S. R., Schjroeder, C. S., & Landesman, S. (1987). Psychological services in educational settings to persons with mental retardation. *American Psychologist, 42,* 805–808.

Schuckit, M. A. (1989). *Drug and alcohol abuse: A clinical guide to diagnosis and treatment* (3rd. ed.). New York: Plenum.

Schultz, D. P., & Schultz, S. E. (1990). *Psychology and industry today.* New York: Macmillan.

Schultz, R., & Alderman, D. (1974). Clinical research on the "stages of dying." *Omega, 5,* 137–144.

Schultz, R., & Decker, S. (1985). Long-term adjustment to physical disability: The role of social support, perceived control and self-blame. *Journal of Personality and Social Psychology, 48,* 1162–1172.

Scogin, F., & McElreath, L. (1994). Efficacy of psychosocial treatments for geriatric depression: A quantitative review. *Journal of Consulting and Clinical Psychology, 62,* 69–74.

Scott, J. P., & Ginsberg, B. E. (1994). The Seville Statement on Violence revisited. *American Psychologist, 49,* 849–850.

Scott, K. G., & Carran, D. T. (1987). The epidemiology and prevention of mental retardation. *American Psychologist, 42,* 801–804.

Scott, M. D., & Pelliccioni, L., Jr. (1982). *Don't choke: How athletes become winners.* Englewood Cliffs, NJ: Prentice-Hall.

Sears, P. S., & Barbee, A. H. (1977). *Career and life satisfaction among Terman's gifted women.* In J. Stanley et al. (Eds.), *The gifted and the creative: Fifty year perspective.* Baltimore: Johns Hopkins University Press.

Segall, M., Dasen, P., Berry, J., & Poortinga, Y. (1990). *Human behavior in global perspective.* Elmsford, NY: Pergamon.

Segall, M. H., Campbell, D. T., & Herskovits, M. J. (1966). *The influence of culture on visual perception.* Indianapolis: Bobbs-Merrill.

Seligman, M. E. P. (1975). *Helplessness: On depression development and death.* San Francisco: Freeman.

Selkoe, D. J. (1990). Deciphering Alzheimer's disease: The amyloind precursor protein yields new clues. *Science, 248,* 1058.

Selye, H. (1956). *The stress of life.* New York: McGraw-Hill.

Selye, H. (1974). *Stress without distress.* Philadelphia: Lippincott.

Selye, H. (1976). *The stress of life.* New York: Knopf.

Serpell, R., & Deregowski, J. B. (1980). The skill of pictorial perception: An interpretation of cross-cultural evidence. *International Journal of Psychology, 15,* 145–180.

Shadish, W. R. (1984). Policy research: Lessons from the implementation of deinstitutionalization. *American Psychologist, 39,* 725–738.

Shadish, W. R., Montgomery, L. M., Wilson, P., Wilson, M. R., Bright, I., & Okwumabua, T. (1993). Effects of marital and family psychotherapies: A meta-analysis. *Journal of Consulting and Clinical Psychology, 61,* 992–1002.

Shaffer, G. S., Saunders, V., & Owens, W. A. (1986). Additional evidence for the accuracy of biographical data: Long-term retest and observer ratings. *Personnel Psychology, 39,* 791–809.

Shaffer, M. (1982). *Life after stress.* New York: Knopf.

Shaver, P., Hazan, C., & Bradshaw, D. (1988). *Love as attachment: The integration of three behavioral systems.* In R. J. Sterberg & M. L. Barnes (Eds.), *The psychology of love.* New Haven, CT: Yale University Press.

Shedler, J., & Block, J. (1990). Adolescent drug use and psychological health: A longitudinal study. *American Psychologist, 45,* 612–630.

Sheehy, R. N. (1976). *Passages: Predictable Crises from Adult Life.* New York: Dutton.

Shekelle, B., Hulley, S. B., Neaton, J. D., Billings, J. H., Borhani, N. O., et al. (1985). The MRFIT behavior pattern study II: Type A behavior and the incidence of coronary heart disease. *American Journal of Epidemiology, 122,* 559–570.

Shekelle, R. B., & Gale, M. (1985). Type A scores (Jenkins Activity Survey) and risk of recurrent coronary heart disease in the Aspirin Myocardial Infarction Study. *American Journal of Cardiology, 56,* 221–225.

Sherman, S. J., Judd, C. M., & Park, B. (1989). Social cognition. *Annual Review of Psychology, 40,* 281–326.

Shertzer, B. (1985). *Career planning* (3rd ed.). Boston: Houghton Mifflin.

Shiffman, L. B., Fischer, L. B., Zettler-Segal, M., & Benowitz, N. L. (1990). Nicotine exposure among nondependent smokers. *Archives of General Psychiatry, 47,* 333–340.

Shimamura, A. P. (1986). Priming effects in amnesia: Evidence for a dissociable memory function. *Quarterly Journal of Experimental Psychology, 38A,* 619–644.

Shipman, P. (1994). *The evolution of racism.* New York: Simon & Schuster.

Shirley, M. C., Matt, D. A., & Burish, T. G. (1992). Comparison of frontalis, multiple muscle site, and reactive muscle site feedback in reducing arousal under stressful and nonstressful conditions. *Medical Psychotherapy, 5,* 133–148.

Shotland, R. L. (1985). When bystanders just stand by. *Psychology Today, 19,* 50–55.

Shulman, H. G. (1971). Similarity effects in short-term memory. *Psychological Bulletin, 75,* 399–415.

Shulman, H. G. (1972). Semantic confusion errors in short-term memory. *Journal of Verbal Learning and Verbal Behavior, 11,* 221–227.

Shweder, R. A., & Sullivan, M. A. (1993). Cultural psychology: Who needs it? *Annual Review of Psychology, 44,* 497–523.

Shwedler, R., & Sullivan, M. (1993). Cultural psychology: Who needs it? *Annual Review of Psychology, 44,* 497–523.

Sibai, B. M., Caritis, S. N., Thom, E., Klebanoff, M., McNellis, D., et al. (1993). Prevention of preeclampsia with low-dose aspirin in healthy, nulliparous pregnant women. *The New England Journal of Medicine, 329,* 1213–1218.

Siegler, R. S. (1983). Five generalizations about cognitive development. *American Psychologist, 38,* 263–277.

Siegler, R. S. (1989). Mechanisms of cognitive development. *Annual Review of Psychology, 40,* 353–379.

Silva, J. M., Hardy, C. J., & Crace, R. K. (1988). Analysis of momentum in intercollegiate tennis. *Journal of Sport and Exercise Psychology*, 10, 346–354.

Skinner, B. F. (1956). A case history in the scientific method. *American Psychologist*, 11, 221–223.

Skinner, B. F. (1957). *Verbal behavior.* Englewood Cliffs, NJ: Prentice-Hall.

Skinner, B. F. (1983). Intellectual self-management in old age. *American Psychologist*, 38, 239–244.

Skinner, B. F. (1984). *A matter of consequence.* New York: Knopf.

Skinner, B. F. (1987). What ever happened to psychology as the science of behavior? *American Psychologist*, 42, 780–786.

Skinner, B. F. (1989). The origins of cognitive thought. *American Psychologist*, 44, 13–18.

Skinner, B. F. (1990). Can psychology be a science of mind? *American Psychologist*, 45, 1206–1210.

Skolnick, A. (1979). *The intimate environment* (2nd ed.). Boston: Little, Brown.

Slobin, D. I. (1979). *Psycholinguistics.* Glenview, IL: Scott, Foresman.

Small, J. G., Klapper, M. H., Kellams, J. J., Miller, M. J., Milstein, V., Sharpley, P. H., & Small, I. F. (1988). Electroconvulsive treatment compared with lithium in the management of manic states. *Archives of General Psychiatry*, 45, 727–732.

Smeaton, G., Byrne, D. & Murnen, S. (1989). The repulsion hypothesis revisited: Similarity irrelevance or dissimilarity bias? *Journal of Personality and Social Psychology*, 56, 54–59.

Smith, A., & Stansfield, S. (1986). Aircraft noise exposure, noise sensitivity, and everyday errors. *Environment and Behavior*, 18, 214–226.

Smith, C. P. (Ed.). (1992). *Motivation and personality: Handbook of thematic content analysis.* Cambridge: Cambridge University Press.

Smith, D. (1987). Conditions that facilitate the development of sport imagery training. *The Sport Psychologist*, 1, 237–247.

Smith, G. B., Schwebel, A. I., Dunn, R, L., & McIver, S. D. (1993). The role of psychologists in the treatment, management, and prevention of chronic mental illness. *American Psychologist*, 48, 966–971.

Smith, P. C. (1976). *Behavior, results, and organizational effectiveness: The problem of criteria.* In M. D. Dunnette (Ed.), *Handbook of industrial and organizational psychology.* Skokie, IL: Rand McNally.

Smith, S. (1979). Remembering in and out of context. *Journal of Experimental Psychology: Human Learning and Memory*, 5, 460–471.

Smith, T. W. (1992). Hostility and health: Current status of a psychosomatic hypothesis. *Health Psychology*, 11, 139–150.

Smither, R. D. (1994). *The psychology of work and human performance.* New York: HarperCollins.

Smyrnios, K. X., & Kirkby, R. J. (1993). Long-term comparison of brief versus unlimited psychodynamic treatments with children and their parents. *Journal of Consulting and Clinical Psychology*, 61, 1020-1027.

Snarey, J. (1987). A question of morality. *Psychology Today*, 21, 68.

Snarey, J. R., Reimer, J., & Kohlberg, L. (1985). Development of social-moral reasoning among kibbutz adolescents: A longitudinal cross-sectional study. *Developmental Psychology*, 21, 3–17.

Snyder, S. H. (1984, November). Medicated minds. *Science*, 84, pp. 141–142.

Snyderman, M., & Rothman, S. (1987). Survey of expert opinion on intelligence and aptitude testing. *American Psychologist*, 42, 137–144.

Sobal, J., & Stunkard, A. J. (1989). Socioeconomic status and obesity: A review of the literature. *Psychological Bulletin*, 105, 260–275.

Somers, V. K., Dyken, M. E., Mark, A. L., & Abboud, F. M. (1993). Sympathetic-nerve activity during sleep in normal subjects. *The New England Journal of Medicine*, 328, 303–307.

Sommer, R. (1969). *Personal space: The behavioral basis of designs.* Englewood Cliffs, NJ: Prentice-Hall.

Sorensen, J. L., Wermuth, L. A., Gibson, D. R., Choi, K., et al. (1991). *Preventing AIDS in drug users and their sexual partners.* New York: Guilford.

Soyka, L. F. & Joffee, J. M. (1980). *Male mediated drug effects on offspring.* In R. H. Schwarz & S. J. Yaffe (Eds.) *Drug and chemical risks to the fetus and newborn.* New York: Alan R. Liss, Inc.

Spanos, N. P., & Barber, T. F. X. (1974). Toward convergence in hypnosis research. *American Psychologist*, 29, 500–511.

Spanos, N. P., Menary, E., Gabora, N. J., DuBreuil, S. C., & Dewhirst, B. (1991). Secondary identity enactments during hypnotic past-life regression: A sociocognitive perspective. *Journal of Personality and Social Psychology*, 61, 308–320.

Sperling, G. (1960). The information available in brief visual presentation. *Psychological Monographs*, 74 (Whole No. 498).

Sperling, G. (1963). A model for visual memory tasks. *Human Factors*, 5, 19–31.

Sperry, R. (1968). Hemispheric disconnection and unity in conscious awareness. *American Psychologist*, 23, 723–733.

Sperry, R. (1982). Some effects of disconnecting the cerebral hemispheres. *Science*, 217, 1223–1226.

Spitz, H. (1986). *The raising of intelligence: A selected history of attempts to raise retarded intelligence.* Hillsdale, NJ: Erlbaum.

Springer, J. P., & Deutsch, G. (1981). *Left brain, right brain.* San Francisco: Freeman.

Squire, L. R., Knowlton, B., & Musen, G. (1993). The structure and organization of memory. *Annual Review of Psychology, 44,* 453–495.

Squire, L. R., & Slater, P. C. (1978). Bilateral and unilateral ECT: Effects on verbal and nonverbal memory. *American Journal of Psychiatry, 135,* 1316–1320.

Stall, R. D., Coates, T. J., & Huff, C. (1988). Behavioral risk reduction for HIV infection among gay and bisexual men: A review of results from the United States. *American Psychologist, 43,* 878–885.

Standing, L. (1973). Learning 10,000 pictures. *Quarterly Journal of Experimental Psychology, 25,* 207–222.

Standing, L., Canezio, J., & Haber, R. N. (1970). Perception and memory for pictures: Single-trial learning 2500 visual stimuli. *Psychonomic Science, 19,* 73–74.

Staw, B. M. (1984). Organizational behavior: A review and reformation of the field's outcome variables. *Annual Review of Psychology, 35,* 627–666.

Stechler, G., & Halton, A. (1982). *Prenatal influences on human development.* In B. B. Woolman (Ed.), *Handbook of developmental psychology.* Englewood Cliffs, NJ: Prentice-Hall.

Steenbarger, B. N. (1994). Duration and outcome in psychotherapy: An integrative review. *Professional Psychology: Research and Practice, 25,* 111–119.

Stein, J. A., Newcomb, M. D., & Bentler, P. M. (1990). The relative infuence of vocational behavior and family involvement on self-esteem: Longitudinal analyses of young adult women and men. *Journal of Vocational Behavior, 36,* 320–328.

Stern, D. (1977). *The first relationship.* Cambridge, MA: Harvard University Press.

Sternberg, R., & Lubert, T. (1993). Creative giftedness: A multivariate investment approach. *Gifted Child Quarterly, 37,* 1–15.

Sternberg, R. J., & Wagner, R. K. (1993). The g-centric view of intelligence and job performance is wrong. *Current Directions in Psychological Science, 2,* 1–5.

Stiles, W. B., Shapiro, D. A., & Elliot, R. (1986). "Are all psychotherapies equivalent?" *American Psychologist, 41,* 165–180.

Stokals, D. (1992). Establishing and maintaining healthy environments. *American Psychologist, 47,* 6–22.

Stokols, D. (1972). On the distinction between density and crowding: Some implications for future research. *Psychological Review, 79,* 275–277.

Stokols, D. (1990). Instrumental and spiritual views of people-environment relations. *American Psychologist, 45,* 641–646.

Stoner, J. A. F. (1961). *A comparison of individual and group decisions involving risk.* Unpublished master's thesis, Massachusetts Institute of Technology, Cambridge, MA.

Streissguth, A. P., Aase, J. M., Clarren, S. K., Randels, S. P., LaDue, R. A., & Smith, D. F. (1991). Fetal alcohol syndrome in adolescents and adults. *Journal of the American Medical Association, 265,* 1961–1967.

Strupp, H. H. (1986). Psychotherapy: Research, practice, and public policy (How to avoid dead ends). *American Psychologist, 41,* 120–130.

Strupp, H. H., & Binder, J. L. (1984). *Psychotherapy in a new key.* New York: Guilford.

Stumpf, H. (1993). The factor structure of the Personality Research Form: A cross-national evaluation. *Journal of Personality, 61,* 27–48.

Stunkard, A. J. (1988). Some perspectives on human obesity: Its causes. *Bulletin of the New York Academy of Medicine, 64,* 902–923.

Stunkard, A. J., Harris, J. R., Pederson, N.L., & McClearn, G. E. (1900). The body-mass index of twins who have been reared apart. *New England Journal of Medicine, 322,* 1483–1487.

Stunkard, A. J., Sorensen, T. I. A., Hanis, C., et al. (1986). An adoption study of human obesity. *New England Journal of Medicine, 314,* 193– 198.

Sue, D. W., & Sue, D. (1990). *Counseling the culturally different: Theory and practice* (2nd ed.). New York: Wiley.

Suinn, R. M. (1980). *Psychology in sports: Methods and applications.* Minneapolis: Burgess.

Surgeon General. (1988). *The health consequences of smoking: Nicotine addiction.* Rockville, MD: U. S. Department of Health and Human Services.

Surwit, R. S., Feinglos, M. N., & Scovern, A. W. (1983). Diabetes and behavior. *American Psychologist, 38,* 255–262.

Swaim, R. C., Oetting, E. R., Thurman, P. J., Beauvais, F., & Edwards, R. W. (1993). American Indian adolescent drug use and socialization characteristics: A cross-cultural comparison. *Journal of Cross-cultural Psychology, 24,* 53–70.

Swedo, S. E., Rapoport, J. L., Leonard, H., Lenane, M., & Cheslow, D. (1989a). Obsessive-compulsive disorder in children and adolescence. *Archives of General Psychiatry, 46,* 335–341.

Swedo, S. E., Shapiro, M. B., Grady, C. L., Cheslow, D. L., et al. (1989b). Cerebral glucose metabolism in childhood-onset obsessive-compulsive disorder. *Archives of General Psychiatry, 46,* 518–523.

Szasz, T. S. (1960). *The myth of mental illness.* New York: HarperCollins.

Szasz, T. S. (1982). The psychiatric will: A new mechanism for protecting persons against "psychosis" and psychiatry. *American Psychologist, 37,* 762–770.

Takanishi, R. (1993). The opportunities of adolescence—research, interventions, and policy. *American Psychologist, 48,* 85–87.

Tandon, R., & Greden, J. F. (1989). Cholinergic hyperactivity and negative schizophrenic symptoms. *Archives of General Psychiatry, 46,* 745–753.

Tannenbaum, S. I., & Yukl, G. (1992). Training and development in work organizations. *Annual Review of Psychology, 43,* 399–441.

Tanner, J. M. (1973). Growing up. *Scientific America, 135,* 34–43.

Tanner, J. M. (1981). Growth and maturation during adolescence. *Nutrition Review, 39,* 43–55.

Taylor, W., Pearson, J., Mair, A., & Burns, W. (1965). Study of noise and hearing in jute weaving. *Journal of the Acoustical Society of America, 4,* 144–152.

Tenopyr, M. L. (1981). The realities of employment testing. *American Psychologist, 36,* 1120–1127.

Teplin, L. A., Abram, K. M., & McClelland, G. M. (1994). Does psychiatric disorder predict violent crime among released jail detainees? A six-year longitudinal study. *American Psychologist, 49,* 335–342.

Thackwray-Emmerson, D. (1989). The effect of self-motivation on headache reduction through biofeedback training. *Medical Psychotherapy, 2,* 125–130.

Thayer, W. P. (1983). *Industrial/organizational psychology: Science and application.* In C. J. Scheirer & A. M. Rogers (Eds.), *The G. Stanley Hall lecture series* (Vol. 3). Washington, DC: American Psychological Association.

Thibault, J. W., & Kelley, H. H. (1959). *The social psychology of groups.* New York: Wiley.

Thomas, M. B. (1992). *An introduction to marital and family therapy.* New York: Macmillan.

Thompson, C. P. (1982). Memory for unique personal events: The roommate study. *Memory and Cognition, 10,* 324–332.

Thompson, J. W., & Blaine, J. D. (1987). Use of ECT in the United States in 1975 and 1980. *American Journal of Psychiatry, 144,* 557–562.

Thorndike, A. L., Hagen, E. P., & Sattler, J. M. (1986). *The Stanford-Binet Intelligence scale, Fourth edition: Technical manual.* Chicago: Riverside.

Thorndike, E. L. (1911). *Animal intelligence.* New York: Macmillan.

Thornton, G. C., III, & Cleveland, J. N. (1990). Developing managerial talent through simulation. *American Psychologist, 45,* 190–199.

Tilley, A. J., & Empson, J. A. C. (1978). REM sleep and memory consolidation. *Biological Psychology, 6,* 293–300.

Tohen, M., Waternaux, C. M., & Tsuang, M. T. (1990). Outcome in mania. *Archives of General Psychiatry, 47,* 1106–1111.

Tolman, C. W. (1969) Social feeding in domestic chicks: Effects of food deprivation of non-feeding companions. *Psychonomic Science, 15,* 234.

Tolman, E. C. (1932) *Purposive behaviorism in animals and men.* Englewood Cliffs, NJ: Prentice-Hall.

Tolman, E. C., & Honzik, C. H. (1930). Introduction and removal of reward and maze performance in rats. *University of California Publication in Psychology, 4,* 257–275.

Tomkins, S. S. (1962). *Affect, imagery, consciousness: Vol. I. The positive affects.* New York: Springer.

Toro, P. A., Trickett, E. J., Wall, D. D., & Salem, D. A. (1991). Homelessness in the United States: An ecological perspective. *American Psychologist, 46,* 1208–1218.

Torrey, T. W., & Feduccia, A. (1979). *Morphogenesis of the vertebrates.* New York: Wiley.

Travis, C. B. (1988). *Women and health psychology: Mental health issues.* Hillsdale, NJ: Erlbaum.

Triandis, H. C. (1990). *Theoretical concepts that are applicable to the analysis of ethnocentrism.* In R. W. Brislin (Ed.), *Applied cross-cultural psychology.* Newbury Park, CA: Sage.

Triandis, H. C. (1993). Collectivism and individualism as cultural syndromes. *Cross-Cultural Research, 27,* 155–180.

Triandis, H. C., Brislin, R., & Hui, C. H. (1988). Cross-cultural training across the individualism-collectivism divide. *International Journal of Intercultural Relations, 12,* 269–289.

Triplett, N. (1898). The dynamogenic factors in pacemaking and competition. *American Journal of Psychology, 9,* 507–533.

True, W. R., Rice, J., Eisen, S. A., Heath, A. C., Goldberg, J., Lyons, M. J. & Nowak, J. (1993). A twin study of genetic and environmental contributions to liability for posttraumatic stress symptoms. *Archives of General Psychiatry, 50,* 257–264.

Tucker, D. M. (1981). Lateral brain function, emotion, and conceptualization. *Psychological Bulletin, 89,* 19–46.

Tulving, E. (1972). *Episodic and semantic memory.* In E. Tulving & W. Donaldson (Eds.), *Organization of memory.* New York: Academic Press.

Tulving, E. (1983). *Elements of episodic memory.* New York: Oxford University Press.

Tulving, E. (1985). How many memory systems are there? *American Psychologist, 40,* 385–398.

Tulving, E. (1986). What kind of a hypothesis is the distinction between episodic and semantic memory? *Journal of Experimental Psychology: Learning, Memory, and Cognition, 12,* 307–311.

Tulving, E., & Schacter, D. L. (1990). Priming and human memory systems. *Science, 247,* 301–306.

Tulving, E., & Thompson, D. M. (1973). Encoding specificity and retrieval processes in episodic memory. *Journal of Experimental Psychology: Learning, Memory, and Cognition, 8,* 336–342.

Tung, R. (1988). *The new expatriates: Managing human resources abroad.* Cambridge, MA: Harper & Row.

Turk, D. C. (1994). Perspectives on chronic pain: The role of psychological factors. *Current Directions in Psychological Science, 3,* 45–48.

Turnbull, C. (1961). Some observations regarding experiences and behaviors of the Bambuti pygmies. *American Journal of Psychology, 74,* 304–308.

Turner, J. A., Deyo, R. A., Loesser, J. D., Von Korff, J. E. & Fordyce, W. E. (1994). The importance of placebo effects in pain treatment and research. *The Journal of the American Medical Association, 271,* 1609–1615.

Turner, J. S., & Helms, D. B. (1987). *Contemporary adulthood.* New York: Holt, Rinehart, and Winston.

Ulrich, R. E., Stachnick, T. J., & Stainton, N. R. (1963). Student acceptance of Generalized Personality Inventory. *Psychological Reports, 13,* 831–834.

Underwood, B. J. (1957). Interference and forgetting. *Psychological Review, 64,* 49–60.

Unger, R., & Crawford, M. (1992). *Women and gender: A feminist psychology.* New York: McGraw-Hill.

U.S. Bureau of the Census. (1991). *Statistical abstract of the United States* (111th ed.). Washington, DC: U. S. Government Printing Office.

U.S. Bureau of the Census. (1994). *Statistical abstract of the United States* (114th ed.). Washington, DC: U. S. Government Printing Office.

USGAO. (1992). *Elderly Americans: Health, housing, and nutritional gaps between the poor and the nonpoor.* Washington, DC: United States General Accounting Office.

Vaillant, G. E. (1983). *The natural history of alcoholism: Causes, patterns, and paths to recovery.* Cambridge, MA: Harvard University Press.

Valenstein, E. S. (1980). *The psychosurgery debate: Scientific, legal, and ethical perspectives.* San Francisco: Freeman.

Valenstein, E. S. (1986). *Great and desperate cures.* New York: Basic Books.

Vallerand, R. J., Colavecchio, P. G., & Pelletier, L. G. (1988). Psychological momentum and performance inferences: A preliminary test of the antecedents-consequences psychological momentum model. *Journal of Sport and Exercise Psychology, 10,* 92–108.

Valliant, G. E., & Valliant, C. O. (1990). Natural history of male psychological health, XII: A 45-year study of predictors of successful aging at age 65. *American Journal of Psychiatry, 147,* 31–37.

van Ijzendoorn, M. H., & Kroonenberg, P. M. (1988). Cross-cultural patterns of attachment: A meta-analysis. *Child Development, 59,* 147–156.

VandenBos, G. R. (1986). Psychotherapy research: A special issue. *American Psychologist, 41,* 111–112.

Vander Wall, S. B. (1982). An experimental analysis of cache recovery in the Clark's nutcracker. *Animal Behavior, 30,* 84–94.

Ventura, J., Nuechterlein, K. H., Lukoff, D., & Hardesty, J. P. (1989). A prospective study of stressful life events and schizophrenic relapse. *Journal of Abnormal Psychology, 98,* 407–411.

Verillo, R. T. (1975). *Cutaneous sensation.* In B. Scharf (Ed.), *Experimental sensory psychology.* Glenview, IL: Scott, Foresman.

Vertes, R. P. (1984). Brainstem control of the events of REM sleep. *Progress in Neurobiology, 22,* 241–288.

Vinacke, W. E. (1974). *The psychology of thinking* (2nd ed.). New York: McGraw-Hill.

Vitz, P. C. (1990). The use of stories in moral development. *American Psychologist, 45,* 709–720.

Voevodsky, J. (1974). Evaluations of a deceleration warning light for reducing rear-end automobile collisions. *Journal of Applied Psychology, 59,* 270–273.

Vroom, V. (1964). *Work and motivation.* New York: Wiley.

Wakefield, H., & Underwager, R. (1992). Recovered memories of alleged sexual abuse: Lawsuits against parents. *Behavioral Sciences and the Law, 10,* 483–507.

Walker, L. J. (1989). A longitudinal study of moral reasoning. *Child Development, 601,* 157–166.

Wallace, P. (1977). Individual discrimination of humans by odor. *Physiology and Behavior, 19,* 577–579.

Wallas, G. (1926). *The art of thought.* New York: Harcourt Brace Jovanovich.

Wallerstein, J. (1989). *Second chances.* New York: Ticknor & Fields.

Walsh, B. T., Hadigan, C. M., Devlin, M. J., Gladis, M., & Roose, S. P. (1991). Long-term outcome of antidepressant treatment for bulimia nervosa. *American Journal of Psychiatry,* 148, 1206–1212.

Walsh, B. T., Kissileff, H. R., Cassidy, S. M., & Dantzic, S. (1989). Eating behavior of women with bulimia. *Archives of General Psychiatry,* 46, 54–58.

Walster, E., Aronson, V., Abrahams, D., & Rottman, L. (1966). Importance of physical attractiveness in dating behavior. *Journal of Personality and Social Psychology,* 4, 508–516.

Walster, E., & Festinger, L. (1962). The effectiveness of "overheard" and persuasive communications. *Journal of Abnormal and Social Psychology,* 65, 395–402.

Walster, E., & Walster, G. W. (1969). The matching hypothesis. *Journal of Personality and Social Psychology,* 6, 248–253.

Walster, E., Walster, G. W., & Bershied, E. (1978). *Equity: Theory and research.* Boston: Allyn & Bacon.

Walters, G. C., & Grusec, J. E. (1977). *Punishment.* San Francisco: Freeman.

Walton, G. E., Bower, N. J. A., Bower, T. G. R. (1992). Recognition of familiar faces by newborns. *Infant Behavior and Development,* 15, 265–269.

Walton, G. E., & Bower, T. G. R. (1993). Newborns form "prototypes" in less than 1 minute. *Psychological Science,* 4, 203–205.

Wamboldt, F. S., & Reiss, D. (1989). Defining a family heritage and a new relationship identity: Two central tasks in the making of a marriage. *Family Processes,* 28, 317–335.

Warrington, E. K., & Weiskrantz, L. (1968). New method of testing long-term retention with special reference to amnesic patients. *Nature,* 217, 972–974.

Warrington, E. K., & Weiskrantz, L. (1970). Amnesic syndrome: Consolidation or retrieval? *Nature,* 228, 629–630.

Watkins, L. R., & Mayer, D. J. (1982). Organization of endogenous opiate and nonopiate pain control systems. *Science,* 216, 1185–1192.

Watkins, C. J. (1981). An evaluation of some aspects of the Steers and Rhodes model of employee attendance. *Journal of Applied Psychology,* 66, 385–389.

Watson, J. B. (1919). *Psychology from the standpoint of a behaviorist.* Philadelphia: Lippincott.

Watson, J. B. (1925). *Behaviorism.* New York: Norton.

Watson, J. B. (1926). What is behaviorism? *Harper's Monthly Magazine,* 152, 723–729.

Watson, J. B., & Raynor, R. (1920). Conditioned emotional reactions. *Journal of Experimental Psychology,* 3, 1–14.

Weaver, C. N. (1980). Job satisfaction in the United States in the 1970s. *Journal of Applied Psychology,* 65, 364–367.

Weekley, J. A., & Gier, J. A. (1987). Reliability and validity of the situational interview for a sales person. *Journal of Applied Psychology,* 72, 484–487.

Weil, A. T., Zinberg, N., & Nelson, J. M. (1968). Clinical and psychological effects of marijuana in man. *Science,* 162, 1234–1242.

Weiner, B. (1985). An attributional theory of achievement motivation and emotion. *Psychological Review,* 92, 548–573.

Weisberg, R. W. (1986). *Creativity: Genius and other myths.* San Francisco: Freeman.

Weiss, C. S. (1992). Depression and immunocompetence: A review of the literature. *Psychological Bulletin,* 111, 475–489.

Weissman, M. M. (1988). The epidemiology of anxiety disorders: Rates, risks and familial patterns. *Journal of Psychiatric Research,* 22, (Suppl. 1), 99–114.

Weissman, M. M. & Klerman, G. L. (1992). The changing rate of major depression. *Journal of the American Medical Association, 268,* 3098.

Weissman, M. M., Klerman, G. L., Markowitz, J. S., & Ouellette, R. (1989). Suicidal idealation and suicide attempts in panic disorders and attacks. *The New England Journal of Medicine,* 321, 1209–1214.

Weldon, E., & Gargano, G. M. (1988). Cognitive loading: The effects of accountability and shared responsibility on cognitive effort. *Personality and Social Psychology Bulletin,* 14, 159–171.

Wellman, H. M., & Gelman, S. A. (1992). Cognitive development: Fundamental theories of core domains. *Annual Review of Psychology,* 43, 337–375.

Wells, G. L. (1993). What do we know about eyewitness identification? *American Psychologist,* 48, 553–571.

Wertheimer, M. (1961). Psychomotor coordination of auditory and visual space at birth. *Science,* 134, 1692.

Wheeler, R. J., & Frank, M. A. (1988). Identification of stress buffers. *Behavioral Medicine,* 14, 78–89.

Whitehurst, G. (1982). Language development. In B. Wolman (Ed.), *Handbook of developmental psychology.* Englewood Cliffs, NJ: Prentice-Hall.

Wickens, C. D. (1992). *Engineering psychology and human performance* (2nd ed.). New York: Harper-Collins.

Wickens, D. D. (1973). Some characteristics of word encoding. *Memory and Cognition,* 1, 485–490.

Wiesner, W. H., & Cronshaw, S. F. (1988). A meta-analytic investigation of the impact of interview format and degree of structure on the validity of the employment interview. *Occupational Psychology,* 61, 275–290.

Wiggins, J. S. (1992). Have model will travel. *Journal of Personality,* 60, 527–532.

Wiggins, J. S. & Pincus, A. L. (1992). Personality: Structure and assessment, *Annual Review of Psychology,* 43, 473–504.

Wilkes, J. (1986). Conversation with Ernest R. Hilgard: A study in hypnosis. *Psychology Today,* 20(1), 23–27.

Williams, K., Harkins, S., & Latané, B. (1981) Identifiability as a deterrent to social loafing: Two cheering experiments. *Journal of Personality and Social Psychology,* 40, 303–311.

Williams, K., Nida, S. A., Baca, L. D., & Latané, B. (1989). Social loafing and swimming: Effects of identifiability of individual and relay performance of intercollegiate swimmers. *Basic and Applied Social Psychology,* 10, 73–82.

Wilson, G. T. (1982). *Adult disorders.* In G. T. Wilson & C. M. Franks (Eds.), *Contemporary behavior therapy: Conceptual and empirical foundations.* New York: Guilford Press.

Winter, D. G. (1987). Leader appeal, leader performance, and the motive profiles of leaders and followers: A study of American presidents and elections. *Journal of Personality and Social Psychology,* 52, 196–202.

Winter, D. G. (1988). The power motive in women—and men. *Journal of Personality and Social Psychology,* 54, 510–519.

Winter, D. G., & Steward, A. J. (1978). *The power motive.* In H. London & J. E. Exner (Eds.), *Dimensions of personality.* New York: Wiley.

Wisensale, S. K. (1992). Toward the 21st century: Family change and public policy. *Family Relations,* 41, 417–422.

Witenberg, S. H., Blanchard, E. B., McCoy, G., Suls, J., & McGoldrick, M. D. (1983). Evaluation of compliance in home and center hemodialysis patients. *Health Psychology,* 2, 227–238.

Wittchen, H., Shanyang, Z., Kessler, R. C. & Eaton, W. (1994). *DSM-III-R* generalized anxiety disorder in the National Comorbidity Survey. *Archives of General Psychiatry,* 51, 355–364.

Wollen, K. A., Weber, A., & Lowry, D. H. (1972). Bizarreness versus interaction of mental images as determinants of learning. *Cognitive Psychology,* 3, 518–523.

Wolpe, J. (1958). *Psychotherapy by reciprocal inhibition.* Stanford, CA: Stanford University Press.

Wolpe, J. (1969). Basic principles and practices of behavior therapy of neuroses. *American Journal of Psychiatry,* 125, 1242–1247.

Wolpe, J. (1981). Behavior therapy versus psychoanalysis. *American Psychologist,* 36, 159–164.

Wolpe, J. (1982). *The practice of behavior therapy* (3rd ed.). New York: Pergamon Press.

Wood, C. (1986). The hostile heart. *Psychology Today,* 20, 10–12.

Woodruff, V. (1994). Studies say the kids are all right. *Working Woman,* October, p. 12.

Worringham, C. J., & Messick, D. M. (1983). Social facilitation of running: An unobtrusive study. *Journal of Social Psychology,* 121, 23–29.

Wright, L. (1988). The Type A behavior pattern and coronary artery disease. *American Psychologist,* 43, 2–14.

Wurtman, R. J. (1985). Alzheimer's disease. *Scientific American,* 247, 62–74.

Yalom, I. D. (1985). The theory and practice of group psychotherapy. New York: Basic Books.

Yaniv, I., & Meyer, D. E. (1987). Activation and metacognition of inaccessible stored information: Potential basis for incubation effects in problem solving. *Journal of Experimental Psychology: Learning, Memory, and Cognition,* 13, 187–205.

Yapko, M. (1993). The seduction of memory. *The Family Therapy Networker,* 17, 42–43.

Yates, A. (1989). Current perspectives on the eating disorders: I. History, psychological and biological aspects. *Journal of the American Academy of Child and Adolescent Psychiatry,* 28, 813–828.

Yates, A. (1990). Current perspectives on eating disorders: II. Treatment, outcome, and research directions. *Journal of the American Academy of Child and Adolescent Psychiatry,* 29, 1–9.

Yates, A. J. (1980). *Biofeedback and the Modification of Behavior.* New York: Plenum.

Yates, F. A. (1966). *The art of memory.* Chicago: University of Chicago Press.

Youngstrom, N. (1991, May). Serious mental illness issues need leadership. *APA Monitor,* p. 27.

Yuille, J. C. (1993). We must study forensic eyewitnesses to know about them. *American Psychologist,* 48, 572–573.

Zajonc, R. B. (1968). Attitudinal effects of mere exposure. *Journal of Personality and Social Psychology,* Monograph Suppl. 9, 1–27.

Zajonc, R. B., & Markus, H. (1982). Affective and cognitive factors in preferences. *Journal of Consumer Research,* 9, 123–131.

Zanna, M. P., & Rempel, J. K. (1988). *Attitudes: A new look at an old concept.* In D. Bartal & A. W. Kruglanski (Eds.), *The social psychology of knowledge.* New York: Cambridge University Press.

Zedeck, S., Tziner, A., & Middlestadt, S. E. (1983). Interviewer validity and reliability: An individual analysis approach. *Personnel Psychology,* 36, 230–237.

Zelnik, M., & Kantner, J. F. (1980). Sexual activity, contraceptive use, and pregnancy among metropolitan-area teenagers: 1971–1979. *Family Planning Perspectives,* 12, 230–237.

Zigler, E. & Hodapp, R. M. (1991). Behavioral functioning in individuals with mental retardation. *Annual Review of Psychology,* 42, 29–50.

Zimmerman, M., & Coryell, W. (1989). DSM-III personality disorder diagnoses in a nonpatient sample. *Archives of General Psychiatry,* 46, 682–689.

Zinbarg, R. E., Barlow, D. H., Brown, T. A., & Hertz, R. M. (1992). Cognitive- behavioral approaches to the nature and treatment of anxiety disorders. *Annual Review of Psychology,* 43, 235–267.

Zohar, D. (1980). Safety climate in industrial organizations: Theoretical and applied implications. *Journal of Applied Psychology,* 65, 96–102.

Zuckerman, B., & Bresnahan, K. (1991). Developmental and behavioral consequences of prenatal drug and alcohol exposure. *Pediatrics Clinics of North America,* 38, 1387–1406.

Zuckerman, M. (1978). Sensation seeking and psychopathology. In R. D. Hare & D. Schalling (Eds.). *Psychopathic Behavior.* New York: Wiley.

CREDITS

Unless otherwise acknowledged, all photographs are the property of Scott, Foresman and Company. Page abbreviations are as follows: (*T*) top, (*C*) center, (*B*) bottom, (*L*) left, (*R*) right.

Chapter 1
Page 13: Gary Hayes/Tony Stone Images; *Page 16:* Drawing by Sam Gross; © 1994/The New Yorker Magazine, Inc. *Page 19:* Will & Deni McIntyre/Photo Researchers; *Page 21:* Archives of the History of American Psychology, University of Akron; *Page 24:* Bettmann Archive; *Page 25:* Historical Pictures/Stock Montage, Inc. *Page 27:* Martin Rogers/Tony Stone Images; *Page 38:* Merlin D. Tuttle/National Audubon Society Collection/Photo Researchers; *Page 42R:* Figure 1.4 "Ascending and Descending" by M. C. Escher, 1960 Cordon Art—Baarn, Holland.

Chapter 2
Page 49: Chronis Johns/Tony Stone Images; *Page 52:* Figure 2.2 Secch-Lecaque/Photo Researchers; *Page 54:* Figure 2.3 from: "Action potentials recorded from inside a nerve fiber" by A. L. Hodgkin & A. F. Huxley, from *Nature*, Vol. 144, No. 3651, 10/21/39; *Page 65:* Bruce Curtis/Peter Arnold, Inc.; *Page 74 (R):* David Young-Wolff/Photo Edit.

Chapter 3
Page 79: Tony Freeman/Photo Edit; *Page 82:* Petit Format/Nestle/SS/Photo Researchers; *Page 84:* Courtesy, American Cancer Society; *Page 87:* Peter Vandermark/Stock Boston, Figure 3.3 from *The First Two Years* by Mary M. Shirley; *Page 88:* Figure 3.4 Enrico Ferorelli Enterprises, Inc.; *Page 92 (All):* George Zimbel/Monkmeyer Press Photo Service; *Page 94:* Figure 3.6 Laura Dwight/Peter Arnold, Inc.; *Page 100:* Jeffrey W. Myers/The Stock Market; *Page 103:* Figure 3.10 from: "Standards from birth to maturity . . ." by Tanner, Whitehouse, & Takaishi, from *Archives of Diseases in Childhood,* Vol. 41, Oct. 1966; *Page 104:* Robert W. Ginn/The Picture Cube; *Page 106:* Ken Kaminsky/The Picture Cube; *Page 112:* Sidney Harris; *Page 113:* SuperStock, Inc.; *Page 115:* Ellis Herwig/The Picture Cube.

Chapter 4
Page 125: David Young-Wolff/PhotoEdit; *Page 128:* J. P. Ferrero/Photo Researchers, Figure 4.1 from: "Contemporary psychophysics" by E. Galanter, from *New Directions in Psychology*; *Page 131:* Figure 4.2 from: "Short term retention of individual verbal items" by L. R. Peterson & J. Peterson, from *Journal of Experimental Psychology*; *Page 138:* E. R. Degginer; *Page 142:* Figure 4.12 MacMillan Science Co., Inc.; *Page 147:* Larry Mulvehill/Photo Researchers; *Page 151:* Tony Freeman/PhotoEdit; *Page 154:* Bob Daemmrich/The Image Works.

Chapter 5
Page 160: Stacy Pick/Stock Boston; *Page 170:* Figure 5.7 Nancy Gerow; *Page 171 (T):* Figure 5.8 J. Sohm/The Image Works; *Page 171 (B):* Figure 5.9 Dennis Kucharzak; *Page 172:* Figure 5.10 De Richemond/The Image Works; *Page 173:* Figure 5.11 Mur-

ray & Associates, Inc.; *Page 174:* Figure 5.12 from: "Pictorial perception and culture" by Jan Deregowski, from *Scientific American,* Nov. 1972; *Page 183:* Alan Hobson/Photo Researchers; *Page 186:* Bart Bartholomew/Black Star; *Page 192 (L):* Rick Friedman/The Picture Cube; *Page 192 (R):* Film Bob Daemmrich/Tony Stone Images; *Page 193:* Claudia Andujar/Photo Researchers.

Chapter 6

Page 201: Andy Sacks/Tony Stone Images; *Page 205:* TASS/SOVFOTO; *Page 209:* VLOO/Stockphotos; *Page 213:* Scott Pauly/Black Star; *Page 216:* Susan Van Etten/PhotoEdit; *Page 227:* Hank Morgan © 1985/Discover Syndication/Walt Disney Publications; *Page 230:* Figure 6.8 from "Introduction and removal of reward, and maze performance in rats" by E. C. Tulman & C. H. Honzik, from *University of California Publications in Psychology*; *Page 232:* Figure 6.9 photos courtesy of Dr. Albert Bandura.

Chapter 7

Page 239: John Eastcott/YVA Momatiuk/The Image Works; *Page 246:* Michael Dwyer/Stock Boston; *Page 247:* D. & I. MacDonald/The Picture Cube; *Page 248:* PhotoFest; *Page 250:* Figure 7.3 from: "The 'general acceptance' of psychological research on eyewitness testimony: A survey of experts" by Kassin, Ellsworth and Smith, from *American Pychologist,* 44, 1089–1098, 1989; *Page 252 (TL):* John Coletti/The Picture Cube; *Page 252 (TR):* Myrleen Ferguson/PhotoEdit; *Page 252 (B):* Doug Menuez/Stock Boston; *Page 256:* Figure 7.4 from: "The conditions of retention" by C. W. Luh, from *Psychological Monographs*; *Page 258:* Figure 7.5 from: "Long-term memory for a common object" by R. S. Nickerson & Marilyn Jager Adams, from *Cognitive Psychology,* 1979, 11, 287–307; *Page 260 (L):* Bettmann Archive; *Page 260 (R):* Ted Soqui/Sygma; *Page 262:* Figure 7.6 from: "Narrative stories as mediators for serial learning" by Gordon H. Bower & Michael C. Clark, from *Psyhonomic Science,* Vol. 14, Figure 7.7 from "Mnemotechnics in second-language learning" by R. C. Atkinson, from *American Psychologist*; *Page 263:* Figure 7.8 From: "Bizarreness vs. interaction of mental images as determinants of learning" by Keith A. Wollen, A. Weber, & D. H. Lowly, from *Cognitive Psychology*; *Page 266:* Figure 7.10 from "The conditions of retention" by C. W. Luh, from *Psychlogical Monographs*; *Page 267:* Figure 7.11 from "Properties of learning curves under varied distribution of practice" by Kientzle, from *Journal of Experimental Psychology,* Vol. 36, No. 3, June 1946; *Page 271:* Figure 7.14 from "Consideration of some problems of comprehension" by J. D. Bransford and M. K. Johnson in W. G. Chase, ed., *Visual Information Processing,* 1973.

Chapter 8

Page 277: Stuart Cohen/Tony Stone Images; *Page 280:* Dennis MacDonald/PhotoEdit; *Page 283:* Figure 8.3 from: "Problem-solving" by Martin Sheerer, from *Scientific American,* p. 124; *Page 284:* Figure 8.4 from: "Reasoning in humans, the solution of a problem and its appearance in conscience" by Maier, from *The Journal of Comparative Psychology*; *Page 286:* Rube Goldberg/Reprinted with special permission of King Features Syndicate; *Page 288:* Burk Uzzle/Magnum Photos; *Page 290:* Four by Five/SuperStock, Inc.; *Page 297:* Courtesy, American Cancer Society; *Page 299:* Custom Medical Stock Photo; *Page 300:* Figure 8.9 from: Manual for the *Wechsler Adult Intelligence Scale,* Revised; *Page 308:* Figure 8.11 from: "Problem solving" by Sheerer, from *Scientific American,* p. 124.

Chapter 9

Page 314: Kindra Clineff/The Picture Cube; *Page 317 (L):* Ron Sanford/Black Star; *Page 317 (R):* Fritz Polking/Peter Arnold, Inc.; *Page 319:* George Goodwin/The Picture Cube; *Page 321 (L):* Starr/Stock Boston; *Page 321 (R):* Francis De Richemond/The Image Works; *Page 323 (L):* Seth Resnick/Stock Boston; *Page 323 (R):* Focus On Sports; *Page 326:* Michael Newman/PhotoEdit; *Page 329:* Tony Freeman/PhotoEdit; *Page 333:* Bob Daemmrich/Stock Boston; *Page 335:* Figure 9.5 Sepp

Seitz/Woodfin Camp & Associates; *Page 337:* Blair Seitz/Picturesque; *Page 343:* George M. Harrison/Grant Heilman Photography; *Page 344:* Figure 9.7 1975/Dr. Paul Ekman/Human Interaction Laboratory.

Chapter 10

Page 350: Billy E. Barnes/PhotoEdit; *Page 359:* Charles Gupton/Tony Stone Images; *Page 369:* Blair Seitz/Photo Researchers; *Page 370:* Peter Steiner/The Stock Market.

Chapter 11

Page 380: Peter Southwick/Stock Boston; *Page 383:* William McCoy/Rainbow; *Page 386:* Figure 11.6 from: "Ten common stressors in the lives of middle-aged adults and college students," from *Comparison of Two Modes of Stress Measurement . . .* by Kanner, Coyne, et al., from *Journal of Behavior Medicine,* 4, 1–39, 1981; *Page 387:* Charles Gupton/AllStock Inc./Tony Stone Images; *Page 392:* William McCoy/Rainbow; *Page 394:* Robert Brenner/PhotoEdit.

Chapter 12

Page 407: V. E. Horne/Unicorn Stock Photos; *Page 409 (T):* Victor Englebert; *Page 409:* Rick Smolan/Reportage Stock; *Page 410:* Figure 12.1 from: "Culture specific syndromes," from *Psychiatric Glossary,* 1984, p. 25; *Page 418 (L):* Jim Harrison/Stock Boston; *Page 418 (R): Dan McCoy/Rainbow;* Page 422: Christopher Morris/Black Star; *Page 428:* Figure 12.5 from: "The 10 warning signs of Alzheimer's disease," from *Is It Alzheimer's? Warning Signs You Should Know*—a pamphlet from the Alzheimer's Association; *Page 435 (All):* Al Vercoutere, Malibu, CA; *Page 436:* Michael Weisbrot/Stock Boston; *Page 438:* Brookhaven National Laboratory and NYU Medical Center.

Chapter 13

Page 444: Zigy Kaluzny/Tony Stone Images; *Page 446:* Erich Lessing/Art Resource, New York; *Page 447:* Scala/Art Resource, New York; *Page 448:* Rick Brown/Stock Boston; *Page 451:* Andy Freeberg; *Page 458:* Michael Newman/PhotoEdit; *Page 466:* Figure 13.2 from: "Reason and emotion in psychotherapy" by Albert Ellis and "A new guide to rational living" by Albert Ellis & Robert A. Harper.

Chapter 14

Page 475: Greenlar/The Image Works; *Page 480:* B. Bachmann/The Image Works; *Page 487:* Mary Kate Denny/PhotoEdit; *Page 489:* Ethan Hoffman/Picture Project, Inc.; *Page 492:* William Vandivert; *Page 493:* Figure 14.4 copyright 1965 by Mrs. Alexandra Milgram, Copyright 1965 by Stanley Milgram. From the film *Obedience,* distributed by The Pennsylvania State University, Audio Visual Services; *Page 498: The Far Side* copyright 1992/Universal Press Syndicate. Reprinted with permission. All Rights Reserved. Farworks, Inc.; *Page 499:* Figure 14.5 from: "When will people help in a crisis?" by Darley & Latanè, from *Psychology Today,* 12/68; *Page 500:* Terry Mckoy/The Picture Cube; *Page 502:* Agence De Presse/Vandystadt/Photo Researchers; *Page 505:* Henley & Savage/Picturesque.

Chapter 15

Page 511: Skjold/The Image Works; *Page 515:* Jeff Isaac/Photo Researchers; *Page 517:* Figure 15.1 from "Training: *Program Development and Evaluation* by Goldstein, p. 18; *Page 518:* Tom Hollyman/Photo Researchers; *Page 520:* Tony Freeman/PhotoEdit; *Page 524:* David Young-Wolf/PhotoEdit; *Page 528 (L):* Mark Richards/PhotoEdit; *Page 528 (TR):* Bob Daemmrich/Stock Boston; *Page 528 (CR):* John Coletti/Stock Boston; *Page 528 (B):* Arthur Grace/Stock Boston; *Page 530 (L):* Stephen Frisch/Stock Boston; *Page 530 (TR):* Marty Heitner/The Picture Cube; *Page 530 (B):* Louis Goldman/Photo Researchers; *Page 533 (L):* Nancy Gerow; *Page 533 (R):* Ken Graham/AllStock Inc./Tony Stone Images.

AUTHOR INDEX

Aase, J. M., 84
Abbott, B. B., 16
Abbott, M., 110
Abbott, R. C., 392
Abboud, F. M., 185
Abel, E. L., 84
Abrahams, D., 488
Abram, K. M., 415
Ackerman, P. L., 294, 516
Acton, H., 100
Adams, G. R., 104
Adams, J. L., 281
Adams, J. S., 520–521
Adams, M. J., 257, 258
Adams, R. M., 535
Adelmann, P. K., 343, 344
Adler, A., 357–358
Adler, N., 393, 395, 396
Adler, N. E., 385
Adler, R., 213
Adler, T., 84, 371, 399
Adrian, C., 431
Aiello, J. R., 526
Aiello, T. D., 526
Aiken, L. R., 370
Ainsworth, M. D. S., 100
Ajzen, I., 478
Alavi, A., 437
Alba, J. W., 264
Albee, G. W., 43
Alderman, D., 117
Allen, M. G., 431
Alliger, R. J., 434, 435
Allport, G., 364–365
Altman, L., 526, 529
Alumbaugh, M. J., 401
Alvir, J., 433, 453
Alzheimer, A., 428
Amabile, T. M., 304
Ames, M. A., 333
Anastasi, A., 295
Andersen, B. L., 399
Anderson, A., 533
Anderson, C. A., 533
Anderson, D. C., 533
Anderson, G., 425
Anderson, J., 251
Anderson, J. C., 408
Andreasen, N. C., 434, 435, 437
Andrews, R. J., 343

Angleitner, A., 110
Angoff, W. H., 303
Anisfeld, M., 293
Anisman, H., 431
Apsche, J., 226
Argyle, N., 415
Arizmendi, T. G., 468
Arnold, M., 189
Aronson, E., 483, 487
Aronson, V., 488
Arthur, R. J., 385
Arvey, R. D., 515
Asch, S., 490–491
Aserinsky, E., 183
Ashcraft, M. H., 241
Asherian, A., 110
Aslin, R. N., 88
Aspinwall, L. G., 392
Atkinson, J. W., 261, 334–336, 335, 336
Atkinson, T., 523
Axelrod, S., 226
Azrin, N. H., 226
Azumi, K., 523

Babor, T. F., 191
Baca, L. D., 502
Back, K., 488
Backman, C. W., 487
Baddeley, A., 254
Baddeley, A. D., 241, 243, 253
Bagby, R. M., 373
Bagozzi, R. P., 478
Bahrick, H. P., 255
Bailey, J. M., 332
Baldwin, M. W., 477
Baldy, R., 437
Baley, S., 515
Ballenger, J. C., 416
Bandura, A., 231–233, 232–233, 361, 464
Barbee, A. H., 304
Barber, J. P., 460
Barber, T. F. X., 187
Barber, T. X., 392
Barefoot, J. C., 396
Bargh, J. A., 477, 487
Barinaga, M., 334
Barker, R., 531
Barlow, D. H., 466

Barnes, M., 110
Baron, R. A., 532, 533
Barr, H. M., 84
Barrett, G. V., 294
Barron, F., 285
Barron, S., 84
Bartell, P. A., 495
Bartoshuk, L. M., 88
Baruzzi, A., 67
Basbaum, A. I., 153
Basso, K., 290
Bates, H. G., 290
Baumeister, A. A., 85, 352
Baumeister, R. F., 305, 499, 503, 535
Beauchamp, G. K., 88
Beauvais, F., 106, 192
Beck, A., 431
Beck, A. T., 416, 465
Beckman, L. J., 110
Bee, H., 100, 101, 111
Beecroft, R., 215
Beers, C., 447
Begg, I., 261
Bekerian, D. A., 249
Bell, P. A., 531
Bellack, A. S., 457
Bellugi, U., 293
Belsher, G., 430
Belsky, J., 101
Benedict, H., 291
Bennett, T. L., 195, 431
Bennett, W., 190
Benowitz, N. L., 190
Bentler, P. M., 106–107, 110
Ben-Yehuda, N., 446
Berg, C. J., 421
Berg, C. Z., 420
Berglas, S., 191
Berkowitz, H., 290
Berkowitz, L., 339, 393
Berlyne, D. E., 320
Bernstein, I., 215
Beroldi, G., 497
Berry, J., 94
Berscheid, E., 254, 476, 477
Bersheid, E., 486
Bertelsen, A., 436, 438
Best, C. L., 421
Beutler, L., 460
Beutler, L. E., 468

Bhawuk, D. P. S., 96
Biaggio, A., 110
Bigelow, L. B., 437
Biggar, R. J., 401
Billings, J. H., 396
Billy, J. O. G., 401
Binder, J. L., 460
Binet, A., 296–299
Birdwhistell, R. L., 343
Birnbaum, I. M., 259
Birnbaum, M. H., 488
Blaine, J. D., 452
Blanchard, D. C., 342
Blanchard, E. B., 399
Blanchard, R. J., 342
Blanco-Villasenor, A., 110
Blank, M., 95
Blashfield, R. K., 427
Blass, E. M., 89
Bleuler, E., 433
Bloch, D., 467
Bloch, G. J., 330
Block, J., 106, 129
Bloodworth, R. C., 195
Bloom, F. E., 432, 433
Blumenthal, J. A., 396
Blyth, D. A., 105
Boer, D. P., 253
Bondareff, W., 429
Booth-Kewley, S., 395
Borbely, A., 182
Bordens, K. S., 16
Borenstein, M., 433, 453
Borhani, N. O., 396
Borman, W. C., 514
Bornstein, R. F., 488
Bouchard, C., 326, 327
Bourne, L. E., 281
Bowden, J., 66
Bower, G., 34
Bower, G. H., 246, 259, 262
Bower, N. J. A., 90
Bower, T. G. R., 88, 90
Bowers, J. S., 257
Bowlby, J., 100
Boyce, T., 385
Boyle, M. H., 408
Bradley, D. R., 167
Bradshaw, D., 486
Bradshaw, J. L., 74
Bransford, J. D., 264, 271

Brasfield, T. L., 401
Bratic, E. B., 84
Braum, A., 397
Braun, P., 457
Breen, M. J., 427
Breier, A., 435
Bremer, D., 259
Bresnahan, K., 84
Brett, J. F., 385
Brief, A. P., 385
Brier, A., 435
Brigham, J. C., 401
Bright, I., 468
Brinkerhoff, R. O., 519
Brislin, R. W., 94, 96, 220, 290, 336, 517
Broca, P., 72
Brodsky, A., 189
Brody, E. M., 114
Brogan, J., 73
Bromley, L. M., 153
Brooks-Gunn, J., 108
Broughton, J. M., 88
Brown, J., 244, 255
Brown, J. D., 392
Brown, J. I., 31, 291
Brown, L., 31
Brown, N. A., 85
Brown, R., 259, 293
Brown, T. A., 466
Browne, M. A., 534
Brownell, K. D., 326, 327, 328, 329
Bruce, M. N., 368
Bruch, H., 329
Bruff, C. D., 521
Bruner, J. S., 41
Buchanan, R. W., 435
Buchsbaum, M.S., 321
Buck, R., 339, 343
Burge, D., 431
Burisch, M., 368
Burish, T. G., 392
Burke, J. D., 212
Burke, M. J., 385
Burney, E., 431
Burnkrant, R. E., 478
Burns, W., 531
Buss, A. H., 427
Buss, D. M., 109–110, 110, 489
Butcher, J. N., 409, 424, 434, 450, 460
Butler, R., 117
Butler, R. N., 429
Butterfield, E. C., 306
Byrd, K. R., 253
Byrne, D., 485, 489

Cacioppo, J. T., 477, 479, 483
Calhoun, J. B., 529
Calkins, M., 22
Campbell, D. T., 177
Campbell, J. P., 519

Campbell, K., 100
Campion, J. E., 515
Canezio, 248
Canezio, J., 248
Cannon, T. D., 435
Cannon, W., 320, 321, 324
Cantril, H., 164
Carey, S., 291
Caritis, S. N., 84
Carlsmith, J. M., 480–482, 483
Caroff, S., 437
Carone, B. J., 433
Carpenter, W. T., 435
Carr, C. R., 399
Carran, D. T., 307
Carson, R. C., 409, 424, 431, 434, 450
Carson, T. P., 431
Carver, C. S., 392
Cash, T. F., 489, 515
Cassidy, S. M., 329
Castelli, W. P., 397
Catron, L. S., 111
Cattell, R., 365, 366
Cavanaugh, J. C., 114, 115
Cavanaugh, P. J., 89
Cazden, C. B., 293
Cermack, L. S., 251
Chaiken, S., 477, 478
Chao, G. T., 515
Charney, D. S., 421
Chase, M. H., 185
Chase, W. G., 265
Chase-Lansdale, L., 108
Chasnoff, I. J., 84
Cheeseman, J., 180
Cheslow, D. L., 419, 421
Chesney, M. A., 385
Chilman, C. S., 107, 110
Chiriboga, D. A., 111
Choi, K., 401
Chomsky, N., 293
Chuang, H. T., 401
Ciaranello, R. D., 414
Clark, D. M., 259, 262
Clark, M. C., 34
Clark, R. A., 334–336
Clark, R. D., 88
Clarkson-Smith, L., 116
Clarren, S. K., 84
Cleary, P. D., 399
Cleveland, J. N., 519
Clifford, B. R., 249
Clinton, J. J., 153
Clore, G. L., 339, 485
Cluss, P. A., 400
Coates, T. J., 401
Cohen, G., 434, 435
Cohen, N., 213
Cohen, N. J., 259
Cohen, R. L., 486
Cohen, S., 385, 399, 531
Colavecchio, P. G., 535
Colby, A., 96

Colditz, G. A., 329
Cole, R. E., 523
Coles, R., 107
Collins, W. A., 100, 339
Conger, J. J., 111
Conner, R., 495
Connett, J. E., 396
Conrad, R., 247
Cooper, J., 482, 483
Cooper, L. A., 247
Coren, S., 167, 177
Cornblatt, B. A., 436
Cornell, K. R., 488
Cornes, C., 430, 469
Cortelli, P., 67
Coryell, W., 427
Costa, P., 117
Costa, P. T., 109, 113, 365, 396
Costello, C. G., 418, 430
Coté, T. R., 401
Coulter, W. A., 305
Council, J. R., 352
Cowan, W. M., 53
Cowen, N., 242
Cox, B. J., 373
Cox, R. H., 534, 535
Coyle, J. T., 429
Coyne, J. C., 386, 393
Cozby, P. C., 290
Crace, R. K., 535
Craik, F. I. M., 251
Cramer, R. E., 495
Crawford, M., 455
Creekmore, C. R., 531, 536
Crews, D. J., 392
Cromwell, R. L., 436
Cronshaw, S. F., 515
Crowder, R. G., 242
Croyle, R. T., 483
Csikzentmihalyi, M., 109
Cunningham, S., 498
Curtis, R. C., 487
Cushner, K., 220
Cutler, W. B., 150

Dahlstrom, W. D., 396
Dahlstrom, W. G., 295
Dallas, M., 180
Dallenbach, K. M., 268, 269
Daniel, T. C., 533
Dann, R., 437
Dannenberg, A. L., 401
Dansky, B. S., 421
Dantzic, S., 329
Darby, B. L., 84
Dare, C., 460
Darley, J., 495
Darley, J. M., 96, 98, 337, 496, 498, 499, 500
Darling, C. A., 107
Darrow, C. M., 113
Darwin, C., 20, 22, 44, 342, 352
Darwin, C. T., 242

Dasen, P., 94
Datan, N., 109
David, G. H., 84
Davidoff, J. B., 177
Davidson, J. K., 107
Davidson, J. M., 330
Davies, M., 420
Davila, G. H., 103
Davis, J. H., 504
Davis, K., 489
Davis, M., 421
Davis, R., 328
Davis, R. M., 398
Davis, W., 102
DeAngelis, T., 411
de Boer, C., 523
DeCaria, C. M., 421
DeCasper, A. J., 88, 89
Decker, S., 391
deCuevas, J., 290
Deffenbacher, J. L., 469
DeGroot, A. D., 265
DeJarlais, D. C., 401
Delaney, H. D., 262
DeLong, M. H., 429
DeLongis, A., 386
Dembroski, T. M., 396
Dement, W. C., 181, 184
Depinett, R. L., 294
Deregowski, J., 174
Derlega, V. J., 489
de Sade, Marquis, 365
Descartes, R., 19–20, 44, 47
Després, J., 326, 327
Deutch, A. Y., 421
Deutsch, G., 72
Devins, G. M., 401
Dewhirst, B., 188
Deyo, R. A., 153
Diamond, M., 332
Digman, J. M., 352, 365, 366, 367
DiMatteo, M. R., 399
Dipboye, R. L., 523
Dirkes, M. A., 285
Dix, D., 447
Dixon, N. F., 180
Dobbins, G. H., 516
Dobkin de Rois, M., 193
Doll, R., 398
Dollard, J., 361, 393
Dominowski, R. L., 281
Domjan, M., 213, 215
Donnenberg, G. R., 98
Doob, L., 393
Doty, R. Y., 150
Doweiko, H. E., 189, 191, 193, 195
Downey, G., 393
Downing, R., 454
Doyal, G. T., 414
Dragna, M., 495
Drakely, R. J., 515
DuBreuil, S. C., 188
Duffy, E., 320

Dumais, S. T., 167
Dunbar-Jacob, J., 400
Duncker, K., 284, 285
Dunham, R. B., 525
Dunn, R. L., 457
Dunnette, M. D., 514
Dunning, E. J., 400
Dweck, C. S., 336
Dworkin, R. H., 434, 435
Dwyer, K., 400
Dyer, J., 435
Dyken, M. E., 185

Eagle, M., 328
Eagly, A. H., 477
Eaker, E. D., 397
Earles, J. A., 294, 516
Early, C., 501
Early, P. C., 96, 517, 521
Eaves, L. J., 431
Ebata, A. T., 102
Ebbinghaus, H., 266
Eckert, E. D., 329
Edelman, G., 55
Edmands, M. S., 93, 328
Edwards, A. L., 371
Edwards, C. P., 96
Edwards, L. K., 371
Edwards, R. W., 192
Egeth, H. E., 249
Ehrhardt, J. C., 434, 435
Eich, J. E., 259
Eisen, S. A., 421
Eisenberg, M., 101
Ekman, P., 339, 343–344
Ellicott, A. M., 109
Ellingboe, J., 191
Elliot, R., 469
Ellis, A., 466
Ellis, H. D., 249
Ellis, L., 333
Ellsworth, P. C., 250
Emery, G., 416
Empson, J. A. C., 185
Emr, M., 429
Endler, N. S., 373
Epstein, L. H., 400
Epstein, S., 179, 180, 352
Erdelyi, M. H., 180, 253
Erez, M., 96, 517, 521
Erikson, E., 89, 98–100, 102,
    105, 109–110, 110,
    114, 119, 123
Erlenmeyer-Kimmling, L., 436
Eron, L., 497
Ervin, F. R., 215
Erwin, E., 468, 469
Esveldt-Dawson, K., 469
Evans, G. W., 526
Eveleth, P., 104
Everett, P. B., 398
Eysenck, H. J., 427, 469

Faber, B., 436
Fackelman, K. A., 429
Fadiman, J., 353

Fairbank, J. A., 421
Fairburn, C. G., 329, 330
Falbo, T., 337
Fantz, R., 90
Farh, J. L., 516
Farrell, M. P., 113
Fassinger, R. E., 468
Fast, J., 343
Fawzy, F. I., 401
Fazio, R. H., 337, 477
Feather, N. T., 336
Federoff, I. C., 328
Feduccia, A., 81
Feeney, J. A., 486
Fein, G. G., 533
Feist, S. C., 467
Fenker, R. M., 536
Fenton, W. S., 435
Ferris, G. R., 522
Festinger, L., 321–322,
    480–482, 483, 488
Fields, H. L., 153
Fifer, W. P., 88, 89
Finnegan, L. P., 84
Fiore, M. C., 398
Fischer, L. B., 190
Fischhoff, B., 533
Fishbein, M., 478
Fisher, A. C., 534
Fisher, J. D., 531
Fisher, S., 359
Fishhoff, B., 102
Fishman, H. C., 467
Fishman, J., 396
Fitzgerald, L., 27
Flagg, P. W., 282
Flament, M. F., 420, 421
Flavell, E. R., 95
Flavell, J. H., 94, 95
Fleishman, E. A., 513
Flexser, A., 257
Folkman, S., 385, 386, 390,
    391
Ford, M. R., 97
Fordyce, W. E., 153
Fosterling, F., 367
Foutz, A. S., 184
Fowles, D. G., 114, 115
Fox, A. C., 185
Frager, R., 353
Frank, E., 430, 468, 469
Frank, M. A., 392
Frankel, F. H., 253
Frazier, T. M., 84
Fredrickson, P. A., 184
Free, M. L., 469
Freedman, D. X., 415
Freedman, J. L., 529, 530
Freeman, A., 466
French, N. H., 469
Freud, A., 102
Freud, S., 24, 31, 47,
    179–180, 185, 197,
    352–357, 423, 455–460
Frey, J., 533
Fribourg, S., 84

Fried, P. A., 84
Friedman, L. N., 532
Friedman, D., 497
Friedman, H. H., 396
Friedman, H. S., 395, 399
Friedman, M., 395
Friedman, M. I., 326
Friedman, R. J., 414
Friedman, S., 89
Friedman, S. R., 401
Frijda, N. H., 339
Frodi, A. M., 100
Frodi, M., 100
Frost, R., 409
Furstenberg, F. F., 108
Furumoto, L., 22

Gabora, N. J., 188
Gabrena, W., 501
Gagné, R. M., 282
Gagnon, J., 331, 332
Gaines, J. G., 392
Gale, M., 396
Gallagher, J. J., 307
Galton, F., 373
Ganchow, J. R., 89
Gans, J. E., 105
Garbarino, J., 102
Garcia, J., 215
Gardner, M., 253
Garfield, S. L., 459
Gargano, G. M., 501
Garner, D. M., 328
Garry, M., 253
Gazzaniga, M. S., 73
Geis, G., 495
Geisler, S., 433, 453
Geller, E. S., 398, 521
Gellhorn, E., 343
Gelman, R., 94
Gelman, S. A., 94
Gelso, C. J., 468
Gemberling, G. A., 215
Genovese, K., 494–495, 500
Gentry, J., 497
George, J. M., 385
George, L., 153
Geracioti, T. D., 329
Gerbert, B., 401
Gerow, J. R., 32
Gest, T., 497
Getzels, J. W., 109
Ghesquire, K., 100
Gibson, D. R., 401
Gibson, E., 88
Gibson, E. J., 88
Gibson, W. M., 514, 516
Gier, J. A., 516
Gilbert, L. A., 111
Gill, M. J., 401
Gillam, B., 176, 177
Gillan, J. C., 259
Gilligan, C., 97–98, 98
Gilligan, S. G., 259
Gillin, J. C., 184

Gilovich, T., 535
Ginsberg, B. E., 497
Girgus, J. S., 177
Giuliano, J. D., 497
Glaser, R., 287, 399
Glasgow, R. E., 399
Glass, A. L., 287
Glass, D. C., 396, 531, 532
Glazer, S., 497
Gleaves, D. H., 253
Glenn, N. D., 109
Glunt, E. K., 401
Golbus, M. S., 84
Gold, P. E., 259
Gold, S. N., 253
Goldberg, 93, 366
Goldberg, B., 253
Goldberg, I. D., 84
Goldberg, J., 421
Goldberg, J. F., 430
Goldbloom, D., 328
Goldfried, M. R., 467,
    468, 469
Goldsmith, H. H., 100, 427
Goldstein, H., 84
Goldstein, I. L., 517
Goleman, O., 304
Goodman, C. C., 41
Goodman, D. W., 41
Goodrich, S., 427
Goodwin, D. W., 259
Gordon, N. C., 153
Gorenstein, E. E., 413
Gormezano, I., 215
Gotlib, I. H., 430
Gottesman, I. I., 436, 438
Gottlieb, B. H., 393
Gottman, J., 111
Gough, H. G., 516
Govoni, L. E., 84
Gowing, M. K., 517
Grady, C. L., 421
Grady, W. R., 401
Graf, P., 256
Graziano, A. M., 15
Greden, J. F., 435, 437
Green, D. M., 129
Greenberg, J., 486
Greenberg, L. S., 338, 339,
    467, 468, 469,
Greenberg, R. P., 359
Greenberg, S., 457
Greenfield, S. F., 191, 194
Greenlick, M. R., 396
Greenwald, A. G., 179, 180
Greer, S., 427
Gregory, R. L., 177
Grice, G. R., 225
Grinspoon, L., 195
Gritz, E. R., 399
Grob, C., 193
Gross, L. P., 327
Grossman, H., 306
Grossman, H. J., 305
Grossman, L. S., 430
Grove, W. M., 438

Groves, P. M., 57, 153
Gruenberg, A. M., 427, 436
Grunberg, N. E., 397
Grusec, J. E., 226
Gudeman, J. E., 457
Guenberg, E., 212
Guilford, J. P., 285, 364
Guion, R. M., 514, 516
Gullotta, T., 104
Gully, R., 421
Gunnar, M. R., 100
Gur, R. C., 437
Gur, R. E., 437
Gurman, A. S., 468
Guthrie, J. F., 328
Guzzo, R. A., 517

Haber, R. N., 248
Hagen, E. P., 297
Hahn, G. L., 401
Hahn, W., 395
Haist, F., 255
Hall, E., 526
Hall, G., 214
Hall, G. S., 102
Hall, J. F., 225
Hall, W. G., 88
Halperin, J., 400
Halton, A., 85
Ham, M., 102
Hamburg, D. A., 104
Hamburger, S. D., 420
Hamer, D. H., 333
Hammen, C., 431
Hammer, L. D., 416
Hancock, E., 109
Haney, T. I., 396
Hanis, C., 327
Hansen, W. B., 401
Hardesty, J. P., 438
Harding, C. M., 434
Hardy, C. J., 535
Hare, R. D., 427
Harkins, S., 501, 502
Harkins, S. G., 501, 502
Harlow, H. F., 327
Harman, C., 100
Harrington, D. M., 285
Harris, B., 211, 212
Harris, D. V., 535
Harris, J. R., 327
Harris, L., 115
Harris, M. M., 515
Harris, P. L., 95, 114
Harris, R. J., 259
Harris, R. L., 109
Harrow, M., 430, 433
Hartley, A. A., 116
Hartup, W. W., 100
Harvey, J. H., 484
Hasher, L., 251, 264
Hassman, H., 454
Hastorf, A. H., 164
Hatsukami, D. K., 329
Hatzlandreu, E. J., 398
Hauser, S. T., 102

Havighurst, R. J., 114
Hawley, P. H., 396
Hayduk, L. A., 526
Hayes, C. D., 108
Hayes, J. E., 84
Hayman, C. A. G., 255
Haynes, S. G., 115
Hayward, C., 416
Hazan, C., 486
Heath, A. C., 421, 431
Hebb, D. O., 320, 322
Heber, S., 425
Heffernan, J. A., 43
Heinrichs, R. W., 433
Hellige, J. B., 73
Helms, D., 112
Helms, J. E., 294, 302
Helzer, J. E., 212, 421
Hennekens, C. H., 329
Hennessy, J., 101
Herbert, T. B., 385
Herek, G. M., 401
Hering, E., 140–141
Heron, A., 94
Herriot, P., 515
Herrnstein, R., 303
Herskovits, M. J., 177
Hertz, R. M., 466
Hester, C., 328
Hetherington, E. M., 111
Higgins, E. T., 477
Hilgard, 187
Hilgard, E. R., 179, 187
Hilgard, J. R., 187
Hill, E. M., 427
Hill, W. F., 392
Hinrichs, J. R., 517
Hinsz, V. B., 504
Hippocrates, 446
Hobfoll, S. E., 381, 393
Hobson, J. A., 183, 185
Hodapp, R. M., 305, 306, 307
Hofferth, S. L., 108
Hoffman, D. D., 177
Hoffman, L. W., 98
Hogan, J., 392
Hogan, R., 364
Hohnecker, L., 253
Hoine, H., 259
Holden, C., 304
Holden, G. W., 192
Holder, A., 460
Hollander, E., 421
Hollis, J. F., 396
Holmes, D. S., 109, 392
Holmes, T. H., 385
Holmes, T. S., 385
Holstein, C., 435
Holyoak, K. J., 180, 287
Holz, W. C., 226
Honzik, C. H., 229
Hood, H. V., 401
Hood, R. D., 85
Hope, R. A., 329
Horn, J. L., 285, 303
Horner, M., 336

Horney, K., 358–359
Horowitz, F. D., 304
Hoshmand, T. L., 17
Hostetler, A. J., 429
Hotstadter, L., 432, 433
Hough, R. L., 421
Houser, B. B., 110
Houston, B. K., 396
Hovland, C. I., 483
Howard, K. I., 468
Howard, R. B., 526
Howe, M. A., 536
Howell, W. C., 523
Howes, C., 101
Hsu, L. K. G., 329
Hu, N., 333
Hu, S., 333
Hubel, D. H., 51
Hudson, J. I., 329
Hudson, W., 174
Huff, C., 401
Huggins, G. R., 150
Hughes, D., 253
Hughes, F., 109
Hughes, F. P., 84
Hugick, L., 399
Hui, C. H., 522
Hull, C., 316–317
Hulley, S. B., 396
Hulsey, M. G., 326, 330
Hunsley, J., 401
Hunt, R. R., 261
Hunter, J. E., 516
Hunter, S., 113
Huston, T. L., 495
Hwang, C. P., 100

Iacono, W. G., 438
Iaffaldano, M. T., 523
Ilgen, D. R., 520
Incontro, C. R., 337
Ingraham, L. J., 436
Insko, C. A., 479
Isard, C. E., 90
Isenberg, D. J., 504
Istvan, J., 85
Izard, C., 339

Jackaway, R., 336
Jackson, D. N., 367
Jacobs, B. L., 194
Jacobsen, B., 436
Jacobson, D. S., 84
Jacoby, L. L., 180
James, M. R., 337
James, W., 22, 44, 178–179,
   197, 316, 447
Janes, H. R., 401
Janis, I., 504
Janis, I. L., 393
Jankiewicz, H., 57, 184
Janoff-Bulman, R., 484
Jansson, L., 436
Jaroff, L., 253
Jarret, D. B., 430
Jarrett, D. B., 469

Jeffery, R. W., 398
Jenkins, C. D., 395
Jenkins, J. G., 268
Jenkins, J. M., 339, 343
Jennison, K. M., 393
Jensen, A. R., 302–303
Jessor, R., 102
Jody, D., 433, 453
Joffee, J. M., 85
John, O. P., 365
Johnson, C. A., 399
Johnson, D. L., 438
Johnson, J., 417
Johnson, M. K., 251, 264, 271
Johnson, S., 457
Johnson, T. R., 519
Johnson, V., 330
Jonas, J. M., 329
Jones, A., 515
Jones, B. A., 396
Jones, E. E., 484, 485
Jones, K. L., 84
Jones, R., 329
Jordan, B. K., 421
Jordan, J., 359
Jordan, M., 409
Joyce, P. R., 452, 453
Judd, C. M., 477
Julien, R. M., 189, 195
Jung, C., 358

Kacmar, K. M., 522
Kagan, J., 100, 364
Kahn, R., 116
Kahn, R. L., 385
Kahn, S., 109
Kale, A. R., 488
Kales, A., 184
Kales, J. D., 184
Kalichman, S. C., 400, 401
Kalikow, K., 420
Kalish, R. A., 117
Kalleberg, A. L., 523
Kalsher, M. J., 521
Kaltman, A. J., 185
Kamin, L., 214, 229
Kamiya, J., 392
Kane, J., 453
Kanfer, R., 294, 516
Kanizsa, G., 167
Kanner, A. D., 386
Kaplan, A., 359
Kaplan, G. M., 392
Kaplan, S., 533
Karlen, A., 332
Karoum, F., 437
Karson, C. N., 437
Kassin, S. M., 250
Kastenbaum, R., 117
Katzell, R. A., 517, 522
Katzman, R., 428
Kay, S. R., 434, 435
Kazdin, A. E., 469
Keating, D. P., 103
Keesey, R. E., 326, 327
Keita, G. P., 430, 457

Keith, P. M., 110
Kellams, J. J., 452
Kelley, H. H., 484, 485
Kelly, J. A., 400, 401
Kempler, D., 73
Kendler, K. S., 427, 431, 436
Kershner, J. R., 285, 303
Kessler, R. C., 212, 386, 408, 415, 416, 431
Kessler, S., 436
Kety, S. S., 436
Key, M. R., 290
Kiecolt-Glaser, J. K., 399
Kientzle, M. J., 266
Kiester, E., 183, 536
Kihlstrom, J. F., 179
Kilcullen, R. N., 515
Killan, J. D., 416
Kilner, L. A., 102
Kilpatrick, D. G., 421
Kilts, C., 421
Kim, J. J., 213
Kimble, G., 39, 40, 220
Kimmel, D. C., 115
Kimmel, H. D., 392
King, M., 523
King, M. J., 185
Kinney, D. K., 436
Kinsbourne, M., 72
Kinsey, A. C., 332
Kirby, D. A., 185
Kirkby, R. J., 468
Kirkpatrick, B., 435
Kirkpatrick, D. L., 519
Kirscht, J. P., 397
Kissileff, H. R., 329
Klapper, M. H., 452
Klebanoff, M., 84
Klein, E. B., 113
Klein, H. J., 520
Kleitman, N., 183
Klepinger, D. H., 401
Klerman, G. L., 416, 417, 430, 469
Klinger, M. R., 180, 181
Knapp, S., 401
Knight, P. A., 523
Kniskern, D. P., 468
Knowles, E. S., 491
Knowlton, B., 241, 247, 255
Kobasa, S. C., 388
Kochansky, G., 457
Koelling, R. A., 215
Koestler, A., 287
Kofoed, L., 427
Kohlberg, L., 89, 96–98, 119, 123
Köhler, W., 280
Kohler, S. S., 371, 513, 515, 516
Kolata, G., 88
Kolb, B., 51, 52
Kontis, T. C., 257
Koop, C. E., 190, 398
Kopata, S. M., 468
Korchin, S. J., 370, 373

Kositcheck, R., 395
Koslow, D. R., 448
Koss, M. P., 460
Kosslyn, S. M., 74
Kotelchuck, M., 100
Kovacic, C. R., 534
Kraepelin, E., 411
Krantz, D. S., 396, 397
Krause, M. S., 468
Krause, N., 116
Krieger, A., 150
Kripke, D. F., 184
Kroonenberg, P. M., 100
Krueger, W. C. F., 266
Krupat, E., 531
Krystal, J. H., 421
Kübler-Ross, E., 116–117
Kuiper, N. A., 391
Kulik, J., 259
Kulka, R. A., 421
Kunst-Wilson, W. R., 488
Kupfer, D. J., 430, 468, 469

Laborit, H., 453
LaDue, R. A., 84
Lafferty, P., 468
Lage, E., 491
Laird, J. M., 344
Lamb, M. E., 100, 101
Lambiotte, J. G., 536
Lamon, M., 344
Lampman-Petraitis, R., 102
Landers, D. M., 392, 535
Landers, S., 108
Landesman, S., 305, 306, 307
Landis, D., 333
Landy, F. J., 371, 513, 515, 516, 525
Lanetto, R., 117
Lang, P. J., 338
Langer, S., 288
Lapidus, L. B., 174
Larsen, R. M., 371
Larson, R., 102
Latané, B., 495, 496, 498, 499, 500, 501, 502
Latham, G., 521
Latham, G. P., 518
Lattal, K. A., 23
Lauer, J., 111
Lauer, R., 111
Laumann, E. O., 331, 332
Lavond, D. G., 213
Lawley, HJ. J., 150
Lawson, W. B., 437
Lazarus, R., 339, 386, 390, 391
Lazarus, R. S., 338, 386
Lazerson, A., 432, 433
Leahey, T. H., 259
Ledger, G., 285, 303
LeDoux, J. E., 73
Lee, I. M., 329
Lefebvre, R., 392
Leger, D. W., 526

Lehman, G. R., 521
Lehrer, P. M., 392
Lempers, J. D., 95
Lenane, M., 419
Lenane, M. C., 420
Lenneberg, E. H., 291, 293
Lenzenweger, M. F., 434, 435
Leonard, J., 399
Leonard, H., 419
Leonard, H. L., 420
Lerner, M. J., 484
Letterman, D., 409
Leupker, R. F., 399
LeVay, S., 67, 333
Leventhal, H., 399
Levin, J. R., 262
Levine, A., 400
Levine, H. Z., 525
Levine, J. D., 153
Levine, J. M., 504
Levine, M., 397, 401, 457, 503
Levine, M. M., 323
Levinson, D., 112, 113
Levinson, D. J., 109, 113
Levinson, M. H., 113
Levinthal, C. F., 325, 342
Lewis, M., 117
Ley, P., 399
Lichtenstein, E., 399
Liddle, R. A., 329
Lidz, T., 437
Lieberman, J., 433, 453
Lieberman, M. A., 393
Lin, T. R., 516
Lincoln, J. R., 523
Linder, D., 487
Lindsley, D. B., 66
Links, P. S., 408
Linnoila, M., 421
Lipsey, M. W., 469
Lish, J. D., 416
Litt, I. F., 416
Litt, M. D., 153
Little Albert, 210–212, 214, 233
Litwin, G. H., 335
Lloyd-Bostock, S., 249
Locke, E. A., 521, 522
Locke, J., 20, 41, 44, 47
Lockhard, J. S., 180
Lockhart, R. S., 251
Loebel, A., 433, 453
Loesser, J. D., 153
Loftus, E., 249
Loftus, E. F., 180, 181, 241, 253, 281
Loftus, G., 249
Lohr, N. E., 427
Long, P., 187
Lonner, W. J., 529
Loomis, R. J., 531
Lord, C. G., 264
Lorenz, K., 526
Lott, A. J., 485
Lott, B. E., 485

Lowell, E. L., 334–336
Lowery, C. R., 97
Lowry, D. H., 262
Lozoff, B., 84
Lubert, T., 286
Lubin, B., 371
Luborsky, I., 460
Lucas, E. A., 184
Lugaresi, A., 67
Lugaresi, E., 67
Lukoff, D., 438
Lykken, D. T., 427
Lyness, S. A., 396
Lynn, D., 100
Lynn, S. J., 187
Lyons, M. J., 421

MacDonald, M. R., 391
MacDougall, J. M., 396
MacFarlane, A. C., 421
Mackenzie, B., 302
Mackintosh, N. J., 215, 303
Mackowiak, P. A., 323
MacLeod, C., 339
MacLeod, M. D., 249
MacMillan, J., 427
Maddi, S. R., 388
Madigan, S., 22
Magid, K., 427
Magnuson, V. L., 333
Magoun, H. W., 66
Magovern, G. J., 392
Maguire, B., 401
Mahoney, M., 535
Mahoney, M. J., 534
Mahowald, M. W., 185
Maier, N. R. F., 284
Mair, A., 531
Malatesta, C. A., 90
Mandler, G., 255
Manning, M. L., 102
Manson, J. E., 329
Mark, A. L., 185
Markowitz, J. S., 416, 417
Marks, G., 400
Marks, I. M., 208
Markus, H., 478
Marmar, C., 467, 468, 469
Marmar, C. R., 421
Marschark, M., 261
Marshall-Goodell, B. S., 479
Martin, G. B., 88
Martin, R. J., 326, 330
Martin, S., 497
Martindale, C., 247
Marx, J., 429
Maslow, A., 25, 45, 317–319, 362–363
Massaro, D. W., 242
Masters, W., 332
Matarazzo, J. D., 42, 371, 397
Mathews, A., 339
Matlin, M. W., 531
Matsumoto, D., 344
Matt, D. A., 392
Matthews, K., 393, 395, 396

Matthews, K. A., 392, 396
Mattson, S. N., 84
Maxman, J. S., 454
Mayer, D. J., 57
Mayer, R. E., 264
McAdams, D. P., 367
McCann, I. L., 109, 392
McCarley, R. W., 185
McCartney, K., 101
McClearn, G. E., 327
McClelland, D. C., 294, 334–336, 516
McClelland, G. M., 415
McClintock, M. K., 150
McCloskey, M., 259
McCoy, G., 399
McCrae, R. R., 365
McCrea, R. R., 109, 113
McDonald, W. T., 270
McDougall, W., 316
McEnvoy, L., 421
McFarland, C., 499
McGaugh, J. L., 259
McGee, R., 408
McGeoch, J. A., 270
McGinnis, J. M., 398
McGlashan, T. H., 435
McGoldrick, M. D., 399
McGonagle, K. A., 212, 408, 415, 416
McGrath, E., 430, 457
McGuire, W. J., 477
McIver, S. D., 457
McKee, B., 113
McKim, W. A., 190, 191
McLaughlin, S. D., 519
McLeod, J. D., 386
McMaster, M. R., 495
McMichael, A. J., 115
McMillan, C. J., 523
McNeil, D., 293
McNellis, D., 84
Mednick, M. T., 98
Mednick, M. T. S., 336
Mednick, S. A., 427, 435
Medori, R., 67
Meer, J., 115
Meichenbaum, D., 391, 399
Melhuish, E. C., 101
Mellers, B. A., 488
Mellstrom, B., 421
Meltzer, H. Y., 430
Melzack, R., 153
Menary, E., 188
Mendelson, J. H., 191
Merikle, P., 180
Messick, D. M., 502
Metcalf, J., 287
Meyer, D. E., 287
Michael, J. L., 221
Michael, R., 331, 332
Michael, S., 331, 332
Michela, J. L., 484
Middlemist, R. D., 521
Middlestadt, S. E., 515

Milgram, S., 491–494, 531
Miller, D. T., 484, 499
Miller, G., 246
Miller, J., 359, 484
Miller, J. G., 367
Miller, K., 191, 487
Miller, M. J., 452
Miller, N., 361, 393
Miller, N. E., 42, 392, 397
Miller, R. R., 214
Miller, W. R., 189
Millstein, S. G., 105
Milstein, V., 452
Minami, H. J., 269
Minuchin, S., 467
Mirin, S. M., 191, 194
Mischel, W., 352
Mitchell, J. E., 329
Mittelmark, M. B., 399
Mittler, M. M., 184
Mobley, W. H., 524
Moffitt, T. E., 427
Moller, J., 399
Molnar, S., 303
Moncher, M. S., 192
Moniz, E., 450
Monson, T. C., 485
Montagna, P., 67
Monteiro, K. P., 259
Montgomery, L. M., 468
Moon, C., 89
Moore, K., 108
Moore, K. L., 81, 83
Moore, M. K., 88
Morales, F. R., 185
Moran, J. S., 401
Moreland, R. L., 504
Morgan, G., 100
Morgan, W. P., 534
Mori, D., 328
Morris, C. W., 288
Morris, L. A., 400
Morrison, D. M., 108
Morrow, H. W., 305
Moruzzi, G., 66
Moscovici, S., 491, 504
Mowday, R. T., 521
Mowrer, O. H., 393
Mshelia, A. Y., 174
Muchinsky, P. M., 515, 523, 524
Mueser, K. T., 457
Mugny, G., 504
Mulác, A., 337
Mumford, M. D., 513, 515
Munn, N. L., 372
Murnen, S., 489
Murphy, D. A., 400, 401
Murphy, D. L., 321
Murphy, D. P., 32
Murray, C., 303
Murray, D. J., 445
Murray, D. M., 399
Murray, H., 334, 374
Murray, M. A., 523
Musen, G., 241, 247, 255

Naffrechoux, M., 491
Nakazima, S., 291
Namir, S., 401
Nash, M., 188
Neale, M. C., 431
Neaton, J. D., 396
Neisser, U., 259
Nelson, C. P., 212, 408, 415, 416
Nelson, J. M., 195
Nelson, K., 254
Nemeth, C., 491
Nettleton, N. C., 74
Neubauer, P. J., 388
Neugarten, B. L., 114, 116
Neugarten, D. A., 114, 116
Newby, R., 257
Newcomb, 106
Newcomb, M. D., 106–107, 110
Newell, A., 285
Nezlek, J., 488
Nichols, I. A., 291
Nicholson, R. A., 364
Nickerson, R. S., 257, 258
Nida, S. A., 498, 501, 502
Nigg, J. T., 427
Nimmer, J. G., 521
Nisan, M., 96
Nisbett, R. E., 326, 485
Nitescu, A., 421
Noble, E. P., 259
Noller, P., 486
Noppe, L. D., 84
Norcross, J. C., 448
Norton, G. R., 425
Novotny, T. E., 398
Nowak, J., 421
Noyes, R., 417
Nuechterlein, K. H., 438

Oatley, K., 339, 343
O'Brien, M., 304
O'Conner, M., 329
Oden, M. H., 304
Oei, T. P. S., 469
Oetting, E. R., 106, 192
Offer, D., 102
Offer, J., 102
Offerman, L. R., 517
Offord, D. R., 408
Ogata, S. N., 427
Ogilvie, B. C., 536
O'Hara, R., 22
Okwumabua, T., 468
Olio, K. A., 253
Oller, D. K., 291
Olmstead, M. P., 328
Olson, J. M., 477, 480
Ones, D. S., 516
Opalic, P., 468
Oppenheim, R. W., 88
Orlinsky, D. E., 468
Orne, M., 187
Ortony, A., 339
Orvaschel, H., 212

Ouellette, R., 417
Owens, J. F., 392
Owens, W. A., 515
Oxley, D., 526
Ozer, D. J., 364, 365, 368, 373

Packard, B., 397
Paffenbarger, R. S., 329
Paivio, A., 261
Palfai, T., 57, 184
Pandey, J., 526, 531
Park, B., 477
Park, D. C., 114, 115
Parker, E. S., 259
Parker, J. D. A., 373
Parnas, J., 435
Parson, A., 153
Pate, J. E., 328
Patel, K. M., 398
Pattatucci, A. M. L., 333
Pauley, J., 409
Paulus, D. L., 180, 369
Paunonen, S. P., 367
Pavlov, I., 204–206, 213, 215, 234
Paykel, E. S., 452, 453
Peake, P. K., 352
Pearce, J. M., 214
Pearson, J., 531
Pearson, J. C., 290
Pederson, D. R., 100
Pederson, N. L., 327
Peele, S., 189
Pelletier, L. G., 535
Pelliccioni, L., Jr., 536
Peplau, L. A., 337
Perel, J. M., 430, 468, 469
Perkins, D. V., 397, 401, 457, 503
Perls, F., 461
Peterman, T. A., 401
Peterson, A. C., 102, 104
Peterson, L. R., 244–245
Peterson, M. J., 244–245
Peterson, R. B., 521
Peto, R., 398
Petty, R. E., 477, 479, 483, 501, 502
Peveler, R. C., 329
Phillips, D., 101
Piaget, J., 89, 90–94, 90–96, 96, 98, 102–103, 119, 123
Pickar, D., 435
Pierce, J. P., 398
Pillard, R. C., 332
Pillemer, D. B., 254
Pincus, A. L., 352, 364, 365, 367
Pinel, P., 447
Pinker, S., 290
Pinsky, J., 397
Pinsof, W. M., 468
Plawin, P., 520
Pliner, P. L., 328

Plomin, R., 436
Plutchik, R., 339, 342
Pogue-Geile, M. F., 435
Polkinghorne, D. E., 17
Pomeroy, C., 329
Pool, R., 332
Poortinga, Y., 94
Pope, H. G., 329
Porter, L. W., 523
Posner, M. I., 281
Powell, B., 259
Powell, L. H., 396
Powell, R. A., 253
Powers, S. I., 102
Powley, T. L., 326, 327
Pressley, M., 262
Preti, G., 150
Price, D. L., 429
Prochaska, J. O., 399
Pumariega, A. J., 328
Putnam, F. W., 425
Pyle, R. L., 329

Quadrel, M. J., 102
Quay, H. C., 427
Quellete, R., 416
Quina, K., 290
Quixote, Don, 365

Radford, A., 291
Rae-Grant, N. I., 408
Rahe, R. H., 385
Raine, A., 427
Ramey, C., 305, 307
Ramon Garcia, C., 150
Randall, T., 153
Randels, S. P., 84
Ransberger, V. M., 533
Rapoport, J. L., 419, 420, 421
Raulin, M. L., 15
Ray, O. S., 191
Rayner, R., 210–212, 235
Rebec, G. V., 57, 153
Rebelsky, F. G., 291
Ree, M. J., 294, 516
Regier, D. A., 212
Reich, J., 415
Reich, R. B., 525
Reilly, R. R., 515
Reimer, J., 96
Reinke, B. J., 109
Reis, H. T., 488
Reise, S. P., 364, 365, 368, 373
Reiss, F. M., 304
Reiss, D., 111
Rempel, J. K., 478
Rescorla, R. A., 213–214, 214, 229
Resnick, H. D., 421
Resnick, S. M., 437
Rest, J. R., 96
Rettew, D. C., 420
Reveley, M. A., 437
Revelle, W., 367
Revely, A. M., 437

Revely, M. A., 437
Revulky, S. H., 215
Reynolds, A. G., 282
Reynolds, B. A., 53
Rhodes, S. R., 112, 522
Rhue, J. W., 187
Rice, J., 421
Rice, M. L., 293
Richardson, J. L., 400
Richmond, C. E., 153
Richmond, C. L., 261
Richters, J., 497
Rickels, K., 454
Riggio, R. E., 513, 522, 525
Riley, E. P., 84
Robins, L. N., 212, 421
Robinson, K., 111
Roche, A. F., 103
Rock, I., 167
Rockert, W., 328
Rodeheaver, D., 109
Rodgers, C. H., 330
Rodin, J., 326, 327, 328, 330, 398, 399, 531
Roediger, H. L., 241, 256, 257
Rogers, C., 25, 45, 362, 460
Rolls, B. J., 328
Rook, K. S., 393
Rorschach, H., 374
Rose, A. S., 95
Rosenbaum, M. E., 489
Rosenberg, S. D., 113
Rosenman, R., 395
Rosenman, R. H., 395
Rosenthal, D., 436
Rosenzweig, M. R., 28
Ross, C. A., 425
Ross, D., 231
Ross, G., 100
Ross, L. D., 484
Ross, M., 484
Ross, S. A., 231
Rossi, A. S., 114
Rossi, J. S., 399
Roth, M., 415
Rothman, S., 301
Rothstein, H. R., 515
Rottman, L., 488
Rotton, J., 533
Rovine, M., 101
Rowe, D. C., 352
Rowe, J., 116
Ruback, R. B., 531
Rubin, Z., 257, 489
Rudd, J. R., 521
Ruggiero, M., 495
Rush, B., 447
Rushton, J. P., 302
Russo, N. F., 430, 457
Ryan, E. D., 534

Saal, F. E., 523
Saari, L. M., 519, 521
Sackeim, H. A., 452

Sadalla, E. K., 526
Saegert, S., 524
Safran, J. D., 338, 339, 469
Sakai, K., 64
Salem, D. A., 457
Salett, E. P., 448
Salovey, P., 398, 399
Salthouse, T. A., 115
Sameroff, A. J., 89
Sampson, P. D., 84
Samuelson, F. J. B., 210
Sandler, J., 460
Santa, J. L., 287
Satir, V., 467
Sattler, J. M., 297
Saunders, B. E., 421
Saunders, V., 515
Sauser, W. J., 523
Scarborough, E., 22
Scarr, S., 101
Sceery, W., 420, 421
Schachter, S., 488
Schacter, D. L., 180, 257
Schacter, D. A., 256
Schacter, D. L., 241, 255
Schacter, S., 327
Schaefer, C., 386
Schaie, K. W., 110, 116
Scharf, B., 531
Scharf, M. B., 184
Scheerer, M., 283
Scheier, M. F., 392
Scheldberg, D., 370
Schelling, T. C., 398
Schenck, C. H., 185
Schiff, B. B., 344
Schiffman, H. R., 142
Schjroeder, C. S., 306
Schlegel, P., 497
Schlenger, W. E., 421
Schmidt, F. L., 516
Schreiber, J. L., 435
Schroeder, C. S., 306
Schroeder, S. R., 306
Schuckit, M. A., 189, 191
Schuldberg, D., 373
Schultz, D. P., 519, 525
Schultz, R., 117, 391
Schultz, S. E., 519, 525
Schultz, T. R., 98
Schwebel, A. I., 457
Schweizer, E., 454
Scott, J. P., 497
Scott, K. G., 307
Scott, M. D., 536
Sears, P. S., 304
Sears, R. R., 393
Secord, P. F., 487
Segall, M., 94
Segall, M. H., 177
Seligman, M. E. P., 431
Selkoe, D. J., 429
Selye, H., 342, 388–389
Serpell, R., 174
Shadish, W. R., 457, 468
Shaffer, D., 420, 483

Shaffer, G. S., 515
Shaffer, G. S., 515
Shaffer, M., 109
Shaker, L. A., 396
Shankster, L. J., 371, 513, 515, 516
Shanyang, Z.
Shapiro, D., 392
Shapiro, D. A., 469
Shapiro, M. B., 421
Shapiro, R., 457
Sharpley, P. H., 452
Shaver, P., 486
Shaw, J. C., 285
Shaw, K. N., 521
Shedler, J., 106
Sheehy, R. N., 113
Shekelle, B., 396
Shepard, R. N., 247
Sher, S. J., 482
Sherman, S. J., 477
Shertzer, B., 112
Shiffman, L. B., 190
Shimamura, A. P., 255, 257
Shipman, P., 303
Shirley, M. C., 392
Shore, M., 457
Shotland, R. L., 498
Shulman, H. G., 247
Shultz, T. R., 96
Shweder, R. A., 29
Shwedler, R., 367
Sibai, B. M., 84
Siegler, R. S., 90
Sigafoos, A. D., 89
Sikkema, K. J., 400, 401
Silk, K. R., 427
Silva, J. M., 535
Silva, P. A., 408
Simmonds, B., 416
Simon, H. A., 265, 285
Simon, R., 467
Simon, T., 296
Singer, J. E., 531, 532
Singh, M. M., 434, 435
Sitko, C., 100
Skinner, B. F., 23, 44, 115, 216–217, 220, 222, 223, 292, 360–361
Skolnick, A., 110
Slater, P. C., 452
Slobin, D., 293
Slobin, D. I., 288
Small, I. F., 452
Small, J. G., 452
Smeaton, G., 489
Smith, A., 531, 532
Smith, C. P., 334
Smith, D., 535, 536
Smith, D. F., 84
Smith, D. W., 84
Smith, E. R., 330
Smith, G. B., 457
Smith, L. B., 88
Smith, P. C., 514
Smith, S., 258–259

Smith, T. W., 396
Smith, V. L., 250
Smither, R. D., 525
Smithers, R. D., 521
Smyrnios, K. X., 468
Snarey, J. R., 96
Snyder, M., 485
Snyder, S. H., 437
Snyderman, M., 301
Sobal, J., 327
Soldatos, C. R., 184
Somers, V. K., 185
Sommer, R., 526
Sorensen, T. I. A., 327
Sorenson, J. L., 401
Southwick, S. M., 421
Soyka, L. F., 85
Spanos, N. P., 187, 188
Spear, N. E., 214
Spearman, C., 294
Spellman, B. A., 180
Sperling, G., 242
Sperry, R., 72, 342
Spitz, H., 307
Springer, J. P., 72
Springston, F., 246
Squire, L. R., 241, 247, 255, 452
Sreff, F. M., 521
St. Lawrence, J. S., 401
Stack, S., 427
Stall, R. D., 401
Standing, L., 248
Stangor, C., 478
Stansfield, S., 531, 532
Staw, B. M., 523
Stechler, G., 85
Steenbarger, B. N., 468
Steers, R. M., 523
Stein, J., 259
Stein, J. A., 110
Steiner, J. E., 89
Steinhilber, A., 535
Stern, D., 100
Sternberg, K. J., 101
Sternberg, R., 286
Sternberg, R. J., 294, 516
Stevens, V. J., 396
Stewart, A. J., 336
Stiles, W. B., 469
Stillman, R. C., 259
Stokals, D., 398
Stokes, G., 107
Stokols, D., 530, 533
Stone, G., 399
Stone, K. M., 401
Stoner, J. A. F., 503
Stoyva, J., 392
Strauss, M. E., 435
Strauss, R., 395
Streissguth, A. P., 84
Stricker, E. M., 326
Strickland, B., 430, 457
Striver, I., 359
Strupp, H. H., 445, 460
Stumpf, H., 367

Stunkard, A. J., 327
Suckow, R. F., 421
Sue, D. W., 448
Suied, M., 520
Suinn, R. M., 536
Sullivan, M., 29, 367
Suls, J., 399
Sundel, M., 113
Surrey, J., 359
Swaim, R. C., 192
Swayze, V. W., 434, 435
Swedo, S. E., 419, 420, 421
Swets, J. A., 129
Symanski, K., 502
Syme, S. L., 385
Szasz, T. S., 413
Szatmari, P., 408
Szymanski, S., 433, 453

Takanishi, R., 102, 104
Tandon, R., 435, 437
Tanfer, K., 401
Tannenbaum, S. I., 517, 519
Tanner, J. M., 103, 104
Tassinary, L. G., 479
Taylor, C. B., 416
Taylor, S. E., 392
Taylor, W., 531
Teasdale, J. D., 259
Teevan, R., 336
Tenopyr, M. L., 370
Teplin, L. A., 415
Terman, L. M., 297, 304
Tessor, A., 483
Thackwray-Emerson, D., 392
Thayer, W. P., 515
Thibault, J. W., 485
Thom, E., 84
Thomas, M. B., 467
Thompson, C. P., 259
Thompson, D. E., 522
Thompson, D. M., 257, 258
Thompson, J. W., 452
Thompson, R. F., 213
Thorndike, A. L., 297
Thorndike, E. L., 217, 220, 222
Thornton, G. C., III, 519
Thurman, P. J., 192
Tice, D. M., 499
Tilley, A. J., 185
Todd-Mancillas, W., 290
Tohen, M., 430
Tolman, C. W., 327
Tolman, E., 229–231
Tolman, E. C., 229–230
Tomkins, S. S., 343
Toro, P. A., 397, 401, 457, 503
Torrey, T. W., 81
Travis, C. B., 455
Tremblay, A., 326, 327
Triandis, H. C., 96, 220
Trickett, E. J., 457
Trimble, J. E., 192
Triplett, N., 502

True, W. R., 421
Trulson, M. E., 194
Trzebinski, J., 367
Tsuang, M. T., 430
Tucker, D. M., 342
Tucker, J. S., 396
Tulving, E., 180, 251–252, 255, 257, 258
Tung, R., 517
Turk, D. C., 153, 399
Turnbull, C., 173
Turner, J., 112
Turner, J. A., 153, 483
Turner, L. H., 290
Turner, T. J., 339
Turvey, M. T., 242
Tuttle, M. L., 524
Tversky, A., 535
Tyroler, H. A., 115
Tziner, A., 515

Uhlman, C. E., 515
Ulleland, C. N., 84
Underwager, R., 253
Underwood, B. J., 270
Unger, R., 455
Unis, A. S., 469

Vaccarino, L. V., 396
Valenstein, E. S., 450
Vallerand, R. J., 535
Valliant, C. O., 116, 192
Valliant, G. E., 116, 192
Vallone, R., 535
Van Avermaet, E., 504
VandeCreek, L., 401
VandenBos, G. R., 468
Vander Wall, S. B., 231
van Ijzendorn, M. H., 100
Van Lancker, D., 73
Varca, P. E., 535
Vavak, C. R., 396
Venables, P. H., 427
Ventura, J., 438
Verillo, R. T., 153
Verrier, R. L., 185
Vertes, R. P., 64
Vinacke, W. E., 285
Vitz, P. C., 96
Voevodsky, J., 525
von Helmholtz, H., 20, 44, 140, 156
Von Korff, J. E., 153
Vroom, V., 520

Wagner, A. R., 214
Wagner, R. K., 294, 516
Wakefield, H., 253
Walk, R., 88
Walker, L. J., 98
Wall, D. D., 457
Wall, P. D., 153
Wallace, P., 150
Wallas, G., 286
Wallerstein, J., 111
Walsh, B. T., 329

Walster, E., 483, 486, 488
Walster, G. W., 486, 488
Walters, G. C., 226
Walton, G. E., 90
Wamboldt, F. S., 111
Wang, Y., 501
Warrington, E. K., 257
Washburn, M. F., 22, 47
Wasserman, S. S., 323
Waternaux, C. M., 430
Watkins, L. R., 57
Watkins, M., 241, 249
Watson, C. J., 523
Watson, J., 44, 210–212, 235
Watson, J. B., 23, 360
Weary, G., 484
Weaver, C. N., 109, 523
Weber, A., 262
Webster, J., 385
Wechsler, D., 294, 299
Weekes, J. R., 187
Weekly, J. A., 516
Weil, A. T., 195
Weiner, B., 339
Weingartner, H., 259
Weisberg, R. W., 304
Weiskrantz, L., 257
Weiss, C. S., 385
Weiss, D. S., 421
Weiss, R. D., 191, 194
Weiss, S., 53
Weiss, W., 483
Weissman, M. M., 212, 415, 416, 417, 430
Weldon, E., 501
Wellman, H. M., 94
Wells, G. L., 249
Wender, P. H., 436
Wenger, N. K., 397
Wermuth, L. A., 401
Wertheimer, M., 26, 88, 173
Wertheimer, W., 48
Werthessen, N. T., 395
Westermeyer, J. F., 433
Wethington, E., 434, 435
Wheeler, L., 488
Wheeler, R. J., 392
Whitaker, A., 420
White, B. D., 326, 330
White, S. H., 254
Whitehurst, G., 292
Wible, C., 259
Wickens, C. D., 525
Wickens, D. D., 247
Wiebe, D., 287
Wiesner, W. H., 515
Wiggins, J. S., 352, 364, 365, 367
Wilkes, J., 187
Williams, K., 501, 502
Williams, K. D., 501
Williams, M., 427
Williams, R. B., 396
Williams, S., 408
Willis, S. L., 110
Wilson, D. B., 469

Wilson, D. M., 416
Wilson, G. T., 330
Wilson, M. R., 468
Wilson, P., 468
Winett, R. A., 398
Wingard, J. A., 290
Winkel, G. H., 524
Winter, D. G., 336, 337
Wisensale, S. K., 111
Witenberg, S. H., 399
Wittchen, H., 415, 416
Woener, M., 433, 453
Wolcott, D. L., 401
Wolf, W., 192
Wolkenstein, J., 401
Wollen, K. A., 262

Wolpe, J., 212, 463
Wood, C., 395
Woodruff, V., 101
Woolf, C. J., 153
Woolfolk, R. L., 392
Worringham, C. J., 502
Wright, L., 396
Wundt, W., 21–22, 44, 47, 178, 339
Wurm, M., 395
Wurtman, R. J., 429
Wyatt, R. J., 437

Yalom, I. D., 468
Yaniv, I., 287
Yapko, M., 253

Yates, A. J., 328, 329, 392
Yates, F. A., 263
York, C. M., 523
Young, T., 140, 156
Youngstrom, N., 457
Yuh, W. T. C., 434, 435
Yuille, J. C., 249, 261
Yukl, G., 517, 519
Yurgelun-Todd, D., 329

Zacharko, R. M., 431
Zajonc, R. B., 343, 344, 478, 488, 503
Zanna, M. P., 477, 478, 480
Zanni, G., 249
Zedeck, S., 515, 516

Zelazo, P., 100
Zettler-Segal, M., 190
Zhao, S., 212, 408, 415, 416
Zidon, I., 521
Ziebell, S., 434, 435
Zigler, E., 305, 306, 307
Zimerle, D. M., 519
Zimmerman, G., 109
Zimmerman, M., 427
Zimmerman, R., 329
Zinbarg, R. E., 466
Zinberg, N., 195
Zir, L. M., 185
Zohar, D., 525
Zubin, J., 435
Zuckerman, M., 84, 321, 427

Page numbers followed by *t* and *f* indicate tables and figures respectively.

ABC (mnemonic), for subject matter of psychology, 17, 351–352, 409, 478
Abilities
  crystallized, 297
  fluid-analytic, 297
  tested by Stanford-Binet Intelligence Scale, 297–298
Abnormality
  classification of, 411–413
  definition of, 409–410, 589
  distress or discomfort caused by, 410
  moral considerations and, 415
  social considerations and, 415
  social/cultural expectations and, 410
  spectrum of, 415
Absolute threshold, 127–128, 128*f*, 129
  definition of, 127, 589
  for hearing, 128*f*
  for smell, 128*f*
  for taste, 128*f*
  for touch, 128*f*
  for vision, 128*f*
Acceptance, in dying person, 117
Accommodation
  Piaget's concept of, 91, 589
  visual, 135, 170, 589
Acetylcholine (ACh), 56–57
  in dementia of the Alzheimer's type, 429
  memory and, 429
Achievement motivation, 334–336
Acquired immunodeficiency syndrome (AIDS), 400–401
  psychological manifestations in, 401

Acquisition
  in classical conditioning, 207, 207*f*, 589
  in operant conditioning, 219, 219*f*, 589
Acrophobia, 417, 418*f*
Action potential, 54, 54*f*, 589
Actor-observer bias, 485, 589
Acupuncture, 153
Adaptation
  dark, 130, 138–139, 139*f*
  Darwin's concept of, 20
  sensory, 129–130, 204
Addiction, drug, 189
ADHD. *See* Attention-deficit/hyperactivity disorder
Adolescence
  challenges of, 102–108
  characteristics of, 101–102
  definition of, 102, 589
  development in, 101–118
  drug use and abuse in, 105–107
  identity formation in, 105
  physical/biological changes of, 103–104
  pregnancy in, 107–108
  sexuality in, 107–108
Adulthood
  development in, 101–118
  early
    definition of, 109
    developmental tasks of, 108–113
  late
    definition of, 109
    developmental tasks of, 114–117
  middle
    definition of, 109
    developmental tasks of, 113–114
Advertising, classical conditioning and, 210, 479
Affect
  definition of, 17, 589
  flattened, in schizophrenia, 432

Affective disorders. *See* Mood disorders
Affiliation motivation, 337–338
Afterimages, negative, 141, 142*f*
Age, mental, 298
Ageism, 115, 589
Aggression. *See also* Violence
  stress and, 393, 394*f*
  temperature and, 533
Aging, successful, 116
Agoraphobia, 417, 418*f*
  definition of, 418, 589
AIDS. *See* Acquired immunodeficiency syndrome
Alarm reaction, in general adaptation syndrome, 388, 389*f*
Alcohol
  blood level, 191–192
  depressant effects of, 191
  effects on fetus, 84
Alcoholism, 192
Algophobia, 418*f*
Algorithm(s), 282, 589
Alienation, and bystander intervention, 495
Alpha activity, in brain, 181–182, 182*f*, 589
Alpha waves, in brain, 181–182, 182*f*
Alzheimer's disease, 428–429
  diagnosis of, 429
  warning signs of, 428*f*
American Psychological Association, 28
  Ethical Principles of Psychologists, 38–39
Amnesia
  definition of, 424
  dissociative, 424
  psychogenic, 424
Amnestic disorders
  definition of, 428, 589
  DSM-IV classification of, 412*t*
Amok, 410*t*
Amphetamines, 191
Amygdala, 66*f*, 67

Anal stage, of psychosexual development, 356
Anger, in dying person, 116–117
Animal(s), research using. *See also* Rats
  ethical guidelines for, 39
The Animal Mind (Washburn), 22
Anorexia nervosa, 328–329
ANS. *See* Autonomic nervous system
Antianxiety drugs, 454–455, 589
Antidepressant drugs, 453–454, 589
Antipsychotic drugs, 453, 589
Antisocial personality disorder, 426
Anxiety
  basic, Horney's concept of, 358
  definition of, 393, 415, 589
  effects on learning, 10–11
  Freud's theory of, 456
  stress and, 393–394
Anxiety disorders, 415–422
  DSM-IV classification of, 412*t*
  prevalence of, 415
  types of, 415
Anxious-ambivalent interpersonal interaction, 486
Apathy, and bystander intervention, 495
Apnea. *See also* Sleep apnea
  definition of, 184
Approach-approach conflict, 383*f*, 383–384
Approach-avoidance conflict, 384, 384*f*
Aqueous humor, 134*f*, 135, 589
Aristotle, 20
Arousal
  definition of, 320, 589
  in motivation, 315, 320–321, 322*f*

Assessment. *See also* Interview(s);
  Observation(s); Psychological tests
  of intelligence, 296–301
  of personality, 367–375
Assimilation, Piaget's concept of, 90–91, 589
Association areas, of cerebral cortex, 69, 69*f,* 71, 72, 589
Astraphobia, 418*f*
Asylums, 446–447
Atheletes, psychological characteristics of, 534
Athletic performance, maximizing, 534–536
Atonia
  definition of, 185, 589
  in sleep, 185
Attachment
  definition of, 100, 589
  father–child, 100
  mother–child, 100–101
  nonparental child care and, 101
  social, development of, 100–101
Attachment theory, of interpersonal attraction, 486
Attention. *See also* Perceptual selectivity
  preferences, neonate's ability for, 90
Attention-deficit/hyperactivity disorder
  in adulthood, 414
  in children, 414
  epidemiology of, 414
  treatment of, 414
Attitudes, 477–483
  affective component, 478
  behavioral component, 478
  change
    central route for, 482–483
    peripheral route for, 482–483
    persuasion and, 480–483
  cognitive component, 478
  components of, 478
  definition of, 477, 589
  formation of, 478–479
  summary of, 506–507
  test yourself, 509–510
Attractions
  interpersonal, 485–489
  summary of, 506–507
  test yourself, 509–510
Attributions
  actor-observer bias and, 485, 589

distorted or biased, 484–485
  external, 483–485, 592
  internal, 483–485, 594
  just world hypothesis and, 484
  self-serving bias and, 484–485, 598
  summary of, 506–507
  test yourself, 509–510
  theory of, 483–485
Audience inhibition, bystander intervention and, 498–499, 589
Audition. *See* Hearing
Authority, obedience to, 491–494, 493*f*
Autobiographical memory, 254
Autonomic nervous system (ANS)
  definition of, 58, 59*f,* 589
  in emotional states, 341–342
  parasympathetic division definition of, 59, 59*f,* 596
    in emotional states, 341–342
  sympathetic division, definition of, 58–59, 59*f,* 599
Autonomy versus self-doubt, Erikson's concept of, 98–99, 99*f*
Autophobia, 418*f*
Average(s), 545
Aversion therapy, 463, 589
Avoidance-avoidance conflict, 384, 384*f*
Avoidant personality disorder, 426
Axon(s)
  myelinated, 51*f,* 51–52
  of neurons, 51, 51*f,* 589
Axon terminals
  of neurons, 51*f,* 52, 589
  vesicles in, 55, 56*f,* 599

Babbling, 291, 589
Babinski reflex, 86*t*
Balance, in motivated behavior, 320–322
Barbiturates, 193
Bargaining, in dying person, 117
Basal ganglia, 64*f*
Base rate, of responding, in operant conditioning, 217
Baseline design, 37, 589
Basic anxiety, Horney's concept of, 358
Basic hostility, Horney's concept of, 358

Basilar membrane, of ear, 146*f,* 147, 589
Bedlam, 446–447, 456
Behavior(s)
  critical thinking about, 74–75
  definition of, 17, 589
  healthy, promotion of, 397–402
  motivated, 316–322
  balance in, 320–322
  Skinner's view of, 216–217
  as subject matter of psychology, 17–18
  summary of, 75–76
  test yourself, 77–78
  verifiable, 17
Behavior therapy, 461–464, 589
Behavioral observation
  definition of, 368, 589
  in personality assessment, 368–370
Behavioral-learning approach to personality, 360–361
  evaluation of, 361
Behaviorism. *See also* Operant conditioning
  definition of, 23, 589
  origins of, 23
  purposive, 230
The Bell Curve (Hernstein and Murray), 303
Bell curve, 303
Benzodiazepines, 455
Bias
  actor-observer, 485, 589
  affecting attributions, 484
  male, in psychoanalytic approach, 358–359
  observer, 27, 595
  self-serving, 484–485, 598
Binocular cues, in perception, 169
Biofeedback, stress reduction and, 392
Biogenic amines, 431
Biomedical treatment, 450–455
Bipolar cells, ocular, 135, 137*f*
Bipolar disorder, 430, 589
  biological factors in, 431
Blindspot, 134*f,* 136–137, 589
  locating your, 137, 137*f*
Blocking, 214
Blood alcohol level, 191–192
Body fat, distribution of, genetics and, 327
Body language, emotion and, 343

Body temperature, regulation of, 323–324
Body weight, regulation of, 326–327
Botulism, 57
Brain
  alpha activity in, 181–182
  cross-laterality in, 63–64, 70, 71–72
  development of, 52–53
  in emotional states, 342–343
  lower brain centers of, 63–67
  nerve impulse transmission to, 70–71
  structures of, 63, 64*f*
Brain stem, 63–64
  cross-laterality in, 63–64
  definition of, 63, 590
Bribery, versus reinforcement, 222
Brightness, 131, 590
Brightness constancy, in perception, 175
British empiricists, 20, 590
Bulimia, 328–329
Bystander effect, 498, 501
Bystander intervention, 494–501
  audience inhibition and, 498–499
  cognitive model of, 496–498, 499*f*
  diffusion of responsibility and, 500–501
  pluralistic ignorance and, 499–500
  social inhibition of helping and, 498

Caffeine, 189–190
California Personality Inventory (CPI), 372–373
Cannabis sativa, 194
Career
  choice of, in early adulthood, 110–113
  in midlife, 114
Case history, 30–31, 590
Cell body, of neurons, 51, 51*f,* 590
Central nervous system (CNS), 58–75. *See also* Brain; Spinal cord
  definition of, 58, 59*f,* 590
Central tendency, 545, 590
  measures of, 546–549
Cerebellum, 64*f,* 64–66
  damage to, 65
  definition of, 64, 590
  functions of, 64–66
  training and, 65, 65*f*
Cerebral cortex, 63, 64*f,* 68–74

association areas, 69, 69f, 71, 72, 589
auditory area, 69, 69f
body sense area, 69f, 69–70
definition of, 68, 590
in emotionality, 342
motor areas, 69, 69f, 70–72, 595
sensory areas, 69f, 69–70, 598
visual area, 69, 69f
Cerebrum. See Cerebral cortex
Chastity, of potential mates, 110
Chemical ions, 53, 590
Chemical senses. See Smell; Taste
Child abuse, repressed memories of, 253
Child care, nonparental, 101
Childhood, definition of, 590
Children
development in, 85–101
cognitive, 89–101
motor, 85–87, 87f
perceptual, 88–89
sensory, 88–89
social, 89–101
development of social attachments, 100–101
divorce's effects on, 111
moral development of, Kohlberg's theory of, 96–98, 97f
Chlamydia, 400
Chlorpromazine, 453
Cholecystokinin (CCK), 329
Chunk(s)
definition of, 245, 590
in short-term memory, 245
Ciliary muscles, of eye, 134f, 135, 590
City life
environmental psychology and, 529–531
positive and negative aspects of, 531
Classical conditioning. See also Behavior therapy
acquisition in, 207, 207f
attitude formation and, 478–479, 479f
definition of, 204, 590
discrimination in, 208
in emotional responses, 209–210
essential procedures in, 204–206
extinction in, 207f, 207–208
generalization in, 208, 208f, 209f

Little Albert and, 210–212, 211f
process of, contemporary understanding of, 212–215
significance of, 209–213
spontaneous recovery in, 207f, 208
summary of, 234–235
test yourself, 237
time interval between CS and UCS in, 215
in treatment of fear, 212–213
Classification, of mental disorders, 411–413
DSM-IV, 411, 412t
problems with, 412–413
Classroom learning
note-taking for, 6–7
preparation for, 5–6
Claustrophobia, 418f
Client-centered therapy, 460, 590
Clinical psychologist, 448–449
Clinical psychology, 28
Clinical social worker, 449
Closure, Gestalt principle of, 167, 590
Clozapine (Clozaril), 453
CNS. See Central nervous system
Cocaine, 57, 190–191
Cochlea, 146f, 146–147
Cognition(s), 278. See also Social cognitions
consonance among, 321
definition of, 17, 590
irrational, maladjustment and disorder due to, 465, 466f
Cognitive abilities, age-related changes in, 115
Cognitive development, 89–101
Piaget's theory of, 90–94
criticisms of, 94–96
Cognitive disorders, DSM-IV classification of, 412t
Cognitive dissonance, 321–322
attitude change and, 480–482
definition of, 480, 590
Cognitive map, 230–231, 590
Cognitive processes. See also Learning; Memory; Perception
higher, 277–312. See also Intelligence; Language; Problem solving
critical thinking about, 307–308

summary of, 308–310
test yourself, 311–312
Cognitive psychology, 29
Cognitive reappraisal, 391
Cognitive restructuring therapy, 465–467, 590
Cognitive therapy, 464–467
Cognitive-behavioral therapy, 464
Collective unconscious, Jung's idea of, 358
Collectivism, 96, 590
Color blindness, 140–142, 142f
prevalence of, 141
Color constancy, in perception, 175
Color vision, 131–132, 132f, 140–142
Young-Helmholtz theory of, 140–141
Common fate, Gestalt principle of, 167, 590
Communication
in family, 467–468
patient–physician, improvement of, 400
persuasive, source of, 482–483
Community mental health centers, 456–457
Comorbidity
definition of, 416, 590
significance of, 416
Competence versus inferiority, Erikson's concept of, 99f, 99–100
Compliance, improvement of, 399–402
Compulsion(s), definition of, 419, 590
Compulsive, definition of, 419–420
Compulsive ritual(s), 419
common, 420f
Conception, 81
definition of, 80, 590
Concrete operations stage, Piaget's concept of, 93, 95f, 590
Conditioned response(s) (CR), 206, 590
emotional, 209–210
Conditioned stimulus (CS), 206, 214, 590
Conditioning. See also Behavior therapy; Classical conditioning; Operant conditioning
definition of, 204
Cones, 135, 137f, 590
in color vision, 140–141, 141f
visual experience provided by, 138–139

Confidentiality, of research participant, 39
Conflict(s)
approach-approach, 383f, 383–384
approach-avoidance, 384, 384f
avoidance-avoidance, 384, 384f
definition of, 383, 590
Freud's theory of, 455
motivational, types of, 383–385
multiple approach-avoidance, 384, 384f
as stressor, 383f, 383–385
Conformity, 490–491, 590
Asch's studies of, 490f, 490–491, 491f
Consciousness, 177–195
altered. See also Hypnosis; Sleep
drug-induced, 188–195
critical thinking about, 195–196
definition of, 161, 177, 590
Freud's theory of, 179f, 179–180, 353
levels of, 178–181, 179f
Freud's ideas about, 353
nature of, 177–181
normal waking, 177–180
characteristics of, 177–178
James's description of, 177–178
summary of, 197–198
test yourself, 200
Conservation, Piaget's concept of, 93, 94f, 95, 590
Constancy, in perception, 174–177, 596
Context, memory and, 257–259
Contiguity, Gestalt principle of, 166, 167f
Contingency contracting, 222, 463–464, 590
Contingency management, 463–464, 590
Continuity, Gestalt principle of, 166, 167f, 590
Continuous reinforcement schedule (CRF), 590
Contrast, in perceptual selection, 162, 590
Control group, 37, 590
Conventional (conforming) morality, 96, 97f
Convergence, visual, 170, 170f, 591
Convergent thinking, 285–286, 287f, 591

Conversion disorder, 423, 591
Cornea, 134, 134*f*, 591
Coronary heart disease, personality and, 395–397
Corpus callosum, 64*f*, 66*f*
  definition of, 73, 591
  functions of, 73
  location of, 73
Correlation
  definition of, 31, 591
  negative, 32*f*, 32–33
  positive, 32, 32*f*
  zero, 32*f*, 33
Correlation coefficient
  calculation of, 32–33
  definition of, 32, 591
  information gained from, 32–33
  negative, 32*f*, 32–33
  positive, 32, 32*f*
  zero, 32*f*, 33
Correlational methods, in psychology, 31–34
Cortex. *See* Cerebral cortex
Couch, Freudian, 458, 458*f*
Counseling psychologist/psychology, 29, 449
Counterconditioning, 213
Counterirritation, 153
CR. *See* Conditioned response
Crack cocaine, 190–191
Crime. *See* Violence
Crises, of development, Erikson's theory of, 98–100, 99*f*
Crisis, midlife, 113–114
Criterion-referenced test(s), 372
Critical thinking, about psychology, 43–44
Cross-laterality
  in brain, 70, 71–72
  in brain stem, 63–64
  definition of, 64, 591
Crowding
  definition of, 530, 591
  effects of, on rats, 529
  population density and, comparison of, 530–531
Crystallized abilities, 297
CS. *See* Conditioned stimulus
Cues
  in perception, 169–174, 174*f*
    binocular, 169
    ocular, 169–170
    physical, 169, 171–174
    pictorial, in perception, 171–174, 174*f*
Cultural psychology, 29
Culture-specific syndromes, 410, 410*t*
Cure, criteria for, difficulties with, 469

Cutaneous senses, 150–152

Dark adaptation, 130, 138–139, 139*f*, 591
Data. *See also* Statistics
  organizing, 543–544
Death
  causes of, 397–398
  premature, 397–398
  preventable, 397–398
Death and dying, 116–117
Death instincts, Freud's theory of, 353, 591
Debrief(ing)
  definition of, 39, 591
  of research participant, 39
Decibel scale, 143–144, 144*f*, 591
Decision making
  in groups, 503–504
  stressors in, 392
Defense mechanisms, Freud's theory of, 354–356, 355*f*, 591
Deinstitutionalization, 456–457
Delirium
  definition of, 428, 591
  DSM-IV classification of, 412*t*
Delta waves, in sleep, 182*f*, 183
Delusion(s)
  definition of, 432
  in schizophrenia, 432
Dementia. *See also* Alzheimer's disease
  definition of, 428, 591
  DSM-IV classification of, 412*t*
Dementia of the Alzheimer's type, 428–429
Dendrites, of neurons, 51, 51*f*, 591
Denial
  as defense mechanism, 355*f*
  definition of, 591
  in dying person, 116
Dependence, drug, 189
Dependent personality disorder, 426–427
Dependent variable(s), 34–35, 591
Depressant(s), 191–193, 591
  definition of, 191
Depression
  biological factors in, 431
  causes of, 430–432
  drug therapy for, 453–454
  in dying person, 117
  major, definition of, 430, 594
  in panic disorder, 416–417

psychological factors in, 431–432
  treatment of, cognitive restructuring therapy and, 465–467
Depth perception, 169–174
Descriptive statistics, 545–549
Development
  in adolescence, 101–118
    summary of, 120–121
    test yourself, 123–124
  in adulthood, 101–118
    summary of, 120–121
    test yourself, 123–124
  in children, 85–101
    summary of, 118–119
    test yourself, 122–123
  cognitive, 89–101
  definition of, 81
  Freud's theory of, 356–357
  human, *critical thinking about,* 117–118
  moral, Kohlberg's theory of, 96–98, 97*f*
  motor, 85–87, 87*f*
  perceptual, 88–89
  prenatal, 80–85
    environmental influences on, 83–84
    nourishment during, 83–84
    paternal influences on, 85
    physical aspects of, 80–83
    summary of, 118
    test yourself, 122
  psychosexual, Freud's theory of, 356–357
  psychosocial, Erikson's theory of, 98–100, 99*f*
  sensory, 88–89
  social, 89–101
Developmental psychology, 28
Diagnosis, definition of, 411, 591
Diagnostic and Statistical Manual of Mental Disorders, 411
  fourth edition (DSM-IV), 411, 412*t*, 591
Dieting, 327–330
Difference thresholds
  definition of, 128, 591
  for senses, 128–129
Diffusion of responsibility, and bystander intervention, 500–501, 591
Direction, in motivation, 315
Discrimination
  in classical conditioning, 208, 591
  in operant conditioning, 227*f*, 227–228, 228*f*

Disorders usually first diagnosed in infancy, childhood, and adolescence, DSM-IV classification of, 412*t*
Disorganized schizophrenia, 434
Displacement, as defense mechanism, 355*f*, 591
Disposition, definition of, 477
Dissociative amnesia, 424, 591
Dissociative disorders, 423–425, 591
  definition of, 423–424
  DSM-IV classification of, 412*t*
Dissociative fugue, 424, 591
Dissociative identity disorder, 424–425, 591
Distance
  intimate, 527, 528*f*
  perception of, 169–174
  personal, 527, 528*f*
  public, 527, 528*f*
  social, 527, 528*f*
Divergent thinking, 285–286, 287*f*, 591
Divorce
  effects on children, 111
  rates, in U.S., 110, 111
Dopamine, 57
Dopamine hypothesis, schizophrenia and, 437, 591
Dorsal, definition of, 60
Dorsal nerve root(s), 60
Down syndrome, 85, 306, 591
Dream(s), 183–185
  Freud's theory of, 185, 459
  interpretation, in psychoanalysis, 459
  latent content, 459
  manifest content, 459
Drinking behavior, factors affecting, 325
Drive(s), 316–319
  definition of, 316, 591
  versus motive, 323
  physiologically based, 323–334
  primary, 317
  psychologically based, 323
  secondary, 317, 598
Drive reduction theory, Hull's, 316–317
Drug(s)
  addiction to, 189
  dependence on, 189
  depressant, 191–193
  maternal, effects on fetus, 84
  for pain management, 153

psychoactive, definition of, 188
stimulant, 189–191
tolerance of, 189
withdrawal from, 189
Drug abuse, 189
definition of, 189, 591
Drug therapy, 452–455
Drug use, by adolescents, 105–107
DSM. *See Diagnostic and Statistical Manual of Mental Disorders*
Dual-career family, 110–111
Dysthymia, 430, 591

Ear, structures of, 146*f*, 146–147
Eardrum, 146, 146*f*, 591
Eating behavior, factors affecting, 325–330
Eating disorders, 328–329
DSM-IV classification of, 412*t*
Ebene, 193*f*
ECT. *See* Electroconvulsive therapy
Educational/instructional psychology, 28
EEG (electroencephalograph), 181, 592
Effexor, 454
Ego, Freud's theory of, 353–354, 455–456, 592
Egocentrism, of preoperational child, 91–93, 95
Ego-integrity versus despair, Erikson's concept of, 99*f*
Elaborative rehearsal, in long-term memory, 250–251, 592
Elderly
demographics of, 114–115
old-old of, 116
young-old of, 116
Electra complex, 357
Electroconvulsive therapy (ECT), 451*f*, 451–452, 592
unilateral, 452
Electroencephalograph (EEG), 181, 592
Electroencephalography, in sleep, 182, 182*f*
Electromagnetic energy, 132*f*
Electromyograph (EMG), 181, 592
Embryo, stage of, 81–83, 82*f*
Emergency, bystander intervention in. *See* Bystander intervention
EMG (electromyograph), 181, 592

Emotion(s)
basic, 339–340
classification of, 339–340
cognitive aspect of, 342
critical thinking about, 345
definition of, 338–339, 592
facial expression and, 343–344, 344*f*
outward expressions of, 343–344
physiology of, 341–343
primary, 339–340, 340*f*
psychology of, 338–344
summary of, 347
test yourself, 349
Emotional experience, components of, 338–339
Emotional responses, conditioned, 209–210
Empathic, definition of, 460, 592
Empiricists
British, 20, 590
definition of, 20
Employee selection, 514–516
Employment interview, 515
structured, 515
Encoding, in memory, 241
context and, 257–259
definition of, 592
long-term, 250–251
retrieval and, 257–265
short-term, 246–247
specificity principle, 257–258, 592
Endler Multidimensional Anxiety Scale, 373
Endocrine system, 59*f*, 59–60, 592
in emotional states, 341–342
Endorphins, 57
Environment, and heredity, interactions of, 40
Environmental psychology, 524–537
city life and, 529–531
critical thinking about, 536
definition of, 524, 592
environmental toxins and, 531–534
interest areas in, 524–526
noise and, 531–534
summary of, 537–538
temperature and, 531–534
test yourself, 540
Episodic memory, 252*f*, 252–254, 259, 592
Equanil, 454–455
Equilibrium
cognitive dissonance and, 321–322
in motivated behavior, 320–322

Equity model, of interpersonal attraction, 486
Equity theory, of work motivation, 520–521, 592
Eros, Freud's theory of, 353
Ethical Principles of Psychologists (APA), 38–39
Ethics, in psychological research, 38–40
Etiology, definition of, 411, 592
Evaluation, definition of, 477
Exams, preparation for, 9–11
Excitatory neurotransmitters, 55–57
Exercise, stress reduction and, 392
Exhaustion stage, in general adaptation syndrome, 388, 389*f*
Expectancy theory, of work motivation, 520, 592
Experience, learning and, 203
Experiment(s)
baseline design for, 37
definition of, 34, 592
random assignment for, 37
with rats, 35–36
stages in, 34–35, 36*f*
Experimental group, 37, 592
Experimental methods, in psychology, 34–38
External attributions, 483–485, 592
Extinction
in classical conditioning, 207*f*, 207–208, 592
in operant conditioning, 219, 219*f*, 592
Extraneous variable(s), 34–35, 592
control of, 37–38
Eye, structures of, 133–134, 134*f*
that focus visual images, 134–135
Eyewitness testimony, 249–250, 250*f*

Facial discrimination, neonate's ability for, 90
Facial expression, emotion and, 343–344, 344*f*
Factor analysis, 365
Failure, fear of, 336
Family
communication in, 467–468
dual-career, 110–111
in early adulthood, 109–110
in late adulthood, 115

in midlife, 114
as system, 467
Family therapy, 467–468, 592
Fantasy, as defense mechanism, 355*f*, 592
Farsightedness, 135, 136*f*
Fatigue, in behaviors, 203
Fear(s). *See also* Phobia(s); Phobic disorder
conditioned, 210–212, 211*f*
treatment, classical conditioning in, 212–213
Fear of failure, 336
Fear of success, 336
Feedback
in learning, 3
stress reduction and, 392
Females
adolescent growth spurt in, 103, 103*f*
moral development of, 97–98
Fertilization, 81, 82*f*
Fetal alcohol syndrome, 84, 592
Fetus, stage of, 83
Fight or flight response, 341
Figure-ground relationship, in Gestalt psychology, 165, 165*f*, 592
Five-Factor Model, of personality traits, 365–367
Fixed reinforcement schedule, 223*f*
Fixed-interval (FI) reinforcement schedule, 224
Fixed-ratio (FR) reinforcement schedule, 224
Flashback(s), in posttraumatic stress disorder, 421
Flashbulb memories, 259, 260*f*, 592
Flooding, 463, 592
Fluoxetine (Prozac), 454
Food, flavor of, versus taste of, 148
Forgetting, 271. *See also* Memory, retrieval of
Formal operations stage, Piaget's concept of, 93–94, 95*f*, 102, 592
Fovea, 134*f*, 136, 592
Fragile X syndrome, 306
Free association, 457–458, 592
Free nerve endings, of skin, 151, 151*f*
Frequency distribution, 543–544, 544*f*, 592
Frustration
coping strategy for, 390
definition of, 382, 592
environmental, 382

personal, 382–383
stress caused by, 382f, 382–383, 383f
Frustration-aggression hypothesis, 393, 394f, 592
Fugue, dissociative, 424, 591
Functional fixedness, problem solving and, 284–285, 592
Functionalism, 22, 593
Fundamental attribution error, 484, 593

g, on intelligence tests, 297, 297f, 301, 593
Ganglion cells, ocular, 135, 137f
Gate-control mechanism, for pain, 153
General adaptation syndrome (GAS), 388, 389f
definition of, 388, 593
General Personality Test, 372
Generalization
in classical conditioning, 208, 208f, 209f
in operant conditioning, 227–228, 593
Generalized anxiety disorder, 416, 593
Generativity versus stagnation, Erikson's concept of, 99f, 110, 114
Genetics, body fat distribution and, 327
Genital herpes, 400
Genital stage, of psychosexual development, 357
Genovese, Kitty, 494–495
Geometrical illusion(s), 175–177, 176f
Gestalt, definition of, 165, 593
Gestalt psychology, 25–26, 593
figure-ground relationship in, 165, 165f
Gestalt therapy, characteristics of, 460
Giftedness, 301–304
Glaucoma, 135
Glove anesthesia, 423
Goal-setting, in work motivation, 521–522
Gonorrhea, 400
Graph(s), 545, 545f
Grasping reflex, 86t
Gray matter, 51–52
spinal, 61, 61f
Group polarization, 504, 593
Group therapy, 467–468
Groupthink, 504, 593
Growing pains, 104

Growth, definition of, 81
Growth spurt, adolescent
in females, 103, 103f
in males, 103f, 103–104
Gustation. See Taste

Habituation, 205, 593
Hair cells, of ear, 146f, 147, 593
Hallucination(s)
definition of, 432, 593
in schizophrenia, 432
Hallucinogens, 193–194, 593
definition of, 193
ritual use of, 193
Hardy personalities, 388
Hassles Scale, 386, 386f
Health, physical
critical thinking about, 402
psychological factors affecting, 395–397
Health psychology, 29, 394–402
critical thinking about, 402
definition of, 395, 593
promotion of healthy behaviors and, 397–402
summary of, 404
test yourself, 405–406
Hearing, 143–147
absolute threshold for, 128f
receptor for, 146f, 146–147
stimulus for, 143–146
summary of, 156–157
test yourself, 159
Heart disease, personality and, 395–397
Hematophobia, 418f
Hemisphere(s)
cerebral, 68, 68f, 69f, 72–74
functional localization in, 73–74
left, functions of, 73–74
right, functions of, 73–74
Hemp, 194
Heredity, and environment, interactions of, 40
Heroin, 192–193
Herpes, genital, 400
Hertz (Hz), 144, 593
Heuristic, definition of, 282, 593
Heuristic problem-solving strategies, 282–283
Hidden observer, in hypnosis, 187–188
Hippocampus, 66f, 67
Histogram, 544–545, 545f, 593
Histrionic personality disorder, 426
HIV. See Human immunodeficiency virus

Holophrastic speech, 291, 593
Homeostasis, 320, 593
Homosexuality/homosexuals, 331–334
causes of, 332–334
definition of, 331, 593
Hormone(s), 59–60
Hostility, basic, Horney's concept of, 358
Hue(s), 131–132, 593
primary, 140
Human immunodeficiency virus (HIV), 400–401
carrier state, 400
infection, prevention of, 400–401
Humanistic psychology, 24–25, 593
Humanistic psychotherapy, 460–461, 462f
Humanistic-phenomenological approach to personality, 362–364
evaluation of, 363–364
Hunger, 325–330
Hyperphagia, 326
Hypnosis, 186f, 186–188
applications of, 186
definition of, 186, 593
Freud's use of, 457–458
memory and, 188
for pain management, 153, 187
susceptibility to, 186–187
Hypochondriasis, 422–423, 593
Hypothalamus, 64f, 66f, 67
in body temperature regulation, 324
definition of, 67, 324, 593
in emotionality, 342–343
functions of, 67
in hunger regulation, 326
location of, 66f, 67, 324f
in thirst regulation, 325
Hypothesis
definition of, 15, 593
scientific, 15–16
Hysteria, 423

Id, Freud's theory of, 353–354, 455–456, 593
Idealistic principle, Freud's theory of, 354, 593
Identity crisis, definition of, 105, 593
Identity formation, in adolescence, 105
Identity versus role confusion, Erikson's concept of, 99f, 102, 105
Illusion(s)
definition of, 175, 593
geometrical, 175–177, 176f
Implantation, 81, 82f

Impossible figures, 177, 177f
Impulses, Freud's theory of, 353
Incentive(s)
for behavior, 319–320
definition of, 319, 593
Incus, 146, 146f, 594
Independent variable(s), 34–35, 593
Individualism, 96–97, 593
Industrial-organizational (I/O) psychology, 16, 29, 512–524
critical thinking about, 536
employee selection and, 514–516
fitting the person to the job and, 513–522
job satisfaction and, 522–524
motivation of workers and, 519–522
personnel training and, 516–519, 517f
summary of, 537
test yourself, 539–540
Industrial/organizational (I/O) psychology, 16, 29
Inferential statistics, 549–552
definition of, 593
Informed consent, of research participant, 39
Initiative versus guilt, Erikson's concept of, 99, 99f
Inner ear, 146f, 146–147
Insanity
definition of, 413, 594
legal implications of, 413
Insomnia, 184
Instinct(s), 316, 594
Freud's theory of, 353
Intelligence, 294–307
creativity and, 285
definition of, 294, 594
extremes of, 301–307
operational definition of, 294
theories of, 294
Intelligence tests, 296–301
Stanford-Binet Intelligence Scale, 296–299, 297f
Wechsler, 299f, 299–301
Intention tremor, 65
Interactive dualism, 19–20, 594
Interference
with memory retrieval, 268–271
proactive, 270f, 270–271, 596
retroactive, 268–270, 269f, 270f, 597
social, 502–503, 598

Intermittent reinforcement schedule, 223, 223*f*, 594
Internal attributions, 483–485, 594
Interneuron(s), 61, 62*f*, 594
in spinal reflexes, 62, 62*f*
Interpersonal attraction, 485–489
anxious-ambivalent, 486
attachment theory of, 486
avoidant, 486
determinants of, 487–489
equity model of, 486
factors affecting, 487–489
matching phenomenon and, 488–489
mere exposure phenomenon and, 488
physical attractiveness and, 488
proximity and, 487*f*, 488
reciprocity and, 487
reinforcement model of, 485
secure, 486
similarity and, 489
social exchange model of, 485–486
theories of, 485–487
types of, 486
Interposition, 171, 171*f*
Interview(s)
definition of, 370, 594
employment, 515
in personality assessment, 370*f*, 370–371
advantages and disadvantages of, 370–371
structured, 515
Intimacy versus isolation, Erikson's concept of, 99*f*, 109
Intimate distance, 527, 528*f*
IQ, 298–299
definition of, 298, 594
mental retardation and, 305
mentally gifted and, 304
scores
distribution in general population, 301
race and, 302–303
Iris, 134, 134*f*, 594

Job(s)
performance criteria, 514
personal characteristics of workers and, matching, 522–524
personnel and, matching, 513–522
worker safety and, 525
Job analysis, 513–514, 594

Job productivity, job satisfaction and, 523–524, 524*f*
Job satisfaction. *See also* Work motivation
definition of, 522, 594
job productivity and, 523–524, 524*f*
personal characteristics of workers and, 522–524
work behaviors and, 523–524
Just noticeable difference (j.n.d.), 128–129, 594
Just world hypothesis, 484, 594

Key word, in learning, 261–262, 262*f*
Kinesthetic sense, 154, 594
Koro, 410*t*

La belle indifférence, 423
Labeling, problems with, 412–413
Language, 288–294
acquisition of, 290–294
biology-oriented theory of, 292–294
learning-oriented theory of, 292–294
theories of, 292–294
characteristics of, 288–289
definition of, 288–289, 594
gender-related differences in, 290
as social process, 289–290
speech and, comparison of, 289
symbols in, 289, 290*f*
Language acquisition device (LAD), 293
Language functions, hemispheric localization of, 72, 73
Latah, 410*t*
Latency stage, of psychosexual development, 357
Latent content, of dream, 459
Latent learning, 229–231, 594
Law of effect (Thorndike's), 217, 594
Learning, 201–238. *See also* Behavioral-learning approach; Classroom learning; Overlearning; Reinforcement
anxiety's effects on, 10–11
cognitive approaches to,

228–233
test yourself, 237
critical thinking about, 233–234
critical thinking and, 4
definition of, 203–204, 594
demonstration of, 203
difficulties in, causes of, 2
experience and, 203
feedback on, 3
goals in, 2
improvement of, methods for, 2–5
key word method in, 261–262, 262*f*
latent, 229–231, 594
motivated by stress, 390
neonate's ability for, 89–90
observational, 231–233, 232*f*, 479. *See also* Social learning theory
performance and, 4–5
practice and, 203
practice in, 2–3
reinforcement of, 2, 3–4
rewards for, 3–4
strengthening, with review, 10
summary of, 234–236
from textbook, 7–9
Lens, of eye, 134*f*, 134–135, 594
Libido, Freud's theory of, 353
Librium, 455
Licensed professional counselor, 449
Life change units, 385
Life events, as stressors, 385–386, 387*f*
Life instincts, Freud's theory of, 353, 594
Life-style, deadly, 397–398
Light, 130–133. *See also* Hue(s)
brightness of, 131
definition of, 130, 594
intensity of, 130–131
monochromatic, 132–133
physical characteristics of, and psychological experience of vision, 130–133, 133*f*, 145*t*
saturation, 133
wave amplitude of, 130–131, 131*f*
wave purity of, 132–133
wavelength of, 131*f*, 131–132
white, 133
Limbic system
constituents of, 66, 66*f*
definition of, 66, 66*f*, 594
in emotionality, 342–343

functions of, 67
location of, 66, 66*f*
Line graph, 545, 545*f*
Linear perspective, 170*f*, 171
Listening skills, development of, 6
Lithium salts, antidepressant effects of, 454
Little Albert, 210–212, 211*f*
Liver, in hunger regulation, 326
Lobe(s)
cerebral, 68*f*, 68–72
frontal, 68, 68*f*, 69*f*
occipital, 68, 68*f*, 69*f*
parietal, 68, 68*f*, 69*f*
temporal, 68, 68*f*, 69*f*
Lobotomy, 450–451, 594
Long-term memory (LTM), 241, 243*f*, 243–244, 248–254
accuracy of, 249–250, 253
capacity of, 248–249
definition of, 248, 594
duration of, 249–250
elaborative rehearsal in, 250–251, 592
encoding information into, 250–251
episodic, 252, 252*f*, 259
procedural, 251, 252*f*, 256–257
recall of, 255, 256*f*
recognition in, 255, 256*f*
retrieval of
factors affecting, 254–271
measures of, 255–257
direct (explicit), 255
indirect (implicit), 255–257
semantic, 251–252, 252*f*
types of, 251–254
Loudness, 143–144, 594
LSD (lysergic acid diethylamide), 194

Maintenance rehearsal, in short-term memory, 244–245, 245*f*, 594
Major depression, definition of, 430, 594
Males
adolescent growth spurt in, 103*f*, 103–104
moral development of, 97–98
Malleus, 146, 146*f*, 594
Mania, 430, 594
Manic depression, 430
Manifest content, of dream, 459
Marijuana, 194–195
Marital therapy, efficacy of, 111

Marriage
in early adulthood,
109–110
successful, predictors of,
111
Maslow's hierarchy of needs,
317–319, 318*f*
Matching phenomenon, interpersonal attraction
and, 488–489, 594
Mean, statistical, 546–547,
594
Meaningfulness, memory
and, 259–261, 594
Median, statistical, 547, 594
Medication(s), compliance
with, improvement of,
399–402
Medulla, 64*f*
definition of, 63, 594
functions of, 63
Melissaphobia, 417
Memory, 239–276
acetylcholine and, 429
autobiographical, 254
critical thinking about, 272
definition of, 241, 594
encoding in, 241
context and, 257–259
definition of, 592
retrieval and, 257–265
specificity principle,
257–258
episodic, 252*f*, 252–254,
259, 592
flashbulb, 259, 260*f*
hypnosis and, 188
improvement of, methods for, 2–5
as information processing, 240–241
long-term (LTM). *See*
Long-term memory
(LTM)
meaningfulness and,
259–261, 594
mnemonic devices and,
261–264
model of, 243, 243*f*
narrative chaining and,
261, 262*f*
neonate's ability for,
89–90
procedural, 251, 252*f*,
256–257, 596
repressed, retrieval of,
253
retrieval of, 241, 597
distribution of practice
time and, 267*f*,
267–268
encoding and, 257–265
factors affecting,
254–271
interference with,
268–271

overlearning and,
265–266, 266*f*
schemas in, 264*f*,
264–265, 271*f*
semantic, 251–252, 252*f*,
598
sensory, 241–242, 598
short-term (STM). *See*
Short-term memory
(STM)
state-dependent, 259, 598
storage in, 71, 241
summary, 272–274
test yourself, 275–276
types of, 241
working, 243
Menarche, definition of,
104, 595
Mental age, 298
Mental disorder(s), 413. *See
also* Psychological disorder(s)
Mental health care, trends
in, 456–457
Mental health technician,
449
Mental illness, 413. *See also*
Psychological disorder(s)
attitudes toward, historical perspective on,
446–448
Mental images, as mnemonic
device, 261
Mental processes, types of, 17
Mental retardation, 305–307
causes of, 306–307
classification of, 305
definition of, 305, 595
Mental set
definition of, 164, 283,
595
and perceptual selectivity,
164, 164*f*
Mentally gifted, 301–304
Meprobamates, 454–455
Mere exposure phenomenon, 488, 595
Method of loci, as
mnemonic device,
262–263, 263*f*, 595
Midlife crisis, 113–114
Miltown, 454–455
Mind, as *tabula rasa,* 20
A Mind That Found Itself
(Beers), 447
Mind-body problem, 19–20
Minnesota Multiphasic Personality Inventory
(MMPI-2), 371–372,
595
Mnemonic device(s)
definition of, 261, 595
key word method as,
261–262, 262*f*
mental images as, 261

method of loci as,
262–263, 263*f*
value of, 261–264
Mode, statistical, 547–548, 595
Modeling, 231–233
in behavior therapy, 464
definition of, 464, 595
Monochromatic light,
132–133, 595
Monophobia, 418*f*
Mood disorders, 429–432
causes of, 430–432
definition of, 429, 595
DSM-IV classification of,
412*t*
types of, 430
Moral development,
Kohlberg's theory of,
96–98, 97*f*
Morality
conventional (conforming), 96, 97*f*
postconventional, 96, 97*f*
preconventional, 96, 97*f*
Moro reflex, 86*t*
Motion parallax, in perception of distance,
172–173, 173*f*
Motion sickness, 154
Motivation, 315–338
arousal in, 315, 320–321,
322*f*
characteristics of,
316–320
critical thinking about, 345
definition of, 315, 595
direction in, 315
and perceptual selectivity,
164
subprocesses of, 315
summary of, 345–346
test yourself, 348–349
Motivational conflict(s),
types of, 383–385
Motive(s), 334–338
definition of, 323, 334
versus drive, 323
Motor areas, of cerebral cortex, 69, 69*f*, 70–72,
595
Motor development, 85–87,
87*f*
rate of, 87
sequence of, 87
Motor neuron(s)
definition of, 60, 595
in spinal reflexes, 62, 62*f*
Movement(s), coordination
of, 64–66
Müller-Lyer illusion, 176*f*,
176–177, 177*f*
Multiple approach-avoidance
conflicts, 384, 384*f*
Multiple personality disorder. *See* Dissociative
identity disorder

Myelin, 51*f*, 51–52, 595
Mysophobia, 418*f*

Nanometer, 131
Narcissistic personality disorder, 426
Narcolepsy, 184
Narrative chaining, 261,
262*f*, 595
Naturalistic observation,
27–30, 38*f*, 595
problems with, 27–30
Nature versus nurture, 40
Nearsightedness, 135, 136*f*
Need(s), 316–319
definition of, 316, 595
esteem, 318
love and belongingness,
318
Maslow's hierarchy of,
317–319, 318*f*
physiological, 318
safety, 318
self-actualization, 318
Need for affiliation,
337–338, 595
Need for power, 336–337,
595
Need to achieve (nAch),
334–336, 595
Negative afterimages, 141,
142*f*
Negative reinforcer(s),
220–221, 595
Nelson Denny Reading Test
(NDRT), 31
Neo-Freudians, 357–360, 595
Neonate, 85, 595
cognitive abilities of,
89–90
reflexes of, 86, 86*t*
sensory capacities of, 88
Nerve cell(s). *See* Neuron(s)
Nerve endings
encapsulated, of skin,
151, 151*f*
free, of skin, 151, 151*f*
Nerve root(s)
dorsal, 60
ventral, 61
Nervous system(s), 58–60,
59*f*. *See also specific system*
critical thinking about,
74–75
summary of, 75–76
test yourself, 77–78
Neural impulse(s), 53, 595
transmission at synapse,
55–56, 56*f*
Neural threshold, 55, 595
Neuron(s), 50–55. *See also* Interneuron(s)
action potential of, 54,
54*f*
axon terminals of, 51*f*, 52

axons of, 51, 51*f*
cell body of, 51, 51*f*
definition of, 50, 595
dendrites of, 51, 51*f*
electrical potential of, 53–54, 54*f*
firing of, 53–55, 54*f*
functions of, 53–55
generation of, 52–53
motor. *See* Motor neuron(s)
myelin sheath of, 51*f*, 51–52
nerve impulse transmission by, 70–71
numbers of, 51
regeneration of, 53
resting potential of, 53
sensory. *See* Sensory neuron(s)
structure of, 51*f*, 51–53
Neurotoxins
definition of, 533, 595
effects on behavior, 533
Neurotransmitter(s). *See also* *specific neurotransmitter*
definition of, 55, 595
excitatory, 55–57
functions of, 55, 56*f*
inhibitory, 55–57
release, 55, 56*f*
Nicotine, 57, 190
Noise
definition of, 531, 595
environmental psychology and, 531–534
neural, 129
predictability of, and effects on cognitive tasks, 531–532, 532*f*
white, 145
Norepinephrine, 57
Normal curve, 552–554, 553*f*, 554*f*, 595
Norms
definition of, 595
for psychological tests, 296
Note-taking, for classroom learning, 6–7
NREM sleep, 183–185
Nutrition, maternal, effects on fetus, 83–84
Nyctophobia, 418*f*

Obedience to authority, Milgram's study of, 491–494, 493*f*
Obesity, 327–330
Object permanence, Piaget's concept of, 91, 92*f*
Observation(s)
naturalistic, 27–30, 38*f*, 595
problems with, 27–30
in scientific method, 15–16

Observational learning, 479
Observational methods, in psychology, 27–31
Observer bias, 27, 595
Obsession(s)
common, 420*f*
definition of, 419, 595
Obsessive-compulsive disorder (OCD), 419–421
biological basis of, 421
definition of, 419, 595
prevalence of, 420
prognosis for, 420
Occupational therapists, 449
OCD. *See* Obsessive-compulsive disorder
Ocular cues, in perception, 169–170
Oedipus complex, 357
Old-old, 116
Olfaction. *See* Smell
Olfactory system, 149*f*, 149–150
On Death and Dying (Kübler-Ross), 116
Operant conditioning, 216–228. *See also* Behavior therapy; Punishment; Reinforcement; Reinforcer(s)
acquisition in, 219, 219*f*
attitude formation and, 479
base rate of responding in, 217
definition of, 216–217, 595
demonstration of, 217–218, 218*f*
discrimination in, 227*f*, 227–228, 228*f*
extinction in, 219, 219*f*
generalization in, 227–228
spontaneous recovery in, 219, 219*f*
stages of, 218–219, 219*f*
summary of, 235–236
test yourself, 237
Operational definitions
definition of, 18, 595
examples of, 18, 18*f*, 19*f*
limitations of, 18
Opiates, 192
for pain management, 153
Opponent-process theory, of color vision, 140–142
Optic nerve, 135, 137*f*, 595
Optical illusions, 175–177, 176*f*
Oral stage, of psychosexual development, 356
Organic mental disorders, 427
Organisms, diversity of, 40
Orienting reflex, 205, 595

Origin of Species (Darwin), 20
Ossicles, auditory, 146, 146*f*, 594
Oval window, 146*f*, 146–147
Overlearning, 265–266, 266*f*, 596
Overregularization, 293, 596
Overweight, 327–330
Ovum/ova, 81

Pain
definition of, 153
expression or display of, 153
management, hypnosis for, 153, 187
management of, 153
sensation
cognitive-behavior theory of, 153
gate-control mechanism for, 153
stimuli for, 153
Panic attacks, 416
Panic disorder, 416–417, 596
Paralysis, 61
Paranoid personality disorder, 426
Parasympathetic division, of autonomic nervous system
definition of, 59, 59*f*, 596
in emotional states, 341–342
Past experience, and perceptual selectivity, 164
Pastoral counseling, 449
Pathophobia, 418*f*
Peak performance, 535
Perception(s), 162–178. *See also* Phenomenology
critical thinking about, 195–196
definition of, 161, 596
of depth, 169–174
of distance, 169–174
as focus of Gestalt psychology, 26
of physical environment, behavior and, 526
summary of, 196–197
test yourself, 199–200
visual, constancy of, 174–177
visual illusions and, 175–177, 176*f*, 177*f*
Perceptual constancies, 174–175, 596
Perceptual development, 88–89
Perceptual organization, 165–169
personal factors in, 168–169, 169*f*
stimulus factors in, 166–168

Perceptual selectivity, 162–165
personal factors in, 163–165
stimulus factors in, 162–163
Performance, learning and, 4–5
Performance criteria, for jobs, 514, 596
Peripheral nervous system (PNS), 58, 59*f*, 596
Personal distance, 527, 528*f*, 596
Personal space
definition of, 526
intimate distance in, 527, 528*f*
personal distance in, 527, 528*f*
public distance in, 527, 528*f*
social distance in, 527, 528*f*
and territory, 526–529
Personal unconscious, Jung's idea of, 358
Personality, 351–379
assessment of, 367–375
behavioral observation in, 368–370
critical thinking about, 375
goals of, 368
interviews in, 370*f*, 370–371
paper-and-pencil tests for, 371–373
projective techniques, 373–375
rating scales in, 369, 369*f*
summary of, 377
test yourself, 379
consistency of, 352
critical thinking about, 375
definition of, 351, 596
dimensions of, Five-Factor Model, 365–367
Freud's ideas about, 352–357
hardy, 388
issues of, 352
structure of, Freud's theory of, 353–354
summary of, 376–377
test yourself, 378–379
theories of, 351–367. *See also* Psychoanalytic approach
Adler's, 357–358
Bandura's, 361
behavioral-learning approach, 360–361
Dollard and Miller's, 361
Horney's, 358–359

humanistic-phenomeno-
logical approach,
362–364
Jung's, 358
Maslow's, 362–363
Rogers,' 362
Skinner's, 360–361
trait approach, 364–367
Watson's, 360
Type A, 395–396
and heart disease,
395–397
Type B, and heart dis-
ease, 396–397
Personality disorders,
425–427
cluster I: disorders of odd
or eccentric reactions,
426
cluster II: disorders of
dramatic, emotional,
or erratic reactions,
426
cluster III: disorders involving anxiety and
fearfulness, 426–427
definition of, 425, 596
DSM-IV classification of,
412t, 425
prevalence of, 427
prognosis for, 427
Personality psychology, 29
Personality trait(s), 364–367
Allport's theory of,
364–365
cardinal, 364–365
Cattell's approach to,
365, 366f
central, 364–365
common, 364
definition of, 364
factor analysis of, 365
Five-Factor Model of,
365–367
personal, 364
secondary, 364–365
source, 365, 366f
surface, 365
Person-centered therapy,
460
Personnel
matching to jobs,
513–522
motivating, 519–522
selection, 514–516
training, 516–519, 517f
effectiveness, measure-
ment of, 519
need for, assessment of,
517–518
techniques for, 518–519
Persuasion
attitude change and,
480–483
central route for,
482–483

perceived expertise and,
483
peripheral route for,
482–483
trustworthiness and, 483
Phallic stage, of psychosexual development,
356–357
Phenomenological. See also
Humanistic-phenome-
nological approach
definition of, 362
Phenomenology, 41, 596
Phenylketonuria (PKU),
307, 596
Pheromones, 150, 596
Phobia(s), 417–418
Phobic disorder(s), 417–418
definition of, 212, 596
prevalence of, 212
prognosis for, 418
treatment, classical condi-
tioning in, 212–213
Photoreceptor cells. See
Cones; Rods
Physical attractiveness, interpersonal attraction
and, 488
Physical cues, in perception,
169, 171–174
Physiological/biological psy-
chology, 28
Piblokto, 410t
Pictorial cues, in perception,
171–174, 174f
Pinna, 146, 146f, 596
Pitch, of sound, 144, 596
PKU. See Phenylketonuria
Placebo effects, 153
Placenta, formation of, 81
Pleasure principle, Freud's
theory of, 354, 596
Pluralistic ignorance, and by-
stander intervention,
499–500, 596
PNS. See Peripheral nervous
system
Pons, 63, 64, 64f
definition of, 64, 596
functions of, 64
Population density
and crowding, compari-
son of, 530–531
definition of, 530, 596
Position senses, 152–154
Positive reinforcer(s),
220–221, 596
Positron emission tomogra-
phy, of brain
in depression, 438f
in schizophrenia, 438f
Postconventional morality,
96, 97f
Posttraumatic stress disorder
(PTSD), 421–422
definition of, 421, 596

Power motivation, 336–337
Practice
distributed, effects on
memory retrieval,
267f, 267–268
effects on memory re-
trieval, 267f, 267–268.
See also Overlearning
learning and, 2–3, 203
massed, effects on mem-
ory retrieval, 267f,
267–268
Pragmatics, 289–290, 596
Preconscious, Freud's theory
of, 179f, 353
Preconventional morality,
96, 97f
Prefrontal lobotomy,
450–451
Pregnancy, adolescent,
107–108
Prenatal development, 80–85
environmental influences
on, 83–84
nourishment during,
83–84
paternal influences on,
85
physical aspects of, 81–83
Prenatal period, definition
of, 81, 596
Preoperational stage, Pi-
aget's concept of,
91–93, 95f, 596
Prevention programs, 398
Primary drives, 317
Primary emotions, 339–340,
340f
Primary hues, 140
Primary reinforcer(s),
221–222, 596
Primary territory, 527, 530f
Principles of Psychology
(James), 22
Proactive interference, 270f,
270–271, 596
Problem(s)
components of, 278
definition of, 278, 596
ill-defined, 278, 279f
representation of, 280f,
280–282, 281f
well-defined, 278
Problem solving, 278–287
creative, 285–287
stages of, 286–287
effective, barriers to,
283–287
functional fixedness and,
284–285, 592
mental set and, 283–285
strategies for, 282–283
algorithms as, 282
heuristic, 282–283
Procedural memory, 251,
252f, 256–257, 596

Process schizophrenia, 434,
596
Prognosis, definition of, 418,
596
Projection, as defense mechanism, 355f, 596
Projective technique(s)
definition of, 373, 596
for personality assess-
ment, 373–375
Proximity
Gestalt principle of, 166,
167f, 596
interpersonal attraction
and, 487f, 488
Psychiatric nurses, 449
Psychiatrist(s), 449
psychologists and, com-
parison of, 28
Psychoactive drugs, 452–453
definition of, 188, 596
Psychoanalysis, 455–460
definition of, 24, 597
dream interpretation in,
459
duration of, 460
Freudian, 457–459
post-Freudian, 459–460
resistance in, 458–459
short-form, 460
time-limited, 460
transference in, 459
Psychoanalyst, 449
Psychoanalytic approach,
352–360
after Freud, 357–359
definition of, 352, 597
evaluation of, 359–360
male bias in, 358–359
neo-Freudian, 357–360
Psychoanalytic psychology,
founding of, 24
Psychodiagnostics, 449
Psycholinguistics, 288, 597
Psychological disorder(s),
408–413
critical thinking about,
438–439
definition of, 408–413
DSM-IV classification of,
411, 412t
summary of, 439–441
test yourself, 442–443
Psychological phenomena,
complexity of, 41–42
Psychological research
ethics in, 38–40
methods for, 26–44
Psychological tests
definition of, 295, 597
in employee selection,
516
of intelligence, 296–301
nature of, 295–296
norms for, 296
reliability of, 295–296

scoring, objective, 295
standardized, 295
validity of, 296
Psychologist(s)
   diversity of, 28–29
   numbers of, 28
Psychology
   applications of, 28–29
      in daily life, 42
   clinical, 28
   cognitive, 29
   correlational methods in,
      31–34
   counseling, 29
   critical thinking about,
      43–44
   cultural, 29
   definition of, 15, 597
   developmental, 28
   educational/instruc-
      tional, 28
   environmental, 524–537
   experimental methods in,
      34–38
   Gestalt. *See* Gestalt psy-
      chology
   health, 29, 394–402
   historical perspective on,
      18–21
   humanistic, 24–25, 593
   industrial-organizational
      (I/O). *See* Industrial-
      organizational (I/O)
      psychology
   modern approaches in,
      26
   observational methods in,
      27–31
   operational definition of,
      26
   personality, 29
   philosophical origins of,
      18–21
   physiological/biological,
      28
   principles of, 40–43
   psychoanalytic. *See* Psy-
      choanalytic psychol-
      ogy
   relevance of, to daily life,
      42–43
   research methods of,
      26–44
   as science, 15–17
      early years of, 21–23
   scientific origins of,
      18–21
   scientist-practitioners in,
      16–17
   social, 29, 475–510
   sports, 534–537, 598
   subject matter of, 17–18
   summary of, 44–46
   test yourself, 47–48
   working definition of,
      14–26

Psychometrics, 29
Psychophysics, 127, 597
Psychosexual development
   anal stage of, 356
   Freud's theory of,
      356–357
   genital stage of, 357
   latency stage of, 357
   oral stage of, 356
   phallic stage of, 356–357
Psychosocial, definition of,
   98
Psychosocial development,
   Erikson's theory of,
   98–100, 99f
Psychosurgery, 450–451, 597
Psychotherapy, 455–469
   behavioral techniques,
      461–464
   client-centered, 460
   cognitive techniques,
      464–467
   effectiveness of, 468–469
   evaluation of, 468–469
   group approaches,
      467–468
   humanistic techniques,
      460–461, 462f
   methods of, comparison
      of, 468–469
   outcome studies, difficul-
      ties with, 468–469
   person-centered, 460
   providers of, 448–449
   psychoanalytic tech-
      niques, 455–460
   Rogerian, 460
   summary of, 471–472
   test yourself, 474
Psychotic disorders, DSM-IV
   classification of, 412t
PTSD. *See* Posttraumatic
   stress disorder
Puberty, 103–105
   definition of, 104, 597
Public distance, 527, 528f
Public territory, 527–529,
   530f
Punishment, 225–227
   definition of, 225, 597
   effective use of, 226
   vicarious, 233
Pupil, 134, 134f, 597
Purposive behaviorism, 230
Pyrophobia, 418f

Race, and IQ scores,
   302–303
Random assignment, 37, 597
Range, 548–549, 597
RAS. *See* Reticular activating
   system
Rational-emotive therapy,
   465, 597
Rationalization, as defense
   mechanism, 355f, 597

Rats
   crowding, effects of, 529
   experiments with, 35–36
Reactive schizophrenia, 434,
   597
Reality principle, Freud's
   theory of, 354, 597
Recall
   definition of, 255, 597
   free, 255, 256f
   serial, 255
Reciprocity, interpersonal attraction and, 487
Recognition, 255, 256f, 597
Recovery, criteria for, difficulties with, 469
Reflex(es)
   definition of, 204, 597
   of neonate, 86, 86t
   spinal, 61–62, 62f
Regression, as defense mechanism, 355f, 597
Reinforcement, 220–225
   versus bribery, 222
   definition of, 220, 597
   schedule, 222–225
      continuous, 223, 223f
      fixed, 223f
      fixed-interval (FI), 224
      fixed-ratio (FR), 224
      intermittent, 223, 223f,
         594
      variable-interval (VI),
         224
      variable-ratio (VR), 224
   vicarious, 233, 479
Reinforcement model, of interpersonal attraction,
   485
Reinforcer(s)
   definition of, 220, 597
   negative, 220–221, 595
   positive, 220–221, 596
   primary, 221–222, 596
   scheduling, 222–225
   secondary, 221–222
Relative size, in perception
   of distance, 171f,
   171–172
Relaxation techniques, stress
   reduction and, 392
Relearning
   definition of, 256, 597
   implicit memory and,
      256
Reliability, of psychological
   tests, 295–296, 597
REM sleep, 183–185, 597
REM sleep disorder, 185
Repression, 253, 597
   as defense mechanism,
      355f
Research. *See* Psychological
   research
Resistance, in psychoanalysis,
   458–459, 597

Resistance stage, in general
   adaptation syndrome,
   388, 389f
Response(s)
   conditioned, 206
      emotional, 209–210
   unconditioned, 205–206
Resting potential, 53, 597
RET. *See* Rational-emotive
   therapy
Reticular activating system
   (RAS), 64f
   definition of, 66, 597
   functions of, 66
Retina, 134f, 135–137, 597
   layers of, 135, 137f
Retinal disparity, 169–170,
   170f, 597
Retirement, 115
Retrieval, in memory, 241,
   254–271, 597
Retroactive interference,
   268–270, 269f, 270f,
   597
Risky shift, in decision making in groups,
   503–504
Rods, 135, 137f, 597
   visual experience pro-
      vided by, 138–139
Rogerian therapy, 460
Role confusion, adolescent's,
   105
Role-playing, in personality
   assessment, 369
Rooting reflex, 86t
Rorschach inkblot test, 374,
   374f, 597
Rubella, birth defects caused
   by, 83

Safety, in workplace, 525
Sample(s), 30, 597
Saturation, of light, 133, 597
Schema(s)
   definition of, 264
   in memory retrieval, 264f,
      264–265, 271f
   Piaget's concept of, 90,
      597
Schizoid personality disorder, 426
Schizophrenia, 432–438
   biochemical factors in,
      437
   causes of, 436–438
   definition of, 432, 598
   delusions in, 432
   disorganized type, 434
   dopamine hypothesis
      and, 437, 591
   drug therapy for, 453
   DSM subtypes of,
      433–434
   DSM-IV classification of,
      412t

hallucinations in, 432
hereditary factors in, 436
incidence of, 433
negative, 434–435
paranoid type, 434
positive, 434–435
process, 434, 596
prognosis for, 433
psychological factors in, 437–438
reactive, 434, 597
residual type, 434
social factors in, 437–438
versus split personality, 433
symptoms of, 432
positive and negative, 434–435
types of, 433–435
undifferentiated type, 434
Science
definition of, 15
psychology as, 15–17
Scientific methods, 15, 598
Scientist-practitioners, in psychology, 16–17
Secondary drives, 317, 598
Secondary personality traits, 364–365
Secondary reinforcers, 221–222
Secondary territory, 527–529, 530f
Self-actualization, 363, 363f
Self-serving bias, attributions and, 484–485, 598
Semantic memory, 251–252, 252f, 598
Semicircular canals, 146f, 154
Senile psychosis, 429
Sensation
basic concepts of, 126–130
definition of, 126, 598
in skin, 150–152
summary of, 155
test yourself, 158
Sensation seekers, 321, 321f
Sense organs, 126
Sense receptors, 126
Senses
chemical, 147–150. See also Smell; Taste
cutaneous, 150–152
position, 152–154
Sensorimotor stage, Piaget's concept of, 91, 92f, 95f, 598
Sensory abilities, age-related changes in, 115
Sensory adaptation, 129–130
definition of, 129, 598
Sensory areas, of cerebral cortex, 69f, 69–70, 598

Sensory development, 88–89
Sensory memory, 241–242, 243–244, 598
capacity of, 241–242
duration of, 242
Sensory neuron(s)
definition of, 60, 598
in spinal reflexes, 62, 62f
Sensory processes. See also Hearing; Smell; Taste; Vision
critical thinking about, 154–155
Sensory thresholds, 127–129
absolute, 127–128, 128f, 129
difference, 128–129
Sentence completion test, 373–374
Septum, 66f, 67
SES. See Socioeconomic status
Set point, 320
The Seville Statement, 497
Sex drive, 330–331
internal and external cues for, 330–331
Sexual abuse, repressed memories of, 253
Sexual behaviors, 330–334
Sexual orientation
determinants of, 332–334
Kinsey's scale of, 332, 332f
spectrum of, 332
Sexuality, adolescent, 107–108
Sexually transmitted disease, 400
Shading patterns, in perception of distance and depth, 172, 173f
Shape constancy, in perception, 175, 175f
Shaping, 218–219, 598
Short-term memory (STM), 241, 242–248
capacity of, 245
chunks in, 245
definition of, 242–243, 598
duration of, 244–245, 245f
encoding in, 246–247
information encoding (representation) in, 246–247
maintenance rehearsal in, 244–245, 245f, 594
tested by Stanford-Binet Intelligence Scale, 297–298
Sightedness, 135, 136f
Signal detection theory, 129, 598
Similarity

Gestalt principle of, 166, 598
interpersonal attraction and, 489
Situational testing, in employee selection, 516
16 PF Questionnaire, 373
Size constancy, in perception, 174–175
Skin
encapsulated nerve endings of, 151, 151f
free nerve endings of, 151, 151f
sensation in, 150–152
structures of, 150–151, 151f
Skinner box, 217–218, 218f
Sleep, 181–186
electroencephalography in, 182, 182f
NREM, 183–185
REM, 183f, 183–185
stages of, 181–183
Sleep apnea, 184
Sleep disorder(s), 184–185
Sleep spindles, 182f, 182–183
Smell, 147–148, 149–150
absolute threshold for, 128f
summary of, 156–157
test yourself, 159
Smoking
cessation, programs for, 398–399
deaths caused by, 398
maternal, effects on fetus, 84
prevention programs, 398–399
secondhand smoke due to, and disease, 398–399
Social cognitions, 476–489. See also Attitudes; Attractions; Attributions
definition of, 476–477
Social development, 89–101
Social distance, 527, 528f
Social exchange model, of interpersonal attraction, 485–486
Social facilitation, 502–503, 598
Social influence, 489–508
summary of, 507–508
test yourself, 510
Social inhibition of helping, 498
Social interaction(s), Horney's concept of, 358–359
Social interference, 502–503, 598
Social learning theory, 231–233, 598

Social loafing, 501–502, 598
Social psychology, 29, 475–510
critical thinking about, 504–505
definition of, 476–477, 598
summary of, 506–508
test yourself, 509–510
Social Readjustment Rating Scale (Holmes and Rahe) (SRRS), 385–386
Social support, stress reduction and, 393
Socioeconomic status (SES)
definition of, 385, 598
stress and, 385–386
Somatic nervous system, definition of, 58, 59f, 598
Somatoform disorders, 422–423
definition of, 422, 598
DSM-IV classification of, 412t
Sound, 143–146
loudness, 143–144
physical characteristics of, and psychological experience of vision, 143–145, 145t
pitch of, 144
timbre of, 145
wave amplitude (intensity) of, 143–144
wave frequency of, 144
wave purity of, 144–145
waves of, 143, 144f
Sound waves, 143, 144f
Space, personal, and territory, 526–529
Speech
holophrastic, 291
language and, comparison of, 289
production, hemispheric localization of, 72, 73
telegraphic, 292
Spinal cord, 60–63, 598
damage to, 61
functions of, 61–63
nerve impulse transmission in, 70–71
structure of, 60–61, 61f
Spinal reflex(es), 61–62, 62f, 71, 598
Split-brain procedure, 73, 598
Spontaneous recovery
in classical conditioning, 207f, 208, 598
in operant conditioning, 219, 219f, 598
Sports psychology, 534–537, 598
critical thinking about, 536
summary of, 537–538
test yourself, 540

SQR3 method, for studying, 11–12
SRRS. *See* Social Readjustment Rating Scale
Standard deviation, 549, 598
Stanford-Binet Intelligence Scale, 296–299, 297*f*
  scores, distribution in general population, 298, 298*f*
Stapes, 146, 146*f*, 594
State-dependent memory, 259, 598
Statistically significant differences, 551, 598
Statistics, 542–554
  descriptive, 545–549
  graphic representations and, 544–545, 545*f*, 546*f*
  inferential, 549–552
  normal curve, 552–554, 553*f*, 554*f*, 595
  organizing data and, 543–544
Stepping reflex, 86*t*
Stimulant(s), chemical, 189–191
  definition of, 189, 598
Stimulus/stimuli
  adaptation to, 163
  closure, in perceptual organization, 167, 167*f*
  common fate, in perceptual organization, 167
  conditioned, 206, 214–215
  contiguity, in perceptual organization, 166, 167*f*
  continuity, in perceptual organization, 166, 167*f*
  intensity, and perceptual selection, 162
  motion, and perceptual selection, 163
  neutral, 205
  in perceptual organization, 166–168
  proximity, in perceptual organization, 166, 167*f*
  repetition, and perceptual selection, 163
  similarity, in perceptual organization, 166
  size, and perceptual selection, 162
  unconditioned, 205–206, 214–215
Storage, in memory, 71, 241
Strategy
  definition of, 282, 598
  for problem solving, 282–283

Stress
  aggression and, 393, 394*f*
  anxiety and, 393–394
  conflict-induced, 383–385
  coping with
    summary of, 403–404
    test yourself, 405–406
    critical thinking about, 402
  definition of, 381, 598
  frustration-induced, 382*f*, 382–383, 383*f*
  life-induced, 385–387
  maternal, effects on fetus, 85
  physiology of, 388–389
  sources of, 381–394. *See also* Stressor(s)
    summary of, 403–404
    test yourself, 405–406
Stressor(s), 381–387
  coping strategies for, 390–393
    emotion-focused, 390–391, 392
    ineffective, 393–394
    problem-focused, 390–391, 392
  definition of, 382, 599
  future, inoculation against, 391–392
  identification of, 390–391
  negation of, 391
  removal of, 391
  responses to, 387–394
    adaptive, 388
    individual differences in, 387–388
    summary of, 403–404
    test yourself, 405–406
Stroke, impairment by, and cross-laterality, 71–72
Structuralism, 22, 599
Structured interview, 515
Studying
  SQR3 method for, 11–12
  textbook, 7–9
    as active process, 8–9
    preparation for, 8
Subjective contours, 167*f*, 167–168, 599
Substance-related disorders, DSM-IV classification of, 412*t*
Success, fear of, 336
Sucking reflex, 86*t*
Sudden infant death syndrome, 184
Suicide
  in HIV-infected (AIDS) patient, 401
  in panic disorder, 417
Superego, Freud's theory of, 353–354, 455–456, 599
Survey(s), 30, 599
Swimming reflex, 86*t*

Sympathetic division, of autonomic nervous system, definition of, 58–59, 59*f*, 599
Synapse(s), 55–58
  definition of, 55, 599
  neural impulse transmission at, 55–56, 56*f*
Synaptic cleft, 55, 56*f*, 599
Synaptic space. *See* Synaptic cleft
Systematic desensitization, 212–213, 461–463, 599
Systems theory, family and, 467

Tabula rasa, mind as, 20
Taste, 147–149
  absolute threshold for, 128*f*
  four basic qualities of, 148–149
    summary of, 156–157
    test yourself, 159
Taste aversion studies, 215
Taste buds, 148, 148*f*, 599
Taylor Manifest Anxiety Scale, 373
Telegraphic speech, 292, 599
Temperature. *See also* Body temperature
  effects on behavior, 532–533
  environmental psychology and, 531–534
  sensation of, 151, 152*f*
Terman-Stanford study, of intellectually gifted, 304
Territoriality, 527–529, 599
Territory
  primary, 527, 530*f*
  public, 527–529, 530*f*
  secondary, 527–529, 530*f*
Test(s). *See also* Intelligence tests; Psychological tests
  criterion-referenced, 372
Tetrahydrocannabinol, 194
Textbook
  learning from, 7–9
  reading, methods for, 8
  study of
    as active process, 8–9
    preparation for, 8
Texture gradients, in perception of distance, 172, 172*f*
Thalamus
  definition of, 67, 599
  functions of, 67
  location of, 67
Thanatophobia, 418*f*
Thanatos, Freud's theory of, 353
THC, 194

Thematic Apperception Test (TAT), 334, 335*f*, 374–375, 599
Theory, definition of, 351, 599
Therapy. *See* Treatment or therapy
Theta waves, 182, 182*f*
Thinking
  convergent, 285–286, 287*f*
  divergent, 285–286, 287*f*
Thirst, 325
Thorndike's law of effect, 217
Threshold(s)
  absolute
    definition of, 127
    for senses, 127–128, 128*f*, 129
  definition of, 127
  difference
    definition of, 128
    for senses, 128–129
  sensory. *See* Sensory thresholds
Timbre, of sound, 145, 599
Time management, 5
Tolerance, drug, 189
Tonic neck reflex, 86*t*
Touch
  absolute threshold for, 128*f*
  sense of, 151
Toxins, environmental, environmental psychology and, 531–534
Trait(s)
  definition of, 364, 599
  personality, 364–367
Trait approach, to personality, 364–367
  evaluation of, 367
Tranquilizers. *See* Antianxiety drugs
Transducer, definition of, 126, 599
Transference, in psychoanalysis, 459, 599
Treatment or therapy. *See also* Biomedical treatment; Drug therapy; Psychotherapy
  compliance with, improvement of, 399–402
    critical thinking about, 469–470
  historical perspective on, 445–448
  providers of, 448–449
    summary of, 470–472
    test yourself, 473–474
Tremor(s), 65, 599
  intention, 65
  at rest, 65

Trial(s), in classical conditioning, 205–206
Trichromatic theory, of color vision, 140–142
Trust versus mistrust, Erikson's concept of, 98, 99f
Two-string problem (Maier's), 284, 284f
Type A behavior pattern
definition of, 395, 599
physical health and, 395–396

UCR. See Unconditioned response
UCS. See Unconditioned stimulus
Umbilical cord, formation of, 81
Unconditional positive regard, 460–461
Unconditioned response (UCR), 205–206, 599
Unconditioned stimulus (UCS), 205–206, 214–215, 599
Unconscious
collective, Jung's idea of, 358
Freud's theory of, 24, 179, 179f, 180, 353
information processing in, 180–181

personal, Jung's idea of, 358
research on, 180–181
Unfinished sentences test, 373–374

Validity, of psychological tests, 296, 599
Validity scales, in MMPI, 372–373
Valium, 455
Variability, 545, 546f, 548f, 548–549, 599
Variable(s)
dependent, 34–35, 591
extraneous, 34–35, 592
control of, 37–38
independent, 34–35, 593
Variance, 549, 599
Ventral, definition of, 61
Ventral nerve root(s), 61
Vesicle(s), in axon terminals, 55, 56f, 599
Vestibular sacs, 146f, 154
Vestibular sense, 154, 154f, 599
Viability, fetal, 83, 599
Vicarious punishment, 233, 599
Vicarious reinforcement, 233, 479, 599
Violence, 496–497
Vision, 130–142. See also Color vision
absolute threshold for, 128f

stimulus for, 130–133
summary of, 155–156
test yourself, 158–159
Visual cliff experiments, 88, 88f
Visual perception, constancy of, 174–177
Vitreous humor, 134f, 135, 599
Vocabulary, acquisition of, 291

Wake Up America: A National Sleep Alert, 184
Walking reflex, 86t
Warm-up, 203
Wave amplitude
definition of, 599
of light, 130–131, 131f
of sound, 143–144
Wave frequency, of sound, 144
Wave purity, of sound, 144–145
Wavelength, of light, 131f, 131–132, 599
Wechsler Adult Intelligence Scale (WAIS and WAIS-R), 299–301, 300f
Wechsler Intelligence Scale for Children (WISC), 299
Wechsler Preschool and Primary Scale of Intelli-

gence (WPPSI), 299
Wechsler Tests, 299f, 299–301
White light, 133, 599
White matter, 51–52
spinal, 61, 61f
White noise, 145, 599
Windigo, 410t
Withdrawal, drug, 189
Women, employment/careers of, 111
Word association, 373
Work. See Industrial-organizational (I/O) psychology; Job(s)
Work motivation, 519–522. See also Job satisfaction
equity theory of, 520–521
expectancy theory of, 520
goal-setting in, 521–522
Working memory, 243
Workplace, safety in, 525

X bar, 546

Young-Helmholtz theory of color vision, 140–141
Young-old, 116

Zoophobia, 418f
Zygote, 81
definition of, 80, 599
stage of, 81